MAGAZINES FOR LIBRARIES

MAGAZINES FOR LIBRARIES

For the general reader and public,
school, junior college,
and college libraries

BILL KATZ
and Berry Gargal, Science Editor

R. R. BOWKER COMPANY, NEW YORK & LONDON 1969

Published by the R. R. Bowker Co.
(A XEROX COMPANY)
1180 Avenue of the Americas, New York, N.Y. 10036

Copyright © 1969 Xerox Corporation
All Rights Reserved.

Standard Book Number: 8352–0221–6
Library of Congress Catalog Card Number: 69–19208

Printed and Bound in the United States of America

For Randy, Janet, students, librarians, and
all others who adventure into love and knowledge.

CONTENTS

→ RIC collection checked 8-3-71

PREFACE

"What a looking-glass to the history and development of this country is the American magazine! Is there any country that has had a more interesting and bedazzling variety of magazines than this? I strongly doubt it. For vigor and variety, I think it would be difficult to equal the performance of the American magazine . . . America's intellectual vigor happily grows greater rather than less, and we may expect this to be paralleled by an increase, rather than a decrease, in the number and quality of its magazines."

Ashley Montagu. (American Way of Life, p. 169–171)

This is a classified, annotated guide to magazines in major, and a few minor subject areas. It represents the views and experiences of the compiler, his science editor, librarians, teachers, subject specialists, students and informed magazine readers. Its purpose is to suggest to the general reader and the librarian the titles best suited for his individual needs. Hopefully, it will introduce him to periodicals which will be stimulating, pleasant and helpful in his quest for knowledge.

The guide is purposefully compiled for all types of readers and libraries. The only exceptions are that it will be of limited use to the specialist in his particular field, and to the librarian building a large, specialized collection.

Emphasis is on the magazine first, the reader second, and the library last. It is a case of the last really being first. This emphasis is believed to be the greatest service to the library in that it gives the librarian the widest base of selection, and does not limit him or her to the necessary qualifications imposed on a list devised for a single type of library. Lists which are put together for a given size, or library type suffer from a major fault—they must by their very nature include or exclude titles which do or do not meet the nebulous needs of what the compiler, no matter how well intentioned or informed, believes is that library's audience. Yet, no library serves a single public, and it would seem most logical to offer a wider choice of magazines, and thereby a less restricted view of the world.

Thus, while each of the periodical entries is keyed for particular types of libraries, the key is only suggestive. There are enough alternatives to offer the librarian a wide choice, a choice which may very well eschew the compiler's notion of what is best suited for this or that type of library. Furthermore, the appendix does include various basic lists for given types of libraries, and this may be of use to the reader or librarian who is either inexperienced or looking for a certain amount of assistance.

In a word, this guide offers the widest possible latitude to reader and librarian. By so doing, the compiler hopes to avoid the necessity of running up the warning flag, i.e., any list of periodicals must be considered from the viewpoint of the community it serves. The compiler has worked on this premise from the first, and while there inevitably will be some titles not included which some reader thinks essential (particularly true of regional magazines), at least the main titles have been annotated.

The compiler is suspicious of any "best" list, particularly for use by librarians and library users. The typical library client, after all, does not require to be told that this or that title is best; he simply wants to know the alternatives within certain limits of value. Conversely, he does require something more than a union list or a bibliography of say, 1,200 titles in one area. In a word, a guide to the field is required. Therefore, the number of titles is purposefully large (although not large enough, and given another edition, the number will be increased).

Finally, despite a consensus of experts, the inclusions or exclusions are admittedly subjective. They can be no other way, for as a wise consultant noted:

"You will do well to recognize that there is *none* of this which is not subjective, and to declare, in the description of your book, that it is directed primarily to librarians seeking *subjective* information for the purchase of periodicals. I naively imagine that they can, with little effort, find all the *objective* information from the dealers with whom they deal."

SELECTION

Anyone remotely familiar with the magazine world recognizes that no one is quite certain how many titles are now available, but world-wide the number is variously estimated at between 60,000 and 100,000. Closer to comprehension, *Ulrich's International Periodical Directory* (12th ed.) lists slightly over 12,000 titles. Approximately 16,000 magazines are published in the United States, and about one half are company magazines or house organs. Still closer to the average library situation, the various American Library Association standards call for from 75 to 150 titles in a small public library; 125 to 175 in a senior high school. Junior colleges, universities and colleges set no particular number, but a collection of 400 to 1,000 titles is considered respectable. Large, special, state university and urban public libraries have holdings in excess of 5,000 titles, but these are the glorious exceptions, not the dismal rule. The check for most small and medium-sized libraries is the *Readers' Guide to Periodical Literature,* which now lists 158 magazines, many of a general or popular nature. It requires no survey, of course, to realize that in the vast majority of libraries—regardless of type—the magazine collection does not measure up even to the limited listing of the *Readers' Guide to Periodical Literature,* and certainly not to A.L.A. standards. Fortunately, matters seem to be improving, but until they do the titles in the average library require particular care in selection. They also require something more than a single index, but that is another story.

Considering what is available (almost infinite) and what the average library purchases (frequently finite) selection was made for this work, as follows:

(1) The major point of departure consisted of polling experts—librarians, teachers, professionals, students, laymen and magazine readers. Each consultant was asked to check a basic list, add and delete. While this procedure was not considered necessary for all areas, it was employed for the major subjects.

(2) Within each subject category, consultants were asked to select titles which were both the "best," and the most often used by the greatest number of their fellow experts. This was not always possible, but it at least eliminated a number of the more esoteric magazines.

(3) Before and after the tentative lists were returned by the consultants, each of the subject areas was checked against previous bibliographies, holdings of representative libraries, use studies, and other standard lists and articles about specific categories. The basic indexes were examined. A list of the other works consulted will be found in the bibliography to this book.

(4) Emphasis is on American magazines with some, but admittedly not enough, attention to Canadian and British publications. A few foreign titles are included, but only in those areas where they are of such importance that exclusion would constitute total provincialism.

(5) The number of titles within each subject area is dictated by the relative number of publications in the area and, more important, by the relative weight (let it be noted, not importance) of the subject in the curricula and day-by-day workings of the average public school, junior college and college and university library. This required eliminating many long, carefully thought out lists submitted by experts, but again, this was necessary to keep the total within balance.

(6) The cutoff date for new titles was early 1969.

(7) Finally, certain subjects were not included, or only in a representative way because they were considered too specialized for this type of general list; e.g., law, medicine, dentistry, at one extreme and at the other, astrology, apparel, building, etc.

SELECTION OF SCIENCE MAGAZINES

Scientific literature today is so highly specialized and so interdisciplinary, that it is difficult to recommend many periodicals that would warrant inclusion in the collections of general libraries. Moreover, the problem is even greater than that of layman vs. specialist. In the case of school and academic libraries, periodicals can be selected for student vs. faculty use or general science journals vs. research journals, depending on the needs of the faculty and the level of sophistication of the institution.

Emphasis should be placed on the fact that little value judgment can be made by the nonspecialist on scientific periodicals which, in the main, are publications of scientific societies or academic institutions, and whose purpose is to promote understanding and to disseminate significant research results among the scientists of the world. Generally, the articles therein are judged by other specialists for the quality of their technical content and rarely reflect editorial bias promoted by the journal itself. The purpose of the commercial trade journals and news organs of societies is to provide announcements of interest to the profession, or to provide tutorials for the members of the profession in fields wherein technical obsolescence can become a fearful certainty.

Moreover, interdisciplinary journals and extremely specialized periodicals are now the trend in all the sciences. The emergence of new societies and new publications with outstanding editorial boards have now adumbrated many of the journals of the past that were once considered vital for any academic or research library. Yet, one can scarcely ignore the periodicals which contributed enormously to the growth of science in the nineteenth century and which still continue to publish high quality papers. With the translation efforts of many scientific societies, much important literature has become accessible from the USSR and Asian countries. These, too, cannot be overlooked.

The following listings do not purport to tap the bulk of the thousands of research journals available. Rather, we have attempted to show, in each discipline, (1) some of the periodicals which could be read by interested laymen or nonspecialists; (2) the main research journals sponsored by distinguished scientific societies in the U.S., Canada, and Great Britain; and (3) some high-quality journals most commonly found in academic libraries.

Inevitably, a title which a reader believes should have been included has been excluded. This does not necessarily mean an oversight or an opinion that it was not worth consideration. It does mean that this is a guide and somewhere, for reasons outlined above, the editorial hatchet had to fall.

RANKING

Within each subject category the magazines are evaluated by a type of ranking. There are two types of ranking. The first is "Rv," or reference value. Here the consideration is how valuable the magazine is for answering reference questions within the subject area—reference, as here used, meaning its usefulness for both the ready reference type query and extended research. The ranking is "H," high in reference value, "M," medium, and "L" low. A number of magazines may be excellent for reference purposes, but within the general collection of only moderate value. Hence, a magazine often will receive an "H" rating for reference, but be pegged at the middle rank for overall general value. This ranking system is used primarily for the librarian who often must decide on a magazine on its utilitarian, rather than its interest value.

The general ranking is shown by letters which follow the abbreviation "Jv," or judgment value. The highest is indicated by the letter "V" and next comes "A." The vast majority of magazines fall within the third range, or "B" category, and a few are listed as "C" or below normal standards, but included either because they are the only ones available in a given area of the subject, or are well known and enjoy a circulation quite beyond their merit.

Ranking, or the ambiguous terms "excellent," "best," "better," "good," "fair," "poor," etc., is a relative business. It takes no perceptive genius to note that *True Story* is not quite up to the *Atlantic Monthly* or that the *Reader's Digest* is not the equivalent of *Current Digest of the Soviet Press.* Conversely, when one compares in terms of rank the *New Republic* and the *New Statesman* or the *Atlantic* and *Harper's,* how is one to say which is best or better? Much, of course, depends upon individual needs, and upon the needs of the library.

Parenthetically, anyone who is familiar with the "New Sensibility" and such items as pop art or popular music recognizes that many of the old standards are now highly suspect for evaluating and ranking. For if *True Story* is not the *Atlantic,* it may quite well serve its reader in some mysterious fashion as well as the *Atlantic* meets the needs of its readers. This, to be sure, is a can of worms which is beyond this work, but one well worth keeping in mind when selecting magazines for a library.

Still, for purposes of the present guide, ranking is based upon the accepted standards, almost the accepted clichés. Such measures as literacy, accuracy, impartiality, trustworthiness of publisher, editor and author, format, purpose, scope and audience are used as a rough value scale.

More important, the pragmatic test has been used in the ranking system; i.e., the question was asked, "Who thinks this is a best, average, or poor magazine?" The score—based upon the opinion of the consultants, use studies and numerous other lists, library holdings and bibliographies—was tallied. As might be expected, there usually was a consensus, particularly as regards the magazines with a "V," "A" or "C" rating. The great middle area, or the "B" area, was more one of how many titles should be included than of quality.

But even this system of evaluation falters when one considers highly specialized subject areas—particularly in the sciences. Here even the weakest magazines may serve the needs of an individual and thus, in his opinion, rocket

it to a "V" rating. There is also the very real consideration that different magazines serve different purposes within the area, and can they all be lumped together and judged? Inevitably, where this has been the situation, the compiler has based the "V" rating as much on intrinsic merit as on its general applicability to a wide audience. Hence, where two magazines in literature may have the same general rating, the question was asked—which one serves the largest audience? The answer then, to a degree at least, determined its place on the "V" or "A" scale.

At best, then, ranking is a dangerous and foolhardy notion. It is employed here only as an initial aid. Hopefully, though, the user will check all of the magazines within the area and make his own decision based upon his own individual need. With this conscientious user in mind, the compiler and his science editor have paid particular attention to the annotations.

One word might be said about the evaluation of popular, general magazines. These are treated for what they are, not for what indexing, circulation or general acceptance would have them. They are, for the most part, superficial, light and certainly harmless reading. Comparatively speaking, they rank low in this work. Here the compiler freely admits to bias, the sincere conviction that most of these should be part of a large library collection, but not included in medium to smaller collections where every dollar counts, where magazines represent an important, often major source of reference. The reasoning here is that most patrons will be taking these magazines at home or certainly can purchase them at a newsstand. Furthermore, if one subscribes to the notion that a library is a place to introduce readers to the world, not to fortify existing biases and prejudices, one might suppose that the periodical dollar would best be used for titles not otherwise available or easily found by the average reader. Not all librarians, to be sure, will agree with this point—but it is a point of view of the compiler, and one which he has assiduously followed throughout.

ANNOTATIONS

All titles are annotated. The annotations represent both an analytical and a critical approach. An effort is made to indicate the purpose, scope and audience for each title. This is done by showing content, often by citing specific articles, editorial biases and types of contributions, departments and specializations. Where the title is esoteric, i.e., extremely limited in interest, the annotation is purposefully brief. This is particularly true in the sciences. Conversely, where the magazine is thought to be of more value to a subject specialist, the annotation is longer.

In preparing the annotations, the compiler has worked on the same principle as applied to selecting the basic lists. At least three or five issues of a magazine have been examined—newer works and a few not available to the compiler, excepted—and the annotations prepared not only with the magazine itself in mind, but, more important, how it fits into the subject area. Where possible the services of people familiar with the magazines—librarians, subject specialists, students—have been employed, either as advisors or as annotators. In this regard, particular thanks go to: Sanford Berman, Univ. Research Library, Univ. of California, Los Angeles; Peter Betz, Assistant Librarian, Fulton Montgomery Community College, Johnstown, N.Y.; Beverly H. Choate & Ann E. Prentice, both of the State University's School of Library Science in Albany, N.Y.; Linda Crismond, San Francisco Public Library; Peter Gellatly, Serials Librarian, Univ. of Washington Libraries; Macy J. Margolis, Coordinator for Research Services, Boston Public Library; Jake Sherman, *Albany Times Union,* Albany, N.Y.; Adeline M. Smith, Hoosick Valley Central School, Schagticoke, N.Y., and Peter Vesenty, Hunter College in the Bronx, N.Y. Some annotations, too, have been taken from the compiler's column in *Library Journal.*

Science area annotations are almost exclusively the work of the compiler's science editor, Miss Berry Gargal, to whom he is deeply grateful. As a science librarian, she has the added advantage of working on a daily basis with many of the magazines annotated.

Finally, my thanks go to the students of the School of Library Science, State University of New York in Albany, who took part in the seminar which initiated this book.

AUDIENCE

Each magazine has an indication of audience, or type of library for which it is best suited. The scale is relatively specific, but in its application purposefully broad. Hence, most magazines have more than one audience symbol, and the more general the magazine, the greater number of potential audiences.

(1) Public Libraries

There is no specific symbol for public libraries, *per se.* The closest is "Ga" or general adult. Small and medium-sized public libraries are kept in mind, in that the term "Ga" is always used in conjunction with a magazine which is suitable for their collections. However, it is reasoned that today's public libraries serve students and specialists as well as a general public, and the librarian must decide which of the magazines marked "Sa," special adult audience, or "E," elementary school, etc., can be used in his or her given situation.

(2) School Libraries

There are three sets of symbols for school libraries: "E," elementary for grades K–6; "Jh" for grades 7–9; "Sh" for grades 10–12. Any recent examination of graded lists for schools indicates a wide variety of opinion, apparently fortified by one list picking up the grading system of another. Obviously, too, grading is arbitrary because the child who is exposed to hours of adult entertainment, news and information on television is logically going to be more advanced (or regressed) than some of the graded magazines allow. Hence, many adult magazines, even those for colleges and universities, may be suitable for senior high school students, or in a given situation, in the junior high schools.

(3) School Teachers and Administrators

The symbols "Ht," high school teacher and "Et," elementary school teacher indicate the audience, but these, also, are magazines which may be suitable for school administrators and interested laymen. These symbols are used only for specialized magazines which advise or assist the teacher or administrator in the school situation. Many of these will constitute the professional collection in a school library.

(4) Junior colleges

The symbol "Jc" is for junior college library collections, but should be considered closely in conjunction with suggestions for academic libraries. Of all the type audiences employed here, this is by far the most difficult, and in the final analysis the librarian should consider the symbol only a tentative indicator. Where there is doubt, he should choose carefully among magazines for academic libraries.

(5) College and Universities

The symbol "Ac," or academic libraries, is employed for college and universities. It is widely used in given areas, particularly in education, where magazines specifically published, say for elementary school teachers, will still be found in a school of education library. Where the symbol is used in conjunction with "Sa," special adult, it is primarily for graduate study in the university or college. Otherwise, it may be considered for students and undergraduates.

(6) Special adult

The symbol "Sa" is used for special audience type magazines, more particularly the learned journals and trade magazines which are published for the professional, the professor, or the graduate student. The symbol is rarely used alone, but where it is, it is primarily a trade magazine of extremely limited use.

Other features include: a) Full bibliographic description for each magazine. The majority of these have been checked by the publisher and represent the situation up to early 1969. Inevitably there will be changes in prices, and this should be checked further. However, prices are given only to indicate the relative cost of the magazine at the time this list was compiled. b) Indexing. All basic indexing services have been consulted and where magazines are indexed this is so indicated. A list of the indexes will be found in "Abbreviations," and they are briefly annotated in the section on "Indexes and Abstracting Services." c) Book reviews. If a magazine has substantial book reviews on a regular basis, this is so noted. The average number of book reviews per issue is given, as is the average length of the reviews. If they are signed, this is indicated. This system was employed primarily to show at a glance the basic reviewing magazines in a subject area, and to avoid the necessity of noting the information repetitiously in each annotation. In the appendices the reader will find a number of quick reference aids, and there is a title index.

ABBREVIATIONS USED IN ENTRIES

TITLE. DATE OF FIRST ISSUE. (1) FREQUENCY. PRICE. EDITOR. PUBLISHER AND ADDRESS. ILLUSTRATIONS, INDEX, ADVERTISING. CIRCULATION. (2) MICROFORM AND/OR REPRINT. (3) INDEXED. BOOK REVIEWS, Average Number, Average Length, Indication of Whether Signed or Not. (4) AUDIENCE. (5) REFERENCE VALUE. (6) JUDGMENT VALUE.

(1) FREQUENCY

ann.	Annual
bi-m.	Bi-monthly
Fortnightly	Fortnightly
irreg.	Irregular
m.	Monthly
q.	Quarterly
semi-ann.	Semi-annual
semi-m.	Semi-monthly
semi-w.	Semi-weekly
w.	Weekly

(2) MICROFORM AND/OR REPRINT

Abrahams	Abrahams' Magazine Service, 56 E. 13th St., New York, N.Y. 10003.
AMC	American Chemical Society, 1155 16th St., N.W., Washington, D.C. 20036.
AMS	AMS Press Inc., 56 E. 13th St., New York, N.Y. 10003. (A branch of Abrahams' Magazine Service)
B&H	Bell & Howell, Microphoto Div., 17003 Euclid Ave., Cleveland, Ohio 44112.
Canner	J. S. Canner & Co., 618 Parker St., Boston, Mass. 02120.
Dawson	William Dawson & Sons, Ltd., 16 West St., Farnham, Surrey, Eng.
Johnson	Johnson Reprint Corp., 111 Fifth Ave., New York, N.Y. 10003.
Kraus	Kraus Reprint Corp., 16 E. 46th St., New York, N.Y. 10017.
Mc	Microcard Editions, Inc., 901 26th St., N.W., Washington, D.C. 20037.

NYPL	New York Public Library, Photographic Service, New York, N.Y. 10018.
PMC	Princeton Microfilm Corporation, P.O. Box 235, Princeton Jct., N.J. 08550.
Rochester	University of Rochester, Rochester, N.Y. 14627.
UM	University Microfilms—A Xerox Co., 300 N. Zeeb Road, Ann Arbor, Mich. 48106.

NOTE: Most questions regarding reprints or microforms of magazines will be found answered in two basic guides: *Guide To Reprints* (1968) and *Guide to Microforms in Print* (1967). Both are published by Microcard Editions, Inc. Items are listed alphabetically by title with publisher, available run, and price. As the vast majority of magazines are microfilmed by University Microfilms, their catalogs are of invaluable help.

(3) INDEXED

For annotations for all of these, and additional indexing and abstracting services, see "Indexing and Abstracting Services," where listings are alphabetical by title rather than by abbreviation.

AbEnSt	Abstracts of English Studies
AbSocWk	Abstracts for Social Workers
AbrRG	Abridged Readers' Guide to Periodical Literature
AmerH	America: History and Life
ArchI	Avery Index to Architectural Periodicals
ArtI	Art Index
ASTI	Applied Science and Technology Index

BioAb	Biological Abstracts	SCI	Science Citation Index
BioAg	Biological and Agricultural Index	SciAb	Science Abstracts
BiogI	Biography Index	SocAb	Sociological Abstracts
BritHum	British Humanities Index	SSHum	Social Sciences and Humanities Index
BritTech	British Technology Index	STAR	Scientific and Technical Aerospace Reports
BusI	Business Periodicals Index		
CanI	Canadian Periodical Index		
CathI	Catholic Periodical and Literature Index		

(4) AUDIENCE

(For additional information see Preface, and subject listings of titles by type of library.)

By type of Library. Public Library Symbols: *E, Ga, Jh, Sa, Sh*. School Library Symbols: *E, Et, Ht, Jh, Sh*. University and College Symbols: *Ac, Sa*. Junior College: *Jc, Ac, Ga*.

ChemAb	Chemical Abstracts
ChildDev	Child Development Abstracts and Bibliography
ColStuPerAb	College Student Personnel Abstracts
DocAb	Documentation Abstracts
EdI	Education Index
EngI	Engineering Index
GeoAb	Geophysical Abstracts
HistAb	Historical Abstracts
IChildMags	Subject Index to Children's Magazines
ICLM	Index to Commonwealth Little Magazines
IMed	Index Medicus
INeg	Index to Periodical Articles By and About Negroes
LegPer	Index to Legal Periodicals
LibLit	Library Literature
LibSciAb	Library Science Abstracts
LMags	Index to Little Magazines
MathR	Mathematical Reviews
Met&GeoAstAb	Meteorological and Geoastrophysical Abstracts
MusicI	Music Index
NucSciAb	Nuclear Science Abstracts
PAIS	Public Affairs Information Service. Bulletin
PerManAb	Personnel Management Abstracts
PhilosI	Philosopher's Index
PhotoAb	Photographic Abstracts
PHRA	Poverty and Human Resources Abstracts
PsyAb	Psychological Abstracts
RelAb	Religious and Theological Abstracts
RelPer	Index to Religious Periodical Literature
RG	Readers' Guide to Periodical Literature

E   Elementary (grades K–6).

Jh   Junior high (grades 7–9).

Sh   Senior high (grades 10–12).

Et   Elementary school teachers and administrators.

Ht   High school teachers and administrators.

Ga   General adult i.e., for public libraries and general reading collections in colleges, universities and junior colleges.

Jc   Junior college.

Ac   Academic, i.e., for colleges and universities.

Sa   Special adult, i.e., for anyone with a special interest in the field. Consequently, for both academic and larger public libraries.

(5) REFERENCE VALUE

(For additional information see Preface.)

H   —High, i.e., will find at least a majority of answers to reference queries in this type of magazine within, of course, the subject area of the magazine.

M   —Medium, i.e., will find at least one-half or more answers.

L   —Low to minimal, will be of little or no use for reference purposes.

(6) JUDGMENT VALUE

(For additional information see Preface.)

V   The best in the field, within its subject category; or, suitable for all public libraries, in the case of highly specialized fields.

A   Among the best, within its subject category; or suitable for most public libraries, in the case of specialized fields.

B   An average magazine within its subject category; or suitable only for specialized or academic collections.

C   A below average magazine within the subject category.

SUBJECT CLASSIFICATIONS

Accounting
Aeronautics
African Studies
Afro-American
Agriculture
Anthropology and Archaeology
Antiques
Architecture
Art
Astronomy
Atmospheric Sciences
Automation
Automobiles

Banking and Finance
Bibliography
Biological Sciences: General, Biochemistry and Biophysics, Botany, Microbiology and Genetics, Physiology, Zoology
Boats and Boating
Book Reviews
Business and Industry

Chemistry
Child Care
Children's Magazines
Cities and Towns
Classical Studies
Comics
Conservation
Crafts and Hobbies
Criminology and Law Enforcement

Dance
Dissident Magazines

Earth Sciences
Economics
Education
Engineering: General, Chemical Engineering, Civil Engineering, Electrical Engineering, Mechanical Engineering
English

Fishing and Hunting
Folklore
Free Magazines (Appendix B)

Games and Sports
Gardening
General
Geography

German Language
History: American History, General History
Home
Indexes and Abstracts
Journalism
Labor and Industrial Relations
Law
Libraries
Linguistics and Philology
Literary and Political Reviews
Literature
Little Magazines

Mathematics
Medical, Nursing and Health Sciences
Men's Magazines
Motion Pictures
Music
Mystery and Detective Stories

Newspapers (Appendix A)

Office and Secretarial Practices
Ornithology

Personnel Management
Pets
Philosophy
Photography
Physics
Poetry
Political Science
Printing
Psychology

Radio, Television and Electronics
Religion and Theology
Romance Languages

Science—General
Science Fiction
Slavic Languages
Sociology

Teenage Magazines
Theatre
Travel

Vocational Guidance

Wit and Humour
Women

MAGAZINES

ACCOUNTING

Indexes and Abstracts

Business Periodicals Index, Education Index, Index to Legal Periodicals, Public Affairs Information Service. (For annotations, see Indexes and Abstracts Section.)

Accounting Review. 1926. q. $9. Wendell Trumbull. Amer. Accounting Assn., 1507 Chicago Ave., Evanston, Ill. 60201. Circ: 18,500. Reprint: Kraus, Abrahams. Illus., index, adv.

Indexed: BusI. *Bk. rev:* 15 to 20 of 1,000 to 1,500 wds, signed. *Aud:* Sa, Ac, Jc, Ht. *Rv:* H. *Jv:* A.

Primarily for accounting teachers from high school through the university with emphasis on teaching methodology. The well documented articles are usually in the form of scholarly research papers which not only discuss accounting, but touch on various aspects of business practice and education. Regular departments include: "Teacher's Clinic," which emphasizes methodology, usually on pragmatic basis; "C.P.A. Examinations," which traces developments and questions in exams; and "Placement Information." The book reviews are among the best in the field. A basic choice for all high school professional collections and colleges and universities.

Cost and Management. 1926. m. Membership (Nonmembers, $7.50). Owen E. Dickman. Soc. of Industrial and Cost Accountants of Canada, Box 176, 154 Main St., E. Hamilton, Ont. Illus., index, adv. Circ: 16,000.

Bk. rev: 2–3, 500 words, signed. *Aud:* Sa, Ac. *Rv:* M. *Jv:* B.

A Canadian business magazine designed as a cross-field technical publication for both the management accountant and manager. It has use in the business and economics collections as well. Articles such as "Education, Economic Growth and the Business Community" and "Some Economic Aspects of Consumer Credit" are of fairly general interest. Most articles are in English, but editorials and some articles appear with English and French versions juxtaposed.

Journal of Accountancy. 1905. m. $8. William O. Doherty. Amer. Inst. of Certified Public Accountants, 666 Fifth Ave., New York, N.Y. 10019. Illus., index, adv. Circ: 122,500. Microform: UM. Reprint: Johnson, Abrahams.

Indexed: BusI, PAIS. *Bk. rev:* 2–3, various lengths, signed. *Aud:* Sa, Ac, Jc, Ht. *Rv:* H. *Jv:* V.

The professional journal of accounting which features major new developments, interpretations and techniques in accounting, auditing, taxation and related business and professional subjects. Contributors are drawn primarily from the fields of public accounting, business, industry and teaching. In addition to four to eight major articles, each issue contains such regular features as "Accounting and Auditing Problems," "Tax Clinic," "Practitioners Forum," "Management Services" and "Education and Professional Training." It is read by public accountants, business and financial executives and government officials. It also will be of interest to teachers and students

Journal of Accounting Research. 1963. semi-ann. with ann. suppl. $7.50. David Green. Inst. of Professional Accounting, Grad. Sch. of Business, Univ. of Chicago, Chicago, Ill. 60637 & London Sch. of Economics and Political Science, Univ. of London. Illus., index. Circ: 2,200.

Bk. rev: 1–2, lengthy, signed. *Aud:* Sa, Ac. *Rv:* H. *Jv:* B.

A scholarly publication covering international aspects of accounting. Articles such as: "Fifteenth and Sixteenth Century Manuscripts on the Art of Bookkeeping" and "Contributions of P. D. Leake to the Theory of Goodwill Valuation" show the theoretical slant of the writers. The two regular issues are supplemented annually by *Empirical Research in Accounting, Selected Studies 19—*, which offers research reports followed by discussions by two or more experts. Of interest to academic libraries, and large public library business collections.

Management Accounting. 1921. m. $10. Stephen Landekich. National Assn. of Accountants, 505 Park Ave., New York, N.Y. 10022. Illus. Circ: 60,000.

Indexed: BusI, EdI, PAIS. *Bk. rev:* 10–16, short, signed. *Aud:* Sa, Ac. *Rv:* H. *Jv:* B.

A technical journal for the professional accountant, graduate student or knowledgeable businessman. Articles on profit planning, organizational communications and systems analysis presuppose considerable background in the areas treated. The usual features: news events, personnel announcements and associations news is published in the second section. For academic Schools of Business and Accounting and large public library business collections.

National Tax Journal. 1948. q. Membership (Non-members, $5). Daniel M. Holland. National Tax Assn., 100 E. Broad St., Columbus, Ohio 43215. Circ: 2,750. Microform: UM. Reprint: Kraus.

Indexed: BusI, LegPer, PAIS. *Aud:* Sa, Ac. *Rv:* H. *Jv:* B.

Although the primary emphasis is on taxes, the authors frequently touch on aspects of economic and business theory. The articles are scholarly, usually technical, and cover private and public finance at both the national and international level. Accountants will consider this a basic journal, but it should be brought to the attention of all teachers of economics and business. And, as many journals in this section, will be of considerable interest to attorneys who practice in this field. Only for large academic business and legal libraries and a few public libraries.

Taxes; the tax magazine. 1923. m. $11. Henry L. Stewart. Commerce Clearing House, Inc., 4025 W. Peterson Ave., Chicago, Ill. 60646. Illus., index. Circ: 17,300. Microform: UM. Reprint: Kraus, Abrahams.

Indexed: BusI, LegPer, PAIS. *Bk. Rev:* notes. *Aud:* Sa, Ac. *Rv:* H. *Jv:* A.

Features articles of a practical rather than a theoretical nature, e.g., articles like "Bequest to an Attorney" and "Tax Savings Accomplished by Proper Election." Sometimes all or a major part of an issue is devoted to a tax conference such as the Annual Federal Tax Conference of the University of Chicago Law School or the University of Pennsylvania Tax Conference. A first choice in most academic and public libraries, particularly as many of the articles are quite within the grasp of the interested layman as well as the professional accountant.

AERONAUTICS

Indexes and Abstracts

Abridged Readers' Guide, Applied Science and Technology Index, British Technology Index, Business Periodicals Index, Chemical Abstracts, Engineering Index, Mathematical Reviews, Meteorological and Geoastrophysical Abstracts, Readers Guide to Periodical Literature, Science Citation Index. (For annotations, see Indexes and Abstracts Section.)

This section comprises both popular and technical periodicals on aviation, aircraft engineering, aeronautics and astronautics, missiles and rockets, and space exploration. Publications are mostly American and British; no attempt has been made to include the highly specialized research journals, but the few which have been selected represent high quality publications.

AIAA Journal; devoted to aerospace research and development. 1963. m. Membership (Non-members, $33). Leo Steg. Amer. Inst. of Aeronautics & Astronautics, 1290 Ave. of the Americas, New York, N.Y. 10019. Illus., index. Circ: 10,900. Microform: UM. Reprint: Abrahams.

Indexed: ChemAb, EngI, MathR, SCI. *Aud:* Sa, Ac, *Rv:* H. *Jv:* B.

Encompasses the entire field of astronautics and aeronautics by publishing original research papers and shorter technical notes of broad and noteworthy applicability to these sciences. Occasional survey papers, which review new research and development, are also included. The Institute also publishes a variety of other journals. The *AIAA Bulletin* (1964. m. Membership) contains programs of meetings, including abstracts of papers presented, and other announcements pertinent to the Institute. *AIAA Student Journal* (1963. 4/yr. $4.), geared toward engineering students, includes contributed papers by scholars, information on careers, and news of student activity in the AIAA. The following specialized journals are concerned with applied, as opposed to basic research: *Journal of Aircraft.* 1964. bi-m. Membership (Non-members, $15). Carl F. Schmidt; devoted to research papers on aircraft subjects. *Journal of Spacecraft and Rockets.* 1964. m. Membership (Non-members, $30). Gordon L. Dugger; consists of reports on research on missiles and spacecraft. *Journal of Hydronautics;* Covers papers on marine systems. Of interest to the non-specialist is yet another AIAA publication, *Astronautics and Aeronautics* (see annotation, this section).

AOPA Pilot. m. $10. Max Karant. Aircraft Owners and Pilots Assn., 4650 East-West Highway, Bethesda, Md. 20014. Illus., adv. Circ: 145,000. Microform: UM.

Bk. rev: 1, 500 words, signed. *Aud:* Ga. *Rv:* H. *Jv:* B.

Official magazine of the Aircraft Owners and Pilots Association. Long, well illustrated articles contain information on general aviation, the latest developments in planes and aircrafts, air traffic systems, radar, landing strips, and legislation pertaining to aircraft. Emphasis on airmanship and air safety. Travel tips included. Extensive use of black and white and color photography.

APRG Reporter. 1962. m. $3.50. Robert J. Gribble. Aerial Phenomena Research Group, 5108 South Findlay St., Seattle, Wash. 98118.

Aud: Sa, Sh. *Rv:* L. *Jv:* C.

With the moon bagged, the question now is "Where do we go from here?" Certainly speculation about UFO's will continue, and become, perhaps, even livelier than it has been. There are, of course, quite a few groups devoted to the study of aerial phenomena, and some of these have their own publications. *The APRG Reporter,* a mimeographed newsletter of some six or eight pages, is one such. This newsletter was originally called the *NICAP* (for National Investigations Committee on Aerial Phenomena) *Reporter.* Made up of tightly-printed stories—most fairly detailed—of sightings of *ignes fatui* and such throughout the world. Recommended for space scientists, science fiction fans and anyone who has a feeling that far-wandering space-probes may be causing comment on places other than earth.

Air Transport World. 1964. m. $5. Joseph S. Murphy. World Aviation Pubns., 806 15th St., N.W., Washington, D.C. 20005. Illus., index, adv. Circ: 20,000.

Aud: Sa. *Rv:* H. *Jv:* B.

Articles for airline management, written both by staff and contributors, discuss new airplane models, air routes, passenger fares, airports, airfreight, etc. Monthly departments regularly include information on new products, statistics of airlines, calendars and personalia. Special issues throughout the year provide reports on such topics as: airline purchasing and supply, airline electronics, market development, air cargo, etc. Many black and white photos, charts, graphs, maps, and the like. The statistical data on airline operations make this high in reference value, and the features assure a wider audience than management.

Aircraft Engineering. 1929. m. $13.75. D. P. L. Scallon. Bunhill Pubns., Ltd., 4 Ludgate Circus, London E.C. 4. Illus., index, adv. Microform: UM.

Indexed: ASTI, BritTech, EngI, SCI. *Bk. rev:* 3–4, 200 words, staff. *Aud:* Sa, Ac. *Rv:* H. *Jv:* B.

Publishing general articles on all aspects of aeronautical engineering, the journal includes reviews of aircraft systems, new materials and equipment. Departments provide thorough coverage of news of the industry, although a large part of this is directed toward British industry.

American Aviation. 1937. semi-m. $8. Wayne W. Parrish. Amer. Aviation Pubns., Inc., 1156 15th St., N.W., Washington, D.C. 20005. Illus., adv. Circ: 49,500. Microform: UM.

Indexed: BusI *Bk. rev:* 4–5, 50–100 words, signed. *Aud:* Sa, Ga, Ac, Jc. *Rv:* H. *Jv:* A.

With the emphasis on the business pulse of the industry, the magazine is nonetheless one of the chief news media for all connected with aviation, whether the interest is in food for passengers, frames for aircraft, or photos of stewardesses. Issues feature: briefs on new aircraft; statistics on airlines; tips for piloting; regulations from Washington; traffic and services; airports; maintenance and operation of aircraft; marketing data; international developments; and myriad other details useful to the professional or interested layman. This periodical includes *Aerospace Technology,* which ceased publication in 1968.

Astronautica Acta. 1954. bi-m. $50. Martin Summerfield. Pergamon Press, Maxwell House, Fairview Park, Elmsford, N.Y. 10523. Illus., index. Reprint: Abrahams.

Indexed: ChemAb, EngI, MathR, SCI. *Aud:* Sa, Ac. *Rv:* H. *Jv:* B.

Sponsored by the International Academy of Astronautics, a division of the International Astronautical Federation, the journal reports original research on most branches of astronautics. Authoritative and high quality papers by international specialists cover such subjects as the physics of space and the atmosphere, astrodynamics, gas dynamics, propulsion, space flight, and guidance. Papers may appear in French and German, as well as English. A few notes of professional interest are also included.

Astronautics and Aeronautics. 1957. m. Membership (Non-members, $10). John Newbauer. Amer. Inst. of Aeronautics and Astronautics, 1290 Ave. of the Americas, New York, N.Y. 10036. Illus., index, adv. Circ: 40,415. Microform: UM. Reprint: Abrahams.

Indexed: ChemAb, EngI, SCI. *Bk. rev:* 3–4, 200–500 words, signed. *Aud:* Sa, Ac, Jc, Ga. *Rv:* H. *Jv:* B.

Intended for a wide readership, the periodical includes "papers that interpret or review new research, engineering . . . and future trends in fields of space flight, rocketry, aeronautics and hydronautics." Articles, often written on a nonspecialist level, include general interest features such as profiles of scientists, tutorials, etc., and are usually illustrated by good photographs. Departments supply ample coverage of aerospace news: Washington reports, news of the profession, calendars, personalia. A noteworthy department is "In the Journals," which does not simply abstract the literature; rather, it culls new research as reported in the more specialized journals and discusses these papers in one evaluative essay. While one of the best general aeronautics magazines, it does require some technical knowledge for full use. At a more popular level, *Space World* is preferable.

Aviation Week and Space Technology. 1916. w. $12. Robert B. Hotz. McGraw-Hill, Inc., 330 W. 42nd St., New York, N.Y. 10036. Illus., adv. Circ: 101,517. Microform: UM.

Indexed: BusI, RG. *Aud:* Sa, Ga, Ac, Jc. *Rv:* H. *Jv:* A.

A most comprehensive news magazine for the aviation aerospace and allied industries. Articles are usually short, crisp, and factual, with occasional in-depth reports on such topics as the aerospace budget. Developments in space technology, air transport, management, aeronautical engineering, and avionics, are discussed in each issue. There is extensive use of photographs and charts to aid in presentations. Departments include "Industry Observer," "Washington Roundup," "News Digest," "Who's Where" and "Aerospace Calendar." A very useful, special marketing directory is issued annually. With emphasis obviously on the industrial aspects, the magazine is suitable both for those connected with the industry and the interested general reader.

Business/Commercial Aviation. 1958. m. $10. James Holahan. Ziff-Davis Publishing Co., 1 Park Ave., New York, N.Y. 10016. Illus., adv. Circ: 51,000.

Bk. rev: 2, 50–200 words, signed. *Aud:* Sa. *Rv:* M. *Jv:* B.

Reviewing the latest developments in both aircraft fleets acquired by corporations and commercial airlines, the publication is directed toward pilots, airport management, and aviation departments of businesses. Articles, written mostly by staff editors, discuss such general topics as air shows and new legislation; some very practical features on piloting; design and performance of aircraft; problems associated with airports, and the like. The magazine is popularly written, tips on piloting are excellent, and its audience could extend to anyone with flying blood.

Flight International. 1909. w. $18. J. M. Ramsden. Iliffe Transport Pubns., Ltd., Dorset House, Stamford St., London S.E.1. Illus., index, adv. Circ: 28,846. Microform: UM.

Indexed: BritTech, EngI. *Aud:* Sa, Ac. *Rv:* M. *Jv:* B.

This weekly is the official organ of the Royal Aero Club (England), who add the byline "First Aeronautical Weekly in the World." Publishes general information and news on aircraft, air transport, spaceflight, etc., much of which deals with the British aerospace industry. Feature articles provide good general reviews of aircraft and special aspects of the aerospace sciences, however. Occasional color photographs of aircraft are excellent. A very useful feature is their annual directory of the world's airlines, covering biographical notes and personnel of some 800 companies. Other departments include sections on "Sport and Business," and "Defense."

Flying. 1927. m. $6. Robert B. Parke. Ziff-Davis Publishing Co., 1 Park Ave., New York, N.Y. 10016. Illus., index, adv. Circ: 231,000. Microform: UM. Reprint: Abrahams.

Indexed: AbrRG, RG. *Aud:* Sa, Ga, Ac, Jc, Sh, Jh. *Rv:* M. *Jv:* V.

A pleasing mixture of technical and popular material on flying, which appeals to children and adults alike. There are comprehensive and informative articles on all phases of aviation, and personal accounts of true life adventures and experiences. The reference value lies in the extensive coverage of the latest developments in planes and aircraft. There are new product listings and news items for everyone interested in flying. The liberal use of photographs and illustrations throughout the magazine makes it a popular browsing item in almost any type of library, though the *text* is somewhat advanced for those in elementary and junior high schools.

Interavia; aviation, astronautics, electronics. 1946. m. $15. E. K. Barnes. 6 Corraterie, 1211 Geneva 11, Switz. Illus., index, adv.

Aud: Sa, Ac. *Rv:* M. *Jv:* B.

Primarily an aviation journal, international in scope, although considerable material is included on electronics and astronautics. Feature articles range from such topics as a discussion of aircraft design to control of natural catastrophes through aviation and space exploration. Articles are general enough to appeal to the nonspecialist. Some elegant photography of aircraft appears in this slightly oversize periodical, which is available in French, Spanish, and German, as well as English.

Planetary and Space Science. 1959. m. $100. D. R. Bates. Pergamon Press, Maxwell House, Fairview Park, Elmsford, N.Y. 10523. Reprint: Abrahams.

Indexed: ChemAb, Met&GeoAstAb, SciAb, SCI. *Aud:* Ac, Sa. *Rv:* H. *Jv:* B.

This international journal publishes mainly original papers on all aspects of planetary and space science and occasionally invited critical essays. The monthly issues contain 11–12 papers that vary in length from 5–30 pages, and research notes in the form of short articles, which are published more rapidly than regular articles. Papers are usually in English, although other languages are represented occasionally.

Royal Aeronautical Society. Journal. 1897. m. Joan Bradbrooke. Royal Aeronautical Soc., 4 Hamilton Place, London W.1. Illus., index, adv. Microform: UM. Reprint: Dawson, Abrahams.

Indexed: ASTI, BritTech, ChemAb, EngI, MathR, Met& GeoAstAb, SCI. *Bk. rev:* 5, 100–250 words, signed. *Aud:* Ac, Sa. *Rv:* H. *Jv:* B.

General news organ of the Society. The 3–4 feature articles encompass trends in aviation, new design, some historical and biographical notes, reviews of aeronautical research—all written on a level which would be intelligible and of interest to the nonspecialist. In addition, each issue contains two or three technical notes and supplementary research papers. Departments include the usual news and notices of the profession, and a student section.

The Society also publishes *Aeronautical Quarterly* (1949. q. E. C. Pike. $10.30), which consists of high-quality research papers in aeronautics and the allied sciences.

Space/Aeronautics; the magazine of aerospace technologies. 1943. 13/yr. Free to qualified personnel; others, $15. John B. Campbell. Conover-Nast Pubns., Inc., 205 E. 42nd St., New York, N.Y. 10017. Illus., adv. Circ: 66,000. Microform: UM. Reprint: Abrahams.

Indexed: ASTI, EngI, SCI. *Aud:* Jc, Ac, Sa, Ga. *Rv:* H. *Jv:* B.

The major articles in this periodical devoted to all the space sciences and technology, take an analytical approach to aerospace missions (including air transport, space exploration, strategic and tactical warfare); vehicles (including launch vehicles, missiles, and related ground systems); and systems and technology (such as propulsion, structures, communications, power, guidance and navigation, etc.). They review the "state-of-the-art," and attempt to forecast future technical directions. Some attention to undersea vehicles and systems is also given. Shorter articles cover significant, individual technical developments. There are also short, nontechnical sections devoted to articles on aerospace budgets and political trends, and departments which provide brief announcements of new products and industrial literature. An annual issue (January), "Aerospace in Perspective," capsulizes recent activities and current trends for major aerospace projects; a midsummer issue reviews current trends for major areas of aerospace technology.

Space World. 1962. m. $7. F. Bremmer. Palmer Pubns., Inc., Amherst, Wis., 54406. Illus., adv. Circ: 25,000. Microform: UM.

Indexed: RG. *Aud:* Jh, Sh, Jc, Ga. *Rv:* M. *Jv:* A.

Of the numerous space magazines, this periodical deserves notice by public libraries and high schools. For what has been buried in the technicalities of the specialty periodicals or in the jargon of the trade journals, largely directed toward professionals, is here digested, elaborated on or reinterpreted for the layman. Feature articles, some of which are contributed by specialists, or reprinted from other periodicals, span advances in space research and technology, new spacecraft, mission accomplishments, reports on astronauts, etc., and are profusely illustrated with black and white photos. Astronaut coverage is quite extensive, incidentally, and might be of particular interest to spacestruck teenagers. An interesting department is "Russian Report," consisting of news issued by the Novosti Press Agency. Other departments include contract awards, reports on satellites, and the like. A first choice for all public and school libraries.

Spaceflight. 1956. m. 30s. Kenneth W. Gatland. British Interplanetary Soc., 12 Bessborough Gardens, London, S.W.1. Illus., adv. Circ: 5,000.

Indexed: BritTech, ChemAb, EngI, SCI. *Aud:* Sa, Ga, Ac, Jc. *Rv:* H. *Jv:* B.

Containing both popular and semi-technical articles, this publication reviews all aspects of space exploration. News coverage is international, ranging from NASA developments to reports from the USSR released by the Novosti Press Agency; European and British news is, in particular, well represented. The nontechnical articles should make informative and entertaining reading for laymen.

The Society also publishes a technical journal, *British Interplanetary Society Journal,* which ceased publication briefly and resumed activities again during 1968. Research reports cover such fields as space medicine and law, propulsion systems, communications, aerospace vehicles, lunar and planetary research, navigation, materials, and extraterrestrial life.

AFRICAN STUDIES

Indexes and Abstracts

British Humanities Index, Public Affairs Information Service, Social Sciences and Humanities Index. (For annotations, see Indexes and Abstracts Section.)

Africa Report. 1956. m. (Oct.–Aug.). $6. Helen Kitchen. African-American Inst., 500 Dupont Circle Bldg., N.W., Washington, D.C. 20036. Illus., adv. Circ: 10,200.

Indexed: PAIS, SSHum. *Bk. rev:* 4–6, 150–500 words. *Aud:* Ga, Ac, Jc. *Rv:* H. *Jv:* V.

One of the few objective current news magazines on Africa, this is closer to a political science journal than the average popular news periodical. Still, it can be recommended highly for its month by month coverage of events on the whole African continent. Often the reports differ sharply from those found in magazines of a wider circulation. Averaging 56 to 70 pages, it includes articles by ex-

perts, a chronology of leading news events, notes on major economic and political developments and some outstanding biographies of leading Africans, both black and white. The book reviews should serve any small to medium sized library which is seeking material in this important area. Differs from *Africa Today* and *African Forum* in that orientation is primarily on current events.

Africa Today. 1965. bi-m. George W. Sheperd & Ezekiel Mphahlele. Africa Today Associates, c/o Grad. Sch. of Intl. Studies, Univ. of Denver, Denver, Colo. 80210. Index, adv.

Indexed: PAIS. *Bk. rev:* 7–8, 200–1500 words, signed. *Aud:* Ga, Ac, Jc, Sh. *Rv:* H. *Jv:* A.

Less scholarly than *African Forum,* this offers intelligent background and commentary about recent news and cultural events. The authors are generally American professors of political science and international studies, and their style is crisp and factual. Editorials discuss Third World development, discrimination and totalitarian practices. There is some poetry as well as reviews of literary and artistic periodicals with an African orientation. By no means concerned exclusively with black Africans. There is enough here to give a good balanced report on all of Africa. Should be found in most libraries, regardless of size or type.

African Forum. 1965. q. $4. John A. Davis. Amer. Soc. of African Culture, 15 E. 40th St., New York, N.Y. 10016. Illus., adv. Circ: 5,000.

Bk. rev: 3–4, 500–700 words, signed. *Aud:* Sa, Ac, Jc, Sh. *Rv:* H. *Jv:* B.

Aimed at Africans and Afro-Americans, this exceptionally well-written journal will interest anyone wanting to know about contemporary Africa. Each issue focuses on a different aspect of African life, e.g., literature, art, institutions, politics, etc. Articles are written by professors at African as well as American and Canadian universities and manage to be well-documented without being pedantic. Along with *Africa Today,* a useful magazine in almost any type of library.

African Historical Studies. 1968. semi-ann. $5. Norman R. Bennett. African Studies Center of Boston Univ. Subscriptions to: 10 Lenox Street, Brookline, Mass. 02146.

Bk. rev: 15, 500–750 words, signed. *Aud:* Sa, Ac. *Rv:* H. *Jv:* B.

Drawing upon university departments of history and anthropology for its authors, this 150- to 175-page journal is made up of three or four major articles, notes and documents, a review article, and first rate book reviews. In the early issues the focus was on all aspects of African history, i.e., "The Campaign Against Malaria in British West Africa, 1898–1910," "English Chief Factors of the Gold Coast, 1632–1753." The material is well documented, represents original research, and is a trifle dull except for the dedicated expert in the field. Librarians will probably find the book reviews the most helpful, especially as the titles examined here rarely find their way into normal review media. For this reason, it is a required item in any academic library where there is interest in Africa. See also, *Journal of African History.*

African Image. 1969. m. $9. Daniel A. Okoronkwo. Center for Advanced African Understanding, 1149 Aldrich Ave., N., Minneapolis, Minn. 55411.

Aud: Ac, Jc, Sh, Ht. *Rv:* H. *Jv:* B.

A particularly useful magazine for teachers from high school through college. The first number included outlines for three lecture programs on Africa, adaptable for various age groups: "Politics in Contemporary Africa," "African History," and "Pan-Africanism." The Center for Advanced African Understanding is a non-profit organization dedicated to making the continent better known to Americans, particularly white Americans, and the magazine is geared primarily for this purpose. The 48-page offset, illustrated magazine also includes articles on political science, art, and culture. There are news notes, recipes, and suggested tours, not to mention fashion notes.

African Literature Today. 1968. semi-ann. $6/four issues. Eldred D. Jones. Africana Center, Intl. Univ. Book sellers, Inc., 101 Fifth Ave., New York, N.Y. 10003. Adv.

Bk. rev: 4–6, 1000 words, signed. *Aud:* Ga, Ac, Jc. *Rv:* H. *Jv:* B.

Devoted to the examination of the literature and the writers of Africa, this pocket-sized, well-printed 60-page journal is edited in the Department of English at the University of Sierra Leone. The first issue featured four articles on themes, poets and poetry in Africa, perceptive book reviews of books by African authors, and an extremely valuable bibliography of current publications (both books and periodical articles) dealing with African literature. This last feature makes it well worth the investment for any interested American library, particularly as it includes items issued in both Africa and England which are not normally found in current, standard bibliographies. An impressive, most useful and needed magazine.

African World. See Business & Industry Section.

Black Orpheus; a journal of African and Afro-American literature. 1958. irreg. About $1.50 an issue. Ulli Beier & Abiola Irele. Longman's of Nigeria, P. M. B. 1036, Ikeja, Nigeria.

Aud: Sa, Ac, Jc. *Rv:* L. *Jv:* B.

Put out by the Mbari Club, in Ibadan, Nigeria, this is an ample, English-language literary magazine, with the emphasis on black writers. Nearly all of the contributors are Africans, although others occasionally appear. Each issue contains large poetry and prose sections, and each runs three or four articles of a critical nature, as well as a fair number of signed reviews. Deserves to be in most large libraries.

Canadian Journal of African Studies/Journal Canadien des Etudes Africaines. 1967. semi-ann. $5. Donald

C. Savage. Loyola College, 7141 Sherbrooke St., W. Montreal 28, Que. Circ: 400.

Bk. rev: 5–10, lengthy, signed. *Aud:* Sa, Ac. *Rv:* H. *Jv:* B.

A publication of the Committee on Africa Studies in Canada, replaces the Committee's earlier *Bulletin of African Studies.* According to an editorial statement in the journal, African studies need more attention than they have been getting, and the hope is that the *Canadian Journal* will help both to stimulate studies on Africa and its problems and to facilitate the exchange of information between Africanists everywhere. Contains a number of substantial articles—some in English, some in French—on such diverse subjects as the Firestone Rubber Company's loan to Liberia in 1927, the role of the UN's Economic Commission for Africa, and the attitude of the black American press toward Africa in the 30's. Also, a number of lengthy book reviews and several sections of notes on happenings of interest to Africanists.

A Current Bibliography on African Affairs. 1962. m. $20. African Bibliographic Center, Box 13096, Washington, D.C. 20009. Circ: 800.

Bk. rev: Almost entire issue is notes. *Aud:* Sa, Ac, Jc, Ht. *Rv:* H. *Jv:* B.

This is primarily a guide to current books and magazine articles concerning Africa. Divided into three parts, it begins with two to three bibliographic articles, moves on to a listing of material under general subjects and concludes with a geographic section. There is an author index. Full bibliographic description is given for each work in the language of the issuing country (all languages are included except for Arabic and the Oriental languages). A 15–30 word content summary is given in English for major listings. Includes a section on juvenile literature. The best single guide of its type now available.

The Jewel of Africa; a literary and cultural magazine from Zambia. 1968. m. $3.50. Mphala Creative Soc., c/o Intl. House 5–13, Univ. of Zambia, P.O. Box 2379, Lusaka, Zambia.

Aud: Ac, Jc. *Rv:* M. *Jv:* B.

A candid, robustly un-academic literary magazine which reflects the warts and dimples of Zambian (and African) society. It's something of a howitzer, too, cannonading against tribal rancor, superstition, intellectual "whores," Western chauvinism, political corruption, and privileged elites. A single issue may feature short stories, poems, plays and essays by high school students and cabinet ministers. Whatever the age or rank, their approach is spirited, sensitive, and often critical. For African collections, and all other libraries desiring an authentic, unpretentious voice from independent Africa.

Journal of African History. 1960. 3/yr. $9.50. Roland A. Oliver & J. D. Fage. Cambridge Univ. Press, 32 E. 57th St., New York, N.Y. 10022. Illus., adv. Circ: 1,923.

Indexed: BritHum, SSHum. *Bk. rev:* 15, lengthy, signed. *Aud:* Sa, Ac, Jc. *Rv:* M. *Jv:* B.

Features scholarly articles on all phases of African history from the Stone Age to present times. The journal attempts to portray African history as a whole rather than to merely describe the last few centuries in which European exploration and settlement took place. The articles frequently are concerned with the history and culture of native races and dynasties. Some pictures and illustrations. Text is in both English and French. While a scholarly journal, the increasing interest in Africa will warrant a place for this journal in medium to large public, as well as all academic libraries.

Journal of Asian and African Studies. See Sociology Section.

Journal of Modern African Studies. 1963. q. $9.50. David & Helen Kimble. Cambridge Univ. Press, 32 E. 57th St., New York, N.Y. 10022.

Indexed: PAIS, SSHum. *Bk. rev:* 10, 1,500 words, signed. *Aud:* Sa, Ac, Jc. *Rv:* H. *Jv:* A.

"The Journal offers a quarterly survey of politics, economics, and related topics in contemporary Africa," and seeks to "promote a deeper understanding of what is happening in Africa today" by selecting authorities from various fields. Political science professors, UN officials, and economics and history teachers, such as Frederick Harbison, John A. Ballard, D.S. Pearson and Peter Robson, give this journal a broad scope. To keep the scholars and librarians up-to-date, a section entitled "Africana" publishes resumes of the work of institutes and centers for African Studies. The critical book reviews are selective and within the scope of the journal's purpose. With its stress upon human and current problems, it is an outstanding choice in academic libraries. Public libraries will probably prefer *Africa Today.*

Pan-African Journal. 1968. q. $10. (Students, $5.). Maina D. Kagombe. 306 W. 93rd St., Suite 35, New York, N.Y. 10025. Circ: 5,000.

Bk. rev: 2–4, 500 words, signed. *Aud:* Ga, Ac, Jc. *Rv:* H. *Jv:* A.

Differs from almost all African reports in that it is published by African students, primarily in the United States. The contributors have included the President of Zambia, Conor Cruise O'Brien, Burundi's Ambassador to the United Nations, and lesser known Africa-experts, both from Africa and the United States. A number of articles are by African students and faculty, particularly those written on such controversial issues as the black power concept, the Nigerian Crisis and the Arab-Israel conflict. The 16 or so articles are balanced by four to five liberal editorials, letters, poetry, and book reviews. The whole is impressive. The journal is devoted to "new methods, techniques and approaches to African problems," and it succeeds well. It will have particular appeal to the young college student,

both Afro-American and white, as well as the interested layman. While much of the material is scholarly in nature, it is presented in a popular, readable style.

Presence Africaine; revue culturelle du monde noir. 1947. q. $5.50. Alioune Diop. 25 bis rue des Ecoles, Paris (5e), France. Circ: 5,000.

Aud: Sa, Ac, Jc, Sh. *Rv:* H. *Jv:* V.

Available both in a French and an English edition, this is the basic journal for a study of African literature and culture. The review is published by Africans, and is intended for all with an interest in the "striking evolution" of the African continent. Its aim is to run articles that contribute to the defining of "African originality." While the review is literary in tone—essays, short stories, poems and reviews appear prominently—a fair amount of space is given over to factual articles on Africa and her people. Thus, one finds in recent issues (each about 200 pages long) articles on African religions, black power in America, black African dancing and politics in Ethiopia. From time to time separately-priced monographs are issued under the imprint "Editions Presence Africaine." This review and its monographs constitute a fine source of information on contemporary African culture, and, to a lesser extent, on social and political events in Africa.

Zuka; a journal of East African creative writing. 1967. semi-ann. $1. P.O. Box 12532, Nairobi, Kenya.

Bk. rev: 1–3, 500–1,000 words, signed. *Aud:* Ga, Ac, Jc, Sh. *Rv:* M. *Jv:* B.

The editors point out the title is a Swahili word meaning "emerge," and the contents of a typical well-printed 54-page issue features emerging new writers. Short stories, poems, critical essays and book reviews are included. The level of both subject matter and style is exceptionally high for what is essentially a little magazine. The American reader will find that the contributors give an accurate picture of an Africa somehow passed over in many learned journals. Equally important, not one of the items is dull. A good representative African literary magazine, and at a price almost any library can afford.

AFRO-AMERICAN

Indexes and Abstracts

Catholic Periodical and Literature Index, Education Index, Index to Periodical Articles By and About Negroes, Psychological Abstracts, Public Affairs Information Service, Readers' Guide to Periodical Literature, Social Sciences and Humanities Index. (For annotations, see Indexes and Abstracts Section.)

Bibliographic Survey: the Negro in print. 1965. bi-m. $11. Beatrice M. Murphy. Negro Bibliographic & Research Center, Inc., 117 R St., N.E., Washington, D.C. 20002.

Aud: Sa, Ac, Jc, Sh, Jh, E. *Rv:* H. *Jv:* A.

The best single source of information on books, periodicals and paperbacks concerned with the Afro-American. Each issue lists titles for adults, teen-agers, and children. Full bibliographic information is given, yet more important are the descriptive (not evaluative) annotations which give the reader or librarian an excellent notion as to content, slant and any particular biases. While most of the information is on recently published works, some issues are devoted to areas such as history and civil rights, which contain a good deal of retrospective material. As all aspects of Afro-American history are considered, and as this is for all ages, it should be an essential book buying tool in any library.

Black Panther. bi-w. $5.50. P.O. Box 841, Emeryville Branch, Oakland, Calif. 94608. Illus., adv.

Aud: Ga, Ac, Jc, Sh. *Rv:* M. *Jv:* B.

The official voice of the militant Black Panther party, this is in tabloid format. The approach, however, is more along the style of a magazine. In addition to current news items, there are regular features from poetry to cartoons, articles on various aspects of the place of the black in American society, and a general forum for anyone who wants to be heard on the issues with which the party is involved. The tone is definitely militant, the emphasis is on political change, and the whole is edited for the black reader who does not read *Ebony* or *Jet.* Its widest appeal is to the young, particularly the blacks who are now plugging for a separate, equal, not integrated society. An important source in that it gives readers, white and black, the unfiltered views of a new approach to social change. Should be found in all academic libraries, and a good number of high schools.

CLA Journal. 1957. 3/yr. $4. Therman B. O'Daniel. College Language Assn., Morgan State College, Baltimore, Md. 21212. Index, adv. Circ: 600.

Indexed: INeg. *Bk. rev:* Various number, lengths. *Aud:* Sa, Ac, Jc. *Rv:* H. *Jv:* B.

Although a language and linguistics publication, emphasis has been on work by and about Afro-American scholars relating to the Afro-American in American literature, and this is one of the few scholarly journals devoted to the area. Conversely, it also includes a wide variety of material (with the text in the language of the author) on all aspects of language and literature. Each issue contains some eight to ten articles, book reviews, and a limited amount of business news about the College Language Association. It is a required item in any academic library where Afro-American literature and linguistics are a consideration, and it will be of value to high school libraries which have programs in this area.

Community. See Sociology Section.

CORE-Lator. 1965. bi-m. $2. Jim Peck. Congress of Racial Equality, 38 Park Row, New York, N.Y. 10038. Illus.

Aud: Ga, Ac, Jc. *Rv:* M. *Jv:* B.

This is the newsletter of the Congress of Racial Equality, a civil rights group that is becoming increasingly militant, at least in its public pronouncements. The primary purpose of the publication is to keep members informed of what various CORE branches are doing. It occasionally contains general articles on the Afro-American situation in America and possible remedies for this. While there are few in-depth reports here, the spirit of the movement is captured. A useful, though not necessary addition for all libraries. See also *Rights & Reviews.*

Ebony. 1945. m. $5. John H. Johnson. Johnson Publishing Co., Inc., 1820 S. Michigan Ave., Chicago, Ill. 60616. Illus., adv. Circ: 1,012,000. Microform: UM.

Indexed: INeg, RG. *Aud:* Ga, Ac, Jc, Sh. *Rv:* M. *Jv:* B.

The photo-feature is the mainstay of this well-known general magazine, a less sophisticated Afro-American version of *Life.* Most articles focus on Afro-American entertainers or atheletes, Afro-Americans in unusual jobs or situations, and the course of the civil rights movement in particular cities. Progress and achievement stories are stressed. No fiction or poetry. Issued by the Johnson Publishing Company, this is only one of several general Afro-American magazines put out by the firm, including *Jet, Tan, Negro Digest,* etc. Except for *Negro Digest,* none of them measure up in either content or spirit to some of the more specialized periodicals in this field. Johnson was among the first to recognize the importance of separate magazines for a public long overlooked by the white press, and he has done much to build his magazine into a middle-of-the-road, respectable voice for the Afro-American. While in most ways no better or worse than other mass circulation magazines, it is at least relevant to the audience it serves. As such, it should be in all libraries, regardless of type or size.

Freedomways; a quarterly review of the Negro freedom movement. 1961. q. $3.50. Esther Johnson. Freedomways Associates, Inc., 799 Broadway, New York, N.Y. 10003. Illus., adv. Circ: 10,000. Microform: UM.

Indexed: INeg. *Bk. rev:* 7–10, 1–3 pages, signed. *Aud:* Ga, Ac, Jc, Sh, Jh. *Rv:* M. *Jv:* V.

A quarterly collection of poetry, fiction, art, and non-fiction concerning the Afro-American freedom movement, primarily in the United States. Articles are generally 10 to 12 pages long. Regular features are an editorial, "Readers' Forum," and "Book Reviews and Recent Books." All books mentioned in "Book Reviews and Recent Books" cover some facet of Afro-American life, either in America or abroad. The book reviews are detailed and critical; the recent books are given brief bibliographic listings. One of the best Afro-American periodicals, and for most libraries.

Harvard Journal of Negro Affairs. 1964. semi-ann. $2. Assn. of African and Afro-American Students at Harvard and Radcliffe, Winthrop E–41, Harvard College, Cambridge, Mass. 02138. Adv. Circ: 2,000.

Aud: Sa, Ac, Jc. *Rv:* H. *Jv:* B.

As befits the Harvard imprint, this has all the trappings of the learned journal—the neat, footnoted format, lengthy articles and weighty opinions. Each issue contains some half-dozen articles, detailed and nicely documented, on Afro-American affairs. Most of the authors are students connected with the sponsoring body, but papers by outside experts are run occasionally. In general, the content is varied, although given issues are turned over to a single topic. One such is the Fall, 1968 number which explores the black power concept. The calibre of writing is indicated by a fine article by Conor Cruise O'Brien on the counter-revolutionary impulse in contemporary society. Recommended for all academic and larger public libraries.

The Hustler. 1967. bi-w. $5. 2 Lansdowne Crescent, London W. 11. Illus., adv.

Aud: Ga, Ac. *Rv:* M. *Jv:* B.

A black magazine in tabloid format of some eight to ten pages, of particular value for the picture it gives of the black community in England. Published with volunteer help, it is dedicated to "exposing the plight of oppressed people in our communities, and fighting in a positive way to relieve these injustices." Material in a typical issue includes short, illustrated news notes, poetry, theater news, education, and interviews. The tone is relatively objective, although a trifle militant, as might be understood by the mission of the publication. The format is good to excellent. A required item for comprehensive collections in this area.

Integrated Education. See Education Section.

Interracial Review. 1934. m. $4. Arthur D. Wright. Catholic Interracial Council of New York, 55 Liberty St., New York, N.Y. 10007. Circ: 4,000.

Indexed: CathI. *Bk. rev:* 7–8, 300 words, signed. *Aud:* Sa, Ac. *Rv:* M. *Jv:* B.

The emphasis in this magazine is on relating Catholic ideas and doctrine to present trends in the civil rights movement. However, each issue will also contain articles on such general subjects as union discrimination, and Afro-American "subculture," which don't necessarily advance the Catholic viewpoint. Editorials discuss civil rights, poverty and Catholic social action. A rather specialized work for large libraries and most medium to large Catholic collections.

Jet. 1951. w. $7. R. E. Johnson. Johnson Publishing Co., Inc., 1820 S. Michigan Ave., Chicago, Ill. 60616. Illus., adv. Circ: 355,000.

Aud: Ga, Sh. *Rv:* M. *Jv:* B.

Pictorial, pocket-sized newsweekly offering a recap of political events, Afro-American accomplishment stories, and scandals involving prominent Afro-American personalities. There is usually a bit of not-too-daring cheesecake. Items are short, the writing snappy, and the whole caters to an audience less well-educated than that approached by *Ebony.*

It is relatively easy to read and geared for an audience overlooked in other magazines of this type. Again, as with *Ebony,* it is not quality that counts so much as coverage, and it is the kind of coverage which should be found in most public and not a few high school libraries. College and university libraries may want it for collections on race relations.

Journal of Black Poetry. See Poetry Section.

Journal of Human Relations. See Sociology Section.

Journal of Religious Thought. See Sociology Section.

The Journal of Negro Education; a quarterly review of problems incident to the education of Negroes. 1932. q. $5. Walter G. Daniel, Howard Univ., Washington, D.C. 20001. Circ: 1,800. Microform: UM.

Indexed: EdI, INeg, PsyAb, PAIS. *Bk. rev:* 3–5, 500–1000 words, signed.
Aud: Sa, Ac, Jc, Ht, Et. *Rv:* H. *Jv:* A.

Perhaps the best respected and established journal in this field, the editors express three goals: the collection and dissemination of facts, the presentation of critical appraisals of these facts and discussion based on them, and the stimulation and sponsorship of research and investigation in the field. The articles cover all levels and all tangents of education. Viewpoints range through the historical, legal, sociological, psychological, and political. An average issue has seven to eight long articles and five shorter ones, usually on a variety of subjects. Articles are documented. The third (summer) issue of the year is the *Yearbook of Negro Education,* giving extensive coverage to a single topic which has been of particular note or concern that year. Essential in college and university libraries, and in elementary and secondary schools with Afro-American students.

The Journal of Negro History. 1916. q. $6. William M. Brewer, 1538 9th St. N.W., Washington, D.C. Circ: 2,200. Microform: PMC, UM.

Indexed: SSHum. *Bk. rev:* 6–12, 250–500 words, signed. *Aud:* Ga, Ac, Jc. *Rv:* H. *Jv:* B.

One of the major voices of the pioneer Association for the Study of Negro Life and History, with a long and successful record of calling attention to the past and present situation of the Afro-American in our society. Of the four to six long articles in every issue, most, but not all, are concerned with the history of the Afro-American in the United States. In addition, there is an excellent section of book reviews and frequent notes on historical news. Of particular note is the fact that the *Annual Report of the Association,* as well as other significant records of current interest, are published in the *Journal.* Especially useful in college and university libraries and large public libraries.

Liberator. m. $3. Daniel H. Watts. Afro-American Research Inst., Inc., 244 E. 46th St., New York, N.Y. 10017. Illus., adv. Circ: 16,000.

Aud: Ga, Ac, Jc, Sh. *Rv:* M. *Jv:* A.

The militant, tough-talking mood of today's Afro-American spokesmen is reflected in this periodical which deals primarily with civil rights and Afro-American goals in housing, education and employment. The magazine has been consistently open to Afro-American writers, artists and photographers. Many writers first published by *Liberator* have since become well known, e.g., Douglas Turner Ward, LeRoi Jones, Ed Bullins, Eldridge Cleaver. The short stories, movie, television and theatre reviews reflect Afro-American interests. Somewhat more to the left than *Freedomways,* yet equally excellent. As a major voice of the black activist movement, it should be found in almost all libraries.

Negro American Literature Forum for School and University Teachers. 1967. q. $2. John F. Bayliss. Dept. of English, Indiana State Univ., Terre Haute, Ind. 47809. *Bk. rev:* 3–5, 250–500 words, signed. *Aud:* Ac, Jc, Ht, Et. *Rv:* H. *Jv:* B.

An overview of all forms of Afro-American literature, from all periods. "Editorial policy is to run the possible gamut in the subject, from kindergarten to university material." A typical mimeographed issue of 10 to 15 pages includes a general article on black literature, a biographical sketch of an author, methods of working with black students, reports on various teaching projects, book reviews and general news notes. The magazine promises to grow, and is one of the few ideally suited for the teacher interested in integrating Afro-American material into school programs. And as it is low priced, relatively objective, and filled with bibliographic information, should be in most school and all academic libraries.

Negro Digest. m. $4. John H. Johnson. Johnson Publishing Co., 1820 S. Michigan Ave., Chicago, Ill. 60616. Illus. Circ: 36,000.

Indexed: INeg. *Bk. rev:* 5, 500 words, signed. *Aud:* Ga, Ac, Jc, Sh. *Rv:* M. *Jv:* V.

The only member of the Johnson publishing family which can be said to accurately and objectively reflect the militant black attitude in America. It has been consistently open to agitation and has maintained a considerably better literary and artistic style than *Ebony, Jet* or *Sepia.* Some point out that this is also the reason for the magazine's relatively low circulation. Contains about four to eight signed articles, plays, short stories and poetry concerning the Afro-American. Features book reviews, cartoons and "Letters to the Editor Not Printed *There,*" which is a column of opinions rejected by other major publications. The April issue is devoted to drama, and the September issue to poetry. A creatively edited periodical that has a place in most libraries.

Negro Educational Review. 1950. q. $5. J. Irving Scott. Florida Memorial College, St. Augustine, Fla. 32084. Index, adv.

Bk. rev: 10–12, 100–600 words, signed. *Aud:* Ac, Jc, Ht, Et. *Rv:* M. *Jv:* B.

Of interest to teachers and administrators, this journal focuses on problems of all levels of education relating to the Afro-American. The racial slant is not nearly as strong as might be expected. Articles are scholarly and frequently utilize statistical tables, etc., to make their points. Books reviewed deal with the problems and progress of the Afro-American, and not necessarily as they pertain to education. A useful and much-needed magazine in schools of education, and certainly in public schools with Afro-American students.

Negro History Bulletin. 1937. m. (Sept.-May). $3. Charles H. Wesley. Assn. for the Study of Negro Life and History, 1538 9th St., N.W., Washington, D.C. 20001. Illus., adv. Circ: 10,000. Microform: UM.

Indexed: INeg, RG. *Bk. rev:* 2–5, one page, signed. *Aud:* Sa, Ac, Jc, Sh. *Rv:* M. *Jv:* V.

The purpose of this magazine is "to promote an appreciation of the life and history of the Negro, to encourage an understanding of his present status and to enrich the promise of the future." Articles are written in popular style, often with photos and illustrations. Among its regular features are the monthly "Calendar of Negro History," and a section on current events of interest to Afro-Americans. Biographical material on such famous Afro-Americans as George Washington Carver is also featured. The book reviews are critical, written by experts in the field. Most books reviewed cover some facet of Afro-American life.

New York Amsterdam News. See Newspapers Section (Appendix).

New South. q. $3. Robert E. Anderson, Jr. Southern Regional Council, 5 Forsyth St., N.W., Atlanta, Ga. 30303. Illus. Circ: 3,000.

Indexed: INeg, PAIS. *Aud:* Ga, Ac, Jc, Sh. *Rv:* M. *Jv:* B.

The focus here is on economic, political, and social problems of the southern Afro-American. Articles document what some (mostly white) Southerners are doing to alleviate these problems, the success they've had and the resistance they've encountered. The publication customarily devotes a whole issue to a single topic such as school desegregation, poverty, voter registrations, etc. The writing is effective and photographs are used for maximum emotional impact. A magazine for all Southern public and high school libraries, as well as a good many of those north of the Mason-Dixon line. As a source of social documentation, should be found in larger academic libraries.

Phylon. 1940. q. $3. Tilman C. Cothran. Atlanta Univ., 223 Chestnut St., S.W., Atlanta, Ga. 30314. Index, adv. Circ: 1,900. Microform: UM.

Indexed: INeg, PAIS, PsyAb, SSHum. *Bk. rev:* 4–5, 500–1,000 words, signed. *Aud:* Ga, Ac, Jc. *Rv:* M. *Jv:* B.

Primarily devoted to scholarly, unbiased articles on Afro-Americans as a social-cultural group. It is very readable and should appeal to anyone interested in thoughtful studies of the reasons behind current racial conflict in America. Seven to nine articles, from 8 to 14 pages long, are presented along with poetry and occasional short articles. The articles are basically of two types. There are historical studies such as those dealing with "The Negro in California from 1849–1859," "The Development of Segregation in the Federal Bureaucracy from 1900 to 1930," and "The Education of Negroes in Virginia during the Civil War." However, the majority are sociological studies dealing with the Afro-American's problems and his relations to the white society: integration in Afro-American colleges, studies of social problems in Afro-American families and communities, and comparative studies of social problems in white and Afro-American groups. The authors are usually academicians from all social science disciplines. The critical book reviews in the section entitled "Literature of Culture and Race" deal with new materials on race, culture, and racial problems, biographies of Afro-Americans, and fiction written by Afro-Americans.

The Quarterly Review of Higher Education Among Negroes. 1933. $2. Winson R. Coleman, Johnson C. Smith Univ., Charlotte, N.C. 28208.

Aud: Ac, Jc, Ht, Et. *Rv:* M. *Jv:* B.

The problems of, and influences on the education of the Afro-Americans are treated here in rather academic fashion. Despite its title, this periodical surveys education at all levels. It is written from the viewpoint of the Afro-American who has already achieved a measure of success and contains a lot of "ought to" rhetoric. Occasional articles deal with civil rights and the position of the Afro-American in general. In most cases the *Negro Educational Review* will take first place, and this would be a strong second for large professional collections in all types of schools.

Race; a journal of race and group relations. See Sociology Section.

Rights & Reviews. 1964. irreg. $2. Doris Innis, National CORE, 200 W. 135th St., New York, N.Y. 10030. Illus., adv. Circ: 2,500.

Bk. rev: Notes. *Aud:* Ga, Ac, Jc, Sh. *Rv:* M. *Jv:* B.

A magazine of the Black Power movement, this is devoted both to the activities of CORE and to the "Movement" in general. It has been supported by such writers as LeRoi Jones, Julian Bond and Floyd McKissick, and represents a factual account of things as they are from the black man's side of the city and the world. There are photographs, cartoons and short book reviews. One of the best of its type. Can be read profitably by anyone from the high school student to the graduate student—not to mention those now actively working for change.

Sepia. 1954. m. $4. Sepia Publishing Co., 1220 Harding St., Ft. Worth, Tex. 76106. Illus., adv. Circ: 57,000.

Indexed: INeg. *Bk. rev:* 3–4, 200 words, signed. *Aud:* Ga, Sh. *Rv:* M. *Jv:* B.

General interest periodical which stresses Afro-American achievement, but also relies heavily on the sensational and the bizarre. Special departments include "Behind the Scenes in Washington," "Mood for Food," "Sound Off," and "Our Men in Vietnam." Also short reviews of books and records. This is in no way a competitor for *Ebony* or *Jet,* both of which are considerably superior in terms of general editorial content and approach. Were it not an Afro-American magazine in a somewhat limited field, the rating would be considerably lower than given here. However, it can be used effectively with poor readers in larger public libraries and some high school libraries.

Southern Education Report. See Education Section.

WCLC Newsletter. 1965. m. Contributions. Western Christian Leadership Conference, 4802 McKinley, Los Angeles, Calif. 90011. Illus., adv.

Bk. rev: Various number, lengths. *Aud:* Sa. *Rv:* M. *Jv:* B.

Features items of interest to members of both WCLC and SCLC. The stress, in general, is on the problem of the Southern Afro-American and what his Western brother can do to help. Advertises and reviews civil rights-related literature.

AGRICULTURE

Indexes and Abstracts

Biological Abstracts, Biological and Agricultural Index, Chemical Abstracts, Education Index, Index Medicus, Readers' Guide to Periodical Literature. (For annotations, see Indexes and Abstracts Section.)

Agricultural Economics Research. 1949. q. $1. E. Lane & R. F. Daly. Economic Research Service, Dept. of Agriculture, Supt. of Documents, U.S. Govt. Printing Office, Washington, D.C. 20402. Illus., index. Circ: 2,500. Microform: UM. Reprint: Johnson, Abrahams.

Indexed: BioAb, BioAg, ChemAb. *Aud:* Sa, Ac. *Rv:* H. *Jv:* B.

A basic government publication in the area of agricultural economics. Each issue gives technical information based upon research and findings of a number of government divisions and departments on various aspects of agricultural economics, e.g., prices, statistics, marketing, methodology, etc. While primarily for the professional, it has some value for both the student of agriculture and the economist.

The Agricultural Education Magazine. 1929. m. $3. Cayce Scarborough. Interstate Printers & Publishers, Inc.,

19 N. Jackson St., Danville, Ill. 61832. Circ: Illus., index. 10,000. Reprint: Johnson, Abrahams.

Indexed: EdI. *Bk. rev:* 6, 300 words, signed. *Aud:* Ht. *Rv:* M. *Jv:* B.

Intended primarily for the high school vocational agriculture teacher and for anyone involved with practical aspects of teaching agriculture. Each issue normally is devoted to one particular area of the subject, and there are some 8 to 12 supporting articles on research, education, practice, etc. The book reviews and abstracts are an excellent way for the teacher to keep up with additional current thinking in the field. While of limited interest to anyone but the high school teacher, it should be in any public or school library where agricultural courses are important.

Agricultural History. 1927. q. Membership (Non-members, $5). James T. Shideler. Periodicals Dept., Univ. of California Press, Berkeley, Calif. 94720. Illus., index, adv. Circ: 800. Microform: UM. Reprint: Abrahams, AMS.

Indexed: BioAg. *Bk. rev:* 10–20, approx. one page, signed. *Aud:* Sa, Ac, Jc. *Rv:* M. *Jv:* B.

Features historical articles on agriculture, which extend to all areas of the world, but the emphasis is on the United States. It usually contains five or six scholarly monographs and a section giving news and notes on the Agricultural History Society's activities and members. Because of its wide scope it is useful to the student of both social and historical problems.

Agronomy Journal. 1907. bi-m. $14. Matthias Stelly. Amer. Soc. of Agronomy, 677 Segoe Rd., Madison, Wis. 53711. Adv., charts, illus. Circ: 5,500. Reprint: Abrahams.

Indexed: BioAb, BioAg, ChemAb. *Aud:* Sa, Ac, Jc. *Rv:* H. *Jv:* B.

A technical journal for the scientist and teacher which is made up of research papers by members of the American Society of Agronomy. The articles touch on all aspects related to the production and growing of field crops. Some attention is given to agronomic teaching and extension education, but this is a minor consideration. Only for large research libraries.

American Agriculturist And The Rural New Yorker. 1842. m. $1. Gordon L. Conklin. A. James Hall, Savings Bank Bldg., Ithaca, N.Y. 14850. Illus., adv. Circ: 230,000. Microform: UM.

Aud: Ga. *Rv:* M. *Jv:* B.

For 125 years a welcome visitor in country homes throughout the Northeast, this offers practical suggestions on how to raise profits in commercial farming. Content is divided between various types of farming from dairy and poultry to field crops. In addition to research, production and marketing, a given amount of space is given over to aspects of rural living which will interest women. A general agricultural magazine which would be a second or first choice in the Northeastern states for all public libraries.

This is only one example of a general, regional farm magazine. Others which tend to stress particular problems and types of farming or ranching in a given area range from the *Alabama Farmer, Arizona Farmer-Ranchman, Arkansas Farmer* to *Wisconsin Agriculturist* and *Wyoming Stockman-Farmer.* Obviously both public and academic libraries in these areas should check for the regional publication of interest to them, all listed in Ulrich's *International Periodicals Directory.*

American Journal of Veterinary Research. 1920. bi-m. Membership. Donald A. Price. Amer. Veterinary Medical Assn., 600 S. Michigan Ave., Chicago, Ill. 60605. Illus., index, adv. Circ: 4,500. Microform: UM., Canner. Reprint: Johnson, Abrahams.

Indexed: BioAb, BioAg, ChemAb, IMed. *Aud:* Sa, Ac. *Rv:* H. *Jv:* A.

Primarily interested in reporting original research in veterinary medicine and related areas such as agriculture and biomedicine. Authors generally are scholars or teachers working in the field, universities, and state extension services. The journal takes on an added dimension in that it not only reports on work in America, but from major countries abroad. A basic periodical for large research oriented libraries, in both veterinary science and agriculture.

Country Guide. 1882. m. $1. Don Baron. The Public Press, Ltd., 1760 Ellice Ave., Winnipeg 21, Man. Illus., adv. Circ: 25,000.

Aud: Ga, Ac, Jc. *Rv:* M. *Jv:* B.

Directed to the interests of the Canadian farmer, providing him with information on improved methods, market forecasts, and problems of an agricultural nature of the various regions of Canada. Ten to twelve feature articles, of 1–3 pages in length, are written in direct, concise style, and are largely the work of field editors of the magazine. A very occasional piece of fiction with regional or topical interest is included. Regular features include sections on beef, hogs, dairy, poultry and soils and crops, with successful practices reported and new methods suggested. A full page is devoted to a weather forecast for the succeeding month, dividing Canada by provinces and giving weekly prognostications for each. The October issues gives several pages of "Outlook" for the following year, with discussions under headings of the various crops generally raised in Canada. Illustrations are ample, of fair quality, and consist mostly of black and white photos. Generous advertising features farm and household products. While directed mainly to Canada's farm population, there is much to commend this for any rural area where livestock is raised, or to schools and colleges with agricultural courses.

Crops and Soils. 1948. m. $3. Steven A. Breth. Amer. Soc. of Agronomy, 677 S. Segoe Rd., Madison, Wis. 53711. Illus., index, adv. Circ: 23,413.

Indexed: BioAb, BioAg. *Aud:* Ac, Jc, Sh. *Rv:* M. *Jv:* B.

This slim, attractive periodical features articles which are highly specialized, yet written in a readable style, stressing practical applications of farm research. They are written by extension agronomists, agronomy specialists and professors in agricultural colleges. An interesting and unusual feature is a box on the title page giving the botanical names of all plants mentioned in the issue. Useful in the high school library as well as in colleges.

Farm Journal. (In 5 editions: Central, Eastern, Western, Southern and Southwestern). 1877. m. $1. Carroll P. Streeter. Farm Journal, Inc., 230 W. Washington Sq., Philadelphia, Pa. 19106. Illus., adv. Circ: 3,000,000. Microform: UM. Reprint: Johnson, Abrahams.

Indexed: RG. *Aud:* Ga, Sh. *Rv:* M. *Jv:* A.

Boasting the largest circulation of any general farm magazine, indexed in *Readers' Guide,* and directed to almost every interest of the farmer and his family, this is probably the best known magazine of its type in America. Approximately two-thirds of each well-illustrated number is turned over to business advice on farm production and management. It rightfully claims to be "the business magazine of farming," and differs from its competitors by the attention it gives to economics as contrasted with the how-to-do-it aspects of other journals. Each issue features material on business forecasts, late Washington news, and the trade involved with farming. "The Farmer's Wife" makes-up about one third of the total, and concentrates on matters of interest to the distaff side and her children. Much emphasis is placed on the role of the woman as a business partner in management of the farm. The overall editorial tone is conservative, but aside from obvious slams at Washington when matters move against the farmer's economic interests, politics plays a minor role in content. There are several regional editions with special material by local correspondents and editors—material not always found in *Readers' Guide,* which indexes only the Central edition. Useful in all public, and high school libraries where agriculture and/or home economics is a major interest.

Farm Quarterly. 1946. 6/yr. $2. Grant G. Cannon. F & W Publishing Corp., 22 E. 12th St., Cincinnati, Ohio 45210. Illus., index, adv. Circ: 300,000. Reprint: Abrahams.

Indexed: BioAg. *Aud:* Ga, Sh, Jh. *Rv:* H. *Jv:* A.

The glamor magazine of agriculture. Its attractive format and striking color photography will captivate the general adult reader as well as the high school student. In a field as specialized as agriculture, it is difficult to find a magazine with so wide an appeal. The articles are authoritative and constructive, with emphasis on management problems that are common to farmers everywhere. Though the *Farm Quarterly* has regional editions for its

advertisements, it has retained its national approach editorially. It is the only farm magazine today attempting to cover the nation with a single editorial edition—the concept being that farmers can profit from studying farm practices of regions other than their own. Though called a quarterly, there are actually six issues a year, two in spring and fall, one each in summer and winter. This would be first for the general collection, although *Farm Journal* is an absolute necessity for specialized farm interests. Should be in all public, many high school and larger academic libraries.

Farmer's Digest. 1937. m. (Oct–May), bi-m. (June–Sept.). $3. Hugh Highsmith. Fort Atkinson, Wis. 53538. Index. Circ: 33,000. Microform: UM.

Aud: Ga. *Rv:* L. *Jv:* C.

Similar in format to more familiar digests, this little magazine serves the same purpose for the busy farmer—a brief overview of current thought in his field. The 25 or so condensed articles are selected from as many periodicals to cover all phases of farm operation. They vary in length from 500 to 2,500 words. Interspersed with them are short comments by experts in farm management. The articles selected are highly practical and are easy to read. A useful, albeit far from necessary acquisition for larger public library collections.

Foreign Agriculture. 1937. w. $7. Alice F. Nelson. Dept. of Agriculture., Supt. of Documents, Washington, D.C. 20402. Illus., index. Microform: UM. Reprint: Johnson, Abrahams.

Indexed: BioAb, BioAg, ChemAb. *Aud:* Sa, Ac, Jc, Sh. *Rv:* H. *Jv:* B.

Usually about 16 pages of tightly packed information, this government publication features brief, signed articles written in a popular style. Its purpose is to give an insight into agriculture practices abroad and to examine the extent of American participation in foreign agriculture. Typical articles: "Food Problems of Developing Countries," "The Future World," "India Moves Closer to Peak Foodgrain Crop." Regular features include "Crops and Markets Short" and a "Crop and Market Index." Not only a useful reference tool on agriculture, but can be used effectively in political and social science classes from senior high school through college and university.

Hoard's Dairyman; the national dairy farm magazine. 1885. bi-w. $1. W. D. Knox. W. D. Hoard & Sons Co., Fort Atkinson, Wis. 53538. Illus., index, adv. Circ: 332,516. Microform: B & H, UM.

Indexed: BioAg. *Aud:* Ga, Ac, Jc, Sh. *Rv:* M. *Jv:* B.

Every article is aimed at helping the farmer get the most out of every hour of labor and dollar spent. The material is written by experts such as agricultural engineers and university professors. A page called "Young Dairymen" offers advice to 4-H members and Future Farmers. The percentage of advertising seems overwhelming, but one subscriber protested, "but we want the ads, too." Tabloid format. The practical approach to problems makes it a must for the libraries of all country areas.

Journal of Dairy Science. 1917. m. $20. E. A. Herried. Amer. Dairy Science Assn., 903 Fairview Ave., Urbana, Ill. 61801. Illus., index, adv. Circ: 5,000. Reprint: Johnson, Abrahams.

Indexed: BioAg, BioAb, ChemAb. *Aud:* Sa, Ac. *Rv:* H. *Jv:* B.

A source of research papers on the dairy industry as a whole, and on specific problems of manufacturing and production. Although the articles are scholarly, usually representing original research, they tend to be more pragmatic in nature than found in most scientific journals. Hence, the publication is not only of value to the teacher, but to the practicing farmer, at least the one with a better than average education. Some space is given over in each issue to developments in teaching and education, and there are the usual news items about personalities and business of the American Dairy Science Association. A basic journal for larger libraries.

National 4-H News. 1923. m. $2. Elwood Shaffer. National 4-H Service Committee, Inc., 59 E. Van Buren St., Chicago, Ill. 60605. Illus., adv. Circ: 120,000.

Bk. rev: Notes, July issue. *Aud:* Ga, Jh, Sh. *Rv:* M. *Jv:* B.

Published "for adult and junior leaders" of a national organization which aims to encourage and develop interest and skills in agriculture, homemaking and rural living. The level of presentation and subject matter make the magazine of interest to rural and suburban teen-age youth. Articles of two to three pages, written by university faculty, home extension agents and 4-H leaders, concerned with descriptions of successful projects and tips for conducting them. Also, material on related subjects from weed control to tractor safety, and from home lighting to clothing construction. Articles are illustrated with well-selected photos and sketches, page design is average, and covers, featuring full color photos, are excellent. A yearly directory in the July issue lists more than 500 free or inexpensive booklets available for use with 4-H groups. This should be a good source of supplemental printed material for the library vertical file, in specialized areas such as agriculture, conservation, citizenship, etc. Either this and/or the *National Future Farmer* should be in all junior and senior high school collections where there is the slightest interest in either farming or animals.

The National Future Farmer. 1952. bi-m. $.75 Wilson W. Carnes. Future Farmers of America, Alexandria, Va. 22306. Illus., adv. Circ: 280,000.

Aud: Jh, Sh. *Rv:* L. *Jv:* B.

Directed to the 14 to 18 year-old boy, although some articles are suitable for more hearty girls. The editorial policy is to point out that the lad should stay down on the farm, and he is encouraged to do so via articles related to organization and how-to-do-it material on farming. There are a number of cartoons, one or two stories, and a few articles of general interest—particularly in the area of outdoor sports. The style is at times over-simplified, but the approach is definitely adult and there is no talking down to the reader. Although primarily for farm youth, it will be of interest to many urban readers who long for the wide open spaces.

Progressive Farmer. 1886. m. $2.00. Alexander Nunn. Progressive Farmer Co., 821 N. 19th St., Birmingham, Ala. 35203. Illus., adv. Circ: 1,250,000.

Aud: Ga. *Rv:* M. *Jv:* B.

A regional, general farm magazine which is primarily concerned with agriculture in the South and Southwest. Emphasis is on practical matters of machinery, crops, livestock, and the economics of farming. Articles tend to be short, informative, and for the practical farmer. A home section, "Southern Farm Living," makes up about one-third of each issue and is devoted to matters of interest to the women and children. The projects for children are excellent and have wider appeal than most of the magazine. Published in five regional editions, it enjoys a circulation second only to *Farm Journal* and *Successful Farming*. A first choice for a general agricultural publication in all libraries south of the Mason Dixon line; but for others, of limited interest.

Rural Sociology. See Sociology Section.

Successful Farming; the magazine of farm business and farm homes. 1902. m. $1. Dick Hanson. Meredith Publishing Co., 1716 Locust St., Des Moines, Iowa 50303. Illus., adv. Circ: 1,300,000. Microform: UM.

Indexed: BioAb, RG. *Aud:* Ga, Sh. *Rv:* M. *Jv:* B.

In many ways this is difficult to tell apart from *Farm Journal*. It professes to emphasize economics as much as its rival, is national in scope, and covers much the same material. Format, writing style and editorial approach is similar. Finally, it, too, is indexed by *Readers' Guide*. Apparently it enjoys many of the same readers as *Farm Journal*.

The articles are practical and informative, and deal with problems solved on working farms. The women's section, "Successful Homemaking," can be used by the suburban and city housewife as well as the farm women. "What's New" is devoted to reports by members of the editorial staff to keep the reader attuned to the latest improvements in all areas of farm business. A choice between this and *Farm Journal* is more a matter of personal taste than anything else. Should be in most public and high school libraries.

Veterinary Medicine/Small Animal Clinician. 1905. m. $12. Carlos M. Cooper. Veterinary Medicine Publishing Co., 144 N. Nettleton, Bonner Springs, Kan. 66012. Illus., index, adv. Circ: 12,500. Microform: UM. Reprint: Abrahams.

Indexed: BioAb, BioAg, ChemAb. *Aud:* Sa, Ac. *Rv:* H. *Jv:* B.

Covers all aspects of veterinary medicine for the specialist and the advanced student, e.g., articles on treatment of cattle, horses, dogs, cats, etc. As this is for the practicing veterinarian, about one-quarter of each issue is given over to management of a vet hospital or clinic, personalities, new products and news of the field. There are many useful features including bibliographies, abstracts, and case histories submitted by readers. Hardly for the amateur, but a necessary addition for any large agricultural or animal collection.

ANTHROPOLOGY AND ARCHAEOLOGY

Indexes and Abstracts

Art Index, Biological Abstracts, British Humanities Index, Chemical Abstracts, Historical Abstracts, Index Medicus, Psychological Abstracts, Public Affairs Information Service, Social Sciences and Humanities Index, Sociological Abstracts. (For annotations, see Indexes and Abstracts Section.)

ANES; journal of the Ancient Near Eastern Society of Columbia University. 1968. bi-ann. $5. The Society, 614 Kent Hall, Columbia Univ., New York, N.Y. 10027.

Bk. rev: 1–2, 1,000 words, signed. *Aud:* Sa, Ac. *Rv:* M. *Jv:* C.

An offset journal of some 70 pages featuring six to seven articles on ancient Near Eastern archaeology, language and culture, art, economics, history, religion, etc. Articles are by students and presuppose a definite knowledge of the subject. In one article alone—"The Three Alephs in Ugaritic"—there were 176 notes for 11 pages. Another piece was titled "Now in Archaeology: The Underground Revealed." Still, not a single hippie in sight. One wonders if journals like this are necessary, but lacking the special knowledge required to even decipher the title, all most librarians can do is pass it by; or order, but only on request from an academic department.

America Indigena. 1940. q. $6. Gonzalo Aguirre Beltran. Instituto Indigenista Interamericano, Ninos Hérdes 139, Mexico 7, D. F. Illus. Circ: 3,000. Reprint: Abrahams.

Indexed: HistAb. *Bk. Rev:* 3 to 4, 1,000 to 1,200 words, signed. *Aud:* Sa, Ac. *Rv:* H. *Jv:* B.

Aims to foster interchange of information on the life of Indians in the Americas and to spread knowledge about the methods, programs, and policies for improving their economic and social condition. Most articles are written in Spanish with English summaries, but some English articles are included. The four to eight articles are not overly technical, and easy to read. There is an annual listing of American and European theses and dissertations in cultural and social anthropology, and each issue lists magazines dealing with anthropology and Indian life. The December issue, entitled the *Indianist Yearbook,* is devoted to news and reports on projects dealing with Indian community development. Valuable for inter-American studies programs and to anyone interested in the social and cultural anthropology of the Indians of the Americas.

American Anthropologist. 1888. bi-m. Membership (Non-members, institutions, $15; personal, $12). Ward H. Goodenough. Amer. Anthropological Assn., 3700 Massachusetts Ave., N.W., Washington, D.C. 20036. Illus., index, adv. Circ: 6,000. Microform: UM, B & H, Canner. Reprint: Kraus, Abrahams.

Indexed: SSHum. *Bk. rev:* 50–60, approx. 800 words, signed. *Aud:* Sa, Ac, Jc, Ht. *Rv:* H. *Jv:* V.

The official organ of the American Anthropological Association is a basic journal. There are from five to six articles per issue which represent original, scholarly research in the entire field of anthropology. Most deal with physical and cultural anthropology, but there are also articles on ethnology comparing past and present cultures. Others deal with the presentation of original theory or the re-study and reformulation of existing ideas, and there are a few articles on archaeology. Authors are professors of anthropology and affiliates of research organizations who are practicing in the field. The "Brief Communications" section in each issue contains five to six short presentations on new ideas, experiments, and methods in the field. In addition to the evaluative book reviews, there is a 1,200-word review of three or four films on anthropology. The "New Publications Received" section lists 100 to 150 new American and foreign titles.

American Antiquity. 1879. q. $12. Robert E. Bell. Univ. of Utah Printing Service, Salt Lake City, Utah 84112. Illus. Circ: 3,000. Reprint: Kraus, Abrahams.

Bk. rev: 15, 300–500 words, signed. *Aud:* Sa, Ac. Jc, Ht. *Rv:* M. *Jv:* B.

The publication of the Society of American Archaeology covers archaeology of the Western hemisphere, and related areas of significance to American archeologists. In addition to scholarly papers, there are detailed obituaries of notable archeologists, a section called "Facts and Comments" contributed by readers and authors, "Current Research," and book review section. Primarily for the scholar and the college student, but the general coverage of the field makes it suitable for professional collections in more advanced high schools.

American Journal of Archaeology. 1885. q. $10. Richard Stillwell. Archaeological Inst. of America, 100 Washington Sq. E., New York, N.Y. 10003. Illus., index. Circ: 3,300. Microform: UM. Reprint: Johnson, Abrahams.

Indexed: ChemAb, SSHum. *Bk. rev:* Approx. 20, 1–2 pages, signed. *Aud:* Sa, Ac, Jc. *Rv:* H. *Jv:* A.

Contains scholarly articles written by American and European archaeologists about excavations in the Near East, Greece, Egypt, and the Mediterranean area. Excellent plates illustrating artifacts and excavations are grouped at the end of the journal. Short notes of progress of digs and special studies. Abstracts of papers presented at annual general meetings of AIA appear each April. Of special interest to students in the fields of archaeology, history, and art. Because of its relatively wide coverage and overlapping in many areas of interest, this should be considered for medium to large public libraries, and certainly for all junior college to graduate university collections. See also, *Archaeology.*

American Journal of Physical Anthropology. 1918. bi-m. $20. Frederick S. Hulse. The Wistar Inst. of Anatomy and Biology, 36th at Spruce, Philadelphia, Pa. 19104. Illus., index, adv. Circ: 1,180. Reprint: Abrahams.

Indexed: BioAb, ChemAb, IMed. *Bk. rev:* 6–14, approx. 500–1,200 words, signed. *Aud:* Sa, Ac. *Rv:* H. *Jv:* B.

Designed for the prompt publication of original articles on comparative human and primate morphology, physiology and genetics, human evolution and fossil man, and the techniques and methods employed in physical anthropology. It presents comprehensive reviews of books and papers, bibliographies of publications, the proceedings of the sponsoring association, and serves as a channel for informal communication. Exceptionally fine photographs illustrate the articles. Only for larger academic collections.

Anthropologica. 1959. semi-ann. $5. Frank Vallee. Canadian Research Center for Anthropology, 223 Main St., Ottawa 1, Ont. Illus.

Indexed: BioAb. *Bk. rev:* 5–14, 150–750 words, signed. *Aud:* Sa, Ac. *Rv:* M. *Jv:* B.

With articles and book reviews in both French and English, this is a technical, scholarly journal published in Canada, but world-wide in scope. A few articles, such as ones on community development and magic in business and industry, may have appeal for students and involved laymen, but on the whole it is for the teacher and expert.

Anthropological Journal of Canada. 1963. q. $4. Thomas E. Lee. Anthropological Assn. of Canada, 1575 Forlan Dr., Ottawa 5, Ont. Illus.

Bk. rev: 1–2, 500–2,500 words, signed. *Aud:* Ga, Sa, Ac, Jc, Sh. *Rv:* M. *Jv:* A.

A 32- to 40-page pocket-sized journal which features one long article and several shorter pieces. Its primary attraction for the nonspecialist is that the writers include both scholars and amateurs, and often the articles are nontechnical, enthusiastic and purposefully written for the interested layman, e.g., an illustrated article on the history of salt. There is equal emphasis on anthropology and archae-

ology, and material is not limited to Canada, but takes in the entire world. In view of the style, it is quite suited for high schools and for many public libraries, as well as for the college and university.

Anthropological Linguistics. See Linguistics and Philology Section.

Anthropos; revue internationale d'ethnologie et de linguistique. 1906. 3/yr. $24.65. Editions St-Paul, P. Arnold Burgmann, S.V.D., Perolles 36, 1700 Fribourg, Switz. Subscriptions to: Stechert-Hafner, 31 E. 10th St., New York, N.Y. 10003. Illus., index. Circ: 1,000. Reprint: Johnson, Abrahams.

Bk. rev: 35–40, 500–1,000 words, signed. *Aud:* Sa, Ac. *Rv:* H. *Jv:* B.

An international journal which covers ethnography, anthropology and ethnology in Europe, Asia, Africa, the Americas and Oceania. Each issue is a collection of 10 to 15 monographs by the world's leaders in the field. (Material is published in the language of the author, i.e., English, French, German). Generally, well illustrated. There are extensive book reviews, plus shorter notes and information on current periodical articles. The 300 or more pages of each issue adds up to an impressive, major journal which is basic in any medium to large academic library.

Antiquity; a quarterly review of archaeology. 1927. q. $8. Glyn Daniel. Antiquity Pubns. Ltd., Heffer & Sons Ltd., St. John's College, Cambridge, Eng. Illus., index, adv. Circ: 3,500. Reprint: Johnson, Abrahams.

Indexed: ArtI, BritHum. *Bk. rev:* 15–16 full page, signed. *Aud:* Ga, Ac, Jc, Sh. *Rv:* M. *Jv:* A.

A highly readable British quarterly review of the latest archaeological discoveries in ancient lands, Europe, and the British Isles. Documented articles on digs, historic monuments, history, and pro and con discussions on the use or meaning of archaeological finds. "News and Notes" section covers a wide field. Good black and white plates depict the artifacts, excavations, and wall drawings. Articles are written by esteemed archaeologists. Of value to students of world archaeology and allied fields, and to the interested layman. Differs from the *American Journal of Archaeology* in its style, which is a bit more popular. Hence, the more suited of the two for the general reading collection and the layman. See also, *Archaeology.*

Archaeology; a magazine dealing with the antiquity of the world. 1948. q. $6. Anna S. Benjamin. Archaeological Inst. of America, 100 Washington Sq. E., New York, N.Y. 10003. Illus., index, adv. Circ: 12,000. Reprint: Abrahams.

Indexed: ArtI. *Bk. rev:* 15–20 full pages, signed. *Aud:* Ga, Ac, Jc, Sh. *Rv:* M. *Jv:* V.

Probably the best archaeology magazine for the nonexpert and the interested layman. The articles are short and written in semi-popular language for a widespread appeal. Articles about excavations and their revealed treasures in the Old World, the New World and the Orient are by well known authorities and experts. There is also a news section with brief notes of activities in the field, museum exhibitions and collections, and new finds. Given a choice between this and others mentioned in the section, it would be first for most medium to large public libraries, and about the only one suitable for almost all high schools. It would, however, be less appealing to the scholar and graduate student, and a second or third choice in larger academic libraries.

Archaeological Reports for 19—. ann. $1.50. Council of the Soc. for the Promotion of Hellenic Studies, 31–34 Gordon Sq., London, W.C. 1.

Aud: Sa, Ga, Ac, Jc, Sh. *Rv:* H. *Jv:* B.

An annual 50- to 60-page report on basic archaeological activities, primarily in the Mediterranean area, for the previous year, e.g., "Excavations at Paphos in Cyprus," "Archaeology in South Italy and Sicily, 1965–66." The reports are extremely well illustrated with black and white photographs. Most of the material is understandable to the layman. An excellent, inexpensive magazine, and for the illustrations alone a second choice for the popular reading collection in public and academic libraries.

Burlington Magazine. See Art Section.

Current Anthropology; world journal of the sciences of man. 1960. 5/yr. $12. Sol Tax. Univ. of Chicago, 1126 E. 59th St., Chicago, Ill. 60637. Illus., index. Microform: UM. Reprint: Johnson, Abrahams.

Indexed: SSHum. *Bk. rev:* 1 or group by single author, 14 pages, signed. *Aud:* Sa, Ac, Jc. *Rv:* H. *Jv:* A.

A general approach to anthropology, supervised by a world-wide community of individual scholars, who participate in a continuous exchange of ideas. It serves as a clearinghouse for new ideas and as an indicator of trends in the profession. The editor encourages and builds a broad, interdisciplinary knowledge base for the study of all aspects of man by choosing topics "relevant to the sciences of man" which are "broad in scope, thoroughly documented and clearly delimited in terms of time, available data and methodology." The format is unusual; each scholarly presentation is accompanied by two or more critical comments by other subject experts which provide insight regarding the article's accuracy and importance. There are three or four articles per issue averaging 10–15 pages with another 8–14 pages devoted to comments and a reply by the author. Book reviews follow the same format and cover one book or a group of books by one author. There is a series of regular features of value to people in the field. Of great value to anthropologists and college students. As one of the few general approaches to anthropology, this is basic to all academic and larger public libraries. While a bit advanced for most high schools, it is worth considering

where there is a major emphasis in this area on the curriculum.

Ethnohistory; devoted to the original research in the documentary history of the culture and movements of primitive peoples and related problems of broader scope. 1954. q. $5. Harold Hickerson. Amer. Soc. for Ethnohistory, 4242 Ridge Lea Rd., Amherst, N.Y. 14226. Illus., index. Circ: 500.

Bk. rev: 4–10, 400–600 words, signed. *Aud:* Sa, Ac. *Rv:* H. *Jv:* B.

Sponsored by the American Society for Ethnohistory, and directed to the scholar and layman interested in the history and culture not only of American Indian tribes, but also of peoples throughout the world at all levels of sociocultural organization, including primitives and peasantries. There are usually two to four articles per issue. All articles are thoroughly documented and contain references to additional sources of information. There are anywhere from four to ten reviews per issue, and "Book Notes" lists additional titles in the field with a general discussion of about 400 words. Only for large academic collections.

Ethnology; an international journal of cultural and social anthropology. 1962. q. Individuals, $5; institutions, $12. George P. Murdock. Dept. of Anthropology, Univ. of Pittsburgh, 4200 5th Ave., Pittsburgh, Pa. 15213. Illus., index. Circ: 2,500. Microform: UM. Reprint: Abrahams.

Indexed: SSHum. *Aud:* Sa, Ac. *Rv:* H. *Jv:* B.

Welcomes articles by scientists of any country on any aspect of anthropology. "Theoretical and methodological discussions will be published only if specifically related to some body of substantive data. . . . Contributions may range in length from 2–50 pages." The articles are written by professors and scholars in the fields of social and cultural anthropology and are mainly descriptive accounts of field studies supported by extensive reading on the subject. They are worldwide in coverage, ranging from studies of the marriage customs of the Moros in the Philippines to sorcery among the Nez Percé. A special feature is the "Ethnographic Atlas" which appears in most issues. This is coded information on many aspects of the culture of various primitive groups and civilized peoples. It is excellent for comparative research and quick factual information for this type of hard to locate material. Along with *Ethnohistory,* a basic journal in this field; only for large academic collections.

Expedition. 1958. q. $3.50. Geraldine Bruckner. Univ. Museum of the Univ. of Pennsylvania, 33rd & Spruce Sts., Philadelphia, Pa. 19104. Illus., index. Circ: 4,500.

Indexed: ArtI. *Aud:* Ga, Ac, Jc, Sh. *Rv:* H. *Jv:* B.

Primary concern with reports on excavation and research. It is currently caught up in the international concern for the restoration and conservation of archaeological sites. In 1966, the University Museum undertook 18 explorations in

14 countries to study ancient and primitive cultures, both extant and extinct. Although the magazine deals with scholarly topics, the articles are well illustrated and readable. Important for students of archaeology, anthropology, and sociology. Should be in most medium to large academic collections.

Human Organization. 1941. q. Individuals, $8; institutions, $10. Marion Pearsall. Soc. for Applied Anthropology, Univ. of Kentucky, Lexington, Ky. 40506. Illus., index. Circ: 2,700. Reprint: Johnson, Abrahams.

Indexed: SSHum. *Aud:* Sa, Ac. *Rv:* H. *Jv:* B.

Devoted to the scientific investigation of the principles of human behavior and the application of these principles to practical problems. Man is viewed holistically as a biological and psychological organism and as a social being existing in a changing physical and cultural environment. Anthropology provides the major framework, but interdisciplinary approaches to problems confronting change agents in many cultures are featured. The fall issue carries the business report of the annual meeting. Of primary interest to behavioral scientists, graduate students, and university libraries.

Israel Exploration Journal. 1950/1. q. $6. M. Avi-Yonah, Israel Exploration Soc., Box 7041, Jerusalem, Israel. Illus., index. Circ: 1,350. Microform: UM.

Bk. rev: About 10 a yr., lengthy, signed. *Aud:* Sa, Ac. *Rv:* H. *Jv:* B.

Features papers in English and occasionally in French on ancient as well as more recent history and archaeology of Israel and the Near East. Articles, mainly written by Israeli scholars cover geography, geology, soil science, and natural history. There are maps and black and white pictures to elucidate the text. In view of the attention given to exploration in this area, the journal will have more than average interest for interested laymen as well as scholars.

Journal of Asian and African Studies. See Sociology Section.

Journal of Egyptian Archaeology. 1914. ann. $8.85. T.G.H. James. The Egypt Exploration Soc., 2 Hinde St., Manchester Sq., London W. 1. Illus., maps, charts. Circ: 1,100. Reprint: Abrahams.

Indexed: ArtI, BritHum. *Bk. rev:* 18–20, lengthy. *Aud:* Sa, Ac. *Aud:* H. *Jv:* B.

Contains articles of a scholarly nature dealing with all aspects of Ancient Egypt, Graeco-Roman Egypt, and Christian Egypt in its earliest phases; also, the Sudan in so far as that country is considered a sphere of Egyptian interest. Features reports of current field-work carried out by the Society. The book reviews are long, critical and among the best in the field. Only for specialized collections.

Journal of Near Eastern Studies. 1884. q. $8. Keith C. Seele. Univ. of Chicago Press, 5750 Ellis Ave., Chicago,

Ill. 60637. Illus., adv. Circ: 1,459. Microform: UM. Reprint: Johnson, Abrahams.

Indexed: SSHum. *Bk. rev:* 5–6, lengthy, signed. *Aud:* Sa, Ac. *Rv:* H. *Jv:* B.

A learned journal concerned with translations of inscriptions of ancient manuscripts and artifacts discovered in archaeological excavations in the Near East. Lengthy studies (10–20 pages) are written by well-known scholars of the Oriental Institute of the University of Chicago. There are numerous charts of hieroglyphics. Supercedes the *American Journal of Semitic Languages and Literatures.* Larger academic libraries will want, but others can pass.

Man. 1966. q. $14.25. Adrian C. Mayer. Royal Anthropological Inst., 21 Bedford Sq., London W.C. 1. Illus., index, adv. Circ: 2,500.

Indexed: BioAb, BritHum. *Bk. rev:* 24, 150 words, signed. *Aud:* Sa, Ac. *Rv:* H. *Jv:* B.

A general anthropological magazine which covers the activities of scientists throughout the world. Articles are scholarly, well documented, and usually illustrated. They are technical, meant primarily for the expert. A basic journal for large collections, but too limited in interest for the average library.

Na'pao; a Saskatchewan anthropology journal. 1968. semi-ann. $3. (Students, $1.50). Dept. of Anthropology and Archaeology, Univ. of Saskatchewan, Saskatoon, Saskatchewan. Illus.

Bk. rev: 2–3, 500 words, signed. *Aud:* Sa, Ga, Ac, Jc, Sh. *Rv:* H. *Jv:* B.

A processed 80- to 100-page student journal of anthropology whose aim is "to help all interested persons to achieve . . . deeper understanding of aboriginal and non-aboriginal peoples, present and past, in Saskatchewan and in adjacent areas." The eight to ten articles are particularly well written, easily within the grasp of the layman or high school student. As might be expected, most of the material concerns the Indians of the area, although other articles touch on all aspects of related interdisciplinary subjects. As the editor points out, a journal of anthropology of this type "is rather uncommon," and particularly in Canada where the number is extremely limited. Anyone who enjoys the *Plains Anthropologist* will welcome this publication as well.

Oceania; devoted to the study of the native peoples of Australia, New Guinea and the Islands of the Pacific Ocean. 1930. q. $9. A. P. Elkin. Univ. of Sydney, New South Wales, Australia. Illus., index, adv. Circ: 750. Reprint: Johnson, Abrahams.

Indexed: PAIS. *Bk. rev:* 12, 250–500 words, signed. *Aud:* Sa, Ac. *Rv:* H. *Jv:* B.

Features four to five technical articles in each issue. The material is fairly well illustrated, and there are a number of worthwhile book reviews. From time to time the publishers issue *Oceania Monographs,* which are listed in each number. Primarily for the professional anthropologist and anyone seriously interested in ethnology.

Plains Anthropologist. q. $3. Alfred E. Johnson. Dept. of Anthropology, Univ. of Kansas, Lawrence, Kan. 66044. Illus. Circ: 670.

Bk. rev: 5, 250–750 words, signed. *Aud:* Ga, Sa, Ac, Jc, Sh, Ht. *Rv:* H. *Jv:* A.

One of the more fascinating anthropology journals which deserves a much wider audience than its circulation indicates. Concerned as it is with the Plains area of the United States, the majority of articles are involved with some aspect of the Indian and his life and habits. Articles, by scholars who write extremely well, touch on everything from Indian wars to burial mounds, arrowheads, and various other artifacts. The whole is adequately illustrated with black and white photographs, maps, charts and diagrams. Although a good part of the information is technical, it is within the grasp of any interested high school student, and much of it may be used by teachers in even lower grades. Laymen who are interested in Indian or American history will welcome an introduction to the magazine.

Southwestern Journal of Anthropology. 1945. q. $5. Harry W. Basehart and Stanley Newman. Univ. of New Mexico, Albuquerque, N.M. 87106. Illus., index. Circ: 2,200. Microform: UM. Reprint: Kraus, Abrahams.

Indexed: BioAb, PsyAb, SocAb, SSHum. *Aud:* Ga, Sa, Ac, Jc, Ht. *Rv:* H. *Jv:* B.

Published by the University of New Mexico in the interest of general anthropology. Designed to include articles on all branches of anthropology relating to peoples and cultures, past and present, in any region of the world. Authors are professors or researchers associated with museums and there are generally five to six articles per issue averaging from 15–30 pages. They deal primarily with social and cultural anthropology. Some attention is given to archaeology, linguistics, and physical anthropology. Necessary for most libraries because of its general coverage of the field and a "must" in larger and specialized collections.

Soviet Anthropology and Archaeology; a journal of translations. 1962. q. $40. International Arts & Sciences Press, 108 Grand St., White Plains, N.Y. 10601. Index. Reprint: Abrahams.

Aud: Sa, Ac. *Rv:* H. *Jv:* B.

Consists of full translations of articles on anthropology and archaeology from eight Soviet journals. The translations appear some 6 to 18 months after original publication, and cover general and theoretical materials, folklore, ethnology and other aspects of the subjects. Translations are reliable, and the selection is particularly good. The high price makes it prohibitive for most libraries, but it deserves a place in any large collection.

ANTIQUES

Indexes and Abstracts

Music Index, Readers' Guide to Periodical Literature. (For annotations, see Indexes and Abstracts Sections.)

Antique Trader. 1957. $4. semi-m. E. A. Babka. Babka Publishing Co., Box 327, 401 E. Division St., Kewanee, Ill. 61443. Illus., adv. Circ: 42,000.

Bk. rev: 3–5, 300–500 words. *Aud:* Ga. *Rv:* L. *Jv:* B.

This newspaper format periodical is a giant advertising medium. It has become the national source for inexpensive advertising of antiques by everyone from the largest by-appointment-only dealer to the smallest, part-time collector. An inadequate subject index is the only guide, after which each "collectable" advertised is divided into "want" and "for sale" sections. Front-page illustrated articles feature private collections. The quality of paper used does not do justice to the photographs. Books are occasionally reviewed, but not on a regular basis. While reference value is virtually nil, patrons of *any* library, public or school, who have any interest in antiques will become regular readers.

Antiques Journal. 1945. m. $6. Don Maust. Antiques Journal Publishing Co., Fayette National Bank Bldg., Uniontown, Pa. 15401. Illus., adv. Circ: 15,000.

Aud: Sa, Ga. *Rv:* M. *Jv:* B.

Caters to an audience which prefers the expensive, rare antiques to the more popular collectables that the average person enjoys. The editorial bias may change. Purchased by the publishers of *Antique Trader* in June, 1968, they state they hope to completely change and broaden the format, so as to increase the magazine's appeal—and its circulation. As the journal is now, its appeal would be to a limited number of patrons, even in a large public library. This is one to watch for future acquisition.

Antiques Magazine. 1922. m. $12. Alice Winchester. Straight Enterprises, 551 Fifth Ave., New York, N.Y. 10017. Illus., index, adv. Circ: 50,000. Microform: UM. Reprint: Abrahams.

Indexed: RG. *Bk. rev:* 4, short, signed. *Aud:* Sa, Ac, Jc. *Rv:* M. *Jv:* B.

All types of antiques, but with emphasis on furniture and furnishings, are treated authoritatively in this magazine. It is aimed primarily at collectors, but is also useful for social historians and interior designers. Emphasis is on American, English, and French styles of the 17th, 18th and 19th centuries, but decorative arts of many other periods and countries are occasionally considered. Also included in the eight or nine articles is information concerning preservation, collectors, exhibits and museums. Articles, which vary from four to eight pages, usually feature excellent photographs. This is not for the majority of collectors whose budgets are limited, or who are involved with mechanical antiques such as banks, guns, clocks, phonographs, etc. A luxury item suited for academic and larger public libraries only.

Appollo. See Art Section.

Auction. See Art Section.

Burlington Magazine. See Art Section.

The Connoisseur. See Art Section.

Hobbies; the magazine for collectors. 1931. m. $4. Pearl A. Reeder. Lightner Publishing Corp., 1006 S. Michigan Ave., Chicago, Ill. 60605. Illus., adv. Circ: 40,000. Microform: UM.

Indexed: MusicI, RG. *Bk. rev:* 4–7, 200–500 words. *Aud:* Ga, Ac, Jc, Sh. *Rv:* M. *Jv:* V.

Despite the title, primarily devoted to popular antiques. Monthly articles and departments cover such major interests as buttons, dolls, glass, books and the like. Guest articles are featured on less universally popular subjects. The writers are authoritative, usually collectors who know and care. In smaller libraries it has long been used as a pacifier; librarians insist that it satisfies a large number of collectors. There is no question that it is the most general magazine of its type, certainly one of the best, and should be in almost every library from public to university. Still, it should be augmented by at least one or two more specific antique journals.

Journal of Glass Studies. See Art Section.

Military Collector & Historian. 1949. q. Membership. Lee A. Wallace, Jr. Company of Military Historians, Inc., 287 Thayer St., Providence, R.I. 02906. Illus., adv. Microform: UM.

Bk. rev: 7–8, brief. *Aud:* Sa, Ac, Jc. *Rv:* H. *Jv:* B.

Despite the title, this journal is restricted to information on flags, uniforms, buttons, weapons, and other collectable items. Papers are well illustrated by photographs or drawings. Separate mimeographed sheets list new members of the Company as well as their special fields of interest, and an exchange for collectors is also included. There are advertisements of interest to the military collector. The editor reports his magazine leaves "the long battle, and biographical articles, to other publications such as *Military Affairs.* Only for specialized collections.

Spinning Wheel; a national magazine about antiques. 1946. 10/yr. $4.50. Marcia Ray. Marjorie M. Smith, Hanover, Pa. 17331. Illus., index, adv. Circ: 21,500. Microform: UM.

Bk. rev: 3–5, 100–350 words. *Aud:* Sa, Ga, Ac, Jc. *Rv:* M. *Jv:* A.

Not a well-known magazine, yet one of the best. Most articles, written by collectors who are perhaps amateur, but good writers, are accompanied by extremely fine, close-up photographs. Some however, give no clue as to authorship, a fact annoying not only for bibliographical purposes, but also to many collectors who commonly carry on correspondence with fellow hobbyists. In no other antiques magazine are there so many related subjects, e.g., "Colonial Williamsburg," "What is a Flea Market?," etc. This is particularly useful for beginning antique buffs. Since regular subject departments are not a part of *Spinning Wheel,* one never knows what to expect in the next issue. In a field where magazine subjects are all too often rigidly controlled by tradition, this is delightful. A fine second for any library that has *Hobbies* and wants another, inexpensive, complementary magazine.

Stained Glass. See Art Section.

Western Collector; pioneer for today's collector. 1963. m. $5. Paul F. Evans. Western World Publishers, Box 9166, San Francisco, Calif. 94129. Illus., index, adv. Circ: 7,000.

Bk. rev: 2–4, 200–400 words. *Aud:* Sa, Ga. *Rv:* L. *Jv:* C.

The title should not deceive. The publishers desire this to be as much a national magazine as any other in the field. Backed up by the usual array of departments dealing monthly with specific subjects such as coins, etc., the majority of the articles are occasional pieces, well written and usually accompanied by good photographs. One might hope that the paper used be improved, as it does not do the photographs credit. Also, the *Reader's Digest* size of the periodical makes this the dwarf of the antique publications. It appears to be a periodical still in the process of growing, not quite worth a subscription for most libraries, but definitely on the way.

ARCHITECTURE

Indexes and Abstracts

Applied Science and Technology Index, Art Index, British Humanities Index, British Technology Index, Canadian Periodical Index, Engineering Index, Public Affairs Information Service, Readers' Guide to Periodical Literature. (For annotations, see Indexes and Abstracts Section.)

American Builder. 1867. m. $6. Joseph W. Kizzia. Simmons-Boardman Publishing Corp., 30 Church St., New York, N.Y. 10007. Illus., index, adv. Circ: 117,632. Microform: UM. Reprint: Abrahams.

Aud: Sa, Ac. *Rv:* M. *Jv:* B.

Advises builders on such subjects as land planning, design, merchandising, new markets, construction technology and labor. Particular emphasis is placed on individual homes, housing developments, townhouses and low-rise apartment projects. There is an annual design competition for single-family homes and multi-family projects. A convenient list of available literature pertaining to building materials and products. Only for the large business or architectural collection.

American Institute of Architects. Journal. 1944. m. $5 (Qualified subscribers). Robert E. Koehler. The Amer. Inst. of Architects, The Octagon, 1725 New York Ave., N.W., Washington, D.C. 20006. Illus., index, adv. Circ: 25,700. Microform: UM.

Indexed: ArtI. *Bk. rev:* 7–8 full column, signed and unsigned book reviews. *Aud:* Sa, Ac. *Rv:* H. *Jv:* B.

A professional journal for the architect and the student. Articles are written by well-known architects and related professionals and reflect the contemporary architects' concern with the building as an integral part of the total environment. "Unfinished Business" page allows refutation of previous essays. "Architects Information Service" provides a convenient way for readers to obtain reprints of articles in current and earlier issues and other pertinent information concerning the AIA. Manufacturers technical data can also be obtained in this easy way. Only for architectural collections.

Architectural Digest. See Home Section.

Architectural Forum. 1892. 10/yr. $12; $6 to students and faculty members of accredited schools of architecture. Peter Blake. Urban America, Inc., 111 W. 57th St., New York, N.Y. 10019. Illus., index, adv. Circ: 40,000. Microform: UM. Reprint: Johnson, Abrahams.

Indexed: ArtI, ASTI, PAIS, RG. *Bk. rev:* 5–6, lengthy, signed. *Aud:* Ga, Sa, Ac, Jc. *Rv:* H. *Jv:* A.

Published by Urban America, Inc., a nationwide, nonprofit educational organization with the goal of improving the total urban environment. In accordance with Urban America's purpose, this well-illustrated publication focuses interest on the physical aspects of building as a part of the whole community, rather than on the individual, isolated structure. Highly readable articles occasionally compare the problems of ancient buildings and villages to modern concepts. The monthly review of notable buildings and a review of events and ideas are regular features. One of three basic architecture magazines for public and academic libraries. See concluding note for *Architectural Record.*

Architectural Record. 1891. m. $5.50. Emerson Goble. McGraw-Hill, Inc., 330 W. 42nd St., New York, N.Y. 10036. Illus., index, adv. Circ: 48,000. Microform: UM. Reprint: Abrahams.

Indexed: ArtI, ASTI, EngI, RG. *Bk. rev:* 2–3 brief, signed. *Aud:* Ga, Sa, Ac, Jc. *Rv:* H. *Jv:* V.

A well-illustrated magazine which contains news and features on building design and technology covering all types of buildings; the latest construction methods and materials, as well as techniques of managing and professional practice. Two-thirds of each issue is composed of advertisements for building materials and building services. While this is primarily for architects and engineers, the abundant illustrations, the frequent emphasis on homes, and the well written articles make it an ideal introduction to architecture for interested laymen. Along with *Architectural Forum* and *Progressive Architecture,* one of three general architecture magazines for all medium to large public and academic libraries. Each fills a different role, with *Architectural Record* being the most general of the trio, hence the most suitable for the average library which can take only one or two magazines in the area. Given this limited choice, the librarian might well consider a more specialized type such as *Domus* for a second acquisition.

The Architectural Review. 1897. m. $10.50. J. M. Richards. Architectural Press Ltd., 13 Queen Anne's Gate, Westminster, London S.W.1. Illus., adv. Circ: 12,275. Microform: UM.

Indexed: ArtI, BritHum, BritTech. *Bk. rev:* Various number, lengths, signed. *Aud:* Sa, Ac. *Rv:* H. *Jv:* B.

One of the world's leading architectural magazines, particularly of value for its stress on modern, often avant-garde trends. While directed to the professional architect and student, the excellent illustrations and text give it an added dimension for the interested layman. The scope is international, although there is considerable emphasis on English building, landscape architecture, and interior design. Also, each issue usually features one or two articles on modern painting and sculpture and furniture, particularly as related to trends in architecture. Occasional issues on special subjects give it particularly high reference value. Definitely a second or third choice in larger academic and junior college libraries, and a first where there is any effort to have a representative architectural collection. The same firm issues *The Architect's Journal* (1895. w. $15.), which provides up-to-date news, reviews and comments on more professionally oriented architectural matters. It is particularly valuable for the technical information section with its detailed cost analyses and studies of specific buildings. The *Journal,* being a more technical approach, is only for the large architecture collection.

Architecture Canada. 1924. m. $7. Walter Bowker. Royal Architectural Inst. of Canada, 160 Eglinton Ave., E., Tor., 12. Illus., index, adv. Circ: 5,279.

Indexed: CanI. *Bk. rev:* 2, 500 words, signed. *Aud:* Sa, Ac. *Rv:* M. *Jv:* B.

The journal of the Royal Architectural Institute of Canada, it averages 40 pages and features articles on the arts allied to architecture, i.e., sculpture, murals, glass, etc. There are review sections on national and international architecture, text and illustrated sections on housing, planning, schools, etc. Work related to schools and Canadian architecture is reported. Although of primary interest to the professional architect, the coverage of related fields gives this an added dimension for general art collections. Should be in all Canadian academic libraries and many medium to large collections in the United States.

Art Bulletin. See Art Section.

Design (American). See Art Section.

Design (English). See Art Section.

Design News. See Art Section.

Domus; architettura arrademanto arte. 1928. m. $23. Editorial Domus, Via Monte di Pietà 15, 20121 Milan, Italy. Illus., adv.

Indexed: ArtI. *Bk. rev:* 1–2, 250–500 words. *Aud:* Sa, Ac. *Rv:* H. *Jv:* A.

A magazine of architecture, interiors and art, this 60- to 70-page Italian periodical is one of the most sumptuously illustrated of any architectural journal. There are a number of well written articles on all aspects of architecture and art, and each is illustrated with oversized black and white and colored photographs. Unlike several of the American entries, it is devoted as much to furniture, graphic arts and better living through new design as to actual building. And "new" is the key word, for the emphasis is definitely *avant-garde* and modern, often presenting ideas which do not pop up in America for months or years after. Except for a few summaries in French and English, the whole is in Italian. Still, the photographs carry most of the message and it is a basic magazine for any library or individual interested in architecture. See concluding statement for *Architectural Record.*

Historic Preservation. 1949. q. Membership; $3. to libraries. Helen Duprey Bullock. National Trust for Historic Preservation, 748 Jackson Place, N.W., Washington, D.C. 20006. Illus., index. Circ: 13,000.

Aud: Ga, Ac, Jc, Sh. *Rv:* M. *Jv:* B.

A publication of the National Trust for Historic Preservation, chartered by an Act of Congress "to facilitate public participation in the preservation of sites, buildings, and objects of national significance or by providing a national trust for historic preservation." Each issue contains 9–10 well-illustrated, brief essays on the preservation or restoration of historic landmarks or natural sites, and presents their historic background in a well-written and readable style. Of interest to general adult students and instructors of architecture and history. See also, *Society of Architectural Historians. Journal.*

House and Home. 1952. m. $6. Richard W. O'Neill. McGraw-Hill, Inc., 330 W. 42nd St., New York, N.Y. 10036. Illus., index, adv. Circ: 115,000. Microform: UM. Reprint: Abrahams.

Aud: Sa, Ac. *Rv:* M. *Jv:* B.

The marketing and management publication of the housing industry, this is a large, glossy, photograph-filled periodical designed to describe and illustrate trends in housing. Builders, investors, realtors, mortgage lenders, and community planners will find the articles readable. Ideas and advice are offered about planning, building, and financing of individual homes and housing developments. Building

successes as well as failures are frequent subject matter. Advertisements are numerous and offer information about new building materials and products. For large business and architecture collections.

Interior Design. See Home Section.

The Japan Architect. 1925. m. $15. Yasugoro Yoshioka. Shinkenchikusha Co., Ltd., 31–2, 2-chome Yushima Bunkyo-ku, Tokyo, Japan. Illus., adv. Circ: 15,000.

Bk. rev: 2–3, full page, signed. *Aud:* Sa, Ac. *Rv:* H. *Jv:* B.

Introduces the imaginative and exciting architecture of modern Japan. Individual homes, housing complexes, industrial, office, ecclesiastic and national buildings are described in detail and photographed from all elevations. The articles are unusually long (10–20 pages) and the illustrations are generous and excellent. There are fewer advertisements than found in American magazines of this type. The publisher holds an annual competition for superior designs in building (the "ideal home" was the subject assigned in 1967). Text is in English with summaries in Spanish. Along with *Domus,* an excellent second or third choice for the library which is not specialized, but which wishes to break out of the limits of general American architectural magazines. A necessary addition for all medium to large architecture collections.

Landscape Architecture. 1910. q. $6. Grady Clay. Publications Board, Amer. Soc. of Landscape Architects, Schuster Bldg., 1500 Bardstown Rd., Louisville, Ky. 40205. Illus., adv. Circ: 7,600. Reprint: Abrahams.

Indexed: ArtI, PAIS. *Bk. rev:* 5, various lengths, signed. *Aud:* Sa, Ac. *Rv:* H. *Jv:* B.

Devoted to all aspects of landscape architecture from national park planning to private gardens. The some 15 articles per issue cover land improvement, city planning, park and natural resource design, and gardens about the home. Emphasis is on the larger municipal and national developments, and the whole is primarily for the professional whether he be a landscape architect, city planner or private developer. Because of the many excellent illustrations it will have some interest for the conservationist and the enthusiastic gardener. Regular departments include a section on designing with plants, and critiques of recent work in the field. A useful addition for business, conservation, architecture and some gardening collections in medium to large public and academic libraries.

Mobilia. See Art Section.

Progressive Architecture. 1920. m. $5. Jan C. Rowan. Reinhold Publishing Corp., 430 Park Ave., New York, N.Y. 10022. Illus., adv. Circ: 65,000. Microform: UM.

Indexed: ASTI, ArtI, ArchI. *Bk. rev:* 3–4, ½ to full page. *Aud:* Sa, Ac. *Rv:* M. *Jv:* A.

Along with *Architectural Forum* and *Architectural Record,* one of the three general magazines in its field. Many architects and even lay readers prefer it because of the emphasis on modern work (as the title implies) and the international scene. The articles tend to be technical, but are well illustrated, and this latter feature gives it particular value for the interested layman. There is some emphasis, too, on the social and ethical responsibilities of the architect and the builder. All aspects are covered from private homes to large industrial complexes and schools. Although written for the professional architect and the student, should be considered for general collections in medium to large public and academic libraries. See concluding comments for *Architectural Record*.

Society of Architectural Historians. Journal. 1940. q. Membership. Robert Branner. c/o Mrs. Rosann S. Berry, Box 94, Media, Pa. 19063. Illus., index, adv. Circ: 3,000. Microform: UM. Reprint: Johnson, Abrahams.

Indexed: ArtI. *Bk. rev:* 5–6, full page, signed. *Aud:* Ga, Ac. *Rv:* M. *Jv:* B.

Membership in the Society is open to all who are interested in furthering the study, enjoyment, and preservation of architecture and its related arts. There are well-illustrated, scholarly, but readable articles (both brief and lengthy) devoted to architectural history, theory, and aesthetics of extant architecture in Europe and America. An allied journal is *Historic Preservation*. Both will be needed in large architectural and historical collections, but of the two, *Historic Preservation* probably will be of most interest to the average layman; therefore, it should be considered by any size of type library where there is an interest in the field.

ART

Indexes and Abstracts

Art Index, British Humanities Index, British Technology Index, Education Index, Index Medicus, Music Index, Psychological Abstracts, Readers' Guide to Periodical Literature. (For annotations, see Indexes and Abstracts Section.)

African Forum. See African Studies Section.

American Artist. 1937. m. (Sept.–June). $8. Norman Kent. Billboard Publishing Co., Inc., 165 W. 46th St., New York, N.Y. 10036. Illus., index, adv. Circ: 55,000. Microform: UM. Reprint: Abrahams.

Indexed: ArtI, PAIS, RG. *Bk. rev:* 3–4 short, signed. *Aud:* Ga, Ht, Et. *Rv:* M. *Jv:* B.

A how-to-do-it approach to art for teachers and students. Articles run the gamut from early to contemporary American artists and describe their subject matter, style, and technique. The essays are written by the professional staff of the magazine, or by the artists, and are informal and descriptive rather than critical. The illustrations are clear and adequate to elucidate the topic and there are frequent profiles of past and present American artists. News of art

competitions and scholarships should interest art students. The advertisements are not excessive and are a good source of information about art materials. Aimed at teachers and a general audience, the magazine is of little value for the scholar or the serious art student. A useful second choice in elementary through high school professional collections, but way down the list for general art collections in public or academic libraries. See concluding remarks for *Art Education*.

Apollo; the international magazine of art and antiques. 1925. m. $24. Denys Sutton. Apollo Pubns., Inc., 720 Fifth Ave., New York, N.Y. 10019. Illus., index, adv. Circ: 14,200. Microform: UM.

Indexed: ArtI, BritHum. *Bk. rev:* 5–7 full page, signed. *Aud:* Sa, Ac. *Rv:* M. *Jv:* B.

This British magazine is an essential and expanding encyclopedia for collectors and connoisseurs of art and antiques of all periods throughout the world. Magnificently illustrated biographical essays and criticisms about artists and their works, on individual works of art, exhibitions, museums and collections are written by experts in their fields. Notes on sales and auctions. Advertisements of galleries, auctioneers and art dealers account for half of the magazine's bulk, 180–200 pages in each issue. In this same area, a periodical of similar worth is *The Connoisseur*. Choosing between one or the other depends primarily upon the size of the budget and the library. Except for large art collections, both are luxuries.

Art and Auctions; international art dealers and collectors guide. Fortnightly. $11.50. Van Kouteren's Publishing Co., Ltd., 40 St. Jobsweg, Rotterdam, Netherlands. Illus., index, adv.

Aud: Sa, Ac. *Rv:* M. *Jv:* B.

The purpose of this international journal is to announce forthcoming art auctions in America and Europe, and after the sales to present the prices for the more important objects of art sold. There are an average of ten black and white illustrations per issue, and while advertising is important, the greatest part is text. A useful feature is the semi-annual index which classifies sales items under the name of the painter and his work. Only for large, specialized collections, the less expensive, more general *Auction* being a better bet for smaller libraries.

Art and Literature. 1964. q. $8. S.E.L.A., 2 Chemin des Trois-Rois, Lausanne, Switzerland. Illus. Circ: 5,000.

Aud: Ga, Sa, Ac. *Rv:* M. *Jv:* B.

A distinguished English-language review of the arts. Emphasis is on avant-garde painting and writing, and much of the material is experimental. However, this is not simply another eclectic magazine. Contributors such as Jean Genet, Cyril Connolly, John Cage, Niccolo Tucci, Stephen Spender and Nelly Sachs give it a major dimension for any library seeking to keep up with current developments in literature and art. Thanks to its prominent contributors and excellent editing, it has become a standard magazine among Europeans and Americans involved with the frontiers of art. Should be found in larger academic and public library collections.

Art Bulletin. 1913. q. Membership. H. W. Janson. College Art Assn. of America, 432 Park Ave. S., New York, N.Y. 10016. Illus. Circ: 4,500. Microform: UM. Reprint: Abrahams.

Indexed: ArtI. *Bk. rev:* 12–20, various lengths, signed. *Aud:* Sa, Ac, Jc. *Rv:* H. *Jv:* B.

Brings serious, learned articles written by faculty members of the Association to students of art history. Its scope includes all facets and periods of the fine arts, from the most esoteric subjects to architecture. The articles are long and well documented studies of aesthetics and theory, with excellent illustrations and drawings. This and *Art Quarterly* are the two major magazines devoted to art history in America, and one or both should be found in larger art collections. See also, *Art Journal.*

Art Direction; the magazine of visual communication, serves the field of advertising art, photography, typography and related graphic arts field. 1950. m. $8. Ralph Thurlow. Advertising Trade Pubns., 19 W. 44th St., New York, N.Y. 10036. Illus., adv. Circ: 12,558. Microform: UM.

Bk. rev: 10, 100 words. *Aud:* Sa, Ac, Jc, Sh, Ht. *Rv:* M. *Jv:* B.

A basic magazine for anyone involved with advertising art. A typical issue includes some 300 pictures and editorial material on every aspect of the subject from illustration, typography and photography to design of posters, television commercials, packaging, direct mail pieces and the like. Most of this will be of interest to the student from high school on up, albeit special departments (taxes, business activity, accounting, legal advice, news of people and events) are directed at the professional.

Art Education. 1948. 10/yr. Membership (Non-members, $5). Charles M. Dorn. National Art Education Assn., 1201 16th St., N.W., Washington, D.C. 20036. Illus., adv. Circ: 9,519. Reprint: Kraus.

Indexed: EdI. *Bk. rev:* 7–8, short, signed. *Aud:* Ac, Jc, Ht, Et. *Rv:* H. *Jv:* B.

One of a number of magazines geared specifically for the art teacher, but not for the layman, artist or serious student of art. Nor for use by students, although some of the periodicals in this field are useful as springboards for classroom projects. *Art Education* deals with the theory and methodology for teaching of art in elementary through high schools. The material tends to be scholarly, albeit well within the grasp of the average teacher. Its particular value is for its studies of the psychology of art in relation to children and for its attention to aesthetics and the theory of

art. There are illustrations both of children's work and of work by recognized artists. All schools should include this in their professional collections, and schools of education in junior colleges and universities will also want to subscribe.

At the more practical, how-to-do-it level, a second or first choice (depending upon need) would be *Arts and Activities, School Arts Magazine* or possibly *Design* and *Artist Junior. Everyday Art* is slight, yet a useful secondary consideration, and *American Artist, Art Journal* and *Bulletin of Art Therapy* are for more specialized situations. It cannot be emphasized too much that all of these are for teachers and adults, not for the students who should be given an opportunity to meet art through the better illustrated, more meaningful adult magazines such as *Art in America.* Granted, the text may be over their heads, but is art a matter of reading or of seeing?

Art in America. 1913. bi-m. $15. Jean Lipman. Art in America Co., Inc., 635 Madison Ave., New York, N.Y. 10022. Illus., adv. Circ: 43,000. Microform: UM. Reprint: AMS, Abrahams.

Indexed: ArtI, RG. *Bk. rev:* 3–4, signed. *Aud:* Sa, Ga, Ac, Jc, Sh. *Rv:* H. *Jv:* V.

The single best general art magazine published in America, this is primarily concerned with the visual arts. It is international in scope, and while there are selected retrospective and historical articles, the emphasis is on contemporary art. Each number, from 128 to 144 pages, features an average of 25 full color plates and scores of black and white reproductions and photographs. Printed on high grade paper, the format is as outstanding as the contents. Painting, sculpture, architecture, design and photography are the magazine's main concerns, and the critics writing on these subjects are among the best in the world—Harold Rosenberg, Elizabeth Hardwick, John Canaday, Brian O'Doherty, Barbara Rose. The style is imaginative, intellectual and always challenging.

Compared with other general art magazines, it is more expensive, yet wider in scope than the equally excellent *Artforum;* more appealing to the layman than the more esoteric *Art International;* better edited and written than *Art News* or *Arts Magazine;* and better suited to American audiences than *Studio International.* Among all of these general periodicals, the average small public library would subscribe first to *Art in America;* medium to large public libraries will select it plus either *Artforum* or *Art International,* in that order. Academic libraries, including the junior college with any kind of an art program, should have all three. Given this general base, the librarian will then wish to explore more specialized works.

High school libraries (not to mention elementary school libraries) should consider *Art in America,* if only for the illustrations, as a first choice. What follows depends upon curriculum, but hopefully the selection will be broader than the standard educational art magazines such as *School Arts.* See concluding comments for *Art Education.*

Art International. 1956. 10/yr. $15. James Fitzsimmons, Via Maraini 17-A, Lugano, Switz. Illus., adv. Circ: 16,500. Microform: UM.

Indexed: ArtI. *Bk. rev:* Various numbers, lengths. *Aud:* Sa, Ac, Jc. *Rv:* H. *Jv:* A.

Considered by many to be the world's leading exponent of contemporary art, this is published in four languages, French, German, Italian, and English. The reproductions are among the finest found in any art magazine, and the articles represent a high level of scholarship matched by equally high standards of literary style. Coverage is international, but in view of trends in art during the past decade, a good amount of the journal is often given over to American art and artists. Should be a first choice for almost any medium to large library, regardless of type. See concluding remarks for *Art in America.*

Art Journal. 1941. q. $5. Henry R. Hope. College Art Assn. of America, 432 Park Ave. S., New York, N.Y. 10016. Illus., index, adv. Circ: 9,000. Microform: UM.

Indexed: ArtI. *Bk. rev:* 8–12, 2–3 pages, signed. *Aud:* Sa, Ac, Jc. *Rv:* M. *Jv:* B.

The major journal devoted to adult level art education. Reports on the College Art Association of America and brings news of exhibitions, recent acquisitions, and additional art buildings on American college and university campuses. Each issue carries news about art educators and some of the problems of teaching the many facets of art in higher education. Several serious, scholarly articles on aesthetics and criticism are included and black and white photographs illustrate the points of interest. A required addition for any junior college or college art collection.

Art News. 1902. m. (Sept.–May); q. (June–Aug.). $11.50. Thomas B. Hess. Newsweek, Inc., 444 Madison Ave., New York, N.Y. 10022. Illus., adv. Circ: 12,000. Microform: UM. Reprint: Abrahams.

Indexed: ArtI, RG. *Aud:* Ga, Ac, Jc, Sh. *Rv:* H. *Jv:* A.

Oldest of the American magazines on art. Serious, well-written criticisms of art movements, works of individual artists, special collections, and exhibitions of interest to the art collector, as well as to artists and to students. Illustrations in black and white and color. Good exhibition calendar is listed by the artist's name. News of important auctions of art collections. Notes on art from London, Chicago, San Francisco, and New York. Information on competitions and scholarships, suggestions on where and when to exhibit, and about new materials is of special concern to the art student. While this remains one of the best general art magazines, more adventuresome librarians might try other lesser known periodicals—particularly those such as *Artforum* (*q.v.*) which stress the modern movements. See concluding remarks for *Art in America.*

The Art Quarterly. 1938. q. $9. The Art Quarterly, Founders Soc., Detroit Inst. of Arts, 5200 Woodward Ave.,

Detroit, Mich. 48202. Illus., adv. Microform: UM. Reprint: Johnson, Abrahams.

Indexed: ArtI. *Bk. rev:* 12–13 brief, signed. *Aud:* Sa, Ac, Rv:* H. *Jv:* B.

Contains lengthy, historical articles on art of all periods, well documented and well illustrated. The magazine has a "Consultative Committee" of some of the most esteemed art scholars in the country. Regular checklist, notes, and illustrations about recent acquisitions of American and Canadian museums and universities offer scholarly comment for art historians, museum curators, dealers, and galleries. Only for larger art collections, but should be a dual selection with *Art Bulletin.*

Art Scene. 1967. m (bi-m, July–Aug.; Dec.–Jan.). $5. Art Scene Co., 200 E. Ontario, Chicago, Ill. 60611. Illus., adv.

Aud: Sa, Ac. *Rv:* M. *Jv:* B.

Primarily a running calendar of events in the Chicago (and environs) art world, each 34- to 40-page issue features articles on artists and their work in the area. Of more than local interest because of the excellent black and white illustrations, the perceptive criticism of both local and international artists, and the wide interpretation of art, including everything from traditional painting and sculpture to handicrafts. A necessary addition to libraries within 200 or 300 miles of Chicago, and should be considered by all large art libraries.

Artforum. 1962. m. $10. Philip Leider. Charles Cowles, 723½ N. La Cienega Blvd., Los Angeles, Calif. 90069. Illus., adv. Circ: 12,000.

Indexed: ArtI. *Bk. rev:* Occasional, lengthy, signed. *Aud:* Ga, Ac, Jc, Sh. *Rv:* H. *Jv:* V.

While some attention is given to retrospective work, the emphasis in this publication is on all forms of 20th century art. Students of art history will find thoughtful analyses and criticisms of contemporary art, as well as film reviews. This is the only popular magazine to devote so much space to profound discussions of aesthetics and theory. The articles are by well-known young critics, many of them formerly with *Art International.* All of the studies are generously illustrated by color and black and white photographs. Formerly especially interested in West Coast art and artists, emphasis has switched, since 1964, to a national orientation. The attention to younger artists and current movements makes this particularly suitable for high school students with a serious interest in art. Among the first choices for any kind of library. See concluding remarks for *Art in America.*

The Artist. 1931. m. $8. Frederick Parkinson. Artist Publishing Corp., 155 W. 15th St., New York, N.Y. 10011. Illus., index, adv. Circ: 21,500. Microform: UM. Reprint: Abrahams.

Aud: Ga, Ht. *Rv:* L. *Jv:* C.

Well-illustrated, both in color and black and white, articles by artists and well-known successful teachers offer practical advice on technique, composition, use of media, color mixing, and practical experience. While useful for the amateur, way down the list for most libraries.

Artist Junior. 1959. m. (Oct.–April, except Dec.). $1. Rachel Baker. 1346 Chapel St., New Haven, Conn. 06511.

Aud: E, Jh, Et, Ht. *Rv:* M. *Jv:* B.

The art magazine for the classroom, is devoted entirely to developing art appreciation in the adolescent. Each issue concerns itself with a type or school of painting, or a principal of art or element of design such as line, color, composition, etc. At least three reproductions in full color plus three or four black and white pictures are featured along with explanatory notes about the artist and his style. This periodical, folder-like in format, consists of eight glossy pages and is sturdy enough to stand up under library circulation. However, this is a teaching tool and not one for casual use by the student. A useful secondary magazine for elementary and junior high schools. See remarks for *Art Education.*

Artist's Proof. 1961. ann. Membership, $10 (Non-members, $12.50). Fritz Eichenberg. Pratt Graphic Art Center, 831 Broadway, New York, N.Y. 10003. Illus., adv. Circ: 5,000. Microform: UM.

Indexed: ArtI. *Aud:* Sa, Ac, Jc, Sh, Ht, Et. *Rv:* M. *Jv:* B.

Edited by one of the world's finest graphic artists, this annual volume is the "only existing publication devoted exclusively to the contemporary print and to its creators." It is definitely aimed at the serious student and not the dabbler. The scope is international, the emphasis is progressive, and contemporary trends are favored. The novel feature is that it allows artists to speak for themselves rather than to be interpreted by critics or art historians. The reproductions are excellent. Highly recommended for elementary and high school teachers, high school students and academic libraries. Public libraries, too, will find a ready audience for this work.

Arts and Activities; creative activities for the classroom. 1937. m. (Sept.–June). $7. Mary C. Emerson. Publisher's Development Corp., 8150 N. Central Park Blvd., Skokie, Ill. 60076. Illus., index, adv. Circ: 35,000.

Indexed: EdI. *Bk. rev:* Notes. *Aud:* Ac, Jc, Et, Ht. *Rv:* H. *Jv:* A.

Along with *Design* and *School Arts,* one of the basic do-it-yourself arts magazines for teachers in elementary and junior high schools. It is particularly useful at the elementary level. Although the only one of the three not indexed in *Readers' Guide,* it is probably a first choice for teachers, particularly those without formal art training. The eight to ten articles are well illustrated, usually with children's art—the ideas for classroom activities seem to be a trifle more imaginative than found in the competitors—and

the emphasis is on the average, not the ideal, classroom situation, where there is often a lack of space, equipment, and even encouragement. There are the usual articles on art education—although not as many as found in *School Arts*—news of the profession, new products and audio-visual aids. The book reviews tend to be short notes, although from time to time there are longer reviews. A useful feature is the section given over to art appreciation which gives the type of information on a masterwork which the teacher can pass on to the student. Another regular department includes outstanding child art. Along with *Design* and *School Arts* this is primarily a magazine to be used by the teacher with the students. It is not for the student—a fine point which is often overlooked in recommended lists of children's magazines.

Arts Magazine. 1926. m. (Nov.–June); bi-m. (Sept.–Oct.). $9.50 (including yearbook, $15.45). Joseph J. Akston. Art Digest, Inc., 41 E. 57th St., New York, N.Y. 10022. Illus., adv. Circ: 25,000.

Indexed: ArtI. *Bk. rev:* 3–4 brief, signed. *Aud:* Ga, Ac, Jc, Sh. *Rv:* M. *Jv:* B.

Respects all points of view and periods of the art world, but has special appeal to those who want to be informed on the latest in contemporary art. The news about the avant-garde is given the most notice and is well-illustrated by both colored and black and white plates. Includes auction news, art market news, exhibition notices, and summaries of art news from abroad. The annual yearbook is familiar to many readers as it features current movements, particular artists and earlier periods. It is well-illustrated, and geared for a more popular audience than the regular issues of the magazine. A useful general art magazine for medium to large collections. See concluding remarks for *Art in America.*

Aspen; a magazine that comes in a box with each article designed as a separate booklet. 1965. 6/yr. $16. Phyllis Johnson. P.O. Box 205, Village Station, New York, N.Y. 10014. Illus., adv. Circ: 20,000.

Aud: Ga, Ac, Jc, Sh. *Rv:* M. *Jv:* B.

Probably the most distinctive general magazine now published in the United States. It is multi-media in every sense. Each issue comes in a box and highlights a given area of modern thought. A double spring number, for example, included four 8mm art and underground films; five records of readings by Marcel Duchamp, William Burroughs, Alain Robbe-Grillet, Samuel Beckett and Merce Cunningham; a cardboard sculpture and a regular typed mag with essays on the arts. Another special "Pop/Underground" number was edited by Andy Warhol and issued in a Fab box. While there is a surprising continuity to what first seems a jumble, and the contributions are good and always imaginative, the overall effect is a controlled happening rather than a magazine. But the editors are no fools, and the contents are representative of some of America's best—or, if you will, worst—thinking. It is a headache for the tidy type of personality, a joy for the creative, particularly the high school student who has difficulty relating to the average magazine. See also, *S.M.S.*

Auction. 1967. m. (Sept.–June). $2. Linda Rosenkrantz. Parke-Bernet Galleries, Inc., 98 Madison Ave., New York, N.Y. 10021. Illus., index, adv.

Bk. rev: 5–10, 150–500 words, signed. *Aud:* Sa, Ga, Ac. *Rv:* M. *Jv:* B.

A 24-page illustrated magazine which generally highlights coming and past auctions at Parke-Bernet and its English co-partner, Sotheby's of London. However, it is more than a newsletter. Each issue features two or three articles, frequently documented, on antiques, art, books, furniture and other matters of interest to the rich collector. Book reviews cover the latest works on antiques, art, and book collecting. An excellent buy for libraries with a limited budget, and required for larger libraries.

Bulletin of Art Therapy; art in education, rehabilitation and psychotherapy. 1961. q. $5. Elinor Ulman. 634 A St., S.E., Washington, D.C. 20003. Illus., index. Circ: 750. Microform: UM.

Indexed: IMed, PsyAb. *Bk. rev:* 6, 1,000 words, signed. *Aud:* Sa, Ac, Ht, Et. *Rv:* M. *Jv:* B.

A forum for professional art therapists, teachers, psychologists, psychiatrists, and others interested in art and its place in the rehabilitation of adults and children. While a highly specialized journal, it offers a new avenue to understanding for both elementary and secondary school art teachers. The two to four articles "include new theoretical formulations, reports of research, descriptions of actual programs, news of opportunities for training and of international developments in the field." Material is concerned with all of the visual arts. A required magazine for larger libraries, and well worth trying in the smaller professional school collection.

The Burlington Magazine. 1903. m. $20. Benedict Nicolson. Burlington Magazine Pubns. Ltd., 258 Gray's Inn Rd., London W.C. 1. Illus., index, adv. Reprint: Kraus.

Indexed: ArtI, BritHum. *Bk. rev:* 6–8, lengthy, signed. *Aud:* Sa, Ac, Jc. *Rv:* M. *Jv:* B.

A basic British art magazine which covers the entire field of art from prehistory to present day in articles of value to the art collector, dealer, scholar, and the knowledgeable museum-goer. Well-illustrated and documented studies on paintings, drawings, and sculpture, and the applied arts. Features include news of recent museum acquisitions, current and forthcoming international exhibitions. The worldwide emphasis makes this one of the standard art magazines in the field, but the high price and English base of publication somewhat limits its use in all but the larger academic art collections.

Carnegie Magazine; dedicated to literature, science, art and music. 1927. 10/yr. $2. James M. Bovard. Carnegie Inst. & Carnegie Library of Pittsburgh, 4400 Forbes Ave., Pittsburgh, Pa. 15213. Illus., index, adv. Circ: 10,000.

Aud: Ga, Ac, Jc. *Rv:* L. *Jv:* B.

Extends the program of the Carnegie Institute and Carnegie Library of Pittsburgh. Each issue includes about ten articles on science, art, literature and music. Holdings of the Institute in the fields of art and natural history form the basis of articles with historical and background material included. Exhibits, festivals, and items of civic improvement and local history are often included. Articles are of high literary quality. Most are signed, and contributors represent the Institute and Library staff and other experts. Illustrations consist of black and white photos and occasional sketches. The broad scope gives it added appeal for all large public and academic libraries.

The Connoisseur. 1901. ann. $16. L. G. G. Ramsey. Joseph T. Butler, 269 Broadway, Dobbs Ferry, N.Y. 10522. Illus., adv. Microform: Mc. Reprint: Abrahams.

Indexed: ArtI, BritHum. *Bk. rev:* 8–10, short to long, signed. *Aud:* Ga, Ac, Jc. *Rv:* M. *Jv:* B.

Connoisseurs and collectors of international works of art of all periods, antique furniture, silver, porcelain, and paintings will be interested in this magazine. Contains authoritative articles, illustrated in color and monochrome, on individual works of art, special collections, biographies of artists, and contemporary art. More than half of each issue is composed of advertisements of art dealers and galleries, European and American. Includes sales news, exhibition news. Special section on exhibitions and recent acquisitions by American museums. While written for the wealthy collector, the illustrations and advertisements make this useful for both dreamer and art enthusiast. See also, *Apollo.*

Craft Horizons. See Crafts and Hobbies Section.

Design. 1949. m. $8.25. J. E. Blake. Council of Industrial Design, The Design Center, 28 Haymarket, London S.W. 1. Illus., index, adv. Microform: UM.

Indexed: ArtI, BritTech. *Aud:* Sa, Ac, Jc. *Rv:* H. *Jv:* B.

Not to be confused with the American magazine of the same name. It aims to promote excellence of design in everything produced by industry, from jewelry to the most mundane household objects. The magazine consists mainly of photographs and descriptions of products which have been chosen for their superior design. Short profiles of industrial designers, and articles about special aspects of business are written by experts in design and industry. News of winners of design competitions, educational progress in design, industrial fairs and exhibitions, and forecasts of the market. Of interest to designers, manufacturers, and students in this field.

Design; the magazine of creative art, for teachers, artists & craftsmen. 1899. bi-m. Beurt R. Ser Vaas. Review Publishing Co., Inc., 1100 Waterway Blvd., Indianapolis, Ind. 46207. Illus., adv. Circ: 8,000. Microform: UM.

Indexed: RG. *Bk. rev:* Notes. *Aud:* Ac, Jc, Ht, Et. *Rv:* H. *Jv:* B.

A useful magazine of practical suggestions for teachers of art, from elementary school through college, interested in pottery, glass, textiles, painting, and sculpture. Deals with art appreciation, instructions, and hints on how to improve techniques and skills used in various crafts. Announcements of forthcoming art exhibits. Competition news. Emphasis is on teaching and differs from the publisher's other magazine *Craft Horizons* which is primarily for the student. Next to *School Arts Magazine,* a useful secondary purchase for elementary and secondary schools, and should be in all school of education collections.

Design News; the design engineer's idea magazine. bi-m. $20. K. F. Kircher. Cahners Publishing Co., Inc. 3375 S. Bannock St., Englewood, Colo. 80110. Circ: 85,026.

Aud: Sa, Ac. *Rv:* H. *Jv:* B.

Primarily for the professional design engineer. Covers every aspect of design from small items to complete machinery. Averaging some 48 short articles per issue, the magazine "provides a wide range of proven design ideas in a concise, graphic form." All articles are illustrated, with four colors used for "perspective" pieces and "special reports." Only for specialized collections.

Design Quarterly. 1946. q. $3.50. Peter Seitz. Walker Art Center, 1710 Lyndale Ave. S., Minneapolis, Minn. 55403. Illus. Circ: 6,000. Microform: UM.

Indexed: ArtI, ICSIDBibl. *Aud:* Ga, Ac, Jc, Sh, Jh, Ht, Et. *Rv:* M. *Jv:* B.

Each issue presents a symposium upon a given theme from the design field. "The subject is previously agreed upon by the writer and editor and written especially for our publication." Writers are authorities in the field. The magazine is particularly valuable for its black and white illustrations—between 55 and 90 for a single number, even more for a double issue. It averages 32 to 36 pages (48–64 for a double number) and does not include advertisements. A useful journal for student, teacher and the professional designer.

Detroit Institute of Arts. Bulletin. 1919. q. $1. 5200 Woodward Ave., Detroit, Mich. 48202. Illus., index. Circ: 5,500. Microform: UM.

Indexed: ArtI. *Aud:* Ga, Ac, Jc. Sh. *Rv:* M. *Jv:* B.

A handsomely printed and illustrated 40- to 50-page report on activities of the Detroit Institute of Art, this covers all phases of the subject from the traditional to the modern. There are usually one or two introductory articles and then a detailed description of several current exhibits. Specialists will want this along with the many other bulletins and programs issued by leading museums, while the numerous black and white illustrations will interest both the layman and the student. One of many museum bulletins, it ranks somewhat behind the *Metropolitan Museum of Art. Bulletin,* yet is among the best in the field. See also *Philadelphia Museum of Art. Bulletin.* A check of *Ulrich's International Periodicals Directory* will show which museums in the library's immediate area issue bulletins; these, of course, should be included in most local or regional collections. Incidentally, those indexed in *Art Index* tend to be better, but this is not always true and each should be checked individually.

Domus. See Architecture Section.

Everyday Art. 1922. 3/yr. $1. Edward Mattil. American Crayon Co., Sandusky, Ohio 44870. Illus. Circ: 30,000. Microform: UM.

Aud: Ga, Ht, Et. *Rv:* L. *Jv:* C.

A trade publication which features pictorial essays on the beauty of the color, forms, and structures found in nature and in everyday surroundings. Colors are related to designs in buildings, bridges, and motifs frequently used by adults and by children in art work. Would be welcomed by art teachers, elementary school teachers, and children.

Graphis; international journal of graphic art and applied art. 1944. bi-m. $22. Walter Herdeg. Graphis Press, P.O. Box 320, New York, N.Y. Illus., adv. Circ: 16,400.

Indexed: ArtI. *Aud:* Sa, Ac, Jc. *Bk. rev:* 2–7, short, signed. *Rv:* H. *Jv:* A.

Published in Switzerland in English, French, and German, this is the best known of all graphic arts periodicals. Each issue is literally a work of art in itself, and the reproductions are among the finest printed in any magazine. All articles are lavishly illustrated, often to the point where it is difficult to concentrate on the text. Coverage extends from exhibitions, artists and awards to typography, posters, advertising and package design. Although directed to the graphic artist, it will be enjoyed by *anyone* in the arts. A required item in large academic and special libraries, and in any type or size library where there is a call for graphic arts material.

Handweaver and Craftsman. 1950. q. $5. Mary Alice Smith. Handweaver and Craftsman, 246 Fifth Ave., New York, N.Y. 10001. Illus., index, adv. Circ: 9,500. Microform: UM.

Indexed: ArtI. *Bk. rev:* Notes. *Aud:* Ga, Ac, Jc, Sh, Jh, Ht. *Rv:* H. *Jv:* B.

Devoted to handweaving and stitchery, this magazine ranges from the how-to of the craft through the history of the art, to the articles describing superior examples of work. There are good black and white illustrations, and news of exhibitions, fairs, and conferences in the field of special projects. Advertisements of supplies and materials, and instruction classes are helpful for both the beginner and the expert. Of interest to amateur and professional weavers and teachers.

Interior Design. 1932. m. $5. Sherman Emery. Whitney Communications Corp., Interior Design Div., 151 E. 50th St., New York, N.Y. 10022. Illus., adv. Circ: 26,111.

Indexed: ArtI. *Bk. rev:* 2–4, 250–500 words *Aud:* Sa, Ac. *Rv:* M. *Jv:* B.

Primarily a trade journal for both professional residential and contract interior decorators, the articles are keyed more towards business than aesthetics. The editors presuppose an educated audience which is interested in source of supply, and current trends in everything from antiques to floor covering. The articles are well illustrated, and as about 40% of the magazine is made up of advertisements it has a much wider appeal to a lay audience than most professional magazines. Whereas the articles will be of limited interest to the general public, on the whole the magazine has appeal for anyone seriously involved with interior design. For all large academic art libraries, and a few small to medium-sized libraries might try it as a change of pace from the usual consumer-type magazine approach to design.

Interiors. 1888. m. $7. Olga Gueft. Whitney Pubns., Inc., 18 E. 50th St., New York, N.Y. 10022. Illus., adv. Circ: 29,214. Microform: UM.

Indexed: ArtI. *Bk. rev:* 5–6, brief, signed. *Aud:* Sa, Ac. *Rv:* H. *Jv:* B.

"Published for the Interior Designers Group which includes: interior designers, architects, and industrial designers, who offer interior designing services, and the interior decorating departments of retail stores." Each issue is devoted to a special topic, and excellent black and white plates illustrate the articles. There are brief news notes of what designers are doing, forthcoming exhibitions, and competitions, and a large advertising section of products used for interiors. Primarily for the professional architect and designer, but useful for graduate students.

Journal of Aesthetics and Art Criticism. 1941. q. Membership (Non-members, $10). Herbert M. Schueller. Wayne State Univ., Dept. of English, Detroit, Mich. 48202. Illus., index. Circ: 2,400. Microform: UM. Reprint: AMS, Abrahams.

Indexed: ArtI, MusicI, PsyAb. *Aud:* Sa, Ac. *Rv:* H. *Jv:* B.

Published by the American Society for Aesthetics to "promote study, research, discussion, and publication in aesthetics." The Society is supported by the major art galleries and universities in America. Long, well-documented articles on the theory of art and literature are written by recognized experts in the field and individual issues are sometimes given over to a single topic. An excellent 25-page (average length) bibliography, arranged by subject, of the previous year's publications in aesthetics and related fields appears in the summer issue. An invaluable study aid and source of reference to students of the arts, and related disciplines,

from a philosophical, scientific, or theoretical standpoint. A useful addition for medium to large academic libraries, particularly as its scope is so broad and can be used in other programs besides art.

Journal of Glass Studies. 1959. ann. $5. Paul N. Perrot. Journal of Glass Studies, The Corning Museum of Glass, Corning Glass Center, Corning, N.Y. 14830. Illus. Circ: 800–1000.

Bk. rev: 2–3, lengthy, signed. *Aud:* Sa, Ac. *Rv:* H. *Jv:* B.

A learned journal devoted to the study of the art and history of glass from prehistoric to present times. The writers are curators, archaeologists, art historians and other experts from the diversified fields which are concerned with glass. A 25-page (average length) bibliography of the previous year's publications of books and articles on glass is of major importance for any library in this or allied fields. Of interest to anyone involved with the arts and design, as well as the serious glass collector.

L'Arte. 1968. q. $16.50. Pennsylvania State Univ. Press, Univ. Park, Pa. 16802. Illus.

Aud: Sa, Ac. *Rv:* H. *Jv:* B.

Published in Milan, this is primarily devoted to art history. Most of the material is in Italian, although articles are summarized in English, French, German and Italian and the original is in the language of the author. Each of the eight to ten articles is liberally illustrated with black and white and some colored plates. The 140 pages are printed on glossy stock, and the format is good, if not impressive. Articles presuppose a knowledge of art, are by authorities, and vary in style from good to excellent. A basic journal in large art collections, but it is a trifle too esoteric for smaller libraries.

Marsyas. 1940. ann. $5. Burr Wallen. J. J. Augustin, Locust Valley, N.Y. 11560. Illus.

Indexed: ArtI. *Aud:* Sa, Ac. *Rv:* H. *Jv:* C.

A scholarly annual devoted to "studies in the history of art" and published by the Fine Arts Department of New York University. It frequently includes masters' theses among its well documented articles. There are numerous black and white illustrations. Several abstracts of unpublished theses appear at the end of each issue. Only for large art collections.

Master Drawings; devoted exclusively to the study and illustration of drawings. 1963. q. $15. Felice Stampfle. Master Drawings Assn., Inc., 33 E. 36th St., New York, N.Y. 10016. Illus., index, adv. Circ: 950.

Indexed: ArtI. *Bk. rev:* 1–2, lengthy, signed. *Aud:* Sa, Ac, Jc. *Rv:* H. *Jv:* B.

On the same high plane as the *Journal of Aesthetics and Art Criticism,* but concerned solely with drawings. There are one or two long (10–20 pages), well documented articles devoted to the study of the drawings and cartoons of an individual artist, a specific collection, etc. Annotated lists of recent publications in the field appear in each issue. In addition, there are about six "notes" (4–5 pages each) dealing with the works of an artist, or with a single project or work of art. Its beautiful typography, good paper, attractive layout, and 50–60 splendid reproductions of drawings make it a quality publication suitable for any library.

Metropolitan Museum of Art. Bulletin, N.S. 1942. 9/yr. Membership (Non-members, $5). Katharine H. B. Stoddert. Metropolitan Museum of Art, Fifth Ave. and 82nd St., New York, N.Y. 10028. Illus., index. Circ: 25,-000. Microform: UM.

Indexed: ArtI. *Aud:* Ga, Ac, Jc, Sh, Jh. *Rv:* M. *Jv:* V.

One of the best art museum bulletins, this contains articles about the museum's own holdings, its activities, news of exhibitions, and special events in the art world. Most articles are too short for reference, but frequently one finds here the only published discussion of the material. The *Bulletin* is never dull and gives an intimate glimpse of what goes on behind the scenes of the nation's largest and richest museum of art. A secondary, important use for high school libraries and up are the fine illustrations and drawings supplementing the text.

Mobilia; for furniture, art handicraft, art and architecture. 1955. m. $23. Svend E. Moeller. Snekkersten, Denmark. Illus., adv. Circ: 6,000.

Aud: Sa, Ac. *Rv:* H. *Jv:* B.

A Danish magazine with text in four languages, including English, this is probably the world's leading journal for new concepts in the design of furniture, handicrafts and materials used in day to day living. Also includes sections on art and architecture. It is a visual delight, as much care going into the design of the multi-colored illustrations and layouts as into the preparation of the articles. The photography is a study in itself. In that the format is almost as important as the contents, this can be compared favorably with *Graphis* as an outstanding example of the graphic arts. A necessity in any medium to large art or advanced home economics or design collection.

Museum. 1948. q. $10. UNESCO, 317 E. 34th St., New York, N.Y. 10016. Illus. Circ (in U.S.): 500. Microform: UM.

Indexed: ArtI. *Aud:* Sa, Ac. *Rv:* H. *Jv:* B.

A magazine on museum management for professionals, and while of interest to teachers of art, is of limited value to the average student. Articles cover every aspect of museum management, report on methods of display, current shows, economic problems and the like. As a UNESCO publication, the scope is international. For the casual reader, of primary interest is the illustrations—some 50 to 75, often oversized, in black and white. The editors also tend to concentrate on one subject such as art and education which may be of interest to teachers as well as museum directors. Most

of the material is in both English and French, with summaries in several languages. One of the few museum publications which is suitable for both the professional and the layman, and might well be considered for medium-sized as well as large public and academic collections.

Museum News. 1952. m. (Sept.–June). $15. Membership. N. Carl Barefoot, Jr. Amer. Assn. of Museums, 2306 Massachusetts Ave., N.W., Washington, D.C. 20008. Illus., index, adv. Circ: 4,200.

Bk. rev: 5–6, one column, signed. *Aud:* Sa, Ac. *Rv:* H. *Jv:* B.

Similar to the British *Museum Journal* in its purpose and scope. It is intended for the museum profession, but has a wide lay readership. Information retrieval, recruitment of staff, education and the museum appear to be universal topics. This magazine offers additional information on aesthetics and solutions to problems of displays and exhibitions with a bi-monthly "Technical Supplement" that discusses various problems in museology. There are many illustrations. Features include announcements of current exhibitions, lists of publications by American museums. Coupled with the book reviews, the last feature makes this a required item for all large art libraries.

Museums Journal. 1901. q. 15s. per issue. Frank Greenaway. The Museums Assn., 87 Charlotte St., London W. 1. Illus., index, adv. Circ: 2,000.

Indexed: ArtI. *Bk. rev:* 6–7, full page, signed. *Aud:* Sa, Ac. *Rv:* H. *Jv:* B.

Presents an exchange of ideas and information among members of the museum profession both in Great Britain and in other countries. Subjects discussed include: information retrieval, education, various newly built—or redesigned —museums or art galleries, problems of display, and preservation, management, etc. Of value to museum and art gallery personnel, specialist and university libraries.

National Sculpture Review. 1951. q. Membership (Non-members, $3). Adolph Block. National Sculpture Soc., 250 E. 51st St., New York, N.Y. 10022. Illus., adv. Circ: 6,000.

Indexed: ArtI. *Bk. rev:* Occasional, brief. *Aud:* Ga, Ac, Jc. *Rv:* M. *Jv:* B.

One of the few periodicals devoted solely to sculpture, meant to spread the knowledge of good sculpture. Each issue reviews work in a particular field or technique. Many high quality photographs and articles. Features news of exhibitions, and award winning examples of sculpture. Primarily for medium to large public and academic collections. Compares favorably with *Sculpture International,* a newer entry in the field.

Oriental Art; devoted to the study of all forms of Oriental art. N.S. 1955. q. $2.50. Peter C. Swann. Oriental Art Magazine Ltd., 12 Ennerdale Rd., Richmond, Surrey, Eng. Illus., index, adv. Circ: 1,000.

Indexed: ArtI. *Bk. rev:* 5–6, full page. *Aud:* Sa, Ac. *Rv:* H. *Jv:* B.

A British publication devoted to all forms of Oriental art. Scholarly articles about individual works of art, history, and legends are written by specialists and well-illustrated with black and white plates. A bibliography section lists books and periodicals by geographic areas of the Orient. Well written essays review exhibitions. A superior reference source for students, and excellent reading for the interested adult.

Philadelphia Museum of Art. Bulletin. 1903. q. $4. 26th & Benjamin Franklin Parkway, Philadelphia, Pa. 19101. Illus. Circ: 10,000. Microform: UM.

Indexed: ArtI. *Aud:* Ga, Sa, Ac. *Rv:* M. *Jv:* B.

Concentrating on a show, artist, period, etc., each issue of this bulletin features one main article with two or three related pieces. Each is illustrated with 50 to 100 black and white reproductions. The low price, and the coverage in depth, assures a place for the *Bulletin* in any medium to large art collection. Art teachers, too, will find the illustrations extremely useful for the class work.

Pictures on Exhibit; world wide reviews of the art shows. 1937. m. (Oct.–June). $4. Charles Z. Offin. Pictures Publishing Co., 30 E. 60th St., New York, N.Y. 10022. Illus., adv. Circ: 23,300.

Aud: Ga, Ac, Jc, Sh. *Rv:* H. *Jv:* B.

This magazine serves a dual purpose. Although primarily a monthly report and criticism of art exhibitions (both here and abroad), it is profusely illustrated with black and white photographs. The illustrations serve to introduce both the student and the general reader to some of the world's finest art. Articles are staff-written, objective and considered quite accurate. Averages some 72 pages per issue and is published in a convenient pocket-size format. A useful addition for larger libraries and, indeed, any library where art is of particular interest to the community.

Prisme International. 1968. bi-m. $2. Overseas Publishers' Representatives, 424 Madison Ave., New York, N.Y. 10017. Illus., adv. Reprint: Kraus.

Aud: Sa, Ac. *Rv:* H. *Jv:* B.

A 72- to 80-page graphic arts French publication with text in French, German and English. But the text is of little importance, as most of each issue is given over to black and white, and some colored illustrations of materials used in advertising posters, packages, typography, logotypes, etc. The scope is international and its primary interest to Americans will be the coverage of European trends. While it does not measure up to the luxurious approach of *Graphis,* it is an excellent second choice for larger academic and specialized libraries.

S.M.S. 1967. bi-m. $100. The Letter Edged in Black Press, Inc., 246 W. 80th St., New York, N.Y. 10024.

Aud: Sa, Ac. *Rv:* M. *Jv:* B.

More an art object than a magazine, which accounts in part for the record high price. Each number is a portfolio of original art, or as the publisher puts it "a portable gallery of contemporary hyper-awareness." The fifth issue included a 45 r.p.m. poem by Diane Wakoski; three ways of making money by Neil Jenny; a cutout ready to be assembled; some bits of tile nicely bagged and boxed; a pop art object to be constructed; an assembly of a nude and a baby ruth bar wrapper—etc., etc. While op and pop art fans will enjoy, as will any art student or artist (regardless of his feelings about the relative worth of the material) it definitely is not for the average layman. And although the objects are fascinating enough, at the price asked, it is an item only for large academic art collections and private collectors. Which is not to knock it, only to wind up with agreement with the publisher—it really isn't a magazine, just a tremendous lot of fun.

School Arts Magazine. 1901. m. 10/yr. $7. George F. Horn. Davis Pubns., Inc., Printers Bldg., Worcester, Mass. 01608. Illus. adv. Circ: 28,723. Microform: UM. Reprint: Abrahams.

Indexed: EdI, RG. *Bk. rev:* Notes. *Aud:* Ac, Jc, Ht, Et. *Rv:* M. *Jv:* B.

"The magazine for art educators," this is primarily valuable to elementary and secondary school teachers as a source of inspiration for creative art projects. The 10 to 12 articles describe a great variety of art techniques and suggest means of presenting them to classes. An occasional article discusses curriculum or educational philosophy. Contributors are drawn from art faculty and museum staff members. General format is pleasing, with each article accompanied by many well-reproduced illustrations consisting of photos and art reproductions in black and white. Full color covers show outstanding examples of student or faculty art work. Each issue has an eight-page center insert, on dull paper of a pastel tint, printed in a darker shade. While this gives an opportunity for more artistic reproductions of some of the illustrative art work, it is more difficult to read because of the comparative lack of contrast between print and paper color. A regular feature, "Items of Interest," gives news of new products, teaching aids, loan service and traveling exhibits. A yearly buyers' guide of supplies and tools, and directory of suppliers appears in the February issue. Book reviews appear irregularly, either in a column of four or five short (50-word) reviews, or in a longer feature of seven to eight signed reviews of 175–200 words. A first or second purchase in all elementary and secondary schools professional collections, and equally important in schools of education. See concluding remarks for *Arts and Activities.*

Sculpture International. 1967. q. $5.50. Fabio Barraclough. Pergamon Press, 44–01 21st St., Long Island City, N.Y. 11101. Illus., adv.

Aud: Sa, Ga, Ac, Jc. *Rv:* M. *Jv:* B.

Featuring some eight to ten articles on sculptors and shows, and profusely illustrated (primarily black and white, with some color). Written as much for the art student as the layman interested in the subject. Emphasis is on modern trends, albeit there are usually one or two articles devoted to a historical study. Although international in tone, the swing is toward shows and artists in England. One of the best magazines available on sculpture, and libraries which now subscribe to the *National Sculpture Review* will want to consider this as well.

Stained Glass; devoted to the craft of painted and stained glass. 1906. q. $5. J. G. Lloyd. Stained Glass Assn. of America, 3600 University Dr., Fairfax, Va. 22030. Illus., index, adv. Circ: 1,400.

Aud: Sa, Ac. *Rv:* M. *Jv:* B.

The only popular periodical devoted exclusively to the ancient craft of stained glass and topics related to it. There are brief articles about craftsmen and outstanding examples of ancient and contemporary work. Illustrations are good to excellent. Ads of suppliers to the trade and convenient list of sources of supplies. Announcements of competitions and scholarship news. Will be of some interest to antique collectors, but primarily for specialized collections. See also, *Journal of Glass Studies.*

Studio International. 1893. m. $15. Peter Townsend. W&J Mackay & Co. Ltd., 37 Museum St., London, W.C. 1. Illus., index, adv. Circ: 14,500.

Indexed: ArtI. *Bk. rev:* Book supplement every 3 months. *Aud:* Ga, Ac, Jc. *Rv:* H. *Jv:* B.

One of the world's oldest art magazines which gives a well balanced report on today's modern art scene. Although published in England and featuring British critics, the coverage is international. It is particularly useful in American libraries for the illustrations—some 60 black and white plates and eight or more color plates per issue. Emphasis is on the 20th century, but there are a number of background articles which focus on the heritage of the past in sculpture, painting, criticism, education, etc. Regular departments include reviews of exhibitions, news of sales, personal notes, and quarterly supplements which cover new art books, prints, graphic design and the like. The style of writing is much above average for an art magazine—i.e., a minimum of jargon and a clarity of thought not often associated with modern art criticism. A worthwhile addition for any medium to large art collection in a public or academic library.

ASTRONOMY

Indexes and Abstracts

Biological Abstracts, Chemical Abstracts, Mathematical Reviews, Meteorological and Geoastrophysical Abstracts, Readers' Guide to Periodical Literature, Science Abstracts, Science Citation Index. (For annotations, see Indexes and Abstracts Section.)

The range of periodicals in this section extends from the very popular to the more sophisticated publications still directed to the amateur astronomer, and includes a sampling of the distinguished journals. Titles have been restricted to those available in English, but academic libraries will probably carry a large number of foreign titles as well. Of particular importance is a new European periodical, *Astronomy and Astrophysics* (Springer-Verlag), scheduled for publication in 1969. Sponsored by the European Southern Observatory, this journal results from the merger of five other publications: *Annales d'Astrophysique, Bulletin of the Astronomical Institutes of the Netherlands, Bulletin Astronomique, Journal des Observateurs* and *Zeitschrift für Astrophysik.*

Astronomical Journal. 1849. 10/yr. $20. L. Woltjer & N. H. Baker. Amer. Inst. of Physics, 335 E. 45th St., New York, N.Y. 10017. Illus., index. Circ: 2,200. Reprint: Johnson.

Indexed: ChemAb, MathR, Met & GeoAstAb, SCI. *Aud:* Sa, Ac. *Rv:* H. *Jv:* B.

Published under the aegis of the American Astronomical Society, the journal reports original research in all phases of astronomy, including such fields as radio astronomy, astrophysics, and instrumentation related to this science. Papers are authoritative and high quality. Reports of observatories, abstracts of papers presented at meetings of the Society, and miscellaneous notices and news formerly published as part of the journal are now reported in a new publication (1969), *Bulletin of the American Astronomical Society.*

Astronomical Society of the Pacific. Publications. 1889. bi-m. Membership ($6.50). D. H. McNamara, c/o Calif. Academy of Sciences, Golden Gate Park, San Francisco, Calif. 94118. Illus. Circ: 1,900. Reprint: Kraus.

Indexed: ChemAb, MathR, SciAb, SCI. *Bk. rev:* 5–6, 250–500 words, signed. *Aud:* Jc, Ac, Sa. *Rv:* H. *Jv:* B.

Short research papers, survey articles of recent developments in the field, and historical and biographical material are presented in this journal. Regular features are: "Comet Notes," abstracts of papers presented at meetings of the Society, and general news of the profession. Also included in the membership fee is *Leaflets,* issued monthly, which supplies nontechnical information and covers general interest topics.

Astrophysical Journal; an international review of astronomy and astronomical physics. 1895. 12/yr. $50. S. Chandrasekhar. Univ. of Chicago Press, 5750 Ellis Ave., Chicago, Ill. 60637. Illus., index. Circ: 3,300. Reprint: Johnson. Microform: Canner; Um.

Indexed: ChemAb, MathR, Met&GeoAstAb, SciAb, SCI. *Aud:* Sa, Ac. *Rv:* H. *Jv:* B.

An important and authoritative research journal, the publication is concerned with current investigations of theoretical and observational astronomy, as well as astronomical physics. Issued monthly in two parts, Part 1 consists of full length papers, a few brief notes, and abstracts of the *Astrophysical Journal Supplement Series* (which also publishes lengthy papers). Part 2 consists of "Letters to the Editor," short, timely reports on research in progress which receive rapid publication.

British Astronomical Association. Journal. 1890. 6/yr. $6. Colin Ronan. British Astronomical Assn., 303 Bath Rd., Hounslow West, Middlesex, Eng. Illus., index, adv. Circ: 6,000.

Indexed: SciAb. *Bk. rev:* 5–6, 300–700 words, signed. *Aud:* Ac, Sa, Jc. *Rv:* H. *Jv:* B.

Since the Society's purpose is to circulate astronomical information and to promote popular interest in the field, papers are less technical and of more general interest than those found in research journals. Feature articles combine studies of recent developments in the field with reports on current research; observational notes with historical and biographical articles. Excellent tutorial departments are: "For the Newcomer," providing tips on telescopes, other instrumentation, etc., and "Notes from Other Journals," digesting some of the important scholarly papers in the literature. The journal also includes news and notices of the Association, personalia, etc.

Icarus. 1962. bi-m. $25. Zdenek Kopal & A. G. Wilson. Academic Press, Inc., 111 Fifth Ave., New York, N.Y. 10003. Illus. Reprint: Abrahams.

Indexed: ChemAb, SciAb, SCI. *Aud:* Ac, Sa. *Rv:* H. *Jv:* B.

An international journal devoted to publication of original research in astronomy, physics, chemistry, or any other scientific discipline which studies the solar system. Papers are both theoretical and observational. Also includes a few announcements on instrumentation. Recommended for research libraries.

Natural Science. See Science—General Section.

The Observatory. 1877. bi-m. C. A. Murray. Royal Greenwich Observatory, Herstmonceux Castle, Hailsham, Sussex, Eng. Illus., index.

Indexed: ChemAb, MathR, Met&GeoAstAb, SciAb, SCI. *Bk. rev:* 4–5, 200–450 words, signed. *Aud:* Ac, Sa. *Rv:* H. *Jv:* B.

One of the older astronomical journals, it publishes short papers on original research, including research on instrumentation, technical correspondence, and brief research notes from observatories. It also reports on meetings and symposia of various societies, and provides some news of the profession.

Review of Popular Astronomy. 1951. bi-m. $4. Donald D. Zahner. Sky Map Pubns., Inc., 111 S. Merame Ave., St. Louis, Mo. 63105. Illus., adv. Microform: UM.

Indexed: RG. *Bk. rev:* 3–5, 50–250 words, signed. *Aud:* Jh, Sh, Jc, Ac, Ga, Sa. *Rv:* H. *Jv:* A.

Popularly written, the periodical should have wide appeal among sky-viewing devotees, whether they are watching by telescope, binoculars, or the naked eye. Issues feature informative essays on topics ranging from studies on celestial objects, observatories, profiles of renowned astronomers, new instruments or equipment. Departments include "Sky Watching," which consists of evening sky maps, notes and news from observers, reports from the American Association of Variable Star Observers, and "Teletopics," which gives details and tips on new equipment. This publication is a continuation of *Monthly Sky Map,* begun in 1904. Less sophisticated in treatment than *Sky and Telescope,* this magazine is nevertheless a good popular item geared toward amateurs and beginning students.

Royal Astronomical Society. Monthly Notices. 1827. irreg. (5/vol; 1½–2 vol/yr.) $30/vol. F. Graham Smith & D. McNally. Blackwell Scientific Periodicals, Ltd., 5 Alfred St., Oxford, Eng. Illus., index. Circ: 1,600. Microform: UM. Reprint: Abrahams.

Indexed: ChemAb, MathR, Met&GeoAstAb, SciAb, SCI. *Aud:* Ac, Sa. *Rv:* H. *Jv:* B.

Monthly Notices is the leading British journal covering all aspects of astronomical research. Papers include studies on observational astronomy, radio astronomy, astrophysics, cosmology, space research, and design of instruments.

The Royal Astronomical Society also issues two other research publications, its *Memoirs,* which comprises research papers including large amounts of mathematical or tabular data, and *Geophysical Journal,* which is devoted to scientific studies on aspects of geophysics.

Royal Astronomical Society. Quarterly Journal. 1960. Free to subscribers of other society publications (Non-subscribers, $9). C. A. Murray, Blackwell Scientific Publications, Ltd., 5 Alfred St., Oxford, England. Index. Circ: 3,200.

Indexed: MathR, SCI. *Aud:* Sa, Ac, Jc. *Rv:* H. *Jv:* B.

Suitable for the non-specialist as well as for the researcher, the *Quarterly Journal* contains around three articles per issue, which are general treatments or review papers covering research and developments of recent astronomical interest. The publication also contains news and notices of the Society, and departments include: "Geophysical Discussions," "Proceedings of Observatories," and a library accessions list.

Royal Astronomical Society of Canada. Journal. 1907. bi-m. $12. Ruth J. Northcott. 252 College St., Toronto 2B, Ont. Illus., index. Circ: 2,250. Microform: UM.

Indexed: ChemAb, SciAb, SCI. *Bk. rev:* 3–4, 400–500 words, signed. *Aud:* Jc, Ac, Sa. *Rv:* H. *Jv:* B.

Available through membership to the Society (which is open to anyone interested in astronomy), the *Journal* provides a good blend, in its four to five feature articles, of the current and the historical, the technical and the tutorial. Departments include reports by Canadian scientists, which are abstracts of papers presented at meetings; reviews or digests of papers published in the more scholarly journals; variable star notes; notes from observatories, and Society news.

Sky and Telescope. 1941. m. $6. Charles A. Federer. Sky Publishing Corp., 49 Bay State Rd., Cambridge, Mass. 02138. Illus., index, adv. Circ: 35,000. Microform: UM. Reprint: Johnson.

Indexed: Met&GeoAstAb, RG. *Bk rev:* 3–5, lengthy, signed. *Aud:* Ga, Ac, Jc, Sh. *Rv:* H. *Jv:* V.

Directed to the amateur astronomer and laboratory scientist who is actively interested in this field. Each issue features four to six articles that are short and lucidly written by experts. There are feature sections, such as "Observer's Page," containing photos and observational articles written by amateurs. "Gleanings for ATM's" is a section of articles by amateurs on telescopes, accessories, observatories, current star and planet charts, celestial calenders, and news notes of interest to astronomers. The leading astronomy magazine for beginners, regardless of age or level of education. Should be in most libraries.

Sun at Work. 1956. q. $2.50. Assn. for Applied Solar Energy, Arizona State Univ., Tempe, Ariz. 85281. Illus., adv. Circ: 1,500.

Indexed: BioAb. *Aud:* Ga, Sh. *Rv:* M. *Jv:* B.

An authoritative, yet semi-popular magazine on all aspects of solar energy. Articles cover various topics from the sun itself to how the sun's power may be harnessed by industry and the individual. Good illustrations. A useful, although not essential magazine for the layman and senior high school student.

Soviet Astronomy-AJ. 1957. bi-m. $55. Amer. Inst. of Physics, Inc., 335 E. 45th St., New York, N.Y. 10017. Illus., index. Circ: 800. Reprint: Abrahams.

Indexed: ChemAb, MathR, Met&GeoAstAb, SciAb, SCI. *Bk. rev:* 2–3, 500–700 words, signed. *Aud:* Ac, Sa. *Rv:* H. *Jv:* B.

Published with the cooperation of the American Astronomical Society, this is a complete translation of the *Astronomicheskii Zhurnal* (*Astronomical Journal of the Academy of Sciences of the USSR*). This leading astronomical journal reports on current research in astronomy and astrophysics, and includes papers on almost all topics. In addition to original contributions, the journal also contains some review articles, detailed reports of conferences, and biographical notes on Russian scientists.

ATMOSPHERIC SCIENCES

Indexes and Abstracts

Biological Abstracts, Chemical Abstracts, Engineering Index, Meteorological and Geostrophysical Abstracts, Read- ers' Guide to Periodical Literature, Science Abstracts, Science Citation Index. (For annotations, see Indexes and Abstracts Section.)

The selection of periodicals for this section has been restricted to titles available in English and to a scant representation of research journals. Academic libraries with an interest in the field would be likely to include such well-known foreign journals as *Météorologie, Meteorologische Rundschau,* and *Zeitschrift für Meteorologie,* among many others.

American Meteorological Society. Bulletin. 1920. m. $15. K. C. Spengler. Amer. Meteorological Soc., 45 Beacon St., Boston, Mass. 02108. Illus., index adv. Circ: 12,000. Reprint: Abrahams.

Indexed: BioAb, ChemAb, Met&GeoAstAb, SciAb, SCI. *Bk. rev:* 2–3, 250 words, signed. *Aud:* Js, Ac, Sa. *Rv:* H. *Jv:* B.

The official organ of the Society. Consists of survey articles covering all aspects of the atmospheric sciences; some general interest features; news and notes of the membership and the profession; occasional summaries of addresses presented before meetings of the Society; and programs and abstracts of papers presented at their meetings. Some feature articles may be of interest to the non-specialist and amateur weatherman. Each issue also contains a directory of consulting meteorologists.

Journal of Applied Meteorology. 1952. bi-m $30. Glenn R. Hilst. Amer. Meteorological Soc., 45 Beacon St., Boston, Mass. 02108. Illus., index. Reprint: Abrahams.

Indexed: BioAb, ChemAb, EngI, Met&GeoAstAb. *Aud:* Sa, Ac. *Rv:* H. *Jv:* B.

Serving as a "medium for the publication of research concerned with the application of the atmospheric sciences to operational and practical goals," the journal deals with applications that are concerned with the health, safety, and economy of the community. Articles are specialized, but of general interest: "Improving Visibility Near Airports During Periods of Fog;" "An Approach to the Classification of Meteorological Satellite Data." Each issue lists forthcoming papers, preliminary research results, informal comments, and discussion of published papers.

Journal of the Atmospheric Sciences. 1944. bi-m. $20. Robert Jastrow & Gordon J. F. MacDonald, Amer. Meteorological Soc., 45 Beason St., Boston, Mass. 02108. Illus., index.

Indexed: BioAb, ChemAb, EngI, SCI. *Aud:* Sa, Ac. *Rv:* H. *Jv:* B.

Following an editorial policy "to encourage papers which emphasize the quantitative and deductive aspects of the subject," the journal publishes research papers concerning atmospheric studies. Articles, averaging five to eight pages in length, are international in scope. Departments consist of notes and correspondence, including informal comment, discussion of published papers, and short notes on results of investigations.

Meteorological Magazine. 1866. m. $10. Meteorological Office, London Rd., Bracknell, Berkshire, Eng. Subscriptions to: H.M.S.O., Atlantic House, Holborn Viaduct, London, E.C. 1. Illus., index, adv. Circ: 1,950. Microform: UM. Reprint: Johnson, Abrahams.

Indexed: Met&GeoAstAb. SCI. *Bk. rev:* 2–3, 300 words, signed. *Aud:* Sa, Ac. *Rv:* H. *Jv:* B.

The scope of this periodical is quite wide. In addition to authoritative research reports and shorter notes covering all the atmospheric sciences, there are general review papers, some historical material, digests of technical symposia, and notices and news of interest to meteorologists.

Monthly Weather Review. 1872. m. $5. James E. Caskey, Jr. Superintendent of Documents, Washington, D.C. 20402. Illus., index. Circ: 3,000. Microform: UM.

Indexed: ChemAb, SCI. *Aud:* Sa, Ac. *Rv:* M. *Jv:* B.

Publication of the U.S. Environmental Science Services Administration. Research articles by meteorologists and other scientists are concerned with various aspects of weather and other atmospheric phenomena. Original contributions vary in length from 2 to 20 pages and, where applicable, contain numerous black and white drawings and charts. Special features are: a picture of the month—a satellite cloud photo with corresponding weather chart; and, of particular interest to American meteorologists, a section dealing with a review of weather and circulation that dates back three months.

Natural History. See Science-General Section.

Royal Meteorological Society. Quarterly Journal. 1871. q. $24.50. H. Charnock. Royal Meteorological Soc., 49 Cromwell Rd., London S.W. 7. Index. Circ: 4,500. Reprint: Johnson, Abrahams.

Indexed: BioAb, ChemAb, Met&GeoAstAb, SciAb, SCI. *Bk. rev:* 5,200 words, signed. *Aud:* Sa, Ac. *Rv:* H. *Jv:* B.

Reports results of original research in the atmospheric sciences, including some studies on geomagnetism and aeronomy, cosmic relationships, as well as general meteorology. Full-length papers, shorter contributions, correspondence, and discussions of papers are included in each issue. Also contains some news of the Society.

Weather. 1946. m. $4.25. D. M. Houghton. Royal Meteorological Soc., 49 Cromwell Rd., London S.W. 7. Illus., index, adv. Circ: 5,500.

Indexed: Met&GeoAstAb. *Bk. rev:* 1–3, lengthy, signed. *Aud:* Ga, Ac, Jc, Sh. *Rv:* H. *Jv:* A.

A popularly written British publication that "welcomes contributions and correspondence on all aspects of weather and meteorology." Each issue averages eight to nine articles of both a historical and current nature, which are usually illustrated with black and white photos and charts. Topics are not restricted to the climatology of the British Isles, but are of general interest. Departments include a separate insert, "Weather Log," a look back on weather in the Brit-

ish Isles, which is complete with statistics and daily weather maps for the North Atlantic and Western Europe; a long-range outlook for the month of issuance; and notices of meetings of various meteorological societies. Nice color photo covers. Roughly equivalent to the American *Weatherwise,* larger libraries will want both; if a choice must be made, the bow should go to the American publication.

Weatherwise; popular weather magazine. 1948. bi-m. $5. David M. Ludlum. Amer. Meteorological Soc., 45 Beacon St. Boston, Mass. 02108. Illus. Circ: 11,631. Microform: UM. Reprint: Abrahams.

Indexed: ChemAb, Met&GeoAstAb, RG. *Aud:* Ga, Ac, Jc, Sh. *Rv:* H. *Jv:* V.

This "popular weather magazine" contains articles of general interest written by experts in a non-technical manner for both the expert and the layman. Averaging five to ten pages in length, the five articles per issue contain plentiful black and white photos, charts and drawings. Each issue features "Weatherwatch," a section devoted to recent weather trends in the United States. Also included in this section are daily weather maps. The February number is an almanac issue and gives weather records and events for the previous year. Dates of AMS meetings and conferences are given in each issue. A good magazine for most libraries, from high school on up.

AUTOMATION

Indexes and Abstracts

Applied Science and Technology Index, British Technology Index, Business Periodicals Index, Chemical Abstracts, Engineering Index, Historical Abstracts, Mathematical Reviews, Science Abstracts, Science Citation Index. (For annotations, see Indexes and Abstracts Section.)

Because of the difficulties involved in making sharp distinctions between overlapping subject areas, the journals in this section have been arbitrarily grouped under one heading to include: periodicals on automatic control and automation of production processes; periodicals concerned with the rather loose term "information processing"; and journals dealing with computers, their design, construction, applications, etc. Thus, the journals range from the fairly general to the highly specialized, already within a highly specialized field. Also, see the Mathematics Section for periodicals dealing with the mathematics of computation.

Association for Computing Machinery. Journal. 1954. q. Membership (Non-members, $20.) Gerard Sacton. ACM, 211 E. 43rd St., New York, N.Y. 10017. Illus., index. Circ: 17,000. Reprint: Johnson, Abrahams.

Indexed: ASTI, BusI, EngI, MathR, SCI. *Aud:* Ac, Sa. *Rv:* H. *Jv:* B.

The corpus of high quality literature on the science of information processing which appears in the *Journal* is more specialized than in *Communications of the ACM,* and treatment is apt to be more theoretical or mathematical.

Occasional survey papers are also published. This is one of the world's foremost journals on the mathematical theory of computing.

Automatica; the international journal of automatic control and automation. 1963. bi-m. $40. George S. Axelby. Pergamon Press, Maxwell House, Fairview Park, Elmsford, N.Y. 10523. Illus., index.

Indexed: SciAb. *Bk. rev:* 1–2, 250 words, signed. *Aud:* Sa, Ac. *Rv:* H. *Jv:* B.

International in character, this disseminates authoritative reports of theoretical and experimental research on all facets of automatic control theory, systems science, and cybernetics. In January, 1969, the journal became the official organ of the International Federation for Automatic Control, and its scope has been broadened to include not only theory and application of systems and components, but to extend these to applications in other fields, such as control of weather, pollution, natural resources, etc. Occasionally, a lengthy, critical, and signed report of a symposium appears. Papers are usually in English, with French, German and Russian summaries.

Automation; the magazine of automatic production operations. 1954. m. $10. (Free to qualified personnel.) R. W. Bolz. Penton Publishing Co., Penton Bldg., Cleveland, Ohio 44113. Illus., adv. Circ: 43,458. Microform: UM. Reprint: Abrahams.

Indexed: ASTI, Engl. *Aud:* Ac, Sa. *Rv:* H. *Jv:* B.

The emphasis in this periodical is on the engineering and manufacturing aspects of automated equipment and systems. Articles include expositions on automatic techniques vs. traditional methods, reviews on pertinent technology from related sciences, the economics of automation, and the like. Written in a style that is comprehensible to a nonspecialist, the magazine should be especially useful to those concerned with clarification of problems or advantages connected with automation in particular fields.

Business Automation. m. $15. Arnold E. Keller. Business Pubns., Inc., 288 Park Ave., West, Elmhurst, Ill. 60126. Illus., adv. Microform: UM.

Aud: Ac, Sa, Jc, Ga. *Rv:* H. *Jv:* B.

Freed from technical language, the three to four main articles in this publication, directed toward administrators of data processing departments, review advances on all aspects of computer technology (equipment, techniques, programming languages, etc.) and their impact with respect to business applications (management decisions, personnel records, sales, etc.). Features profile not only novel usage of computing equipment tailored to individual organizations, but also describe applications in such fields as education and medicine. Contributions are both by staff writers and specialists, are popularly written, and emphasize the practical. Several departments provide adequate coverage of developments in the industry and reviews of new prod-

ucts, including other business machines. New equipment is well illustrated by photos. A salary schedule for all levels of data processing personnel is published yearly, and a useful annual reference guide lists manufacturers, suppliers of software, computer characteristics, other business machines, etc. Useful for business school students as well as the specialist, the periodical is also easily read by any interested layman.

Communications of the A.C.M. 1958. m. Membership (Non-members, $20). M. Stuart Lyren. Assn. for Computing Machinery, 211 E. 43rd St., New York, N.Y. 10017. Illus., index, adv. Circ: 21,000. Reprint: Johnson.

Indexed: SCI. *Aud:* Jc, Ac, Sa. *Rv:* H. *Jv:* B.

Spanning the spectrum of the computing sciences, this excellent publication provides articles of interest to its entire membership and should be indispensable to anyone in any aspect of information processing. Papers deal with both basic research and applications, and range from mathematical analyses, theoretical scientific applications and computer systems, to business applications, information retrieval, and programming techniques. Some tutorial papers are included. The periodical also serves as a news medium for activities of the Society.

Computer Bulletin. 1957. 6/yr. 52s. P. Spooner. British Computer Soc., 23 Dorset Sq., London N.W. 1. Illus., adv. Circ: 7,500.

Indexed: BritTech, MathR, SCI. *Bk. rev:* 10, 100–500 words, signed. *Aud:* Ac, Sa, Jc, Ga. *Rv:* H. *Jv:* B.

Reflecting the interests of the British Computer Society (comparable to America's Association for Computing Machinery), the periodical serves as news organ for the Society and reviews trends and developments in all the computing sciences. Much of the material has a nontechnical tone, and general articles on such topics as the computer and society, or computer applications to other disciplines would be of interest to and within the grasp of the interested layman. Departments include reports on meetings, calendars, equipment and the like, with the emphasis, of course, on British industry. More technical papers appear in the Society's *Computer Journal.*

Computer Journal. 1958. q. $12.60. E. N. Mutch. British Computer Soc., 23 Dorset Sq., London N.W. 1. Illus., index, adv. Circ: 7,500.

Indexed: BritTech, MathR, SCI. *Bk. rev:* 5, 300 words, signed. *Aud:* Ac, Sa. *Rv:* H. *Jv:* B.

Authoritative, research-level papers and technical correspondence on every facet of computers are published in the *Journal.* Studies range from mathematical and engineering investigations to practical applications. Essays on such general topics as computers and the law are also included regularly. On occasion, an algorithms supplement, which has been compiled from references appearing elsewhere in the literature, is published. Book reviews are dispersed throughout the text, rather than included in a separate department.

Computers and Automation. 1951. m. $15. Edmund C. Berkeley. Berkeley Enterprises, Inc., 815 Washington St., Newtonville, Mass. 02160. Illus., index, adv. Circ: 10,500.

Indexed: BusI, SCI. *Bk. rev:* 10, 100 words, unsigned. *Aud:* Jr, Ac, Sa, Ga. *Rv:* H. *Jv:* A.

Featuring articles which reflect the state-of-the-art in a multitude of areas (design, programming, applications, education, even art produced by computers), the periodical is a good choice for a general magazine on computers, data processing, automation. Although ostensibly written on an intermediate level, much of the material is still intelligible to the interested layman. Market reports, newsletters, a monthly computer census, new patents, announcements of government contracts, etc., also make this a valuable addition to any library serving patrons concerned with computers. Of particular note is the June directory, which consists of a roster of organizations, equipment, products, services, and a glossary.

Computers and the Humanities. 1966. bi-m. $7.50 ($10 for institutions). Queens College of the City Univ. of N.Y., Flushing, N.Y. 11367

Indexed: HistAb. *Bk. rev:* 1–3, 700 words, signed. *Aud:* Sa, Ac. *Rv:* H. *Jv:* A.

Articles written for and by scholars in history, literature, music, visual arts and the social sciences, all concerned with uses of computers in their fields of interest. The editors presuppose some basic knowledge of computers, but require neither the technical jargon nor the mathematical background necessary for understanding most computer/ automation journals. Material tends to stress the use of computers for bibliography, compilation of indexes and concordances, etc. Articles such as "Computer Study of Medieval German Poetry," "The Computer as Art Cataloger," and "The Systems Designs and Devices Used to Process *The Random House Dictionary,*" indicate the scope. In addition to book reviews, each issue abstracts 12 to 20 articles from books and periodicals in the area. There is also an annual directory of scholars and their work in the field, an annual listing of literary materials in machine-readable form, and an annual bibliography. An extremely useful journal for almost any scholar who is actively engaged in research. Should be found in all academic libraries, and the wise librarian will do well to scan each issue for developments which may influence his library.

Control Engineering; instrumentation and automatic control systems. 1954. m. $10. Byron K. Ledgerwood. Reuben H. Donnelly Corp., 466 Lexington Ave., New York, N.Y. 10017. Illus., adv. Microform: UM. Reprint: Johnson, Abrahams.

Indexed: ASTI, EngI, SciAb, SCI. *Bk. rev:* 2, 100 words, signed. *Aud:* Ac, Sa. *Rv:* H. *Jv:* B.

Circulated without charge to engineers, management, technical libraries and institutions responsible "for the design, application and test of automatic control systems," the trade journal is replete with ads, photos, and short announcements of new products and installations valuable to the specialist. But its two or three general interest features, which view the computer technology field broadly on such topics as automation of factories, or control of urban crises through automation in education, transportation, and pollution, make interesting reading for the nonspecialist as well. Each issue also contains useful tutorials on such subjects as programming, mathematical tools for computers, as well as articles on specific control systems. News sections supply brief notes on technical developments, business perspectives, and device previews. A small abstracts department also includes digests of one or two technical papers.

Datamation; the automatic handling of information. 1957. m. $15 (Free to qualified personnel). Robert B. Forest. F. D. Thompson Pubns., Inc., 94 S. Los Robles Ave., Pasadena, Calif. 91101. Illus., index, adv. Circ: 72,111. Microform: UM.

Indexed: SCI. *Bk. rev:* 1, 250–500 words, signed. *Aud:* Jc, Ac, Sa, Ga. *Rv:* H. *Jv:* A.

The popularity of this magazine among those associated with computer technology is well deserved; yet its scope is wide enough so that the periodical should be informative and interesting to any layman wishing details on the intricacies of information processing. Feature articles range from the economics and history of computers to reviews or tutorials on programming languages, algorithms, systems, etc. Market coverage, both U.S. and foreign, is exhaustive; technical meetings are also reported in detail. Contributions by the editorial staff are evaluative, rather than expressive of the platitudes of the trade, and the prose is often lively. Also included are news briefs, reports from Washington, sections on new products and literature, gossip of the trade, and personalia. This should be a good choice for a trade journal dealing with hardware and software, business and science, and may also be valuable for high schools in which a data processing curriculum has been established.

Data Processing Magazine; the publication of computers and information technology. 1958. m. $8.50. M. Nussbaum. North American Publishing Co., 134 N. 13th St., Philadelphia, Pa. 19107. Illus., adv. Circ: 55,000. Microform: UM.

Bk. rev: 8, 50 words, unsigned. *Aud:* Sa, Ga. *Rv:* M. *Jv:* B.

A practical periodical directed toward the EDP (electronic data processing) profession. The two to three feature articles cover such topics as guidelines for, or applications of data processing techniques, surveys of systems and equipment, designs for programs, analysis of personnel requirements for EPD departments. The language is fairly non-technical. An interesting monthly section is on data processing applications to education. Departments include thumbnail reviews of current developments in the field, studies of U.S. and foreign markets, surveys of hardware and software, and the usual personalia, forthcoming events, new products and services.

IBM Journal of Research and Development. See Science-General Section.

IBM Systems Journal. 1962. q. $3. M. T. Cook. Intl. Business Machines Corp., Armonk, N.Y. 10504. Illus., index.

Indexed: SCI. *Aud:* Ac, Sa. *Rv:* H. *Jv:* B.

Contributions to this journal are from the scientific staff of the various divisions of the IBM complex, and comprise research papers on all aspects of system design, including such fields as computer systems, mathematical programming techniques, language design, control systems, simulation, etc. Each issue also contains pertinent abstracts of recent papers by other IBM authors.

IEEE Transactions on Automatic Control. 1956. bi-m. George S. Axelby. Inst. of Electrical and Electronics Engineers, Inc., 345 E. 47th St., New York, N.Y. 10017. Illus., index.

Indexed: ASTI, ChemAb, EngI, MathR, SciAb, SCI. *Bk. rev:* 3, 250–350 words, signed. *Aud:* Ac, Sa. *Rv:* H. *Jv:* B.

The major articles, short notes and technical correspondence of this research journal are concerned with theoretical studies of control systems and their applications. Some review papers also appear.

IEEE Transactions on Computers. 1953. m. $36. Harry D. Huskey. Inst. of Electrical and Electronics Engineers, Inc., 345 E. 47th St., New York, N.Y. 10017. Illus., index. Circ: 14,000.

Indexed: ASTI, ChemAb, EngI, MathR, SciAb, SCI. *Bk. rev:* 2, 250 words, signed. *Aud:* Ac, Sa. *Rv:* H. *Jv:* B.

Directed towards engineers and supervisors in the computer field, this research journal publishes articles, notes and correspondence relating to the theory, design and applications of all types of computers. Regular features include lengthy and signed reviews of papers appearing elsewhere in the literature, as well as reviews of books. Short abstracts of the current computer literature, prepared by the Cambridge Communications Corporation (publishers of several abstracting journals), with author and subject indexes to the abstracts, are also supplied in each issue.

IEEE Transactions on Systems Science and Cybernetics. 1965. irreg. $12.75 to public libraries and colleges; others, $17.00. John N. Warfield. Inst. of Electrical and Electronics Engineers, Inc., 345 E. 47 St., New York, N.Y. 10017. Illus., index.

Indexed: ASTI, ChemAb, EngI, MathR, SciAb, SCI. *Aud:* Ac, Sa. *Rv:* H. *Jv:* B.

The scope of this interdisciplinary journal covers "the closely interrelated fields of system science, systems engineering, and cybernetics." Research papers on systems science are concerned with large technological systems (e.g., transportations systems or complete factories), rather than specific control systems and their components, and include such areas as the economics, operation and utilization, as well as the engineering design of the system. The contributions on cybernetics emphasize the methodology of these technological systems to biological, behavioral, sociological, political, legal and economic systems. A few announcements are also included.

Information and Control. 1957. bi-m. $18. Academic Press, Inc., 111 Fifth Ave., New York, N.Y. 10003. Illus., index, adv. Reprint: Abrahams.

Indexed: ChemAb, EngI, MathR, SciAb, SCI. *Aud:* Ac, Sa. *Rv:* H. *Jv:* B.

The research papers published in this journal cover theory of automatic control, communications, and computers. Articles tend to be highly specialized, and treatment is often mathematical.

Information Storage and Retrieval. 1963. q. $35. B. M. Fry. Pergamon Press, Inc., Maxwell House, Fairview Park, Elmsford, N.Y. 10523. Illus., index, adv. Reprint: Abrahams.

Indexed: LibSciAb, MathR, SCI. *Aud:* Ac, Sa. *Rv:* H. *Jv:* B.

Primarily directed toward the intellectual problems associated with "the task of recovering information from those who produce it for transmission to those who need it," the journal pays special attention to information storage and retrieval of scientific literature. Research papers, concerned with both theory and technique, explore such areas as information gathering methods, new approaches to indexing, classification and notation, methods for handling the stored information, and techniques for selection, reproduction and transmission, both with mechanical and electronic selectors. Some investigations on mechanical translation are also published, as well as papers with applications to other fields, such as psychology, linguistics, logic, etc. The three to four articles in each issue may represent comprehensive studies of over 40 pages in length and, reflecting the international character of the journal, may appear in French, German and Italian, as well as English. Occasionally, the entire proceedings of significant symposia are published.

Journal of Computer and System Sciences. 1966. q. $20. Academic Press, Inc., 111 Fifth Ave., New York, N.Y. 10003.

Aud: Ac, Sa. *Rv:* H. *Jv:* B.

Stressing mathematical theory and its applications to computer and system sciences, the journal publishes research papers on such subjects as: automata theory, theory of formal languages and systems, computer programming theory, mathematical theory of systems, mathematical programming, and the application of mathematics to the study of complex systems.

Journal of Data Management. 1963. m. $5. R. Calvin Elliott. Data Processing Management Assn., 505 Busse Highway, Park Ridge, Ill. 60068. Illus., adv. Circ: 21,000. Microform: UM.

Bk. rev: 2, 200 words, signed. *Aud:* Ac, Sa. *Rv:* H. *Jv:* B.

"Representing the data processing and computer community," the official publication of the Association not only publishes general articles reviewing hardware and software developments in all areas of data processing, but bears special emphasis on applications to auditing, banking, education, engineering, insurance, publishing, retailing, and transportation. Departments include Association notes and personalia, news of the industry, new products, tips of the trade, etc.

The Association also publishes a quarterly, *DPMA Quarterly* (1964. q. Circ: 20,000), which is a small bulletin containing articles on education for EDP departments, their management, and reviews of equipment and techniques. Very often the articles are reprints of addresses presented before meetings of the society.

Simulation. 1964. m. $28. John H. McLeod. Simulation Councils, Inc., P.O. Box 2228, La Jolla, Calif. 92037. Illus., index, adv. Circ: 2,200. Microform: UM.

Indexed: Engl. *Bk. rev:* 2–3, 100 words, unsigned. *Aud:* Ac, Sa. *Rv:* H. *Jv:* B.

The journal considers simulation of systems by the use of mathematical or physical analogies performed by computers or other devices. Research papers, and review and tutorial articles thus cover both the theory, design and construction of these computing devices, their applications to simulation systems, and techniques suitable for simulation. Special departments include notes on techniques, educational demonstrations, reviews of meetings, informal news of the society and the profession, and a literature review supplies short abstracts of recent and significant technical articles.

AUTOMOBILES

Indexes and Abstracts

Abridged Readers' Guide, Applied Science and Technology Index, British Technology Index, Business Periodicals Index, Engineering Index, Metals Abstracts, Psychological Abstracts, Readers' Guide to Periodical Literature.

Antique Automobile. 1947. bi-m. $5. William S. Jackson. Antique Automobile Club of America, Inc., Box 678, State College, Pa. 16801. Illus., index, adv. Circ: 26,000.

Bk. rev: 4–5, approx. 50–400 words, signed. *Aud:* Ga, Sh. *Rv:* M. *Jv:* B.

Primarily devoted to reporting winners and showing pictures of show class winners at various competitions of the Antique Automobile Club of America, and information about its activities and members. Some issues feature articles on the history of a particular automobile manufacturer or on restoration. Other articles note the going market price for antique cars. The magazine provides a good place to advertise and exchange cars, parts, and information. It has reasonably good reference value for the history of various cars with minimal value on restoration and mechanical repair information. A useful, although not necessary magazine for both the adult and the high school student, not to mention a few college professors and their students. Buy where needed.

Auto Topics. 1900. m. $5. Floyd Clymer, 222 N. Virgil Ave., Los Angeles, Calif. 90004. Illus., adv. Circ: 65,000.

Aud: Ga. *Rv:* M. *Jv:* B.

An above average general automotive magazine which provides good coverage of a wide range of automotive subjects including safety, traffic, highways, and history. Technical articles are well detailed. There are two road tests reported in each issue, but these are mainly driver impressions with limited technical data. One issue each year gives a brief review of new car models from all manufacturers. Regular monthly departments are: "Publisher's Opinion" —a quick survey of world-wide events in the auto industry; "New Products"—introduces new products and new catalogs of auto parts; and "Industry Statistics"—gives current two week production figures for all American car models and compares the current year's figures with last year's figures. A general interest magazine for the adult, and while good for a secondary purchase, should not be considered until more basic magazines in the field are ordered.

Autocar. 1895. w. $19.50. Maurice A. Smith. Iliffe Transport Publns. Ltd., Dorset House, Stamford St., London S.E. 1. Illus., index, adv. Circ: 140,830.

Indexed: BritTech. *Aud:* Ga, Ac, Jc, Sh. *Rv:* H. *Jv:* V.

Probably the best single magazine for information about foreign cars, and English automobiles in particular. It is recommended as a source of accurate, unbiased information by *Consumer Bulletin,* and the American who has any question regarding the performance, and overall quality of a foreign car should turn here first. It has the distinct advantage of appearing weekly and so is able to carry more road tests than its American counterparts *Road and Track and Car and Driver.* In addition to the appraisal of new cars, each issue includes information of particular interest to the racing fan and those who look upon cars as a serious hobby. Special numbers are given over to large automobile shows, and once a year the London Show number covers almost every major new development in the industry. Particularly noteworthy for the detailed illustrations which include cutaways of the car being studied. Although an expensive item, highly recommended for any type of library where there is an interest in foreign automobiles and racing. Should be a required reference item in larger academic and public library collections.

Automobile Quarterly. 1962. q. $21. L. Scott Bailey. Automobile Quarterly, Inc., 515 Madison Ave., New York, N.Y. 10017. Circ: 31,862.

Aud: Ga, Sa, Ac, Jc, Sh, Jh. *Rv:* H. *Jv:* A.

This is to the automobile fan what *American Heritage* is to the amateur historian, i.e., a hardbound, advertiserless collection of both black and white and color illustrations fitted into a series of nontechnical articles on automobiles. Emphasis is historical, and each issue usually features one manufacturer or type of car from yesteryear. This is balanced with data on new, superior cars in terms of design and individuality. The writing is as basically sound as the marvelous illustrations. It will be welcomed by anyone who looks to a car for more than simple transportation, and the pictures make it suitable for enthusiasts from junior high on up. Although the price is a bit high, the fact that it is hardbound means that a run virtually constitutes an ongoing history of automobiles, and many librarians simply catalog each issue as a book. By and large the best of its type, and should be in most school, public, college and university libraries.

Automotive Industries. 1899. semi-m. $5. Hartley W. Barclay. Chilton Co., Chestnut & 56th Sts., Philadelphia, Pa. 19139. Illus., adv. Circ: 38,815. Microform: UM.

Indexed: ASTI, BusI, EngI. *Aud:* Sa, Ac. *Rv:* M. *Jv:* C.

For students of engineering, vehicle design, management and production in the automotive industry. A large number of articles written by the staff review design and engineering trends in the industry—new models, assembly line techniques, quality control, etc. Many ads by suppliers to the automotive industry, with an index to advertisers. Definitely pro-Detroit. Only for specialized collections.

Car and Driver. 1956. m. $6. David E. Davis. Ziff-Davis Publishing Co., 1 Park Ave., New York, N.Y. 10016. Illus., adv. Circ: 281,139. Microform: UM.

Bk: rev: Notes. *Aud:* Ga, Ac, Jc, Sh. *Rv:* H. *Jv:* A.

Competes with *Road & Track* as the best general automotive magazine in America. Written for foreign car and high performance American car enthusiasts with a definite bias for foreign cars. It is generally anti-Detroit in tone, and editorials show interest in promoting car racing into a major league sport. Most of the articles are written by the staff with an occasional guest expert. Results of their own road tests are reported in detail. An occasional article appears on a personality in the racing field. Special monthly departments give information on new cars and related products, short detailed results of races (3 month lag) and a racing calendar listing big attraction races world-wide. Many fine black and white photographs with occasional color ones. *Car and Driver* issues a yearbook, not included

in the subscription price, which gives road test reports on foreign cars, sports cars, and a few American cars. Definitely not for the lover of the average American car. A third choice for school and public libraries after *Road & Track* and the Detroit oriented *Motor Trend.*

Car Craft. 1953. m. $5.00. Dan Roulston. Peterson Publishing Co., 5959 Hollywood Blvd., Hollywood, Calif., 90028. Illus., adv. Circ: 200,000. Microform: Um.

Aud: Jh, Sh. *Rv:* L. *Jv:* B.

A magazine written for the teen-ager interested in drag racers, stock cars and hot rods. Articles, written by the staff and contributors, are semi-technical and feature information on suspension, modifying engines, how to build chassis, street rods and drag racers. Results of drag races throughout the United States are reported. Every issue features new car road and drag tests, plus a motorcycle test. Regular monthly features include "Straight Scoop"—latest gossip from racing circles; "CC/Shops"—a look at new products; and "CC/Gassers"—a page of jokes. There are many black and white color action photos throughout the magazine. While this has many enthusiastic readers in the younger set (and not a few adults), it would be a second or third choice for public or school libraries. *Hot Rod Magazine* is adequate for most situations.

Car Life. 1954. m. $5. Dennis Shattuck. Bond Publishing Co., 834 Production Pl., Newport Beach, Calif. 92663. Illus., index, adv. Circ: 128,000.

Aud: Ga, Sh. *Rv:* M. *Jv:* C.

Concentrates mainly on American cars with coverage of new foreign models as they are introduced on the market. There are usually three road tests a month, which seem to be fairly objective. Each issue has one brief fiction article, and there is an occasional article on vintage cars. Technical articles have good basic information easily understood by the layman. Many black and white photos and occasional color photos with relatively few advertisements make this an attractive magazine. Popular monthly features such as "New Products"—pictures with brief information; a calendar of auto shows and races; "Motor City"—information about what's new in Detroit; "Autos Abroad"—news about the foreign car industry; "Nuts and Bolts"—answers to readers' car problems. Useful for high schools and public libraries, but should not be purchased before major magazines in this area are considered.

Cycle. 1952. m. $5. Gordon Jennings. Ziff-Davis Publishing Co., 1 Park Ave., New York, N.Y. 10016. Illus., adv. Circ: 168,000.

Aud: Ga, Sh. *Rv:* L. *Jv:* B.

News of famous motor cyclists, racing events, and technical information on how and what to buy. Particularly good for its relatively objective road tests and reports on individual makes. Follows the pattern of another Ziff-Davis magazine, *Car and Driver.* The approach is sensible, and can be used in any public or school library where there is an audience for the subject. See also, the two related English publications, *Motor Cycle* and *Motor Cycle News*.

Driver. q. $.50. United States Air Force, U.S. Superintendent of Documents, Washington, D.C. 20402. Illus.

Aud: Ga, Sh. *Rv:* M. *Jv:* B.

A well-illustrated, 28-page government magazine which stresses safe driving. Articles cover everything from summer trips and automobile law, to how to survive in a crash. There is a minimum of government material, and the whole is quite suitable for both adults and high school students who may be beginning drivers.

Fleet Owner. 1928. m. $3. Carroll W. Boyce. McGraw-Hill Publishing Co., 330 W. 42nd St., New York, N.Y. 10036. Illus., adv. Microform: UM.

Indexed: BusI, EngI. *Aud:* Sa. *Rv:* M. *Jv:* B.

Supplies information, opinion, news, and know-how service to managers who administer, operate, and maintain motor vehicle fleets. Covers all aspects of operating a fleet of trucks or autos. Articles deal with management, operations, maintenance and safety. Occasionally there is an article on related businesses like air transport. Well-illustrated with many black and white photos and advertisements. Only for specialized and business collections.

Foreign Car Guide; featuring the Volkswagen. 1955. m. $5. Angus Laidlow. Rajo Pubns., Inc., 215 Park Ave. S. New York, N.Y. 10003. Illus., adv. Circ: 31,551.

Aud: Ga, *Rv:* L. *Jv:* C.

Primarily of interest to Volkswagen owners, as many of the articles are devoted to simple repairs and additions for that car. Accompanying illustrations often show poor coordination with the text. Regular monthly features are "Tech Tork"—answers to readers' problems; "Bits and Pieces"—letters and odd items of special interest to all small car lovers; "Small Car Scoops"—all about cars from around the world; and "Wagenaids"—new products, ideas, services and activities for Volkswagens. Volkswagen owners will love, but except for the largest collections, it can be bypassed by most libraries.

Hot Rod Magazine. 1948. m. $5. Ray Brock. Petersen Publishing Co., 5959 Hollywood Blvd., Hollywood, Calif. 90028. Illus., adv. Circ: 701,123. Microform: UM.

Indexed: AbrRG, RG. *Aud:* Ga, Sh, Jh. *Rv:* M. *Jv:* A.

One of the most popular automobile magazines for the teen-ager, this appeals to drag race enthusiasts. The editor shows concern about the image of drag racing off the streets. The monthly issues feature at least one road test, racing gossip, a calendar of custom rod shows, technical advice to readers, and an index of advertisers. Most articles are written by the staff and give technical information on engine modifications, and building and construction of various classes of drag cars. Also features articles on

motorcycles and racing boats. There are many black and white and color photos. The language used throughout is in the vernacular of hot-rodding. A basic magazine in any size or type library, even the academic, where there is a given amount of interest in such things.

Model Car and Science. See Crafts and Hobbies Section.

Motor; the automotive business magazine. 1903. m. $5. Edward Ford. Hearst Corp., 250 W. 55th St., New York, N.Y. 10019. Illus., index, adv. Circ: 139,800. Microform: UM.

Aud: Sa, Ga. *Rv:* M. *Jv:* B.

A trade magazine for service station owners or students of automobile mechanics. About one-half of the articles are devoted to technical information and tips on servicing cars. The rest is given over to management information for the individual service station owner or for the larger service operation employing many mechanics. Some of the monthly features include "What Detroit Is Thinking"—rumors and statements about future automobiles; "Engineers at Work"—new design ideas; "New Products"—a survey of new products; and "New Literature"—brief descriptions of new service charts, parts catalogs, handbooks, etc. Many advertisements and black and white pictures and cartoons. A valuable source of information to the mechanic who needs to become familiar with various models of cars and special problems encountered in certain makes and models. Can be of great value to the do-it-yourself home mechanic, and should be in larger public libraries, certainly in all technical and specialized collections.

Motor Cycle. 1903. w. $10. Harry W. Louis. Illiffe Specialist Pubns., Ltd., Dorset House, Stamford St., London S.E. 1. Circ: 109,711. Microform: UM.

Indexed: BritTech. *Aud:* Ga, Sh. *Rv:* M. *Jv:* C.

A British weekly, in tabloid format, covering motorcycle news and major sporting events from all parts of the world. Informative articles with expert commentary provide up-to-date accounts of new machines and models, technical developments, and famous personalities in the cycling world. Includes many practical hints and suggestions for the cycling enthusiast. Liberally illustrated with dramatic action photographs in black and white. Especially interesting for the young adult group, but in America, only after a subscription has been entered for *Cycle*.

Motor Cycle News. 1956. w. $7.60. Brian McLoughlin. East Midland Allied Press Ltd., Newspaper House, Broadway, Peterborough, Eng. Illus., adv. Circ: 104,025.

Aud: Ga, Sh. *Rv:* L. *Jv:* C.

Another British weekly which deals with all aspects of motor cycles, with the sporting side predominating. It, too, is in newspaper form. Covers current motorcycling activity throughout the world, including the United States. Road tests on new models and equipment; latest technical developments related, readers' technical queries answered.

Geared primarily to the young adult audience. Liberal use of action photographs in black and white, weekly readers' photo contest. Either this or *Motor Cycle* is a good addition where there is a particular interest in the subject, but otherwise most libraries can pass by.

Motor Trend Magazine. 1949. m. $5. D. MacDonald. Petersen Publishing Co., 5959 Hollywood Blvd., Los Angeles, Calif. 90028. Illus., index, adv. Circ: 535,344. Microform: UM.

Indexed: RG. *Aud:* Ga, Sh. *Rv:* M. *Jv:* A.

A magazine for American, as opposed to foreign sport car enthusiasts, which covers all facets of the automobile industry and auto ownership. Monthly road tests cover six to eight American cars, mainly high performance, as well as new foreign sedans and economy cars. Comparisons are in language understandable to the average person who is not technically oriented. Each issue features: vintage cars, racing, news from Europe, new car announcements, etc. There are many black and white illustrations and occasional color photos. Special issues throughout the year —June deals with the used car market, November with the new cars and February is an awards issue, devoted to recognition of the most significant automotive achievements by the industry and the people in it. Editorial policy is opposed to government regulation of automobile safety engineering and smog control systems. In view of its editorial policy it is the verso of what is preached in *Road & Track* or *Car and Driver.* Libraries should try to cover both sides of the argument, and for this reason it is the basic magazine in all size and type libraries.

National Speed Sport News. 1932. w. $5. Chris Economaki. Kay Publishing Co., Box 608, Ridgewood, N.J. 07451. Illus., adv. Circ: 57,583.

Aud: Ga, Sh. *Rv:* M. *Jv:* C.

A weekly newspaper for the auto racing enthusiast. Gives fairly prompt and detailed coverage of professional oval track and road races, foreign and domestic, racing cars, and people in racing. A greater coverage of races than the daily newspapers and faster than monthly magazines. Where there are fans this is a must, but most school and public libraries can probably pass.

Road & Track. 1947. m. $6. Dean Batchelor. Bond Publishing Co., 834 Production Place, Newport Beach, Calif. 92660. Illus., index, adv. Circ: 263,855.

Bk. rev: 2,300 words, signed. *Aud:* Ga, Ac, Jc, Sh. *Rv:* H. *Jv:* V.

One of the best automobile magazines for people who are seriously concerned with driving and cars. It has appeal for intellectuals and the men who can hardly read a road sign. Emphasis is on foreign-made cars, particularly the sports models. Every issue gives detailed road test results on at least two cars. There is generally an article on a personality in the racing field. Regular departments pre-

sent non-technical information about the motor industry, a calendar of motor sports events and technical advice to those readers who write for help. Black and white and some color photographs. Issues an annual which includes all road tests for the year. Either this, or this and *Car and Driver,* should be in every library where there is an automobile enthusiast about. Of course, the Detroit oriented readers should be equally served with *Motor Trend.* The librarian who has to make the choice between the two is advised to first consult readers to ascertain where major interest lies.

Road Test. 1963. m. $6. Ocee Ritch. Motor Sports Pubns., P.O. Box 22253, Los Angeles, Calif. 90022. Illus. Circ: 120,000.

Aud: Ga. *Rv:* M. *Jv:* B.

Prepared to help the average American driver select a new car. About ten American and foreign car road tests reported in each issue. The tests are objective and thorough, and evaluations are based on the panel decision of a group of experts. Other articles evaluate automobile products and occasionally safety features. No advertisements by automobile manufacturers or accessory manufacturers are accepted. Black and white pictures throughout. A useful addition for public libraries.

Rod & Custom. 1953. m. $4.25. Don Typond. Quinn Pubns., Inc. 5959 Hollywood Blvd., Los Angeles, Calif. 90028. Illus., adv. Circ: 122,975. Microform: UM.

Aud: Sh, Jh. *Rv:* L. *Jv:* C.

A magazine directed to the junior high and high school crowd interested in customizing cars and hot rods. Articles, written by the staff and contributors, cover shows and competitions, and how to build chassis and various types of hot rods and go-karts. Pictures and a page of cartoons help to keep the amount of text at a minimum. A second or third choice, but a passable one where there is a heavy demand for such magazines. See also *Car Craft* and *Hot Rod Magazine.*

SAE Journal. 1917. m. Membership (non-members, $12). Otto W. Vathke. Soc. of Automotive Engineers, Inc., 485 Lexington Ave., New York, N. Y. 10017. Illus., index, adv. Circ: 28,000. Microform: UM.

Indexed: ASTI, EngI, MetAb. *Aud:* Sa, Ac, Jc. *Rv:* H. *Jv:* B.

Directed to automotive engineers and students of engineering, covering: automobiles, trucks, airplanes, trains, fuels, tires, computers, space, and management. Articles, written by engineers in the field, are generally followed by a bibliography of publications which can be ordered from *SAE Journal.* There is a special section on the Society of Automotive Engineers—reports from committees, a calendar of meetings, and news of appointments and promotions of members. In the back of each issue there is an annotated list of various papers of the latest technical information on different subjects developed by SAE. Only for technical and business libraries.

Sports Car Graphic. 1961. m. $5. James E. Alexander. Petersen Publishing Co., 5959 Hollywood Blvd., Hollywood, Calif. 90028. Illus., adv. Circ: 150,000. Microform: UM.

Aud: Ga, Sh. *Rv:* M. *Jv:* B.

Written for sports car, competition racing and rallying enthusiasts, this has many cartoons, and black and white and color photos. The staff writes most of the technically oriented articles. Tests and reports on about two to four cars a month, primarily foreign. Regular departments: calendar of major racing events; "Washington Report"— information on pending federal legislation; "Rally Scene" —a quick wrap-up on what's going on in rallying; "New Products"—photos and brief information on new car items. A third choice, after *Car and Driver* and *Road & Track,* for public and school libraries.

Super Stock & Drag Illustrated. 1964. m. $5. James W. Davis. Eastern Publishing Co., 522 Pitt St., Alexandria, Va. 22314. Illus., adv. Circ: 111,494.

Aud: Ga, Sh. *Rv:* M. *Jv:* B.

Differs from the normal "hot rod" magazine, in that emphasis is on late model, stock cars which are employed in authorized races—races which are now held in almost every community throughout the country. As the title suggests, there are numerous pictures of drivers and cars, racing events and new products. No fiction. Articles concentrate on technical material on how to turn an average American car into a stock machine, news of national and local races, personalities, and general information on the automobile industry. The writing is relatively simple, well within the grasp of the high school student or interested adult. In that it is more specialized, limited to a given sports event and type of car, it is no replacement for the better known *Hot Rod Magazine;* yet, wherever there is particular interest in cars this will be a good choice for many high school and public libraries. Kimtex Corporation (P.O. Box 26, Southwest City, Missouri, 64863) publishes two similar magazines: *Drag Strip* (1963. m. $5. Illus., adv. Circ: 89,000) and *Drag Racing* (1963. m. $5. Illus., adv. Circ: 79,000), which are neither as well illustrated or as authoritative, yet for fans fill a definite need. Librarians might bring them to the attention of those who enjoy *Super Stock* or *Hot Rod.*

Traffic Safety. 1927. m. $4.50. Angela Maher. National Safety Council, Inc., 425 N. Michigan Ave., Chicago, Ill. 60611. Illus., index, adv. Circ: 16,500. Microform: UM.

Indexed: PsyAb. *Aud:* Sa, Ac, Jc, Ht. *Rv:* M. *Jv:* B.

Issued by the National Safety Council for the purpose of bringing together the latest information on accident prevention. The journal is not for the layman, but primarily for the educator, traffic specialist, and police officer. Ar-

ticles are geared for the expert, moving from traffic control methods to safety devices. Particularly useful is the 30- to 40-page "Research Review" which summarizes all activity in this field. Teachers of driver education will find articles of value. The National Education Association and its American Driver and Traffic Safety Education Division issues *Safety-Administration, Instruction, Protection,* for members. It is free, and reports on safety instruction at the secondary level.

Trailering Guide. 1962. q. $2. George S. Wells. Rajo Pubns. Inc., 215 Park Ave. S., New York, N.Y. 10003. Illus., adv.

Aud: Ga. *Rv:* L. *Jv:* C.

Edited for owners or prospective owners of travel trailers, pick-up truck campers and motor homes. Also includes helpful information on travel. Articles, written by the staff and contributors, draw on experiences of people in building and living aboard trailers. There is at least one how-to-do-it article for trailer owners. Regular monthly features are "Meals on Wheels"—recipes and tips for trailer cooks; "Technical Tips"—answers to readers' problems; "Calendar of Events"—a listing of shows, rallies, caravans, and motorcades; "Rolling Along"—news of new products. The many black and white pictures help make this quick and easy to read. For public libraries where demand warrants—others can pass. See also *Wheels Afield.*

Ward's Quarterly. 1965. q. $15. Robert B. Powers. Powers & Co., Inc., 550 W. Fort St., Detroit, Mich. 48226. Illus., index, adv. Circ: 40,000.

Bk. rev: 6, 100–400 words. *Aud:* Sa, Ac. *Rv:* H. *Jv:* B.

A beautifully illustrated magazine of the automobile industry. Articles, written by the staff, give the history of motor transportation, the inside news of the auto industry, safety, cars and trucks, and news on personalities in the field. Regular features provide production figures and forecasts for United States and foreign manufacturers, and news of promotions in the field. Only for specialized collections.

Wheels Afield. 1967. m. $5. James E. Potter. Petersen Publishing Co., 5959 Hollywood Blvd., Los Angeles, Calif. 90028. Illus., adv.

Aud: Ga. *Rv:* L. *Jv:* B.

Comprehensive coverage of the field of recreational vehicles and their use and handling for safer, more comfortable trips. Each issue has four to five road tests of various types of recreational vehicles—vans, cars and trailers, trucks and piggy-backs, and motor homes. The reports are objective and designed to help the prospective buyer choose the proper combination for his particular needs. Technical articles are oriented toward the do-it-yourself handyman with information on modification and improvements for comfort and safety. Some of the regular monthly departments are "Date Book"—a calendar of trailer club rendezvous; "Is It Legal?"—a column by the Public Information officer of the California Department of Motor Vehicles; "Cycles Afield"—information about recreational cycles to be used along with campers; "The Woman's Angle"—helpful advice on the woman's area of responsibility: children, food supplies, and clothing. Many black and white and color photos. Differs from *Trailering Guide* in that more emphasis is put on travel. A useful, although not necessary acquisition for larger public libraries.

BANKING AND FINANCE

Indexes and Abstracts

Business Periodicals Index, Canadian Periodical Index, Public Affairs Information Service.

The Appalachian Financial Review. 1966. semi-ann. $3. Donald A. Fergusson. Duquesne Univ., Pittsburgh, Pa. 15219. Circ: 1,200. Microform: UM.

Aud: Sa, Ac, *Rv:* M. *Jv:* B.

This is not about the poverty belt. The name comes from the 11-state area where members of the Appalachian Finance Association work. The teaching of banking and finance was considered in the first issue, and economics of pensions plans in the second. Articles are scholarly, well documented, and very much down-to-business. Should be in all medium to large business collections in the Appalachian area, and might be considered by other libraries because of the wide scope of the articles.

Bank of England Quarterly Bulletin. 1960. q. Issued free to libraries, financial institutions, economists, etc. Economic Intelligence Dept., Bank of England, London E.C. 2. Index.

Indexed: PAIS. *Aud:* Sa, Ac. *Rv:* H. *Jv:* B.

This journal is an invaluable guide to the British banking scene, and the British economy as a whole. At the beginning of each issue, there is a fairly lengthy commentary section, which reviews the British economy during the preceding three months. A specialized journal for large academic libraries, although it may be useful in other situations where there is a particular interest in the politics and economics of Britain.

The Bankers' Magazine. 1844. m. $6.30. G. W. Maynard. Waterlow & Sons Ltd., Waterlow House, Worship St., London, E.C. 2. Illus., index, adv. Circ: 5,300. Microform: UM.

Indexed: BusI, PAIS. *Bk. rev:* 2–4, short, signed. *Aud:* Sa, Ac. *Rv:* M. *Jv:* B.

The British counterpart of the American journal of the same name. Articles cover every aspect of British money, finance, banking and the economy in general. Material tends to be technical and presupposes at least a basic knowledge of the field. American students will profit from the section which gives model answers for the banking examination. Only for large business collections.

Bankers Magazine. 1846. q. $24. Theodore L. Gross. Warren, Gorham & Lamont, Inc., 89 Beach St., Boston, Mass. 02111. Illus., adv. Circ: 5,100. Microform: UM.

Bk. rev: 15–20, short, signed. *Aud:* Sa, Ac. *Rv:* M. *Jv:* B.

One of the oldest professional journals in America devoted to aspects of banking such as planning, economics, business trends, and counseling. The articles are scholarly, prepared by professors, accountants, and lawyers with a banking background. Government officials and bankers also contribute. While highly specialized, from time to time it publishes articles of more general interest in the field of economics and history. Primarily for business collections and academic libraries, where there is a major business school.

Bankers Monthly, national magazine of banking & investments. 1884. m. $6. Alvin M. Younquist, Jr. Rand McNally & Co., Box 7600, Chicago, Ill. 60680. Illus., adv. Circ: 27,289.

Indexed: BusI. *Aud:* Sa, Ac. *Rv:* M. *Jv:* B.

Prepared for top management in banks and investment houses, this is primarily concerned with how money is invested. Interestingly enough, the writing style is good to excellent, the otherwise technical material relatively easy to understand for a student of economics. Serious investors will find it of value for the advice on stocks and bonds. There is an annual report on finance companies, and a section giving brief comments about people in the profession. Obviously not everyone's reading matter, but an important item in business collections and schools of business.

Banking. 1908. m. $6. William P. Bogie. 90 Park Ave., New York, N.Y. 10016. Illus., index, adv. Circ: 40,431. Reprint: Abrahams.

Indexed: BusI, PAIS. *Aud:* Sa, Ac. *Rv:* M. *Jv:* B.

The journal of the American Bankers Association is primarily for members of the banking profession and teachers and students of advanced economics. The writing style is popular, yet the material is well documented. All areas of banking are covered including the investment market, consumer credit, and world business. There are numerous diagrams, charts, and graphs. Only for special collections.

Burroughs Clearing House; for bank and financial officers. 1916. m. Controlled circulation. Harry V. Odle. Box 299, Detroit, Mich. 48232. Illus., adv. Circ: 104,000. Microform: UM.

Indexed: BusI. *Aud:* Sa, Ac, Jc. *Rv:* M. *Jv:* B.

A pragmatic approach to banking and finance for bank and financial officers. Emphasis is on personalities, and "how-to-do-it" feature articles. The style and contents are popular and readable. There are sections devoted to "Trends in Finance," "Washington View-Point," "International and Personality Spotlight." And surprisingly there are some cartoons—bankers are not quite as stuffy as their popular image. The "controlled circulation" means there are no paid subscribers and that the magazine profits via advertising and assuring the advertisers that their ads will be seen. Libraries might inquire for copies, but only for large business collections.

Canadian Banker. 1893. q. $2. D. W. Slater. Canadian Bankers Assn., 50 King St., W., Toronto, Ont. Illus. Circ: 12,000.

Indexed: CanI, PAIS. *Bk. rev:* 4–6, short, signed. *Aud:* Sa, Ac. *Rv:* M. *Jv:* B.

The Canadian equivalent to *Banking,* covering much the same type of material and interests. Most articles are in English, with occasional contributions in French. There are sections on foreign banking; a "Banker's Diary," giving news events in the banking profession, and a section on legal decisions that affect banking in Canada. Only for the special or large business collections.

Exchange. 1939. m. $2. William D. Horgan. New York Stock Exchange, 11 Wall St., New York, N.Y. 10005. Illus. Circ: 130,600. Reprint: Johnson, Abrahams.

Indexed: PAIS. *Aud:* Ga, Ac, Jc. *Rv:* H. *Jv:* B.

A small magazine written in a popular style for the "amateur" as well as for the "pro" in the market. The six articles per issue range from industry surveys to economic forecasts, discussions of industries of the future, far-out scientific developments, portfolio analysis, trends in dividends, stock splits, odd lots. Two features: "Investors' Notebook," a capsule discussion of widely used business and financial terms; and "Who's New on the Big Board," brief sketches of companies newly listed on the Stock Exchange. Considering the low subscription price, a good investment/business magazine for almost any library.

Most periodicals in this section are primarily for the specialist, and aside from *Exchange,* the average public, junior college, or college library will probably only be interested in magazines of wider scope. Although each has a particular audience and purpose, the three more generalized banking and finance magazines are *Finance, Financial World,* and *Magazine of Wall Street.* The latter, along with *Exchange,* is probably the most helpful for the private investor; the first two are for the average businessman.

Federal Reserve Bank of New York. Monthly Review. 1919. m. Free. Federal Reserve Bank of New York, 33 Liberty St., New York, N.Y. 10005. Microform: UM.

Indexed: BusI, PAIS. *Aud:* Sa, Ac. *Rv:* H. *Jv:* B.

This short periodical is of importance primarily because it is the voice of the Federal Reserve Bank of New York, the major member of twelve regional banks. It normally contains three or four articles, reviews current domestic and international economic and financial developments, with occasional articles on select subjects in banking and finance. Charts and tables often accompany the text. The *Review* is intended for economists, bankers, businessmen, and teachers and students of economics and banking. It often includes the texts of major addresses by top officials of the Reserve Bank. Regular features are "The Business Situation" and "The Money and Bond Markets," reviewing the prior month. The other eleven regional banks also publish free periodicals. These periodicals are invaluable in giving a picture of U.S. banking as well as the entire U.S. economy. All are useful additions to the *Federal Reserve Bulletin,* and should be found in large reference collections.

Federal Reserve Bulletin. 1915. m. $6. Board of Governors, Federal Reserve System, Washington, D.C. 20551. Index. Circ: 26,500. Microform: UM. Reprint: Kraus, Abrahams.

Indexed: BusI, PAIS. *Aud:* Sa, Ac. *Rv:* H. *Jv:* A.

Directed primarily to members of the banking profession, but is of value to economists and graduate students. Each issue contains an unsigned article on some aspect of economics or banking; a section, "Staff Economic Studies," which summarizes, or sometimes gives an entire version of, papers written by members of the staff of the Federal Reserve System; and a summary of new laws, and interpretations of laws, as they apply to banking. Over one-half of each issue is devoted to tables containing data on various aspects of the U.S. economy under such headings as: bank credit, mortgage and consumer credit, credit markets, government and corporate finance, production, prices, and international trade and finance. The tables are an invaluable guide to the changes in the American economy. A basic item for large reference collections in both public and academic libraries. For a discussion of regional bulletins, see *Federal Reserve Bank of New York. Monthly Review.*

Finance; the magazine of money. 1941. m. $12. Gardner Jack Frost. 25 E. 73rd St., New York, N.Y. 10021. Illus., adv. Circ: 28,000.

Indexed: PAIS. *Aud:* Ga, Ac. *Rv:* M. *Jv:* B.

A highly readable general financial report, covering all aspects of the field, with particular emphasis on personalities. The style is quite similar to *Time* magazine—from cover stories about leading businessmen to its attractive layout. Most of the average eight to nine articles per issue, on industries, business trends, and investments, are unsigned. There are sections giving financial information from Washington about insurance, and stocks, and also a section on people in the financial field. The magazine has a slightly conservative editorial policy. While directed to corporate officials, will be of interest to most businessmen and students of finance. Should be in larger public and academic business collections. See concluding remarks for *Exchange.*

Financial Analysts Journal. 1945. bi-m. $6.50. P. R. Bretzy. Financial Analysts Federation, 82 Beaver St., New

York, N.Y. 10005. Index, adv. Circ: 17,000. Reprint: Abrahams.

Indexed: BusI. *Bk. rev:* 2–3, 150 words, signed. *Aud:* Sa, Ac. *Rv:* M. *Jv:* B.

Written specifically for fund managers and teachers of finance, with some material for the private investor. The strength of the magazine is its unbiased reports on the corporate and economic outlook and techniques of money management. Other articles cover a wide range of topics from foreign investments to an overview of investment literature (an excellent feature for large business libraries) and short book reviews. The analyses of various industries make it a worthwhile addition for any size or type library where there is more than passing interest in the stock market. Only for large libraries and academic business collections.

Finance and Development. 1964. q. Free. Intl. Monetary Fund. 19th & H Sts., Washington, D.C. 20431. Illus. Circ: 85,000. Microform: UM.

Indexed: PAIS. *Bk. rev:* 3–5, 250 words, signed. *Aud:* Ga, Ac, Jc. *Rv:* H. *Jv:* B.

Despite the sponsor and title, the editors assert this is not for the specialist, but for a wider audience. The seven to eight articles are purposefully written for the layman who is seeking knowledge of activities of the International Monetary Fund and the World Bank. The authors presuppose some knowledge of business and finance, but manage to avoid jargon. Material covers such things as business in Europe, the problems of new nations, world wide inflation, sales taxes—and almost anything concerned with international finance and development. Features include a summary of recent activities of the International Bank for Reconstruction and Development and the International Monetary Fund. As the magazine is free, and as the scope is wide, it should be found in both academic and public libraries.

Financial Executive. 1932. m. $8. Ben Makela. Financial Executives Inst., 50 W. 44th St., New York, N.Y. 10036. Illus., index, adv. Circ: 11,103.

Indexed: BusI, PAIS. *Aud:* Sa, Ac. *Rv:* M. *Jv:* B.

As the title of the magazine suggests, it is aimed at top corporate financial executives. There is an average of six articles per issue, and the editorial material is written almost entirely by financial executives. The "Research Notes" give information on taxes, government activities, and mergers. Extensive graphs and charts. An esoteric approach, and only for the largest business libraries.

Financial World. 1902. w. $24. R. J. Anderson. 17 Battery Pl., New York, N.Y. 10004. Illus., index, adv. Circ: 64,000. Microform: UM.

Indexed: PAIS. *Aud:* Ga, Ac. *Rv:* M. *Jv:* B.

A weekly which is directed primarily toward the private investor, and is a basic magazine (along with *Exchange,*

Finance and *The Magazine of Wall Street*) in this area. Each issue includes "Special Studies" of topics of interest in the field, reviews of industries with trend forecasts, as well as profiles of specific companies. In the first issue of each month, there is a section rating up to 1,900 stock issues. Extensive graphs and charts are used to illustrate certain points, and to give further information. The periodical has a definite conservative editorial policy. For all academic business collections, and for most medium to large public libraries.

International Monetary Fund Staff Papers. 1950. 3/yr. $6. ($3 to universities). J. Keith Horsefield. Intl. Monetary Fund, 19th & H Sts., N.W., Washington, D.C. 20431. Circ: 2,000. Microform: UM.

Indexed: BusI, PAIS. *Aud:* Sa, Ac. *Rv:* M. *Jv:* B.

A well-written collection of papers by the staff of the International Monetary Fund concerned with world monetary policies in regard to international trade, exchange rates, balance of payments and inflation. Many of the staff members are foreign nationals working in the Washington bank, thus adding variety to the viewpoints expressed. Only for large collections.

Journal of Finance. 1946. 4/yr. $10. Dudley G. Luckett. Robert A. Kavesh, Grad. Sch. of Business Admin., New York Univ., 100 Trinity Pl., New York, N.Y. 10006. Index, adv. Circ: 5,500. Reprint: Kraus, Abrahams.

Indexed: BusI, PAIS. *Bk. rev:* 20, 200 words, signed. *Aud:* Sa, Ac. *Rv:* M. *Jv:* B.

The scholarly journal of the American Finance Association is aimed at teachers, as well as the professional financier. Articles touch on every aspect of finance from international banking to consumer credit. The book reviews are short, but give a relatively current check on new works in the field. Dissertation abstracts and proceedings of the annual meeting are published. A basic magazine for schools of business at all academic levels, and for large public libraries.

Journal of Financial and Quantitative Analysis. 1966. q. $5. Stephen H. Archer. 105 Mackenzie Hall, Univ. of Washington, Seattle, Wash. 98105. Index, adv. Circ: 900.

Aud: Sa, Ac. *Rv:* H. *Jv:* B.

A joint publication of the Western Finance Association and UW's Graduate School of Business Administration, it specializes in the uneasy art of predicting stock market trends. More, however, than merely a handbook for market buffs, it contains much general information on the market, finance and banking. The publication's tone is, on the whole, heavily learned, and even at times esoteric. Yet for those with the right vocabulary, it is not likely to prove oppressive. Recent articles include reports on the liquidity and stabilization effects of savings deposits, stock evaluation theory and the use of investment portfolios to alter risk-patterns.

The Magazine of Wall Street. 1907. Fortnightly. $25. S. J. Paul. Ticker Publishing Co., Inc., 120 Wall St., New York, N.Y. 10005. Illus. index, adv. Circ: 10,000. Microform: UM.

Indexed: BusI. *Aud:* Ga, Ac, Jc. *Rv:* M. *Jv:* B.

Quite successfully fulfills its editorial policy: "to provide a publication written and produced by the experts in their fields, but presented in a way to make it useful to the average investor as well as the professional." The average eight unsigned articles per number will be readable to the layman, and are concerned primarily with the investment scene. There are also sections devoted to "Inside News" of Washington and Wall Street, as well as columns of analyses and information on investments. Along with *Exchange, Finance,* and *Financial World,* a good (and necessary) purchase for larger business collections in both public and academic libraries.

BIBLIOGRAPHY

Indexes and Abstracts

Abstracts of English Studies, Bibliographical Index, Biography Index, British Humanities Index, Historical Abstracts, Library Literature, Library Science Abstracts, Public Affairs Information Service, Social Sciences and Humanities Index. (For annotations, see Indexes and Abstracts Section.)

AB Bookman's Weekly. 1948. w. $13.50. Sol M. Malkin. Box 1100, Newark, N.J. 07101.

Indexed: LibLit. *Bk. rev:* 10–30, 50 words. *Aud:* Sa, Ac, Jc. *Rv:* H. *Jv:* V.

Devoted to news about the antiquarian book trade and libraries, this is in two parts. The first section features news of libraries, collectors, book sales, developments in the antiquarian book trade, sales tips, brief book reviews, and personnel information. Usually there are one or two lead articles on an aspect of the book trade or libraries, and several issues a year are devoted to special subjects, meetings and conventions, or personalities or authors. The second section, which makes-up two thirds of every issue, consists of lists of books wanted by various dealers. Other dealers check the wanted book section and quote prices for the desired items. The last pages normally are turned over to a listing of books for sale. There is also an annual *Bookman's Yearbook* which consists primarily of advertisements from the world's used book dealers, nicely indexed by subject. This latter feature makes it possible to check on who sells everything from Americana to books on zoology. The weekly magazine and yearbook are very much the work of editor Sol Malkin and his wife, who write most of the copy. The result is a highly individualized, intelligent, and always literate approach to the book world. By and large the best magazine of its type, and should be in every library where the librarian or the collector has the slightest interest in books. Differs from the other national book magazine, *Pub-lishers' Weekly,* in its emphasis on antiquarian and rare books.

American Book Collector. 1950. 10/yr. $6. W. B. Thorsen, 1822 School St., Chicago, Ill. 60657. Illus., index, adv. Circ: 2,000.

Bk. rev: 5–10, 50–150 words, signed. *Aud:* Ga, Ac, Jc. *Rv:* M. *Jv:* B.

Averaging 32 pages, this is the only American magazine devoted solely to articles of interest to book collectors. Editor Thorsen usually features checklists and three to four articles per issue to a given author. The value of the magazine is that the featured writer is usually little known, deserving of more attention. Contributors vary from journalists and librarians to bibliographers and book enthusiasts. The style is always within the grasp of the lay reader. The range of interest is wide, albeit Western literature and travels are often favored. The magazine deserves support by libraries, and certainly should be brought to the attention of collectors. It nicely augments *AB Bookman's Weekly* and *Publisher's Weekly,* but in no way replaces or competes with their particular fields of interest.

Bibliographic Survey: The Negro in Print. See Afro-American Section.

Bibliographical Society of America. Papers. 1904. q. Membership. William B. Todd. P.O. Box 397, Grand Central Station, New York, N.Y. 10017. Reprint: Kraus, Abrahams.

Indexed: LibLit, LibSciAb, SSHum. *Bk. rev:* 6–10, 500–2,000 words, signed. *Aud:* Sa, Ac, Jc. *Rv:* H. *Jv:* V.

There is no other American publication quite like this, and it stands well above the average bibliographic journal. Each issue contains four to five articles by experts on various aspects of bibliography, both analytical and historical. While the contributions tend to be a trifle esoteric, there are usually one or two items of interest to anyone remotely involved with books and publishing. The book reviews are the best available in this field, and following the lengthy critical remarks there are extensive notes by the review editor, Lawrence S. Thompson. Averaging some 150 to 200 pages, the whole boasts a pleasing format. A required item in all medium to large public and academic libraries.

Bibliography, Documentation, Terminology. 1960. bi-m. Free. Unesco, Place de Fontenoy, Paris, 7e. Circ: 3,000.

Aud: Sa, Ac. *Rv:* H. *Jv:* B.

Divided into three sections—"News from Unesco," "Bibliographic Services Throughout the World," "International and National Activities"—this 40- to 45-page bulletin contains current information of interest to large academic and public libraries. An invaluable tool for alerting librarians and scholars to the latest information from all parts of the world. Primarily for large research and reference collections in both public and academic libraries.

Bodleian Library Record. 1938. irreg. (Usually once or twice a year). 3s.6d. per issue. Bodleian Library, Oxford. Eng. Illus.

Aud: Sa, Ac. *Rv:* H. *Jv:* B.

About one-quarter of this 56-page journal is devoted to news and notes about the Bodleian Library; the remainder consists of our to five articles of bibliographic and historical interest. The whole is scholarly, documented and of primary value to the subject expert. This is one of a number of library based magazines which go considerably beyond being public relations vehicles, and are actually contributions to the scholarship of bibliography. In American academic and public library collections they fill an important role—primarily as adjuncts to the two basic bibliographic journals, *Bibliographical Society of America. Papers* and the English *The Library.* A representative group is indicated in this section, but for large research collections and library school needs the librarian should check *Ulrich's International Periodicals Directory.* See also select lists in the appendices concluding this work. For the average public or academic collection preference should be given to the two basic bibliographical journals mentioned above, followed by the *Harvard Library Bulletin,* the *New York Public Library Bulletin,* and possibly the *Library of Congress Quarterly Journal.*

The Book Collector. 1952. q. $6.50. Nicolas Barker. The Collector Ltd., 58 Frith St., London, W.1. Illus., index, adv. Reprint: Kraus, Abrahams.

Indexed: BritHum, LibLit, LibSciAb. *Bk. rev:* 5–8, 250–1,000 words, signed. *Aud:* Sa, Ac, Jc. *Rv:* H. *Jv:* A.

Among dedicated bibliographies, this is considered to be the best general journal of book collecting. Published in England, it is notable for its handsome format, frequent illustrations, and international interests. Each issue features news notes on the world of books; three to five articles on authors, typography, illustrations, collectors, libraries and the like; bibliographical notes and queries; excellent book reviews and shorter annotations for books received. The authors are prominent scholars, librarians, book dealers and bibliographers. The style is pleasing and comprehensible to the interested layman. This should be in every library, regardless of size, if only for the joy and edification of the book-loving librarian.

Books and Bookmen. 1955. m. $4. Stephanie Nettel. Hansom Books, 16 Buckingham Palace Rd., London S.W. 1. Illus., adv. Circ: 17,000.

Aud: Sa, Ac. *Rv:* H. *Jv:* B.

News and gossip about writers, publishers, and awards, but primarily of value for combination book reviews, i.e., two to four related titles examined by an authority in an essay of 500 to 1,000 words. Books of the British Commonwealth are noted, and subdivided by type and age group. About 100 titles are mentioned in each issue, and the reviews are both descriptive and critical. One of the best

mediums for British books, and should be included in all academic and larger libraries. Using a similar format and approach, Hansom Books also issues magazines in seven other areas. Each of these is well illustrated, excellent for an overview of the particular subject. And while the bias is definitely English, usually there is enough material of an international nature to warrant consideration by many American libraries. The magazines, self-descriptive by title, are: *Art and Artists, Dance and Dancers, Films and Filming, Music and Musicians, Plays and Players, Records and Recording, Seven Arts.* All are prepared by subject experts, exceptionally well-illustrated and written as much for the layman as the expert. Interested libraries should ask the publisher for sample copies.

The Bookseller; the organ of the book trade. 1858. w. $11.40. Edmond Seagrave. J. Whitaker & Sons, Ltd., 13 Bedford Sq., London, W.C. 1. Illus., adv. Circ: 13,000.

Aud: Sa, Ac, Jc. *Rv:* H. *Jv:* M.

Somewhat the English equivalent of *Publishers' Weekly.* Covers news of the booktrade, publishing and libraries, and lists all new British books, with a monthly cumulation. The cumulated lists become *Current Literature and Whitaker's Cumulative Book List,* i.e., the cousins of the *American Book Publishing Record* and the annual volume of same. Advertising, as in *PW,* composes a large part of each issue and there are special features such as "Under Review" which quotes from and digests reviews of new titles. A required item in any medium to large academic or public library.

British Book News; a guide to book selection. 1940. m. $4.25. Patricia Bingham. British Council, 65 Davies St., London W.1. Illus., index, adv. Circ: 10,000.

Indexed: BritHum, LibSciAb. *Aud:* Sa, Ac, Jc. *Rv:* M. *Jv:* B.

An English publication which briefly reviews some 250 titles published in the Commonwealth. The reviews are succinct, descriptive, and usually critical. Dewey number is given for each title. Special sections for young people, lists of forthcoming books, and highlights in given areas. Each issue has its own index. Normally there are one or two biographical articles. A useful item for larger libraries.

Bulletin of Bibliography and Magazine Notes. 1897. 3/yr. $7. Walter T. Dziura. F. W. Faxon Co., 515–525 Hyde Park Ave., Boston, Mass. 02131. Index, adv. Circ: 1,005. Microform: UM. Reprint: Johnson.

Indexed: LibLit, LibSciAb. *Aud:* Sa, Ac. *Rv:* M. *Jv:* B.

Although averaging only some 20 to 30 pages per issue, this is of major importance for detailed bibliographies of authors. A typical issue includes a checklist of James Baldwin's work and critical articles about him, a bibliography of Richard Wright and usually a continuing series on writings about an author such as Herman Melville. Over its long history the magazine has included almost every major

American and foreign author in its bibliographies. Of lesser help is the "Birth, Deaths and Magazine Notes" which is a simple listing by title (with bibliographical information) on new and deceased magazines, as well as notes on changes in title. An occasional short book review or two rounds out each issue. From time to time a single article on some aspect of bibliography may be published, but this is the exception. For all academic literature collections, and for larger academic and public reference and acquisition departments.

Cambridge Bibliographical Society. Transactions. 1949. ann. $4.25. Cambridge Univ. Press, 32 E. 57th St., New York, N.Y. 10022.

Indexed: BritHum. *Aud:* Sa. *Rv:* H. *Jv:* B.

Unlike other bibliographical society publications, emphasis here is almost exclusively on esoteric bibliographical research which has limited appeal except for the subject expert. One of five parts is issued each year, the volume cumulating at the end of the fifth year. Only for large collections.

Cornell Library Journal. 1966. 3/yr. $4.50. George H. Healey. 106 Olin Library, Cornell Univ. Library, Ithaca, N.Y. 14850. Illus. Circ: 1,200.

Indexed: HistAb. *Aud:* Sa, Ac. *Rv:* H. *Jv:* B.

A handsome publication on the pattern of the Harvard and New York Public Library bulletins. Brings news of the Cornell Library, particularly concerning the library's life and growth, and offers investigators using the library a means of publishing reports on their findings. Articles have appeared on the early days of the library, on Coleridge's "16-page pamphlet" of sonnets, and on recent exhibitions from outstanding acquisitions.

The Courier. 1964. irreg. $2 per issue. John S. Mayfield. Syracuse Univ. Library, Syracuse, N.Y. 13210. Illus.

Aud: Sa, Ac. *Rv:* M. *Jv:* B.

Published by the Syracuse University Library Associates, this is one of the better magazines of its type. The typography and illustrations are unusually pleasing. Includes articles covering all aspects of bibliography, literature and history. News notes on the activities of the library and the Associates. For larger collections.

A Current Bibliography on African Affairs. See African Studies Section.

Harvard Library Bulletin. 1947. q. $10. Howard Mumford Jones. Harvard Univ. Press, 79 Garden St., Cambridge, Mass. 02138. Illus. Circ: 1,000. Reprint: Johnson.

Indexed: LibLit. *Aud:* Sa, Ac. *Rv:* H. *Jv:* A.

Among the scores of journals and bulletins issued by large academic American libraries, this is the best. Having ceased publication in 1960, it began again in 1967 and within its 200 or so pages now offers outstanding articles on bibliography, literature, history and material connected in some way with interests of the Harvard library. In view

of its wide scope, it should be found in all medium to large libraries.

Huntington Library Quarterly; a journal for the history and interpretation of English and American civilization. 1937. q. $6. John M. Steadman. The Huntington Library and Art Gallery. San Marino, Calif. 91108. Illus., index, Circ: 950. Microform: UM. Reprint: Kraus, Abrahams.

Aud: Sa, Ac. *Rv:* H. *Jv:* B.

Primarily contains scholarly articles of original research with emphasis on literature and history. In addition to the main articles, there are the usual news notes and shorter items about the library and its collection. Ranks among the top ten such publications in this country, and deserves serious attention by any academic library.

Inter-American Review of Bibliography. 1951. q. $3. Armando C. Pacheco. Pan American Union, Div. of Philosophy and Letters, Washington, D.C. 20006. Illus., index, adv. Circ: 3,000. Microform: UM. Reprint: Johnson, Abrahams.

Indexed: HistAb. *Bk. rev:* Various number, lengths. *Aud:* Sa, Ac, Jc, Ht. *Rv:* H. *Jv:* A.

Used heavily by historians and students of literature, this is a journal devoted to all aspects of the humanities as found in the Americas. Articles are scholarly, well documented and represent some of the leading authorities in the field. The title, unfortunately, seems to frighten the student who might find much of value here for term papers and basic information on Latin America. The book reviews consider books from all nations, often touching on titles not mentioned in the more common review media. Also, there are usually good to excellent bibliographies. In view of its particular interest and its forthright treatment of materials, it is preferable for serious work to the more propagandistic *Americas.* It deserves a place in all medium to large academic and public libraries, and could be well used by teachers and advanced students in high schools.

John Rylands Library. Bulletin. 1903. semi-ann. $3.65. John Rylands Library, Deansgate, Manchester 3, Eng. Illus. Reprint: Kraus, Abrahams.

Indexed: BritHum, LibSciAb. *Aud:* Sa, Ac. *Rv:* H. *Jv:* B.

In scope and interest this is somewhat equivalent to the *Harvard Library Bulletin.* Each issue contains news and notes of the library, and eight to ten articles on literature, bibliography, linguistics, history, and almost anything of interest to the literary scholar. The writing is good to excellent, but presupposes a basic understanding and knowledge of bibliographic practices. It tends to be extremely esoteric, e.g., "Some Traces of Heterodox Theology in the Samaritan Book of Joshua." Of interest to any large academic library.

Library. 1899. q. Membership (Non-members, 50s.). R. A. Sayce, Worcester College, Oxford. Subscriptions to: Oxford Univ. Press, Ely House, Dover St., London W.1. Circ: 1,250. Microform: UM. Reprint: Kraus, Abrahams.

Indexed: LibSciAb. *Bk. rev:* 2–5, 1,000–2,400 words. *Aud:* Sa, Ac. *Rv:* H. *Jv:* B.

Next to the *Papers of the Bibliographical Society of America,* this publication of the Bibliographical Society of England would be a second choice in most American libraries. Personal subscribers would want both, particularly as emphasis here is on all aspects of not only English, but international history of books, publishing, printing, libraries, and book collecting. The articles are scholarly, yet boast a quite pleasant style. Emphasis is on historical, descriptive and analytical bibliography in the longer articles and in the notes. The book reviews, while limited in number, are excellent.

Library of Congress. Quarterly Journal. 1943. q. $2.50.
Sarah L. Wallace. Supt. of Documents, U.S. Govt. Printing Office, Washington, D.C. 20402. Illus., index. Microform: UM.

Aud: Sa, Ac, Jc. *Rv:* H. *Jv:* B.

This is a "best buy" for any library or interested student from the standpoint of price and content. The 100-page magazine not only is beautifully designed and illustrated, but covers a variety of interests as reflected by the activities of the Library of Congress. The articles by scholars and members of the L.C. staff touch on every base from education and motion pictures to biography and music. Certain issues are given over in part to a particular field, e.g., papermaking, orientalia, etc. Each issue concludes with an annotated listing of "Some Recent Publications of the Library of Congress," a valued checklist for any librarian. Although primarily for the specialist, the informed laymen will enjoy being introduced to this journal, and considering its low price it should be in most libraries.

New York Public Library. Bulletin. 1897. 10/yr. $5.
David V. Erdman. New York Public Library, Fifth Ave. & 42nd St., New York, N.Y. 10018. Illus. Circ: 1,700.

Indexed: AbEnStud, BiblI, BiogI, LibLit, PAIS. *Aud:* Sa, Ac. *Rv:* H. *Jv:* A.

One of the best printed, certainly one of the most interesting of the bibliographic library publications. Each issue contains articles on various aspects of bibliography from rare books and typography to manuscript holdings and music. Anyone who enjoys the eccentric, the out-of-the-way type of reading matter is sure to find at least one or two issues of deep interest. It is particularly useful for its many bibliographies, check lists and notes on little known material either recently acquired, or recently discovered in the stacks. It will appeal to all serious students, librarians, and even laymen. A must for medium to large public and academic libraries.

Newberry Library Bulletin. 1944. irreg. Free to qualified
personnel. James M. Wells. The Newberry Library, 60 W. Walton St., Chicago, Ill. 60610. Illus., index. Circ: 2,500.

Aud: Sa, Ac. *Rv:* H. *Jv:* B.

While relatively small in format, this is handsomely printed, nicely edited, and usually contains three to four short articles based on some aspect of the Newberry Library collection or interests. It is particularly useful for information on the humanities, typography and, on occasion, Americana. The articles are by the staff, or by scholars who have used the facilities of the library. Of interest to bibliographers, and students of English and history.

Princeton University Library Chronicle. 1939. 3/yr.
$5. Mrs. Mina R. Bryan. Friends of the Library, Princeton Univ. Library, Princeton, N.J. 08540. Illus., index. Circ: 1,600. Microform: UM. Reprint: Johnson, Abrahams.

Indexed: LibLit. *Aud:* Sa, Ac. *Rv:* M. *Jv:* B.

Each issue usually features two or three long bibliographic articles on either the University or the holdings of the library. There are library notes, news, and information on the Friends of the Princeton library. The whole is well documented, illustrated, and nicely printed. A more esoteric item for larger academic libraries.

Private Library. 1957. q. Membership (Non-members,
$8.50). Roderick Cave. Private Libraries Assn., 41 Cuckoo Hill Rd., Pinner, Middlesex, Eng. Illus., adv. Circ: 1,000.

Indexed: LibLit, LibSciAb. *Bk. rev:* 5–10, 300–500 words, signed. *Aud:* Sa, Ac, Jc. *Rv:* M. *Jv:* B.

Somewhat a junior version of the older *Book Collector,* this has a deceptive title. The contents have nothing to do with libraries or librarians, *per se,* emphasis being on book collecting, typography, and more particularly private press books. (An annual checklist of such titles, *Private Press Books,* is published by the Association annually, and constitutes the best current source of information in the field.) The 40- to 50-page pocket-sized magazine features a round-up article on the interests of members, and contributions on everything from private collections to typography and illustrations. Although small, it is nicely printed. In addition to the regular book reviews, a special section is given over to short announcements of "Recent Private Press Books." After the *Book Collector,* a first choice for anyone interested in books.

Publishers' Weekly; the book industry journal. 1872.
w. $16.50. Chandler B. Grannis. R. R. Bowker Co., 1180 Ave. of the Americas, New York, N.Y. 10036. Illus., index, adv. Circ: 26,700. Microform: UM.

Indexed: BusI, LibLit, RG. *Bk. rev:* 75–100, 50–100 words. *Aud:* Sa, Ac, Jc, Sh, Jh, E. *Rv:* H. *Jv:* V.

The basic American book trade journal. Features news of publishers and booksellers, lists of new and forthcoming American publications, and editorials and articles which concentrate on the business activities of the book world. Important to all libraries for two reasons. First, the "Weekly Record," an alphabetical listing by authors of books published the previous week in America. Full bibliographical data is given for each title, plus a short descriptive note.

This represents the base of the major American trade bibliography which cumulates monthly as a separate publication, *The American Book Publishing Record,* and in an annual volume. Adjacent features in each issue include: "PW Forecasts," detailed, often critical annotations of forthcoming fiction, nonfiction, children's books and paperbacks. There are, also, announcement issues for the spring and fall which give detailed information on publisher's lists of forthcoming works. The second reason for having *PW* in all libraries is it is the only publication which gives complete information on the booktrade from statistics to a monthly issue devoted to book design and production. Every number features several articles on publishing, libraries, book selling and the like. Of lesser interest to libraries are regular departments on personnel changes, tips on sales, and brief news notes. In addition to announcement numbers there are special issues devoted to children's books, religion and scientific and technical works, and an annual summary number of statistics, trends and awards. Should be in every library regardless of size or type.

Studies in Bibliography and Booklore; devoted to research in the field of Jewish bibliography. irreg. 1953. $4. Library of Hebrew Union College, Jewish Inst. of Religion, Cincinnati, Ohio 54220. Illus., index. Circ: 1,300.

Aud: Sa, Ac. *Rv:* H. *Jv:* B.

A scholarly journal devoted primarily to Jewish bibliography, publishing, booksellers, etc. While most of the articles are in English, many references are made in Hebrew. Issues tend to concentrate on a given area, e.g., Jewish Persian studies. There are numerous black and white illustrations. A superior bibliographic journal for the specialist and for all large collections.

Yale University Library Gazette. 1926. q. $4. Donald C. Gallup. Yale Univ. Library, New Haven, Conn. 06520. Illus., index.

Indexed: LibLit. *Aud:* Sa, Ac. *Rv:* M. *Jv:* B.

While the primary emphasis of this journal is on the resources of the Yale library, it has much wider application for the student of history and bibliography. The four to five articles, written for the most part by faculty and librarians at Yale, are universal in interest. For example, a typical issue might include material on French illustrated books, books relating to Colonial Latin America, and information on special collections. Usually there are a number of excellent illustrations. The concluding "Recent Acquisitions," a descriptive listing of some six to eight pages, highlights important new manuscripts, books, broadsides and the like acquired by the library. A must for the serious bibliographer and all library schools.

BIOLOGICAL SCIENCES

Indexes and Abstracts

Biological and Agricultural Abstracts, Biological Abstracts, Chemical Abstracts, Education Index, Index Medicus, Psy- *chological Abstracts, Science Citation Index.* (For annotations, see Indexes and Abstracts Section.)

The biological sciences probably contain more subfields and areas of specialization than any other science. Research developments in the last decade have altered the emphasis in the study of modern biology so that sharp delineations can no longer be made between subfields. Journals included in this section have been grouped into six major areas. (1) General, covering more than one subfield and including a sampling of periodicals on ecology, evolution, cytology, and developmental biology; (2) Biochemistry and Biophysics; (3) Botany; (4) Microbiology and Genetics; (5) Physiology; and (6) Zoology. Selections of research journals for academic libraries have been severely limited, mostly to U.S. publications. Unless noted otherwise, these represent authoritative, high-quality publications of distinguished scientific societies and well-known commercial publishers. Moreover, each research report submitted for publication is usually reviewed critically by one or two referees. Thus, the annotations which follow are brief, general descriptions of the periodicals, rather than evaluative comments, which only subject specialists are qualified to make. The American Institute of Biological Sciences Subcommittee on Facilities and Standards has published a list of first-choice journals for biological libraries (*BioScience,* v. 13, no. 6, 1963, pp. 14–19). Their basic selection of essential periodicals are: *American Journal of Botany, American Zoologist, Biological Abstracts, Biological Bulletin, Ecology, Genetics, Journal of Bacteriology, Journal of Experimental Biology, Journal of Experimental Zoology, Nature, Physiological Reviews, Quarterly Review of Biology, Science,* and *Scientific American.* Several additional journals (many of which are included here) were also suggested for possible choices.

General

American Biology Teacher. 1938. 9/yr. Membership (Non-members, $10). National Assn. of Biology Teachers, 1420 N St., N.W., Washington, D.C. 20005. Illus., index. Circ: 12,000.

Indexed: BioAb, EdI. *Bk. rev:* 5–10, 500 words, signed. *Aud:* Ac, Jc, Ht. *Rv:* H. *Jv:* B.

The professional journal for high school biology teachers, yet it may be used effectively by college teachers at the beginning course level. The 12 to 15 articles, written by educators and scientists, are concerned with better methods of teaching, new research, teaching aids, technological changes, etc. A basic item for all high school libraries, and most college libraries.

American Midland Naturalist. 1909. q. $12.50. Joseph A. Tihen. Univ. of Notre Dame, Notre Dame, Ind. 46556. Illus., index. Circ: 968. Reprint: Johnson. Microform: Canner, UM.

Indexed: BioAg, BioAb, ChemAb, SCI. *Bk. rev:* Notes. *Aud:* Sa, Ac, Jc. *Rv:* H. *Jv:* B.

A general biological journal reporting original research in any of the biological sciences. Ecological studies are frequently presented. Papers mostly concern, but are not restricted to the natural history of the mid-West. Occasional critical papers on specialized topics are also included.

American Naturalist; devoted to the advancement and correlation of the biological sciences. 1867. bi-m. $12.50. E. C. Lewontin and W. K. Baker. Univ. of Chicago Press, 5750 Ellis Ave., Chicago, Ill. 60637. Illus., index. Circ: 2,000. Reprint: Johnson. Microform: Princeton, UM.

Indexed: BioAb, BioAg, ChemAb, SCI. *Aud:* Sa, Ac, Jc. *Rv:* H. *Jv:* B.

One of the older U.S. biological journals and the official organ of the American Society of Naturalists. Review articles and research papers emphasize broad biological studies and a view of organic evolution. Short discussions or "Letters to the Editor" are also included, as are occasional general addresses, essays or papers presented at symposia.

Biological Bulletin. 1898. bi-m. $18. W. D. Russell Hunter. Marine Biological Laboratory, Woods Hole, Mass. 02543. Illus., index, adv. Circ: 2,500. Microform: Canner.

Indexed: BioAb, BioAg, ChemAb, SCI. *Aud:* Sa, Ac, Jc. *Rv:* H. *Jv:* B.

Covering research papers ranging from biochemical studies to zoology, the journal is an excellent publication representative of overall studies in the biological sciences. The periodical also carries reports of the Marine Biological Laboratory and abstracts of papers presented at special symposia there.

Biological Reviews of the Cambridge Philosophical Society. 1923. q. $18.50. Sydney Smith. 32 E. 57th St., New York, N.Y. 10022. Illus., index. Circ: 1,394.

Indexed: BioAb, ChemAb, SCI, IMed. *Aud:* Sa, Ac. *Rv:* H. *Jv:* B.

Reviewing specific topics in biology, the journal comprises critical and authoritative summaries of current research problems. Each issue contains three to four lengthy articles which, although constituting a high degree of specialization, are still styled as tutorials for the nonspecialist biologist. Reviews contain detailed tables of contents, excellent bibliographies, and resumés which are not merely short abstracts, but which detail the main facts and conclusions of the paper. Occasional lectures presented before the Society are also published.

BioScience. 1951. m. Membership only, institutions $18. David M. Prescott. Amer. Inst. of Biological Sciences, 3900 Wisconsin Ave., Washington, D.C. 20016. Illus., index, adv. Circ: 35,000.

Indexed: BioAb, ChemAb, SCI. *Bk. rev:* 6–8, lengthy, signed. *Aud:* Sa, Ac, Jc, Sh. *Rv:* H. *Jv:* A.

The official publication of the American Institute of Biological Sciences. Covers developments in the biological, medical and agricultural sciences both from the standpoint of research and education as well as news and commentary.

Contains full length articles, research reports, as well as information articles on new developments in all the life sciences and bibliographies of pertinent research areas of biology. Significant news and comment on biologists, congressional legislation, scientific meetings, including a calendar of events, government programs and awards are a regular feature of each issue. Reviews all important new books in biology and, in addition to extended reviews, includes brief reviews and lists of new book titles.

Developmental Biology. 1959. bi-m. John W. Saunders, Jr. Academic Press, Inc., 111 Fifth Ave. New York, N.Y. 10003. Illus., index.

Indexed: BioAb, BioAg, ChemAb, IMed, SCI. *Aud:* Sa, Ac. *Rv:* H. *Jv:* B.

Focusing attention on developmental problems from both botanical and zoological approaches, this international journal publishes research papers "dealing with embryonic and postembryonic development of plants and animals." The majority of articles appear in English, with occasional papers in French and German.

Ecology; all forms of life in relation to environment. 1920. bi-m. $18. Monte Lloyd, Peter Frank, Ralph L. Dix. Duke Univ. Press, Box 6697, College Station, Durham, N.C. 27708. Illus., index. Circ: 5,200.

Indexed: BioAb, BioAg, ChemAb, SCI. *Bk. rev:* 5–8, lengthy, signed. *Aud:* Sa, Ac, Jc. *Rv:* H. *Jv:* B.

Published for the Ecological Society of America, the journal contains research papers and shorter papers. The stress is on basic ecological problems, rather than applied studies. Articles are restricted in length to less than 20 pages, and priority in publication is given to members of the Society.

Longer research papers (over 20 pages) and studies larger in scope appear in the Society's other journal, *Ecological Monographs; a journal for all phases of biology* (1931. q. $9. W. D. Billings and Alan E. Stiven. Duke Univ. Press, Box 6697, College Station, Durham, N.C. 27708. Illus., index. Circ: 2,300. Microform: UM. Reprint: Johnson). About 3–4 monographs appear in each issue.

Evolution; international journal of organic evolution. 1947. q. $15. Ralph G. Johnson. Soc. for the Study of Evolution. R. E. Beer. Entomology Dept., Univ. of Kansas, Lawrence, Kan. 66044. Illus., index. Circ: 3,200. Microform: UM.

Indexed: BioAb, ChemAb, SCI. *Bk. rev:* 1–2, lengthy, signed. *Aud:* Sa, Ac. Jc. *Rv:* H. *Jv:* B.

Papers that concern "facts, conclusions, or ideas of primary interest to students of evolution" are published in this journal. The subjects cover a wide biological spectrum, both flora and fauna. Authorship is international and the 10–15 papers usually range in length from 10–20 pages. "Notes and Comments" is a section devoted to short articles commenting on previously published articles or notes on research.

Experimental Cell Research. 1950. m. $29/v. Ed bd. Academic Press, Inc., 111 Fifth Ave., New York, N.Y. 10003. Illus., index.

Indexed: BioAb, ChemAb, IMed, SCI. *Aud:* Ac, Sa. *Rv:* H. *Jv:* B.

The official journal of the International Society for Cell Biology publishes original research reports on experimental studies of the general organization and operation of cells. Investigations range from the molecular level to cell interactions, and include such areas as physical and chemical aspects of cellular and intercellular structure, environmental relations and adaptation, biosynthesis with reference to cell growth, subcellular particles, etc. International in scope, papers may appear in English, French or German.

Human Biology: an international record of research. 1929. q. $8. Gabriel W. Lasker. Wayne State Univ. Press, Detroit, Mich. 48202. Reprint: Kraus.

Indexed: BioAb, BioAg, ChemAb, PsyAb, SCI. *Bk. rev:* 6, lengthy, signed. *Aud:* Sa, Ac. *Rv:* H. *Jv:* B.

A publication of the Society for the Study of Human Biology. Studies frequently are concerned with genetic and environmental factors effecting human variations, and embrace such fields as ecology, genetics, demography and physical anthropology. Each issue contains some 6 to 9 articles, "Notes on International Activities," and long, critical book reviews as well as an annotated list of books on human biology.

Journal of Experimental Biology. 1923. bi-m. $14/v. (2v./yr.) V. B. Wigglesworth & J. A. Ramsay. Cambridge Univ. Press, Bentley House, 200 Euston Rd., London, N.W. 1. Illus., index. Circ: 1,369. Reprint: Johnson.

Indexed: BioAb, BioAg, ChemAb, IMed, PsyAb, SCI. *Aud:* Sa, Ac. Jc. *Rv:* H. *Jv:* B.

The papers in this journal cover a broad variety of topics, including marine biology, neurophysiology and entomology, as related to experimental zoology, physiology, physiology, and biochemistry. Investigations are largely concerned with invertebrates. About 14 articles, varying in length from 10–20 pages, appear in each issue; authorship is international. Since its scope is wide, the publication is a valuable one for undergraduate libraries.

Life Sciences; an international medium for the rapid publication of preliminary communications in the life sciences. 1962. Fortnightly. $75. Pergamon Press, Maxwell House, Fairview Park, Elmsford, N.Y. 10523. Illus., index.

Indexed: BioAb, ChemAb, IMed, PsyAb. *Aud:* Sa, Ac. *Rv:* H. *Jv:* B.

Supplying early research reports the journal is issued in two parts. Part I includes short research reports on bio-

chemistry, general and molecular biology; Part II comprises studies on physiology and pharmacology. Its scope is international, and text may be in French or German, as well as English. Necessary for research libraries. (Note: Parts I or II may be purchased separately.)

Quarterly Review of Biology. 1926. q. $10. H. Bentley Glass. Stony Brook Foundation, Inc., State Univ. of New York, Stony Brook, N.Y. 11790. Illus., index, adv. Circ: 3,000. Microform: UM.

Indexed: BioAg, BioAb, ChemAb, IMed, PsyAb, SCI. *Bk. rev:* 2–3 major; 90 notes, signed. *Aud:* Sa, Ac, Jc. *Rv:* H. *Jv:* B.

Addressed to both the researcher and the general biologist, the journal provides about 4–5 "critical reviews of recent research in all special fields of biological sciences." A very useful section is "New Biological Books," which often comprises half the journal. Classified by field of specialization, the book reviews constitute both lengthy appraisals as well as notices of new literature. An excellent review publication for any academic library.

Society for Experimental Biology and Medicine. Proceedings. 1903. m. (except Sept.) $17. L. J. Cizek. Academic Press, Inc., 111 Fifth Ave., New York, N.Y. Illus., index, adv. Circ: 7,400. Reprint: Johnson.

Indexed: BioAb, ChemAb, IMed, PsyAb, SCI. *Aud:* Ac, Sa. *Rv:* H. *Jv:* B.

Specializing in short, timely research reports (2–3 pages), the journal is concerned with problems of importance to both the biological and medical community. Papers have dealt with such topics as endocrinology, enzymology, hematology, immunology, virology, and many other facets of biochemistry, microbiology, pharmacology, physiology, and pathology. A valuable journal for research libraries.

Stain Technology. 1925. bi-m. $6.50. H. A. Davenport. Biological Stain Commission, 428 E. Preston St., Baltimore, Md. 21202. Illus., index. Circ: 3,003. Microform: UM. Reprint: Johnson.

Indexed: BioAb, ChemAb, IMed, SCI. *Bk. rev:* 1–2, lengthy, signed. *Aud:* Sa, Ac, Jc. *Rv:* H. *Jv:* B.

International in scope, this publishes original articles relating to the nature and use of staining agents in the studies of microscopic structure of tissues of organisms, and other histological techniques. "Notes of Technics" consists of short reports less than two pages in length. The periodical is particularly important for undergraduate laboratory training.

Biochemistry and Biophysics

In recent years the chemical and physical aspects of biological studies have assumed major significance. Although most of the general research journals contain biochemical or biophysical papers, some of the important journals devoted exclusively to these fields are listed below.

Archives of Biochemistry and Biophysics. 1942. m. $25/v. Ed bd. Academic Press, Inc., 111 Fifth Ave., New York, N.Y. 10003. Illus., index.

Indexed: BioAb, ChemAb, IMed, SCI. *Aud:* Sa, Ac. *Rv:* H. *Jv:* B.

The journal publishes scholarly research papers on current biochemical and biophysical problems underlying aspects of biological processes in animal and plant systems. Studies have been concerned with such topics as protein synthesis, nucleic acids, lipids, enzymes, vitamins, etc. Both comprehensive research reports and "Communications" (2 pages or less) of more limited scope are included. A companion publication, *Biochemical and Biophysical Research Communications,* issued semi-monthly since 1959, presents very short (1,200 words or less), but highly significant new research results. To facilitate rapid publication, the journal reproduces authors' manuscript copies by offset printing.

Biochemical Journal. 1906. semi-m. $76.80 for 4 vols; $19.20 additional vols. Ed bd. Chemical Soc., Burlington House, Picadilly, London, W.1. Illus., index. Microform: MF. Reprint: Dawson.

Indexed: BioAb, ChemAb, IMed, SCI. *Aud:* Sa, Ac. *Rv:* H. *Jv:* B.

A prestigious publication, this is the official organ of the Biochemical Society (London). Research papers comprise both fundamental studies on chemical and physico-chemical aspects of life processes, and some methodological and clinical studies related to biochemistry. Topics under investigation have included carbohydrates, lipids, proteins, enzymes, energy metabolism, etc. Some short reports on colloquia sponsored by the Society are also published.

Biochemistry. 1962. m. $32. Hans Neurath. Amer. Chemical Soc., 1155 16th St., N.W., Washington, D.C. 20036. Illus., index. Circ: 5,500. Microform: AMC.

Indexed: ChemAb, SCI. *Aud:* Sa, Ac. *Rv:* H. *Jv:* B.

All areas of fundamental research in biochemistry are explored in this high quality journal. Emphasis is placed on the chemical aspects of biological processes, and the relationship of chemistry to the biological sciences. Research papers deal with such subjects as enzymes, proteins, lipids, nucleic acids, protein synthesis, and metabolism. In addition to tables and charts, the journal is illustrated with some excellent color stereophotography.

Biochimica et Biophysica Acta; international weekly of biochemistry and biophysics. 1947. w. $336. E. C. Slater. Elsevier Publishing Co., Box 211, Amsterdam, Netherlands. Illus., index, adv. Circ: 3,200. Reprint: Johnson.

Indexed: BioAb, ChemAb, IMed, SCI. *Aud:* Ac, Sa. *Rv:* H. *Jv:* B.

The journal is published in several sections: (1) "General subjects," (2) "Nucleic acids and protein synthesis," (3) "Lipids and lipid metabolism," (4) "Enzymology," (5) "Protein structure," (6) "Bio-energetics," and (7)

"Bio-membranes." Each section contains research papers of average length, shorter communications, and preliminary research notes averaging 1–2 pages. Subscriptions to individual parts are also available.

Biophysical Journal. 1960. m. $30. Fred M. Swell. Rockefeller Univ. Press, 66th St. & York Ave., New York, N.Y. 10021. Illus., index. Circ: 1,777.

Indexed: BioAb, ChemAb, IMed, SCI. *Aud:* Sa, Ac. *Rv:* H. *Jv:* B.

Research papers of the official journal of the Biophysical Society are concerned with the application of the methodology of physics to studies of processes in living organisms, and the physics of these processes. Authoritative studies include both molecular biophysics and biological ultrastructure. Both full-length investigations and short, timely "Letters to the Editor" are published. A special annual issue contains abstracts of papers presented at meetings of the Society.

Journal of Biological Chemistry. 1905. semi-m. $45. W. H. Stein. American Soc. of Biological Chemists, Mount Royal & Guilford Aves., Baltimore, Md. 21202. Illus., index. Microform: UM. Reprint: Johnson.

Indexed: BioAb, ChemAb, IMed, SCI. *Aud:* Sa, Ac. *Rv:* H. *Jv:* B.

One of the oldest publications devoted exclusively to chemical problems in life processes. The research papers in the official journal of the Society deal with any branch of biochemistry, and include studies on enzymes, proteins, lipids, nucleic acids, metabolic processes, and the like. In comparison to a publication such as the ACS's *Biochemistry,* emphasis in this journal tends somewhat more toward the biological rather than the chemical. Both full-length studies and some communications are included. An important journal for any biochemical collection.

Journal of Molecular Biology. 1959. m. $22/v. J. C. Kendrew. Academic Press, Ltd., Berkeley Sq. House, London W.1. Illus., index.

Indexed: BioAb, ChemAb, IMed, SCI. *Aud:* Sa, Ac. *Rv:* H. *Jv:* B.

Containing research papers and short communications concerning the nature, production, and replication of biological structure at the molecular level, the journal covers many of the activities now motivating contemporary biology. Studies under investigation have included the structure of muscle, nerve and tissue, structure of proteins, nucleic acids, and carbohydrates, structure of viruses, and molecular genetics.

Botany

The journals included below deal broadly with the entire range of the botanical sciences, and include papers on: systematic botany, plant morphology, plant physiology, plant ecology, economic botany, phytopathology, and paleobotany.

American Journal of Botany; devoted to all branches of plant sciences. 1914. m. (bi-m. May–June, Nov.–Dec.). $21.50. Charles Heimsch. Botanical Soc. of America, Inc., c/o Bus. Mgr., Lawrence J. Crockett, City College, Convent Ave., New York, N.Y. 10031. Illus., index, adv. Circ: 5,000, Reprint: Johnson.

Indexed: BioAb, BioAg, ChemAb, SCI. *Aud:* Sa, Ac, Jc. *Rv:* H. *Jv:* B.

The official journal of the Botanical Society of America. It publishes original research reports in this broad field and, occasionally, an invited review paper. Abstracts of papers presented at meetings of the association are also provided. An important journal for most collections in the biological sciences.

Annals of Botany. 1887. 4/yr. $16.00. J. F. Sutcliffe. Oxford Univ. Press, Ely House, 37 Dover St., London W.1. Illus., index, adv. Circ: 1,600. Reprint: Dawson. Microform: Princeton.

Indexed: BioAb, BioAg, ChemAb, SCI. *Aud:* Sa, Ac. *Rv:* H. *Jv:* B.

The scholarly research contributions to this journal, which is one of the leading botanical publications, are concerned with every aspect of plant science. Will be found in every research collection.

Botanical Gazette; a journal embracing all departments of botanical science. 1875. q. $10. Charles E. Olmsted. Univ. of Chicago Press, 5750 Ellis Ave., Chicago, Ill. 60637. Illus., index, adv. Circ: 1,572. Microform: Canner.

Indexed: BioAb, BioAg, ChemAb, SCI. *Aud:* Sa, Ac, Jc. *Rv:* H. *Jv:* B.

The journal publishes both research-level papers in areas of current interest and some short studies on apparatus appropriate to the science. Many articles contain lengthy bibliographies.

Botanical Review; interpreting botanical progress. 1935. q. $12. Pierre Dansereau. New York Botanical Garden, Bronx, N.Y. 10458. Circ: 2,500. Microform: UM. Reprint: Johnson, Stechert-Hafner.

Indexed: BioAb, BioAg, ChemAb, SCI. *Aud:* Sa, Ac, Jc. *Rv:* H. *Jv:* B.

The two or three lengthy papers in this journal represent authoritative and comprehensive reviews, with emphasis on providing exhaustive descriptions of the plant world, or new interpretations of plant life. Contributions, by invitation from the editor, are by distinguished specialists in the field. The reviews are not only excellent tutorials, but frequently pose questions for additional research; bibliographies give fine reviews of the literature. Occasionally, various phases of a single topic may be treated in one issue.

Canadian Journal of Botany. 1929. m. $9. Michael Shaw. National Research Council of Canada, Ottawa 7, Ont. Illus., index. Circ: 2,000.

Indexed: BioAb, BioAg, ChemAb, SCI. *Aud:* Sa, Ac. *Rv:* H. *Jv:* B.

Contributions, mostly from Canadian universities, reflect all aspects of research in the botanical sciences. Articles may appear in English or French. Although many studies are concerned with Canadian species, papers are not necessarily restricted to that locale.

Economic Botany; devoted to plant botany and plant utilization. 1947. q. $10. R. Evans Shultes. New York Botanical Garden, Bronx, N.Y. 10458. Illus., adv. Circ: 1,700. Microform: UM.

Indexed: BioAb, BioAg, ChemAb, SCI. *Bk. rev:* 10, 300–1000 words, signed. *Aud:* Sa, Ac, Jc. *Rv:* H. *Jv:* B.

Investigating the "past, present and future uses of plants for man," the journal comprises both research papers on various botanical studies and some purely descriptive essays on such topics as medicinal folk healing. The range, thus, extends from the scholarly to the entertaining and informative. Book reviews are to be particularly commended. Also includes news and notices of the Society for Economic Botany.

Journal of Experimental Botany. 1950. q. $14. L. J. Adus. Oxford Univ. Press, Ely House, Dover St., London W.1. Illus., index, adv. Circ: 1,800. Microform: UM.

Indexed: BioAb, BioAg, ChemAb, SCI. *Aud:* Ac, Sa. *Rv:* H. *Jv:* B.

The research papers in this important journal are concerned with plant physiology, biochemistry, biophysics, and related fields. Official organ of the Society of Experimental Biology.

Phytopathology; an international journal. 1911. m. $25. Amer. Phytopathological Soc., Heffernan Press, Inc., Worcester, Mass. 01601. Illus., adv. Microform: UM.

Indexed: BioAb, BioAg, ChemAb, SCI. *Aud:* Sa, Ac. *Rv:* H. *Jv:* B.

Devoted to the study of plant diseases, the journal contains reports of research being conducted on such subjects as the nature and causes of plant diseases, host parasite physiology, genetics, ecology and plant disease control. Summaries are given in French and Spanish. An abstracting section includes papers presented to the society during the year.

Plant Physiology. 1926. m. $35. Martin Gibbs. Amer. Soc. of Plant Physiologists, Box 5706, Washington, D.C. 20014. Illus., index. Circ: 4,400. Microform: Canner.

Indexed: BioAb, BioAg, ChemAb, SCI. *Aud:* Sa, Ac, Jc. *Rv:* H. *Jv:* B.

Both pure and applied research studies are published in this international journal devoted to all phases of plant physiology. Papers and short communications have been concerned with such topics as photosynthesis, respiration, growth and development, plant anatomy, and mineral and nitrogen metabolism.

Torrey Botanical Club. Bulletin (**Including** *Torreya*). 1870. bi-m. Membership (Non-members, $12). Murray F. Buell. New York Botanical Garden, Bronx, N.Y. 10458. Illus., index, adv. Circ: 1,350. Reprint: Johnson. Microform: UM.

Indexed: BioAb, BioAg, ChemAb, SCI. *Bk. rev:* 1–4, 500 words, signed. *Aud:* Sa, Ac, Jc. *Rv:* H. *Jv:* B.

"The oldest botanical journal in this hemisphere" publishes research papers varying from short reports to lengthy studies of over 20 pages. All aspects of the botanical sciences are represented. Each issue also supplies a classified index to American botanical literature. Annotated bibliographies of the floristic publications of New Jersey covering the years 1753–1965 are contained in the 1944 and 1966 volumes. *Torreya,* a news bulletin, consists of news of the activities of the club and its membership.

Microbiology and Genetics

This section deals with journals concerned exclusively with microbiology (studies of bacteria, microfungi, etc., and their biological activity) and genetics. Journals devoted solely to aspects of virus research have not been included, but attention is drawn to such high-quality publications as the English *Journal of General Virology, Journal of Virology,* which formerly constituted the virology section of *Journal of Bacteriology,* and *Virology.*

Applied Microbiology. 1953. bi-m. $20. J. C. Sylvester. Williams & Wilkins Co., 428 E. Preston St., Baltimore, Md. 21202. Illus.

Indexed: BioAb, BioAg, ChemAb, IMed, SCI. *Aud:* Sa, Ac, Jc. *Rv:* H. *Jv:* B.

Sponsored by the American Society for Microbiology, the journal publishes research papers and short notes dealing with "applied knowledge concerning microorganisms." More fundamental studies appear in the Society's other research journal, *Journal of Bacteriology.*

Bacteriological Reviews. 1937. q. $8. Edward A. Adelberg. Amer. Soc. for Microbiology, 4715 Cordell Ave., Bethesda, Md., 20014. Illus. Circ: 11,240.

Indexed: BioAb, BioAg, ChemAb, IMed, SCI. *Aud:* Sa, Ac, Jc. *Rv:* H. *Jv:* B.

The journal contains authoritative and critical reviews on the current state of research in all aspects of microbiology, and some monographs, which are extensive and definitive studies of specialized topics. Historical analyses may appear occasionally. Articles range from 3–8 in number and vary in length from 10–100 pages. This journal is included with a subscription to *Journal of Bacteriology.*

Genetics; a periodical record of investigations bearing on heredity and variation. 1916. m. $14. Ernst W.

Caspari. Genetics, Drawer U, University Station, Austin, Tex. 78712. Illus., index. Circ: 4,400.

Indexed: BioAb, ChemAb, IMed, SCI. *Aud:* Sa, Ac. *Rv:* H. *Jv:* B.

Publishes papers on "original research in genetics proper, or in any scientific field, if of primary genetic interest." Each issue contains a section entitled "Genetics Literature," which is a reproduction of the tables of contents of current periodicals of genetic interest (prepared by the Institute of Scientific Information).

Heredity; an international journal of genetics. 1948. semi-ann. $14. Oliver & Boyd, Ltd. Tweedle Court, Edinburgh, Scotland. Illus., adv. Circ: 1,350.

Indexed: BioAb, BioAg, ChemAb, IMed, SCI. *Bk. rev:* 5–6, lengthy, signed. *Aud:* Sa, Ac, Jc. *Rv:* H. *Jv:* B.

Included in this research journal, which covers various aspects of heredity, are reports in the fields of experimental breeding, cytology, statistical and biochemical genetics, and evolutionary theory. Papers may also be historical studies or review articles. Also publishes abstracts of the papers read at the meetings of the Genetical Society of Great Britain.

Journal of Bacteriology. 1916. m. $30. William B. Sarles. Williams & Wilkins, 428 E. Preston St., Baltimore, Md. 21202. Illus., adv. Circ: 8,547. Microform: UM.

Indexed: BioAb, BioAg, ChemAb, IMed, SCI. *Aud:* Ac, Sa. *Rv:* H. *Jv:* B.

Devoted to the "advancement and fundamental knowledge concerning bacteria and other microorganisms," the official journal of the American Society for Microbiology includes research papers on such studies as: taxonomy, ecology, morphology and structure, and microbiological methods; infection and immunity; genetics and molecular biology; microbial physiology and metabolism. The virology section of the journal is now issued as a separate publication, *Journal of Virology.* A subscription to *Bacteriological Reviews* is also included with the price of this journal.

Journal of General Microbiology. 1947. 4 vol./yr—ea. vol., $70. B. C. J. G. Enight, A.F.B. Standfast. Cambridge University Press, 32 E. 57th St., New York, N.Y. 10022. Illus., index, adv. Circ: 4,600.

Indexed: BioAb, BioAg, ChemAb, IMed, SCI. *Bk. rev:* Occasional. *Aud:* Ac, Sa. *Rv:* H. *Jv:* B.

Published for the Society for General Microbiology, the journal includes papers of original research concerned with fundamental aspects of microorganisms. Proceedings of the general meeting of the Society and abstracts of the papers presented are also provided.

Journal of Heredity. 1910. bi-m. $15. Barbara Lake. Amer. Genetic Assn., 1507 M St., N.W., Washington, D.C. 20005. Illus., index, adv. Circ: 4,300.

Indexed: BioAb, BioAg, ChemAb, IMed, SCI. *Bk. rev:* Occasional. *Aud:* Sa, Ac, Jc. *Rv:* H. *Jv:* B.

The short papers published in the journal, which is the official publication of the Association, are concerned with "knowledge of the laws of heredity and their applications to improvement of plants, animals, and human welfare." A section on news, notes, and reviews includes one to two page research studies, commentaries and the like. The occasional book review is critical and lengthy.

Physiology

The physiology journals listed here report on all branches of physiology and include papers on: comparative and general physiology, renal and electrolyte physiology, gastrointestinal physiology, neurophysiology, circulation, respiration, endocrinology and metabolism, environmental psychology and exercise, and hematology.

American Journal of Physiology. 1898. m. $40. Amer. Physiological Soc., Rockville Pike, Bethesda, Md. 20014. Illus., index, adv. Circ: 3,780. Microform: UM, Canner. Reprint: Johnson.

Indexed: BioAb, BioAg, ChemAb, IMed, PsyAb, SCI. *Aud:* Ac, Sa. *Rv:* H. *Jv:* B.

Dealing with all aspects of physiology, with emphasis on physiological mechanisms or actions, the journal reports results which are both very short one-or two-page studies and full-length papers. More applied studies are published in the Society's other publication, *Journal of Applied Physiology.*

Canadian Journal of Physiology and Pharmacology. 1929. bi-m. $6. J. A. F. Stevenson. National Research Council of Canada, Ottawa 7, Ont. Illus. Circ: 1,600.

Indexed: BioAb, ChemAb, IMed, SCI. *Aud:* Sa, Ac. *Rv:* H. *Jv:* B.

Covering both physiology and pharmacology, the research studies reported in this journal represent both full-length papers and brief notes, which comprise preliminary investigations. Papers may appear in French or English.

Journal of Applied Physiology. 1948. m. $35. Sara F. Leslie. Amer. Physiological Soc., 9650 Rockville Pike, Bethesda, Md. 20014. Illus., index, adv. Circ: 3,080. Microform: Canner, UM. Reprint: Johnson.

Indexed: BioAb, BioAg, ChemAb, IMed, PsyAb, SCI. *Aud:* Ac, Sa. *Rv:* H. *Jv:* B.

Less fundamental than the Society's other research journal, *American Journal of Physiology,* the publication contains research papers on the applications of physiological principles, with special emphasis on environmental and respiratory physiology. "Special Communications" reports on new methods, new apparatus, and techniques applicable to research.

Journal of Cellular Physiology. 1932. bi-m. $30. Angus F. Graham. Wistar Inst. Press, 36th St. at Spruce, Philadelphia, Pa. 19104. Illus. Circ: 1,543. Reprint: Johnson.

Indexed: BioAb, ChemAb, IMed, SCI. *Aud:* Sa, Ac. *Rv:* H. *Jv:* B.

Formerly *Journal of Cellular and Comparative Physiology.* The research papers are concerned with "physiology at the cellular level: the biochemical and biophysical mechanisms concerned in the regulation of cellular growth, function and reproduction." Short studies are published in its section "Comments and Communications."

Journal of General Physiology. 1918. m. $25. Paul F. Cranefield. Rockefeller Univ. Press, New York, N.Y. 10021. Illus., index. Circ: 2,000. Microform: UM. Reprint: Johnson.

Indexed: BioAb, BioAg, ChemAb, IMed, SCI. *Aud:* Ac, Sa. *Rv:* H. *Jv:* B.

Official organ of the Society of General Physiologists. High-quality research papers cover all branches of physiology, although emphasis is placed on cellular studies. Some issues contain proceedings of symposia.

Journal of Physiology. 1878. 18/yr. $114. Ed bd. Cambridge Univ. Press, 32 E. 57th St., New York, N.Y. 10022. Illus. Microform: Mc, UM. Reprint: Dawson.

Indexed: BioAb, ChemAb, IMed, PsyAb, SCI. *Aud:* Ac, Sa. *Rv:* H. *Jv:* B.

Published for the Physiological Society of London, the journal reports high quality studies on physiological research. The journal comprises both full-length papers and a "Proceedings" section, divided into "Demonstrations" (reports of talks given at society meetings) and "Communications" (brief and preliminary reports of research in progress).

Physiological Reviews. 1921. q. $15. Ray G. Daggs. Amer. Physiological Soc., 9650 Rockville Pike, Bethesda, Md. 20014. Illus., index, adv. Circ: 5,120. Microform: Canner, UM. Reprint: Johnson.

Indexed: BioAb, ChemAb, IMed, SCI. *Aud:* Ac, Sa, Jc. *Rv:* H. *Jv:* B.

Critical, comprehensive reviews of topics in physiology are reported by scientists prominent in the field. Each issue contains three to five lengthy (20–50 pages) reviews. Bibliographies are exhaustive, and each review has a prefatory outline and a detailed and informative summary. An excellent journal for most biological collections.

Zoology

No attempt has been made to incorporate any of the subfields such as entomology, mammalogy, etc. Rather, the following is representative of general zoological research journals available, and some journals concerned with anatomy, most of which are U.S. publications. Reference works such as *Zoological Record,* an annual bibliography which would be found in any zoological collection are, of course, beyond the scope of this study.

✓*American Zoologist.* 1961. q. Membership (Non-members, $9). Howard L. Hamilton. Amer. Soc. of Zoologists, 104 Liberty St., Utica, N.Y. 13503. Illus., index, adv. Circ: 4,500. Microform: UM.

Indexed: BioAb, BioAg, SCI. *Aud:* Sa, Ac, Jc. *Rv:* H. *Jv:* B.

Including all aspects of zoological research, this journal publishes both research and review papers. Two issues each year are devoted exclusively to research papers centering around one specialized topic of zoology (usually papers presented at a special symposium organized by the Society). The other two issues contain the entire programs and abstracts of papers presented at annual and summer meetings of the Society, as well as some research reports on a special symposium. (Originally, the abstracts appeared as a supplement to *Anatomical Record*.) Necessary for all zoology collections.

✓*Anatomical Record.* 1906. m. $37.50. Aaron J. Ladman. Wistar Inst. of Anatomy and Biology, 36th St. at Spruce, Philadelphia, Pa. 19104. Illus., index, adv. Circ: 1,564.

Indexed: BioAb, ChemAb, IMed, SCI. *Aud:* Ac, Sa. *Rv:* H. *Jv:* B.

Reflecting the research interests of anatomists, and important to zoologists, the journal publishes original research articles and an occasional review essay on descriptive or experimental vertebrate anatomy. Some methodology studies are also included. Papers are of short to moderate length, not exceeding 20 pages. As the official journal of the American Association of Anatomists, the publication also contains abstracts of papers and proceedings of meetings of the society.

Longer and more extended studies are reported in the other research journal of the Association devoted to vertebrate anatomy, *American Journal of Anatomy.* (1901. bi-m. $30. Donald Duncan. Circ: 1,288. *Indexed:* BioAg, BioAb, ChemAb, SCI.)

✓*Animal Behavior.* 1952. 3/yr. $20. L. R. Aronson & P. G. Bateson. Bailliere, Tindal & Cassell, Ltd., 7 Henrietta St., London W.C.2. Illus., index, adv. Circ: 3,000.

Indexed: BioAb, IMed, PsyAb, SCI. *Bk. rev:* 4–6, 500 words, signed. *Aud:* Ga, Ac, Jc, Sh. *Rv:* H. *Jv:* B.

Published for the Association for the Study of Animal Behavior, this extremely readable British periodical has appeal for both those with an elementary knowledge of the field, as well as for the specialist. Aspects of animal behavior are discussed in a nontechnical manner, and scientific studies of animal learning and behavior in the experimental setting are also included. Of value to physiologists and psychologists, as well as zoologists.

✓*Canadian Journal of Zoology.* 1929. bi-m. $6. T. W. M. Cameron. National Research Council of Canada, Ottawa 2, Ont. Illus., index. Circ: 1,500.

Indexed: BioAb, BioAg, SCI. *Aud:* Ac, Sa. *Rv:* H. *Jv:* B.

A general zoology publication, the *Journal* reports on all aspects of zoological research, largely from Canadian research centers. Papers may appear in French or English. In addition to full length articles, brief notes are published on new investigations.

✓*Journal of Experimental Zoology.* 1904. m. $37.50. Clement L. Markert. Wistar Inst. of Anatomy and Biology, 36th St. at Spruce, Philadelphia, Pa. 19104. Illus., index, adv. Circ: 1,515.

Indexed: BioAb, BioAg, ChemAb, IMed, SCI. *Aud:* Ac, Sa, Jc. *Rv:* H. *Jv:* B.

Published under the auspices of the American Society of Zoologists, this important journal reports results of experimental or analytical zoological research at all levels of biological organization, from the molecular to the organismal. A high quality journal for any academic collection.

Journal of Morphology. 1887. m. $37.50. Marcus Singer. Wistar Inst. of Anatomy and Biology, 36th St. at Spruce, Philadelphia, Pa. 19104. Illus., adv. Circ: 1218.

Indexed: BioAb, ChemAb, IMed, SCI. *Aud:* Ac, Sa. *Rv:* H. *Jv:* B.

Original research articles of moderate length are published in the field of general morphology, as well as studies on cytology, embryology, and protozoology.

✓*Physiological Zoology; a quarterly journal of zoological research.* 1928. q. $12. Thomas Park. Univ. of Chicago Press, 5750 Ellis Ave., Chicago, Ill. 60637. Illus., index, adv. Circ: 962. Microform: Princeton, UM, Canner.

Indexed: BioAb, SCI. *Bk. rev:* 1, 400–500 words, signed. *Aud:* Ac, Sa. *Rv:* H. *Jv:* B.

Emphasis in the research papers reporting zoological research is on the physiological aspects of organisms. The few book reviews are scholarly.

✓*Systematic Zoology.* 1952. q. Membership (Non-members, $8). Richard F. Johnston. Soc. of Systematic Zoology, c/o U.S. National Museum, Washington, D.C. 20560. Illus. Circ: 2,104.

Indexed: BioAb, SCI. *Bk. rev:* 1, 300 words, signed. *Aud:* Ac, Sa. *Rv:* H. *Jv:* B.

Contributions to the journal comprise research papers and short notes concerned with both principles and methodology of systematics. Articles also include studies on evolution, morphology, zoogeography, paleontology and genetics. A section entitled "Points of View" provides a forum for short discussions of papers that have either appeared in the journal or elsewhere in the literature. Some notices of meetings, publications, or other news of interest to the Society.

BOATS AND BOATING

Indexes and Abstracts

Readers' Guide to Periodical Literature. (For annotations, see Indexes and Abstracts Section.)

Each of the magazines listed in this section performs a distinct service for various types of sportsmen, and probably all would be found in a public, school, or academic library where there is particular interest in boats. Where a choice must be made for the general collection, *Boating* would be first (except in high schools where *Motor Boating* would be preferable), followed by *Rudder, Yachting,* and *Motor Boating.* Others would be purchased as needed, and some areas have regional magazines which probably come second or third in selection (see *Sea and Pacific Motor Boat*).

Boating. 1956. m. $6. Moulton H. Farnham. Ziff-Davis Publishing Co., 1 Park Ave., New York, N.Y. 10016. Illus., index, adv. Circ: 196,000. Microform: UM.

Bk. rev: 2–3, short, signed. *Aud:* Ga, Ac, Jc. *Rv:* M. *Jv:* A.

"America's most widely read boating magazine." All about boats; inboard, outboard, and sail. Geared to the pleasure boater and the racing and cruising enthusiast. While not particularly suitable for the school library, the amateur and skilled boatsman would appreciate the many articles on seamanship, navigation, boat design, and detailed instructions on construction and maintenance. Photographs, diagrams and charts are used throughout. Some true adventure stories included. Trip ideas, news of nautical interest and buying information provided. One of the best general boating magazines for any library near water enough to float a canoe.

Motor Boating. 1907. m. $6. Walter R. Juettner. Hearst Corp., C. F. Chapman, 959 Eighth Ave., New York, N.Y. 10019. Illus., index, adv. Circ: 105,000.

Indexed: RG. *Bk. rev:* 3–5, grouped. *Aud:* Ga, Ac, Jc, Sh. *Rv:* M. *Jv:* A.

Long articles, well illustrated with color and black and white photography, cover the broad spectrum ranging from outboards to yachts. Boatmen with wide and varied experience write expertly on boats, engines, navigation, regattas, cruising and sailing, racing, and sport fishing. The Boat Show Annual gives a preview of new products in inboards, outboards, stern drives, sailboats, houseboats, cruisers, trailers, equipment, electronics, paints and finishes. Buying information, complete with pictures and descriptions are provided. In view of its wide scope and authoritative articles, it is one of the best general boating magazines for almost any type of library.

National Fisherman. 1919. m. $3. Russell W. Bruce. Journal Publishing Co., Belfast, Me. 04915. Illus., adv. Circ: 40,000.

Aud: Sa, Ga, Ac. *Rv:* H. *Jv:* B.

Although the national journal of the fishing industry, this is an example of a trade journal which has a wider scope. Not only does it report the news of the industry, but it is loaded with fascinating contemporary and historical material on the fisherman's life, boatbuilding, and many related topics. Each issue is of great interest to the boating enthusiast and marine historian of all ranges of scholarly and recreational interest. Published in newspaper format, it is on excellent paper and profusely illustrated. It features more than 75 expert writers who report on activities throughout the United States. While at one level for the specialist, at another level it is ideal for the average reader of boating magazines and books. Should be considered by any public or academic library where there is more than passing interest in fishing, boating or marine architecture.

Rudder. 1890. m. $5. Mark Penzer. Fawcett Pubns., Inc., 67 W. 44th St., New York, N.Y. 10036. Illus., adv. Circ: 104,000.

Bk. rev: 1–2, 500 words, signed. *Aud:* Ga, Ac, Jc, Sh. *Rv:* M. *Jv:* B.

A "magazine for the yachtsman" covering the whole world of pleasure boats and boating, this is written for the reasonably informed sailor. Contains tight, informative articles on navigation, small-boat handling, marine electronics, and marine products. Expert comments on diesel, gas, out-drive and outboard engines. Special features are devoted to boat designs, racing, cruising, construction, money management, and maintenance of boats. Additional departments concentrate on maritime law, living aboard, problem clinics and mail order products. Both the style and content are geared for the serious amateur, not necessarily the rich one. A good magazine for most libraries.

Sea and Pacific Motor Boat. 1908. 9/yr. $6. Robert E. Walters. Miller Freeman Pubns., Inc., 3648 Long Beach Blvd., Long Beach, Calif. 90807. Illus., adv. Circ: 51,500. Microform: UM.

Aud: Ga. *Rv:* L. *Jv:* B.

Covers family boating, racing, cruising, and sailing of all types of boats in 13 Western states, western Canada, Alaska, and Mexico. Excellent articles, amply illustrated with maps, charts, and photographs, detail sailing adventures, cartographic history, and harbor activities. A special issue is devoted to outfitting for Spring. A monthly "Trade-winds" section covers news of interest to subscribers and a "Plan and Design" section features instructions for cruiser construction, racing sloops, ketches, trimarans, etc. Probably a second or third choice in Western public and school libraries. Another regional magazine of this type is *Lakeland Boating; mid-America's freshwater yachting magazine* (1946. m. $4. 416 Longshore Dr., Ann Arbor, Mich. 48107. Illus., adv. Circ: 20,000) for the Great Lakes and upper Mississippi region.

Skipper. 1947. m. $6. H. K. Rigg. 2nd St. at Spa Creek, Annapolis, Md. 21404. Illus., adv. Circ: 34,000.

Bk. rev: 3–7, 150–300 words, signed. *Aud:* Ga. *Rv:* M. *Jv:* B.

A yachting magazine whose principal appeal is to adults only. Contains articles of interest to boatmen (both power and sail), manufacturers of boating equipment, and designers. Fresh, well written narratives, approximately 75% by free lance contributors, cover topics pertaining to the sea, sailing, and good nautical fiction. True adventure stories are sometimes included. Special departments given over to news, and notes and comments from around the world. Expert commentary on boat and engine design. The "Marine Trader" carries items of interest to all interested in boating. The cover is usually graced with very fine paintings and photographs of boats, birds, etc. All articles are well-illustrated with excellent photographs. The addition of fiction and the relatively popular style make this particularly suited for men who may or may not have a boat. An excellent second or third choice for most libraries.

Watersport. 1967. q. Membership, $5. A. W. Limburg. Boat Owners Council of America, 534 N. Broadway, Milwaukee, Wis. 53202. Illus.

Aud: Ga, Sh. *Rv:* M. *Jv:* B.

A colorfully illustrated 34- to 40-page magazine devoted to all aspects of boating. A typical issue includes a report on a trip by boat "Up the Inside Passage to Alaska," a descriptive and critical article on life preservers, a seascape painter's work, a nontechnical view of a hydrofoil, and a raft trip. The whole is written for popular consumption, albeit the information is accurate and sound. Probably fits best into most public and high school libraries where there is a tremendous demand for such things, particularly illustrations of travel and boats. In a word, a good second choice for the boating enthusiast.

Yachting; power and sail. 1907. m. $7. William W. Robinson. Yachting Publishing Corp., 50 W. 44th St., New York, N.Y. 10036. Illus., adv. Circ: 105,000. Microform: UM.

Indexed: RG. *Bk. rev:* 3–6, 150–500 words, signed. *Aud:* Ga, Ac, Jc. *Rv:* M. *Jv:* B.

The luxury magazine of boating, primarily for dreamers and men of above average incomes. Long articles, written by experienced yachtsmen, cover the nautical horizon, including both power and sail, and racing and cruising boats. Special departments are devoted to various racing classes; marine tools, gadgets, and equipment; nautical publications of the Federal government; monthly digests of yachting and yachting industry news; and harbor centers of yachting activity. Detailed plans and specifications for boat construction are included in the section on boat design. In addition to reviewing books, the reader is alerted to books that may be reviewed in forthcoming issues. The Annual Show Issue contains over 500 pages of information on the latest inboats, engines and equipment, and purchasing information. Articles and illustrations indicate that this is not a magazine directed to those of ordinary means, and while indexed in *Readers' Guide,* it should be third choice for most public libraries.

BOOK REVIEWS

Indexes and Abstracts

British Humanities Index, Library Literature, Readers' Guide to Periodical Literature, Social Sciences and Humani-

ties Index, Subject Index to Children's Magazines. (For annotations, see Indexes and Abstract Section.) Almost without exception, all of the books listed here are indexed in *Book Review Digest* and *Book Review Index.* Consequently, in this section, these two works are not mentioned in the annotations.

AB Bookman's Weekly. See Bibliography Section.

ASLIB Book List; a monthly list of recommended scientific and technical books. 1935. m. 40s. ASLIB Pubns. Office, 3 Belgrave Sq., London S.W. 1. Circ: 2,890.

Aud: Sa, Ac. *Rv:* H. *Jv:* B.

The English equivalent of *New Technical Books,* it consists of a recommended monthly listing of new scientific and technical books. Emphasis is on British and continental titles, and while of great value to the English librarian, it is of limited interest to any but the largest, or more specialized, American library.

Appraisal: children's science books. 1967. 3/yr. $3.00. Children's Science Book Review Committee, Harvard Grad. Sch. of Education, Longfellow Hall, Appian Way, Cambridge, Mass. 02138.

Aud: Sa, Sh, Jh, E. *Rv:* H. *Jv:* B.

A dual approach is offered here to evaluate some 45 to 60 science books suitable for elementary through junior high school, and some for grades 10–12. First, a subject expert places the work within his area. Second, a librarian describes how it will fit in a total collection. The two 50- to 100-word annotations frequently overlap, and there is some disagreement—the end result is that the reader may still wonder as to the worth of the volume. A rating from Excellent to Unsatisfactory is given for each work. Sponsored by the Harvard Graduate School of Education and New England librarians, the reviewers represent both school and public libraries. Despite its minor faults, it is the best general science reviewing service for this age group now available. Should be in all public and school libraries.

Bestsellers. 1946. m. $3. A. Chris Nuessle. National Bestsellers Inst., Inc., 134 N. 13th St., Philadelphia, Pa. 19107. Illus., adv. Circ: 50,000. Microform: UM.

Aud: Sa, Ac. *Rv:* M. *Jv:* C.

Primarily tips on how to sell popular paperbacks and some magazines. Written for the dealer, whether he be at the corner drugstore or in a large bookstore, it has some value for librarians in that it includes an up-to-date listing of paperbacks. The letters column, which tells what readers like or dislike in paperbacks and magazines, affords librarians and social scientists an informal view of reading habits found almost nowhere else. Still, way down the list for libraries who would be better off with a current review media and *Paperbound Books in Print.* (This magazine should not be confused with *Best Sellers* issued by the University of Scranton, Scranton, Pa. Here all types of books are reviewed in terms of what moral or lack of moral values they contain. Indexed in the *Catholic Periodical Index.*)

Bibliographic Survey: The Negro in Print. See Afro-American Section.

Bookbird. 1962. q. $3.80. Richard Bamberger and Jella Lepman. Verlag für Jugend und Volk, Tiefer Graben 7–9, Vienna 1, Austria. (U.S. Subscriptions: Package Library of Foreign Children's Book, Inc., 119 Fifth Ave., New York, N.Y. 10003.) Illus. Circ: 2,000.

Aud: Sa, Sh, Jh, E. *Rv:* H. *Jv:* B.

Published by the International Board on Books for Young People and the International Institute for Children's Juvenile and Popular Literature, this is a news magazine of what is going on in the world of children's literature and libraries. In that it champions understanding via books, and suggests titles for translation, it is excellent. Moreover, as one of the few book reviews devoted to covering books internationally, it fulfills a great need for a representative review of the children's book field.

Books. 1964. m. $3. Jerome B. Agel. Agel Publishing Co., Inc., 598 Madison Ave., New York, N.Y. 10022. Illus., adv.

Aud: Ga, Ac, Jc, Sh. *Rv:* L. *Jv:* B.

The "underground" book publishing magazine. The newspaper format is orthodox enough for a book reviewing medium, but the editor is something else. Rather than feature the usual reviews, he spotlights personalities, and events in both the writing and the publishing world. An article may turn up on Dylan or Knopf, or Cerf or New Directions. They all have one thing in common—a breezy, at times sensational exposé tone which tends to be flip and filled with gossip. The running commentary by the editor is apt to touch on anything from the bars and restaurants of New York to the latest film hit. Cartoons, advertisements and a listing of current paperbacks and other books (with, to be sure, some regular book reviews) rounds out each issue. The paper is particularly geared for the teen-ager or reader under thirty. It may shock or dismay the average book review reader, but there is no denying that it has impact, particularly for the young who may equate reviews only with the *New York Times.* As such it could be a welcome addition in the liberal high school library, or the general reading collection in a junior college or university. Of limited use to libraries for book selection.

Booklist and Subscription Books Bulletin; a guide to current books. semi-m. $8. Edna Vanek. Amer. Library Assn., 50 E. Huron St., Chicago, Ill. 60611. Circ: 32,663. Microform: UM.

Aud: Sa, Ac, Jc, Sh, Jh, E. *Rv:* M. *Jv:* B.

This is really two magazines in one. The *Subscription Books Bulletin* is the standard reviewing medium of reference works—usually two or three encyclopedias, dictionaries, atlases and the like are given penetrating, detailed reviews in each issue. They are a trifle pedantic and pedestrian, yet always objective, and accurate. Prepared by a board of experts they are the last word for criticism. Their only failure

is that they often do not appear until months after the reference work has been issued and possibly purchased. The inclusion of this important reviewing service makes the magazine a must for any size or type library. *The Booklist* is another matter.

The second part, and by far the largest part of the magazine, consists of classified reviews of books for adults, young adults and children. Special sections are devoted to pamphlets, foreign language books, and specialized interests. All reviews are written by the staff of *The Booklist* at ALA headquarters, and are unsigned. Acceptance for review means the title has passed the standards established by ALA and the editor, and as a consequence they are rarely critical. The 50- to 150-word comments tend to compare, summarize contents and give highlights of audience interest. In that they alert the librarian to books otherwise passed by in many reviewing media, they are good. Conversely, because of the rules established for acceptance, some controversial works, particularly in the field of fiction and areas considered "dangerous" by librarians, are not reviewed or noted. Unfortunately, smaller libraries tend to rely on *The Booklist* for a good part of their guidance. The result is often a fair, middle-of-the-road collection, lacking any indication of thought to the right- or left-of-center. Conversely, the children's and young adult reviews are excellent, both in terms of presentation and what is selected for consideration. Librarians who recognize *The Booklist's* limitations will find it useful, but only in conjunction with other standard reviewing media. It should never be used as the single major source for reviews.

Book Buyer's Guide. 1897. m. $6. Francis Ludlow. Book Buyer's Guide, Inc., 1405 N. Broad St., Hillside, N.J. Illus., adv.

Aud: Sa, Ac, Jc, Sh. *Rv:* C. *Jv:* C.

One of the better-known book alerting services issued by a book jobber. It serves the purpose of informing the librarian about books recently or just about to be published, book club selections, and miscellaneous information on both national and regional publishing. Unfortunately, while many readers believe the service to be critical—it is not. The brief annotations are simply publisher's blurbs, and while indicative of content are non-evaluative. There is a recommended list of books in each issue for libraries with budgets of $50, $100 etc., but these tend to be the more ephemeral, popular titles. While a legitimate advertising medium, it is emphatically not a legitimate reviewing service and should never be used as such by librarians or readers.

Book World. w. $7. Postrib Corp., 230 W. 41st St., New York, N.Y. 10036. Illus., adv.

Aud: Ga, Ac, Jc, Sh. *Rv:* B. *Jv:* B.

The former *World Journal Tribune Book Week.* The format and approach is somewhat similar to the *New York Times Book Review,* and reviewers represent the same general cross section of authors, subject specialists, journalists and laymen. Unlike its rival, the reviews are considerably more incisive, critical and literate. Not as many titles are scanned, but there is more emphasis on grouping a number of works for purposes of comparison, e.g., three books on the police, three new studies of Picasso. Regular features include news of paperbacks, letters to the editor, a topical column or two, and a series, "Portrait of a Man Reading," which is an interview with an author. This latter department is worth the price of the paper. Because it is not as general in scope as the *New York Times Book Review*, nor as scholarly as the *New York Review of Books*, it would be a third choice in most libraries.

Books Abroad; an international literary quarterly.
1927. q. $4. Ivar Ivask. Univ. of Oklahoma, Norman, Okla. 73069. Circ: 1,850. Microform: UM. Reprint: Abrahams.

Indexed: SSHum. *Aud:* Sa, Ac, Jc. *Rv:* H. *Jv:* B.

In two parts—the first devoted to articles about foreign publishing, writers and movements; the second to 200- to 300-word reviews of new original works published abroad. Emphasis is on the review of literary and liberal arts titles, and they are representative of all nations. Reviews are by scholars and subject experts, and in English. A minor criticism is that most of the comments are favorable, the less acceptable titles not being considered. As a current source of information on international literature this has no equal, at least in the number of titles covered. Conversely, for all but the largest libraries much the same result would be obtained via a subscription to *The Times Literary Supplement*. A necessity for large academic and junior college libraries, but down the list for public and smaller libraries.

Catholic Bookseller & Librarian. 1958. bi-m. $4. Michael Glazier. Catholic Bookseller & Librarian Publishing Co., 100 N. Village Ave., Rockville Centre, N.Y. 11570. Illus., adv. Circ: 7,500.

Aud: Sa. *Rv:* M. *Jv:* C.

A trade journal for Catholic bookstores, and of some value to Catholic libraries. On a more modest scale it follows much the same pattern as *Publishers' Weekly* and the Protestant *Christian Bookseller*. While short articles on sales promotion, management and trends in Catholic publishing will be of major interest to dealers, the regular non-critical reviews of Catholic and other religious books gives it a certain amount of value for librarians. Titles discussed cover all age groups and interests of readers. Also, there are special issues devoted to paperbacks, bibles and prayerbooks, and regular announcement numbers. While the average Catholic school, public or university library should first subscribe to basic review media, this is a useful supplement.

Center for Children's Books. Bulletin. 1945. 11/yr. $4.50. Sena Sutherland. Univ. of Chicago Grad. Library Sch., Univ. of Chicago Press, 5750 S. Ellis Ave., Chicago, Ill. 60637. Index. Circ: 7,300.

Aud: Sa, Sh, Jh, E. *Rv:* H. *Jv:* A.

The single best source for reviews of children's books, this publication covers some 50 to 70 titles per issue. While material for readers from primary through 12th grades is included, the main emphasis is on the elementary and junior high school levels. The reviews follow a definite pattern: each title is rated in terms of reading level, the importance within the field, and its usefulness for both the child and the library or classroom situation. Editor Sutherland, who edits a children's book column in *Saturday Review*, includes both recommended and not recommended works. The December number includes a list of the best books of the year. A helpful feature is the bibliography of suggested readings for teachers and librarians which is usually included in each issue. In view of the high critical standards, the succinct, literate reviews, and the degree of coverage, this and *School Library Journal* will be the first choices in any library dealing with younger readers. *Horn Book* or *School Library Journal* would be a second choice, *Booklist* a third.

Choice. 1964. 11/yr. $20. Peter M. Doiron. Amer. Library Assn., 50 E. Huron St., Chicago, Ill. 60611. Circ: 2,700. Reprint: Abrahams.

Indexed: LibLit. *Aud:* Sa, Ac, Jc, Sh. *Rv:* H. *Jv:* V.

Among the book reviewing media specifically geared for librarians, this is one of the two best. Although ostensibly limited to interests of colleges and junior colleges, its 75- to 150-word reviews of some 500 to 600 books a month make it a required item in all medium to large high school and public libraries. Emphasis tends to be on scholarly books, but its some 30 subject categories are open to titles of a more popular nature. Furthermore, many of the books are not reviewed in any other general reviewing medium and this is the one single place where librarians may be sure of finding out about the titles which might otherwise escape their notice. There are some 1,900 reviewers, primarily teachers and subject experts, who are asked to write critical comments and where possible compare the book with other titles in the same area. This last feature is invaluable where the librarian is attempting to determine advisability of purchasing still another work in a given subject area. While the names of the reviewers are given at the end of the magazine, the reviews are unsigned. Next to the *Library Journal*, this is the best general source of book reviews, and would be a second choice for all public and high school libraries—a first for college and academic libraries. The price is high, yet the returns for librarians are even higher.

Christian Bookseller; the business magazine of the church supply stores. 1955. m. $6. Robert Walker. Christian Life Pubns., Inc., Gundersen Dr. & Schmale Rd., Wheaton, Ill. 60187. Illus., adv. Circ: 5,533.

Aud: Sa. *Rv:* M. *Jv:* C.

Primarily for Protestant religious bookstores, this is a kind of *Publishers' Weekly* for a specialized audience. It is of interest to readers and librarians in that it not only includes news and selling tips, but information on new books from dictionaries and Bibles to texts and general reading materials. The information tends to be non-critical; at best it might indicate what will or will not sell. Conversely, it covers titles often not found in other publications, and certainly should be checked regularly by those interested in religious books.

Christianity Today. See Religion Section.

Horn Book Magazine; about children's books and reading. 1924. bi-m. $6. Paul Heins. Horn Book Inc., 585 Boylston St., Boston, Mass. 02116. Illus., index, adv. Circ: 22,314. Microform: UM. Reprint: Abrahams, AMS.

Indexed: IChildMags, LibLit, RG. *Aud:* Sa, Jh. E. *Rv:* H. *Jv:* A.

Primarily a book reviewing medium for children's titles (kindergarten through 8th grade), this includes three to five articles on writers, books, illustrators and libraries. The writing tends to be considerably above average, and has a reputation for being "literate," and of a higher quality than found in most library periodicals. The 75 to 100 signed reviews usually run from 75 to 200 words, are critical, and grouped by picture books, age group and various subjects. Usually only recommended titles are noted. Recordings are often listed, and from time to time books of interest to adults working with children. Among the best of the general reviewing media, certainly among the top five for its articles, this should be found in all libraries dealing with the younger set.

International P.E.N. Bulletin of Selected Books. 1950. q. $2.30. Kathleen Nott. 62 Blebe Pl., London S.W. 3. (Subscriptions to: Stechert-Hafner, 31 E. 10th St., New York, N.Y. 10003.) Index.

Aud: Sa, Ac. *Rv:* M. *Jv:* B.

Published in cooperation with UNESCO, this includes some 10 to 12 long reviews of selected foreign titles in each issue. The reviews are good to excellent, often covering titles not included in regular reviewing media. Text in French and English, no advertising. A supplement to, but not a replacement for, *Books Abroad.*

Junior Bookshelf. 1936. bi-m. Marsh Hall, Thurstonland, Huddersfield, Yorkshire, Eng. Illus., index, adv. Microform: UM.

Indexed: LibLit, LibSciAb. *Aud:* Sa, Jh, E. *Rv:* H. *Jv:* B.

An English combination of *Hornbook* and *Center for Children's Books Bulletin.* Succinct, hard hitting reviews which are among the best published anywhere. There is really no American equivalent, particularly as to the style of writing which is often beautifully blunt and outspoken. Some 125 to 150 titles are noted in each issue. The majority are works published in England. In addition, there are excellent articles on writers, illustrators and anyone connected with children's books. While of limited use to smaller American libraries, should be a first choice where an effort is made to go beyond the bounds of the American publishing scene.

Library Journal. See Library Section.

New Book Review (Formerly: *Herder Book Supplement*). 1966. q. $2. Maureen Sullivan. Herder & Herder Inc., 232 Madison Ave., New York, N.Y. 10016. Illus., adv. Circ: 62,000.

Aud: Sa, Ac, Jc. *Rv:* M. *Jv:* B.

Devoted entirely to essays and reviews of religious books, with the emphasis on Catholic publishers. Approximately 250 titles per year are examined. Of these, about ten per issue are the subject of long signed essay articles, and the remainder are 200- to 500-word unsigned, critical notes. The tone is generally objective, even liberal, and the reviews are good to excellent in that they do not hesitate to point up the weaknesses of the books. The only exception seems to be the titles issued by the founder of the book review medium, i.e., the publisher, Herder & Herder. On the whole, one of the best all-around current reviews of dominantly Catholic books. Recommended for all Catholic libraries and larger religious collections in junior college and university libraries.

New Technical Books. 1915. 10/yr. $5. Robert Krupp. New York Public Library, Fifth Ave. at 42nd St., New York, N.Y. 10018.

Aud: Sa, Ac, Jc. *Rv:* H. *Jv:* B.

An annotated list of science books which have already been purchased by the New York Public Library. Most of the titles are for adults, and the reviewing service tends to complement the children's *Appraisal* and the frequent American Academy for the Advancement of Science's science lists. The majority of books are highly technical, and of limited use in all but the largest libraries. Still, as a valuable checkpoint for titles not often found in common reviewing media, this is unexcelled. Another useful work, albeit more of a reference aid along the lines of *Book Review Digest,* is *Technical Book Review Index* (1935. m. Special Libraries Assn., 31 E. 10th St., New York, N.Y. 10003). As the title suggests, this indexes reviews found in scientific and specialized journals. Each title is also usually followed by a short excerpt from the review and therefore can be used as an alerting device.

New York Review of Books. 1963. bi-w. $7.50. Robert B. Silvers and Barbara Epstein. New York Review, Inc., 250 W. 57th St., New York, N.Y. 10019. Illus., index, adv. Circ: 73,000. Microform: Mc.

Aud: Ga, Ac, Jc, Sh. *Rv:* H. *Jv:* V.

The most sophisticated book review medium in the United States, this is the closest American cousin to *The Times Literary Supplement.* The 10 to 15 reviews are often long essays, the book under question serving only as a springboard for the thoughts of the reviewer. Usually, too, there are one or two essays on some aspect of the current political or social scene. Among the distinguished writers are the literary establishment from Mary McCarthy and Edmund Wilson to W. H. Auden and Dwight Macdonald. The letters to the editor easily rival those found in the English counterpart, both for wit and cutting comments. Readers who are accustomed to short, snappy journalistic review notes are often confused by the more scholarly, thoughtful style of the *New York Review of Books*. In a word, this is for the reader with an above average education, an appreciation of literary style, left to radical left politics, and some background in literature and the arts. A must for all medium to large libraries, and not a few high school libraries.

The New York Times Book Review. 1896. w. $7.50. New York Times Co., Times Sq., New York, N.Y. 10036. Illus., adv.

Aud: Ga, Ac, Jc, Sh. *Rv:* M. *Jv:* A.

Possibly the best-known book review medium in the United States, this has the reputation for publishing generally favorable comments on almost anything noted. The writers, who are authors, journalists and subject specialists, rarely find much to condemn. The 20 to 30 reviews per issue cover the whole spectrum of interests from fiction to poetry, from art to politics. There are good reviews of children's and teen-ager books, and excellent notes on new mysteries. A lead essay, "Speaking of Books," is usually by a prominent writer about an aspect of the publishing world. Since the advent of *The New York Review of Books* and rather severe criticism in the early 1960's, the general tone of *The New York Times Book Review* has improved. Still, it is aimed at a large, general audience which it attempts to alert to the best being published, and the overall impression is one of middle-brow culture. In that the reviews are prompt and well-written, in that it is read by over a million readers each week, this deserves a place in most libraries—if only to alert the librarian to requests on Monday.

Publishers' Weekly. See Bibliography Section.

Quinzaine Litteraire. 1966. semi-m. 50 F. François Erval & Maurice Nadeau. 13, due de Nesle, Paris (6e). Illus., index, adv. Circ: 50,000.

Aud: Ga, Sa, Ac, Jc. *Rv:* H. *Jv:* B.

A French *New York Times Book Review,* having no connection with a daily newspaper. As a newspaper itself, this is the only one put out in France that is devoted exclusively to literary criticism and information about new books. Although a large part of its space is given over to critical articles on new books, it also contains: interviews with authors; articles on writers and painters; poems; lists of best-sellers; recommended books and new books in general. Nicely produced on improved, white newspaper stock, with many illustrations and the occasional use of colored type.

Scholarly Books in America; a quarterly bibliography of University press publications. 1959. q. Free. Thomas Lloyd. Amer. Univ. Press Services, Inc., 1 Park Ave., New York, N.Y. 10016. Circ: 250,000.

Aud: Sa, Ac. *Rv:* H. *Jv:* B.

A medium of the American University Press Service, this offers a complete annotated list of all books, serials and journals published by members of the American Association of University Presses, i.e., the majority of American university presses. There are usually one or two opening articles of general interest. Titles are arranged by broad subject classification. An excellent method of alerting librarians and laymen to new publications, particularly as a number of the more esoteric works are either never reviewed, or reviewed only in highly specialized journals. The brief annotations are descriptive, and in no way critical.

School Library Journal. See Library Section.

Science Books; a quarterly review. 1965. q. $4.50. Amer. Assn. for the Advancement of Science, 1515 Massachusetts Ave., N.W., Washington, D.C. 20005. Circ: 1,200.

Aud: Ga, Ac, Jc, Sh, Jh. *Rv:* H. *Jv:* B.

Approximately 100 to 150 relatively popular science books are reviewed, including both recommended and not recommended titles. The selection and the reviews are purposefully directed to the layman, not to the specialist. Titles for all ages, from junior high through adult, are considered, and a series of symbols indicates the various age levels. This is one of a number of works issued by the Association, and librarians who need assistance in this area should write for the complete listing of the AAAS services. *Science Books* would be a first choice for most small to medium-sized libraries, while *New Technical Books* would be a first choice in larger libraries.

Stechert-Hafner Book News. 1946. 9/yr. Free to libraries. Stechert-Hafner, Inc., 31 E. 10th St., New York, N.Y. 10003. Circ: 5,000. Microform: UM.

Indexed: LibLit. *Aud:* Sa, Ac. *Rv:* H. *Jv:* B.

Primarily an advertising medium for Stechert-Hafner book jobbers, this 15-page publication begins with a three-page article on some aspect of librarianship or bookselling by a scholar or subject expert. After the essay there are regular features "Book News and Commentary," a discursive discussion of new works, and "The New Books," a classified listing with full bibliographic detail of titles mentioned in the previous section. Most books are for larger academic libraries. As the publication is free, it is well worth a request, if only for the opening essay.

The Times Literary Supplement. 1902. w. $12. Times Newspapers of Great Britain, Inc., 201 E. 42nd St., New York, N.Y. 10017. Illus., index, adv. Circ: 43,000. Microform: Recordak. Reprint: Abrahams, Bowker.

Indexed: BritHum, SSHum. *Aud:* Ga, Sa, Ac, Jc. *Rv:* H. *Jv:* A.

Probably the best single review medium in the English language, the *TLS* sets standards for excellence, considerably ahead of most of its American counterparts (*The New*

York Review of Books is an exception). The writing is scholarly, well within the grasp of any educated man or woman, and the style is both varied and lively. Major books in every language are considered, and it is in no way limited to British publishers. In fact, some of the best reviews of major American titles will be found here. In addition to the lead essay article, there is a leader column devoted to a current event, and letters to the editor which are as fascinating as they are informative. Irregular columns appear on little magazines, paperbacks, and items of literary or historical importance. Usually, too, one page is given over to important reference and bibliographical titles. Several issues a year are devoted to special topics and in these there are long signed articles by some of the world's leading scholars. Yet, one major criticism of the *TLS* is that none of the reviews are signed, and it is a guessing game as to who either tore a book apart or did a bit of log rolling for the author. Often, too, the fiction reviews are much too brief and the treatment of American scholarship tends to be a trifle less than sacred. The overall level of sophistication is high, and quite a pleasant shock for the reader who equates reviews with *The New York Times* or *Saturday Review*. While of limited value for small or medium-sized libraries seeking advice on new titles, it should be found in all libraries as a source of information and intellectual stimulation for readers.

Virginia Kirkus' Service. 1933. semi-m. $25. Virginia Kirkus. 317 W. 4th St., New York, N.Y. 10012. Index.

Aud: Sa, Ac. *Rv:* M. *Jv:* C.

One of the oldest, continuous commercial book reviewing services in America, this twice a month loose-leaf publication has one major asset—it frequently reports on books weeks to sometimes months ahead of the better known media. Some 4,000 to 5,000 titles are noted each year. Originally it began as a service to tip off booksellers as to what might or might not sell, but soon became a handy tool for librarians. It is divided into fiction, non-fiction and books for younger readers sections, with a religious book supplement. The indexing is cumulated four times a year, but between numbers the subscriber must use a series of gummed sheets to make-up his own index. The reviews are unsigned and written by ex-librarians and publishing staff members. They are frequently clever, concise and downright critical. However, the major problem has been that the reviewer has chosen to mark with a "Q" any work which might offend for one reason or another. This results in timid users assiduously passing by some rather good titles, and is a form of self-imposed censorship which may have a place commercially, but not in a library. Then too, some pot boilers which may sell well are marked for special consideration. All and all, a review service which should be far down the list for any library—certainly not recommended for small- to medium-sized libraries with limited budgets or personnel.

Wilson Library Bulletin. See Library Section.

BUSINESS AND INDUSTRY

Indexes and Abstracts

Applied Science and Technology Index, British Humanities Index, Business Periodicals Index, Chemical Abstracts, Education Index, Engineering Index, Psychological Abstracts, Public Affairs Information Service, Science Abstracts, Social Sciences and Humanities Index, Sociological Abstracts, Readers' Guide to Periodical Literature. (For annotations, see Indexes and Abstracts Section.)

Academy of Management. Journal. 1958. q. $6. Stanley C. Vance. Academy of Management, Sch. of Business Admin., Univ. of Oregon, Eugene, Ore. 97403. Illus., index, adv. Circ: 2,100. Reprint: Abrahams.

Indexed: BusI, PAIS. *Aud:* Sa, Ac. *Rv:* H. *Jv:* B.

A scholarly publication covering research, organization theory and management in an era of technological change. A section on dissertation abstracts is an aid to bibliographic control. The approach is often sociological and psychological, with such articles as "A Behavioral Science Approach to Personnel Selection," "An Input-Output Model of Employee Behavior" and "The Manager and His Job Skills." Only for specialized collections. *Administrative Management* or *Management Review* is considerably better for the general public or academic business library.

Administrative Management; the magazine of methods, personnel and equipment. 1940. m. $5. Lewis Lachter. Geyer-McAllister Pubns., 51 Madison Ave., New York, N.Y. 10010. Illus., index, adv. Circ: 53,200. Microform: UM. Reprint: Abrahams.

Indexed: BusI. *Bk. rev:* 4–5 short, unsigned. *Aud:* Sa, Ac, Jc. *Rv:* M. *Jv:* B.

A useful, general management magazine for most libraries. Its editorial position is reflected in its treatment of personnel problems—"Gradual Retirement Plan Eases Transition" and "Solving the Problems of Incompatibility." Methodology is discussed in titles like "Handling Your Workload Fluctuation Crises," "Three-Part Form Simplifies Expense Accounting" and "New Controls Help Insure Quality." The attention to equipment is particularly good with articles on typewriters, new filing equipment and paper supplies. Because of equipment purchase coverage and use, this magazine should be in the libraries of junior colleges and secretarial schools training office workers, as well as those libraries with a management clientele.

Administrative Science Quarterly. 1956. q. $7.50. Thomas M. Lodahl. Grad. Sch. of Business and Public Admin., Cornell Univ., Ithaca, N.Y. 14850. Illus., index, adv. Circ: 3,000.

Indexed: BusI, PAIS, PsyAb, SocAb. *Bk. rev:* 8–9, 1–3 pages. *Aud:* Sa, Ac. *Rv:* M. *Jv:* B.

"Dedicated to advancing the understanding of administration through empirical investigation and theoretical analysis." Besides the rather lengthy book reviews, a listing of publications received, as well as abstracts of relevant publications are included. Primarily for the advanced administrator and graduate students.

Advanced Management Journal. 1936. q. $8. William Mumpower. Soc. for the Advancement of Management, 16 W. 40th St., New York, N.Y. 10018. Illus., index, adv. Circ: 20,000. Microform: UM. Reprint: Abrahams, AMS.

Indexed: BusI. *Bk. rev:* 2–5 of 500 words, signed. *Aud:* Sa, Ac. *Rv:* H. *Jv:* B.

An excellent source of management advice from outstanding and successful managers. Contributors are business and corporate executives who offer many "how to" suggestions for new techniques and innovations in business administration. Recent titles include "On Decision Making," "The Risks of Management," and "Planning—Elements and Problems." Although the articles are short and practical rather than scholarly, this periodical is valuable both in university business schools and in public libraries for the working administrator.

Advertising Age; the national newspaper of marketing. 1930. w. $6. James V. O'Gara. Advertising Pubns., Inc., 740 N. Rush St., Chicago, Ill. 60611. Illus., adv. Circ: 60,000.

Indexed: BusI, PsyAb. *Aud:* Sa, Ac, Jc. *Rv:* H. *Jv:* B.

Presents all that is recent and upcoming in the field of national sales and advertising and international news concerning television, radio and printed advertising. Personnel shifts, account changes, important rating figures, new products, and convention news are given through regular columns. There is often coverage of controversial subjects, interviews and speeches which makes the magazine useful for students. During the year, six to eight large topical issues concentrate on a single subject such as: "Market Data" or "Leading Advertisers."

African World. 1902. m. $4.20. African Pubns., Ltd. 21/22 St. Bride Inst., Bride Lane, London E.C.4. Illus., index, adv. Circ: 5,000. Reprint: Johnson, Abrahams.

Aud: Sa, Ga, Ac, Jc, Sh. *Rv:* M. *Jv:* B.

One of the oldest, basic economics and business magazines about Africa. Covers the whole of the African economic scene from banking and finance to mining and tea raising. The articles are prepared by staff and experts, and, while written for the interested executive, they are nontechnical. The tone is objective, and a run of several issues gives the layman—including the high school student—an accurate picture of the economic side of today's Africa. A few illustrations.

American Druggist. 1871. Fortnightly. $10. Dan Rennick. Hearst Corp., 1790 Broadway, New York, N.Y. 10019. Illus., adv. Circ: 66,543.

Aud: Sa, Ac. *Rv:* M. *Jv:* C.

Oriented toward the retail drug trade. The articles cover a wide range of topics—current news, forthcoming legis-

lation, pharmaceutical research and product development, and market research on drug store operations. Information on the wide variety of products sold in drug stores—including prescriptions, cosmetics, toiletries, photographic products, packaged medicines and surgical supports.

American Import and Export Bulletin. 1934. m. $5. John F. Budd. Budd Pubns., Inc., 26 Beaver St., New York, N.Y. 10004. Illus., index, adv. Circ: 5,184. Microform: UM.

Aud: Sa, Ac, Jc. *Rv:* M. *Jv:* B.

A valuable guide for all those interested in foreign trade. Includes: statistical information on trade and tariffs, government activities, personalities in the import-export field, and port and railroad activities. One bad feature is overcrowded pages. A useful addition for both business and political science collections in large academic and public libraries.

Barron's National Business and Financial Weekly. 1921. w. $15. Robert Bleiberg. Dow Jones & Co., Inc., 200 Burnett Rd., Chicopee, Mass. 01021. Adv.

Indexed: BusI. *Aud:* Sa, Ac. *Rv:* M. *Jv:* B.

This newspaper publication of Dow Jones (which also publishes the *Wall Street Journal*) has a decidedly conservative point to make. Almost every issue starts out with a long editorial, either pro-armament, anti-communist or anti-riot, and their sometimes evangelical tone casts considerable doubt on their value. It contains objective articles on specific businesses or industries—merchandising, oil, electronics, for example—which spell out the financial ups and downs of each. There is much business advertising, investment information, a book review of interest to financiers, a Wall Street section—"Up and Down Wall Street—and a statistical section with weekly national and international market data. Political viewpoint aside, this is one of the two or three basic business newspapers which should be taken by larger libraries.

Business Abroad; the international trade review. 1919. Fortnightly. $10. Michael G. Duerr. Dun & Bradstreet Pubns. Corp., 466 Lexington Ave., New York, N.Y. 10017. Illus., adv. Circ: 11,500.

Indexed: PAIS. *Bk. rev:* Notes. *Aud:* Sa, Ac, Jc. *Rv:* H. *Jv:* B.

For students of international trade and investment. In addition to articles there are special sections on new developments, personnel news, as well as news from Washington concerning international trade and tariffs. One especially valuable feature is "World Trade Data" that gives foreign exchange rates, trade rates, and other statistical data. A useful addition to the government's *International Commerce,* but only for relatively specialized collections in economics and political science.

Business Education Forum. 1947. m. Membership

(Non-members, $5). National Business Education Assn., 1201 16th St., N.W., Washington, D.C. 20006. Circ: 13,500.

Indexed: EdI. *Aud:* Ac, Jc, Ht. *Rv:* H. *Jv:* B.

Primarily for high school teachers of business and anyone dealing with the education of business teachers. Each number highlights one aspect of instruction in the field, e.g., shorthand, business law, typewriting, accounting, office practices, etc., and includes regular features on all areas of the subject. New equipment, classroom techniques, curriculum development and the like. Association news and some book reviews conclude each number. Most school libraries will also want a subscription to *Business Education World.* The NBEA also publishes *National Business Education Quarterly* (1932. q. Membership; Non-members, $3), which is more theoretical and scholarly, articles constituting almost individual monographs on business teaching. Useful for summaries of research and the annual directory of supervisors of business education.

Business Education World. 1919. 10/yr. $4.50. James Bolger. McGraw Hill Book Co., Gregg Div., 330 W. 42nd St., New York, N.Y. 10036. Illus., index, adv. Circ: 20,700. Microform: UM. Reprint: Johnson, Abrahams.

Indexed: EdI. *Aud:* Ac, Jc, Ht. *Rv:* H. *Jv:* B.

Somewhat similar to *Business Education Forum,* differing in that articles are prepared by staff and business teachers more often than by professional educators. In many ways the style is better, the tone more relaxed than its competitors. Coverage is about the same, e.g., most of the space is given over to practical teaching methods, problems and solutions, new equipment and professional matters. Teachers will wish to try both this and *Business Education Forum,* although they may automatically be receiving the latter publication as members of NBEA. A third choice, but only for larger libraries and for business schools, is: *Journal of Business Education* (1928. m. (Sept–May). $5. Robert C. Treadway. 15 S. Franklin St., Wilkes-Barre, Pa.). Covers a good deal of the same ground as the other two.

Business History Review. 1926. q. $10. James P. Baughman. Harvard Grad. Sch. of Business Admin., 214–16 Baker Library, Soldiers Field, Boston, Mass. 02163. Illus., index, adv. Circ: 1,800. Microform: UM. Reprint: Kraus, Abrahams.

Indexed: BusI, PAIS. *Bk. rev:* 14–16, 500 words, signed. *Aud:* Sa, Ac, Jc. *Rv:* M. *Jv:* B.

Features scholarly articles, of interest to both students of business and history, on the historical evolution of business in the United States and abroad. Current events are noted in the "Editor's Corner." An added value for libraries is the book review section. All reviews are by experts and are critical. Not an essential magazine, but one for larger collections.

Business Horizons. 1958. q. $6.50. William G. Ryan. Indiana Univ. Grad. Sch. of Business, 1205 E. 10th St., Bloomington, Ind. 47401. Illus., index, adv. Circ: 11,000. Microform: UM.

Indexed: PAIS. *Bk. rev:* 2–3, lengthy, signed. *Aud:* Sa, Ac, Jc. *Rv:* H. *Jv:* B.

More readable for the average layman than most graduate school quarterlies. Presents lengthy articles on new approaches to management and marketing, studies of the business situation in specific countries, accounting, banking, business education, unions, and corporation mergers. Little emphasis is placed upon foreign and governmental topics. Many articles are written by men in the business world as well as professors. Of special note is the regular feature "Research Clearinghouse," which indicates current research projects that are of interest to business executives. A useful addition for most medium to large academic and public business libraries.

Business Today. 1968. q. $6. Jonathan S. Perel. Princeton Business Review Publishing Co., 171 Broadmend Road, Princeton, N.J. Illus., adv. Circ: 200,000.

Bk. rev: 1–3, 250 words, signed. *Aud:* Sa, Ac. *Rv:* H. *Jv:* A.

Edited by the students of Princeton University, this has a format resembling *Business Week,* and a style which is closely identified with the popular press rather than with learned journals. However, it is no hybrid, and the voice is uniquely that of today's college students, or at least those in business school. The 10 to 12 articles are by businessmen and educators, normally trying to explain their interests to students and laymen, i.e., "Responsibility, A Two Way Street," by the vice-chairman of American Telephone & Telegraph; "Can We Afford Not to Support Good Research?" by the president of the National Academy of Science. The students appear in a number of feature editorials, reports on trends in finance, communication, advertising, etc. Then, too, there are usually one or two articles which are student written, i.e., "Gas Games: Fraud on the Consumer?" Regular columnists include Ralph Nader, Art Buchwald and Drew Pearson. Almost every economic and business interest is considered, usually on a more long-range basis than found in commercial journals of this type. An impressive magazine for all college and university libraries, and a good number of public libraries.

Business Week. 1929. w. $8. Elliott V. Bell. McGraw-Hill, Inc., 330 W. 42nd St., New York, N.Y. 10036. Illus., index, adv. Circ: 555,000. Microform: UM. Reprint: Abrahams.

Indexed: BusI, PAIS, RG. *Aud:* Ga, Sa, Ac, Jc, Sh. *Rv:* H. *Jv:* V.

One of four basic, general business magazines for most libraries. (The others are: *Forbes, Fortune* and *Nation's Business*). As its cousins, *Business Week* is conservative yet objective and reasonable when it comes to anything which deals with the dollar. All the material smacks of big money, and the underlying premise is that what is good for business is good for the country. American and foreign items are included, with increasing emphasis upon those that have the greatest effect upon worldwide business. Regular departments, edited by experts in the field, investigate the significant developments and outlooks in labor, production, marketing research, finance, foreign business, and other allied areas. The articles covering the whole area of general business are up-to-date, concise and well written. Illustrations, graphs, charts and statistical tables are graphically clear and well placed. Written in terms easily understood by the informed layman. As the most general of the four, it is the business magazine for all libraries from senior high school through the university. A second choice would be *Fortune,* followed by *Nation's Business* and then *Forbes.*

C. L. U. Journal. 1946. q. $6. Kenneth Black, Jr. Amer. Soc. of Chartered Life Underwriters, 270 Bryn Mawr Ave., Bryn Mawr, Pa. 19010. Illus., adv. Circ: 19,500.

Aud: Sa, Ac. *Rv:* M. *Jv:* B.

A substantial, specialized magazine for the health and life insurance industry, with material centered around trusts, management, estate planning, business insurance, psychology and human relations, taxes, personnel selection and training. Only for large libraries.

California Management Review. 1958. q. $6.50. Wayne L. McNaughton. Grad. Sch. of Business Admin., Univ. of Calif., Los Angeles, Calif. 90024. Illus., index, adv. Circ: 3,600. Microform: UM. Reprint: Abrahams.

Indexed: BusI, PAIS. *Aud:* Sa, Ac, Jc. *Rv:* M. *Jv:* B.

Directed to "active managers, scholars and teachers, and others concerned with management," with articles of fairly general business interest. Contributors come from economics, insurance companies, and the labor relations field as well as university business management departments. It leans rather heavily on California contributors, but the material covered is not limited geographically. Only for large collections. *Administrative Management* or *Management Review* are better suited to the average business library.

Commerce. 1882. 30s. Sam Black. London Chamber of Commerce, 69 Cannon St., London E.C.4. Illus., adv. Circ: 13,350.

Bk. rev: Notes. *Aud:* Sa, Ac. *Rv:* M. *Jv:* B.

Emphasis is on the industry and trade of Great Britain and world economics. There are sections on trade fairs, news of overseas trade, and various aspects of business which will interest the specialist and student. Not a required magazine, but for its limited area of coverage, a good one.

The Commercial and Financial Chronicle. 1865. semi-w. $90. William B. Dana Co., 25 Park Place, New York, N.Y. 10007. Circ: 20,000.

Indexed: BusI. *Aud:* Sa, Ac. *Rv:* M. *Jv:* B.

This newspaper is for those interested in business, economics, and the international monetary system; it is definitely for a more specialized audience than that of the *Wall Street Journal.* A general news and advertising issue comes out every Thursday, and a complete statistical issue, containing market quotation records, securities, mutual funds, corporation news, bank clearings, state and city bond proposals, and the like, appears every Monday. Articles in the Thursday issue, written by professors of economics, corporation executives, and government economists, are long, theoretical, and deal with current problems.

Conference Board Record. 1964. m. $15. National Industrial Conference Board, Inc., 845 Third Ave., New York, N.Y. 1002. Illus., adv.

Indexed: BusI, PAIS. *Aud:* Sa, Ac. *Rv:* H. *Jv:* B.

Sponsored by "non profit fact finding laboratories," this is an effort to report objective, original research in the fields of business management and economics. There is little or no bias, a somewhat unique feature for a journal which is primarily read by business executives and professional economists. Hence, it is ideal for the student seeking basic information on a variety of topics from anti-trust and consumer economics to employment and economic trends. Such articles as "The Drinking Employee," "Profiling the New Car Market," or "Getting a Measure on the Married," indicate the broad interest of the editors. There are usually some 12 articles per 64-page issue, and in 1968 approximately one-half the material was staff written. The other articles are by business executives and professional researchers. All material is supported by documentation, charts and statistics. A basic journal for larger business and economics collections.

Cost and Management. See Accounting Section.

Dun's Review. 1893. m. $5. Raymond Brady. Dun & Bradstreet Pubns. Corp., 466 Lexington Ave., New York, N.Y. 10017. Illus., index, adv. Circ: 135,000. Microform: UM. Reprint: Abrahams.

Indexed: BusI, RG. *Bk. rev:* 1–2, 1 column, signed. *Aud:* Ga, Ac, Jc. *Rv:* H. *Jv:* B.

A general business magazine more for the expert than the layman. Well-written feature articles discuss business from the financial angle in a readable style for the general adult reader and student, as well as the business executive. Management, marketing, accounting, specific industries and positions, labor, employee relations, investment advice, and new techniques in industry are discussed in the excellent longer articles. Regular features include: "The Economy," which reports on the strength of business, effects of government spending and activities; "Business Failures," which gives the number of failures and the size of the debts, with an accompanying article on various aspects of business failures; "The Washington Desk," which supplies brief reports of the Administration's economic decisions. Summaries of employment, economic, investment and governmental activities are given in the "Business Situation" section. Because it is one of the few financial magazines indexed by *Readers' Guide,* and the reference value is high, it should be given first consideration for medium-sized business collections, and should be in all larger libraries. However, for a general collection it would rank below *Business Week, Nation's Business, Fortune* and *Forbes.*

Economist. 1843. w. $19.50. J. W. A. Burnet. 25 St. James's St., London S.W. 1. Illus., index, adv. Circ: 84,200. Microform: UM, Canner. Reprint: Abrahams.

Indexed: BritHum, BusI, SSHum. *Bk. rev:* 6–8, 400 words, signed. *Aud:* Ga, Ac, Jc, Sh. *Rv:* H. *Jv:* A.

The most international of the business magazines, covering the political and economic news of the entire world. The analysis of the news offered on a world-wide scale is helpful to all students. British trade and industry are reviewed, as are the business conditions of various countries and regions. The "American Survey" offers a look at ourselves as others see us. Statistics concerning production, products, and earnings are published, though a knowledge of the British monetary system is often required to understand the charts and graphs. Should appear on the shelves of all medium to large college, university, and public libraries as well as many senior high schools.

Modern Manufacturing (Formerly: Factory.) 1891. m. $2. Lester R. Bittel. McGraw-Hill Inc., 330 W. 42nd St., New York, N.Y. 10036. Illus., index, adv. Circ: 85,000. Microform: UM.

Indexed: BusI, ChemAb, EngI. *Aud:* Sa, Ac. *Rv:* H. *Jv:* B.

A practical approach to the business, engineering and maintenance needs in industrial plants. Articles discuss improved techniques, latest data and comprehensive surveys of the manufacturing world. Newsletters report recent developments, legislation, seminars and conferences. Cost indexes suggest the latest prices of facilities, materials, labor, and equipment. Ten "Casebooks" present the specific ideas of the month including practical views on troublesome problems, helpful pamphlets and new techniques, while "Billboards" introduce new products. With change in name and format, the magazine tends to put as much emphasis on engineering and design as on operations, but the primary purpose remains the same. A basic item for all large business collections.

Forbes. 1917. semi-m. $7.50. James Michaels. Forbes Inc., 60 Fifth Ave., New York, N.Y. 10011. Illus., index, adv. Circ: 450,000. Microform: UM.

Indexed: BusI. *Aud:* Ga, Ac, Jc, Sh. *Rv:* M. *Jv:* A.

This is somewhat the *Time* of the general business magazine world—particularly in writing style, which is both popular and a trifle breezy. The material, however, is usually accurate and unbiased. The political slant, when it shows, is reasonably conservative, but the editors are never above looking behind the public relations' face of business. In fact, it is one of the few general business magazines which cuts through the news releases and gets down to the essential facts about operations, executives and general practices. Particularly noteworthy for personal profiles and candid business case histories. A good magazine for both the specialist and the reader who has only a peripheral interest in the world of business. After *Nation's Business* and *Fortune,* an excellent choice for the general medium to small public and academic collection. Useful, too, in most high schools.

Fortune. 1930. 14/yr. $14. Louis Banks. Time, Inc., Time-Life Bldg., New York, N.Y. 10020. Illus., adv. Circ: 450,-000. Microform: UM. Reprint: Johnson, Abrahams.

Indexed: BusI, PAIS, RG. *Aud:* Ga, Ac, Jc, Sh. *Rv:* H. *Jv:* V.

Without a doubt, the most ambitious of all business periodicals, dealing with business and general interest topics on a grand scale. It is designed to appeal to students, top management men and those on the way up, analyzing news from a broader point of view than the strictly business scene. World affairs, political questions, new industries and products are discussed. Biographies presented in "Businessmen in the News" are valuable, supplying facts that cannot be found any place else. Social, economic, and political aspects of industries, regions and countries are traced and forecasts attempted. The material is presented in a vivid manner, making use of colorful illustrations and easily-read graphs and charts. Supplies the background material which can be used with factual statistics and data discovered in more technical magazines. Unlike other Luce publications, *Fortune* is relatively objective and demonstrates only a mildly conservative bias. Recommended for all types of libraries.

France Actuelle. 1952. semi-m. $4. (Academic use, $2). Comité France Actuelle, 221 Southern Bldg., Washington, D.C. 20005. Illus.

Aud: Ga, Ac. *Rv:* M. *Jv:* B.

The Comité France Actuelle is a private association of French businessmen, and the purpose of their well-illustrated magazine is to promote French society and industry in the United States. It is both an attempt to win approval and investments. A section in each issue is devoted to current notes on French internal and external economics. While geared for the businessman, it is quite suitable for general adult use. It is in English and usually runs eight to twelve pages.

Harvard Business Review. 1922. bi-m. $10. Edward C. Bursk. Harvard Univ., Grad. Sch. of Business Admin., Soldiers Field, Boston Mass. 02163. Illus., index, adv. Circ: 95,000. Microform: UM. Reprint: Kraus, Abrahams.

Indexed: BusI, PAIS, RG. *Aud:* Sa, Ac, Jc, Ht. *Rv:* H. *Jv:* A.

This periodical is designed for the serious student of the current business scene, and thoughtful businessmen, teachers, and scholars will find the lengthy articles concerning trends, predictions, and developments of great interest and value. All phases of business, management through labor, as well as the political, social, and economic developments which affect business are topics for study. Primarily written by scholars rather than business executives, the articles are the result of extensive research. The authors, unbiased by ties to a certain industry or company, are able to give an objective analysis of the problems researched. Each article is accompanied by a foreword which describes contents and provides biographical data about the author. The periodical also includes such feature items as "Thinking Ahead" which lists and discusses future outlooks for a specific industry.

Industrial Marketing; selling and advertising to business and industry. 1935. m. $3. Leo Anderson. Advertising Pubns., Inc., 200 E. Illinois St., Chicago Ill. 60611. Illus., index, adv. Circ: 20,000. Microform: UM.

Indexed: BusI. *Bk. rev:* Notes. *Aud:* Sa, Ac. *Rv:* M. *Jv:* B.

Deals with all phases of marketing, advertising, and sales promotion, in the industrial field. Overall business trends and activities and governmental regulations affecting business are discussed. Problems of specific companies and reports of their results with advertising are included. Departments: "Factfile," advertising volume in business publications, managing market information, and marketing meetings; "American Industrial Advertisers," newsletter; "Washington Report;" and "Market Guide Information," where to locate specific information pamphlets. Annually issues a supplement, *Market Data and Directory Number,* which gives current descriptive information and latest statistics outside the range of industry. Facts on agriculture, mining, construction, utilities, finance and others are provided. Considerably more general than *Journal of Marketing* or *Journal of Marketing Research,* and a first choice for libraries, where there is an audience for this type of material.

Inter-American Economic Affairs. 1947. q. $9. Simon G. Hanson. Box 181, Washington, D.C. 20044. Index.

Indexed: PAIS, SSHum. *Aud:* Sa, Ac. *Rv:* H. *Jv:* B.

Presents materials concerning financial activities in all the American countries. Inter-American political and economic agreements, governmental regulations and practices, political elections and activities, credit programs, and the development of specific companies are discussed. Many of the papers are historical and theoretical rather than practical studies. Some issues present several articles (or the entire issue) devoted to the various economic aspects of a single country or field. Primarily for large business and economics collections.

International Commerce. 1940. w. $16. U.S. Dept. of Commerce, Superintendent of Documents, Washington, D.C. 20402. Microform: UM.

Indexed: BusI. *Aud:* Sa, Ga, Ac. *Rv:* M. *Jv:* B.

A government report which covers all phases of international trade and commerce. It is directed to private industry in this country, and attempts to help U.S. firms make best use of overseas goods and markets. Included are such articles as, "Saudi Economic Recovery Just Around the Corner," and "Ivory Coast Prosperity Seen Reaching into '70's." Perhaps of greater interest than the articles are the listings of U.S. overseas trade promotions, export opportunities and investment opportunities. These sections list potential markets for American products as well as areas where U.S. investment is needed. A listing of new books and reports in the field of international commerce along with brief annotations is included.

International Railway Journal. 1950. m. $9. Joseph Asher. Simmons-Boardman, 30 Church St., New York, N.Y. 10007. Illus., adv. Circ: 11,000.

Aud: Sa, Ac. *Rv:* M. *Jv:* B.

Written to keep railroad management abreast of what's new and what's planned in railroad construction around the world. Articles all have brief abstracts in French, German and Spanish, and are generously illustrated with maps and pictures. Regular monthly features are "World Market," "World Report" and "New Products." Only for large collections, *Railway Age* being a better choice for smaller libraries.

Journal of Advertising Research. 1960. q. Membership (Non-members, $45). Charles K. Ramond. Advertising Research Foundation, 3 E. 54th St., New York, N.Y. 10022. Illus. Circ: 3,000. Microform: UM.

Indexed: BusI. *Bk. rev:* 5–6, lengthy notes. *Aud:* Sa, Ac. *Rv:* H. *Jv:* B.

Teachers, students and businessmen engaged in advertising and marketing will find valuable information and data in this periodical. Articles, contributed by professors and businessmen, are carefully prepared and well-written. Objective and impartial findings are reported to develop new practices, techniques and standards in the field of advertising and research. The staff is responsible for several regular features: "Research in Review," and "Federal Statistics in Advertising." The last examines a particular set of governmental statistical figures discussing its influence upon the advertising field.

Journal of Business. 1928. q. $8. Irving Schweiger. Univ. of Chicago Press, 5750 S. Ellis Ave., Chicago, Ill. 60637. Illus., index, adv. Circ: 3,573. Microform: Canner, UM. Reprint: Johnson, Abrahams.

Indexed: BusI. *Bk. rev:* 15–25, lengthy, signed. *Aud:* Sa, Ac. *Rv:* H. *Jv:* B.

Published by the Graduate School of Business, University of Chicago, this journal features four or five scholarly research papers each issue. Contributed by professors and leading professionals in the field, the studies are more technical than those found in the *Harvard Business Review.*

Knowledge of advanced analytic methods is necessary to understand the findings. An abundance of technical tables, charts, symbols and formulae accompany most articles. Business books, covering all topics, are reviewed by university scholars and some businessmen. The reviews are lengthy and critical, often suggesting appropriate uses and users. Only for large libraries.

Journal of Marketing. 1936. q. $10. Eugene J. Kelly. Amer. Marketing Assn., 230 N. Michigan Ave., Chicago, Ill. 60601. Illus., index, adv. Circ: 18,000. Microform: UM. Reprint: Kraus, Abrahams.

Indexed: BusI, PAIS. *Bk. rev:* 15,300 words, signed. *Aud:* Sa, Ac. *Rv:* H. *Jv:* B.

Scholarly articles, contributed by teachers and researchers, discuss international marketing facts and the impact of government policy on the field, others suggest improved theories and techniques and study the ethical and historical facets of marketing. Accompanied by biographical sketches of the authors and statements of purpose, the articles contain many graphs, charts, tables, and statistical formulae. Special sections give information on current marketing questions, leaders in marketing and legal developments. All material is relevant and presented in an extremely well-written and interesting manner. A required item in large public and academic business collections, but others may pass.

Journal of Marketing Research. 1964. q. $10. Robert Ferber. Amer. Marketing Assn., 230 N. Michigan Ave., Chicago, Ill., 60601. Index, adv. Circ: 6,600. Microform: UM.

Indexed: BusI, PAIS. *Bk. rev:* 5–6, 500 words, signed. *Aud:* Sa, Ac. *Rv:* H. *Jv:* B.

For students of marketing and businessmen involved in improving the current techniques of marketing products, this journal offers sophisticated papers describing the latest research. It is considerably more technical than its sister publication, *Journal of Marketing,* and readers must have a good basic knowledge of research methods as well as marketing principles. The contributions discuss new methods of research, systems of evaluation, and comparisons of marketing and research methods. Also included are studies of current trends, review articles on different aspects of marketing research, and experiments in social psychology and other behavioral sciences relating to marketing. Only for special collections.

Journal of Retailing. 1925. q. $3.50. Sallie W. Sewell. New York Univ., Inst. of Retail Management, Commerce Bldg., Washington Sq., New York, N.Y. 10003. Illus., index. Circ: 2,200. Microform: UM. Reprint: Kraus, Abrahams.

Indexed: BusI, PAIS. *Bk. rev:* 8, lengthy. *Aud:* Ga, Ac, Jc. *Rv:* H. *Jv:* A.

The homemakers of the country would do well to become acquainted with this periodical. Analyzing the broad aspects of retailing and current developments, the scholarly studies are designed for students and teachers of retailing, and managers in chain, department and specialty shops. Articles concern shopper habits, price strategies, trends in stores, and the labor market. Factual and readable studies of the trading stamp mystery, the decline of department stores and why the check-out girl in the food market seldom lasts more than a month. Articles are not overburdened with statistics and are, on the whole, fascinating. One of the few technical journals which deserves a wider, general reading public. Better educated and interested consumers will welcome this, as will students of the subject.

Kiplinger Washington Letter. 1923. w. $24. Austin H. Kiplinger. Kiplinger Washington Editors, Inc., 1729 H St., N.W., Washington, D.C. 20006.

Aud: Ga, Sa, Ac. *Rv:* M. *Jv:* B.

One of the earliest business newsletters, this is a weekly four-page report on current activities in Congress and government. It is written in a stacatto fashion to keep the businessman up-to-date on bills before Congress, new rules and regulations, tax changes and proposals, contracts, etc. The facts are accurate enough, but the editorial line is definitely conservative. Political views aside, the newsletter is valuable for its currency and inside information on personalities and matters which rarely make the average newspaper. It is of interest to both the businessman and the general student of government. The firm, best known for *Changing Times,* also issues a number of other newsletters, i.e., *Kiplinger Agricultural Letter, Book Report, Florida Letter, Tax Letter.* Only for large business collections in public and academic libraries.

Management Review. 1923. m. Members, $7.50 (Nonmembers, $12.50). Patricia Haskell. Amer. Management Assn. Inc., 135 W. 50th St., New York, N.Y. 10020. Illus., index. Circ: 45,000. Microform: UM. Reprint: Kraus, Abrahams.

Indexed: BusI, PsyAb. *Bk. rev:* 1, 1200 words, signed. *Aud:* Sa, Ac. *Rv:* H. *Jv:* B.

Picks up articles of interest to managers from sources such as *Harvard Business Review* (q.v.), *Wall Street Journal* (q.v.) and *Management of Personnel Quarterly* (q.v.). The articles are usually condensed and revised in an easy-to-read form. It also includes two or three original articles, sometimes devoting one section to a single theme. Since there are also 15 or 20 short summaries of other journal articles, it provides a quick overview of current management literature for students and busy executives. One of the best general management magazines, despite the digest approach, for medium to large academic and public business libraries.

Management Services; a magazine of planning, systems and controls. 1964. bi-m. $10. Robert M. Smith. Amer. Inst. of Certified Public Accountants, 666 Fifth Ave.,

New York, N.Y. 10019. Illus., index, adv. Circ: 24,573. Microform: UM.

Indexed: PAIS. *Bk. rev:* 3–10, notes. *Aud:* Sa, Ac. *Rv:* H. *Jv:* B.

Interdisciplinary coverage of accounting and management, which is of value in both business and academic situations. Contributors are practicing accountants, managers, or teachers. Thus, the numerous scholarly articles are balanced with some of general appeal. "People, Events, Techniques" is a valuable section to keep the administrator up-to-date on news in the field. This journal makes an effort to review periodical literature through use of Ph.D. candidates in fifteen universities who scan the literature and present five to ten of the best articles in 100- to 300-word summaries. The latter services give it added reference value for larger academic and public business collections.

Marketing. 1931. m. Membership (Non-members, $12.60). Subscription Dept., Inst. of Marketing, Haymarket Publishing Group, 9 Harrow Rd., London W.2. Illus., adv. Circ: 15,000.

Bk. rev: 6, 300 words, signed. *Aud:* Sa, Ac, Jc. *Rv:* M. *Jv:* B.

The official journal of the English Institute of Marketing. It has a double purpose: the first, to keep members up with news of the organization and activities in their field; the second, to acquaint top management with the need for consulting marketing experts. The average issue features six to seven articles, seven to eight features. Particularly impressive for the jargon-free English, and attractive format. A useful addition for larger business collections.

Marketing/Communications (Formerly: **Printer's Ink.**) 1888. m. $10. Decker Communications, Inc., 501 Madison Ave., New York, N.Y. 10022. Illus., adv. Circ: 41,546. Microform: UM.

Indexed: BusI, PAIS. *Bk. rev:* Notes: *Aud:* Sa, Ac. *Rv:* M. *Jv:* B.

One of the oldest, continuous magazines devoted to advertising in the United States, *Printer's Ink* changed its title and emphasis in the 1960's. At one time there was considerable interest in printing practices and problems, but no more. The usual issue is directed to the individual buying advertising and those seeking the best method to plug their products, discussing packaging, the advantage or disadvantage of a given type of media for advertising, and methods of merchandising. Legislation which affects advertisers is considered. Book reviews are short, but good. Similar material, although with more emphasis on media and advertising, is covered in *Media/Scope,* and, of the two, the latter is preferable for libraries which support strong advertising oriented courses. Conversely, *Marketing/Communications* has a wider scope and will be of more value for the general business collection.

Media Decisions. 1965. m. $5. (Controlled circulation). Norman R. Glenn. 4 East 53rd St., New York, N.Y. 10022. Illus., adv. Circ: 12,000.

Aud: Sa. *Rv:* M. *Jv:* B.

A general news magazine for "key media personnel" (and, incidentally, free to them). The purpose is to report on activities of magazines, television, radio, and advertising in general. Six to eight articles follow the month's past developments, and there are regular columns on radio, newspapers, magazines and television. There are a number of magazines in this field, but the needs of most academic and public libraries will be met by *Advertising Age* and/or *Editor & Publisher.*

Media/Scope; for buyers of advertising. 1957. m. $6. (Controlled circulation.) Carroll J. Swan. Standard Rate & Data Service Inc., 5201 Old Orchard Rd., Skokie, Ill. 60076. Illus., index, adv. Circ: 18,000.

Indexed: PAIS. *Bk. rev:* 2–3, notes. *Aud:* Sa, Ac. *Rv:* H. *Jv:* B.

A guide to advertisers and advertising men issued by the same firm which issues the "Bible" of advertisers, the various Standard Rate and Data Services. There are a number of general feature stories on media and advertising, but the primary importance of the service are the departments which keep readers up on current developments in their given areas of interest. Regular departments include: ad-chart service which gives scores by experts on the effectiveness of an advertisment; personnel; advertising agency account changes; consideration of some 13 various types of media and their effectiveness, coverage, rates, etc. An added value for the non-specialist is the current reports on commercial magazines. A basic magazine in the area, but not as broad in scope as *Editor & Publisher,* and should be considered only for large collections which would also include *Advertising Age, Media Decisions,* and *Marketing Communications.*

Mergers & Acquisitions. 1965. bi-m. $35. Richard L. Gilbert, Jr., Stanley F. Reed. Mergers & Acquisitions, Inc., 54 Wall St., New York, N.Y. 10005. Illus.

Aud: Sa, Ac. *Rv:* M. *Jv:* B.

Discusses the philosophy and industry and business trends concerning mergers and acquisitions. Rather lengthy feature articles offer well documented essays concerning the history and current development of mergers, practices of American investors, government agencies, and regulations relating to the subject. Articles include many charts, graphs, and photocopies of pertinent material. Actual techniques of specific companies are analyzed and evaluated. Only for special collections.

Nation's Business. 1912. m. $19.75. 3/yrs. Jack Wooldridge. Chamber of Commerce of the United States, 1615 H St., N.W., Washington, D.C. 20006. Illus., index, adv. Circ: 800,000. Microform: UM.

Indexed: BusI, RG. *Aud:* Ga, Ac, Jc, Sh. *Rv:* M. *Jv:* B.

Like *Business Week* and *Forbes,* discusses the latest news and developments in the field of business from the businessman's point of view. As the official publication of the

Chamber of Commerce, an organization of professionals and businessmen, it often represents government and labor as the villains, while business and industry are represented favorably. Through its regular features, it presents capsule comments about news and trends in government, world affairs, and all areas of business. Particular concern is given to panning almost all types of government spending and taxation. Brief articles discuss the activities of business or the progress of a specific industry. Interviews with leaders in the field give biographical sketches, emphasizing ideas, background and accomplishments. Very literate and enjoyable columns by signed authors discuss local developments, aspects of congressional or executive roles, schools, books, and the ideas and feelings of the younger generation. A healthy, biased magazine of business which can be understood by high school students and adults. A third or fourth choice, in medium to large public and academic libraries, after *Business Week, Fortune,* and possibly *Forbes.*

Public Relations Journal; a journal of opinion in the field of public relations practice. 1945. m. $7.50. Thomas J. Kraner. Public Relations Soc. of Amer., Inc., 845 Third Ave., New York, N.Y. 10022. Illus., index, adv. Circ: 7,600. Reprint: Kraus, Abrahams.

Indexed: BusI, PAIS. *Bk. rev:* 3, 2,500 words, signed. *Aud:* Ga, Ac, Jc. *Rv:* H. *Jv:* B.

Deals with the wider aspects, trends and policies of public relations in all fields. Articles, written by active businessmen, are timely and literate, containing very few statistics and charts. Problems in all areas are discussed with possible solutions offered. Most of the articles are specific, exemplified by actual cases rather than theoretical studies. National agencies, federal regulations and current news are given in the regular feature, "Washington Focus," with the foreign scene being covered in the "International Focus." Other material supplied by the magazine are new devices, progress reports and news of conferences and symposiums. A specialized periodical for larger collections, although all librarians might take a close look for their own public relations programs.

Public Relations Quarterly. 1957. q. $6. Howard P. Hudson. Richard Toohey, Public Relations Aids, Inc., 305 E. 45th St., New York, N.Y. 10017. Circ: 4,500.

Bk. rev: Various number, lengths. *Aud:* Sa, Ac. *Rv:* H. *Jv:* B.

The leading semi-scholarly magazine in the field of public relations. Each issue includes not only pragmatic examples of successful p.r., but contributions from teachers, sociologists, and psychologists on various aspects of what constitutes a viable method of winning or losing public approval. Much of the material is of value to the student of the behavioral sciences. Good book reviews, and features on current trends, programs and the like.

Railway Age. 1856. w. $6. Luther S. Miller. Simmons-Boardman Publishing Corp., 30 Church St., New York,

N.Y. 10007. Illus., index, adv. Circ: 14,000. Microform: UM.

Indexed: BusI, EngI, PAIS. *Aud:* Sa, Ac. *Rv:* H. *Jv:* B.

Articles, written by the staff, discuss problems in railway operations and management, urban rapid transit, new diesel designs, use of computers, railroad communications, etc. Most issues are devoted to a special area like freight traffic, railway engineering, transit, or special reports to management. Regular features: "New Products Report;" "People in the News;" "Market Outlook"—sales information and statistics; "Lines on Labor." Many black and white pictures and indexed advertisements.

Sales Management; the magazine of marketing. 1918. semi-m. $12. Sales Management, Inc., 630 Third Ave., New York, N.Y. 10017. Illus., adv. Circ: 33,000. Microform: UM.

Indexed: BusI, PAIS. *Aud:* Sa, Ac, Jc. *Rv:* H. *Jv:* B.

For the general business executive and student as well as the marketing manager, the sales manager, advertising director and salesman, *Sales Management* offers information on all phases of the marketing process. Unsurpassed in its field, it concentrates on the strategies and the tactics of marketing; including the research and evaluation of markets for products and services, the operations involved in bringing them to the consumer, and the building of effective sales teams. Most of the articles are short reports of developments in business and selling or descriptions of individual campaigns, selling techniques and use of media. Of particular note is the annual service issue, *Survey of Buying Power,* which factually and statistically reports the current estimated figures in buying power, showing population, sales and income changes. Definitions, descriptions, sources, methods and application of the data are also supplied. This enables the reader to use the facts for his own specific needs. Although specialized, it will be useful in most public and academic libraries.

Sweden Now. 1967. 10/yr. $9. Tell G. Dahllof. 161 E. 42nd St., New York, N.Y. 10017. Illus., adv. Circ: 30,000.

Aud: Sa, Ac, Jc. *Rv:* M. *Jv:* B.

An English language business magazine which touches lightly on Swedish social life, concentrates on Swedish business and new products. (Also, published in several other languages for businessmen from Japan to Switzerland.) After four or five well-illustrated general articles, departments discuss new products, finance, company news, etc. Thanks to the illustrations and the semi-popular writing style, the whole will be of value to both layman and businessman alike. Not an essential item, but worthwhile for general and business collections in larger academic and public libraries.

Steel; metalworking weekly. 1882. w. Free to qualified personnel, others $25. Walter J. Campbell. Sal F. Marino, Penton Publishing Co., Penton Bldg., Cleveland, Ohio 44113. Illus., index, adv. Microform: UM.

Indexed: ASTI, BusI, EngI. *Aud:* Sa, Ac. *Rv:* H. *Jv:* B.

Brief articles, illustrated with photographs, diagrams and charts, discuss maintenance problems, costs, developments, personnel and specific steel companies. New technology, products and literature are presented in a practical manner. Auto production, problems and developments are supplied as a regular feature. Especially useful are the production indexes, trends, and outlooks presented. Labor problems and government activities round out the information offered. Since the developments and trends reported affect all phases of business and the economy, the reading audience should include readers in many allied fields. A basic industrial magazine for all medium to large public and academic libraries.

Stores. 1918. m. $8. John S. Kelly. National Retail Merchants Assn., 100 W. 31st St., New York, N.Y. 10001. Illus., adv. Circ: 13,000.

Indexed: BusI, PAIS. *Aud:* Sa, Ac. *Rv:* M. *Jv:* B.

Provides association news, merchandising information, and financial and political news of interest to retailers. Strictly concerns the American scene with little reference to international aspects. Regular features supply comments on current marketing and retailing practices, governmental trends, statistics and congressional activities. Hearings and regulations of the Federal Trade Commission are reported and discussed and the economy as it concerns retailers is carefully analyzed. Brief articles discuss vital and current developments; how to improve credit legislation, business and government conflicts, research in retail management and techniques for improved retailing. Only for specialized collections.

Survey of Current Business. 1921. m. Murray F. Foss. U.S. Dept. of Commerce, Office of Business Economics, Supt. of Documents, Washington, D.C. 20402. Illus. Circ: 15,000. Microform: UM. Reprint: Johnson, Abrahams.

Indexed: BusI, PAIS. *Aud:* Ga, Ac, Jc. *Rv:* H. *Jv:* A.

A governmental periodical devoted to a monthly review of employment, economic activity, government spending, production, construction, and personal income for the past month. Forecasts for the general trends of business for the immediate future are given. Supported by charts and tables, business volume growths and failures are described. Concluding the first section are two or three lengthy, authoritative articles, treating studies of business in general or surveys of specific industries. "Current Business Statistics" is the second major section. It updates the *1965 Business Statistics,* and is a compilation of statistics for the significant fields of business activities. Indexes and tables relate prices, personal consumption and expenditures, private and domestic investment, employment, finance, foreign trade, labor, and production. A basic acquisition in all medium to large public and academic libraries.

Traffic World; a working tool for traffic and transportation men. 1907. w. $42. J. C. Scheleen. Traffic Service Corp., Washington Bldg., Washington, D.C. 20005. Illus., index, adv. Circ: 10,500. Microform: UM.

Aud: Sa, Ac. *Rv:* M. *Jv:* B.

Directed to transportation managers in the manufacturing industries, and to water, motor, rail, and air carriers. Articles give world-wide coverage to all aspects relating to the movement of goods. Regular features include ICC decisions, applications, petitions and hearings; FAB News; Maritime Commission News; Court News; international transportation; legislative news; statistics, etc. There are some black and white pictures and many advertisements. While a specialized trade journal, the scope is wide enough to warrant consideration in many medium to large public and academic libraries.

Wall Street Journal. See Newspaper Section.

CHEMISTRY

Indexes and Abstracts

Applied Science and Technology Index, Biological Abstracts, British Technology Index, Business Periodicals Index, Chemical Abstracts, Engineering Index, Mathematical Reviews, Science Abstracts, Science Citation Index. (For annotations, see Indexes and Abstracts Section.)

Most of the periodicals represented in this section are research journals appropriate for academic libraries. As is usually the case with scholarly publications of scientific societies or well-established, commercial research journals, editorial boards consist of prominent specialists in the field, and the contributions are generally high-quality studies. Moreover, in every journal listed herein which reports on original research, each paper has been submitted to the scrutiny of one or two subject specialists who determine the caliber of the research effort according to their respective fields. No attempt has been made to incorporate the vast number of periodicals necessary for a good research library, nor to include those covering the more specialized branches of chemistry. Rather, we have tried to select: (1) titles available in English of some of the highly distinguished general chemistry journals; (2) the important review journals; (3) a representative sampling of periodicals available in analytical, inorganic, organic, and physical chemistry; (4) a few foreign titles of historical importance; (5) and some magazines or trade publications of interest to students and laymen. Most academic libraries will carry several of the important publications of the American Chemical Society, the number depending on the size of the library, the curriculum offered by their institution, and the specific needs of their faculty. Libraries supporting full research programs would naturally subscribe to many more titles, including the prestigious publications of foreign chemical societies, such as *Acta Chemica Scandinavica, Bulletin de la Société Chimique de France, Helvetica Chimica Acta, Recueil des Travaux Chimique des Pays-Bas,* and *Bulletin of the Chemical Society of Japan,* to name a very few.

Accounts of Chemical Research. 1968. m. $10. J. F. Bunnett. Amer. Chemical Soc., 1155 16th St., N.W., Washington, D.C. 20036. Illus., index. Circ: 110,000. Microform: AMC.

Indexed: ChemAb. *Aud:* Sa, Ac, Jc. *Rv:* H. *Jv:* B.

Publishing "concise, critical reviews of areas currently under active investigation," the journal reports on work being carried out on the very frontiers of chemical research. All branches of chemistry are represented. Although the articles (5–6 pages in length) are not of the exhaustive nature associated with review papers, bibliographies are fairly comprehensive. Contributions by specialists are usually at the invitation of the editorial board. A valuable and authoritative journal for short reviews on specialized subjects.

American Chemical Society. Journal. 1879. semi-m. Membership (Non-members, $32). Marshall Gates. Amer. Chemical Soc., 1155 16th St., N.W., Washington, D.C. 20036. Illus., index, adv. Circ: 16,000. Microform: AMC, Mc, Princeton. Reprint: Johnson.

Indexed: ASTI, BioAb, ChemAb, EngI, SciAb, SCI. *Bk. rev:* 1–2, 800 words, signed. *Aud:* Sa, Ac. *Rv:* H. *Jv:* B.

In the last three decades, the *Journal,* which is the oldest publication of the Society, has emerged as one of the world's most important chemical publications. Significant research papers report on all branches of fundamental chemistry; articles are selected on the basis of broad chemical interest, and the journal avoids those which merely report routine measurements. Divided into sections comprising physical, inorganic, organic, and biological chemistry, the periodical also devotes a section to "Communications to the Editor," which consists of short, preliminary studies of importance and timeliness. The book reviews are excellent.

Analyst. 1876. m. $60. J. B. Attrill. Soc. for Analytical Chemistry, 9/10 Savile Row, London W.1. Illus., index, adv. Circ: 7,319. Microform: UM. Reprint: Johnson.

Indexed: BioAb, BritTech, ChemAb, SCI. *Bk. rev:* 7–8, 300–500 words, signed. *Aud:* Sa, Ac. *Rv:* H. *Jv:* B.

International in scope, this British journal publishes original research papers, along with some lengthy review articles, in all branches of analytical chemistry. Incorporated in the price of the periodical is a subscription to *Analytical Abstracts,* which supplies coverage of the world's literature in the field, and *Proceedings of the Society for Analytical Chemistry.* Although an excellent choice for libraries with a strong interest in analytical chemistry, the small academic library may find its needs sufficiently served by its American counterpart, *Analytical Chemistry.*

Analytical Chemistry. 1929. m. Membership (Non-members, $5). H. A. Laitinen. Amer. Chemical Soc., 1155 16th St., N.W., Washington, D.C. 20036. Illus., index, adv. Circ: 30,000. Microform: AMC.

Indexed: ASTI, BioAb, ChemAb, EngI, SciAb, SCI. *Bk. rev:* 7, 300 words, signed. *Aud:* Sa, Ac, Jc. *Rv:* H. *Jv:* B.

All aspects of analytical chemistry are represented in this publication. Papers and reports, both theoretical and me-

thodological, range from studies of operations, instrumentation, measurements, to chemical reactions. Very thorough news coverage of research, product developments, chemicals, and professional activities is also given. Two special issues appear annually: an April supplement provides excellent and comprehensive reviews of the literature; and a laboratory guide, issued in July, gives detailed information on new equipment, services, and the like. This is the best U.S. source for authoritative and comprehensive information on analytical chemistry.

Angewandte Chemie. International Edition. 1962. m. $38. H. Grunewald. Academic Press, Inc., 111 Fifth Ave., New York, N.Y. 10003. Illus., index, adv. Circ: 3,000.

Indexed: ChemAb, SCI. *Bk. rev:* 7, 250 words, signed. *Aud:* Sa, Ac. *Rv:* H. *Jv:* B.

The International Edition, sponsored by the Gesellschaft Deutscher Chemiker, is a translation of the German edition which originated in 1888. The journal features extended, authoritative review articles covering all facets of chemical research; "Communications," a section devoted to brief research reports; selected abstracts; reports of presentations at conferences; and book reviews. The latter two sections are especially useful, since they provide a current-awareness program of unpublished results presented at European conferences, and announcements of new chemical texts appearing abroad.

Biochemical Journal. See Biological Sciences Section ("Biochemistry and Biophysics").

Biochemistry. See Biological Sciences Section ("Biochemistry and Biophysics").

Canadian Journal of Chemistry. 1929. semi-m. $15. C. T. Bishop & J. A. Morrison. National Research Council of Canada, Ottawa 7, Ont. Illus., index. Circ: 5,200. Microform: Princeton.

Indexed: BioAb, ChemAb, SCI. *Aud:* Sa, Ac. *Rv:* H. *Jv:* B.

Covering all areas of chemistry, the journal reports the results of original research investigations, including studies in biochemistry, as well as analytical, inorganic, organic, and physical chemistry. Contributions are, in large part, from Canadian universities and research establishments. In addition to full-length papers and research notes of limited scope, the periodical includes very short communications which receive prompt publication. Papers may appear in English or French.

Chemical Abstracts. See Indexes and Abstracts Section.

Chemical and Engineering News. 1923. w. $6.00. Gordon H. Bixler. Amer. Chemical Soc., 1155 16th St., N.W., Washington, D.C. 20036. Illus., index, adv. Circ: 114,580. Microform: AMC.

Indexed: ASTI, BioAb, ChemAb, *Aud:* Sa, Ga, Ac, Jc. *Rv:* H. *Jv:* B.

The weekly newsmagazine runs the gamut from the latest developments in industrial, academic, and governmental research to announcements of new products and technology. As the American Chemical Society's "newsmagazine of the chemical world," and with its frequent editorial comment on policies and practices in the profession, it is a valuable publication for any chemistry or chemical engineering collection. Special reports reviewing selected aspects of chemistry and written in fairly nontechnical language would also recommend the periodical for interested laymen. Features which make the magazine high in reference value are: market surveys, chemical prices, salary schedules, education notes, and professional opportunities. Two special issues— "Career Opportunities" appearing in the spring, and "Facts and Figures" issued each September—summarize these data. Also included are the usual news and notices of the profession. Checklists of new books are published regularly. Quarterly and annual indexes must be purchased separately.

Chemical Reviews. 1924. bi-m. $20. H. Hart. Amer. Chemical Soc., 1155 16th St., N.W., Washington, D.C. 20036. Illus., index. Circ: 6,100. Microform: AMC, UM. Reprint: Johnson.

Indexed: BioAb, ChemAb, SciAb, SCI. *Aud:* Sa, Ac. *Rv:* H. *Jv:* B.

"Authoritative critical reviews and comprehensive summaries of recent research in theoretical chemistry" are contributed by distinguished scientists (usually at the invitation of the editor) in areas representing all branches of chemistry. Generally, the topics under discussion have not been reviewed in a readily available publication for at least five years, although exceptions are made if developments in a field have been particularly rapid, or if new insight can be achieved through further evaluation of a subject. The timely articles, averaging 10–20 pages in length, and exhaustive bibliographies make the journal an invaluable reference for both advanced students and researchers.

Chemical Society, London. Journal. 1848. m. $168. L. C. Cross. The Chemical Soc., Burlington House, London W.1. Illus., index. Microform: UM, Mc, Princeton. Reprint: Johnson.

Indexed: ChemAb, SCI. *Aud:* Sa, Ac. *Rv:* H. *Jv:* B.

An outstanding research publication, the *Journal* is one of the world's major chemical periodicals. Recently, it has been fragmented into four parts. Section A publishes research on inorganic, physical, and theoretical chemistry and is issued monthly; Section B covers research on physical organic chemistry on a monthly basis; and Section C, published twice monthly, is devoted to organic chemistry. Articles comprise full-length, definitive studies.

"Urgent preliminary accounts of important new work" appear semi-monthly in Part D, *Chemical Communications,* which formerly constituted the "Communications" section of the defunct *Proceedings of the Chemical Society.* The reports included herein are very short (1–2 pages).

All of the above sections are received with the price of a full subscription; individual parts may be purchased separately.

The Chemical Society also puts out a current-awareness publication, *Current Chemical Papers,* which is a classified list of titles of significant papers culled from the international literature on pure chemistry.

Chemical Week. 1914. w. $5. H. C. E. Johnson. McGraw-Hill, Inc., 330 W. 42nd St., New York, N.Y. 10036. Illus., index, adv. Circ: 60,000. Microform: UM.

Indexed: BusI. *Aud:* Sa, Ga. *Rv:* H. *Jv:* B.

The trade publication spots the news: in legislation emerging from Washington; from high-level executive suites; from production lines in the Far East or USSR; from research laboratories; from corporate battles in the courtroom to pickets on the streets. Of course, the magazine is directed toward professionals in the chemical process industries, but its content and scope are broad enough to appeal to a layman with an interest in the field, particularly since the prose is so readable. Some issues feature special reports—comprehensive resumés of state-of-the-art—on topics which range from plant sites to pollution control. Regular departments include business (sales, growth, mergers); international activities; technology (new products, instrumentation); marketing (including price indexes and surveys); and people (profiles of executives). A buyers' guide is issued annually. Indispensable for the desktops of investors or sales executives for its news and statistics, it may also serve some of the clientele of public libraries.

Chemische Berichte. 1868. m. $85. Gesellschaft Deutscher Chemiker. Verlag Chemie GmbH, Weinheim/Bergstr., Germany. Illus., index. Circ: 3,600. Microform: UM, Mc. Reprint: Johnson.

Indexed: BioAb, ChemAb, SCI. *Aud:* Sa, Ac. *Rv:* H. *Jv:* B.

The publication is a continuation of the very renowned *Berichte der Deutschen Chemischen Gesellschaft* which, prior to 1945, was, if not the leading general chemical journal, certainly one of the most prestigious. Currently, high-quality research papers in the journal are concerned with both inorganic and organic chemistry, although in recent years it has leaned heavily toward studies in organic chemical research. In addition to full-length papers, the publication contains a few research notes of more limited scope.

Chemistry. 1927. m. $4.00. O. Theodor Benfey. Amer. Chemical Soc., 1155 16th St., N.W., Washington, D.C. 20036. Illus., index, adv. Circ: 31,000. Microform: AMC, UM.

Indexed: ChemAb, RG. *Bk. rev:* 2, 300–500 words, signed. *Aud:* Sh, Jc, Ac, Sa, Ga. *Rv:* H. *Jv:* V.

"Why grow old?" "How were the elements named?" These are some of the questions answered on a nontechnical level in this periodical directed at introducing chemistry to beginning students at any level. The 3–4 features in each issue probe into such areas as the application of chemical research in our daily lives, supply historical or biographical notes from the annals of chemistry, and explore and interpret new research. Articles, usually by highly distinguished scientists, are written in general, readable prose, are lavishly illustrated, often with some extremely good photography, and make entertaining as well as informative reading. To further the educational end, special departments are included such as "Lab Bench," which describes experiments which have been, and can be, undertaken at the high school level; or "Language Corner," which provides articles in German or French to assist students in learning technical terminology. An exceptional title for high school libraries, the magazine is worthwhile for any public library seeking more than a general science periodical.

Chemistry and Industry. 1881. w. $20. T. F. West. Soc. of Chemical Industry, 14 Belgrave Square, London S.W.1. Illus., index, adv. Circ: 9,988.

Indexed: ASTI, BioAb, BritTech, ChemAb, SCI. *Bk. rev:* 12, 100–200 words, signed. *Aud:* Sa, Ac. *Rv:* H. *Jv:* B.

An important section of this periodical, which also serves as the news organ for the Society, is its "Communications," which publishes brief reports on original chemical research. Other valuable features are: essay reviews; short accounts of methods and apparatus in product and process developments; resumés of current chemical literature. A buyers' guide to chemicals and equipment (mostly English) is issued annually.

Chemistry in Britain. 1965. m. $14.50. P. J. Farago. Chemical Soc., Burlington House, London W.1. Illus., index, adv. Circ: 37,500.

Indexed: BritTech, ChemAb. *Bk. rev:* 12–13, 150–250 words, signed. *Aud:* Sa, Ac, Jc. *Rv:* H. *Jv:* B.

Incorporating the *Journal of the Royal Institute of Chemistry* and the *Proceedings of the Chemical Society,* this periodical supplies the majority of British chemists with the "raw gossip" of their profession—personalia, salaries, news bits, calendar. The publication also contains some very worthwhile features for U.S. libraries. Articles discuss trends in research, education, government, and industry. Specialists review their areas of research either in essays or in a "Current-Awareness" series, both of which supply excellent tutorials to the general chemist. Since many of the reports are written in nonspecialist language, the periodical should also be useful to undergraduates. Occasional, essay-type book reviews (500–600 words) are good.

Electrochemical Society. Journal. 1948. m. $40. Cecil V. King. Electrochemical Soc. Inc., 30 E. 42nd St., New York, N.Y. 10017. Illus., index, adv. Circ: 6,500. Microform: UM. Reprint: Johnson.

Indexed: ASTI, ChemAb, EngI, SciAb, SCI. *Bk. rev:* 1–2, 250 words, signed. *Aud:* Sa, Ac. *Rv:* H. *Jv:* B.

Although directed toward the specialist, this important journal, which publishes both fundamental and applied research in electrochemistry, is interdisciplinary in character and incorporates papers from all the sciences concerned with

electrochemical phenomena. Since 1969, it has been divided into four sections. "Electrochemical Science" includes fundamental research studies on electrochemical phenomena in chemistry, physics, biology, and medicine. "Solid State Science" emphasizes papers dealing with the solid state in areas of physics, electronics, chemistry, biology and medicine. "Electrochemical Technology" is concerned with the applications of electrochemical phenomena to products and systems, both in science and engineering. "Reviews and News" publishes both invited and contributed papers summarizing current problems in chemistry, physics, electronics, metallurgy, medicine, and engineering, as they relate to electrochemical phenomena. Also included in this section twice annually are abstracts of papers presented at meetings of the Society, as well as news, personalia, book reviews, etc.

Faraday Society. Transactions. 1905. m. 124s. F. C. Tompkins. Aberdeen Univ. Press Ltd., Farmers Hall, Aberdeen, Scotland. Illus., index. Circ: 5,000. Microform: Mc, Princeton. Reprint: Johnson.

Indexed: BioAb, ChemAb, EngI, MathR, SciAb, SCI. *Bk. rev:* 7, 250 words, signed. *Aud:* Sa, Ac. *Rv:* H. *Jv:* B.

The original focus of this learned society was "to promote the study of sciences lying between chemistry, physics and biology." Currently, the *Transactions* publishes research papers mostly in the field of physical chemistry; yet, these reports are of interest to a large body of specialists in the physical sciences because either the theory or experimental methods overlap from one science to another.

The Society also sponsors two other publications, its *Discussions* and *Symposia.* The *Discussions,* issued semiannually, comprises research papers read at meetings of the organization and includes discussions thereon by the scientists in attendance. Papers center around one specific subject. *Symposia,* published annually, are also the reports presented at special conferences held under the aegis of the Society, and again are focused on one topic. Discussions on these papers are also included. *Discussions* and *Symposia* may be purchased separately or can be obtained in combination with a subscription to the *Transactions.*

Industrial and Engineering Chemistry. See Engineering Section ("Chemical Engineering").

Inorganic Chemistry. 1962. m. $28. M. Frederick Hawthorne. Amer. Chemical Soc., 1155 16th St., N.W., Washington, D.C. 20036. Illus., index, adv. Circ: 5,200. Microform: AMC.

Indexed: ChemAb, EngI, SCI. *Aud:* Sa, Ac. *Rv:* H. *Jv:* B.

Both experimental and theoretical research papers are published in this journal devoted exclusively to all phases of inorganic chemistry. Authoritative studies cover such areas as synthesis of new compounds, their properties, reaction mechanisms, quantitative investigations of structures, and thermodynamics. In addition to full-length papers, the journal also carries brief notes describing research of a more limited scope, and a "Correspondence" section largely consisting of comments on other research reported in the journal, or new observations. Since the periodical is a primary medium for reporting new results in inorganic chemistry, it is an important addition for academic libraries supporting curricula in this field, and an essential item in any research library.

Journal of Applied Chemistry. 1951. m. $50.40. T. E. Symes. Soc. of Chemical Industry, 14 Belgrave Sq., London S.W.1. Illus., index. Circ: 4,000.

Indexed: ASTI, BritTech, ChemAb, EngI, SCI. *Aud:* Sa, Ac. *Rv:* H. *Jv:* B.

Consisting of original research papers on most aspects of the applied chemical sciences, the journal also publishes occasional review articles on specialized topics and includes a large abstracts section. Abstracts cover selected literature in the fields of chemical engineering: fuel and fuel products; industrial inorganic chemistry (incl. metals, glass, ceramics, etc.); industrial organic chemistry (incl. dyestuffs, photographic materials, some pharmaceuticals); fats (incl. oils, waxes, detergents, rubber, leather, etc.); fibres (incl. textiles, paper, plastics, paints); and apparatus.

Journal of Biological Chemistry. See Biological Sciences Section ("Biochemistry and Biophysics").

Journal of Chemical Documentation. 1961. q. $14. Herman Skolnik. Amer. Chemical Soc., 1155 16th St., N.W., Washington, D.C. 20036. Illus., index. Microform: AMC.

Indexed: ChemAb, SCI. *Bk. rev:* 2–3, 250 words, signed. *Aud:* Sa, Ac. *Rv:* H. *Jv:* B.

Dealing with far more than the problems of handling the chemical literature, this publishes studies of subjects involved with the science of documentation, its results and methodology. Papers, varying in levels of sophistication, cover such topics as classification systems, indexing, abstracting, chemical nomenclature, information processing, storage and retrieval systems, machine translations, technical writing, etc. Frequently, contributions are based on papers presented at the American Chemical Society's Division of Chemical Literature, for which the journal is the official publication. Because of the broad variety of subject matter, the journal belongs on the professional reading list of any librarian concerned with the technical literature and its documentation.

Journal of Chemical Education. 1924. m. $4. W. T. Lippincott. Amer. Chemical Soc., 20th & Northampton Sts., Easton, Pa. Illus., index, adv. Circ: 22,000. Reprint: Johnson.

Indexed: BioAb, ChemAb, SCI. *Bk. rev:* 10, 300–400 words, signed. *Aud:* Sa, Ac, Jc, Ht. *Rv:* H. *Jv:* A.

Perhaps every chemistry library and every chemical educator is a subscriber, but this is one publication which ought to find its way into high school collections as well. Papers encompass the full range of chemistry—ideas, theory,

method, laboratory experimentation, philosophy, and history. Levels of sophistication vary, and articles are useful to both students and teachers. Reports covering the technical problems of teaching—administration, curricula, lecture demonstrations, and methods of presentation—are featured regularly. Several monthly departments review new instruments, chemicals, products, safety in the chemical laboratory, and the like. Appearing each September is a comprehensive, classified checklist of new technical books. The journal also incorporates the *Report of New England Association of Chemistry Teachers* and the *Proceedings of the California Association of Chemistry Teachers.*

Journal of Chemical Physics. See Physics Section.

Journal of General Chemistry of the USSR. 1949. m. $175. Consultants Bureau, 227 W. 17th St., New York, N.Y. 10011. Illus., index. Microform: The publisher.

Indexed: ChemAb, SCI. *Aud:* Sa, Ac. *Rv:* H. *Jv:* B.

The journal is a complete translation of *Zhurnal Obshchei Khimii,* the leading chemical journal of the USSR, and a publication of their well-known Academy of Sciences. Comparable in scope and quality to *Journal of the American Chemical Society,* the periodical reflects the current chemical interests of reputable Russian scientists. Research papers deal with all branches of chemistry and include studies on analytical, biochemical, inorganic, organic, and physical chemistry. (Note: Consultants Bureau publishes in translation a large number of authoritative journals pertinent to chemical interests.)

Journal of Inorganic and Nuclear Chemistry. 1955. m. $175. Ed bd. Pergamon Press, Maxwell House, Fairview Park, Elmsford, N.Y. 10523. Illus., index.

Indexed: ChemAb, SCI. *Bk. rev:* Occasional, 250 words, signed. *Aud:* Sa, Ac. *Rv.* H. *Jv:* B.

An international publication, this journal comprises research reports and short notes both in nuclear and inorganic chemistry. Investigations include synthesis of new compounds and their reactions, structures, mechanisms, solution complexes, and studies of stable and radioactive isotopes. Shorter research communications in need of faster publication appear in its monthly, letter-type supplement, *Inorganic and Nuclear Chemistry Letters* ($60/yr.). The papers are high quality, and the editorial boards represent a distinguished body of international specialists. Both the *Journal* and the *Letters* are necessary for any library emphasizing research in inorganic chemistry; the smaller academic library, however, will find the American Chemical Society's publication, *Inorganic Chemistry,* adequate for its needs.

Journal of Organic Chemistry. 1936. m. $32. Frederick D. Greene. Amer. Chemical Soc., 1155 16th St., N.W., Washington, D.C. 20036. Illus., index, adv. Circ: 10,400. Microform: AMC, UM. Reprint: Johnson.

Indexed: BioAb, ChemAb, SCI. *Aud:* Sa, Ac. *Rv:* H. *Jv:* B.

Devoted to "original contributions on fundamental researches in all branches of the theory and practice of organic chemistry," the *Journal* publishes both comprehensive research papers and short notes of a more limited scope. Studies include investigations on organic reactions, mechanisms, natural products, synthesis of new compounds, theoretical organic chemistry, and some aspects of spectroscopy related to organic chemistry. If a library is limited to a single publication in this field, this publication would be a first choice.

Journal of Physical Chemistry. 1896. m. $32. F. T. Wall. Amer. Chemical Soc., 1155 16th St., N.W., Washington, D.C. 20036. Illus., index. Circ: 6,400. Microform: AMC, UM, Mc. Reprint: Johnson.

Indexed: ChemAb, EngI, SciAb, SCI. *Aud:* Sa, Ac. *Rv:* H. *Jv:* B.

Dealing with "fundamental aspects of physical chemistry," the journal publishes articles, notes, and communications particularly involving "new concepts, techniques and interpretations." High quality papers represent thorough and complete studies; notes are of a more limited nature; and communications include both reports of preliminary results, and comments on the work of others. The theoretical and experimental articles treat such topics as atomic and molecular phenomena, quantum mechanical calculations, magnetic resonance spectroscopy, and molecular electronic spectroscopy. This publication would be essential to any collection supporting either a graduate or undergraduate chemistry program.

Justus Liebigs Annalen Der Chemie. 1832. irreg. 10v./ yr. R. Kuhn. Verlag Chemie GmbH, Pappelallee 3, Weinheim, Bergstr., Germany. Illus., index. Circ: 2,450. Microform: UM, Mc. Reprint: Johnson.

Indexed: ChemAb, SCI, *Aud:* Sa, Ac. *Rv* H. *Jv:* B.

Annalen is one of the oldest chemical journals still in print and one which, through a series of highly distinguished chemists who acted as editors, made valuable contributions to the development of chemistry in the 19th century. Originally an outgrowth of two pharmaceutical journals, it expanded its scope to all phases of chemistry, with a strong emphasis on organic chemistry. Today the journal is devoted exclusively to organic chemistry, including natural products, and though it may be equalled in quality and content by many other research publications, it is still a distinguished addition to an academic library emphasizing this field.

Quarterly Reviews. 1947. q. $12.60. L. C. Cross. Chemical Soc., Burlington House, London W.1. Illus., index. Circ: 13,000.

Indexed: ChemAb, SCI. *Aud:* Sa, Ac. *Rv:* H. *Jv:* B.

The scope of this important review journal includes selected and timely topics in general, physical, inorganic, and organic chemistry. Papers, by well-known authorities, are geared toward researchers but are still of a general nature, with some specialist articles of particular interest included from time to time. About seven reviews, approximately 30 pages in length, appear in each issue; bibliographies are comprehensive. An excellent publication for most academic libraries.

Russian Chemical Reviews. 1960. m. $60. Ed bd. Chemical Soc., Burlington House, London W.1. Illus., index. Circ: 820.

Indexed: ChemAb, SCI. *Aud:* Sa, Ac. *Rv:* H. *Jv:* B.

With the exception of a few articles, the journal is a cover-to-cover translation of *Uspekhi Khimii,* a monthly publication of the Academy of Sciences of the USSR. Comparable in scope and purpose to *Chemical Reviews,* it publishes review papers by leading Russian scientists in all branches of current chemical research. The few exceptions which have not been translated are papers which originally appeared in other review journals (e.g., *Quarterly Reviews, Angewandte Chemie,* etc.) and were subsequently translated into Russian. Reviews are authoritative and critical, and cover selected topics in inorganic, analytical, physical, and organic chemistry, with some biochemical studies included. Although there is a significant time lag in translation (more than six months), an important feature of this journal for research libraries is that the comprehensive bibliographies frequently bring to light little known publications from the USSR. Note: The Chemical Society of London also sponsors two other translations of specialized research journals: *Russian Journal of Inorganic Chemistry (Zhurnal Neorganicheskoi Khimii)* and *Russian Journal of Physical Chemistry (Zhurnal Fizicheskoi Khimii).*

Tetrahedron. 1957. semi-m. $225. Pergamon Press, Maxwell House, Fairview Park, Elmsford, N.Y. 10523. Illus., index. Circ: 3,500.

Indexed: BioAb, ChemAb, SCI. *Aud:* Sa, Ac. *Rv:* H. *Jv:* B.

The emphases in this international journal dealing exclusively with research papers on organic chemistry are: organic reactions, natural products, studies of mechanism, and spectroscopy. Its supplement, *Tetrahedron Letters* ($175/yr), communicates shorter reports which are in quick need of dissemination in a letter-type journal (60/yr). The cost of these publications can clearly be a prohibitive factor for small, academic libraries, whose needs may be met by the ACS periodical, *Journal of Organic Chemistry.* Nevertheless, the journals are essential for any institution with an active research program in organic chemistry.

CHILD CARE

Indexes and Abstracts

Abridged Readers' Guide, Biological Abstracts, Education Index, Index Medicus, Nutrition Abstracts and Reviews, Psychological Abstracts, Public Affairs Information Service,

Readers' Guide to Periodical Literature. (For annotations, see Indexes and Abstracts Section.)

Adolescence. 1966. q. $10. Ernest Harms & Robert Meister. Libra Pubns., Inc., 1133 Broadway, New York, N.Y. 10010. Illus., adv. Circ: 3,500.

Bk. rev: Various numbers, lengths. *Aud:* Sa, Ac. *Rv:* H. *Jv:* B.

Primarily directed to the experienced psychologist and sociologist who is involved with the education and the problems of adolescents. Articles are well documented, for the most part represent original research or observation, and are usually illustrated with necessary charts. While an interdisciplinary journal for the specialist, the better educated parent and the interested teacher will find much here of value. The wide scope guarantees an interest in this unique periodical in larger psychology, sociology and education collections in academic libraries.

Baby Talk. 1935. m. $4. Deirdre Carr. Leam Publishing Corp., 149 Madison Ave., New York, N.Y. 10016. Illus., adv. Circ: 900,000.

Aud: Ga. *Rv:* L. *Jv:* C.

Information for mothers of babies and young children as well as the expectant mother. Articles are of practical value and center on such items as a research report on thumbsucking; a series based on Lawrence K. Frank's scholarly book on infant development, *On the Importance of Infancy;* and a sketch called "Journey to Childhood" in cooperation with the Pediatrics Department of Duke University Medical Center. The usual departments on maternity fashions, baby products and readers' suggestions are included. The magazine is distributed by maternity and/or infant departments in stores as well as by diaper services and in offices of obstetricians, general practitioners and pediatricians. Librarians may be able to pick up complimentary copies or a subscription. Similar (and equally good) publications include: *My Baby* and *Your New Baby,* the latter probably being more suitable for most libraries. Although a paperback, and not generally considered a magazine, Dr. Benjamin Spock's *Baby and Child Care* (semi-ann. $.95/copy. Pocket Books, Inc., 630 Fifth Ave., New York, N.Y. 10020) is many parent's "bible" in this area. It does carry advertising which apparently allows the publisher to make semi-annual revisions incorporating the latest information on child care. Needless to say, it is a required purchase for any public library.

Child Development. 1930. q. $20. Alberta E. Siegel. Univ. of Chicago Press, Chicago, Ill. 60637. Circ: 3,000. Reprint: Kraus, Abrahams.

Indexed: BioAb, EdI, IMed, PsyAb. *Aud:* Sa, Ac. *Rv:* M. *Jv:* B.

Published by the Society for Research in Child Development, Inc., this is one of the best journals devoted to publishing original research articles which cover all phases of

the field. The articles are scholarly and include medical, psychological, and mathematical concepts and terminology. Only for the specialist and research student.

Child Development Abstracts and Bibliography. See Indexes and Abstracts Section.

Child Welfare. 1922. m. (Oct.–July). $5. E. Elizabeth Glover. Child Welfare League of America, Inc., 44 E. 23rd St., New York, N.Y. 10010. Circ: 8,700. Microform: UM. Reprint: Kraus, Abrahams.

Aud: Sa, Ac, *Rv:* M. *Jv:* B.

Concerned primarily with the social-economic issues of caring for children. Articles represent current data, original research, trends and education programs. Particularly of value to the sociologist, but in this day of ever-increasing interest in guaranteed incomes for the poor, it has considerable value for the economist.

Childhood Education. See Education Section.

Children; an interdisciplinary journal for the professions serving children. 1954. bi-m. $1.25. Kathryn Close. U.S. Dept. of Health, Education and Welfare, Social Rehabilitation Service, Children's Bureau, 330 Independence Ave., S.W., Washington, D.C. 20201. Illus., index. Circ: 30,000. Microform: UM. Reprint: Abrahams.

Indexed: EdI. *Bk. rev:* Notes. *Aud:* Ac, Jc, Ht, Et. *Rv:* M. *Jv:* B.

The purpose of this journal is to bring to the professions intelligence concerning all aspects of service to children. Its scope is broad, as is indicated by a random sampling of titles: "The Prevention of Oral Diseases in Preschool Children," "Teaching Emotionally Disturbed Children," and "A Guide for Collaboration of Physician, Social Worker, and Lawyer." The style ranges from popular to scholarly. Special departments: "Here and There," "In the Journals," "Readers' Exchange," "U.S. Government Publications," "Films on Child Life." *Children* is designed more for the social worker and child psychologist than the teacher, albeit the latter will find it useful.

Exceptional Children. 1934. m. (Oct.–May). $7. June B. Jordan. Council for Exceptional Children, 1201 16th St., N.W., Washington, D.C. 20036. Circ: 16,500. Reprint: Abrahams, AMS.

Indexed: EdI, PsyAb. *Aud:* Sa, Ac, Jc, Ht. *Rv:* H. *Jv:* B.

Covers not only the bright child and his educational problems, but is concerned with any exceptional child, i.e., handicapped psychologically or physiologically. Experienced educators and teachers contribute articles on curriculum planning, classroom hints, organization of programs, and report on current developments in all areas; also included is information on new teaching aids, news notes, a calendar of events, and some book reviews. While primarily for the educator, the journal should be introduced to parents of above average education who have exceptional children of one type or another. The National Association for Gifted Children issues a more specialized journal, *Gifted Child Quarterly* (1957. q. $10. Ann F. Isaacs). This is concerned with both the education of proven brilliant children and methods of developing special talents in the young.

Happier Marriage and Planned Parenthood. See Sociology Section.

My Baby. 1932. m. $3.50. Peg Rivers. Crane Publishing Co., Inc., 175 Glen Rock, N.J. 07452. Illus., adv. Circ: 750,000.

Aud: Ga. *Rv:* L. *Jv:* B.

Provides articles of general family interest, on child and baby care, to mothers of pre-schoolers as well as to new mothers. Articles about the pre-schooler include "What Is Wrong with Nursery Education Today" and "Colds—The Bugaboo of Early Childhood." New mothers would be interested in "Planning Your Family," "Obstetric Teams," and "Why Measles Vaccine." Also includes features similar to those in the general women's magazines, such as menu suggestions, recipes and beauty suggestions. Often given away free by the distributors of baby products, it provides information about new equipment and includes a coupon for ordering free and inexpensive information and samples.

Parents' Magazine and Better Homemaking. 1926. m. $4. Dorothy Whyte Cotton. Parents' Magazine Enterprises, Inc., 52 Vanderbilt Ave., New York, N.Y. 10017. Illus., index, adv. Circ: 2,000,000. Microform: UM.

Indexed: AbrRG, PAIS, RG. *Bk. rev:* Notes, signed. *Aud:* Ga, Sh. *Rv:* M. *Jv:* A.

Parents who raise children by the book will find much of value here. Health, education, personality, and discipline are considered in an intelligent and authoritative fashion. Family and marital relationships are discussed. Finally, there are articles which encourage the parent and the child to take an active role in social matters. The eight to ten articles are counterpointed by such features as "Family Movie Guide," "Family Quiz Guide," "Family Clinic," and the like. Mature teenagers as well as more thoughtful parents will find this is a good down-to-earth approach to the whole business of children and families.

Teaching Exceptional Children. 1968. q. $5. Council for Exceptional Children, National Education Assn., 1201 16th St., N.W., Washington, D.C. 20036.

Aud: Sa, Ac, Ht, Et. *Rv:* H. *Jv:* B.

While the Council's other magazine in this same field (see *Exceptional Children*) is concerned with all aspects of the child, this is primarily a journal for the teacher of the gifted or handicapped. Articles are technical, well documented and deal with teacher-oriented aspects of the subject, from diagnostic techniques to instructional methods and materials. Several features are given over to the exchange of ideas and questions and answers by teachers. Early issues did not include book reviews, but they are

promised for the future. The library which takes *Exceptional Children* will unquestionably want to subscribe to its companion.

Your New Baby. 1942. m. Free to readers; sold in bulk to exclusive franchisers. Maja Bernath. Parents' Magazine Enterprises, Inc., 52 Vanderbilt Ave., New York, N.Y. 10017. Illus., adv. Circ: 1,050,000.

Bk. rev: Occasional notes. *Aud:* Ga. *Rv:* L. *Jv:* A.

Features about five articles of inspiration and advice to new mothers. Coverage includes fashions for infants and toddlers, maternity fashions, new products, layette needs and good ideas from other mothers. While articles are primarily concerned with practical baby care, contents are balanced with concern for broader issues, for example "Milk, Medicine and a Plea for Peace," a description of the world-wide work of UNICEF. It is distributed to stimulate sales of baby products and its main value is in educating inexperienced mothers. *Parents' Magazine* also issues two similar type magazines which many libraries may wish to consider. *Baby Care Manual* (1940. q. Free) is presented to new mothers in the hospital and includes practical material on what to do next. *Expecting* (1967. q. Free) is devoted exclusively to the needs of expectant mothers. Libraries wanting any of these are advised to contact the publisher. While all cater to advertising, they are among the most reliable publications of this type.

CHILDREN'S MAGAZINES

Indexes and Abstracts

Subject Index to Children's Magazines. (For annotation, see Indexes and Abstracts Section.)

American Girl. 1917. m. $4.50. Pat di Sernia. Girl Scouts of the U.S.A., 830 Third Ave., New York, N.Y. 10022. Illus., index, adv. Circ: 600.

Indexed: IChildMags. *Bk. rev:* Short notices. *Aud:* E, Jh. *Rv:* L. *Jv:* C.

A compact low-keyed magazine designed for the young girl. Officially an organ of the Girl Scouts of America, some regular features are so oriented, but the publication is not limited in scope. Articles emphasize hostess hints, fashion, movie and record news. Special reports range from studies of Vista to career discussions. Two or three stories help span the age range by including material of interest for the pre-teen and older girls. Advertising is tasteful and appropriate to the group it serves.

American Junior Red Cross News. 1919. m (Oct.–May). $1. Maurice Flagg. Amer. National Red Cross, 18th & D Sts., N.W., Washington, D.C. 20006. Illus. Circ: 450,000.

Indexed: IChildMags. *Aud:* E. *Rv:* M. *Jv:* A.

Intended to be used by elementary school Red Cross youth volunteers, this is useful also as a classroom supplement in the areas of science and social studies. Reports of successful projects are presented as suggestions for action by other youngsters. General interest articles and good stories with world interest encourage concern for others in this country and throughout the world. These are written by qualified, sometimes well-known people, such as Margaret L. Crawford, noted children's writer. Each issue contains a "Primary Graders' Book" about 3 pages in length, illustrated, and set in type somewhat larger than that of the rest of the magazine. Excellent articles on science are usually included, written and illustrated for elementary grades. An occasional skit on the topic of one of the articles makes an interesting way of making science more meaningful in the elementary classroom. Some verse by contributors in grades 4 to 6, a fun page, and a classroom calendar of notable dates are other features. The format is appealing, from the well-designed, colorful cover to the good clear type and the photos and drawings illustrating the contents.

Boys' Life. 1911. m. $4. Robert Hood. Boy Scouts of America, U.S. Highway No. 1, New Brunswick, N.J. 08903. Illus., adv. Circ: 2,410,000.

Indexed: IChildMags. *Aud:* E, Jh. *Rv:* M. *Jv:* A.

The best all-around magazine published for the adolescent male. It is not, however, recommended for advanced or sophisticated boys, although even they may find sections of interest. Boy Scout-oriented, it ranges far afield from prosaic camping advice to articles on soaring and sailing. Regular features include a hobby column, patrol ideas, stamp and coin collecting and a full page of jokes. Special features offer well-written, signed articles on nature, chess, autos and even tips on getting along with girls. Essays vary in reading level and interest and include something for everyone from 9 to 16. Two or three stories. Discriminating advertising, color and black and white photographs and illustrations enhance this attractive periodical.

Catholic Boy. 1932. m (Sept.–May). $3. Rev. Russell J. Huff, C.S.C., Holy Cross Fathers of Notre Dame, South Bend, Ind. 46556. Illus. Circ: 79,350.

Aud: E, Jh. *Rv:* L. *Jv:* B.

The foremost magazine for those boys of ages 11–15, who are Catholic Church oriented. An attractive format includes full page photographs, slick paper and compactness with discreet advertising. Articles range from sports to careers and science. A "Teen Panel" discusses religious topics, from learning to love, falling in love, to be alive, to growing and faith. The articles are well written and geared for the teenager. Regular features include "What's On" (film reviews) and "Jokes'N Stuff." The limited fiction attempts to span the age differences. A good periodical for youngsters, but its church affiliation prohibits use in most public school libraries.

Catholic Miss of America. 1942. m (Sept.–May). $3. K. Joyce Panchot. Holy Cross Fathers of Notre Dame, South Bend, Ind. 46556. Illus.

Aud: Jh, E. *Rv:* L. *Jv:* B.

The sister publication of *Catholic Boy,* for girls 11 to 15. In fact, monthly issues are identical in the "Teen Panel" article—a series devoted to young people and their relationship to others and their God. Other articles include one on a cheerleading school, finances and teen celebrities such as figure skater Peggy Fleming. Regular features are "Dear Editor," "Charm," "In the Kitchen," and film and TV reviews. At least three stories run the gamut from the romantic to those of school adjustments. Tasteful advertising, exciting illustrations and general attractiveness make this an appealing magazine for the adolescent female. Like its counterpart, it is also limited in use because of its religious affiliations.

Child Life. 1921. m (Sept.–June), bi-m (June–Sept.). $5.95. B. R. SerVass. 1100 Waterway Blvd., Indianapolis, Ind. 46202. Illus. Circ: 210,000.

Indexed: IChildMag. *Aud:* E. *Rv:* L. *Jv:* B.

A magazine created for children from pre-readers to sixth graders. Equally divided among fiction, arts, crafts, and miscellanea, it features poems, trading posts, letters to the editor, jokes, riddles and activity pages. A reading guide keynotes the articles for reading levels. Inside each cover, a well-known encyclopedia publisher features learning units, such as "Trees—Their Products and Uses." Every issue is done in monochrome, i.e., one month's issue printed in all shades of blue and white, and another in brown and white. Generally appealing to elementary school children.

Children's Digest. 1950. m (except June and Aug). $5. Parents' Magazine Enterprises, Inc., 52 Vanderbilt Ave., New York, N.Y. 10017. Illus., index, adv. Circ: 1,000,000.

Indexed: IChildMags. *Bk. rev:* 6–8, short, signed. *Aud:* E. *Rv:* L. *Jv:* B.

Published under the direction of *Parents' Magazine, Children's Digest* presents, in conventional digest format of 100 pages, material from a variety of sources, for children ages 6 to 12. Old and new fiction (reprints and excerpts) accounts for the bulk of each issue, plus some articles on science, nature and history. Authors of classic works for children, such as Kipling, Stevenson, Milne and others are represented, along with some of the leading present day writers for young people. A current picture book (using all of text and 90% of art) is reprinted monthly, and covers 19 to 21 pages. Book reviews are especially well done for the age group intended, and should tempt young readers to explore some of the new books. Short features of one to two pages include games, hobbies, play activities, puzzles and jokes. All material is well illustrated, in one color, and in some cases illustrations are reproduced from the original book. The digest format includes dull paper with a light green "eye ease" tint, and a specially designed binding which is intended to lie flat when open. Advertising in limited amounts is chiefly confined to offerings of Parents' Magazine Press. Two other publications by the same publisher are *Humpty Dumpty's Magazine* and *Young Miss.*

Children's Playmate Magazine. 1929. 10/yr. $3.95. Review Publishing Co., 1100 Waterway Blvd., Indianapolis, Ind. 46202. Illus., adv. Circ: 150,000.

Indexed: IChildMags. *Aud:* E. *Rv:* L. *Jv:* B.

Directed to ages 6 to 10, features the usual type of illustrated stories and articles. While directed to both boys and girls, the emphasis is feminine. There are games, and things to make, with contents and material submitted by young readers. The illustrations are mediocre and show little or no relationship with what has come to be known as imaginative work for children. In no way a competitor to *Jack and Jill,* it is a fair second choice in school libraries.

Elizabethan. 1947. m. $4. Lewis Sheringham. 355 Ashford Rd., Box 7, Stanes, Middlesex, Eng. Illus., adv. Circ: 20,000.

Indexed: IChildMags. *Aud:* Sh, Jh. *Rv:* L. *Jv:* B.

A general English girl's magazine for ages 10 to 17, it has definitely more possibilities for the girls in the lower age bracket. Anyone over 13 who reads *Seventeen* or any of the American teen mags will find it, as one young lady put it, "a drag." Using somewhat the same approach as *American Girl,* it pays considerably more attention to current events than most periodicals of this type. The format is good, the writing style good to excellent. The problem for American girls is to relate to the material which is often entirely English centered, right down to the vernacular and personalities. Only for large collections.

Golden Magazine for Boys and Girls. 1964. m. $5. R. D. Bezucha. Golden Press, Inc., North Rd., Poughkeepsie, N.Y. 12601. Illus., index, adv.

Indexed: IChildMags. *Bk. rev:* Notes. *Aud:* E. *Rv:* L. *Jv:* B.

A cheerful magazine published for the sole purpose of providing a special form of reading matter for boys and girls from ages 7–12. The magazine emphasizes four different types of material: fiction, informative, things-to-do and jokes and games. The fiction ranges from the well-known *Seward's Folly* in installments, to *The King Who Moved the Mountain,* a Hawaiian myth. Colorful sketches by well-known illustrators enhance the pages. The "How-To" section runs the gamut from cooking fun to first lessons in German. A parent-teacher guide inside the front cover is an added inducement for adult approval.

Highlights for Children. 1946. 10/yr. $7.95. Dr. & Mrs. Garry C. Myers, 2300 W. Fifth Ave., Columbus, Ohio 43216. Circ: 800,000.

Indexed: IChildMags. *Aud:* E. *Rv:* M. *Jv:* A.

Edited by leading child specialists, educators and scientists, this is to assist the pre-school and elementary child "gain in creativeness, ability to think and reason and worthy ways of living." There is reading material suitable for all elementary levels in a wide variety of subject areas, including social studies, biographies, science, and literature. Games, tricks and teasers, word fun, parties and craft ideas are aimed at stimulating thinking. Signed, informative articles by eminent scientists such as Dr. Donald Menzel of the Harvard College Observatory, Dr. Jack Myers of the University of Texas and Dr. Joel Hildebrand of the University of California; by prominent leaders such as Supreme Court Justice William Douglas and news commentator Walter Cronkite; and by educators such as Dr. Paul Witty make *Highlights* an up-to-date authoritative source of valuable information. There is no paid advertising. A reading guide for parents and teachers is an added feature. The sturdy format makes it a prime candidate for circulation, and the contents recommend it to most school libraries.

Hi-Venture (Formerly: *Canadian Boy*). 1964. 9–10/yr. Can. $2.50. Norman Brown. Boy Scouts of Canada, Box 5151, Station F., Ottawa 5, Ont. Illus., adv. Circ: 306,000.

Aud: E, Jh. *Rv:* M. *Jv:* B.

The Boy Scout magazine for boys in Canada. Eye-catching covers with tempting titles beckon the 10 to 16 year-old inside where he'll find regular features which comment on movies, cars, records, stamps and contests. Stories range in scope from out-door life to science fiction. Articles such as "Time Trip to 1967," "Survival" or "The Future" are well written and informative. Comic Strip educational pieces, science articles and Boy Scout news round out this excellent periodical. Compact, well-illustrated with related tasteful advertising, this magazine should be welcome in those public libraries and schools in areas close to Canada.

Humpty Dumpty's Magazine; magazine for little children. 1952. m (except June & Aug.). $5. Alvin Tresselt. Parents' Magazine Enterprises, 52 Vanderbilt Ave., New York, N.Y. 10017. Illus., adv. Circ: 1,379,111.

Indexed: IChildMags. *Aud:* E. *Rv:* L. *Jv:* B.

A publication of Parents' Magazine (*Young Miss, Children's Digest*), written and illustrated for children from 3 to 7 years of age. Many consider this the best of the children's mags—the circulation is impressive—primarily because it is a sincere effort to both entertain and educate. Stories, articles and features are written to develop reading and vocabulary, if not an interest in the world of reality. Although printed on "eye ease" paper, the format is reminiscent of yesterday's newspaper; the illustrations are no better. On the plus side, the large type, the lack of advertisements (except for the publisher's products), and the pocket size make it attractive for the younger set. Contents, though, is nothing more than can be found in most good children's story books readily available in libraries. A second choice for most collections.

Jack and Jill Magazine. 1938. m. $3.95. Karl K. Hoffmann. Curtis Publishing Co., Independence Sq., Philadelphia, Pa. 19105. Illus., index, adv. Circ: 875,000.

Indexed: IChildMags. *Aud:* E. *Rv:* L. *Jv:* B.

A variety magazine with material presented on various levels to suit the reading ability and interests of children ages 5–12. Each issue contains six or seven stories and an equal number of articles, with a variation in type size and reading level from grades 1 to 6. Both fiction and non-fiction are of equally high quality. Many single page items are included in each issue. Games, riddles and puzzles, projects, picture features, jokes and contests serve the purpose of providing individual and group amusement. Some simple recipes are usually included, perhaps suggested by the theme of one of the articles or stories. "Let's Discover America" is one of the best features, and describes points of interest which families might visit. Color photos for these articles are good, and well-chosen. The series "My Father Is" helps young boys and girls understand the finer facets of the American way of life. Illustrations throughout the magazine consist mainly of drawings and are colorful, generally good and well arranged.

Vacation Fun; summer magazine for leisure reading and for pleasure. 1961. w (June–Aug.). $50. Tony Simon. Scholastic Magazines Inc., 50 W. 44th St., New York, N.Y. 10036. Illus. Circ: 100,000.

Aud: E. *Rv:* L. *Jv:* C.

One of three summer magazines issued by Scholastic, this is a 16-pager for grades 4 and 5 and includes the usual type of material featured in classroom newspapers published by the same firm. More emphasis is placed on "fun," less on learning, but the style, format, and approach is about the same. The magazine does have useful games, a few rather pedestrian stories, and suggestions on where and what to do around the home.

Two other periodicals of the same type are published by Scholastic for the summer months: *Merry-Go-Round,* for grades 2 and 3 and *Summertime,* for grades 6 and 7. Parents may be grateful to be introduced to one more ploy to keep the children happy during the long summer, but librarians can skip with ease.

Wee Wisdom. 1893. m. $2. Anna Thompson. Unity School of Christianity, Lee's Summit, Mo. Illus. Circ: 110,000.

Indexed: IChildMags. *Aud:* E. *Rv:* L. *Jv:* B.

Although the publisher asserts this is for boys and girls ages 5 to 13, its primary appeal is to the girl under 10. And while issued by a religious organization, there is a minimum of moralizing and religious teaching. In fact, it is one of the better children's magazines, combining four to six stories, poems, and various activities in a single issue. The illustrations are indifferent, albeit no worse than most in this genre. A useful second magazine for any school or public library.

Young Miss (Formerly: ***Calling All Girls***). 1955. 10/yr. $5. Rubie Saunders. Better Reading Foundations, 52 Vanderbilt Ave., New York, N.Y. 10017. Illus., adv. Circ: 500,000.

Indexed: IChildMags. *Aud:* Jh, E. *Rv:* L. *Jv:* B.

A compact, low keyed magazine designed for young girls. Regular features include fashions, food, personality articles and a fiction novelette. There are also articles on careers, self-help (getting along with siblings, parents, etc.) and parties. Short fiction, of interest to girls from 11 up to about 14, is also included. "Letters to the Editor" is a popular column in which the reader tells her problem and a possible solution is given. Advertising is tasteful and oriented to the group it serves.

CITIES AND TOWNS

Indexes and Abstracts

Art Index, Business Periodicals Index, Engineering Index, Index to Legal Periodicals, Public Affairs Information Service, Social Sciences and Humanities Index. (For annotations, see Indexes and Abstracts Section.)

In this section, readers will find two kinds of magazines. One ("Urban Affairs") comprises the magazines dealing with general problems and situations endemic to all urban or suburban communities, such as land economics or city management. The other, primarily a phenomena of the last five or ten years, is "City Magazines," dealing with the activities and problems within specific communities. There are, of course, magazines of long standing within this category, but the proliferation in the late fifties and early sixties reflects a growing concern with the complexities and dilemmas of urban life.

At one time primarily voices of goodwill for various chambers of commerce, several of the "city" magazines have expanded into genuine 50- to 100-page general news and cultural periodicals. A number are now operated by private companies which function the same as any non-government sponsored publisher. While the primary purpose of almost all the magazines is to plug community welfare, entertainment, business, and good living, a few have gone beyond this to penetrating, often controversial articles on all aspects of urban life from the slums to questionable politics and politicians. The trend, in fact, seems to be moving away from the goody-two-shoes approach to the more objective type of journalism.

Almost without exception the "city" magazines are of value for: (a) the historical and biographical material they offer; (b) the illustrations, usually superior photographs and original art work; (c) the picture, biased or otherwise, they give of 20th century urban living; (d) the up-to-date, sometimes critical information on business, entertainment, cultural activities etc. Libraries, within the city or its environs, regardless of size or type, will wish to subscribe to their local publication. Larger academic libraries will want the key magazines for the ongoing, contemporary comment on modern city life.

While, in format, they run from good to excellent, the two best city magazines, in terms of content and approach, are *Seattle Magazine* and *Philadelphia Magazine.* No effort is made here to grade or to more than suggest editorial policy, only to indicate the major audiences—usually the business or the general community.

Urban Affairs

American City Magazine. 1911. m. $7. William S. Foster. Buttenheim Publishing Corp., 757 Third Ave., New York, N.Y. 10017. Illus., index, adv. Circ: 34,000. Microform: UM. Reprint: Abrahams.

Indexed: EngI, PAIS, RG. *Aud:* Sa, Ac. *Rv:* H. *Jv:* B.

Next to *Nation's Cities,* one of the most useful municipal publications. Emphasis here is more on techniques and how-to-do-it than in its competitor, and it tends to be more pragmatic in its approach to everyday problems. Planning and finance account for only a relatively small part of each issue, the main sections dealing with practical methods of coping with water, sewage, street, traffic and parks problems. Of primary interest to the specialist, particularly city engineers and managers. While *American City Magazine* well suits the needs of city officials, in a general library situation two other general magazines would be preferable. *City,* because of its broad interests, is the leader, followed by *Nation's Cities,* with *American City* coming in last. The judgement is not so much one of quality as one of the "best magazine for the greatest number of people."

American County Government. 1936. m. $10. Bernard F. Hillenbrand. National Assn. of Counties, 1001 Connecticut Ave., N.W., Washington, D.C. 20036. Illus., index, adv. Circ: 16,182.

Indexed: PAIS. *Aud:* Sa, Ac, *Rv:* M. *Jv:* B.

Discusses common political and economic problems of county government in a semi-popular style. The relatively short articles usually pinpoint a specific situation and explain what decision should or should not have been made. Experiences of personnel from the elected officials to the appointed county planners are highlighted. Rapid urbanization, crime and delinquency, new equipment, finance, legal problems, and even civil defense make up a good part of the material covered in each issue. While written for the official, there is enough here of general interest to warrant consideration in any medium to large public or academic library where there is emphasis on government and political science.

American Institute of Planners. Journal. 1935. bi-m. Membership (Non-members, $8). David R. Godschalk. Amer. Inst. of Planners, 917 15th St., N.W., Washington, D.C. 20005. Illus. Circ: 8,000. Microform: UM. Reprint: Abrahams, Kraus.

Indexed: ArtI, PAIS. *Bk. rev:* 5–10, 1,000 words, signed. *Aud:* Sa, Ac. *Rv:* H. *Jv:* B.

A scholarly journal concerning city planning, with special emphasis on the social problems of urban areas. Each of the six to ten signed articles is well written, generally by professors, architects, city planners, social scientists or other experts in the field. The book reviews cover scholarly works in the field. Of value to professionals and students in the various planning fields.

City. 1967. bi-m. Membership (Non-members, $5). Donald Canty. Urban America Inc., 1717 Massachusetts Ave., N.W., Washington, D.C. 20036. Illus. Circ: 12,000. Microform: UM.

Bk. rev: 1–3, 1,000 words. *Aud:* Ga, Ac, Jc, Sh. *Rv:* H. *Jv:* A.

The first choice for most libraries, this is published by Urban America Inc., a non-profit organization "dedicated to improving the quality of life in the nation's cities." The 40- to 50-page magazine covers matters of urban interest—congressional action, housing, land management, city planning and government, etc. Most articles are prepared by staff members, or experts on urban planning. All are authoritative, liberal and extremely well written. The object is to educate the reader to the pressing needs of cities, and it is intentionally geared for the layman. Much of the material, too, is appropriate for high school students. Because of its approach it is among the best magazines in this field for any library.

From the State Capitals. General Bulletin. 1946. semi-m. $30. Bethune Jones. 321 Sunset Ave., Asbury Park, N.J.

Aud: Sa, Ac. *Rv:* H. *Jv:* B.

Issued in concise, mimeographed, time-saving news digest form, this provides a continuing source of factual data on current and prospective legislative, administrative and judicial action at the state and local levels in the area of labor, public works, taxes, civil service and all matters relating to public management and planning. The concern also issues a number of more specialized newsletters: *From the State Capitals—Housing and Redevelopment;—Off-Street Parking;—Civil Defense,* etc. These are primarily for the professional civic employee or dedicated politician, yet are extremely useful in a more general way for research in depth on particular issues.

Land Economics; a quarterly journal devoted to the study of economic and social institutions. 1925. q. $8. Mary Amend Lescohier. Social Science Bldg., University of Wisconsin, Madison, Wis. 53706. Circ: 3,500. Microform: UM. Reprint: Kraus, Abrahams.

Indexed: BusI, PAIS. *Aud:* Sa, Ga, Ac, Jc. *Rv:* H. *Jv:* B.

"Reflects the growing emphasis on planning for the wise use of urban and rural land to meet the needs of an expanding population." It usually contains about eight articles on such topics as housing, air and water use, and land reform. Emphasis is on public action. Of interest to public service-minded citizens as well as to public officials.

Landscape Architecture. See Architecture Section.

Mayor and Manager; the magazine of municipal management. 1958. m. $5. Don Jefferson. 5826 Dempster St., Morton Grove, Ill. 60053. Illus., index, adv. Circ: 11,161.

Bk. rev: 2–3, ½ to 1 column, signed. *Aud:* Sa, Ac. *Rv:* M. *Jv:* B.

Largely devoted to providing information and new ideas to municipal executives. Some regular features are "Munici-Pulse," a column of short news items from across the country; "Legal Briefs," legal developments in municipal affairs; and the "Municipal Digest," a section containing digests and excerpts from a variety of sources. These abstracts are from one to two pages in length and there are usually four to five per issue. Each issue also carries one longer essay from four to six pages in length. Some of the topics covered have been "How to Make Your Budget Work for You"; "New Towns—A Third Alternative"; "The Policies Plan"; etc. This would be of use in urban libraries and academic collections.

Metropolitan Area Digest. 1957. 6/yr. Joseph F. Zimmerman. Grad. Sch. of Public Affairs, State Univ. of New York at Albany, 179 Partridge St., Albany, N.Y. 12203.

Bk. rev: Notes. *Aud:* Sa, Ac. *Rv:* M. *Jv:* B.

A 12-page newsletter which includes many short, unsigned articles on happenings and trends in public affairs in cities all over the country. Besides the book reviews, there is a section of "Recent Publications in Metropolitan Problems" listing articles and pamphlets. This publication is typical of many newsletter type publications issued by various universities and governmental agencies. Librarians should check to see what may be available in their immediate area.

National Civic Review. 1911. m. (Sept.–July). $5. Alfred Willoughby. National Municipal League, 47 E. 68th St., New York, N.Y. 10021. Circ: 5,485. Microform: UM. Reprint: Abrahams.

Indexed: BusI, LegPer, PAIS. *Bk. rev:* 3–5, 200 words. *Aud:* Ga, Sa, Ac, Jc. *Rv:* H. *Jv:* A.

Intended for civic leaders, public officials and students of state and local government and intergovernmental relations. Each 60-page issue contains three or four articles, 2,500–3,000 words in length, concerning problems of state and local government with emphasis on definition of problems, proposed solutions and action taken. Half of each number is devoted to "News in Review" with reports on significant developments reported in the following sections: "City, State and Nation," "Representation," "Metropolitan Areas," "County Government," "Taxation and Finance," "Citizen Action," and "Researcher's Digest." A detailed annual index is published which makes this a basic reference source on the chronology of state and local government reform and reorganization widely cited in textbooks.

Nation's Cities. 1963. m. $6. Patrick Healy. National League of Cities, 1612 K St., N.W., Washington, D.C. 20006. Illus., index, adv. Circ: 64,000.

Indexed: PAIS. *Bk. rev:* Notes. *Aud:* Sa, Ac, Jc. *Rv:* M. *Jv:* A.

The third general magazine devoted to city government, but unlike *American City Magazine,* there is considerably more emphasis on social-economic questions. Also, it is the official organ of the National League of Cities and, as such, tends to stress theory and philosophy more than its competitor. In fact, no now how-to-do-it articles are included, albeit there is pragmatic advice on such matters as preparing for a municipal bond issue, surveying low-cost housing, and the best method of providing slum clearance, health care, recreational facilities and the like. The tone tends to be both knowledgeable and liberal, and the seven to ten articles are prepared by experts in the fields discussed. Regular departments include news from Washington, traffic and public relations. And while not a regular feature, several issues a year feature candid interviews with people of interest to municipal planners. There are a number of photographs, and charts and tables. In view of its broad scope, it would be a first choice in all general library collections where there is any interest in municipal government. The social-political-economic emphasis will give it added value for all academic libraries.

Parking. 1952. q. Membership. Norene Dann Martin. National Parking Assn., Inc., 1101 17th St., N.W., Washington, D.C. 20036. Illus., adv. Circ: 7,500.

Indexed: PAIS. *Aud:* Sa, Ac. *Rv:* M. *Jv:* B.

A small, attractive magazine intended for those involved with the problem of parking facilities in large cities. Improvements and trends in parking are supported by attractive illustrations. There are about 10 signed articles in each issue, 2 to 5 pages long. Helpful to students, municipal executives, and city officials.

Public Administration Review. 1940. q. $15. Dwight Waldo. Amer. Soc. for Public Admin., 1329 18th St., N.W., Washington, D.C. 20036. Index, adv. Circ: 8,600. Microform: UM. Reprint: Kraus, Abrahams.

Indexed: LegPer, PAIS, SSHum. *Bk. rev:* 6, 1,500 words, signed, notes. *Aud:* Sa, Ac. *Rv:* H. *Jv:* B.

Designed to provide public executives and other administrative officers with news of research and public policy activities. It usually contains six to ten signed articles. The book reviews are critical and arranged in groups having the same general subject. This would be useful to students, to urban libraries and in special collections.

Public Management; devoted to the conduct of local government. 1919. m. $4. Orin F. Nolting & David S. Arnold. Intl. City Manager's Assn., 1140 Connecticut Ave., N.W., Washington, D.C. 20036. Index, adv. Circ: 11,380. Microform: UM. Reprint: Abrahams.

Indexed: PAIS. *Bk. rev:* Notes. *Aud:* Sa, Ac. *Rv:* M. *Jv:* B.

As the official publication of The International City Managers' Association, *Public Management* has as its primary purpose service to the urban administrator. There are usually about three articles, of about 1,000 words, concerning a wide range of topics of interest to civic leaders. Of value to students, as well as to civic minded general readers.

Reviews in Urban Economics. 1968. q. $5. Communication Service Corp. in cooperation with the Inst. for Urban and Regional Studies of Washington Univ., 1150 Connecticut Ave., N.W., Washington, D.C. 20036.

Bk. rev: Notes. *Aud:* Sa, Ac. *Rv:* H. *Jv:* B.

Published for professional economists and individuals working in urban economics and planning, the purpose of this journal is to explore "the new and largely undefined character of urban economics as an academic discipline." The first issue featured three articles with exhaustive references and two pages of brief book reviews. Only for large academic collections.

State Government. See Political Science Section.

Urban Affairs Quarterly. 1965. q. $8. (Institutions, $12). Marilyn Gittell. Sage Pubns., Inc., 276 South Beverly Drive, Beverly Hills, Calif. 90212. Circ: 1,740.

Indexed: PAIS. *Bk. rev:* 1–3, long, signed. *Aud:* Ga, Ac, Jc. *Rv:* M. *Jv:* B.

An omnibus journal of city problems with excellent credentials, sponsored by the City University of New York. The Editorial Advisory Board has such experts as Nathan Glazer, Daniel P. Moynihan, and Oscar Lewis. Each issue has five to eight long articles, often devoted to different views of a single topic such as race relations or urban renewal. The number of subjects covered in a span of just a few issues is quite large: poverty, crime, police, riots, urban renewal, education, race, interest groups, urban planning, taxes, distribution of funds, law and politics. A worthwhile addition to any college and university library, and particularly to urban public libraries.

Urban Land; news and views in city development. 1941. m. (except July and Aug.). Membership. Max S. Wehrly. Urban Land Inst., 1200 18th St., N.W., Washington, D.C. 20036. Illus., index. Circ: 4,400.

Indexed: PAIS. *Bk. rev:* 2, short, signed. *Aud:* Sa, Ac. *Rv:* M. *Jv:* B.

Devoted to news items and articles on urban development such as revival of downtown shopping centers, slum clearance, population trends, parking problems—in fact, anything of interest to the city dweller. There are usually one or two long articles in this eight- to twelve-page newsletter. Only for large or specialized collections.

City Magazines

Atlanta. 1961. m. $8. John W. Lange, Atlanta Chamber of Commerce, 1104 Commerce Bldg., Atlanta, Ga. 30303. Illus., adv. Circ: 22,000.

Directed to a wide audience, not just the business community. In addition to well-illustrated articles on problems of the city, often includes photo-essays on Southern writers, politicians, civic leaders, and towns in the immediate Atlanta area. One of the first city magazines to consider social issues, this has featured articles on everything from the rate of suicide to subtle slams at those who still plug for discrimination in Southern communities. The tone is definitely upper-middle class liberal, and as one of the better Southern city magazines it should be a first consideration for libraries south of the Mason-Dixon line. It is among the top five for all libraries seeking more than one or two representative magazines of this type. (The other four of the five are *Los Angeles Magazine, Philadelphia Magazine, Seattle Magazine* and *Washingtonian Magazine.*)

Baltimore Magazine. 1907. m. $6. William Stump. Chamber of Commerce of Metropolitan Baltimore, 22 Light St., Baltimore, Md. 21202. Illus., adv. Circ: 10,000.

One of the oldest general city magazines, with a broad base of interest from sports to cultural events in Baltimore. It puts a strong emphasis on interests of Chamber of Commerce members and the business community, and features the usual calendar of events on entertainment, stories on Maryland history, and notes on personalities. Considerably less reform oriented than many magazines in this area, yet useful for the current material on the city and the state.

Boston Magazine. 1962. m. $6. Jerrold Hickey. James Kelso, 125 High St., Boston, Mass. 02110. Illus., adv. Circ: 11,000.

A general magazine which carries authoritative articles on current events in Boston and the immediate area with the usual attention to the arts. Particularly good for objective, well-illustrated materials on economics of the city and environs. The editors have long plugged urban renewal projects and can take considerable credit for many innovative changes in greater Boston. Among the more liberal, far-sighted of the city magazines.

Chicago Magazine. 1964. q. $2.50. David L. Watt. New Chicago Foundation, 22 W. Monroe Street, Chicago, Ill. 60603. Illus., adv. Circ: 90,000.

Of general interest, directed to upper-income groups with emphasis on non-controversial aspects of Chicago and mid-Western history, culture, business and retail trade. Extremely well-produced, it averages some 100 pages, featuring outstanding graphics, and professional writers. Should be found in all Chicago and environ libraries, if only because of the excellent coverage of current cultural events and the superior format which features Chicago artists and photographers.

Dayton U.S.A. 1964. bi-m. $3.50. J. Kay Timmons. Dayton Area Chamber of Commerce, 210 N. Main St., Dayton, Ohio 45402. Illus., adv. Circ: 10,500.

Directed primarily to the business community of the Dayton area. Articles are generally non-controversial, touching on industry, education, government, entertainment, and prominent civic leaders. The tone is optimistic, but from time to time the editors have not pulled any punches in explaining to readers what is necessary for the city to grow and improve. A good example of a smaller city magazine with more than average editorial skill evident in its format and content.

Honolulu Magazine. 1966. m. $10. David & Cynthia Eyre. Paradise Publishing Co., P.O. Box 80, Honolulu, Hawaii 96810. Illus., adv. Circ: 21,000.

Emphasis is on general material of interest to the whole community from gardening to the arts. Each issue devoted to a number of articles on business, government and politics of Honolulu and greater Hawaii. A special fall number is given over to Hawaii as a place for tourists, and in view of the wide mainland interest in the Islands, should be a useful addition for any library.

Houston Magazine. 1930. m. $7.21. Floyd Martin. Houston Chamber of Commerce, Box 53600, Houston, Tex. 77052. Illus., adv. Circ: 13,500.

Primarily a business magazine for the upper echelon managers. Emphasis is on industry, commerce, finance, construction, and general business news in the greater Houston area. Excellent format. This is a good example of a city magazine which has pretty much adhered to the traditional Chamber of Commerce line. Consequently, this side of the greater Houston area it has limited appeal for anyone except the business executive.

Los Angeles Magazine. 1960. m. $7.50. David R. Brown. Pacific West Publishing Co., Inc., 271 North Canon Drive, Beverly Hills, Calif. 90210. Illus., adv. Circ: 62,000.

Despite the title, of interest to other than Los Angeles readers. Directed to all Southern Californians, it concentrates on urban problems, culture, travel and personalities. Often controversial, relatively sophisticated, and much above the average for this type of magazine. In fact, it boasts one of the largest circulations of any of the genre, primarily because its editor intentionally attempts to touch on materials which will be of interest to any Californian or anyone interested in the area. One of the five best, and should be a major consideration for all medium to large western libraries.

Louisille Magazine. 1950. m. $4. Helen C. Henry. Louisville Chamber of Commerce, 300 W. Liberty St., Louisville, Ky. 40202. Illus., adv. Circ: 5,000.

A general business magazine with emphasis on trends, economics and industry. Some historical and current events materials. Although a required item in Kentucky libraries, southern libraries will find *Atlanta* a much better bet.

Milwaukee Magazine. 1955. m. $5. Robert J. Riordan. Schmidt Pubns., 720 N. Jefferson St., Milwaukee, Wis. 53202. Illus., adv.

A folksy, yet often penetrating look at the Milwaukee area. Articles are geared for community leaders and businessmen, but the editor is not above pointing out faults in the city, and the magazine has considerable appeal for the sophisticated, better educated reader.

New York Magazine. See General Section.

Philadelphia Magazine. 1908. m. $6. Alan Halpern. Municipal Pubns., Inc. 1500 Walnut St., Philadelphia, Pa. 19102. Illus., adv. Circ: 43,000.

One of the few city magazines which is as quick to point out the faults of the community as its glories. The reporting is good to excellent, coverage includes every aspect of city life from the slums to the suburbs. Various issues have considered such controversial subjects as homosexuality, extra-marital activities among the suburbanites and richer city families, dishonest real-estate practices, and errors in urban planning. This type of coverage and reporting is better than found in many American general magazines. The whole is professionally edited, the format is superior and an average issue will run to some 150 to 200 pages. A must magazine for any library in the greater Philadelphia area, and one of the best in the United States for almost any library.

San Diego Magazine. 1948. Edwin F. Self, San Diego Magazine Publishing Co., 3254 Rosecrans, San Diego, Calif. 92110. Illus., adv. Circ: 16,500.

Of more than local interest as it often features travel articles on Mexico, Central America, and the Pacific. Relatively sophisticated writing on all aspects of the area from sports and amusements to city and country planning. In conservative Southern California it is considered a liberal magazine, and it has done much to balance a somewhat reactionary press in the city. Any library which subscribes to the *Los Angeles Magazine* will want to consider this one, too. It definitely should be included in all libraries in and around San Diego.

San Francisco Magazine. 1963. m. $6. John A. Vietor, San Francisco Magazine, Inc., 120 Green St., San Francisco, Calif. 94111. Illus., adv. Circ: 22,000.

Geared primarily to the upper-income classes with emphasis on architecture, art, fashions, theatre, travel and good food. Some politics, but concentrates more on the social scene. Except for the immediate San Francisco area, a better bet for Californians would be the *Los Angeles Magazine.*

Seattle Magazine. 1954. m. $7. King Broadcasting Co., 320 Aurora Ave., Seattle, Wash. 98109. Illus., adv. Circ: 30,000.

An unusual city magazine in that it often concentrates in depth on controversial issues, offers critical evaluations of both sides of a current political or social problem, and features major articles on all aspects of life in the Pacific Northwest, not just Seattle. The art, music and drama sections are excellent. It has gained a reputation for crusading.

The editors were among the first in the area to point out that the freeways could be a mixed blessing, and a downright headache unless checked. Subtle segregation, real estate manipulations and job discrimination against Afro-Americans has been considered. This consistently bold policy has earned the magazine a national reputation, and in the West is somewhat equivalent to the *Philadelphia Magazine* in the East. A basic city magazine for most libraries.

Washingtonian Magazine. 1965. m. $6. Laughlin Phillips. Washington Magazine Inc., 1218 Connecticut Ave., Washington, D.C. 20036. Illus., adv. Circ: 36,000.

A city magazine which has more than local or state appeal. Feature articles have touched on everything from the lobbyist to national political figures. The reporting is professional, the style good to excellent, the tone liberal. There are regular columns on entertainment, fashion, restaurants, etc. Feature stories have considered every element of modern living from the need to improve education to the antics of the psychedelic devotees. One of the nation's five best, and a consideration for any library regardless of location.

CLASSICAL STUDIES

Indexes and Abstracts

British Humanities Index, Education Index, Social Sciences and Humanities Index. (For annotations, see Indexes and Abstracts Section.)

American Journal of Philology. 1880. q. $8.50. Henry T. Rowell. Johns Hopkins Press, Baltimore, Md. 21218. Index, adv. Circ: 1,300. Microform: UM. Reprint: Abrahams.

Indexed: SSHum. *Bk. rev:* 12–18, 1,000 words, signed. *Aud:* Sa, Ac. *Rv:* H. *Jv:* B.

"Publishes original contributions in the field of Greco-Roman antiquity, especially in the areas of philology, literature, history, and philosophy." Articles are generally interpretive, with analyses of literary works, historical documents, and inscriptions—all involving close examination of original texts, corruptions, and new discoveries. Of primary interest to the classical scholar. See, also, *Classical Philology.*

Archaeological Reports for 19—. See Anthropology and Archaeology Section.

Arion; a quarterly journal of classical culture and the humanities. 1962. q. $5. Donald Carne-Ross. Univ. of Texas Press, Austin, Tex. 78712. Illus., index. Reprint: Abrahams.

Indexed: SSHum. *Aud:* Sa, Ac. *Rv:* H. *Jv:* B.

Published to reestablish the classics as a humanizing force in education and intellectual life in general. It is interested in items with an interdisciplinary appeal, and while not ignoring what it refers to as the "specialisms" of philology and criticism, it attempts to display these subjects in the broadest possible context. The usual items of textual and historical criticism appear, but there are many more philosophical and literary items here than in other publications. There are also original literary works—but, of course, with a classical content. Typical offerings: an examination of Petronius as artist and moralist, a discussion of the future of classical teaching and a collection of Martial poems in a new translation. Recommended for large public and university libraries.

Classical Journal. 1905. m. (Oct.–May). $4.25. W. Robert Jones. Classical Assn. of the Middle West and South, Inc., Dept. of Classical Languages, Ohio State Univ., Columbus, Ohio. 43210. (Subscriptions to: Prof. Paul R. Murphey, Ohio Univ., Athens, Ohio 45701). Illus., index, adv. Circ: 5,000. Microform: UM. Reprint: Johnson, Abrahams.

Indexed: EdI. *Bk. rev:* 8–12, 1,300 words, signed. *Aud:* Sa, Ac, Jc, Ht. *Rv:* H. *Jv:* A.

Probably the best general classical journal in the field for teachers. In addition to the usual two to four articles, there are notes of the Association, and the "Forum," a source of helpful hints for teachers in secondary schools. An annual feature, "From Other Journals," constitutes a survey of articles which have appeared on classical subjects. It is invaluable for the teacher as well as the student, and is a handy checklist for the librarian attempting to build a meaningful periodical collection in this area. The book reviews by distinguished classical scholars are authoritative, critical, and detailed. A first choice for most school, academic and public libraries. See also, *Classical World.*

Classical Outlook. 1936. m. (Sept.–May). $5. Konrad Gries. Amer. Classical League, Miami Univ., Oxford, Ohio 45056. Index, adv. Circ: 6,500. Microform: UM.

Bk. rev: Various number, lengthy. *Aud:* Ac, Jc, Ht. *Rv:* M. *Jv:* B.

Primarily geared for teachers of classics in high schools and colleges. The text is in English, Greek and Latin and the editorial policy is to promote the teaching of the classics. Features an annual verse writing contest for students, and news of the Junior and Senior Classical Leagues. Special features are "Letters from Our Readers," "Notes and Notices," a placement service, and a service bureau which offers for sale materials such as posters, tapes, stationery, and mimeographs. Book reviews are generally written by the editors. The more pragmatic approach gives this added appeal for some teachers, but if a choice is to be made between it and *Classical Journal,* libraries should first purchase the latter. (Most teachers will receive *Classical Outlook* with membership in the American Classical League.)

Classical Philology; devoted to research in the languages, literatures, history and life of classical antiquity. 1906. q. $8. Richard T. Bruere. Univ. of Chicago

Press, 5750 S. Ellis Ave., Chicago, Ill. 60637. Circ: 1,261. Microform: Princeton, UM. Reprint: Johnson, Abrahams. *Indexed:* SSHum. *Bk. rev:* 20, lengthy, signed. *Aud:* Sa, Ac. *Rv:* H. *Jv:* B.

For the scholar and the advanced student of Greek and Latin. Each issue contains several long studies, shorter articles, and lengthy book reviews. Articles are usually original and critical analyses of texts, tracings of myths and motifs, studies of the use of language, and historical and comparative studies. Supplements the *American Journal of Philology,* but only for large academic collections.

Classical Quarterly. 1906. semi-ann. $6.75 (with *Classical Review,* $13). K. J. Dover & D. A. Russell. Oxford Univ. Press, Ely House, Dover St., London W.1. Index, adv. Circ: 1,550. Microform: UM. Reprint: Abrahams.

Indexed: BritHum. *Aud:* Sa, Ac. *Rv:* H. *Jv:* B.

The English equivalent of the *Classical Journal,* issued by England's Classical Association, whose objectives are "to promote and sustain interest in classical studies, to maintain their rightful position in universities and schools, and to give scholars and teachers opportunities of meeting and discussing their problems." The signed articles are generally lengthy, and contributors are almost exclusively British scholars. Primarily for the teacher in England, it has limited value for his American counterpart. See also, *Greece and Rome.*

The Classical Review. 1886. 3/yr. $7.25. C. J. Fordyce & H. Tredennick. Oxford Univ. Press, Ely House, Dover St., London, W.1. Circ: 1,378. Reprint: Johnson.

Indexed: BritHum, SSHum. *Aud:* Sa, Ac, Jc. *Rv:* H. *Jv:* A.

Primarily the review medium for *Classical Quarterly,* but with considerably wider appeal because of the critical coverage of new titles in the field. Most of the journal is composed of signed, often essay length reviews of some 40 to 60 titles per issue. About half as many shorter notices also are included. Living up to the best British tradition, the comments are detailed, comparative, extremely well written, and rarely superfluous. Although the majority of titles represent English publishers, a number are from American and continental presses. While for the average library the book reviews in the *Classical Journal* will be sufficient—and usually more current—*The Classical Review* is a basic selection medium in larger, specialized libraries. See also, *Greece and Rome.*

Classical World. 1907. m. (Sept.–June). $4.25. Edward A. Robinson. Classical Assn. of the Atlantic States, Rutgers Univ., 12 James St., Newark, N.J. 07102. Index, adv. Circ: 3,200. Microform: UM. Reprint: Kraus, Abrahams.

Bk. rev: 16–22, 250 words, signed. *Aud:* Sa, Ac, Jc, Ht. *Rv:* M. *Jv:* B.

The eastern seaboard equivalent of *Classical Journal* which features brief, signed scholarly articles, with useful bibliographies. An annual aid is the list of audio-visual materials, Greek and Latin college textbooks, and inexpensive titles for the teaching of the classics. High school teachers find the occasional list of historical fiction with classical themes for young adults particularly helpful. Finally, there are the usual conference and news notes. A useful item wherever the classics constitute a part of the curriculum. While required in most eastern libraries, a second choice for others, after the more scholarly *Classical Journal.*

Greece and Rome. 1931. 2/yr. $2.50. G. T. W. Hooker & E. R. A. Sewter. Oxford Univ. Press, Ely House, Dover St. London W.1. Illus., adv. Microform: UM. Reprint: Johnson, Abrahams.

Indexed: BritHum. *Bk. rev:* 40, short, signed. *Aud:* Sa, Ac. *Rv:* M. *Jv:* B.

Whereas the Classical Association's *Classical Review* is for the scholar, this is the review medium for the teacher at the high school and beginning college level. The reviews rate books according to four categories: "Recommended for school libraries," "For advanced students," "For non-Greek readers," and "Include bibliographies." Each note gives a concise and useful evaluation. There is a limited amount of textual material and some fine art. For reviewing purposes, a third or fourth choice in most American libraries.

Greek Heritage; the American quarterly of Greek culture. 1963. q. $20. Kimon Friar. The Athenian Corp., 360 N. Michigan Ave., Chicago, Ill. 60601. Illus.

Bk. rev: Notes. *Aud:* Ga, Ac, Jc, Sh, Jh. *Rv:* H. *Jv:* A.

Following the same general approach and format as *American Heritage,* the editors concentrate on all aspects of ancient and modern Greece. Articles are semi-popular, yet written by experts. The majority of contributions are concerned with the history, literature and art of the country. For the most part the current controversial political scene is side-stepped. All material is beautifully illustrated in both color and black and white. Usually each issue has an annotated bibliography of current and retrospective literature for adults and children. While the price is high, it is a good investment. Many libraries or individuals can treat each copy as a book, and a run constitutes an excellent basic source of information on Greek culture. The best single classical magazine for the layman; should be in most libraries.

Greek, Roman and Byzantine Studies. 1958. q. $7. William H. Willis. Box 144, Cambridge, Mass. 02138. Circ: 425. Reprint: Johnson.

Aud: Sa, Ac. *Rv:* M. *Jv:* B.

A general journal of the classics, but differs from others in that it contains a fair amount of material on the Byzantine Empire. Each issue presents six or eight long articles, some with illustrations, on any subject of classical or Byzantine interest. The tone is learned, but not formidable. Any reader of cultivated taste is bound to find articles here that catch his attention. Some recent articles are concerned with a new inscription of Arrian, Byzantine bronze coins and judicial awards in ancient Athens. Recommended for large public and academic libraries.

Phoenix. 1946. q. $6. Classical Assn. of Canada, Univ. of Toronto Press, Toronto, Ont. Illus., index, adv. Circ: 950.
Bk. rev: 7–10, 250–500 words, signed. *Aud:* Sa, Ac. *Rv:* M. *Jv:* B.

A general classical journal which has much the same aims as *Arion.* Rather than limit itself to philology, it includes articles on literature, philosophy, archaeology and history. The interdisciplinary approach gives it added interest, but as all contributors are scholars writing for their fellows, it is difficult reading. And while the official voice of the Classical Association of Canada, contributors are international and the amount of news notes and material for teachers is limited. The book reviews cover much the same ground as *Classical Journal* and *The Classical Review,* albeit more emphasis is placed on French language publications. Articles are in either French or English. A basic acquisition for Canadian Academic libraries, but only for large American collections.

Quarterly Check List of Classical Studies. See Literature Section, *Quarterly Check List of Literary History.*

COMICS

The following is a representative list of comic magazines prepared by Mrs. Beverly H. Choate and Mrs. Ann E. Prentice, both of the State University of New York, School of Library Science, at Albany.

The titles are selective, representative of the subject matter and interests in this field. Unlike other sections of this book, there is no grading system employed. The genre does not suit itself to the "good, better, best" type of categorization. However, indication is given by grouping as to the probable age group to which the magazine will have the most appeal.

In that comics are a medium of enjoyment for some 70 percent of the reading population, including many adults, they are of importance in our culture. Although it is not suggested they be used by all libraries, they are an excellent introduction to reading for some types of youngsters—particularly teen-age dropouts, or children with reading or concentration problems. The average comic has a simple vocabulary, a fast moving plot, and (at least those listed here) a minimum of violence, sex and the like. In fact, all of the titles recommended are almost too free of reality—the policemen, judges and officials are inevitably the good guys; no criminal ever escapes unpunished, and profanity is forbidden.

Standards

Batman. m. No subscriptions. National Periodical Pubns., Inc., 2nd & Dickey Sts., Sparta, Ill. 62286.

Batman is technically not a Super-Hero. He has no hidden powers other than the new sex-appeal that writer Frank Robbins is developing for him. The Caped Crusader is in reality millionaire Bruce Wayne, who with his ward Dick Grayson, gets his kicks by running around at night in a mask and leotard. The villains they track are far from conventional—the Joker, the Penguin, Katwoman—all of them with a single goal in mind, to put pun back in life. A typical plot will find the Caped Crusader and Robin patroling Gotham City in the Batmobile. Crimes are prevented; crimes are detected; crimes are solved. It's all in a night's work for the Dynamic Duo, and the series has a fanatical following.

Spiderman. m. $1.75 (12 issues). Magazine Management Co., 625 Madison Ave., New York, N.Y. 10022.

At last there is a super-hero for paranoids and henpecked students. Peter Parker, alias Spiderman, was literally bitten by the super-hero bug in 1962. A huge radioactive spider bit him, leaving him with the strength of spider of human proportions. Unfortunately, Peter has only the strength of a super-hero and none of their god-like bearing. His suit is subject to rips, he has a widowed aunt who is subject to heart attacks, and the newspapers hate him. Besides all these troubles, he, unlike other superheroes, has to make a living. With great bravado he takes free-lance photographs of his best crime smashing and tries to sell them to the local newspaper which, of course, usually refuses to print them. Spiderman gets altogether too much publicity as it is. Unappreciated and suspecting that no one really likes him, Spiderman has begun to call for a super-hero union that will insure equal treatment and a minimum wage. The *Spiderman* magazines are among the best available. Thanks to editor, Stan Lee, he is very much in tune to the world around him. Spiderman has taken part in demonstrations and is currently opposing the Vietnam war. The vocabulary is excellent and the plots are sophisticated social satires.

Superboy. m. No Subscriptions. National Periodical Pubns., Inc., 2nd & Dickey Sts., Sparta, Ill. 62286.

Even Superman was young once. *Superboy* fills in the early years for those who may be interested in a super-powered childhood. Superman was a hard worker even then, patrolling around Smallville all night, only pausing for an hour's rest each day from 5:30 to 6:30 A.M. The Kent family, who rescued the sole survivor of the planet Krypton, have been raising 'Clark' as their son. He is, to the uninitiated, a typical small town kid living in the Mid-West during the 1930's. The brightest character in the series is Krypto the faithful superdog. In the best tradition of 1930's fiction, the devoted dog rescues and defends his master from a never ending line of crooks who long to see a crime on every street corner and a mugging in every park. This comic is recommended for anyone who is interested in the background of a super-hero. It is especially recommended for amateur psychologists who may discover something in his childhood to explain Superman's hangup about taking off his clothes in phone booths.

Superman. m. No Subscriptions. National Periodical Pubns., Inc., 2nd & Dickey Sts., Sparta, Ill. 62286.

One of the oldest comics and the basis for the whole Super-Hero cult. Adventures usually involve Lois Lane, Jimmy Olsen, and Clark Kent (Superman), all reporters for the *Daily Planet.* Typically, some force of evil disrupts "Metropolis," and Lois, Jimmy, and Clark win honors for further complicating the situation. Superman, of course, restores "law and order." The plots however can literally take place anywhere. The Kryptonian is faster than the speed of light and moves forward and backward in time as well as hopping into parallel dimensions. The trend is also toward transferring villains and characters from one comic series to another. For example, the April 1969 issue of *Superman* employs the villains Luther and Brainiac from *The World's Finest,* (a comic featuring both Superman and Batman) to save Superman from the disintegration rays of the Dimension Master. After approximately thirty years of existence, the Superman situation has grown so complex that background reading may be necessary for the serious student of comics literature. It will be impossible to function knowledgeably in the Super-Hero world without knowledge of this comic and of its affiliates.

Elementary Grades through Junior High

Anthro. bi-m. No subscription. National Periodical Pubns., Inc., 2nd & Dickey Sts., Sparta, Ill. 62286.

A newcomer to the comic world, Anthro is a man of Ice age Europe trying to find food and shelter for his family. Their long journey to the Land of the Sun provides the adventures. The concept of Anthro is more in the Tarzan vein than in the super-hero mold. The situations and characters are very like the early Edgar Rice Burroughs *Tarzan* adventures. The action is fast, the research is passable, and the dialogue good. It is a new comic with appeal to young readers studying the dinosaur age or passing through ancient history.

Bomba the Jungle Boy. bi-m. $1.75 (12 issues). National Periodical Pubns., Inc., 2nd & Dickey Sts., Sparta, Ill. 62286.

A teenage Tarzan type, Bomba makes the Amazon jungle safe for the good and sends the evil ones fleeing. His success is due to his jungle cunning and the help he can expect from Kokor the Jaguar, Kawkaw the Condor, Tiki the Parrot, Doto the Monkey, etc.

Casper. m. $1.50 (10 issues). Harvey Pubns., Inc., Sparta, Ill. 62286.

Casper is right in keeping with Code regulations. He is a good little ghost and manages to keep the bad spooks to a minimum. One issue finds him at the circus trying desperately to find the villain who is trying to murder the clown and take over the circus. The clown has had about all he can take. He has fallen from a tight rope, been shot from a cannon without a net, and fallen from the high trapeze. Casper solves the mystery. The ugly magician, Mr. Snarl, was behind the accidents. Casper is a favorite with young readers.

The Lone Ranger. q. $.50 (4 issues). Western Publishing Co., Inc., North Rd., Poughkeepsie, N.Y. 12602.

The Lone Ranger has been around for several decades and is still going strong. It is a well constructed story with some of the glory going to the Indian, Tonto. Tonto speaks with the usual Indianese "Ughs," but he is also shown to be an intelligent, able partner for the Ranger. An above average comic with particular appeal to boys from the elementary grades through junior high school.

Tomahawk. bi-m. No subscription. National Periodical Pubns., Inc., 2nd & Dickey Sts., Sparta, Illinois 62286.

Tomahawk and his trusty rangers fight Indians and the British in tales from early America. In one issue, Tomahawk is on petticoat detail. The rangers must guide six women across the plains to Fort Shelter. Behind the hills the Indians are waiting in ambush. There is the usual skirmish and Tomahawk and the Indian chief square off against each other in hand-to-hand combat. Tomahawk is knocked to the ground forcing Bill Howell, a green recruit, to discover that he is not a coward after all. Howell drives off the Indians single-handedly and the patrol reaches its destination. *Tomahawk* is one of the best comics in that it provides insight into its characters and fleshes out the figures that people the tales. It is particularly suited for the young boy or girl in elementary grades and junior high, or for older boys with reading problems.

Tom and Jerry. q. $.50 (four issues). Western Publishing Co., Inc., North Road, Poughkeepsie, N.Y. 12602.

Tom is an un-cat cat and Jerry is the smart little mouse that makes his life miserable. A typical episode concerns who is dumb enough to believe that Jerry and Tuffy (a smaller Jerry) have submitted Tom's name for a Nobel Prize. He doesn't believe in Sweden, but when he receives occupant mail giving him a free dance lesson he lets the mice go and packs his bags. He returns later that night after discovering there is no bus service to Stockholm. This comic is most suitable for younger children.

Junior High Through High School—Girls

Falling in Love. m. No Subscription. National Periodical Pubns., Inc., 2nd & Dickey Sts., Sparta, Ill., 62286.

Girls have to be careful about their reputations. That's what Kim found out the hard way. She had been hanging around with a guy with long hair and a motorcycle. Whatever else she had been doing we will never know, but we are told by Kim that no boy will ever want her. But her mother tells her she isn't a criminal, and can therefore change her ways. Kim does it, and becames a bona fide prude. Now the guys are afraid to go out with her. She is too good for them. Eh bien.

Falling in Love is typical of the emotions of very young adolescents. The problem is that the persons involved in the story are much older than fourteen and are shown handling their problems in adolescent terms. Life and love are not that simple; the girl does not always get the dreamy boy. Recommended for confirmed teen-age girl escapists only.

Lois Lane, Superman's Girl Friend. m. No subscription. National Periodical Pubns., Inc., 2nd & Dickey Sts., Sparta, Ill. 62286.

Lois Lane is a series which began as an off-shoot of a more famous comic, *Superman*. For years Lois has been waiting for Superman to marry her. In her dreams she forgets the man from Krypton and marries Bruce Wayne, better known as Batman. Meanwhile, Gimmick Master has taken over as leader of Gotham City's crime syndicate, and masterminds a plan to rid the world of all the superheroes starting with Batman. The comic is especially well drawn and the dialogue is good. New ideas and references to other media are common, as with the mention of the Opera *Carmen* in this issue of the series. As a spin off of a more famous comic, *Lois Lane* is obviously another way to bring money and has a thrown together quality missing in the master comics, *Superman* and *Batman*. It is still enjoyable reading, but of less distinction than the older mags. Among a given set of pre teen-age girls it is usually a winner.

Junior High Through High School—Boys

G. I. Combat. bi-m. No subscription. National Periodical Pubns., Inc., 2nd & Dickey Sts., Sparta, Ill. 62286.

The comics are still fighting the Second World War. The Nazis are as bad as ever. The theater is in the African desert. In a typical episode, action is supplied by Jeb Stuart and the Haunted Tank. Jeb is sent to command the defense of the Oasis of Seven Skulls. His backup crew is composed of three big Pershing Tanks driven by three self-confident brothers. Early in the story the brothers and the Pershings are wiped out, leaving Jeb to defend himself.

G. I. Combat can be seen as an attempt to glorify war for would-be GI's. This is how the comic looks to the adult reader. The Americans always win, and the bloodshed is kept to a minimum. However, the kids themselves, as evidenced by their letters to the editor, are more interested in the equipment and the drawing techniques than in the gory details. Not for children whose parents object to war toys or indication of war in any form, but suitable for junior high and up, and for many teen-age dropouts.

Doctor Solar, Man of the Atom. q. $.45/yr. K. K. Pubns., Inc., North Road, Poughkeepsie, N.Y. 12602.

Science fiction is the dominant theme in this comparatively new entry into the comic book field. Man of the Atom, disguised as a good scientist, battles Nuro, the evil one who has transferred his brain to the body of an indestructible robot. Guess who triumphs?

Hawkman. bi-m. $1.75/yr. National Periodical Pubns., Inc., 2nd & Dickey Sts., Sparta, Ill. 62286.

Hawkman and his wife-partner, Hawkgirl, use their super-strength and flying skill to protect civilization from the ilk of Dr. Malevolo and his super-powered scientific inventions. Machines which would destroy lesser beings temporarily scramble Hawkman's brain on occasion, but Hawkgirl, with the help of the U.S. government, manages to restore him in time to thwart evil plans. Adversaries include pterodactyls, a tyrannosaurus rex, and various reptile mutants; so violence is in the land of the outlandish.

I Spy. irreg. $.12/copy. K. K. Pubns., Inc., North Road, Poughkeepsie, N.Y. 12602.

Kelly and Scotty meet espionage adventure in the romantic corners of the earth. The underlying good-humored friendship of the two men carries over into the comics. Plot, dialogue, and action parallel the show.

Justice League of America. 8/yr. $1.75 (12 issues). National Periodical Pubns., Inc., 2nd & Dickey Sts., Sparta, Ill. 62286.

Flash, Green Arrow, Hawkman, and Snapper Carr seek out the unfortunate, the unhappy and semi-alienated who have been unjustly treated by society, and help them to help themselves. One issue is concerned with helping a Negro and an Apache regain self-confidence and pride in their heritage through success in capturing the enemy. Another episode takes place in India in which an American philanthropist, trying to help a village grow its own food, gets into trouble by being too successful. A nearby village, seeing the rich harvest, decides to attack and capture it. The fairly sophisticated solution is reached when Hawkman pelts the aggressors with the harvest of rice, beans, and melons, telling them between direct hits that "the fruits of others' labor shall leave a bad taste in your mouths!" The two villages agree to share their labor, one hunting and one farming, and divide the food.

Our Army at War. m. (Semi-monthly in Feb.) $1.75 (12 issues). National Periodicals Pubns., Inc., 2nd & Dickey Sts., Sparta, Ill. 62286.

Sgt. Rock of Easy Co., a heart-of-gold tough soldier, recounts World War II episodes. Easy Co. has its share of cowards, heroes, and ordinary Joes, all of whom help win that war. The bad guys lose and some are killed. Just plain hard working soldiers are even found on the enemy side, sometimes. War is portrayed as noisy, dirty, and dangerous, where doing a job and surviving is more important than one-man heroics.

Sad Sack and the Sarge. bi-m. $1.50 (10 issues). Harvey Hits, Inc., Sparta, Ill. 62286.

Sarge is featured in his own comic. He has it rough in the world of tough non-coms. Nothing he tries to do turns out quite the way he has planned. Sad Sack and Slobinski see to that, if Sarge himself doesn't beat them to it. Who but Sarge could ask for promotion to lieutenant and end up on a torture course in Slimesville Jungle, or buy out a surplus supply of stripes and chevrons from a phony gypsy? *Sarge* is a friendly jab at army life which is not completely fanciful. The final episode in one issue concerns a professor who was able to destroy all weapons the army had. He was sure wars would stop forever. He destroyed all weapons, that is, but the master sergeant's ultimate weapon, his ability to sear. A nice combination of anti-war sentiment with true, blue patriotism. Good for all ages, and not a few adults.

CONSERVATION

Indexes and Abstracts

Biological Abstracts, Biological and Agricultural Index, Chemical Abstracts, Engineering Index, Public Affairs Information Service, Readers' Guide to Periodical Literature, Science Citation Index. (For annotations, see Indexes and Abstracts Section.)

American Forests. 1895. m. $6. James B. Craig. Amer. Forestry Assn., 919 17th St., N.W., Washington, D.C. 20006. Illus., index, adv. Circ: 48,000. Microform: UM.

Indexed: BioAb, PAIS, RG. *Bk. rev:* 5–6, approx. 500 words. *Aud:* Ga, Ac, Jc, Sh. *Rv:* H. *Jv:* B.

A general conservation magazine issued by a national organization which is independent and non-political. Much of the material on how to best conserve and use the forests is suitable for the non-expert, and the illustrations and photographs give it an added dimension for high school students. As the voice of the American Forestry Association, it is not always in accord with conservation moves suggested in Congress. In many ways it serves as the counter-voice to material found in such magazines as *National Parks Magazine* and *Conservation News*. Not an essential purchase, but a useful one for any type of library serving forestry and conservation interests.

American Midland Naturalist. See Biological Sciences Section.

American Naturalist. See Biological Sciences Section.

Appalachia. See Games and Sports Section.

Conservation News. 1937. semi-m. free. Willard J. Johns. National Wildlife Federation, 1412 16th St., N.W., Washington, D.C. 20036.

Bk. rev: 6–8, 200–750 words, signed, short notes. *Aud:* Ga, Ac, Jc, Sh, Jh. *Rv:* M. *Jv:* B.

Covering every aspect of conservation which is of interest to the issuing agency—the National Wildlife Federation—this is primarily important for the current coverage of pending and recent federal legislation. The book reviews and notes are one of the best sources available to the librarian for objective news about books in the field. The style of writing is semi-popular, and the appeal ranges from junior high school to the general adult. Best of all, it is free to any library.

The Conservationist. 1946. bi-m. $2. James E. Gavagan. New York State Conservation Dept., State Campus, Albany, N.Y. 12226. Illus. Circ: 105,000.

Indexed: BioAb, RG. *Aud:* Ga, Ac, Jc, Sh, Jh. *Rv:* H. *Jv:* A.

Although a New York state publication, this magazine has national appeal. It covers all phases of conservation. School librarians will find it helpful for its lively presentation of conservation reference material and for the beautiful color photography. Several full page reproductions of nature paintings appear in each issue. A centerfold spread is devoted to color drawings of wildlife and natural history. Pond fish, edible wild plants, and winter birds have been typical subjects. *The Conservationist* is an outstanding example of a government publication and is valuable to libraries outside of New York state since plants and animals know no state lines.

Defenders of Wildlife News. 1926. q. $5. Mary Hazell Harris. Defenders of Wildlife, 731 Dupont Circle Bldg., 1346 Connecticut Ave., N.W., Washington, D.C. 20036. Illus., index. Circ: 10,500.

Bk. rev: 10–12, 500 words, signed. *Aud:* Ga, Sh. *Rv:* H. *Jv:* B.

"A magazine of wildlife issues and educational articles for the whole family." Since it is dedicated to the preservation of all forms of wildlife, the articles and comments are slanted in this direction, but information pertaining to the other side of the picture is presented realistically. Articles dealing with factual material and proposed legislation are supported by bibliographies. Special articles are particularly educational and often deal with various endangered species; occasional poetry. Primarily for the dedicated conservationist, and while the message is worthwhile, it would be a third or fourth choice in most general school and public library collections.

Environment. See Science—General Section.

Journal of Forestry; a journal reporting on all phases of professional forestry. 1902. m. $12. Arthur B. Meyer. Soc. of Amer. Foresters, 1010 16th St., N.W., Washington, D.C. 20036. Illus., adv. Circ: 17,000.

Bk. rev: Various number, lengths. *Aud:* Sa, Ac. *Rv:* H. *Jv:* B.

The basic, scholarly journal in the field of forestry. Emphasis is on technical aspects of conservation, timberlands, lumbering, land management, etc. Articles, by teachers and professional foresters, tend to stress long range planning, economic and scientific problems. Here it differs from the more commercial oriented *American Forests,* which is primarily geared for the man working in the field. It is particularly useful to librarians because of the departments which cover all major new books in the area, monographs and other literature of forestry. A required item in any academic library where there is an interest in the subject. Conversely, *American Forests* would be a first in more business oriented collections.

Journal of Soil and Water Conservation. 1946. bi-m. Membership (library subscriptions, $7.50). Max Schnepf. 7515 N. E. Ankeny Rd., Ankeny, Iowa 50021. Illus., index, adv. Circ: 12,000. Reprint: Abrahams.

Indexed: BioAb, BioAg. *Aud:* Ac, Jc. *Rv:* H. *Jv:* B.

Issued by the Soil Conservation Society of America, this periodical will be found useful in high school, public and college libraries as a source of supplementary material in the field of conservation. It covers such subjects as the sources of soil and water pollution and the steps being taken by public and private agencies to abate the destruction of our natural resources. Although the articles are written by experts, they are popular in approach and are well illustrated. Film reviews are a distinctive feature, and will interest librarians in instructional materials centers. A specialized conservation magazine primarily for the academic library.

Journal of Wildlife Management. 1937. q. $15. Thomas S. Baskett. Wildlife Soc., 3900 Wisconsin Ave., N.W., Washington, D.C. 20016. Illus., index. Circ: 6,000. Microform: UM. Reprint: Johnson, Abrahams.

Indexed: BioAb, BioAg, ChemAb, SCI. *Bk. rev:* 6, 350 words, signed. *Aud:* Sa, Ac, Jc. *Rv:* H. *Jv:* B.

An official publication of the Wildlife Society (an international professional organization) which reflects the attitude of its parent. The level of scholarship is high and the material is specialized. The subjects covered include habitat management, the effects of various toxic agents on plants and animals, and studies of animal behavior and life histories. The detailed charts and graphs, as well as the few photographs, enrich and clarify the material. Each article is signed and accompanied by an extensive bibliography. In addition to the critical book reviews, there are some two pages devoted to listings of recently published books in the field. A helpful reference tool for college and large public libraries. The Society also issues occasional lengthy papers in the *Wildlife Monographs* and current events in the bi-monthly *Wildlife Society News.*

The Living Wilderness. 1935. q. Membership (Nonmembers, $3.). Michael Nadel. Wilderness Soc., 729 15th St., N.W., Washington, D.C. 20005. Illus., index. Circ: 35,000.

Indexed: RG. *Bk. rev:* 2–3, 400 words, signed. *Aud:* Ga, Ac, Jc, Sh, Jh. *Rv:* H. *Jv:* A.

Next to *National Wildlife,* probably the best general conservation magazine for teen-agers and adults alike. Its major concerns are: (a) the need to preserve national, state and local wilderness areas; (b) public support for such preservation; and (c) the necessity for scientific studies concerning the wilderness. Although the editorials and articles are slanted in accordance with the Society's policies and aims, news, forthcoming legislation and the pros and cons of various issues are objectively presented. Reports of citizen-conservationist studies and opinions, as well as government authorized studies on national forests, parks and wildlife refuges as they are affected by the proposed inroads of civilization upon wild lands, are interspersed with narrative articles, wilderness experience essays, occasional poetry, and future activities of the Society. The format is enhanced by clear maps and artistic photographs. An excellent magazine for all libraries from junior high school up.

National Parks Magazine. 1919. m. Membership (Nonmembers: individuals, $.50 per issue; schools and libraries, $5.). Paul M. Tilden. National Parks Assn., 1300 New Hampshire Ave., N.W., Washington, D.C. 20036. Illus., index, adv. Circ: 33,500.

Indexed: RG. *Bk. rev:* 1–5, 300– 1000 words, signed. *Aud:* Ga, Ac, Jc, Sh, Jh. *Rv:* H. *Jv:* A.

Since the National Parks Association is a completely independent, private, non-profit, public-service organization, it can and does offer constructive criticism of government and private agencies. The Association's primary aim is to protect the great national parks and monuments of America, but its interests extend to the protection of the natural environment generally, including work in watershed management and river basin planning. Each issue carries beautifully illustrated stories of famous parks, little known beauty spots and areas of special natural interest, some of which lie within easy traveling distance of our cities. A feature is the "Conservation Docket" which lists bills relating to conservation in the legislatures and official government actions. Editorials comment on current national conservation issues, and "News and Commentary" relates news items. In view of format, content and non-partisan sponsorship, this is an excellent magazine for almost all libraries.

National Wildlife. 1962. bi-m. $5. John Strohm. National Wildlife Federation, Inc., 1412 16th St., N.W., Washington, D.C. 20036. Illus. Circ: 220,000.

Indexed: RG. *Bk. rev:* Notes. *Aud:* Ga, Sh, Jh. *Rv:* H. *Jv:* V.

The major conservation magazine for all libraries, particularly school and public. (Academic libraries will probably give first choice to more specialized publications such as *Defenders of Wildlife News* and *Journal of Wildlife Management*). Issued by the world's largest conservation organization, each issue contains some 10 to 12 articles on animals, natural scenery, outdoor recreation, or personalities. Most are prepared by professional writers, including naturalists and scientists, but there is normally a first-person narrative about some outstanding experience. While emphasis is on the interdependence of mankind and earth's resources, there is a given amount of material on how to camp, photograph animals, and related areas. All articles are beautifully illustrated both in color and black and white. Regular features include current views on conservation, legislation at the national and state level, and the Washington Report on aspects of conservation. The tone, while factual and objective, is popular and intentionally at the level of the interested layman. The approach is suitable for most high school students. For all libraries regardless of size or type. The publisher also issues *Ranger Rick's Nature Magazine* for elementary grades.

Natural History. See Science—General Section.

Nature and Science. See Science—General Section.

Our Public Lands. 1951. q. $.60. Dwight F. Rettie. Supt. of Documents, Washington, D.C. 20402. Illus.

Aud: Ga, Ac, Jc. *Rv:* M. *Jv:* B.

Issued by the Bureau of Land Management, Department of the Interior, this government publication will be found helpful in conservation education. Articles are popularly written, mostly by BLM specialists, but also by other government and private authors interested in conservation. Subjects range through the human and natural history of the land as well as through all aspects of the management and public use of the nation's 467 million acres of public lands. A regular feature, listing public lands for sale, will interest the general adult reader. While it does not have the high reference value of many other conservation periodicals, it fills a need for non-technical information.

Outdoor World. 1968. bi-m. $5.75. Ernest S. Booth. Preston Pubns., Inc., 1600 Tullie Circle, N.E. Atlanta, Ga. 30329. Illus.

Bk. rev: 5–10, 50–100 words. *Aud:* Ga, Sh, Jh. *Rv:* M. *Jv:* B.

Illustrated in accurate colors, the 34- to 40-page magazine touches on all aspects of outdoor life from canoeing to desert plants and mushrooms. It differs from its competitors primarily because of its much wider scope, and its focus on nature in all countries, not only America. It rightfully claims to use some of the best outdoor writers, photographers and artists. The text accompanying the pictures is purposefully written for the layman, and most of it will be understood by the youngster from junior high school age on up. Each issue features an insert such as a brief guide to hiking, canoeing, outdoor photography, etc., which is separately bound and paged so it may be removed for use in a vertical file. One of the better outdoor magazines which should be found in most general library collections.

Parks & Recreation; journal of park and recreation management. 1903. m. $5. Walter M. Kiplinger, Jr. National Recreation and Park Assn., 1700 Pennsylvania Ave., N.W., Washington, D.C. 20006. Illus., index, adv. Circ: 19,400. Microform: UM.

Indexed: RG. *Bk. rev:* 3–4, 150–500 words, signed. *Aud:* Ga, Ac, Jc, Sh. *Rv:* M. *Jv:* B.

Concerned with providing information on all phases of the park, recreation and conservation movements. Each issue usually contains 12 to 15, one- to three-page articles with illustrations. Contributed articles are signed. Some topics covered include: new and unusual facilities; education and training; federal, state and local legislation; working with special groups such as the handicapped, mentally retarded, senior citizens, etc., and other subjects related to the use of leisure time, conservation of natural resources, and beautification of the American environment. Occasionally, there is a special issue devoted to just one of these topics. For professional and lay leaders in the field, teachers, students, and the general public. A third choice after *National Parks Magazine* and *American Forests*.

Ranger Rick's Nature Magazine. 1967. 10/yr. Membership, $6. Trudy Dye Farrand. National Wildlife Federation, 1412 16th St., N.W., Washington, D.C. 20036. Circ: 100,000.

Bk. rev: 4, 150 words. *Aud:* E. *Rv:* M. *Jv:* B.

The children's version of *National Wildlife,* designed to give boys and girls a program of activities, adventure and knowledge which will help them appreciate and enjoy nature. The color photography and illustrations draw the eye to the information-packed pages. Stories and articles, games and puzzles are of graded difficulty and interest levels. The type sizes are also adjusted to the age of the reader. "Ranger Rick's Book Nook" selects and reviews four books each month which may be purchased through the magazine at a discount from publishers' list prices. These, too, are chosen with differing ages and reading abilities in mind. A good magazine for elementary schools and children in that age group.

Sierra Club Bulletin. 1915. m. Membership (Non-members, $5.). Hugh Nash. Sierra Club, 1050 Mills Tower, San Francisco, Calif. 94104. Circ: 34,835.

Aud: Ga, Ac, Jc, Sh, Jh. *Rv:* H. *Jv:* A.

Rapidly becoming a contender for second or third place in most libraries after *National Wildlife* and *Living Wilderness.* The Sierra Club is the premier outdoors club in the U.S., and its *Bulletin,* edited first by John Muir, the Club's founder, is beyond question among the finest such publication anywhere. Each issue, which is from twenty to fifty large, glossy pages long, is made up of articles, many illustrated, on matters of concern to people interested in preserving America's remaining wilderness and in keeping naturally beautiful areas beautiful. Originally, much material was given on mountain climbing, but since the appearance in 1967 of *Ascent,* the Club's mountaineering annual, this subject has been set aside. The *Bulletin's* emphasis is now on conservation, a matter of which the Club has become the country's chief advocate. Occasional special issues of the *Bulletin* come out. These issues, which are book-sized, with color illustrations (and about as luxurious as the Club's justly famous monographs), are supposed to come out annually, but the Club admits that in this case annual can mean biennial or triennial.

Soil Conservation. 1935. m. $1.75. F. B. Harper. Supt. of Documents, Washington, D.C. 20402. Illus., index. Microform: UM.

Indexed: BioAg. *Bk. rev:* 2–5, 250 words. *Aud:* Sa, Ac, Jc. *Rv:* H. *Jv:* B.

The official organ of the Soil Conservation Service of the Department of Agriculture, this is devoted to the wise use of land and water resources. Although only about 25 pages, a prime source of information about current conservation projects and research being carried on by the Federal government. Under "New Publications" there are notes on current government bulletins. Only for medium to large collections.

World Wildlife Illustrated. 1966. bi-m. $5. Virginia A. Barber. World Wildlife Publishing Co., 1 Lincoln Ave., Holden, Mass. 01520. Illus.

Aud: Ga, Sh, Jh, E. *Rv:* M. *Jv:* B.

About one-half of this 25- to 30-page magazine is devoted exclusively to black and white or color photographs of animals. The articles, for the most part staff written, are short, popular in style and concentrate on habits and physical aspects of animals. Several pieces have a boxed summary of the animal features, i.e., common name, scientific name, feeding habits, coloration, etc. No advertising. After *Ranger Rick's Nature Magazine,* probably a first choice at the elementary school level, not so much for the text as the pictures. Other school and public libraries should subscribe, but only after *National Wildlife, Living Wilderness,* and the *Sierra Club Bulletin.*

CRAFTS AND HOBBIES

Indexes and Abstracts

Abridged Readers' Guide, Art Index, Biological Abstracts, Readers' Guide to Periodical Literature, Subject Index to Children's Magazines. (For annotations, see Indexes and Abstracts Section.)

American Aircraft Modeler (**Formerly:** *American Modeler*). 1928. m. $6. William J. Winter. Potomac Aviation Pubns., Inc., 1012 14th St., N.W., Washington, D.C. 20005. Illus., adv. Circ: 85,000.

Indexed: IChildMags. *Aud:* Jh, Sh, Ga. *Rv:* M. *Jv:* B.

Although primarily an adult's magazine, the sophisticated child or teen-ager who knows something about aircraft models will find it useful. A typical issue puts considerable emphasis on radio-directed models and, to a lesser degree, scale models of historical and present day aircraft. The whole is well-illustrated, with detailed plans, and a center spread given over to a colored drawing of an important airplane. Other articles cover flying in general, design and construction. In fact any lover of airplanes, whether he builds models or not, will find something of interest in an average issue. Compared with *Flying Models* it is preferable for younger readers, primarily because it is somewhat better illustrated, has a wider scope and the articles tend to be a trifle more simplified. It would be a second for children, if the choice had to be made between it and *Model Airplane News.*

American Philatelist; journal of the American Philatelic Society. 1887. m. $8. James M. Chemi. Amer. Philatelic Soc., Box 800, State College, Pa. 16801. Illus., adv. Circ: 17,000.

Bk. rev: 2–7, 100–400 words. *Aud:* Ga, Sh. *Rv:* H. *Jv:* B.

For those with a sincere interest in philately, this furnishes authoritative articles on the many phases of philately as well as news of interest to Society members. Worldwide in coverage, more than half the articles deal with countries other than the United States (e.g., "Laos: Its Musical Instruments on Stamps" by Robert Morefield, Oct., 1967). Of special merit is the "New Issues Chronicle," which advises readers as to which stamps may have questionable market value. "World Wide Listing of Philatelic Periodicals of Regular Issue" (James M. Chemi, Oct., 1967), while unannotated, is a worthwhile reference for readers who seek a long listing of philatelic periodicals.

Aquarium. 1932. m. $4.50. Albert J. Klee. Pet Books, Inc., 87 Rt. 17, Maywood, N.J. 07607. Illus., index, adv. Circ: 12,000.

Indexed: BioAb. *Bk. rev:* 1, 130–150 words, unsigned. *Aud:* Ga, Sa, Sh. Jh. *Rv:* M. *Jv:* B.

A magazine for the hobbyists and the dealers in tropical fish and related pets. There are numerous articles and short notes on specific types of fish and how to care for them, as well as new discoveries which have been made. Also contained are long feature articles such as "An Amazonian Adventure" and "A History of the Aquarium Hobby in America." Other features are the "Editor's Letter;" "Views and Reviews," which may or may not contain book reviews, and "This is my Problem," in which readers may receive answers to the problems that they have encountered regarding their fish. While some of the material is a bit technical, and there is emphasis on the trade, it is one of the best fish magazines for anyone from junior high school on up.

Ceramics Monthly. 1953. m. (except July and Aug.). $6. Thomas Sellers. Professional Pubns., Inc., 4175 N. High St., Columbus, Ohio 43214. Illus., index, adv. Circ: 14,604. Microform: UM.

Indexed: RG. *Aud:* Ga, Ac, Jc, Sh. *Rv:* H. *Jv:* B.

A popular magazine for craftsmen engaged in the making of pottery. Practical articles clearly explain, with text and photographs, how-to-do everything in ceramics from the wedging of the clay to the final decoration of the pottery. Many types of ceramic products are discussed as well as the methods used in making them. The regular features are: list of back issues available; "Answers to Question"— CM staff answers questions from those with technical problems; "CeramActivities"—lists award winners and exhibitions; "Suggestions"—shares discoveries of other craftsmen to improve techniques, "Summer Workshops" (Spring issues), and Biennial Ceramic Film and Slide Issue. As is true with most hobby magazines, this one can only be recommended where there is an interest in the subject, or where the school curriculum includes the subject.

Coin World; the weekly newspaper of the entire numismatic field. 1960. w. $6. Margo Russell. Sidney Printing & Publishing Co., 119 E. Court St., Sidney, Ohio 45365. Illus., adv. Circ: 10,000.

Bk. rev: Short notes. *Aud:* Ga, Sh. *Rv:* H. *Jv:* B.

Advertised as the coin collectors' only weekly newspaper, this features articles covering a broad range of subject material of interest to U.S. and Canadian collectors. The material is written by such foremost numismatic authorities as Eric Newman, Edward Gans, and Dr. V. Clain Stefanelli of the Smithsonian. Valuable reference material appears (e.g., the bibliography of major numismatic groups, Nov. 22, 1967, and the in-depth reports on specific coins in the "Collectors' Clearinghouse" column). Mint reports and trends keep readers abreast of current additions and alert to changes in coin values. A basic addition to any library where there are more than a few collectors. Particularly useful with hobby groups in high schools.

Coinage. 1964. m. $6. James L. Miller. Behn-Miller Publishers, 15840 Ventura Blvd., Encino, Calif. 91316. Illus., adv. Circ: 140,000.

Aud: Ga, Sh, Jh. *Rv:* H. *Jv:* B.

All avenues of numismatics are given coverage, including the investment phase (e.g., "The Best Coin Investments" by George Haylings, April, 1967), which is usually ignored in magazines devoted to numismatics as a hobby. While the main concern is with U.S. coins, medals and currency, an occasional article treats an interesting facet of foreign issues (e.g., "The Saga of the British Counterfeit Currency" by George Rony, June, 1967). Included are articles for the beginning collector as well as material for the knowledgeable numismatist or the reader interested in specialty collecting. An important feature is the complete retail listing of current coin prices. It differs from *Coin World* in frequency (monthly as compared to the latter's weekly edition) and format. In view of weekly issues *Coin World* will be a first choice for libraries with serious collectors, while *Coinage* may be more suitable for general coverage of the subject area.

Craft Horizons. 1941. bi-m. $8. Rose Slivka. Amer. Craftsmen's Council. 16 E. 52nd St., New York, N.Y. 10022. Illus., adv. Circ: 26,000. Microform: UM.

Indexed: ArtI, RG. *Bk. rev:* 2–5, 150–1,000 words, signed. *Aud:* Ga, Ac, Jc, Sh, Ht. *Rv:* M. *Jv:* A.

A magazine for the craftsman, artist, teacher, and buyer interested in ceramics, weaving, metal and wood working, jewelry, glass, mosaics, and enameling. Articles cover the wide range of handicrafts, exhibitions, and market places. The style is semi-popular and can be understood by the teen-ager. At least two biographical sketches of famous artists, early and modern, are included. Contributors are themselves practicing craftsmen and/or teachers in leading schools and universities. High quality paper, a pleasing layout, liberal use of artistic color, and black and white photography combine to make this a beautiful magazine. It is useful for both the layman and the student of design and crafts. As the one general handicraft magazine, it should be found in all types of libraries, from high schools to universities.

Earth Science. See Earth Sciences Section.

The Family Handyman. See Home Section.

Flying Chips and Deltagram. 1932. semi-m. $1.75. A. M. Warkaske. Rockwell Manufacturing Co., 400 N. Lexington Ave., Pittsburgh, Pa. 15208. Illus. Circ: 36,000.

Aud: Ga, Sh, Jh. *Rv:* L. *Jv:* B.

A trade publication issued by a prominent power tool manufacturer, this features detailed plans for projects (utilizing stationary and power tools) for home workshop enthusiasts, school shop classes, and professional woodworkers. There is a limited amount of plugging for the sponsor's product. An inexpensive, useful magazine for most school and general adult collections.

Flying Models; the model builder's How-To-Do-It magazine. 1927. m. $5. Don McGovern. Rajo Pubns., Inc., 215 Park Ave. S., New York, N.Y. 10003. Illus., index, adv. Circ: 36,000.

Aud: Ga, Sh, Jh. *Rv:* M. *Jv:* B.

A magazine for teenagers and adults interested in constructing and designing flying model airplanes. Contains design information and articles about airplane modelers and their machines. All types of airplanes are covered—radio control models, sports planes, free flight, helicopters, gliders, rubber powered designs, etc. The visual quality of the articles is enhanced by numerous photographs, finely detailed drawings, and charts. Famed designer-contributors include editor Don McGovern, Joe Bilgri, Paul Del Gatto, Harry English, and many others. Somewhat more adult in its approach than either *Model Airplane News* or *American Aircraft Modeler,* but still a notch below the latter for most libraries.

The Gibbons-Whitman Stamp Monthly. 1967. m. $4.50. Whitman Publishing Co., 1220 Mound Ave., Racine, Wis. 53404. Illus., adv.

Aud: Ga, Sh, Jh. *Rv:* M. *Jv:* B.

Averaging some 36 colorfully illustrated pages, this is for almost any stamp collector. Each issue begins with a number of articles on subjects from airmail stamps to the new nine-colored stamp printing press. The last half consists of illustrated and priced additions to the *Gibbons-Whitman Postage Catalogue*—a commercial twist which probably accounts for the low subscription price and the frequent use of color. A competitor of *Scott's Monthly Stamp Journal,* but a second choice next to that.

Handweaver & Craftsman. See Art Section.

Hobbies. See Antiques Section.

Home Craftsman. See Home Section.

Lapidary Journal. 1946. m. $5.75. Hugh N. Leiper. Lapidary Journal, Inc., P.O. Box 2369, San Diego, Calif. 92112. Illus., index, adv. Circ: 43,619.

Aud: Ga, Sh. *Rv:* M. *Jv:* B.

Tells amateur gem cutters and rock hounds how to cut, make and refine the stones they so highly value. The well-illustrated articles include news of gem finds of interest to amateur "prospectors," famous collections of jewels, and stories of people who have turned their hobbies into profitable businesses. A complete calendar of events lists all forthcoming exhibitions of minerals, rocks, gems and jewelry. There are numerous ads and an advertising index, as well as classified ads for lapidary supplies. The annual April *Rockhound Buyers Guide* ($1.75) presents similar features, but is unique because of its carefully indexed lists of clubs, dealers, suppliers, and 7,700 "Where to Find It" product listings. A basic rock hound magazine for any library where there are people interested in the subject.

Linn's Weekly Stamp News. 1928. w. $3.50. Carl P. Rueth. Rueth Pubns., Inc., 324 S. St., Sidney, Ohio 45365. Illus., adv. Circ: 70,370.

Bk. rev: Occasional. *Aud:* Ga, Sh. *Rv:* M. *Jv:* A.

This weekly newspaper covers the international stamp world more thoroughly than any other stamp periodical. It is among those with the highest circulation, and is an old standby for avid collectors. Frequent publication keeps philatelists informed of the latest issues and happenings in the stamp world. Many regular columns discuss geographic areas (e.g., "London Thoughts on the Stamp World," by Edgar Lewy) or specific aspects of philately (e.g., "Precancel News," by Kenneth Gierhart), and at regular intervals the entire issue is devoted to various societies of specialist collectors (e.g., John F. Kennedy Philatelic Society). Both the display and classified advertisements are important for collectors who take a serious interest in purchase, or wish to compare prices. In view of the low price, the frequency, and the reputation, should be in any library where stamps are a factor.

Mechanix Illustrated. 1928. m. $3. Robert G. Beason. Fawcett Pubns., Inc., Fawcett Bldg., Greenwich, Conn. 06830. Illus., adv. Circ: 1,412,000. Microform: UM.

Indexed: RG. *Aud:* Ga, Sh, Jh. *Rv:* M. *Jv:* B.

Written primarily for the amateur handyman and mechanically inclined teen-ager. Features articles of about 2,000 words on the latest developments in automobiles, aviation, inventions, and other mechanical and scientific areas. Largest portion of magazine's contents is devoted to cars, followed by home improvements, sports and recreation and hobbies and other forms of transportation. Special areas covered at times include money management for the family, advice on careers and advancement, health and medicine, photography, electronics. One four-color photographic essay usually included in each issue; other photographs in black and white; diagrams and drawings include black and one color. It is sometimes difficult to tell the differences among this, *Popular Mechanics,* and *Popular Science Monthly.* The latter two have the advantage of age and a somewhat better format, but on the whole the material covered is almost identical, as is the approach and reading level. While final decision on which one to subscribe to is a matter of personal preference (most libraries carry them all), this compiler suggests *Popular Science, Popular Mechanics* and *Mechanix Illustrated,* in that order.

McCall's Needlework and Crafts. See Women's Magazines Section.

McCall's Patterns. See Women's Magazine Section.

Minkus Stamp Journal. 1966. q. $2. Belmont Fairies. Minkus Stamp Journal, Inc., 116 W. 132nd St., New York, N.Y. 10001. Illus., adv.

Aud: Ga, Sh, Jh. *Rv:* M. *Jv:* B.

A quarterly which keeps the *Minkus Stamp Index* current. It illustrates and gives technical information about the newly issued stamps of the world; describes unique collections, and new series of stamps; and gives a history of biographical sketch of people or things commemorated by the stamps. There is full purchase information for each stamp shown.

Model Airplane News. 1929. m. $5. Walter L. Schroder. Air Age, Inc., 551 Fifth Ave., New York, N.Y. 10017. Illus., adv. Circ: 70,740.

Aud: Ga, Sh, Jh, E. *Rv:* L. *Jv:* B.

A popular magazine for children and adults with special interest in model aviation. Detailed charts, diagrams, and directions make this an excellent guide for constructing models of various types of airplanes, about half of them radio controlled. Short articles on related aviation activity are easily understandable to the young reader and the layman. Features up-to-date news about the aviation world, and gears its advertising to the young reader's pocketbook. Extensive use of photographs enhances the magazine's usefulness and appeal. This would be a first choice before *Flying Models,* although older readers may prefer its competitor.

Model Car and Science. 1962. m. $5. Raymond E. Hoy. Delta Magazines Inc., Argus Pubns. Group, 171 S. Barrington Place, Los Angeles, Calif. 90049. Illus., adv. Circ: 130,420.

Aud: Ga, Sh, Jh. *Rv:* L. *Jv:* B.

Covers both the model and the rebuilt full-sized car, but emphasis is on the former. Articles are of two basic types. The first reports on model races, radio-controlled cars, personalities and general news. The second is a how-to-do-it approach for both beginner and advanced hobbyist. The "Science" in the title accounts for not only car models, but articles on boats, trains, airplanes and rockets. The style is direct, the illustrations plentiful, and the advertising a delight for beginner and expert. Should be in any library where there is an avid interest in automobiles, or model making.

Model Railroader. 1934. m. $6. Linn E. Wescott. Kalmbach Publishing Co., 1027 N. 7th St., Milwaukee, Wis. 53233. Illus., index, adv. Circ: 87,165.

Aud: Ga, Sh, Jh. *Rv:* L. *Jv:* B.

The single best magazine for the model railroad fan, regardless of age. Illustrated articles are for both the beginner and the sophisticated Casey Jones. Instructions are frequently given as to how to build, buy or dream about a particular train or layout. There is news of others bitten by the bug, and anecdotes. A good bet for any library from the junior high level to the old folk's home.

Numismatic Scrapbook Magazine. 1935. m. $4. Lee F. Hewitt. Hewitt Brothers, 7320 Milwaukee Ave., Chicago, Ill. 60648. Illus., index, adv. Circ: 18,000. Microform: UM.

Bk. rev: Notes. *Aud:* Ga. *Rv:* M. *Jv:* B.

For the serious collector or the interested amateur, this furnishes mint reports, reviews of world coins and authoritative articles on various aspects of numismatics. Articles of one to eight pages appear with some lengthy research continued over a period of up to five months. Advertisements constitute a major portion, of content. A serious drawback is the lack of a table of contents. Only for larger public libraries.

The Numismatist. 1888. m. Membership (Non-members, $7.50). Edward C. Rochette. Amer. Numismatic Assn., Box 2366, Colorado Springs, Colo. 80901. Illus., index, adv. Circ: 28,000.

Bk. rev: 3–5, 400–600 words, signed. *Aud:* Ga, Sh, Jh. *Rv:* M. *Jv:* B.

This well-illustrated monthly serves as the official publication for the American Numismatic Association. It boasts of subscribers in 60 countries, and its coverage of foreign coins and currency is extensive. A regular report from the U.S. Mint gives an official tally of coinage struck. Many knowledgeable contributors (not necessarily members) furnish information about items of interest to the numismatist. A regular feature called "For the Juniors" praises young numismatists who have won awards. Official news is prominent. Probably a second choice in public and high school libraries after *Coin World* or *Coinage*.

Pack-o-Fun. 1951. m. (Sept.–June). $4. Edna N. Clapper. Clapper Publishing Co., Inc., 148 S. Northwest Highway, Barrington, Ill. 60010. Illus., adv. Circ: 256,828.

Aud: E, Et. *Rv:* M. *Jv:* B.

A pocket-sized magazine for children, parents and teachers who are seeking imaginative ideas on hobby crafting. The short, well illustrated articles are geared to demonstrate how scrap materials may be used by and with children to make toys, games, gifts and decorations. Specific, detailed information is given for each item. Most are within the grasp of children from preschool age through the fifth or sixth grades. The writing style is aimed at the child who can read and follow instructions. Teachers and parents will find the material equally useful. Each issue also includes sections on pen pals, children's activities, stunts and games, an exchange of ideas, and hints for the group leader. An extremely useful magazine for both school and public libraries serving children and leaders of children's groups.

Popular Mechanics. 1902. m. $4. Robert P. Crossley. Hearst Magazines, 250 W. 55th St., New York, N.Y. 10019. Illus., adv. Circ: 1,409,179. Microform: UM.

Indexed: AbrRG, IChildMags, RG. *Aud:* Ga, Sh, Jh. *Rv:* H. *Jv:* A.

A "how-to-do-it" magazine which popularizes science and mechanics for all age levels. Emphasis is on practical application rather than theory. Filled with amply illustrated articles on: automobiles, science, inventions and explorations, shop and craft, radio and TV, home and yard, photography, boating, and outdoor recreation. Contains many easy-to-follow directions for numerous useful projects such as sewing centers, patios, sailboards, etc. Tips are given on the care of automobiles, driving, and how to build, repair and use equipment. Occasional picture stories where the illustrations tell the story with little reliance on text. Approximately 14 pages of classified advertising appear each month. Editions are available in Australia, Brazil, the Caribbean, Denmark, France, Mexico, and Sweden. See concluding comments for *Mechanix Illustrated*.

Popular Science Monthly. 1872. m. $4. Ernest V. Heyn. Popular Science Publishing Co., 355 Lexington Ave., New York, N.Y. 10017. Illus., adv. Circ: 1,400,000. Microform: UM.

Indexed: AbrRG, RG. *Aud:* Ga, Sh, Jh. *Rv:* H. *Jv:* V.

Articles are written in simple language for the enjoyment of the weekend mechanic and hobby fan. It is divided into sections representing his varied interests: "Car and Driving," "Science and Invention," "Space and Aviation," "Home and Shop," "Electronics," "Boating," and "Photography." In addition there are many special feature articles. Neither too general nor too technical for the average hobbyist. Illustrations and diagrams are plentiful and ingeniously simplified. Possibly there is more emphasis here on science than in its two competitors, *Popular Mechanics* and *Mechanix Illustrated*, but the difference is not great. On the whole, the editorial style, illustrations and general treatment of material is somewhat better than either of the others, and for that reason it is preferred by this compiler. However, they are all so close that a conclusion as to merit can only be relative. See concluding comments for *Mechanix Illustrated*.

Rocks and Minerals. See Earth Sciences Section.

Scale Modeler. 1965. m. $5.50. Challenge Pubns., Inc., 7805 Deering Ave., Canoga Park, Calif. 91304. Illus., adv. Circ: 55,000.

Aud: Ga, Sh. *Rv:* M. *Jv:* B.

One of the best general model magazines, although rarely found in libraries. It stresses, as the title implies, building models to an accurate scale and scoffs at efforts and kits which void this sacred rule. Primarily concerned with ships, airplanes, and military models from miniatures to armour. There are historical articles to support many of the projects, beautiful illustrations, often in color, and each issue is usually devoted to a single basic theme or type of model. Instructions on everything from painting to construction are monthly features. A bit advanced for the younger set, but certainly for high school students and serious adults.

Scott's Monthly Stamp Journal; articles on stamps and philately; chronicle of new issues updates Scott Catalogues each issue; topical listings. 1920. m. (July–Aug.). $4. Scott Pubns., 461 Eighth Ave., New York, N.Y. 10001. Illus., adv.

Aud: Ga, Sh, Jh. *Rv:* M. *Jv:* A.

The main purpose of this journal is to update *Scott's Catalogues*. In addition to the new issues section, there are usually two articles of 4 to 7 pages, concerning some aspect of philately, written by informed collectors. Each issue features a section of topical listings, and news about a particular stamp; why it was issued and something about the designer. Illustrations include photocopies of stamps, cartoons and photographs, all in black and white. Some articles may interest the general public but the journal is, by and large, intended to serve the serious philatelist. Most stamp collectors desire information more frequently than once a month, but this is a good supplement.

Stamps. 1932. w. $3.90. H. L. Lindquist Pubns., 153 Waverly Place, N.Y. 10014. Illus., adv. Circ: 30,000.

Bk. rev: Occasional. *Aud:* Ga, Sh, Jh. *Rv:* M. *Jv:* B.

A weekly newspaper for the new and veteran collector. Covers the world-wide concerns of philatelists: developments in collecting, and new issues and discoveries. Calendars of events and approaching sales are useful to serious collectors, and "Stamp Market Tips" by John G. Ross serve investor interests. In addition to short news items there is usually a two-page feature article on some interesting or unusual phase of philately. Reviews of stamp catalogues serve a limited reference purpose. There are black and white illustrations of new stamps.

Western Stamp Collector. 1931. semi-w. $2.50. William W. Wylie. Van Dahl Pubns., Box 10, Albany, Ore. 97321. Illus. Circ: 33,877.

Bk. rev: Notes, critical. *Aud:* Ga, Sh, Jh. *Rv:* M. *Jv:* B.

A newspaper of some 12 to 28 pages which covers the whole of the world of stamps but places emphasis on the issues of the United States, United Nations and Canada. Short articles are primarily concerned with current issues. Some present historical background, e.g., "The First Official United States Air Mail." An editorial column, "It's Worth Mentioning," furnishes odds and ends of interest to stamp collectors, ranging from new catalog announcements to notes about clubs and collectors. The editor is quite competent and the general writing style can be appreciated by anyone from the expert to the beginning collector in the grade schools. While not as large or as extensive in coverage as *Linn's Weekly Stamp News*, this has the advantage of more frequent publication.

Workbasket. 1935. m. $1.50. Mary I. Sullivan. Modern Handcraft, Inc., 4251 Pennsylvania Ave., Kansas City, Mo. 64111. Illus., adv. Circ: 1,450,000.

Aud: Ga. *Rv:* L. *Jv:* B.

While this is primarily for women who sew (knitting and sewing account for the title), it goes somewhat beyond the traditional workbasket. In addition to the illustrated needlework projects and instructions for specific types of sewing, there are short articles on gardening, home ceramics and recipes. The magazine is keyed for the woman who is looking for practical help, not advice or suggestions on how to improve the world. Because it includes more than sewing, and is monthly instead of semi-annual, it is a serious contender in libraries for the position held by *McCall's Needlework & Crafts*.

CRIMINOLOGY AND LAW ENFORCEMENT

Indexes and Abstracts

British Humanities Index, Chemical Abstracts, Index to Legal Periodicals, Psychological Abstracts, Public Affairs Information Service. (For annotations, see Indexes and Abstracts Section.)

American Journal of Correction. 1920. bi-m. $2. Roberts J. Wright. Amer. Correctional Assn., 2642 University Ave., St. Paul, Minn. 55114. Illus., index, adv. Circ: 7,685. Reprint: Kraus, Abrahams.

Indexed: PAIS. *Bk. rev:* Various numbers, lengths. *Aud:* Sa, Ac. *Rv:* H. *Jv:* B.

The official publication of several organizations dealing with prisons and prisoners (National Jail Assn., etc.). Contributors are almost always those actively engaged in prison work. The emphasis is decidedly progressive with a good part of each issue going to innovations and new programs for rehabilitation. Of considerable value to the serious student and one of the most reliable sources of information in this field.

British Journal of Criminology; delinquency and deviant social behaviour. 1950. q. $11. Edward Glover, Emanual Miller & J. E. Hall-Williams. Fred B. Rothman & Co., 57 Leuning St., South Hackensack, N.J. 07606. Index, adv. Circ: 1,500.

Indexed: BritHum, PAIS, PsyAb. *Bk. rev:* 7–10, 500 words, signed. *Aud:* Sa, Ac. *Rv:* H. *Jv:* A.

With a decided emphasis on the psychology and sociology of juvenile delinquency, this British journal is of use in colleges and universities as well as to correction officers. Has a good section, "Current Survey and Methodology," which includes several research reports. Its approach is considerably more international than that of most American journals, e.g., "Drug Offenders in Israel, A Survey," and "Crime and Social Class in Denmark." Although admittedly for the specialist, it is of such high general quality as to be considered by any academic or public library.

Criminologist. 1966. q. $4.20. Nigel Morland. Forensic Publishing Co., Ltd., 9 Old Bailey, London E.C. 4. Illus., index, adv.

Bk. rev: Various numbers, lengths. *Aud:* Ga, Sa, Ac, Jc. *Rv:* M. *Jv:* B.

"The views and the experiences of the world's leading authorities on all matters relating to crime." Features some 14 articles by scholars who write with verve and style. The editor strikes a nice balance between professional interests and matters fascinating to any detective story fan, e.g., the article "Anatomy of the Lock" is a combination history and advisory piece, and "Post Mortem Fingerprinting" notes certain problems after rigor mortis. Correspondence and book reviews round out the magazine. An invaluable periodical for experts as well as mystery fans.

FBI Law Enforcement Bulletin. 1931. m. Free. Federal Bureau of Investigation, U.S. Dept. of Justice, Washington, D.C. 20535. Illus.

Aud: Sa, Ac. *Rv:* M. *Jv:* C.

This covers scientific crime detection, legal aspects of importance to arresting officers, and practical ideas useful to the efficient operation of police departments. Each issue contains a message from J. Edgar Hoover emphasizing theory and policymaking aspects of law enforcement. Scientific detection is reflected in such titles as "Handgun Cartridge Texts," "Document Examination from a Photocopy," and "A Look at Codes and Ciphers." Articles like "Fingerprint Records for the Small Department" and "Stake Out Teams" have practical suggestions for the working policeman. Recent articles have covered the importance of legal aspects of making arrests. The low rating here is not so much because of the quality of the magazine, but rather as a warning that within the field there are much better general works, as well as scholarly periodicals. Because of the publicity generated by Hoover and the FBI, too often this has been picked up simply because of the name, not because of content. It is good (and, it should be noted, free), but comparatively speaking, way down the list except for special libraries, or large collections.

Federal Probation; a journal of corrective philosophy and practice. 1936. q. Free. Victor H. Evjen. Administrative Office of the United States Courts, in cooperation with Bureau of Prisons of the U.S. Dept. of Justice, Supreme Court Bldg., Washington, D.C. 20544. Illus, index. Circ: 23,000. Microform: UM. Reprint: Kraus, Abrahams.

Indexed: LegPer. *Bk. rev:* 11–13, 1,000 words, signed. *Aud:* Ga, Sa, Ac, Jc. *Rv:* H. *Jv:* V.

The correctional approach to crime prevention and control, of use to sociologists, psychologists, social workers, educators and correctional officers. Broadens its appeal by including occasional articles on theory, for example: "A Multiple Theory of Juvenile Delinquency," "Trends in Theories Regarding Juvenile Delinquents and Their Implications for Treatment Programs," and "A Look at Prison History." It has excellent reviews of current literature as well as abstracts of significant articles in the leading periodicals of the field. Abstracts of articles in foreign journals and of those appearing in the popular press are also included. The fact that it is free, coupled with the broad scope, makes it an ideal acquisition for almost any type or size library where there is an interest in this area.

International Police Academy Review. 1967. q. Free. Office of Public Safety, Agency for International Development, Dept. of State, Washington, D.C. 20523. Illus. Circ: 4,000 English; 3,000 Spanish.

Aud: Sa, Ac, Jc. *Rv:* M. *Jv:* B.

Reflects the increased attention to criminology and criminal apprehension in a mass society. While its main purpose is stated to be to "provide an academic environment for discussion of police problems," its primary value lies in its emphasis on the international aspects of crime control. Typical articles include: "Resources Control in Vietnam," "Marijuana Eradication," "Feminine Police Corps" and "The Blue Berets of the Somali Republic." Its appeal is more to practicing policeman and police department executive, but scholarly criminologists would find informative its descriptions of international situations.

Issues in Criminology. 1965. semi-ann. $4. Thomas Murton. Sch. of Criminology, 101 Haviland Hall, Univ. of California, Berkeley, Calif. 94720. Illus., index. Circ: 700. Microform: UM.

Bk. rev: 4–5, lengthy, signed. *Aud:* Sa, Ac. *Rv:* H. *Jv:* B.

Reflects the increasing movement of crime control and detection into the university. Includes historical papers, philosophical discussions of modern jurisprudence and emphasis on abnormal behavior. Each issue has a main topic, for example: "Criminal Responsibility" and "Police and the Community."

Journal of Criminal Law, Criminology and Police Science. See Law Section.

National Sheriff. 1948. bi-m. Membership, $2; Non-members, $5. Ferris E. Lucas. National Sheriff's Assn., Inc., 1250 Connecticut Ave., N.W., Washington, D.C. 20036. Illus., index, adv. Circ: 21,022.

Aud: Sa, Ac. *Rv:* M. *Jv:* C.

The type of professional journal rarely seen by laymen, but of interest because of its position on issues. It seeks to instill in its readers the viewpoint that the individual who commits a crime should be punished for that crime, and tends to look askance at sociological and psychological theories which would absolve the criminal of his guilt. Summed-up by the editor :"While the root causes of crime may someday be eliminated from society, until then the suggestion of Messrs. Gilbert and Sullivan that the punishment fit the crime may have to suffice." Presentation is direct, honest and of value for anyone who seeks a broader understanding of law enforcement.

DANCE

Indexes and Abstracts

Music Index, Readers' Guide to Periodical Literature. (For annotations, see Indexes and Abstracts Section.)

Ballroom Dance Magazine. 1960. m. $4. Helen Wicks Reid. Rudolf Orthwine, 268 W. 47th St., New York, N.Y. 10036. Illus., adv. Circ: 50,000.

Bk. rev: Irreg., signed. *Aud:* Sa, Ga. *Rv:* L. *Jv:* B.

Written for interested laymen and ballroom dance instructors. The articles, the regular feature "What's in the News," and other columns cover such topics as the latest dance crazes, news of social events and dance clubs, dancers, contests, opinions concerning the state of ballroom dancing, where to dance and instructions for learning steps. Anything of interest to people who like to dance is included. Record suggestions and hints for teaching are provided to help the dance instructor. A nice combination of education and fun, and recommended for at least a trial subscription where there is an interest in dance.

Ballet Today. 1946. 6/yr. $3.50. Mrs. Estelle Herf. I. E. Herf, 21 Parkside, Wimbledon, London S.W. 19. Illus., adv. *Bk. rev:* 5–8, ½ page, signed. *Aud:* Ga, Ac, Jc, Sh. *Rv:* H. *Jv:* B.

A British review which presents comprehensive international coverage of the dance. There probably is no better single source of current dance reviews. The reviews are frank, balanced and evaluative. Articles which vary in length from a paragraph to several pages cover news about dancers, companies and choreographers. Biographies appear frequently and record reviews are a regular feature. Despite its British emphasis, the magazine has wide appeal for anyone of any age interested in the ballet.

Balletopics; la revue du ballet nationale. 1953. q. $2. George MacPherson. National Ballet Guild of Canada, 66 Temperance St., Toronto 1, Ont. Illus., adv. Circ: 10,000.

Aud: Sa, Ac, Jc. *Rv:* L. *Jv:* B.

The purpose of this Canadian report is to record "the day-to-day history, the triumphs, the heartaches and high hopes of the National Ballet of Canada." Eight pages of articles include news concerning the company's performances, explanations of their work and short biographies of the ballet's members. Primarily a regional magazine, recommended for Canadian libraries and larger American collections.

Dance and Dancers. 1950. m. $8.50. Peter Williams. Hansom Books Ltd., 16 Buckingham Palace Rd., London S.W. 1. Illus., adv. Circ: 19,000.

Aud: Sa, Ga, Ac, Jc. *Rv:* M. *Jv:* B.

A nicely illustrated 50-page magazine, issued in England but international in its coverage of ballet and modern dance. Excellent reviews of recitals, articles on dance and dancers, education, and all topics of interest to both the professional and the viewer. Particularly useful for the many illustrations, usually photographs, which make up a good part of the content. News notes, record reviews and some general gossip. In view of its scope, of interest to students and laymen alike, and a good acquisition for medium to large public and academic libraries.

Dance Magazine. 1926. m. $8. Lydia Joel. Dance Magazine, Inc., 268 W. 47th St., New York, N.Y. 10036. Illus., adv. Circ: 32,000. Microform: UM.

Indexed: RG. *Bk. rev:* irreg., various lengths, signed. *Aud:* Ga, Ac, Jc, Ht. *Rv:* M. *Jv:* V.

Coverage of ballet, modern, variety and ethnic dancing. Each issue contains approximately ten articles, three or four pages in length, which treat the theory and practice of dance. Reviews of performances and excellent formal and informal photographs of dancers are always included. "Presstime News" provides international information about the activities of dance companies, specific dancers and schools. Biographies of dancers are featured monthly. While primarily for adults, some high school students will find it of interest, and it should be in any library serving teachers of the dance from senior high schools to universities.

Dance News. 1942. m. $3. Anatole Chujoy. 119 W. 57th St., New York, N.Y. 10019. Illus., adv. Circ: 14,500.

Aud: Sa, Ac, Jc. *Rv:* M. *Jv:* B.

International coverage of the current dance scene in tabloid format. Comprehensive news concerning performances, dancers, choreographers, schools, colleges and companies and other related items of interest to dance fans is presented. The paper which runs approximately 20 pages also contains evaluative reviews of performances. An excellent source for dance news, and should be in all larger academic and public library collections.

Dance Perspectives. 1959. q. $7. Selma J. Cohen. Dance Perspectives Foundation, 29 E. 9th St., New York, N.Y. 10003. Illus. Circ: 1,500.

Indexed: MusicI. *Aud:* Sa, Ac, Jc. *Rv:* M. *Jv:* A.

Publishes critical and historical monographs and symposia. Usually an entire issue is devoted to a single topic treated by several authors, or often a single author writes the entire issue except for an introduction. The authors are notable personalities in the dance or in other fields—including designers, musicians and sociologists. Frequently, the author discusses and explains his own work. The cover design, illustrations, typography, etc., are arranged with care to produce a handsome format. This will be of value not only to dance collections, but to any general collection.

Northern Junket. 1950. q. $2.50. Ralph G. Page. 117 Washington St., Keene, N.H. 03431. Circ: 1,000.

Aud: Ga. *Rv:* L. *Jv:* C.

Directed to New England callers and square dancers, this is a typical local publication for dance groups. It presents approximately 40 pages of news, articles, dances and calls and even anecdotes and a few recipes. Usually included are two or three, five- or six-page articles related to square dancing. Hardly essential for most libraries, it serves to indicate the type of material which may be available in the region.

Sets in Order; the magazine of square dancing. 1948. m. $5. Bob Osgood. 462 N. Robertson Blvd., Los Angeles, Calif. 90048. Illus., adv. Circ: 22,463.

Aud: Ga, Sh. *Rv:* L. *Jv:* B.

Published "for and by square dancers and for the general enjoyment of all." In approximately 15 articles per issue, news about club activities, ideas for parties, advice to teachers and opinions on subjects concerning square dancing are presented. Regular features include international notes on square dancing, record reviews, "Caller of the Month," "Feature Fashion" and dances and calls. A yearbook containing the dances presented in *SIO* is available every year. Either, or both, it and *Square Dance Magazine* should be in public and school libraries where there is an interest in the subject.

Square Dance; square dance and round dance. 1945. m. $5. Arvid Olson. Amer. Squares, 1622 N. Rand Rd., Arlington Heights, Ill., 60004. Illus., adv. Circ: 20,000.

Aud: Ga, Sh. *Rv:* L. *Jv:* B.

A good general magazine for the square dance enthusiast, regardless of age. Five or six, two- or three-page articles usually present various aspects of round and square dancing as well as hints for teachers and callers. Many calls and dances are included in each issue. Regular features include record reviews and "National News and Events." Somewhat difficult to differentiate between this and *Sets in Order,* and for most libraries it is a matter of personal taste. The library with square dance enthusiasts should definitely try one, if not both.

DISSIDENT

Indexes and Abstracts

Catholic Periodical and Literature Index, Historical Abstracts, Public Affairs Information Service. (For annotations, see Indexes and Abstracts Section.)

For the most part this list represents the best of the radical dissident publications, whether right, left or off center. "Radical" should be stressed, for such magazines as *The Nation, The New Republic,* the *National Review,* etc., are so well established as to be accepted voices of the liberal or conservative establishment.

The source for objective information on radical works is Robert H. Muller's *From Radical Left to Extreme Right* (Ann Arbor, Mich.: Campus Publishers, 1967). Some 163 publications are annotated with a non-partisan analysis of content. Titles by Muller are indicated by: (*Muller, p.—*) following the annotation. Almost all the annotations here are the work of Mr. Sanford Berman (Formerly the Periodicals Librarian, Research Library, Univ. of California at Los Angeles, now at the Univ. of Zambia).

In selecting and preparing the annotations Mr. Berman was asked to write a brief introduction:

"None of these variously enraged, visionary, discontented, and rebellious magazines represents the American mainstream. None would win a national popularity contest. Few, if any, appear in doctors' waiting rooms. Depending on the reader's viewpoint, some might be derisively termed Fascist, racist, Red, unpatriotic, godless, utopian, Neanderthal, jingoist, reactionary, creeping Socialist, revolutionary, flag-waving, or crackpot. None, however—and this, paradoxically, may be all they have in common—is really happy with the way things are. Moreover, although almost all appeared in Muller's survey, few have ever been stocked by public libraries. And the percentage in most colleges is probably low. Well, then, why bother with them at all? Simply because America is not all mainstream. It is not only Democrats and Republicans, capitalists and trade unionists, Catholics and Presbyterians, *but also* Wobblies and populists, socialists and tycoons, fundamentalists and atheists, white supremacists and egalitarians. In sum, America is diversity and ferment. It is a running battle between tradition and change. It is two unresolved questions: What is the 'good society'? and What are we all about?

Bluntly put, the library that fails adequately to reflect the widespread and long-standing dissidence in American life is a lie. Worse, it is profoundly un-American, for it denies that very vitality, conflict, and color that help to make this country unique.

A word to the hesitant, anxious librarian. While a majority of patrons will certainly find these titles distasteful, the Constitution clearly underwrites such expressions of opinion. As Charles Rembar observes in *The End of Obscenity* (Random House, 1968), "When First Amendment freedoms are involved . . . the majority does not rule. Our fundamental law is designed to protect the dissident and the unpopular."

To conclude on an upbeat. The open-minded reader, even if he can't agree fully with the dissidents, will nonetheless discover in their newspapers and journals much incisive criticism, many creative proposals, a host of genuine grievances that otherwise go unventilated, and often some inspired, engrossing prose.

Civil Libertarian

Censorship Today. 1968. bi-m. $6. Doris Fleishman. 1680 Vine St., Suite 700, Taft Bldg., Hollywood, Calif. 90028. Illus. Circ: 500 now, but expected to reach 5,000.

Bk. rev: 7–8, 10–25 words. *Aud:* Ga. *Rv:* H. *Jv:* B.

Designed to report both "victories—and defeats—in the war concerning freedom of speech and expression," this—in the publisher's words—"is a news magazine that will keep you abreast of the varying interpretations, and the practical results that stem therefrom, of the First Amendment and fundamental belief that censorship is the deadly enemy of freedom and progress." Then follows a datelined roundup of censorship news under such rubrics as "Film," "International," "Publishing," "State," and "Television." Pieces by Stanley Fleishman, the well-known censorship attorney, and the late Alexander Meiklejohn, former President of Amherst College, highlighted the maiden issue. Broader in scope than the *Newsletter on Intellectual Freedom,* but where a choice must be made, the *Newsletter* is preferable for most libraries.

Civil Liberties. 1931. m. (except for Mar.–Apr., and June). 5¢ per issue. Claire Cooper. Amer. Civil Liberties Union, 156 Fifth Ave., New York, N.Y. 10010. Illus., adv. Circ: 125,000.

Bk. rev: 0–5, 125–250 words. *Aud:* Ga, Ac, Jc, Sh. *Rv:* H. *Jv:* B.

Founded in 1920, the ACLU believes "that no one should have the privilege of deciding who is deserving of the rights guaranteed to us under the Constitution. These rights belong to all—*without exception.*" The 8- to 12-page newsletter documents the organization's continuing struggle on behalf of "freedom of inquiry and expression, due process of law, and equality before the law." A typical number reports on the progress of ACLU court cases, details the group's position on issues like abortion and loyalty oaths, and presents symposia on current questions, from juvenile rights and civil disobedience to migrant labor and congressional investigations. (*Muller, p.62.*)

The Ladder; a lesbian review. 1956. m. $5. Barbara Gittings. Daughters of Bilitis, Inc., 3470 Mission St., San Francisco, Calif. 94110. Illus.

Bk. rev: Grouped, 5–6, signed. *Aud:* Ga, Ac, Jc. *Rv:* M. *Jv:* B.

Published by a woman's organization "for the purpose of promoting the integration of the homosexual into society by education of the lesbian . . . education of the public . . . encouragement of and participation in responsible research

dealing with homosexuality." Each pocket-sized 32- to 40-page issue contains fiction, poetry, book reviews, and one or two articles on some aspect of the lesbian in society. The stories are fair, the book reviews excellent, and the articles instructive—particularly for the average layman who may have little or no understanding of the problems faced by lesbians in our society. The almost total lack of reliable information in this area, at least in terms of magazines, warrants serious consideration of a subscription by many libraries. The publishing group has issued a graded bibliography: *The Lesbian in Literature* (Gene Damon & Lee Stuart, 1967. 80p. pap. $2.) which is unannotated and arranged by author. It is a reliable, well constructed work which should be in a number of libraries. See also, *Tangents.*

Newsletter on Intellectual Freedom. 1952. bi-m. $3. LeRoy C. Merritt. Amer. Library Assn., 50 E. Huron St., Chicago, Ill. 60611. Index. Circ: 1,953.

Bk. rev: 3–4, 500 words, signed. *Aud:* Ga, Ac, Jc. *Rv:* H. *Jv:* B.

Reporting on all matters about censorship, but particularly those items which affect libraries, the *Newsletter* offers the best single source of current information on intellectual freedom for librarians. A typical issue covers national news about attempts to remove this or that book from a library, new laws or interpretations of the law, and a number of succinct reviews of new books on the problems of censorship and intellectual freedom. There is a minimum of ALA business, although usually full enough reports on the activities of the ALA Committee on Intellectual Freedom which sponsors the publication. Should be in all libraries, regardless of size or type.

Tangents (Formerly: *One Magazine*). 1953. m. $7.50. Don Slater. One, Inc., 3473½ Cahuenga Blvd., Hollywood, Calif. 90028. Illus., index. Circ: 5,000.

Bk. rev: 2–3, 250 words, signed. *Aud:* Ga, Sa, Ac, Jc. *Rv:* M. *Jv:* B.

A pocket-sized 32-page magazine devoted to the homosexual and his position in our society. The tone is serious, the level of writing fair to excellent, the editorial point of view clear: the homosexual is a human being who should not be treated as a criminal or a far-out sexual deviate. The four to five articles survey legal problems, the portrayal of the homosexual in films and books, meetings of local groups, and the ever recurring censorship and harassment by the law. The book reviews usually deal critically with some aspect of sex studies, and from time to time there is a short poem or story. Letters, understandably not signed, finish off each issue. As the editor points out: "More than 17 million American citizens form a minority group which is considered outcast." The magazine attempts to fight for these individuals, to call for freedom of sexual expression, and to give readers a sense of belonging to "a significantly large minority of our citizens." An important magazine for many libraries, particularly academic and large public. See also, the sister publication, *The Ladder.*

Peace

News Notes. 1949. bi-m. Free. Arlo Tatum. Central Committee for Conscientious Objectors, 2016 Walnut St., Philadelphia, Pa. 19103. Circ: 10,000.

Aud: Sa, Ac, Jc. *Rv:* H. *Jv:* B.

In four to six pages, *News Notes* matter-of-factly describes individual cases of draft resistance and conscientious objection, indicates changes in Selective Service law and procedure, reports on pacifist activity in the U.S. and overseas, cites evidence of disaffection within the Armed Forces, and in the "Court Reporter" section lists arrests, indictments, and convictions of objectors and noncooperators. The Committee, whose chief purpose is "to maintain freedom of conscience," publishes a *Handbook for Conscientious Objectors,* now in its 9th edition, which has sold more than 70,000 copies. (*Muller, p.82.*)

The Peacemaker. 1948. Every 3 wks. $3. Ernest R. Bromley. Peacemaker Movement, 10208 Sylvan Ave. (Gano), Cincinnati, Ohio 45241. Illus. Circ: 2500.

Aud: Ga, Ac, Jc, Sh. *Rv:* M. *Jv:* B.

A well-printed, eight-page newsletter which reports on civil disobedience, primarily to the draft, and nonviolent action against war. The paper is particularly useful to those who advocate noncooperation with the draft, and features a national "Resistance Calendar" which gives names and addresses of nonregistrants, acts of draft severance, arrests, trials and sentences. Fuller news items report on major activities of the draft resisters, and include letters from those sentenced or about to make the long trip to jail. The whole gives a certain amount of unity to the movement, a feeling of identity for the reader who may be contemplating draft resistance or suffering the results of failure to register; those who have little feeling for the matter one way or another cannot help but be impressed by the sincerity and usually the sacrifice of the young men who follow the philosophy of the organization to the jail cell. The newsletter also reports on the continuing fight against paying income tax to support the war, activities of the FBI and other law enforcement agencies in harassing members and sympathizers, and shorter notes on violations of civil rights. An important addition for all high school, public and most academic libraries. (*Muller, pp.50–51.*)

Peace News. w. $10. Roger Barnard, Peter Willis, Bob Overy, Kevin McGrath. 5 Caledonian Rd., Kings Cross, London N.1. Illus., adv. Circ: 6,000.

Bk. rev: 0–3, 400–550 words. *Aud:* Ga, Ac, Jc. *Rv:* H. *Jv:* B.

"An international weekly newspaper for people who are interested in world affairs and prepared to consider radical solutions to social and international problems," *Peace News* concentrates on anti-war activity but also deals with nonviolence, political repression (e.g., in Greece and South Africa), racial discrimination, urban problems, "pop" culture, and worldwide turmoil (e.g., the Biafra secession and French student revolt). Staffers and contributors are mainly English and American.

Reporter for Conscience's Sake. 1942. m. $1. National Service Board for Religious Objectors, 550 Washington Bldg., 15th & New York Ave., N.W., Washington, D.C. 20005. Circ: 5,000.

Aud: Sa, Ac, Jc, Sh. *Rv:* M. *Jv:* B.

A four-page newsletter, published for the information of conscientious objectors. The sponsoring group is an organization founded during World War II, made up of Quakers, Mennonites and Brethren. Articles touch on every matter of concern to a C.O. or anyone involved with the situation, e.g., law and regulations affecting conscientious objectors, procedures available to them, their experiences in the processes of classification and alternate service assignments, court cases, and general news. The whole is objective, certainly of considerable interest to any young man who may have questions concerning the draft law. Should be of particular value in any library serving youth, particularly high schools. (*Muller, p.85.*)

Sane World. 1961. m. $3. National Committee for a Sane Nuclear Policy, 17 E. 45 St., New York, N.Y. 10016. Circ: 20,000.

Bk. rev: 1, 600 words, signed. *Aud:* Ga, Ac, Jc, Sh. *Rv:* M. *Jv:* B.

A six-page newsletter "of action on disarmament and the peace race." The organization takes a left-liberal position on international affairs, urging the United States away from the position of "self-appointed" world policeman and toward a position of greater international cooperation and efforts in disarmament. Each number includes news concerning various aspects of disarmament, the Vietnam War, politics, etc. Members are nonpartisan, from every walk of life and political party, but united in the drive for peace. A worthwhile addition for any library. (*Muller, p.86.*)

WRL News. 1940. bi-m. Free. Jim Peck. 5 Beekman St., New York, N.Y. 10038. Circ: 8,000. Microform: UM.

Aud: Sa, Ac, Jc, Sh. *Rv:* M. *Jv:* B.

Published by the War Resisters League (which early in 1968 affiliated with the Committee for Nonviolent Action), this is a four- to six-page newsletter. Other than its advocacy of nonviolence, WRL does not posit a definite political or social program; the beliefs of its members vary widely, and the League "encourages the widest experimentation" within the boundaries of pacifism. The newsletter generally contains short articles and news items on various aspects of the peace movement. (*Muller, pp.88–89.*)

War/Peace Report. 1961. m. $5. Richard Hudson. 300 E. 46th St., New York, N.Y. 10017. Illus., adv. Circ: 6,000. Microform: UM.

Indexed: PAIS. *Bk. rev:* 2–6, 200 words, signed. *Aud:* Ga, Ac, Jc, Sh. *Rv:* M. *Jv:* B.

Published by the Center for War/Peace Studies, a program of the New York Friends Group. Its editor sums up its purpose as a platform for "reports on world crisis areas and analysis of the long-term problems of achieving peace. It also serves as a forum for the airing of various views on foreign policy and international affairs. It is the only American magazine devoted solely to the question of peace." The whole is objective, authoritative, and has featured such outstanding writers as Hans J. Morgenthau, Reinhold Niebuhr, Norman Thomas, Erich Fromm, Norman Cousins and Juan Bosch. In addition to short reviews, it carries one or two essay reviews in each issue. There are short reports, too, on organizational activities relating to world peace. An excellent magazine with a definite point of view which deserves a place in most libraries. (*Muller, p.87.*)

WIN Magazine. 1965. semi-m (except July, Aug., Dec., when m). $5. Paul Johnson. War Resisters League, 5 Beekman St., New York, N.Y. 10038. Illus., adv. Circ: 5,000.

Bk. rev: 2, 500 words. *Aud:* Ga, Ac. *Rv:* H. *Jv:* A.

"Joy, affirmation, chaos, flowers to the enemy. Political non-violence, psychedelic pacifism, terror to the Old Left, *WIN* is a radical-pacifist magazine written for and by the front line activists of the peace and non-violent movement in America." So *WIN* characterizes itself. Produced by the 45-year-old WRL, in cooperation with the N.Y. Workshop in Nonviolence, and hostile to "bureaucratic statism," each issue · fuses analysis of national and world affairs with *engagé* poetry, accounts of civil disobedience and imprisonment, news of deserters and draft resisters, and appraisals of the "now scene," from rock music to offbeat cinema. The League also issues a free, bi-monthly bulletin *WRL News*, rich in pacifist philosophy as well as nitty gritty reports from the streets and induction centers. (*Muller, p.88.*)

Left of Center

ADA World. 1947. m. Membership (Non-members, $5). Americans for Democratic Action, 1223 Connecticut Ave., N.W., Washington, D.C. 20036. Circ: 26,000.

Aud: Ga, Ac. Jc. *Rv:* M. *Jv:* B.

A tabloid which is the official voice of Americans for Democratic Action, this features from three to five articles per issue. The other half is given over to news items, an editorial column and letters. Through legislative and political action and education, the ADA supports liberal foreign and political policies. In view of its major links with the Democratic party, it should be found in most medium to large libraries. (*Muller, p.15.*)

Catholic Worker. 1939. m. (Sept.–June, bi-m). $25. Dorothy Day, 36 E. 1st Street, New York, N.Y. 10003. Illus. Circ: 80,000.

Indexed: CathI. *Aud:* Ga, Ac, Jc. *Rv:* M. *Jv:* B.

The official organ of the Catholic Worker Movement, it preaches a peaceful revolution of Christian communism

akin to many conceptions of the early church. It is not supported by the Church, but is the voice of a radical political offshoot of the Church. It is anti-Vietnam, pro-black, and has a long history of interest in migrant workers' problems. It is often interesting and has frequent striking woodcuts. However, it has little detail that is not available from many other sources. Its major interest is as an example of a particular genre of political/moral thought. (*Muller, p.20.*)

CAW! 1968. bi-m. $5 for 12 issues. Jerry Badanes. Students for a Democratic Society, Box 332, Cooper Station, New York, N.Y. 10003. Illus., adv.

Aud: Ac, Jc, Sh. *Rv:* H. *Jv:* B.

The first national magazine for the militant student group reflects the varied interests of the members, from revolution to poetry. A typical 86-page issue included songs; a report on the Foreign Policy Association and its fingers in the educational packet; "Great Decisions"; an essay on civil disobedience by Bertolt Brecht; Walter Lowenfels on "The Poem and Revolution"; a brief survey of the street theatre in New York and China; a review of *Black Poetry;* a fascinating account of Vietnamese Le Van Luong as a prisoner of the French; and a long piece by Fidel Castro on intellectual property. The whole is printed on newsprint with a scattering of songs and poetry. While badly in need of editing, the thoughts come through well enough, and it is a much above average publication for young people. In view of the diversified approach to politics and art, it should be found in all academic libraries, and in many high schools.

Dissent. 1954. bi-m. $3.50. Irving Howe. Dissent Publishing Corp., 509 Fifth Ave., New York, N.Y. 10017. Circ: 7,500. Microform: UM. Reprint: Kraus, Abrahams.

Bk. rev: 3–5, 800–3,100 words. *Aud:* Ga, Ac, Jc. *Rv:* H. *Jv:* V.

"Devoted to the ideas and values of democratic socialism," including "public ownership and control of basic sectors of the economy," *Dissent* prints "full-scale, fundamental essays," as well as "topical comment, reportage," and "short criticisms of movies, plays, books." Among its editors and contributors are poverty-warrior Michael Harrington; novelists Norman Mailer and Jeremy Larner; psychoanalyst-philosopher Erich Fromm; anthropologist Stanley Diamond; labor specialist Paul Jacobs; and Norman Thomas, long-time Socialist Presidential candidate (now deceased). The broad subject scope encompasses union democracy, the "Negro Revolution," developments within the Communist sphere, the concentration of corporate wealth, American foreign policy, and ghetto education. Just as the title-page announces, "There is no effort made to exact editorial concensus or uniformity." However, the emphasis is largely humanistic, anti-authoritarian, skeptical, and pragmatic.

The journal has registered many *coups*, literary and political alike, printing the first English versions of Gunter Grass' "Open Letter to Chancellor Kiesinger"; "Hands," a short story by Nikolai Arzhak; and Andrei Sinyavsky's controversial essay, "On Socialist Realism"; as well as Claude Brown's "Harlem, My Harlem" and Mailer's "White Negro." A collection of *Dissent* articles, selected by Howe, appeared as *The Radical Imagination* (New American Library, 1967). (*Muller, p.23*)

Despite Everything. 1964. q. $2. P. S. MacDonald and Alan Dutscher. 1937½ Russell St., Berkeley, Calif. 94703. Illus. Circ: 1,000. Microform: UM.

Aud: Ga, Ac, Jc, Sh. *Rv:* M. *Jv:* B.

A 30- to 50-page lithographed magazine which champions the politics of the New Left, university revolutionary movements, the civil rights action groups, etc. The July, 1968, issue included a detailed article on the Black Panther Party by Eldridge Cleaver, documents of the German student protest by F. Lohenbill, an exchange of letters by Alan Dutscher and M. Grossman on resistance to the draft and a translation of a statement made by a German university student to the court. The whole is primarily the work of young men and women in their late teens and early twenties, and it is exceptionally well written and thought out, and ably presented. That not all readers will agree with the left-of-center views is to be expected, but all younger people (and not a few oldsters) who wish to keep up with student political action movements will find this is a major sounding board. It should be particularly popular in colleges and universities, and will have an audience among more thoughtful high school students, regardless of their political persuasions. (*Muller, p.22.*)

The Guardian. 1948. w. $7. Jack A. Smith. Weekly Guardian Associates, Inc., 197 E. 4th St., New York, N.Y. 10009. Illus., adv. Circ: 28,000. Microform: UM. Reprint: Abrahams.

Bk. rev: 0–1, 1,000–1,600 words. *Aud:* Ga, Ac. *Rv:* H. *Jv:* B.

Originally established as the *National Guardian* to promote the Independent Progressive Party and Henry Wallace's presidential campaign, the 20-page tabloid has now become a major organ for the New Left, reporting events along the whole spectrum from SDS and SNCC to Progressive Labor and the Black Panthers. Columns on "The Movement" and "World in Revolution" appear weekly, together with film, music, theater, and book reviews. Correspondents and columnists include Irwin Silber, editor of *Sing Out;* Carl Braden of the Southern Conference Educational Fund; Wilfred Burchett, an authority on Southeast Asia; SNCC's Julius Lester, who writes "From the Other Side of the Tracks"; Anna Louise Strong in Peking; William J. Pomeroy in London; and Jaime Alvarez del Vayo, once a minister in the Spanish Republican Government.

A "coordinating committee" runs the paper, which "sees its role as helping to develop a radical movement for social change as opposed to a liberal reform movement within the United States." Politically, according to a May 18, 1968 editorial, the *Guardian* is "dedicated to the principle that the capitalist system which governs the United States and exploits the world must be dismantled and replaced by a socialist model . . ." (*Muller, p.35.*)

I. F. Stone's Weekly. 1952. bi-w. (since Jan., 1968). $5. I. F. Stone. 5618 Nebraska Ave., N.W., Washington, D.C. 20015. Circ: 30,000.

Aud: Ga, Ac, Jc, Sh. *Rv:* H. *Jv:* B.

Essentially a one-man operation, the *Weekly* embodies the unique viewpoint and background of a veteran journalist and independent radical whose "leading heroes" are Spinoza and Bertrand Russell. Stone, an avowed "peacenik" and champion of the underdog—whether poor Appalachian white, Mexican-American farm worker, or black Mississippi sharecropper—employs the essay, direct quote, trenchant caption, and telling juxtaposition as means to highlight issues and expose what he regards as doubletalk or hypocrisy. In addition, he often prints valuable material otherwise played down or ignored by the mass media: excerpts from Congressional debates and committee hearings, foreign press dispatches, official briefings, and research on unpopular or troubling topics. The most enduring of Stone's *Weekly* articles, together with his many contributions to the *New York Review of Books,* have been confected into two books, *The Haunted Fifties* (Random House, 1963) and *In Time of Torment* (Random House, 1967). For more data on the *Weekly*'s origin and influence see: "I. F. Stone: The Journalist as Pamphleteer," by Sol Stern in the Feb., 1968, *Ramparts*. (*Muller, p.28*)

Independent Socialist. 1967. m. $1. Kit Lyons. Independent Socialist Clubs of America, P.O. Box 910, Berkeley, Calif. 94701, or P.O. Box 481, Cooper Station, New York, N.Y. 10003. Illus., adv. Circ: 5,000.

Bk. rev: 0–2, 375–2,200 words. *Aud:* Ga, Ac. *Rv:* H. *Jv:* B.

Aggressively Marxist, but undoctrinaire; committed to "collective ownership and democratic control of the economy"; down on Washington, yet equally disenchanted with Moscow and Peking, the eight-page *Independent Socialist* functions as a conduit for ISCA thought, "a rallying point for the rebirth of 'socialism-from-below,'" and a source of hard-to-get information on grass roots militancy among workers, students, and minorities. Not a large group, the ISCA has nevertheless emerged as the most influential single force in creating "Peace and Freedom" parties, especially in California and New York, and numbers in its ranks such nationally-known opinion makers as Mike Hannon, recent candidate for Los Angeles County District Attorney; Hal Draper, co-editor of *New Politics;* Mario Savio, leader of the Berkeley "Free Speech Movement"; Marvin Garson, publisher of the "underground" San Francisco *Express-Times;* and Kim Moody, a labor organizer. Subscribers also receive occasional pamphlet supplements.

LID News Bulletin. 1960. irreg. Membership, $7.50. League for Industrial Democracy, 112 E. 19th St., New York, N.Y. 10003.

Aud: Ga, Ac, Jc. *Rv:* M. *Jv:* B.

With increasing polarization on both ends of the political spectrum, "moderately Radical" groups and ideas tend to be overlooked or minimized. The League for Industrial Democracy, chaired by poverty-warrior Michael Harrington, fits this neglected category. Its *News Bulletin,* featuring reports and articles by Bayard Rustin, Director of the A. Philip Randolph Institute and leading proponent of the "Freedom Budget"; Tom Kahn, who some time ago authored the incisive "Economics of Equality"; Irving Howe, editor of *Dissent;* and labor historian Thomas R. Brooks, explores such immediate issues and problems as teacher strikes, coalition politics, unemployment, union democracy, ghetto schools, air polution, and urban rot—all from the viewpoint of the non-Communist Left. Membership includes not only the *News Bulletin,* but also timely pamphlets.

Leviathan (Formerly: *Viet Report*). 1965. 9/yr. $5. 133 W. 72nd St., New York, N.Y. 10023. Illus., adv. Circ: 35,000.

Aud: Ga, Ac, Jc, Sh. *Rv:* H. *Jv:* B.

Known as *Viet Report* until March 1, 1969, this began primarily as an anti-war report on Vietnam of some 20 to 50 pages. The editors and authors represent all political views, but are united on one major point: the war must be ended, and the total American policy in Asia must be shifted to peaceful methods of helping peoples and nations. Although early issues of the magazine concentrated solely on Vietnam, it has broadened its focus to include all of American policy, foreign *and* domestic, and in so doing has emerged as a magazine with distinct and coherent leftist politics. Classified by some as the voice of the New Left, it is considerably more than that, and some of the views expressed are held by those who might not sympathize with the more extreme of the New Left ideologies. On the whole an objective treatment of material not often found in other American magazines and newspapers, and of considerable value for the most public, academic and senior high school libraries. (*Muller, p.51.*)

Liberation; an independent monthly. 11/yr. $7. Dave Dellinger. 5 Beekman St., New York, N.Y. 10038. Illus., adv. Circ: 9,000. Microform: UM.

Indexed: INeg, PAIS. *Bk. rev:* 1, 1,500 words. *Aud:* Ga, Ac, Jc. *Rv:* H. *Jv:* A.

An editorial in the March, 1968, issue proclaimed that "the money changers and money makers, and the military and civilian militarist establishment which they have spawned, have fashioned a culture that spews alienation, dehumanization, racism and imperialism. . . . To us at this moment in history is given little choice, for we have no healthy society, free of war and exploitation, to opt into. Unless we and tens of millions of others first opt out of the diseased one no healthy one will ever be constructed." Accordingly, news and analyses underscore revolutionary experiments abroad (e.g., Cuba), nuclear disarmament, the effects of American foreign policy (especially on Vietnam

and the Dominican Republic), and forces for change in the U.S.: "peace-and-freedom" politics, war resistance, and organization among the poor.

Barbara Deming, Paul Goodman, Sidney Lens, and Staughton Lynd compose the Editorial Board (the pacifist-preacher, A. J. Muste, had chaired it until his death in early 1967), while such figures as James Baldwin, Nat Hentoff, poet Lawrence Ferlinghetti, Dorothy Day, editor of the *Catholic Worker,* the late Dr. Martin Luther King, Jr., Lewis Mumford, Nobel Prize-winner Linus Pauling, and Tom Hayden have contributed. Recent numbers included verbatim testimony from the Russell War Crimes Tribunal, "Hanoi Poems" by Father Daniel Berrigan, an eyewitness report from North Vietnam by Dellinger, and a lively exchange on "sex and caste." In 1966, George Braziller published *Seeds of Liberation,* an anthology culled by Paul Goodman from the magazine's first ten years. Murray Kempton, in reviewing the collection, commented: "Who could have thought that there would be so much irony and beauty in what is, at bottom, a trade magazine for persons who practice the art which seems to us the impossible one, the politics of solitary resistance to massed power?" (*Muller, p.32.*)

The Militant; in the interests of the working people. 1928. w. $3. Barry Sheppard. Militant Publishing Assn., 873 Broadway, New York, N.Y. 10003. Illus., adv. Circ: 9,000.

Aud: Sa, Ac. *Rv:* H. *Jv:* C.

Issued by the Trotskyite Socialist Workers Party and proponent of "Revolutionary Socialism," the *Militant* includes a column-long editorial and three regular features—"Black Liberation Notes," "The National Picketline" (a potpourri of labor news), and "The Great Society" (sour vignettes from the bourgeois world)—plus lengthy accounts of fraternal movements abroad; worker, student, and minority-group unrest at home; and rifts between American left-wing activists. Communist parties, whether foreign or domestic, prove frequent objects for criticism. Coverage of the mid-1968 "French Revolution," with an accent on the JCR (Revolutionary Communist Youth), was notably extensive and the editorial stance toward that uprising nearly ecstatic. In remarking on the French experience, the *Militant* endorsed as a general revolutionary formula "the formation of a network of factory committees and committees of action which can organize their combat against capitalism and blaze the trail to a Socialist Republic." (*Muller, p.32.*)

The SWP's youth organization, Young Socialist Alliance, also publishes a bi-monthly magazine, *Young Socialist* (*viz.*).

The Modern Utopian. 1967. bi-m. $4. Richard Fairfield. Tufts Univ., Box 44, Medford, Mass. 02155. Illus., adv.

Aud: Ga, Ac, Jc. *Rv:* H. *Jv:* B.

A 36- to 40-page digest "of the major activities and progress of liberal social change agencies and intentional communities." Each issue includes reports on community living, a digest of social change (covering developments in birth control, capital punishment, civil liberties, etc.), "The hip side of life" (excerpts from various underground newspapers), notes on religion, the music scene, peace movements, activities of Students for a Democratic Society, etc. The method is primarily to use brief excerpts, with proper citations to sources, and include two to four original short articles. As an overview of social activities it is excellent, but falters in that there is little in-depth material. Still, it will serve the sociologist, student, political scientist, educator and anyone who has neither the time nor the inclination to go to the original source material. A useful addition for most academic and medium to large public libraries.

Monthly Review; an independent socialist magazine. 1949. 11/yr. $6. Leo Huberman & Paul M. Sweezy. Monthly Review, Inc., 116 W. 14th St., New York, N.Y. 10011. Index, adv. Circ: 9,000.

Indexed: PAIS. *Bk. rev:* 0–2, 2,200–2,700 words. *Aud:* Ga, Ac. *Rv:* H. *Jv:* B.

Vehemently anti-capitalist, *MR* is "an independent magazine devoted to analyzing, from a socialist point of view, the most significant trends in domestic and foreign affairs." It espouses a complete material restructuring of society, supports "national liberation" movements in the Third World, attacks "American imperialism," looks kindly upon the Soviet Union, and draws heavily upon Frantz Fanon, Che Guevara, Mao Tse-tung, and Regis Debray for insight and inspiration. The editors direct much attention to both Cuba and Vietnam, approving Castro's innovations and favoring an NFL victory. Recent contributors include Eldridge Cleaver, Black Panther Minister of Information; one-time "Wobbly" Harvey O'Connor; Trotsky-biographer Isaac Deutscher; literary critic Maxwell Geismar; Prof. Herbert Marcuse; and CORE leader Floyd B. McKissick. The only continuing feature is Scott Nearing's "World Events" column. An omnibus November, 1967, number joyfully commemorated the 50th anniversary of the Russian Revolution. (*Muller, p.34.*)

People's World. 1938. w. $5. 81 Clementina St., San Francisco, Calif. 94105. Circ: 8,149.

Bk. rev: 1, 500 words, signed. *Aud:* Sa. *Rv:* M. *Jv:* B.

The West Coast counterpart of *The Worker,* this is a tabloid, radical news weekly which speaks for a combination of Communists and, according to the editor, "non-Communists of the Left." While it is primarily a newspaper, it usually carries several in-depth articles (1,000–1,500 words) on politics, the Black Power movement, labor, foreign affairs, anti-war activities, and Mexican-American activities. Two of its 12 pages are devoted to book and film reviews, with occasional reviews of music, theater and the graphic arts. As might be expected, advertising constitutes only 5% of the whole, a near record low for any newspaper, and a bonus feature for the reader who wants news. There are news photos, an occasional drawing, and one sports fea-

ture per issue. The editor reports that "its purpose is to help create a viable, mass political movement on the Left," and its goal, "the socialist reconstruction of American society." While representative of Communistic viewpoints, it is not necessarily a Communist newspaper. (*Muller, pp.43–44.*)

Progressive Labor. 1962. bi-m. $2.50. Milton Rosen. Box 808, Brooklyn, N.Y. 11201. Illus., adv. Circ: 9,000.

Bk. rev: 0–1, 3,200–12,000 words. *Aud:* Ga, Ac. *Rv:* M. *Jv:* B.

Bête noire as much of the orthodox Left as the Right and Center, the Progressive Labor Party seeks to spearhead "the fight for a new way of life—where working men and women own and control their homes, factories, the police, courts, and the entire government on every level." Its magazine proclaims "Non-violence is dead," advocating "humane revolutionary violence" in its place; praises the "Proletarian Cultural Revolution" in China; quotes Mao Tse-tung approvingly; believes that war with China would produce the "total defeat of U.S. imperialism"; comments upon "the fascist takeover in Poland and Czechoslovakia"; charges "collusion between the government . . . companies, and union officials against the workers" in the Anaconda copper strike; acclaims Daniel De Leon as "the towering figure of the early American socialist movement"; describes American elections as "a quadrennial swindle"; claims that the Soviet Union is controlled by "neo-bourgeois counter-revolutionaries"; and resolves to "build a socialist U.S.A." based on "communist principles and the science of Marxism-Leninism." (*Muller, p.47.*) The PLP also issues a monthly, Spanish-English newspaper, *Challenge/Desafio,* priced at $2.00 per year. (*Muller, p.21.*) The Bay Area Branch in California mimeographs a scrappy 18-page newsletter, available free from 948 Market St., San Francisco, Calif. 94102.

Radical America. 1967. bi-m. $3. Paul Buhle. Students for a Democratic Soc., c/o Paul Buhle, 1237 Spaight St., Madison, Wis. 53703. Circ: 2,000.

Bk. rev: 1, 2,500 words. *Aud:* Ga, Ac. *Rv:* H. *Jv:* B.

"New Left"—especially SDS—ideologues and activists not only undertake an earnest and unblinkered assessment of America's recent past, but also seek to fashion a revolutionary program for the future. The editor notes that "particular emphasis is laid upon the Left in its past and present forms, but neo-Marxist and aesthetic-cultural studies are also published." Topics range from "radical theater" and the abortive organizing drive among unemployed miners in Hazard, Kentucky, to Debsian Socialism and the role of intellectuals during the "Red Scare." Although jargon-prone and almost painfully self-critical, *Radical America* well reflects the spirit, strategy, and tactics of the angry young militants hell-bent on turning society inside-out.

Weekly People. 1891. $2. Eric Hass. Weekly People, 116 Nassau St., New York, N.Y. 11201. Circ: 13,000.

Aud: Sa, Ac. *Rv:* M. *Jv:* C.

This paper exists to push the aims and programs of the Socialist Labor Party. The articles are anti-capitalist, anti-communist, and solicitous of a new society. All of the articles tend to build polemical arguments for socialism around specific events or personalities in the news. Obviously propaganda, but sometimes thought provoking. Only for larger library collections. (*Muller, p.53.*)

The Worker. 1922. bi-w. $7. Box 28, Madison Sq. Station, New York, N.Y. 10010. Circ: 17,000.

Aud: Sa, Ac. Rv: M. Jv: B.

Founded as the voice of the Communist Party of the United States, *The Daily Worker* became *The Worker* in 1958, when it changed to twice-weekly status. With the break-up of world-wide Communist ideology, the newspaper found itself in an interesting philosophical position, and its editor now claims that it is a liberal newspaper, definitely *not* an organ of the Communist Party. Be that as it may, much of the material follows the lead of the international group. It is particularly valuable for its accounts of Party activities in France, Italy, and the rest of Europe. The reporting is obviously in left field, and is less trustworthy for its notes on American domestic affairs. Civil rights, labor, politics and the war in Vietnam figure heavily in most issues. This is an essential item for any large library, but can be passed by in favor of more objective, liberal magazines and newspapers in small and medium-sized libraries. (*Muller, p.55.*)

Young Socialist. 1957. m. $1.25. Mary-Alice Waters. Box 471, Cooper Station, New York, N.Y. 10003. Illus., adv. Circ: 10,000.

Bk. rev: 1–2, 1,000–1,500 words, signed. Aud: Ac, Jc, Sh. Rv: L. Jv: B.

The Young Socialist Alliance's magazine for high school and college youth. The 30 pages consist mainly of interviews with people sympathetic to the cause. Carries news of future or past conventions and demonstrations, and an annotated list of causes to support. Articles on controversial topics—the Vietnamese war, Southern elections, Negro voting rights, labor strikes, etc.—form the magazine's feature section. "Young Socialist Notes," relating news from college campuses and the news media, and "Meet Young Socialists in Your Area" are regular columns. The chief value of this magazine is as an information and updating service for members of Socialist organizations, or as means of exposing students within the classroom to current viewpoints of young socialists. (*Muller, p.56.*)

Right of Center

American Mercury. 1924. q. $10. La Vonne Doden Furr. P.O. Box 1306, Torrance, Calif. 90505. Illus., index, adv. Circ: 10,000. Microform: UM. Reprint: Johnson, Abrahams.

Bk. rev: 1, 400–1,600 words. Aud: Ga, Ac. Rv: M. Jv: B.

Originally founded by H. L. Mencken and George Jean Nathan, the magazine in June 1966 incorporated *Western*

Destiny, Folk, and *Northern World.* It describes itself as "bold and unafraid to tell the truth—with a galaxy of authors—America's greatest and most courageous personalities—standing up, as always, for true-blue Americanism." An organ of ultra-Conservatism, the *Mercury* advocates racial purity, "strong, substantial tariff walls," heightened nuclear armament, and "universal nationalism"; denounces water fluoridation, TV, Zionists, the "no-win strategy" in Vietnam, the Warren Commission, liberalized immigration, the progressive income tax, the Federal Reserve System, LSD, the Anti-Defamation League, the GOP's "Eastern Establishment," William F. Buckley, democracy ("a degenerate form of government"), synthetic fertilizers, and "unwashed decadents"; and extols the Pilgrims, Leif Erikson, covered wagons, and Father Coughlin. Occasional pieces also suggest how to combat Communism and offer popular health advice. Writers include Sir John Glubb; Calif. State Sen. John Schmitz; Horace Greeley, Jr.; Phyllis Schafly, author of the best-selling *A Choice Not An Echo;* and Brig. Gen. Clyde J. Watts (Ret.), espouser of "Fourth Dimensional Warfare." Subscribers automatically receive the semi-monthly, 4-page *Washington Observer Newsletter.* (*Muller, p.102.*)

American Opinion. 1958. m. $10. 395 Concord Ave., Belmont, Mass. 02178. Illus., adv. Circ: 36,000. Microform: UM.

Aud: Ga, Ac, Jc. Bk. rev: 5–10, 250–500 words, signed. Rv: L. Jv: B.

The official organ of the John Birch Society. "Official" is used advisedly, for according to *Muller* (p.104) editor Robert Welch states it is not an official Birch publication, "and less than half of its subscribers are members of the John Birch Society." Be that as it may, the tabloid sized magazine plugs the well known radical right notions of the Birchers, and is geared for the man or woman who is ultra conservative. A typical issue features four to five articles on various social, political and economic issues and reports from correspondents in key European and American cities. The style of writing is semi-popular, sometimes satirical. The magazine is informative in that it does give viewpoints rarely found in most magazines of political opinion. The book reviews, often of titles by lesser known publishers, serve to alert the librarian to the more conservative authors and books. Regardless of how the librarian may feel about the John Birch Society, the group has generated enough interest, pro and con, to make her consider the magazine for purchase. As one of the more representative conservative periodicals it deserves a place in any well balanced collection. (*Muller, p.103.*)

Christian Economics. 1948. semi-w. Free. Howard Kirschner. 250 W. 57th St., New York, N.Y. 10019. Circ: 215,000.

Bk. rev: 2, 500 words, signed. Aud: Ga, Ac, Jc, Sh. Rv: L. Jv: B.

The editor reports on this right of center magazine that the magazine "upholds the Constitution of the United States and the limited government which it inaugurated. It favors the free market and the faithful application of Christian principles to economic activities. It is concerned with the application of the Christian ethic to the economic and social problems confronting our country." As the title and statement imply, most of the writing is by Protestant ministers or economists with deep religious convictions. That they are fundamentalists, at least in one area, has gained them a healthy readership. While not everyone can be expected to agree with the approach, it is an interesting one which should be of value to any serious student of economics, politics, or, for that matter, religion. (*Muller, p.108.*)

The Citizen. 1955. m. $4. W. J. Simmons. Citizens Councils of America, 315–325 Plaza Bldg., Jackson, Miss. 39201. Illus., adv. Circ: 40,000.

Bk. rev: 0–1, 1,000 words. *Aud:* Ga, Ac. *Rv:* M. *Jv:* C.

Combining white supremacy with ultra-Conservatism, *Citizen* authors—like John J. Synon, operator of the Patrick Henry Press; Sen. Strom Thurmond; South Carolina industrialist William Lowndes; and Rev. T. Robert Ingraham, a Director of the Association for Christian Schools—inveigh against "latter-day abolitionism," "the white Liberal sickness," and public schools. "The wages of integration and 'black power,'" an editorial maintains, "are violence, anarchy, and death." The Citizens Councils endorse "separate development" as "the way to racial peace," holding that "integration, mixing the unmixable, is the way to race war." The magazine favored George Wallace, candidate of the American Independent Party, for President in 1968. Medford Evans, Managing Editor, also serves as Associate Editor of *American Opinion,* to which he contributes a book column, "De Libris." (*Muller, p.90.*)

The Dan Smoot Report. 1955. w. $10. P.O. Box 9538, Lakewood Station, Dallas, Tex. 75214. Index. Circ: 35,000. Microform: UM.

Aud: Ga. *Rv:* L. *Jv:* B.

A weekly right-wing four-page newsletter which has gained fame because of Mr. Smoot's radio and television broadcasts. Each issue covers a single topic (usually with at least one to four footnotes), e.g., Jan. 29, 1968, a report that "the socialist government of England strangled that once-mighty nation . . . ;" May 27, 1968, a report on slum clearance. The editor is opposed to most federal controls, advocates abolishing income taxes, and is convinced the Civil Rights movement is Communist controlled. In view of the slim contents and relatively high price, not for most libraries, but should be accepted should anyone wish to give a gift subscription. (*Muller, p.110.*)

The Freeman; a monthly journal of ideas on liberty. 1950. m. On request. Paul L. Poirot. Foundation for Eco-

nomic Education, Inc., Irvington-on-Hudson, N.Y. 10533. Illus., adv. Circ: 50,000. Microform: UM, Canner.

Indexed: PAIS. *Bk. rev:* 2–3, 550–1,500 words. *Aud:* Ga, Ac. *Rv:* M. *Jv:* B.

Committed to the market economy and private property, "libertarian" spokesmen like John Chamberlain, Dr. Clarence B. Carson, Erik v. Kuehnelt-Leddihn, Henry Hazlitt, and Dr. Howard Kershner, editor of *Christian Economics,* argue for unrestricted trade and travel, support individual decision-making instead of "government compulsion," claim that "price wars" result from "strikes and other forms of violence" rather than "open competition," and protest "interventionism," whether in the guise of Medicare, protective tariffs, or municipal garbage collection. Unlike some Conservatives, *Freeman* writers do not deny that poverty exists, but maintain that it can be cured through "capitalization." (*Muller, p.115.*)

Human Events. 1944. w. $12.50. Thomas W. Winter. Human Events, Inc., 422 First St., S.E., Washington, D.C. 20003. Illus., adv. Circ: 100,000. Microform: UM. Reprint: Johnson.

Bk. rev: 150 words. *Aud:* Ga, Ac, Jc, Sh. *Rv:* H. *Jv:* V.

"*Human Events,*" according to its masthead, "aims for accurate presentation of the facts. But it is *not* impartial. It looks at events through eyes that are biased in favor of limited constitutional government, local self-government, private enterprise, and individual freedom." Together with such regular features as "This Week's News from Inside Washington," "Capitol Briefs," "Politics '68," and "Spotlight on Congress," each number contains up to a dozen articles by syndicated columnists, among them Ralph de Toledano, author of *Seeds of Treason;* Russell Kirk, outstanding Conservative philosopher; Raymond Moley; Dr. Max Rafferty, California State Superintendent of Public Instruction; Victor Riesel; Henry J. Taylor; and Alice Widener, who publishes the bi-weekly *U.S.A.* Far more moderate in tone than many other Conservative publications, *Human Events* opposes disarmament and school integration, deplores "mob rule" and "academic guerrillas," categorizes the Poor People's Campaign as a "hoax," criticizes public housing for the same reason that most radicals do (that one slum merely replaces another), regards the UN trade and travel blockade against Rhodesia as unjust, warns about "Soviet spy expertise," demands that the U.S. resume bombing North Vietnam, and laments the inaction of the Subversive Activities Control Board. (*Muller, p.120.*)

Liberty Letter. 1960. m., during Congressional sessions. $2. 300 Independence Ave., S.E., Washington, D.C. 20003. Circ: 200,000.

Bk. rev: 3, 300 words, signed. *Aud:* Ga, Ac, Jc, Sh. *Rv:* M. *Jv:* B.

A right of center four- to six-page newsletter, this reports on legislation pending before Congress. It is opposed to all liberal causes, supports the belief that the Communists are behind most of our woes. A recent issue cited Congressmen on an "honor roll" who voted against the Civil Rights Act of 1968, and another number plugged a 12-page tabloid backing George C. Wallace. As it faithfully records Congressional action, the letter has value not only for those who accept its beliefs, but those who are most opposed to its policy—the reader soon becomes familiar with where Congressmen stand on what piece of legislation. (*Muller, p.127.*)

Modern Age. 1957. q. $4. Eugene Davidson. Foundation for Foreign Affairs, Inc., 154 E. Superior St., Chicago, Ill. 60611. Index, adv. Circ: 6,000. Microform: UM. Reprint: Johnson, Abrahams.

Indexed: CathI, HistAb, PAIS. *Bk. rev:* 8–15, 990–3,100 words. *Aud:* Ga, Ac, Jc, Sh. *Rv:* M. *Jv:* B.

Scholarly in form, leisurely and aristocratic in tone, *Modern Age* is the very embodiment of genteel, tradition-rooted, well-schooled Conservatism. Up to 30 pages of rigorous and often scathing book reviews follow lengthy essays by such highly-articulate writers as Frank S. Meyer; Mario Pei, Professor of Romance Languages at Columbia; Francis Russell, author of *Tragedy at Dedham;* Wolfe Mays, Professor of Philosophy at the University of Manchester; and Thomas Molnar, Professor of French Literature at Brooklyn College. Concerns span the contradictions within Communist societies; Cardinal Newman's effect upon English Catholicism; the connection between Tolkien, St. Francis, and Hippies; Soviet letters; postwar art; the *New York Times'* attitude toward Fidel Castro; Paul Goodman's pedagogic theories; and mutations in Marxist-Leninist philosophy. An editorial in the Spring 1968 issue notes with tough-minded satisfaction that "increasingly," whites "are refusing to live with the Negro and the Negro to live with the whites"; one contributor denotes the *political* Bertrand Russell a "total imbecile," dismissing his War Crime Tribunal as a "notorious prank," while another prescribes for the Freudian-author of *Friendship and Fratricide* "a good dose of classical education *cum* discipline from grammar school up"; a reviewer of the Carmichael-Hamilton opus, *Black Power,* talks of "agitators, posing as victims of persecution," who "roam the college campuses and tour the churches, speaking for fat fees on how the souls of black folks are being scarred by race prejudice and proscription"; and James McClellan derides the Warren Court as "the most incompetent . . . ever assembled at any one time." (*Muller, p.131.*)

National Decency Reporter. m. $5. Citizens for Decent Literature, Inc., 5670 Wilshire Blvd., Suite 1680, Los Angeles, Calif. 90036.

Bk. rev: Notes. *Aud:* Ga, Ac. *Rv:* L. *Jv:* C.

Deeply concerned with what it believes to be the growing problem of "pornography" and "sexual perverseness," the *Reporter* chronicles the nationwide campaign by police, legislators, churchmen, and CDL itself against "smut peddlers" and "dirty books." A piece in the May–June, 1968, number severely castigated the several Supreme Court justices who "consistently vote for reversal in obscenity cases."

The New Guard. 1961. m. (except June and Aug.). $4. Arnold Steinberg. Young Americans for Freedom, Inc., 1221 Massachusetts Ave., N.W., Washington, D.C. 20005. Illus., adv. Circ: 25,000. Microform: UM.

Bk. rev: 1–6, 90–1,000 words. *Aud:* Ac. *Rv:* M. *Jv:* B.

To quote a *New Guard* contributor, YAF—established in 1960—seeks to "resist the collectivism and statism that emanate from indigenous Liberalism and simultaneously to repel and overcome the Communist attack upon Western civilization." Oriented toward the Conservative (i.e., Goldwater-Reagan) wing of the Republican Party, the magazine lauds broadcasters Fulton Lewis III and William F. Buckley, contends that Sen. Joseph McCarthy "and his allies proved that the Liberal monolith could be beaten," maintains that former Alabama Governor George Wallace "simply does not qualify as a Conservative, but rather as a Populist-Segregationist," has published essays on the distinction between "traditionalist" and "libertarian" Conservatives, cautions against American universities becoming "havens for revolutionaries and subversives," hails the growth of a two-party system in the South, encourages "a strong foreign policy for the United States," and advocates "private enterprise" plus "individual responsibility." "Report on the Left" and "YAF Around the Nation" are constant features, while recent contributors have included Alan Mackay, National YAF Chairman, and David Friedman, founder of the Harvard Society of Individualists, who declared that "what we must get from the left is the ability to recognize real problems, and the will to find and implement such solutions as may be possible." (*Muller, p.133.*)

The Objectivist. 1962. m. $5. Ayn Rand. 120 E. 34th St., New York, N.Y. 10016. Circ: 21,056.

Aud: Ga, Ac, Jc, Ht. *Rv:* L. *Jv:* B.

Edited by well-known author Ayn Rand, this conservative 16-page magazine features two or three 3,000-word theoretical articles on Objectivism. Special features include events of interests to students of the Nathaniel Branden Institute, and a column on movies, books and current cultural trends. The philosophy of the magazine and the Institute supports individual freedom and initiative and, by extension, *laissez faire* capitalism. The group is violently opposed to what the editor terms "appalling indifference to the wholesale atrocities" of Soviet Russia and Red China. In view of the wide interest in both the author and her philosophy, this is a magazine which will appeal to both laymen and students. (*Muller, p.136.*)

Through to Victory. 11/yr. $2. Rev. Paul C. Neipp. 731 N. Sanders, Ridgecrest, Calif. 93555. Illus., adv.

Aud: Sa. *Rv:* H. *Jv:* B.

Editor Neipp conducts a vigorous, 12-page tabloid crusade—partly through reprints from other rightist journals—against the Communist menace, domestic disorder, liberal theology, ecumenism, moral "permissiveness," hippies, civil disobedience, Black Power, and collectivism. Each issue of this "Conservative monthly publication for Lutheran Laymen for Christ and Country" features a number of keynote slogans, e.g., "Socialism = Communism = Slavery"—"Never forget: all roads to freedom lie through Communism's defeat"—"Register Reds, not rifles." Contributors include Rep. James B. Utt; Edith Kermit Roosevelt, syndicated Hearst columnist; Dr. George S. Benson, President of the National Education Program; FBI Director J. Edgar Hoover; Dr. Fred Schwarz, President of the Christian Anti-Communism Crusade; Los Angeles TV commentator, George Putnam; and the Cardinal Mindzenty Foundation. Specific targets include Ralph Bunche, the World Council of Churches ("a radical, revolutionary, pro-Marxist and unscriptural organization"), the Kerner Commission, SDS ("professional troublemakers and non-students . . . disloyal to the United States of America"), Dick Gregory, and the Reuther brothers.

EARTH SCIENCES

Indexes and Abstracts

Applied Science and Technology Index, Biological Abstracts, British Technology Index, Chemical Abstracts, Engineering Index, Meteorological and Geoastrophysical Abstracts, Science Citation Index. (For annotations, see Indexes and Abstracts Section.)

The periodicals in this section are, in the main, research journals commonly found in most academic libraries. Concentration has been largely on high quality U.S. publications covering aspects of geology, geochemistry, geophysics, mineralogy, oceanography, paleontology, petrology, and petroleum geology. The selections are but a sampling of the distinguished journals required by sizable research libraries. A few titles of a less technical nature or of popular interest have also been included.

Abstracts of North American Geology. See Indexes and Abstracts Section.

American Association of Petroleum Geologists. Bulletin. 1917. m. $30. John D. Haun. Box 979, Tulsa, Okla. 74101. Illus., index, adv. Circ: 15,750. Microform: UM, Canner. Reprint: Johnson, Abrahams.

Indexed: ASTI, BioAb, ChemAb, EngI. *Bk. rev:* 5, 250–500 words, signed. *Aud:* Ac, Sa. *Rv:* H. *Jv:* B.

Although mainly concerned with studies of geology as related to petroleum and natural gas, the periodical also contains some general geological material, as well as numerous papers on geophysics and physical oceanography. Research papers tend to be lengthy, and shorter investigations are published as geological notes. Noteworthy departments are "Association Round Table," which includes abstracts of papers presented at various meetings, together with the proceedings of the Association; and the book review section, which supplies a long checklist, by country, of recent publications. The June issue annually publishes statistical data pertinent to the North American oil and gas industry for the previous year, and the August issue supplies similar information for the oil and gas industry exclusive of North America. Also publishes news of professional interest, calendars, and personalia.

American Geophysical Union. Transactions. 1919. m. $5. Waldo E. Smith. 2100 Pennsylvania Ave., N.W., Washington, D.C. 20036. Illus., index, adv. Circ: 9,000. Microform: Canner. Reprint: Johnson.

Indexed: BioAb, EngI, Met&GeoAstAb, SCI. *Bk. rev:* 7, 300–500 words, signed. *Aud:* Sa, Ac. *Rv:* H. *Jv:* B.

Treatment of material in this periodical devoted to problems concerned with the figure and physics of the earth is less technical than that supplied in the main research journals of the AGU, namely *Journal of Geophysical Research* (q. v.) and *Reviews of Geophysics* (q.v.). Articles which regularly review progress and achievements in geophysical research are often written in a chatty vein and may be of interest to science teachers, non-specialists, and qualified laymen. For the professional, the *Transactions* also carry reports on activities of the AGU, news notes and personalia. Abstracts of papers presented at meetings are also published, as is a membership directory. A fairly large section reports on new publications and supplies translations of tables of contents of foreign journals.

American Journal of Science; devoted to the geological sciences and to related fields. 1818. m. (except July & Sept.). $15. John Rodgers & John H. Ostrom. Yale Univ., New Haven, Conn. 06520. Illus., index. Circ: 2,510. Microform: UM, Princeton, Canner. Reprint: Johnson, Jaeger.

Indexed: BioAb, ChemAb, EngI, SCI. *Bk. rev:* 1–3, lengthy, signed. *Aud:* Sa, Ac. *Rv:* H. *Jv:* B.

Originally entitled *Silliman's Journal,* the periodical was the first scientific journal published in the U.S. Although it had a brief career as a general science periodical, it became exclusively a geology journal shortly thereafter. Papers now report original research in all the geological sciences, with predominance on geology; some significant review articles appear occasionally. Recommended for academic collections.

American Mineralogist. 1916. bi-m. $15. William T. Holser. Mineralogical Society of America. Subscriptions to: Marjorie Hooker, Treas., U.S. Geological Survey, Washington, D.C. 20242. Illus., index, adv. Circ: 4,200. Reprint: Kraus, Abrahams.

Indexed: ASTI, ChemAb, EngI, SCI. *Bk. rev:* 3–4, signed, 250–300 words. *Aud:* Ac, Sa. *Rv:* H. *Jv:* B.

The research papers published in this official journal include studies in the general fields of mineralogy, crystallography, petrology and allied sciences. Investigations of smaller scope are published as mineralogical notes. Included as a regular feature is "New Mineral Names," which gives brief résumés of new minerals as reported elsewhere in the literature. Also includes news and notices for the profession and the Society.

Bibliography and Index of Geology Exclusive of North America. See Indexes and Abstracts Sections.

Canadian Journal of Earth Sciences. 1964. bi-m. $6. J. W. Ambrose, National Research Council of Canada, Ottawa 7, Ont. Illus., index. Circ: 1,500.

Aud: Sa, Ac. *Rv:* H. *Jv:* B.

The journal publishes research papers and short notes in any branch of the geosciences. Among the subjects covered are geophysics, geochemistry, mineralogy, crystallography, and petrology. Contributions, reflecting the research interests of Canadian laboratories, are not limited geographically, although most geological studies are of North America. Papers may appear in English and French.

Earth Science; the rockhound's national magazine. 1946. bi-m. $2.50. Ben Hur Wilson. Midwest Federation of Mineralogical Societies, Earth Science Publishing Co., Box 550, Downers Grove, Ill. 60515. Illus., index, adv. Circ: 5,000. Microform: UM. Reprint: Johnson, Abrahams.

Bk. rev: 5–8, 100–200 words. *Aud:* Ga, Ac, Jc, Sh, Jh. *Rv:* M. *Jv:* B.

This is an "educational and hobby periodical . . . devoted to all aspects of each science." The 5–8 articles, usually by people in the field, are non-technical and are easily understood by student, hobbyist, or initiate. They are amply illustrated by black and white photos and charts. Of special interest to hobbyists are the pages of club news and notes. According to the editors, about 20% of the subscribers are universities, colleges, and senior and junior high schools.

Earth Science Reviews; international magazine for geoscientists. 1966. q. $12.50. Elsevier Publishing Co., Box 211, Amsterdam, Netherlands. Illus., index, adv. Reprint: Abrahams.

Bk. rev: 7, 250–500 words, signed. *Aud:* Ac, Sa. *Rv:* H. *Jv:* B.

International in scope and including all aspects of the geosciences, the journal comprises two sections. One is devoted to a few comprehensive review papers averaging 40–50 pages and including lengthy bibliographies. The second section consists of *Atlas,* its news supplement, which often carries special reports of research being conducted in various parts of the world. Features include "Between Stone and Hammer," a section of short, critical notes of new developments; some general interest articles for the profession;

occasional profiles of scientists; a few scientific letters to the editor; and news and notices.

Economic Geology and the Bulletin of the Society of Economic Geologists. 1905. 8/yr. $8.50. Alan M. Bateman. Economic Geology Publishing Co., Box 26, Blacksburg, Va. 24060. Illus., index. Circ: 5,816. Microform: UM. Reprint: Johnson, Abrahams.

Indexed: ASTI, ChemAb, EngI, SCI. *Bk. rev:* 5, 150–200 words, signed. *Aud:* Sa, Ac. *Rv:* H. *Jv:* B.

Papers on economic and applied geology, particularly as applicable to mining, are published in this international journal. The eight to ten papers per issue may vary in length from 5 to 50 pages. Other sections include "Scientific Communications," discussions containing letters referring to previously published papers, notices of interest to Society members, and books reviewed and listings of books received.

Geochimica et Cosmochimica Acta. 1950. m. $75. A. A. Levinson. Pergamon Press, Maxwell House, Fairview Park, Elmsford, N.Y. 10523. Illus., index. Reprint: Abrahams.

Indexed: ChemAb, SCI. *Bk. rev:* 1–3, 400 words, signed. *Aud:* Sa, Ac. *Rv:* H. *Jv:* B.

The journal is a publication of the Geochemical Society (international membership). High-quality papers report on all aspects of geochemistry, including studies of meteorites, and the chemical composition of extra-terrestrial matter. Investigations of smaller scope appear as short research notes, or as letters to the editor, which receive prompt publication. International in scope, papers may appear in German and French, as well as English.

Geological Magazine. 1864. bi-m. $12. Ed bd. Mimram Books, Ltd., Caxton Hill, Hertford, Herts, Eng. Illus., index, adv. Circ: 1,375. Microform: UM. Reprint: Dawsons.

Indexed: BioAb, BritTech, ChemAb, EngI, SCI. *Bk. rev:* 3–4, 300 words, signed. *Aud.* Sa, Ac. *Rv:* H. *Jv:* B.

Although a fair portion of this publication devoted to general geological studies represents contributions from the British Isles, investigations are of general interest and are not necessarily limited geographically. Research papers usually do not exceed 20 pages, and more limited studies are published as research notes or correspondence. In addition to regular book reviews, lengthy essay reviews are often included.

Geological Society of America. Bulletin. 1888. m. $40. Edwin B. Eckel. Geological Soc. of America, P.O. Box 1719, Boulder, Colo. 80302. Illus., index. Circ: 8,000. Microform: Canner. Reprint: Johnson; Jaeger.

Indexed: ASTI, BioAb, ChemAb, EngI, SCI. *Aud:* Sa, Ac. *Rv:* H. *Jv:* B.

The official publication of the Society is concerned with original research on any facet of geology, including geochemistry, geophysics, mineralogy, and the like. Studies are international and are not restricted to North America. In addition to full length papers, short articles describing instrumentation or providing critical comments and timely data are included under a "Notes and Discussions" section. The journal is fully illustrated with plates, photos, and fold-out maps. Necessary for any academic collection.

Geological Society of London. Quarterly Journal. 1845. q. $23.25. H. K. Lewis & Co., Ltd., 136 Gower St., London W.C.1. Illus., index, adv. Reprint: Kraus, Abrahams.

Indexed: BioAb, EngI. *Aud:* Ac, Sa. *Rv:* H. *Jv:* B.

The scholarly contributions to this research journal represent investigations in all branches of geology. Although many papers are restricted geographically to the British Isles, it would be a sophisticated addition to a good collection. The Society also publishes, irregularly, its *Proceedings,* which consists of notices of meetings, abstracts of papers presented at symposia of the Society, and discussions.

Geophysics. 1936. bi-m. $15. Carl H. Savit. Soc. of Exploration Geophysicists, Box 3098, Tulsa, Okla. 74101. Illus., index, adv. Circ: 7,200. Microform: UM, Canner, Soc. Exploration Geophysicists. Reprint: Abrahams.

Indexed: ASTI, BioAb, ChemAb, EngI, SciAb, SCI. *Bk. rev:* 6, 250 words, signed. *Aud:* Sa, Ac. *Rv:* H. *Jv:* B.

The technical papers published in this journal stress the applied aspects of geophysical studies, including mining, and geophysical prospecting. In addition, the official publication of the Society serves as a current awareness medium for its membership. Issues frequently carry review articles or general essays, abstracts of papers presented at their meetings or discussions of the papers read, selected abstracts of papers from some Russian journals, and the usual news and notices of the Society, new product announcements, etc.

Geotimes; news of the earth sciences. 1956. 8/yr. Membership (Non-members, $2.). Wendell Cochran. Amer. Geological Inst., 1444 N St., N.W., Washington, D.C. 20005. Illus., index, adv. Circ: 35,000. Reprint: Johnson, Abrahams.

Bk. rev: 4–5, lengthy, signed. *Aud:* Sa, Ac, Ht. *Rv:* M. *Jv:* B.

"Published as a service to scientists belonging to AGI societies." Short articles and news items to keep scientists abreast of earth science activities such as meetings, conferences and symposia. Features include: editorials, which deal with current issues, such as selective service, as well as scientifically-oriented issues such as "Translation Services" and "Support for Seismology"; calendar of events; news notes and an annotated list of books received.

International Geology Review. 1959. m. $110. Martin Russell. Amer. Geological Inst., 1444 N St., N.W. Washington, D.C. 20005. Illus., index. Circ: 700. Reprint: Kraus, Abrahams.

Indexed: ChemAb. *Aud:* Ac, Sa. *Rv:* H. *Jv:* B.

The publication represents translations into English of the significant foreign literature in all branches of geological research, and incorporates a variety of other material. A "Papers" section translates a large body of Russian papers taken from some of their most distinguished journals, and frequently includes Chinese and Japanese literature. A "Review" section reports on nonserial works, parts of which may be translated by this journal; very often entire scientific treatises are published. A "Reference" section features prepublication announcements of forthcoming Soviet literature. For research libraries.

Journal of Geological Education. 1951. 5/yr. $5. Robert E. Boyer. Natl. Assn. of Geology Teachers, c/o Roy L. Ingram, Dept. of Geology, Univ. of North Carolina, Chapel Hill, N.C. 27514. Illus., index. Circ: 2,600.

Indexed: GeoAb. *Bk. rev:* 8–10, lengthy, signed. *Aud:* Ac, Jc, Ht. *Rv:* H. *Jv:* B.

Primarily for professional educators and teachers at the college and secondary level. Each issue features an average of four 5-page articles, some of which will be of equal interest to geology students. There is also an average of two to three brief reports. A section on classroom ideas (techniques) is usually included, as well as sections for notices and NAGT transactions. The book review section includes reviews of texts and laboratory manuals as well as popular geology books.

Journal of Geology. 1893. bi-m. $18. Peter J. Wyllie. Univ. of Chicago Press, 5750 S. Ellis Ave., Chicago, Ill. 60637. Illus., index, adv. Circ: 2,712. Microform: UM, Canner. Reprint: Johnson, Abrahams.

Indexed: ASTI, BioAb, ChemAb, Engl, SCI. *Bk. rev:* 2–3, lengthy, signed. *Aud:* Ac, Sa. *Rv:* H. *Jv:*B.

An authoritative, international research journal concerned with original studies in all aspects of geology. The five to six lengthy reports represent comprehensive studies, which may either be theoretical in nature or applications of new approaches to geological problems. Shorter investigations are published as notes. Occasionally special issues of the journal are devoted to a single subject. Many book reviews constitute long, scholarly critiques. An important and prestigious addition to any geology collection.

Journal of Geophysical Research. 1896. semi-m. $35. A. J. Dessler & O. L. Anderson. Amer. Geophysical Union, 2100 Pennsylvania Ave., N.W., Washington, D.C. 20031. Illus., index, adv. Circ: 9,500. Reprint: Johnson, Abrahams.

Indexed: BioAb, ChemAb, Met&GeoAstAb., SciAb, SCI. *Aud:* Sa, Ac. *Rv:* H. *Jv:* B.

Devoted to original contributions dealing with the "full spectrum of the physics of the Earth and its environment in space," this publication is the world's leading journal of geophysical research. Papers represent comprehensive and authoritative studies by distinguished scientists;

shorter investigations are published in a "Letters" section. Semi-monthly since 1963, the first monthly issue is concerned with space physics, and the second reports research on the fluid and solid parts of the earth and other bodies in space.

Journal of Marine Research. 1937. 3/yr. $15. Yngve H. Olsen. Sears Foundation for Marine Research, Box 2025, Yale Station, New Haven, Conn. 06520. Illus., index. Circ: 1,200.

Indexed: BioAb, ChemAb, Met&GeoAstAb. *Aud:* Sa, Ac. *Rv:* H. *Jv:* B.

Articles of previously unpublished investigations concerning problems of the sea, both theoretical and descriptive, are presented in this scholarly journal. Both biological and oceanographic studies are published. Most entries are short (eight to ten pages) and primarily from American authors, albeit a few foreign contributors are included. An important journal for the graduate student or scholar in marine studies.

Journal of Paleontology. 1927. bi-m. $28. Box 979, Tulsa, Okla. 74101. Illus., index, adv. Circ: 2,674. Microform: UM, Canner. Reprint: Johnson.

Indexed: BioAb, ChemAb. *Bk. rev:* 5, lengthy, signed. *Aud:* Sa, Ac. *Rv:* H. *Jv:* B.

The publication is sponsored jointly by the Paleontological Society (Jan.–May–Sept. issues) and the Society of Economic Paleontologists and Mineralogists (Mar.–July–Nov. issues.) Research papers touch on most branches of paleontology, and include studies on both vertebrates and invertebrates, micropaleontology, paleobotany, stratigraphic paleontology, paleoecology, and paleobiogeography. Occasional review papers, items on nomenclature, and notes and announcements are included. Illustrations are superior. Useful for both geological and biological studies, the journal is an excellent vehicle for publications concerning the occurrence, relationship, and evolutionary development of organisms through geologic times.

Another high quality journal covering the same field is *Paleontology,* a publication of the Paleontological Association (London).

Journal of Petrology. 1960. 3/yr. $12. Ed bd. Oxford Univ. Press, Ely House, London, Eng. Illus., index. Circ: 1,500. Reprint: Dawson.

Indexed: ChemAb, SCI. *Aud:* Sa, Ac. *Rv:* H. *Jv:* B.

The journal publishes research papers which fall under the broad term "petrology," including studies on the physics and chemistry of rocks, mineralogy, dating of rocks by natural radioactivity, and the like. The scholarly contributions usually deal with fundamental science and are not simply regional studies. A high quality, international periodical for any academic library concerned with this aspect of the geological sciences.

Journal of Sedimentary Petrology. 1931. q. $18. G. M. Friedman. Soc. of Economic Paleontologists and Mineral-ogists, Box 979, Tulsa, Okla. 74101. Illus., index, adv. Circ: 2,567. Microform: UM, Canner. Reprint: Johnson.

Indexed: BioAb, ChemAb, SCI. *Bk. rev:* 3–4, lengthy, signed. *Aud:* Sa, Ac. *Rv:* H. *Jv:*B.

One of the research publications issued by the Society of Economic Paleontologists and Mineralogists. Papers, exploring the entire field of sedimentation, deal with such subjects as the physical and chemical characteristics or origins of sediments, and certain aspects of mineralogy, petrography, and lithology. Studies are not limited geographically. Both full-length papers and some research notes are included.

Lapidary Journal. See Crafts and Hobbies Section.

Limnology and Oceanography. 1956. q. $12.50. Dr. Francis Richards. Allen Press, Lawrence, Kan. 66044. Illus., index. Circ: 2,300.

Indexed: BioAb, ChemAb, Met&GeoAstAb. *Bk. rev:* 3, lengthy, signed. *Aud:* Sa, Ac. *Rv:* H. *Jv:* B.

Papers of original research in every area of limnology and oceanography are published in this journal. The 14–17 articles average ten pages in length and are mainly by Canadian or American authors. A section of notes and comments is concerned with apparatus or non-theoretical reports of research done or observations of phenomena. This section consists of 2– to 4–page articles and may constitute up to one-third of the journal.

Oceanology International. 1966. 7/yr. $10. ($5 to libraries; free to scientists). Neil P. Ruzic. Industrial Research Pubns., Beverly Shores, Ind. 46301. Circ: 30,000. Microform: UM.

Bk. rev: 3, 100–200 words, unsigned. *Aud:* Sa, Ga, Ac, Jc. *Rv:* H. *Jv:* B.

Directed both toward the professional associated with oceanic activity, and the interested student or layman, the magazine acts as a news and review medium for the former, and an introduction to physical and biological oceanography for the latter. Feature articles, contributed by specialists and staff writers, run the gamut from underwater archaeology to submersible electric motors. A "News" section reports on national, international, and Washington trends. Most issues contain special reports on instrumentation, conferences, and the like, which describe advances in the fields. A distinguished editorial advisory board includes such names as Arthur C. Clarke and Jacques-Yves Cousteau. The text is readable, lucid, and aptly illustrated with black and white photographs; covers, in full color, are striking. Also published annually is a useful *Yearbook/Directory.*

Reviews of Geophysics. 1963. q. $10. Gordon J. F. Macdonald. Amer. Geophysical Union, 1145 19th St., N.W., Washington, D.C. 20036. Illus., index, adv. Circ: 2,300. Reprint: Abrahams.

Indexed: SciAb, SCI. *Aud:* Ac, Sa. *Rv:* H. *Jv:* B.

Authoritative and critical, the reviews discuss current and timely problems in geophysical research and occasionally in the planetary sciences. Comprehensive bibliographies are included. Some reviews are tutorial in nature and would be of value to the advanced student, as well as to the specialist in the field.

Rocks and Minerals; minerology, geology, lapidary.
1926. m. $4. Peter Zodac, Box 29, Peekskill, N.Y. Illus., adv. Circ: 12,000.

Indexed: ChemAb. *Bk. rev:* 3–4, 100 words, unsigned. *Aud:* Jh, Sh, Ga, Sa. *Rv:* M. *Jv:* B.

The official journal of the Rocks and Minerals Association, and "America's oldest and most versatile magazine for the mineralogist, geologist, lapidary," the publication carries a variety of informally written articles in these areas. Some features represent little tutorials by those knowledgeable in the field; others may be notes on equipment; some contain histories of gems; and yet others may be chatty reports on field trips, etc. Departments include current events, bits from club bulletins, a swap column, information on mineral localities, new equipment, and a miscellany of personals, ads, or comments from contributors. Would be a good choice for schools with mineral or geology clubs, and is also popular enough in tone for interested public libraries.

Sea Frontiers. 1954. bi-m. F. G. W. Smith. Intl. Oceanographic Foundation, 1 Rickenbacker Causeway, Virginia Key, Miami, Fla. 33149. Illus., index. Circ: 52,000.

Indexed: BioAb, Met&GeoAstAb, RG. *Bk. rev:* 9–12, 200 words, signed. *Aud:* Ga, Sh, Jh. *Rv:* H. *Jv:* B.

An authoritative oceanography magazine with articles by experts and scholars, yet written in a semi-popular fashion for the layman and high school student. Material covers every scientific aspect of the sea from fish to ocean topography, and the whole is illustrated with suitable graphs and maps. A helpful aid is the insert "Sea Secrets," which includes questions and answers about various aspects of oceanography. One of the few authoritative, yet popular magazines in this ever growing scientific area, it is a first choice for most libraries.

Seismological Society of America. Bulletin. 1911. bi-m. $12. Bruce A. Bolt. Waverly Press, Inc., Baltimore, Md. 20207. Illus., index. Circ: 2,000. Reprint: Abrahams.

Indexed: SciAb, SCI. *Bk. rev:* 3, signed, 200 words. *Aud:* Ac, Sa. *Rv:* H. *Jv:* B.

Research papers are devoted to fundamental studies of earthquakes, including analyses of historical, as well as recent, seismic activity, all illustrated by clear black and white photographs. Departments include "Seismological Notes," concerned with recordings of shocks; a few professional announcements, and some scientific "Letters to the Editor."

Tectonophysics. 1964. m. $12.50. Ed bd. Elsevier Publishing Co., Box 211, Amsterdam, Netherlands. Illus., index.

Bk. rev: 3–4, 250 words, signed. *Aud:* Sa, Ac. *Rv:* H. *Jv:* B.

The literature in this journal deals with the subject of tectonics, that is, structural geology and the physics of the interior of the Earth. A fairly wide variety of material is published: original research papers and short communications; occasional review articles; notices of significant developments, or brief news of interest to the profession; book reviews. International in scope, research papers may appear in French and German, as well as English. An editorial board of distinguished geoscientists assures high quality papers. To facilitate rapid dissemination of information, the publication is produced by offset printing.

Water Resources Research. 1965. q. $13. Walter B. Langbein & Charles W. Howe. Amer. Geophysical Union, 2100 Pennsylvania Ave., N.W., Washington, D.C. 20036. Illus., index. Circ: 4,217.

Aud: Sa, Ac. *Rv:* H. *Jv:* B.

Concerned with all the sciences dealing with water, the journal offers an interesting combination of scientific contributions from the physical, biological, and social sciences, including such fields as hydrology, fluid mechanics, geochemistry, economics, and water law. Research papers provide a blend of studies on topics such as thermal pollution of river ice, with biological investigations of water, and economic analyses of lakeshore property value. Papers are authoritative and scholarly. A valuable publication for any academic library involved with research on environmental studies, as well as earth sciences.

ECONOMICS

Indexes and Abstracts

British Humanities Index, Business Periodicals Index, Legal Periodicals Index, Public Affairs Information Service, Social Sciences and Humanities Index, Sociological Abstracts. (For annotations, see Indexes and Abstracts Section.)

American Economic Review. 1911. 5/yr. Membership (Non-members, $10). John G. Gurley. Amer. Economic Assn., 629 Noyes St., Evanston, Ill. 60201. Index, adv. Circ: 20,500. Microform: UM. Reprint: Johnson, Abrahams.

Indexed: PAIS, SSHum. *Bk. rev:* 50–75, one to two pages, signed. *Aud:* Sa, Ac, Jc, Ht. *Rv:* H. *Jv:* V.

Outstanding both for its extensive book reviews and its forthright articles. The reviews, which take-up a good half of the magazine, are arranged under economics subject headings, e.g., methodology, price and allocation theory, history, statistical methods, etc. In addition, there is usually a listing of 250–300 new books in the field and notes on periodicals. Articles, often with bibliographies, range from wages and employment to marketing and welfare. Comments and letters make up a good part of each issue, and there is an annual list of doctoral dissertations. Appointments, research grants, deaths and promotions are noted. A basic journal for a beginning or advanced collection in this area.

American Journal of Economics and Sociology. 1941. q. $5. Will Lissner. Amer. Journal of Economics and Sociology, Inc., 50 E. 69th St., New York, N.Y. 10021. Illus., index. Circ: 1,062. Microform: UM. Canner. Reprint: Abrahams, Kraus.

Indexed: PAIS, SSHum, SocAb. *Bk. rev:* 1–2, lengthy, signed. *Aud:* Sa, Ac. *Rv:* H. *Jv:* B.

Aims at a "constructive synthesis in the social sciences" through the reporting of the results of original research aimed at achieving an understanding of contemporary economic and social processes. It could be used effectively by the scholar, college student or interested layman who is seeking analysis of economic problems and situations; or by one who is seeking studies of the interrelationships between economics and sociology, history and political science. Two important areas covered are the sociological aspects of economic institutions and the economic aspects of social and political institutions. Besides studies of the United States, material concerns foreign situations. While the articles are thoroughly documented, the style is non-technical. Authors are professors and government officials. Each issue contains one or more lengthy reviews of important recent works along with briefer book notices. A basic journal for medium to large collections.

Antitrust Bulletin; journal of American and foreign antitrust and trade regulations. 1955. q. $25. James M. Clabault. Federal Legal Pubns., Inc., 95 Morton St., New York, N.Y. 10014. Index, adv. Circ: 1,100.

Indexed: LegPer, PAIS. *Bk. rev:* 3–4, several pages, signed. *Aud:* Sa, Ac. *Rv:* H. *Jv:* B.

A specialized technical journal edited for persons interested in economics and antitrust matters. Current cases or specific issues are discussed. The periodical is strictly for the use of directly involved lawyers and economists, though very advanced students in the field will find it useful.

Canadian Journal of Economics. 1968. q. $10. Canadian Economics Assn., Univ. of Toronto Press, Toronto 5, Ont.

Indexed: CanI, SSHum. *Bk. rev:* 5, 500–1000 words, signed. *Aud:* Sa, Ac. *Rv:* H. *Jv:* B.

Formerly part of the *Canadian Journal of Economics and Political Science* (1935–67), now a separate publication of some 150 pages. Articles are primarily concerned with general economic issues, are written by economists and teachers, and appear in French and English. Material more relevant to the Canadian scene appears in shorter items as "Notes." There is usually a bibliographic article,

and the whole is the best academic approach to the subject available in Canada.

Challenge, The Magazine of Economic Affairs. 1952. bi-m. $6. Inst. of Economic Affairs, New York Univ., 475 Fifth Ave., New York, N.Y. 10017. Illus. Circ: 15,000. Reprint: Kraus, Abrahams.

Indexed: PAIS. *Bk. rev:* Various numbers, lengthy. *Aud:* Sa, Ac, Jc, Sh, Ht. *Rv:* H. *Jv:* A.

One of the few economics magazines specifically written for the layman, not for the specialist or scholar. An effort is made to concentrate on issues currently in the news, and the scope is broad enough to take in all aspects of economic policy and related subjects, e.g., public affairs, business, government, ethics, political science, etc. The magazine is particularly interesting because the contributors tend to be scholars, practicing economists (in private industry and government); yet they are able to maintain a style of writing which is both authoritative and well within the grasp of the average reader. An air of objectivity, rarely found in popular business or economic journals; discussions which usually cover controversial matters in depth, giving both sides; good book reviews of semi-popular material, all add up to a first-rate magazine for most libraries from high school through university. It is particularly useful as a counterbalance in high school to the general news magazines and school papers.

Chinese Economic Studies. 1967. q. $40. (Personal subscriptions $15) Fred Ablin. Intl. Arts and Sciences Press, Inc., 108 Grand St., White Plains, N.Y. 10601.

Aud: Sa, Ac. *Rv:* H. *Jv:* B.

Contains four to five translations from some ten Chinese newspapers and journals, often no more than a few months after publication. "The aim of the journal is to present the more important Chinese studies in this field in the light of the interest of those who are professionally concerned with it." Unfortunately, the institutional price will limit this to large academic and public libraries. Interested individuals may receive it for considerably less. IASP issues a number of translation journals covering China, the Soviet Union and the immediate area, and other parts of the world. Most are equally high priced for institutions. Nevertheless, they serve a valuable purpose and should be brought to the attention of scholars in the field. See also, *Eastern European Economics.*

Eastern European Economics; a journal of translations from Bulgaria, Czechoslovakia, East Germany, Hungary, Poland, Rumania and Yugoslavia. 1962. q. $35. Intl. Arts & Sciences Press, 108 Grand St., White Plains, N.Y. 10601. Index. Reprint: Abrahams.

Indexed: PAIS. *Aud:* Sa, Ac. *Rv:* H. *Jv:* B.

Includes "selected articles from scholarly journals of Eastern Europe in English translation." There are usually four to five articles from the Eastern European press for scholars in this country. It is of invaluable assistance for research in this area.

Econometrica. 1933. q. $16. Robert H. Strotz. North-Holland Publishing Co., Amsterdam, Netherlands. Index, adv. Circ: 6,500. Reprint: Abrahams.

Indexed: SSHum. *Bk. rev:* 14, 200 words, signed. *Aud:* Sa, Ac. *Rv:* H. *Jv:* B.

A highly specialized and scholarly journal "for the advancement of economic theory in its relation to statistics and mathematics." The articles are written mainly by faculty members of American universities. Material is technical, and would have interest only for the expert in the expert in the field.

Economic Development and Cultural Change. 1952. q. $8. Bert F. Hoselitz. Research Center in Economic Development & Cultural Change, Univ. of Chicago. (Subscriptions to: University of Chicago Press, 5750 S. Ellis Ave., Chicago, Ill. 60637.) Index, adv. Circ: 3,000. Microforms: UM, Canner. Reprint: Johnson, Abrahams.

Indexed: PAIS. *Bk. rev:* 5, 300 words, signed. *Aud:* Sa, Ac. *Rv:* H. *Jv:* B.

A well-written journal primarily concerned with developments in the emerging nations of the world. Economic, political and cultural activities are examined, and an effort is made to link all factors relevant to development. The material is technical, but because it covers such a wide range of social and political issues, it will be of interest to a great number of scholars and graduate students. Should be in most medium to large economics, sociology, and political science collections.

Economic History Review. 1927. 3/yr. Membership (Non-members, $9). D. C. Coleman & R. M. Hartwell. Broadwater Press Ltd., Welwyn Garden City, Herts., Eng. Reprint: Kraus, Abrahams.

Indexed: BritHum, PAIS, SSHum. *Bk. rev:* 40–50, one page, signed. *Aud:* Sa, Ac, Jc. *Rv:* H. *Jv:* B.

Published by the Economic History Society, Cambridge, England, and devoted to economic history in all its aspects, with special emphasis placed upon Great Britain. Each issue usually contains ten scholarly articles and occasional essays and short articles. It is particularly useful in libraries for the 40 to 50 relatively long and critical book reviews which cover new books in any way connected with economic history. See also, *Journal of Economic History.*

Economic Journal. 1891. q. 50s. Royal Economic Soc., Sidgwick Ave., Marshall Library, Cambridge, Eng. Index, adv. Circ: 10,000. Microform: UM. Reprint: Abrahams.

Indexed: BritHum, PAIS, SSHum. *Bk. rev:* 35, 200 words, signed. *Aud:* Sa, Ac. *Rv:* H. *Jv:* B.

Features articles written primarily by faculty members of British, American, and Canadian universities. There is an excellent section devoted to recent periodicals and new

books. Contents of approximately 150 periodicals in the field are listed. In view of this, the journal serves as a type of quarterly index to major magazines, and is extremely useful for larger libraries.

Economica. 1921. q. $6.75. B. S. Yamey. London Sch. of Economics and Political Science, Economica Publishing Co., Houghton St., Aldwych, London W.C.2. Index, adv. Circ: 3,300. Reprint: Abrahams.

Indexed: BritHum, PAIS, SSHum. *Bk. rev:* 15, 150 words, signed. *Aud:* Sa, Ac. *Rv:* H. *Jv:* B.

Limited to "economics, economic history, statistics and closely related problems." Approximately half of the articles are written by non-British faculty members, primarily Americans. Since the subject matter is theoretical and universal, there is no special emphasis on the British economy. There is an extensive bibliography in each issue giving a list of the new books in the field. Primarily for graduate students and scholars.

The Economist. See Business and Industry Section.

European Community. 1954. m. Free. Leonard Tennyson. European Community Information Service, 808 Farragut Bldg., Washington, D.C. 20006. Illus. Circ: 35,000.

Indexed: PAIS. *Bk. rev:* Varies, short. *Aud:* Ga, Sa, Ac, Jc. *Rv:* M. *Jv:* B.

Covers the economics affairs of the Common Market countries including discussions on tariffs, agriculture, customs unions, social fund grants, etc., in relationship with each other and with the rest of the world. Some political concerns are mentioned, but politics is not stressed. The editorial treatment is semi-popular, intentionally more informative than scholarly. As the publication is free, it is worth trying in any library. For a more scholarly approach, see *Journal of Common Market Studies.*

German Economic Review. 1963. q. $6. Wissenschaftliche Verlagsgesellschaft, Postfach 40, Stuttgart, Germany. Circ: 4,000.

Bk. rev: 15, 200 words, signed. *Aud:* Sa, Ac. *Rv:* H. *Jv:* B.

The audience for this English language quarterly is primarily professional economists. The average of one to two articles per number are translations of papers written by faculty members of German universities and there are reviews of German books and abstracts of material from various German periodicals. There is also a selected bibliography of books and periodicals on various aspects of economics, and a section devoted to news of economic developments in Germany.

International Development Review. 1959. q. Membership (Libraries only, $7.50). Andrew E. Rice. Soc. for Intl. Development, 1346 Connecticut Ave., N.W., Washington, D.C. 20036. Adv. Circ: 6,000. Microform: UM. Reprint: Johnson, Abrahams.

Indexed: PAIS. *Bk. rev:* 15, 200 words, signed. *Aud:* Sa, Ac, Jc. *Rv:* H. *Jv:* B.

A well-written, readable journal devoted to the economic development of the emerging nations. Articles are practical, documented and usually in English. Those in French or Spanish have English abstracts. News of the United Nations, film reviews and short, perceptive book reviews round out the average issue. Valuable magazine for difficult-to-find information on smaller nations.

International Economic Review. 1960. 3/yr. $9. P. J. Dhrymes. Kansai Economic Federation, Shin-Osaka Bldg., Dojima-Hamadori, Kita-ku, Osaka, Japan. Index, adv. Circ: 4,500.

Indexed: PAIS. *Aud:* Sa, Ac. *Rv:* H. *Jv:* B.

Published in Japan with the text in English. The emphasis is primarily on quantitative economics. Over half of the average seven articles per issue are written by American university faculty members. Only for large libraries.

Journal of Common Market Studies. 1962. q. $5.88. U. W. Kitzinger. Basil Blackwell, Broad St., Oxford, Eng. Circ: 1,054.

Indexed: PAIS. *Aud:* Sa, Ac. *Rv:* H. *Jv:* B.

A British journal for specialists of the European Common Market, as well as other regional economic trading groups. The average four articles per number deal with social and political issues within the Common Market, and trade in general; there is a register of current research being done in the field. Primarily for large academic libraries.

The Journal of Developing Areas. 1966. q. $4. Spencer H. Brown. Western Illinois Univ. Press, 900 W. Adams St., Macomb, Ill. 61455. Circ: 550.

Indexed: HistAb. *Bk. rev:* 15–20, 150–750 words, signed. *Aud:* Sa, Ac, Jc. *Rv:* H. *Jv:* B.

Concerned with the problems of underdeveloped countries, this journal takes more of an interest in the general type of development problems than in the problems of particular countries. The approach is not purely economic but attempts to deal with all potentially relevant aspects of changing societies, from tangible variables such as wage structures, schools, the military, unions, and trade to intangible ones such as goal orientation and values in their relations to change. There is much data given on many different areas and a regular news and notes section.

Journal of Economic History. 1941. q. $6. Hugh G. J. Aitken. Grad. Sch. of Business Admin., New York Univ., 100 Trinity Pl., New York, N.Y. 10006. Circ: 2,800. Microform: UM, Canner. Reprint: Kraus, Abrahams.

Indexed: PAIS, SSHum. *Bk. rev:* 20–25, 1 page, signed. *Aud:* Ac, Jc. *Rv:* H. *Jv:* B.

The journal of the Economic History Association, this is the American equivalent of *Economic History Review,*

devoted to articles on the history of economic life in all its phases. The articles are not confined to any one country or period of history, and cover such subjects as transportation, taxation, investment and the history of business and industry. The book reviews are critical and a particularly excellent guide for librarians. Although an academic journal, the material is broad enough in scope to be of interest to teachers or graduate students in economics, history, sociology, and related areas. A basic journal for medium to large academic and public library economics collections.

Journal of Economic Issues. 1967. q. Membership. (Non-members, $6) Forest G. Hill. Assn. for Evolutionary Economics, The Univ. of Texas, Austin, Tex. 78712.

Bk. rev: 20–25, 250 words, signed. *Aud:* Sa, Ac. *Rv:* H. *Jv:* B.

Written by and primarily for professors of economic theory, each issue includes some six or seven articles on a variety of economic issues, e.g., the gold-dollar problem, the political economy of poverty, wages in historical context. There are comments of a shorter nature, and critical book reviews as well as a listing of new books received. Emphasis tends to be on general economic theory, and the magazine unquestionably has a wide appeal for anyone who teaches the subject or for graduate students.

Journal of Law and Economics. See Law Section.

Journal of Political Economy. 1892. bi-m. $10. Robert A. Mundell. Univ. of Chicago Press, 5750 S. Ellis Ave., Chicago, Ill. 60637. Illus., index, adv. Circ: 4,120. Microform: UM, Canner. Reprint: Johnson, Abrahams.

Indexed: PAIS, SSHum. *Bk. rev:* Various numbers and lengths. *Aud:* Sa, Ac. *Rv:* H. *Jv:* B.

Written primarily for professional economists. The average ten articles per number are written almost exclusively by faculty members of various universities. There are occasional review articles as well as periodic supplementary issues devoted to one topic—usually one discussed at a conference. There is also a list of books that have been received, and several short notices of new books. For large academic collections.

Kyklos; internationale Zeitschrift für Sozialwissenschaften. 1948. q. $7.50. Kyklos-Verlag, Postfach 785, Basel 2, Switz. Circ: 3,000. Reprint: Johnson, Abrahams.

Indexed: PAIS. *Bk. rev:* 40, 150–750 words, signed. *Aud:* Sa, Ac. *Rv:* H. *Jv:* B.

An international review of the social sciences, this is issued by the List Society, "a forum of leading representatives in the fields of political science, economics, business and public administration." It boasts subscribers from over 76 countries and carries the type of data and articles which are interdisciplinary, but lean heavily towards economics, e.g., "Intellectual Sources of Karl Marx" and "Soviet Views on American Unemployment." While the text is in English, French and German, the majority of the seven to eight articles appear in English. An intellectual journal for only the largest economics and social sciences collections.

Law and Contemporary Problems. See Law Section.

National Tax Journal. See Accounting Section.

Oxford Economic Papers. 1937. 3/yr. $6. J. F. Wright. Oxford Univ. Press, Ely House, London W. 1. Circ: 2,250. Microform: UM. Reprint: Abrahams.

Indexed: BritHum, PAIS. *Aud:* Sa, Ac. *Rv:* M. *Jv:* B.

A general review of economics, primarily for the professional and graduate student. The material shows a definite sophistication, particularly as much of it is written by the Oxford faculty. From time to time, leading American economists contribute. Coverage is universal, both in terms of country and time. The six to eight articles frequently include a long book review, although there is no book review section. One of the best overall economic journals for the large library.

Quarterly Check List of Economics and Political Science. See Literature Section, *Quarterly Check List of Literary History.*

Quarterly Journal of Economics. 1886. q. $6. Gottfried Haberler. Harvard Univ. Press, 79 Garden St., Cambridge, Mass. 02138. Adv. Circ: 5,400. Microform: UM. Reprint: Kraus, Abrahams.

Indexed: PAIS, SSHum. *Aud:* Sa, Ac. *Rv:* M. *Jv:* B.

Authors represent the leaders in the American and international schools of economics. The authoritative articles tend to examine the implications of the long rather than the short movements in prices, labor, public finance, and industrial development. Coverage is international, and while no particular theory of economics is championed, the tone is definitely liberal, at all times free of either national or political overtones. Its wide scope gives it a place of importance in any library serving the teacher, professional economist, or graduate student.

Quarterly Review of Economics and Business. 1961. q. $4. (Organizations, $5). Herbert I. Schiller. Bureau of Economic and Business Research, Urbana, Ill. 61801. Circ: 1,500. Microform: UM. Reprint: Johnson, Abrahams.

Indexed: BusI, PAIS, SSHum. *Bk. rev:* 5–6, 250–500 words, signed. *Aud:* Sa, Ac. *Rv:* M. *Jv:* B.

Useful not only to the serious student and teacher, but businessmen as well. The seven or eight articles emphasize business in practice as much as in theory. There is a good deal of original research and theoretical material on economics, usually related to contemporary problems. The book reviews are excellent, and on the whole it is a much above average journal for the medium to large business and economics collection.

Review of Economic Studies. 1933. q. $8. M. J. Farrell & F. H. Hahn. Faculty of Economics, Sidgwick Ave.,

Cambridge, Eng. (Subscriptions to: Oliver & Boyd Ltd., Tweeddale Ct., 14 High St., Edinburgh 1. Scotland. Circ: 2,500. Microform: UM. Reprint: Kraus, Abrahams.

Indexed: BritHum, PAIS, SSHum. *Aud:* Sa, Ac. *Rv:* M. *Jv:* B.

Originally founded by a group of young British and American economists, the Economic Study Society encourages research in theoretical and applied economics. Although now older, the magazine still encourages work from younger men. There are an average of nine articles per issue, and each contribution is documented and usually supported by extensive graphs and charts. Emphasis tends to be international. A useful journal for medium to large academic and public business and economics collections.

Review of Economics and Statistics. 1919. q. $9. Otto Eckstein. Harvard Univ. Press, 79 Garden St., Cambridge, Mass. 02138. Illus., index, adv. Circ: 4,500. Reprint: Kraus, Abrahams.

Indexed: BusI, PAIS. *Bk. rev:* Various numbers, lengthy. *Aud:* Sa, Ac. *Rv:* M. *Jv:* B.

Emphasis is on economic statistics, and the average 10 articles per number are written primarily by American scholars and government business economists, although major foreign scholars are represented. Concentrates on economic analysis with particular reference to issues of public policy. One interesting feature is symposia by economists on various issues of the day. There is a bibliography of books that have been received, and a few lengthy critical reviews. Primarily for the large, specialized business and economics collections.

Reviews in Urban Economics. See Cities and Towns Section.

Social Security Bulletin. 1938. m. $2.75. Josephine Merican. Social Security Admin., Office of Research and Statistics. Supt. of Documents, Washington, D.C. 20402. Illus., index. Microform: UM.

Indexed: BusI, PAIS. *Aud:* Sa, Ac, Jc. *Rv:* M. *Jv:* B.

This official publication of the Social Security Administration presents current data and statistics on retirement; health insurance programs; disability insurance; Medicare, Medicaid and other help for the aged; aid for the blind and disadvantaged; and the poverty programs. Contributors are associated with the administration's Office of Research and Statistics or are officials with the specialized programs discussed. The two to four articles per issue range from four to six pages in length. Most of each issue is devoted to a statistical presentation of the administrations' current operations broken down by time period and types of programs. These are cumulated quarterly. Of use in most libraries because of subjects discussed. Necessary in larger collections specializing in social science or related to economics and welfare programs.

Southern Economic Journal. 1933. q. $8. Robert E. Gallman. Southern Economic Assn., Univ. of North Carolina, Carroll Hall, Chapel Hill, N.C. 27514. Index, adv. Circ: 2,500. Microform: UM. Reprint: Kraus, Abrahams.

Indexed: PAIS, SSHum. *Bk. rev:* 7, 250 words, signed. *Aud:* Sa, Ac, Jc. *Rv:* M. *Jv:* B.

Contents are not concerned with the South alone, or written from a Southern viewpoint. In fact, most of the ten articles per issue are written by faculty members of non-Southern schools. Emphasis is as much on applied as theoretical economics, and the contributions cover both national and international problems. Occasionally there are review articles of previously written papers. An extensive list of new books in the field, and short book previews. Only for larger academic and public libraries.

Soviet Studies. 1949. q. $8.40. A. Nove, D. J. I. Matko, J. Miller, D. J. R. Scott, S. V. Utechin. Inst. of Soviet & East European Studies, Univ. of Glasgow, Glasgow, Scotland. Adv. Circ: 1,750. Microform: UM. Reprint: Johnson, Abrahams.

Indexed: BritHum, PAIS, SSHum. *Bk. rev:* 16, 400–500 words, signed. *Aud:* Sa, Ac. *Rv:* H. *Jv:* M.

A scholarly journal, covering social sciences, as well as economics of the Soviet and East European nations. In each issue there is an extensive bibliography of books in the field. "Information Supplement," a separate quarterly publication distributed with the journal, is an annotated bibliography of selected materials. Primarily from current Soviet periodical literature. There is also an "Information Bulletin" on research in progress in the field. Because it is not limited entirely to economics, this will be of interest to scholars in a number of related disciplines, and is a useful acquisition for the medium to large academic library.

Taxes. See Accounting Section.

Yale Economic Essays. 1961. semi-ann. $4. Dept. of Economics, Yale Univ., Box 1905a, Yale Station, New Haven, Conn. 06509. Microform: UM.

Indexed: PAIS. *Aud:* Sa, Ac. *Rv:* M. *Jv:* B.

Publishes "either in full or in extended summary . . . all doctoral dissertations at Yale University" and provides "a medium for economic comment and analysis by faculty, students, and graduates in economics at Yale University." Greater emphasis seems to be on the former. An average of about five to six dissertations are presented in each issue. Because of the wide range of topics of dissertations done at Yale, the essays are quite varied in content. Primarily for the large academic library.

EDUCATION

Indexes and Abstracts

Abstracts for Social Workers, Canadian Periodical Index, Catholic Periodical and Literature Index, Chemical Ab-stracts, Education Index, Historical Abstracts, Index to Periodical Articles By and About Negroes, Psychological Abstracts, Public Affairs Information Service. (For annotations, see Indexes and Abstracts Section.)

AAUP Bulletin. 1915. q. Membership (Non-members, $4.50). Warren C. Middleton. Amer. Assn. of Univ. Professors, 1785 Massachusetts Ave., N.W., Washington, D.C. 20036. Circ: 85,000. Microform: UM.

Indexed: EdI, PAIS. *Aud:* Sa, Ac, Jc. *Rv:* M. *Jv:* B.

As the voice of the teachers and research scholars on the faculties of approved American colleges and universities, this journal has three main features. First, it includes four to six articles per issue on various aspects of the profession and teaching; second, it documents cases against censured college and university administrations, and gives the present standing of such censure; finally, the summer issue is primarily devoted to a detailed analysis of faculty salaries and compensation. While the latter item is of limited interest to laymen, the forthright reports on education and matters of academic freedom make it an invaluable aid for anyone interested or involved with the field. Should be in all college and university libraries, and in many public libraries.

AAUW Journal. 1882. q. Membership (Non-members, $3.50). Amer. Assn. of Univ. Women, 2401 Virginia Ave., N.W., Washington, D.C. 20037. Circ: 195,645. Microform: UM.

Indexed: PAIS. *Aud:* Sa, Ac, Jc. *Rv:* M. *Jv:* B.

One of the few women's magazines devoted entirely to education without a whisper of home economics (other than as a college subject) or fashions. Articles report on activities of the Association, but each issue includes more general material on the education of women, social and economic problems, and progress and regression in making a way in the world. While not precisely militant, it is a champion of the second sex, and men are advised to give this a closer look for a better understanding of the aspirations of the modern woman. Should be in most education collections, and in general collections.

Accounting Review. See Accounting Section.

Adolescence. See Child Care Section.

Adult Education. 1950. q. Membership (Non-members, $7.50) Thurman White. Adult Education Assn. of the United States of America, 1225 19th St., N.W., Washington, D.C. 20036. Circ: 4,300. Microform: UM. Reprint: Abrahams.

Indexed: EdI, PAIS. *Bk. rev:* 4–6, 740–2,400 words, signed. *Aud:* Sa, Ac, Jc. *Rv:* M. *Jv:* B.

The journal of the Adult Education Association, this reports research and provides news and views of interest to adult education administrators. Sample articles: "Doctorates in Adult Education Awarded in 1966," "Research and Investigations in Adult Education," "Differences Between Adults and Youth Affecting Learning," "Study of Classroom Factors Related to Drop Outs." There are usually about five articles which range in length from two to eighteen pages, and the writing style is semi-popular to scholarly. All articles are by professionals in the field.

Agricultural Education Magazine. See Agriculture Section.

American Artist. See Art Section.

American Biology Teaching. See Biological Sciences Section.

American Education. (Formerly: *Higher Education and School Life.*) 1965. 10/yr. $3.75. Supt. of Documents, Washington, D.C. 20402. Illus. Microform: UM. Reprint: Abrahams.

Indexed: EdI, PAIS, RG. *Aud:* Ga, Ac, Jc, Sh, Jh. *Rv:* M. *Jv:* B.

Published by the U. S. Department of Health, Education and Welfare, Office of Education, this presents statistics on federal legislation and broader aspects of American education. A random sampling of articles indicate its scope: "Mama Goes to Nursery School," "The Instant Campus: Yesterday a Barn, Today a Junior College," "Presidential Scholars," "Behind the Riots." The style of writing is popular and the content is frequently of interest to laymen as well as educators. Special departments: "Federal Funds," "Statistics of the Month," "Recent Publications" (unannotated), "Research Report." Most articles are by professionals, and are signed.

American Educational Research Journal. 1964. q. $6 (Annual rate to libraries for one regular and one bindery issue, $6). Robert W. Heath. Amer. Educational Research Assn., Natl. Education Assn. 1201 16th St., N.W., Washington, D.C. 20036. Illus., adv. Circ: 6,455. Microform: UM.

Bk. rev: 4–6, 500 words, signed. *Aud:* Ac, Jc, Ht, Et. *Rv:* M. *Jv:* B.

A more scholarly publication of the NEA which covers general research at all levels in education. Articles touch on almost every base from teaching methods and testing to administration. In some way it is a bit too diffuse, and in most cases individuals and librarians would be better advised to subscribe to more specialized publications. Still, a worthwhile consideration for large professional and educational collections. See also, *NEA Research Bulletin.*

American School and University. 1881. m. $8. Georgette N. Manla. Buttenheim Publishing Corp., 757 Third Ave., New York, N.Y. 10017. Illus., index, adv. Circ: 35,000. Microform: UM.

Indexed: EdI. *Aud:* Sa, Ac, Jc. *Rv:* M. *Jv:* B.

The journal for the executives and the administrators in the American elementary, secondary, and university system. Articles pertain to public, private, and parochial schools and deal with buildings and supplies, teacher-administration relationships, food service, and maintenance. A large part of this publication is devoted to advertisements, and information about the latest products that would be useful in either administration or maintenance of school buildings. Aside from major education collections, useful for school administrators who may wish to enter a personal subscription where library budget does not allow purchase.

American School Board Journal; a periodical of school administration. 1891. m. $4.50. William C. Bruce. Bruce Publishing Co., 400 N. Broadway, Milwaukee, Wis. 53211. Illus., index, adv. Circ: 35,000. Microform: UM. Reprint: Abrahams.

Indexed: EdI, PAIS. *Bk. rev:* 5–8, short to 1,500 words. *Aud:* Ac, Jc, Ht, Et. *Rv:* M. *Jv:* B.

Contains "articles on the work of boards of education and on problems of school administration, school business, fiscal and architectural subjects." It is a "market place for the objective examination of the significant issues, innovations, problems and points of view dealing with education today." The style of writing is semi-popular. Articles are written by professional educators for administrators and school board members at the primary and secondary levels. For large collections, but should be brought to the attention of administrators and board of education members even in the smallest community.

American Teacher. 1912. 10/yr. $5. David Elsila. Amer. Federation of Teachers, 716 N. Rush St., Chicago, Ill. 60611. Illus., adv. Circ: 160,000. Microform: UM.

Aud: Ac, Jc, Ht, Et. *Rv:* M. *Jv:* B.

The journal of the American Federation of Teachers, in tabloid format, strives to keep its members abreast of union activities and accomplishments. All facets of public school education are examined in the four to five major articles in each issue, but the emphasis is on today's chaotic and fast-moving drive to organize teachers. In that it includes up-to-date data on current controversies, e.g., "Ten-Hour Sit-In Results in First D.C. Teachers' Pact," it is of much wider interest and value than the title indicates. Lay readers, particularly the involved student or parent, will find it informative. A good item not only for education collections, but also related areas in public and school libraries. See also, *Changing Education.*

Arithmetic Teacher. See Mathematics Section.

Art Education. See Art Section.

Art Journal. See Art Section.

Artist Junior. See Art Section.

Arts and Activities. See Art Section.

Athletic Journal. See Games and Sports Section.

Bulletin of Art Therapy. See Art Section.

Canadian Education and Research Digest. 1961. q. Membership (Non-members, $3). Carol Warrington. Canadian Education Assn., 151 Bloor St., W. Toronto 5, Ont. Index, adv. Circ: 2,300.

Indexed: CanI, EdI. *Aud:* Sa, Ac, Jc. *Rv:* M. *Jv:* B.

Information is provided on current educational developments in Canada as well as in other parts of the world. The articles are designed to relate recent research in education. An outstanding feature is the bibliographies for at least two articles in each issue. One of the quarterly numbers lists abstracts from research studies made during the previous year as well as listings of summaries of graduate theses in education. In America, only for large education collections, but for almost any education-oriented curriculum, or medium to large school in Canada.

Catholic Educational Review. 9/yr. $5. Eugene Kevane. Catholic Univ. of America Press, 620 Michigan Ave., N.E., Washington, D.C. 20017. Index, adv. Circ: 5,120. Microform: UM. Reprint: Abrahams.

Indexed: CathI, EdI. *Bk. rev:* 5–6, 300–600 words, signed. *Aud:* Sa, Ac. *Rv:* H. *Jv:* B.

Written for professional educators by specialists in the field, the journal is noted for a high level of relatively conservative scholarship. All facets of Catholic education are considered, and while it may be of some interest to the teacher, its primary audience is in the Catholic school of education or among high-level principals and supervisors (*Catholic School Journal* is better suited to the day-by-day needs of the practicing teacher). As a vehicle for opinion and research it should be found in all large Catholic and non-Catholic education libraries. Most others may pass it by.

Catholic School Journal. 1901. m. (Sept.–June). $4. William H. Conley. Bruce Publishing Co., 400 N. Broadway, Milwaukee, Wis. 53201. Illus., index, adv. Circ: 13,025. Microform: UM. Reprint: Abrahams.

Indexed: CathI, EdI. *Bk. rev:* 10–12, various lengths, signed. *Aud:* Ac, Jc, Ht, Et. *Rv:* M. *Jv:* B.

The basic journal for Catholic elementary and secondary school teachers. Articles are "on any subject related to education and welfare of Catholic schools, e.g., methods of teaching, child study, curriculum making, school administration, school building construction and upkeep." Contents are divided into five sections: "Educational Issues," "Grade School Features," "High School Features," "Management Features," "Departments." The style of writing is semi-popular. Regular departments include "News of Educators," "New Books," "Evaluations of Audio Visuals." Articles are signed and aimed at the professional educator. Should be found in all Catholic schools, and in larger non-Catholic education collections.

Changing Education. 1967. q. $5. (in combination with the *American Teacher*). Patricia Strandt. Amer. Federation of Teachers, AFL-CIO, 1442 Brush St., Detroit, Mich. 48226. Illus., adv. Circ: 160,000. Microform: UM.

Bk. rev: 1–2, lengthy, signed. *Aud:* Ac, Jc, Ht, Et. *Rv:* M. *Jv:* B.

Whereas the *American Teacher* is a monthly "battle" report on issues of interest to the teachers' union, this quarterly sets a more leisurely, cool-headed pace. The longer range concerns are examined, e.g., "Racism in Education, the Role of the AFT in School Desegregation," ". . . Can a Teachers' Union Be Professional?" A good part of this is both informative and persuasive propaganda, yet is never dull or pedantic. It has wider implications for all those involved or interested in education. As it comes with a subscription to *American Teacher,* the reader or librarian actually has two magazines for the price of one. They are both well worth the subscription.

Childhood Education; a journal for teachers, administrators, church-school workers, librarians, pediatricians. 1924. m. (Sept.–May). $6. Margaret Rasmussen. Assn. for Childhood Education Intl., 3615 Wisconsin Ave., N.W., Washington, D.C. 20016. Illus., index, adv. Circ: 56,888. Microform: UM. Reprint: Johnson, Abrahams.

Indexed: EdI. *Bk. rev:* 15–20, short, signed. *Aud:* Ga, Ac, Jc, Et. *Rv:* H. *Jv:* V.

Directed to both teacher and parent of the child from nursery school through the elementary grades (i.e., two to twelve years) and written in language understandable to layman and professional alike. Generally, each issue is devoted in part to a single theme, e.g., Head Start, Outdoor Education, Parents As Educators, etc. The tone is liberal, the style relatively popular, the content accurate and pragmatic. As the emphasis is on child development, equal attention is given to problems faced daily by the teacher or parent. Yet, it is not parochial, and a major asset of the magazine is its proper emphasis on international developments in education. Coupled with short childrens' and adult book reviews and data on magazine articles, it is an ideal, all-around education/childhood magazine for almost any size or type of library.

The Chronicle of Higher Education. 1966. bi-w. (Oct.–May). $10. Corbin Gwaltney. 3310 N. Charles St., Baltimore, Md. 21218. Illus.

Aud: Ac, Jc. *Rv:* H. *Jv:* A.

Gives both national and international coverage. Objective and knowledgeable reportage on events, trends, reforms, speeches, meetings, government actions, legislation, polls, and studies dealing with higher education. There is special concern with recent student activism. The standard issue is in newspaper format, with a number of signed articles and regular features such as deaths, promotions, and appointments, and a calendar of coming events. Necessary in the college and university library, and recommended in any library which meets needs of users interested in higher education.

Clearing House; a journal for modern junior and senior high faculties. 1925. m. (Sept.–May). $5. Joseph

Green. Fairleigh Dickinson Univ., Teaneck, N.J. 07666. Illus., index, adv. Circ: 8,000. Microform: UM. Reprint: Abrahams.

Indexed: EdI. *Aud:* Ac, Jc, Ht. *Rv:* M. *Jv:* B.

For teachers, guidance counselors, and administrators working in secondary schools, this journal offers the latest trends and developments in curriculum practices. The articles are written principally by college professors rather than practitioners in the field. They are fairly brief, seldom exceeding 2,500 words. Interesting experiments, research findings and new slants on persistent problems in education are reported. Unburdened by statistical formulas and complicated charts and tables, the articles are concise and easily read. The emphasis is upon practical application to problems in courses of study, teaching methods, student activities, the library, guidance work, and other areas relating to programs, services and personnel. Regular departments offer current information in the fields of the humanities and instructional media. A useful addition for almost all professional teacher collections at the junior high through high school level.

College and University. 1925. q. $3. Robert E. Mahn. George Banta Co., Menasha, Wis. 54952. Illus., index. Circ: 4,500. Microform: UM. Reprint: Johnson, Abrahams.

Indexed: EdI. *Aud:* Sa, Ac, Jc. *Rv:* M. *Jv:* B.

Although issued by the American Association of Collegiate Registrars and Admissions Officers, this contains many articles of general interest to anyone concerned with higher education. In addition to statistical and research data in the field of the Association's interest, there is material on the average type of college student, problems of enrollment, difficulties of securing top rated students, what to do with the drop-outs, etc. Proceedings and news of the organization are included in each issue.

College and University Journal; devoted to the advancement of higher education. 1962. q. Membership (Non-members, $7.50). Amer. College Public Relations Assn., 1785 Massachusetts Ave. N.W., Washington, D.C. 20036. Illus., index, adv. Circ: 4,000. Microform: UM.

Indexed: PAIS. *Aud:* Sa, Ac, Jc. *Rv:* M. *Jv:* B.

Not to be confused with *College and University,* this is, nevertheless, a magazine for administrators and more particularly, the public relations experts who are fundamental in raising funds for the schools. In its 48 pages, a good three-quarters of the space is devoted to some aspect of money. The remainder is turned over to everything from publicity for the cafeteria to how to get along with college trustees and presidents. Of limited use in most libraries, although it gives a side of administration rarely covered in other educational journals.

College Board Review. 1947. q. $2. S. Donald Karl. College Entrance Examination Board, 475 Riverside Dr., New York, N.Y. 10027. Circ: 20,000. Reprint: Johnson.

Indexed: PAIS, PsyAb. *Aud:* Sa, Ac, Jc, Ht. *Rv:* M. *Jv:* B.

Basically reports on activities of the College Entrance Examination Board, yet has some value for the nonspecialist in that it includes articles and news on guidance, developments and changes in curriculum, government activities related to education, finance for students, etc. Often there are items on entrance requirements which affect the counselor in the high schools. Not an essential, but a useful item for school libraries.

College Management. 1966. m. $8. Paul Abramson. Management Publishing Group, Inc., 22 W. Putnam Ave., Greenwich, Conn. 06830. Illus., adv. Circ: 24,000. Microform: UM.

Aud: Sa, Ac, Jc. *Rv:* M. *Jv:* B.

The purpose of this school administration magazine is to give college officials information on how to run their schools effectively—and, one assumes, avoid a student strike. Divided by sections, experts write on such things as budgets, personnel, buildings, business and finance, and, of course, student activities. The administrative side of curriculum is considered, too. Considerable emphasis on new mechanical innovations. An esoteric journal for large education collections, and most college and university officials, who will be pleased to find it in the library.

College Student Personnel Abstracts. See Indexes and Abstracts Section.

College Student Survey; an interdisciplinary journal of attitude research. 1967. 3/yr. $5. P.O. Box 125, Oshkosh, Wis. 54901. Circ: 1,000.

Aud: Sa, Ac, Jc. *Rv:* M. *Jv:* B.

Edited by James Croake of the University of South Dakota, this boasts an editorial board of five professors. In a word, it is authoritative, and contains "factual information about college student attitudes, values and opinions." There is an article on the student view of the ideal student, and well-documented pieces on everything from the influence of fraternity rituals to reasons for college attendance. Anyone involved with students will find this informative as well as interesting. It may help a few parents, too.

Comparative Education Review. 1956. 3/yr. $5. Harold J. Noah. Comparative Education Soc., 525 W. 120th St., New York, N.Y. 10027. Circ: 2,000.

Indexed: EdI. *Bk. rev:* Various numbers, lengthy, signed. *Aud:* Sa, Ac. *Rv:* H. *Jv:* B.

One of the basic journals in comparative and international education. Each number averages ten to fifteen articles of both a descriptive and analytical nature. The level of scholarship is high, the style relatively difficult. As the magazine stresses international coverage, it has some interest for political scientists and sociologists, but the primary audience is the professional educator. Only for large collections.

Contemporary Education. 1967. (Formerly: *The Teachers College Journal.*) 1929. m. Free. M. Dale Baughman. 217 Alumni Center, Indiana State Univ., Terre Haute, Ind. 47809. Illus., index. Circ: 3,500. Microform: UM.

Indexed: EdI. *Bk. rev:* 1–2, 400 words, signed. *Aud:* Sa, Ac, Jc. *Rv:* M. *Jv:* B.

"*Contemporary Education* seeks to present competent discussions of professional problems in education and toward this end usually restricts its contributing personnel to those of training and experience in the field." Most issues of CE concentrate on a theme; "Teacher Education: Pressure and Problems"; "Education for Peace." In view of its contents and the fact that it is free, it is certainly worth trying in almost any library.

Counselor Education and Supervision. 1961. q. $6. Edward C. Roeber. Amer. Personnel & Guidance Assn., 1605 New Hampshire Ave., N.W., Washington, D.C. 20009. Circ: 2,767. Microform: UM.

Aud: Sa, Ac, Jc, Ht, Et. *Rv:* M. *Jv:* B.

A guidance journal for the professional or the graduate student, emphasis here is as much on training the counselor as on the work he performs. It definitely is not meant for discovering what is wrong or right with the average student in a typical school situation. It is directed at those who educate counselors and, as such, is of limited interest or value except for the largest education collections.

Education Digest. 1935. m. (Sept.–May). $6. Lawrence Prakken. Prakken Pubns., Inc., 416 Longshore Dr., Ann Arbor, Mich. 48107. Index, adv. Circ: 36,000. Microform: UM. Reprint: Abrahams.

Indexed: EdI, RG. *Bk. rev:* 5, 120 words. *Aud:* Ga, Ac, Jc, Ht, Et. *Rv:* M. *Jv:* B.

Drawing upon what the editors consider to be the best and most representative articles on education, this magazine condenses or publishes in full some 15 to 20 contributions each month. The scope is broad, moving through the elementary grades to graduate school, and the magazine is purposefully geared for the generalist. The articles average two to four pages in length, and the style of writing depends to a degree upon the original source—*PTA Journal, Time, Saturday Review, Harvard Education Review,* etc. The editors claim they check-out some 300 magazines a month for articles. Regular features include: "With Education in Washington," "Education Briefs," "Dates of the Month," "New Educational Materials" and a limited number of short book reviews. This is primarily for the library with little demand for educational news and research. It will not satisfy the professional educator or the serious student, but admittedly is a handy overview of more important educational issues.

Education Summary; a new semi-monthly report on new developments, trends, ideas and research in education. 1947. semi-m. $18. David H. Foerster. Croft Edu-cational Services, 100 Garfield Ave., New London, Conn. 06320. Circ: 12,000.

Bk. rev: Various numbers, lengths. *Aud:* Sa, Ac. *Rv:* H. *Jv:* B.

A loose-leaf newsletter issued semi-monthly to keep subscribers advised of latest developments. The service is particularly useful for keeping up with current federal and state activities, and is good as an up-to-date reference source. Not only for education collections, but for any medium to large reference department where there are recurrent questions in the area.

Educational Administration Quarterly. 1964. 3/yr. $5. Van Miller. Univ. Council for Educational Admin., Ohio State Univ., 65 S. Oval Dr., Columbus, Ohio 43210. Illus. Circ: 1,135.

Aud: Sa, Ac. *Rv:* M. *Jv:* B.

An interesting journal of administration woes and delights at the college and university level. While a number of the contributions are of a practical nature, some of those from people in and outside the administrative framework are theoretical and concerned with larger problems of education, from student revolt to the future of colleges. Serious students of education will find much here not otherwise touched on by other journals, and a given amount of frankness which is enlightening.

Educational and Psychological Measurement. See Psychology Section.

Educational Leadership. 1943. m. (Oct.–May). $5.50. Robert R. Leeper. Assn. for Supervision and Curriculum Development, 1201 16th St., N.W., Washington, D.C. 20036. Illus., index, adv. Circ: 14,800. Microform: UM. Reprint: Abrahams.

Indexed: EdI. *Bk. rev:* 6, 400 words., signed. *Aud:* Ac, Jc, Ht, Et. *Rv:* M. *Jv:* B.

Curriculum and all its implications are involved here, with particular emphasis on the administrative, professional educator's, or teacher's view of curriculum in elementary and secondary schools. Usually, each issue is devoted to a major theme, with an occasional general piece on education and regular departments concerned with various developments in research and new innovations in education. The whole is a trifle dull, yet as the voice of a major division of the NEA, it deserves a place in larger school and education collections.

Educational Product Report (Formerly: *Epie Forum*). 1968. m. (Oct.–June). $35. Educational Products Information Exchange Inst., 386 Park Ave., S., New York, N.Y. 10016. Illus.

Aud: Ac, Jc, Ht, Et. *Rv:* H. *Jv:* A.

Published by the EPIE Institute, a nonprofit, non-industry, non-government professionals' cooperative which conducts impartial studies of the effectiveness of instructional materials, equipment and systems. A much-needed consumer's report for the education administrator who must select equipment and materials for schools from the elementary through high grades. (Some of the equipment, however, is used in colleges and universities—particularly schools of education—and therefore the magazine is almost as valuable at this level.) Issues have dealt with programmed instruction, science kits, 8mm projectors, study carrels, textbooks, and the like. Comparative data is given for price, grade level, content or design, and producer's warrantees in a self-contained section. Informative articles, interviews, analyses and guidelines are presented in the main portion of each issue. A required magazine for almost every situation where a decision must be made regarding the purchase of materials for education.

Educational Record. 1920. q. $6. Edward Joseph Shoben, Jr. Amer. Council on Education, 1785 Massachusetts Ave., N.W., Washington, D.C. 20036. Illus. Circ: 8,000. Microform: UM. Reprint: Abrahams.

Indexed: EdI. *Bk. rev:* 15 (fall & summer issues), 500–2,500 words. *Aud:* Ac, Jc. *Rv:* H. *Jv:* B.

Covering the general education field, emphasis is on material of interest to the college and university administrator, school of education personnel and, to a limited extent, faculty. The content and style are scholarly, yet pragmatic in that specific suggestions are often given on everything from legal and governmental regulations to how to train the junior college teacher. The increasing importance of the American Council on Education gives the *Record* added interest, since the activities of the Council are reported in full. Only for larger libraries.

Educational Theatre Journal. See Theatre Section.

Educational Theory; a medium of expression for the John Dewey Society and the Philosophy of Education Society. 1951. q. W. O. Stanley, Education Bldg., Univ. of Illinois, Urbana, Ill. 61801. Index, adv. Circ: 1,625. Reprint: Johnson, Abrahams.

Indexed: EdI. *Bk. rev:* 1–2, lengthy. *Aud:* Sa, Ac. *Rv:* M. *Jv:* B.

"The general purposes of this journal are to foster the continuing development of educational theory and to encourage wide and effective discussion of theoretical problems within the education profession." Scholarly articles further this end, touching not only on education, but on education's relations to anthropology, sociology, psychology, etc. While primarily directed to teachers and graduate students in schools of education, its broad scope makes this journal useful to scholars in a number of disciplines. A required item in all schools of education, and for larger academic collections.

Elementary School Journal. 1900. m. (Oct.–May). $6. Kenneth Rehage. Univ. of Chicago Press, 5750 S. Ellis Ave., Chicago, Ill. 60637. Index, adv. Circ: 17,500. Microform: UM. Reprint: Abrahams.

Indexed: EdI. *Bk. rev:* Occasional. *Aud:* Ac, Jc, Et. *Rv:* H. *Jv:* B.

Strives to keep elementary school educators abreast of new developments and provide them with practical in-service education. Generally its scope emphasizes what should go on in the classroom, but occasionally there are other types of articles exemplified by such titles as "Enter Funding—Exit Curriculum Planning," and "The Community School in Historical Perspective." Each issue contains approximately 8 to 10 articles. More scholarly than *Childhood Education,* and some of the writers have a tendency to lapse into an educational jargon which is rather stiff, even for professional educators. A basic journal for almost all education school libraries, but others are better served by *Childhood Education.*

Everyday Art. See Art Section.

French Review. See Romance Language Section.

Grade Teacher. 1882. m. (Sept.–May). $5.50. Paul Abramson. Teachers Publishing Corp., Darien, Conn. 06820. Illus., adv. Circ: 195,000. Microform: UM. Reprint: Abrahams.

Indexed: EdI. *Bk. rev:* 8, 75–150 words, signed. *Aud:* Ac, Jc, Et. *Rv:* M. *Jv:* B.

Next to *The Instructor,* this is the most popular, large circulation magazine for elementary and junior high school teachers. Emphasis is almost entirely on how to teach, and the 20 or so articles move from new innovations in geography to politics and audio-visual. Most material is of the step-by-step variety which can be translated into classroom projects and innovations. There are a number of departments which review new books and materials in the field. While the intellectual content is limited, the how-to-do-it approach is done quite well, and teachers find it a valuable aid. There is a considerable amount of advertising. Most school libraries will want both this and *The Instructor,* but if a choice is to be made, the latter has a slight edge.

Harvard Educational Review. 1931. q. $6. W. Charles Read. Grad. Sch. of Education, Harvard Univ., Longfellow Hall, 13 Appian Way, Cambridge, Mass. 02138. Illus., index, adv. Circ: 10,000. Microform: UM. Reprint: Johnson, Abrahams.

Indexed: EdI, HistAb, PAIS. *Bk. rev:* 12, lengthy, signed. *Aud:* Sa, Ac, Jc. *Rv:* H. *Jv:* V.

The intellectual teacher's magazine, certainly the basic journal for anyone remotely connected with the education and supervision of teachers. Here, as in the less ambitious *Educational Theory,* the emphasis is on the theoretical, long-range topics which concern not only educators but all of society, e.g., teaching about religion, humanism vs. the sciences, intellectuals and the schools. Special issues often are devoted to a single topic, and many of the contributors are from fields outside of education. The tone is scholarly, always critical, always challenging, and rarely dull. A major journal for all medium to large libraries where education and its many facets are important.

Hispanica. See Romance Languages Section.

Home Economics. See Home Section.

Improving College and University Teaching; international quarterly journal. 1953. q. $4. Delmer M. Goode. Oregon State Univ., 101 Waldo Hall, Corvallis, Ore. 97331. Illus., adv. Circ: 2,000.

Indexed: EdI. *Bk. rev:* Various numbers, lengths. *Aud:* Sa, Ac, Jc. *Rv:* H. *Jv:* A.

A major journal for the teacher at the junior college, college, or university level. As the title indicates, the emphasis is pragmatic, the articles usually reflecting practical experience, ideas, problems and suggestions for improvement of teaching. While there are longer articles on ongoing research, most of the 20 or so contributions are relatively brief. Teachers of many subjects report on successes and failures in classroom procedures. Reports come from various type and size schools from all parts of the United States, Canada and, recently, the world. Rarely an issue goes by in which the teacher cannot find at least two or three items to help him with his classes. The book reviews, too, represent the best single source for locating material in this field. As one fan puts it, the magazine "promotes a continuous awareness of the need for constant self-evaluation, reappraisal . . . and innovation which characterizes the effective teacher." It hardly holds all the answers, but faculty members will thank the librarian who brings it to their attention.

Independent School Bulletin. 1941. q. $3.50. Esther Osgood. Natl. Assn. of Independent Schools, 4 Liberty Sq., Boston, Mass., 02109. Index, adv. Circ: 7,800.

Aud: Ac, Jc, Ht, Et. *Rv:* M. *Jv:* B.

Although for teachers and educators who are interested in independent school education, much of the material will interest public school teachers and students of education. Directed to elementary and secondary school teachers and administrators, it stresses the peculiar benefits, and few of the drawbacks, of a private or independent school education. A greater emphasis is found here on creative teaching and thinking than in many other educational publications. For all libraries serving private education and larger education collections.

Industrial Arts and Vocational Education; the shop teachers' professional magazine. 1914. m. (except July & Aug.) $4. John L. Feirer. Bruce Publishing Co., 400 N. Broadway, Milwaukee, Wis. 53201. Illus., index, adv. Circ: 30,500. Microform: UM. Reprint: Abrahams.

Indexed: EdI. *Bk. rev:* 14–16, 100 words. *Aud:* Ht, Et. *Rv:* M. *Jv:* B.

For the instructor at the advanced vocational, high school and elementary school levels. Articles support the need for industrial and vocational courses and give specific advice of a how-to-do-it nature. There is emphasis, too, on how to assist young boys, unique tools and methods, and a number of departments: "Teacher's Notebook," "Equipment," "News in the Field," and short book reviews. A must in any school with an industrial arts program.

The Instructor. 1891. m. (Sept.–June). $7. Elizabeth F. Noon. F. A. Owen Publishing Co., 5 Bank St., Dansville, N.Y. 14437. Illus., index, adv. Circ: 239,322. Microform: UM. Reprint: Abrahams.

Indexed: EdI. *Bk. rev:* 20–25, short, signed. *Aud:* Ac, Jc, Et. *Rv:* H. *Jv:* A.

An approach somewhat similar to that of *Grade Teacher,* differing in that there is considerably more advertising, a larger format, and, more important, some stress on social issues rather than the how-to-do-it emphasis of the *Grade Teacher.* In addition to practical materials and techniques, the editors usually open each issue with a series of articles on educational developments and philosophy. With this out of the way, they then move over the familiar territory of the *Grade Teacher,* i.e., sections on arts and crafts, foreign languages, history, folklore geography, etc. Each area is nicely supplemented with diagrams, illustrations and photographs. Finally, there are reviews of books, curriculum materials and reference works. The amount of advertising may "turn off" some readers, but the editorial content is solid enough. While some teachers consider neither magazine intellectually stimulating or overly imaginative, of the two, this would be a first choice.

Integrated Education. 1963. bi-m. $4. Meyer Weinberg. Integrated Education Associates, 343 S. Dearborn St., Chicago, Ill. 60604.

Indexed: INeg, PAIS. *Aud:* Ga, Ac, Jc, Sh. *Rv:* H. *Jv:* B.

Begun by teachers interested in integrated education, this is a non-partisan report on current developments in the integration of the nation's schools. Each issue includes a bibliography of current books and articles on the subject, and the ten pages or so arranged under 16 subject headings are an invaluable guide to integration and related topics. The bibliography is preceded by articles, a chronicle of integration on a state by state basis, and pertinent court decisions and documents. The May–June number featured, "The Indian in American History Textbooks," and a document, "Black and White at Northwestern University." Should be a basic periodical in any public or academic library.

International Review of Education. 1955. q. $8.90. Martinus Nijhoff Publishing, Lange Voorhout 9–11, 's-Grauenhage, P.O.B. 269, Netherlands.

Indexed: EdI. *Bk. rev:* 10–30, average length, signed. *Aud:* Sa, Ac, Jc, Ht, Et. *Rv:* M. *Jv:* B.

Dedicated to achieving international intercommunication on all aspects of education. Highly technical articles in English, French, and German are typical. The average issue has 3–8 long articles, varying numbers of shorter articles, and book reviews. There is often a particular concern with experimental programs, such as the use of computers in teaching. An occasional issue is devoted to a special topic, usually under a guest editor, and including a bibliography on the topic. UNESCO sponsored, the *Review* has a board of editors selected from a number of countries. School, college, and university libraries could use this journal.

Italica. See Romance Languages Section.

Jewish Education. 1929. q. $5. Samuel Dinin. National Council for Jewish Education, 101 Fifth Ave., New York, N. Y. 10003. Index, adv. Reprint: Abrahams.

Indexed: PsyAb. *Bk. rev:* 8, 50–750 words, signed. *Aud:* Ac, Jc, Ht, Et. *Rv:* M. *Jv:* B.

Deals exclusively with the problems and directions of Jewish education in America and abroad. The core of the publication is comprised of scholarly articles. Topics vary from "Creativity, Culture and the Synagogue School" to "Jewish Education in Western Europe" and "Notes on the Relation of Governments to Jewish Day Schools." Periodically, there is an added section for the younger set. A required item in large school of education collections, and will be appreciated in any community with a large Jewish population.

JGE; Journal of General Education. 1946. q. $5. Henry W. Sams. Pennsylvania State Univ. Press, University Park, Pa. 16802. Illus., index, adv. Circ: 1,856. Microform: UM. Reprint: Kraus, Abrahams.

Indexed: EdI. *Bk. rev:* 2–4, 500 words, signed. *Aud:* Ac, Jc. *Rv:* M. *Jv:* B.

Primarily a journal for school of education faculties, each issue features seven or eight scholarly, somewhat theoretical articles on a wide variety of subjects. Emphasis is on the humanities, although such articles as "Larger Implications of Computerization" tend to broach all fields. Faculty members will welcome librarians bringing this to their attention.

Journal of American Indian Education. 1961. q. $3.50. George A. Gill & Bruch Meador. Indian Education Center, College of Education, Arizona State Univ., Tempe, Ariz. 85281. Circ: 1,000.

Bk. rev: 2–3, 300 words, signed. *Aud:* Sa, Ac. *Rv:* M. *Jv:* B.

A slim magazine with articles by tribal leaders, educators and anthropologists dealing with current Indian problems, programs and proposed solutions. Most deal with the field of education, and many are applicable to the study of education among other ethnic and under-privileged groups. Emphasis is on the American Southwest. Articles evaluate educational programs and describe new projects like "Project Awareness" among the Chippewas or "Teaching English as a Foreign Language to the Eskimos." "From the Bookshelf" offers reviews of newly released titles on Indian

history and contemporary life. Useful in most larger libraries, especially those in the Southwest or with specialized collections on Indian education or Indian affairs.

Journal of Chemical Education. See Chemistry Section.

Journal of College Placement; the international magazine of placement and recruitment. 1940. q. $10. Warren E. Kauffman. College Placement Council, Inc., 35 E. Elizabeth Ave., Bethlehem, Pa. 18018. Illus., index, adv. Circ: 4,400. Microform: UM.

Indexed: EdI, PAIS. *Aud:* Ac, Jc. *Rv:* M. *Jv:* B.

A professional journal for college placement directors and vocational counselors and employer representatives who recruit and hire college graduates. It usually contains about 12 four- to fifteen-page articles on topics pertaining to placement techniques and new or different career fields. The employer advertising is valuable to both counselors and students.

Journal of Creative Behavior. 1967. q. $8. Eugene A. Brunelle. Creative Education Foundation, Inc., State Univ. College, 1300 Elmwood Ave. Buffalo, N.Y. 11422. Illus., index, adv. Circ: 5,000. Microform: UM.

Bk. rev: 3–4, 400–1,000 words, signed. *Aud:* Ac, Jc, Ht, Et. *Rv:* M. *Jv:* B.

Although the subject scope here is limited to "the general area of creativity, intelligence and problem solving," the magazine has wide appeal for teachers sharing some of the editor's interests. The six to eight articles are scholarly, reporting on various research activities, yet are well within the grasp of the more involved elementary, secondary or university teacher. Admittedly a narrow area, but one well worth space in more advanced school libraries and in almost all larger schools of education.

Journal of Education. 1875. q. $3. Thomas H. Eames. Boston Univ. Sch. of Education, 765 Commonwealth Ave., Boston, Mass. 02115. Illus. Circ: 2,000. Microform: UM. Reprint: Johnson, Abrahams.

Indexed: EdI. *Aud:* Ac, Jc, Ht, Et. *Rv:* H. *Jv:* B.

Devoted to the in-service education of school teachers. Each issue focuses on a particular theme, e.g., "Classroom Tested Learning Games for Use in Urban Elementary Education," "Metagenesis—A Need for Teachers of Teachers." There are usually five articles which are well-documented, but semi-popular in style, and each issue is almost a book in itself. Noted for its well ordered format and the practical nature of its articles, it is a must for any library concerned with elementary or secondary education.

Journal of Educational Psychology. 1910. bi-m. $10. Raymond G. Kuhlen. Amer. Psychological Assn., Inc., 1200 17th St., N.W., Washington, D.C. 20036. Illus., index, adv. Circ: 7,300. Microform: UM. Reprint: AMS, Abrahams.

Indexed: BioAb, EdI, PsyAb. *Aud:* Ac, Jc, Ht, Et. *Rv:* H. *Jv:* B.

This journal "publishes original investigations and theoretical papers dealing with problems of learning, teaching, and the psychological development, relationships, and adjustment of the individual." The editors give preference "to studies of the more complex types of behavior, especially in or relating to educational settings." The articles "concern all levels of education and all age groups." The style of writing is scholarly, and requires a solid background in psychology.

The Journal of Educational Research. 1920. 10/yr. $7.50. Wilson Thiede. Dembar Educational Research Services, Inc., Box 1605, Madison, Wis. 53701. Illus., index, adv. Circ: 6,800. Microform: UM, Canner. Reprint: AMS, Abrahams.

Indexed: EdI, PsyAb. *Bk. rev:* 1–2, 500–1,500 words, signed. *Aud:* Ac, Jc, Ht, Et. *Rv:* H. *Jv:* B.

In that this covers all aspects of current educational research, usually in the form of short, concise articles, here is an overall view for anyone involved seriously with educational research. It moves from elementary school problems through graduate study. Each article is well documented, normally accompanied by useful charts, tables and graphs. The basic journal in this field, and, as such, should be found in all large libraries and schools of education. Progressive elementary and secondary school libraries will also wish to subscribe.

Journal of Experimental Education. 1932. q. $10. John Schmid. Dembar Educational Research Services, Inc., Box 1605, Madison, Wis. 53701. Illus., index, adv. Circ: 1,400. Microform: UM, Canner. Reprint: Abrahams, AMS.

Indexed: EdI. *Aud:* Sa, Ac. *Rv:* M. *Jv:* B.

Similar to *Journal of Educational Research* in scope, but a trifle more esoteric, as more emphasis is placed upon new and experimental tests and procedures. Articles range from "A Scale to Measure Teacher Student Interaction," to "The Empirical Validity of Major Properties of a Taxonomy of Affective Education Objectives." Extensive use is made in the articles of graphs, charts and statistics. Only for the largest public library and the teacher education oriented college; a third choice, the second being *Review of Educational Research*.

Journal of Health, Physical Education, Recreation. 1930. 9/yr. Membership (Non-members, $15). Nancy Rosenberg. American Assn. for Health, Physical Education, and Recreation, 1201 16th St., N.W., Washington, D.C. 20036. Illus., index, adv. Circ: 50,000. Microform: UM.

Indexed: EdI. *Bk. rev:* 20, notes. *Aud:* Sa, Ac, Jc, Ht, Et. *Rv:* H. *Jv:* B.

The basic journal for teachers at all levels involved with physical education, health classes and recreation—including the dance. The well-illustrated 88-page magazine is usually composed of three parts: a special feature with a number of supporting articles, e.g., teaching aids, tennis, physical education in 1977; shorter contributions on problems of teaching; a considerable number of regular columnists covering everything from news of the organization to dance and coming events. There is an annual convention number.

The Journal of Higher Education. 1930. m. (Oct.–June). $6. C. Grey Austin. Ohio State Univ. Press, 164 W. 19th Ave., Columbus, Ohio 43210. Index, adv. Circ: 2,400. Microform: Canner, UM. Reprint: Johnson, Abrahams.

Indexed: AbSocWk, ChemAb, EdI, PsyAb. *Bk rev:* 5, 500 words, signed. *Aud:* Ac. *Rv:* H. *Jv:* B.

A general education magazine directed to faculty in universities and colleges, yet considerably more limited in coverage than either the *AAUP Bulletin* or the administration-directed *Educational Record*. Useful because of well-written, topical articles which range from a study of The University of Zambia to "Organization of the Liberal Arts in the Large University." Editorials take strong stands on important issues, e.g., the Clark Kerr episode and government relations with education. The book reviews are relatively short, but critical.

Journal of Industrial Arts Education. 1939. 5/yr. Membership (Non-members, $6). A. P. Bornstein. Amer. Industrial Arts Assn., Inc., 1201 16th St., N.W., Washington, D.C. 20036. Illus., index, adv. Circ: 14,000. Microform: UM.

Indexed: EdI. *Bk. rev:* Notes. *Aud:* Jc, Ht. *Rv:* M. *Jv:* B.

An important magazine in that it covers developments in not only technical education, but in technology which may change or replace current employment patterns. The advice is sound, often months or years ahead of what may be found in the popular press. The bread-and-butter material is primarily centered around methods of teaching, news in the field, personalities and the like. The whole is well written, supplemented by useful advertisements on everything from shop training devices to summer school programs. While of primary interest to high school and trade school teachers, it should also be found in larger public libraries.

Journal of Learning Disabilities. 1967. m. $7. Martin Topaz. Professional Press, 5 N. Wabash Ave., Chicago, Ill. 60602. Illus., adv.

Bk. rev: 1–3, 500 words, signed. *Aud:* Sa, Ac. *Rv:* H. *Jv:* B.

Claiming to be the first "multi-disciplinary exchange of international information in the field," the journal represents 24 disciplines, from anthropology to speech. Each is supported by a member of a large editorial advisory board, primarily made-up of professors and doctors. The four to five articles touch every level, from adult education to techniques used in diagnosing a learning disability in a child. Obviously for the professional educator and specialist, yet will have considerable interest for the average elementary school through college teacher who works in this area.

Journal of Negro Education. See Afro-American Section.

Journal of Research and Development in Education. 1967. q. $7. Evelyn J. Blewett, 122 Baldwin Hall, College of Education, Univ. of Georgia, Athens, Ga. 30601.

Aud: Sa, Ac, Jc. *Rv:* M. *Jv:* B.

Each issue of this 140- to 150-page journal is turned over to a given subject, e.g., mathematics in the first number. Normally it includes papers delivered at a conference of professional educators on the subject treated. There are one or two main papers, responses, and summaries. Detailed references accompany each article. As a series of what amounts to verbatim reports of conferences on the theory of education the journal is valuable for all schools of education. Teachers at the high school level and up may find it of interest.

Journal of Teacher Education. 1950. q. $5. D. D. Darland. Natl. Education Assn., 1201 16th St., N.W., Washington, D.C. 20036. Illus., index, adv. Circ: 5,500. Microform: UM. Reprint: Kraus, Abrahams.

Indexed: EdI, PsyAb. *Bk. rev:* 7, 400–600 words, signed. *Aud:* Ac, Jc. *Rv:* H. *Jv:* B.

As the title suggests, of limited interest except to professional educators. The 12 to 15 scholarly articles normally are concerned with a current issue in teacher education. An essential addition to university or junior colleges with any type of teacher education program.

Junior College Journal. 1930. m. $4. Roger Yarrington. Amer. Assn. of Junior Colleges, 1315 16th St., N.W., Washington, D.C. 20036. Illus., index, adv. Circ: 22,000. Microform: UM. Reprint: Johnson, Abrahams.

Indexed: EdI. *Aud:* Jc. *Rv:* M. *Jv:* B.

Although limited to interests of faculty and administrators in junior colleges, every base within the field is touched. A typical issue will discuss music, art, the library, salaries, administrative problems, and even general living conditions. Articles are sound and semi-popular in style. A useful feature is the report on dissertations in progress, or completed, which have anything to do with junior colleges. A basic journal for all junior colleges.

Lovejoy's Guidance Digest. 1947. 10/yr. $15. Clarence E. Lovejoy's Guidance Services, 443 Broad St., Red Bank, N.J. 07701. Illus., adv. Circ: 4,500.

Aud: Ga, Ac, Jc, Sh. *Rv:* M. *Jv:* B.

This monthly supplement to Lovejoy's familiar *College Guide* provides up-to-date news of colleges and schools to prospective students, their parents, and guidance counselors. It's 20 pages contains newsy short articles concerning scholarship information, innovations in colleges and education, how to get into college, and a great deal of advertising from colleges and prep schools. There are two regular monthly features of interest to students: "Career Corner," a description of a specific occupation, and "Lovejoy's Educational and Vocational Guidance Research Service," free advice from Lovejoy's Education Center to subscribers.

Mademoiselle Gymnast. See Games and Sports Section.

Mathematics Teacher. See Mathematics Section.

Modern Language Journal. See Linguistics and Philology Section.

NEA Research Bulletin. 1923. q. $2. Beatrice C. Lee. National Education Assn., Research Div., 1201 16th St., N.W., Washington, D.C. 20036. Circ: 110,000. Microform: UM.

Indexed: EdI, PAIS. *Aud:* Ac, Jc, Ht, Et. *Rv:* H. *Jv:* B.

This is statistical data reported to NEA and then passed on to the membership in short, concise, staff-written articles. The style is semi-popular, well within the grasp of the lay reader. Material touches all aspects of problems and discussions in current education. While it lacks the depth and research of other magazines in the field, the concise nature of the reports make it an excellent addition to any medium to large library, and is particularly useful for answering queries within the lay community.

National Association of Secondary School Principals. Bulletin. 1917. m. (Oct.–May). $15. Warren C. Seyfert. National Assn. of Secondary Sch. Principals, 1201 16th St., N.W., Washington, D.C. 20036. Illus., index, adv. Circ: 30,000. Microform: UM. Reprint: Kraus, Abrahams.

Indexed: EdI. *Bk. rev:* 2, 11 pages, signed. *Aud:* Ac, Jc, Ht. *Rv:* M. *Jv:* B.

This NEA bulletin seeks to "highlight some one or at most two subjects or topics" for the information and edification of secondary school principals. It covers a broad spectrum, e.g., "Some Challenges of Curricular Change," "Radio & Television in the Secondary School," "Secondary Education and Human Resources." Articles are written by professional educators and the style is somewhat dull. Larger school libraries will want this, but in most cases the principal can well subscribe to this item himself.

National Catholic Educational Association. Bulletin. 1904. q. $5. Russell Shaw. Natl. Catholic Educational Assn., 1785 Massachusetts Ave., N.W., Washington, D.C. 20036. Circ: 16, 807. Microform: UM. Reprint: Abrahams.

Indexed: CathI, EdI, PAIS. *Bk. rev:* 4, 750 words, signed. *Aud:* Ac, Jc, Ht, Et. *Rv:* H. *Jv:* B.

A thoughtful, scholarly approach to Catholic education in America, here is a fascinating magazine for both Catholic and non-Catholic alike. The tone is generally liberal, although the conservative voice is often found in letters or in replies to articles. The scope is broad, unusually candid and aware of problems associated with Catholic education. While it covers all facets of the subject, emphasis tends to be on higher education. Normally, each issue is devoted to a main topic, e.g., "Needed Research in Catholic Education," Collective Bargaining in Catholic Education." It nicely complements *Catholic Educational Review,* yet would be the first choice between the two in Catholic schools and large non-Catholic school and public libraries.

The National Elementary Principal. 1921. bi-m. (Sept.–May). Membership. Dorothy Neubauer. Elementary School Principals Dept., National Education Assn., 1201 16th St., N.W., Washington, D.C. 20036. Illus., adv. Microform: UM.

Indexed: EdI. *Bk. rev:* 4, 600 words, signed. *Aud:* Ac, Jc, Et. *Rv:* M. *Jv:* B.

Similar in approach to the *Bulletin of the National Association of Secondary School Principals,* i.e., articles stress practice more than theory. A typical issue will discuss findings regarding class sizes, reading instruction, staff and salary negotiations. Unquestionably of interest to its target readers, but again, one which should be subscribed to by the principal. Larger school and educational libraries, of course, should subscribe.

Nation's Schools; the magazine of better school administration. 1928. m. $12. Aaron Cohodes. McGraw-Hill Pubns., Circ. Dept., 1050 Merchandise Mart, Chicago, Ill., 60654. Illus., index, adv. Microform: UM.

Indexed: EdI. *Aud:* Ac, Jc, Ht, Et. *Rv:* M. *Jv:* B.

A trade magazine whose advertisements and editorial copy are directed primarily at the elementary through high school administrator. Concentration is on personnel, finance, equipment and buildings. Articles of a wider scope are usually connected with the curriculum, and involve innovations which require new equipment or teaching methods. Particularly useful for the non-administrator are reports on activities in Washington and in the courts which directly affect education. The reports are candid and accurate. A required item for most school libraries, and should be distributed to teachers as well as administrators.

Negro American Literature Forum for School and University Teachers. See Afro-American Section.

Negro Educational Review. See Afro-American Section.

PTA Magazine. 1906. m. (Sept.–June). $2. Eva H. Grant. National Congress of Parents and Teachers, 700 N. Rush St., Chicago, Ill. 60611. Illus., index. Microform: UM.

Indexed: EdI, RG. *Aud:* Ga, Ac, Jc, Ht, Et. *Rv:* M. *Jv:* A.

A sounding board for anyone involved with the PTA. All aspects of elementary and secondary education are considered in a semi-popular style. Features include: "Our Life and Times," "Happenings in Education," "The President's Message," TV and motion picture reviews. Designed for anyone interested in education and their children's future. Although it is not *the* source for educational information, it is useful to active parents and teachers. This magazine's high rating is due rather to its wide scope and reader interest, than because of its intrinsic value.

Perceptual Cognitive Development. See Psychology Section.

Phi Delta Kappa. 1918. m. (Sept.–June). $5. Stanley Elam. Phi Delta Kappa, Inc., 8th St. & Union Ave., Bloomington, Ind. 47401. Index, adv. Circ: 80,000. Microform: UM. Reprint: Kraus, Abrahams.

Indexed: EdI. *Bk. rev:* 5, 500–1500 words, signed. *Aud:* Ac, Jc, Ht. *Rv:* H. *Jv:* B.

Published by the professional fraternity for men in education, this journal's purpose is "the promotion of leadership in education." Its scope embraces aspects of education at all levels; however, emphasis is on research and the secondary school. The level of the 10 to 12 articles is consistently high; not loaded with the educationist's jargon. A good, solid addition for most school libraries.

Physics Teacher. See Physics Section.

Quarterly Review of Higher Education Among Negroes. See Afro-American Section.

Research Quarterly. See Games and Sports Section.

Review of Educational Research. 1931. 5/yr. Membership (Non-members, $10). Jacob T. Hunt, National Education Assn., 1201 16th St., N.W. Washington, D.C. 20036. Index. Circ: 6,000. Microform: UM. Reprint: Abrahams, AMS.

Indexed: EdI, PsyAb. *Aud:* Ac, Jc, Ht, Et. *Rv:* H. *Jv:* B.

Published by the American Educational Research Association, this is primarily of value in schools of education, but will be useful for all teachers. Differs from the equally good *Journal of Educational Research* in that each issue focuses on a particular aspect of education, e.g., "Educational Organization, Administration, and Finance;" "Philosophical and Social Framework of Education;" "Methodology of Educational Research;" "Educational Programs: Adolescence, Educational and Psychological Testing." Where school libraries may not wish to subscribe, it is advisable to watch for topics highlighted. Often a single issue order will satisfy some faculty need.

Scholastic Coach. See Games and Sports Section.

School and Society. 1915. semi-m. (Oct.–May). $9.50. William W. Brickman. Soc. for the Advancement of Education, 1860 Broadway, New York, N.Y. 10023. Index, adv. Circ: 7200. Microform: UM. Reprint: Johnson, Abrahams.

Indexed: EdI, PsyAb, RG. *Aud:* Ac, Jc, Ht. *Rv:* M. *Jv:* B.

A somewhat jargon-ridden approach to the topics of current secondary and higher education, although the coverage is broad enough to overcome the style. Articles cover every conceivable facet of current secondary and advanced education, e.g., "Presidential Leadership in Academe," "The

Group Case Study Method in Political Education," "Admissions and the Private College." The six to eight articles are semi-popular and the journal has expanded news coverage in education, including pictorial reporting. Special departments; events, special book preview (excerpts from forthcoming books). Way down the list, except for the large school of education or general professional collection.

School Arts. See Art Section.

The School Review; a journal of philosophical and theoretical policies and practices in education. 1893. q. $8. Univ. of Chicago Press, 5750 S. Ellis Ave., Chicago, Ill. 60637. Index, adv. Circ: 3,800. Microform: UM. Reprint: Abrahams.

Indexed: EdI. *Aud:* Ac, Jc, Ht. *Rv:* H. *Jv:* A.

"The purpose of *The School Review* is to encourage reflection and discussion by all persons who are interested in or concerned about education." This does, and has become, through time and reputation, the bastion of scholarship for articles on secondary education and education in general. The writing style varies from pompous to excellent, the content from the theoretical to the practical. Considerably above the average educational journal, this should be in all schools of education and read by teachers.

School Safety. 1965. q. $3.60. Joan Crosbie. National Safety Council, 425 N. Michigan Ave., Chicago, Ill. 60611. Illus. Circ: 17,000.

Indexed: EdI. *Aud:* Et. *Rv:* M. *Jv:* B.

Issued by the National Safety Council as a teaching aid in the elementary schools. Features articles, simplified instructional materials, and hints on how to instill the importance of safty in youngsters. Useful as an added magazine for health and safety classes, but not essential.

School Shop; for industrial education teachers. 1942. m. (Sept.–June). $4. L. W. Prakken, Prakken Pubns., 416 Longshore Dr., Ann Arbor, Mich. 48107. Illus., index, adv. Circ: 38,000. Microform: UM.

Indexed: EdI. *Bk. rev:* Notes. *Aud:* Sa, Ht. *Rv:* M. *Jv:* B.

A magazine of hints, suggestions and some inspiration to shop teachers at the secondary and vocational school level. Primarily given over to articles on teaching techniques and detailed reports of successful projects. News items on Washington legislative action affecting vocational training, new products and personnel and the profession. A basic periodical for most secondary and vocational schools.

Social Education. 1937. m. Membership (Non-members, $6). Lewis Paul Todd. National Council for the Social Studies, 1201 16th St., N.W., Washington, D.C. 20036. Illus., adv. Circ: 25,000. Microform: UM.

Indexed: EdI. *Bk. rev:* 9–12, 500 words, signed. *Aud:* Ac, Jc, Ht, Et. *Rv:* M. *Jv:* B.

For the teacher of history, geography, and other social science subjects at elementary and secondary levels. Articles include new techniques, current trends, changes and problems involved in teaching. Authors are high school teachers, professors of education, and social scientists from all over the country. Special features include annual reviews of curriculum materials; annual reviews of research in the social studies; bi-monthly presentations of recent Supreme Court decisions prepared for classroom use; reviews of pamphlets; and the regular department "Sight and Sound," which reviews 20 to 30 movies, providing full bibliographic information, source information, grade level and a 60-word annotation.

Social Studies. 1909. m. (Oct.–Apr.) $5. Leonard B. Irwin. McKinley Publishing Co., 112 S. New Broadway, Brooklawn, N.J. 08030. Index, adv. Circ: 4,800. Microform: UM.

Indexed: EdI, PAIS. *Bk. rev:* 10–15, ½ page. *Aud:* Ac, Jc, Ht. *Rv:* M. *Jv:* B.

Similar in scope and approach to *Social Education,* yet articles tend to be briefer and the whole is about one-half the size of its competitor. Features articles on the teaching of history and current affairs. Material is presented in a semi-popular style. There is considerable effort to describe instructional materials like films and records. The book reviews are good to excellent. A useful magazine for schools of education, and for high school and junior high libraries, but only after a subscription has been entered for *Social Education.*

Sociology of Education. 1927. q. $7. Martin A. Trow. Amer. Sociological Assn. 1001 Connecticut Ave., N.W., Washington, D.C. 20036. Illus., index, adv. Circ: 2,400. Microform: UM.

Indexed: EdI, PAIS, PsyAb. *Aud:* Sa, Ac, Jc. *Rv:* H. *Jv:* B.

Serves as a forum for the study of education by scholars in all the social sciences. The editorial board reflects this international and inter-disciplinary nature, and the presentations use the perspectives of history, anthropology, education, political science, psychology and sociology to analyze educational institutions. The four 15–25 page articles are research studies on such subjects as investment in education and economic growth; teacher attitudes toward academic freedom; the relation of education, mobility, social values, and expectations. Until 1963 was entitled the *Journal of Educational Sociology.* A specialized magazine for schools of education and larger school professional collections.

Southern Education Report. (Formerly: **Southern School News**). 1965. 10/yr. Robert F. Campbell. Southern Education Reporting Service, Box 6156, Nashville, Tenn. 37212. Illus., index. Circ: 14,100.

Indexed: INeg. *Aud:* Ac, Jc, Ht, Et. *Rv:* M. *Jv:* B.

"Southern Education Report is the official publication of the Southern Education Reporting Service, an objective, fact-finding agency established by Southern newspaper editors and educators with the aim of providing accurate, unbiased information on developments in education, with emphasis on programs for the education of the culturally disadvantaged in the 17 Southern and border states and the District of Columbia." There are usually six to nine articles which range in length from 1 to 12 pages. Objective articles on school desegregation are published regularly. The style of writing is popular. A good magazine for the layman and teacher from elementary through high school. Librarians in other areas of the country should check to see what regional magazines are published in their areas.

Soviet Education; selected articles from Soviet education journals in English translation. 1958. m. $75. Seymour M. Rosen. Intl. Arts and Sciences Press, 108 Grand St., White Plains, N.Y. 10601.

Indexed: EdI, PAIS. *Aud:* Sa, Ac, Jc, Ht, Et. *Rv:* H. *Jv:* B.

Translated articles from basic Soviet education journals and government documents, usually about one year behind actual date of publication. All material is unabridged, and covers the entire educational spectrum. The 55-page magazine normally concentrates on one major area—elementary and secondary education, programmed instruction, language study, etc.—with two to four articles of a more general nature. An excellent journal, although the understandably high price makes it prohibitive for all but the largest libraries.

Speech Monographs. 1934. q. $12.50. Speech Assn. of America, Statler-Hilton Hotel, 33rd St. & Seventh Ave., New York, N.Y. 10011. Circ: 2,375.

Indexed: EdI, PsyAb. *Aud:* Sa, Ac, Jc. *Rv:* H. *Jv:* B.

Primarily a vehicle for reports on ongoing research in speech at all levels, from philosophy to literature. Articles are by and for scholars and students of speech, particularly educators. The scope is broader than the title implies, and much of the material will be of value to the advanced student of literature, or theater. High in reference value because it includes an annual bibliography, "Graduate Theses: An Index to Graduate Work in Speech," which lists titles of completed M.A. and Doctoral dissertations. The bibliography is cross-indexed, and is particularly useful for the detailed subject index. Another bibliography lists doctoral dissertations in progress for a given year. The August issue also features "Abstracts of Dissertations in the Field of Speech." The two compilations represent an excellent key to research, and should be brought to the attention of anyone working in speech, literature or the theatre.

Studies in Philosophy and Education. 1960. q. $3.25. Francis T. Villemain. Studies in Philosophy and Education, Inc., Southern Illinois Univ., Edwardsville, Ill. 62025. Illus., adv. Circ: 1,000.

Bk. rev: 3–5, lengthy, signed. *Aud:* Sa, Ac. *Rv:* H. *Jv:* B.

A scholarly journal which attempts to explore the philosophy and methodology of teaching at all levels. An annual issue reviews the current status of the philosophy of education. The book reviews are detailed, critical and a bit esoteric. Included here, as it represents one of the few education journals given over entirely to the theoretical aspects of education and society. It enjoys a small circulation which deserves to be larger, and certainly should be supported by schools of education.

Teachers College Record; a professional journal of ideas, research and informed opinion. 1900. m. (Oct.–May). $7.50. Maxine Greene. Teachers College, Columbia Univ., 525 W. 120th St., New York, N.Y. 10027. Adv. Circ: 6,200. Microform: UM.

Indexed: EdI, PsyAb. *Bk. rev:* 8, 800 words, signed. *Aud:* Ac, Jc, Ht, Et. *Rv:* M. *Jv:* A.

An excellent general magazine on the philosophy and methodology of education. It has appeal for students and teachers at all levels. As the editors explain, "it is a forum for articulate discussion by those engaged in the teaching activity." There are usually some five to six articles, and a number of special departments which survey the literature and current opinions. A good deal of emphasis is placed on the humanities and the behavioral sciences, giving it a considerably broader appeal than the related *Journal of Teacher Education*. While this may be difficult going for the average reader, it is among the best of its kind for the involved educator—therefore the high rating and the recommendation that it be in all school libraries.

Theory into Practice. 1962. 5/yr. $3.75. Ohio State Univ., College of Education, Arps Hall, 1945 N. High St., Columbus, Ohio 43210. Reprint: Kraus. Microform: UM.

Indexed: EdI. *Bk. rev:* 2–3, 100–900 words, signed. *Aud:* Ac, Jc, Ht, Et. *Rv:* H. *Jv:* B.

"Committed to the point of view that there is an integral relationship between educational theory and practice." Each issue, of eight to ten articles, focuses on a specific theme, e.g., research, independent study, Title I, planning for education change. The format is above average, and the general style of writing and research makes it a worthy addition for all school of education libraries and large elementary and high school teachers' libraries.

This Magazine Is About Schools. 1967. q. $3.50. Robert Davis. P.O. Box 876, Terminal "A," Toronto 1, Ont. Illus., adv. Circ: 3,500.

Aud: Ga, Ac, Jc, Ht, Et. *Rv:* H. *Jv:* V.

Probably the best written, liveliest and most up-to-date education magazine now being published. Although published in Canada, the material is useful to anyone involved with elementary and secondary education: parent, teacher or administrator. The tone is progressive, and the emphasis is on innovation and improvement. There are usually 10 to 12 articles per 150-page issue, as well as poetry, provocative letters and short notes, and essays on controversial books, magazine articles, and public pronouncements by educators. Authors vary from a professor of religion and a free-lance photographer to a music expert and a professor of English at Columbia. Material ranges from a study of films in schools to the meaning and use of rock music in education. The emphasis on media uses shows the strong influence of the best of McLuhan. Highly recommended not only for educators, but also for their brighter charges in high school.

Today's Education (Formerly: ***NEA Journal***). 1913. m. (Sept.–May). Membership (Non-members, 80¢ per no.). Mildred S. Fenner. National Education Assn. of the United States, 1201 16th St., N.W., Washington, D.C. 20036. Illus., index, adv. Circ: 1,100,000. Microform: UM.

Indexed: EdI, PsyAb, RG. *Bk. rev:* Various numbers & lengths, and notes. *Aud:* Ga, Ac, Jc, Ht, Et. *Rv:* H. *Jv:* V.

The official journal of the largest educational association in the U.S., this is directed at public school teachers and administrators. Included are articles of a general interest within the education profession, e.g., "The Disturbed Child in the Classroom," and "Teaching in Inner-City Schools." New developments in education and news of the National Education Association are featured. Some issues focus on special subjects, such as "The Average Child" or "The Inner-City." A list of new NEA publications is included, and there are book reviews of various lengths from time to time. At one time this was a relatively conservative journal, but in the past few years it has taken on a more militant attitude towards teaching and education. Laymen who are interested or involved with education will find it of almost as much value as teachers do. It belongs in every school library, and in medium to large public libraries.

Educational Aids

American Education Publications, Wesleyan Univ., 55 High Street, Middletown, Conn. 06457. Various dates. w. (32 issues). $1 to $1.40.

GRADE	TITLE	CIRCULATION
K	*My Weekly Reader Surprise.* 1959	1,489,000
1	*My Weekly Reader Picture Reader.* 1930	2,147,577
2	*My Weekly Reader News Reader.* 1934	2,514,000
3	*My Weekly Reader News Story.* 1929	2,312,000
4	*My Weekly Reader News Parade.* 1928	2,070,000
5	*My Weekly Reader World Parade.* 1930	1,688,000
6	*Senior Weekly Reader.* 1947	1,416,000
7–8	*Current Events.* 1902	1,052,264
9–10	*Everyweek.* 1936	381,000
9–12	*Our Times.* 1935	190,545

The fifth, sixth, seventh and eighth of these magazines are indexed in IChildMags.

The largest single curriculum-oriented news magazine publisher in the United States, American Education Publications began as the child of a non-profit University—Wesleyan. It is now a subsidiary of the Xerox Corporation. While it only publishes a limited number of magazines other than those listed here (*Current Science, Read,* and *Science & Math Weekly*), it exceeds in total circulation almost all of the Scholastic Magazines publications. The reasons are two fold—first it got off to an earlier start, and, second, the prestigious backing of Wesleyan University created a favorable climate among educators.

Although the two companies are rivals for the goodwill of the teachers, it is sometimes difficult to tell the products apart. The *My Weekly Reader* series seems to have an edge in the number of pictures and guides it employs for helping the student to build vocabulary and critical thinking, and on the whole the format tends to be a trifle more appealing. There are usually one or two feature articles geared for the interest and reading level of the grade, and a number of special sections on everything from science and social studies to art and literature. In the more advanced papers, e.g., *Everyweek* and *Our Times,* a serious effort is made to present controversial issues, more so than in the Scholastic group, and both feature "Voice of the Press", a good cross section of editorials, cartoons and columnists' viewpoints from various American newspapers. Lacking the magazine format of the Scholastic publications, these tend to be more like newspapers. That they often contain fewer features and articles is balanced by somewhat better coverage. Finally, unlike its competitor, it carries no advertising. In that most of the papers are intentionally class oriented, they are of dubious value for the average school or public library.

Civic Education Service. 1733 K St., N.W., Washington, D.C. 20006. Various dates. w. (32 issues). $1.50 to $2.

GRADES	TITLE	CIRCULATION
7–9	*Junior Review.* 1927	498,000
9–11	*Weekly News Review.* 1923	234,800
10–12	*American Observer.* 1930	431,083

Junior Review is indexed in IChildMags.

The smallest of the big three in classroom news magazine publishing, Civic Education Service is also one of the best. Of their publications, the *American Observer* is typical enough. It strives to be "compact . . . yet comprehensive enough to provide adequate material for a thorough study of great problems of the day," and succeeds very well in this objective. Its articles, written by a staff of educators and journalists, present major issues in an unusually clear and straightforward style, and supplement the headline facts with historic and geographic background, and with short biographies of key persons where appropriate. "Here and Abroad" devotes 2 or 3 paragraphs to each of several timely events of interest to high school students, and includes an occasional film review. Suggestions for further reading, included in some issues, refer mainly to recent articles in leading news periodicals. Illustrations consist of good-quality, well-chosen photos, charts and maps. A good to excellent classroom paper, yet is a last choice for school and public libraries who would do better to subscribe to more fullsome, national news magazines.

The New York Times Student Weekly. 1967. w. (30 issues). $2.40. The New York Times, College & School Service, Times Square, New York, N.Y. 10036. Illus. Circ: 400,000.

Aud: Jh, Sh. *Rv:* H. *Jv:* A.

A tabloid-size classroom newspaper, this is by and large one of the best available and is preferable to those issued for junior and senior high by other publishers. Each issue consists of a 12-page roundup of the week's major events, much on the same style as "The Week In Review" in the regular Sunday edition. It differs in that the style is somewhat less rigorous, there are more photographs, maps and illustrations, and the whole is geared specifically for the student. A second section of varying size is a "Background Supplement," which consists of exploring a given area in depth. Issued each month, the latter has covered such topics as "Political Parties," "Mass Communications," "Japan and India," and "Europe's New Look." Finally once a month there is a perceptive "News Quiz" for review purposes. The reporting, both in depth and coverage of controversial issues, equals anything found in the regular edition of *The New York Times.* Also, there is less emphasis on popular culture and the teen-ager as a consumer than in competing journals of the same type. One of the few classroom newspapers which should be in every school, and most public libraries. (*School Weekly,* the same publication under a different name, covers only the Eastern states. The rest of the country is covered by the *Student Weekly.*)

Scholastic Magazines, Inc. 50 W. 44th St., New York, N.Y. 10036. Various dates. Except where noted: w. (30–32 issues). $1 to $2.

GRADE	TITLE	CIRCULATION
K	*Let's Find Out.* 1966. m (8)	
1	*News Pilot.* 1960	333,434
2	*News Ranger.* 1960	394,000
3	*News Trails.* 1960	455,000
4	*News Explorer.* 1957	646,000
5	*Young Citizen.* 1940	279,000
6	*Newstime.* 1952	1,075,101
6–8	*Junior Scholastic.* 1937	1,479,000
8–10	*World Week.* 1942	509,000
10–12	*Senior Scholastic.* 1920	563,000

With the exception of *Senior Scholastic* (Indexed in RG), all of the last six of the above-listed magazines are indexed in IChildMags.

The second largest single publisher of classroom general news magazines, Scholastic Magazines, Inc., is rivalled only by the familiar *My Weekly Reader* series published by

American Education Publications. The firm issues a total of some 24 magazines for children, including 10 foreign language periodicals in French, Spanish, German and Russian. Three book clubs for various grade levels are part of the company, along with free book selection magazines covering current selections. Finally, there are a number of specialized publications for students and teachers, e.g., *Practical English, Scholastic Teacher, Senior Science, Science World,* etc. A privately owned corporation, with a prestigious advisory board, it plugs its products through the teacher and librarian. Each of the various sized magazines (in tabloid format) are written for a given reading level, and assume basic educational-curriculum levels for subject matter ranging from recreation and art to world affairs and national politics. The whole, as in almost all classroom publications of this type, is informative, accurate, and generally about as exciting as warmed over mush. Most shy clear of controversial subjects, although in recent years the pressure of more involved teachers has forced at least the recognition that all is not milk and honey. The two more popular ones in public and school libraries tend to be *Junior Scholastic* and *Senior Scholastic.* Both are closer to magazines than newspapers and approach the news in much the same fashion. They digest the main events of the week, and the former carries a long "Theme Article," usually on a country; a "Language Page;" "American issues;" "Frontiers of Science," and "Turning Points in American History." There are crossword puzzles, a joke page and quizzes. Most material is staff written. *Senior Scholastic* follows the overall editorial policy of "promoting education for enlightened citizenship of students in the schools of the U.S.A.," and features two or three articles on various topics of the day. One section gives a brief resume of "The Headline," and explanatory background material is found in "What's Behind It." There are columns on films and records, television and the arts.

Advertising is carried in many of the magazines, more particularly in three of the new periodicals, e.g., *Junior Scholastic, World Week* and *Senior Scholastic.* This teen-age consumer group is the darling of the business side of the company, and has resulted in some rather fascinating in-fighting among educators.

Possibly the best summary will be found in an exchange of opinion in *The ACCE Reporter* (March, 1966. p.115–119; published by American Council for Curricular Evaluation, 829 Woodruff Drive, Ballwin, Mo. 63011).

While the products of Scholastic Magazines, Inc., may serve a purpose in the curriculum, they are of questionable use in any school or public library. The librarian, or for that matter the teacher, would be better advised—at least in junior high school through high school—to subscribe to several national news magazines of different political slants.

State Education Association Publications

Every state education association, except Rhode Island, issues its own publication. Most concentrate on activities of the teachers (from elementary school through college), supervisors, principals, counselors, PTA and school board members. A few, such as the *California Journal of Educational Research,* are broader in scope and present original research type articles.

In view of the similarity of purpose and scope, it seems pointless to annotate the individual publications. Librarians within each state will wish to take their own education association magazine. Larger libraries may wish those from adjoining states; education libraries will concentrate primarily on those indexed, many in the *Education index.*

All of the magazines are indexed in considerably more depth in: *State Education Journal Index.* semi-ann. (Feb. & July). $15. P.O. Box 1030, Fort Collins, Colo. 80522.

Alabama Education Assn., 422 Dexter Ave., Box 4177, Montgomery, Ala. 36104. *Alabama School Journal.* 1921. m. (Sept.–May). Membership (Non-members, $4). C. P. Nelson. Illus., index, adv. Circ: 27,850.

Alaska Education Assn., Room 207, Seward Bldg., Juneau, Alas. 99801. *Alaska Teacher.* 1953. 7/yr. Membership (Non-members, $2). Illus., adv. Circ: 2,900. Bk rev.

Arizona Education Assn., 2102 W. Indian School Rd., Phoenix, Ariz. 85015. *Arizona Teacher.* 1914. 5/yr. $2. Ed bd. Illus., index, adv. Circ: 15,500. *Indexed:* EdI.

Arkansas Teachers Assn., 924 Ringo St., Little Rock, Ark. 72201. *Bulletin of the Arkansas Teachers Assn.* 1898. q. $1.40. Adv. Circ: 3,600. Bk rev.

California Teachers Assn., 1705 Murchison Dr., Burlingame, Calif. 94011. *California Journal of Educational Research.* 1950. 5/yr. $6. Garford C. Gordon. Index. Circ: 1,374. Bk rev. *Indexed:* EdI, PsyAb.

Colorado Education Assn., 5200 S. Quebec St., Englewood, Colo. 80110. *Colorado School Journal.* 1885. 4/yr. (Sept.–May). $3. Allan L. Johnson. Illus., adv. Circ: 24,000.

Connecticut Education Assn., 21 Oak St., Hartford, Conn. 06106. *Connecticut Teacher.* 1932. 8/yr. Membership (Non-members, $1.50). Norman E. Delisle. Illus., adv. Circ: 20,000. Bk rev.

Delaware State Education Assn., 113 S. Bradford St., Dover, Del. 19901. *Delaware School Journal.* 1934. 5/yr. $2.50. Edward J. Richter. Illus., adv. Circ: 5,500 Bk rev.

Florida Education Assn., 208 W. Pensacola St., Tallahassee, Fla. 32301. *Florida Education.* 1923. m. (Aug.–June). $3. Gayle E. Norton. Illus., index, adv. Circ: 70,000. Bk rev.

Georgia Education Assn., G.E.A. Bldg., 197 Central Ave., S.W., Atlanta, Ga. 30303. *Georgia Education Journal.* 1908. m. (Sept.–May). $8. Frank M. Hughes. Illus., adv. Circ: 27,361.

Hawaii Education Assn., 1649 Kalakaua Ave., Honolulu, Hawaii 96800. *HEA News Flash.* 1939. 9/yr. Free. Circ: 6,900.

Idaho Education Assn., Inc., Box 2638, Boise, Idaho 83701. *Idaho Education News.* 1926. m. (Sept.–May). $1.75. Donovan Douglas. Illus., adv. Circ: 8,500.

Illinois Education Assn., 100 E. Edwards St., Springfield,

Ill. 62704. *Illinois Education.* 1855. m. (Sept.–May). $2. Francine Richard. Illus., adv. Circ: 80,000. *Indexed:* EdI. Bk rev.

Indiana State Teachers Assn., 150 W. Market St., Indianapolis, Ind. 46204. *Indiana Teacher.* 1856. bi-m. (Sept.–June). Membership (Non-members, $4). Robert H. Wyatt. Illus., adv. Circ: 53,046.

Iowa State Education Assn., 4025 Tonawanda Dr., Des Moines, Iowa 50312. *ISEA Communique.* 1963. m. (Sept.–June). Membership (Non-members, $1.35). Illus. Circ: 42,000.

Kansas State Teachers Assn., 715 W. 10th St., Topeka, Kan. 66612. *Kansas Teacher.* 1914. m. (Sept.–May). $3. Anna M. Murphy. Illus., adv. Circ: 40,000.

Kentucky Education Assn., 101 W. Walnut St., Louisville, Ky. 40202. *Kentucky School Journal.* 1922. m. (Sept.–May). Membership (Non-members, $2). Gerald Jaggers. Illus., adv. Circ: 34,000. *Indexed:* EdI. Bk rev.

Louisiana Teachers Assn., 1755 Nicholson Dr., Box 1906, Baton Rouge, La. 70821. *Louisiana Schools.* 1923. m. (Sept.–May). $2. Illus., adv. Circ: 22,500.

Maine Teachers Assn., 184 State St., Augusta, Me. 04330. *Maine Teacher.* 1940. 4/yr. Membership (Non-members, $1.25). John H. Marvin. Illus., adv. Circ: 11,000.

Maryland State Teachers Assn., Inc., 344 N. Charles St., Baltimore, Md. 21201. *Maryland Teacher.* 1944. m. Membership (Non-members, $2). Milson C. Raver. Illus., adv. Circ: 28,000. *Indexed:* EdI. Bk rev.

Massachusetts Teacher Assn., 14 Beacon St., Boston, Mass. 02108. *Massachusetts Teacher.* 1914. m. (Sept.–May). Membership (Non-members, $2.25). William J. Kilroy, Jr. Illus., adv. Circ: 45,988.

Michigan Education Assn., Box 673, Lansing, Mich. 48903. *Michigan Education Journal.* 1923. semi-m. (Sept.–May). Membership (Non-members, $4). Arthur H. Rice, Jr. Illus., index, adv. Circ: 80,000. *Indexed:* EdI. Bk rev.

Minnesota Education Assn., 41 Sherburne Ave., St. Paul, Minn. 55103. *Minnesota Journal of Education.* 1920. m. (Oct.–May). $2. Donald N. Nelson. Illus., index, adv. Circ: 30,000. *Indexed:* EdI. Bk rev.

Mississippi Education Assn., 219 N. President St., Box 826, Jackson, Miss. 39205. *Mississippi Educational Advance.* 1911. m. (Oct.–May). Membership (Non-members, $2). C. A. Johnson. Illus., adv. Circ: 15,500.

Missouri State Teachers Assn., Teachers Bldg., Columbia, Mo. 65201. *School and Community.* 1915. m. (Sept.–May). $4. Inks Franklin. Illus., index, adv. Circ: 45,000. *Indexed:* EdI. Bk rev.

Montana Education Assn., 1232 E. Sixth Ave., Box 1690, Helena, Mont. 59601. *Montana Education.* 1924. q. $4. Adv. Circ: 8,000.

Nebraska State Education Assn., Box 1428, Lincoln, Neb. 68501. *Nebraska Education News.* 1946. w. (Sept.–May).

Membership (Non-members, $2). Conrad Good. Illus., adv. Circ: 20,000.

Nevada State Education Assn., 151 Park St., Carson City, Nev. 89701. *Nevada Education Journal*. 1966. q. Membership (Non-members, $2). Charles Fleming. Illus., adv. Circ: 5,500.

New Hampshire Education Assn., 103 N. State St., Box 272, Concord, N.H. 03301. *New Hampshire Educator*. 1920. 4/yr. Membership (Non-members, $2). Illus., adv. Circ: 5,200. Bk rev.

New Jersey Education Assn., 180 W. State St., Trenton, N.J. 08608. *New Jersey Educational Review*. 1927. m. (Sept.–May). Membership (Non-members, $3.50). Marvin R. Reed. Illus., adv. Circ: 78,000. Bk. rev.

New Mexico Educational Assn., Box 729, Santa Fe, N.M. 87501. *New Mexico School Review*. 1921. q. Membership (Non-members, $2). David F. Miller. Illus., adv. Circ: 11,752. Bk rev.

New York State Teachers Assn., 152 Washington Ave., Albany, N.Y. 12210. *New York State Education*. 1914. m. (Oct.–May). Membership (Non-members, $2). G. Howard Goold. Illus., adv. Circ: 120,000: *Indexed*: EdI, PsyAb. Bk rev.

North Carolina Education Assn., Box 350, Raleigh, N.C. 27602. *North Carolina Education*. 1906. m. $2. W. Amos Abrams. Adv. Circ: 42,350. Bk rev.

North Dakota Education Assn., Box J, Bismark, N.D. 58501. *North Dakota Teacher*. 1959. m. (Sept.–May) Membership only. Stella E. Arnaud. Illus., adv. Circ: 9,000. Bk rev.

Ohio Education Assn., 225 E. Broad St., Columbus, Ohio 43215. *Ohio Schools*. 1923. m. (Sept.–May). Membership (Non-members, $3.50). William E. Henry. Illus., adv. Circ: 90,000. *Indexed*: EdI.

Oklahoma Education Assn., 323 E. Madison, Oklahoma City, Okla. 73105. *Oklahoma Teacher*. 1919. m. (Sept.–May). Membership (Non-members, $4). Illus., index, adv. Circ: 37,000. Bk rev.

Oregon Education Assn., 1530 S.W. Taylor, Portland, Ore. 97205. *Oregon Education*. 1926. semi-m. (Sept.–May). Membership (Non-members, $3). Richard H. Barss. Illus., adv. Circ: 20,000. Bk rev.

Pennsylvania State Education Assn., 400 N. Third St., Harrisburgh, Pa. 17101. *Pennsylvania School Journal*. 1852. Fortnightly (Oct.–May). Membership (Non-members, $3.50). Ralph C. Swan. Illus., adv. Circ: 95,000. *Indexed*: EdI. Bk rev.

Rhode Island. No publication.

South Carolina Education Assn., 1510 Gervais St., Columbia, S.C. 29201. *South Carolina Education News*. 1966. 8/yr. Membership (Non-members, $3). Margaret J. Reagan. Illus., adv. Circ: 20,000.

South Dakota Education Assn., Box 939, Pierre, S.D. 57501. *SDEA Journal*. 1925. 5–yr. Membership (Non-members, $3.50; Includes *SDEA News*. 14/yr). Clarence Drenkhahn. Illus., adv. Circ: 11,500.

Tennessee Education Assn., 598 James Robertson Parkway, Nashville, Tenn. 37219. *Tennessee Teacher*. 1934. m. (Sept.–May). Membership (Non-members, $1.50). Sara S. Nolan. Illus., adv. Circ: 40,000. Bk rev.

Texas State Teachers Assn., Inc., 316 W. 12th St., Austin, Tex. 78701. *Texas Outlook*. 1917. m. Membership (Non-members, $4). Charles H. Tennyson. Illus., index, adv. Circ: 126,253. *Indexed*: EdI. Bk rev.

Utah Education Assn., 875 East 5180 South, Box 7500, Murray, Utah 84107. *Utah Educational Review*. 1906. bi-m. (Sept.–May). $1.50. John C. Evans, Jr. Illus., index, adv. Circ: 13,500. Bk rev.

Vermont Education Assn., 5 Baldwin St., Montpelier, Vt. 05602. *The Vermont Blackboard*. 1933. m. (Oct–May). $2. Circ: 5,000.

Virginia Education Assn., 116 S. 3rd St., Richmond, Va. 23219. *Virginia Journal of Education*. 1907. m. (Sept.–May). Membership only. Robert F. Williams. Illus., index, adv. Circ: 40,000. *Indexed*: EdI. Bk rev.

Washington Education Assn., 910 Fifth Ave., Seattle, Wash. 98104. *Washington Education*. 1889. m. (Oct.–May). $3.50. (Available only with joint subscription to *WEA Action*; combined cost, $5). Index, adv. Circ: 36,667.

West Virginia Education Assn., 1558 Quarrier St., Charleston, W.Va. 25311. *West Virginia School Journal*. 1881. m. (Sept.–May). Membership (Non-members, $2). Illus., index, adv. Circ: 20,300. Bk rev.

Wisconsin Education Assn., Insurance Bldg., 119 Monona Ave., Madison, Wis. 53703. *Wisconsin Journal of Education*. 1856. m. Membership (Non-members, $3). R. H. Munger. Illus., adv. Circ: 44,500. *Indexed*: EdI.

Wyoming Education Assn., 115 E. 22nd St., Cheyenne, Wyo. 82001. *Wyoming Education News*. 1935. m. (Sept.–May). $1. Illus., adv. Circ: 5,343.

ENGINEERING

Indexes and Abstracts

Applied Science and Technology Index, Biological Abstracts, British Technology Index, Business Periodicals Index, Chemical Abstracts, Engineering Index, Science Abstracts, Science Citation Index. (For annotations, see Indexes and Abstracts Section.)

It would be difficult to include, within the scope of this study, even a minimum selection of journals in a field which not only consists of applications of other sciences (e.g., mathematics, physics, chemistry, etc.) but which, by itself, contains many specialties, such as navigational, marine, materials engineering, to name a few. Moreover, with the exception of technical institutes, many college libraries do not support engineering curricula. The following, then, represents a sampling of periodicals in general, chemical, civil, electrical and mechanical engineering, many of which are the publications of U.S. technical societies, as well as a few general engineering magazines which cross over into all these areas. There are a number of periodicals which, in interpreting scientific and technological advances to the layman, include most aspects of engineering in their scope; these have been reviewed in the Science-General section. See also the RSD Science and Technology Reference Services Committee List mentioned in the introduction to Science-General, and sections on Aeronautics, Automation, and Physics for additional titles.

General

Design News. See Art Section.

Engineer. 1856. w. $16. A. Conway. Morgan Brothers, 28 Essex St., Strand, London W.C.2. Illus., index, adv. Circ: 8,300. Microform: UM.

Indexed: ASTI, BritTech, EngI, SciAb. *Aud:* Sa, Ac. *Rv:* H. *Jv:* B.

The weekly states that it is directed toward "everyone involved in engineering—technologist, technician, inventor, designer, research worker, executive, applied scientist." Thus, any interpretations of technological developments are written in terminology common to all. Most fields of engineering are covered, as well as those closely allied to engineering problems, and industrial advances are comprehensively reviewed. The emphasis in the magazine is on the news development, rather than the lengthy tutorial; and although a great deal involves British engineering and industry, European and U.S. coverage is more than adequate.

Engineer. 1960. bi-m. $2. Peter J. Brennan. Engineers Joint Council, 345 E. 47th St., New York, N.Y. 10017. Illus., adv. Circ: 455,000.

Bk. rev: 1, 500–600 words, signed. *Aud:* Sa, Ga, Ac, Jc. *Rv:* M. *Jv:* B.

Whereas the English publication by the same title provides capsules of technological advances, the U.S. *Engineer,* a slim publication of not more than 30 pages, devotes an article or two toward identifying the image of the profession and interpreting its role in society, and a feature on some topic of recent engineering interest. Circulated gratis by the Engineers' Joint Council (which comprises many U.S. engineering societies) to its member groups, the periodical ranges in subject matter from status reports on salaries to predictions on the design of future trains, bridges, and the like. Although the EJC disavows editorial emphasis in its articles, essays carrying such provocative and amusing titles as "Help Stamp Out Engineering Schools" and "Too Many Engineers Go Wrong" to create cause for skepticism. Informal and entertaining reading for professionals, the one or two general interest papers could also be informative for laymen. The few book reviews are concerned with general

works, as opposed to highly technical monographs, and are well written. A directory of short engineering courses and briefs on new products are also regular departments.

Engineering. 1866. w. $16. F. B. Roberts. Engineering Ltd., 36 Bedford St., London, W.C. 2. Illus., adv. Circ: 8,700. Microform: UM.

Indexed: ASTI, BritTech, EngI, SciAb. *Aud:* Ac, Sa. *Rv:* H. *Jv:* B.

Comparable to the English *Engineer,* this weekly reviews news in the applied sciences. On the whole, the material in this publication is concerned with engineering advances in machinery, instrumentation, or other equipment developed for a wide variety of industries. Mechanical aspects are stressed, but materials and other new products are fairly well covered. Although the scope of the periodical is international, surveys deal mainly with British state-of-the-art; adequate coverage of European engineering is also given.

Engineering Index. See Indexes and Abstracts Section.

Technology and Culture; devoted to the study of the development of technology and its relation with society and culture. 1960. q. $10. Melvin Kranzberg. Univ. of Chicago Press, 5750 Ellis Ave., Chicago, Ill. 60637. Illus., index, adv. Circ: 1,350.

Bk. rev: 20, 500–600 words, signed. *Aud:* Ac, Sa, Jc. *Rv:* H. *Jv:* B.

Published for the Society for the History of Technology, the journal is concerned with the history of technological devices or processes and their relations to any aspect of society—politics, economics, humanities, etc. Long, scholarly articles and research notes range in epoch and culture from Greek catapults and early electric motors in India to a study of the first concrete skyscraper and a review of aeronautics/astronautics and rocketry programs. Although the research investigations by distinguished historians and specialists are clearly not intended for breezy reading, the journal provides fascinating material for those with a historical bent and a respect for the technical contributions of the past, as well as authoritative source material for students and scholars. Organizational notes and announcements are also included in each issue. Excellent book reviews comprise a good portion of the periodical.

Chemical Engineering

A.I.CH.E. Journal. 1955. bi-m. $25. Harding Bliss. Amer. Inst. of Chemical Engineers, 345 E. 47th St., New York, N.Y. 10017. Illus., index, adv.

Indexed: ASTI, ChemAb, EngI, SCI. *Aud:* Sa, Ac. *Rv:* H. *Jv:* B.

The chief research journal of the Institute, and one of the leading publications in its field. High-quality research papers are devoted to fundamental studies in all areas of chemical engineering. Subjects under investigation have included fluid mechanics, chemical thermodynamics, reaction kinetics, heat and mass transfer, and process control. Both full-length papers of significant scope and short "Letters to the Editor" of a more limited nature are published. The A.I.Ch.E. also puts out another excellent research journal, *International Chemical Engineering,* which comprises translations of important foreign papers representing research from the USSR, Eastern Europe and Asia (mostly from Japan). See also, *Chemical Engineering Progress.*

Chemical and Engineering News. See Chemistry Section.

Chemical Engineering. 1902. Fortnightly. $4. Calvin S. Cronan. McGraw-Hill, Inc., 330 W. 42nd St., New York, N.Y. 10036. Illus., index, adv. Circ: 62,000. Microform: Mc, UM. Reprint: Johnson.

Indexed: ASTI, ChemAb, EngI. *Bk. rev:* 1 major, 300 words, signed; 20 short, 50 words, unsigned. *Aud:* Ac, Sa. *Rv:* H. *Jv:* B.

McGraw's trade journal for the chemical process industries covers not only the latest technical achievements from industrial, academic and governmental laboratories, but also provides political, social, and economic comment, both by staff writers and leading industrialists or specialists. Lengthy feature reports, averaging over 20 pages, investigate special aspects of chemical engineering and constitute excellent tutorials, as do the shorter feature articles and departments geared toward supplying refresher courses for the less-than-recent graduate. All areas of chemical engineering are considered, including applications to other sciences. Each issue also supplies useful articles on professionalism (i.e., how to get ahead, salary schedules), as well as abundant news coverage. The balance of the magazine is good, extending from highly technical papers, to practical engineering tips, management essays, market studies and news flashes. New products and materials are given thorough coverage, both through special departments and more than liberal advertising.

Chemical Engineering Progress. 1947. m. $25. Larry Resen. Amer. Inst. of Chemical Engineers, 345 E. 47th St., New York, N.Y. 10017. Illus., index, adv. Microform: Canner, UM. Reprint: Johnson.

Indexed: ASTI, ChemAb, EngI, SCI. *Aud:* Ac, Sa. *Rv:* H. *Jv:* B.

Issued as the general organ of the Institute to its membership, the journal supplies interpretive news and reviews of the latest developments in chemical engineering and peripheral disciplines. Each issue contains a number of review or tutorial papers, contributed by specialists, which cover timely research topics; frequently a body of papers will investigate a subject from various viewpoints, such as all engineering aspects of air pollution. Regular features include: a professional interest section, which discusses subjects such as job mobility; industry developments, which review advances in technology in more abbreviated form; and a wealth of announcements concerning new publica-

tions, activities of all sections of the society, forthcoming meetings, courses, and the like. Of particular note is "Research Roundup," which lists Ph.D. theses available in chemical engineering or notes on research in progress.

Industrial and Engineering Chemistry. 1909. m. $5. David E. Gushee. Amer. Chemical Soc., 1155 16th St., N.W., Washington, D.C. 20036. Illus., index, adv. Circ: 24,000. Microform: AMC. Reprint: Johnson.

Indexed: ASTI, ChemAb, EngI, SciAb, SCI. *Bk. rev:* 3, 350 words, signed. *Aud:* Sa, Ac, Jc. *Rv:* H. *Jv:* B.

Intended for the chemical engineer and chemist, the journal publishes surveys, critiques, and reviews of current research in both applied chemistry and chemical engineering. (Highly specialized papers appear in the journal's three quarterlies listed below.) Too technical for the layman, the periodical is, nonetheless, useful to the nonspecialist in supplying authoritative information on trends, state-of-the-art, etc. An interesting section in each issue is "Research Results," containing abstracts of papers submitted to the journal for publication; manuscript copies of these papers can be purchased before publication. Issues also summarize current trends in the field and papers which appear in the *I&EC* quarterlies.

The research papers formerly published in *Industrial and Engineering Chemistry* have, in the past several years, been contained in three distinct journals: *I&EC Fundamentals* "publishes papers in the broad field of chemical engineering research;" *I&EC Process Design and Development* "reports on design methods and concepts and their application to the development of processes and process equipment;" *I&EC Product Research and Development* "publishes papers reporting findings on the preparation of new or improved chemical products."

Civil Engineering

American Society of Civil Engineers. Proceedings. 1873. Price varies. William D. French. Amer. Soc. of Civil Engineers, 345 E. 47th St., New York, N.Y. 10017. Illus. Circ: 105,000 (total journals).

Indexed: ASTI, ChemAb, EngI. *Aud:* Ac, Sa. *Rv:* H. *Jv:* B.

The scope of the Society's interests is enormous, and each division of this association publishes its own highly specialized research journal (too numerous in number to describe here). Fields represented by these publications are: aerospace transport; professional activities; construction; urban planning and development; engineering mechanics; highways; hydraulics; irrigation and drainage; pipelines; power; sanitary engineering; soil mechanics and foundations; structure; surveying and mapping; and waterways. Generally, each publication contains original research papers and discussions of current papers. Reference "cards" for each article, containing keywords and abstracts, are also included. Periodicity and price vary from journal to journal.

Civil Engineering; magazine of engineered construction. 1930. m. $5. Hal W. Hunt. Amer. Soc. of Civil Engineers, 345 E. 47th St., New York, N.Y. 10017. Illus., adv. Circ: 70,500. Microform: Mc, UM.

Indexed: ASTI, ChemAb, EngI. *Bk. rev:* 12, 50 words, signed. *Aud:* Ac, Sa. *Rv:* H. *Jv:* B.

Twofold in purpose, the society's general news organ publishes both review papers to supply civil engineers with latest technical developments in and out of their fields, and current awareness articles on activities in the profession, the society, and the like. Feature articles, written in very general language, extend from such topics as goals in professional cooperation to construction details. Frequently, applications of civil engineering to other technologies are stressed. Liberal coverage is given to new products and materials, engineering education, spot news of the industry, etc.

Engineering News-Record. 1874. w. $7. Arthur J. Fox, Jr. McGraw-Hill, Inc., 330 W. 42nd St., New York, N.Y. 10036. Illus., adv. Circ: 92,000. Microform: UM.

Indexed: ASTI, BusI, EngI, SciAb. *Bk. rev:* 1, 200 words, signed. *Aud:* Ac, Sa. *Rv:* H. *Jv:* B.

The publication is one of the chief announcement bulletins for the construction and related industries. Brief reports highlight latest developments in business, labor, engineering. A significant portion of the weekly is devoted to contract statistics, i.e., highway contracts awarded, or announcements of large construction programs in the planning and bidding stages. Materials, equipment, and new product briefs also receive ample coverage.

Electrical Engineering

Bell System Technical Journal. See Physics Section.

Electrical and Electronics Abstracts (Series B of Science Abstracts). See Indexes and Abstracts Section.

Electronics. 1930. semi-m. Donald Christiansen. McGraw-Hill, Inc., 330 W. 42nd St., New York, N.Y. 10036. Illus., adv., Circ: 71,000. Microform: Canner. Reprint: Kraus, Johnson.

Indexed: ASTI, BioAb, ChemAb, EngI, SciAb, SCI. *Bk. rev:* 4, 200 words, signed. *Aud:* Sa, Ac, Jc. *Rv:* H. *Jv:* B.

One of the best periodicals for supplying concise, yet thorough and worldwide coverage of the news of the electronics industry; authoritative, yet nonspecialist interpretations of developments in electronics technology, including applications to other sciences; and technical articles, reviews, and tutorials ranging from advanced circuit design to tips for professional development. Feature articles, contributed by both U.S. and foreign specialists and staff writers, deal with electronics in avionics and space, communications and computers, consumer usage in TV, appliances, etc. Special reports may be as general as a study of socioeconomic problems in business and urban crises, or as detailed as comprehensive marketing statistics. The prose is informal, ex-

tremely readable, and well illustrated by graphic techniques; new products and processes are particularly well represented by excellent color photographs. Statistical data and news, provided by the widespread research bureaus of the Mc-Graw complex, are extremely reliable. Departments cover the usual technical, business and governmental news, and a technical abstracts section briefly reviews five or six pertinent papers. A large buyers' guide, issued annually, is a valuable reference source for information on electronic components and services. Necessary for electronics engineers and interested special libraries, the magazine may also be a welcome choice for faculty of vocational schools or public libraries serving a technical clientele.

IEEE Proceedings. 1913. m. Membership (public libraries and colleges $16.50; others, $22). M. E. Van Valkenburg. Inst. of Electrical and Electronics Engineers, Inc., 345 E. 47th St., New York, N.Y. 10017. Illus. Circ: 45,000.

Indexed: ASTI, ChemAb, EngI, MathR, SciAb, SCI. *Aud:* Sa, Ac. *Rv:* H. *Jv:* B.

The *Proceedings* of this professional society are devoted to research papers deemed of broad applicability or interest to the membership. Invited and excellent review papers or surveys by specialists are also published. Frequently, an entire issue will investigate one special topic, such as transportation, and the research or review papers will explore particular facets of the field as related to engineering. The journal also carries "Letters," or very brief reports of timely and important research. These fall under such categories as: circuit theory and design, electromagnetics; electronic devices; communications theory and technology; computers, etc. There are also a very few departments which report briefly on association meetings, new products, etc.

The Institute also publishes 31 *Transactions* and two other research journals which reflect the specialized interests of their 31 professional groups. The publications range from such high degrees of technicality as *IEEE Transactions on Information Theory* and *IEEE Transactions on Antennas and Propagation* to more general ones concerned with education, engineering writing and speech, engineering management. Periodicity, price, and format vary according to publication: some carry a few notes on the professional group, occasional book reviews, entire proceedings of their special symposia, abstracts of the pertinent literature, as well as technical papers; others are devoted exclusively to research papers.

IEEE Spectrum. 1964. m. Membership ($13.50 to public libraries and colleges; others, $18). J. J. G. McCue. Inst. of Electrical and Electronics Engineers, Inc. 345 E. 45th St., New York, N.Y. 10017. Illus., index, adv. Circ: 144,000.

Indexed: EngI, SCI, SciAb. *Bk. rev:* 3–4, 250–350 words, signed. *Aud:* Ac, Sa, Jc. *Rv:* H. *Jv:* B.

This periodical is as fine a publication as that offered by any technical society as a news organ to its general membership. Whether the emphasis is on relating scientific developments in electrical engineering to other fields (sonar for ocean exploitation), relating technology to culture (electronics and urban crisis), providing historical essays (Wheatstone—forgotten genius) or tutorial articles on specialty fields within the discipline (planetary radioastronomy), the approach in the feature articles is always creative, informative, and well written. Contributions, frequently on a nontechnical level, are usually by distinguished scientists. Association, educational, and professional news are covered by a variety of departments; and technical correspondence airs opinions from the membership. Useful and informative departments also supply advance abstracts of research papers that will appear in the society's highly technical journals, the *IEEE Proceedings and Transactions,* and in several foreign journals published in translation by the Institute; a section entitled "Scanning the Issues" gives longer reviews of significant papers that have already appeared in these journals. Members of the IEEE probably make the journal cover-to-cover reading, but the audience for this publication should extend much further than its membership, including public libraries with an informed clientele.

IEEE Transactions. Automatic Control; Computers; Systems Science & Cybernetics. See Automation Section.

RCA Review. See Physics Section.

Mechanical Engineering

American Society of Mechanical Engineers. Transactions. 1880. q. Membership (Non-members, $15). J. J. Jaklitsch, Jr. American Soc. of Mechanical Engineers, 345 E. 47th St., New York, N.Y. 10017.

Indexed: ASTI, ChemAb, EngI, SCI. *Aud:* Sa, Ac. *Rv:* H. *Jv:* B.

Published in separate journals for many years, the six series of the *Transactions* represent the basic research interests of the Society. Some of the areas of study, though by no means all, covered by these specialized journals are indicated briefly.

Series A: *Journal of Engineering for Power* publishes "significant papers on power generation and usage; design, operation, and applications of gas turbines; nuclear engineering; solar energy, etc."

Series B: *Journal of Engineering for Industry* contains "contributions on problems of aviation; machine design, maintenance and plant engineering; areas of the petroleum field, etc."

Series C: *Journal of Heat Transfer* discusses "problems on radiation, conduction, convection; thermophysical problems; design techniques; insulation, etc."

Series D: *Journal of Basic Engineering* includes "developments in lubrication; fluid mechanics; research in hydrodynamics; metalforming processes; plastic flow."

Series E: *Journal of Applied Mechanics* pertains to "studies in the fields of elasticity, plasticity, dynamics, vibration, flow and fracture, stress analysis, etc."

Series F: *Journal of Lubrication Technology* specializes in "papers on friction and wear, bearing technology, lubricants, etc."

Applied Mechanics Review. See Indexes and Abstracts Section.

Chartered Mechanical Engineer. 1954. m. Membership (Non-members, $5.40). E. G. Semler. Institution of Mechanical Engineers, 1 Birdcage Walk, Westminster, London S.W.1. Illus., index, adv. Circ: 64,784.

Indexed: BritTech, ChemAb, EngI. *Aud:* Sa, Ac. *Rv:* H. *Jv:* B.

More than a review of the society's news and other recent advances in mechanical engineering, the periodical discusses any topics which concern the scientific community. Feature articles delve into such general areas as problems of creativity, science teaching and education, and the like. Of course many articles are topical—Britain's weather, brain drain, patent system. Occasional essays on the history of engineering are excellent. For the membership of the Institution, the publication attempts to view the field from several focal points: management techniques; materials and methods; design and development; education and training; as well as world news.

Mechanical Engineering. 1906. m. $7. J. J. Jaklitsch, Jr. Amer. Soc. of Mechanical Engineers, 345 E. 47th St., New York, N.Y. 10017. Illus., index, adv. Circ: 65,400. Microform: Mc, UM.

Indexed: ASTI, ChemAb, EngI, SciAb, SCI. *Bk. rev:* 1, 250–500 words, signed. *Aud:* Sa, Ac. *Rv:* H. *Jv:* B.

With the intent of publishing surveys on trends and developments in both mechanical engineering and related sciences, the periodical serves, in addition, as a general news organ for the ASME. Features include tutorials and reviews on special aspects of the field, and some general articles on management, economics, and education. Its special departments provide exhaustive coverage of news and literature: abstracts of recent ASME meetings; digests of the current technical literature; briefs on engineering developments, both U.S. and foreign; programs of forthcoming meetings; announcements of new equipment and products; Society notes and personalia. The publication should be informative and useful to nonspecialists, as well as to members of the profession.

ENGLISH

Indexes and Abstracts

British Humanities Index, Education Index, Psychological Abstracts, Readers' Guide to Periodical Literature. (For annotations, see Indexes and Abstracts Section.)

College Composition and Communication. 1950. 5/yr. $3. William F. Irmscher & James R. Squire. Membership (Non-members, $3). National Council of Teachers of English, 508 S. 6th St., Champaign, Ill. 61820. Circ: 5,476. Microform: UM.

Aud: Ac, Jc, Ht. *Rv:* M. *Jv:* A.

The sister to *College English* and *English Journal,* differing only in that the major emphasis is on composition and communication rather than literature *per se.* Most articles deal with methodology, problems, students, curriculum and the like. While geared for college teachers a good deal of the material is useful for high school teachers of English courses.

College English. 1939. m. (Oct.–May). $7. Richard Ohmann. National Council of Teachers of English, 508 S. 6th St., Champaign, Ill. 61820. Circ: 17,000. Microform: UM.

Indexed: EdI. *Bk. rev:* 1–5, 500–2,000 words, signed. *Aud:* Ac, Jc, Ht. *Rv:* H. *Jv:* B.

A leading journal in the field of English education, which is generally used by college English teachers and many high school teachers. Keeps readers up-to-date in the latest studies both on techniques and views of teaching English and on critical studies of literary works. The bulk of each issue is devoted to four or five scholarly articles concentrating on one particular theme. For instance, the January, 1968, issue is entitled "Language, Forming, Meaning." Several features keep the reader tuned in to current happenings. "Comment and Rebuttal" gives statements on articles that have previously appeared in the journal and rebuttals by the author of the article. "News and Ideas" features new criticisms and findings about literary works and introduces new journals in the field. The "Counciletter" is a comment and report on the proceedings of the National Council of Teachers of English. A humorous feature, "Rhetoric Prize," prints responses sent in by readers to hypothetical situations, and shows modern rhetoric at its laughable best. There are excellent, critical book reviews. Should be in large high school, and all school of education libraries, and medium to large public libraries.

Elementary English; a magazine of the language arts. 1925. 8/yr. (Oct.–May). $7. William A. Jenkins. National Council of Teachers of English, James R. Squire, Ex. Secy., 508 S. 6th St., Champaign, Ill. 61820. Illus., index, adv. Circ: 4,097. Microform: UM. Reprint: Kraus.

Indexed: EdI. *Bk. rev:* Various lengths. *Aud:* Ac, Jc, Et. *Rv:* H. *Jv:* B.

Concentrates on the elementary school language arts curriculum. It is directed to elementary school teachers and librarians and to their college instructors. Articles range from critical examinations of children's literature and audiovisual material, to the use of structural linguistics and usage in the elementary school, and educational theory. Generally, 10–15 short articles appear in each issue, and are well written and useful. Book reviews appear in two sections: generally 15 reviews of children's books, averaging 150 words; 1–4 reviews of professional and reference tools, averaging 400 words. While a must for all elementary

school libraries, should be considered in public libraries where there is an interest in personal and remedial reading.

English; literature, criticism, teaching. 1906. 3/yr. Membership (Non-members $3.50). Margaret Willy. Oxford Univ. Press, Press Rd., Neasden, London N.W. 10. Index, adv. Microform: UM.

Indexed: BritHum. *Bk. rev:* 4–7, 500 words, signed. *Aud:* Ac, Jc, Ht. *Rv:* H. *Jv:* B.

The journal of the English Association, Great Britain's counterpart of the National Council of Teachers of English. It combines the functions of the literary, critical, and teaching periodical in one journal with a high standard of scholarly content and a popular format. Articles are short, ranging from original critical readings, and theories of education, to surveys of reading tastes and writing in the Commonwealth. Poetry, prose compositions, reviews of drama and recordings, association news, and lists of classroom and professional materials are included. Issues have been devoted to studies of T. S. Eliot and W. B. Yeats. Contributors have included Cleanth Brooks and Kenneth Watson. Should be in all school of education libraries as well as larger high school collections.

English Journal. 1912. 9/yr. (Sept.–May). $7. Prof. Richard S. Alm. National Council of Teachers of English. Robert F. Hogan, Ex. Secy., 508 6th St., Champaign, Ill. 61820. Index, adv. Circ: 54,722. Microform: UM. Reprint: Kraus.

Indexed: EdI, RG. *Bk. rev:* Various types and lengths. *Aud:* Ac, Jc, Ht. *Rv:* H. *Jv:* A.

Features articles for teachers of English in junior and senior high schools. Topics include curriculum methods in the teaching of language, composition, and literature, as well as general topics in the field of English, and professional problems. Generally 12 to 16 articles appear in each issue. Contributors are primarily English teachers. The book reviews appear in three sections. "Book Marks" appears irregularly, with reviews, in essay form, of a group of young adult books. "Teaching Materials" features 6–8 reviews, 350 words in length, of textbooks and audiovisual material. "Professional Publications" features 4–5 reviews of scholarly releases, averaging 1,300 words. As the high school equivalent of *College English,* it is a basic magazine for schools of education and secondary school libraries.

English Progress. 1967. 3/yr. $5. Gordon Dennis. Pergamon Press, 44–01 21st St., Long Island City, N.Y. 11101.

Bk. rev: Extensive—almost entire issue. *Aud:* Ac, Jc, Ht, Et. *Rv:* H. *Jv:* B.

Edited by Gordon Dennis of Westminster College, Oxford, this is primarily a review of books suitable for use in english classes in elementary and secondary schools. Close to 200 titles are critically annotated. Almost all works are from British publishers, but a good number are suitable for American schools. Following a 12-page editorial, the material is divided by poetry, prose, speaking, and drama, English as a second language, specialist English, studies of individual writers or works, topics, and finally, libraries. The 100- to 300-word reviews are generally excellent. Any teacher of English and any elementary or high school librarian should welcome this as a most useful guide.

Journal of Reading (Formerly: *Journal of Developmental Reading*). 1968. 8/yr. Membership $7, (Nonmembers, $8). Margaret J. Early & Harold L. Herber. Intl. Reading Assn., Box 695, Newark, Del. 19711. Illus., index, adv. Circ: 12,000. Microform: UM. Reprint: Johnson.

Indexed: EdI, PsyAb. *Bk. rev:* 2, lengthy, signed. *Aud:* Ac, Jc, Ht. *Rv:* H. *Jv:* B.

Features suggestions for the improvement of reading in high school, college, and adult programs. Members of the International Reading Association have the option of receiving either this or *The Reading Teacher,* which emphasizes reading in the elementary schools. Each issue contains about five or six signed articles, which range in length from five to ten pages. Special departments: "President's Letter," "Reviews of Professional Publications," "Reviews of Instructional Materials," News from Washington," "News from the States," "International News," "Conversation," "Readers' Reactions." A required journal for most schools of education and for high school teachers in the area of reading development and improvement.

Literary Cavalcade. 1948. m. 8/yr. $1.25. Scholastic Magazines, Inc., 50 W. 44th St., New York, N.Y. 10036. Illus. Circ: 170,000.

Bk. rev: Notes. *Aud:* Sh, Ht. *Rv:* M. *Jv:* B.

A 40-page Scholastic publication which serves the dual purpose of assisting the senior high school English teacher (grades 10–12) and introducing modern writers to students. Examples of drama, fiction and poetry are offered with a detailed analysis of techniques, social meaning, and biographical information on authors. The selections are good, sometimes notable, but always "safe" in that they are devoid of violence, sex and politics. Also features student writing, and guidance for the college directed. One issue a year, usually in May, features student award winners of Scholastic-sponsored contests in art, photography and writing. Useful, short book reviews, particularly of paperbacks. Primarily for classroom use.

Quarterly Journal of Speech. 1915. q. $12.50. Robert G. Gunderson. Speech Assn., of America, William Work, Secy., Statler Hilton Hotel, New York, N.Y. 10001. Circ: 7,000. Microform: UM. Reprint: Johnson.

Indexed: EdI. *Bk rev:* 30, 250–500 words, signed. *Aud:* Sa, Ac, Jc, Ht. *Rv:* M. *Jv:* B.

For the most part, directed to college and university teachers of speech and specialists in speech pathology. Articles tend to be long monographs and cover every aspect of the subject, from the theatre and rhetoric to interpreta-

tion of what contemporary personalities are really saying. Of limited, yet valuable use for the high school teacher who wishes to keep up with research in the field. A first for colleges and universities, a second for secondary schools, where *The Speech Teacher* would be generally more useful.

Read Magazine (Incorporating, *Young America*). 1951. semi-m. $2.40. Victor Salvatore, Jr. Amer. Education Pubns., 1250 Fairwood Ave., Columbus, Ohio 43216. Illus. Circ: 400,000.

Aud: Jh. *Rv:* M. *Jv:* B.

A competitors answer to *Literary Cavalcade,* but at the junior high level. Material is selected to meet youthful interests and to develop tastes for good, relatively conservative, current literature. Regular features include the current scene, life in other lands, people of our times, language history, and a poetry corner. Students are urged to contribute poems and short prose pieces to the "Readers Write" pages, and jokes to the joke page. The components of reading skills are strengthened by features showing a fresh approach to word study. Etymology is stressed, in small doses, and suggestions appear in frequent issues to encourage the writing of rhymes and poetry. Articles, choral readings, and plays average three to five pages and are usually staff-written. The short story in each issue is reprinted from current fiction. Photos and sketches, and a 32-page newsprint format with a small type size. While primarily for classrooms, public libraries might consider subscribing.

Reading Improvement. 1963. 3/yr. $3.50. Hugo Hartig. Box 125, Oshkosh, Wis. 54901. Adv. Circ: 1,500.

Bk. rev: Notes. *Aud:* Ac, Jc, Ht. *Rv:* H. *Jv:* A.

"Devoted to the idea that English teaching in high school and college is essentially the teaching of reading, since the act of reading underlies nearly all learning in composition and literature." The material covers all aspects of reading from censorship to initiating a reading program. Each issue contains about six articles which range in length from 2 to 5 pages, and are written in a semi-popular style. Special departments: "Selected Abstracts from Current Literature," "New Materials for Reading Improvement." This is a must for high school libraries and high school English teachers. Differs from *College English, English Journal* and *Journal of Reading* in that it has a wider scope and a somewhat more interesting method of presentation. As such, it is useful in all types of school libraries, schools of education and might be considered in larger public libraries.

Reading Teacher. 1947. 8/yr. Membership (Institutions, $8). Roy A. Kress and Marjorie Seddon. Intl. Reading Assn., 6 Tyre Ave., Newark, Del. 19711. Circ: 45,000. Microform: UM. Reprint: AMS.

Indexed: EdI. *Bk. rev:* 5, 50–400 words. *Aud:* Sa, Ac, Jc, Ht, Et. *Rv:* H. *Jv:* B.

Deals with all aspects of the teaching of elementary and secondary reading, but concentrates on the elementary level. Each issue has from 12 to 15 signed articles which range from scholarly studies of reading habits to semi-popular contributions on the woes and joys of teaching the subject. Regular departments include notes on current research, articles from magazines and books worth examining, a list of materials particularly suited for children, and the usual organizational news. Particularly useful for the teacher who is searching for new methods of improving reading.

Scholastic Scope. 1964. w. (Sept.–June). $1.65. Roy Hemming. Scholastic Magazines, Inc., 50 W. 44th St., New York, N.Y. 10036. Illus., adv. Circ: 350,000.

Aud: Sh, Ht. *Rv:* L. *Jv:* B.

The primary purpose of this 32-page general senior high school magazine is to present news, sports, job tips, biographies and other topics in a fashion easily grasped by the student with below normal reading abilities. While the reading level is geared to the fourth to sixth grade, the approach is adult. Teachers will find the various language exercises helpful. Best used in a classroom situation, but can be seriously considered for public and school libraries without remedial reading courses, or those serving the urban slum areas.

The Speech Teacher. 1952. q. Membership (Non-members, $10). Speech Assn. of America, Statler Hilton Hotel, New York, N.Y. 10001. Illus., index, adv. Circ: 3,500.

Indexed: EdI, PsyAb. *Bk. rev:* Various numbers, lengths. *Aud:* Sa, Ac, Jc, Ht, Et. *Rv:* M. *Jv:* B.

Another journal of the Speech Association of America (see *Quarterly Journal of Speech*) more directed to the teaching of the subject than to research. Articles tend to be methodological, giving information on debate, rhetoric and general communications. A helpful feature is the review of new audio-visual equipment, pertinent articles published in other journals, and book reviews which relate to the subject of teaching speech. Some of the articles will be of interest to high school students. A basic journal in the field for all elementary and secondary professional collections.

Today's Speech. 1953. q. Membership (Non-members, $2.50). Allan B. Karstetter. Dept. of Speech, Rm. 354, Sparks Bldg., Pennsylvania State Univ., University Park, Pa. 16802. Reprint: Johnson. Microform: UM.

Bk. rev: 6–8, 400 words. *Aud:* Ac, Jc, Ht. *Rv:* H. *Jv:* B.

Although essentially a professional organ (Speech Association of Eastern States), this touches on all phases of speech: classroom approaches, public speaking, drama, therapy, business and professional communication and semantics. The editor makes every effort to stir up discussion and rebuttal, e.g., articles and letters on contemporary usage, the communication process, as well as critical appraisals of the status quo of teaching methods. In some

ways superior in style and liveliness to either *Speech Teacher* or *Quarterly Journal of Speech*. High school students, as well as teachers, will find much of value and interest, and it should be found wherever there is an active speech department.

FISHING AND HUNTING

Indexes and Abstracts

Abridged Readers' Guide, Canadian Periodical Index, Readers' Guide to Periodical Literature. (For annotations, see Indexes and Abstracts Section.)

The American Rifleman. 1885. m. $5. Ashley Halsey, Jr. National Rifle Assn. of America, 1600 Rhode Island Ave., N.W., Washington, D.C. 20036. Illus., index, adv. Circ: 879,000.

Bk. rev: 4–7, 500–1000 words, signed. *Aud:* Ga. *Rv:* H. *Jv:* A.

The *American Rifleman* has one essential reference function for *any* library which receives calls for information on gun control legislation, for it includes a monthly report on *all* state and federal laws, proposed or passed, as well as expanded articles on significant legislation. Articles are usually on the technical, historical, or how-to-do-it aspects of shooting and hunting. Close-up photography is excellent. The factual, journalistic style of presentation will discourage all but the most interested readers of any age group. However, this is still the best general gun magazine for public libraries, followed by *Sporting Times* and *Guns*. In high school libraries where there is a need for a gun magazine, *Sporting Times* should be the first choice.

American Sportsman. 1967. q. $20. Jerry Mason. 239 Great Neck Rd., Great Neck, N.Y. 11021. Illus. Circ:

Aud: Ga, Sh, Jh. *Rv:* M. *Jv:* V.

One of the most handsome outdoor sporting magazines available, this features illustrated articles on all aspects of hunting and fishing. An early issue had stories on salmon, leopards, water-fowl, shotguns, white tailed deer and whaling as practiced a century ago. The magazine is issued in conjunction with the American Broadcasting Company, and more particularly its well-known "American Sportsman" television series. Several of the television program stills and revised dialogue are employed in each issue. Differs from *Field and Stream, Outdoor Life* and *Sports Afield* in its superior format and emphasis on the history and joy of outdoor life (usually with the supposition of an unlimited budget), rather than the how-to-do-it approach of the three other magazines. At the subscription price a bit of luxury, but well worth it.

Angling Times. 1953. w. $5.80. Jack Thorndike. East Midland Press Ltd., Newspaper House, Broadway, Peterborough, Eng. Illus., adv. Circ: 146,712.

Aud: Ga, Sh, Jh. *Rv:* M. *Jv:* B.

An informative and well-illustrated publication devoted to the sport of angling with rod and line in Great Britain and Ireland. Latest equipment and methods for capturing freshwater, sea or game fish are covered in detail. Advocates intelligent and responsible use of public and private waters. Provides answering service for reader's queries and clues to good fishing around the coast. Features the "Kingfisher Page" for young anglers under 16. Newspaper format. The publisher also issues two other related journals: *Trout & Salmon* and *Fishing*. Both are excellent sources of information for the fishing enthusiast.

Field and Stream. 1895. m. $4. Clare Conley. Holt, Rinehart & Winston, Inc., 383 Madison Ave., New York, N.Y. 10017. Illus., adv. Circ: 1,371,430.

Indexed: AbrRG, RG. *Aud:* Ga, Sh, Jh. *Rv:* M. *Jv:* B.

One of the major American outdoor sporting magazines, this puts primary emphasis on "where to go" and "how to do it." It has appeal for all men and boys who enjoy hunting, fishing and boating. The editors have a strong commitment to conservation, which is reflected in many of the articles and illustrations. One or two personal accounts of hunting and fishing experiences are usually included. The advertisements are informative and geared to the specialized audience. This side of an all-girl's school (and it might be enjoyed even there), this is a required magazine in almost any type of library from the junior high to the public library.

Gun Report; dedicated to the interests of gun enthusiasts everywhere. 1955. m. $6. Kenneth W. Liggett. World-Wide Gun Report, Inc., P.O. Box 111, Aledo, Ill. 61231. Illus., index, adv. Circ: 8,000.

Aud: Ga. *Rv:* H. *Jv:* B.

The official publication of the Florida Gun Collectors Association and the Vermillion Trail Historical Arms Association this is a "must" for the gun and cartridge collector. News and articles of interest are written by experts in the field. Historical material is liberally illustrated. Important features are the "Antique Arm Prices" and the "Collectors Cartridge Prices," which are derived from reports of bona fide sales at collectors' meetings and from recent catalogs. Handsome photographs in black and white, charts, and diagrams throughout.

Guns. (Formerly: *Guns Magazine.*) 1955. m. $7.50. J. Rakusan. Publishers' Development Corp., 8150 N. Central Park Ave., Shokie, Ill. 60076. Illus., adv. Circ: 130,000.

Bk. rev: 10–12, 50–200 words, signed. *Aud:* Ga. *Rv:* M. *Jv:* B.

Informative articles on modern and antique guns, ballistics, technology, patents, and how-to-material related to guns and shooting. Special departments are devoted to guns and the law, answering queries from correspondents, gun collecting, gunsmithing tips, and the guns market. Useful, but not always critical book reviews. Liberal use

of handsome color photographs along with regular pictures in black and white. This is a more popular, general approach than *Gun Report,* and probably would be first choice in most libraries, although the latter has a higher reference value for pricing guns.

Guns & Ammo. 1958. m. $5. Tom Siatos. Peterson Publishing Co., 5959 Hollywood Blvd., Los Angeles, Calif. 90028. Illus., index, adv. Circ: 200,000.

Bk. rev: 3–5, 400–700 words, signed. *Aud:* Ga. *Rv:* M. *Jv:* B.

This is the "glamour" gun publication, catering to the off-beat, do-it-yourself, esoterica of shooting and hunting. *G&A* can serve one valued reference function as the purveyor of a series of accurate, well-written and illustrated articles on historical arms and arms collecting, written by veteran collector Arnold M. Chernhoff. Thus *G&A*, backfiles included, can be an excellent substitute for assembling an expensive collection of books on guns. The magazine is not recommended for high school collections. Many articles border on the sensational, and the gun legislation controversy is much more objectively handled by other magazines. An illuminating discussion of this magazine's role in gun legislation will be found in a *New Yorker* article "Annals of Legislation. If You Love Your Guns" (April 20, 1968, particularly pages 122–128).

Guns & Hunting. 1958. m. $6. Mel Bookstein. Maco Publishing Co., 757 Third Ave., New York, N.Y. 10017. Illus., adv. Circ: 106,000.

Aud: Ga. *Rv:* M. *Jv:* B.

More oriented to the hunter than the gun enthusiast, although there are a number of articles on collecting. Particularly useful for reliable reports on new equipment. Techniques of hunting, dogs, and some book reviews are included. The whole is nontechnical, written for the layman who wishes to learn, and is a good, useful addition for larger libraries, or where there is a heavy demand for this type of magazine.

Outdoor Life. 1898. m. $4. William E. Rae. Popular Science Publishing Co., Inc., 355 Lexington Ave., New York, N.Y. 10017. Illus., adv. Circ: 1,450,000. Microform: UM.

Indexed: RG. *Aud:* Ga, Sh. *Rv:* M. *Jv:* A.

A magazine similar to *Field and Stream,* equally geared to hunting and fishing. The 11 to 15 articles, 3,000 to 4,000 words long usually detail real life adventures and experiences of hunters and fishermen. Information on conservation, game laws and regulations is included, as well as practical tips on sporting equipment. The articles are by staff specialists and non-staff contributors. Stories are illustrated with drawings and photographs. In addition, regular departments are devoted to boating, archery, fresh and saltwater fishing, camping, dogs, woodcraft, and firearms. The type of articles featured, the quality of the illustrations, and the novelty of the items advertised make this an appealing magazine for all age levels. Between this and *Field and Stream,* the latter probably will be favored in junior high schools for a somewhat similar approach. But at the adult and senior high level, *Outdoor Life* has a slight edge.

Outdoors Calling. 1966. m. $5. Hans Tanner. Floyd Clymer Pubns., 222 N. Virgil Ave., Los Angeles, Calif. 90004. Illus., adv. Circ: 150,000.

Aud: Ga. *Rv:* M. *Jv:* B.

Camping, fishing, snowmobiling, exploring, and mountain climbing are covered in this magazine. The long articles, fully illustrated, are written by seasoned experts. Each issue offers the reader tips on camping, food preparation, new products and equipment, tackle, and select fishing locations. Answers questions on subjects of interest to readers. A good third after libraries have both *Outdoor Life* and *Field and Stream.*

Rod & Gun in Canada; the outdoor man's magazine. 1899. m. $4. Maxwell J. Seeley. 1475 Maxwell St., Montreal, Que. Illus., adv. Circ: 73,000.

Indexed: CanI. *Aud:* Ga, Sh, Jh. *Rv:* M. *Jv:* C.

Devoted primarily to hunting and fishing in Canada. Strong emphasis is placed on conservation of wildlife and natural resources. Principles of wildlife management are stressed, and personal accounts of real life adventures related. Safety suggestions and tips, including first aid, are given prominent attention. Canadian libraries should make this a first choice in the field, and large American collections might want it after subscribing to the main American magazines.

Salt Water Sportsman. 1939. m. $4. Frank Woolner. Salt Water Sportsman, Inc., 10 High St., Boston, Mass. 02110. Illus., index, adv. Circ: 65,000.

Aud: Ga. *Rv:* L. *Jv:* C.

"The voice of the coastal sport fisherman." Written and edited for saltwater fishing and fishermen, this features factual articles on methods, tackles, and lures. Staff writers provide answers to questions about sport fishing and fishing tackle, boats, boating, marine biology, and related subjects. Liberal use of photographs throughout this magazine. The reader is alerted to what fish are in season and where. The magazine also attempts to keep the public informed about conservation issues affecting saltwater anglers.

Shooting Times. 1882. w. $14.50. P. B. Brown. Burlington Publishing Co. Ltd., Braywick House, Braywick Rd., Maidenhead, Berks., Eng. Illus., adv. Circ: 28,093.

Bk. rev: 3, 300 words, signed. *Aud:* Ga. *Rv:* L. *Jv:* C.

The official organ of two of the best known shooting clubs: Wildfowlers Association of Great Britain and the Clay Pigeon Shooting Association. Primarily a publication for shooters and fishermen. Long articles, well-illustrated with photographs in black and white, cover fishing, clay pigeon shooting, guns, gun dogs, and wildfowling. Illustra-

tions on various types of weapons and birds. Some personal narratives included.

Sporting Times. 1959. m. $5. R. A. Steindler. Peoria Journal Star, Inc., News Plaza, Peoria, Ill. 61601. Illus., adv. Circ: 36,000.

Bk. rev: 3–5, 400–700 words, signed. *Aud:* Ga, Sh. *Rv:* H. *Jv:* A.

A magazine which has established national circulation only in recent years, *Sporting Times* may not be familiar to many libraries which could use it. The title is misleading, as the magazine emphasizes shooting as it is involved with the allied fields of hunting, camping, and conservation, and it thus becomes an excellent magazine for high school libraries that don't need the reference value of *The American Rifleman,* nor the sensational approach of *Guns & Ammo.* Articles are aimed at discussing and solving the problems of the average hunter, target shooter, or conservation-minded sportsman. Quality of photographs varies, but otherwise it is the "best buy" of the gun magazines. Not to be confused with the older, English periodical by the same name.

Sports Afield. 1888. m. $4. Ted Kesting. Hearst Publishing Corp., 959 Eighth Ave., New York, N.Y. 10019. Illus., adv. Circ: 1,350,000.

Aud: Ga, Sh. *Rv:* M. *Jv:* B.

Not limited to fishing and hunting, this takes in all types of activities from conservation to camping. It is particularly good for down-to-earth tips on outdoor living. The style is simple, direct, and easily understood by the high school student. It is extensively illustrated, but the photographs are only poor to good. The more sophisticated fisherman or hunter probably would put this somewhere behind *Outdoor Life* and *Field and Stream.* But the differences are few, and a choice among the three is more a matter of personal bias than objective judgment. A library might try one after the other for a number of years.

FOLKLORE

Indexes and Abstracts

Music Index, Social Science and Humanities Index. (For annotations, see Indexes and Abstracts Section.)

Folklore Institute. Journal. 1964. 3/yr. $4. Richard M. Dorson. Folklore Inst., Indiana Univ., 714 E. 8th St., Bloomington, Ind. 47401. Circ: 1,000. Microform: UM.

Aud: Sa, Ac, Jc. *Rv:* H. *Jv:* B.

Until 1964 entitled *Midwest Folklore.* With the title change it has broadened its coverage from articles of local interest to the whole subject field. Presents materials on different aspects of folklore centered on a selected topic. Articles are non-technical discussions of the present state of the topic and its specialized aspects. They are written by those reporting on actual research and observations of different aspects of folk-life. The 75-page issues have been devoted to how folklore affects culture, folklore and folk-life studies in Great Britain and Ireland, and folklore in Eastern Europe.

Journal of American Folklore. 1888. q. Membership (Non-members, $8). John Greenway. Amer. Folklore Soc., Univ. of Texas Press, Austin, Texas. 78712. Illus., index, adv. Microform: UM. Reprint: Kraus.

Indexed: MusicI, SSHum. *Bk. rev:* 15–20, 500–800 words, signed. *Aud:* Ga, Ac, Jc, Sh, Ht. *Rv:* H. *Jv:* V.

The basic journal in this field, and should be in every library including high school collections. The articles are written in a non-technical style, and will appeal to the general reader as well as the scholar. The full range of folklore, including local customs, traditions, music and dance, art, literature, and occasional biographies of interesting people is covered. A few articles are technical and frequently compare literary themes, textual illusions, themes, forms, and language used in written and orally transmitted folk-literature. Each issue contains short contributions, new discoveries, and queries requesting information or verification. The evaluative book reviews are arranged topically, and there is frequently a section devoted to noting and reviewing reprints and new editions of important works. Annual features include a "Folklore Bibliography" of new books and articles and an excellent title, author, and detailed subject index broken down by characters, incidents, ethnic and regional groups, and tale types.

Kentucky Folklore Record. 1955. q. $2. Kenneth W. Clarke & Mary W. Clarke. Kentucky Folklore Soc. & Western Kentucky State College, Bowling Green, Ky. 42101. Circ: 450. Reprint: Johnson.

Indexed: MusicI. *Bk. rev:* 2–4, 400 words, signed. *Aud:* Ga, Ac, Jc, Sh. *Rv:* M. *Jv:* B.

Typical of the many smaller journals of local folklore. Each issue contains three to five articles on ghost-tales, folk-tales, superstitions and legends of the area, folk expressions, historical events or local folk songs. Regular features are "News and Notes," concerning meetings and the membership, and the book reviews. Occasionally there will be a review of three or four records which contain music of the area. Contributors are both professional and amateur. There is a yearly bibliography of Kentucky folklore and a "Discography" section of notable records. Of value to libraries in the area and to specialists and special collections on the region or on American folklore.

New York Folklore Quarterly. 1945. q. Membership (Non-members, $4). William G. Tyrrell. New York Folklore Soc., The Farmers Museum, Cooperstown, N.Y. 13326. Illus., index, adv. Circ: 650. Microform: UM.

Indexed: MusicI. *Bk. rev:* 20–30, 150 words, signed. *Aud:* Ga, Ac, Jc, Sh. *Rv:* M. *Jv:* B.

Articles are designed to have general appeal, and while most deal with New York State, many have wider applicability, even at the junior high level. Included in the field of interest are "customs, festivals, songs, ballads, folkmusic, art, proverbs, superstitions, ghost stories, witchcraft, the history of place names, local customs and architecture, homemaking and cooking, the lore of the Indians, frontier and rural life and folkways, and the contributions of the foreign born to New York's folk heritage." Book reviews reflect the general interests of the journal and are a good source for books about New York State, pioneer life, and early American customs. For all libraries in the New York state area.

Northwest Folklore. 1965. semi-ann. $2.50. J. Barre Toelken. Univ. of Oregon Pubns., Friendly Hall, Eugene, Ore. 97403. Circ: 750.

Aud: Ga, Ac, Jc, Sh. *Rv:* M. *Jv:* B.

This journal, which replaces the smaller, mimeographed *Oregon Folklore Bulletin,* publishes the "raw materials of folklore . . . the actual collected superstitions, tales, songs, etc., of oral traditions in the Northwest." It also publishes short investigative and critical articles on the area's folklore. Items in the first few issues are concerned with such things as the tales of an early Idaho Munchausen, the derivation of children's songs and the superstitions of military flyers. A fine, lively attempt to record the folkways of an area, which despite relative newness, has plenty of ghosts and ancient whimsy tucked away in odd corners. Recommended for academic and large public libraries.

Southern Folklore Quarterly. 1937. q. $4.50. Butler H. Waugh. Univ. of Florida in cooperation with the South Atlantic Modern Language Assn., Gainesville, Fla. 32601. Circ: 630. Microform: UM.

Indexed MusicI, SSHum. *Bk. rev:* 2–3, 500 words, signed. *Aud:* Sa, Ac, Jc. *Rv:* M. *Jv:* B.

Not confined to the Southern United States, but international in scope. Devoted to the historical and descriptive study of folklore. Primarily interested in literary and historical analysis of oral and written folk-literature; the comparison of their origins, content, themes, and other similarities; and the method of using literature to learn the folkways of the past. There are frequent analyses of the use of folk materials in an author's work. Each June there is an extensive "Folklore Bibliography" on books and articles which have appeared during the previous year. Primarily for academic, junior college and large public libraries.

Tennessee Folklore Society Bulletin. 1935. q. $2. Ann Farris. Tennessee Folklore Soc. Middle Tennessee State Univ., Murfreesboro, Tenn. 37130. Circ: 246.

Indexed: MusicI. *Bk. rev:* 5–7, 40 words, signed. *Aud:* Sa, Ac, Jc, Sh. *Rv:* M. *Jv:* B.

Most of the three to four articles deal with the folk-materials of the Tennessee-Kentucky region. Some general articles on other areas of the world such as India, Guam, and Germany. Book reviews deal with all aspects of folklore, and there are occasional reviews of five or six country-music records. Special sections of "Events and Comments" and "Tales and Superstitions." Of use in larger libraries or specialized collections and of value to all libraries, including high schools, in the area.

Western Folklore. 1942. q. $5. Albert B. Friedman. Univ. of California Press, Berkeley, Calif. 94720. Circ: 675. Microform: UM. Reprint: AMS.

Indexed: MusicI. *Bk. rev:* 20, 300–500 words, signed. *Aud:* Ga, Ac, Jc, Sh. *Rv:* H. *Jv:* A.

A publication of the California Folklore Society. One of the folklore journals of wide interest and applicability, which should be in most libraries because of the popular nature of the material and its style of presentation. The five to seven articles cover all aspects of folklore—popular folk-literature and figures, literary analysis and comparison, weather lore and all types of folk beliefs and superstitions, songs and music, colloquial expressions, close-ups of folklore organizations, and cross-cultural comparisons of all of these aspects. The journal has an excellent series of regular features which include: "Notes and Queries" presenting small items and questions and answers; Peter Tamony's column on Western words in which various terms, phrases, and sayings reflecting the folklore and cultural history of the West are discussed; "Folklore and Folklorists," presenting news in the field. In addition to the topically arranged, evaluative book reviews there are four to six pages of discussion on new record releases, which are usually devoted to particular types of music or individual artists. Useful in public libraries and in high school and college collections.

GAMES AND SPORTS

Indexes and Abstracts

Abridged Readers' Guide, Biological Abstracts, Psychological Abstracts, Readers' Guide to Periodical Literature. (For annotations, see Indexes and Abstracts Section.)

Alaska Sportsman. 1935. m. $5. Bob Henning. Alaska Northwest Publishing Co., Box 1271, Juneau, Alas. 99801. Illus., adv. Circ: 92,000.

Bk. rev: 3 to 5 , 100–400 words. *Aud:* Ga, Sh, Jh. *Rv:* M. *Jv:* B.

"The magazine of the state of Alaska," this covers all phases of living in Alaska, the Yukon, British Columbia, and the North Pacific. Factual articles on history, hunting and fishing, scenic trails, and current happenings provide rich sources of information for the interested reader. No fiction. Many true life adventures. All articles supported by photographs, many in color. Although the magazine's appeal is primarily to the general adult, it has value for the high school student and scholar.

Amateur Athlete. 1929. m. H. O. Zimman. Amateur Athletic Union of the U.S.A., 156 Broad St., Lynn, Mass. 01901. Illus., adv. Circ: 12,000.

Aud: Ga, Ac, Jc, Sh. *Rv:* M. *Jv:* B.

A reporting medium for amateur sports, and particularly useful for detailed accounts of the Olympic games. A scoreboard tallies results in a variety of sports from swimming to skating. A number of articles on changes in rules and regulations, medical considerations, and individual games. Much of the basic material is covered in other sporting magazines, but this is a handy type reference tool for larger collections. See also, *Comité International Olympique Newsletter.*

Amateur Wrestling World. 1968. m. $4. William E. Pendleton. Pendleton Pubns., Box 24751, Los Angeles, Calif. 90824. Illus., adv.

Bk. rev: Notes, signed. *Aud:* Ga, Ac, Jc, Ht, Sh. *Rv:* M. *Jv:* B.

Directed to college and high school wrestlers and their coaches with four to six articles on national events, methods of teaching and outstanding amateur wrestlers. The first issues are thin, some 22 pages, but promise to grow. Each article is well illustrated, and the style is semi-popular. Should appeal to most coaches and their eager students from high school through university.

Appalachia. 1876. m. $6. Bradford F. Swann. Appalachian Mountain Club, 5 Joy St., Boston, Mass. 02108. Illus., index, adv. Circ: 10,000.

Indexed: BioAb. *Bk. rev:* 18–20, 50–600 words, signed. *Aud:* Ga, Sh. *Rv:* M. *Jv:* B.

A magazine for the mountain climbing and hiking enthusiast of all age levels. Long articles, well-illustrated and written by club members, detail climbing adventures in the U.S., Canada, and around the world. Great emphasis is placed on conservation of natural resources and the preservation of the wilderness. Contains many suggestions for new trial cutting and the maintenance and care of existing ones. Includes tips on safety precautions for climbing and hiking, and reports on the condition of various trials. Most suitable for Eastern libraries interested in the subject, but in the West and for others interested in this kind of magazine, the *Sierra Club Bulletin* (see Conservation Section) should be the first choice.

Archery World (**Incorporating: *TAM***). 1952. m. $4. Sherwood Schoch. Archers' Magazine Co., 24 S. Reading Ave., Boyertown, Pa. 19512. Illus., adv. Circ: 50,000.

Bk. rev: 12–15, 50–100 words. *Aud:* Ga, Ac, Jc. *Rv:* L. *Jv:* B.

The official publication of the National Archery Association of the United States, this is the best of two or three magazines in the field. It contains articles on hunting, major tournaments and interviews with famous bowmen.

There are how-to-do-it features, and book reviews which offer news of titles rarely found in most journals. Suitable for the back-yard amateur or the professional, and a good bet for schools where archery is part of the physical education program. See also, *Bow and Arrow.*

Athletic Journal. 1921. m. (Sept.–June). $3. M. M. Arns. Athletic Journal Publishing Co., 1719 Howard St., Evanston, Ill. 60602. Illus., index, adv. Circ: 27,500.

Indexed: EdI. *Bk. rev:* 15–20 notes. *Aud:* Ac, Jc, Ht. *Rv:* M. *Jv:* B.

Covers the broad spectrum of high school and college sports and appeals to the coach, player and non-player alike. Well written articles with photographs, charts and diagrams, are by high school and college coaches and physical education specialists. Various experiments and theories for the development, training and conditioning of high school and college athletes are treated. Special departments devoted to coaching clinics and new ideas in equipment and products. More emphasis is placed upon physical education in *Scholastic Coach,* but in many ways the two are similar. Of the two, the general school library will prefer *Athletic Journal,* while larger libraries will want both.

Baseball Digest. 1942. m. (10 issues). $3.50. Herbert F. Simons, 1708 2nd St., Highland Park, Ill. 60035. Illus., adv. Circ: 100,000.

Aud: Ga, Jh, Sh. *Rv:* M. *Jv:* B.

Dedicated primarily to reporting on all aspects of professional baseball, from the major and minor leagues to profiles of major and minor players. The style of writing presupposes some knowledge of what baseball is all about, but it is simple enough to be well within the grasp of the more than average baseball-oriented junior high school student. Not essential, but a good one in any community where baseball is a major concern. See also, *Softball Illustrated.*

Black Belt Magazine. 1960. m. $5. Anthony De Leonardis. Black Belt, Inc., 5650 W. Washington Blvd., Los Angeles, Calif. 90016. Illus., adv. Circ: 91,000.

Bk. rev: 1–2, 500 words, signed. *Aud:* Ga, Sh, Jh. *Rv:* L. *Jv:* C.

Primarily devoted to judo, karate, gung fu, etc. Informative and well-illustrated articles feature the art of self-defense as well as historical coverage. Personalities, tournaments, and techniques are highlighted. Young boys and adults make up the audience for this magazine. As the material is presented in an intelligent fashion, it can be recommended for most school and public libraries. Librarians who dread violence in any magazine are advised that all the violence here is presented in terms of health and the victory of good over evil.

Bow and Arrow. 1963. bi-m. $3. Bob Said. Gallant Publishing Co., 116 E. Badillo Ave., Covina, Calif. 91722. Illus., adv. Circ: 73,000.

Bk. rev: 1–2, 250 words, signed. *Aud:* Ga, Sh. *Rv:* L. *Jv:* B.

Although a somewhat more popular approach than *Archery World,* this magazine takes about the same tack. There are a considerable number of illustrations and advertisements, and tips on new products. Certainly one of the most useful features is the testing of new equipment. This is done in the field and the results appear to be quite objective. A handy guide for both the coach and the serious archer. Articles range from the use of the bow in war to backyard target practice. Some historical emphasis. For both the beginner and the expert, and suitable for high schools as well as public libraries. See also *The Woman Bowler.*

Bowling Magazine. 1934. m. $3. Edward L. Marcou. Amer. Bowling Congress, Inc., 1572 E. Capital Dr., Milwaukee, Wis. 53211. Illus., adv. Circ: 125,000.

Aud: Ga. *Rv:* L. *Jv:* B.

The official publication of the American Bowling Congress, this stresses membership news, items regarding events and personalities, and new legislation and equipment. A given amount of space is turned over to detailed tournament results. There is a strong editorial bias favoring the sport as a legitimate expression of Americanism. Little how-to-do-it type material. Primarily for the dedicated bowler.

Camping Guide. 1959. m. $5. George S. Welles. Rajo Pubns., Inc., 215 Park Ave. S., New York, N.Y. 10003. Illus., adv. Circ: 70,000.

Aud: Ga, Sh. *Rv:* M. *Jv:* B.

One of several general camping magazines devoted to family camping, from mountain climbing to setting up a tent in the local park. Most of the emphasis is on tenting and on trailers, and there are consumer reports on the latest camping equipment: tent-trailers, car top carriers, small boats and smaller products. Articles cover every part of the country and are geared for the middle-income group which has a two-to-three-week vacation and free weekends. This is much to be preferred to *Camping Magazine,* a professional journal. Somewhat different in its approach is: *Camping Journal* (m. $6. Davis Pubns., 229 Park Ave. S., New York, N.Y. 10003. Illus., adv. Circ: 125,000). This can be recommended for the same audience, but is a bit broader in scope than *Camping Guide.* It puts more emphasis on the outdoor life, with tips on where to camp, fish and hunt, reports from various camping areas (both U.S. and Canada), fishing tips, camp cooking, and hiking. Of the three, *Camping Journal* is probably preferable for the active outdoorsman and high school, while *Camping Guide* may be of more interest to the less active, more equipment minded camper.

Camping Magazine. 1926. m. (Jan–June); bi-m. (Sept–Dec). Membership (Non-members, $6). Howard Galloway.

Galloway Corp., 5 Mountain Ave., N. Plainfield, N.J. 07060. Illus., adv. Circ: 9,152. Microform: UM.

Indexed: RG. *Bk. rev:* 4–6, 50–100 words. *Aud:* Sa, Ht, Et. *Rv:* M. *Jv:* B.

Published by the American Camping Association and primarily directed to administrators and staffs of professional camps, particularly those for children. In that a number of articles are devoted to various outdoor activities, e.g., sports, drama, crafts, it has some value for high school and elementary school teachers. The writing style is popular, the material authoritative, and the ideas imaginative, if not always original. Parents may find it useful for tips on what to do on a camping trip, but on the whole, the material is for the camp director who is involved with such things as supervision, administration, purchasing and insurance. Way down the list for most libraries.

Chess Life. 1946. m. Membership (Non-members, $6.50). Burt Hochberg. United States Chess Federation, 479 Broadway, Newburgh, N.Y. 12550. Illus.

Aud: Ga, Ac, Jc, Sh. *Rv:* H. *Jv:* B.

Each 40- or so page issue offers the dedicated chess player three important services. First, the non-profit sponsoring organization gives worldwide news of chess matches, and features "Tournament Life," a three- to four-page calendar of tournaments scheduled in the United States for the two months ahead. Second, detailed studies—right down to moves and chess board illustrations—are reported for every major match. Finally, there are a number of theoretical articles on various aspects of the game. It is hard to imagine a good chess player who doesn't know this magazine, but it is rarely found in libraries. While it is not for the novice, the material is of such importance that it should be in any library, from the senior high school through the university, where there is more than a single chess player about. If the library can't find a place in its budget for this magazine, be sure to bring it to the attention of the chess lover.

Chess Review; the picture chess magazine. 1933. m. $7.50. I. A. Horowitz & Jack Straley Battell. I. A. Horowitz, 134 W. 72nd St., New York, N.Y. 10023. Illus., index, adv. Circ: 12,000.

Aud: Ga, Ac, Jc, Sh. *Rv:* M. *Jv:* B.

Edited by the well-known author and chess columnist for the *New York Times,* this magazine has great appeal for anyone interested in chess. It covers international regional, and interstate chess news, and is written for the expert player as well as the novice. Authorities discuss outstanding games, diagrammed plays, Solitaire Chess, and correct opening strategy. Correspondents are located in 30 states, the District of Columbia, and Canada. Contains game reports and ratings, names of new players, prize winners, and news of coming events in the U. S. and Canada. *Chess Life* is probably a first choice for most libraries, but both are equally good.

Coach & Athlete; magazine for coaches, players, trainers, officials. 1938. m. (Aug.–June). $3. Dwight Keith, Jr. Coach & Athlete, Inc., 1421 Mayson St., N.E., Atlanta, Ga. 30324. Illus., adv. Circ: 18,500.

Aud: Ac, Jc, Sh. *Rv:* M. *Jv:* B.

The official publication of some 20 associations from the Arizona High School Coaches Association to the National Junior College Athletic Association. It is primarily geared for the professional high school or college coach, and includes articles by and for them on various technical aspects of every sport from baseball to wrestling. Features such as a profile of the college of the month and news on various regional activities will make the magazine of some interest to sports fans. A limited number of non-specialized articles broadens the potential audience. However, for most libraries it will be of value to those directly involved with coaching or training. As many of the associations it represents are in the southern and southeastern United States, it will be of special interest to libraries in those areas.

Comité International Olympique. Newsletter. 1967. m. $6. Comité International Olympique, Mon Repos, Lausanne, Switzerland. Illus. Circ: 2,100.

Aud: Sa, Ga, Ac. *Rv:* H. *Jv:* B.

Published in both an English and French edition, includes five to six non-partisan articles on all facets of the Olympics from history to "Thoughts on Doping." About one-quarter of the 56-page magazine is turned over to official information, news, brief notes on publications, and personalities. During the Olympic games a given number of issues are devoted to the results, and in considerably more detail than found in most publications—hence, its high reference value. A few illustrations. As the official organ of the International Olympic Committee, it occupies a unique place, and should be considered by larger public and academic libraries.

Contract Bridge Bulletin. m. Membership (Non-members, $3). Richard L. Frey, Amer. Contract Bridge League, Inc., 125 Greenwich Ave., Greenwich, Conn. 06830. Illus., adv. Circ: 150,000.

Aud: Ga, Ac, Jc. *Rv:* H. *Jv:* B.

Approximating, both in size and format, *The Bridge World,* this has a considerably wider audience because it is the official publication of the American Contract Bridge League. It tends to stress more "what the folks are doing" than its competitor, featuring articles on clubs and activities throughout the United States. It is filled with pictures of members. Information on the game itself is limited to a few articles and regular departments. The player who is more involved with the game than with the League may prefer *The Bridge World,* and for the library the latter is definitely preferable as it stresses the finer points of bridge rather than personalities.

Gambling Illustrated. 1965. m. $10. H. R. David. President Pubns., P. O. Box 425, Ojus, Fla. Illus., adv. Circ: 100,000.

Aud: Ga. *Rv:* M. *Jv:* B.

Dedicated to the proposition that gambling is more a matter of mathematical "money management" than chance, the publisher plugs a "Club for the Improvement of Bettors." The 64-page professional format includes 10 to 12 articles directed to the serious $2 bettor. One issue, for example, included articles on differences among casinos in Nevada, how a computer can give odds, greyhound bettors, horse racing and a number of features on various methods of wagering. The whole is illustrated, and balanced with advertisements. The tone is popular, yet serious. It is well documented with facts rather than conjecture, and there is a refreshing honesty of approach. If the letters to the editor are any indication, it is a magazine which is faithfully read by every type of gambler from those who follow the nags to card players. It would be a good choice for any library where there is a gambler within betting distance.

Golf Digest. 1950. m. $5.95. Richard Aultman. Golf Digest, Inc., 88 Scribner Ave., Norwalk, Conn. 06850. Illus., adv. Circ: 330,000.

Aud: Ga. *Rv:* L. *Jv:* B.

Published by the New York Times Company, and claiming to be the "world's leading golfing publication," this is directed to an upper-income audience. It is written and edited for the beginning and professional golfer. Detailed and thorough instruction in good golfing principles and techniques from professionals such as Snead, Nelson, Player, Casper, Boros, etc. Informative articles highlight profiles of promising and established golfing personalities, interesting and unusual golfing situations and feats, records, predictions, and biographies. Includes "Golf Information Directory," vacation tips, and a complete guide to courses that can be played. Liberal use of charts, diagrams, and photographs (black and white and color) throughout. See final comments for *Golf.*

Golf Magazine. 1959. m. $7. John M. Ross. Universal Publishing and Distributing Corp., 235 E. 45th St., New York, N.Y. 10017. Illus., adv. Circ: 350,000.

Aud: Ga. *Rv:* L. *Jv:* B.

For the recreational golfer and those interested in improving their game. Contains expert instruction and commentary by professional golfers and special contributors. Offers tips and suggestions for handling all types of golfing situations and difficulties. Answers questions on techniques, tactics, and rules of the game. Spotlights the latest in golfing attire, tournaments, and equipment. Golf vacation guide included. Between this and *Golf Digest* the decision is simply a matter of personal preference. Librarians might try them both, or one after the other.

Mademoiselle Gymnast. 1966. q. $3. Barbara and Glenn Sundby. Sundby Pubns., 410 Broadway, Santa Monica, Calif. 90406. Illus., adv. Circ: 2,475.

Bk. rev: Notes. *Aud:* Ac, Jc, Sh, Ht. *Rv:* L. *Jv:* B.

Specifically geared for the instructor in women's gymnastics (high school and adult), this features articles on the importance of programs, methodology, and world-wide activities in the field. The articles are illustrated with photographs, sketches and diagrams, which are particularly good for teaching purposes. Features include news of workshops and clinics, association activities, and short book reviews and notices. Attention is given to participants, and anyone actively interested in the sport will enjoy the magazine almost as much as the teacher.

Modern Gymnast. 1957. 10/yr. $5. Glenn Sundby. Sundby Pubns., 410 Broadway, Santa Monica, Calif. 90406. Illus., adv. Circ: 9,500.

Aud: Sa, Ac, Jc, Ht. *Rv:* H. *Jv:* B.

A glossy, well-illustrated magazine of some 28 to 40 pages, which covers all aspects of amateur gymnastics. About three-quarters of every issue is given over to complete reports on national, Canadian and international events. The other quarters include regular features which cover developments in gymnastics for teachers and students alike. Emphasis is primarily on men's activities, from high school through the university. A fundamental purchase for any high school or university where gymnastics are a concern. Large public libraries may also wish to consider.

Pool N' Patio. See Home Section.

Research Quarterly. 1930. q. $5. Nancy K. Rosenberg. Amer. Assn. for Health, Physical Education and Recreation, 1201 16th St., N.W., Washington, D.C. 20036. Illus. Circ: 11,000. Microform: UM. Reprint: Kraus, Abrahams.

Indexed: PsyAb. *Aud:* Sa, Ac, Jc, Ht. *Rv:* L. *Jv:* B.

This periodical is devoted to exploring various aspects of physical education and recreation. Articles such as "Sixteen Personality Factor Profiles of Collegiate Wrestlers," and "The Effect of Varied Instructional Emphasis upon the Development of a Motor Skill," indicate the rather narrow range of interest or value for the educational aspect of recreation and physical education.

The Ring; world's official boxing magazine. 1922. m. $4. Nat S. Fleischer. 120 W. 31st St., New York, N.Y. 10019. Illus., adv.

Aud: Ga. *Rv:* M. *Jv:* B.

Featured articles, fully illustrated with photographs and drawings, cover the whole boxing universe. One or two articles on wrestling and wrestlers is featured each month. Fight reports from all parts of the world, boxing personalities present and past, and news of interest to the boxing world are included. The deliberate inclusion of some articles by editors and boxing notables is designed to evoke controversy and interest. Contains world rating of various fighters and tips on fighters of promise. Appeal limited to those interested in boxing.

Scholastic Coach. 1931. m. (Sept.–June). $3.50. Scholastic Magazines, Inc., 50 W. 44th St., New York, N.Y. 10036. Illus., index, adv. Circ: 33,000. Microform: UM.

Indexed: EdI. *Bk. rev:* 4–7, 50–250 words. *Aud:* Ac, Jc, Ht. *Rv:* M. *Jv:* B.

A trade journal for coaches, athletic directors and physical educators in high schools, colleges and universities. The technical aspects of coaching, physical education, medical problems, trends in facilities and equipment—all are subjects of rather exhaustive, well-written articles. Only for the professional, and librarians should know that about one-half the circulation represents free copies sent to professionals.

Skating. 1923. 8/yr. $4. Marjorie Martin. United States Figure Skating Assn., 178 Tremont St., Boston, Mass. 02111. Illus., adv. Circ: 10,422.

Aud: Ga, Sh. *Rv:* L. *Jv:* B.

Geared to the competitive and the recreational skaters of all ages. Includes skating tips for the beginning, figure, dance, and free style skater, with appropriate illustrations. Spotlights ice show reviews and itineraries, and fashion news. Special section of the magazine, for subscribers only, devoted to the Association-affiliated skater. Contains lists of tests passed in the U.S. and Canada. Profiles of skating personalities, meet results, and technical articles, are included in a separate section. Of its type, probably the best magazine available, and a good addition for all kinds of libraries.

Ski. 1935. 8/yr. $4. John Fry. Universal Publishing and Distributing Corp., 235 E. 45th St., New York, N.Y. 10017. Illus., adv. Circ: 215,000.

Aud: Ga, Sh, Jh. *Rv:* M. *Jv:* B.

Editors claim this is the "world's largest ski magazine." Informative articles, lavishly illustrated, spotlight activities throughout the ski world. Contains "where to go and where to stay" information, both for the U.S. and abroad. Expert advice and instruction from nationally and internationally famous masters. Profiles of famous ski personalities and great moments in racing. Offers winter driving tips, up-to-date equipment ideas and ski fashions. Many exciting action photographs of skiers on the slopes or in competition. Appeal limited to those in middle or upper-middle income brackets, but for skiers of all ages and experience.

Skiing. 1947. bi-m. (Oct–Mar). $3. Doug Pfeiffer. Ziff-Davis Publishing Co., 1 Park Ave., New York, N.Y. 10016. Illus., adv. Circ: 210,000.

Bk. rev: Notes. *Aud:* Ga, Sh. *Rv:* L. *Jv:* B.

There are close to 20 magazines published in the United States devoted entirely to skiing. Along with *Ski,* this is the most popular. It is geared to a less affluent audience than its competitor, and pays more attention to how-to-do-it type information. There are the usual articles on resorts, competitions and feature stories. The illustrations are good

to excellent. High school libraries may prefer this to *Ski,* but any library with enthusiastic skiers will want both.

Skin Diver Magazine; devoted to the underwater world. 1951. m. $5. Paul J. Tzimoulis. Petersen Publishing Co., 5959 Hollywood Blvd., Los Angeles, Calif. 90028. Illus., index, adv. Circ: 59,698.

Aud: Ga, Sh. *Rv:* M. *Jv:* B.

An action-packed magazine devoted to skin diving and the whole underwater world. Excellent articles range the broad spectrum from ocean science to spear fishing, travel and boats. Famous shipwrecks, sunken treasure, diving techniques, and true life experiences stimulate the reader's interest and imagination. Brilliantly illustrated with full color and black and white photographs. The "Diver's Directory" serves the local and travelling diver. Suggestions and tips on "where-to-go" and "what-to-do" are included for the diving enthusiast. Should delight the teen-ager as well as the adult audience.

Softball Illustrated. 1967. q. $3. Don Sarno & Milton Stark. P.O. Box 1081, Whittier, Calif. 90603. Circ: 10,000.

Aud: Ga. *Rv:* L. *Jv:* B.

A glossy, standard-sized 50-page magazine, this is filled with photographs and advice on softball. Such items as "Starting a New League, Here's How," and "The Drop Ball Grips," will have appeal for anyone interested in the sport. Covers all aspects of softball: activities of the industrial leagues, how to organize children's teams, how to improve a woman's game, even a section entitled "National Tournament Review." Should be particularly useful to urban libraries in areas where there are several teams, or in high schools and colleges where the game is played regularly.

Sport. 1946. m. $6. Al Silverman. MacFadden-Bartell Corp., 205 E. 42nd St., New York, N.Y. 10017. Illus., adv. Circ: 800,000.

Bk. rev: 3–4, 50–100 words, signed. *Aud:* Ga, Sh, Jh. *Rv:* L. *Jv:* A.

Emphasis is on the "fan" approach to sports, and the well-illustrated articles feature what this or that baseball player or football star thinks about the game. The writing style is in the tradition of sports journalism, heavy on jargon and the "stars," light on intellectual content. Each issue is balanced by special features and news of current sporting events. It differs radically from its competitor *Sports Illustrated* in that it stresses the nitty gritty of the sporting life, and pays little or no attention to the gentlemanly aspects. As such it offends the sensitive, disturbs the dedicated sportsman, and is a constant joy for teenagers and less sophisticated adults. A good bet to lure the non-reading male into the library, and a first choice for junior high and high school libraries.

The Sporting News; the nation's oldest sports publication. 1886. w. $12. Lowell Reidenbaugh. The Sporting

News, 2012–2018 Washington Ave., St. Louis, Mo. 63166. Illus., adv.

Aud: Ga, Sh. *Rv:* M. *Jv:* B.

This informative, entertaining, easy-to-read newspaper is America's oldest national sports weekly. Interesting and exciting articles cover baseball, basketball, golf, soccer and other sports in season. Special departments include both professional and collegiate football. Filled with statistics, stories, gossip, and action photographs (black and white and color) that capture and hold the reader's interest. Capsule treatment of sporting news of yesteryear. For sports fans of all ages, although the format and relatively high price dictate inclusion only in larger collections, or where there is a particularly strong interest in the subject.

Sports Illustrated. 1954. w. $8. Hedley Donovan. Time Inc. 540 N. Michigan Ave., Chicago, Ill. 60611. Illus., index, adv. Circ: 1,250,000. Microform: UM.

Indexed: AbrRG, RG. *Bk. rev:* Occasional. *Aud:* Ga, Ac, Jc, Sh, Jh. *Rv:* H. *Jv:* A.

America's best known general sports magazine, this is the Time/Life approach to the "wide world of sports." Covers the usual spectator sports (baseball, basketball, boxing, football), and features lengthy articles (2,000–5,000 words) on mountain climbing, big game hunts, horse racing, boating, and major sports personalities. Lists sports records, "backs" and "players of the week," and reports timely news of current interest to the sporting world. Primarily staff written, articles have also been commissioned from writers including Robert Frost, Catherine Drinker Bowen, and John Steinbeck. Extensive use is made of paintings and black and white and color photography. Even readers with a limited interest in sports will find something of interest here. Should be in all libraries.

Strategy & Tactics; a journal of American wargaming. 1966. m. (except Feb. and April), $6. Project Analysis Corp. Box 11–187, Loudonville, N.Y. 12211. Illus.

Aud: Sa. *Rv:* L. *Jv:* C.

If the reader believes war can be set up in terms of games, this is his magazine. The 32 pages includes such items as "The Battle of Britain," the inside story on how the Gamescience Corporation developed a set which includes a mapboard, 130 pieces showing diagrams of aircraft, a commander's manual, all for $7. Other articles discuss the battle of Stalingrad and rules for naval wargames. All of this apparently interests a special type of adult (not always a military man), but it is not the usual game for the children. Most libraries can skip, and it is included here as an admittedly unique publication of interest to a few readers.

Surfer Magazine; the international surfing magazine. 1960. bi-m. $4. John Severson Pubns., P.O. Box 1028, Dana Point, Calif. 92629. Illus., adv. Circ: 101,000.

Aud: Ga, Sh, Jh. *Rv:* M. *Jv:* B.

One of the best magazines devoted to surfing, with a not too serious approach to what is downright fun for the younger set. Particularly good for the how-to-do-it articles, and information on the best surf. This latter feature makes it a type of travel magazine, and the well-illustrated articles—many in color—on the waters of France, South America and the eastern and western United States (to mention a few spots covered) give it some appeal for nonswimmers. The limited fiction and cartoons are a bit weak, but harmless enough. A good bet for any school or public library where there is interest in the sport.

While this magazine tends to stress surfing in the Western United States, another equally good entry in this field puts more emphasis on the world scene. This is the *International Surfing Magazine* (1965. bi-m. $4. Avant Publishing Co., 8155 Van Nuys Blvd., Panorama City, Calif. 91402). It covers all major and minor international surfing meets, and features fine photographs, fast-moving articles, and authoritative information for amateur and expert alike.

A third surfing magazine, and a third choice for most libraries, is *Atlantic Surfing Magazine* (m. $2.50. Atlantic Surf Pubns., P.O. Box 96, Dyker Heights, Brooklyn, N.Y. 11228). The scope is indicated by the title, and like the other two, it is profusely illustrated. Unlike them, it is for the expert and semi-expert, and there is little or no "how-to-do-it" information.

Swimming World. 1960. m. $5. Albert Schoenfield. 12618 Killion St., North Hollywood, Calif. 91607. Illus., index, adv. Circ: 13,866.

Bk. rev: Occasional. *Aud:* Ga, Ac, Jc, Sh. *Rv:* M. *Jv:* B.

Geared to the interests of dedicated swimmers and coaches, this is the official magazine of the American Swimming Coaches Association, the National Interscholastic Swimming Coaches Association and the College Swimming Coaches Association. A great deal of space is devoted to listing conference dates and record holders, All-Americans and national champions. One or two articles per issue stress diving, swimming, body building (conditioning) or stroke techniques and are written by coaches of universities and colleges. Individual champions and record holders are interviewed and photographed. Prolific advertising devoted entirely to the related field—anything from wheat germ to diving boards. For the competitive swimmer, diver and water polo player, and a consideration for most libraries.

Tennis U.S.A. 1937. m. $3. Hal Steger. Popular Pubns., Inc., 205 E. 42nd St., New York, N.Y. 10017. Illus., adv. Circ: 27,000.

Aud: Ac, Jc, Sh, Ht. *Rv:* M. *Jv:* B.

Primarily for tennis coaches and serious players, this is the official publication of the United States Lawn Tennis Association. Emphasis is on how to promote, teach and to an extent, play the game. Particularly useful in reference collections because it gives full reports on national and international tournaments, many supported by the Association. Features include court and equipment reports, profiles of national champions, news of the organization, and rule changes. Differs from *World Tennis* in that it concentrates on amateur efforts, while the other tennis magazine considers professional play equally important. Of the two, *Tennis U.S.A.* will be of more direct benefit to teachers and players from high school through college, while *World Tennis* will have greater appeal for fans of all ages.

Track & Feld News. 1948. m. $4. Cordnor Nelson. Track & Field News, Inc., P.O. Box 296, Los Altos, Calif. 94022. Illus., adv. Circ: 10,600.

Bk. rev: 5–10, 100–250 words. *Aud:* Ga, Ac, Jc, Sh. *Rv:* H. *Jv:* B.

The favored field magazine among enthusiasts, but not among librarians. "We are in our 20th year," the publisher observes, "but are not well known outside the immediate world of track and field." It deserves wider attention, particularly as it offers high reference value (methodical worldwide coverage, with statistics, data and anything connected with the sport), and current news, photos and columns which have wide appeal for anyone from the high school runner to the college or university coach.

The Woman Bowler. 1936. m. (except May & July). $2. Charles W. Westlake. Woman's Intl. Bowling Congress, Inc., 1225 Dublin Rd., Columbus, Ohio 43212. Illus., adv. Circ: 125,000.

Aud: Ga. *Rv:* L. *Jv:* C.

Details activities and events involving women bowlers, and includes some discussion of rules and regulations pertinent to the sport. Outstanding games and performances are spotlighted along with leading prize winners and personalities in various tournaments. Photographs, color and black and white, are widely used throughout and bowling fashion news and equipment are featured.

World Tennis. 1953. m. $5. Gladys M. Heldman. World Tennis Magazine, 82 Beaver St., New York, N.Y. 10005. Illus., adv. Circ: 44,000.

Aud: Ga, Ac, Jc, Sh. *Rv:* M. *Jv:* B.

"World's largest tennis magazine," this contains news and features for anyone interested in the sport. Valuable tennis instruction is accompanied by action photographs, diagrams, and some picture stories are included. Articles are written by well known professionals. Features: tennis news from around the world; lists of the world ranking of outstanding tennis stars; happenings of "25 years ago"; answers to questions posed by correspondents. Tips on tennis fashions, tournaments, and equipment. Probably the best tennis magazine for the general collection, although *Tennis U.S.A.* is preferable for amateur players and their coaches.

GARDENING

Indexes and Abstracts

Biological Abstracts, Biological and Agricultural Index. (For annotation, see Indexes and Abstracts Section.)

American Rock Garden Society. Bulletin. 1934. q. Membership. Albert M. Sutton. Lawrence Hocheimer, Ridge Farms Rd., Norwalk, Conn. 06850. Illus., index, adv. Circ: 1,200.

Aud: Ga. *Rv:* B. *Jv:* B.

Designed for the rock garden enthusiast, but is also valuable for those interested in wild flowers. Usually there are about four, two- to five-page articles concerning plants in their natural rock environments or about rock gardening. Contributors are experienced gardeners and horticulturists. Only for larger collections. See concluding statement for *American Rose Magazine.*

American Rose Magazine. 1933. m. Membership (Nonmembers, $4.50). O. Keister Evans, Jr. Amer. Rose Soc., Inc., 4048 Roselea Pl., Columbus, Ohio 43214. Illus., index, adv. Circ: 16,000.

Aud: Ga. *Rv:* M. *Jv:* B.

Well suited for beginning and advanced rose growers and "rosarians." The one- or two-page articles cover such diverse topics as the histories of particular types of roses, research on rose diseases and new varieties, famous rose gardens, exhibitions, care of cut roses and arrangement and practical gardening advice for rose growers in various parts of the United States. Frequently, articles are written by amateurs about their work with roses. Rose growing in foreign countries is occasionally discussed. As this is a specialized magazine for society members (the same is true of the *American Rock Garden Society. Bulletin* and the *Fairchild Tropical Garden Bulletin*), it is only for large libraries. However, the smaller library may well be able to find an interested subscriber who would be willing to donate copies.

Fairchild Tropical Garden Bulletin. 1945. q. $3. John Popenoe. 10901 Old Cutler Rd., Miami, Fla. 33156. Illus.

Aud: Ga. *Rv:* L. *Jv:* B.

Although mainly a news bulletin for the Garden, it contains information concerning tropical plants and gardens not usually found in other garden publications. Ordinarily, there is one three- or four-page article on a particular garden or group of plants found in a tropical setting.

Flower and Garden. **(Eastern, Mid-America and Western eds.)** 1957. m. $3. Rachel Snyder. Mid-America Publishing Corp., 4251 Pennsylvania Ave., Kansas City, Mo. 64111. Illus., index, adv. Circ: 580,000.

Bk. rev: Notes. *Aud:* Ga. *Rv:* M. *Jv:* B.

Written for amateur gardeners who are interested primarily in flowers and other decorative plants. Within each regional edition, gardening information is given for more specific areas in the "Regional Reports." Many how-to-do-it articles on general gardening practices, techniques for specific plants, landscaping, flower arranging and drying are presented in non-technical language. Other articles discuss interesting gardens of amateurs and famous botanical gardens as well as garden equipment and horticultural developments. The most useful regular features include "The Beginning Gardener," "In House and Greenhouse," and a column answering readers' questions. An active competitor to other general gardening publications such as *Home Garden and Flower Grower* and *Popular Gardening and Living Outdoors*. It ranks somewhat behind *Home Garden* in overall appeal, but ahead of *Popular Gardening*. Selection, though, will depend upon reader interest and the wise librarian will try each of them out for a while. Where gardening is a serious matter, it would be a good idea to take one of these general magazines and then a specialized publication such as the *Garden Journal of the New York Botanical Garden*.

Garden Journal of the New York Botanical Garden.

1951. bi-m. $3. Dorothy E. Hansell. New York Botanical Garden, Bronx Park, N.Y. 10458. Illus., index, adv. Circ: 4,500. Microform: UM.

Indexed: BioAg. *Bk. rev:* 5–7, half page, signed. *Aud:* Ga, Ac, Jc, Sh. *Rv:* M. *Jv:* A.

Written for the informed layman "who has an abiding interest in plants." The articles, averaging 12 per issue, present in non-technical language such diverse subjects as famous gardens throughout the world, historical aspects of plant use, conservation, ecology and plant growth. The occasional how-to-do-it material about cuttings and grafting is for the advanced gardener, and some of the articles are well suited for students of elementary botany. The contributors are professional gardeners, writers and professors of horticulture. Regular features include "Courses, Lectures and other Garden Events" and "News, Notes and Comments." The format of *Garden Journal* is more attractive than most other garden periodicals and no distasteful advertising appears. An excellent, all around gardening magazine for the serious gardener. Should be in most public libraries, and in high school and academic libraries in support of the botany program.

Garden News.

1958. w. $7.60. Tony Ireson. Garden News Ltd., Newspaper House, Broadway, Peterborough, Eng. Illus., adv. Circ: 59,350.

Aud: Ga. *Rv:* M. *Jv:* B.

Aimed primarily at the British gardener, the 24 to 26 pages, presented in newspaper format, offer news concerning shows, garden societies, flowers, house plants, vegetables, fruit growing and much practical gardening advice. Whether British or not, a person interested in new varieties of flowers and plants will find the coverage of the latest

horticultural developments an excellent alerting device. Landscaping, greenhouses and historical research involving plants and gardens are also frequently discussed. Regular features include questions and answers for English gardeners, and classified ads and gardening positions. While a good addition for libraries, the English emphasis limits it primarily to large collections.

Home Garden and Flower Grower.

1914. m. $3.50. Carroll C. Calkins. Home Garden, 1031 Broadway, Albany, N.Y. 12201. Illus., adv. Circ: 400,000. Microform: UM.

Indexed: BioAb, BioAg, RG. *Aud:* Ga. *Rv:* M. *Jv:* A.

Written for amateur gardeners and homeowners in all locales of the United States. The eight or nine short articles offer, in non-technical language, how-to-do-it information for gardening and landscaping. Frequently, house plants are discussed as well as famous gardens, flower arrangement and the latest in garden equipment. The emphasis is on decorative gardening and landscape design but travel, cooking, conservation and beautification, considered from the gardener's point of view, are included. Regular features include "Garden Events" and "Question Box," in which readers' questions are answered by an expert. The color photographs are excellent. One of the best all around gardening magazines for most libraries. See concluding comments for *Flower and Garden*.

Horticulture.

1904. m. $4. Edwin F. Steffek. Massachusetts Horticultural Soc., Horticultural Hall, 300 Massachusetts Ave., Boston, Mass. 02115. Illus., adv. Circ: 102,000. Microform: UM.

Indexed: BioAb, BioAg, RG. *Bk. rev:* 7–13, short, signed. *Aud:* Ga, Sh. *Rv:* M. *Jv:* B.

A single example of a local publication, this is published by the Massachusetts Horticultural Society, and presents a wide range of information about gardening and flora in all parts of the world. Material is semipopular and by recognized authorities. The information is general enough to be of interest to gardeners in almost any part of the United States, as well as high school biology students. Excellent color photographs accompany the articles. Librarians are advised to check for local horticultural publications. Almost every area publishes one or two, and they are extremely useful for gardeners.

Horticultural Research; a journal for the publication of scientific work on horticulture.

1961. semi-ann. $5. C. A. Wood & W. W. Fletcher. Oliver & Boyd Ltd., Tweeddale Court, 14 High St., Edinburgh, Scotland. Illus., index. Circ: 700.

Indexed: BioAb, BioAg. *Bk. rev:* 2–3, lengthy, signed. *Aud:* Sa, Ac. *Rv:* H. *Jv:* B.

Aimed at advanced researchers and specialists. Seven to nine "research papers and research reviews on subjects connected with horticultural plants and practices" from all parts of the world are presented in each issue. The research concerns such subjects as plant breeding, genetics, plant physiology, plant pathology and soil science, all as related to horticulture. Only for larger academic collections.

The National Gardener. 1930. bi-m. $1. Mrs. James N. McClure. National Council of State Garden Clubs, Inc., 4401 Magnolia Ave., St. Louis, Mo. 63110. Illus., adv. Circ: 40,000.

Bk. rev: 2, half-page, signed. *Aud:* Ga. *Rv:* L. *Jv:* B.

Published primarily for news about state garden clubs. The 12 or 13 brief articles describe various civic projects such as beautification and conservation schemes. International projects are sometimes included. Although not a how-to-do-it magazine, there are occasional articles dealing with flower arranging and related activities. Useful, but way down the list for most libraries.

Organic Gardening and Farming. 1942. m. $5. Robert Rodale. Rodale Press, 33 E. Minor St., Emmaus, Pa. 18049. Illus., adv. Circ: 340,000.

Aud: Ga, Sh, Jh. *Rv:* L. *Jv:* B.

Nature is the message, chemicals the villain, and the result is a how-to-do-it approach to gardening which has vast appeal. The editor-owner stresses the natural maintenance of nutrients in the soil by careful use of organic wastes for compost, cover crops and the like. Emphasis is on the garden, and the small farm. Even those who fail to go all the way with the editor's viewpoint will find much of value in suggestions for how to garden. Advertisements and illustrations round out the message. Useful, too, at the junior and senior high school level.

Plants and Gardens. 1945. q. Membership (Non-member, $3). Brooklyn Botanic Garden, Brooklyn, N.Y. 11225. Illus., index. Circ: 9,500.

Indexed: BioAb, BioAg. *Bk. rev:* occasional. *Aud:* Ga, Ac, Jc. *Rv:* H. *Jv:* A.

Aimed chiefly at the more experienced gardener. Each of three of the four issues is written as a comprehensive handbook on a particular topic. For example, "weed control," "orchids," "garden pests," "rock gardens," etc., have appeared. The information in the ten or eleven, four- or five-page articles is practical and detailed. Often many pages of useful, easy-to-consult charts are presented. Research reports and suggestions concerning equipment and reading matter are included. The pamphlet and book suggestions are not always annotated, but the reader is told where they are available. The contributors are university professors, entomologists, pathologists, writers of garden books and horticulturists. The year-end issue (no. 4) includes the 10 to 15 articles judged by the Editorial Board to be the most significant gardening (or horticultural) articles published during the year in other periodicals. The library which finds a large reader interest in the *Garden Journal of the New York Botanical Garden* should try a subscription to this equally worthwhile magazine.

Popular Gardening and Living Outdoors. 1950. q. $2. Mary E. O'Brien. Holt, Rinehart & Winston, Inc., 383 Madison Ave., New York, N.Y. 10017. Illus., adv. Circ: 330,000.

Indexed: RG. *Aud:* Ga. *Rv:* M. *Jv:* B.

The third, large subscription, general gardening magazine. (See also, *Flower and Garden, Home Garden.*) Each issue consists of approximately 12 articles, three to seven pages in length, which offer practical how-to-do-it information on gardening, landscaping and building greenhouses, driveways, patios and walks. Gardening equipment, gardens of special interest and house plants are also frequently discussed. Regular features include tips for "Regional Gardening" and questions of readers answered. In that this emphasizes such items as patios, games, barbeques, etc., it is somewhat broader in scope than its two competitors, yet this emphasis limits the amount of garden coverage. All of which is to say, it is a good general magazine for the garden enthusiast and weekend man about the house. For a comparison of the various general gardening magazines see the concluding comments on *Flower and Garden.*

GENERAL

Indexes and Abstracts

Abridged Readers' Guide, British Humanities Index, Canadian Periodical Index, Music Index, Public Affairs Information Service, Readers' Guide to Periodical Literature, Social Sciences and Humanities Index. (For annotations, see Indexes and Abstracts Section.)

The majority of general, non-specialized consumer magazines are well enough known by laymen and librarians. And, in compiling this section, it seemed logical to include those publications commonly referred to as "news magazines," e.g., *Time, Newsweek,* etc., because their coverage of the news is general in scope, including their weekly feature stories. The annotations which follow are more analytical than descriptive, more comparative and critical than necessarily objective. They represent one man's viewpoint, and regardless of whether or not the reader agrees, it is hoped that he will at least take a second look at the magazine which he has possibly assumed must be good because of wide circulation.

Other general magazines of a more sophisticated literary and political content, such as *Atlantic Monthly, Encounter,* or *Saturday Review,* will be found in the Literary and Political Reviews Section.

American-German Review. 1934. bi-m. Lewis F. Gittler. Natl. Carl Schurz Assn., Inc., 339 Walnut St., Philadelphia, Pa. 19106. Illus., index, adv. Circ: 3,800. Microform: UM.

Aud: Ga, Ac, Jc, Sh. *Rv:* M. *Jv:* B.

Written for the interested layman, not the expert, this is a general magazine of German-American culture. Emphasis is on promoting better relationships between the two peoples by highlighting the artistic, social, and business life of the German speaking peoples. Articles, both in German and English, touch on almost every phase of modern life from art and music to architecture, trade and economic developments. There is some political material, but this is limited almost entirely to noncontroversial subjects. The illustrations are good, and even younger children might enjoy browsing here.

The American Legion Magazine. 1919. m. $2. Robert B. Pitkin. 720 Fifth Ave., New York, N.Y. 10019. Illus., adv. Circ: 2,523,000.

Bk. rev: 1–2, 500–600 words, notes. *Aud:* Ga. *Rv:* L. *Jv:* B.

While veteran's affairs and problems are stressed, this is much closer to a general interest magazine than the title suggests. Each issue contains five or more articles on a variety of subjects from international affairs to tips on buying a home or an automobile. While middle-of-the-road to conservative in editorial matters, the magazine features opposing views on major issues and tends to represent a broad section of public opinion. There are some book reviews, travel tips, consumer information and the like. The writing is never exciting, but the circulation indicates more than a passing interest by many members of the Legion.

American-Scandinavian Review. 1913. q. $6. Erik J. Friis. American-Scandinavian Foundation, 127 E. 73rd St., New York, N.Y. 10021. Illus., index, adv. Circ: 7,000. Microform: UM.

Indexed: PAIS. *Aud:* Ga, Sh, Jh. *Rv:* M. *Jv:* B.

Well-illustrated accounts of cultural and political life in Denmark, Finland, Iceland, Norway, and Sweden, and regular news of noted "Scandinavians in America." Scandinavian poetry and short stories in translation. The style is popular and the magazine will be of interest to travelers, and teen-agers studying the Scandinavian countries.

Americas. 1949. m. $4. Dept. of Public Information, Pan American Union, Washington, D.C. 20006. Illus. Circ: 80,000. Microform: UM.

Indexed: PAIS, RG. *Aud:* Ga, Sh. *Rv:* L. *Jv:* B.

This is the official publication of the Pan American Union, and while it is beautifully illustrated and well written, it is essentially biased. Most of the articles are of the *National Geographic* type, i.e., travel, peoples and the happy life led by all in the lands south of the border. The features on the arts, literature and music are excellent. The lack of material on pressing political and economic unrest is something else again. Where there is an indication of poverty or political unrest, this is usually capped by what the present political leaders or businessmen are doing to cure the situation. Controversy, then, is a thing which the magazine tends to avoid. As far as it goes, it can be recommended for most collections, but it badly needs balancing by other magazines and books. Editions also available in Portuguese and Spanish, and Spanish teachers often find it a nice addition for the classroom.

Arab World. 1954. m. $2. Arab Information Center, 757 Third Avenue, New York, N.Y. 10032. Illus. Circ: 26,000.

Indexed: PAIS. *Aud:* Ga, Sh. *Rv:* M. *Jv:* B.

Important primarily for the biased point of view, a view which is not often found in American newspapers and magazines. Issued by the Arab Information Center, it includes illustrated articles on travel, art, people and the like. All pleasant and accurate enough, but its true worth as a reference source is the reporting of the Near East conflict. The Arab side is given either directly or by implication, and it is an argument which should not be overlooked. Academic libraries have other resources at hand for this type of material, but the typical small to medium sized public library or high school library will profit from a subscription.

Army Times. 1940. w. $8.50. Tony March. Army Times Publishing Co., 2201 M. St. N.W., Washington, D.C. 20037. Illus., adv. Circ: 168,000. Microform: UM.

Bk. rev: Notes. *Aud:* Sa. *Rv:* M. *Jv:* B.

Published in national and international editions for members of the army and their families. Primary value is semi-official information on activities of the army, proposed changes in pay, promotion procedures, housing allowances and the like. However, it has a broader scope, including articles on all aspects of the army from the newest weapons to reports from the battlefronts. A given number of pages are devoted to business, amusement, and even a woman's section. As it is edited for professional army personnel, the tone is understandably biased in its coverage of news. The same company publishes similar works for other armed forces personnel, i.e. *Air Force Times* (1947. w. $8.50. Circ: 154,000) and *Navy Times* (1951. w. $8.50. Circ: 101,026). All are consistently reliable in their coverage and have gained a reputation for reporting news days or weeks before it breaks in the popular press. While of limited interest to most libraries, one or all should be found in libraries serving a large group of the military.

Atlas; the magazine of the World Press. 1961. m. $8. Marvin Barrett. World Press Co., 1180 Ave. of the Americas, New York, N.Y. 10036. Illus. Circ: 100,000.

Indexed: PAIS, SSHum. *Bk. rev:* 5–6, 300–500 words, signed. *Aud:* Ga, Ac, Jc, Sh. *Rv:* H. *Jv:* B.

This monthly (about the size of the *Saturday Review*) operates on the principle that to understand events occurring in other parts of the world, it is not sufficient to read the American press, no matter how well it is edited here or served by foreign correspondents abroad. What is required is to read periodicals published in the various nations of the world for the citizens of those countries. And *Atlas* makes this possible by supplying its readers with English translations of a selection of articles from the world press (newspapers and magazines). It does not limit itself to political matters, but includes articles from the field of arts and letters as well. A recent issue included material selected from newspapers and magazines published in Montevideo, Paris,

Frankfurt, Zagreb, Vienna, Bombay, Peking, Tokyo, and Pnom-Penh. Besides the excellent illustrations liberally interspersed among the articles, the cartoons from the foreign press will strike American readers as unusual both in style and message.

Avant Garde. 1967. bi-m. $10. Avant Garde Media, Inc., 110 W. 40th St., New York, N.Y. 10018. Illus., adv.

Aud: Ga. *Rv:* L. *Jv:* C.

Ralph Ginzburg's venture is a cross between his successful *Fact Magazine* and *Eros,* though the first issue owes more to the former than to *Eros.* Such articles as "What *Makes Nixon Run*" and *"The Hate Mail of Captain Levy"* are well enough written, but straight from *Fact.* The photography is excellent, but not overly consequential. The overall impression is one of a Madison Avenue whiz kid serving up bohemia for suburbia.

Coronet. 1963. m. $4. Thetis Powers. 315 Park Ave. S., New York, N.Y. 10010. Illus., adv. Circ: 392,000.

Aud: Ga. *Rv:* L. *Jv:* C.

Not to be confused with the now defunct *Coronet* of pre-World War II days, this is a general pocket sized magazine which appeals to the mildly sensational and follows the same general style as *Readers' Digest.* Articles, as short as the sentences and the thoughts, cover everything from how-to-do-it type materials to personalities and crime. There is relatively little intellectual content, nothing which is politically or socially controversial. Appeal is primarily to the man or woman with a limited education who looks to reading to help kill time.

Country Life. 1897. w. $27.50. George Newnes Ltd., Tower House, Southampton St., London W.C.2. Illus., adv. Microform: UM.

Indexed: BritHum. *Aud:* Ga. *Rv:* L. *Jv:* C.

Not to be confused with the long defunct American title, this is a luxury English magazine, conservative in tone, dedicated to exploring the activities of the rich and the society world. Emphasis is on England, but the tone is generally international. Particularly useful for the daydreamer who enjoys looking at advertisements for castles and estates, and wishes to follow who is in or out at this or that event. On the serious side, it has good to excellent coverage of the arts, and current events which are culturally meaningful. But at the high price a last choice for most. (Satirized by Colleen Brooks: "Post Pastoral," *The New Yorker,* June 1, 1968, p. 29.)

Cue Magazine. See Theatre Section.

Cultural Affairs. 1968. q. $3. Associated Councils of the Arts, 1564 Broadway, New York, N.Y. 10036.

Aud: Ga, Ac, Jc. *Rv:* H. *Jv:* B.

Issued by a non-profit organization, dedicated to all aspects of American culture, this is one of the few general magazines which objectively discusses the arts in America.

Articles, essays, news items tend to emphasize the political, social and economic aspects of the arts. It serves an important function for the general reader in that it stresses the importance of culture to a nation's well being and growth, but always in terms he can understand, i.e., excerpts from the semi-popular Jacques Barzun's "The American University." Aside from the more general editorial material, libraries will find it useful for information on grants, education, community activities, and news of individuals in the arts.

Current. 1960. m. $8. Ira S. Glasser & Grant S. McClellan. Eliot D. Pratt, 905 Madison Ave., New York, N.Y. 10021. Illus., index. Circ: 18,000. Microform: UM.

Indexed: RG. *Aud:* Ga, Ac, Jc, Sh. *Rv:* M. *Jv:* A.

This is an unbiased "digest" approach to current events, which is useful for the layman, and high school and college students who want to keep abreast of new information and ideas about the central national and international problems of our time. The magazine staff examines over 600 periodicals, books, newspapers, reports and speeches and then reprints excerpts from this material. Each issue presents six to twelve of these "current" topics. The excerpts represent the present state of controversy on a topic; there is no bias in selection. Examples from recent issues are Vietnam, the making of foreign policy, understanding China, labor's role in American society, civil liberties, race relations, and the role of the church in society. Also included is an editorial which presents a thought-provoking idea relating to some item in the news. On the back cover of each issue is "Current Readers Service," which lists free materials on matters of "Current" concern for which the reader can write.

East. 1964. bi-m. $5.40. Tohru Morita. Mikawadai Heights, 121, 7 Mikawadai-Machi, Minatoku, Tokyo, Japan. (Subscriptions to: Appex Natl. Assn., P.O. Box 20768, Los Angeles, Calif. 90006). Illus., index, adv. Circ: 52,000.

Aud: Ga, Sh, Jh. *Rv:* M. *Jv:* B.

A general magazine about travel and life in Japan which is nonpolitical, and relatively objective in its Chamber of Commerce way about the country. Articles cover every aspect of national life from education and art to literature and economics. The illustrations are fair to good, and the whole is a useful source of information for the layman, and particularly the junior high or high school student. See also, *Japan Illustrated.*

Ebony. See Afro-American Section.

Expanse; an annotated guide to current magazines and books. 1965. m. $10. Wilfred Bockelman. Expanse Pubns., 1330 Jersey Ave., S. Minneapolis, Minn. 55426.

Aud Ga. *Rv:* L. *Jv:* C.

This is the ultimate in digests, in that it simply annotates some 100 articles from popular magazines. Apparently this is to whet the reading appetite of the reader and send him to the original. Not a bad notion, but it falters in that the "most significant articles of current interest" are almost exclusively from popular magazines which are readily available either at home, or in the local library. There are, and have been a number of such attempts, and within a limited area of interest they are relatively useful, e.g., the free *Tangley Oaks Reading Guide* (United Educators, Inc., Lake Bluff, Ill. 60044) to "current and upcoming articles in library science." This four-page newsletter lists some 15 to 20 lead articles in library science or education magazines. Descriptive annotations are usually furnished by the editor.

French News. 1957. q. Request. Cultural Services of the French Embassy, 972 Fifth Ave., New York, N.Y. 10021. Illus. Circ: 12,000.

Bk. rev: 100–150, 250 words. *Aud:* Ga, Ac, Jc, Sh. *Rv:* M. *Jv:* B.

A combination art and literary review magazine, its chief value will be for the librarian or student attempting to keep-up with significant, yet relatively popular French books. The perceptive book reviews, all in English (as is most of the magazine), cover current works in history and social science, philosophy and religion, belles-lettres, science, theatre, art, poetry and fiction. A "Theatre and Arts" section contains reviews of exhibits, theatre performances in and outside of Paris, concerts, schedules of French musicians on tour in the United States and notes on historical places of interest, sculpture and trends in the arts. In view of its wide scope, it is particularly useful for anyone—student, expert or layman—interested in French culture.

Global Dialogue. 1968. m. $8. E. Weinfeld, S. Martin Johnson & Co., Ltd., 11 Fifth Avenue, Pelham, N.Y. 10803.

Aud: Ac, Jc, Sh. *Rv:* H. *Jv:* B.

A pocket-sized, 30-page, advertising free magazine which reports on current political and social activities on a worldwide basis. A given amount of each issue is turned over to a central theme, i.e., the population explosion, the Catholic Church and birth control, Nigeria, etc. Articles are relatively objective, and by authorities who may or may not be identified by position. The tone is definitely intellectual and liberal. The editor claims that the majority of readers of the short articles are college students, more particularly those involved with debate on a formal or informal level. However, high school debating groups will find the magazine equally useful, and it is well worth the rather steep price.

Ideals. 1944. bi-m. $7.50. John H. Hafemeister. 11315 Watertown Plank Rd., Milwaukee, Wis. 53201. Illus.

Aud: Ga, Sh, Jh. *Rv:* L. *Jv:* B.

A general magazine whose editorial aim is to present homespun fiction, articles, photos, poems and anything else which the editor thinks is inspirational, patriotic or religious. Particularly good for the abundant illustrations,

both in color and black and white. The pictures follow the theme of the magazine which is based on the seasons, e.g., a single issue is given over to Spring, Summer, Fall, Winter, Easter and Christmas. While the literary level is a trifle monotonous, and the theme not for the sophisticated, something is to be said for the illustrations and the calm attitude of it all. A useful, if not precisely educational magazine for secondary schools and for a certain type of adult. Elementary teachers, too, will find the seasonal aspects of the magazine helpful for filling in discussions.

Illustrated London News. 1842. w. $24. John H. Kisch. Illustrated London News and Sketch, Ltd., Elm House, 10–16 Elm St., London W.C. 1. Illus., index, adv.

Indexed: BritHum. *Aud:* Ga, Ac. *Rv:* M. *Jv:* B.

The precursor of *Life* and a number of illustrated magazines, at one time this offered readers a view of world events. The drawings and text contained in early issues are of value to the social historian. Today the magazine emphasizes London social life and personalities, with less attention to world affairs; the photographs are dull by American standards. Primarily valuable for its reviews of theatre, cinema and social activities. Some attention, too, is given to motoring, fishing and chess. Hardly an essential, but a good magazine for browsing, and of reference value for its coverage of personalities.

Israel Magazine; the Israel independent monthly. 1968. m. $10. Maurice Carr. 11401 Roosevelt Blvd., Philadelphia, Pa. 19154. Illus.

Aud: Ga, Ac, Jc, Sh. *Rv:* M. *Jv:* B.

A glossy, well-illustrated magazine dedicated to putting the best foot forward for the Israeli government and people. The articles, while admittedly biased in favor of the country, are well-written and tailored for the average reader from high school through college. The information is accurate, at least within the context of the base of operation. A recent issue, for example, contained several articles in depth on genocide with special reference to activities in Biafra; the Six Day War, and immigration and manpower problems in Israel. An occasional literary and historical article serves to balance the predominantly current political and social material. A useful magazine for most general collections.

Italian Quarterly. 1957. q. $4.50. Carlo L. Golino. College of Letters & Science, Univ. of California, Riverside, Calif. 92502. Circ: 650.

Bk. rev: 1–10, 1,300 words, signed. *Aud:* Sa, Ac. *Rv:* M. *Jv:* B.

A literary quarterly covering the entire spectrum of Italian literature and culture. Occasional issues with color illustrations are devoted to important literary figures. A regular feature is "Trends," which deals with the current Italian scene. There are critical reviews of books about Italian literature, art, and politics, and "Items," an eclectic list of brief news items about Italy and Italians. A useful journal not only for language and linguistics purposes, but for social and historical reasons. Should be in most medium to large academic libraries.

Jamaica Journal. 1967. q. $3.50. Alex Gradussov. Inst. of Jamaica, 12–15 East St., Kingston, Jamaica, West Indies.

Aud: Ga, Ac, Jc, Sh. *Rv:* H. *Jv:* B.

A national magazine which covers a particularly wide field—history, science, art, literature and music. The glossy, oversized 80 pages are nicely illustrated, and the pictures will be suitable for use in schools and public libraries where there is little enough material from this area of other than the travel bureau variety. The level of writing is high, and while the magazine is obviously tailored to make Jamaica look its best, the material seems to give a well-balanced picture of the country. Hardly required, but in view of its low price, format, and generally intelligent presentation, should be welcomed for both recreational and reference purposes in larger public, academic and some high school libraries.

Japan Illustrated. 1962. q. $3.50. Mitsuo Suzuki. Japan Pubns. Trading Co., Ltd., Box 722, Tokyo, Japan. Illus., adv.

Aud: Ga, Ac, Jc, Sh, Jh, E. *Rv:* L. *Jv:* B.

The Japanese counterpart of *Soviet Life,* this is another (see *East*) chamber of commerce approach to Japan. It features beautifully oversized illustrated articles on non-controversial topics such as the Japanese New Year, and life in Hokkaido, "land of promise." The major pieces are primarily a matter of black and white and colored photographs with some minor comments. As such, it is suitable for use in almost any type of schoolroom activity on Japan. It will be enjoyed by adults, as well, but it in no way contains anything of interest to a serious student of the country.

Life. 1936. w. $7.75. Thomas Griffith. Time, Inc., 1271 Ave. of the Americas, New York, N.Y. 10020. Illus., adv. Circ: 8,000,000. Microform: UM.

Indexed: AbrRG, RG. *Bk. rev:* Notes. *Aud:* Ga, Ac, Jc, Sh, Jh. *Rv:* M. *Jv:* B.

The best known picture weekly in the world, this is a middle-of-the-road to conservative general publication which touches on almost every base of reader interest. Working on the same principal as *Time,* that the news can be entertaining, photographers work over the week's activities in about the same fashion. In recent years there has been considerably more emphasis on features, from homes and cooking to art and babies. The strengths of the magazine are two fold: first, the photographs are some of the best published anywhere; second, the popularization of art through fair to good reproductions has been a major factor in making art an acceptable feature in American homes. Conversely, it is weak in that the photos are often sup-

ported by superficial commentary, the juxtaposition of murder and war on one page with a movie star or pot of stew on the next does dim the senses a bit, and, finally, the editorial treatment of some social issues is often loaded in favor of the middlebrow reader's biases. Yet, in all fairness, it has from time to time come out for such unpopular issues as integration, a reasonable approach to drugs, etc. As a source of accurate information on the news, it is questionable. As a source of entertainment and easily digested information it is good.

The Listener and British Broadcasting Corporation Television Review. 1929. w. $11. British Broadcasting Corp., Broadcasting House, London W.1. Illus., adv.

Indexed: BritHum. *Bk. rev:* 7, 150–250 words, signed. *Aud:* Ga, Ac, Jc, Sh. *Rv:* M. *Jv:* B.

Although this is the printed voice of the British Broadcasting Corporation, it is much wider in scope and purpose than the sponsor would indicate. It does publish a number of talks from BBC's "third program," but the subject approach is purposefully less limited. Articles cover such diverse topics as Galbraith's new industrial state, the Rhodesian neurosis, pot—the opium of the people, Egyptian pyramidology, belly dancing, and Petula Clarke. Editorially, it takes a middle-of-the-road approach, but the book, film, television and radio reviews are refreshingly candid and critical. The tone is definitely intellectual, the writing style superb, and the whole an extremely worthwhile general weekly for almost any type of library, from senior high school on up.

Look. 1937. bi-w. $4. Cowles Communications Inc., 488 Madison Ave., New York, N.Y. 10022. Illus., adv. Circ: 8,212,000.

Indexed: AbrRG, RG. *Aud:* Ga, Ac, Jc, Sh. *Rv:* M. *Jv:* A.

Emphasizing more editorial matter than photographs, *Look* is a mature, somewhat more sophisticated approach to the same world covered by *Life.* It, too, concentrates on news events, but is less interested in yesterday's topical happenings, more concerned with the larger social, economic, and political issues behind these occurrences. Hence, the magazine's primary value is the good to excellent background article, usually tastefully illustrated, on everything from world affairs to sports. A byline is a normal thing in *Look* (rarely used in *Life,* except for the one or two longer articles), and among its writers it has counted some of the leading international figures from Bertrand Russell to Ernest Hemingway. The editorial policy is liberal, and the magazine has from time to time broken new ground in social and political areas, e.g., a realistic look at China, the habits of teen-agers in love and drugs. There are a number of regular features on food, clothing and the home. Comparatively speaking, *Life* and *Look* are two distinct approaches which offer the average reader a wide lens world view. Of the two, though, *Look* should be a first choice in libraries. It is by far the more reliable, the more likely to approach a story in depth.

Maclean's; Canada's national magazine. 1905. m. $2. Borden Spears. Maclean-Hunter Publishing Co., Ltd., 481 University Ave., Toronto 2, Ont. Illus., adv. Circ: 563,955.

Indexed: CanI, PAIS. *Bk. rev:* 3–4, 180 words, signed. *Aud:* Ga, Sh. *Rv:* M. *Jv:* B.

The general magazine of Canada, which combines some of the features of *Life, Post* and *Time.* While many articles are primarily concerned with Canadian problems such as Quebec separation and antiquated liquor laws, it also discusses Vietnam, urban riots and other U.S. problems, as well as issues of international interest, e.g., the "Pill," sports and fashions. This should be in all U.S. school and public libraries for the purpose of increasing cross-cultural contact. One of its best features is a book review section which alerts readers to new Canadian books.

New York Magazine. 1968. w. $8. New York Magazine Co., 207 E. 32nd St., New York, N.Y. 10016. Illus., adv. Circ: 100,000.

Aud: Ga, Ac, Jc. *Rv:* M. *Jv:* B.

A general periodical, which is technically a city magazine because a good part of the features are given over to activities in and around the city of New York. Conversely, as *The New Yorker*—which it attempts in part to challenge—it has a much wider scope and will be of interest to the better than average educated adult. Each well-designed and illustrated number features some 20 to 30 pages of articles on everything from the Cosa Nostra to commuter trains and personalities. There is a considerable amount of satirical social commentary, and the writers, editors, and illustrators are definitely independent in their assessment of the American social scene. The "Lively Arts" is a section devoted to reviews of film, music, art, theatre and literature by such national figures as Richard Goldstein, Judith Crist and John Simon, to name a few. Two regular features, "In and Around Town" and "Best Bets," point out where New Yorkers or visitors can find everything from nightclubs to the best shows and exhibits in town. The style of writing is sophisticated, the format imaginative, and the whole a useful general magazine for all libraries—not only those in the New York area.

The New York Times Magazine. 1896. w. $28.50. The New York Times Co., 229 W. 43rd St., New York, N.Y. 10036. Illus., adv. Circ: 1,550,000. Microform: UM.

Indexed: NY Times Index. *Aud:* Ga, Ac, Jc, Sh, Jh. *Rv:* H. *Jv:* V.

Probably the best known "Sunday supplement" to a newspaper in America, this is the size of many commercial magazines, and has articles on virtually every topic related to the news: religion, crime, science, music, business, education and political science. There are regular departments in "Fashion," "Food," and "Home." Written by the *Times'*

staff, and including such outstanding contributors as Martin Mayer, Aubrey Menen, Irving Kristol, J. Kenneth Galbraith, and Isaac Asimov, The *Times Magazine* stresses current and significant topics. The many and excellent illustrations and advertisements make the magazine as useful for browsing as for research and is equally at home in a high school, general, or college library. There is no comparison in quality, size or importance between this and the other Sunday supplements such as *Family Weekly, Parade,* or *This Week Magazine* (see Newspapers Section). The *Times Magazine* is the only one worth subscribing to for libraries.

The New Yorker. 1925. w. $8. William Shawn. The New Yorker Magazine, Inc., 25 W. 43rd St., New York, N.Y. 10036. Illus., adv. Circ: 464,119.

Indexed: MusicI, RG. *Bk. rev:* 10–20, essay notes of 50–100 words. *Aud:* Ga, Ac, Jc, Sh. *Rv:* H. *Jv:* V.

Boasting a readership of nearly 75% college graduates whose median income is $18,000 a year, *The New Yorker* is the general magazine of the upper middle classes. (*The Saturday Evening Post* might once have occupied the middle bracket, with *The Reader's Digest* taking over the chief lowbrow place.) The categorization is meaningful only in that it helps to establish the degree of sophistication of writing, the depth of content and the general approach to everything from advertising to cartoons. *The New Yorker* is as well-known as the *Digest*, albeit the circulation is considerably below the *Digest's* 17 million. This is understandable in that the fiction, the weekly main article on travel, politics, history, social problems, personalities and the like are for an audience with a command of language and taste far above the readers of the average mass magazine. Many of the *New Yorker* pieces are later incorporated or expanded into book form, e.g., Truman Capote's *In Cold Blood* and Jonathan Schell's *The Village of Ben-Suc.* The art, music, drama, motion picture and book columns are written by some of the sharpest critics in America. In scope, it is more general than *Harper's, Atlantic, Saturday Review;* below the intellectual acuteness of *Commentary* and *Partisan Review.* Comparisons, though, are invidious; *The New Yorker,* as any magazine of impact—for good or bad—has quite an individual character. It suffers from oversophistication, (indeed, an over-simplification of certain situations) and a curious format induced by yards of advertisements, but on the whole is a basic periodical for any library from senior high on up, regardless of size or location.

Newsweek. 1933. w. $9. Osborn Elliot. Newsweek, Inc., 444 Madison Ave., New York, N.Y. 10022. Illus., adv. Circ: 2,128,000. Microform: Newsweek, UM.

Indexed: AbrRG, RG. *Bk. rev:* 5–8, 300–1,000 words. *Aud:* Ga, Ac, Jc, Sh. *Rv:* H. *Jv:* V.

In format and approach somewhat similar to *Time,* yet considerably more objective, better written, and certainly more middle-of-the-road to liberal in its approach to domestic and international affairs. Inevitably, it covers the same general news as its competitor, the essential difference being that at least some of the material is attributed to an author, e.g., movie, music, theatre and book reviews are signed. An occasional signed report is featured, such as comment on Vietnam by *Newsweek's* Bureau Chief in Saigon. Regular editorial comments are by Kenneth Crawford, Milton Friedman, and less often by Walter Lippmann. The balance between the conservative and the liberal columnists is nicely maintained. Then, too, in regular news features, there is no mistaking the opinion of the editor, which is frankly stated, rather than suggested, as in *Time,* by loaded comments. Unfortunately, the vast majority of national and international news represents a composite job of editing, and here the magazine suffers from the same faceless reporting as *Time.* Feature cover stories tend to follow the *Time* pattern, but often are done with more depth, and sincerity, and a feeling for the subject which is indicative of sympathy rather than showmanship. An instructive method of indicating the difference between the two magazines is to compare the length, the adverbs and adjectives, and the overall bias of three of four stories on the same news event. Neither will be overly objective, neither will give the type of reporting synonymous with the caution and skill of *The New York Times,* but *Newsweek* usually will come off as at least making an effort to give both sides. Certainly for both personal and library collections, *Newsweek* will be a first choice, particularly in high schools.

Pageant. 1944. m. $6. Macfadden-Bartell Corp., 205 E. 42nd St., New York, N.Y. 10017. Illus., adv. Circ: 473,168. Microform: UM.

Aud: Ga. *Rv:* L. *Jv:* B.

A general family magazine for the younger generation, styled after *Reader's Digest,* strong on photographs, weak on editorial content. Although considerably better than others of this genre, (*Coronet et al.*) it suffers from the editorial bias that most young marrieds are interested in three major items: how to succeed and make money without being taken; how to conduct a happy sex life; and how to emulate pious, sometimes colorful and not so colorful national personalities. While all of this may be true (some 400,000 readers seem to agree), the overall effect is a trifle dismal. To its credit, the magazine is quite quick to point up crooked advertising and tricks of merchants who prey on the inexperienced and uneducated, reports on community action programs, and occasionally runs a piece which tends to question current social practices. Obviously for the lesser educated, it is all harmless enough, and may deserve a place in the library seeking to bring some form of reading to an otherwise uninterested public. The editorial policy, if not always acceptable to a given type of reader, is at least forthright and honest—hence the somewhat higher rating.

Peking Review; a magazine of Chinese views and news. 1958. w. Price not reported. Pai Wan Chuang, Peking, 37, China. Circ: 000

Indexed: PAIS. *Aud:* Ga, Sa, Ac, Jc, Sh. *Rv:* H. *Jv:* B.

Somewhat equivalent in purpose to the Russian *Sputnik,* but without benefit of national agreement between the United States and China. Published in English, French, Japanese, German and Spanish, it is primarily a vehicle for official reprints of policy statements, a summary of news, editorials, and a regular cultural events calendar, "What's On in Peking." Although obviously following the party line, the material is less outright propaganda than most magazines of this type. Frequently, it is the one source of complete statements from China, which may be quoted only in part by the American or British press. As such, it represents an extremely valuable reference source. A more blatantly propaganda type magazine, closer in makeup and the "goody-two-shoes" approach of *Soviet Life* is *China Pictorial* (1951. m. Guozi Shudian, Box 399, Hsitan Bldg., Peking, China. Price not given.) This is published in 12 languages, and the general emphasis is pictorial, with smiling Chinese in various attitudes of work, play and the arts. Published in English, French and Spanish, *China Reconstructs* (1952. m. $3. China Welfare Inst., Wai Wen Bldg., Peking, 37, China.) is similar to *China Pictorial,* but adds features for children, and a fascinating column of letters from people all over the world who are in sympathy with the cause. Of these three, *Peking Review* is by far the most important for the sinologists, if only for its official statements of policy. The other two serve to give Americans a different view of China than found in the average American publication.

Reader's Digest. 1922. m. $3.97. DeWitt Wallace & Lila A. Wallace. Reader's Digest Assn., Pleasantville, N.Y. 10570. Illus., adv. Circ: 17,000,000.

Indexed: AbrRG, RG. *Aud:* Ga. *Rv:* L. *Jv:* C.

The most popular general magazine in America, this is based on the sure fire formula of the big gate feature film, the soap opera, or the large audience television Western, i.e., little strain, intellectual effort, or meaningful controversy. (If there is anything debatable, it is loaded in favor of what the editor, usually quite correctly, assumes will be the biases of his readers.) In view of its vast circulation, it is redundant to outline content or emphasize the well-known conservative editorial stance. Since taking on advertising this tendency has increased, as has, in recent years, the number of articles geared for the general, how-to-do-it approach to life. By now, it is no longer "digesting" many articles, a good three-quarters of them being staff written or on commission. Possibly impressed by its circulation, the compilers of lists inevitably include the magazine as a choice for libraries. Admittedly, the simplified style has an appeal, as do the jokes, humorous pieces and the occasional well-meaning article on some sport or fashion fad. Conversely, the oversimplification, the often facile treatment of personalities and problems and the condensation of books is a poor example for any student. That the magazine is also published in 14 other languages and distributed abroad as an example of American journalism is enough to make any serious critic pause. That librarians and selectors should continue to carry on the myth of its worth is sad, indeed. Unquestionably, it does have a place in general public library collections, but should be a last choice for smaller and medium sized public, school, and academic libraries. Even librarians who take issue with this summary might consider that it is probably the one magazine in almost every American home—why repeat it in the library?

Realities. 1946. m. $20. Alfred Max. Société d'Etudes et de Publications Economiques, 13 rue Saint-Georges, Paris (9e), France. Illus., index, adv. Circ: 174,369.

Indexed: PAIS. *Bk. rev:* 1–2, lengthy. *Aud:* Ga, Sh. *Rv:* L. *Jv:* B.

Published in French and in a number of other languages (English among them), *Realities* includes all the categories common to our general periodicals: recent events in world affairs, science, fashion, sports, travel, literature, art. Each month a major question is fully treated, e.g., child psychology. The format is outstanding, being studded with brilliant full-color photographs on high-quality glossy paper. The art section particularly benefits, and the exquisite reproductions are worth the price of the magazine. The literature section concentrates on one author's work or works, often extending to five or eight pages for a thorough presentation and evaluation.

Saturday Night; Canada's leading magazine of comment and opinion. 1887. m. $2.50. Arnold Edinborough. Saturday Night Pubns., Ltd., 55 York St., Toronto 1, Ont. Illus., adv. Circ: 95,000.

Indexed: CanI, PAIS. *Bk. rev:* 5–7, lengthy or notes, signed. *Aud:* Ga, Ac, Jc, Sh. *Rv:* M. *Jv:* A.

This is Canada's answer to the *Time-Newsweek* syndrome. Sections on sports, religion, movie reviews, business, travel, etc., provide capsuled overviews similar to most news magazines. The international picture is presented in the form of essays on current issues rather than news items. "New York Letter" may cover drugs or black power. "Paris Letter" has discussed contraception and anti-Americanism; "London Letter," the eleven-plus exam. Recent articles have emphasized the Vietnam War and special status for Quebec. The magazine strongly reflects its editor, Arnold Edinborough, but its editorial slant should broaden in the future because Peter Desbarats, a former editor of the now defunct *Parallel,* has joined the staff. Contributors like Marshall McLuhan and Mordicai Richler make this important internationally. Should be in all high school, college and public libraries, if only to counteract American influence.

Soviet Life. 1956. m. $3.50. Georgi I. Issachenko. Embassy of the USSR in the USA, 1706 18th St., N.W., Washington, D.C. 20009. Illus. Circ: 52,000.

Indexed: MusicI, PAIS. *Aud:* Ga, Ac, Jc, Sh. *Rv:* L. *Jv:* C.

A cross between *Life,* the *Illustrated London News* and the *National Geographic,* this is low keyed propaganda for the U.S.S.R. It is published via a reciprocal agreement whereby the U.S.A. is allowed to sell a similar magazine, *American Illustrated,* within the Soviet. (Incidentally, the American Russian-language entry cannot be purchased here.) The English language magazine is so bland as to be practically useless for an accurate picture of economic or political attitudes. It does serve a useful purpose in that its beautiful illustrations, often in color, give Americans a view of the culture, peoples and arts of the Soviet. Recreation and sports are other favored areas. It is all harmless enough, showing that Russian editors are no different in their attitudes towards general magazines than their American counterparts.

Spectator. 1828. w. $17. Spectator Ltd., 99 Gower St., London W.C.1. Microform: UM.

Indexed: BritHum. *Bk. rev:* Notes, 3–4 essays, signed. *Aud:* Ga, Ac, Jc. *Rv:* H. *Jv:* A.

One of the world's oldest magazines of commentary. While not strictly comparable to anything in the United States, it is (somewhat) a cross between *Newsweek* and the *New York Times Magazine.* It represents a strong independent view on politics and social matters and generally gives arguments on both sides of any major question. Coverage tends to be primarily English and European, but larger issues are considered on a world-wide basis. Perhaps of more interest to Americans are the contributors who are among the world's leading "popular" intellectuals, i.e., Denis Brogan, Murry Kempton and Auberon Waugh—to name a few. Special departments include an objective treatment of everything from finance to books, theatre, art and music. The book reviews are particularly good, and vary from the essay type to shorter notes. Also, special issues are given over to reviews of books for the seasons ahead. Particularly useful for college, university and larger public libraries. Some high school libraries also may want.

Sputnik. 1967. m. $5. Sputnik Novosti Press, 2 Pushkin Sq., Moscow, U.S.S.R. (Subscriptions to: Eastern News Distributors, Inc., 155 W. 15th St., New York, N.Y. 10011). Illus.

Aud: Ga, Ac, Jc, Sh. *Rv:* L. *Jv:* B.

A somewhat more sophisticated approach than *Soviet Life,* this English language periodical has about the same format as *Reader's Digest.* Emphasis is on brief, entertaining articles which are purposefully non-political and non-controversial. There are numerous illustrations, but nowhere near the number in *Soviet Life.* A typical issue covers a bit of Russian history, recent scientific achievements, the arts, literature, poetry, and even cartoons. A "Teach Yourself Russian" feature is a trifle elementary, yet should have appeal for high school students. This is primarily an adult magazine, yet the style is quite suited to teenagers. And while the literary quality is fair to good, it is so obviously an effort to improve the world's view of the Soviet that it must be labelled essentially a propaganda piece. This does not detract from its information value, which is considerably greater than its sister publication. Should be in most libraries, and certainly a first choice over *Soviet Life*.

Sunset; the magazine of Western living. 1898. m. $3. Proctor Mellquist. Lane Magazine & Book Co., Menlo Park, Calif. 94025. Illus., adv. Circ: 807,410.

Indexed: RG (Central ed.). *Aud:* Ga. *Rv:* M. *Jv:* B.

This is a national phenomenon in that it is one of the few regional magazines which enjoys a circulation larger than many national periodicals. Within its covers, it combines the better features of *Better Homes and Gardens* and *Holiday*. It is directed primarily to the Western home owner, and gives tips on everything from how to buy a house to how to repair it. However, it attracts a more generalized audience by running features on travel through the West, foods and handcrafts. The articles are short, explicit and popular. A highlight is the abundant number of photographs. While not sold on newstands outside of the West, it is frequently a subscription item in libraries throughout the country.

TV Guide. 1953. w. $7. Merrill Panitt. Triangle Pubns., Inc., Box 400, Radnor, Pa. 19088. Illus., adv. Circ: 12,-342,732.

Aud: Ga, Ac. *Rv:* M. *Jv:* B.

The largest-selling weekly magazine in America, this is directed to the general television viewer. It is made up of two parts: national and regional. The national section carries about six 1,000- to 2,500-word articles by both staff members and such well-known contributors as S. J. Perelman, Henry Steele Commager, Margaret Mead, Jacob Javits, and H. Allen Smith, on the state of TV in general and background information about its performers. New York and Hollywood sections give brief items about performers and forthcoming programs. Complete program listings are given in the regional section, which sometimes covers a large geographical area. Seventy-nine regional editions are published each week. Also included here are a critical column on the week's TV movies by Judith Crist, television criticism by Cleveland Amory, a report on network doings, and a page of readers' letters. The magazine "is widely used as a reference or teaching aid in many schools, colleges and universities," the publisher reports. He adds that "almost none of the non-programming material appears in newspapers. Repeated studies have shown that *TV Guide's* program information is far more complete and accurate," than found in newspapers. Over the years it has

moved from an unsophisticated listing to become a magazine that is relatively critical. Its daily purpose is best-suited to the home, but a run of the magazine will prove a valuable reference and research aid in the years to come. Larger academic and public libraries certainly should consider it for its long-range research aspects.

Time; the weekly newsmagazine. 1923. w. $10. Hedley Donovan. Time, Inc., 1271 Ave. of the Americas, New York, N.Y. 10020. Illus., adv. Circ: 3,710,000. Microform: Mc, UM.

Indexed: AbrRG, RG. *Bk. rev:* 4–8, 100–1,000 words. *Aud:* Ga. *Rv:* M. *Jv:* C.

The first general American news magazine, this really consists of two parts. The first section is devoted to classified news, the second to departments from religion and education to business and books. Inevitably, anyone with judgment will comment that "I never read the first part, only the second." Although with the death of its founder, Henry Luce, the magazine may change, it has gained a reputation for biased news (i.e., part one), a decided conservative viewpoint, and a style which is clever, yet inevitably tiresome when the reader seeks fact rather than a good story. The news sections tend to be loaded, with material either added or excluded, or adjectives or adverbs dropped in or out to shade the meaning of an event. A given amount of this is inevitable, but when a story is written by not one, but a dozen writers, the end result is calculated mush. Even the second part suffers somewhat the same fate, although here it is less noticable, and in all fairness the magazine does excel at bringing to attention little known, yet important events and personalities. Some sections have gained deserved fame, as the art, movie and from time to time the book review sections. The frequent colored inserts in the art section are good, and the general level of photography throughout the magazine is equally commendable. Yet, the major fault is that it is faceless, written by Time, Inc., and the reader ends with the opinions filtered through a giant machine rather than a personality. (Credit, however, is often given the reporter of the week's feature item, not with a byline, but rather with an "inside" story on his activities.) As a source of entertainment and easily digested data the magazine has gained a wide audience. That it is used in schools as a legitimate source of news is not only questionable, but reprehensible. It definitely is not recommended for any school library—except, perhaps, as a case study—and in public libraries it should be balanced with more objective, or at least obviously biased news media.

Town and Country. 1846. m. $9.50. Anthony Mazzola. Hearst Corp., 572 Madison Ave., New York, N.Y. 10022. Illus., adv. Circ: 112,000. Microform: UM.

Aud: Ga. *Rv:* M. *Jv:* C.

One of the oldest prestige periodicals in America, this is among the few general magazines left which are addressed primarily to the affairs of high society. That the majority of readers are not of that social group, but interested in the gossip, fashions, travels, homes and festivities, is what makes the relatively high circulation possible. At one time it featured some of the more sophisticated writers in the world, but now is primarily geared along the lines of *Holiday* and *Harper's Bazaar,* i.e., emphasis on travel and the history of the world's leading communities, and the social life of those able to purchase the originals in *Harper's Bazaar.* The illustrations are often outstanding, but the chatter is a bit irrelevant. Good clean amusement, particularly the advertisements, but a last purchase for most libraries.

UNESCO Courier; a window open on the world. 1945. m. (combined issue, July/Aug.). $5. Sandy Koffler. UNESCO Pubns. Center, 317 E. 34th St. New York, N.Y. 10016. Illus. Circ: 12,000. Microform: UM.

Indexed: RG. *Aud:* Ga, Ac, Jc, Sh, Jh. *Rv:* H. *Jv:* V.

As indicated by the sub-title, this periodical strives for greater international understanding. Each issue focuses on a particular country or area and some aspect of the educational, scientific and cultural life there, or on some problem common to men everywhere. For example, one issue focused on "Africa and the African genius," stressing the emergence of new nations and cultural changes. Another issue featured "Noise Pollution." Still another was devoted to showing how the religious and cultural life of the whole of India is influenced by two great epic poems. The articles are signed and are contributed by authorities around the world. Politics are avoided; opinions stated do not necessarily reflect those of the United Nations or UNESCO. Some issues have many pages in full color; generally most of these are the center pages and may be beautiful photographs or maps. The inclusion of bibliographies makes many issues exceptionally good teaching aids. The December issue includes an index of the year's issues, giving the topic of the issue and the names of the articles and their authors. Excellent format, paper, photography, and writing. Teachers should buy at least two copies, using one as material for bulletin boards, vertical files, etc.

U.S. News & World Report. 1933. w. $10. David Lawrence. U.S. News & World Report, Inc., 2300 N St., N.W., Washington, D.C. 20037. Illus., adv. Circ: 1,550,000. Microform: UM.

Indexed: AbrRG, PAIS, RG. *Aud:* Ga, Ac, Jc, Sh. *Rv:* H. *Jv:* B.

Unlike its sisters, *Time* and *Newsweek,* this obviously conservative magazine is devoted entirely to reporting and analyzing the news of national and international affairs— the news of what is happening in the fields of government, politics, economics, education, labor, religion, business, social progress, etc., in this country and the world, which affects the people of the United States. The arts, theater, and the like are rarely mentioned. Editor David Lawrence is a political conservative, and through careful selection and emphasis beats the drum for his cause. Yet, considering this context, the news coverage is good, particularly for statements and documents. A highlight of each issue is the interview, usually with an important public figure or authority in some field of current interest. There are also regular features, such as "Newsgram," which present in newsletter-form the salient developments of the week. Within the frame of its bias, it is a magazine which should be considered for most libraries.

Yankee. 1935. m. $3. Robb Sagendorph. Yankee Inc., Dublin, N.H. 03444. Illus., adv. Circ: 325,000. Microform: UM.
Aud: Ga, Sh. *Rv:* L. *Jv:* B.

Issued by the publishers of America's oldest almanac (*Old Farmers' Almanac,* 1792–   .), this is a general magazine for the New Englander and anyone else interested in the area. In that it includes fiction, crafts, humor, biographical sketches, poetry, food and travel articles it is considerably more than a regional publication. The historical articles are particularly good. It is well illustrated with photographs, many in color, and there is a monthly double-page print of a typical New England scene. The "sitting around the cracker barrel style," tends to be a bit tiresome, but not for young and old devotees of the early American spirit. The classified advertisement section, "Trading Post," and the "Shopper's Guide" offer a useful aid for anyone interested in antiques and crafts. A must for anyone in or near New England, and a diversion for public or school libraries looking for something a bit different.

GEOGRAPHY

Indexes and Abstracts

Abridged Readers' Guide, Biological Abstracts, British Humanities Index, Canadian Periodical Index, Chemical Abstracts, Education Index, Public Affairs Information Service, Readers' Guide to Periodical Literature, Social Sciences and Humanities Index, Subject Index to Children's Magazines. (For annotations, see Indexes and Abstracts Section.)

Arctic. 1948. q. Members, $5. Mrs. Anna Monson. Arctic Inst. of North America, 3458 Redpath St., Montreal 25, Que. Illus., adv. Circ: 2,800. Microform: UM. Reprint: Johnson.

Indexed: BioAb, CanI, ChemAb. *Bk. rev:* 3–5, 350–1,000 words, signed. *Aud:* Sa, Ac. *Rv:* H. *Jv:* B.

Features scientific papers on subjects related to the Arctic, the Subarctic, and Antarctica, contributed by specialists in both the natural and social sciences. The main papers are abstracted in English, French and Russian. Also contains reports, notes, news items and commentaries of more general interest on the exploration or study of the polar regions. A scholarly journal for only the large academic library.

Association of American Geographers. Annals. 1911. q. $10. Joseph E. Spencer, Assn. of Amer. Geographers, General Office, 1146 16th St., N.W., Washington, D.C. 20036. Illus., index. Circ: 6,000. Microform: PMC. Reprint: Kraus.

Indexed: BioAb, SSHum. *Bk. rev:* 2–4, lengthy, signed. *Aud:* Sa, Ac, Jc. *Rv:* H. *Jv:* A.

A general, scholarly approach by professional geographers on any geographical subject—human, historical, economic, cultural, etc. Each article is extensively footnoted and illustrated with maps, photographs, tables, graphs and charts. Material ranges from the technical to the semi-popular, and while most presuppose more than passing knowledge of the field, its excellent illustrations can be appreciated by almost everyone. (See also, *Professional Geographer.*) Abstracts of papers presented at annual meetings of the Association are given. Each issue has a review article which covers several studies on a particular subject. Symposia which are beyond the normal coverage of the journal are covered in special issues. This is the basic journal in the field for all academic and junior college libraries, as well as large public libraries.

Canadian Geographer/Geographe Canadien. 1951. q. $12. William G. Dean. Univ. of Toronto Press, Front Campus, Univ. of Toronto, Toronto 5, Ont. Illus. Circ: 850.

Bk. rev: 4–6, 25–1,400 words, signed. *Aud:* Sa, Ac. *Rv:* H. *Jv:* B.

Dedicated to the advancement of geographical knowledge and to the dissemination of information on the geographical resources and people of Canada. Scholarly articles, written by experts in the field, and dealing mainly with Canadian geography, are followed by extensive bibliographies. Charts, maps, and black and white pictures are used, when necessary, to elucidate the text of the articles. The journal is bilingual and abstracts of the articles are given in both English and French. For all Canadian academic libraries and for large American collections.

Canadian Geographical Journal. 1930. m. $6. William J. Megill. Royal Canadian Geographical Soc., 488 Wilbrod St., Ottawa 2, Ont. Illus., adv. Circ: 21,121. Microform: UM.

Indexed: CanI, PAIS, SSHum. *Bk. rev:* 2–3, 200–600 words, signed. *Aud:* Ga, Ac, Jc, Sh. *Rv:* H. *Jv:* B.

A popularly written magazine, which is the Canadian counterpart of *National Geographic*. Most of the articles cover different areas, peoples, and natural resources of Canada. However, in each issue there is always one article about a foreign land. All material is written by guest experts. The cover has an attractive color picture, but other illustrations are black and white. Once a year there is a report on the annual meeting of the Royal Canadian Geographical Society. Anyone who enjoys the American cousin to this publication will thank the librarian for bringing it to his or her attention.

Current Geographical Publications; additions to the research catalogue of the American Geographical Society. 1938. m. (Sept.–June). $10. Amer. Geographical Soc., Broadway & 156th St., New York, N.Y. 10032. Circ: 1,200.

Aud: Sa, Ac. *Rv:* H. *Jv:* B.

A straight listing by title of new books, pamphlets and journals added to the collection of the American Geographical Society. Divided by general titles and those in given areas of study. A basic checklist for large libraries, but of limited value for smaller collections.

Economic Geography. 1925. q. $8. Raymond E. Murphy. Clark Univ., Worcester, Mass. 01610. Illus., index. Circ: 37,000. Microform: UM. Reprint: Johnson.

Indexed: BioAb, PAIS, SSHum. *Bk. rev:* 8, 300–1,300 words, signed. *Aud:* Sa, Ac, Jc. *Rv:* H. *Jv:* B.

A journal for geographers, economists, businessmen and others interested in the intelligent utilization of the world's resources. It is the only magazine of its type in English, and one of the few geographical journals comprising so many fields. Articles, written by experts in the field, are devoted to economic and urban geography. Maps, tables, graphs, and occasional black and white pictures are used to illustrate the text. The book reviews vary in length, but are uniformly excellent. A basic magazine for larger collections, and one worth considering for most business and/or political science and history departments.

Focus; presenting a brief, readable, up-to-date survey of a country, region or resource, helpful in understanding current world events. 1950. m. (Sept.–June). $2. Alice Taylor. Amer. Geographical Soc., Broadway & 156th St., New York, N.Y. 10032. Circ: 16,000. Microform: UM.

Indexed: PAIS, RG. *Aud:* Ga, Ac, Jc, Sh, Jh. *Rv:* H. *Jv:* A.

A twelve-page report that concentrates on one country or region in each issue, giving information about the peoples and their customs, the agricultural and mineral resources, and the industry and trade. It is written by an expert on the particular country, usually a professor of geography, in language that can be understood at the junior high school level. There are always several maps, black and white photographs, and an annotated bibliography. Although relatively elementary in style, the material is precise and it may be used to advantage in basic social studies in universities and junior colleges. Public libraries will find it helpful as an excellent reference source.

Geographical Journal. 1893. q. $10.90. L. P. Kirwan. Royal Geographical Soc., 1 Kensington Gore, London S.W. 7. Illus., index, adv. Circ: 9,500. Microform: UM.

Indexed: BritHum, PAIS, SSHum. *Bk. rev:* Numerous, various lengths. *Aud:* Sa, Ac, Jc. *Rv:* H. *Jv:* A.

Probably the world's leading scholarly geographical journal, particularly noteworthy for its original maps and articles on exploration. Articles, with extensive bibliographies, include original papers presented at Society meetings and usually cover exploration, and physical geography, with material on allied sciences. There are charts and maps to elucidate the text, but very few illustrations. A substantial part is devoted to reviews of geographical books, atlases, and a number of travel books of general interest. The reviews alone are well worth a subscription by any library which has more than a passing interest in the subject. Summary issues devoted to various subjects such as the state of exploring, and maps give it added value for research in depth. Given a choice between this and the *Annals of the Association of American Geographers,* the English entry would come in first. And while primarily for academic and junior college collections, it will be of value in medium to large public libraries.

Geographical Review. 1916. q. $9.50. Wilma B. Fairchild. Amer. Geographical Soc., Broadway & 156th St., New York, N.Y. 10032. Illus., index, adv. Circ: 7,200. Microform: UM, Canner.

Indexed: PAIS, SSHum. *Bk. rev:* 14, 300–1,400 words, signed. *Aud:* Sa, Ac, Jc. *Rv:* H. *Jv:* B.

Scholarly articles cover the whole spectrum of geography, from the historical to current exploration. All material is extensively footnoted and illustrated with black and white pictures, maps and charts. The book reviews (including new maps and atlases) are of the same scholarly, critical nature as those found in the *Geographical Journal.* The "Geographical Record" feature serves as a review medium of new journals, reports, monographs and news about personalities and events in the field. In terms of reviews, more valuable than the *Annals of the Association of American Geographers,* and for this reason may be preferred by some libraries. Otherwise, the latter journal is somewhat more extensive in its coverage. Both are needed for medium to large academic and junior college collections.

Journal of Geography. 1897. m. $7. Herbert H. Gross. National Council for Geographic Education, Rm. 1532, 111 W. Washington St., Chicago, Ill. 60602. Illus., index, adv. Circ: 6,800. Reprint: Kraus. Microform: UM.

Indexed: EdI, PAIS. *Bk. rev:* 5, 300–800 words, signed. *Aud:* Ac, Jc, Ht, Et. *Rv:* H. *Jv:* A.

The official organ of the National Council for Geographic Education is directed at teachers of elementary school and high school geography. It emphasizes methods of teaching geography, suggesting techniques and audio-

visual aids, but also contains some professional articles. Written by teachers in the field, the articles are generally brief, with footnotes and occasionally a bibliography. Regular features include a section in which the editor answers questions sent in by teachers, and a preview of films available for teaching geography. For all school and school of education libraries.

National Geographic Magazine. 1888. m. Membership (Non-members, $8). Melville Bell Grosvenor. National Geographic Soc., 17th & M Sts., N.W., Washington, D.C. 20036. Illus., index, adv. Circ: 5,000,000. Microform: Princeton.

Indexed: AbrRG, RG. *Aud:* Ga, Ac, Jc, Sh, Jh, E. *Rv:* H. *Jv:* V.

Few magazines serve as many audiences and so many purposes as this old standby. It can be enjoyed by the elementary school child as well as by the professional geographer. Its reference value is particularly high, and it is one of the few magazines which should be in every library. In each issue, five or six clearly written articles, profusely illustrated with color photographs, tell of interesting people, places, customs, activities, animals, and plant life; staff writers, contributors, and scientists range all over the world. Scientists often write about discoveries, such as the fossils of earliest known man, made with National Geographic support. Maps help the reader understand the text's geography; larger, supplemental maps are world-famous. As one critic put it, this is "a voyeur's dream . . . for gazing on all sorts of exotic delights." No more need be said.

National Geographic School Bulletin. 1922. w. (during sch. yr.) $2. Ralph Gray. National Geographic Soc., N.W., Washington, D.C. 20036. Circ: 430,000.

Indexed: IChildMags. *Aud:* Jh, E. *Rv:* H. *Jv:* B.

Geared for elementary school and junior high students who want to read as well as look, this is a pocket-sized version of the monthly parent magazine. Written in a simplified style, it boasts a number of small maps and illustrations, and prepares the reader for a subscription to the *National Geographic.* There are a number of features, and the whole is in a tasteful format of some 10 to 20 pages. While it hardly replaces the larger work, it can be used by children who wish to follow text as much as pictures. A useful, inexpensive addition for almost all school and public libraries.

Professional Geographer. N.S. 1949. bi-m. $5. Hallock F. Raup. Assn. of Amer. Geographers, 1146 16th St., N.W., Washington, D.C. 20036. Illus., adv. Circ: 5,000. Reprint: Johnson.

Bk. rev: 30, 150–500 words, signed. *Aud:* Sa, Ac. *Rv:* M. *Jv:* B.

Includes short scholarly articles covering most aspects of geography. Maps, charts, and tables are used throughout. The short book reviews are exhaustive and, while not always critical, serve as a check list for libraries. From time to time the publication carries lists of recent geography dissertations and theses. Primarily, as the title suggests, for the teacher at the university level. Only for large collections.

Scottish Geographical Magazine. 1885. 3/yr. $3. Alfred Jefferies. Royal Scottish Geographical Soc., 10 Randolph Crescent, Edinburgh 3, Scotland. Illus., adv. Circ: 4,000. Microform: UM.

Indexed: BioAb, BritHum. *Bk. rev:* 8–9, 250–800 words, signed. *Aud:* Sa, Ac. *Rv:* H. *Jv:* B.

An example of the numerous geographical magazines primarily devoted to a single nation. One article in each issue deals with a foreign country. There are many maps and some black and white photographs. News of meetings and lecture programs of the Royal Scottish Geographical Society is reported. As almost every nation issues its own geographical review (usually, to be sure, with some attention given to broader problems), colleges and universities may wish to subscribe to those which will not only meet the needs of the geography department, but complement other areas such as history and political science. Another approach is offered by a magazine like *Soviet Geography.*

Soviet Geography: Review and Translation. 1960. m. (Sept.–June). $10. Theodore Shabad. Amer. Geographical Soc., Broadway & 156th St., New York, N.Y. 10032. Circ: 900. Microform: UM.

Indexed: PAIS. *Aud:* Sa, Ac, Jc. *Rv:* H. *Jv:* B.

Despite the title, this is an American publication. Includes: 1) English translations of current Soviet research in geography taken from the principal Russian geographic journals; 2) brief abstracts preceding each article; 3) tables of contents of the current issues of the Russian journals. Readers are invited to suggest articles of general interest for translation. News notes on geographic changes in the Soviet Union are provided. Special issues are devoted to translations of the legend matter and text of important Soviet atlases and to a directory of Soviet geographers. Occasional review articles by American scholars summarize Soviet work in a particular field of geography. Obviously, only for the large academic collection, although it may be useful in smaller schools where Soviet studies are emphasized.

GERMAN LANGUAGE

Indexes and Abstracts

British Humanities Index, Education Index, Social Sciences and Humanities Index. (For annotations, see Indexes and Abstracts Section.)

Archiv für das Studium der Neuren Sprachen und Literaturen. 1946. bi-m. $14.50. Georg Westermann Verlag, Georg-Westermann-Allee 66, Braunschweig, Germany. Circ: 700.

Bk. rev: 10–15, av. 500 words, signed. *Aud:* Sa, Ac. *Rv:* H. *Jv:* B.

Devoted to the study of the Germanic, Romance and Slavic languages and literatures on an advanced level of scholarship. Emphasis is on criticism and interpretation. Articles are generally long, averaging from 7,000 to 9,000 words, and the text is in English, French, German, Italian, and Spanish. While extremely esoteric in terms of a general collection, this is a superior journal for graduate study.

Dimension; contemporary German arts and letters. 1968. 3/yr. $6. A. Leslie Willson. The Univ. of Texas Press, P.O. Box 7819, Austin, Tex. 78712.

Aud: Ac, Jc. *Rv:* H. *Jv:* A.

Averaging some 200-well printed pages, this is an outstanding journal of current German thought and will be useful for both the student and the specialist in German literature. Each issue offers contributions in German with the English translation and the German original printed side by side. Material varies from poetry to critical comments on current writers, political events, and social developments. A good one-half of each issue includes material heretofore not issued elsewhere. The critical style is definitely academic (poetry and prose aside), but the wide selection of current German writings makes it a suitable addition for any type of library where there is more than passing interest in the country or its writers.

Frankfurter Hefte; zeitschrift fuer kulture und politik. 1946. m. $9.25. Eugene Kogon, Reichenbachweg 21, 6243 Falkenstein, W. Germany. Circ: 8,000.

Bk. rev: 4–7, various lengths, signed. *Aud:* Sa, Ac. *Rv:* H. *Jv:* B.

One of the few independent political-literary magazines in Germany, this is somewhat similar in format and purpose to *Der Monat.* Emphasis tends to be on social and political issues, the tone is left of center, and the writing style is semi-popular. All aspects of the national and international scene are covered, and there are short, penetrating pieces on various developments in domestic affairs. While not quite so lively as *Der Monat,* it brings another dimension to the German political scene, which should make it one of the basic journals for medium to larger academic collections.

German Life and Letters. 1936. q. $7.20. L. W. Forster. Basil Blackwell, Oxford, Eng. Circ: 704. Microform: UM. Reprint: Johnson.

Indexed: BritHum. *Bk. rev:* 15–35, 500 words, signed. *Aud:* Ga, Ac. Jc. *Rv:* H. *Jv:* A.

Somewhat equivalent to the American-German Review, only British-based. Published with both English and German text, this scholarly journal stresses German literature with one or two long articles on other aspects of German life and intellectual history, e.g., "Notes on the West German Army." Articles are not heavily footnoted and many are of general interest. The extensive book review section has excellent critical reviews by British scholars. Books reviewed are from continental, British, and American presses. As this has more emphasis on literature than the *American-German Review* (See General Section), and is considerably more scholarly, it would be a first choice in academic and junior college libraries. Conversely, the American, more general, counterpart would be suitable for most public libraries.

German Quarterly. 1928. 5/yr. Membership (Non-members, $7.50). Robert R. Heitner. Amer. Assn. of Teachers of German, Adolph Wegener, Treas., Muhlenberg College, Allentown, Pa. 18104. Index, adv. Circ: 5,200.

Indexed: EdI. *Bk. rev:* 20, 600 words, signed. *Aud:* Ac, Jc, Ht, Et. *Rv:* H. *Jv:* B.

A literary and teaching journal in English and German devoted to the Germanic languages and literatures. Published by the American Association of Teachers of German, it is of interest to all teachers of German, from the elementary to college levels, to students from the secondary through graduate levels, and to scholars. In two sections: the first includes critical and interpretive articles, historical studies, discussions of literary theories and movements, personal philosophies of authors, and linguistic studies. Twentieth century literature receives a good deal of attention, although all periods are covered; the second part deals with teaching methods, professional problems, linguistics, textual studies, literary attribution, and chronology. Special sections are devoted to elementary languages education. A required item in high school and college libraries where German is an important part of the curriculum.

Germanic Review; devoted to studies dealing with the Germanic languages and literatures. 1926. q. $6. Joseph Bauke. Columbia Univ. Press, 440 W. 110th St. New York, N.Y. 10025. Index, adv. Microform: UM.

Indexed: SSHum. *Bk. rev:* 5–8, 1,000 words, signed. *Aud:* Sa, Ac. *Rv:* H. *Jv:* B.

Features scholarly writing, primarily in English, with articles of 5,000 to 7,000 words emphasizing close examination of source material. Literary studies focus on all Germanic literatures except English. Articles range from original interpretations to historical and biographical studies, history of ideas, criticism, and comparative studies. Linguistic studies of the Germanic languages appear occasionally. Only for large collections.

Journal of English and Germanic Philology. 1897. q. $7.50. Univ. of Illinois Press, Urbana, Ill. 61801. Index. Circ: 1,350. Microform: UM.

Indexed: SSHum. *Bk. rev:* 40, 760–1,000 words, signed. *Aud:* Sa, Ac. *Rv:* H. *Jv:* B.

Devoted to studies of the English, German, and Scandinavian languages and literatures. Published under the auspices of the Graduate College of the University of Illinois, it features a wide range of studies—original and scholarly —of interest to undergraduates as well as to scholars. Ar-

ticles are of medium length, and range from criticism and interpretation, textual studies, and discussion of literary forms to linguistics, historical studies, sources, dating and chronology of works, and analysis of style. The annual "Anglo-German Literary Bibliography" appears in the July issue. Somewhat less esoteric than the *German Review,* but, again, only for large academic collections. An exception might be where a smaller academic or public library will find the book reviews in this area useful—here the *Journal* is without equal.

Monat. 1948. m. $3.75. Gesellschaft für internationale Publizistik GmbH, Schlorlemer-Allee 28, Berlin 33, Germany. Circ: 20,000.

Bk. rev: 6, 3–7 pages, signed. *Aud:* Ga, Sa, Ac. *Rv:* H. *Jv:* A.

Both in format and approach this is similar to the English *Encounter.* Emphasis is on the passing social-political scene, and the contributors are international, although the majority are scholars and journalists from West Germany. The writing is some of the liveliest in the current German press, and the book reviews are exceptionally well done. There are the usual notes on other cultural developments from recordings to the theatre. It is a basic journal in any library where there is a demand for a German language periodical. In fact, it is probably the best single, general magazine of its type now available. Considerably more esoteric, with emphasis on literature and the fine arts is *Merkur* (1947. $10. Verlag Kiepenheuer & Witsch, Rondorfer Str. 5, 5 Koln-Marienburg, Germany). It, too, features review type analysis of books, and includes contributors from throughout Europe. Larger libraries will wish both, but first choice is *Monat.*

Monatshefte; a journal devoted to the study of German language and literature. 1899. q. $5. J. D. Workman. Univ. of Wisconsin Press, Box 1379, Madison, Wis. 53701. Index, adv. Circ: 1,261. Reprint: Kraus. Microform: UM.

Bk. rev: 20, 400 words, signed. *Aud:* Sa, Ac, Jc. *Rv:* H. *Jv:* B.

Published under the auspices of the Department of German, at the University of Wisconsin, for advanced students, scholars, and teachers of German. All periods of German literature are covered, with much attention to the recent period. The professional interests of teachers of German are emphasized. Articles are generally short and interpretive. Coverage includes literary theories, literary sources, history of ideas, and biography. More specialized technical articles also appear—generally textual analyses of manuscripts, new documents, and personal papers. Linguistic studies appear occasionally. An annual listing of members of the German departments of U.S. colleges and universities and a listing of dissertations appear in the Fall issue. A basic journal for all junior college, college and university libraries.

Neue Rundschau. 1890. q. $7. Golo Mann, S. Fischer Verlag, Mainzer Landstr, 10–12 Frankfurt am Main, W. Germany. Index, adv. Circ: 8,000.

Bk. rev: Various numbers, lengths. *Aud:* Sa, Ac. *Rv:* H. *Jv:* A.

The outstanding, "old guard" literary magazine of Germany, which over the past few years has attempted to modernize its approach. On the whole, though, it occupies a position in Germany somewhat similar to America's traditional little, campus-sponsored literary magazines. Emphasis is on the literary essay, dully footnoted, a trifle ponderous, but usually meaningful. Aside from literature—fiction, poetry, drama—about one half of each issue is turned over to the arts, history, and politics. During its long history it has boasted publication of almost every major European figure from Thomas Mann to Hofmannsthal. In addition to books received, there are usually penetrating essays on writers and current titles. A run of the magazine is an absolute must for any academic library where German or European literature is a consideration.

Der Spiegel. 1947. w. $25. Spiegel-Verlag, Pressehaus, 2 Hamburg 1, W. Germany. Subscriptions to: German News Co., 218 E. 86th St., New York, N.Y. 10028. Illus., adv. Circ: 900,000.

Aud: Ga, Ac, Jc, Sh. *Rv:* M. *Jv:* B.

One of the major news magazines in the chain held by the now famous Axel Springer. In 1968 the "Luce of West Germany" was forced to sell some of its holdings because of a government report critical of his control of the West German press. However, *Der Spiegel* remains a basic Springer product. It is, in format and approach to news, quite similar to *Time.* At first sight, it appears to be a translation of the American magazine. The reporting is a trifle more accurate than in *Time,* but just as biased in its middle-class way. And, at least as seen from some quarters, considerably more militant in the fight against any right-wing or left-wing elements in Germany or abroad. The magazine has consistently kept a careful watch on the government, been subject to suits and threats, but always emerges the darling of the average German reader. Given its peculiar biases, it is a required item for anyone who wishes to understand the passing scene in Germany and how the Germans observe Europe and the rest of the world. It can be useful for advanced German classes in high schools, but some explanation of the Springer philosophy might be given its young readers. (Articles on Springer are numerous, as a check of *Reader's Guide* will show, and a biographical sketch of him will be found in the *1969 Encyclopaedia Britannica Yearbook.*)

On the pictorial side, a popular German magazine similar to *Life* is *Scala International* (1961. m. $2.70. Verlagshaus Frankfurter Societaets-Druckerei, Frankenallee 71–81, Frankfurt am Main, W. Germany. Subscriptions to: German News Co., 218 E. 86th St., New York, N.Y. 10028). Again, it may be used by German speaking readers and by advanced students of the language in high schools and colleges. The layout and approach is similar to the American magazine, although there tends to be more text than pictures. The editorial slant is middle-of-the-road.

Zeitschrift für Deutsche Philologie. 1869. q. $13.50. Hugo Moser & Benno Von Wiese. Erich Schmidt Verlag, Berlin 30, Genthiner Str. 30g, Germany. Illus., index, adv. Circ: 900. Reprint: Johnson.

Bk. rev: 5–10, 1,000 words, signed. *Aud:* Sa, Ac. *Rv:* H. *Jv:* B.

The primary German publication devoted to studies of the Germanic languages and literatures. Intended for the advanced student and the scholar, features technical writing on specialized problems of language and interpretation, with emphasis on the examination of original texts and manuscripts. Articles include critical discussions of theory and history of criticism, analysis of literary forms and periods, biography and history, textual studies—especially those dealing with literary provenance and newly-discovered texts—and structural linguistics. The text is in German, and the articles are of medium length, averaging 3,500 words.

Classroom Aids

In addition to the German-language periodicals listed below, *Reader's Digest, True Story,* and the *UNESCO Courier* are available in German editions.

Monatspost. m (during school year). $1.50. 237–8 Andrews St., Rochester, N.Y. 14604.

For students of German at the lower levels, and at junior high school level in terms of interest. The 8-page format is somewhat familiar to the Scholastic Magazines efforts, but much of the material is closer to current events. The usual illustrations, puzzles, cartoons, and a page of vocabulary are used in the paper. Primarily a classroom tool, and not for most libraries. It is, however, considered to be one of the best of its type, and should be called to the attention of all teachers.

Scholastic Magazines Inc. 50 W. 44th St., New York, N.Y. 10036. Various dates. m (during school year). $1 to $1.50.

	LANGUAGE LEVEL	INTEREST LEVEL	CIRCULATION
Das Rad.	1–2	E, Jh	37,000
Schuss	2	Jh, Sh	15,000
Der Roller	2–4	Sh	21,000

All of the Scholastic foreign-language classroom magazines follow a definite pattern. First and foremost, they are prepared by Mary Glasgow & Baker, Ltd., an outstanding British publisher. Working with American specialists, the firm has developed an 8-page format which is geared specifically to the needs and curricula of schools. The format and content are equally attractive. An effort is made to familiarize the student, via the short conversations, expository material, cartoons, crossword puzzles and games, with the German people. The material is quite understandably non-controversial, but honest in that the approach is imaginative and intelligent. The many photographs and line drawings show an appreciation for aesthetics, as well as for education, on the part of the editors.

A particularly good feature in each issue is the vocabulary page. Here, the foreign word is given with the English translation on a page-by-page basis as found in the magazine. The vocabulary becomes progressively more difficult with each issue in the series.

Unike many of the Scholastic classroom papers, the language papers are uniformly excellent, always at the top of most recommended lists. It is doubtful whether they would be of much use in a library, but they should certainly be considered by any language teacher in elementary through high school.

Taking full advantage of the situation, the firm also issues photograph records of most of their magazines' contents. A monthly teacher edition includes the student edition plus a two- or four-page supplement with background on the major articles, questions, crossword puzzle solutions, etc.

Der Spiegel. See this section.

Unsere Zeitung. m (school year). $2. German News Co., 218 E. 86th St., New York, N.Y. 10028.

A teaching aid for advanced senior high German students, (levels 4–6), this is a cross between the *Reader's Digest* and the Scholastic classroom newspapers. Each 6-page issue features digested articles from German newspapers, photographs, and line drawings. The format is attractive, and the contents are of considerable interest to the student. On each page, translations of the more difficult words are given in English, Spanish, French, or simple German. While the whole is pedagogically excellent, it is primarily for classrooms. Libraries should consider German magazines for students at this relatively advanced level.

Die Welt. See Newspaper Section (Appendix).

HISTORY

Indexes and Abstracts

Abridged Readers' Guide, America: History and Life, British Humanities Index, Canadian Periodical Index, Catholic Periodical and Literature Index, Historical Abstracts, Philosopher's Index, Public Affairs Information Service, Readers' Guide to Periodical Literature, Social Sciences and Humanities Index, Subject Index to Children's Magazines. (For annotations, see Indexes and Abstracts Section.)

For reasons of size and, more importantly, convenience for the reader, this section has been divided into two parts, "American History," and "General History." If the periodi-

cal in question is devoted primarily to American history, it will be found in the first part; otherwise, in the second.

American History

American Heritage; the magazine of history. 1954. bi-m. $16.50. Oliver Jensen. Amer. Heritage Publishing Co., Inc., 551 Fifth Ave., New York, N.Y. 10017. Illus., index. Circ: 300,000. Microform: UM.

Indexed: AbrRG, AmerH, HistAb, RG. *Bk. rev:* Averages 2, approx. 1,500 words, signed. *Aud:* Ga, Ac, Jc, Sh, Jh. *Rv:* H. *Jv:* V.

An outstanding historical journal which has succeeded in presenting scholarly material at a popular level. Articles by such authorities as Bruce Catton, Carl Carmer, Richard M. Ketchum and Allan Nevins cover every conceivable aspect of American history from major to minor events and personalities. It is particularly noteworthy for the attention it gives to social, educational, and cultural trends in America's past. And if one article is concerned with a major military figure or battle, another may turn to a little known artist, teacher, writer or inventor who helped to change the course of our history. From time to time an entire issue is given over to a period, state or important series of events. There is no advertising, which accounts in part for the relatively high price. The magazine's primary attraction to adults and young people alike is the handsome format and the numerous illustrations and photographs, many in color. The hard-covered periodical is often catalogued and shelved by librarians as a book. The "package" is expensive, but worthwhile for any type library from junior high school up.

American Historical Review. 1895. q. $15 (students, $7.50). Henry R. Winkler. Macmillan Co., 866 Third Ave., New York, N.Y. 10022. Circ: 20,000. Microform: UM.

Indexed: AmerH, HistAb, RG. *Bk. rev:* Approx. half the journal, lengthy, signed. *Aud:* Sa, Ac, Jc, Sh, Ht. *Rv:* H. *Jv:* V.

The official organ of the American Historical Association, this is valuable both for its scholarly articles and its extensive book reviews. Contributions represent original research, are usually some 6,000 to 10,000 words long, and may move from a study of the right-wing in America to a monograph on some aspect of communism. The style is better than most journals of this type, although the writers presuppose some basic knowledge of historiography on the part of the reader. The 150 to 200 reviews are arranged according to period and area of historical interest, thus making them an invaluable book selection aid for libraries. Major articles, monographs and documents are classified in much the same manner. Should be in every scholarly library, and in larger high school libraries.

American History Illustrated. 1966. 10/yr. $10 ($8.50, educational rate). Robert Fowler. Edward J. Stackpole, Telegraph Bldg., Harrisburg, Pa. 17101. Illus., index, adv. Circ: 25,000.

Indexed: AmerH, HistAb. *Bk. rev:* 4–8, approx. one-half page each, signed. *Aud:* Ga, Ac, Jc, Sh. *Rv:* H. *Jv:* A.

"Articles will range over events as recent as the Korean War to the days when only prehistoric creatures inhabited the continent." The contributions are devoted to all phases of American history and are written by historians or actual participants in the events described. One of the strong points of the magazine is the excellent use it makes of photographs and illustrations to document its articles. It would be a second choice after its sister type magazine, *American Heritage.*

American Jewish Historical Quarterly. 1893. q. $10. Isidore S. Meyer. Amer. Jewish Historical Soc., 150 Fifth Ave., New York, N.Y. 10011. Illus., index, adv. Circ: 2,755.

Indexed: AmerH, HistAb. *Bk. rev:* 7–10, 1–2 pages, signed. *Aud:* Sa, Ac. *Rv:* H. *Jv:* B.

Features two to three scholarly articles on some aspect of Judaism in the United States. There are notes and comments which are somewhat shorter articles on more esoteric aspects of the settlement and history of Jews in America. Although only for the largest libraries, it will be welcome in any library where there is a large Jewish audience.

The American West. 1964. q. $7. Wallace Stegner. Amer. West Publishing Co., 577 College Ave., Palo Alto, Calif. 94306. Illus., adv. Circ: 38,000.

Indexed: AmerH, HistAb, SSHum. *Bk. rev:* Notes. *Aud:* Ga, Ac, Jc, Sh. *Rv:* M. *Jv:* B.

The magazine of the Western History Association describes itself as "a magazine devoted to the story of the Great West, past and present." While strong on historical scholarship, it is designed for the general reader as well as the specialist. It is particularly attentive to the value of pictorial history. There are eight or nine well-illustrated articles in each issue. They range from literary criticism and historical narrative to the subject of conservation. Authors represent a broad spectrum of professions and interests. One of the few scholarly magazines which is suitable for the non-specialist adult or teen-age reader, and will be welcome in most public and school libraries, as well as college and junior college collections.

The American West Review. 1967. q. $2. (Free to subscribers of *The American West.*) Roger Olmsted. Amer. West Publishing Co., 577 College Ave., Palo Alto, Calif. 94306. Illus., adv.

Bk. rev: Extensive, entire issue. *Aud:* Ga, Ac, Jc. *Rv:* H. *Jv:* B.

Following one or two general essays on the literature of the American West, the entire magazine is devoted to between five and ten lengthy reviews and some 50 shorter notes on both current and reissued works. The reviewers are remarkably lucid; reviews are evaluative, and all are

signed. While the major books reviewed will be examined in general reviewing media, the magazine touches upon many works which otherwise might not come to notice. A must for medium to large history and general reading collections.

Badger History. 1948. q. (during school yr.). $4. Howard W. Kanetzke. Wisconsin State Historical Soc., 816 State St., Madison, Wis. 53706. Illus. Circ: 25,000.

Indexed: IChildMags. *Aud:* E. *Rv:* H. *Jv:* B.

One of several local historical magazines indexed by *Subject Index to Children's Magazines,* and both because of indexing and scope, of more than purely local interest. (See also, *Gopher Historian, Illinois History, Junior Historian* and *The Yorker.*) Since 1965, *Badger History* has been specifically written for the 4th grade. Each issue is extremely well illustrated and runs some 60 or 70 pages. The material is of enough general interest to warrant consideration by many public and school libraries, e.g., an issue on Wisconsin Indians consisted of articles on ways of life, buildings, recreation, religion, sports and the like. The writing style is simple, yet never insulting. The content is both meaningful and interesting—even for the older reader.

California Historical Society Quarterly. 1922. q. Membership (Non-members, $15). 2090 Jackson St., San Francisco, Calif. 94109. Illus., index, adv. Circ: 3,800.

Indexed: AmerH, HistAb. *Bk. rev:* 10–15, 250–750 words, signed. *Aud:* Ga, Sa, Ac, Jc, Sh. *Rv:* H. *Jv:* B.

Features five or six articles, both by scholars and amateur historians, on California history. Many of the pieces are illustrated and they range from the story of printing or a personality to economic and political issues. The book reviews usually concentrate solely on works relating to California or the West. The journal is particularly well printed, and a required item in all California libraries, and in larger historical collections.

There are two other West Coast historical journals of note, both of which follow the same general pattern, i.e., concentration on a local area with a nod now and then to larger issues and national events. These are: *Oregon Historical Quarterly* (1900. q. $7.50. Oregon Historical Society, Portland, Ore.) and the *Pacific Northwest Quarterly* (1906. q. $3.50. Washington Historical Soc., c/o Parrington Hall, Univ. of Washington, Seattle, Wash. 98105). Both have excellent book reviews, and in the past few years the Oregon journal has assumed an extremely attractive format, often featuring maps and excellent illustrations.

Civil War History; a journal of the middle period. 1955. q. $5. John T. Hubbell. Univ. of Iowa, Iowa City, Iowa 52240. Circ: 1,800. Reprint: Johnson.

Indexed: AmerH, HistAb. *Bk. rev:* 10–15, one page, signed. *Aud:* Sa, Ac, Jc. *Rv:* M. *Jv:* B.

Devoted to scholarly articles dealing with the American Civil War and Reconstruction, this considers all aspects and views of a popular reading period in history. Its editorial board is composed of eminent authorities on the Civil War such as T. Harry Williams and Robert T. Johannsen. Each issue contains four or five articles, with occasional review articles and bibliographical information. There are critical book reviews, and a regular feature is one or two pages of book notes. Only for large collections.

Civil War Times Illustrated; a magazine for people interested in American History, particularly in the Civil War period. 1959. 10/yr. $10. Robert H. Fowler. Edward J. Stackpole, Telegraph Bldg., Harrisburg, Pa. 17101. Illus., index, adv. Circ: 18,000.

Indexed: AmerH, HistAb. *Aud:* Ga. *Rv:* M. *Jv:* B.

Another special-period historical journal with emphasis on authentic photographs and illustrations. The articles are written by historians or are narratives of actual participants in the war, and concern all phases of the conflict. Considerable coverage is given to biographies of leading figures in the war. A semi-popular historical magazine, this is particularly suited for the layman. But as is the case with the more scholarly *Civil War History,* it can only be recommended for large libraries, or where there is a particular interest in the subject.

Daughters of the American Revolution Magazine. 1892. 10/yr. $3. Mary Rose Hall. National Soc. Daughters of the Amer. Revolution, 1776 D St., N.W., Washington, D.C. 20006. Illus., adv. Circ: 48,500.

Aud: Ga. *Rv:* L. *Jv:* C.

The voice of the D.A.R., this is interesting for the viewpoint, usually conservative, and the few historical articles, which are not necessarily limited to the period of the American Revolution. The magazine makes frequent use of pictures and illustrations. A large part is given over to official news of the D.A.R. and is primarily of interest to communities with large D.A.R. chapters. It is not recommended for most libraries.

Frontier Times. 1958. bi-m. $4. Pat Wagner. J. A. Small, Box 3668, Austin, Tex. 78704. Illus., index, adv. Circ: 177,337.

Bk. rev: Notes. *Aud:* Ga, Sh. *Rv:* L. *Jv:* B.

A popular man's magazine which features factual, authentic stories of the Old West. Photographs and illustrations of the period are used to give greater authenticity to the material. The articles are popularly written rather than scholarly, but every effort is made to present the facts as they happened. The articles deal with Indians, outlaws, lost gold and many other facets of Western history. On occasion there are features on Mexico and Alaska and some modern looks at ghost towns, mining camps and other points which may interest the tourist. An above average "Western" type magazine which will appeal to adults and teenagers. It should be found in collections where there is any effort to lure the reader normally "turned off" by more scholarly history magazines. See also, *Old West.*

Gopher Historian; the junior historical magazine of Minnesota. 1946. 3/yr. $1.50. A. H. Poatgieter. Minnesota Historical Soc., Historical Bldg., St. Paul, Minn. 55101. Illus., index. Circ: 4,000.

Indexed: IChildMags. *Aud:* Jh, E. *Rv:* M. *Jv:* B.

Similar in purpose and scope to other state historical magazines geared for children, this is somewhat better than most in that it has good to excellent pictures. Many of the articles, while centered on Minnesota subjects, are applicable to other parts of the country, e.g., forests, Indians, conservation, etc. Primarily for those between 10 and 12 years of age.

Harvard Journal of Negro Affairs. See Afro-American Section.

Illinois History; a magazine for young people. 1947. m. (Oct.–May). $1.25. (Free to libraries and schools in Illinois.) Olive S. Foster. Illinois State Historical Soc., Centennial Bldg., Springfield, Ill. 62706. Illus., index.

Indexed: IChildMags. *Aud:* Jh, E. *Rv:* M. *Jv:* B.

While written by specialists for an age group between 7 and 12, contents is above average for magazines of this type. In fact, the information is basic to any understanding of either Illinois or much Midwest history. Normally, a given issue is turned over to a single historical theme with a number of well-illustrated articles. Regular features include puzzles, contributions from students and a brief section on additional reading. It will be of limited value outside of the Midwest, but there it should be found in every elementary, junior high, and not a few senior high school libraries.

Journal of American History. (Formerly: Mississippi Valley Historical Review). 1914. q. $8. Martin Ridge. Organization of Amer. Historians, Box 432, Abilene, Kan. 67410. Circ: 11,700. Microform: UM.

Indexed: AmerH, HistAb, SSHum. *Bk. rev:* 75–120, ½ to 1 page, signed. *Aud:* Sa, Ac, Jc. *Rv:* H. *Jv:* A.

One of the best American historical journals, and of particular value to the librarian, as over half of each issue is devoted to extensive book reviews. The scope is almost entirely American, and articles move from historical theory to biographical sketches. The writing is scholarly and primarily for the professional historian or student of history. Included are sections devoted to news on appointments, promotions, grants, aids and other items about the Organization of American Historians. A basic journal for any medium to large historical collection.

Journal of American Studies. 1967. semi-ann. $7.50. Dennis Welland. Cambridge Univ. Press, 32 E. 57th St. New York, N.Y. 10022.

Indexed: AmerH, HistAb. *Bk. rev:* 15–20, 500–1,000 words, signed. *Aud:* Sa, Ac. *Rv:* M. *Jv:* B.

The purpose of this British journal is to "promote the study of history, institutions, literature and culture of the

United States." The orientation is essentially literary. There are three to four long reviews and the shorter notes consider both historical and literary publications. Useful for both the scholar and student of American history and literature, not to mention the individual who seeks the British viewpoint in these areas.

Journal of Negro History. See Afro-American Section.

Journal of Southern History. 1935. q. Membership (Non-members, $2). S. W. Higginbotham. Southern Historical Assn., Tulane Univ., New Orleans, La. 70118. Index, adv. Circ: 3,500.

Indexed: AmerH, HistAb, SSHum. *Bk. rev:* 50, page, signed. *Aud:* Sa, Ac, Jc. *Rv:* H. *Jv:* B.

A non-partisan magazine that concentrates on the history of the Southern United States. It usually contains three or four scholarly monographs by leading historians, who often are not from the region. In addition, it lists book notes and prints historical news and notices. The book reviews are more general in scope, and often makeup a good one-quarter or one-half of the journal. They are long, critical and required reading for any library with even a modest history collection. There are frequent bibliographical notes ranging from library acquisitions to detailed lists of materials in given areas of Southern history. A basic magazine for all medium to large research libraries.

Journal of the West. 1962. q. $6. Lorrin L. Morrison & Carroll S. Morrison. 1915 S. Western Ave., Los Angeles, Calif. 90018. Illus., index, adv. Circ: 3,500.

Indexed: AmerH, HistAb, SSHum. *Bk. rev:* 30–50, one page, signed. *Aud:* Sa, Ac. *Rv:* M. *Jv:* B.

Devoted to the history and geography of the American West. The editors welcome articles dealing with such related fields as anthropology and archaeology. Every issue has some ten scholarly articles written by historians or experts in other disciplines. The articles frequently contain maps and illustrations. An outstanding feature is the book review section, which is comprehensive, lengthy and covers the whole of American Western history and geography. While a good addition to most libraries, it would be a second choice after *The American West,* and also possibly after the more popularly written *Frontier Times.* Larger libraries should automatically subscribe.

Junior Historian. 1941. 6/yr. Joe B. Frantz. Texas State Historical Assn., Box 8059, University Station, Univ. of Texas, Austin, Tex. 78712. Illus. Circ: 2,500.

Indexed: IChildMags. *Aud:* Sh, Jh. *Rv:* H. *Jv:* B.

The *Junior Historian* movement "is designed to put its major emphasis on youthful inquiries into the way of life in the various Texas communities and fostering the most sound American patriotism of which we have any knowledge." Articles are contributed by members of the Junior Historian Chapters, which are high school groups. Quite scholarly in approach, they range from the history of the

Santa Fe R.R. to a feature on the oil boom in Texas. Strictly a literary magazine, it carries no advertising, but some pictures and reports of local chapters. Articles are well written, informative, and especially interesting to those who live in the Southwest or are students of that area. Other local historical societies frequently publish journals or reports for young readers, and these should be considered before a library buys sometimes better known, but less regional magazines such as *Junior Historian.*

Military Affairs; devoted to American military (including Naval and Air) history. 1937. q. Membership (Non-members, $6). Victor Gondos, Jr. Amer. Military Inst., P.O. Box 568, Benjamin Franklin Station, Washington, D.C. 20044. Illus., index. Circ: 1,800.

Indexed: AmerH, HistAb. *Aud:* Ga, Ac, Jc. *Rv:* M. *Jv:* B.

A scholarly journal of military history which concentrates on detailed articles by both professional historians and members of the armed forces. Emphasis tends to be on American military affairs, but the magazine is international in scope. All branches of the armed forces are considered, and most of the material is well documented. A glance at *Ulrich's International Periodicals Directory,* 12th ed., will reveal a number of historical journals in this area, but this is the standard American publication.

Montana, The Magazine of Western History. 1951. q. $5. Vivian A. Paladin. Montana Historical Soc., 225 N. Roberts, Helena, Mont. 59601. Illus., index, adv. Circ: 14,000.

Indexed: AmerH, HistAb. *Bk. rev:* 15–20, 500–1,000 words, signed. *Aud:* Ga, Ac, Jc. *Rv:* M. *Jv:* B.

One of the better known regional history magazines, this is also one of the best produced. The five or six well-written, well-documented articles are supported by an excellent format, including a number of photographs and illustrations. Emphasis is on Montana and bordering states, but the subject matter is diverse: ranching, mining, homesteading, Indians, fur trade, etc. The book reviews are good to excellent, but as in many magazines of this type they tend to lag months behind publication date. A useful magazine for almost any library. As is true with other junior historian magazines of this type, the librarian should first subscribe to his own regional historical magazine.

Negro History Bulletin. See Afro-American Section.

New England Quarterly; an historical review of New England life and letters. 1928. q. $8. Herbert Brown, Hubbard Hall, Bowdoin College, Brunswick, Me. 04011. Index. Circ: 1,550. Reprint: AMS.

Indexed: AmerH, HistAb, SSHum. *Bk. rev:* 15–20, lengthy, signed. *Aud:* Sa, Ac. *Rv:* M. *Jv:* B.

Devoted to the history and culture of New England, with emphasis on literary history. Among its editors are such distinguished scholars as Samuel Eliot Morison, Oscar Handlin and Bernard Bailyn. There are usually four or five scholarly articles, a section on memoranda and documents, and, until 1967, an annual bibliography on writings about New England. The book reviews are critical and cover all aspects of New England. As this covers such a wide range of interests, it can be subscribed to by many libraries as much for its literary as its historical value. While the main appeal will be to New England libraries, the material is usually of value to anyone interested in American culture and life. It deserves at least a trial subscription by medium to large academic and public libraries throughout the country.

Old West. 1964. q. $2. Pat Wagner. Joe A. Small, Box 3668, Austin, Tex. 78704. Illus., adv. Circ: 150,000.

Bk. rev: Notes. *Aud:* Ga, Sh. *Rv:* L. *Jv:* B.

As is also true with *Frontier Times,* this is an above average "western" for the historically inclined reader who desires more fact than fiction and is devoted to popular stories concerning Western history. Frequent use is made of authentic photos, and the subject matter touches such varied facets of Western life as ghost towns, lost treasure, Indians and descriptions of colorful frontier characters. Among the contributors are the noted western writers J. Frank Dobie and S. Omar Barker. Each issue carries a reprint of a rare book that is costly or not available to the average reader. While a trifle more serious than *Frontier Times,* it is in the same genre and should be considered by high school and public libraries that feel a need for such material.

Pacific Historical Review. 1932. q. $5. John W. Caughey. Univ. of California Press, Berkeley, Calif. 94720. Index, adv. Circ: 1,250. Microform: UM.

Indexed: AmerH, HistAb, SSHum. *Bk. rev:* 6–10, one page, signed. *Aud:* Sa, Ac. *Rv:* M. *Jv:* B.

About equally divided between articles on American western history and countries bordering on the Pacific basin, including islands. Although coverage extends from the 16th century, most of the recent material has concentrated on developments in the 19th and early 20th centuries. There are normally six to seven scholarly articles, news items about historians and reports of the Pacific Coast branch of the American Historical Association. A required item in Western libraries and in larger academic historical collections.

The Palimpsest. 1920. m. 50¢ per copy. William J. Petersen. State Historical Soc. of Iowa, Iowa City, Iowa 52240. Illus., index. Circ: 10,500.

Indexed: AmerH, HistAb. *Aud:* Sa, Ac. *Rv:* M. *Jv:* B.

A somewhat different approach to local history by the State Historical Society of Iowa. Each issue is entirely devoted to covering one aspect of Iowa's history: the biography of a pioneer, the story of a college or railroad. It treats such diversified subjects as Indians, government and

politics and social and cultural history. Photos and illustrations enliven the articles. A useful addition for not only Iowan, but all Midwestern medium to large academic libraries.

Real West. 1957. bi-m. $1.50. William T. Kish. Charlton Pubns. Inc., Charlton Bldg., Derby, Conn. 06418. Illus., adv. Circ: 100,000.

Bk. rev: Notes. *Aud:* Ga, Sh. *Rv:* L. *Jv:* B.

A popular Western magazine for the general reader. Articles are authenticated by the use of photos and illustrations from the period and lists of reference sources. The subject matter covers all aspects of Western history, but particular attention is given to many of the more colorful Western characters like Buffalo Bill, Wyatt Earp and Wild Bill Hickok. Differs from other Western magazines listed here, in that there is more emphasis on photographs, and the whole is a trifle more scholarly than usual. And while a few photographs may upset conservative librarians, it is a good choice for the library seeking to attract the slow reader or the adult with a limited interest in most books and magazines.

True West. 1957. bi-m. $4. Pat Wagner. J. A. Small, Box 3668, Austin, Tex. 78704. Illus., index, adv. Circ: 210,414.

Aud: Ga, Sh. *Rv:* L. *Jv:* B.

A popular man's magazine, this features authentic non-fiction stories dealing with all facets of the Old West. Such colorful figures as famous lawmen, outlaws and Indians are among the subjects featured. The well-known Western writer, Walt Coburn, is a frequent contributor, and on the whole the level of writing is good to excellent. The approach is similar to that of the publisher's other magazines, *Frontier Times* and *Old West,* and one or all would be equally good for most libraries.

Virginia Cavalcade. 1951. q. $2. Edward F. Heite. Virginia State Library, Richmond, Va. 23219. Illus. Circ: 15,208.

Indexed: AmerH, HistAb. *Aud:* Sa, Ac. *Rv:* M. *Jv:* B.

Devoted to all periods of Virginia history, and biographical articles on Virginia-born historical figures. Articles are accompanied by numerous illustrations in black and white and color. Historical documents frequently are reproduced. As a historical magazine from one of the oldest regions in the United States, much of the material has more than local interest. A necessary addition for large academic libraries.

William and Mary Quarterly; a magazine of early American history. 1892. q. $5. Thad W. Tate. Inst. of Early Amer. History and Culture, Box 220, Williamsburg, Va. 23185. Illus., index, adv. Circ: 3,100. Reprint: Kraus. Microform: UM.

Indexed: AmerH, HistAb, SSHum. *Bk. rev:* 15–25, lengthy, signed. *Aud:* Sa, Ac. *Rv:* M. *Jv:* B.

One of the earliest magazines devoted to the notion of culture as an important aspect of history, this is a scholarly approach to the American scene before 1815. Articles range from biographies to bibliographies, and many border on literary essays. The book reviews are broad in scope, critical, and quite reliable for both the historian and the teacher of comparative literature.

The Yorker. 1942. bi-m. (Sept.–June). $1.50. Milo V. Stewart. New York State Historical Assn., Cooperstown, N.Y. 13326. Illus. Circ: 11,000.

Indexed: IChildMags. *Aud:* Sh, Jh. *Rv:* M. *Jv:* B.

Student-written articles which are commendable for their high quality of writing and for their accurate and imaginative presentation of New York State's history. Among senior and junior high school pupils, historical buildings, industries, and organizations are favorite topics. The articles, averaging 3,000 words or more, appear to be well researched, but are not documented. Most of them represent awards given by the Association in writing competitions held annually. Illustrations consist of old prints, documents, maps, portraits, etc., in black and white, sometimes with the addition of one color. Reports of the activities of "Yorker" chapters, conventions, trips, projects and other activities are included in each issue. A useful addition for most eastern school libraries. Of limited value to others.

General History

African Historical Studies. See African Studies Section.

Agricultural History. See Agriculture Section.

American Journal of Legal History. See Law Section.

The Americas; a quarterly review of inter-American cultural history. 1944. q. $6. Fr. Mathias C. Kiemen, O.F.M. Academy of Amer. Franciscan History, Box L, Washington, D.C. 20014. Circ: 925.

Indexed: HistAb, SSHum. *Bk. rev.* 10–15, approx. one page, signed. *Aud:* Sa, Ac, Jc. *Rv:* M. *Jv:* B.

Devoted to the history of Latin America, with emphasis on cultural history. The period covered is from the beginning of European colonization until the twentieth century. Bibliographical and cultural news of interest to its readers is contained in a regular feature called "Inter-American Notes." While this is a limited circulation, scholarly journal, it does cover an area which is difficult to find in English, especially without political or economic bias. The religious sponsorship is rarely reflected in the articles and, on the whole, the magazine is quite objective. Should be considered by any library, from medium size public to academic, where an intelligent coverage of this area would be appreciated. See also, *Hispanic American Historical Review.*

The Beaver; a magazine of the North. 1920. q. $2. Malvina Bolus. Hudson's Bay Co., Hudson's Bay House, Winnipeg 1, Manit. Illus., index.

Indexed: CanI, HistAb, IChildMags. *Bk. rev:* 6–8, one page, signed. *Aud:* Ga, Ac, Jc, Sh. *Rv:* M. *Jv:* B.

Somewhat similar in editorial approach to Canadian history as *American Heritage* is to American history. Although considerably more modest in size, the style of writing is similar, and the llustrations are carefully selected to augment all of the articles. Authors are historians and scholars, but gear their material to a lay audience. Articles are concerned with the Canadian Western frontier, the fur trade, exploration, and Indian and Eskimo life. While this magazine is often recommended for elementary grades, the reading level is well beyond the average grade school child. Its primary value for the child is the illustrations and use by the teacher in the classroom. Conversely, it is an excellent choice for senior high. A required item in Canadian libraries and a good second for most American libraries.

Business History Review. See Business and Industry Section.

Canadian Historical Review. 1920. q. $6. G. Ramsay Cook. Univ. of Toronto Press, Toronto, Ont. Circ: 2,700.

Indexed: CanI, HistAb, SSHum. *Bk. rev:* 20–25, 1–2 pages, signed. *Aud:* Sa, Ac, Jc. *Rv:* H. *Jv:* A.

Concentrates on Canadian history, with special emphasis on political history and foreign relations. Each issue features three or four scholarly monographs written by professional historians. The book reviews cover, selectively, all fields of history, and are lengthy and evaluative. A regular feature is several pages listing recent publications relating to Canada. Both the scope and the nature of the book reviews makes this a required journal in history departments and large libraries. It will be a necessary purchase for all types of Canadian libraries, even high school libraries.

Canadian Journal of African Studies. See African Studies Section.

Canadian Journal of History (Canada)/Annales Canadiennes D'histoire. 1966. semi-ann. Ivo N. Lambi. $3.50. Journal of History Co. Ltd., 717 Arts Bldg., Univ. of Saskatchewan, Saskatoon, Sask.

Indexed HistAb. *Bk. rev:* 25, 1–2 pages, signed. *Aud:* Sa, Ac. *Rv:* H. *Jv:* B.

Despite the title, this is not concerned with Canadian history but is world-wide in scope. The four to five well-documented articles cover all periods and countries. Most are in English, one or two in French. There is usually a review article on one or more books, and then some 25 to 30 shorter notices of other general historical works. As many of the titles are issued abroad, this is an excellent checklist for the large history library.

Catholic Historical Review. 1915. q. $7. Robert Trisco. Catholic Univ. of America Press, Washington, D.C. 20017. Illus., index, adv. Circ: 2,290. Microform: UM. Reprint: Kraus.

Indexed: CathI, HistAb, SSHum. *Bk. rev:* 50, 350 words. *Aud:* Ga, Sa, Ac, Jc. *Rv:* H. *Jv:* B.

The official publication of the Catholic Historical Association. Emphasis is on Catholic church history, although it is of interest to both the general historian and the non-Catholic religious student. There are some five articles per issue, which are international in scope and period. The book reviews are excellent, and often cover material not found elsewhere. For all religious and large historical collections.

Comparative Studies in Society and History. See Sociology Section.

Economia E Storia; rivista Italiana di storia politica e sociale. 1954. q. $4.50. Amintore Fanfani. Casa Editrice Dott. A. Giuffre, Via Statuto 2, 20121. Milan, Italy. Illus., index, adv. Circ: 2,000.

Indexed: HistAb. *Bk. rev:* Various numbers, lengths. *Aud:* Sa, Ac. *Rv:* H. *Jv:* B.

An Italian historical journal, but with summaries in English and French, and includes the work of American historians and scholars. Emphasis is on the Mediterranean region, and this journal is considered by authorities to be one of the best for the area. A must for medium to large history collections.

Economic History Review. See Economics Section.

Éire-Ireland; a journal of Irish studies. 1966. q. $10. Eoin McKiernan, Irish American Cultural Inst., Box 5026, College of St. Thomas, St. Paul, Minn. 55101. Circ: 1,000. *Bk. rev:* 10–12, 500–1,500 words, signed. *Aud:* Ga, Ac, Jc. *Rv:* M. *Jv:* B.

The editor probably rightfully claims this is "the only intelligent Irish magazine published in the United States." In that it is free of wild stories and worship of the old country, he is quite correct. In fact, contributors are teachers, authors and historians who give an unbiased account of everything from the Irish theatre to the Irish revolt. The writing style, while scholarly, is easily within the grasp of the average layman, and the scope is wide enough to appeal to anyone remotely interested in Irish culture. Emphasis is on history, literature and the arts, particularly in the critical book reviews, notes, queries, and bibliographies. A good acquisition for the general or fine arts collection in most medium to large public and academic collections.

English Historical Review. 1886. $12. J. M. Wallace-Hadrill & J. M. Roberts. Longmans Green & Co. Ltd., 48 Grosvenor St., London W.1. Adv. Circ: 2,200. Microform: Canner. Reprint: Johnson.

Indexed: BritHum, HistAb, SSHum. *Bk. rev:* Numerous, one page, signed. *Aud:* Sa, Ac, Jc. *Rv:* H. *Jv:* V.

Deals with history of all periods, with some emphasis on Great Britain and the British Empire. It usually contains four or five scholarly articles and shorter notes and documents. A valuable feature is its annotated list, in each July issue, of periodical articles primarily, but not exclusively dealing with European history. The book reviews are some of the best in the field, usually long, penetrating and highly critical. A basic journal for the university and junior college library. Laymen with more than a passing interest in history will appreciate the public librarian who introduces them to this outstanding review.

Greek Heritage. See Classical Studies Section.

Hispanic American Historical Review. 1918. q. $6. Robert E. Quirk. Duke Univ. Press, Box 6697, College Station, Durham, N.C. 27708. Index, adv. Circ: 1,900.

Indexed: HistAb, SSHum. *Bk. rev:* 50, lengthy or 400–500 words, signed. *Aud:* Sa, Ac. *Rv:* M. *Jv:* B.

Devoted to Latin American history, particularly from the 17th to the 19th centuries. Each issue contains four or five scholarly articles, with some emphasis on politics and government. There is an extensive book review section in which the reviews are classified by subject and period. Among the journal's regular features are sections on professional news and dissertations. Nicely complemented by the somewhat broader scope of *Americas,* but of the two, this one is more valuable for its book reviews. The library that feels a need for one should try both.

Historian; a journal of history. 1938. q. $6. William D. Metz. Phi Alpha Theta National Honor Soc. in History, D. B. Hoffman, 2812 Livingston St., Allentown, Pa. 18104. Index, adv. Circ: 8,500.

Indexed: HistAb, SSHum. *Bk. rev:* 60–70, 400–500 words, signed. *Aud:* Sa, Ac, Jc. *Rv:* H. *Jv:* A.

Covering the whole field of history, and excluding no period or time, this is one of the best scholarly, general historical journals available. The writing style is consistently high, although at times a bit too deep, and articles are accepted from students, teachers and interested laymen. News of the Society is included. Particularly valuable for the large number of book reviews. While not widely circulated, this quarterly can be of great value to any university or large public library.

Historic Preservation. See Architecture.

Historical Studies. 1940. semi-ann. $4.50. F. B. Smith & N. D. Mclachlan. Sch. of History, Univ. of Melbourne, Parkville, Victoria 3052, Australia. Circ: 1,100.

Indexed: BritHum, HistAb, PAIS. *Bk. rev:* 15–20, lengthy, signed. *Aud:* Sa, Ac. *Rv:* M. *Jv:* B.

Features the political, economic, and social history of Australia, New Zealand, and the Pacific. The articles may cover any period from early discovery and settlement to the present. Articles in other fields, notably British Empire, American and European history, by historians working in Australia, are occasionally published. The magazine also carries laws of professional interest. Recently completed research is listed. A specialized work for larger libraries.

History. 1912. 3/yr. Membership (Non-members, $4.50). Historical Assn. 59a Kensington Park Rd., London S.E.11. Index, adv. Circ: 7,000.

Indexed: BritEd, BritHum, HistAb, SSHum. *Bk. rev:* 80–90, lengthy, signed. *Aud:* Sa, Ac. *Rv:* H. *Jv:* B.

Deals with all aspects of history, but concentrates on the European scene. There are usually five to six scholarly articles. The primary value for librarians is the book review section, which makes up most of the journal. Reviews are long, critical and particularly helpful for their wide coverage. It should be considered by any library with a particular interest in history, but, in America, the same type of specialized book review service is available in *Historian.*

History and Theory; studies in the philosophy of history and historiography. 1960. 3/yr. $6. George H. Nadel. Wesleyan Univ. Press, Wesleyan Station, Middleton, Conn. 06457. Illus., index. Circ: 2,000.

Indexed: HistAb, SSHum. *Bk. rev:* 6–9, lengthy, signed. *Aud:* Sa, Ac. *Rv:* H. *Jv:* B.

Primarily concerned with the philosophy of history and historiography. The editorial committee is composed of prominent historians such as Crane Brinton and Pieter Geyl. There are three to five scholarly monographs, and six to nine book review essays. An example of a highly specialized kind of historical journal which is excellent for its purposes, but should be limited to large academic collections.

History Studies. 1968. 3/yr. $7. C. K. Francis Brown. Pergamon Press, Inc., Maxwell House, Fairview Park, Elmsford, N.Y. 10523.

Indexed: HistAb. *Aud:* Sa, Ac. *Rv:* H. *Jv:* B.

Sponsored by University Hall, Buckland, Berkshire, England and devoted "to papers on ancient, medieval and modern history." The tone is scholarly, the scope limited primarily to English and European history. Each issue features five to eight well-documented articles. Only for large academic libraries, or for smaller libraries which have a particular interest in English history.

History Today. 1951. m. $8.50. Peter Quennell & Alan Hodge. Bracken House, Cannon St., London E.C. 4. Illus., index, adv. Circ: 31,989.

Indexed: BritHum, HistAb, SSHum. *Bk. rev:* Various numbers, lengths. *Aud:* Ga, Ac, Jc, Sh. *Rv:* M. *Jv:* A.

One of the few historical magazines geared for the general reader and beginning student. Each issue contains some six to seven illustrated articles, written in a semi-popular style by professional historians. All periods and places are covered, although the emphasis is on the English speaking nations. The book reviews are good to excellent. Students from senior high through college will find that the "Notes for Further Reading" at the end of each article are helpful guides in preparing papers. While *American Heritage* and *Horizon* are preferable, if only for their illus-

trations, *History Today* is a good second or third choice— in fact, where budget problems might prohibit the other two quite costly magazines, *History Today* would be a very satisfactory first choice.

Horizon. 1958. q. $16. Joseph J. Thorndike. Amer. Heritage Publishing Co., Inc., 551 Fifth Ave., New York, N. Y. 10017. Illus. Circ: 160,000.

Indexed: HistAb, RG. *Aud:* Ga, Ac, Jc, Sh. *Rv:* M. *Jv:* A.

The first cousin to *American Heritage,* this has a similar hard cover and glossy format. It is replete with striking colored photographs and drawings, and is to be looked at as much as read. Although its primary target is world history, it is much broader in scope. A typical issue may consider all subjects related to the humanities from literature and art to archaeology and the performing arts. The articles are prepared by authorities, and are styled to be read with a minimum of effort. Some accuse it, as *American Heritage,* of a quasi-scholarly approach, but this is only to say it is not for the professional historian. It is for the high school and college student and for most adults who do not require footnotes with their history.

Historical Journal. 1958. q. $10.50. F. H. Hinsley, Cambridge Univ. Press, 200 Euston Rd., London N.W. 1. Index, adv. Circ: 1,800.

Indexed: BritHum, HistAb. *Bk. rev:* 8–10, lengthy, signed. *Aud:* Sa, Ac. *Rv:* M. *Jv:* B.

The successor to the *Cambridge Historical Journal.* Each issue features six to eight long, well-documented articles, and two to three review pieces. Social and political issues of England and Europe are the primary concern, and the authors span almost the whole time period from the Middle Ages to the present, e.g., "The Guildhall Declaration of 11 December 1688" to "The Importance of Energy in the First and Second World Wars." The book reviews are usually essay form, and may include several related titles. The whole is written and edited for the professional historian. Only for large academic libraries.

Institute of Historical Research Bulletin. 1923. semi-ann. 30s. A. G. Dickens. Athlone Press, 2 Gower St., London W.C.1. Index, adv.

Indexed: BritHum, HistAb. *Aud:* Sa, Ac. *Rv:* H. *Jv:* B.

Features articles on medieval and modern history, as well as shorter notes often accompanied by documents. As it is one of the few journals which prints documents, reference value is particularly high. Other regular features are news of professional interest, summaries of completed London theses and selected lists of historical manuscripts recently offered for sale. Occasional special supplements are issued to subscribers. Only for large academic libraries.

Journal of African History. See African Studies Section.

Journal of Asian History. 1967. semi-ann. $8. Denis Sinor. Otto Harrassowitz, Postfach 349, Wiesbaden, W. Germany. Illus., adv. Circ: 2,000.

Indexed: HistAb. *Bk. rev:* 10–12, 500 words, signed. *Aud:* Sa, Ac. *Rv:* H. *Jv:* B.

Covers historical research on any period and all the regions of Asia, with the exception of the Ancient Near East. Contributions are published in the language of the author, but the emphasis is on English. The material is universal in scope, ranging from a well illustrated monograph on "Asian Elephants in Renaissance Europe," to "Soviet-Japanese confrontations in Outer Mongolia." Book reviews seem to concentrate on American university presses. A specialized journal for scholars and graduate students who have any interest in Asia, historical or otherwise.

Journal of Contemporary History. 1966. q. $7. Walter Laqueur & George L. Mosse. Weidenfeld & Nicholson, 5 Winsley St., London W.1. Index. Microform: UM.

Indexed: HistAb. *Aud:* Sa, Ac, Jc, Ht. *Rv:* M. *Jv:* B.

A publication of the Institute of Contemporary History, this British journal is dedicated to the promotion of "research mainly in twentieth-century European history." The 12 to 15 articles are written by scholars and normally have a central focus, e.g., "Education and Social Structure." A separate insert, of particular value to librarians, is the "Quarterly Select List of Accessions of the Wiener Library"—divided by subject and country, this gives a full bibliographic description for each book. Limiting itself to the twentieth-century, and then to Europe, this journal is of less general use than *Journal of Modern History,* which has a much wider scope. Conversely, the emphasis on special topics of general interest make it a required item in larger libraries and in many high school professional collections.

Journal of Economic History. See Economics Section.

Journal of Modern History. 1929. q. $8. Charles & Hanna Gray. Univ. of Chicago Press, 5750 Ellis Ave., Chicago, Ill. 60637. Index, adv. Circ: 3,279. Microform: UM. Reprint: Johnson.

Indexed: HistAb, SSHum. *Bk. rev:* Numerous, signed. *Aud:* Sa, Ac, Jc, Ht. *Rv:* H. *Jv:* B.

Emphasis is on scholarly articles covering European history from the Renaissance to the present. Here it differs radically from the English *Journal of Contemporary History,* which deals only with twentieth-century history. Contributors are among the world's leading historians, and the magazine has reached an honored place in its field. All philosophical approaches to history are represented, and each article is thoroughly documented. Important documents are often published, in full or in parts, with critical comments. The book reviews are excellent, and cover thoroughly the scope of the journal's interest. A required magazine for all medium to large historical collections.

Journal of Pacific History. 1966. ann. $4. Australian National Univ., P.O. Box 4. Canberra, A.C.T., Australia.

Indexed: HistAb. *Bk. rev:* Notes. *Aud:* Sa, Ac. *Rv:* H. *Jv:* B.

A part of the world sure to receive increasing attention as time goes on is the Pacific Islands. This journal publishes articles concerned with the history, archaeology and government of the Islands (which, incidentally, include Hawaii), and says it is willing to publish articles on other regions, particularly Africa and Southeast Asia, when the point discussed has relevance to Island affairs. The articles are wide-ranging in subject and treatment, but all readable, and some of more than passing interest. Following the articles are sections on current developments, manuscript collections and recent publications. The usual issue is fat—250 pages—a circumstance that suggests a more-than-lukewarm interest in the Islands.

Journal of Social History. 1967. q. $10. Peter N. Stearns. Univ. of California Press, Berkeley, Calif. 94720.

Indexed: HistAb. *Bk. rev:* Various numbers, lengths. *Aud:* Sa, Ac. *Rv:* M. *Jv:* B.

Articles are of a scholarly nature, interdisciplinarian, and geared to fill the need for a bridge between political and social historians, e.g., social history, sociological history, trends in American social history. Authors tend to be specialists' writing with various degrees of clarity and thought. A few of the entries are quite understandable to the layman, but most require at least some academic background.

Journal of Southeast Asian History. 1960. semi-ann. $5.70. Chiang Hai Dung & R. Suntharalingam. Univ. of Singapore, History Dept., Singapore 10. Circ: 1,800.

Indexed: HistAb. *Bk. rev:* 15–20, 250–500 words, signed. *Aud:* Sa, Ac. *Rv:* H. *Jv:* B.

Though published in English, more than half of the contributors to the *Journal* are of Asian origin, all of them scholars. Most articles are on twentieth century history, but this is balanced with a number of contributions from the disciplines of anthropology, philology, sociology, economics, and social psychology. The data is available in few other sources, at least to the Westerner. A significant publication, considering the increasing need for objective knowledge of this area of the world. Excellent for college and university libraries, and suitable for large public library collections.

Journal of World History. 1953. q. $15. UNESCO, Editions de la Baconniere S.A., Neuchatel, Switzerland. Index, adv. Circ: 1,500. Microform: UM.

Indexed: HistAb, SSHum. *Aud:* Sa, Ac, Jc. *Rv:* M. *Jv:* B.

Published by UNESCO—International Commission for a History of Scientific and Cultural Development of Humanity. Articles by scholars from many countries. The text is primarily in English and French with some Spanish. Particular emphasis is placed on the history of science and on cultural institutions. Special numbers are issued from time to time on such subjects as "Science in Italy" or "Spanish Cultural History." In view of its broad scope it is particularly suited for both undergraduate and graduate study. In most cases, however, the *Journal of the History of Ideas* will meet the needs of the average library.

Journal of the History of Ideas; a quarterly devoted to cultural and intellectual history. 1940. q. $6. Philip P. Wiener. The City College, City Univ. of New York, New York, N.Y. 10031. Index, adv. Circ: 3,000. Reprint: Johnson. Microform: Publisher.

Indexed: HistAb, PhilosI, SSHum. *Bk. rev:* 1, 2,000 words, signed. *Aud:* Ga, Ac, Jc. *Rv:* H. *Jv:* B.

Contributors to this journal, professionals in their fields, seek to isolate and explain the germinal ideas behind significant intellectual movements. Many articles are concerned to show the influences of one important figure or school of thought upon another. Devoted to "cultural and intellectual history," it usually contains eight or ten contributions dealing with the history of philosophy, of literature and the arts, of the natural and social sciences and of religion and political and social movements. The lengthy book reviews are critical. Among the editors are such distinguished scholars as Hans Kohn and Marjorie H. Nicholson. Not only of value to the student of intellectual history, but to anyone seeking to understand current developments in the theoretical basis of an academic discipline. For the educated general reader as well as the student.

Journal of the Society of Architectural Historians. See Architecture Section.

Labor History. See Labor and Industrial Relations Section.

Law and Contemporary Problems. See Law Section.

Mankind (U.S.); the magazine of popular history. bi-m. $4.50. 8060 Melrose Ave. Los Angeles, Calif. 90046. Illus., adv.

Bk. rev: 5–6, 100–250 words. *Aud:* Ga, *Rv:* L. *Jv:* C.

The American answer to the British magazine, *History*. It is profusely illustrated with color and black and white, averages out to some 10 to 12 articles per 100-page issue, and covers every aspect of world history, although emphasis is on the European scene. The writing style is oversimplified, and there is neither documentation nor bibliographies. While the effort to bring history to the average man is commendable, the treatment is too shallow. Not for most libraries, and certainly no substitute for the British periodical.

Past and Present; a journal of historical studies. 1952. 3/yr. 25s. T. H. Aston. Corpus Christi College, Oxford, Eng. Index, adv. Circ: 3,300.

Indexed: BritHum, HistAb. *Aud:* Sa, Ac, Jc. *Rv:* M. *Jv:* B.

An English general historical magazine, yet considerably more scholarly than *History Today*. It covers historical, social and the historical aspects of literary and artistic movements in all countries and times. Emphasis, however, is on social and economic history, class structure, social mobility, and the organization of society. There are usually six to seven articles, a section devoted to a current debate among historians, and from time to time a single, long book review. While particularly suited to the professional historian and graduate, some material is helpful for undergraduates at both the college and junior college level. (This magazine should not be confused with *Past and Future,* another English publication which is directed primarily at a popular audience. It has limited use for American libraries.)

School of Oriental and African Studies. Bulletin. 1917. 3/yr. $28.60. Univ. of London (Subscriptions to: Luzac & Co., Ltd., 46 Great Russell St., London W.C.1). Illus., index.

Indexed: BritHum, HistAb. *Bk. rev:* 80, 100–500 words, signed. *Aud:* Sa, Ac. *Rv:* H. *Jv:* B.

Concerned with both modern and ancient history, art and archaeology, this is a highly thought of journal for experts in Orientalia and related areas, i.e., religion, literature, anthropology, etc. The five to eight technical articles are all by scholars, primarily British. The primary use of the journal for the librarian and non-expert is found in the book review section. Here, some 80 to 100 titles are noted each issue, and the signed reviews are both descriptive and critical. Two somewhat similar journals are published at Yale for American scholars, although, as with the English periodical, they are used extensively by students of the area regardless of nationality. There, too, there are good book reviews. A minor point of interest is that one, the *American Oriental Society Journal,* is one of the oldest magazines in the United States, first published in 1843. The second, established in 1919, is the *American School of Oriental Research Bulletin.*

The Smithsonian Journal of History; an illustrated scholarly quarterly of general history. 1966. q. $7.50. Walter Cannon. Smithsonian Inst. (Subscriptions to: P.O. Box 1001, Berkeley, Calif. 94701). Illus. Circ: 2,500.

Indexed: HistAb. *Aud:* Ga, Ac, Jc, Sh. *Rv:* M. *Jv:* B.

While in one respect a general historical journal, this concentrates on interests of the Smithsonian, i.e., history related to art, anthropology, archaeology, technology, and the general sciences. The articles are written by scholars, are well documented, and even better illustrated. Fortunately, the editor has avoided the pedantic approach, and the style usually matches the fascination of the topic. Although primarily for the educated adult, this can be enjoyed by the brighter high school student.

Social Education. See Education Section.

Social Studies. See Education Section.

Technology and Culture. See Engineering Section.

HOME

Indexes and Abstracts.

Abridged Readers' Guide, Art Index, Biological Abstracts, Chemical Abstracts, Education Index, Public Affairs In-

formation Service, Readers' Guide to Periodical Literature, Subject Index to Children's Magazines. (For annotations, see Indexes and Abstracts Section.)

American Home. 1928. 10/yr. $4. Hubbard H. Cobb. Curtis Publishing Co., Philadelphia, Pa. 19105. Illus., adv. Circ: 3,400,000. Microform: UM.

Indexed: RG. *Bk. rev:* 3–4, plus about 5–10 on booklets of 35–75 words. *Aud:* Ga, Sh. *Rv:* L. *Jv:* B.

A comprehensive home magazine for "active young homemakers," *American Home* stresses the enjoyment of living. Like *Better Homes and Gardens,* the ideas are intended for people of modest means, but *American Home* emphasizes the esthetic aspects of homemaking more than does the more pragmatic *Better Homes and Gardens.* It relies on outside contributors for some of its 40–50 articles, ranging in length from a short description of 200 words to a few essays of 1,500 to 2,000 words. Foods receive the most coverage with home building and decorating close behind. Almost any topic related to family living is included (e.g., "Space and Gadgets," "Leisure: How to Make the Most of It"). Important features include a question and answer clinic on decorating, and tested recipes (arranged for easy clipping). The beautiful color photos are sometimes more important than the accompanying article.

Architectural Digest; the quality guide to decorating ideas. 1920. q. $10.50. Bradley Little. John C. Brasfield Publishing Corp. 680 Wilshire Place, Los Angeles, Calif. 90005. Circ: 45,000.

Aud: Ga, Ac. *Rv:* M. *Jv:* B.

Not an architecture magazine *per se,* but a general periodical in the interior decorating field. This is specifically edited for the layman with expensive tastes. It features up to 100 illustrations per issue, almost one-third of these in color. They are rivaled only by the advertising, some 25% of the whole, which assumes the reader is in the upper income brackets. Feature articles take the reader to the homes of national figures, and explain how they are decorated, designed and furnished. Other articles report on new products, trends and history, restorations, foreign homes, and art and antiques. Useful on two counts: the sketches of the famous owners are quite revealing on personality; the design ideas are often applicable for the homeowner with a limited budget, but a good imagination. Not a necessary purchase, but should be in all larger art and design libraries.

Better Homes and Gardens. 1922. m. $3. (Regional editions for eight different areas of the country.) Bert Dieter. Meredith Publishing Co., 1716 Locust St., Des Moines, Iowa. 50303. Illus., adv. Circ: 7,000,000.

Indexed: AbrRG, RG. *Aud:* Ga, Ac, Jc, Sh. *Rv:* M. *Jv:* A.

One of the general magazines covering the field of homes and gardens, *Better Homes and Gardens* calls itself "the ideal magazine for better homes and families." It caters to the middle class homemaker stressing gardening and foods,

but handyman articles aré included as well. Money management is always a feature, as is an illustrated section called "Shopping Editor's Choice," which introduces new products. Evidence of the policy of addressing articles to those with an average income are such articles as "Where Does Money Trouble Start?," and the annual collection of "100 Ideas under $100." Almost all articles are written by the editorial staff. Very practical and attractively illustrated, *Better Homes* should be in almost any collection.

Changing Times; the Kiplinger magazine. 1947. m. $6. Robert W. Harvey. Kiplinger Washington Editors, Inc., 1729 H St., N.W., Washington, D.C. 20006. Illus., index, adv. Circ: 1,220,000. Microform: UM. Reprint: Abrahams.

Indexed: AbrRG, PAIS, RG. *Aud:* Ga, Sh, Jh. *Rv:* M. *Jv:* B.

A service for families who like to plan their finances, *Changing Times* presents short accurate articles concerning problems faced in everyday life. New research and activities in religion, education, science, medicine and the arts are reported. Concise discussions of current business developments enable the hurried businessman to stay aware of the latest events. Also included are practical articles concerning ways to earn, buy and save. Simple graphs, charts, and statistics are provided to clarify and illustrate the more difficult topics discussed. Capsule news items and fresh ideas are supplied each issue in a regular section, "The Months Ahead," to act as a guide for families in planning their future budgets. Appeals to the do-it-yourself economist.

Co-ed. 1956. 10/yr. $2.40. Margaret Hauser. Scholastic Magazines, Inc., 50 W. 44th St., New York, N.Y. 10036. Illus., adv. Circ: 1,000,000.

Indexed: IChildMags. *Aud:* Sh, Jh. *Rv:* L. *Jv:* B.

Co-ed is the only magazine of homemaking for young women. Its editorial policy is "expressly designed to enrich every area of the home economics program in junior and senior high schools," which it does by reaching teen-age girls at their own interest levels. Articles of two to three pages in length, dealing with grooming, fashions, homemaking arts and finance, friends and family, are presented in simple, straightforward style. Often included is a description of the career of someone successful in the field of home economics. Each issue includes one or two short stories, of good quality, of interest to high school girls, useful in classes on personal and family relationship. Features are illustrated with sketches and photos, in simple and effective arrangement. Advertising is screened and not excessive, tastefully presenting products for the teen-age market. In general this magazine is well done, and is of interest to high school girls, with a special appeal to older girls preparing for business or homemaking careers.

Consumer Bulletin. 1928. m. $5. F. J. Schlink. Consumers' Research Inc., Washington, N.J. 07882. Illus., index. Circ: 100,000. Microform: Mc, UM.

Indexed: RG. *Aud:* Ga, Ac, Jc, Sh. *Rv:* H. *Jv:* A.

The oldest of the consumer magazines, *Consumer Bulletin* reports ratings of tested brand-name products. Ratings of recommended, intermediate and not recommended are applied to hundreds of items which have been laboratory tested or, in some cases, judged by qualified experts. The research involved is highly impartial and results are reported accurately; simple enough for understanding by the novice, yet with enough further technical information to satisfy the more informed reader. Regular departments include editorials, and reviews of classical and popular recordings. Motion picture recommendations and ratings based on motion picture reviews in 15 periodicals, and news items of special interest to the consumer and to teachers of economics, consumer buying, consumer problems, consumer economics, home economics, etc. Short articles provide information concerning nutrition, health, food adulteration, appliance hazards and descriptive recommendations of new products considered as meriting special attention by consumers. A second choice after *Consumer Reports* for medium-sized libraries, but should be a joint purchase for larger libraries.

Consumer Reports. 1936. m. $6. Patricia Jenkins. Consumers Union of U.S., Inc., 356 Washington St., Mount Vernon, N.Y. 10550. Illus., index. Circ: 825,000. Microform: UM.

Indexed: AbrRG, PAIS, RG. *Bk. rev:* Notes, signed. *Aud:* Ga, Ac, Jc, Sh. *Rv:* H. *Jv:* V.

Provides consumer information on goods and services through ratings of brand name products which have been laboratory and use tested as well as expertly inspected. Estimated overall quality is either judged acceptable, with variations from good to poor, or not acceptable. Products which have a high overall quality coupled with a low price are judged best buys. The testing is thorough and qualitative with the results reported impartially. A regular feature, "Once Over," comments upon news items, prices, products, advertising and recommendations for the best use of certain products. Other columns report government actions to enforce consumer protection laws and discuss government legislation and judicial decisions which have a healthy or unhealthy effect upon the consumer economy. Articles are as technically accurate as *Consumer Bulletin,* but have a more diversified appeal. Broader topics are discussed in an informative manner conducive to reading for pleasure. A first choice for all size and types of libraries.

FDA Papers. 1967. m. $5.50. Govt. Printing Office, Washington, D.C. 20402. Illus.

Aud: Ga, Ac, Jc, Ht. *Rv:* H. *Jv:* B.

This is an example of a government periodical which gives objective, non-biased information on consumer products. The official voice of the Food and Drug Administration, it is concerned with matters close to everyone's environment. One issue, for example, included articles on testing drugs, standards for antibiotics, child protection, food

radiation, and "notices of judgment," which spell out, with names and addresses, manufacturers guilty of some misdeed or other. The housewife who values the two national consumer magazines will find additional help here. Equally useful in classroom situations.

Family Economics Review. q. Free. Consumer and Food Economics Research Div., Agricultural Research Service, U.S. Dept. of Agriculture, Washington, D.C. 20250.

Aud: Sa, Ac, Sh, Ht. *Rv:* H. *Jv:* B.

A government publication directed primarily to home demonstration agents and specialists, but of some use to the high school teacher and student. There are succinct reports on the past quarter's or year's activities in such diverse matters as cost of living and its effect on home economics, food prices and distribution, etc. From time to time summarizes findings of other government reports which will be of value to readers. The numerous charts and the direct, easy-to-understand style give it relevance for some high school students, especially those living in farming communities.

The Family Handyman; the do-it-yourself magazine. 1950. bi-m. $3. Morton Waters. Universal Publishing & Distributing Corp., 235 E. 45th St., New York, N.Y. 10017. Illus., index, adv. Circ: 400,000.

Aud: Ga. *Rv:* H. *Jv:* B.

The popular do-it-yourself magazine for howeowners covers practical suggestions for remodeling homes, fabricating built-in furniture and accessories, hints on gardening and decorating. Detailed building plans accompany articles on storage units and furniture to make in the home workshop. Many ads for tools and building materials. Year's index in each issue is a convenience to readers who are looking for a solution to a specific problem. An excellent guide to every phase of maintenance and improvement of the house, both inside and out. Probably the best magazine of its kind, suitable for public libraries and, possibly, useful to schools with shop courses.

Flying Chips & Deltagram. See Crafts and Hobbies Section.

Forecast for Home Economics. 1952. 9/yr. $5. Eleanor Adams. Scholastic Magazines, Inc., 50 W. 44th St., New York, N.Y. 10036. (Subscriptions to: Forecast, 902 Sylvan Ave., Englewood Cliffs, N.J. 07632.) Illus., index, adv. Circ: 70,000. Microform: UM.

Indexed: EdI. *Aud:* Ht. *Rv:* L. *Jv:* B.

This "comprehensive, professional magazine for every home economist" is primarily edited for teachers, and its purpose is to insure the continued usage of *Co-ed* by approximately 1,000,000 girls taking home economics courses in junior and senior high schools. It provides articles ranging from theories of learning to practical homemaking hints. *Forecast* strives to be an updated teaching text by providing lively, topical coverage of every homemaking area. Each issue includes several articles co-ordinated with those in *Co-ed* and a copy of *Co-ed* itself. An obvious choice for libraries in junior and senior high schools where home economics is taught.

Gourmet; a magazine of good living. 1941. m. $6. Lamar Hoover. Gourmet Inc., 777 Third Ave. New York, N.Y. 10017. Illus., index, adv. Circ: 340,000. Microform: UM.

Aud: Ga, Ac, Jc. *Rv:* M. *Jv:* B.

Covers all aspects of fine food and wine. The emphasis is definitely on the reader who has the money to enjoy the best, or dreams about travel to fabulous restaurants. It is geared for those who wish to gain knowledge about what makes a fine wine, an exceptional dish, or tips on regional products. Although the publisher claims some 900 recipes are published each year, few of them are for the average housewife. All concentrate on the best in eating, usually equated with expense. Supporting articles plug the good life from travel to hunting and fishing. Some fiction. The whole is nicely illustrated, and will be a delight to either the man or the woman who sees the kitchen as an art gallery. Of some use for more imaginative high school and college and university home economics courses. Not a necessary item for libraries, but one sure to be enjoyed.

The Home Craftsman. 1932. bi-m. $2.50. Gibco, P.O. Box 1288, Alexander, Va. 22314. Illus., adv. Circ: 168,700.

Aud: Ga. *Rv:* L. *Jv:* C.

Numerous advertisements, a crowded format, and poor paper work against this otherwise fair how-to-do-it magazine. Describes various projects from bookshelves and kitchen units to conversion of a basement into a family room. Diagrams, lists of materials and steps for carrying out the job are given. For the man, woman, beginner or expert, this is a useful, although not essential item. Should be purchased only after other magazines in the field have been considered.

Homemaker's Digest. 1968. bi-m. Free (Controlled circulation). Consumer Communications Corp., 444 Madison Ave., New York, N.Y. 10022. Illus., adv. Circ: 10,000,000.

Aud: Ga. *Rv:* L. *Jv:* B.

Claiming to have the largest controlled circulation of any magazine, this is directed to women with two or more children, living in their own homes, and with incomes of $8,000 a year or more. It is free, the profit coming from advertising, which the publisher garners by promising advertisers the audience mentioned above. It has an attractive, well illustrated format, features short articles on all aspects of homemaking from interior decorating to recipes and suggested shopping hints. The intellectual content is low, the do-it-yourself emphasis high. As it is tailored for the four regional markets and a number of metropolitan areas, there are a variety of editions. Hardly a required item for a library, but as it is free, it might be welcomed where there is a limited magazine budget.

House and Garden. 1901. m. $6. Harriet Burket. Conde Nast Pubns., Inc., 420 Lexington Ave., New York, N.Y. 10017. Illus., adv. Circ: 1,293,000. Microform: UM.

Indexed: RG. *Aud:* Ga. *Rv:* M. *Jv:* B.

A guide to the ultimate in luxurious living in which the decorating arts predominate. Beautiful photographs, artistically presented, should inspire students and general readers. Articles feature analysis of homes by leading architects and decorators. The editorial policy dictates that ideas for homes and hobbies fit the personality. A few pages are devoted to music and travel and each issue features a cookbook section. Suggestions are directed toward those with a cultivated interest in fine homes, furnishings and decor. Although geared for the upper income groups, the magazine has a value for any reader with imagination and the ability to adapt expensive ideas to a modest home, or checkbook. Depending on the reader's philosophy of life and his income, it may be more useful than *Better Homes and Gardens,* but for most libraries it would be a second choice.

House Beautiful. 1896. m. $6. Sara Lee. Hearst Corp., 250 W. 55th St., New York, N.Y. 10019. Illus., adv. Circ: 862,227.

Indexed: RG. *Aud:* Ga. *Rv:* L. *Jv:* B.

A close competitor for the same audience as *House and Garden,* this is designed for those who can afford and enjoy the "good life." Colorfully illustrated articles supply ideas concerning designing and building new homes, remodeling old ones, decorating in the modern and traditional styles. Landscaping, gardening, home furnishings and accessories, gourmet cooking, menu planning, travel and entertainment are all discussed. Ideas and plans offered are seldom original; usually they are copies of work done for some famous celebrity or wealthy personality. The magazine is noted for its extensive offering of purchasing sources and prices of unusual items. The "Decorator's Diary," a regular feature, offers some useful and new ideas and techniques in home decoration and care. Similar to *House and Garden,* and the choice between the two is a matter of personal preference.

Journal of Consumer Affairs. 1967. semi-ann. $6 (Includes subscription to the *CCI Newsletter*). Gordon E. Bivens. Council on Consumer Information, Gwynn Hall, University of Missouri, Columbia, Mo. 65201. Illus., adv. Circ: 1,100.

Bk. rev: 8–10, 500–1000 words, signed. *Aud:* Ga, Ac. *Rv:* H. *Jv:* B.

Devoted to "the dissemination of research results on consumer education, protection and public issues affecting the consumer." Directed to the teacher, sudent, and, to a degree, the interested layman. The 150 pages are divided among five or six articles, shorter pieces and news-notes, and book reviews. Written by professors of sociology, business, home economics, etc., the articles vary from technical to relatively easily understood overviews of everything from wages, food prices and financing to trading stamps. The discussions are both practical and theoretical. The objective treatment of matters concerning almost every American product give it an added dimension for the lay reader who wants to go beyond the standard *Consumer Reports* or *Consumer Bulletin*. A good bet for all academic libraries, and a number of public libraries.

Journal of Home Economics. 1909. m. $10. Ruthanna Russel. Amer. Home Economics Assn., 1600 20th St., N.W., Washington, D.C. 20009. Illus., index, adv. Circ: 30,374.

Indexed: BioAb, ChemAb, EdI, PAIS. *Bk. rev:* 3–6, 100–250 words, signed. *Aud:* Ac, Jc, Ht. *Rv:* H. *Jv:* A.

As the official organ of the American Home Economics Association, this journal assumes responsibility for stressing new trends in home economics curricula at both the secondary and college level. The six to eleven articles, often based on research, also offer "newest developments in family relations and child development, family economics—home management, housing, furnishings, and equipment, food and nutrition, institution administration and textiles and clothing. A valuable reference tool is the annual listing in the March issue of "Titles of Theses in Home Economics and Related Fields" for the preceding academic year. Notes on booklets, bulletins, and films are informative, not critical. A publication of major importance for anyone concerned with home economy in education, business, extension, health and welfare, and homemaking.

Pool 'N Patio. 1961. semi-ann. Free. Faye Coupe. General Pubns. Ltd., 3923 W. 6th St., Los Angeles, Calif. 90005. Circ: 100,000.

Aud: Ga. *Rv:* M. *Jv:* B.

A free publication (formerly known as *California Pool*), which is edited for pool owners in all parts of the country, not just California. The average issue features articles on how to care for the pool, landscaping methods for enlarging an existing facility or planning for a new one, types of entertainment and parties to build around a pool, and usually one or two items on water safety. A regular feature gives non-evaluative advice on new products. Meant to be given out by pool dealers, the magazine has considerable value and interest for libraries where the outdoor sport is popular. As it is free, all public libraries should try it, and certainly many pool owners will be grateful to learn about the magazine.

Workbench. 1957. bi-m. $2. Modern Handcraft Inc., 4251 Pennsylvania Ave., Kansas City, Mo. 42111. Illus., adv. Circ: 300,000.

Aud: Ga, Sh. *Rv:* L. *Jv:* B.

This is for the do-it-yourself fan who wishes illustrated, explicit instructions on how to build everything from a bird house to an addition to the family mansion. There are numerous tips on home improvement, often tied in with the advertisements. The style of writing is pleasant, clear and quite understandable for the high school student interested in crafts and carpentry. A good second choice after *The Family Handyman*.

INDEXES AND ABSTRACTING SERVICES

There is no single index or abstracting service which meets the need of every library. A glance at the Library of Congress' *A Guide to the World's Abstracting and Indexing Services in Science and Technology* (Washington, D.C., 1963. 183p.) will indicate the scope of the services available. The bibliography lists 1,855 titles from 40 countries. And that was several years ago.

What follows, then, is highly selective. It is composed of indexes and abstracts which most frequently are cited as listing the magazines included in this work.

It is, of course, difficult to recommend one or more indexes for all libraries, but for certain types and sizes of libraries a suggested *minimum* list by title follows. Titles are listed in order of preference:

A. PUBLIC LIBRARIES

(1) Small

Readers' Guide to Periodical Literature, RG; *Subject Index to Children's Magazines*, IChildMags.

(2) Medium

RG, and *Social Sciences and Humanities Index*, SSHum; IChildMags, *Public Affairs Information Service. Bulletin*, PAIS; *New York Times Index*.

(3) Medium to Large

RG, SSHum, IChildMags, PAIS, and *New York Times Index*. One or more subject indexes in fields of interest to the greatest number of users, i.e., *Biological and Agricultural Index, Business Periodicals Index*, etc.

Note: Canadian libraries would first take the *Canadian Periodical Index* if the body of the magazine collection was made up of Canadian periodicals. Ideally, the small and medium Canadian library would include both the *Canadian Periodical Index* and the *Readers' Guide*. The *Abridged Readers' Guide* is not recommended for any library. See annotation.

B. SCHOOL LIBRARIES

(1) Elementary

Readers' Guide to Periodical Literature, RG, *Education Index*, EdI; *Subject Index to Children's Magazines*, IChildMags.

(2) Secondary

RG, EdI, and, *Social Sciences and Humanities Index,* SSHum. And, various subject indexes in fields associated with the curriculum and needs of students and teachers.

(3) Larger secondary schools

RG, EdI, SSHum, and, *Public Affairs Information Service. Bulletin,* PAIS; *New York Times Index.* Subject indexes in field allied to the curriculum and needs of teachers and the students.

C. JUNIOR COLLEGE LIBRARIES

Here the list would be the same as for the "Medium to Large" public libraries (see A3), but with a notable exception. More emphasis should be placed upon subject indexes in fields allied to the subject areas of the college.

D. COLLEGES AND UNIVERSITIES

No list is possible. The only rule here is to include as many indexing and abstracting services as needed.

It cannot be stressed too much that even where a library lacks the magazines indexed or abstracted, the index or abstract serves a worthwhile purpose. It indicates to the user what is available to him for his particular interests. And in this day of cooperation among local, county, state and national networks of libraries, the index or abstract is often the only key the user has to materials which may be readily available to him for the asking.

Finally, simply because a magazine is not indexed is no reason to dismiss it from consideration. This is particularly true if it is not found in that basic war horse, the *Readers' Guide to Periodical Literature.*

Many magazines serve the casual reader in that they introduce him to new ideas, concepts and personalities. Having "fugitive" magazines available, even if not indexed, will frequently meet the objectives of the library.

ABC Pol Sci (*Advance Bibliography of Contents: Political Science and Government.* 1969. 8/yr. $6.50. (Institutions, according to size of book fund, $30 to $50). Lloyd Garrison. ABC-CLIO Inc., Rivera Campus, 2010 Alameda Padre Serra, Santa Barbara, Calif. 93103.

The publishers of *Historical Abstracts* and *America: History and Life* offer a simple presentation of tables of contents from some 260 journals in political science and government. Arrangement is alphabetical, by journal title, with an author index. Early issues are limited in use for lack of a subject index, but this is promised on an annual (and eventually an issue-by-issue) basis. The subject index failure accounts for not including this index in the listings of political science journals in the present work. Also, there is some questions as to the validity of such a difference in price for libraries and individuals.

Abridged Readers' Guide to Periodical Literature. 1935. m. (except June, July, Aug.). $11. Zada Limerick. H. W. Wilson Co., 950 Univ. Ave., Bronx, N.Y. 10452. Circ: 19,960.

A cutdown version of the *Readers' Guide to Periodical Literature.* Indexes 40 magazines, all of which appear in the larger version. Although the price is less than one-half that of unabridged work, it is not recommended. With the increase in duplicating services, inter-library loans and cooperation between libraries, the user should have access to the full index. Magazines not carried by the library may be borrowed or, at best, the user may find the material he needs and go to a larger library. See also, *Readers' Guide to Periodical Literature.*

Abstracts for Social Workers. 1965. q. $10. National Assn. of Social Workers, 49 Sheridan Ave., Albany, N.Y. 12210.

Classified arrangement of abstracts of articles in social work and allied areas. Author and subject indexes.

Abstracts of English Studies. 1958. 10/yr (Sept.–June). $7. National Council of Teachers of English, 508 S. 6th St., Champaign, Ill. 61820. Circ: 3,422.

Abstracts articles on English and American literature from some 300 journals. Journals employed have varied over the years, but the index is particularly useful as it often abstracts items from periodicals not often associated with English studies. Issue and annual subject index. A primary reference aid for larger junior college and all academic libraries.

Abstracts of North American Geology. 1966. m. $5. Geological Survey, U.S. Dept. of the Interior. Subscriptions to: Supt. of Documents, U.S. Govt. Printing Office, Washington, D.C. 20402.

Covering the significant literature concerned with the geology of North America, including Greenland, West Indies, Hawaii, Guam, and U.S. island possessions, this publication also incorporates books and citations of maps, as well as technical papers. Journal references are usually culled from domestic publications, although some foreign work is cited if the papers are of a general nature. Entries are arranged alphabetically by author, and each issue contains a subject index. Necessary for any geology collection.

Abstracts of Photographic Science & Engineering Literature. 1962. m. $200 ($40 to educational institutions & public libraries). Kevin R. Gilson. Soc. of Photographic Scientists & Engineers, c/o Engineering Index, Inc., 345 E. 47th St., New York, N.Y. 10017.

Aud: Sa, Ac. *Rv:* H. *Jv:* B.

Abstracts the significant technical literature related to photography, including its physics and chemistry, photographic theory and materials, photographic apparatus, and applied photography. Over 3,000 informative abstracts are published annually, and over 300 international journals are screened. The literature covered is predominantly from periodicals and patents. Entries are arranged under four broad classifications subdivided by a large number of specific subject headings. In addition to full bibliographic citation, each entry contains descriptors which further delineate the subject matter. Cross references appear under each classification. Each issue contains an author and patent index; an annual index is issued with each volume, but multivolume indexes must be purchased separately. Academic and special libraries concentrating in this field will need both this and the older *Photographic Abstracts*.

America: History and Life; a guide to periodical literature. 1964. q. Price based on annual book fund of library ($35–$115). Eric H. Boehm. Amer. Bibliographical Center, Clio Press, 2010 Alameda Padre Sierra, Santa Barbara, Calif. 93103. Circ: 1,250.

Abstracts from some 650 American and Canadian periodicals and 950 foreign periodicals cover all aspects of the nation's history and life from earliest times to current events. Arrangement is classified: "North America;" "Canada;" "U.S. to 1745;" "U.S. 1945 to Present;" "U.S. Regional, State and Local History;" "History, the Humanities and Social Sciences." There are annual subject and personal name indexes. A major reference aid for larger public and academic libraries. See also, *Historical Abstracts*.

Applied Mechanics Reviews. 1947. m. $80. S. Juhasz. Amer. Soc. of Mechanical Engineers, 345 E. 47th St., New York, N.Y. 10017. Circ: 5,000. Microform: UM. Reprint: Johnson.

The Society's excellent review and abstracting journal provides coverage of the international literature on applied mechanics and allied sciences, as culled from over 900 engineering periodicals. Fields incorporated within the scope of the publication are not only mechanical engineering, but extend to aerospace, chemical, and civil engineering, as well as applied mathematics. Each issue contains one short survey paper reporting on research of timely and widespread interest. The reviews themselves are, on the average, lengthy, critical, signed, and include books and reports, as well as periodicals.

Applied Science and Technology Index; a cumulative subject index to periodicals in the fields of aeronautics, automation, chemistry, construction, electricity and electronics. 1913. m. Elsa Toom. Service basis. H. W. Wilson Co., 950 Univ. Ave., Bronx, N.Y. 10452. Circ: 3,887.

Following the format and policies of the other Wilson indexes, the publication screens some 160 periodicals in all the engineering and applied sciences, and includes articles, books and pamphlets. Coverage is largely U.S., with much of the material of a semi-technical or general nature. Entries are arranged under alphabetical subject headings; only a

bibliographic citation is provided. Cumulative indexes are issued every three months, as well as in an annual bound volume. Would be a first-choice selection for libraries needing some index to the technical literature, yet not requiring the exhaustive bibliographic control supplied by the more sophisticated abstracting journals.

Art Index; a cumulative author and subject index to fine arts periodicals and museum bulletins covering archaeology, architecture, arts and crafts, ceramics, decorations and ornaments. 1929. q. Service. Mary Schmidt. H. W. Wilson Co., 950 Univ. Ave., Bronx, N.Y. 10452. Circ: 1,412.

Author-subject index which analyzes contents of 110 periodicals and museum bulletins. Coverage is international and wider than the title indicates. A basic reference aid in all university, college, junior college, and medium to large high school and public libraries.

Avery Index to Architectural Periodicals. 1963. a. $65. G. K. Hall & Co., 70 Lincoln St., Boston, Mass. 02111.

Since the publication of the 12-volume set in 1963 ($745), there have been annual supplements. Indexes all major architectural periodicals found in the Columbia University Avery Architectural Library. Particularly useful as it includes other major disciplines: art, furniture, city planning, landscape architecture, etc. Should be purchased by any large library interested in the arts, if only to supplement the *Art Index*.

Bibliography and Index of Geology Exclusive of North America. m. $150. Geological Soc. of America (pub. in cooperation with Amer. Geological Inst.), Colorado Bldg., P.O. Box 1719, Boulder, Colo. 80302. Index.

Formerly an annual, and now issued as a monthly abstract journal, the *Bibliography* covers the geological literature of South America, Europe, Asia, Africa, Australia, Iceland, and islands of the eastern Atlantic and Western Pacific. (Its complement is *Abstracts of North American Geology*.) Literature by foreign scientists is included regardless of place of publication, and some general geological papers published in foreign journals are also cited, regardless of the authors' nationalities. Entries are grouped by field of interest. In the case of foreign titles, an English translation follows the original language. Each issue contains its own subject-author index; a two-part annual index includes a listing of all citations by author, and a comprehensive subject index referring to these citations.

Biography Index; a quarterly index to biographical material in books and magazines. 1946. q. $20. H. W. Wilson Co., 950 Univ. Ave., Bronx, N.Y. 10452. Circ: 5,302.

An index to biographical material in the some 1,600 magazines indexed elsewhere by Wilson; and collective biography and individual biographical volumes as published. Obituaries as reported in the *New York Times* are included. Each entry indicates illustrations, bibliographies, and portraits when they appear with the indexed piece. The whole is arranged alphabetically by name with a useful professions and occupations index. Quarterly issues are cumulated annually and then every three years.

Although considered reference sources issued serially rather than magazines, there are two basic biographical serials for all types and sizes of libraries. (No magazine *per se* is given over solely to biography, geneological magazines excepted.)

Current Biography. (1940. m. (Sept.–July). $8. H. W. Wilson Co.) The monthly issues, cumulated annually and sold as separate *Yearbooks* for $8.00, include some 30 to 40 biographies of approximately two pages each. An effort is made to feature personalities from all walks of life who are currently in the news. The sketches are objective, usually in a style within the grasp of anyone from junior high school to an adult. Basic data for each entry includes sources of information, pronunciation of the name, date of birth, occupation, and address. The whole is arranged alphabetically with an index by occupation.

Contemporary Authors. (1962. semi-ann. $25. Gale Research Co., Book Tower, Detroit, Mich. 48226.) Brief sketches of some 2,000 authors a year in almost every field from technical books to fiction. In addition to background information the work includes: a list of writings completed, works in progress, and other biographical sources where available. In view of its wide scope it often is the single source for information about a little known, or new writer. Should be found in all libraries from junior high through university.

Biological Abstracts; reporting the world's biological research literature. 1926. semi-m. $340 to qualified personnel; $600 to others (cumulative index $160–$200; not included in subscription). P. V. Parkins. 2,100 Arch St., Philadelphia, Pa. 19104.

As the major abstracting service for the biological sciences, the publication also includes coverage of the literature in agriculture and basic medicine. Approximately 7,400 serials, as well as books, government reports, and symposia, are screened annually to produce 130,000 abstracts. Entries are arranged under broad subject headings, with many subdivisions; most abstracts are informative. Titles of foreign references appear in translation, followed by the title in its original language.

In addition to an author index and list of subject headings employed, each issue contains two other indexes. A "Biosystematic Index" coordinates abstracts under lists of taxonomic categories. Following the name of the organism, additional abbreviated notations (based on the subject headings) appear; these terms delineate the exact nature of the study. A "CROSS Index" (Computer Rearrangement of Subject Specialties, comprises an alphabetical list of subject headings under which pertinent abstract numbers have been posted in 10 columns (location determined by the last digit of the abstract number). Since most entries appear under as many subject headings as are necessary, this index is used as a coordinating tool (particularly in combination with the "Biosystematic Index") to locate subject material as broadly or as narrowly required, by comparing abstract numbers. All indexes are composed by computer.

The main subject index to *Biological Abstracts* is *B.A.S.I.C.* (*Biological Abstracts Subjects In Context*), issued semimonthly as another publication. *B.A.S.I.C.* consists of a computer-produced keyword-in-context index, arranged alphabetically, and includes additional subject words both preceding and following the keyword.

The total subscription price to *Biological Abstracts* (with *B.A.S.I.C.*) includes a third publication, *BioResearch Index,* which provides, annually, rapid access to some 84,000 research papers not covered in *Biological Abstracts*. Each citation appears in an alphabetically permuted subject index, includes editorially expanded titles, and uses the same subject terminology as that employed in the other indexes. Issues also contain an author index and a bibliographic section which publishes the title of each journal and its table of contents.

Cumulative indexes to *Biological Abstracts* (incl. *B.A.S.I.C.*, "Biosystematic Index," "CROSS," and *BioResearch Indexes*) must be purchased separately ($200 annually). Sections of *Biological Abstracts, B.A.S.I.C.,* and *BioResearch Indexes* can be purchased as individual items.

The BioSciences Information Services of *Biological Abstracts* also supply several custom-searching services.

Biological and Agricultural Index. 1916. m. (except Sept.). Service basis. H. W. Wilson Co., 950 Univ. Ave., Bronx, N.Y. 10452. Circ: 943.

A subject index to approximately 148 magazines. While many of the periodicals are highly specialized, a number in the areas of agriculture, biology, botany, forestry and conservation, nutrition and soil sciences have a wider appeal. Recommended where the subject matter is an important part of the curriculum or the library is in a predominantly agrarian area. May be used profitably by large high school libraries.

Book Review Digest. 1905. m. (except Feb. & July). Service basis. H. W. Wilson Co., 950 Univ. Ave., Bronx, N.Y. 10452. Circ: 12,639.

An index to reviews which have appeared in some 70 English and American periodicals. Arranged alphabetically by author with subject and title index. Cumulated annually, and every five years there is a cumulated index. Probably more important for most libraries, the index includes excerpts from enough reviews to give a balanced opinion of the book. Approximately 5,000 titles—primarily of a general nature—are listed each year. As the United States alone is now publishing over 25,000 titles a year, the index is highly selective. For a wider approach, larger and specialized public and academic libraries will also want the *Book Review Index*.

Book Review Index. 1965. m. $24. Gale Research Co., Book Tower, Detroit, Mich. 48226.

Indexes some 80,000 reviews of approximately 40,000 new titles each year. Unlike *Book Review Digest,* it does not include excerpts from the review, but stresses source of the review—a major difference, and of particular importance, as the number of reviews indexed is many times more than that found in *Book Review Digest.* Some 250 American, Canadian and British periodicals are indexed. There are cumulations every three months and annually. A basic index for larger public and academic libraries.

British Humanities Index. 1962. q. 204s. Library Assn., 7 Ridgmount St., Store St., London W.C.1.

This is somewhat equivalent in Britain to our *Readers' Guide to Periodical Literature.* The scope is now narrower than the earlier work, *Subject Index to Periodicals* (1915–1961), but the quarterly issues cover "all materials relating to the arts and politics." The quarterly numbers are by subject only, but there is an author index to the annual cumulations. Some 275 magazines are included.

British Technology Index; a current subject guide to articles in British technical journals. 1962. m. $65. E. J. Coates. Library Assn., 7 Ridgemount St., Store St., London W.C.1.

The Library Association's "current subject-guide to articles in British technical journals" consists of citations only, does not include an author index, and is restricted in coverage to over 275 selected periodicals published in England. (Many of the journals are international publications, however.) Within its framework are included all aspects of engineering and chemical technology, and related fields such as chemistry and physics. Entries (some 30,000 annually) are arranged under very detailed alphabetical subject headings; cross references are more than liberal. Because of its high degree of specificity, the *Index* is helpful for narrowing subject searches, particularly for articles which emphasize applications and processes. Its usefulness for U.S. libraries, with the exception of technical libraries, would, of course, be quite limited.

Business Periodicals Index; a cumulative subject index to the fields of accounting, advertising, banking & finance, general business, insurance, labor & management. 1958. m. (except July). Service basis. Lucille V. Craumer. H. W. Wilson Co., 950 Univ. Ave., Bronx, N.Y. 10452. Circ: 2,848.

A subject index to some 170 magazines in business and related fields, i.e., advertising and public relations, automation, economics, applied engineering etc. Because of its wide scope it is useful for considerably more than either business or economics.

Canadian Periodical Index. 1948. m. Rates on request. Canadian Library Assn., 63 Sparks St., Ottawa, 4, Ont.

The Canadian equivalent to the *Readers' Guide to Periodical Literature.* An earlier version (by the same name) ran from 1928 to 1947, when the name was changed to *Canadian Index to Periodicals and Documentary Films.* In 1964, the name was changed back to the current one. A subject index to some 90 Canadian magazines, many in French.

Catholic Periodical and Literature Index. 1930. q. Service basis. M. Richard Wilt. Catholic Library Assn., 461 W. Lancaster Ave., Haverford, Pa. 19041. Circ: 1,927.

Indexes some 200 periodicals published here and abroad. Subject coverage is universal, and in no way limited solely to theological interests. A good general index, even for the non-Catholic library.

Chemical Abstracts. 1907. bi-w. $700 to members, colleges and universities; others, $1,200. Fred A. Tate. Amer. Chemical Soc., 1155 16th St., N.W. Washington, D.C. 20036. Circ: 6,600. Microform: AMC.

Unquestionably, this is the world's most important abstracting journal. The publication now reviews some 12,000 journals, covering 50 languages, and patents from 25 countries, as well as books, conference proceedings, theses, and government reports. Moreover, the scope is not confined to chemistry, but extends to all the scientific and technical literature which includes some chemical or chemical engineering aspect in the study. The abstracts, numbering over 240,000 annually, are informative, rather than indicative; that is, they are extremely detailed and include actual data. Each issue of the journal contains (1) a keyword index, with entries derived from both titles and text; (2) a patent index and concordance; and (3) an author index. Subject, author, patent indexes, concordance, formula, ring, and "HAIC" (Hetero-Atom-In-Context) indexes are issued twice annually. Collective indexes (decennial and quinquennial through 1966) may be purchased separately. Selective sections of the abstracts can be obtained, if the entire journal is not desired. The journal is also available in 16 mm. cartridge microfilm; in combination with a reader-printer, this medium is developing a fast and facile method for performing literature searches.

The Chemical Abstracts Service also provides other important reference tools and services. Computer-based current-awareness journals, covering special subject areas, are available. Magnetic tapes of the *Abstracts,* or special sections thereof, can be purchased. Custom computer searches will also be performed. An invaluable reference is the *List of Periodicals,* which provides a 60-year cumulative listing of the periodicals abstracted, including title changes, and locations of the journals in the world's major research libraries. In addition, CAS supplies a photocopying service of original Russian papers which are very often difficult to locate in U.S. libraries.

Another noteworthy publication from the Chemical Abstracts Service is *Chemical Titles* (1961. bi-w. $50.), a keyword and author index covering selected chemical journals. This bi-weekly picks significant research papers from roughly 650 chemical and chemical engineering journals, and a concordance to the papers is made by a keyword-in-context index. There are three points of access to the journal: (1) the keyword index arranged alphabetically; (2) a bibliographic listing of titles in the form of tables of contents, and (3) an author index. One of the unavoidable weaknesses in *Chemical Abstracts* has been the time lag between date of publication of a paper in a journal and its subsequent appearance as an abstract. Inclusion of current papers in *Chemical Titles* is rapid, since many publishers submit advance copies of their tables of contents to the journal before publication. Magnetic tapes and custom computer searches of this journal are also available.

Child Development Abstracts and Bibliography. 1927. 3/yr. $10. Dale Harris. Univ. of Chicago Press, 5750 S. Ellis Ave., Chicago, Ill. 60637. Index. Circ: 2,127. Reprint: Kraus, Abrahams.

Another publication of the Society of Research in Child Development (see also, *Child Development*). Lists abstracts of articles which have appeared in psychological, educational, medical, and other kinds of journals which have any relationship to the study of children. Also includes notices of new books, pamphlets and periodicals in the field. An invaluable research tool for anyone involved in this field. Should be in all larger collections.

Christan Science Monitor Subject Index. See Newspapers Section (Appendix).

College Student Personnel Abstracts. 1965. q. $14. Jonathan R. Warren. 165 E. 10th St., Claremont, Calif. 91711. Circ: 1,700.

Abstracts of articles concerning college students and their problems, largely from the point of view of college administrators. Accent is on student services as housing and eating plans. It is broken up into general subject categories such as admissions, housing, campus organizations, sex behaviour, and so forth. Main entry within a category is alphabetical by title. There are also author and subject indexes.

Computer Abstracts. 1957. m. $96. B. A. Fancourt. Technical Information Co., Ltd., Martins Bank Chambers, P.O. Box 59, St. Heller, Jersey, British Channel Islands. Index. Reprint: Abrahams.

Over 3,000 abstracts covering the world literature on computing science (including applications to business, education, information retrieval) are produced annually by the journal. Abstracts, arranged by subject classification, incorporate books, patents, and U.S. government R&D reports, as well as journals. Pages are printed on one side to facilitate clipping. Each issue contains an author and patent index, followed by an annual subject-author-patent index.

Computing Reviews. 1960. m. $25. J. F. Lubin. Assn. for Computing Machinery, 211 E. 43rd St., New York, N.Y. 10017. Index. Circ: 30,000. Reprint: Abrahams.

The literature selected for review in this publication touches on every aspect of the computing sciences, as well as applications to the humanities, social and behavioral sciences, natural sciences, and engineering. Although the journal does not purport to supply complete coverage, its scope is international and it attempts to include much of the significant literature in the field. The reviews, ranging from one line to excellent, 1000-word annotations, are evaluative, signed, and incorporate journals, books, theses, conference proceedings, as well as some government reports. An annual computer-produced index includes an author index, index of reviewers, and a bibliography; subject approaches are provided by a permuted index and a classification scheme.

Documentation Abstracts. 1966. q. $25. (Special Libraries Assn. Members, $15). Amer. Documentation Inst., Amer. Chemical Soc., Special Libraries Assn., Documentation Abstracts, P.O. Box 9018, Southeast Station, Washington, D.C. 20003.

Takes in journals, books, conference proceedings, reports, and other publications. Coverage is worldwide, although primarily confined to works in English. Both technical and popular items are noted. Arrangement is by a classified scheme with author index. There is an annual, extensive subject index.

Education Index. 1929. m. (Sept.–June). Service basis. Julia Enrenreich. H. W. Wilson Co., 950 Univ. Ave., Bronx, N.Y. 10452. Circ: 3,994.

A subject approach to not only magazines, but yearbooks, bulletins and monographs in education. Covers the United States, Canada, and Great Britain. Every aspect of education from adult to international education is indexed, as well as from elementary grades through graduate study. An absolute necessity in any large public or college library, and highly desirable in the medium to large elementary school high school library.

Engineering Index; a guide to the current technological literature of the world. 1962. m. Price varies by sections. 345 E. 47th St., New York, N.Y. 10017.

Engineering Index is a major bibliographic tool for technical libraries and is available in several formats; all branches of engineering, as well as the applied sciences, are represented.

Engineering Index Monthly Bulletin ($350/yr; $250 to academic institutions) includes approximately 59,000 abstracts culled annually from 2,000 periodicals, books, reports, translations and patents. Access to the *Index* is either through alphabetically arranged subject fields (which comprise the body of the publication), under which are grouped pertinent abstracts, or through an author index supplied in each issue. Assignment of many subject headings and abundant cross references further assist the subject approach, but entries are not given a unique accession number, as is the case in many other abstracting journals. Foreign titles appear in the original language, but are not translated.

Annual, bound volumes, consisting of cumulations of the monthly indexes, can be purchased separately ($150/yr; $125 to academic institutions).

Electronics and plastics monthly bulletins, with computer-produced indexes, are also available as separate publications.

A weekly card service is also provided ($1500 for complete service; $750 to academic institutions). Approximately 60,000 abstract cards, which comprise the input to the monthly bulletins, are issued annually. Separate subject categories may be subscribed to individually. Magnetic tape services are offered as well.

Geophysical Abstracts. 1929. m. $7. Geological Survey, U.S. Dept. of Interior. Subscriptions to: Supt. of Documents, Govt. Printing Office, Washington, D.C. 20402.

Aud: Sa, Ac. *Rv:* H. *Jv:* B.

The journal specializes in abstracts of the literature related to the physics of the solid earth, geophysical exploration, and applications of techniques and physical methods to geophysics. Publications screened are largely books and technical papers; coverage is international. Entries are arranged by accession number under alphabetical subject headings. Each issue contains its own subject and author indexes, and an annual, cumulated index is issued at the end of each volume. Necessary for most academic libraries with collections in the earth sciences.

Historical Abstracts; bibliography of the world's periodical literature, 1775–1945. 1955. q. Service basis ($35–$115), based on annual book fund of subscribers. Eric H. Boehm. Amer. Bibliographical Center, Clio Press, 2010 Alameda Padre Serra, Santa Barbara, Calif. 93103. Circ: 1,450.

World wide in scope; covered U.S. and Canada prior to 1964, but thereafter both countries indexed in *America: History and Life* (see annotation). Arrangement is classified, and there is an annual subject, author and biographical index. Five year cumulations. An absolute necessity for any medium to large history collection, and an invaluable source of supporting materials for anyone working in allied disciplines.

Index Medicus. 1960. m. $63. National Library of Medicine, 8600 Rockville Pike, Bethesda, Md. Subscriptions to: Supt. of Documents, Govt. Printing Office, Washington, D.C. 20402.

Encompassing the world's biomedical literature, the Index is produced by the National Library of Medicine's MEDLARS (Medical Literature Analysis and Retrieval System), which is a computer-based system screening approximately 2,500 journals and consisting of about 175,000 citations annually. Computer-produced monthly issues consist of "Subject-Author" sections, which are the *Index* proper, and "Bibliography of Medical Reviews Subject-Author" sections, which represent surveys of the current biomedical literature. The scope of the journal is limited to the periodical literature; symposia, congresses, etc. are not included unless the proceedings have been published in the actual journals. If the reference is from a foreign journal, the title is translated into English in the subject section; under the author index, the title appears in its original language. An interesting feature is the grouping of citations by the original language of the text, with English appearing first, followed by other languages arranged alphabetically, and then arranged alphabetically by the journal in which they appear. The January issue contains "Medical Subject Headings," the subject authority list which controls the vocabulary and subject access to MEDLARS, and a complete list of journal titles. A cumulated *Index Medicus* may be purchased separately.

The MEDLARS system, and its regional centers, supplies many additional bibliographic services for researchers, including computer-produced literature searches.

Index to Commonwealth Little Magazines. 1964/1965. bi-ann. $7.50. Stephen H. Goode. Alan Swallow, Denver, Colo.

Similar in purpose to the *Index to Little Magazines.* Author-subject index to some 34 little magazines published in England and English Commonwealth countries. Eventually, the compiler intends to go back to 1900 in his indexing.

Index to Legal Periodicals. 1908. m. (Oct.–Aug.). Service basis. Mildred Russel. H. W. Wilson Co., 950 Univ. Ave., Bronx, N.Y. 10452. Circ: 1,800.

The basic law index to some 305 periodicals, journals of bar associations and journals of judicial councils. A three part arrangement; subject and author index, table of cases, and book reviews. Annual and three year cumulations.

Index to Little Magazines. 1948. ann. $7.50. Alan Swallow, Denver, Colo.

An author-subject approach to some 40 to 45 little magazines. Volumes now issued cover the period 1943 through 1965. (A retrospective index, 1943–1947, was issued in 1965). Hopefully the work will continue, although Alan Swallow's death makes the index's future uncertain.

Index to Periodical Articles By and About Negroes (Formerly: Index to Selected Periodicals). 1950. ann. $12. G. K. Hall & Co., 70 Lincoln St., Boston, Mass. 02111.

The only index which limits itself exclusively to what the title indicates. About 20 magazines are indexed, primarily by subject and author. The majority are not indexed elsewhere. A one-volume decennial cumulation for 1950–1959 is available ($35). An absolute necessity for any library serving a Negro population; and for the average college or university collection.

Index to Religious Periodical Literature. 1949. ann. $30. Amer. Theological Library Assn., Princeton, N.J. 08541.

Primarily a Protestant index, with a scattering of Jewish and Catholic periodicals. International in scope, analyzing some 105 magazines. Useful, too, for indexing in related fields, i.e., archaeology.

Information Processing Journal; a reference journal devoted to the theory, fabrication and application of computers. 1962. m. $60. Geoffrey Knight, Jr. Cambridge Communications Corp., 1612 K St., N.W., Washington, D.C. 20006. Circ: 826.

"Devoted to the theory, fabrication and application of computers," the journal provides abstracts of the literature on such topics as components, systems, logic, programming, mathematics, information theory, as well as applications to science, engineering, business, education, medicine, government, military. The abstracts cover periodicals, books, patents, government reports, and conference proceedings. The classification scheme is fairly elaborate, and cross references are abundant. Author-subject indexes are supplied in each issue, as well as at the end of the volume.

International Aerospace Abstracts. 1961. semi-m. $54. John J. Glennon. AIAA Technical Information Service, 750 Third Ave., New York, N.Y. 10017.

Sponsored by the American Institute of Aeronautics and Astronautics, this provides informative abstracts of the published literature related to the space sciences and technology, and aeronautics. Coverage is international and includes books, periodicals, proceedings of conferences, meeting papers, and translations. (Abstracts of the report literature are not included but are available in a companion publication, *Scientific and Technical Aerospace Reports,* published by NASA). Entries, carrying full bibliographic citations, are arranged by accession number under fairly broad subject categories. Each issue includes a subject index, through which cross references are effected, as well as personal author, contract number, meeting paper or report number, and accession number indexes. Cumulated indexes must be purchased separately ($30/yr). Since the coverage is very broad (including such basic sciences as chemistry, physics, mathematics, the life sciences), its usefulness should extend to many more libraries than those dealing solely or largely with the aerospace literature.

Journal of Economic Abstracts. 1963. q. $2. Littauer Center M-12, Harvard Univ., Cambridge, Mass. 02138.

A two-part abstracting service. The first section includes the contents pages of some 35 to 50 journals. Part two consists of the rather long abstracts arranged by subject. There is an annual author index. Only for large academic collection—the more popular economic journals are indexed in the standard indexes.

Library Literature; an author and subject index to selected material on library science and librarianship. 1933. q. Service basis. Jane Stevens. H. W. Wilson Co., 950 Univ. Ave., Bronx, N.Y. 10452. Circ: 1,853.

Close to 180 periodicals, concerned directly or indirectly with library science, are indexed. Also includes: films, film-strips, microcards, library school theses and "all books and pamphlets dealing with libraries and librarianship that come to the attention of the editor." Emphasis is on American publications, although major foreign works included. Only for library schools and large libraries.

Library Science Abstracts. 1950. q. $10. H. A. Whatley. Library Assn., Chaucer House, 7 Ridgmount St., Store St., London W.C.1. Circ: 1,700.

An excellent abstracting service for library schools and large libraries. Material is classified, and there is an annual author and subject index. Although prepared in England, the coverage is international and the editor examines a good number of American books, pamphlets, periodicals and reports.

London Times Index. See Newspapers Section (Appendix).

Mathematical Reviews; a reviewing journal covering the world literature of mathematical research. 1940. m. $290. Ed bd. Amer. Mathematical Soc., P.O. Box 6248, Providence, R.I. 02904. Circ: 6,000.

Essential for any good mathematics collection, *Reviews* publishes abstracts and reviews of mathematical literature comprising nearly 1,200 journals and books, conference proceedings, and translations. Sponsored by some of the world's leading mathematical societies, the publication is international in scope and is the most comprehensive source for reviews in this field. Reviews are signed, critical, and range in length from short abstracts to excellent 1,000-word essays; many appear in French and German, as well as English. Entries are grouped under general subject headings, and an author index is provided for each issue. Cumulative author and subject heading indexes are published twice a year, but detailed subject indexes are not supplied.

Meteorological and Geoastrophysical Abstracts. 1950. m. $400. ($200 to education institutions and public libraries.) Malcolm Rigby. Amer. Meteorological Soc., 45 Beacon St., Boston, Mass. 02108.

Covering thoroughly the current literature directly concerned with the atmospheric sciences (meteorology, climatology, aeronomy, planetary atmospheres, solar-terrestrial relations), the journal includes, as well, selected abstracts of the literature from many related fields (e.g. aeronautical, astronomcial, earth and engineering sciences). Nearly 10,000 informative abstracts, culled annually from over 300 serials, cover, in addition to technical papers, some reports, conference proceedings, books, along with a very few theses, patents, and citations of maps. Each issue has an author and subject index, as well as an index of geographic locations. Annual, cumulative indexes are also published.

Music Index. 1949. m. $195. Florence Kretzschmar. Information Coordinators, Inc., 1435 Randolph St., Detroit, Mich. 48226. Circ: 600.

Indexes approximately 180 periodicals from all English speaking countries and 15 non-English speaking language nations. Entries from the latter are generally in the language of the country in which they originated. Author-subject approach, and includes obituaries, first performances and music reviews.

New York Times Index. See Newspapers Section (Appendix).

Nuclear Science Abstracts. 1948. semi-m. $42. U.S. AEC Div. of Technical Information, P.O. Box 62. Oak Ridge, Tenn. 37830. Subscriptions to: Supt. of Documents, Govt. Printing Office, Washington, D.C. 20402. Index. Circ: 7,500. Microform: Canner, Princeton, UM. Reprint: Johnson.

With the intent of providing comprehensive coverage of the world literature on nuclear science and technology, the abstract journal encompasses the following fields: chemistry, physics, earth sciences, life sciences, engineering, instrumentation, metallurgy. The periodical not only abstracts the technical report literature produced by research sponsored by the Atomic Energy Commission, but also pertinent reports of other government agencies, universities, and foreign research establishments. Books, journals, conference proceedings, and patents also fall within its scope. Entries are arranged by accession numbers under subject categories. Each issue contains corporate author, personal author, subject and report indexes; cumulative indexes must be purchased separately ($38/yr.).

Personnel Management Abstracts. 1955. q. $10. William H. Price. Bureau of Industrial Relations, Grad. Sch. of Business Admin., Univ. of Michigan, Ann Arbor, Mich. 48104. Illus., adv. Circ: 5,600.

An index to periodical literature in the areas of management, personnel policies, manpower, and industrial relations. Approximately 80 magazines are indexed, and there are 15 to 20 abstracts of current books.

The Philosopher's Index; an international index to philosophical periodicals. 1967. q. $8.50. Richard H. Lineback. Bowling Green Univ., Bowling Green, Ohio 43402.

A relatively new, badly needed index. Includes more than 80 American and a select number of foreign philosophical journals. A "Key-Word-In-Context" approach for subject and author.

Photographic Abstracts. 1921. bi-m. $20. Royal Photographic Soc. of Great Britain, Maddox House, Maddox St., London W.1. Circ: 850.

Arranged by the Universal Decimal Classification system with author, patent and subject index. Contains abstracts of the whole of the world's literature, including patents, on the science and technology of photography, and its numerous applications in industry, medicine and commerce.

Emphasis is placed on original material, and elementary articles on familiar topics are excluded. Not to be confused with *Abstracts of Photographic Science and Engineering Literature,* an American publication produced by the Society of Photographic Scientists and Engineers.

Poverty and Human Resources Abstracts. 1966. bi-m. $40. Louis A. Ferman, Univ. of Michigan, P.O. Box 1567, Ann Arbor, Mich. Circ: 1,200.

Published by the Institute of Labor and Industrial Relations, University of Michigan—Wayne State University. Each issue is in several sections. The first two are "Trend" and "Washington Notes." "Trend" is a single, long article dealing with some current questions on manpower, job training, the working poor, and so forth. "Washington Notes" deals with federal legislation, policies, and actions, on all departmental and agency levels. The "Abstracts" section is further divided into two sections, "Poverty" and "Manpower," and is subdivided within these sections along broad subject lines. Useful in college, university, and business libraries.

Public Affairs Information Service. Bulletin. 1915. w. (Sept.–July); fortnightly (Aug.). Weekly and cumulated *Bulletins* (5/yr.), $100; cumulated *Bulletins* including *Annual* $50; Annual cumulated *Bulletin,* $25. Robert S. Wilson. Public Affairs Information Service, Inc., 11 W. 40th St., New York, N.Y. 10018.

This side of the *Readers' Guide to Periodical Literature* and the *Social Sciences and Humanities Index,* this is the best basic index for most libraries. Given all three indexes, a library could answer all but the most esoteric questions. Indexes magazines, books, pamphlets, documents and other materials related to the social sciences, i.e., economics, political science, government, sociology etc. Libraries may purchase the weekly, monthly or annual service separately.

Psychological Abstracts. 1927. m. $30. Amer. Psychological Assn., Inc. 1200 17th St., N.W. Washington, D.C. 20036. Circ: 9,300.

New books and major periodical articles are listed here by subject. There is an author index for each monthly issue and a combined author-subject index for the annual volume. G. K. Hall issued a cumulative subject index for 1927–1960 in 1966 (2 vols., $650), and supplements are planned. The same company offers a cumulative author index. Because of the low price, and the extensive abstracting, which covers many related fields from education to zoology, this is an excellent abstracting service for even the medium sized non-specialized library.

Quarterly Check-list of Literary History; international index of current books, monographs, brochures and separates. 1958. q. $8.50. Amer. Bibliographic Service, Darien, Conn. 06820.

An author listing of books and monographs published on American, English, German and French literature.

There are no annotations, but complete bibliographical data is provided, including a list of publishers. The fourth issue of each year gives a cumulative author, translator, and editor index. While other than western language works are listed, emphasis is on material in these areas. An annual run covers some 1,000 titles, often not found in regular reviewing sources. The lack of annotations is a handicap for the novice, but the author approach makes the listing useful for the knowledgeable professor trying to keep up with his field. Should be found in all larger academic collections.

The American Bibliographic Service issues similar check lists in a variety of subjects: *Quarterly Check List of: Classical Studies* (1958. q. $6.); *Economics and Political Science* (1958. q. $8.50.); *Linguistics* (1958. q. $4.); *Medievalia* (1958. q. $7.); *Musicology* (1959. q. $4.); *Oriental Studies* (1959. q. $7.50); *Renaissance Studies* (1959. q. $4). The approach is similar in all, again with emphasis on western language books, and monographs.

Readers' Guide to Periodical Literature. 1900. semi-m. (Sept.–June), m. (July–Aug.). $28. Zada Limerick. H. W. Wilson Co., 950 Univ. Ave., Bronx, N.Y. 10452. Circ: 16,385.

The basic periodical index in any library. The author-subject approach to 158 magazines serves as the primary key to current materials for everyone from the elementary school student to the graduate student. Magazines are selected for indexing by librarians. Titles represent the best (and some of the worst) magazines published in America. Emphasis is on popular, consumer magazines. There is a decided de-emphasis on controversial materials, and the orientation is to middle-class tastes. While often hailed as a model of indexing (which it is), it is rarely criticized for its lack of imagination in selection. Unfortunately, as it often is the only index in a library, it is the basic periodical buying guide for librarians. To a point this is commendable, but any library seeking a broader range of interests and subjects must subscribe to other indexes. For a suitable rejoinder and justification of current selection policies see the explanation by Edwin B. Colburn, vice president of H. W. Wilson Company, in the Feb. 1, 1968 issue of *Library Journal*, p. 527.

Religious and Theological Abstracts. 1958. q. $12. 301 S. College St., Myerstown, Pa. 17067. Circ: 1,000.

International in scope, this is the basic abstracting service in the area. It is nonsectarian, and abstracts for Christian, Jewish and Muslim journals appear in language of publication. Author-subject biblical index. Six months to one year in arrears of indexing.

Science Abstracts. 1898. Institution of Electrical Engineers, Savoy Place, London W.C.2.

Originally issued in two sections (Series A & B, *Physics* and *Electrical & Electronics Abstracts,* respectively), the publication added a third section (Series C, *Computer and Control Abstracts*) in 1966. These are now part of the

INSPEC (Information Service in Physics, Electrotechnology and Control) publications, produced in cooperation with the American Institute of Physics, the Institute of Physics and Physical Society (London), the Institute of Electrical and Electronics Engineers (U.S.), the Institution of Electronic & Radio Engineers (London), and the International Federation of Automatic Control.

Series A: *Physics Abstracts* (1898. m. $192. Circ: 7,500). The major abstracting journal for physics; includes such overlapping fields as mathematical physics, physical chemistry, biophysics, geophysics, astrophysics. Some 50,000 abstracts are issued, screened annually from 1,000 of the world's journals.

Series B: *Electrical and Electronics Abstracts* (1898. m. $120. Circ: 4,000). Provides coverage of all branches of the electrical sciences and includes related fields such as engineering mathematics, aerospace and earth technology, computers. About 30,000 abstracts are published yearly.

Series C: *Computer and Control Abstracts* (1966. m. $60). ". . . . covers cybernetics, the electrical, electronics, mechanical, pneumatic, and hydraulic aspects of automatic control, computers, and all applications."

Entries in all issues of *Science Abstracts* are arranged under classified subject headings, delineated in a Table of Contents. Abstracts are usually informative, and include papers, books and conference proceedings. An alphabetical "Subject-Chapter Code Index" supplements the table of contents with more specific headings, and an alphabetical combined list of subject headings in *Science Abstracts* refers the user to related headings in other sections of the publication. Each issue also contains an author index. Cumulative subject-author indexes are issued for each volume; 5-year indexes are also available.

The following companion *INSPEC* publications are also issued to provide an even faster current-awareness service. *Current Papers in Physics,* published semimonthly, lists titles of significant research papers; *Current Papers in Electrical and Electronics Engineering,* a monthly, supplies important references in electrical engineering and electronics, and *Current Papers on Computers and Control* disseminates titles on new research in this field.

Science Citation Index. 1963. q. $1950. ($1250 to educational institutions). Eugene Garfield. Inst. for Scientific Information, 325 Chestnut St., Philadelphia, Pa. 19106.

The *SCI*, first initiated as an experimental project in the early sixties and sold on a regular subscription basis since 1963, has been described and discussed in the literature in elegant detail. Very briefly, it consists of the following. It is a computer-produced index, issued quarterly and cumulated annually, covering some 2,000 source journals in all the sciences, and cited U.S. and foreign patents. Divided into several parts, it includes the actual "Citation Index," arranged by author; lists of journals, which include breakdown by geography and subjects; "Corporate Index;" "Patent Index;" an index of anonymous titles; a "Source

Index," giving full bibliographic details, and a "Permuterm Index," which indexes titles by keywords in pairs.

The uniqueness of the *SCI,* as opposed to other retrieval systems, is that it is actually a list of references to which citations have been made during a particular time period. In other words, if, in searching for particular subject material, one knows an author working in the field or, even better, a key paper or review article on the subject, one consults the "Citation Index" under the author. Beneath his name, listed in chronological order, is each of his cited works, together with the citations that have referred to these works during that particular time span. Thus, if one continues to check these other citations by author, a cyclical process takes place, often with mushrooming results.

Of course, its other subject approach is through the "Permuterm Subject Index," an alphabetically arranged subject index which is derived from words appearing in the titles of source articles. Each significant word has been pre-coordinated with other terms to produce all possible permutations of pairs of terms.

The following is not a discussion of the multiplicity of approaches—history, concepts, methodology—for which the index can be used; nor of its coverage, which is multi-disciplinary, which includes the main research journals of every aspect of science and technology, and which lists over 3 million citations annually. Rather, this emphasizes its practical utility for a reference librarian. Since its cost is clearly a prohibitive factor, the SCI will hardly be a first-choice selection for a librarian whose reference work is minimal, and for whom the standard indexes are perfectly adequate. But if libraries are active in reference work, particularly in interdisciplinary fields, and if speed and currency of material are vital, the following points can be made.

(1) At some time or other, every librarian searches the literature backward by the citation principle; the SCI allows one to move *forward* in time. (2) In most cases, more than one abstracting journal or index must be consulted; the SCI, by coordinating references through its multidisciplinary approach, very often obviates this need. (3) Particularly when there is lack of familiarity with subject terminology, the SCI can eliminate gropings for synonyms, related terms, etc. (4) It provides a resume of one author's work (for what author does not cite his previous research?) (5) It supplies current references often before they have been included in the standard abstracting services. (6) Its pyramidal effect can be huge; relevancy of citations is large. (7) Most importantly, it can give a lead into the literature in a few minutes—the amount of time it takes to check an author's name and scan the column.

It seems evident, then, that this very clever and powerful bibliographic tool should be an absolute necessity in every academic institution and in every organization in which research is being conducted.

The Institute for Scientific Information also supplies the *SCI* on magnetic tape and provides other important publications and custom-alerting services. *ASCA (Auto-matic Subject Citation Alert)* a weekly service, gives citations based on user-profiles. *Current Contents,* available for the life, physical and chemical sciences, provides a weekly table of contents of pertinent journals. *Index Chemicus,* a weekly indexing-abstracting journal, contains graphic data on new chemical compounds which frequently have not yet been listed by other abstracting services.

Scientific and Technical Aerospace Reports (STAR). 1963. semi-m. $54. National Aeronautics and Space Admin., Scientific and Technical Information Div., Washington, D.C. 20546. Subscriptions to: Supt. of Documents, Govt. Printing Office, Washington, D.C. 20546.

The journal publishes abstracts of the report literature dealing with the broad field of space science and technology, and aeronautics. Coverage is worldwide and includes not only reports issued by NASA and its contractors, but also pertinent documents from other government agencies, universities, foreign research establishments, and the like. Thus, coverage may extend to some theses, translations, conference proceedings, etc. Informative abstracts are grouped under fairly general subject headings; a detailed subject index in each issue provides the necessary cross references. In addiiton to full bibliographic citation, entries contain a statement of the availability of the document to the public. Each issue contains personal author, corporate author, subject, contract number, report number and accession number indexes; cumulated indexes must be purchased separately ($30/yr). Necessary for any library dealing with the aerospace literature. A corollary publication providing abstracts of the published literature, i.e., books, journals, is *International Aerospace Abstracts,* issued by the American Institute of Aeronautics and Astronautics.

Social Sciences and Humanities Index (Formerly: *International Index*). 1907. q. Service basis. J. Doris Dart. H. W. Wilson Co., 950 Univ. Ave., Bronx, N.Y. 10452. Circ: 2,473.

Next to the *Readers' Guide to Periodical Literature,* this is the closest thing to a general periodical index. It should be included in most libraries because of its broad coverage— 206 English language periodicals—in many fields: "anthropology, archaeology, classical and area studies, economics, folklore, geography, history, language and literature, music, philosophy, political science, religion and theology, sociology and theatre arts, plus many periodicals of general scholarly interest."

Sociological Abstracts. 1952. 8/yr. Institutions and libraries, $100. (Individuals by special arrangement with professional societies only). Leo P. Chall. 2315 Broadway, New York, N.Y. 10024. Circ: 2,000.

Covers a wide range of sociological journals in a typical classified arrangement. The coverage is international in scope, but emphasis is on periodicals in the English language.

Subject Index to Children's Magazines. 1949. m. (except June and July). $9. Meribah Hazen. 310 Palomino Lane, Madison, Wis. 53705.

The only index devoted solely to children's magazines. (Primarily, but not exclusively, grades 1–8.) Some 50 magazines are analyzed under subject headings familiar to teachers and librarians, as well as most students. Titles range over those suitable for elementary through senior high school. Unfortunately, several of the magazines, including *Popular Mechanics, Popular Science,* etc., are also indexed in the *Readers' Guide to Periodical Literature.* Nevertheless, the index is an absolute must in any school, at least for elementary grades. For high schools the unabridged *Readers' Guide* is preferable.

U.S. Government Research & Development Reports. 1965. semi-m. $30. Clearinghouse for Federal Scientific and Technical Information, Springfield, Va. 22151.

The journal publishes abstracts of government-sponsored research and development reports, many of which are for sale to the public. The documents abstracted have been prepared under contract to the Dept. of Defense, Atomic Energy Commission, NASA, as well as other government agencies, and some foreign research establishments. Also incorporated are government-sponsored translations formerly announced in *Technical Translations* (no longer published). All aspects of science and technology are covered. Entries are arranged under subject categories; cross references in overlapping areas are liberal. In addition to bibliographic details and abstracts, information on availability and price of documents are also provided. Subject, personal and corporate author, contract and accession/report indexes appear in corresponding issues of *U.S. Government Research & Developments Reports Index,* which must be subscribed to separately ($22/yr). Quarterly and annual cumulative indexes are also available. (Note: Published for many years prior to 1965, the journal has undergone a series of title changes.)

Wall Street Journal Index. See Newspapers Section (Appendix).

JOURNALISM

Indexes and Abstracts

Business Periodicals Index, Canadian Periodical Index, Catholic Periodical and Literature Index, Psychological Abstracts, Public Affairs Information Service, Readers' Guide to Periodical Literature. (For annotations, see Indexes and Abstracts Section.)

Advertising Age. See Business Section.

American Press; the monthly feature magazine for newspaper management. 1882. m. $5. Edwin G. Schwenn. Michael & Ginsburg Publishing Co., 1215 Wilmette Ave., Wilmette, Ill. 60091. Illus., adv. Circ: 13,570.

Aud: Sa, Ac, Jc. *Rv:* M. *Jv:* B.

"The nation's only independent journal for the entire newspaper management," useful in journalism departments of colleges and universities. "Newspaper Production," a special interest section, is applicable to the smaller publishers. It includes two or three articles plus columns on "Offset and Photomechanics" and "Look at Letterpress." "Suburban Publisher" is a person-to-person account of one publisher's improvement or success story. Among the other departments are an "Idea Swapshop," "The Photojournalist," and a column by Don Robinson.

Canadian Author and Bookman. 1923. q. Membership (Non-members, $2.50). Gladys Taylor. Canadian Authors' Assn., Yorkville Public Library, 22 Yorkville Ave., Toronto 5, Ont. Adv. Circ: 1,200.

Indexed: CanI. *Bk. rev:* 3–5, short, signed. *Aud:* Ga, Ac, Jc, Sh. *Rv:* M. *Jv:* B.

The writer's magazine for the Canadian publishing trade, also the official organ of the Canadian Authors' Association. It incorporates the functions of literary magazine and gossip sheet with that of craft organ. Small and informal in format, the magazine offers articles on Canadian authors, Canadian literary trends, and literary and publishing history, as well as advice on writing and submitting manuscripts, and information on markets, contests, and prizes. Poetry and purely literary pieces, often by new authors, are featured.

Catholic Journalist. 1945. m. $3. James A. Doyle. Catholic Press Assn., 432 Park Ave. South, New York, N.Y. 10016. Illus., adv. Circ: 2,500.

Indexed: CathI. *Bk. rev:* 5–10, notes to 250 words. *Aud:* Ga, Ac, Jc. *Rv:* M. *Jv:* B.

Boasting close to 150 newspapers, 400 magazines and miscellaneous publications, the Catholic press in the United States is the largest for any religious group. And the growth rate continues to rise. Serving the editors and publishers of this large segment of the journalism world, *Catholic Journalist* emphasizes material which will help the key executive make a profitable thing of his enterprise. In a sense, then, this is a combination of *Editor & Publisher* and *Advertising Age.* The emphasis is on current news about publishing markets, how-to-do-it, and there is little of a scholarly or, for that matter, crusading nature. It is primarily a trade journal. Although the material is keyed to Catholic publications, much of it is applicable to all newspapers and magazines. The book reviews, which run from notes to longer pieces, cover both Catholic and lay titles for journalists and advertising men. Even in Catholic libraries, a much better general choice would be either *Journalism Quarterly* or the *Columbia Journalism Review.*

Columbia Journalism Review. 1962. q. $6. James Boylan, Grad. Sch. of Journalism, Columbia Univ., New York, N.Y. 10027. Illus. Circ: 8,260.

Indexed: PAIS. *Aud:* Ga, Ac, Jc, Sh. *Rv:* H. *Jv:* A.

One of the best magazines published for and by journalists. Articles deal with all aspects of the profession from reporting to broadcasting, and are for working members of the press, students, and laymen. It is particularly outstanding for review articles of specific magazines and newspapers. The style of writing is well within the range of the senior high school student and layman, and, more important, the crusading, objective reports should be of interest to anyone who picks up a daily newspaper or a magazine. From time to time the quarterly has taken on the "giants," and it features ongoing material on the failures of the press to accurately report given news stories. Since its inception it has become the conscience of the working press. In a word, a major magazine for most libraries, not simply journalism collections. It ranks as an equal to *Journalism Quarterly,* although the latter is of more interest to the professional and the scholar. In a general collection, the Columbia magazine would be a first choice; in a journalism collection, both would be required.

Columbia Scholastic Press Advisers Association. Bulletin. 1942. q. $1.50. Bryan Barker. Box 11, Low Library, Columbia Univ., New York, N.Y. 10027. Circ: 2,500.

Bk. rev: Various numbers, lengths. *Aud:* Sa, Ht, Et. *Rv:* H. *Jv:* B.

Primarily for high school and some elementary school teachers who teach journalism and direct the activities of the school paper and yearbook. A number of practical articles give advice, solve problems, suggest methods of improvement, both in the papers and in methods of teaching. Examples are usually cited, and case histories are common. Larger problems of censorship, the role of the school newspaper, etc., are considered. A basic teaching aid for all school libraries.

Editor & Publisher—The Fourth Estate; spot news and features about newspapers, advertisers & agencies. (Annual numbers: *International Year Book; Market Guide*). 1884. w. $8. Robert U. Brown. Editor & Publisher Co., 850 Third Ave., New York, N.Y. 10022. Illus., adv. Circ: 25,822. Microform: B&H.

Indexed: BusI. *Bk. rev:* Notes. *Aud:* Sa, Ac, Jc. *Rv:* H. *Jv:* B.

The newspaperman's trade journal, this weekly reports on all aspects of journalism from reporting to advertising. The behind-the-scenes stories of newspapers and personalities make it of value to both journalism students and informed laymen. Background stories about reporters and photographers, and articles on the sometimes difficult task of getting the news are well written. Editorials are short, pointed, and directed toward the improvement of newspapers and the reduction of abuses both by and of them. Regular features cover various areas: layout and design, the advertising, circulation, printing equipment, photography, syndicated features. As both a trade and a professionl journal, it is a required item in any journalism/advertising collection. The less specialized collection will turn first to the *Columbia Journalism Review* or *Journalism Quarterly.*

Gazette; international journal of the science of the press. 1955. q. $7. H. E. Stenfert Kroese N.V., Pieterskerkhof 38, Leiden, Netherlands. Illus., index, adv.

Indexed: PAIS. *Bk. rev:* Various numbers and lengths. *Aud:* Sa, Ac. *Rv:* M. *Jv:* B.

A scholarly journal devoted to the international press, and all aspects of communications. Its primary value for an American audience is the record of research it offers through good bibliographies, both separately published and with articles. Social scientists and psychologists will find it useful for the study of propaganda, in its various forms, which often makes up a good part of a particular issue. The magazine is published in English, French and German editions.

Journal of Advertising Research. See Business Section.

Journalism Quarterly; devoted to research in journalism and mass communications. 1924. q. $8. Edwin Emery, Sch. of Journalism, Univ. of Minnesota, Minneapolis, Minn. 55455. Illus., index, adv. Circ: 3,000. Microform: UM.

Indexed: PAIS, PsyAb. *Bk. rev:* 20–40, various lengths, signed. *Aud:* Sa, Ac, Jc, Ht. *Rv:* H. *Jv:* V.

Although of primary interest to journalists, the scope and purpose of the journal is much broader than the title implies. Scholarly articles are devoted to almost every aspect of communication from women's magazines to public opinion polls. Each of the contributions is well-documented, normally written in a fashion intelligible to any educated layman. There are, to be sure, pragmatic contributions on how to do this or that well, but the emphasis is on research and scholarship. The full book reviews are excellent, the best single source of information on new publications in every aspect of communications. In addition, there are selected bibliographies of articles, book lists, and summaries of major doctoral and master's theses. Research in progress, methods of teaching journalism, statistics on enrollment, etc., are included. In view of its broad field of interest, this is a magazine which should be found in all medium to large public and academic libraries.

Marketing/Communications. See Business Section.

Media/Decisions. See Business Section.

Media/Scope. See Business Section.

Nieman Reports. 1947. q. $3. Dwight E. Sargent. Soc. of Nieman Fellows, 77 Dunster St., Cambridge, Mass. 02138. Circ: 2,500.

Bk. rev: Various numbers and lengths. *Aud:* Sa, Ac. *Rv:* H. *Jv:* B.

A liberal, working journalist's point of view is reflected here. Nieman Fellows are selected for a year at Harvard on the basis of their education and achievements. Only a chosen few are picked each year, and the *Nieman Reports* represents the writings of both present and past Fellows. Every topic of interest to a journalist is covered, from propaganda and politics to the reporting of the arts and bathing beauty contests. The book reviews are some of the best available, and this side of *Journalism Quarterly,* offer the widest, fullest selection for the librarian or journalist. Another feature which makes it particularly useful for reference is the republishing of major statements on the press by national and international leaders.

Public Relations Journal. See Business Section.

Public Relations Quarterly. See Business Section.

Quill; a magazine for journalists. 1912. m. $5. Clarence O. Schlaver. Sigma Delta Chi, 35 E. Wacker Dr., Chicago, Ill. 60601. Illus., index, adv. Circ: 19,500. Microform: UM.

Bk. rev: 1–2, 300–500 words, notes, signed. *Aud:* Sa, Ac. *Rv:* M. *Jv:* B.

The publication of the honorary journalism society, Sigma Delta Chi, this features news of the organization and its members. It has wider interest in that there are frequently articles on the ethics of the press, censorship, biographies, advertising, radio, television, photography and free lance writing. Emphasis is on the philosophy that journalism is a profession, not simply a trade.

Quill and Scroll. 1926. q. $1.50. Quill and Scroll Soc., Sch. of Journalism, Univ. of Iowa, Iowa City, Iowa 52240. Illus., adv. Circ: 31,750.

Bk. rev: 3–4, short. *Aud:* Sh, Jh. *Rv:* M. *Jv:* B.

A junior edition of *Quill,* this concentrates on how to improve the high school newspaper and other publications. The other side of the magazine consists of news, biographies and reports of events in school newspapers and school publications throughout the country. Again, emphasis is as much on the ethics of journalism as on its practice. A must for any school where there is a publications program. While a first choice over *Scholastic Editor,* both should be purchased where there is more than a minimum journalism or publishing program in the high school.

Scholastic Editor. 1921. m. $5. Kathleen K. Leabo. Journalism Bldg., Univ. of Minnesota, Minneapolis, Minn. 55455. Illus., adv. Circ: 5,000.

Aud: Ac, Jc, Sh, Jh. *Rv:* H. *Jv:* B.

A how-to-do-it magazine for editors and teachers who have anything to do with school publications. Articles, usually derived from personal experience or the training of experts, tell how to put together newspapers, yearbooks, and magazines. Other articles give tips on how to succeed as a journalist or editor, methods of writing, markets and the like. While this processed magazine includes information at the college level, the primary emphasis is on the high school student effort. One of the few publications

geared at this level, it is one of the best for all journalism classes. See also, annotation for *Quill and Scroll.*

The Writer 1887. m. $6. A. S. Burack. The Writer, Inc., 8 Arlington St., Boston, Mass. 02116. Index, adv. Circ: 41,000. Microform: UM.

Indexed: RG. *Aud:* Ga, Ac, Jc, Sh. *Rv:* M. *Jv:* A.

America's oldest and most prominent writer's magazine, this features practical advice and instruction on how to get published. Six or eight 1,000–3,000 word articles by successful authors or editors tell how to write for publication. Some do's and don't's by such writers as Anya Seton, Ray Bradbury and B. J. Chute give advice in a most enjoyable manner, but waste no words and pull no punches. The market listing for manuscript sales is primarily for the magazine and book fields, and explains the type of material each wants, usual rates, etc. Each issue has a special market list devoted to a specific field, i.e., books, articles, fiction, fillers and short humor, poetry, and drama. The Writer, Inc., also publishes *The Writer's Handbook,* an annual collection of writing instructions and market listings, as well as books on all writing fields. One of the best general writer's magazines, this should be in libraries where there is any interest in the subject.

Writer's Forum; a new magazine for writers and literary enthusiasts. 1965. q. $4.75/12 issues. Newton Berry. Writer's Forum, Inc., 910 Riverside Dr., New York, N.Y. 10032. Illus., index, adv.

Aud: Ga, Ac, Jc, Sh. *Rv:* M. *Jv:* A.

A combination literary magazine and writer's magazine whose aim is to set standards for serious contemporary writing. It is intended primarily for authors. Articles examine literary figures, works, and trends by means of interviews, presentation of pieces of contemporary short fiction and accompanying commentary, and essays and features dealing with ideas and problems in contemporary work. Excerpts from works of past notable authors are also presented. Fiction, poetry, and music receive the major attention, with some articles on the drama. The magazine also publishes poetry.

LABOR AND INDUSTRIAL RELATIONS

Indexes and Abstracts

Business Periodicals Index, Public Affairs Information Service, Readers' Guide to Periodical Literature, Social Sciences and Humanities Index. (For annotations, see Indexes and Abstracts Section.)

The American Federationist; official monthly magazine of the American Federation of Labor and Congress of Industrial Organizations. 1894. m. $2. George Meany. AFL-CIO at the AFL-CIO Bldg., 815 16th St., N.W., Washington, D.C. 20006. Illus. Circ: 140,000.

Indexed: PAIS. *Bk. rev:* 1–2, lengthy, signed. *Aud:* Sa, Ac, Jc. *Rv:* M. *Jv:* A.

A small, 24- to 32-page attractive magazine, designed for the leadership levels of the trade union movement starting with the local shop steward and moving up through the ranks. Articles deal with various problems and issues confronting the trade unions, both here and abroad, covering a wide range of topics. Economic issues dominate, but it does not concern itself in any specific sense with working conditions, occupations, and the like. Sources are listed for pamphlets, films, and other information concerning Social Security, finance, voter registration and other contemporary issues. Only for larger collections. A much better title for general libraries is *American Labor Magazine*.

American Labor Magazine. 1968. m. $7. Jay Victor. ComCor, Inc., 101 W. 57th St., New York, N.Y. 10022. Illus., adv.

Aud: Sa, Ac, Jc, Sh. *Rv:* H. *Jv:* A.

The editors claim this to be the first independently published labor magazine: "There are two sides to every labor-management discussion. We're reporting labor's side. It's as simple as that." The format and approach is somewhat similar to such business oriented publications as *U.S. News and World Report,* but the orientation is definitely labor. The usual issue features five to eight articles on current items in the news, a profile of a personality, and regular departments such as "Labor Month," "Labor Indicators," and "Labor International." These latter, staccato-like features make it of particular value to the reference librarian. The writing style is good to excellent, the illustrations pertinent, and on the whole the authors are objective within their given direction. Deserves a place in almost all libraries, and certainly should be subscribed to as a balance to the standard business publications.

British Journal of Industrial Relations. 1963. 3/yr. $8. B. C. Roberts. London Sch. of Economics and Political Science, Houghton St., Aldych, London W.C.2. Illus., index, adv. Circ: 1,500.

Indexed: PAIS. *Bk. rev:* 15–20, short, signed. *Aud:* Sa, Ac. *Rv:* H. *Jv:* B.

A scholarly, theoretical British journal primarily for those involved in the academic side of labor and industrial relations, as well as labor and management leaders. Articles are primarily written by faculty members of British universities, although many are written by Americans, Canadians, and Australians. A "Chronicle" section gives first: statistical information about the business and labor picture in the United Kingdom, and then a listing of events such as strikes and government economic policy for a four-month period. Only for specialized collections.

Industrial and Labor Relations Review. 1947. q. $6. Robert H. Ferguson. New York State Sch. of Industrial and Labor Relations, Cornell Univ., Ithaca, N.Y. 14850. Illus., index, adv. Circ: 4,400. Microform: UM. Reprint: Kraus.

Indexed: BusI, PAIS. *Aud:* Sa, Ac. *Rv:* M. *Jv:* B.

This interdisciplinary journal in the field of industrial and labor relations publishes articles covering such topics as personnel administration, industrial sociology and psychology, labor economics, labor history and labor law. Approximately six articles appear in each issue, the vast majority being written by faculty members of various universities. Every number has a section on research, and occasionally there is a "Discussions" section, where current topics of interest are considered by leading experts, with a symposium of several essays written by the "pro's." Periodically a list of new books in the field is compiled by the library staff of the school. For the academic and professional leaders in the area of industrial relations.

Industrial Relations; a journal of economy and society. 1961. 3/yr. $4.50. George Strauss. Inst. of Industrial Relations, Univ. of California, Berkeley, Calif. 94720. Illus., index, adv. Circ: 2,500.

Indexed: PAIS. *Aud:* Sa, Ac, Jc. *Rv:* H. *Jv:* B.

An interdisciplinary approach to the social, political, legal and economic aspects of employment, labor relations and personnel management. Its tendency to rely on university contributors gives it a predominantly theoretical slant. Each issue contains a symposium on a special industrial relations problem of general interest and four or five 20-page articles. Typical symposium subjects have been: "British Incomes Policy," "Manpower Projections," "Labor Education" and "Work and Leisure in Modern Society." The broad approach and the highly literate quality of the contributors makes it of almost general business interest and especially good for students.

International Labour Review. 1921. m. $6. Intl. Labour Office, Geneva, Switzerland. Dist. in U.S. by ILO., 917 15th St., N.W., Washington, D.C., 20005. Circ: 5,000. Microform: UM.

Indexed: PAIS. SSHum. *Bk. rev:* 15, 100 words, signed. *Aud:* Sa, Ac. *Rv:* H. *Jv:* B.

Addressed particularly to students of social policy, whether in government, universities or industries. Published in English, French and Spanish, the articles cover every aspect of international labor. Current information about meetings of labor organizations, a bibliography section, and short book reviews are regular features.

Labor History. 1960. 3/yr. $5. Milton Cantor. Tamiment Inst., 7 E. 15th St., New York, N.Y. 10003. Adv. Circ: 1,400. Microform: UM. Reprint: Johnson.

Bk. Rev: 10, 100 words, signed. *Aud:* Sa, Ac. *Rv:* M. *Jv:* B.

Those interested in the history and development of the labor movement will find this well-written journal invaluable. Emphasis is international, and on both past and contemporary labor studies and social history. In addition to an average of six articles per issue, there often are bibliographies of periodical articles, and books. As one of the few journals that devotes itself exclusively to labor history, it should be a major consideration in history, business, and economics libraries.

Labour Monthly. 1921. m. R. Palme Dutt. Trinity Trust, 134 Ballards Lane, London N.3. Index, adv. Circ: 10,000. Reprint: Johnson.

Indexed: PAIS. *Bk. rev:* 3, various lengths, signed. *Aud:* Sa, Ac, Jc. *Rv:* M. *Jv:* B.

A readable British journal of opinion with generally Marxist leanings. The "Labour" in its title derives from the working class to whom it is directed. There are usually about five articles concerned with world and labor problems. In every issue there is a "Notes of the Month" section written by the editor, which gives his views on the British and international scene. There is a well-written, readable section that reviews the theatre, films, television, and the other arts. Its down-to-earth approach to international labor problems will assure it a wide readership among non-specialists and students who are seeking non-technical material in this field.

Monthly Labor Review. 1915. m. $7.50. Lawrence R. Klein. U.S. Bureau of Labor Statistics. Subscriptions to: Supt. of Documents, U.S. Govt. Printing Office, Washington, D.C. 20402. Index. Circ: 13,000. Reprint: Kraus.

Indexed: BusI, PAIS, RG. *Bk. rev:* 10, 350 words, signed. *Aud:* Ga, Ac, Jc, Sh. *Rv:* H. *Jv:* A.

Issued by the U.S. Bureau of Labor Statistics, this is an authoritative monthly record of various economic developments which have anything to do with labor. There are a number of articles on wages, unions, prices, building, labor practices, and the like. Regular departments discuss court decisions affecting labor, news in the field, a chronology of events, research in progress and objective book reviews. One invaluable feature is the 40-page statistical section. It covers the labor force, labor turnover, earnings, consumer and wholesale prices, work stoppages and job injuries. An extremely useful magazine for almost all libraries.

LAW

Indexes and Abstracts

Index to Legal Periodicals, Library Literature, Library Science Abstracts, Public Affairs Information Service, Social Sciences and Humanities Index. (For annotations, see Indexes and Abstracts Section.)

American Bar Association Journal. 1915. m. Membership (Non-members, $5). Richard Bentley. Amer. Bar Assn., 1155 E. 60th St., Chicago, Ill. 60637. Illus. Circ: 128,799. Microform: UM.

Indexed: LegPer, PAIS. *Bk. rev:* 5–10, various lengths, signed. *Aud:* Sa, Ac. *Rv:* M. *Jv:* B.

Directed to the practicing lawyer, this features sections on "Recent Supreme Court Decisions," "What's New in the Law," "Tax Notes," and abstracts of periodical articles, all of these geared to keeping the lawyer up-to-date. Contributions come from a wide range of professionals: lawyers, district attorneys, judges, insurance experts and law librarians and include recent messages from Hubert Humphrey and Lyndon B. Johnson. While primarily the lawyers' professional news medium, it has some broader appeal in such articles as: "The Legality of the United States Position in Vietnam," "The Developing Law for Outer Space," and "Toward a Supranational Law: The Common Market Experience."

American Journal of International Law. 1907. q. Membership (Non-members, $15). William W. Bishop, Jr. Amer. Soc. of Intl. Law, 2223 Massachusetts Ave., N.W., Washington, D.C. 20008. Illus., index, adv. Circ: 6,000. Reprint: Johnson. Microform: UM.

Indexed: LegPer, SSHum, PAIS. *Bk. rev:* 10–15 of approx. 600 words, signed. *Aud:* Sa, Ac. *Rv:* H. *Jv:* A.

A scholarly, yet readable journal on international law which is of value to anyone concerned with current worldwide problems in political science, economics and, of course, law. Articles have touched on: "The Lawfulness of Military Assistance to the Republic of Vietnam," and "Legal Aspects of the French Nuclear Tests." The book reviews are well-written and include a number of foreign publications. Of special importance are the sections devoted to publications of the United Nations, the United States, judicial decisions involving international law, and the contemporary practice of the United States in international legal matters.

American Journal of Legal History. 1957. q. $7.50. Erwin C. Surrency. Temple Univ. Sch. of Law, 1715 N. Broad St., Philadelphia, Pa. 19122. Circ: 675.

Indexed: LegPer. *Bk. rev:* 2–3, 500–1,500 words. *Aud:* Sa, Ac. *Rv:* M. *Jv:* B.

This claims to be the only journal in the English language which deals exclusively with legal history. As such it deserves a wider audience than lawyers, and should be in most large history collections. Articles cover every aspect of the law and the peripheral interests such as publishing, social aspects, literary works, personalities and the like. The style varies, but is usually scholarly, and most of the articles are well-documented.

Columbia Law Review. 1901. m. (Nov.–June). $9.50. Columbia Law Students, 435 W. 116th St., New York, N.Y. 10027.

Indexed: LegPer, PAIS. *Bk. rev:* 4–6, 350–750 words, signed. *Aud:* Sa, Ac. *Rv:* M. *Jv:* B.

Following the classic design of a review journal, there are two to three articles on current problems of interest; notes and comments which are really short articles; and a few, highly topical book reviews. The whole is written by both professors and lawyers, and much of the material in the notes section is of interest to those in related areas, e.g., articles on developments in censorship, advertising, proposed constitutional changes and the like. Law librarians consider this a must for any legal collection, and it has wider use in universities and colleges with strong political science departments.

Criminal Law Bulletin. 1964. m. $22. Neil Fabrikant. Criminal Law Bulletin Inc., 52 Vanderbilt Ave., New York, N.Y. 10017. Index.

Indexed: LegPer. *Aud:* Sa, Ac. *Rv:* H. *Jv:* B.

While written for lawyers and students, there is much here of interest to laymen dealing in areas of controversy. For example, articles touch on the war in Vietnam, e.g., "Permissible Dissent or Treason," and there is a full section given over to "Recent Decisions" which have wide effects in civic affairs. A "Criminal Law Bulletin Quiz" presents one or two model cases with suggestions as to where answers may be found.

Harvard Law Review. 1887. 8/yr. (Nov.–June). $10. Harvard Law Review Assn., Gannet House, Cambridge, Mass. 02138. Index, adv. Circ: 11,000.

Indexed: LegPer, PAIS. *Bk. rev:* 2–3, 1,000–2,000, 400 words, signed. *Aud:* Sa, Ac, Jc. *Rv:* H. *Jv:* A.

Besides being *the* scholarly publication for lawyers, this periodical covers legal aspects of problems of general interest to social scientists. Articles like "The Geneva Convention and the Treatment of Prisoners of War in Vietnam," "Neighborhood Law Offices: The New Wave in Legal Services for the Poor," "Firearms: Problems of Control," and "Law in Colonial New York: The Legal System of 1691" appeal to political scientists, sociologists and historians. The one or two main articles are often highly literate and exhaustive studies of almost monograph length and quality. Contributors such as Felix Frankfurter have lent it added prestige. Every university and many colleges should have it available for faculty and students.

The Journal of Criminal Law, Criminology and Police Science. 1910. q. $9. Fred C. Imbau. Williams & Wilkins Co., 428 E. Preston St., Baltimore, Md. 21202. Illus., index. Microform: UM.

Indexed: ChemAb, LegPer, PAIS, PsyAb. *Bk. rev:* 5–6, 1,000–2,500 words, signed. *Aud:* Sa, Ac, Jc. *Rv:* H. *Jv:* V.

An interdisciplinary journal of use to students, lawyers, criminologists and police officers. Emphasis is on court procedure, legal administration of evidence and protection of civil liberties. Articles such as "Closing Argument for the Defense," "The Informer Privilege," "Estimating Speed of a Motor Vehicle in a Collision," as well as abstracts of recent cases are of interest to the trial attorney. In a second section, the police science field is covered in such titles as "Detection and Identification of Ibogaine and Heroin," and "Specialized Photographic Techniques." The articles reflect the necessary cooperation required in modern criminal justice. Issued by the Northwestern University School of

Law, this is one of the best journals in the field and a first choice for larger collections.

Journal of Law and Economics. 1958. bi-ann. $5. Univ. of Chicago Law Sch., Univ. of Chicago Press, 5750 S. Ellis Ave., Chicago, Ill. 60637. Circ: 750.

Indexed: LegPer. *Aud:* Sa, Ac. *Rv:* H. *Jv:* B.

A journal of equal interest to economists, lawyers and students of business. The nine to twelve articles, written primarily by faculty, emphasize the legal aspects of both national and international economic issues, e.g., "Mergers and Public Policy in Great Britain," "Cookware: A Study in Vertical Integration." Each piece is well documented, interpretive and of considerable value for the specialist.

Journal of Legal Education. 1948. q. $10. Eugene F. Mooney. Univ. of Kentucky, School of Law Assn., Lexington, Ky. 40506. Circ: 5,000.

Indexed: LegPer. *Bk. rev:* 4–5, 500–1,000 words. *Aud:* Sa, Ac. *Rv:* M. *Jv:* B.

As the title implies, this is primarily for the law teacher, and is edited by professional legal educators. The articles are both specific and general, dealing with the problems of a law education and the process of law. A journal which is received as a matter of course by any university with a law program.

Law and Contemporary Problems. 1933. q. $10. Clark C. Havighurst. Duke Univ. Sch. of Law, Duke Station, Durham, N.C. 27706. Illus., adv. Circ: 1,850. Microform: UM.

Indexed: LegPer, PAIS, SSHum. *Aud:* Ga, Ac, Jc. *Rv:* H. *Jv:* A.

While technically a law periodical this is actually a series of symposiums on contemporary problems. Each issue covers a specific subject, e.g., "Antipoverty Programs," "Privacy," "Banking." Contributors tend to be economists, sociologists, and philosophy professors as well as law experts. Recent contributors include Hubert Humphrey; Terry Sanford, former governor of North Carolina; and Mitchell Ginsberg, Commissioner of Welfare for New York City. This is a must for college and university libraries and of importance to public libraries.

Law and Society Review. 1967. q. Membership ($12). Richard D. Schwartz. Sage Pubns., 275 Beverly Drive, S. Beverly Hills, Calif. 90212.

Indexed: LegPer. *Bk. rev:* 4–5, grouped, 7–8 pages, signed. *Aud:* Sa, Ac, Jc. *Rv:* M. *Jv:* B.

Differs from most law journals in that the editors attempt to stress the relationship between law and the social sciences. Issues have covered school segregation as seen from a lawyer's viewpoint and the same question as viewed by a sociologist, political scientist and educator. Other topics have touched on such varied subjects as speeding laws, witchcraft, and population control. Special bibliographies often are featured, e.g., a 28-page subject break-down of books and articles on law and society. In view of its broad scope, this will be of interest to students and teachers of the social sciences as well as law students.

Law Library Journal. 1908. q. $10. Richard C. Dahl. Amer. Assn. of Law Libraries, 53 W. Jackson Blvd., Chicago, Ill. 60604. Circ: 1,250.

Indexed: LibLit, LibSciAb, LegPer. *Bk. rev:* Various numbers. *Aud:* Sa, Ac. *Rv:* B. *Jv:* A.

The official journal of the American Association of Law Libraries, this is of a general enough nature to warrant inclusion in any library which has a small to medium-sized law collection, or an interest in the subject. Hence, its high rating—in this case as much for its applicability to many situations as for its intrinsic worth. In addition to the regular news of meetings, and members, it provides fair to good articles on the problems besetting the librarian. There are frequent bibliographies on selected subjects—and these are usually considerably better than some of the articles. A regular feature is a running check on current state reports, statutes and session laws. The bibliographic features insure a broader audience than the other more specialized journals.

Michigan Law Review. 1902. m. (Nov.–June). $9. Michigan Law Review Assn., Ann Arbor, Mich. 48105. Index, adv. Circ: 3,000.

Indexed: LegPer, PAIS. *Bk. rev:* 5, 4–8 pages, signed. *Aud:* Sa, Ac. *Rv:* H. *Jv:* B.

One of the basic law review journals, useful not only in law collections, but in libraries which have a strong interest in political science, economics and government. Each issue features scholarly articles, often in the form of a symposium, on all aspects of law and society. Some are frequently news, e.g., Stanley Siegel's suggestion for reorganization of the U.S. Post Office, and the "Symposium on Article V Convention Process." In addition to detailed book reviews there is a "Periodical Index," which arranges, by subject, articles from other major law reviews.

Yale Law Journal. 1891. 8/yr. (Nov.–Jan.; Mar.–Jul.). $10. William D. Iverson. Yale Law Journal Co., Inc. 127 Wall St., New Haven, Conn. 06520. Illus., index, adv. Circ: 4,000. Reprints: Fred B. Rothman Co. Microform: UM.

Indexed: PAIS. *Bk. rev:* 3–4, 2300 words, signed. *Aud:* Sa, Ac. *Rv:* H. *Jv:* B.

A legal journal of use to social scientists and scholars. Long articles (sometimes 100 pages) are devoted to topics of general interest, e.g. "International Law and the United States Role in Vietnam: A Reply," "National Economic Policy in an Interdependent World Economy," and "Government Housing Assistance to the Poor." It has an excellent policy of occasionally having more than one reviewer report on the same book. Book reviews are long and complete and often of general interest books, for example:

"Rush to Judgment" and "The Right to Bear Arms." A scholarly and literate addition for the college and university library.

LIBRARY PERIODICALS

Indexes and Abstracts

Business Periodicals Index, Canadian Periodical Index, Catholic Periodical and Literature Index, Documentation Abstracts, Education Index, Historical Abstracts, Library Literature, Library Science Abstracts, Public Affairs Information Service, Readers' Guide to Periodical Literature. (For annotations, see Indexes and Abstracts Section.)

The American Library Association issues 28 serials, some of which are mentioned in this section. However, for a complete, unannotated listing, see the *ALA Bulletin,* April, 1969 (p. 503).

A.L.A. Bulletin. 1907. m. (bi-m., July–Aug.). Members only. Gerald R. Shields. Amer. Library Assn., 50 E. Huron St., Chicago, Ill. 60611. Illus., adv. Microform: UM. Reprint: Johnson.

Indexed: EdI, LibLit, RG. *Aud:* Sa. *Rv:* M. *Jv:* B.

This is the librarian's own, and aside from trustees and interested laymen, the audience is purposefully selective. Its purpose is to report the official and semi-official activities of the Association's multiple divisions, sections, committees, sub-committees, and officers. It features topical articles, news items on personalities, legislation and equipment, an intellectual freedom column, a report from the Director, and a number of classified advertisements. As the official voice of the American Library Association, this has two major faults. First, it tends to mouth official opinion, which is quite often so solid as to be dense. Second, it tends to follow rather than innovate. The editor, of course, sits in the dragon's den, as do most editors of national association publications, and cannot be expected to exert any more independence than, say, the editor of *Pravda* or the *Peking Review.* Yet, there is hope. At this writing a new editor has been appointed who seems to be exerting a personality, a less than sanctimonious approach to ALA or libraries and librarians. He is not only covering official business—a quite legitimate task for a journal of this type—but is reaching out for innovative, imaginative articles on all aspects of librarianship. The format, never exciting, shows sign of improvement. Librarians tend to be hard on their own, and while in some ways this is commendable, let it be said that the *Bulletin* is no worse, and in fact, is better in many ways than a good number of other official association voices. For what it is supposed to do, it does well enough, and has promise of doing much better. Needless to add, it should be a major magazine in every librarian's own collection. *Every* cannot be overstressed. It is only for ALA members, and free at that. And every librarian should be a member.

APLA Bulletin. 1919. q. $3 (Institutions, $4). Subscriptions to: Pauline Home, Halifax Memorial Library, Halifax, Nova Scotia.

Indexed: LibLit, LibSciAb, CanI. *Aud:* Sa. *Rv:* M. *Jv:* B.

The official publication of the Atlantic Provinces Library Association, comprising Nova Scotia, New Brunswick, Prince Edward Island, Newfoundland. Emphasis is on activities of librarians in this area, but the articles tend to touch on material of interest to all librarians, regardless of location. The level of writing is high for this type of journal, the articles above average, and the editor includes items of value to all types of librarians. Some material in French.

ASLIB Proceedings. 1949. m. (Non-members, 90s). Assn. of Special Libraries and Information Bureaus, 3 Belgrave Sq., London S.W.1. Illus., index, adv. Circ: 3,500.

Indexed: LibLit, LibSciAb. *Bk. rev:* Notes. *Aud:* Sa, Ac, Jc. *Rv:* M. *Jv:* B.

This is the English counterpart of the American *Special Libraries.* As the official organ of the Association, it usually features two to three long, often illustrated articles on computers, documentation, indexing and bibliographic control. The style of writing is good to excellent, the contributors among the leaders in the field. Of particular value to Americans is the regular feature "Selections from the Recent Literature," an unannotated listing of books, pamphlets and articles of three to five pages.

The American Archivist. 1938. q. $10. Ken Munden. Soc. of Amer. Archivists, Wayne State Univ., Detroit, Mich. 48202. Reprint: Johnson.

Indexed: LibLit, LibSciAb, PAIS. *Bk. rev:* 10–12, 150–700 words, signed. *Aud:* Sa, Ac. *Rv:* H. *Jv:* B.

Two or three of the four annual issues of this official publication of the Society are usually turned over to special areas, e.g., automation in archives and manuscript collections, archives of the arts. Other issues feature six to ten articles on every aspect of archival librarianship from cataloging to collecting. While of limited interest to the generalist, it has high reference value for both the librarian and historian. Book reviews cover the art of the profession and reference works employed by archivists.

American Documentation. 1950. q. Membership (Non-members, $18.50). Arthur W. Elias. Amer. Documentation Inst., Information Science, 2000 P St., N.W., Washington, D.C. 20036. Illus., index, adv. Circ: 3,600. Microform: UM. Reprint: Kraus.

Indexed: ChemAb, LibLit, LibSciAb. *Bk. rev:* 5–10, 200–1000 words, signed. *Aud:* Sa, Ac. *Rv:* H. *Jv:* B.

The scholarly American journal devoted to documentation, broader in scope than the *Journal of Library Automation,* narrower in view than the English *Journal of Documentation.* The 10 to 15 articles are technical, written by subject experts and librarians, and presuppose considerable background in the field. The style varies, but the journal's primary value is that it encourages exploratory research and

philosophical queries considerably above the intellectual level of most magazines of this type. An absolute necessity for the large library, the library school, and the specialist.

Annual Report of the Librarian of Congress. 1866. q. $3. Library of Congress. Subscriptions to: Supt. of Documents, U.S. Govt. Printing Office, Washington, D.C. 20402.

Aud: Sa, Ac. *Rv:* H. *Jv:* B.

Although not precisely a magazine, this annual report is an invaluable serial for any type of library. As a summary of Library of Congress activities over the previous year, it covers all departments and areas, all new developments, in fact, anything which has a bearing upon present library practices. It is becoming increasingly important as the library slowly assumes more and more leadership in centralized cataloging, reference service, and the like. And while a good part of it is routine and dull enough, there are enough important facts and data to make it a reference point for librarians. Fortunately, it is well indexed and much of the superficial material may be avoided.

The Assistant Librarian. 1898. m. Membership (Non-members, $3.50). Tony Shearman. Assn. of Assistant Librarians, Central Library, Surrey St., Sheffield 1, Eng. Illus., index, adv. Circ: 11,000.

Indexed: LibLit, LibSciAb. *Bk. rev:* 4–7, 150–250 words, signed. *Aud:* Sa. *Rv:* M. *Jv:* B.

The official journal of the Association, a division of the English Library Association. The format is somewhat confusing, the contents a potpourri of ideas, suggestions and gripes by the younger members of the English library profession. It is a delight to read, primarily because unlike many similar American publications it takes a dim view of the establishment, is quick to chastise, and even quicker to shatter sacred ideas and notions. It should be required reading for all younger American librarians, and not a few older ones.

British Columbia Library Quarterly. 1937. Membership (Non-members, $5). Alan Woodland. British Columbia Library Assn., New Westminster Public Library, New Westminster, B.C. Illus., adv. Circ: 500. Microform: UM.

Indexed: CanI, LibLit, LibSciAb. *Bk. rev:* 5–8, 200–500 words, signed. *Aud:* Sa, Ac. *Rv:* M. *Jv:* B.

A superior local publication, this 40-page periodical includes two to three articles on Canadian libraries, literature and history. The signed book reviews offer an excellent source of information on Canada. Typographically, it is one of the best of its kind. A required item for all Canadian libraries, certainly for most large American collections.

CU Voice. 1965. irreg. Free. Allan Covici, Univ. Federation of Librarians, Berkeley Campus, Univ. of California. Subscriptions to: P.O. Box 997, Berkeley, Calif. 94701.

Aud: Sa. *Rv:* M. *Jv:* B.

An 8-page newsletter issued by the AFT (AFL-CIO) Local 1795 to bring news of union organizing to members and would-be members of the organization. Of more than passing interest because it is: well-edited and includes items of value to those outside of the California system; normally has one or two longer articles on issues confronting anyone involved with the library-union movement, and is satirically militant. In view of the increasing interest, pro and con, in the movement towards unions, it should appeal to both camps.

California Librarian. 1939. q. Membership (Non-members, $6.). Richard D. Johnson. California Library Assn., 1741 Solano Ave., Berkeley, Calif. 94707. Illus., index, adv.

Indexed: LibLit, LibSciAb. *Aud:* Sa, Ac, Jc. *Rv:* H. *Jv:* B.

Almost every state and regional library association published its own journal. The majority are suitable for local consumption, yet fairly poor in terms of returns for the general librarian or student. Among the exceptions is this publication of the California Library Association. While a given amount of each issue is given over to parochial news items, the majority of the five to six articles are of interest to any bibliographer or librarian. The writers are much above average and deal with everything from book collecting and printing to common problems and solutions in library administration. The format is outstanding. The California Association of Schools also publishes an excellent journal devoted to school libraries, *California School Libraries* (1929. q. $3). Among others of near equal quality which should be considered by larger libraries and library schools are: *Bay State Librarian* (1911. q. Non-members, $2); *The Bookmark* (1940. 10/yr. $1), a publication of the New York State Library, useful for its reviews; *Illinois Libraries* (1919. m. Free); *PNLA Quarterly* (1963. q. Non-members, $5), a publication of the Pacific Northwest Library Association; *Wisconsin Library Bulletin* (1905. bi-m. $). All libraries, of course, should subscribe to the local publication of the state association and/or state library. Most of these are indexed in *Library Literature*. Where other state or regional publications are considered, the *California Librarian* would be a first choice in the United States, the *British Columbia Library Quarterly* in Canada.

Call Number. 1967. m. Free. Don Draganski. Library Staff, Univ. of Illinois at Chicago Circle, Chicago, Ill. 60680.

Aud: Sa. *Rv:* H. *Jv:* B.

A mimeographed staff news letter which is much above average because of its editor, Don Draganski. He manages to take a traditional, usually dull enough form, and turn it into a useful, often imaginative and entertaining report on library activities broad enough in scope to be of value to many academic and public librarians. Aside from the usual notes on staff there is usually a major article on some aspect of librarianship, a suggestion box with answers, and a number of miscellaneous items on everything from reference to cataloging. In view of its non-existent price, certainly should be tried by many librarians.

Canadian Library; Canada's national library journal. 1944. bi-m. Membership (Non-members, $4). Elizabeth H. Morton. Canadian Library Assn., 63 Sparks St., Ottawa 4, Ont. Illus., adv. Circ: 4,000.

Indexed: CanI, LibLit, LibSciAb. *Aud:* Sa. *Rv:* M. *Jv:* B. 19041. Illus., adv. Microform: UM.

The Canadian counterpart of the *American Library Association Bulletin,* this has considerable more life, controversy, and downright good writing than its American cousin. There are the usual news items about the Association, and some six to ten articles on Canadian libraries and related areas of the profession. The "related areas" are of import to American librarians, particularly those dealing with the international aspects of the field. Pragmatic tips on how to run a library are extremely helpful, and have much wider application than simply to libraries north of the border. A good choice for any medium to large American collection, and a must for all Canadian libraries.

Catholic Library World. 1929. m. (Sept.–May). Membership (Non-members, $6). Jane F. Hindman. Catholic Library Assn., 461 W. Lancaster Ave., Haverford, Pa. 19041. Illus., adv. Microform: UM.

Indexed: CathI, LibLit, LibSciAb. *Bk. rev:* 50–100, 40–50 words. *Aud:* Sa, Ht, Et. *Rv:* M. *Jv:* C.

This 50- to 60-page journal is divided between articles on librarianship, news of the Association, and short book reviews of titles suitable for elementary through college libraries. The reviews are the primary value for the non-Catholic. Articles tend to be a trifle repetitious of the form, if not the content, of those found in scores of other library periodicals. The writing is poor to good, but rarely outstanding. While a must in any Catholic library, it can be passed over by all but the largest libraries.

College and Research Libraries. 1939. bi-m. Membership (Non-members, $10). David Kaser. Assn. of College & Research Libraries, Amer. Lib. Assn., 50 E. Huron St., Chicago, Ill. 60611. Circ: 10,000. Microform: UM. Reprint: Kraus.

Indexed: LibLit, LibSciAb, PAIS. *Bk. rev:* 5–10, 500–1,500 words, signed. *Aud:* Sa, Ac, Jc. *Rv:* H. *Jv:* A.

In many ways the best of the American Library Association publications, this is professionally edited and contains articles and features not only of interest to college and university librarians, but anyone dealing with problems of bibliography, cataloging, acquisitions and the whole range of professional librarianship. The articles tend to be uniformly good, usually thought provoking, and often controversial. There is a minimum of repetition, a maximum of new insights into old problems. Regular features include excellent book reviews, additions to the current edition of *Guide to Reference Books,* notes on new magazines, and news items on individuals and events. A monthly newsletter (*NEWS.* 1966. Membership; Non-members, $10), keeps abreast of meetings, changes in personnel and general current topics not covered in the regular publication. A useful item for all college and university and many public and special libraries.

Drexel Library Quarterly. 1965. q. $10. Donald H. Hunt. Graduate Sch. of Library Science, Drexel Inst. of Technology, Philadelphia, Pa. 19104. Microform: UM.

Indexed: LibLit, LibSciAb, PAIS. *Aud:* Sa, Ac. *Rv:* M. *Jv:* B.

Plotted on somewhat the same lines as *Library Trends,* each number is given over to a single subject handled by a variety of authors, e.g., film librarianship, law librarianship, education, etc. There are critical reviews of professional literature, and other titles pertaining to librarianship. A required item for all large libraries and smaller libraries might check individual numbers for subjects of particular interest to their situation.

The Journal of Documentation; devoted to the recording, organization and dissemination of special knowledge. 1945. q. 39s (Non-members, 70s). H. Coblans. Assn. of Special Libraries and Information Bureaus, 3 Belgrave Sq., London S.W.1. Circ: 3,200. Reprint: Johnson, Kraus.

Indexed: LibLit, LibSciAb. *Bk. rev:* 12–15, 1 to 2 pages, signed. *Aud:* Sa, Ac. *Rv:* H. *Jv:* A.

Within a field notable for jargon and sloppy writing, this is a primary example of the exception. Articles by librarians and specialists are not only clear, but literate. Although usually technical, most are within the grasp of the interested librarian or laymen. All aspects of documentation are covered, "including translations, abstracts, indexes, and other bibliographic aids." Although published in England, contributors and articles are international in scope, and in no way limited to an English audience. The book reviews are good to excellent. Each issue also includes a "Documentation Survey," which consists of some 30 to 50 subject-arranged abstracts of books, reports and articles. This indexing service is highly selective, and can in no way be considered a substitute for the standard library science and documentation indexes. Emphasis tends to be on the sciences, but subject bibliography and cataloging are equally stressed. An absolute must for any library interested in the subject.

Journal of Education for Librarianship. 1960. q. $5. Bill Katz. Sch. of Library Science, State Univ. of New York, 1400 Washington Ave., Albany, N.Y. 12203. Circ: 1,500.

Indexed: LibLit, LibSciAb. *Bk. rev:* 2–3, 500–1,500 words. *Aud:* Sa, Ac. *Rv:* M. *Jv:* B.

Published by the Association of American Library Schools, this is an effort to cover material of interest to teachers in library schools. The five to eight articles per issue touch on every aspect of library education from the doctoral program to methods of teaching. Regular features include a column on research, book reviews, teaching methods and a calendar of events. The winter number is a directory of teachers and schools. The writing is popular to scholarly. A specialized magazine for a highly specialized group of readers.

Journal of Library Automation. 1968. q. $10. Frederick G. Kilgour. 1415 Kirkley Rd., Columbus, Ohio 43221. Illus., adv.

Indexed: LibLit, LibSciAb. *Aud:* Sa. *Rv:* H. *Jv:* B.

The journal of the Information Science and Automation Division, A.L.A., this usually features three or four articles on some technical aspect of how automation can be, or is used in libraries. The first issue included information on the book catalog at Stanford, comparative costs of converting shelf lists to machine readable form, and administrative procedural changes due to automation. The writers normally are librarians, and while the style is not always pleasing it is at least clear. Primarily a magazine for the technician and advanced student.

Journal of Library History; philosophy and comparative librarianship. 1966. q. $10. Louis Shores. Library Sch., Florida State Univ., Tallahassee, Fla. 32306. Circ: 1,150.

Indexed: HistAb, LibLit. *Bk. rev:* 4–5, 500–1,500 words, signed. *Aud:* Sa, Ac. *Rv:* H. *Jv:* A.

Presents the librarian, bibliophile, and interested layman with richly detailed articles on the history of librarianship, publishing, and books. It is international in scope, including articles on its chosen subjects from and about any area on earth. "Oral History" provides transcripts of interviews with leaders in librarianship and library history. Each issue reviews four or five titles concerned with library history. Indicates that librarianship can be significant and intellectually stimulating.

The Library Association Record. 1899. m. $20. E. Dudley. 7 Ridgmount St., Store St., London W.C.1. Circ: 15,000. Microform: UM.

Indexed: LibLit, LibSciAb. *Bk. rev:* Various numbers and lengths. *Aud:* Sa, Ac, Jc. *Rv:* H. *Jv:* B.

The English equivalent of the *American Library Association Bulletin.* As the official journal of the Library Association, it includes the usual articles on news of the organization, personalities, meetings, and the like. The writing tends to be pedestrian and, as with the *ALA Bulletin,* it suffers a bit from being an official publication. (*The Assistant Librarian* stands in marked contrast to its senior partner). Articles cover all aspects of the field and there are a number of items of international interest. American librarians may learn from the experiences and ideas put forth by their English cousins. A basic journal for library school collections, and useful for academic and public library staffs who think it necessary to read more than the American professional library magazine.

The Library-College Journal; a magazine of educational innovation. 1968. q. $8. Library-College Associates, Box 173, Brockport, N.Y. 14420.

Aud: Sa, Ac, Jc. *Rv:* H. *Jv:* B.

This is a specialist journal with a difference. Its subject is actually a specialty of a specialty—the teaching function of the academic library. The purpose of the publication, as its editors make clear, is to "give meaning to the unique role which the academic library can play in the learning process." Whatever contribution it is able to make in this direction, it already forms an interesting adjunct to the LEDS Newsletter and the *Journal of Education for Librarianship.* Among its distinguished contributors so far have been Louis Shores, Robert Blackburn and E. J. Josey.

Library Journal. 1876. semi-m. (Sept.–June); m. (July–Aug.). $10. John N. Berry III. R. R. Bowker Co., 1180 Ave. of the Americas, New York, N.Y. 10036. Illus., index, adv. Circ: 35,832. Microform: Mc, UM.

Indexed: LibLit, LibSciAb. *Bk. rev:* 200–250, 125 words, signed. *Aud:* Sa, Ac, Jc, Sh, Ht, Et. *Rv:* H. *Jv:* V.

The oldest of U.S. library periodicals, this is a multi-purpose journal running the gamut of library activities. (Bound in once a month is a reprint of *School Library Journal;* see annotation, this section.) Articles frequently speak controversy, as do the forthright editorials. A principal feature is the review section, which provides about two hundred reviews per issue, arranged by subject. Ten to twenty record reviews are provided in each issue. Other features include: a large "News" section providing coverage of the library and publishing worlds; "Magazines," introducing the reader to new serials; a checklist of free or inexpensive items of interest to the librarian; a buyer's guide to new equipment for use in libraries; a calendar of upcoming events of importance, and a lively "Letters to the Editor" department. Each year there are a number of special issues, e.g., foreign libraries, equipment, lists of forthcoming titles in various subject areas or formats (paperbacks). Advertising often swamps the magazine, although it rarely intrudes into the text of the main articles. As a general journal of librarianship, nothing surpasses it.

The Library Quarterly; a journal of investigation and discussion in the field of library science. 1931. q. $8. Howard W. Winger. Univ. of Chicago Press, 5750 Ellis Ave., Chicago, Ill. 60637. Circ: 3,300. Microform: UM.

Indexed: LibLit, LibSciAb, PAIS. *Bk. rev:* 10–15, 500–1,500 words, signed. *Aud:* Sa, Ac. *Rv:* H. *Jv:* A.

Considered by both teachers and librarians to be the outstanding library school publication, this long-standing quarterly concentrates on research and investigation type articles. There are usually three to four per issue, and one number a year is given over to the proceedings of the annual GLS conference. The critical reviews by librarians are excellent. Sometimes the writing is a bit pedestrian, but the content is usually thought provoking. A must for anyone who sees librarianship as a profession.

Library Resources and Technical Services. 1955. q. Membership (Non-members, $5). Resources and Technical

Services Div., Amer. Library Assn., 50 E. Huron St., Chicago, Ill. 60611. Index, adv. Circ: 7,000. Microform: UM.

Indexed: LibLit, LibSciAb. *Bk. rev:* 5–10, 500–1,500 words, signed. *Aud:* Sa. *Rv:* H. *Jv:* B.

Concerned primarily with technical services—acquisitions, serials, but particularly cataloging and classification—this is one of the better ALA divisional publications. Articles are well documented, and there is a nice balance between the pragmatic how-to-do-it type and the scholarly research approach. There is a limited amount of jargon, but at times the writers go off the deep end of the catalog by stating problems in terms which are hardly understandable to anyone but the expert. Fortunately, this does not happen often. A required item for the technical services section of any library, and certainly for all students.

Library Trends. 1952. q. $6. Herbert Goldhor. Univ. of Illinois Graduate Sch. of Library Science, Urbana, Ill. 61801. Subscriptions to: Univ. of Illinois Press, Subscription Dept., Urbana, Ill. 61801. Circ: 3,800.

Indexed: LibLit, LibSciAb, PAIS. *Aud:* Sa, Ac, Jc. *Rv:* H. *Jv:* V.

Each issue is devoted to a single theme in library science. There is a guest editor and some 7 to 12 contributors who offer survey type articles with usually extensive bibliographies. Through the years the editors have touched on almost every subject of interest to librarians (and not a few laymen), from rare books and periodicals to special libraries and government documents. Coverage of the topic varies with the editor and with the contributors, but on the whole it is complete enough. The main advantage of *Library Trends* is that it serves as a vehicle for updating and reviewing material usually found only in sometimes dated texts or scattered periodical articles. Individual issues are frequently used as texts in library schools, and librarians find it useful for both practical and theoretical approaches to common problems. A required item for almost any library.

Libri: International Library Review. 1951. q. $17.50. Palle Birkelund. Munksgaard, A/S Prags Blvd. 47, Copenhagen S, Denmark. Illus. Circ: 1,100.

Indexed: LibLit. *Bk. rev:* 5–10, 100–1,500 words, signed. *Aud:* Sa, Ac. *Rv:* H. *Jv:* A.

This is the one foreign library science journal which most library schools and medium to large libraries honor with a subscription. Published as the official organ of the International Federation of Library Associations (IFLA), it features original, well-documented studies on all aspects of libraries and bibliography. There are usually four or five articles per issue, and while the style is not brilliant, the material is usually original, the thought speculative, and the overall impression one of scholarship. The book reviews, which run from mere notes to essays, cover the entire field of international library work. There are the usual news items and announcements. Conveniently published in English, French, or German editions.

M.L.A. Quarterly. 1939. q. Membership (Non-members, $4). John G. Burke. Missouri Library Assn., Univ. of Missouri Library, Columbia, Mo. 65201. Circ: 1,300.

Indexed: LibLit. *Bk. rev:* 2 to 3, 3 pages, signed. *Aud:* Sa, Ac. *Rv:* H. *Jv:* B.

A handsome, above-average state library association publication which not only features information on the sponsoring group, but interviews with authors, book reviews, and special issues, such as the June, 1968 number on "Library Service to the Inner City." Contributors tend to be from libraries throughout the United States. Deserves a place among the top ten of its type in the country.

Mountain Plains Library Association Quarterly. 1956. q. Membership (Non-members, $2). Ford A. Rockwell. Wichita City Library, Wichita, Kan. 67202. Illus., adv.

Indexed: LibLit. *Aud:* Sa. *Rv:* L. *Jv:* C.

Members of the Mountain Plains Library Association include librarians and laymen from Kansas, Nebraska, North and South Dakota, Wyoming, Colorado, Utah and Nevada. A considerable amount of each 28- to 36-page issue is given over to Association events and personalities. There are usually two or three short general articles, e.g., "Fiction and History," "Subscription Agencies at Second Glance." The format is fair, and while the whole is of value to the Association membership, it is not a library journal for most libraries outside of the area.

Mousaion. 1955. 6 to 8/yr. Exchange. H. J. de Vleeschawer. Univ. of South Africa, 808 George Ave., Pretoria, S.A. Illus. Circ: 400. Microform: UM.

Indexed: LibLit, LibSciAb. *Aud:* Sa, Ac. *Rv:* M. *Jv:* B.

Somewhat similar in purpose to the University of Illinois *Occasional Papers.* Each number concentrates on research in a given area of librarianship, and if involved enough, may continue on for several issues. While prepared for working librarians, the pamphlet-like magazine is often used in library schools. Much of the material is esoteric, at least in terms of American students. Subscriptions not accepted, and must be received on exchange.

NELA Newsletter. 1969. bi-m. $4. Lee Ash. New England Library Assn. Subscriptions to: Mrs. Nan Berg, P.O. Box 609, Peabody, Mass. 01960.

Aud: Sa. *Rv:* M. *Jv:* B.

The official voice of the New England Library Association (comprising Connecticut, Massachusetts, Maine, New Hampshire, Rhode Island and Vermont). The first pocket sized 16-page issue (Jan. 1969) was nicely printed, primarily limited to short news items and the by-laws of the Association. Both its editor, Lee Ash, and the NELA President, Lawrence E. Wikander, indicate it will grow in content and scope. Longer articles of 1,500 to 2,000 words are promised for future issues. According to Mr. Wikander the publication is intended "to inform a growing membership about the work of the Association, to provide a forum

for reporting and discussion of inter-state regional library functions, to report on States' major library activities, and especially to encourage a regional cohesiveness among New England's thousands of libraries." Both gentlemen emphasize that the new publication is not an attempt to supplant other library publications. (*North Country Libraries,* issued since 1957, is primarily the state library magazine for New Hampshire, Vermont and Maine. The new entry has a broader base, and a different purpose.)

North Country Libraries. 1957. bi-m. Free. Louise Hazelton. 20 Park St., Concord, N.H. 03301. Illus. Circ: 4,500.

Indexed: LibLit. *Bk. rev:* 80–100, 40 words, signed. *Aud:* Sa. *Rv:* L. *Jv:* C.

A joint publication of three state agencies: the Maine State Library, the New Hampshire State Library, and the Free Public Library Service of Vermont. Differs from many such publications in that it is geared primarily for the non-professional without any formal library training, and for trustees. Usually contains two or three short, informative articles on libraries and personalities, followed by news notes about the three sponsoring agencies. Each issue features short annotations of "Books About the North Country," and equally brief, annotated reviews of general books divided by adult fiction, non-fiction, children, and teen-age. There is often an author profile, a bibliography on anything from conservation to current biographies, and film reviews. The reviews are good, yet of questionable value to any library subscribing to more basic reviewing services. Within its expressed purpose and scope, a useful magazine for the audience served. Libraries outside the area, however, may find it of limited help.

Occasional Papers. 1949. irreg. Free. Herbert Goldhor. Univ. of Illinois Graduate Sch. of Library Science, Urbana, Ill. 61801.

Indexed: LibLit, LibSciAb. *Aud:* Sa, Ac. *Rv:* H. *Jv:* B.

Usually a mimeographed report of some 20 to 30 pages, this irregular series deals with all aspects of librarianship from studies of reference to censorship. The series was founded to issue papers which normally might not be published elsewhere because of specialization, length or detail. Individual issues are of extreme value for an overview of a given area. Librarians should certainly ask to be put on the free list, although some issues are sold at a nominal cost.

PNLA Quarterly. 1936. q. Membership (Non-members, $5). Perry D. Morrison. School of Librarianship, Univ. of Oregon, Eugene, Ore. 94703. Illus., adv. Circ: 1,000.

Indexed: LibLit, LibSciAb. *Bk. rev:* 6–10, 250–500 words, signed. *Aud:* Sa, Ac, Jc. *Rv:* H. *Jv:* A.

The official voice of the Pacific Northwest Library Association, which includes Washington, Oregon, Idaho, Montana and British Columbia. An average 56-page issue features four or five articles on librarianship at all levels, written by practicing librarians. The material tends to be considerably better written and livelier than that found in most official publications, and is broad enough in scope to interest any librarian. Of particular value to the bibliographer and historian is the ongoing "Checklist of Books and Pamphlets Relating to the Pacific Northwest." This is comprehensive, scholarly, and in many ways a model of its kind for regional bibliography. One of the few library magazines which can be recommended for any medium to large library.

RQ. 1960. q. Membership. Bill Katz. ALA Reference Services Div., 50 E. Huron St., Chicago, Ill. 60611. Circ: 5,000.

Indexed: LibLit. *Bk. rev:* 40–60, notes, signed. *Aud:* Sa, Ac, Jc, Sh. *Rv:* H. *Jv:* A.

Published by the Reference Services Division, American Library Association, this touches on various aspects of reference service and bibliography. The 90- to 100-page magazine normally contains some four to six articles, and regular columns on government documents, reference research, difficult reference questions, and short book reviews of reference titles. The editor makes an effort to obtain articles by theorists and those working in the field, and attempts to balance each issue with both scholarly and sometimes humorous articles. Sometimes the mixture fails, but there is usually enough good, new writing to make it at least mildly interesting for anyone involved with reference.

School Libraries. 1951. q. Membership (Single copies $.50). Frances Fleming. Amer. Assn. of School Librarians, Amer. Library Assn., 50 E. Huron St., Chicago, Ill. 60611. Illus., adv. Circ: 12,000. Microform: UM.

Indexed: LibLit, LibSciAb. *Bk. rev:* 1–3, 200–300 words. *Aud:* Sa, Ht, Et. *Rv:* L. *Jv:* C.

Informs Association members of news and changes in their world, as well as including a number of general articles on librarianship, children, and reading. Special features include a list of National Education Association publications, brief reviews of professional materials, and news of personalities. Advertisements comprise a good part of the reading matter. The writing is over-simplified, the approach often a trifle juvenile, and the whole considerably below the level of other magazines for this same audience. While it has value to members, it is somewhat low on the list for required items in a school library.

School Library Journal; the journal of library work with children and young people. 1954. m. (Sept.–May). $5. Evelyn Geller. R. R. Bowker Co., 1180 Ave. of the Americas, New York, N.Y. 10036. Illus., index, adv. Circ: 25,846. Microform: UM.

Indexed: LibLit, LibSciAb. *Aud:* Sa, Sh, Jh, E. *Rv:* H. *Jv:* V.

Included as both a part of the *Library Journal* (last issue of the month) and separately, this serves school librarians and those dealing with children. Articles are from experts in the field, and tend to emphasize what is currently of interest to the majority of its readers. On the whole, the writing is somewhat better than found in school library periodicals; it certainly is considerably more controversial, primarily because the editor believes strongly in raising rather than hiding important issues. There are more extensive reviews here than in any other publication. Appraisals are made by experienced librarians and always in terms of current needs and expanding ideas about social and political relations. Consequently, the reviews tend to be considerably more realistic as to children's and young people's interests than more theoretical publications. Book reviews are critical, signed, and cover almost every title issued below the adult level. Should be in every medium to large library. The news coverage, though, makes it a first for all libraries, regardless of size; certainly for those not taking *Library Journal.*

Southeastern Librarian. 1950. q. Membership (Nonmembers, $4). Jerrold Orne. Univ. of North Carolina Library, Chapel Hill, N.C. 27514. Illus., adv. Circ: 3,000.

Indexed: LibLit, LibSciAb. *Bk. rev:* 1–2, 500 words, signed. *Aud:* Sa. *Rv:* M. *Jv:* B.

The voice of the Southeastern Library Association, covering Alabama, Florida, Georgia, Kentucky, Mississippi, North Carolina, South Carolina, Tennessee, and Virginia. About evenly divided among four to five articles on librarianship and features news notes, reports from the various state memberships, bibliographies, and the annual proceedings of the Association. The articles are much above average, and cover such subjects as integration, faculty-library relationships, special collections and other topics of interest to librarians in any part of the country or world. Bibliographies such as "Good Reading for Disadvantaged Youth," and author profiles give it an added dimension. Should be found in all Southern libraries, and in larger libraries and library schools.

Special Libraries. 1910. 10/yr. $20. Guy R. Bell. Special Libraries Assn., 31 E. 10th St., New York, N.Y. 10003. Illus., index, adv. Circ: 8,592. Microform: UM. Reprint: Kraus.

Indexed: BusI, LibLit, LibSciAb, PAIS. *Bk. rev:* 20–30, 40 words. *Aud:* Sa, Ac. *Rv:* M. *Jv:* B.

There are usually four to five articles, and of late these have tended to concentrate on documentation and automation. The second one-quarter or half is given over to news of the Association, and "Recent References" (short, annotated notes about new books). The magazine tends to be extremely uneven in content, the articles a trifle bland, and its primary value for librarians is the occasional good article and the news features. Only for larger libraries.

Synergy. 1967. m. Request. Daniel Tatko. Bay Area Reference Center, San Francisco Public Library, Civic Center, San Francisco, Calif. 94102.

Bk. rev: 7–10, 150–500 words. *Aud:* Sa. *Rv:* H. *Jv:* A.

An unorthodox library publication which shows a sense of humor, social responsibility and intellectualism rarely associated with the genre. The official publication of the S. F. Bay Area Reference Center, it is processed newsletter approach of 20 to 40 pages. Usually each issue features one or two articles, i.e., the Nov.–Dec. 1968 number was devoted to an introductory essay on, and an annotated list of underground newspapers. (Incidentally, this single issue is one of the more authoritative, objective lists in the area of underground press.) Regular features include out-of-the-way reference questions and their answers, as well as unanswered queries; new sources of reference, primarily in the form of book reviews; and an invaluable updating service which lists new names to be added or deleted to standard annuals such as the Congressional Directory, World Almanac, etc. A basic library periodical, particularly as it is free, for all types of libraries.

Top of the News. 1942. q. Membership (Non-members, $1.25). Doris Stotz. American Library Assn., Children's Services Div. & Young Adult Services Div., 50 E. Huron St., Chicago, Ill. 60611. Illus., adv.

Indexed: LibLit, LibSciAb. *Bk. rev:* 15–20, 30–50 words, signed. *Aud:* Sa, Ac, Jc, Ht, Et. *Rv:* H. *Jv:* A.

Usually features some six to eight articles of interest to librarians and educators working with elementary and high school students. The writing is uneven, the philosophy middle-of-the-road to sometimes iconoclastic, the content good to excellent. There is a minimum of the goody two shoes approach, a maximum of practical advice. The authors, for the most part practicing librarians, tend to take a realistic rather than idealistic view of their charges. The short book reviews, by a different librarian in each issue, are succinct, current and among the best available. This feature, coupled with reviews of magazines for children and young adults, makes it a required magazine for all libraries and certainly for most teachers.

UNESCO Bulletin for Libraries. 1947. bi-m. $3.50. Unesco Pubns. Center, 317 E. 34th St., New York, N.Y. 10016. Illus. Circ: 1,000.

Indexed: LibLit, LibSciAb. *Bk. rev:* 20–30, 50–100 words. *Aud:* Sa, Ac, Jc. *Rv:* H. *Jv:* A.

Aside from *Libri,* this is the basic international journal of librarianship. It tends to be more pragmatic than the former, stressing daily operations of various type libraries, problem solving, and articles on bibliography, reference, documentation, archives, etc. The contributors are usually practicing librarians who offer basic advice on setting-up and operating a library. The "New Publications" section comprises short reviews of a variety of works in librarianship, and the "News and Information" department is one of the best single sources for data on international developments in the field. Published in Russian, French, Spanish and English editions. A major publication for student and librarian alike.

Wilson Library Bulletin. 1914. m. (Sept.–June). $5. William R. Eshelman. H. W. Wilson Co., 950 Univ. Ave., Bronx, N.Y. 10452. Illus., index, adv. Circ: 38,100. Microform: B&H, Mc, UM.

Indexed: LibLit, LibSciAb, RG. *Bk. rev:* Reference books only. *Aud:* Sa, Ac, Jc, Ht, Et. *Rv:* H. *Jv:* A.

Next to the *Library Journal,* this is the only other national library magazine published by an independent publisher. There the comparison ends. Under the able editorship of Kathleen Molz, the *Bulletin* developed a style of featuring one major topic per issue—censorship, bibliography, children's work, the art of the book, etc. Miss Molz then secured the services of such national figures as Susan Sontag, Kenneth Clark and Dwight Macdonald, to name but three, to write on the subject at hand. There were usually a number of substantiating articles by leaders in the library profession. From time to time, too, there were symposiums on various subjects. This is written in the past tense, because as of June, 1968, a new editor (William Eshelman) was appointed and the style of the magazine is apt to change. Nevertheless, the magazine is equally valuable for its departments and features, particularly the caustic wit of Jesse Shera, Dean of the Library School at Case Western Reserve, and the perceptive reviews of current reference books by Frances Cheney of Peabody. (No other books are reviewed.) There are news notes, but here the *Library Journal* has been far ahead of this one. While the *Library Journal* would be a first choice as a general magazine for the library, the *Bulletin* runs a close second. It certainly should be found in all medium to large libraries, regardless of type, and often is useful for teachers as well as librarians.

State Library Association Publications

Almost all state library associations issue a publication, and they are listed here on a state by state basis. Major state periodicals that are indexed are also included. (School library association publications are listed separately.) Reference is also made to the regional periodicals, all of which are annotated in the main listing.

With some notable exceptions, content is rather parochial, limited to immediate interests of the state association—personal notes, business activities, meetings, etc. For purposes of purchase, all libraries within a state will want their own association publication, plus the regional magazine. Beyond that, publications from adjoining states are sometimes helpful. For all around information, the best are (not necessarily in this order): *California Librarian, D.C. Libraries, Illinois Libraries, Bay State Librarian, Maryland Libraries, Minnesota Libraries, MLA Quarterly* (Missouri), *NYLA Bulletin, Pennsylvania Library Assn. Bulletin, Texas Library Journal, Wisconsin Library Bulletin.*

Alabama Library Assn., 4265 Amherst St., Montgomery, Ala. 36111. *Alabama Librarian.* 1949. q. Membership (Non-members, $1.50). Luther E. Lee, Illus., adv. Circ: 750.

Indexed: LibLit, LibSciAb. Bk rev. (See also, *Southeastern Librarian*)

Alaska State Library Assn., Alaska Methodist Univ. Library, Anchorage, Alas. 99504. *Newsletter.* 1962. q. Free. Elizabeth Carroll.

Arizona State Library Assn., Arizona State Univ. Library, Tempe, Ariz. 85281. *Arizona Librarian.* 1940. q. Membership (Non-members, $2). Kenneth Slack. Adv. Bk rev. Circ: 800. *Indexed:* LibLit.

Arkansas Library Assn. & Arkansas Library Commission, 506½ Center St., Little Rock, Ark. 72201. *Arkansas Libraries.* 1944. q. Membership. LaNel Compton. Illus. Bk rev. Circ: 809. *Indexed:* LibLit.

California Library Assn., 1741 Solano Ave., Berkeley, Calif. 94707. *California Librarian.* 1939. q. Membership (Non-members, $6). Richard D. Johnson. Illus., index, adv. Bk. rev. Circ: 3,500. *Indexed:* LibLit, LibSciAb.

California State Library, Box 2037, Sacramento, Calif. 95809. *News Notes of California Libraries.* 1906. q. Free. Natalie Smith. Circ: 1,700. *Indexed:* LibLit, LibSciAb.

Colorado Library Assn., College & Univ. Section, Univ. of Denver Libraries, Denver, Colo. 80210. *Colorado Academic Library.* 1963. q. Membership (Non-members, $2). Leo Natanson & Mell Klatt. (See also, *Mountain Plains Library Quarterly*)

Connecticut Library Assn., 38 Elgin St., Hamden, Conn. 06514. *CLA News & Views.* 1959. 5/yr. $5. Catherine Maybury. Illus., adv. Circ: 1,000. (See also, *NELA Newsletter.*)

Delaware Library Assn., Dept. of Public Instruction, Dover, Del. 19401. *Delaware Library Association. Bulletin.* 1946. semi-ann. Free. Helen Bennett.

District of Columbia Library Assn., 2104 Cascade Rd., Silver Spring, Md. 20902. *D.C. Libraries.* 1929. q. Membership (Non-members, $4). Merle Goldberg. Adv. Circ: 850. *Indexed:* LibLit.

Florida Library Assn., 722 Ivanhoe Rd., Tallahassee, Fla. 32303. *Florida Libraries.* 1949. q. Membership (Non-members, $2). Mary Alice Hunt. Illus., adv. Circ: 1,400. *Indexed:* LibLit, LibSciAb. Bk rev. (See also, *Southeastern Librarian*)

Georgia Library Assn., 112 State Office Bldg., Atlanta, Ga. 30303. *Georgia Librarian.* 1964. semi-ann. Membership (Non-members, $1). (See also, *Southeastern Librarian*)

Hawaii Library Assn., Box 3941, Honolulu, Hawaii 96816. *Hawaii Library Association Journal.* 1944. semi-ann. Don McNeil. Illus., adv. Circ: 500. *Indexed:* LibLit, LibSciAb.

Idaho Library Assn. & Idaho State Library, 615 Fulton St., Boise, Idaho 83706. *Idaho Librarian.* 1945. q. Membership (Non-members, $3). Illus. Circ: 800. *Indexed:* LibLit. (See also, *PNLA Quarterly*)

Illinois Library Assn., 4944 Paxton Rd., Oak Lawn, Ill. 60453. *ILA Reporter.* 4/yr. Free. Mrs. Robert Ihrig. Illus. Circ: 4,900.

Illinois State Library, Springfield, Ill. 62706. *Illinois Libraries.* 1919. m. Free. Irma Bostian. Illus. Circ: 7,200. *Indexed:* LibLit. Bk rev.

Indiana Library Assn., Bureau of Public Discussion, Owen Hall, Indiana Univ., Bloomington, Ind. 47405. Subscriptions to: Public Library, Evansville, Ind. *Focus on Indiana Libraries.* 1947. q. Membership (Non-members, $2). Edward Howard. Illus., adv. *Indexed:* LibLit.

Indiana State Library, Indianapolis, Ind. 46204. *Library Occurrent.* 1906. q. Free. Edgar W. Chamberlain. Illus. Circ: 2,500. *Indexed:* LibLit.

Iowa Library Assn., Earlville, Iowa 52041. *Catalyst.* 1946. bi-m. Free. Louis Hunt. Adv.

Iowa State Travelling Library, Des Moines, Iowa 50319. *Iowa Library Quarterly.* 1901. q. Ernestine Grafton. Circ: 14,000. *Indexed:* LibLit.

Kansas State Libraries, Public Library Extension, 801 Harrison St., Topeka, Kan. 66612. *Kansas Library Bulletin.* 1932. q. Free. Claire Vincent. Circ: 3,900. *Indexed:* LibLit. (See also, *Mountain Plains Library Quarterly*)

Kentucky Library Assn., Box 141, Univ. Station, Murray, Ky. 42071. *Kentucky Library Association Bulletin.* 1963. q. Membership (Non-members, $3). Jean Wiggins. Adv. (See also, *Southeastern Librarian*)

Louisiana Library Assn., P.O. Box 131, Baton Rouge, La. 70821. *Louisiana Library Association Bulletin.* 1937. q. Membership (Non-members, $4). Mrs. Carl Thomas. Illus. Circ: 1,300. *Indexed:* LibLit. Bk rev.

Maine Library Assn., Univ. of Maine Library, Orono, Me. 04473. *Maine Library Association Bulletin.* 1939. q. Membership (Non-members, $1). John Burnham. Adv. *Indexed:* LibLit. Bk rev. (See also, *North Country Libraries* and *NELA Newsletter.*)

Maryland Library Assn. & Assn. of School Librarians, Mrs. Frank Levin, 115 W. Franklin St., Baltimore, Md. 21201. *Maryland Libraries.* 1932. q. Membership (Non-members, $2). Norman Finkler. Adv. Circ: 1,500. *Indexed:* LibLit. Bk rev.

Massachusetts Library Assn., P.O. Box 7, Nahant, Mass. 01908. *Bay State Librarian.* 1911. q. Membership (Non-members, $2). Robert Wagenknecht. Adv. Circ: 1,800. *Indexed:* LibLit. (See also, *NELA Newsletter.*)

Michigan Library Assn., 1480 South Shore Drive, Holland, Mich. 49423. *Michigan Librarian.* 1935. 4/yr. Membership (Non-members, $2). Mrs. G. S. MacKenzie. Adv. Circ: 1,725. *Indexed:* LibLit.

Minnesota. No library association publication.

Minnesota State Dept. of Education, Library Div., 117 Univ. Ave., St. Paul, Minn. 55101. *Minnesota Libraries.* 1904. q. Free. Hannis S. Smith. Circ: 1,933. *Indexed:* LibLit, LibSciAb. Bk rev.

Mississippi Library Assn. & Mississippi Library Commission, 405 State Office Bldg., Jackson, Miss. 39201. *Mississippi*

Library News. 1937. q. Membership (Non-members, $5). Lelia Clark. Adv. Circ: 1,200. *Indexed:* LibLit. (See also, *Southeastern Librarian*)

Missouri Library Assn., Univ. of Missouri Library, Columbia, Mo. 65201. *MLA Quarterly.* 1939. q. John G. Burke. Illus., adv. *Indexed:* LibLit.

Montana. No library association publication.

Montana State Library, 930 E. Lyndale Ave., Helena, Mont. 59401. *Montana Libraries.* 1947. q. Free. Ruth O. Longworth. Illus. Circ: 2,500. *Indexed:* LibLit. Bk rev. (See also, *PNLA Quarterly*)

Nebraska. No publication. (See also, *Mountain Plains Library Quarterly*)

Nevada Library Assn., State Library, Carson City, Nev. 89701. *Nevada Libraries.* 1964. q. Membership (Non-members, $2). Barbara Mauseth. Adv. (See also, *Mountain Plains Library Quarterly*)

New Hampshire Library Assn., Woodbury Memorial Library, 9 Bell Hill Rd., Bedford, N.H. 03102. *Newsletter.* 1940. 3/yr. Free. Doris Peck. (See also, *North Country Libraries* and *NELA Newsletter.*)

New Jersey Library Assn., 800 Rathway Ave., Woodbridge, N.J. 07095. *New Jersey Libraries.* 1966. q. Membership (Non-members, $1). Edwin P. Beckerman. Illus., adv. *Indexed:* LibLit. Bk rev.

New Mexico Library Assn. & State Library, P.O. Box 1629, New Mexico State Library, Santa Fe, N.M. 78501. *New Mexico Library Bulletin.* 1932. q. Dorothy J. Watkins. Circ: 559. *Indexed:* LibLit. Bk rev.

New York Library Assn., Box 521, Woodside, N.Y. 11377. *NYLA Bulletin.* 1953. bi-m. $3. Mrs. R. K. Baum. Illus., adv. *Indexed:* LibLit, PAIS.

New York State Library, N.Y. State Education Dept., Albany, N.Y. 12224. *The Bookmark.* 1949. m. (Oct.–July). $1. Circ: 5,000. *Indexed:* LibLit, PAIS. Bk rev.

North Carolina Library Assn., Drawer W, Greensboro, N.C. 27402. *North Carolina Libraries.* 1942. q. Membership (Non-members, $3). Mrs. Stella Townsend. Circ: 2,000. *Indexed:* LibLit, LibSciAb. Bk rev. (See also, *Southeastern Librarian*)

North Dakota. No publication. (See also, *Mountain Plains Library Quarterly*)

Ohio Library Assn., Suite 400, 43 South St., Columbus, Ohio 43215. *Ohio Library Association Bulletin.* 1937. q. $3. Gerald R. Shields. Adv. *Indexed:* LibLit.

Oklahoma Library Assn., Box 53245, Oklahoma City, Okla. 73105. *Oklahoma Librarian.* 1950. q. Membership (Non-members, $3). Josh Stroman. Illus., adv. Circ: 774. *Indexed:* LibLit.

Oregon Library Assn., 801 Southwest 10th Ave., Portland, Ore. 97205. *Oregon Library News.* 1954. q. Free. Jimmy Takita. (See also, *PNLA Quarterly*)

Pennsylvania Library Assn., 200 S. Craig St., Pittsburgh, Pa. 15213. *Pennsylvania Library Association Bulletin.* 1945. q. Membership (Non-members, $3). Hilda Reitzel. Illus., adv. Circ: 3,000. *Indexed:* LibLit, LibSciAb.

Rhode Island. No publication. (See *NELA Newsletter.*)

South Carolina Library Assn., Box 5193, Spartanburg, S.C. 29301. *South Carolina Librarian.* 1956. semi-ann. Membership (Non-members, $1). Herbert Hucks. Illus. Circ: 550. *Indexed:* LibLit. Bk rev. (See also, *Southeastern Librarian*)

South Dakota Library Assn., Camegie Library, Pierre, S.D. 57501. *South Dakota Library Association News.* 1950. q. Free. Esto Hatfield.

South Dakota State Library Commission, Pierre, S.D. 57501. *South Dakota Library Bulletin.* 1914. q. Free. Circ: 1,500. *Indexed:* LibLit. (See also, *Mountain Plains Library Quarterly*)

Tennessee Library Assn., Univ. of Tennessee Library, Knoxville, Tenn. 37916. *Tennessee Librarian.* 1948. q. $2. John Dobson. Illus., adv. Circ: 1,500. *Indexed:* LibLit. (See also, *Southeastern Librarian*)

Texas Library Assn., Box 7763, Univ. Station, Austin, Tex. 78712. *Texas Library Journal.* 1924. q. Membership (Non-members, $2). Mary Pound. Illus., adv. Circ: 2,700. *Indexed:* LibLit.

Texas Library & Historical Commission, Drawer DD, Capitol Station, Austin, Tex. 78711. *Texas Libraries.* 1906. q. Free. W. P. Westmoreland, Jr. Circ: 1,950. *Indexed:* LibLit. Bk rev.

Utah Library Assn., 2555 Washington Blvd., Ogden, Utah 84401. *Utah Libraries.* 1957. semi-ann. Membership (Non-members, $1). J. M. Sorensen. Illus., adv. Circ: 600. *Indexed:* LibLit. Bk rev. (See also, *Mountain Plains Library Quarterly*)

Vermont. No publication. (See also, *North Country Libraries* and *NELA Newsletter.*)

Virginia Library Assn., Fairfax County P.L., 3915 Chain Bridge Rd., Fairfax, Va. 22030. *Virginia Librarian.* 1954. q. Membership (Non-members, $1). Orland Wages. Circ: 1,250. *Indexed:* LibLit, LibSciAb. Bk rev. (See also, *Southeastern Librarian*)

Washington. No library association publication. (See *PNLA* Quarterly.)

Washington State Library, Olympia, Wash. 98501. *Library News Bulletin.* 1932. q. Free. Harris C. McClaskey. Circ: 3,500. *Indexed:* LibLit. Bk rev.

West Virginia Library Assn., West Virginia Univ., Morgantown, W.Va. 26506. *West Virginia Librarian.* 1948. q. Membership (Non-members, $1) Charles D. Patterson. Circ: 1,250. *Indexed:* LibLit. Bk rev.

Wisconsin Library Assn., Public Library, Madison, Wis. 53703. *President's Newsletter.* bi-m. Free. Bernard Schwab.

Wisconsin State Dept. of Public Instruction, Div. for Library Services, Madison, Wis. 53702. *Wisconsin Library Bulletin*. 1905. bi-m. $2. Beryl E. Hoyt. Illus. Circ: 4,000. *Indexed:* LibLit. Bk rev.

Wyoming Library Assn., Wyoming State Library, Cheyenne, Wyo. 82001. *Wyoming Library Roundup*. 1945. q. Free. Mary Rogers. Illus. Circ: 750. Bk rev. (See also, *Mountain Plains Library Quarterly*)

State School Library Association Publications

There are few adequate publications from state school library associations (or, for that matter, from state departments of education). The only indexed magazine is *California School Libraries,* and it is by and large the best of the group. Conversely almost all the publications are free, and for this reason certainly worth trying. The following is an unannotated state by state list. Most of the bulletins, newsletters and periodicals concentrate on local affairs, but a number do carry articles, from time to time, of interest to all school librarians. School libraries within a state issuing such a work will want to subscribe, and many school librarians should subscribe to publications in adjoining states.

Alabama Department of Education, Montgomery, Ala. 36104. *School Library Bulletin*. 1946. semi-ann. Free.

Alaska. No publication.

Arizona. No publication.

Arkansas Department of Education, Little Rock, Ark. 72207. *Library Bulletin*. 1967. q. Free. Bk rev.

California Assn. of School Librarians, 2369 Glenada Ave., Montrose, Calif. 91020. *California School Libraries*. 1929. q. Membership (Non-members, $3). Illus., adv. Circ: 1,800. *Indexed:* LibLit.

Colorado. No publication.

Connecticut School Library Assn., Early Jr. High School Library, Wallingford, Conn. 06492. *Connecticut School Library Association Newsletter*. 1963. 5/yr. Free. Robert O'Neill. Bk rev.

Delaware. No publication.

District of Columbia. No publication.

Florida Assn. of School Libraries, 1410 N.W. Second Ave., Miami, Fla. 33132. *Bookcase*. 1958. Free. Gus Adams. Bk rev.

Georgia. No publication.

Hawaii. No publication.

Idaho. No publication.

Illinois Assn. of School Librarians, 1823 C. Valley Rd., Champaign, Ill. 61820. *IASL News for You*. 1948. q. Free. Cora Thomassen.

Indiana School Librarians Assn., N. Central High School Library, 1801 E. 86th St., Indianapolis, Ind. 46240. *Hoosier School Libraries*. 1962. q. Membership (Non-members, $2). W. Duane Johnson. Illus., adv. Circ: 825. Bk rev.

Iowa Assn. of School Librarians, Franklin Jr. High School,

Des Moines, Iowa 58510. *Library Lines*. 1961. 3/yr. Free. Alice Darling.

Kansas Assn. of School Librarians, 965 Lexington St., Wichita, Kan. 65218. *Kansas Association of School Librarians. Newsletter*. 1952. 3/yr. Free. Aileen Watkins. Adv. Bk rev.

Kentucky Assn. of School Librarians, 4027 St. Germaine Ct., Louisville, Ky. 40207. *Kentucky Association of School Librarians. Bulletin*. 1965. semi-ann. $2. Eleanor Koon. Adv.

Louisiana. No publication.

Maine School Library Assn., 78 Hill St., Orono, Me. 04473. *Maine School Library Association Bulletin*. 1939. q. $1. John Burnham, Adv. Bk rev.

Maryland State Dept. of Education, 301 W. Preston St., Baltimore, Md. 21210. *Library Newsletter*. 1964. q. Free. Nettie Taylor.

Massachusetts. No publication.

Michigan Assn. of School Librarians, Bureau of School Services, Univ. of Michigan, Ann Arbor, Mich. 48104. *Forward*. 1951. 3/yr. Free. Illus.

Minnesota. No publication.

Mississippi. No publication.

Missouri. No publication.

Montana. No publication.

Nebraska. No publication.

Nevada. No publication.

New Hampshire. No publication.

New Jersey School of Library Councils Assn., 162 Palmer Ave., South Plainfield, N.J. 07080. *Library Council—ER*. 1954. q. Free. John Cordner.

New Mexico. No publication.

New York Board of Education, 110 Livingston St., Brooklyn, N.Y. 11201. *School Library Bulletin*. 1908. m. Free. Helen Sattley.

North Carolina Dept. of Public Instruction, Raleigh, N.C. 27602. *Educational Media Bulletin*. 1950. 3/yr. Free.

North Dakota. No publication.

Ohio Assn. of School Librarians, 7001 Reading Rd., Cincinnati, Ohio 45237. *Ohio Association of School Librarians. Bulletin*. 1955. $3. Anna Borchin. Adv. Bk rev.

Oklahoma. No publication.

Oregon. No publication.

Pennsylvania Dept. of Public Instruction, Harrisburg, Pa. 17126. *Instructional Materials Intercom*. 1964. q. Free.

Rhode Island. No publication.

South Carolina State Dept. of Education, Columbia, S.C. 29201. *S.C. State Dept. of Education—Division of Instruction and Library Services. Newsletter*. 1946. 3/yr. Free.

South Dakota. No publication.

Tennessee. No publication.

Texas. No publication.

Utah. No publication.

Vermont. No publication.

Virginia Education Assn., Richmond, Va. 23219. *Libra-chat.* 1960. semi-ann. Free.

Washington State Association of School Librarians, 3217 N. 29th St., Tacoma, Wash. 98407. *Library Leads.* 1951, q. $3. Helen Bumgardner. Adv.

West Virginia. No publication.

Wisconsin. No publication.

Wyoming. No publication.

LINGUISTICS AND PHILOLOGY

Indexes and Abstracts

Education Index, Psychological Abstracts, Social Sciences and Humanities Index. (For annotations, see Indexes and Abstracts Section.)

American Journal of Philology. See Classical Studies Section.

American Speech; a quarterly of linguistic usage. 1925. q. $6. James Macris. Columbia University Press, 440 W. 110th St., New York, N.Y. 10025. Index, adv. Circ: 1,200. Reprint: Johnson. Microform: UM.

Indexed: SSHum. *Bk. rev:* 1–3, average 450 words, signed. *Aud:* Sa, Ac, Jc. *Rv:* H. *Jv:* B.

A highly respected journal in the field of applied linguistics, presenting both general and scholarly studies of the English language in North America. Among the areas it covers are: dialect geography, current usage, semantics, structural linguistics, phonetics, vocabulary, names and special nomenclatures, and dialects. Occasional studies of foreign languages spoken in North America appear. There is a featured section on new words. Primarily for large university and junior college collections.

Anthropological Linguistics. 1959. 9/yr. $3.50. Florence M. Voegelin. Archives of Languages of the World, Anthropology Dept., Rawles Hall 108, Indiana Univ., Bloomington, Ind. 47401. Illus. Circ: 1,000. Reprint: Kraus.

Aud: Sa, Ac. *Rv:* H. *Jv:* B.

A processed publication of the Archives. Occasionally publishes scholarly research articles based on the taped resources available at the archives, with the aim of making these resources more widely available to scholars in the field. Theoretical and methodological papers, especially symposia papers, are also published. All articles are specialized and technical, and are the result of field work among the groups described. They employ the standard format of linguistic analysis. The three to four articles per

issue usually range from 10 to 15 pages. Only for the specialist and the larger academic libraries.

CLA Journal. See Afro-American Section.

Canadian Modern Language Review. 1944. q. $5. G. A. Klinck. Ontario Modern Language Teachers' Assn., 34 Butternut St., Toronto 12, Ont. Illus., index, adv. Circ: 1,800.

Bk. rev: Notes. *Aud:* Sa, Ac, Jc, Ht, Et. *Rv:* H. *Jv:* B.

A basic journal of information on teaching for elementary and secondary teachers of modern languages. Articles cover business of the Association—usually a minimum of the total—and various aspects of the profession from content analysis to methodology. Particularly valuable for the short notes on books—dictionaries, readers, guides, and literature which is suitable for classroom use, or for the further education of the teacher. The reviews are grouped by language. Articles appear in English, French, Italian, German, Russian, and Spanish. While primarily of value to Canadians, the reviews often cover material not mentioned in American professional journals.

Classical Philology. See Classical Studies Section.

Current Slang; a quarterly glossary of slang expressions presently in use. 1966. q. Free to institutions. Stephen H. Dill & Clyde Burkholder. Dept. of English, Univ. of South Dakota, Vermillion, S.D. 57069.

Aud: Sa, Ac. *Rv:* H. *Jv:* B.

A free mimeographed report of some dozen pages on current slang expressions of a given group or type. Issues, for example, have examined the slang of the U.S. Air Academy, the Midwest and the Blacks in Watts, California. The procedure is to give the slang term, its definition, the place or places it is most often used, and information about the users. This is a handy way of keeping up with modern talk, and for reference librarians an excellent method of keeping the slang dictionary up-to-date.

English Language Notes. 1963. q. $4. William G. Lane. Univ. of Colorado, 1200 Univ. Ave., Boulder, Colo. 80302. Index. Circ: 700.

Bk. rev: 12–14, 1,400 words, signed. *Aud:* Sa, Ac. *Rv:* H. *Jv:* B.

An expansion of the "Notes" sections appearing in most philology journals, *English Language Notes* is a scholarly and specialized journal presenting the results of historical and textual research in English and American languages and literatures. Articles are brief and informative, covering incidents in authors' lives, literary sources and parallels, word usage, and corrupt texts. Contributors generally cite newly-discovered documentary evidence—original manuscripts and historical documents. "The Romantic Movement: A Selective and Critical Bibliography" appears annually as a supplement to the September issue (from 1937 to 1950 it appeared in *English Literary History;* from 1951 to

1964, in *Philological Quarterly*). Useful in larger academic libraries, but teachers of literature and English at almost any level will find much of value.

English Studies; a journal of English letters and philology. 1919. bi-m. $10. R. W. Zandvoort. Swets en Zeitlinger, Keizergracht 471, Amsterdam, Netherlands. Index, adv. Circ: 1,600.

Indexed: SSHum. *Bk. rev:* 9–12, 900 words, signed. *Aud:* Sa, Ac, Jc. *Rv:* H. *Jv:* B.

A Dutch journal devoted to English language and literature, including American English. It covers all periods and forms of English writing and speech, with a highly-readable presentation appealing to undergraduates as well as scholars. Featured are long articles of original criticism, and linguistic analysis of early and modern English. Shorter articles include textual and historical studies of literature, structural and applied linguistics. Contributors are from America, England, and the continent. The book reviews are highly critical, and considered among the best in the field. The June and August issues feature two annual bibliographic essays: "Current Literature" in prose, poetry and drama, and "Current Literature" in criticism and biography.

ETC; a review of general semantics. 1943. q. $4. S. I. Hayakawa. International Soc. for General Semantics, 540 Powell St., San Francisco, Calif. 94108. Illus., index, adv. Circ: 8,600. Microform: UM.

Indexed: PsyAb. *Bk. rev:* 4–6, 500 words, signed. *Aud:* Ga, Ac, Jc. *Rv:* H. *Jv:* A.

The official organ of the International Society for General Semantics, a group concerned with communication and the relations of language and symbols to all aspects of human behavior. Attitude, format, and content combine to make this the "little magazine" of the general semantics field, with a wide reader appeal. Articles cover the arts, science, and all fields of social science. Broad scope finds unity in the magazine's dedication to the "permanent Et cetera," the rejection of all dogmatic, period and stop attitudes. Generally five to six medium length articles appear per issue, ranging from explanations of current word usage to theoretical essays and research. Sample titles are: "Language of the Oil Fields," "General Semantics Orientation in Dentist-Patient Relations," "Pre-Socratics and the Rationalist Tradition," and "Semantic Aspects of Abortion." Style is semi-popular, and always interesting. Poetry and line drawings are regularly included. A bibliography on general semantics appears irregularly.

International Journal of American Linguistics. 1917. q. $5. C. F. Voegelin. Waverly Press, Inc., Mt. Royal & Guilford Ave., Baltimore, Md. 21202. Subscriptions to: Alice Zorn, Indiana Univ., Bloomington, Ind. 47405. Index. Circ: 2,250.

Indexed: SSHum. *Bk. rev:* 3–5, 1,500 words, signed. *Aud:* Sa, Ac. *Rv:* H. *Jv:* B.

A joint publication of the Linguistic Society of America and the American Anthropological Association. This journal issues results of research in North American Indian languages. Articles include both scholarly and field research as well as some general and theoretical material, and descriptive linguistics and classification of languages receive the greatest emphasis. Intended for a select audience of specialists in North American language, culture, and anthropology.

Italian Quarterly. See General Section.

Journal of English and Germanic Philology. See German Language Section.

Language and Speech. 1958. q. $15. D. B. Fry. Robert Draper Ltd., Kerbihan House, 85 Udney Park Rd., Teddington, Middlesex, Eng. Circ: 750.

Indexed: PsyAb. *Aud:* Sa, Ac. *Rv:* H. *Jv:* B.

A British journal publishing the results of research into all aspects of the spoken word. Articles are usually presented as formal reports, with summaries, background, and description of the methodology. Typical topics are: transmission of speech, perception of speech, language structure, patterns of speech, and the relations between linguistics and psychology, social factors, and cognitive activities. Also covered are problems of mechanical translation and mechanical speech recognition, language statistics, and abnormalities of language and speech. Four to six articles appear in each issue. While a technical journal, will have some appeal for more seriously involved teachers of speech and anyone interested in communications from the specialist to the graduate library school student.

Language Learning; journal of applied linguistics. 1948. q. $2. (Libraries and schools, $3). John C. Catford. North Univ. Bldg., Univ. of Michigan, Ann Arbor, Mich. 48104. Circ: 3,000. Microform: UM.

Indexed: EdI. *Bk. rev:* 2–4, 1200 words, signed. *Aud:* Sa, Ac, Jc, Ht. *Rv:* H. *Jv:* B.

The main focus is on the teaching of English as a second or foreign language on the college level. Articles are generally reports of case studies which indicate results achieved through teaching approaches which utilize structural analyses, linguistic theory, and the related fields of psychology and anthropology. Generally 8–10 articles of medium length appear in each double issue. Treatment is simplified and non-technical, with clear explanations of linguistic concepts. Regular features are announcements, brief reviews of bibliographies in the field, and a list of new publications. Of interest to all college and university language instructors, and of some, though limited value to high school teachers.

Lingua; international review of general linguistics. 1947. 8/yr. $13. Ed bd. North-Holland Publishing Co., Box 103, Amsterdam, Netherlands. Index. Circ: 850. Reprint: Publisher.

Bk. rev: 5–8, 600 words, signed. *Aud:* Sa, Ac. *Rv:* H. *Jv:* B.

A general linguistics journal, presenting "such studies as are likely to be of interest to any linguist, whatever his own specialization." Intended for the scholar, the journal tends to be a forum of opinion, presenting new approaches, critical articles, and rebuttals of previously published work. Generally two to four specialized, monographic articles appear in each issue. The text is in English, French, and German. Regular features are "Publications Received," a bulletin of new titles and reprints, and a special section of review articles, featuring long and critical reviews of important new books, as well as state of the art reports, which are interesting to language students.

Linguistics; an international review. 1963. 9/yr. $3. per no. Mouton & Co., Herderstraat 5, The Hague, Netherlands. Illus., index, adv. Circ: 1,500.

Bk. rev: 6, 1000 words, signed. *Aud:* Sa, Ac. *Rv:* H. *Jv:* B.

A magazine for the advanced researcher in all fields of linguistics. It presents scholarly studies in descriptive, historical, structural, and applied linguistics, as well as theoretical articles of a more general interest. Articles are rather long and monographic, often with charts. The text is in English, French, and German. The occasional supplement, "Linguistic Abstracts," contains short, informative abstracts of books, articles, and dissertations.

Modern Language Journal. 1916. m. (Oct.–May). $4. Robert F. Roeming. George Banta Co., Curtis Reed Plaza, Menasha, Wis. 54952. Illus., index, adv. Circ: 11,000. Microform: UM.

Indexed: EdI. *Bk. rev:* 25, 750 words, signed. *Aud:* Ac, Jc, Ht, Et. *Rv:* H. *Jv:* V.

Published by the National Federation of Modern Language Teachers Associations, and is "devoted primarily to methods, pedagogical research, and to topics of professional interest to all language teachers" from the elementary to graduate levels. Articles are usually case studies in teaching materials, methods and effects; the most recent issues focus on studies of the audio-lingual method. Linguistic analysis, critical discussions, theory, and occasional articles of literary interest also appear. Professional problems are a major focus of the journal, particularly the question of the formation of the American Council on the Teaching of Foreign Languages. Among the regular features are review essays, abstracts of articles from related periodicals, professional news, academic reports, "Books Received," an annual list of doctoral degrees awarded, and a directory of state, county and city foreign language supervisors. A basic journal for any school or academic library where foreign languages are a major concern of the curriculum.

Modern Language Quarterly. 1940. q. $4. William H. Machett. Univ. of Washington, Parrington Hall, Seattle, Wash. 98105. Index, adv. Circ: 1,450. Reprint: Johnson.

Indexed: SSHum. *Bk. rev:* 5–10, 800 words, 1 or 2 review articles. *Aud:* Sa, Ac, Jc, Sh. *Rv:* H. *Jv:* B.

Presents critical studies of literary works and forms in the English, Germanic, and Romance languages. Articles focus on the use of language and form in literary works. Some historical studies appear. Well-written and non-technical, the journal has an attractive format. Generally seven to ten articles appear in each issue, averaging 4,500 words each. Contributors are primarily American, Canadian, and British. Among the regular features are a comparative review of several recent books on a single topic, and a listing of new books. Of interest to all general literature students from the advanced high school to the university level.

Modern Language Review. 1905. q. $16.75. Ed bd. Modern Humanities Research Assn., Downing College, Cambridge, Eng. Index, adv. Circ: 2,200. Reprint: Dawson.

Indexed: BritHum, SSHum. *Bk. rev:* 60, 450 words, signed. *Aud:* Sa, Ac. *Rv:* H. *Jv:* A.

Publishes "original articles . . . on language and literature, embodying the results of research and criticism" for the advanced researcher in the English, Germanic, Romance, and Slavonic languages. A majority of the articles deal with historical, textual, linguistic, and critical approaches to literature. Occasional linguistic studies appear. Approximately one-quarter to one-half of the journal is devoted to critical book reviews. The rating here is based upon the general approach of the magazine to the field, and the extensive book reviews which are useful for any individual or library attempting to keep up with publications in the areas of literature, linguistics and philology. See also, *English Studies.*

Modern Philology; a journal devoted to the study of medieval and modern literature. 1903. q. $8. Univ. of Chicago Press, 5750 Ellis Ave., Chicago, Ill. 60637. Index, adv. Circ: 1,500. Reprint: Johnson. Microform: Canner, Princeton, UM.

Indexed: SSHum. *Bk. rev:* 15–20, 1200 words, signed. *Aud:* Sa, Ac. *Rv:* H. *Jv:* B.

The journal's main emphasis is on research into literary sources, literary indebtedness, comparative studies, historical criticism, and textual studies. All articles are well documented. English literature receives the most attention, with studies of Romance and Germanic works appearing occasionally. American and Canadian scholars contribute the three to five monographic articles which appear in each issue. A regular feature is a "Notes and Documents" section of short reports on the dating of works, attribution, newly-discovered manuscripts, and clarifications of facts in an author's life.

Philological Quarterly; devoted to scholarly investigation of the classical and modern languages and literature. 1922. q. $5. Curt A. Zimansky. Univ. of Iowa, Dept. of Pubns., Iowa City, Iowa 52240. Circ: 2,000. Microform: Canner, UM. Reprint: Johnson.

Indexed: SSHum. *Bk. rev:* Occasional, lengthy. *Aud:* Sa, Ac, Jc. *Rv:* H. *Jv:* B.

Predominantly studies of English literature, especially the Neoclassic period. The journal's primary concern is with investigation into textual and historical problems in the interpretation of literary works. Literary figures, literary history and theories, trends and conventions are also covered. A department for brief notes on sources, newly-discovered texts, dating and authenticity of texts is included. An important bibliography, "English Literature, 1660–1800," appears annually in the July issue. It includes notes on reviews (maximum length, 1,000 words) of almost all articles and books on English neoclassicism. The writing is not as technical as that in most philology journals, and the content is interesting to all students of literature—from the advanced high school to college level.

Quarterly Check List of Linguistics. See Literature Section (*Quarterly Check List of Literature*).

Studies in Philology. 1906. 5/yr. $6. Osborne B. Hardison. Univ. of North Carolina Press, Box 510, Chapel Hill, N.C. 27514. Adv. Circ: 1,600. Microform: UM. Reprint: Johnson.

Indexed: SSHum. *Aud:* Sa, Ac. *Rv:* H. *Jv:* A.

Presents textual and historical research in the classical and modern languages and literatures. Intended for the scholar and prepared under the auspices of the graduate faculty of the language and literature departments of the University of North Carolina. All forms and periods of literature are covered. Articles are long, averaging 5,000 words, and include: analysis of poetic language—imagery, structure, etymology; examination of newly-discovered texts and original manuscripts, and historical studies. Occasional extra series are published in honor of distinguished retired or deceased scholars. The April or May issue contains a comprehensive bibliography of the literature of the Renaissance. Somewhat comparable in purpose, if not scope, to *Modern Philology,* but rated higher here because of the annual bibliography.

Word. 1945. 3/yr. $7.50. (Students, $5). Louis G. Heller. Linguistic Circle of New York, Inc., Compton 102, City College of New York, New York, N.Y. 10031. Index.

Bk. rev: 10, 4000 words, signed. *Aud:* Sa, Ac. *Rv:* H. *Jv:* B.

Presents a wide range of linguistic studies for the advanced student and researcher. Text is in English and French. Articles are divided equally among research, theory and history, and original studies. Fields of coverage include descriptive linguistics, all phases of structural analysis, and mentalistic or formal linguistics, which emphasizes the relationship between language and psychology. Articles are lengthy, averaging 5,000 words, and are contributed by the Circle's international membership.

LITERARY AND POLITICAL REVIEWS

Indexes and Abstracts

Abstracts of English Studies, Abridged Readers' Guide, Biological Abstracts, British Humanities Index, Canadian Periodical Index, Catholic Periodical and Literature Index, Chemical Abstracts, Historical Abstracts, Index to Commonwealth Little Magazines, Index to Little Magazines, Music Index, Psychological Abstracts, Public Affairs Information Service, Science Abstracts, Social Sciences and Humanities Index, Sociological Abstracts. (For annotations, see Indexes and Abstracts Section.)

The terms "literary review" and "political review" are admittedly ambiguous, but they can be defined broadly enough to allow their being given a separate section. Literary reviews are generally distinguished by limited circulations, scholarliness (not to be automatically equated with dullness), and the inclusion of all types of quality fiction and non-fiction. In any single edition of one of these reviews, the reader can find several poems—perhaps by an established poet, perhaps not—a short story or excerpts from a novel or play, as well as critical articles covering politics, sociology, literary criticism, etc. In terms of content, the literary review is quite often the sounding board for some of the best thought available. And, interestingly enough, most tend to be liberal, particularly in their approach to politics.

Many literary reviews began as little magazines, e.g., *Evergreen Review* and *Paris Review.* They fall into a new category when the circulation exceeds 1,500, editing becomes more precise (and sometimes pedantic and stifling), support is guaranteed by subscriptions or university or foundation grants, and considerably more attention is paid to older, well-established writers. For the average reader the distinction may be unimportant, but the literary reviews, or as some put it, the "big littles," are a breed apart from the average "little" magazine, and it is important that the librarian know the difference. A library may consider itself quite advanced in taking a few of the reviews, with no representation from the little magazines. Without this representation, however, the library is incomplete, as well as unfair to those of its patrons (most notably the younger ones) who read these regularly.

"Political reviews" are a little more easily defined, the most obvious characteristic being the intelligence of approach in, say, *The Nation,* or *The New Statesman.* Where *Time* would simply report, in its standard, dulling fashion, the *New Republic* or *The National Review* would report and analyze, speculating on the why's, wherefore's and what's of a political event. And, each of these reviews takes a selective approach to the news, including only what the editors consider to be the important events. They are far more obviously political than the "news" magazines (see *General Magazines*), and are represented all across the political spectrum, from *The National Review* to *Ramparts.* They can be caustic, insulting, frustrating or simply annoying, but they are rarely dull, staffed by men who realize that political events are nothing until you've taken the time to find out what really happened, and why.

For related magazines, see *Dissident Magazines* and *Little Magazines.*

American Scholar; a quarterly for the independent thinker. 1932. q. $5. Hiram Haydn. United Chapters of

Phi Beta Kappa, 1811 Q St., N.W., Washington, D.C. 20009. Illus., index, adv. Circ: 42,000.

Indexed: PAIS, SSHum. *Bk. rev:* 3–4, 500–1,000 words, signed. *Aud:* Ga, Ac, Jc. *Rv:* M. *Jv:* A.

Published by Phi Beta Kappa, this is a nice combination of scholarship and popular writing directed to the general, intelligent reader. It offers the frank opinions of such scholars as Alfred Kazin, Jacques Barzun, August Heckscher, and Loren Eisley. Topics cover both cultures and are of interest to anyone who is intellectually alert. In the "Revolving Bookstand" section, there are reviews of important new books. In his column, "If You Don't Mind My Saying So," Joseph Wood Krutch has offered his opinion on such subjects as civil rights and technology. A section called "Arts and Letters" often appears. A recent topic discussed was Vietnamese music. An excellent magazine for almost all libraries.

Antioch Review. 1941. q. $3.50. Paul H. Rohmann. Antioch Press, Yellow Springs, Ohio 45387. Index, adv. Circ: 2,200. Reprint: AMS. Microform: UM.

Indexed: AbEnStud, HistAb, PAIS, SocAb, SHI. *Bk. rev:* 2, 2,000–2,500 words, signed. *Aud:* Ga, Ac, Jc, Sh. *Rv:* H. *Jv:* A.

A wide-ranging literary magazine which touches on social and political issues. The articles and short stories are of the calibre found in the best of the older reviews, and appeal primarily to the intelligent layman, and student. There are excellent book reviews of novels, poetry and literature, which are usually in the form of short essays. Often a single issue centers on a given theme, as for example, Greek philosophers. One of the better literary magazines, and should have appeal for most libraries.

Appalachian Review. 1966. q. $6. Lloyd Davis. West Virginia Univ., Morgantown, W.Va. 26505. Illus. Circ: 853.

Bk. rev: 4 or 5, various lengths, signed. *Aud:* Ga, Ac, Jc. *Rv:* L. *Jv:* B.

Initiated to help develop a sense of unity and direction for an Appalachia moving from a rural into an urbanized society, the *Review* publishes the best of the region's literature, art, ideas, and opinions. Book reviews and a bibliography are included in each issue. It will appeal mostly to intellectuals, but all libraries in Appalachia and others concerned with the region should subscribe to the *Review.*

Atlantic Monthly. 1857. m. $8.50. Robert Manning. Atlantic Monthly Co., 8 Arlington St., Boston, Mass. 02116. Adv. Circ: 290,000. Microform: UM.

Indexed: AbrRG, RG. *Bk. rev:* 5–10 lengthy, 10–20 notes, signed. *Aud:* Ga, Ac, Jc, Sh. *Rv:* M. *Jv:* A.

One of the best and oldest of the general interest review magazines, this presents informative and entertaining articles by accepted authorities, stories and poetry by established writers and talented newcomers. Regular features include the "Reports," candid studies of important political

activities and other foreign and domestic developments; "Accent," amusing provocative essays upon varied subjects; "Places," thoughts about unusual places and travel; "Music," critical comments and record reviews; and "Books," excellent reviews of current books. Articles, sometimes commissioned, explore controversial political and social questions, scientific and technical innovations, and the whole range of the arts. Quality literature and literary criticism earn a place for *The Atlantic* in the lists of literary magazines.

The Aylesford Review; a literary quarterly sponsored by English Carmelites. 1955. q. $4.50. Rev. Brocard Sewell. St. Albert's Press, Aylesford Priory, Aylesford, Maidstone, Kent, Eng. Circ: 700–1,000.

Indexed: ComLMags 1964–65. *Bk. rev:* 2–3, lengthy, 10–14 notes, signed. *Aud:* Ac, Jc. *Rv:* M. *Jv:* B.

An established "above-ground" small review published by the English Carmelite fathers. Features work, both traditional and "concrete," by new English poets, and lengthy articles on current problems and developments within the Roman Catholic Church. Although leaning heavily on British poets for its creative portion, *Aylesford* has published Americans as well. A "big little" magazine of primary interest to the academic audience.

Bulletin of the Atomic Scientists; a journal of science and public affairs. 1945. m. (Sept.–June). $7. Eugene Rabinowitch. Educational Foundation for Nuclear Science, 935 E. 60th St., Chicago, Ill. 60637. Illus., index, adv. Circ: 20,000. Microform: UM.

Indexed: BioAb, PAIS, PsyAb, RG. *Bk. rev:* 4–8, 900 words, signed. *Aud:* Ga, Ac, Jc, Sh. *Rv:* H. *Jv:* A.

Despite its title, this is a general magazine directed toward the intelligent layman who believes there is a bridge between Snow's "two cultures." This offers such a bridge, and its subtitle indicates the wide scope. In a recent issue international affairs, disarmament, problems of world agriculture, racial questions, economic planning and the relationship of the growth of science and technology to environment and institutions are discussed. All articles are by experts, are written in an intelligible manner, and decidedly liberal. None require a scientific background, and all show the close relationships among science, the humanities and politics. An ideal magazine for the scientist or the humanist who seek to understand one another's thinking. Suited for most high schools.

Canadian Forum. 1920. m. Milton Wilson. Canadian Forum Ltd., Univ. & King Sts., Toronto, 1, Ont. Illus., index, adv. Circ: 2,200.

Indexed: CanI. *Bk. rev:* Various numbers, lengths. *Aud:* Ga, Ac, Jc. *Rv:* M. *Jv:* B.

Canada's oldest and most distinguished "independent journal of opinion and the arts." It covers all aspects of the arts—play reviews, television, films—and has articles on various aspects of Canadian and international politics, economics, and social activities. Each issue usually contains a number of poems, short stories, and book reviews. The latter vary in number and length, but are particularly good for keeping up with general Canadian books and many English based titles. A required item for any Canadian library and certainly should be in the larger American public and academic libraries.

The Carleton Miscellany. 1960. q. $3.50. Erling Larsen. Carleton College, Northfield, Minn. 55057. Index, adv. Circ: 1,300. Microform: UM.

Indexed: LMags. *Bk. rev:* 4–6, 1,500 words, signed, critical. *Aud:* Ac, Jc. *Rv:* M. *Jv:* B.

Fiction, poetry and criticism are featured in this college-based literary review. The material is consistently good and of a well-made, academic, variety. While the imaginative quality is not always high, the critical articles, which concern both contemporary and historical literary subjects, are excellent and readable. A basic magazine for any large academic collection of literary periodicals.

Center Magazine. 1967. bi-m. $10. John Cogley. Center for the Study of Democratic Institutions, Box 4608, Santa Barbara, Calif. 93103. Circ: 50,000.

Bk. rev: 3–6, 500–1,500 words, signed. *Aud:* Ga, Ac, Jc, Sh. *Rv:* H. *Jv:* A.

Edited by a former editor of the *New York Times,* drawing upon the talents of the leading scholars of the world, including those at the Center, directed to an intelligent, lay audience-all of this adds up to a truly distinguished magazine of comment, touching all of the vital issues of the day. The style of writing is lucid, and presupposes no particular specialized knowledge on the part of the reader. A typical issue may examine the student revolt, the Vietnam war, race relations, and city planning. The contributors are well known, and have included such people as Bishop James Pike, Harry Ashmore, Michael Harrington, Edward Engberg, and Thomas Merton. The approach is objective, liberal, and in the best tradition of such long-standing magazines as *American Scholar* and *Encounter*. While a bit difficult for the average high school student, it will be of considerable interest and value to better, more involved juniors and seniors. Should be in all medium to large public and all academic libraries.

The Chicago Review. 1946. $3.50. Eugene Wildman. Univ. of Chicago, Chicago, Ill. 60637. Illus., index, adv. Circ: 3,000. Reprint: AMS.

Indexed: LMags, SSHum. *Bk. rev:* 2–3, 1,500–3,000 words, signed. *Aud:* Sa, Ac, Jc, Sh. *Rv:* M. *Jv:* A.

A little review which has shown remarkable staying power, primarily because of its consistent high quality. Each issue is divided between creative writing and critical essays. Stories are longer than in many other little magazines and show better development. Poetry is usually traditional and

workmanlike. Critical articles, which are sound without being pedantic, and not limited to the work of contemporary writers, make the magazine valuable to the student of literature as well as to the intelligent layman.

Christian Century. 1884. w. $8.50. Kyle Haselden. Christian Century Foundation, 407 S. Dearborn St., Chicago, Ill. 60605. Adv. Circ: 45,000. Microform: UM.

Indexed: RG. *Bk. rev:* 10–12, 200–900 words, signed. *Aud:* Ga, Ac, Jc, Sh. *Rv:* M. *Jv:* A.

A non-denominational Protestant weekly, that is similar in purpose to *Commentary* (Jewish) and *Commonweal* (Catholic), i.e., it is closer to a liberal, general literary/ political magazine than a religious periodical. While its writers are among the leading theological thinkers in the world, the scope of the magazine is broad. It covers foreign policy, the arts, literature, social problems and general news. The book reviews cover religious works, but are just as apt to discuss any current novel or non-fiction title. The editorial policy is definitely liberal, although not as outspoken at times as *Commentary*. Probably the best summary of the magazine was made by John Cogley in the *New York Times* (Aug. 15, 1965, p.E5): "It is steadfastly urbane, highly respected and, cutting across denominational lines as it does, is probably the most influential of all Protestant publications." A first choice for any library.

Columbia University Forum; a journal of fact and opinion. 1957. q. Controlled. Lee Ambrose. Records Control Center, 632 W. 125th St. New York, N.Y. 10027. Circ: 115,000. Microform: UM.

Indexed: PAIS. *Aud:* Ga, Ac, Jc, Sh. *Rv:* H. *Jv:* A.

Free upon request, this alumni magazine is one of the best in the United States. It has appeal for any perceptive adult, and is in no way limited to Columbia University interests. An alumni magazine, it seeks to "give a hearing to divergent ideas in the interests of thought and discussion" without taking any one viewpoint or position. The breadth and depth of the many contributors in the areas of social, economic, scientific and political thought produce a thought provoking and interesting journal. The style of writing is excellent and semi-popular. As evidence of its scholarly audience a section of "Letters" reveals the names Henry Steele Commager, Stuart Chase and Robert Ogden, Jr. In many ways it is broad enough in subject and scope to qualify for an honorable place alongside such magazines as *Commentary* and *Encounter*. A "best buy" for almost any type of library.

Commentary; journal of significant thought and opinion on Jewish affairs and contemporary issues. 1945. m. $9. Norman Podhoretz. Amer. Jewish Committee, 165 E. 56th St., New York, N.Y. 10022. Circ: 45,000.

Indexed: PAIS, RG. *Bk. rev:* 5–8, 500–1,500 words, signed. *Aud:* Ga, Ac, Jc, Sh. *Rv:* M. *Jv:* V.

Numbering among its contributors the principal thinkers of America, and directed at the liberal reader, this is one of three mirrors of the American intellectual establishment, the other two being the *Partisan Review* and *The New York Review of Books*. Articles cover the whole general range of current interest, from politics and literature to sex and art. All are not only extremely well written, but are often months to years ahead of thinking in the popular press. The book reviews are among the best available. Although sponsored by the American Jewish Committee, there is little religious material included—normally no more than one or two articles, and these usually in reference to social, economic or literary matters. While in some ways equivalent to *Commonweal* and the *Christian Century*, the emphasis is considerably more literary than the other two. A magazine for almost any library that has an educated public.

Commonweal. 1924. w. $10. Edward S. Skillin. Commonweal Publishing Co., Inc., 232 Madison Ave., New York, N.Y. 10016. Illus., adv. Circ: 45,000. Microform: UM.

Indexed: CathI, RG. *Bk. rev:* 6–8, 900 words, signed. *Aud:* Ga, Ac, Jc, Sh. *Rv:* H. *Jv:* A.

Independently edited by laymen for the better educated Catholic and non-Catholic, this reports on all current affairs and events which have any relationship to the Catholic church. Sometimes the relationship is a bit tenuous, at least from the viewpoint of more conservative church members and particularly as regards the editors' liberal ideas in the social and political fields. There are usually three to five long articles by eminent scholars and lay experts, editorials, briefer comments, and regular departments covering books, records, film and drama. The writing style is excellent, the coverage nicely augments what is found in general magazines of news and comment, and the overall impression is one of a much above average publication. Should be in almost all libraries, certainly in those serving a Catholic community.

Contemporary Review Incorporating the Fortnightly. 1866. m. $12.25. Dominic Le Foe. Contemporary Review Co., Ltd., 36 Broadway, Westminster, London S.W.1. Adv. Microform: UM.

Indexed: BritHum, SSHum. *Bk. rev:* 8–10, 150–500 words. *Aud:* Ga, Ac, Jc. *Rv:* M. *Jv:* B.

A famous, old British magazine which features a collection of commentaries on today's world happenings and on many events of the past. It is written in a semi-popular manner, but emphasis is on material which will appeal only to the educated and the literary. The journal divides its entries into various sections including "Forum Features," "World Vistas," "Literature," "Arts," "History," and a "Literary Supplement." Books are reviewed in an interesting but not too critical style. The overall tone is relatively conservative, the emphasis is on established literary figures. It is an ideal magazine for libraries where a combination literary review and magazine of opinion is sought which will shock almost no one.

Daedalus. 1955. q. $6.50. Amer. Academy of Arts and Sciences, 280 Newton St., Brookline Station, Boston, Mass. 02146. Circ: 58,000.

Indexed: BioAb, ChemAb, PAIS, PsyAb, SSHum, SciAb. *Aud:* Sa, Ac, Jc, Sh. *Rv:* H. *Jv:* A.

Concentrating on one particular social, political or literary topic, each issue offers a current report on an aspect of American life. Contributors are leaders in the area covered, and normally there is a brief introductory essay with some 15 to 20 supporting articles. Topics range from "Students and Politics" to "Historical Population Studies" and "The Negro American." (Librarians who recognize the approach of *Library Trends* will find the same general monographic method here.) A run of *Daedalus* is equivalent to an updating service of texts and full length book studies found on the shelves. Many libraries and individuals tend to bind the copies and catalog them in the subject area. In view of its authority, the frequency of comment on an issue by the American press, and the topical nature of its coverage, this should be found in all libraries.

Dalhousie Review; a Canadian quarterly of literature and opinion. 1921. q. $4. C. L. Bennett. Review Publishing Co., Ltd., Dalhousie Univ., Halifax, Nova Scotia. Index, adv. Circ: 900.

Indexed: CanI, PAIS. *Bk. rev:* 20–25, various lengths, signed. *Aud:* Ac, Ga, Jc. *Rv:* M. *Jv:* B.

Articles are concerned with current affairs, the humanities, literature, and particularly with Canadian history and politics. Books are treated in long review articles, and in a section devoted to shorter reviews, often treating several books under one unifying theme (cf. *The New York Review of Books*). Some poetry is published, and an occasional short story. Despite its limited circulation and its university base, this is not a typical scholarly magazine. The style assumes a good education, but it is semi-popular and geared for the layman rather than the specialist. As one of the best Canadian literary reviews, it should be found in all Canadian libraries, along with *Saturday Night*. A necessary addition, too, for larger American academic collections.

Delta; a review of arts, life and thought in the Netherlands. 1958. q. $5. Delta Intl. Pubn. Foundation, 41 J.J. Viottastraat, Amsterdam, Netherlands. Illus., index. Circ: 6,000.

Indexed: PAIS. *Aud:* Ga, Ac, Jc, Sh. *Rv:* M. *Jv:* B.

Not to be confused with the English *Delta* (or a half dozen other publications by the same name), this is an extremely literate voice of European social, political and literary commentary. The tone is avant-garde yet the approach is always thoughtful and intelligent (even a bit conservative, some would say). The editors stand detached from the subject matter, giving an objective, thorough report, e.g., issues devoted to the Provos (a short-lived Dutch, radical hippie movement), art, music, and the fate of many intellectuals under the Nazi occupation. By and large, one of the best literary reviews coming out of Europe. As it is in English, it can be recommended for almost all libraries, and the more advanced high school collections.

Encounter. 1950. m. $10. Nigel Dennis & Melvin J. Lasky. British Pubns., Inc., 30 E. 60th St., New York, N.Y. 10022. Circ: 34,000. Microform: UM.

Indexed: BritHum, PAIS, SSHum. *Bk. rev:* 2–5, 3–5 pages, signed. *Aud:* Ga, Sa, Ac, Jc, Sh. *Rv:* M. *Jv:* V.

A British magazine with close American ties, this is somewhat similar in purpose to *Commentary,* the *Partisan Review* and other general literary-political reviews. Although contributors are representatives of some of the world's leading scholars, the tone is not academic. Emphasis is on wit, style and a sense of proportion between the ivory tower and the marketplace. Articles cover a wide field, from social and political studies to literary and philosophical considerations. The April, 1968 issue is typical enough, with four articles ranging from "The Philby Affair" by Hugh Trevor-Roper to "Greek Mythologies" by Leslie Fiedler, poetry, notes on Germany's young left, two book reviews, and commentary from the Fiji Islands. The writers presuppose a better than average educated audience with a liberal viewpoint. From its beginnings it was one of the more influential international periodicals, particularly under the editorship of Stephen Spender and Frank Kermode. Both quit in 1967 when it was found that funds had been channeled by the Central Intelligence Agency to the magazine. Then it was said that the "editors alone have always been responsible for what they published," and it had always "enjoyed complete independence in its editorial policy." There is no indication that this is not the case, and it remains an important general magazine for all types of libraries.

Evergreen Review. 1957. m. $9. Barney Rosset. Evergreen Review, Inc., 80 Univ. Place, New York, N.Y. 10003. Illus., index, adv. Circ: 125,000. Microform: UM.

Indexed: LMags. *Aud:* Ga, Ac, Jc. *Rv:* M. *Jv:* A.

The leading "big little" magazine which is both a literary review and a purveyor of the "Underground" to Everyman. Growth has not vitiated *Evergreen's* strength. Featuring contemporary writers such as Gregory Corso, Allen Ginsberg, Hubert Selby, Paul Blackburn, and Nat Hentoff, it has added satire, camp, comics and extended jazz notes in a dizzying spiral of multi-color presentations. In the past, *Evergreen* has presented excerpts from *Naked Lunch, Our Lady of the Flowers, The Tin Drum* and other important fictional works. Although unlimited in geographical scope, it is an "All-American" with a strong New York flavor. For the intelligent adult whose politics are liberal and who is not shocked by an occasional Anglo-Saxon monosyllable or nude photograph. Senior high school librarians who take a realistic view of their charge's intelligence and taste might try a subscription, too.

Form. 1966. q. $5. Philip Steadman, 78 Norwich St., Cambridge, Eng. Illus. Circ: Microform: UM.

Aud: Ga, Sa, Ac. *Rv:* H. *Jv:* B.

A 32-page English avant-garde magazine, covering a range from modern music and art to architecture and education. The writing is scholarly, yet exceptionally lucid. A regular feature is "Great little magazines," which devotes several pages to the history of outstanding littles. The series on "Black Mountain College" describes it from the point of view of its early teachers. This has achieved wide success in England, and while hard to classify—it seems to touch on every base—it should have a ready audience in American libraries.

Hard Times (Formerly: *Mayday*). 1968. w. (bi-w, July & Aug.). $10 (Students, $6). 617 N. Carolina Ave., S.E., Washington, D.C. 20003.

Aud: Ga, Ac, Jc, Sh. *Rv:* H. *Jv:* B.

A four-page weekly edited by some of the more lucid writers of the left-liberal camp, including Andrew Kopkind, James Ridgeway and Robert Sherrill. Consulting editors include Ralph Nader and Fred Gardiner, with Richard Grossman as publishing consultant. This high-calibre group usually devotes each issue to short notes on current affairs and one or two longer articles on a generally overlooked issue, e.g., James Ridgeway's study of the plight of the American Indian, "Teddy at Little Tin-Horn." Notes on publishing show Grossman's hand, and from time to time there are slams at consumer exploitation by Ralph Nader. The style is lively, often amusing, and consistently iconoclastic. Thanks to the frequency of publication, it is a good springboard for discussions in high school, and a source of up-to-date reference material for college and university libraries.

Harper's Magazine. 1850. m. $8.50. Willie Morris. Harper's Magazine, Inc., 2 Park Ave., New York, N.Y. 10016. Illus., index, adv. Circ: 282,064. Microform: UM.

Indexed: AbrRG, RG. *Bk. rev:* 4–5, lengthy, book notes. *Aud:* Ga, Ac, Jc, Sh. *Rv:* M. *Jv:* V.

One of the oldest general cultural magazines in the United States, this is usually considered a must for all types of libraries. The articles and fiction are carefully selected and well-written by established authors and specialists. There are candid discussions of international affairs, politics, business and industrial problems, legislative and judicial activities, education, and science. In a lighter vein, profiles of literary and entertainment personalities are presented. The book reviews are outstanding, and show thoughtful selection coupled with descriptive, comparative criticism. Discussion and criticism of music, records, and current drama are also included.

Harvard Review. 1963. q. $4.50. Harrison H. Young. Room 206, 52 Dunster St., Cambridge, Mass. 02138.

Bk. rev: Occasional long featured reviews. *Aud:* Ac, Jc. *Rv:* M. *Jv:* B.

The general goal here is to provide an articulate but not too highly academic forum for debate on topics selected by the editors as being particularly timely. Each issue takes a special area, such as law, drugs, revolution, the Middle East, or the American City, and presents several varied and often opposing articles on the subject. It very often attracts top-notch contributors such as Daniel Bell, Reinhold Niebuhr, Daniel P. Moynihan, and Paul Goodman. The approach is successful and stimulating. Good for college, university, and large public libraries.

The Hudson Review. 1948. q. $5. Frederick Morgan. The Hudson Review, Inc., 65 E. 55th St., New York, N.Y. 10022. Index, adv. Circ: 3,000. Microform: UM. Reprints: AMS.

Indexed: SSHum. *Bk. rev:* 30, various lengths, signed. *Aud:* Ga, Ac, Jc. *Rv:* M. *Jv:* A.

An outstanding literary periodical with perceptive coverage of cultural life in the U.S. and abroad. Well-known writers and scholars contribute articles on criticism, aesthetics, and literary topics. Regular coverage of the British scene by Anthony Burgess. Stimulating articles on architecture, art, ballet, film, music, and theater. Original fiction and poetry of the highest quality. Book reviews are well written, substantial, and critical. An unusually large number of poetry books are reviewed regularly in "Poetry Chronicle." Frequent illustrations. Ranks favorably among the top dozen relatively long-standing literary magazines in this country, and should be a serious consideration for all libraries.

Kenyon Review. 1939. 5/yr. $5. Robie Macauley. Kenyon College, Box 73, Gambier, Ohio 43022. Circ: 6,000. Reprint: AMS.

Indexed: SSHum. *Bk. rev:* 5, 1,500 words, signed. *Aud:* Ga, Ac, Jc. *Rv:* M. *Jv:* A.

One of the long-time favored literary quarterlies, this is famous for its emphasis on literary criticism. Its editors have included distinguished critics and writers, and to have a contribution accepted is to win a place in a rather select inner circle. The book reviews are, more often than not, literary essays, reminiscent of many of the articles (and of the *N.Y. Review of Books*). Poetry, essays on the arts (from music to the theatre), and scholarly comments counterpoint the literary criticism. Frequent illustrations. Special features are "Department KR," and "Excursion," with briefer comments, tributes, and reminiscences. A basic journal for most libraries.

London Magazine. 1954. m. $10. Alan Ross. 30 Thurloe Pl., London W.C.1.

Bk. rev: 10–15, 1,000 words, signed. *Aud:* Sa, Ac, Jc. *Rv:* M. *Jv:* B.

A monthly of the arts from Britain. A high proportion of its content is devoted to poems, stories, and art. New writers as well as established ones are featured, and it maintains an excellent level of poetry for a magazine of this type. The special editorial aim is to discuss individual writers and painters out of season, and to keep literary contact with Europe, Africa, America, and the Commonwealth. Regular features are the sections on theater, cinema, music, art, architecture, poetry, and "Reminiscences." Book reviews are of scholarly works, poetry, and fiction. A first choice in academic libraries over *Contemporary Review,* but for public libraries it would probably have less appeal than the other English magazines.

Massachusetts Review. 1959. q. $6. Jules Chametzky & John H. Hicks. Massachusetts Review, Inc., Univ. of Massachusetts, Amherst, Mass. 01002. Illus., index, adv. Circ: 2,000.

Indexed: LMags, SSHum. *Bk. rev:* 4–8, 2,500 words, signed. *Aud:* Ga, Ac, Jc. *Rv:* M. *Jv:* B.

One of the best printed, prestigious literary periodicals. Devotes a large number of its pages to original fiction, plays, and poetry. Writers range from the youngest to the well-established. The "Signature Series" generously features individual poets. Frequent review articles on contemporary American and British poetry and fiction. Some of today's most distinguished scholars of literature, including Harold Bloom, R. W. B. Lewis, and Conor Cruise O'Brien contribute articles to each issue. Various aspects of cultural life here and abroad are treated, e.g., drama and film. The fine arts, in particular, receive excellent coverage, complete with superb illustrations. American and international politics are another concern of the *Review.* Book reviews cover a similar range of topics, including fiction, poetry, art, and politics. Along with the equally handsome and relatively new *Tri-Quarterly,* it should be considered by those large public and academic libraries which may be in a rut with the traditional publications such as the *Hudson Review, Kenyon Review, Sewanee Review,* etc.

Midway. 1960. q. $7. Morris Philipson. The Univ. of Chicago Press, 5750 Ellis Ave., Chicago, Ill. 60637. Illus., adv. Circ: 8,843.

Aud: Ga, Ac, Jc. *Rv:* H. *Jv:* B.

Although published since 1960, it has only been since 1967 that this college-based magazine has attracted attention. Under editor Morris Philipson the format was revamped and the scope enlarged to include significant articles on almost every aspect of society, from the Secret Service to poetry, the militant blacks, and films. Articles are often by University of Chicago faculty, but regardless of origin, represent the established intelligentsia of this country. The style is scholarly, yet lucid, the content original, usually thought-provoking. It presupposes a good university background, an interest in social problems and the liberal arts. The format, right down to the cover and graphics, is much above average. Normally thought of as a literary magazine, it is closer to a general periodical for intellectuals. Should be found in any medium to large academic collection.

The Minnesota Review. 1960. q. $3. Alvin Greenberg. Box 4066, Highland Station, St. Paul, Minn. 55116. Illus. Circ: 1,000.

Indexed: LMags. *Bk. rev:* 2–5, lengthy, signed. *Aud:* Ac, Jc. *Rv:* M. *Jv:* B.

An experienced teacher, poet and author, the editor demonstrates the importance of editorship for the success of a literary magazine. Professor Greenberg strikes a nice balance between fiction, poetry and commentary—some by new talent, much by professionals such as Ted Enslin, Paul Carroll and Margaret Randall, to name only a few of the contributors. An excellent general little literary magazine. For larger libraries.

The Nation. 1865. w. $10. Carey McWilliams. Nation Co., Inc., 333 Sixth Ave., New York, N.Y. 10014. Illus. Circ: 33,000. Microform: UM.

Indexed: PAIS, RG. *Bk. rev:* 5–6, 1,500 words, signed. *Aud:* Ga, Ac, Jc, Sh. *Rv:* H. *Jv:* V.

A journal of opinion which pledges (as stated in its third issue) that it "will not be the organ of any party, sect, or body. It will, on the contrary, make an earnest effort to bring to the discussion of political and social questions a really critical spirit, and to wage war upon the vices of violence, exaggeration and misrepresentation by which so much of the political writing of this day is marred." The independent liberal character of the publication appeals to students and informed adults. Well-documented articles concerned with foreign affairs, civil liberties, domestic policies, disarmament, etc., are presented with clarity and simplicity. Important events and significant undertakings are discussed in its pages sometimes long before they appear in other news media, e.g., the Bay of Pigs affair. Its list of outstanding contributors has included Henry and William James, H. L. Mencken, Carl Van Doren, Harold Laski, Bernard Fall, Fred J. Cook, Robert Sherrill, and Alexander Werth. Its scholarly appraisal of the theatre, the arts, and literature contributes to its position of respect. Almost devoid of advertising, the magazine depends upon contributions and subscriptions for its support. Should be in all libraries, regardless of size or type.

National Review; a journal of fact and opinion. 1955. bi-w. $9. William F. Buckley, Jr. William A. Rushev, 150 E. 5th St., New York, N.Y. 10016. Illus., adv. Circ: 96,000. Microform: UM.

Indexed: RG. *Bk. rev:* 3–4, one page, notes, signed. *Aud:* Ga, Ac, Jc, Sh. *Rv:* M. *Jv:* A.

The intellectual voice of conservatism in America, this is the outspoken critic of most liberal or progressive ideas. In coverage and scope it is somewhat similar to the *New Republic* and the *Nation.* Here the analogy ends. First and foremost, it is the child of its editor, William Buckley, a controversial editor who has brought a degree of respectability to the conservative school. No friend of either the reactionary right wing or the progressive left, he blasts both with a telling wit and a style which is sometimes flippant, sometimes penetrating. The flag of bias is not only evident, it is flown in pride. Among contributors are Russell Kirk, James Burnham, Hugh Kenner, and Will Herberg. All are representative of a depth of thought and opinion rarely associated with the popular notion of conservatism. Except for the *National Review,* the conservatives have failed to produce a major journal of news of political commentary. (The publications of the radical right, as those of the radical left, stand only on the fringes—see "Dissident Magazines" section.) Christopher Lasch gives one possible reason why there are a dozen liberal magazines to only one *National Review.* There are so few, he notes, because, "the opinions represented by the *National Review* are not dissenting opinions at all but opinions which are readily endorsed, in whole or in part, by the mass media and, on at least one recent occasion by one of the major political parties" (*New York Times Magazine,* July 18, 1965, p.33). Librarians and readers may no more agree with the *National Review* than they do with the *New Republic,* but because of its intellectual approach, this magazine should be in every library, from senior high school to academic.

New American Review. 1967. 3/yr. $1.25 an issue. Theodore Solotaroff. New American Library, 1301 Ave. of the Americas, New York, N.Y. 10019.

Aud: Ga, Ac, Jc. *Rv:* M. *Jv:* A.

This thrice yearly literary-social journal is in the form of a paperback, and looks more like a book than a magazine. Nevertheless, it follows the tradition of such items as *New World Writing* (defunct) and the *New Directions Annuals* (still very much with us). The mass-market paperback form and the frequency of issue is almost a ploy to catch readers who otherwise might avoid the "little magazines," which it emulates. The contents follow the best tradition of the littles—six or seven works of short fiction, seven or eight essays on everything from literature to social issues, and a considerable amount of verse. It differs from a number of literary magazines by its quality—exceptionally high—and its relatively well known authors, from Philip Roth to Donald Barthelme. The material is imaginative, represents discussion of issues of interest to the "now" generation, and is served up in a format which will attract almost any literate reader. Should be found in most public and academic libraries, and possibly in a few advanced high school collections.

New Leader; a bi-weekly of news and opinion. 1927. bi-w. $8. Myron Kolatch. Amer. Labor Conference on Intl. Affairs, 212 Fifth Ave., New York, N.Y. 10010. Illus., adv.

Indexed: PAIS. *Bk. rev:* Various numbers, lengths. *Aud:* Ga, Ac, Jc, Sh. *Rv:* M. *Jv:* B.

A moderately liberal magazine of opinion which has somewhat the same political-social leanings as *The New Republic* and *The Nation,* yet is somewhat closer to a center position than either. The editor and the contributors frequently chastise both the left and the right wing, maintaining a staunchly independent policy in national and international affairs. The literary and fine arts reviews are excellent, often taking quite a different tack than found in many regular reviewing services. A second choice for high school, college and public libraries.

New Left Review. 1957. 6/yr. $5.50. Perry Anderson. Subscriptions to: B. de Boer, 188 High St., Nutley, N.J. 07110.

Indexed: BritHum, PAIS. *Aud:* Sa, Ac. *Rv:* M. *Jv:* B.

A sounding board for English and European intellectuals who prescribe to views indicated in the title. It is considerably more to the left than the *New Statesman,* yet has been highly critical of Soviet- or Chinese-oriented Communism. The particular value of the journal for Americans is that its articles give an intelligent, highly topical view of issues on the left which are of interest to those who follow the New Left in the United States. A normal number consists of two or three articles, poems, literary criticism, art, and music criticism, documents and short essays or discussions. From time to time a single issue is given over to a theme, e.g., "Festival of the Oppressed—France 1968." A solid addition for larger academic libraries.

The New Republic; a journal of opinion. 1914. w. $10. Gilbert A. Harrison. 1244 19th St., N.W., Washington, D.C. 20036. Subscriptions to: New Republic, Subscription Dept., 381 W. Center St., Marion, Ohio 43302. Illus., index, adv. Circ: 125,000. Microform: UM.

Indexed: RG. *Bk. rev:* 3–5, 1,500 words, signed. *Aud:* Ga, Ac, Jc, Sh. *Rv:* H. *Jv:* A.

A refreshing and thought-provoking periodical which pulls no punches in representing the moderate and liberal point of view on current political, economic and social problems. Acting as a social conscience, *The New Republic* adds intelligent thought to the all too frequently dull journalistic world. With men like Robert Coles, Stanley Kauffman and Robert Schwartz lending their prestige and literary talents, it presents its left-of-center political philosophy in an interesting and exciting way. The book reviews are uniformly excellent, as are the comments on the film and arts. Differs only from *The Nation* in a somewhat more left-of-center viewpoint. The two magazines supplement one another, and both should be found in most libraries.

New Statesman; an independent political and literary review. 1913. w. $11. Paul Johnson. Statesman & Nation Publishing Co., 10 Great Turnstile, London W.C.1. Circ: 91,408. Microfilm: UM.

Indexed: BritHum, SSHum. *Bk. rev:* 20–25, 800–1,500 words, signed. *Aud:* Ga, Ac, Jc, Sh. *Rv:* H. *Jv:* A.

Roughly equivalent to *The Nation* and *The New Republic,* this British-based review has a world-wide reputation for its excellent political and literary satire. Here it is considerably ahead of its American counterparts. A weekly with a tabloid format, it discusses economic, religious, social, cultural and political matters. Although it champions

the liberal point of view, the criticism strikes liberal as well as conservative policy. The book reviews are of major importance; beautifully written, highly critical and always useful for American librarians. For better high school students, and should be included in all adult library situations.

New York Review of Books. See Book Review Section.

The North American Review. 1964. q. $4. Univ. of Northern Iowa, Cedar Falls, Iowa 50613. Illus. Circ: 800.

Indexed: SSHum. *Bk. rev:* 4–6, 500 words, signed. *Aud:* Ga, Ac, Jc. *Rv:* L. *Jv:* B.

Although based on the original *North American Review* (1815–1940) the revived magazine has a character peculiar to itself. Each number features political-cultural reports from Latin America and the United States, three to four social or literary articles, two or three short stories, poetry, and book reviews. Once a year there is a special number devoted to fiction or poetry. The 64-page magazine supports new writers, a liberal policy and is edited for the above average educated reader. Early in 1969 the magazine changed ownership, but there is every indication the content will remain much the same. It should be stressed that this is not to be confused with the original publication which at one time enjoyed a circulation of close to 100,000 and boasted such writers as Mark Twain, Daniel Webster and U. S. Grant. The current publication is good, considerably more modest, and definitely aimed at a select rather than a general audience.

The Paris Review. 1952. q. $4. George A. Plimpton. 45–39 171st Place, Flushing, N.Y. 11358. Illus., adv. Drawings, photos. Circ: 19,000. Microform: UM. Reprint: Johnson.

Indexed: LMags, SSHum. *Aud:* Ga, Ac, Jc, Sh. *Rv:* H. *Jv:* A.

Famous for its founder, George Plimpton, now a successful author and man-about-town; its longevity, one of the oldest of the "littles"; and its interviews with prominent authors. The interviews have been published in book form, and the techniques are of much interest as the content. Publishes new poetry and fiction. During the past year, Diane DiPrima, Ted Berrigan, Kenneth Koch and John Ashberry have had poetry printed along with the fiction by such writers as Christina Stead and John Phillips. Among those interviewed have been Vladimir Nabokov, Jorge Luis Borges and Edward Albee. A fine magazine with a mixed bag of excellent literary material. For the general adult reader as well as the college student, and most advanced high school libraries. (If the students aren't interested, it should certainly be brought to the attention of literature teachers.)

Partisan Review. 1934. q. $4.50. William Phillips. American Committee for Cultural Freedom, Inc., Rutgers Univ., New Bruswick, N.J. 08903. Index, adv. Circ: 15,500. Reprints: AMS. Microform: UM.

Indexed: SSHum. *Bk. rev:* 5–15, 1,300 words, signed. *Aud:* Sa, Ac, Jc, Sh. *Rv:* M. *Jv:* V.

One of the most influential literary reviews in America, or anywhere else, this is a testing ground for new political, social, artistic, and literary ideas. Writers including Susan Sontag and Leslie Fiedler represent the best America has to offer in intellectual thought, although admittedly at a semi-popular rather than detailed scholarly level. Delights in an intellectual or political cause celebré. Creative criticism of current literature, and occasionally art and theater. Outstanding fiction and poetry. Book reviews are equally divided between literary topics and politics. As the leading voices for the avant-garde in the U.S. and abroad, contributors are a more select group than those writing for other leading literary periodicals, e.g., *Hudson Review, Kenyon Review,* etc. There are frequent stimulating symposiums or exchanges on the American political and social scenes, and a lively "Letters to the Editor" section. This should be in every medium to large library, and in some advanced senior high school libraries.

Progressive. 1909. m. $6. Morris H. Rubin. Progressive, Inc., 408 W. Gorham, Madison, Wis. 53703. Illus., index, adv. Circ: 40,000.

Indexed: PAIS. *Bk. rev:* 5–7, 1,000 words, signed. *Aud:* Ga, Ac, Jc, Sh. *Rv:* M. *Jv:* B.

One of the oldest liberal, independent magazines in America, founded in 1909 by the late Senator R. M. LaFollette, Sr. as a voice for his then advanced political views. The magazine ceased publication for a time, then began anew in 1948 and now carries some eight to ten articles per issue. The editor is concerned with national and world affairs, and contributors are correspondents on the scene or prominent educators who are specialists in a given field. The magazine is particularly strong in its condemnation of present American foreign policy, but no more so than other liberal voices. The writing is authoritative, calm and objective. There are some 10 pages of editorials, regular columns, and fascinating letters to the editor. The book reviews are excellent and range from politics to works on the social sciences and fine arts. All and all, an impressive magazine of opinion which should be found in most libraries, and a good number of high school libraries as a supplement to the better-known *Nation* and *The New Republic.*

The Public Interest. 1965. q. $5. Daniel Bell & Irving Kristol. Basic Books, 404 Park Ave. S., New York, N.Y. 10018.

Indexed: HistAb. *Aud:* Ga, Ac, Jc. *Rv:* H. *Jv:* B.

Sponsored by the Freedom House, a liberal non-partisan organization, this is a general magazine of social commentary, somewhat on the order of the *American Scholar,* yet with more emphasis on political-economic issues, less on literature or art. Its distinguished editors attract some of the best writers in America today: Daniel Moynihan on "Crisis in Welfare," followed by articles on the American

university, European disunion, and a piece on class in America by Christopher Jencks and David Riesman. While there are few book reviews, generally one or two titles are the object of, a long, analytical piece, such as "To Suburbia With Love." A much above average magazine which should find a place in medium to large library collections.

The Public Life; a biweekly journal of politics. 1968. bi-w. $6. Walter Karp & H. R. Shapiro, 29 Fifth Ave., New York, N.Y. 10003.

Aud: Ga, Ac, Jc. *Rv:* H. *Jv:* B.

A four-page newsletter dedicated to more self-government for Americans, considerably less centralization of power. A typical issue features two long articles, boxed quotes and a short editorial. The editors, according to *The New York Times,* describe themselves "as the first Jeffersonians since the Populists in 1890." The style is refreshing, candid, intelligent, and a major step towards a definition of new politics within the terms of humanistic goals. It is bound to upset both the radical and the conservative, but it is one of the few political publications which will have meaning for the man or woman who is looking for realistic answers instead of hollow rhetoric or promises. As the editors are grinding no accepted political party's axe, they can swing their own individual hatchet. It is an impressive effort and one which most libraries should consider for purchase.

The Quest. 1966. q. $3.50. Ed bd. P.O. Box 207, Cathedral Station, New York, N.Y. 10025. Index, adv. Circ: 3,000.

Aud: Ga, Ac, Jc. *Rv:* M. *Jv:* B.

The "quest" of this literary magazine, as an accompanying flyer describes it (there is no editorial intrusion in the magazine itself), is for an emphasis on content as well as form in the literary work. This no-nonsense (or, no "absurd") approach to contemporary literature is apparent in the somewhat conservative format and layout of the magazine, the presence of W. H. Auden's name in a prominent position among the list of contributors, and a generally serious tone in the poetry, fiction and occasional essays. Contrary to the flashiness of many present-day flash-in-the-pan little magazines, *The Quest* is solid and quietly attractive, and fit to appear on the shelf beside such well-established quarterlies as *Massachusetts Review* or *Carleton Miscellany.* There appears to be no regional bias, nor any concentration upon one group of writers. The most frequent names to appear are those of Auden, John Tagliabue, Dilys Laing, and V. S. Yanovsky (a Russian émigré whose works have been widely published in Europe). Also notable is the presence of Elizabeth Daryush, daughter of Robert Bridges, whose work has rarely appeared in this country.

Ramparts. 1962. bi-w. $15. Robert Scheer. 495 Beach St., San Francisco, Calif. 94133. Illus., adv. Circ: 270,000.

Indexed: PAIS, RG. *Bk. rev:* 1–2, 500–6,000 words. *Aud:* Ga, Ac, Jc, Sh. *Rv:* H. *Jv:* V.

Established by Edward Keating as a renegade voice for lay Catholics, *Ramparts,* in seven years, has metamorphosed into the nation's prime muckraking journal. Unparalleled in modern American journalism, it does not merely convey news; it is news. Among its staffers are Editor-in-Chief Robert Scheer, a vote-getting Congressional "peace" candidate and "New Politics" leader; Eldridge Cleaver, prominent Black Panther and author of *Soul on Ice;* Society Editor Paul Krassner, who also produces the intemperate, New York-based *Realist;* Donald Duncan, a former Special Forces sergeant whose revelations concerning the "Green Berets" were shocking to many people; Stanley Sheinbaum, now with the Center for the Study of Democratic Institutions, who first exposed CIA infiltration of the "Vietnam Project" at Michigan State University; Andrew Kopkind, volatile U.S. correspondent for the *New Statesman,* associated with the recently founded *Mayday* (now changed to *Hard Times*), and Conor Cruise O'Brien, once U.N. chief in the Congo and former Vice-Chancellor of the University of Ghana. A typical *Ramparts* number, bright and zestful in layout, may include articles on Leonard Baskin, Luis Bunuel, Che Guevara, the Warren Commission, draft-card burning, the Arab-Israeli crisis, U.S. oil companies, or Bob Dylan. Many will find this distasteful, some even hateful, but its quality and uniqueness demand its placement in all libraries. For a full analysis of the magazine, see "O'er Ramparts We Watch," in the April, 1967, edition of *Holiday.*

Saturday Review. 1924. w. $8. Norman Cousins. Saturday Review, Inc., 380 Madison Ave., New York, N.Y. 10017. Illus., adv. Circ: 450,000.

Indexed: AbrRG, MusicI, RG. *Aud:* Ga, Ac, Jc, Sh. *Rv:* M. *Jv:* B.

At one time devoted almost exclusively to book reviews, this is now a general literary and arts magazine which features regular departments on films, music reviews, education, science, plays, politics, poetry and just about everything of interest to the suburban, liberal reader. The normal issue is in three parts—the first, a series of features and lead articles on politics or social issues; the second, book reviews; and the third, a monthly department on communication, education, music or science. The reviews tend to be squeezed between the other material, but are noteworthy for the fine and fair fiction notes by Granville Hicks. Journalists and subject specialists examine other titles (including paperbacks) of interest to the educated, fairly sophisticated reader. The reviews tend to be timely, somewhat critical, and unusually accurate in summation of overall value. Both as a reviewing medium and as a literary magazine this should be in most library collections.

Sewanee Review. 1892. q. $5. Andrew Lytle. Univ. of the South, Sewanee, Tenn. 37375. Circ: 4,200. Microform: UM. Reprint: Kraus.

Indexed: SSHum. *Bk. rev:* 10–30, grouped 3,000 words, signed. *Aud:* Sa, Ac, Jc, Sh. *Rv:* M. *Jv:* A.

The oldest literary magazine in the United States, yet remarkably up-to-date, and often ahead of the times. Each issue contains original fiction, outstanding poetry, and, in the "Arts and Letters" section, book review essays, occasional correspondence, and review articles covering recent criticism on a single literary figure. Essays vary in length from 2,000 to 10,000 words, and deal predominantly with contemporary literature and literary criticism. Contributors are international scholars and writers in English. Primarily for larger academic collections, but public libraries (as well as high schools with advanced programs) subscribing to the basic reviews will want to seriously consider this one.

The Southern Review. 1965 (originally published: 1935–1942). q. $4. Lewis P. Simpson & Donald E. Stanford. Louisiana State Univ., Drawer D, Univ. Station, Baton Rouge, La. 70803. Circ: 4,000. Microform: UM. Reprint: Kraus.

Indexed: LMags. *Bk. rev:* Grouped, lengthy, signed. *Aud:* Ga, Ac, Jc. *Rv:* M. *Jv:* B.

A literary periodical with essays, creative writing, and book reviews. There are five to eight signed scholarly articles, with emphasis on twentieth century literature. Essays that deal with the culture and history of the South are also published. Original poems, translations, and short stories emphasizing technical discipline by important writers from the South and other regions of the U.S. and abroad. Eight to eleven substantial, critical, signed book review articles which discuss, *in toto,* approximately fifty books each issue. Books reviewed include fiction, poetry, drama, and scholarly works from the U.S. and abroad. New series promises to maintain high quality of original series edited by Robert Penn Warren and Cleanth Brooks. Only for large collections, although both public and academic libraries will wish to examine for possible subscriptions.

Tri-Quarterly; a national journal of arts, letters and opinions. 1964. 3/yr. $4. Charles Newman. Univ. Hall 101, Northwestern Univ., Evanston, Ill. 60201. Illus., index, adv. Circ: 5,000. Reprint: Johnson.

Bk. rev: Occasional. *Aud:* Ga, Ac, Jc. *Rv:* M. *Jv:* A.

A handsomely printed literary periodical usually devoted to one or more themes, e.g., "Creativity in the Soviet Union," "Writers Under 30," "New French Writing," "Recent American Historiography," etc. The Fall-Winter, 1968–1969 edition, probably one of the most outstanding so far, is devoted wholly to "Contemporary Latin American Literature," a realm all too often neglected in our schools and periodicals. The theme is supported by articles on art, music, drama, theater, and literary criticism. Also includes outstanding original fiction and poetry as well as translations of poems, plays, fiction and criticism, all by relatively well-established contributors. Beautifully illustrated throughout. Occasional supplements are monographs devoted to the work of one artist or writer, e.g., "Hans Haacke's Wind and Water Sculpture," William Gass' "Willie Masters' Lonesome Wife." As separate publications, the supplements represent some of the best in modern culture, and are an added bonus for subscribers. Although relatively new, the magazine has rapidly acquired a large audience, and should be a major consideration for any public or academic library where there is an interest in literature and the arts.

Twentieth Century. 1887. q. $7. Michael Wynn Jones. Twentieth Century Magazine Ltd., 25 Queen Anne's Gate, London S.W.1. Illus., index, adv. Microform: UM.

Indexed: BritHum, SSHum. *Bk. rev:* 5, 300–500 words, signed. *Aud:* Ga, Ac, Jc. *Rv:* M. *Jv:* B.

This somewhat conservative magazine offers a direct look at different aspects of contemporary life, from economics and politics to literature and art. Although published in Britain, the comments and reviews can be appreciated by the American reader. A major topic is covered, along with three or four smaller articles, in each issue. Recent numbers have dealt with "Aggression," "Provincial Culture," and "Pornography." The book reviews are often lengthy and usually contain a bit of that infamous British satire. Not a required magazine for most collections, but a useful and enjoyable one for larger libraries.

Virginia Quarterly Review; a national journal of literature and discussion. 1925. q. $5. Charlotte Kohler. Univ. of Virginia, 1 W. Range, Charlottesville, Va. 22903. Index, adv. Microform: UM.

Indexed: PAIS, SSHum. *Bk. rev:* 70–90, 100–300 words. *Aud:* Ga, Ac, Jc. *Rv:* M. *Jv:* B.

Along with the *Sewanee Review* and the *Southern Review,* one of the three basic literary magazines published in the South. It is less parochial than the *Southern Review,* more popular in style and content than the *Sewanee.* Differences aside, it covers much the same general area as its competitors—literature, social sciences, politics, art, etc. Particularly valuable for all libraries because of the short notes on current books (preceded by several critical essays), and a section, "List of Reprints and New Editions." The reviews are as broad in scope as the magazine, i.e., fiction, history, poetry and the like. Because of its somewhat broader scope, it would be slightly ahead of the *Southern Review* for library purchase, yet not up to the *Sewanee.* Southern public and academic libraries will want all three, others may choose in the order suggested here.

Yale Review. 1911. q. $5. J. E. Palmer. Yale Univ. Press, 92-A Yale Station, New Haven, Conn. 06520. Microform: UM.

Indexed: PAIS, RG. *Bk. rev:* Group reviews, various lengths. *Aud:* Ga, Ac, Jc. *Rv:* M. *Jv:* B.

One of the earliest national literary and political reviews, this tends to be more general in content than other literary magazines noted here. It has the usual amount of fiction, poetry and good to excellent book reviews, but is particularly noted for the outstanding articles on current problems in economics, politics and world events. Its contributors include some of the best minds in America, and while the

tone is generally liberal, it is more middle of the road than the usual literary review. The moderate, yet penetrating viewpoint gives it a substantial base which has wide appeal for both informed laymen and intellectuals. A good purchase for most general library collections.

LITERATURE

Indexes and Abstracts

Art Index, British Humanities Index, Canadian Periodical Index, Index to Little Magazines, Public Affairs Information Service, Social Sciences and Humanities Index. (For annotations, see Indexes and Abstracts Section.)

African Forum. See African Studies Section.

African Literature Today. See African Studies Section.

American Literary Realism, 1870–1910. 1967. bi-ann. $3. Clayton L. Eichelberger. Dept. of English, Univ. of Texas, Arlington, Tex. 76010.

Bk. rev: 3–5, 500 words, signed. *Aud:* Sa, Ac. *Rv:* H. *Jv:* B.

The purpose of this bibliographic journal is to "emphasize the compilation and publication of comprehensive annotated bibliographies of secondary comment on those literary figures of the designated period." The article on George Washington Cable, for example, lists sources of critical estimates, bibliographies, and additions to published works about the author. Some 15 to 20 authors are covered in each 100 pages or so an issue. One of the two issues usually emphasizes the work of one or two authors (Fall, 1969 on Sarah Orne Jewett and W. D. Howells). A valuable reference aid for any large library.

American Literature; a journal of literary history, criticism and bibliography. 1929. q. $5. Clarence Gohdes. Duke Univ. Press, 6697 College Station, Durham, N.C. 27708. Index, adv. Circ: 5,500. Reprint: Kraus. Microform: UM.

Indexed: SSHum. *Bk. rev:* 15–30, average 750 words, signed. *Aud:* Sa, Ac, Jc. *Rv:* H. *Jv:* V.

Sponsored by the American Literature Section of the Modern Language Association (MLA), this is a scholarly journal, with research articles on the history, criticism, and bibliography of American literature. Contains both substantial, critical book reviews, and annotated listings of recent books not reviewed. Special features are research in progress, a listing of dissertations completed and in progress and other projects underway, and an index to articles on American literature appearing in current periodicals, with short annotations. While a basic journal for any academic library, it should interest secondary school English teachers and may be a suitable publication for larger professional collections in high schools.

American Notes & Queries. 1962. 10/yr (Sept–June). $6.50. Lee Ash. 31 Alden Road, New Haven, Conn. 06515. Index.

Bk. rev: 10–15, various lengths, signed. *Aud:* Sa, Ac. *Rv:* H. *Jv:* B.

Somewhat similar to its British counterpart—*Notes and Queries*—and normally made-up of several well defined sections: three to four short items on literature; queries, and replies to questions regarding research and esoteric bibliographical problems; the editor's comments and readings; reviews of recent foreign reference books by Lawrence Thompson, and shorter book notes. The whole usually is 16 pages, and while small in format it is large in the amount of help it renders to students of literature. A necessary reference aid—and just good reading—for any academic library where there is serious interest in literary research and bibliography.

American Quarterly. 1949. q., and 1 supplement/yr. $8. Hennig Cohen. Univ. of Pennsylvania Trustees, Box 46, College Hall, Philadelphia, Pa. 19104. Illus., adv. Circ: 4,000. Microform: UM.

Indexed: SSHum. *Bk. rev:* 3–5, average 1,000 words, signed. *Aud:* Sa, Ac, Jc. *Rv:* H. *Jv:* B.

As the journal of the American Studies Association, features scholarly articles on American politics, society, history, art, belles-lettres etc. Supplement contains a selected, annotated interdisciplinary bibliography of current articles on American Studies, dissertations in progress, writings on the theory and teaching of American Studies, a list of college and university programs in American Studies, financial aid available to graduate students, and a membership directory. Supplement also contains year's list of short reviews, descriptive in nature, approximately 175 words in length, and signed.

Anglia; Zeitschrift für englische Philologie. 1878. q. DM. 76. Ed bd. Max Niemeyer Verlag, Pfrondorfer Str. 4, Tübingen 74, Germany. Circ: 750. Microform: Mc.

Bk. rev: 20, average 500 words, signed. *Aud:* Sa, Ac. *Rv:* H. *Jv:* B.

A German journal (text in German and English) of English studies, presenting the results of scholarly investigation in the English and American languages and literatures. Includes criticism, interpretation, textual studies, literary sources and traditions, and linguistics. All periods from Old English to the 20th century are represented, and emphasis is on examination of original or newly-discovered works and manuscripts. Only for large academic libraries.

Art and Literature. See Art Section.

Aspen. See Art Section.

Australian Literary Studies. 1963. semi-ann. $3.30. L. T. Hergenhan, Univ. of Tasmania, Dept. of English, Box 252c, G.P.O., Hobart, Tasmania, Australia. Adv. Circ: 1,200.

Indexed: PAIS. *Bk. rev:* 3–5, 250–500 words, signed. *Aud:* Sa, Ac. *Rv:* H. *Jv:* B.

Usually three to four articles on Australian writers and literature are included with a bibliographical article, i.e. "Price Warung: Some Bibliographical Details and a Checklist of Stories." In addition to reviews of books in the area (published world wide) there are bibliographical notes. Useful in larger academic American libraries not only for the wide scope, but for the "Annual Bibliography of Studies In Australian Literature," which usually appears in the May number, and the "Research In Progress In Australian Literature." The bibliography includes a general section and one devoted to works by and about individual authors.

Black Orpheus. See African Studies Section.

Blackwood's Magazine. 1817. m. $12. G. D. Blackwood. Blackwood & Sons, Ltd., 45 George St., Edinburgh, 2, Scotland. Adv. Circ: 15,364. Microform: UM.

Bk. rev: 5, 250 words. *Aud:* Ga, Ac. *Rv:* L. *Jv:* C.

Although at one time this was a leading literary periodical, it will have little appeal for American audiences. Material is somewhat equally divided between insipid short stories and articles on travel and literary personalities. There is a section of comment on international affairs which is the best part of the magazine, but this 10- to 15-page section hardly justifies a subscription. Libraries taking the magazine will wish to continue, but a last choice for all others.

Cambridge Quarterly. 1965. q. $5. Ed bd. New Hayes, Huntingdon Rd., Cambridge, Eng. Circ: 2,000.

Bk. rev: 4, long, featured, signed. *Aud:* Ac. *Rv:* L. *Jv:* B.

A small and somewhat idiosyncratic English literary magazine, published, distributed, and often written by the editorial board. The articles range over literature, art, music, movies, and sometimes get out into politics, values, and so forth. In addition to two to four articles and the book reviews, there is usually some interesting and articulate correspondence.

Canadian Literature/Litterature Canadienne; a quarterly of criticism and review. 1959. q. $4. George Woodcock. Univ. of British Columbia, Vancouver, B.C. Circ: 1,200.

Indexed: CanI. *Bk. rev:* 8–10, 1,000 words, signed. *Aud:* Sa, Ac, Jc. *Rv:* H. *Jv:* A.

One of the best Canadian literary periodicals. Differs from *Prism International* and the *Malahat Review* in that it stresses the traditional as well as the modern. Special issues, for example, have discussed explorers as writers, the Federation of Letters and early Canadian journals. Includes essays in English and French on new and established Canadian writers, discussions of the writer's problems, autobiographical essays by Canadian writers, and studies of past and present trends in Canadian literature. Unobtrusive editorials on Canadian literature or some phase of the Canadian publishing industry. Contributors include distinguished Canadian scholars and authors and also important foreign critics. In addition to the "Books in Review" section each issue also contains three to five longer critical analyses in the "Review Articles" section, averaging 1,200–2,000 words in length. Books reviewed are Canadian books in the fields of poetry, fiction, drama, criticism, biography, history and *belles lettres*. Special features are the "Chronicle" section, with its "Letters from London," "Montreal," "Vancouver," etc., reporting on the current scene in these cities, and an annual checklist of the past year's Canadian literature, appearing in the April issue. It is the standard unannotated source in this field. See also, *University of Toronto Quarterly*. A necessary purchase for all Canadian academic and larger public libraries, and certainly should be found in most American junior college, college and university libaries.

Carnegie Magazine. See Art Section.

Chinese Culture. 1957. q. $7. Chang Chi-yun. Inst. for Advanced Chinese Studies, Box 12, Yang Ming Shan, Taiwan.

Aud: Sa, Ac. *Rv:* M. *Jv:* B.

Published in English, a Taiwan-based literary magazine of some 120 poorly-printed pages. Contributors are mostly from Taiwan university; a few are American based. Coverage moves from religion and art to fiction and poetry. There is a minimum of political material, although from time to time such articles as "The People's Commune in Communist China" do appear. On the whole a scholarly, esoteric magazine for the subject specialist.

Comparative Literature. 1949. q. $3.50. Chandler B. Beall. Univ. of Oregon Books, Eugene, Ore. 97403. Index, Circ: 2,212. Microform: UM.

Indexed: SSHum. *Bk. rev:* 4–7, lengthy, signed. *Aud:* Sa, Ac. *Rv:* H. *Jv:* B.

Long, critical articles, averaging 6,000 words, deal with the "manifold relations of literatures," covering theory of literature, literary movements, themes, genres, periods, and authors—from the earliest times to the present. International themes and the tracing of influences from the literature of one country to another are also presented. Of interest to all advanced students of general literature.

Contemporary Literature (Formerly: *Wisconsin Studies in Contemporary Literature*). 1960. q. $4. L. S. Dembo. Journals Dept., Univ. of Wisconsin Press, Box 1379, Madison, Wis. 53701. Adv. Circ: 1,500. Microform: UM.

Indexed: SSHum. *Bk. rev:* 4–6, 1,000 words, signed. *Aud:* Sa, Ac, Jc. *Rv:* H. *Jv:* B.

Devoted to studies of all areas of Anglo-American and continental literature—poetry, fiction, drama, and criticism —chiefly but not exclusively since the second World War. The journal features well-written, original critical articles and reviews, ranging in coverage from analyses of writers— both the established and the little-known—to explications,

essays on poetry, critical theory and practice, and continental literature. Generally six to eight articles appear in each issue, averaging 5,000 words each. Frequently issues revolve around a central theme ("Austrian Literature," "Literature and Science," for example) or an author (Vladimir Nabokov). Two basic bibliographies are issued annually: "Criticism: A Review," and "Poetry." The former is an essay on criticism and books of criticism about American and British authors; the latter, compiled by Samuel French Morse, evaluates 20 to 30 major English and American books of contemporary poetry. Useful in all academic libraries, and should be considered by larger public libraries.

The Critical Quarterly. 1959. q. $5. C. B. Cox & A. E. Dyson. Oxford Univ. Press, Press Rd., London, N.W.10. Index, adv. Circ: 3,000.

Indexed: BritHum. *Bk. rev:* 3–4, 1–3 pages, signed. *Aud:* Sa, Ac. *Rv:* M. *Jv:* B.

An English literary quarterly which features new poetry and criticism of both American and British authors. Poets have included Audin, Hecht, Stead and Wain; articles run from The "Shakespearean Lie-Detector" to "Do We Need the Terms 'Image' and 'Imagery'?" There is an annual poetry supplement which highlights modern contributors. The society also issues *The Critical Survey*, which is included in the subscription. Issued twice a year, the latter is a review of new novels and poetry, and is particularly useful to teachers, as it includes material on the teaching of literature at all grade levels.

Criticism; a quarterly for literature and the arts. 1959. q. $6. Emerson R. Marks. Wayne State Univ. Press, 5980 Cass Ave., Detroit, Mich. 48202. Circ: 620.

Indexed: SSHum. *Bk. rev:* 6–8, 1,000 words, signed. *Aud:* Sa, Ac, Jc, Sh. *Rv:* H. *Jv:* B.

Devoted to the study of literature and the fields of fine art and music. Evaluation and explication of artists and their works. Examines the arts and literatures of all periods and nations, either individually or in their interrelationships, and critical theory regarding them. Contributors are U.S. and foreign scholars. Formal aesthetics and more technical studies in philology and linguistics are not included. Book review section has critical and authoritative reviews of vital books in the humanities. An excellent purchase for junior college, college and university libraries.

Critique: Studies in Modern Fiction. 1957. 3/yr. $2.50. James Korges. Bolinbroke Society, Inc., Box 4063, University Station, Minneapolis, Minn. 55414. Index. Circ: 1,200.

Bk. rev: 2–3, 3–4 pages, signed. *Aud:* Sa, Ac. *Rv:* H. *Jv:* B.

Covers both English and American modern fiction, and is particularly useful for extended coverage of a single author, e.g., Iris Murdoch and a checklist of her works. The tone is scholarly, yet not overly academic. The style is considerably better than many other literary magazines of this type.

As it concentrates on writers of most interest to the modern generation, librarians and even lay readers will find much here which will give an added dimension to their reading.

Delos; a journal on and of translation. 1968. irreg., but limited to 12 numbers. $12.50 for the 12/$5 for four issues. D. S. Carne-Ross, National Translation Center, 2621 Speedway, Austin, Tex. 78705. Illus.

Bk. rev: 5–7, 500–2,000 words, signed. *Aud:* Sa, Ac, Jc. *Rv:* H. *Jv:* A.

A beautifully produced 250-page journal devoted to translations and the problems of translators. Funded by the Ford Foundation, the Center claims it will issue only 12 numbers. The first issue contains works by translators on Osip Mandelshtam, Franz Mon and Cesare Pavese. Poetry includes a translation from Brecht by Auden, and Pasternak by Weiss, among others. A report on "Translation and the Publisher," by Andre Schiffrin of Pantheon Books, points up the problems of a publisher finding either adequate translations or translators. Experiences of translators are documented, and the book reviews touch on various translations of Russian, German, and classical poetry and prose. The whole is impressive yet a trifle uneven; while some parts are easy enough to read, others are bogged down in the academic style. A major magazine for all literature and language collections in most public and academic libraries.

El Grito; a journal of contemporary Mexican-American thought. 1967. q. $4. Andres Ybarra. Quinto Sol Pubns. Inc., 2214 Durant, Suite 2, Berkeley, Calif. 94704. Illus.

Aud: Ga, Ac, Jc. *Rv:* M. *Jv:* B.

A 50-page, nicely illustrated pocket sized magazine in English. Emphasis is almost equally divided among fiction, poetry and social commentary. Also, there is normally a small, well-printed portfolio of a Mexican-American artist's work. The primary purpose is to acquaint readers with the talents, not to mention the social-economic problems, of Mexican-Americans in the United States. The tone is liberal, yet objective. The overall quality is quite high, and the total picture is one with which more Americans—particularly those living in California and the Southwest—should be familiar. For medium to large libraries with an interest in social science, Mexico, and the liberal arts.

Dickensian. 1905. 3/yr. 25s. Leslie C. Staples. Dickens Fellowship, 48 Doughty St., London W.C.1. Illus., index, adv. Circ: 2,250.

Aud: Ga, Ac, Jc. *Rv:* M. *Jv:* B.

The longest established journal devoted to an English novelist, this literary magazine is the best of its type. The *Dickensian* boasts substantial issues of estimable quality, and while contributors in the past years have been scholars, there is an indication that more amateur Dickens fans will be involved. As the voice of a literary cult, the magazine has cousins such as: *Johnsonian News Letter, Baker Street*

Journal and *Mark Twain Journal*. Any reader devoted to a given author will welcome this type of periodical. He, or the librarian, is advised to turn to the section on literature in *Ulrich's.* Most are for both the general reader and the scholar. See also, *Shakespeare Newsletter.*

Eighteenth Century Studies. 1967. q. $5. Robert H. Hopkins & Arthur E. McGuinness. Univ. of California Press, Periodicals Dept., 2223 Fulton St., Berkeley, Calif. 94720. Index.

Aud: Sa, Ac. *Rv:* M. *Jv:* B.

Employing somewhat the same approach as *Renaissance Quarterly,* this is a general magazine which uses literature as a base and explores, as well, art, intellectual history, painting and music. The only limitation is that each article must have some bearing on the 18th century. Particularly useful in medium sized libraries where it is not possible to subscribe to many literature magazines and it is desirable to touch a number of academic bases.

English Literary History/ELH. 1934. q. $4. Don Cameron Allen. Tudor and Stuart Club, Johns Hopkins Univ., Baltimore, Md. 21218. Circ: 868. Reprint: Kraus, Johnson.

Indexed: SSHum. *Aud:* Sa, Ac. *Rv:* H. *Jv:* A.

ELH is an esoteric scholarly journal covering the entire spectrum of English literature. Signed articles by contributors from the U.S. and abroad are of the highest quality. Articles are presently restricted to criticism or aesthetics and are concerned mainly with English literature, only occasionally with American literature. In recent years no biographical, bibliographical or source studies have been included unless they relate to textual study or criticism. There are from seven to nine articles of moderate length in each issue. Primarily for large academic libraries.

English Literature in Transition, 1880–1920, (Formerly: English Fiction in Transition). 1957. irreg. $2.50. Helmut E. Gerber. Dept. of English, Purdue Univ., W. Lafayette, Ind. 47907. Circ: 700. Reprint: Kraus.

Aud: Sa, Ac. *Rv:* M. *Jv:* B.

Concentrates on the fusing genres and categories of the late Victorian and early modern period. *ELT* includes articles on aesthetics, literary history, all varieties of criticism, and "appreciations" of minor figures. Articles vary in length from issue-long bibliographies to short notes. A major concern is the publishing of bibliographies of primary works, of abstracts of writings about some 100 authors of the period, and manuscript location lists. While earlier emphasis was on fiction, *ELT* is now primarily interested in poets, dramatists and critics. Since 1964 "Special Series" on individual authors and topics have appeared irregularly as a bonus to subscribers. One of the few self-supporting scholarly periodicals, *ELT*'s new photo offset printing process is not entirely satisfactory, being difficult to read plus slightly reducing coverage.

Essays in Criticism; a quarterly journal of literary criticism. 1951. q. $5. Ed bd. The Editors, Brill, Aylesbury, Eng. Circ: 2,200

Bk. rev: 3–6, 2,500 words, signed. *Aud:* Sa, Ac. *Rv:* H. *Jv:* B.

A scholarly journal of literary criticism with articles of from 4,000 to 5,000 words, but with limited footnotes. Editorial policy is concerned with avoiding the mechanization of literary scholarship. Emphasis is on English and continental literatures rather than on American. International contributors provide articles on all aspects of literary criticism and individual authors. Preference is given to articles arising from earlier discussion in the journal. A regular feature is "Critical Forum," devoted to similar discussions but in a shorter, "Letters-to-the-Editor" format. The book reviews are classics of their type—long scholarly articles similar to *The Times Literary Supplement* in style and depth.

Explicator. 1942. 10/yr. $2. J. Edwin Whitesell. Richmond Professional Inst., 901 W. Franklin St., Richmond, Va. 23220. Index. Circ: 2,300. Reprint: Kraus. Microform: UM.

Aud: Sa, Ac, Jc. *Rv:* H. *Jv:* B.

A scholarly publication devoted exclusively to *explication de texte* of English, American, and Continental literature. The literature under discussion is reprinted whenever it is short enough. Generally short, concise signed notes, but occasionally somewhat longer articles. Comments and queries are included. Footnotes are incorporated in the body of the article. Contributors are American and foreign scholars. Bibliographical issue in June includes a checklist of the past year's explication of British and American writings. List includes "items of unquestioned explicatory merit and substance, but it has omitted nothing merely because it is brief or its subject . . . of doubtful literary importance." A basic journal for all types of academic libraries.

The Jewel of Africa. See African Studies Section.

The Journal of Commonwealth Literature. 1965. biann. $6.50. Arthur Ravenscroft. Heinemann Educational Books Ltd. & Univ. of Leeds, 48 Charles St., London W.1. Circ: 700.

Indexed: AbEnSt, ComLMags. *Bk. rev:* Various numbers and lengths, signed. *Aud:* Sa, Ac. *Rv:* M. *Jv:* B.

Although it has been said that there is no such thing as a "Commonwealth literature," this magazine provides a much needed forum for "scholars throughout the world about creative writing in English from all Commonwealth countries except Great Britain." Contents encompass critical, scholarly articles and reviews, together with bibliographies of Commonwealth countries (for the previous year) contributed by respected and mostly well-known scholars. Subscriptions should be held by any library with an English language and literature collection.

Journal of Popular Culture. 1967. q. $4. Ray B. Browne. Univ. Hall, Bowling Green State Univ., Bowling Green, Ohio 43402.

Bk. rev: 3–4, 250–500 words, signed. *Aud:* Ga, Sa, Ac, Jc. *Rv:* M. *Jv:* B.

Recognition of the importance of popular culture is evident in special columns in news magazines, reviewing media, and even in the curricula of some colleges and universities. Yet, there has been a lag in concentrated study of the area, at least in terms of a single journal. Boasting an editorial board of such notables as Northrop Frye and Leslie Fiedler, the backing of the Modern Language Association, and the talents of a number of scholars, the *Journal* hopes to fill this gap. The four to five articles per issue touch such topics as the audiences of *Playboy* and the detective stories, and "Some Vestiges of Ritual Charms in Beowulf." The articles are well written, and usually as lively as the material itself. While directed to the student and teacher, the magazine should have wide appeal among more involved adults as well.

Kansas Quarterly. 1968. q. $5. Harold W. Schneider. The Univ. Press of Kansas, 358 Watson Library, Lawson, Kan. 66044.

Aud: Ga, Ac, Jc. *Rv:* M. *Jv:* B.

The successor to the *Kansas Magazine,* founded in 1872, this is a literary review which pays particular attention to the talents of regional writers in mid-America. Emphasis is on creative work, and the first issue featured ten prose pieces and over 50 poets, few of them well known, but almost all with passable to excellent command of the muse. A small part of each number is given over to critical essays. The whole is nicely printed and well edited. While not an essential magazine for anyone this side of the Kansas borders, it should be welcomed by larger academic libraries seeking publications representative of less well-known literary directions in America.

Literature and Psychology; a quarterly journal of literary criticism as informed by depth psychology. 1951. q. $6. Morton Kaplan. Dept. of English, Farleigh Dickinson Univ., Teaneck, N.J. 07666. Circ: 550. Microform: UM.

Bk. rev: 1–5, 750–1,000 words, signed. *Aud:* Sa, Ac. *Rv:* M. *Jv:* B.

Beginning as a cheaply produced newsletter, *L&P* has developed into a quite respectable and innovative interdisciplinary journal. Its purpose is to apply the techniques of depth psychology to literary analysis and criticism, while trying to "not do violence to the peculiar life and character of the text." It has apparently used well a practice of self-criticism and conscious change. An established yet absorbing experiment in interdisciplinary applications which looks like it is not going to fall into a rut in the forseeable future. At last notice, a regular supplementary bibliographic issue was planned to begin in the early part of 1969. Good for college and university libraries.

Literature East & West. 1954. q. $4. Alfred H. Marks. Conference on Oriental-Western Literary Relations of the Modern Language Association of America. State Univ. College, Div. of Literature and Philosophy, New Paltz, N.Y. 12561. Index. Circ: 2,000.

Bk. rev: 35–40, notes or 500–1,000 words, signed. *Aud:* Sa, Ac, Jc, Ht. *Rv:* M. *Jv:* B.

The editor's stated purpose is to "encourage study of the literature of Asia and Africa and especially study in comparative literature." Usually each issue is devoted to the works of a single country, and in addition to critical essays there are excerpts from books and poetry. The book reviews are usually grouped by subject. i.e., two or three titles of a similar nature considered by the same reviewer, and afford the librarian one of the best single sources of information in this area. A secondary purpose is to "encourage the greater use of non-Western literature in Western classrooms," and the adventuresome high school teacher will find something of value here for his or her classes.

The Malahat Review. 1967. q. $5. John Peter & Robin Skelton. Univ. of Victoria, Victoria, B.C. Illus. Circ: 1,000.

Bk. rev: 2–3, 2,000 words, signed, critical. *Aud:* Ga, Ac, Jc. *Rv:* H. *Jv:* B.

This thick Canadian journal correctly styles itself as "international": its list of contributors includes writers from Canada, the United Kingdom, continental Europe, America, Latin America, Asia, the Middle East and Australia. For example, American poets who have appeared in its pages are James Dickey, Anne Sexton, Stanley Kunitz, Paul Blackburn and May Sarton. Names like these are a virtual assurance of high quality. These same comments apply to the short fiction, drama and literary criticism. Line drawings, photos, and photos of art are beautifully reproduced on glazed stock in each issue. Poetry worksheets, drama and original letters and journals are announced as a special interest of the review. For the student and general reader. Should also be considered a basic choice for larger Canadian libraries.

Michigan Quarterly Review. 1962. q. $5. Sheridan Baker Adm. Bldg., Univ. of Michigan, Admin. Bldg., Ann Arbor, Mich. 48104. Illus., index, adv. Circ: 3,000.

Bk. rev: 10–12, 1 page, signed. *Aud:* Ga, Sa, Ac, Jc. *Rv:* H. *Jv:* B.

One of the more sophisticated, and certainly one of the best university literary reviews. Features an excellent format and articles of both topical and literary interest, e.g., a symposium on Vietnam and many pieces on modern poetry. The writing is skillful, well within the grasp of the average educated layman who seeks an overview of current thought in the humanities and social sciences. Some fiction, a good deal of excellent poetry. In addition to the regular book reviews, there is generally one longer essay type article on

a current work, such as Robert Bly's incisive analysis of Robert Lowell's *Near The Ocean.* Among the top three or four in its class, and a first choice for medium to large libraries.

Modern Fiction Studies; a critical quarterly devoted to criticism, scholarship and bibliography of American, English, and European fiction since about 1880. 1955. 4/yr. $3. Maurice Beebe. Purdue Univ. Dept. of English, Lafayette, Ind. 47907. Circ: 3,200. Microform: UM. Reprint: Kraus.

Indexed: SSHum. *Bk. rev:* 23, 500 words. *Aud:* Sa, Ac, Jc. *Rv:* H. *Jv:* B.

Each issue contains six to eight signed scholarly articles of from 2,500 to 7,000 words. Works of fiction, writers, or problems in fictional technique are covered in two of the four issues. The other two are devoted to a series of articles on an individual novelist, followed by a checklist of criticism by the editor. Book reviews appear in the "Newsletter" section of the two issues not devoted to individual novelists. They cover primarily American and British, and occasionally continental fiction, and special subjects. Useful in almost any type or size academic library, and in high schools with advanced literature programs. See also, *Nineteenth Century Fiction.*

Modern Language Notes/MLN. 1886. bi-m. $15. Rene N. Girard. The Johns Hopkins Press, Baltimore, Md. 21218. Index, adv. Circ: 1,700. Reprint: Johnson. Microform: UM.

Indexed: SSHum. *Bk. rev:* 4–10, 600 words, signed. *Aud:* Sa, Ac. *Rv:* H. *Jv:* B.

Publishes articles of literary criticism and discussions of problems in criticism of comparative literature. Each volume contains six issues devoted, in order of publication, to Italian, Spanish, German, French, again German, and comparative literature. All types and periods of the national literature are considered. Articles are generally original and critical. There is an emphasis on critical theory, and the history and problems of criticism. Occasionally the results of textual research are presented. Generally four to six articles appear in each issue, averaging 6,000 words each. Review articles and a section of short notes presenting literary research and linguistics also appear. Only for large collections.

New Mexico Quarterly. 1931. q. $5. Roland Dickey. Univ. of New Mexico Press, Albuquerque, N. M. 87106. Illus., index, adv. Circ: 800.

Aud: Ga, Sa, Ac. *Rv:* M. *Jv:* B.

Although a major journal of the Southwest, a good deal of the material in this magazine is general enough to warrant inclusion in almost any type library. The six to eight articles are usually excerpts from books to be published by the University press. Emphasis is on history, literature and art, although there is a limited amount of poetry and fiction. Contributors write in terms any layman can understand, and a good deal of it is nicely illustrated.

Nineteenth-Century Fiction. 1945. q. $4. Blake Nevius. Univ. of California Press, Berkeley, Calif. 94720. Circ: 1,600. Reprint: AMS.

Indexed: SSHum. *Bk. rev:* 3–10, 1200 words. *Aud:* Sa, Ac. *Rv:* H. *Jv:* B.

Covers English and American fiction of the entire nineteenth century. The critical and bibliographical studies cover both major and minor figures. The reviewing section occasionally prints "notes" or spirited discussions following from the reviews. The book reviews are specialized, and critical. An obvious consideration for any academic library where nineteenth century studies are a strong consideration in the curriculum.

Notes and Queries; for readers and writers, collectors and librarians. 1849. m. $11. J. C. Maxwell & E. G. Stanley. Oxford Univ. Press, Ely House, 37 Dover St., London, W.1. Circ: 1,000. Microform: UM.

Indexed: BritHum, SSHum. *Bk. rev:* 6–16, 800 words. *Aud:* Sa, Ac. *Rv:* H. *Jv:* B.

Contains information on source materials, bibliographical data, English genealogy and heraldry, lexicography, textual emendations, literary parallels, etc. Each month's issue is devoted to a particular literary period, which is announced in advance in the "Memorabilia" section. Queries about literary and historical subjects are also included, with answers appearing in later issues. *American Notes & Queries* is the same approach, only with more emphasis on queries from the United States. Both magazines provide excellent means of tracing an elusive quotation or bit of information. While both are written primarily for the scholar, the reference desk of any medium to large academic or public library should be aware of the publications.

Novel: A Forum on Fiction. 1967. 3/yr. $6. Box 1984, Brown Univ., Providence, R.I. 02912.

Bk. rev: 6–10 joint reviews; 6–15 1,000 words, notes, signed. *Aud:* Sa, Ac, Jc, Ht. *Rv:* M. *Jv:* B.

"Our journal takes its title and its justification from the amazing surge of interest in the novel since the last world war." Opposed to the usual pedantic dullness of literary studies, this concentrates on presenting six to eight articles on all aspects of fiction—primarily by popular scholars such as Carlos Baker and Leslie Fielder. The reviews are divided into two sections, the first built around a common theme, e.g., "Three Americans," and "Visions and Epistles" and the second around perceptive notes on recent fiction. All libraries will find the reviews helpful, and imaginative teachers will discover much here to spark a dull class. One of the few literary journals which can be used for high schools, and should be found in most professional collections.

PMLA. 1884. 7/yr. Membership (libraries $18). John Hurt Fisher. Modern Language Assn. of America, 60 Fifth Ave., New York, N.Y. 10011. Adv. Circ: 28,000. Microform: UM. Reprint: Kraus.

Indexed: SSHum. *Aud:* Sa, Ac, Jc. *Rv:* H. *Jv:* V.

As the journal of the MLA, *PMLA* presents " the most distinguished contemporary scholarship and criticism in the modern languages and literatures." Unmatched in scholarship and authority, its articles serve researchers and teachers of literature. The journal is issued quarterly with three added numbers. Each regular issue contains from 15 to 20 articles with professional news and notes and a section of critical comment. More than one critic has accused it of being exceedingly dull, particularly as emphasis is on esoteric literary and critical matters of interest only to the most dedicated scholar. Its large circulation seems more due to the sponsor than the content, and the bibliographic data more than the style. The annual bibliography appears in the special June issue, a comprehensive listing of the previous year's publications of interest to scholars in the modern language field. The other two yearly supplements contain the directory and the program. Both feature articles and addresses on language education. No large library can afford to be without a subscription. Small and medium sized libraries may wish only the annual bibliography.

Papers on Language and Literature; a quarterly journal. 1965. q. $5. Nicholas Joost. Southern Illinois Univ., Edwardsville, Ill. 62025. Circ: 900.

Aud: Sa, Ac. *Rv:* H. *Jv:* B.

Deals with English, American, and the various European literatures. Literary history, analysis, stylistics, and evaluation, as well as original materials relating to belles lettres—letters, journals, notebooks, and similar documents. While five to six papers of substantial length fill each issue, a section of brief notes also appears. Special features include review essays, which appear in alternate issues and are devoted to an individual writer. Occasional supplements feature a series of papers on an individual writer or subject. Only for large libraries.

Prairie Schooner. 1927. q. $3. Bernice Slote. Nebraska Hall 215, Univ. of Nebraska, Lincoln, Neb. 68508. Index, adv. Circ: 1,000.

Bk. rev: 6–8, 1–3 pages, signed. *Aud:* Sa, Ac, Jc. *Rv:* M. *Jv:* B.

A general literary review magazine of some standing which publishes non-academic material. Each issue usually features one or two articles of general interest, but concentrates on short stories, poetry and literary essays. The amount of poetry is impressive, and the reviews frequently concentrate in this area. Contributors tend to be teachers from all parts of the country. One of the better general reviews for libraries with a large literary collection.

Prism International; a journal of contemporary writing. 1959. q. $3.50. Jacob Ziller. Univ. of British Columbia, Creative Writing Dept., Vancouver 8, B.C. Illus., adv. Circ: 1,000.

Aud: Ga, Ac, Jc. *Rv:* M. *Jv:* B.

One of Canada's major literary magazines, divided evenly between fiction and poetry (with occasional critical essays), with the prose usually illustrated. Although it originates in British Columbia, contributors are not necessarily limited to Canada, and there are always a number of translations. (Contributors have included Malcolm Lowry, Cesar Pavese, Uggo Betti, Gunter Grass, William Stafford and Jorge Luis Borges; the Spring, 1968 issues featured two plays by the German, Ernst Barlach.) Conversely, every effort is made to give Canadian writers a platform, and through the years it has published almost every new voice. The format is as pleasing as the content. A necessary purchase for all medium to large Canadian libraries and most American academic libraries, along with the equally fine *Malahat Review*.

The University creative writing department also publishes *Contemporary Literature in Translation* (1968. 3/yr. $4.), which includes both fiction and poetry. While a far cry from the work found in *Delos* or *The Sixties,* it is of value to large academic libraries who wish to augment the two basic translations' journals now being published.

Quarterly Review of Literature. 1943. 2/yr. $4. for 2 double no's. Theodore Weiss. Bard College, Box 287, Annandale-on-Hudson, N.Y. 12504. Index, adv. Circ: 2,000.

Indexed: LMags. *Aud:* Ga, Ac, Jc. *Rv:* M. *Jv:* A.

An international literary magazine of modern creative work, this is one of the leaders in presenting significant writers, from Nobel Prize winners to lively newcomers. Publishes poetry, short stories, plays, and novellas. Features unpublished or little known work of older American writers (Whitman, Jones, Very, H.D.), and distinguished writers' translations, from Dutch, German, Italian, French, Japanese, Greek and Spanish, of new and older writers. It has considerably wider interest than most of the literary journals in this section, and because it stresses the work of the artist rather than the criticism, can be enjoyed by any sophisticated adult reader. Hence, it should be found in many medium to large public libraries, as well as in all academic collections.

Readers & Writers. 1966. bi-m. $1.50. Stanley Beitler. S. S. Beitler, Inc., 130–21 224th St., Jamaica, N.Y. 11413. Illus., adv.

Aud: Ac, Jc, Sh, Ht. *Rv:* L. *Jv:* B.

Geared for the imaginative teens to early twenties, this well-illustrated magazine includes articles on modern films, art, literature, and (of most interest to beginning writers) some three to four short stories by students or professors. "Payment is $50 per story." There also are news notes from various campuses. In view of the low price, the high level of content, and the potential audience, this can be recommended for both college and high school teachers seeking to spark an interest in writing in their students.

Red Clay Reader. 1964. ann. $4. Charleen Whisnant. Rt. 2, Sharon Hills Rd., Charlotte, N.C. 28210. Illus.

Aud: Ga, Ac, Jc. *Rv:* M. *Jv:* B.

Featuring a regular hard binding and issued annually, this is more of an anthology than a normal magazine.

It modestly calls itself "one of the most important literary magazines in America," which it is not, but it does deserve kudos for the excellent format, the concentration on Southern writers—well known and otherwise—and an imaginative editorial policy which concentrates on off-beat material, from essays to poetry. In issue number five, the article on Meher Baba and his center in South Carolina dedicated to an Indian-based spiritualism is worth every penny of the $4. The columnist J. A. C. Dunn writes about the man who hasn't spoken for 43 years with understanding and humor. The poetry selection is equally good, but the fiction is only fair. Libraries may wish to consider this annual as a book, and catalog for the regular collection. Not essential, yet useful in larger literary collections and for many Southern public and academic libraries.

Renaissance Quarterly (Formerly: Renaissance News). 1954. q. $8. Elizabeth S. Donno. Renaissance Soc. of America, 1161 Amsterdam Ave., New York, N.Y. 10027. Index, adv. Circ: 2,707.

Indexed: ArtI. *Bk. rev:* 20–30, 2–3 pages, signed. *Aud:* Sa, Ac, Jc. *Rv:* H. *Jv:* B.

A general magazine, limited only to some aspect of Renaissance study. Scholarly articles range from art and music to literature and history. Most of the writing touches on more than one area, and emphasis is on the synthesis of a theory or idea about a particular period, place, or personality. There are extensive book reviews in each issue, and a bibliography of publications in the field, arranged by subject. In view of its wide interests, it is a must for medium to large academic libraries.

Review of English Studies. 1925. q. $7.25. J. B. Bamborough. Oxford Univ. Press, Ely House, 37 Dover St., London W.1. Circ: 2,000.

Indexed: BritHum, SSHum. *Bk. rev:* 25–35, 1,000 words, signed. *Aud:* Sa, Ac, Jc. *Rv:* H. *Jv:* B.

A journal of English Literature and the English language, which concentrates on book reviews. The reviews are detailed and critical. Many of the books are from British presses, but at least one third are scholarly publications from the United States. A few continental titles appear. Each issue contains a "Summary of Periodical Literature" listing the contents of various journals in English literature and philology. Alternate issues contain a "List of Publications Received." Literature of all periods is covered in 3,000- to 4,500-word signed scholarly articles. While primarily for larger libraries, the reviews may make it worthwhile for smaller libraries where there is a particular need for detailed work in this area.

SMS. See Art Section.

Saint Louis Quarterly. 1963. q. $6. Esther C. Mendoza. St. Louis Univ., Baguio City, Philippines. Illus., adv. Circ: 1,000.

Bk. rev: 7–10, 250–500 words, signed. *Aud:* Sa, Ac. *Rv:* H. *Jv:* B.

A Catholic university literary magazine of more than passing interest because it publishes outstanding material by both Philipino lay and religious writers. Emphasis is on research in literature, philosophy, language, i.e., "Keat's 'Ode to a Nightingale': Aesthetic and Myth;" history as related to the church and the area, "Former Spanish Missions in the Cordillera," and a limited amount of theology. Book reviews are perceptive, and cover all aspects of literature, history and education. Beginning in 1968, it was to be indexed in the *MLA International Bibliography*. The level of writing is uniformly high, the format good, and the place of origin such that it warrants a place in any large academic library.

Shakespeare Newsletter. 1951. 6/yr. (Sept.–May). $1.50. Louis Marder. Dept. of English, Univ. of Illinois at Chicago Circle, Chicago, Ill. 60680. Index, adv. Circ: 1,800. Reprints: Johnson.

Aud: Sa, Ac, Jc. *Rv:* M. *Jv:* B.

Here is Shakespeareana in a newspaper format. Contains: reports on conferences and current productions; international coverage, with special emphasis on writings of English and German Shakespearean scholars; short articles on Shakespearean scholars; short articles on Shakespeare and related drama, history, social life, etc.; brief biographies of Shakespeare scholars; reprints, digests, and reviews of journal articles and book reviews; a list of books received; and queries. Advertising in quantity, which provides information on forthcoming books, etc. *SN* is mainly the product of the editor whose interests range over all aspects of Shakespeare scholarship. He is currently promoting the use of computers by Shakespeare scholars. A useful adjunct to scholarship and a supplement to scholarly Shakespearean journals.

Shakespeare Quarterly. 1950. q. Membership (Non-members, $10). James G. McManaway. Shakespeare Assn. of America, Inc., Box 2653, Grand Central Station, New York, N.Y. 10017. Illus., index. Circ: 2,500. Reprint: AMS.

Indexed: SSHum. *Bk. rev:* 6–12, 600 words, signed. *Aud:* Sa, Ac. *Rv:* H. *Jv:* B.

Generally contains six to eight critical articles by Shakespearean scholars, and is one of the few scholarly journals with illustrations. Articles are concerned with all phases of Shakespeare's life and work. Reviews of festivals and the London and New York state productions are an annual feature. The Renaissance period in general is covered in the book reviews. "Queries and Notes" also appear. Only for large libraries.

South Atlantic Quarterly. 1902. q. $5. William B. Hamilton, Duke Univ. Press, 6697 College Station, Durham, N.C. 27708. Circ: 1,000.

Indexed: PAIS. SSHum. *Bk. rev:* Various numbers and lengths, signed. *Aud:* Sa, Ac, Jc. *Rv:* H. *Jv:* B.

A general literary magazine, which covers public affairs, history, social studies, the arts, etc. It boasts that it is the second oldest review in the United States—the *Sewanee Review* (1892) being the first. Many of the contributors are from the South, and the emphasis is on Southern affairs, although not exclusively. (It is considerably broader in scope, for example, than *The Southern Review*.) Articles tend to be scholarly, yet maintain a style which can be appreciated by any educated adult. Should be found in most Southern libraries, and in the larger college and university collections nationally.

Southwest Review. 1915. q. $3.50. Margaret L. Hartley. Southern Methodist Univ. Press, Dallas, Tex. 75222. Index, adv.

Bk. rev: Various numbers and lengths, signed. *Aud:* Sa, Ac, Jc. *Rv:* M. *Jv:* B.

Primarily a literary magazine that issues articles by scholars on modern American writing and authors. There is some short fiction and poetry and critical articles on the social scene. Although neither regional in content nor in contributors, a given amount of emphasis is on the Southwest. A good magazine for libraries in the area, but a second choice for other medium to large collections.

Speculum; a journal of medieval studies. 1926. q. Membership (Non-members, $12). Van Courtlandt Elliott. Mediaeval Academy of America, 1430 Massachusetts Ave., Cambridge, Mass. 02138. Index, adv. Circ: 4,300. Microform: UM.

Indexed: SSHum. *Bk. rev:* 30–40, lengthy, signed. *Aud:* Sa, Ac, Jc. *Rv:* H. *Jv:* A.

This is an interdisciplinary approach to history, art, music, literature, in fact, anything within a medieval scholar's interest. In recent years emphasis has been on literature and linguistics. Each issue contains several monographs, and all of these are of a uniformly high quality. The subject matter may be a trifle esoteric for the general reader, but frequently the writing style is as brilliant as the scholarship. Possibly of more importance to the librarian is the feature, *Bibliography of American Periodical Literature*. Under various names, this has appeared in the journal since 1934. It consists of a classified arrangement of articles on medieval subjects from journals published in North America. There are also extensive book reviews and a regular listing of books received. A basic magazine for the academic or large public library.

Studies in English Literature 1500–1900. 1961. q. Individuals, $6; institutions, $7. Carroll Camden. Rice Univ., Houston, Tex. 77001. Circ: 1,000. Microform: UM. Reprint: Johnson.

Indexed: SSHum. *Aud:* Sa, Ac. *Rv:* H. *Jv:* B.

A scholarly journal with each seasonal issue devoted to a particular period and genre of English literature: "Nondramatic Prose and Poetry of the English Renaissance" (Winter); "Elizabethan and Jacobean Drama" (Spring); "Restoration and Eighteenth Century" (Summer); "Nineteenth Century" (Autumn). There are 10 to 12 articles of moderate length, which present the results of historical research, are concerned with matters of interpretation, and offer conclusions which involve scholarly criticism. Each number contains a review covering the significant scholarship of the year in the area of the issue's concentration. While primarily for the advanced scholar, the bibliographic feature gives it an added dimension for all teachers from the junior college to the university level.

Studies in Romanticism. 1961. q. $4. Edwin B. Silverman, 236 Bay State Rd., Boston, Mass. 02115.

Indexed: SSHum. *Aud:* Ac. *Rv:* M. *Jv:* B.

Published by the Graduate School of the Boston University, the subject matter is more specific than its name implies. Its first concern is English literature of the period, and its second is poetry, particularly that of Byron and Shelley. Each issue has three to five long scholarly articles on Romantic literature and thought. A degree of familiarity is required to read it intelligently. Good for college and university libraries.

Studies in Short Fiction. 1963. q. $5. Frank L. Hoskins. Newberry College, Newberry, S.C. 29108. Circ: 350.

Bk. rev: 5–10, 500–1,000 words, signed. *Aud:* Ac, Jc, Ht. *Rv:* M. *Jv:* B.

Devoted to filling a major gap left by the standard journals of literature, which are preoccupied with the longer established forms of writing. Each issue has several long articles, frequently showing a special concern with the history of the short story, but not ignoring contemporary contributions to the form. Book reviews include coverage of recent anthologies and collections. Good in college and university libraries. Can be used to supplement high school English courses.

Symposium; a quarterly journal in modern foreign literatures. 1946. q. $6. J. H. Matthews. Syracuse Univ. Press, Box 87, Univ. Station, Syracuse, N.Y. 13210. Adv. Circ: 750. Reprint: Kraus.

Indexed: SSHum. *Bk. rev:* 2–5, 1,200 words, signed. *Aud:* Sa, Ac. *Rv:* M. *Jv:* B.

A scholarly journal devoted primarily to modern foreign literature. The five to eight articles, of moderate length, are generally written by American scholars. Dramatists, novelists, and poets are covered in the articles. Many of the substantial reviews, some of them remarkably thorough, are written by members of the editorial board. An occasional review of critical writings about one author appears in the "Book Review" section. An annual feature, usually in the Fall issue, is the bibliography "Relations of Literature and Science: Selected Bibliography for ———." Text mainly in English but includes French, German and Spanish at times and less often Portuguese, Italian, Russian, Modern Greek, and Arabic. Useful for both literature and foreign language collections in large academic libraries.

Tamarack Review. 1956. q. $4. Robert Weaver. Box 159, Postal Station K, Toronto, Ont.

Indexed: CanI. *Bk. rev:* Various numbers and lengths. *Aud:* Ga, Ac, Jc. *Rv:* M. *Jv:* B.

One of the longest lived, best Canadian literary magazines. (Others are *The Malahat Review* and *Prism*). It has included work by Brian Moore, Mordecai Richler and Robert Fulford, and is open to all promising new Canadian writers. There is a nice balance of fiction, poetry and critical reviews, and the level is usually quite high. It is a required item in almost all Canadian libraries—there simply are not enough first class Canadian literary magazines to warrant its exclusion—and should be in larger American academic and public libraries.

Texas Quarterly. 1958. q. $4. Harry R. Ransom. Univ. of Texas, Box 7517, Univ. Station, Austin, Tex. 78712. Illus., index. Circ: 4,000.

Indexed: PAIS, SSHum. *Aud:* Ga, Sa, Ac, Jc. *Rv:* H. *Jv:* A.

Drawing heavily upon holdings of the University of Texas Library, yet calling for contributions on an international scale, this is an impressive literary review. Both in format and size it measures up to its state of origin. Thanks in part to a relatively high payment for authors, it boasts excellent writers who, while being scholars, are still able to express themselves in terms understandable to any well-educated reader. Coverage is general, yet concentrates on literature and the humanities, e.g., a symposium issue on Ezra Pound and another on Isaac Newton. Social criticism centers around the area of origin, and there are frequent articles on American-Mexican relationships. The whole is balanced with one or two short stories, some poetry and a few illustrations. A major magazine for medium to large literature and social science collections.

Texas Studies in Literature and Languages; a journal of the humanities. 1959. q. $4. Ernest J. Lovell, Jr. Univ. of Texas, Austin, Tex. 78712. Circ: 600. Reprint: Johnson.

Aud: Sa, Ac. *Rv:* M. *Jv:* B.

A scholarly journal featuring articles on the humanities. Emphasis is on English and American literature, language, philosophy, and fine arts. A few articles consider continental literature, and social studies. The eight to ten articles may be critical, textual, bibliographical, or explication. International contributors. Somewhat esoteric, and only for the large academic library.

Twentieth Century Literature; a scholarly and critical journal. 1955. q. $4. Fallon Evans. IHC Press, 2021 N. Western Ave., Los Angeles, Calif. 90027. Index, adv. Circ: 1,200.

Indexed: SSHum. *Aud:* Sa, Ac. *Rv:* H. *Jv:* B.

Covers 20th century authors of all nations, particularly those out of favor or overlooked by the traditional literary journal. Scholarly articles examine essays, novels, poetry, and all forms of literature. High in reference value because of its "Current Bibliography," which appears in each issue. This is an abstract of periodical articles on 20th century literature that have appeared in American, British and European journals. Due to its frequency it nicely augments the annual *MLA Bibliography,* and is useful for its relative currency. A major journal for any large academic or specialized literature collection in this field.

Broader in scope, but covering the same period, is *20th Century Studies* (1969. semi-ann. $3. Faculty of Humanities, Eliot College, Univ. of Kent, Eng.). The magazine features literary, philosophical and historical studies. One issue, for example, featured lively essays on Sir Oswald Mosely, Thomas Mann, and the differences between British and Continental concepts of philosophy.

University of Toronto Quarterly; a Canadian journal of the humanities. 1931. q. $6. W. F. Blissett. Univ. of Toronto Press, Toronto 5, Ont. Circ: 2,500.

Indexed: CanI. *Bk. rev:* 5–15, 2,400 words, signed. *Aud:* Sa, Ac, Jc. *Rv:* H. *Jv:* B.

A Canadian literary periodical with three issues devoted to approximately six scholarly articles on English, American, French, and German literature. Long, critical book reviews are primarily of scholarly works devoted to English literature. The July bibliographical issue has one or two critical articles, but the rest is given over to long review articles on the past year's work in Canadian literature including poetry, fiction, humanities, social studies, "livres en francais," and publications in other languages (chiefly Icelandic, Ukrainian, and German). Contributors are Canadian, English, and American scholars. A basic purchase for all medium to large Canadian public and academic libraries, but only for the large American junior college or college or university collection.

Victorian Poetry. 1963. q. $4. John F. Stansky. 129 Armstrong Hall, West Virginia Univ., Morgantown, West Va. 26505.

Bk. rev: 2–5, essay length, signed. *Aud:* Ac, Jc. *Rv:* M. *Jv:* A.

Devoted to criticism of Victorian poetry, and requires some knowledge of the author or work being discussed. Each issue has five to eight articles of some length, and several shorter articles. The former are devoted to extended discussions, whereas the latter are more often concerned with the presentation of esoteric items of scholarship. Some of the book reviews are delightful, all of them excellent. An annual review "The Year's Work in Victorian Poetry," appears in the summer issue. The special Fall-Winter 1968 commemorative issue of the publication of *The Ring and the Book,* by Robert Browning, is of special note. Essential for the college and university library.

A broader approach to the period and its literature will be found in *Victorian Studies* (1958. q. $6. Indiana Univ.,

Bloomington, Ind. 47401). This covers all aspects of the period, from science to literature. The June number features an annotated bibliography of books, dissertations, and articles.

LITTLE MAGAZINES

Indexes and Abstracts

Abstracts of English Studies, Index to Commonwealth Little Magazines, Index to Little Magazines. (For annotations, see Indexes and Abstracts Section.)

There is no completely satisfactory definition of a little magazine. Tradition has it that any magazine which is mimeographed, boasts a circulation of less than 1,500, is open to all comers (usually without benefit of payment), and is on a hazardous financial footing is a little magazine. Much of this applies to other types of magazines, yet "littles" are unique in that they pioneer new forms of writing, give inexperienced authors an opportunity to publish, and, most important, establish standards of taste based on the editor's notion of aesthetics, rather than on what the general public or the advertiser wants. Finally, readers tend to be confined either to that famous group under 30 years of age, or to oldsters who have the patience to seek out gems in what admittedly can be a rugged and uneven content.

Most little magazines become another breed when they find success, i.e., more than 1,000 or 2,000 subscriptions and financial support. Inevitably the nature of the publication changes, sometimes for the best, and a literary review is born.

Given these generalizations, it will be noted here that there are exceptions to each and every statement made. A few have large circulations; many are well printed; a number set severe standards for acceptance and even pay authors; and almost all will inevitably include poetry or prose by an older literary figure who for one reason or another has yet to break into the so-called literary establishment.

The difficulty of categorization or definition best explains the typical little magazine. It is an adventure in thought—an adventure not all readers will enjoy, but one which they should, at least, be aware of. This seems particularly important for the younger readers, who somehow fail to find their generation faithfully mirrored in the more popular magazines.

It should be noted that many of the little magazines are recommended for high schools. Not a single title, however, is listed in the ALA's *Periodicals for School Libraries.* Behind this exclusion is the traditional belief that liberal or radical politics and avant-garde literature will corrupt our young. Perhaps, but the high school that fails to include any of the little magazines is, in the editor's opinion, failing the brighter, more imaginative students.

As little magazines are notoriously short-lived, the policy here is to include primarily those first published prior to mid-1967 and those still being published as of 1969. This eliminates some excellent titles, most of which can be picked up in the author's magazine column in *Library Journal*.

The *Ulrich's* of little magazines is Len Fulton's *Directory of Little Magazines* (1965. ann. $2. Len Fulton. 5218 Scottwood Rd., Paradise, Calif. 95969). Mr. Fulton also issues an updating service and reviews of new little magazines and little magazine publications in his *Small Press Review* (1968. q. $3.50).

Emphasis in this section has been placed on magazines of a literary nature. Those more political are covered in the section on *Dissident Magazines* and, in part, on *Newspapers*. Graduates of the "little magazine phase" will be found in the *Literary and Political Reviews* section. Those devoted almost exclusively to poetry will be found in the section of the same name.

Agenda. 1959. q. $4. William Cookson. 5 Cranbourne Court, Albert Bridge Rd., London S.W.11. Circ: 1,500.

Indexed: ComLMags, 1964–1965. *Bk. rev:* 6–8, 300–1,000 words, signed. *Aud:* Ga, Ac, Jc. *Rv:* M. *Jv:* A.

An established, better magazine of new poetry and literary criticism. The poetry is of traditional format but well representative of the best of this kind of writing by new British and American poets. Critical articles, which are well-argued, are addressed to contemporary poetry and shun the usual fustian of the scholarly journals. Special numbers (such as the Spring-Summer 1957 issue devoted to David Jones) deal with a single artist or topic and are published regularly. Of value to the sophisticated adult reader interested in today's English-language poetry.

Ambit; a quarterly of poems, short stories, drawings and criticism. 1959. q. $2. M. C. O. Bax. 62 Hornsey Lane, London N.6. Illus., adv. Circ: 1,250.

Indexed: ComLMags, 1964–65. *Bk. rev:* 5–10, various lengths, signed. *Aud:* Ga, Ac, Jc, Sh. *Rv:* L. *Jv:* A.

One of the more solid avant-garde English magazines, *Ambit* is devoted to original material: poems, short stories, groups of drawings. Most contributors are young, but several of the poets are beginning to be widely known: Edwin Brock, Anselm Hollo, George Macbeth, Tony Connor, and Bob Sward, to name a few. The eternal topics, the state of man and the world are treated in the idiom of the sixties—dead-pan, ironic, aloof, illusionless. *Ambit* resembles the American "little" more than most English small-press magazines and should prove popular with young people who wish to find out about the new literature across the water.

Ante. 1964. q. $3.50. Vera Hickman. Echo Press, P.O. Box 29915, Los Angeles, Calif. 90029. Illus., adv. Circ: 1,000.

Aud: Ga, Ac, Jc, Sh. *Rv:* M. *Jv:* B.

Preserves a neat balance between short fiction and poetry, by newcomers as well as by such names as Ted Enslin and David Cornel DeJong. Poetry is of traditional form. The short stories are consistently of higher quality than those found in the majority of comparable little magazines. There are occasional book reviews and critical essays on art, politics, etc. In all, a superior small literary magazine. For all readers interested in new American writing. Letter-press produced and handsomely designed.

Avalanche. 1966. q. $1.75. Richard Krech & Shelley Silliman. 2315a Russell St., Berkeley, Calif. 94702. Illus. Circ: 500–1,000.

Aud: Ac, Jc, Sh. *Rv:* L. *Jv:* B.

A combination poetry/literary little magazine with a left-of-center political orientation and a sure sense of what is best in new poetry. Contributors have included Gene Fowler, Charles Bukowski, Doug Blazek and George Bowering as well as many others not so well known. From time to time interviews are published, such as with Gerard Malanga and Andy Warhol. Parts of new novels, photographs, and some art work rounds out each issue. The hip tone and rhetoric will make it primarily of interest to younger readers. Offset.

Boss. 1966. semi-ann. $2. Reginald Gay. Box 231, Village Station, New York, N.Y. 10014. Illus.

Aud: Ga, Ac, Jc. *Rv:* L. *Jv:* B.

"Exciting" is hardly an exaggeration. In nearly 100 pages, editor-publisher Reginald Gay assembles a high-quality, highly readable potpourri of leading movement trends, and figures in contemporary art and literature. No. 2 alone encompasses poetry by Gerard Malanga, Phillip Whalen, and Fug-bard Tuli Kupferberg; a stimulating interview with the French Happening-impresario, Jean Jacques Lebel; an extensive review of the Living Theatre's "Frankenstein," and several fine photographs. In the Black Mountain-Big Table tradition, this is a worthy item for any library interested in today's rampaging avant-garde. Offset.

Chelsea; a magazine for plays, stories, poetry and translation. 1958. q. $3.50. Ed bd. Box 242, Old Chelsea Station, New York, N.Y. 10011. Circ: 1,000.

Bk. rev: Occasional, average 500 words, signed. *Aud:* Ga, Sa, Ac, Jc. *Rv:* L. *Jv:* B.

A magazine of continuing vitality. The guest-editorship policy has produced fine translations of European poets and short story writers as well as "special" double numbers devoted to a designated artistic theme. Poetry published has been both traditional and avant-garde in form. Among the many poets published, the names David Ignatow, May Swensen, Galway Kinnell, and Denise Levertov should indicate adequately the high quality of the contributions. The poetry is balanced with prose, both foreign and American, which ranges from literary essays to interviews and fiction. For the student of contemporary literature as well as the intelligent adult reader. Letterpress.

City Lights Journal. 1963. irreg. $2.50. Lawrence Ferlinghetti. City Lights Books, 261 Columbus Ave., San Francisco, Calif. 94133. Illus.

Aud: Ga, Ac, Jc, Sh. *Rv:* H. *Jv:* A.

Edited by poet Lawrence Ferlinghetti, this appears every year (21 to date) or so as collection of critical essays, poetry and fiction by the authors associated with Ferlinghetti and his City Lights Book Store. Emphasis tends to be on the San Francisco school, although the representation is international. The level of writing is uniformly high, and the editing is excellent. Featuring such writers as Allen Ginsberg, Julian Beck, Michael McClure and Charles Olson, this is a journal which should be found in every library, including high schools. Due to the relative infrequency of its appearance, its format (almost an anthology), and the fact that it is bound like a paperback (and sold as such in book stores), librarians might consider cataloguing this as a book. Letterpress.

December; a magazine of the arts and opinion. 1957. irreg. $5/4 issues. Curt Johnson. Box 274, Western Springs, Ill. 60558. Illus., adv. Circ: 1,200.

Indexed: AbEnStud, IChildMags. *Aud:* Ga, Ac, Jc, Sh. *Rv:* L. *Jv:* B.

Fiction and film reviews are *December's* main strength. Short stories are given adequate breathing space and do not suffer the lack of development common to those appearing in many other little magazines. The editor quite often comments incisively upon the current state of American publishing. A long "Movies" section is a regular feature. An important bonus to subscribers is the publication of long excerpts from novels which would otherwise be overlooked by commercial publishers. Has featured work by Henry Roth, William Stafford and Richard Hugo. Suitable for senior high schools. Letterpress.

Delta. 1953. 3/yr. $1.25. Roger Gard. 12 Hardwick St., Cambridge, England. Circ: 1,000.

Indexed: BritHum. *Bk. rev:* 2–5 lengthy, signed. *Aud:* Ga, Ac, Jc. *Rv:* M. *Jv:* B.

Publishes original articles, fiction, poetry and a considerable amount of literary criticism. Considered to be one of the better small circulation English literary reviews, the primary emphasis is on new or little publicized novelists. Not to be confused with the Dutch based *Delta* (See Literary and Political Reviews Section).

Dust. 1964. q. $3.50. Leonard V. Fulton. Dustbooks, 5218 Scottwood Rd., Paradise, Calif. 95969. Illus., adv. Circ: 1,500.

Aud: Ga, Ac, Jc, Sh. *Rv:* L. *Jv:* B.

A vehicle for American new poets, *Dust* has featured Gene Fowler, Doug Blazek and William Wantling among many others. The poetry is good to excellent, and its hip posture makes the magazine attractive mainly to a younger audience. Short stories are constructed around problems of current interest to members of the avant-garde generation. It is more "with" the underground than the accented voices of the establishment. *Dust* publisher Len Fulton is the compiler, editor and publisher of the valuable annual

Directory of Little Magazines and quarterly *Small Press Review.* A good, representative little magazine for school and public libraries. Offset.

Exit. 1965. bi-m. $3. (Students $2). Martin J. Martin. G.P.O. Box 1812, New York, N.Y. 10001.

Aud: Ga, Ac, Jc. *Rv:* M. *Jv:* B.

A combination literary, left-of-center, 30- to 40-page contribution from freethought enthusiasts. The few stories and poems are relatively good; the articles on everything from drugs and sex to civil rights are familiar and well-intentioned efforts. Probably of more general value is the free newsletter, which comes with a subscription to *Exit.* This is *Index Repartee,* "opinion and discourse in the open-letter tradition —no subject or topic excluded." Issued ten times a year, the four- to six-page mimeographed communication has covered everything from scientific morality to the contributions of Robert Ingersoll to free thought. The emphasis here is definitely lack of belief in dogma. From time to time the editor also includes copies of other magazines which champion the same cause. Quite a package for $3, and probably well worth it to the more involved college student.

Fishpaste. 1966. irreg. $3/21 issues. 97 Holywell St., Oxford, Eng. Illus.

Aud: Ga, Ac, Jc. *Rv:* L. *Jv:* B.

This rightfully claims to be "the smallest little magazine in Western Europe." It is a bilingual postcard. One side is an original colored drawing, usually by Rigby Graham, and the other a poem. Not essential, but a fascinating series.

Kauri. 1964. 6/yr. $2. (Institutions, $4). Will Inman. 362 E. 10th St., Apt. 4W, New York, N.Y. 10009. Illus., adv. Circ: 1,000.

Aud: Ga, Ac, Jc. *Rv:* L. *Jv:* B.

A magazine of much poetry, occasional kinetic drama and little short fiction, *Kauri* is dedicated to publishing new writers. To enumerate those whose work has appeared here would be of dubious value; most are unknown, many will write little more. What counts is that they are among today's lively voices. Editor-poet Inman's magazine is a real service to those who are more interested in reading and enjoying poems rather than in studying "poetic form" or otherwise operating upon the printed page. For young and old alike. Mimeographed, quarto-size.

Lillabulero; being a periodical of literature and the arts. 1966. q. $2.75. Russell Banks. Lillabulero Press, Box 67, Aurora, N.Y. 13026. Illus., index. Circ: 2,300.

Bk. rev: 4–6, 1–2 pages, signed. *Aud:* Ac, Jc. *Rv:* M. *Jv:* B.

Features poetry, an occasional story, articles and critical reviews of little-press poets and novelists. Lesser known authors are balanced by the leading young writers in America. The tone is intelligent, the style winning, and the format offset and nicely done. The press, as its counterparts on the West Coast, also publishes poetry pamphlets and broadsides. One of the leading "littles," this takes its place among the top 20 or so little magazines now being published in the United States. Offset.

The Literary Times (Formerly: *Chicago Literary Times*). 1961. m. $3. Jay R. Nash. Box 4327, Chicago, Ill. 60680. Illus., adv. Circ: 38,000. Microform: B&H.

Bk. rev: Critical notes. *Aud:* Ac, Jc. *Rv:* H. *Jv:* A.

A great grab-bag of information on new writers, magazines, and news of the literary scene (or scenes). Interviews with writers, critics and musicians are featured, as well as poetry and fiction, all of high quality. Chicago-oriented, but many columns by contributors keep readers informed of literary happenings all over the United States and Europe. Highly opinionated, consistently interesting comments by the editor. One of the best magazines available to those seeking to keep up with poetry and small-press publishing in the United States. Newspaper format.

Maguey; a bridge between worlds. 1968. q. $3.50. Jed Linde & Maria Esther Manni. P.O. Box 385, El Cerrito, Calif. 94530. Illus., adv.

Aud: Ac, Jc. *Rv:* M. *Jv:* B.

A bi-lingual (Spanish/English) 65-page literary approach, which is of interest on two counts. First, it offers Spanish speaking peoples some of the best poetry and prose by Americans now often found only in American little magazines. Second, while nowhere as comprehensive as *El Corno Emplumado,* it nicely augments that Mexican based little magazine by publishing Latin American writers in good to excellent translations. Given this dual attack, it may be used effectively in any Spanish speaking American community, certainly in most libraries where there is any interest in the language or the peoples. Prose writers have included Emma Dolujanoff, Juan Jose Arreola, and Michael Rosenberg; among the poets have been D. R. Wagner, Thomas McKeown, Margaret Randall and John Tagliabue. Letterpress and a good format.

Manhattan Review (Formerly subtitled: *a magazine of emerging poetry and fiction*). 1966. 3/yr. $3./4 no's. Eric F. Oatman & Edythe Dimond. 229 E. 12th St., New York, N.Y. 10003. Circ: 1,000.

Aud: Ga, Ac, Jc. *Rv:* L. *Jv:* B.

In 1967 this little magazine turned to publishing fiction exclusively. Since writers of the caliber of James Boyer May, Franklin Stevens and Henry Roth (among others) have put good short stories in past issues, *Manhattan Review* is a magazine to watch for good new fiction. A journal of promise for those interested in contemporary American prose. Offset.

The Newsletter on the State of the Culture. 1968. m. (Sept.–June). $10. Harry Smith. 5 Beekman St., New York, N.Y. 10038.

Aud: Sa, Ac, Jc. *Rv:* H. *Jv:* B.

A 4-page monthly report on cultural activities, more precisely the state of literary and little magazine publishing as seen by Harry Smith, editor of *The Smith.* Inside information is given on everything from activities of the National Endowment for the Arts to personal notes on well known figures in the business. Examples: "Seymour Krim left *Evergreen* because of Barney Rosset's unresponsiveness to new writers;" "*EVO* & *The Rat* use The Dun & Bradstreet Collection Service to police delinquent accounts." Of particular value to librarians for news of changes and prospective changes in publishing. Somewhat equivalent on a literary level to the market-oriented (and equally excellent in its own area) *Magazine Industry Newsletter.*

The Outsider. 1963. ann. $5. Jon & Lou Webb. Loujon Press, 1009 E. Elm, Tucson, Ariz. 85719. Illus.

Aud: Ga, Ac, Jc, Sh. *Rv:* H. *Jv:* A.

The first issue of what is one of the best edited, best produced little magazines in America was published in New Orleans. The Webbs put out three numbers (now collector's items) featuring the whole stellar parade of modern American and European avant-garde writers from Henry Miller to Robert Creeley. After almost five years during which time they produced a limited number of handsome poetry volumes, the Webbs again began publishing their magazine as an annual, in 1968. The first annual volume is devoted to the work of Kenneth Patchen, the unsung American poet and essayist who recently has been taken over by the younger generation, despite the fact he is not only over 30, but pushing to his sixties. The issue also includes the work of other poets, writers, film makers, etc. The whole is produced on a handpress, is nicely edited, and in many ways more of a book than a magazine. All libraries, including sophisticated high school libraries, should subscribe.

Paunch. 1963. 3/yr. $4. (Students $2.50). Arthur Efron. 19 Claremont Ave., Buffalo, N.Y. 14222. Circ: 400.

Indexed: AbEngSt. *Aud:* Sa, Ac, Jc. *Rv.* M. *Jv:* B.

Named after Sancho Panza and "his notable gut," this differs from most little mags in that the orientation is more literary, and the editor seeks material within the scope of Romantic criticism "in the radical sense defined . . . in the work of Alex Comfort, Paul Goodman, Wilhelm Reich, Norman O. Brown, Herbert Marcuse, A. S. Neill, and even John Dewey." Which adds up to a much above average base for criticism, poetry, prose and special issues devoted to such subjects as the modern film, the novel and Chaucer. Contributors are primarily from academic circles, but show no particular reverence for the traditional If anything, the editor and his writers demonstrate that literary criticism need not be dull, that the province of the little mag is not necessarily the hip and the hip only, and that worthwhile prose can flow from the mimeograph machine. (Issues normally number 60 to 100 pages.) A good addition for all academic collections, and should be shown to struggling and discouraged English students.

Quixote. 1965. m. $5. (Institutions, $10). Morris Edelson. 315 N. Brooks, Madison, Wis. 54306. Illus. Circ: 1,000.

Aud: Ga, Ac, Jc. *Rv:* L. *Jv:* B.

Features poetry, fiction and parts of novels in progress. Most is student writing, but small-press writers such as Doug Blazek, Tuli Kupferberg and Curt Johnson have appeared. Supplements (two to five per year, included in subscription price) have been of uneven quality, the best being translations of European poets who would otherwise remain unknown in the United States. Many typographical errors. Offset. Size varies.

The Review. 1962. q. $3.50. Ian Hamilton. 72 Westbourne Terrace, London W.2.

Aud: Sa, Ac, Jc. *Rv:* H. *Jv:* V.

A pocket-sized, well-printed, English magazine of some 70 pages which has gained a place as one of the more outstanding of its type. It is primarily concerned with poetry and criticism. The writing is almost at an academic level, and is considerably more astute than that found in the traditional little magazine. A recent issue, for example, featured an article on Wittgenstein as a poet, a tribute to R. P. Blackmur by A. Alvarez, five poems by Michael Fried, and long reviews of Thom Gunn's and Robert Lowell's work. This is balanced by a telling wit and a degree of humor, e.g., a short bit on the "death" of Poet Laureate Cecil Day Lewis who "died of boredom while listening to a broadcast of his own poems." A first choice for libraries and individuals, particularly those concerned with modern poetry.

The Smith. 1964. q. $3.50. Harry Smith. Horizon Press, 156 Fifth Ave., New York, N.Y. Circ: 1,500.

Aud: Ga, Ac, Jc. *Rv:* M. *Jv:* V.

Started in 1964, this has the advantage of a highly personalized editorial approach and has a professional touch uncommon among little magazines. The well-printed pages include contributions from James T. Farrell, Robert Girourard, John Tagliabue and takes in novellas, a play, commentaries, short stories, poems and reviews. Material is uneven, but strong on satire, i.e., "*The Smith* wishes to thank the Cultural Division of the C.I.A. for the $8,000 which made this issue possible." There is something here for everyone. Letterpress.

Some/Thing. 1965. semi-ann. $2. David Antin & Jerome Rothenberg. Hawk's Well Press, 600 W. 163rd St., New York, N.Y. 10032. Illus. Circ: 500

Aud: Ac, Jc. *Rv:* L. *Jv:* B.

A major vehicle for the presentation of new American poetry. The poetry of the editors, both well known on the contemporary scene, as well as that of Ted Berrigan,

Jackson MacLow, Clayton Eshleman, Margaret Randall and many others has been featured. Prose works and kinetic theater "happenings" have also appeared. A very exciting magazine which should prove of interest to both the student and the intelligent adult reader. Letterpress produced and quite attractively designed.

Spero. 1965. semi-ann. $4. Douglas & Kathleen Casement. 1517 Jonquil Terrace, Chicago, Ill. 60626. Illus. Circ: 1,000.

Aud: Ga, Ac, Jc, Sh. *Rv:* L. *Jv:* A.

Among better-known poets contributing to this little magazine have been d.a. Levy, William Wantling, Diane Di Prima, Gerard Malanga and LeRoi Jones. Good short fiction by Henry Roth and William Sayers has appeared, as well as part of a William Burroughs novel. Woodcuts by Naomi Blossom and John Randle and finely-produced silkscreens make the illustrations more interesting than those in most other literary magazines. Some of the poetry has been printed with pouchbooks—independent small volumes contained within the cover flaps. While the magazine is basically produced by photo-offset process, one portion of each issue is handset and printed by letterpress. For young adult and adult readers of contemporary American literature.

Stand. 1952. q. $2.40. Ed bd. Stand Magazine, 58 Queens Rd., Newcastle-upon-Tyne 2, Eng. Illus., adv. Circ: 6,000.

Indexed: ComLMags. *Bk. rev:* Grouped, 20–25 pages, signed. *Aud:* Ga, Ac, Jc. *Rv:* L. *Jv:* A.

One of the English "established" little mags, this is also one of the best in terms of content. Each issue features short stories, articles, poems and perceptive reviews of fiction and poetry. The authors are from both sides of the Atlantic, usually in the forefront of the best of the young talent. Particularly noteworthy for translations of European poets and novelists, e.g., Babel, Eluard, Quasimodo, Vallejo, the Turkish poet Nazim Hikmet, and others of unusually high quality. Handsome letterpress with drawings, photographs, etc. Should be in most libraries where modern literature and criticism are considerations.

Tlaloc. 1964. irreg. $1/6 issues. Cavan McCarthy. BCM/ CAVAN, London W.C.1. Circ: 500.

Bk. rev: 2–3, 500 words, signed. *Aud:* Ac, Jc. *Rv:* H. *Jv:* B.

Featuring visual/concrete/computer poetry, *Tlaloc* has published many of the better-known new poets of the United Kingdom—Anselm Hollo, Edwin Morgan, Jim Burns, Tom McGrath, etc. Although the broadside format makes it somewhat inconvenient for the library, the material contained as well as the librarian-editor's unrelenting reporting on new U.K. and continental little magazines (he's also the U.K. compiler for DUSTbooks' *Directory of Little Magazines*) make it worth-while. New volumes of poetry are the invariable subject of the reviews section. The magazine is to shorten its title to *Loc* in the future.

For all who want news of the small-press scene and wish to keep up with what's happening in new poetry. Mimeographed on foolscap.

Trace; a chronicle of living literature, including original work, articles, reviews and comprising current chronicles for bibliographers. 1952. q. $4. James B. May. Villiers Pub. Ltd., Ingestre Rd., London N.W.5. Subscriptions to: Box 1068, Hollywood, Calif. 90028. Illus., index, adv. Circ: 2,500.

Bk. rev: 10–12, 400–500 words. *Aud:* Ga, Ac, Jc. *Rv:* M. *Jv:* B.

A magazine of short fiction, new poetry, art and critical comment on literature and films. David Cornel DeJong, Fil Orlovitz, Gene Fowler, John Tagliabue, and David Margolis have been among American poets contributing to recent issues. Translations of European poets also appear regularly. Particularly interesting to librarians and others seeking information about small-press publishing is the section "The Chronicle—An Evolving Directory," which lists general theme and bibliographic details of many small press books and little magazines, published throughout the world, received by *Trace* or reported by correspondents. Editor May's concern with small press publishing is reflected not only in the "Chronicle" section, but in frequent articles concerning little magazines. Film fans will find a bonus in the reviews and discussions (often with photos) of American and foreign films of note. A fine little review of interest to students of contemporary literature and film as well as to the educated adult reader. Letterpress.

Unicorn Journal. 1968. bi-ann. $4. ($7, hardbound). Teo Savory. Unicorn Press, El Paseo, Studios 126 and 127, Santa Barbara, Calif. 93101. Illus., adv.

Aud: Ga, Ac, Jc. *Rv:* M. *Jv:* A.

Probably one of the best printed little magazines now available, and with content quality to match. Under the editorship of poet Savory the first number included a series of paintings by Arthur Secunda on Watts; concrete poetry by Gomringer and Rothenberg; a series of photographs; an essay by Erich Kahler and more poetry by Merton and Goll. There is more, the emphasis being on poetry published by the Unicorn Press, which supports the magazine. As one of the major new poetry publishers in the United States, the press is rapidly assuming importance for both original work and translations. Their journal adds to the dimension, and it should be in all medium to large public and academic libraries. (Each issue is available in hardbound as well as paper, and the former is probably the best buy for most libraries.)

Voyages; a national literary magazine. 1967. q. $5. William Claire. 2034 Allen Pl. N.W., Washington, D.C. 20009.

Aud: Ac, Jc. *Rv:* M. *Jv:* A.

The first of its type to be published in the national capital. Outstanding contributors, an obviously intelligent editor

and a professional format assure an above-average literary review. The first issue paid homage to poet Ben Belitt, and had an interview with Carolyn Kizer and a one-act play by Edward de Grazia. The content is general enough to appeal to anyone interested in literature and the arts. Letterpress.

Works; a quarterly of writing. 1967. q. $3.50. John Hopper & Richard Brotherson. AMS Press, Inc., 56 E. 13th St., New York, N.Y. 10003.

Bk. rev: 2–3, lengthy, signed. *Aud:* Ga, Ac, Jc. *Rv:* M. *Jv:* B.

Set in two columns (poetry and plays aside), the 125-page *Works* is another form of *New American Review* in true magazine format. Edited by John Hopper and Robert Brotherson, the pattern is that new or relatively unknown writers are first introduced by a short essay, followed by examples of their work. For example, Michael Smith writes of Tom Sakey, and then the latter's marvelous play, "The *Golden Screw*," is published in full. Howard Moss introduces the poetry of Louis Moyles and Richard Howards rings in David Taylor. Fiction and poetry by better known writers are included also. Social commentary and book reviews are added features. Letterpress.

Zuku. See African Studies Section.

MATHEMATICS

The periodicals in this section can roughly be classified into three main groups: research journals for academic libraries, periodicals embracing all aspects of mathematics education and teaching, and a few publications aimed at students. Clearly, the choice of research journals has been severely limited, mostly to publications of U.S. societies. Were one to supply even a modest list for academic libraries, one would naturally include such renowned foreign publications as *Mathematische Annalen, Mathematische Nachrichten,* and *Mathematische Zeitschrift,* representing some important German journals; the French *Journal Mathematiques Pures et Appliquees* and the *Bulletin de la Societe Mathematique de France;* the English *Quarterly Journal of Mathematics;* the Swiss publication *Commentarii Mathematicii Helvetecii; Acta Mathematica,* representing Scandinavian research in mathematics; some distinguished Russian journals, many of which are available in translation; the large body of Japanese journals, etc., as well as the high-quality publications of some of our universities, such as *Illinois Journal of Mathematics, Michigan Mathematical Journal,* or MIT's *Journal of Mathematics and Physics.* Specialized research periodicals, representing the subfields of mathematics, e.g., *Journal of Algebra, Journal of Combinatorial Theory, Topology,* etc., have, of necessity, been excluded.

There are, as well, a number of publications, modest in scope, format, and price, which are concerned with high school or undergraduate mathematics and, more importantly, which are directed toward, or encourage publication by, students. Many are the news organs of mathematics clubs, honor societies, or schools. The ones included in this section comprise only a random selection of the number available. High school and junior college libraries with enthusiastic math classes would be well advised to supplement their collections with a few titles.

American Journal of Mathematics. 1878. q. $15. W. L. Chow. Amer. Mathematical Soc. & Johns Hopkins Press, Baltimore, Md. 21218. Index. Circ: 1,240. Microform: UM. Reprint: Johnson.

Indexed: MathR, SCI. *Aud:* Ac, Sa. *Rv:* H. *Jv:* B.

As the oldest mathematics periodical published in the U.S., the journal makes a distinguished addition to a research library. Theoretical papers, covering all branches of mathematical research, often represent extended studies and may average 40 to 50 pages in length.

American Mathematical Monthly. 1894. 10/yr. $15. R. A. Rosenbaum. Mathematical Assn. of America, SUNY at Buffalo, N.Y. 14214. Index, adv. Circ: 22,000. Reprint: Johnson.

Indexed: MathR, SCI. *Bk. rev:* 10–15, 200–500 words, signed. *Aud:* Jc, Ac, Sa. *Rv:* H. *Jv:* B.

Aimed at college-level mathematics, this is an excellent choice for junior college libraries and upward. Papers and notes are both of a research and an expository nature and, thus, should be equally useful to faculty and students. For mathematics teachers, a section on "Classroom Notes" is included in each issue as a teaching aid. A "Problems and Solutions" section invites reader participation both on an elementary and advanced level. In addition to detailed book reviews, a good checklist for librarians is "Telegraphic Reviews," which indicates the exact audience at which a publication is directed. As the official journal of the Mathematical Association of America, it also includes the usual official news and notices.

American Mathematical Society. P.O. Box 6248, Providence, R.I. 02904.

The American Mathematical Society is one of the chief publishers of distinguished mathematics journals, including a number of Russian journals in translation and, beginning in 1969, a current-awareness journal entitled *Contents of Contemporary Mathematical Journals.* Some of their publications are similar enough in title to cause confusion.

Bulletin. 1894. bi-m. Membership (Non-members, $12.). Ed bd. Index. Circ: 13,700.

Indexed: MathR, SCI. *Bk. rev:* 1–2, 500–700 words, signed. *Aud:* Ac, Sa. *Rv:* H. *Jv:* B.

This is the official organ of the society. As well as the usual reports and announcements of meetings, it publishes long, expository articles which are usually invited addresses presented before the Society. Also included are research announcements, which are brief notes on mathematical studies in progress.

Memoirs. 1950. irreg. Price varies. Ed bd.

Indexed: MathR, SCI. *Aud:* Ac, Sa. *Rv:* H. *Jv:* B.

Each issue, which may be purchased separately, consists of one, long research monograph, often part of a Ph.D. dissertation.

Notices. 1953. 8/yr. Membership (Non-members, $12.). Everett Pitcher & G. L. Walker. Adv. Circ: 12,000.

Indexed: MathR. *Aud:* Ac, Sa. *Rv:* M. *Jv:* B.

Announces programs of forthcoming meetings, activities of other associations, new publications, news of interest to the profession, and personalia. Also publishes abstracts of papers presented at meetings of the Society.

Proceedings. 1950. bi-m. $12. Ed bd. Circ: 6,000.

Indexed: MathR, SCI. *Aud:* Ac, Sa. *Rv:* H. *Jv:* B.

Consists of reports of research on pure and applied mathematics. Publishes papers, which are of moderate length, and brief notes.

Transactions. 1900. 5/yr. $12. Ed bd. Circ: 1,800. Reprint: Johnson.

Indexed: EngI, MathR, SCI. *Aud:* Ac, Sa. *Rv:* H. *Jv:* B.

Papers longer than those in the *Proceedings,* devoted entirely to pure and applied mathematical research.

Annals of Mathematics. 1884. bi-m. $18. Ed bd. Princeton Univ. & Inst. for Advanced Study, Box 708, Fine Hall, Princeton, N.J. 08540. Circ: 2,000. Microform: UM. Reprint: Kraus.

Indexed: MathR, SCI. *Aud:* Ac, Sa. *Rv:* H. *Jv:* B.

This scholarly publication containing research papers in all fields of mathematics will probably be too sophisticated for small collections, but should be found in all research libraries. The six or seven papers in each issue reflect exhaustive studies and frequently range from 40 to 50 pages in length.

Arithmetic Teacher. 1954. m. (Oct.–May). $7. Marguerite Brydegaard. National Council of Teachers of Mathematics, 1201 16th St., N.W., Washington, D.C. 20036. Illus., index, adv. Circ: 45,000. Microform: UM. Reprint: AMS.

Indexed: EdI. *Bk. rev:* 3, 250–500 words, signed. *Aud:* Jc, Ac, Sa, Et. *Rv:* H. *Jv:* B.

Although "devoted to the interests of elementary school personnel," the scope of this periodical is much wider. It should be found in all libraries connected with teacher education programs, and in mathematics material for potential teachers of elementary school. Main articles are both expository and reports of research. Feature departments, such as "In the Classroom," "Focus on Research," and "Forum on Teacher Preparation," promote an exchange of ideas which ought to be both stimulating and informative to anyone involved in this vital area of education. The magazine is also the official journal of the Council and reports on its activities.

Canadian Journal of Mathematics/Journal Canadienne de Mathematiques.
1949. bi-m. $18. H. A. Heilbronn & J. H. H. Chalk. Canadian Mathematical Congress, Univ. of Toronto, Toronto, Ont. Circ: 1,450.

Indexed: MathR, SCI. *Aud:* Ac, Sa. *Rv:* H. *Jv:* B.

Largely reflecting the current research interests in Canadian universities and organizations, the journal publishes quality papers in all fields of mathematical research. Text is in both French and English. (Another publication of the Congress is *Canadian Mathematical Bulletin.*) Appropriate for a good undergraduate mathematics library.

Communications on Pure and Applied Mathematics.
1948. bi-m. $15. Interscience Publishers, Div. of John Wiley, 605 Third Ave., New York, N.Y. 10016. Reprint: Kraus.

Indexed: MathR, SCI. *Aud:* Ac, Sa. *Rv:* H. *Jv:* B.

Published for the Courant Institute of Mathematical Sciences of New York University, the journal consists of research papers in the fields of applied mathematics, mathematical physics and mathematical analysis. Contributions are mainly from the Institute or are solicited under its auspices from other organizations. Many of the papers are outgrowths of technical reports sponsored under government contracts. Although the publication may be too specialized and sophisticated for small college collections, it should be found in most research libraries.

Delta Epsilon.
1960. irreg. Free. Dept. of Mathematics, Carleton College, Northfield, Minn. 55057.

Bk. rev: 1, 250 words, signed. *Aud:* Jc, Ac, Sa. *Rv:* M. *Jv:* B.

Issued by the students and faculty at Carleton, the publication is devoted to undergraduate mathematics: expository papers, unusual solutions of familiar problems, problem proposals and solutions. The tone is informal—as is the format (about 8–10 multilithed, stapled pages)—and the editors also supply some news of mathematics colloquia, research in progress, and a few alumni notes. Contributions from students include book reviews: reviewers are conscientious, critical, and highly articulate—more so than some who review in the more sophisticated journals.

Duke Mathematical Journal.
1935. q. $12. J. R. Shoenfield. Duke Univ. Press, College Station, Box 6697, Durham, N.C. 27708. Index. Circ: 1,200. Reprint: Johnson. Microform: Academic Archives, Inc.

Indexed: MathR, SCI. *Aud:* Ac, Sa. *Rv:* H. *Jv:* B.

Research papers in this journal cover both pure and applied mathematics. About 20 papers of average length appear in each issue. A good, general mathematics journal, and a good choice for academic libraries.

The Fibonacci Quarterly; a journal devoted to the study of integers with special properties.
1963. q. $4. Brother U. Alfred, St. Mary's College, Calif. 94575.

Indexed: MathR. *Aud:* Ac, Jc, Sa. *Rv:* M. *Jv:* B.

The official publication of the Fibonacci Association. Though it is relatively specialized and definitely inaccessible to the layman with little mathematical background, it makes a strong effort to orient itself to the larger possible audience. To this end it encourages contributions from mathematics students and teachers, has a special section on problems at the elementary level of this branch of mathematics, and tries to present sections useful for class work. The mathematics involved is for the most part on the college level, yet can be understood by amateur mathematicians interested in the subject. A typical issue has 10–15 articles of varying lengths, and a number of problems and proofs submitted by readers.

Journal of Recreational Mathematics.
1968. q. $9. J. S. Madachy. Greenwood Periodicals, Inc., 211 E. 43rd St., New York, N.Y. 10017. Illus.

Bk. rev: 3, 300 words, signed. *Aud:* Sh, Jc, Ac, Sa, Ga. *Rv:* M. *Jv:* A.

For that portion of the population which delights in mathematical tricks, games, mindteasers, curiosa, etc., this publication will be a welcome addition. Feature articles and a problems section include such topics as magic designs, geometric diversions, "alphametics" (letter arithmetic problems), chess problems, and the like. And for that portion of the world which trembles at the mere thought of number manipulation, the periodical can also be fun, since it offers a variety of pleasurable reading by way of historical notes, articles on math in relationship to other fields, "Mathematical Browsing," i.e., items on unusual events, meetings, recent literature gossip, etc. The value of recreational mathematics, as the editor expresses it, is to "stimulate an interest in mathematics and in education," and, indeed, a periodical of this sort will find wide audiences in public, high school, and undergraduate libraries. The tone is chatty, and the typography is large and clear.

London Mathematical Society. Journal.
1926. q. $25.50. G. E. H. Reuter. C. F. Hodgson & Son, Ltd., Pakenham St., Kingsway, London W.C.1. Index. Reprint: Dawson.

Indexed: MathR, SCI. *Bk. rev:* 10, 250–500 words, signed. *Aud:* Ac, Sa. *Rv:* H. *Jv:* B.

Covering all aspects of pure and applied mathematics, the *Journal* of this distinguished society limits its research papers to a length of not more than 10 pages. Shorter investigations appear as mathematical notes. Occasionally, brief notices of the Society are also published.

London Mathematical Society. Proceedings.
1865. 4/yr. J. D. Weston. Oxford Univ. Press, Amen House, Warwick Square, London E.C.4. Reprint: Dawson.

Indexed: MathR, SCI. *Aud:* Ac, Sa. *Rv:* H. *Jv:* B.

The *Proceedings* first made its appearance when the Society was founded in 1865 for "the promotion and extension of mathematical knowledge." Now in its third series, the publication devotes itself to research papers longer in length and larger in scope than those appearing in the *Journal*.

The Society will issue a third publication, the *Bulletin*, beginning in Spring, 1969, which will provide faster dissemination of short research reports.

Mathematical Gazette. 1894. 4/yr. $4.20. E. A. Maxwell. G. Bell & Sons, Ltd., York House, Portugal St., London W.C.2. Illus., index adv. Microform UM. Reprint: Johnson.

Indexed: MathR. *Bk. rev:* 50, 200–500 words, signed. *Aud:* Et, Ht, Ac, Jc, Sa. *Rv:* H. *Jv:* B.

Published by The Mathematical Association, an "association of teachers and students of elementary mathematics." Although primarily concerned with mathematics education and teaching in the English classroom, the publication should not be overlooked by U.S. libraries. The variety of expository papers, ranging from elementary to more advanced mathematics, the creative approaches described in teaching methods, and the interesting general atricles make the journal a splendid choice for mathematics collections. Departments include: "Notes on Mathematics Education;" "Notes for the Classroom;" news of the Society and the profession; and a large and comprehensive book review section which provides a good checklist for foreign publications.

Mathematical Log. 1957. 3/yr. $1. Josephine & Richard V. Andree. Mu Alpha Theta, Dept. of Mathematics, Univ. of Oklahoma, Norman, Okla. 73069. Illus. Circ: 18,000.

Aud: Sh, Jc. *Rv:* M. *Jv:* B.

Mu Alpha Theta, the National High School and Junior College Mathematics Club, supplies a good bit of educational and diversional material in its 4-page news organ. As well as notes on its meetings and chapters, it publishes short essays and problems contributed by educators and members, and occasionally reprints problems from other publications. Includes discussions on educational and employment opportunities for students. (Copies are circulated, in quantity, without charge, to chapters of this society.)

Mathematical Reviews. See Indexes and Abstracts Section.

Mathematics Magazine. 1926. bi-m. $3. Roy Dubisch. Mathematical Assn. of America, SUNY at Buffalo, N.Y. 14214. Illus., index, adv. Circ: 5,200. Microform: UM.

Indexed: MathR. *Bk. rev:* 2–3, 300–500 words, signed. *Aud:* Sh, Jc, Ac, Sa. *Rv:* H. *Jv:* B.

An excellent general mathematics magazine. Catering to varying levels of sophistication and interest in undergraduate mathematics, the periodical should be equally enjoyable to faculty, both of colleges and secondary schools, students, and professionals. Papers and shorter notes are largely expository, and include fresh insights into familiar problems, as well as original works. There are, occasionally, general articles (some written with a touch of humor) which range from the pedagogical—discussions of mathematics curricula

and the like—to the historical and philosophical. A problems and solutions section ensures a wide audience by posing problems from the elementary to more advanced levels.

Mathematics of Computation. 1943. q. $16. E. Isaacson. Amer. Mathematical Soc., Box 6248, Providence, R.I. 02904. Illus., adv. Circ: 3,200. Microform: Mc.

Indexed: MathR, SciAb, SCI. *Bk. rev:* 20, 100–1000 words, signed. *Aud:* Ac, Sa. *Rv:* H. *Jv:* B.

Research journal devoted to original papers on computational mathematics. A large and very useful section is that containing reviews and descriptions of books and tables. Grouped by subjects, the longer reviews very often represent tutorial essays in themselves. A novel addendum to recent issues is a microfiche, placed into a pocket on the back cover, which contains specialized data described in one of the articles or reviews.

Mathematics Student Journal. 1954. q. $2. National Council of Teachers of Mathematics, 1201 16th St., N.W., Washington, D.C. 20036. Illus. Circ: 80,000.

Aud: Jh, Sh. *Rv:* M. *Jv:* B.

Geared for students from the 7th through 12th grade, this periodical provides a variety of instructional and recreational material for this age group. Features include both math projects and a problems section, to which students are invited to send both queries and solutions.

Mathematics Teacher. 1908. m. $5. (Institutions, $7). Irvin Brune. National Council of Teachers of Mathematics, 1201 16th St., N.W., Washington, D.C. 20036. Illus., index, adv. Circ: 44,000. Microform: UM. Reprint: AMS.

Indexed: EdI, MathR. *Bk. rev:* 4–10, 350–800 words, signed. *Aud:* Ht, Jc, Ac. *Rv:* H. *Jv:* B.

Concerned with mathematics and education on a secondary level, the periodical provides articles by leading educators on current practices and trends, testing, some expository papers, historical reviews, and reports of research or descriptions of novel experimental programs. (Elementary school teachers will find their needs served by the other publication of the Council, *Arithmetic Teacher*.)

Pacific Journal of Mathematics. 1951. m. $32. Ed bd. 103 Highland Blvd., Berkeley, Calif. 94708. Index. Circ: 1,400.

Indexed: MathR, SCI. *Aud:* Ac, Sa. *Rv:* H. *Jv:* B.

Publishes research papers in all branches of pure and applied mathematics. Contributions to the journal often come from some of the supporting institutions of the periodical, namely western U.S. and Canadian universities, and some Japanese universities.

Pi Mu Epsilon. 1949. semi-ann. Membership (Non-members, $2.). Kenneth Loewen. Dept. of Mathematics, Univ. of Oklahoma, Norman, Okla. 73069. Illus. Circ: 4,000.

Aud: Sh, Jc, Ac, Sa. *Rv:* M. *Jv:* B.

The publication, which is the official journal of the honorary mathematical fraternity, Pi Mu Epsilon, supports the expressions of mathematical inclination and creativity by undergraduates, as well as faculty or professionals. Features range from expository papers to general interest articles on such topics as the etymology of mathematical terms, historical reviews, addresses presented before meetings of the organizations, etc. Departments include a "Problems and Answers" section designed for both intermediate and more advanced levels, and a section on recommended undergraduate research projects.

Quarterly of Applied Mathematics. 1943. q. $8. Ed bd. Brown Univ., 182 George St., Providence, R.I. 02912.

Indexed: EngI, MathR, SCI. *Bk. rev:* 10, 250 words, signed. *Aud:* Ac, Sa. *Rv:* H. *Jv:* B.

The research papers in this journal specialize in "applied mathematics which have an intimate connection with application in industry or practical science."

SIAM Review. 1959. q. $14. Ed bd. Society for Industrial and Applied Mathematics, 33 S. 17th St., Philadelphia, Pa. 19103. Illus., adv. Circ: 5,000.

Indexed: MathR, SCI. *Bk. rev:* 5–6, 300–500 words, signed. *Aud:* Jc, Ac, Sa. *Rv:* H. *Jv:* B.

The journal covers the broad field of applied mathematics comprising expository papers, survey articles on new research, and essays on general interest topics for the profession, such as historical reports, reviews of pedagogical techniques, and discussions of mathematical curricula. Short research notes on mathematical techniques are also published. Features include a "Problems and Solution" section, and news and notices. Abstracts of papers presented at meetings of the Society also appear regularly.

The Society for Industrial and Applied Mathematics, devoted to promoting the application of mathematics to science and industry, sponsors other more specialized research publications:

SIAM Journal on Applied Mathematics. 1953. bi-m. $20. Ed bd. Circ: 5,500. *Indexed:* ChemAb, EngI, MathR, SCI.

"Contains research papers in mathematics having relevance to the solution of applied problems."

SIAM Journal on Control. 1963. q. $14. Ed bd. Circ: 1,100. *Indexed:* MathR, SCI.

"Research articles on mathematical theory of control and applications."

SIAM Journal on Numerical Analysis. 1964. q. $14. Ed bd. Circ: 1,300. *Indexed:* MathR.

"Research articles on the development and analysis of numerical method."

School Science and Mathematics. See Science—General Section.

Scripta Mathematica. 1933. q. $4. A. Gelbart. Yeshiva Univ., Amsterdam Ave. & 186th St., New York, N.Y. 10033. Illus., index. Reprint: AMS Press.

Indexed: MathR, SCI. *Bk. rev:* 40, 150–500 words, signed. *Aud:* Jc, Ac, Sa. *Rv:* H. *Jv:* B.

Although originally devoted to the "philosophy, history and expository treatment of mathematics," including such entertainments as mathematical curiosa, the periodical has, in the last several years, concerned itself with research papers of varying levels of sophistication. Well-written expository papers often supply historical and biographical material, which make fascinating reading. The book review section, easily representing about one-quarter of each issue, emphasizes the exotic, drawing attention to many foreign mathematical works not generally found in the average U.S. library, thus punctuating the international scope of the journal. A rather large section on "Books and Pamphlets Received," supplies brief annotations. Purportedly a quarterly, the publication has been rather erratic in producing issues (Spring 1965 issued in Spring 1967) but is well worth the delay. Moreover, beginning collections would do well to collect back volumes.

Washington State University. Mathematics Notes. 1958. q. Free. Dept. of Mathematics, Washington State Univ., Pullman, Wash. 99163.

Bk. rev: Occasional. *Aud:* Sh, Jc, Ac, Sa. *Rv:* M. *Jv:* B.

Although only a leaflet this small publication contains a variety of interesting material. The main article may consist of a short historical essay or biographical note on some mathematician, a review of famous and familiar problems, or a discussion of some events of professional interest. A section on problems and solutions is included, and, occasionally, a book review.

MEDICAL, NURSING AND HEALTH SCIENCES

Indexes and Abstracts

Abridged Readers' Guide, Biological Abstracts, Chemical Abstracts, Education Index, Index Medicus, International Pharmaceutical Abstracts, Psychological Abstracts, Public Affairs Information Service, Readers' Guide to Periodical Literature, Science Citation Index. (For annotations, see Indexes and Abstracts Section.)

In a field where the literature is so highly specialized, requiring some knowledge of medicine and medical practices, there are few medical periodicals which would be appropriate for, or of interest to laymen or even academic libraries. The medical journals chosen for this section represent only a small sampling of those available; some are pertinent to collections in the biological sciences, and others will be useful to libraries supporting medical technology programs.

The nursing and health periodicals, on the other hand, are a little more accessible to the informed layman, and the former will be found useful in nursing school libraries, college libraries where a nursing program is being supported, and community libraries in the vicinity of a large public or private hospital, while the latter could be found in all of these, as well as in high school libraries.

American Journal of Medicine. 1946. m. $14. A. B. Gutman. Reuben H. Donnelley Corp., 466 Lexington Ave., New York, N.Y. 10017. Illus., index, adv. Circ: 22,671. Microform: UM.

Indexed: BioAb, ChemAb, IMed, NuAb, SCI. *Aud:* Sa, Ac. *Rv:* H. *Jv:* B.

The journal publishes research and clinical reports in the broad fields of the medical and biological sciences. Sections include clinical studies, review papers, clinico-pathologic conferences, and case reports. Editorial comments on timely or controversial medical research are also provided.

American Journal of Nursing. m. $6. Barbara G. Schutt. Amer. Journal of Nursing Co., 10 Columbus Circle, New York, N.Y. 10019. Illus., index, adv.

Indexed: IMed. *Bk. rev:* 5–6, 250 words, signed. *Aud:* Sa, Ac, Jc. *Rv:* H. *Jv:* B.

Ranging from material concerned with the highly specialized to the highly topical, this official magazine of the American Nurse's Association is geared toward both student and professional. Fifteen or so articles in each issue include contributions by medical specialists on new medical techniques or equipment, articles on professionalism, case studies or clinical reports, and short pieces on patient-nurse relations. An extensive news section touches on every aspect of nursing-education, legislation, service, professional practice—and special departments provide as good a current-awareness program on research and nursing trends as any periodical in the field. Of particular note are "Drug Data," listing information on new pharmaceuticals, and "Medical Highlights," digesting new findings from the medical journals. Recommended for any library supporting a nursing program or any collection concerned with this aspect of medical practice.

American Journal of Public Health and The Nation's Health. 1911. m. $15. Amer. Public Health Assn., 1790 Broadway, New York, N.Y. 10019. Illus., index, adv. Circ: 18,281. Microform: UM.

Indexed: ASTI, BioAb, ChemAb, IMed, NuAb, PAIS, SCI. *Bk. rev:* 15, 100–150 words, signed. *Aud:* Sa, Ac. *Rv:* H. *Jv:* B.

Covers all aspects of public health, and while written primarily for the expert, has a given amount of general information for the interested layman, e.g., a symposium on health planning and an evaluation of regional medical programs. It should be consulted by anyone outside of the profession who is dealing with current issues in health as related to society and politics. In addition to the book reviews, there is a selected public health bibliography of magazine articles. The usual amount of organizational news and items on personalities. A useful journal for all large public and academic libraries.

American Medical Association. Journal. 1848. w. $23. John H. Talbott. Amer. Medical Assn., 535 N. Dearborn St., Chicago, Ill. Illus., adv. Circ: 11,800. Microform: Univ. of Rochester.

Indexed: BioAb, ChemAb, IMed, NuAb, PAIS, SCI. *Bk. rev:* 6–7, 200 words, signed. *Aud:* Sa, Ac. *Rv:* H. *Jv:* B.

The official journal of the A.M.A. comprises a review of current research, clinical trials, and advances in the field of medical science. Each issue contains sections on "Original" and "Special Communications," as well as selected abstracts of the world's medical literature. "The Book Forum" describes and evaluates current literature. One of the chief publications for news, views and reviews of the profession, the *Journal* includes, as well, information on such topics as law and medicine, and current legislation. Useful for the medical collections of academic libraries.

Annals of Internal Medicine. 1922. m. $15. Edward C. Rosenow, Jr. Amer. College of Physicians, 4200 Pine St., Philadelphia, Pa. 19104. Illus., index, adv. Circ: 37,500. Microform: UM.

Indexed: BioAb, ChemAb, IMed, NuAb, SCI. *Bk. rev:* 25, 250–600 words, signed. *Aud:* Sa, Ac. *Rv:* H. *Jv:* B.

Containing original articles, case reports and reviews of current research interest, the journal covers the "broad field of internal medicine and allied sciences." Special articles of a general or review nature are frequently included. Editorial notes, medical news, questions and answers on particular aspects of internal medicine, and letters and comments are also regular features. Book reviews are short but good.

British Medical Journal. 1832. w. $21. Martin Ware. British Medical Assn., B.M.A. House, Tavistock Sq., London W.C.1. Illus., index, adv. Microform: UM.

Indexed: BioAb, ChemAb, IMed, SCI. *Bk. rev:* 8–9, 250–300 words, signed. *Aud:* Sa, Ac. *Rv:* H. *Jv:* B.

The official journal of the British Medical Association comprises digests or commentaries on recent advances in medicine and related fields, reports on original research, clinical studies, and news and notes within its community.

Canadian Nurse. 1905. m. $5. Virginia A. Lindabury. Canadian Nurses' Assn., 50 The Driveway, Ottawa 4, Ont. Illus., index, adv. Circ: 71,000. Microform: UM.

Indexed: IMed. *Bk. rev:* 8–10, 250–500 words, signed. *Aud:* Sa, Ac, Jc. *Rv:* H. *Jv:* B.

Worldwide in scope, this periodical is available in both English- and French-language editions. The objective editorials deal with current topics and aim at stimulating interest in the profession's problem areas. The articles range from the technical to popular; some have bibliographies. Featured departments are the recent additions to the CNA's library accession list, new products and occasional research abstracts.

Index Medicus. See Indexes and Abstracts Section.

Journal of Nursing Education. 1962. q. Free to qualified academic personnel and institutions. Elizabeth E. Kinzer. McGraw-Hill Book Co., 330 W. 42nd St., New York, N.Y. 10036. Illus., index, adv. Circ: 8,500.

Indexed: IMed. *Aud:* Sa, Ac, Jc. *Rv:* H. *Jv:* B.

Directed toward nursing educators, the publication features articles emphasizing nursing education, techniques, teaching programs, new courses and materials. Reports are short (2–3 pages) yet informative.

Journal of Practical Nursing. 1953. m. $4. V. L. Conley. National Assn. for Practical Nurse Education and Service, Inc., 535 Fifth Ave., New York, N.Y. 10017. Illus., index, adv. Circ: 40,000.

Aud: Sh, Jc, Ac, Sa. *Rv:* H. *Jv:* B.

The "voice of practical/vocational nursing," although primarily directed toward the licensed practical nurse, contains information which should be valuable to nursing students or the nursing profession at large. Four to five articles in each issue vary in content and in levels of sophistication. Authoritative, technical articles, by leading medical specialists, review current progress or practices in the medical sciences and represent excellent tutorials; current trends in continuing education for practical nurses, or professional attitudes are featured regularly; and informally written articles, contributed by LPN's, on nursing experiences, practical nursing notes and the like, are also included. Useful departments are: "Modern Medications," which reviews new drugs; "NAPNES Newsletter," which gives thumbnail reports on current medical news; and "Washington News and Views," which deals with legislation affecting the profession. Other departments are concerned with general news of the profession or of the Association, for which the periodical is the official organ. A good choice for vocational schools with medical technology programs.

Journal of School Health. 1927. m. (Sept.–June). Membership (Non-members, $5). Amer. School Health Assn., 515 E. Main St., Kent, Ohio 44240. Circ: 11,000.

Indexed: EdI, IMed. *Aud:* Ac, Jc, Ht, Et. *Rv:* H. *Jv:* B.

A journal for anyone dealing with health problems in elementary and secondary schools and colleges, e.g., the school nurse, doctor, dentist, psychologist and, to a degree, the teacher of health education. While most of the journal is given over to articles which deal with professional problems of these people, there are a few articles which are helpful to the teacher—particularly those concerning new developments in medicine and health education.

Lancet. 1823. w. $15. Ian Douglas-Wilson. Lancet Ltd., 7 Adam St., London W.C.2. Subscriptions to: Little, Brown & Co., 34 Beacon St., Boston, Mass. 02106. Illus., adv. Circ: 46,000.

Indexed: BioAb, ChemAb, IMed, SCI. *Bk. rev:* Occasional, lengthy, signed; several, brief, unsigned. *Aud:* Sa, Ac. *Rv:* H. *Jv:* B.

Intended for those who have some knowledge of medicine and medical practices, the journal publishes articles dealing with medical postulates, methods, results and discussions. Signed articles vary in the degree of technicality. An "Annotation Section" presents brief discussions of topics which deal with the relationship between medicine and the current problems of mankind. Editorial pages are informative, unbiased, and occasionally witty.

Medical Economics. 1923. bi-w. $15. R. C. Lewis. Medical Economics, Inc., Oradell, N.J. 07649. Illus., index, adv. Circ: 186,000. Microform: UM.

Indexed: PAIS. *Aud:* Sa, Ga. *Rv:* M. *Jv:* B.

Purportedly the periodical most widely read by physicians, this is the *Changing Times* of the medical world, and a guide for laymen to what the doctor does with the dollar, how he handles his practice and what fees he might charge. More precisely, it is directed to the affluent physician, telling him how he should live with his money. Articles such as "Playing It Cool in a Nervous Market," and "The Latest Fees in Five Major Fields," indicate the scope and purpose. Some give pause, e.g., "Why Surgeons are Real Swingers," but then this is not meant for the uninitiated.

New England Journal of Medicine. 1812. w. $8. Franz J. Ingelfinger. Massachusetts Medical Soc., 10 Shattuck St., Boston, Mass. 02115. Illus., index, adv. Circ: 104,000. Microform: UM.

Indexed: BioAb, IMed, SCI. *Bk. rev:* 3–6, 450 words, signed. *Aud:* Sa, Ac. *Rv:* H. *Jv:* B.

One of the leading medical journals, the weekly includes both original research papers (about 4–5 per issue), a review paper covering recent medical advances, some short case studies, and case records of the Massachusetts General Hospital. Special articles are frequently included on general topics such as the nation's health or medical education. Brief editorials on medical topics and technical correspondence are also included, as are summaries of statistics of the Massachusetts Department of Public Health. Official publication of the Massachusetts Medical Society.

Nursing Forum. 1961. q. $6.50. Alice R. Clarke. Nursing Pubns., Inc., Box 218, Hillsdale, N.J. 07642. Illus., index, adv. Circ: 8,000.

Indexed: IMed. *Aud:* Sa, Ac, Jc. *Rv:* H. *Jv:* B.

A journal for those actively engaged in general hospital nursing. The signed and authoritative articles cover a wide range of topics—research, nursing techniques and goals, patient-nurse relationships and the nursing problems that arise in the care of the physically and mentally handicapped. Also included are editorials dealing with current or controversial problems in nursing.

Nursing Outlook. 1953. m. $5. Alice M. Robinson. Amer. Journal of Nursing Co., 10 Columbus Circle, New York, N.Y. 10019. Illus., index, adv. Circ: 24,417. Microform: UM.

Indexed: IMed, PsyAb. *Bk. rev:* 3–5, 250 words, signed. *Aud:* Sa, Ac, Jc. *Rv:* H. *Jv:* B.

Aimed at educators, and valuable for all nurses, the official magazine of the National League for Nursing covers the entire field. Eight to nine feature articles in each issue report on various topics of current interest: the profession, education, the community and public health, nursing problems in specialized areas such as physical therapy, and case studies. Regular departments provide news and information on teaching aids, new products, educational programs, calendars, and the like.

Nursing Research. 1952. bi-m. $12. Lucille E. Notter. Amer. Journal of Nursing Co., 10 Columbus Circle, New York, N.Y. 10019. Illus., index, adv. 6,400. Microform: UM.

Indexed: IMed, PsyAb. *Aud:* Sa, Ac. *Rv:* H. *Jv:* B.

Sponsored by the National League for Nursing and the American Nurse's Association, the publication stresses original research activities undertaken by the profession. Articles report on studies of nursing education, professional attitudes, experimental studies on nursing procedures, and clinical studies on nursing practices. Many of the papers are portions of Master's theses. Selected abstracts of the literature and brief reports on nursing techniques are featured regularly.

R N; a national magazine for nursing. 1937. m. $3.50. Eleanor B. Dowling. R N Pubns., Inc., Oradell, N.J. Illus., adv. Circ: 183,500.

Aud: Sa, Ga, Ac, Jc. *Rv:* M. *Jv:* B.

Not of the technical caliber of many other nursing publications, the magazine is still a readable periodical which may be of interest to the layman as well as to the professional. Signed articles cover all aspects of nursing. Valuable information is also found in the special departments and features, such as "On the Clinical Horizon," "Nursing Tips," and "What's New in Drugs." Objective presentation of material is found both in the "Letters to the Editor" and the editorial comments.

Social Science & Medicine; an international journal. 1967. $10 (Libraries and other institutions, $30.). Pergamon Press, 44-01 21st St., Long Island City, N.Y. 11101.

Bk. rev: Various numbers, lengths. *Aud:* Sa, Ac. *Rv:* H. *Jv:* B.

A first-rate scholarly journal, focusing on the interrelationship between various social sciences and medicine, including epidemiology, medical education, psychiatry, and public health. The scope and editorship is international. Each paper concludes with abstracts, 500–600 words in length, in French, German, and Spanish. The book reviews are extensive. Additional features include proceedings of symposia, monograph supplements, and a "Current Research" section.

Today's Health. 1923. m. $4. Elliott H. McCleary. Amer. Medical Assn., 535 N. Dearborn St., Chicago, Ill. 60610. Illus., index, adv. Circ: 710,000. Microform: UM.

Indexed: AbrRG, BioAb, PAIS, RG. *Aud:* Ga, Ac, Jc, Sh, Jh. *Rv:* H. *Jv:* B.

An informative and well-written health periodical for the layman. The signed articles and special feature departments cover all facets of health, hygiene and inter-personal relationships. Certain issues deal with particular topics, as schools and education. Travel articles, question and answer departments, "Today's Health News," and "First Aid" are among the special features which are included in most issues. Although published by the American Medical Association, all material, even that of a controversial nature, appears to be presented in an objective manner.

WHO Chronicle. 1947. m. $3. World Health Organization, Geneva, Switzerland. Subscriptions to: Columbia Univ. Press, 2960 Broadway, New York, N.Y. 10027. Circ: 15,000. Microform: UM.

Indexed: BioAb, IMed, SCI. *Aud:* Ga, Ac, Jc, Sh. *Rv:* H. *Jv:* A.

Although published for the medical and public health professions, this periodical is of value and interest to the layman. It "provides a monthly record of the principal health activities undertaken in various countries with WHO assistance." One of its aims is the achievement of better world health, and in conjunction with this, worldwide health problems are discussed. Published in Chinese, English, French, Russian and Spanish.

Weight Watchers Magazine. 1968. m. $4.50. W/W Twenty-first Corp., 1790 Broadway, New York, N.Y. 10019. Illus., adv. Circ: 300,000.

Aud: Ga. *Rv:* M. *Jv:* B.

One of a number of magazines geared to show readers how to exercise and take off weight. Although some men will find it useful, the primary audience is the woman. Articles are by doctors, psychologists and experts on diet. They tend to be direct, easy to understand, and apparently medically sound. Regular features include items on recipes, fashion, beauty, travel, and success stories by women who lost pounds. There is a limited amount of fiction. The format is pleasing, if not exciting, and the whole will have a given amount of appeal to affluent readers.

Placing more emphasis on exercise than losing weight per se, *Fitness for Living* will have a wider appeal for men (1967. bi-m. $3. Rodale Press, Inc., 33 E. Minor St., Emmaus, Pa. 18049. Circ: 118,000). This pocket-sized, illustrated magazine stresses the need for walking, jogging and using the bike. Other articles cover nutrition and reports on those who have succeeded in maintaining waistline and health through proper exercise.

World Health; an illustrated magazine for the general public giving an idea of WHO activities throughout the world and showing some of the more striking aspects of public health work. 1947. m. $5. World Health Organization, Geneva, Switzerland. Subscriptions to: Columbia Univ. Press, 2960 Broadway, New York, N.Y. 10027. Illus. Circ: 105,000.

Aud: Ga, Ac, Jc, Sh, Jh. *Rv:* H. *Jv:* B.

A World Health Organization magazine for the general public, suitable for the high school student. Articles are authoritative, yet written in a popular style. Covers all aspects of public health on an international basis. Each issue is devoted to a particular theme, country, or personality. Well-illustrated with drawings and photographs. In view of the pictures and the wide scope of the magazine, it may be used at almost any level for a better understanding of the world's peoples.

MEN'S MAGAZINES

Indexes and Abstracts

Readers' Guide to Periodical Literature. (For annotation, see Indexes and Abstracts Section.)

Argosy. m. $5. Henry Steeger. Popular Pubns., Inc., 205 E. 42nd St., New York, N.Y. 10017. Illus., adv. Circ: 1,523,000.

Aud: Ga, Sh. *Rv:* L. *Jv:* B.

For the man of action, this magazine provides articles and fiction suited to his needs and interests. Following a rather conservative editorial policy, fiction and articles stress the attributes of the All-American male. Fiction, including a full-length novel, is of the adventurous variety, action and heroics being the main themes. Illustrated articles include true exciting experiences in war, sports and travel, as well as informative pieces on cars, guns, boats, hunting and fishing. Special departments offer coverage of new products, techniques and ideas for cars, camping, hunting, fishing, hobbies, clothes, entertainment and home repairs. In the genre, *True* tends to be a bit more sophisticated, but in any public or high school library where there are reluctant male readers, this is bound to be popular.

Cavalier. 1951. $6. Douglas Allen. Arizill Publishing Co., 145 E. 49th St., New York, N.Y. 10017. Subscriptions to: Box 29, Mt. Morris, Ill. 61054. Illus., adv. Circ: 50,000.

Bk. rev: 7–10, 50–250 words, signed. *Aud:* Ga. *Rv:* L. *Jv:* B.

This is a considerably more sophisticated edition of the *Playboy* ploy—even the pinups are a trifle more realistic. Articles deal with issues and personalities of interest to teenagers and men under 30. Most are well written by journalists, well-known authors and subject experts. The magazine is particularly strong on special features, which include movie reviews by Paul Krassner (*The Realist* editor), television by Leonard Feather, and even a column on cooking by Donald Kramer. A considerable amount of space, in fact, is given over to the arts, music, books and the theatre. One suspects the girls are a lead-on, and if this is what it takes to stir interest in culture, it is well worth serious consideration by librarians—particularly those in senior high schools with reluctant readers. The magazine is not to be confused with the typical girlie approach, and if a choice were to be made between it and *Playboy,* it would be the winner.

Dare. 1965. m. $5 (Controlled circulation). John G. Cashin. 1626 Magnolia Ct., Cleveland, Ohio 44106. Illus., adv.

Aud: Ga. *Rv.* L. *Jv:* C.

A free, controlled-circulation college man's magazine, which accounts for the fact that it is found in almost every school barbershop. The title seems to come from the type of articles—usually biographical and short items about men who excel at sports. The style of writing is popular, and between the lines there is emphasis on being an all-American boy of the *Playboy* variety. But there is one major exception; sex is played down and there are no illustrations which will turn a librarian's head. Regular departments cover (somewhat superficially) fashions, records, books, business, etc. Some short fiction. The whole seems as much geared for the advertiser as the reader.

Elks Magazine. 1922. m. Membership (Non-members, $2.). Ed bd. B.P.O. Elks of U.S.A., 425 W. Diversity Parkway, Chicago, Ill. 60614. Illus., adv. Circ: 1,400,000.

Aud: Ga. *Rv:* M. *Jv:* B.

A number of men's fraternal magazines include material other than that geared for its members. This is a good example, for in addition to news about individuals and lodges throughout the United States, there are general articles on travel, world events and editorials that frequently go beyond fraternal matters. Others in this group are *Lion* (Circ: 550,000), the official organ of Lions International, and *Kiwanis Magazine* and the *Rotarian,* both discussed in this section. On the whole, these tend to be middle-of-the-road in their attitudes, the writing style is fair to good, and the imaginative content somewhat below average. Nevertheless, they perform an important function, and because of their wide coverage of world events, people and places, are to be recommended for larger libraries as well as smaller ones, which may have a particularly strong fraternal organization in the community. Best to have a member give the library a copy or subscription.

Esquire. 1933. m. $7.50. Harold Hayes. 488 Madison Ave., New York, N.Y. Illus., adv. Circ: 956,000. Microform: UM.

Indexed: RG. *Bk. rev:* 3–5, 150–2,000 words, signed. *Aud:* Ga, Ac, Jc, Sh. *Rv:* M. *Jv:* A.

The best "man's magazine" now available, and in many ways a leading contender for a front place among literary and politically-oriented periodicals. Librarians who remember it many years ago as the haven for the "pretty girl" need have no fears. After all, it did make *Readers' Guide,* and the "girlie" aspect of the magazine lost out some time ago in favor of literate articles on everything from the current presidential candidates to the latest in pop art. Among the regular features are political reviews by Dwight McDonald, and film and book reviews by some of the leading critics in the United States. In addition to topical articles there are the usual run of features on fashion, sports, travel and personalities. A few short stories or excerpts from novels, again by leading writers. Cartoons and skilled photography round out each issue. The style is readable and the spirit is a nice combination of youth and intellect. A basic man's magazine for all libraries from high school on up, particularly the latter, where *Playboy* may be a bit too "advanced" for either the librarian or the community.

Gentlemen's Quarterly. 1957. 8/yr. $8. Everett Mattlin. Esquire Inc., 488 Madison Ave., New York, N.Y. 10022. Illus., adv. Circ: 75,000.

Aud: Ga. *Rv:* L. *Jv:* B.

A man's high fashion magazine, this is unique in that it is one of the few fashion periodicals devoted solely to masculine interests. It is probably read as much by clothing salesmen and dealers as by the general public, but an effort is made to attract the man next door with special features, such as John Wayne speaking out on box office and movies, and where to dine and dance. A typical issue may touch on what color and type shirt to wear with six button double-breasted styling. Not for every library, or every reader, but it has more than passing interest, both for men and the women who help the male to purchase his clothes.

Kiwanis Magazine; published for community leaders. 1915. m. $2. R. P. Merridew. Kiwanis Intl., 101 E. Erie St., Chicago, Ill. 60611. Illus., adv. Circ: 276,000. Microform: UM.

Aud: Ga. *Rv:* L. *Jv:* B.

The official publication of Kiwanis International is devoted to "the principle of service and the advancement of individual community, and national welfare, and to the strengthening of international goodwill." It is written primarily for business and professional men who play an active part in civic affairs, but many of the articles deal with social, political and economic matters of wide interest to those who are not members. The authors tend to be objective, accurate, and unusually thorough. There is no overt political philosophy, though most of the material is middle-of-the-road in tone. A few humorous and pedestrian articles

counter the more serious material. One of the better organizational magazines, it is useful in many public libraries where there may be a limited number of journals on cities and government. See comments for *Elks Magazine.*

Knight; the magazine for the adult male. bi-m. $6. Jared Rutter. Publishers Service Inc., 8060 Melrose Ave., Los Angeles, Calif. 90046. Illus., adv. Circ: 275,000.

Aud: Ga. *Rv:* L. *Jv:* B.

While this is a bit stronger on pin-ups than *Cavalier,* the level of its articles and particularly its fiction is the same. The editor often features new writers, and a number of their efforts will have strong appeal to younger adults. Science fiction is also stressed, and established writers such as Pietro Di Donato contribute. There are the usual number of features on the good life, e.g., sports cars, dining out, dress, personalities. Again, not to be confused with the run-of-the-mill girlie magazine.

Modern Man. m. $9. Publishers' Development Corp., 8150 N. Central Park Ave., Skokie, Ill. 60076. Illus., adv. Circ: 115,000.

Aud: Ga. *Rv:* L. *Jv:* C.

This is a single example of the so-called "girlie magazine" that replies almost exclusively on the charms of the girls to lure the reader to put down his money. There are a number of simplified articles on crime, adventure, and the hippie scene, and the usual pedestrian bits of fiction. Anyone who has an esthetic eye will be baffled by the editor's notion of feminine beauty. While a magazine of this type is of no value to librarians, it should not be confused with more legitimate efforts such as *Playboy, Cavalier* or *Knight.* In the woman's field, a rough equivalent, sans the photographs, is the soap opera true confessions type magazine.

Playboy. 1953. m. $8. Hugh Hefner. H.M.H. Publishing Co., Inc., Playboy Bldg., 919 N. Michigan Ave., Chicago, Ill. 60611. Illus., adv. Circ: 5,040,000. Microform: UM.

Aud: Ga, Ac, Jc, Sh. *Rv:* M. *Jv:* B.

Subtitled *Entertainment for Men,* yet probably read by almost one-third as many women, *Playboy* surveys the interests of the worldly man: girls, travel, music, entertainment, books, sports, clothing, gourmet cooking, world affairs, and sex. Authored by the best of contemporary writers, articles and fiction are candid, thought-provoking, and superior in literary technique if not always content. The humor, both in word and picture, pokes fun at the human foibles concerning sex and moral behavior. The philosophy is consumer-oriented, but no more so than many magazines for women. The intellectual level is more ersatz than real, yet keyed to an above-average reading ability. A monthly interview with a well-known and controversial figure offers candid and solid conversation. The illustrations provide appreciation of the female torso, stressing that "it's what's up front that counts." The photography and drawings are pointed, creative and eye-catching. It is the rare individual reading this magazine who turns to the literature before gazing at all the illustrations. Deserves to be in most libraries, but the colorful illustrations cause many to pass it by. If student preference is any indication, it is favored among teen-age boys. (The majority of readers are in their teens or early to middle twenties.) High school librarians in liberal communities will wish to consider.

Rotarian. 1911. m. $2. Karl L. Krueger. Rotary Intl., 1600 Ridge Ave., Evanston, Ill. 60201. Illus., index, adv. Circ: 419,000. Microform: UM.

Aud: Ga, Ac, Jc, Sh. *Rv:* M. *Jv:* B.

One of the better known organizational magazines—it inevitably tops the pile in a dentist's office—this is, also one of the best. Although middle-of-the-road to conservative in tone, it has outstanding articles on international business and government (one emphasis of the organization is to broaden understanding of the world), and community and civic problems. The writing style is understandable to anyone from high school on up, but has a (degree) of sophistication not usually associated with this type of publication. A given amount of space is turned over to Rotarian business. A good general magazine for most libraries. A Spanish edition is available at $3.75.

True; the man's magazine. 1937. m. $5. Douglas S. Kennedy. Fawcett Pubns., Inc., 67 W. 44th St., New York, N.Y. 10036. Illus., adv. Circ: 2,500,000.

Bk. rev: 10–12 notes. *Aud:* Ga, Sh. *Rv:* M. *Jv:* A.

Using the approach of *Argosy,* distinctively a man's magazine appealing to his interest in factual material rather than fiction. Articles concern adventures, news, sports, hunting, fishing, travel, personalities, science and unusual events. They are well-written, accurate and illustrated with the man in mind. Many are commissioned for publication by the magazine. Humor, especially in the cartoons, appeals to men. Short regular features include book, film, and record reviews, shopping guides and frank answers to readers questions. "It's a Man's World" supplies a monthly commentary by the editors on all types of topics, to keep the man informed and entertained and to keep the little woman firmly in her place. One of the better men's magazines, this is about on the level of *Redbook* or *Cosmopolitan.* If a library thinks the general male reader as important as the female, it will subscribe. Suitable, too, for high schools.

True Detective. See Mystery and Detective Stories Section.

True West. See History Section.

MOTION PICTURES

Indexes and Abstracts

Applied Science and Technology Index, Art Index, British Humanities Index, Chemical Abstracts, Education Index, Photographic Abstracts. (For annotations, see Indexes and Abstracts Section.)

AV Communication Review. 1953. q. $6. William H. Allen. Dept. of Audiovisual Instruction, 1201 16th St., N.W., Washington, D.C. 20036. Illus., index, adv. Circ: 7,000. Microform: UM.

Bk. rev: Various numbers, lengths. *Aud:* Sa, Ac, Jc. *Rv:* M. *Jv:* B.

A journal devoted to theoretical aspects of the audiovisual field. Not for the average teacher, but for the administrator, behavioral scientist and school of education professor. Librarians who direct audiovisual programs will find it of some value. Rather technical articles deal with application and development of audio-visual aids to augment new approaches to learning. Features include book reviews and abstracts of research, and departments on teaching machines and programmed instruction, and world communications.

Action. 1966. bi-m. $4. David I. Zeitlin. Directors Guild of America, 7950 Sunset Blvd., Hollywood, Calif. 90046. Illus., adv. Circ: 6,500.

Bk. rev: Yearly summary, 30–40, notes, Christmas issue (Dec.–Nov.). *Aud:* Sa, Ac. *Rv:* M. *Jv:* B.

The magazine of the Guild, directed to professional directors, with articles by them. Topics relate the motion picture industry to international, social, and political issues. A regular feature is the "News of the Guild." Typical articles cover such topics as TV coverage of the 1968 election year, a film-maker's report on the Arab-Israeli War, and an article by Gregory Peck on the purposes of the American Film Institute. Helpful for the industrial and professional slant to movies. Only for large collections.

American Cinematographer. 1919. m. $5. Herb A. Lightman. Amer. Soc. of Cinematographers, Inc., 780 N. Orange Dr., Hollywood, Calif. 90028. Illus., adv. Circ: 8,013. Microform: UM.

Bk. rev: 1, 300–500 words, signed. *Aud:* Sa, Ac. *Rv:* M. *Jv:* B.

Trade journal directed at cameramen and others concerned with the technical side of moviemaking, both here and abroad. Typical articles deal with the latest in equipment advances and explains examples of special effects. Includes interviews with top cameramen and listings of current workshops, conferences, and film locations. Written with a minimum of technical jargon, it is of general interest to the film buff.

Audiovisual Instruction. 1956. m. (Sept.–June). $6. Anna L. Hyer. National Education Assn., Dept. of Audiovisual Instruction, 1201 16th St., N.W., Washington, D.C. 20036. Illus., adv. Circ: 15,000. Microform: UM.

Indexed: EdI. *Bk. rev:* 4–6, 300–500 words, signed. *Aud:* Ac, Jc, Ht, Et. *Rv:* H. *Jv:* B.

Concerned with educational technology for teachers and media specialists. Ten or twelve articles of varying length give practical information about audiovisual equipment and used techniques. Articles have included good coverage of closed-circuit television in the field of education. Its "News Notes" reviews films, records, and new equipment, along with news items in the field. One of its best features is an index to audiovisual reviews in other publications. A good general addition for the primary and secondary school's professional collection, and schools of education. Second only to *Educator's Guide to Media and Methods.*

Audio Visual Media/Moyens Audio Visuels. 1967. q. $10. Intl. Council for Education Films, c/o Pergamon Press, 44-01 21st St., Long Island City, N.Y. 11101. Illus. *Bk. rev:* 4–5, 300–400 words. *Aud:* Ac, Jc, Ht, Et. *Rv:* M. *Jv:* B.

Free to members of the Council, this international journal offers articles in French and English by leading media experts. Material is geared for the teacher. "Training to Use Television as a Teacher," and "The Language Master in the Classroom" typify the subject matter of the seven or eight articles. Some illustrations and book reviews. A sophisticated approach, considerably above the average audiovisual magazine. Between this and *Audiovisual Instruction,* it is to be preferred where there is as much emphasis on theory as on techniques and equipment. The latter, however, has the pragmatic edge for most everyday problems in schools. Hopefully, both can be included.

Business Screen. 1938. 8/yr. $3. O. H. Coellin, Jr. Brookhill Pubns., 402 W. Liberty St., Wheaton, Ill. 60817. Illus., adv. Circ: 8,000. *Aud:* Sa, Ac. *Rv:* M. *Jv:* B.

Despite the title, this is not only the principal business magazine for the motion picture industry, but also takes in almost all of the audio-visual field. It has well illustrated articles on films, slides, film strips, etc., and is concerned with the techniques of making, distributing and marketing products. A regular feature, "Right Off the Newsreel," reports forthcoming conferences, film festivals, and news of prominent people and corporations in the field. Annually, *Business Screen* publishes a review of production in the field, including a list of producers of specialized equipment in the United States and abroad; a geographical index lists producers by location. "Guide to Writers" lists script writers, including their addresses and titles of recently produced scripts. A major magazine for medium to large film or audio-visual libraries.

CTVD/Cinema TV Digest; a quarterly review of the serious foreign-language cinema-TV press. 1961. q. $3. Ben Hamilton. Hampton Books, Hampton Bays, N.Y. 11946. Illus., adv. *Bk. rev:* 1–2, 200 words, signed. *Aud:* Sa, Ac. *Rv:* M. *Jv:* B.

Consists of condensed articles from domestic and foreign journals pertaining to new developments in cinema and

television. Films discussed range from the commercial to the experimental with special emphasis on international film festivals. A few specific films are reviewed, but in general contributors display a knack for writing around the movies rather than about them. Comparatively little attention is paid to TV. Primarily for the expert and the larger academic library.

Cahiers du Cinema. 1951. m. $9.50. J. L. Comolli & J. L. Ginibre. 8 rue Marbeuf, Paris, 8e, France. Illus., index, adv. *Aud:* Ga, Ac, Jc. *Rv:* M. *Jv:* A.

The best known French film magazine. (Unfortunately, the English-language edition, edited by Andrew Sarris, is no longer being published.) Emphasis is upon the French film-making scene of the *nouvelle vague,* featuring those directors of the Cahiers Circle such as Godard, Truffaut, and Chabrol. Coverage includes biofilmographies, scenarios, and interviews, with generous double-page stills and photographic spreads. There are ratings of recent films by the "Council of 10" film critics. Also, the 20 best films of the previous year are listed as selected both by the Cahiers staff and by the readers. Underground film-making is given coverage (e.g., one issue had an Andy Warhol spread). Brief annotations of a few film journals may sometimes be included. Considered by many to be the leading avant-garde film magazine, this is a must for most libraries.

Canadian Film and TV Bi-Weekly (Formerly: *Canadian Film Weekly*). 1942. bi-w. $7.50. Stan Helleur. Film Pubns. of Canada, Ltd., 175 Bloor St., E. Toronto 5, Ont. Illus., adv. Circ: 2,500. *Aud:* Sa, Ac. *Rv:* M. *Jv:* B.

A trade newsletter keeping abreast of notable goings-on in the commercial film and television industries of Canada and the United States. Short items such as "Montreal-born Starlet Inks Hollywood Contract," "CBS Launches New Music Series," etc., give general flavor. Somewhat equivalent to *CTVD,* and only for large libraries.

Cineaste. 1967. q. $2. Gary Crowdus. 27 W. 11th St., New York, N.Y. 10011. Illus., adv. *Bk. rev:* 5–6, 150–250 words, signed. *Aud:* Ga, Ac, Jc. *Rv:* H. *Jv:* B.

A processed 35- to 40-page report on all aspects of the film. The five to seven articles, usually by younger members of the *nouveau* film circuit, are critical, perceptive, and well written. A typical issue carried an article by a young film maker on the economics of the business, an appraisal of Andy Warhol and an excellent review of a Godard movie. Of particular interest to librarians are the ongoing columns on new books, magazines and explanations of equipment in terms any layman can grasp. Although the format is nothing flashy, this allows a low price which should bring it within the budget of any library. A sound offbeat magazine to balance such traditionals as *Film Quarterly* or the typical audio-visual magazines.

Cinema. $4.50. Spectator Intl., 9667 Wilshire Blvd., Beverly Hills, Calif. 90241. Illus.

Aud: Ga, Ac, Jc. *Rv:* M. *Jv:* B.

Offers international coverage and reviews of films from Japan to England and the Continent. Probably as impressive for its fine format and numerous, tasteful illustrations as for the editorial material. The reviews tend to lean toward the popular commercial movies, and for this reason it will be of more interest to the casual film-goer than to the student of the form. The writing is good to excellent, and the wide coverage gives it an assured, although not a major place, in larger film-magazine collections.

Educational Screen and Audio-Visual Guide. 1922. m. $4. Henry C. Ruark. Trade Periodicals, Inc., 434 S. Wabash, Chicago, Ill. 60605. Illus., index, adv. Circ: 11,000. Microform: UM.

Indexed: EdI. *Bk. rev:* Notes. *Aud:* Ac, Jc, Ht, Et. *Rv:* H. *Jv:* B.

Geared to the user rather than the producer, this will be of value to the media specialist and teacher. Regular sections on "Av in Religion," "Filmstrips," "Film Evaluations," and "Audio" and "Local Production" include editorial discussion and reviews. Sometimes the whole issue is devoted to one subject, such as films on religion or the organization of I.M.C. Departments. Several special information series were underway in 1968, including features on outstanding media preparation programs for specialist, significant new developments in media utilization, etc. The new materials section evaluates films, lists them by subject and gives complete information including prices for purchase. A trade directory and the "Annual Blue Book," a list of all new AV materials (both published in the August issue), are especially good features. A second or third choice after *Audio-Visual Instruction* and/or *Audio-Visual Media,* although where there is a large audio-visual department, it should be a major purchase.

Educator's Guide to Media and Methods. 1964. m. (Sept.–May). $5. Frank McLaughlin. Media & Methods Inst., Inc., 134 N. 13th St., Philadelphia, Pa. 19107. Illus., adv. Circ: 65,000.

Bk. rev: 15, short, signed. *Aud:* Ac, Jc, Ht. *Rv:* H. *Jv:* V.

In many ways, the best general audio-visual magazine available. Emphasizes practical, how-to articles about creative and effective methods and media in the high school classroom. It also publishes stimulating, challenging theory. Each issue contains 12 to 14 articles in the following categories: "Editorials," "Teaching and Theory," "Paperbacks," "Films and Media Mix," "Television, Records and Tapes." Special departments: "Feedback" (letters to editor), "Have You Discovered?" (materials review), "Recommended Shorts," "Earsights" (a column of sound observations), and "Audiofile" (tapes & records review). A must for high school libraries, English teachers, social studies teachers, and schools of education.

Eight MM. Magazine. 1960. m. $9. Anthony Page. Haymarket Press, Ltd., Gillon House, 9 Harrow Rd., London W.2. Illus., index, adv. Circ: 23,000.

Aud: Ga, Sh. *Rv:* M. *Jv:* B.

An English how-to publication aimed at the home moviemaker. Typical articles deal with choosing the right camera, shooting from a moving car, capturing those long-to-be-remembered events, i.e., baby's first steps, graduation, weddings, etc. Generally, not of interest to the filmmaker as artist. Test reports on various makes of film, cameras and projectors, plus tips on camera care. Also 3–4 film reviews, 75–100 words, signed. Unfortunately, most of the equipment is English and some of the material is not applicable to American situations. Still, as one of the few magazines which concentrates on eight-mm. films, it is a necessary addition to any library where there is a film program, or young film makers.

Fame. 1933. Annual. $3. William R. Weaver. Quigley Publishing Co., 1270 Sixth Ave., New York, N.Y. Illus., adv. Circ: 7,000.

Aud: Ga, Ac. *Rv:* M. *Jv:* C.

Consists largely of photos of Hollywood stars selected for their box-office appeal, i.e., fame. Lists year's top ten money-making films with complete credits; also top ten money-making actors, actresses and directors. No discussion of either individual films or film as art. Of interest primarily to the movie fan at one extreme, or the film historian at the other. A run constitutes a valued record of the industry and, as such, will be a consideration for large academic libraries.

Film. 1952. 3/yr. $1. Peter Armitage. Federation of Film Societies, 102 Dean St., London W.1. Subscriptions to: Larchwood Rd., St. John's Woking, Surrey, Eng. Illus., adv. Circ: 10,000.

Bk. rev: 6–10, 150–350 words, signed. *Aud:* Ga, Ac, Jc. *Rv:* M. *Jv:* B.

A pocket-sized, well-illustrated English film magazine, which many consider the best buy for the money of any film periodical published. At only $1 a year it offers three 40- to 50-page issues, which cover all aspects of the modern movie scene, not only in England, but throughout the world. The four to six articles are written by experienced critics, often in a style considerably more lively and imaginative than in better known film magazines. The black and white illustrations are used liberally throughout, and are always pertinent to the text. Finally, the book reviews are some of the best available. In view of its modest price, style and coverage, it should be one of the first choices for most libraries.

Film and Television Daily (Formerly: *Film Daily*). 1918. 5/wk. $25. Gene Arneel. Wid's Films and Film Folk, Inc., 1600 Broadway, New York, N.Y. 10019. Illus., adv. Circ: 6,500.

Aud: Sa, Ac. *Rv:* M. *Jv:* B.

Emphasis on the business activities and developments of the motion picture and broadcasting industries. Among the regular features of this small (under 15 pp.), but highly informative newspaper are: a "Coming and Going" section, which tells of the latest activities of motion picture and broadcasting executives and personalities; "Hollywood Hotline," and obituaries. Topics covered include the activities of the Federal Communications Commission (FCC), major motion picture studios, TV and radio networks, and recording companies. Other features relate to producers, directors, and film stars. Only for large, special collections.

Film Comment. 1963. q. $3.75. Gordon Hitchens. 838 West End Ave., New York, N.Y. 10025. Illus., adv.

Bk. rev: 15–20, lengthy, signed. *Aud:* Ga, Ac, Jc, Sh. *Rv:* H. *Jv:* V.

Directed to the scholarly, well-informed film buff interested in motion pictures and television. It relates many aspects of the contemporary film to pertinent social and political issues. Topics range widely from such items as U.S. Information Agency films, Viet Cong and Right-Wing films, Civil Rights, Japanese Underground films, film festivals, interviews, as well as historical articles studying the development and techniques of the great movie-makers (one issue contained a 13-page article on the work of D. W. Griffith). A valuable feature for librarians is the substantial book review section, which may run to 16 full pages of insightful reviews of up to 20 books. William Sloan, film librarian at the New York Public Library, is the Book Editor. As an additional bonus, an issue may contain a half-column or more devoted to "New Books of Interest to Librarians and Teachers of Film" (e.g., Fall/Winter 1967), and evaluations of reference book guides to the film. Along with *Cahiers du Cinema* and *Film Culture,* one of the basic movie magazines for any type of library where the film is considered important. Relative ranking is a matter of opinion and interest, and any good library will have all three.

Film Culture. Revived with No. 24, Spring, 1962. q. (Erratic). $4. Jonas Mekas. Box 1499, G.P.O., New York, N.Y. 10001. Illus. Circ: 11,000.

Bk. rev: Occasional notes. *Aud:* Ga, Ac, Jc, Sh. *Rv:* M. *Jv:* A.

Edited by one of the world's leading exponents of independent film making (Mekas is also a regular contributor to New York's *Village Voice*). Geared to an audience seriously interested in the personal, independent (Underground) film movement in New York and San Francisco. The format is imaginative and unusual in appearance. Articles deal with such topics as cinematic style, commercial distribution of independent films, experimental art theatres, art today as it relates to films, etc. There are interviews with film-makers, filmographies, stills and full-page photographic spreads, personal letters by film-makers and their notes, and articles of historical interest. The activities of the Film-

Makers' Cooperative, which handles distribution, plays an important part by reporting its news and latest developments to the magazine. In addition, there is coverage of film festivals and critical notes. In a special New York Film Festival issue, there were transcripts from film symposia. Each year the magazine presents the "Independent Film Award" (for original American contributions) to a film-maker. There is a bibliographic listing of books received in each issue, which may include 20 to 30 (or more) items in a full-page. A major film magazine for all libraries.

Film Fan Monthly. 1961. m. $3.50. Leonard Maltin, 254 Merrison St., Teaneck, N.J. 07666. Illus., adv.

Bk. rev: 3–5, average 150 words. *Aud:* Ga. *Rv:* L. *Jv:* C.

Concentrates on stories and stars of old films, primarily the Hollywood variety. Pamphlet size (15 pp.), in small print, it includes such features as interviews, news items (e.g., obituaries of early movie stars); sometimes lengthy filmographies (which may number up to 85 items), and book reviews. A "Profile" section in each issue is devoted to the films of a particular actor/actress or moviemaker (e.g., Feb. 67 was a special tribute to Walt Disney). Of interest to libraries are notes about 8-mm. home movies, 16-mm. sound and silent releases, and items of news from the movie studios and local neighborhood theatres. Long on nostalgia, the magazine is useful for serious students of film history.

Film Français-Cinematographie Française (Formerly: *Cinematographie Française*). 1918. w. $18. Maurice Bessy. 40 rue du Cherche Midi, Paris (6e), France. Illus., adv. Circ: 7,200.

Aud: Sa. *Rv:* M. *Jv:* B.

Trade journal aimed at French movie-theatre owners. Includes illustrated articles on new and remodeled theatres, a complete list of films currently being shown in France and short, descriptive film reviews intended as a booking aid. Also brief notes on new theatres and theatre owners. A special journal, and only for the largest research or business library.

Film Heritage. 1965. q. $2. F. Anthony Macklin. Film Heritage, Box 42, Univ. of Dayton, Dayton, Ohio 45409. Illus., adv.

Bk. rev: 1–2, 1,000 words, signed. *Aud:* Ga, Ac, Jc. *Rv:* M. *Jv:* B.

Sponsored and written predominantly by the academic community, and directed to students and others who have an intellectual-cultural interest in the film. Each issue is devoted to the study of a particular film or film critic of significance (e.g., Winter 1967–68: "Bonnie & Clyde" issue; Fall/67 "James Agee" issue). Essay type articles are written by noteworthy film critics (e.g., Dwight Macdonald, Arthur Knight). Other quality features sometimes included are interviews with film-makers and examinations of a story and its film script. Good quality photographs, which often have not been previously published. Although the approach is sometimes a bit academic, the whole is excellent, and the magazine ranks with *Film Comment, Film Culture,* etc.

Film Library Quarterly. 1967. Membership (Non-members, $8.). William Sloan. Film Library Information Council, 101 W. Putnam Ave., Greenwich, Conn. 06830. Illus., adv.

Bk. rev: 4, average 100 words, signed. *Aud:* Sa, Ac, Jc, Sh. *Rv:* H. *Jv:* A.

Primarily for the public film librarian, this serves as a forum for articles, columns, reviews and general news of the field. It is the child of the Film Library Information Council, organized in May, 1967, and material is divided between the traditional and the newer approaches to films in libraries. Articles are considerably above average, both in content and style. Frank appraisals, the various critical film and book reviews, and the intelligent style recommends this for all libraries.

Film News. 1939. bi-m. $4. Rohana Lee. Film News Co., Editorial & Advertising Office, 259 W. 57th St., New York, N.Y. 10019. Illus., adv. Circ: 10,000. Microform: UM.

Bk. rev: 8–10, 75 words, signed. *Aud:* Sa, Ac, Jc, Ht, Et. *Rv:* H. *Jv:* B.

A somewhat conservative and traditional magazine for users of educational film strips, TV, etc., with special attention to classroom possibilities. Contains five to six, 1000-word, by-lined articles on uses of film, usually in educational context. Lists available films, what's being shown and where, distribution agencies and some rental prices. Four to five 100- to 400-word signed reviews of feature-length films per issue, as well as short reviews of documentary and educational films. Also "New Films" and "What's New in Equipment." Second to *Sightlines* as a good working tool for teachers and librarians. Should be augmented by at least one non-education directed film magazine such as *Film Comment* or *Film Quarterly.*

Film Quarterly. 1958. q. $4, $7.20/yr. Ernest Callenbach. Univ. of California Press, Berkeley, Calif. 94720. Illus., adv. Circ: 5,600. Microform: UM. Reprint: AMS.

Indexed: ArtI, RG, SSHum. *Bk. rev:* 4–6, 150–500 words, signed. *Aud:* Ga, Ac, Jc, Sh. *Rv:* H. *Jv:* A.

The only serious film magazine indexed by *Readers' Guide,* this has a reputation for critical, objective, scholarly, yet extremely well-written reviews of films and film makers. Several long reviews under the "Features" section thoroughly cover direction, techniques, plot, performances and dialogue. There are "Short Notices" for films of only passing interest, and a section of "Short Films" reviews appears occasionally. Two or three long, scholarly articles appear in each issue, often concerned with historical or biographical aspects of moving picture production. Recent titles include "Luis Bunuel: Spaniard and Surrealist," and

"Orson Welles: Of Time and Loss." The book notices are equally well done and stress the academic rather than the popular. Although not the most exciting film magazine, it is among the most scholarly and is certainly a required addition for any library.

Film Society Review. m. (Sept.–May). $5. William Starr. Amer. Federation of Film Societies, Inc., 144 Bleecker St., New York, N.Y. 10012. Illus., adv.

Bk. rev: 2–4, lengthy, signed. *Aud:* Sa, Ac, Jc, Ht, Et. *Rv:* M. *Jv:* B.

This small (5″ × 8″), handy-sized and compact magazine is directed to those who want to keep up with the latest roundup of news about developments in the film medium. There is an emphasis on screen education, as reflected in the special section "Film Study Section," which focuses on such things as workshops and applications of film to the training of media center specialists. Will be particularly helpful for elementary and secondary teachers as well as anyone interested in the film as an educational tool.

Films and Filming. 1954. m. $8.50. Peter G. Baker. Hansom Books, Artillery Mansions, 75 Victoria St., London S.W.1. Illus., adv. Circ: 30,000.

Aud: Ga, Ac, Jc, Sh. *Rv:* M. *Jv:* B.

Well-illustrated with stills from current motion pictures, written in an intelligent, perceptive style, this magazine can be recommended for the general adult and teen-age reader who has an interest in both popular and art films. Each issue covers several general topics, e.g., violence in movies, the choice of titles for a box-office hit, current trends in erotic films, etc. More important to the average moviegoer are the excellent reviews (by David Austen, Raymond Durgnat, Michael Armstrong, to name a few), which make up a good part of every number. While published in England, selection is international, interests are popular to intellectual, and the whole is one of the better methods of keeping up with what is going on. A good magazine for school libraries, although some of the illustrations from current flicks may frighten the more modest.

Films in Review. 1950. m. (Oct.–May); bi-m. (June–July; Aug.–Sept.). $6. Henry Hart. National Board of Review of Motion Pictures, Inc., 31 Union Sq., New York, N.Y. 10003. Illus., adv. Circ: 5,300.

Bk. rev: 4–5, 100–300 words, signed. *Aud:* Ga, Ac, Jc. *Rv:* M. *Jv:* B.

Brief but meaty reviews of about 10 current films form the nucleus of each issue. Also at least one well-researched biographical profile of a leading cinema actor or actress. Special departments include TV films, 8- and 16-mm. films and a movie sound track, each rating a 500-word (or thereabouts) essay. Reviews of film books and a lengthy section of "Letters-to-the-Editor." The magazine enjoys a relatively wide distribution, has an attractive format, and the reviews often run counter to opinion found in more esoteric and scholarly journals. Its primary value for libraries is this very bias, which balances other film magazines. However, it should not be the single choice for any library.

Kaleidoscope. 1963. 3/yr. $2. Don Shay & Ray Cabana, Jr. 95 Dearborn St., East Longmeadow, Mass. 01028. Illus. Circ: 1,000.

Aud: Ga, Ac, Jc. *Rv:* M. *Jv:* B.

Small (approximately 34pp.—6½″ x 8½″) and informative, this identifies itself as "a serious amateur publication . . . out to please ourselves" (its editors). However, its contents evidence a professional quality. Frequent features include lengthy, exclusive interviews with outstanding film personalities. Sometimes an entire issue is devoted to a single actor with a filmography, e.g., an interview with Buster Crabbe, and a comprehensive Buster Crabbe Film List. Articles may cover background information behind the making of a film: "Murder, Mythology, and Mother Goose," about the detective novels of Willard Huntington Wright (pseudonym of S.S. Van Dine), whose novels were made into movies. The photographs are plentiful and of good quality, taken from scenes of films. Well-organized and thoughtfully-written, this will be of interest to film enthusiasts. A trifle on the esoteric side for many libraries, but where film is a serious matter, it should be on the subscription list.

Making Films in New York. 1967. bi-m. $3. 120 E. 56th St., New York N.Y. 10022.

Aud: Ga, Ac, Jc. *Rv:* H. *Jv:* B.

Devoted almost exclusively to New York film makers. However, has more than passing interest for anyone seriously involved with the making of films. A typical issue not only covers the current New York scene, but features relatively technical articles on how to make films, equipment, distribution and the like. It assumes some basic knowledge of the field, but can be used effectively by anyone this side of amateur status. At a somewhat less technical level is the *New York Film Maker's Newsletter* (1967. m. $2. Film Makers' Distribution Center, 175 Lexington Ave., New York, N.Y. 10016). This includes reports on equipment and film-making, but also takes in more general articles on the history and the aesthetics of 8-mm and 16-mm films. It is particularly useful for brief items on festivals both here and abroad, as well as news about personalities and events in the New American Cinema. On the West Coast, the equivalent is Bruce Baillee's *Canyon Cinema News* (1966. m. $3. 263 Colgate, Berkeley, Calif. 94708). This well-known experimental film-maker's newsletter reports not only on activities in his area, but is one of the best single sources for accurate information on film festivals of interest to non-commercial film fans. Although none of the publications is essential for libraries outside of the immediate geographic areas covered, all should be found in larger, representative film magazine collections.

Modern Screen. 1930. m. $4. Richard H. Heller. Dell Publishing Co., 750 Third Ave., New York, N.Y. 10017. Illus., adv. Circ: 1,000,000.

Aud: Ga. *Rv:* L. *Jv:* C.

Contains the usual intimate glimpses into the private lives of both movie and TV actors. Ten to fifteen articles and feature stories plus gossip columns form the main basis of the publication. Dorothy Manners writes one of the gossip columns and answers questions sent to her by fans. The movie review section rates the films reviewed on a basis of four stars for the best pictures, resorting to half-stars for finer points of judgment. The reviews also state their suitability to audiences of adults, adults and mature young people and family with a coding of A, Am and F. One of the oldest Hollywood film magazines, rivalled only by *Motion Picture Magazine* and *Photoplay*. Useful in two types of collections: the academic, where there is a serious drive to collect all materials on movies, and the popular public or school library collection where the teen-agers (and anyone else) are still fascinated by the Hollywood mythos. In this genre, preference should go to *Motion Picture Magazine,* and then *Photoplay*, but all three are pretty much the same.

Montage. 1967. irreg. Free. Rodney Sheratsky. Center for Film Production, Northern Valley Regional High School, 150 Knickerbocker Rd., Demarest, N.J. 07627.

Aud: Jh, Sh, Ht. *Rv:* M. *Jv:* B.

Primarily of interest because it is a newsletter reporting on a unique high school film program. The Center, under the supervision of Mr. Sheratsky, offers high school students regular courses in making 8-mm films and in the appreciation of the film. The newsletter contains reports on the project as well as articles and reviews by high school students. The information is invaluable for any high school teacher or librarian working in this area, and it serves as a model which others might follow. Interested librarians should write for free copies.

Motion Picture Magazine. 1911. m. $3. Barbara Janes. MacFadden-Bartell Corp., 205 E. 42nd St., New York, N.Y. 10017. Illus., adv. Circ: 500,000.

Aud: Ga, Sh. *Rv:* L. *Jv:* C.

Probably the best of the movie fan magazines for escape reading, this periodical contains a feature story, "scoop" articles and 10 or 12 articles about the private lives of TV actors, movie stars and public personalities, e.g., the romance and wedding of Lynda Bird Johnson. Several regular features vary from the standard format: a "Bulletin Board" column listing births, deaths, marriages and announcements; rather complete obituaries of actors recently deceased; a "Letters to the Editor" column, and "Ask Debbie," an advice-to-readers column. The usual gossip columns are included, one by Sheilah Graham. One of its best features for movie fans is the generous number of full page color "pin-ups," (which is also a disadvantage if one is trying to encourage the non-reader). See concluding comments for *Modern Screen.*

Moviegoer. 1964. q. $4. James Stoller. Moviegoer, Box 128, Stuyvesant Station, New York, N.Y. 10009. Illus., adv. Circ: 2,500.

Bk. rev: 1–2, 1,000 words, signed. *Aud:* Sa, Ac. *Rv:* M. *Jv:* B.

In-depth studies of films, film-makers and the art of films by academicians, students, and well-respected critics. Films are discussed on a moral and philosophical plane and within the broad context of the cinema rather than reviewed in the narrow, journalistic sense. Movies considered may be either current or historic. Some knowledge of the history of cinema a prerequisite. An excellent review, but as with *Film Heritage,* primarily for the serious student of motion pictures and not for the casual moviegoer. Should be in all large academic libraries.

Movie Life. 1937. m. $3. Diana Lurvey. Ideal Publishing Co., 295 Madison Ave., New York, N.Y. 10017. Illus., adv. Circ: 210,000.

Aud: Ga. *Rv:* L. *Jv:* C.

Contains beauty tips from the "stars," gossip columns, and extended treatment of the latest scandals and other Hollywood lore. Also short film reviews that are generally plot summaries written with limited vocabulary. While one would wish for a more intelligent approach, this is the kind of publication that can have some use in a library where there is a concerted drive to meet poor readers at their own level. Otherwise, libraries can do without it.

Photoplay. 1911. m. $5. Jack J. Podell. Macfadden-Bartell Corp., 205 E. 42nd St., New York, N.Y. 10017. Illus., adv. Circ: 1,800,000.

Aud: Ga. *Rv:* L. *Jv:* C.

Claims to be first with news about the "stars," and has the usual features to appeal to fans. Nearly twenty short articles examine the personal lives of movie and TV actors and actresses or of personalities in the news, e.g., Lynda Bird Johnson, Jackie Kennedy and the Beatles. Many pictures and some articles have particularly sensational titles like "A Hollywood Doctor Opens his Files on Love, Sex and Dope." Regular features include a taped interview with a prominent screen personality, news of new cosmetics, gossip columns by Cal York and Pamela Mason and editorial comment. For those women, teens and up, who enjoy reading about the fortunes, and misfortunes, of those in the Hollywood limelight. See concluding comments on *Modern Screen.*

SMPTE Journal. 1916. m. Membership (Non-members, $16.) Victor H. Allen. Soc. of Motion Picture and Television Engineers, 9 E. 41st St., New York, N.Y. 11017. Illus., index, adv. Circ: 9,647.

Indexed: ASTI, ChemAb, EdI, PhotoAb. *Bk. rev:* 5–6, 500 words, signed. *Aud:* Sa, Ac. *Rv:* M. *Jv:* B.

Directed to the society membership, the purpose of this well-written periodical is to keep its specialist membership abreast of current technological advancements and education in the varied, but related fields of motion pictures, TV, instrumentation, and high-speed photography. Articles cover scientific investigations into applications to the audio-visual field, recommended practices, SMPTE Technical Conferences, as well as a variety of technical problems. Appraisal of the latest equipment is also covered, e.g., "A New 16mm Sound News Camera." In addition to the substantial book review section, there are other sections dealing with the current literature, books, booklets and brochures; abstracts of papers from other journals; new products and developments; employment service, and the "Journals Available/Wanted" section, which provides a useful service for the librarian seeking to sell or buy out-of-print journals (this title or others in the audio-visual field). Contains summaries in French, German and Spanish. There is also a calendar of meetings schedule. A technical, well-indexed journal for large library collections. Not for the average film buff or even the film historian.

Screen Facts; the magazine of Hollywood's past. 1963. bi-m. $5.50. Alan G. Barbour. 123-40 83rd Ave., Kew Gardens, N.Y. 11415. Illus., adv. Circ: 2,000.

Bk. rev: Occasional, average 150 words, signed. *Aud:* Ga, Ac, Jc. *Rv:* M. *Jv:* B.

This small (5½″ x 8″), enthusiastically written, magazine is for nostalgic fans of Hollywood movies. Each issue is usually devoted to the films of a particular movie star, with a filmography included. Articles may historically trace a particular theme in the movies e.g., "Christ on the Screen." There are photos of scenes from the movies as well as publicity shots of movie stars. Somewhat above the level of *Film Fan Monthly,* and will be enjoyed by those who take the efforts of Hollywood seriously (even if only from a cultural/critical viewpoint). Primarily for the serious film historian, although it can be enjoyed by the nostalgic adult as well.

Sight and Sound; the international film quarterly. 1932. q. $4. Penelope Houston. British Film Inst., 81 Dean St., London W.1. Circ: 27,500.

Indexed: ArtI, BritHum. *Bk. rev:* 1–2, lengthy, signed. *Aud:* Ga, Ac, Jc, Sh. *Rv:* M. *Jv:* V.

One of the world's most famous film magazines, this is directed to the cultivated, sophisticated adult. It is printed on fine paper, contains numerous stills from films, and the editor, Penelope Houston, is one of the best film critics now writing. Articles are uniformly excellent and cover all aspects of the current scene. The magazine tends to take a middle-of-the-road policy. Features include film festival round-ups with their ratings; interviews; coverage of the underground film movement, and such topics as copyright problems, politics, and film schools. Should be in every library where the film is even a minor consideration.

Sightlines. 1967. bi-m. $8. Esme Dick. Educational Film Library Assn., 250 W. 57th St., New York, N.Y. 10019. Illus.

Aud: Sa, Ac, Jc, Ht, Et. *Rv:* H. *Jv:* B.

This is a pragmatic approach to the film for librarians and teachers who work with, or order films for the public. It absorbs the separate EFLA *Filmlist,* and incorporates reviews and information on 16-mm and 8-mm films. Usually, each issue is centered around a particular theme, e.g., the outlook for films in the next decade. Articles are written by educators and librarians, and the style is clear if not always exciting. A few illustrations. A useful guide for any library where films are purchased or rented. While good as far as it goes, it should definitely be augmented by several more scholarly, less education-directed periodicals.

Soviet Film. 1959. m. $13. Armen Medveder. Mezhdunarodnaya Kniga, Smolenskaya Sennayo 32/34, Moscow G-200, U.S.S.R. Illus., index.

Aud: Ga, Ac, Jc. *Rv:* M. *Jv:* B.

Coverage is focused upon the current Soviet film-making scene, particularly documentary and epic-type films. There are interviews with major Soviet directors, leading film-stars, and cameramen. A feature entitled "On Location" describes the making of an up-and-coming film. A sampling of articles includes such topics as: "Soviet Cinema in 1967," "They Filmed Lenin," "Cinema of Revolution in Retrospective," and such events as the 7th International Comedy Films Festival in Vienna. War is a favorite recurring theme, with frequent allusion to the "Great Patriotic War." There is a number of good quality photos throughout, depicting scenes from films as well as full-page portraits of particular film-stars. International Film Festivals are illustrated with numerous photos of guests in attendance. An English edition is available, but it is also published in Arabic, French, German and Spanish. Propaganda is limited to boosting Soviet films. A fascinating magazine not only for the serious film student, but for anyone interested in Soviet culture. Should be in all academic libraries, and in larger public libraries.

Take One; the Canadian film magazine. 1966. bi-m. $1.50. P. Lebensold. Unicorn Publisher, Box 1778, Station B., Montreal 2, Que. Illus.

Aud: Ga, Ac, Jc. *Rv:* H. *Jv:* B.

An avant-garde Canadian film publication which is of value for reviews,, and news of Canadian film-makers, particularly in the Montreal-Toronto circle. The independents take up considerable space, but some of the best general reviews of commercial and foreign films published anywhere will be found in its pages. The writers seem to specialize in the same type of critical, caustic comments asso-

ciated with such Americans as Jonas Mekas and Andrew Saris. The format is good, the price is low, and it is one of the best buys for all Canadian and many American libraries.

University Film Producers Association. Journal. 1949. q. Membership (Non-members, $4.). Robert W. Wagner. Univ. Film Producers Assn., Ohio State Univ., Dept. of Photography, 190 W. 17th Ave., Columbus, Ohio 43210. Illus., index. Circ: 700 regularly, special issues 3,000-5,000.

Bk. rev: Occasional, 20, average 75-500 words, signed. *Aud:* Sa, Ac, Jc. *Rv:* M. *Jv:* A.

Directed to the teaching of film production, cinematography, and photography at the university level. Conferences on film-makers and film-teachers are covered, and articles deal with such topics as "The University Film Director and Cinema Verité," and "A Liberalized Concept of the Teaching of Film Production." Technical aspects of film-making and photography are also explored in articles on multi-media, e.g., "Research Cinematography." The projects of university film units form an important part of the reportage. While a good deal of the content is technical or education-bound, there is a freshness about the whole which makes it required reading for anyone working actively with films and students. High school teachers may welcome the librarian bringing this to their attention, and it should be considered for all academic collections.

Variety. See Theater Section.

MUSIC

Indexes and Abstracts

Abridged Readers' Guide, British Humanities Index, Education Index, Music Index, Readers' Guide to Periodical Literature. (For annotations, see Indexes and Abstracts Section.)

Acta Musicologica. 1928. q. Membership (Non-members, $9.). Hellmut Federhofer. Barenreiter-Verlag, Neuweilerstr. 15, CH 4000 Basel 15, Switzerland, Illus.

Indexed: MusicI. *Aud:* Sa, Ac. *Rv:* H. *Jv:* B.

Fully-documented research papers of musicological interest are published in this official journal of the Societe Internationale de Musicologie. The erudite articles, reporting historical and theoretical hypotheses, often include valuable bibliographies. Considered the standard international musicological journal, papers are presented in the language of the author's choice. For use in the United States, this periodical would be far more useful if there were summaries in English of the articles in other languages (text is in English, French and German). Only for large academic libraries.

American Choral Review. 1958. q. Membership (Non-members, $7.50). Alfred Mann. American Choral Foundation, Inc., Assn. of Choral Conductors, 130 W. 56th St., New York 10019. Illus., adv. Circ: 2,000.

Indexed: MusicI. *Bk. rev:* 1–3, 250–1,000 words, signed. *Aud:* Sa, Ac, Ht. *Rv:* H. *Jv:* B.

Published for composers, conductors, musicologists and students of choral music, this usually runs to 56 pages, with three to four major articles dealing with choral music and related subjects. There are numerous musical examples. In addition to the regular book reviews, there are featured columns on choral music and the conductor, in the music curriculum, in the liturgy, performances, and recent records and scores. The style presupposes a knowledge of the field, but content-wise it is of great value to any serious student or teacher of choral music.

American Music Teacher. 1951. bi-m. Membership (Non-members, $3.). Frank S. Stillings. Music Teachers National Assn., 2209 Carew Tower, Cincinnati, Ohio 45202. Illus., adv. Circ: 14,000. Microform: UM.

Indexed: EdI, MusicI. *Bk. rev:* Occasional. *Aud:* Sa, Ac, Jc, Ht. *Rv:* M. *Jv:* B.

Features articles on and reviews of keyboard, vocal, organ and string music. The Association represents many private and studio teachers as well as secondary school and college music faculties. Articles are geared to assist the teacher, e.g. "Tone Quality, a Pragmatic Approach for High School Choirs," and keep readers advised of association activities. Occasional bibliographies add to the magazine's reference value. Because of its emphasis on individual teaching, this nicely augments the basic journal in the field of music education, *Music Educator's Journal.* Both would be advisable for secondary school and college music teachers, as well as libraries serving them. However, both stress the how-to-do-it approach, as contrasted with the more scholarly *Journal of Research in Music.* In elementary through secondary schools, the *Music Educator's Journal* would be a first choice, followed by *American Music Teacher.* Academic libraries of any size or type will wish to take all three, although *American Music Teacher* would be last on the list.

American Musicological Society. Journal. 1948. 3/yr. Membership (Non-members, $10). James Haar. William Byrd Press, 2901 Byrdhill Rd., Richmond, Va. 23228. Illus., index.

Indexed: MusicI. *Bk. rev:* Various numbers, lengths. *Aud:* Sa, Ac. *Rv:* H. *Jv:* B.

The leading learned journal in American music. The scholarly articles, usually with examples and extensive bibliographies, concentrate on American music and musicians, but not excluding material international in scope. The journal is particularly useful for the extensive book reviews, and information on new editions of music and recordings. There are reports on doctoral dissertations, and abstracts of papers presented at various meetings of the organization throughout the United States. Only for large collections.

American Record Guide; incorporating the American Tape Guide (Formerly: *The American Music Lover*). 1934. m. $4.50. James Lyons. American Record Guide, Box 319, Radio City Station, New York, N.Y. 10019. Illus., adv. Circ: 28,000.

Indexed: MusicI, RG. *Bk. rev:* 1–3, average 500 words. *Aud:* Ga, Ac, Jc, Sh. *Rv:* H. *Jv:* A.

Probably the best single review medium for recordings and tapes. As the oldest of its kind in the field, it aims for "encyclopedic, unbiased coverage of classical recordings by critics qualified to compare all new releases with all competitive versions." One major artist's work is studied each month, and there is a section on jazz recordings. "Sound Ideas," an equipment review by Larry Zide, is the only concession to the hardware aspect. The rest is devoted to such features as discographies, e.g., "Beecham Discography-IV" by Ward Botsford, and serious reviews of music and drama recordings. Sometimes one recording is compared with another, and two reviewers will sometimes present opposing views on the same recording. The anniversary issue includes articles, an expanded book review section and all the regular features as well. The whole has vast reference value for any type of library, particularly where recordings are an important part of the collection. An essential item for all libraries.

Audio. 1947. $5. North American Publishing Co., 134 N. 13th St., Philadelphia, Pa. 19107. Illus., adv. Circ: 25,000.

Indexed: MusicI. *Aud:* Ga, Ac, Jc, Sh. *Rv:* H. *Jv:* B.

This is the primary journal for serious students and hobbyists who are as much concerned with audio equipment as the sounds it reproduces. New products, installation, construction (particularly of kits), and maintenance are stressed. The analytical reviews of new stereo and video products are honest, and unusually dependable. Usually there are one or two articles on the theory of sound, and these are geared for both the advanced and the amateur who may wish to learn about fundamentals. There are three record review sections—classical, popular, and jazz—and from time to time information on the making of recordings. *Audio* differs from its two main competitors, *Hi Fi/Stereo Review* and *High Fidelity,* in that equipment is more important than the music covered in the other two magazines. Next to these two, it will be a second choice among general music magazines for any small to medium sized library, and an automatic necessity in all larger libraries.

Audio and Record Review. 1961. m. $6. Peter Gammond. Heathcock Press Ltd., Heathcock Court, Strand, London W.2. Illus., adv. Circ: 20,000.

Bk. rev: 3–4, 300 words, signed. *Aud:* Sa, Ac, Jc. *Rv:* M. *Jv:* B.

Not to be confused with the American *Audio,* this is a British journal which concentrates on "all aspects of gramophone record collecting, mainly from the musical point of view." In addition to its critical monthly reviews of recordings, there are articles on equipment, musicians and related subjects. Nicely supplements, but does not replace *Gramophone*.

Billboard; the international music-record news-weekly. 1894. w. $20. Leo Zhito. Billboard Publishing Co., 2160 Patterson St., Cincinnati, Ohio 45214. Illus., adv. Circ: 28,000.

Indexed: MusicI. *Aud:* Sa, Ac. *Rv:* M. *Jv:* B.

A newspaper primarily for the businessman and advertiser concerned with publishing, recording and selling music. Its value to laymen lies in its comprehensive coverage of almost anything to do with music. In fact, the eager teenager will find it the best single source of information on new albums, tapes, performers and pop music. There are also sections on country, gospel and classical music; musical instruments; audio retailing; machines, and "Hits of the World," arranged by country, which follows the long "International News Reports." The writing style is somewhat similar to that of *Variety,* and while of limited value to smaller libraries, it is a must in larger public and academic libraries. High school librarians with a little extra money and imagination might try it for a season too. It is bound to be a hit.

Brass and Woodwind Quarterly; devoted to articles, research studies, bibliographies and reviews concerning wind instruments and their music. 1957. q. $6.50. Mary Rasmussen. Box 111, Durham, N.H. 03824. Illus., index, adv. Circ: 1,000.

Indexed: MusicI. *Aud:* Sa, Ac, Jc, Ht, Et. *Rv:* M. *Jv:* B.

Devoted to long articles on brass and woodwind instruments, their history, music, performance, practice, etc. There are usually one to three articles per issue. Its principal value for teachers, however, rests in the frequent bibliographies on musical instruments, performance practice, and music for wind instruments. Features include "Current Publications" and "Briefly Noted," a review column which lists new works of interest to the readers. Worthwhile for both the serious student and the teacher of music from the elementary grades through college and university.

Choral and Organ Guide; a magazine for choral and organist-directors. 1957. 10/yr. $5. Roy Anderson. Music Enterprises, Box 714, Mt. Vernon, N.Y. Illus., adv. Circ: 34,000.

Indexed: MusicI. *Bk. rev:* 4–5, 50–500 words, signed. *Aud:* Sa, Ac, Jc, Ht, Et. *Rv:* M. *Jv:* B.

A 26- to 30-page pocket-sized magazine which reports on concerts, music interpretation, teaching methods and anything to do with choral and organ music. Each issue also contains the score for a new piece of music. Its primary value rests on the critical reviews of new choral and organ music, a feature particularly helpful to teachers.

Clavier; a magazine for pianists and organists. 1962. 9/yr. $5. Dorothy Packard. Instrumentalist Co., 1418 Lake St., Evanston, Ill. 60201. Illus., adv. Circ: 21,700.

Indexed: MusicI. *Bk. rev:* 3, 150–200 words. *Aud:* Sa, Ac, Jc, Ht. *Rv:* M. *Jv:* B.

The leading scholarly journal of piano and organ, prepared primarily for advanced students and teachers. Articles include interviews with concert performers, "suggestions for improving keyboard technique, analytical discussion of the literature, and teaching methods." There is a regular review of materials for teachers and other musicians, descriptions of new products, and reviews of records, piano and organ music, and books. An interesting feature is the complete piece or pieces of music in each issue, together with a lesson on interpretation. In this same field, *Piano Quarterly* (1952. q. $6. Box 3881, Grand Central Station, New York, N.Y. 10017) is directed almost exclusively to the teacher. It is particularly useful as it lists pieces of music and books by grades. *Clavier* would be a first choice, but for elementary piano teaching, the former magazine is somewhat better.

Current Musicology. 1965. semi-ann. $4. Columbia Univ. Dept. of Music, New York, N.Y. 10027. Illus. Circ: 1,100.

Aud: Sa, Ac. *Rv:* M. *Jv:* B.

Edited by the graduate students and published by the Department of Music of Columbia University, this is directed to other graduate students and faculty members. Contains reports on curricula, seminars, meetings and usually six well-documented articles per issue dealing with musical subjects in depth. A special feature is a dissertation review section which covers all areas of musical study both in American and foreign universities. No advertising, and illustrations are confined to musical examples or musical instruments. Only for large academic libraries.

Crawdaddy. 1967. m. $5. Paul Williams. Crawdaddy Magazine Inc., 383 Canal St., New York, N.Y. 10013. Illus., adv.

Aud: Ga, Ac, Jc, Sh, Jh. *Rv:* M. *Jv:* A.

Subtitled "the magazine of rock," this features some ten illustrated articles in each issue on personalities, music, concerts, and the controversial matter of many teen-age songs. Unlike a number of popular music mags, the emphasis is on analysis, often at a relatively high level, of what makes this or that song or musician a success. There is considerable attention given to related social issues that have had a bearing on either the musician or his music. Each 50-page number features a revealing interview with a major musical figure, e.g., Jimi Hendrix. The black and white photography is outstanding. This is not for the average young reader, but for the student who takes his music and his musicians seriously. Should be included in most school libraries, certainly in well rounded music collections in all libraries. See also, *Rolling Stone*.

Diapason; devoted to the organ and the interests of organists. 1909. m. $3. Frank Cunkle. Royal Canadian College of Organists, 434 S. Wabash Ave., Chicago, Ill. 60605. Illus., adv. Circ: 21,000.

Indexed: MusicI. *Bk. rev:* 6–8, 75–100 words, signed. *Aud:* Sa, Ac. *Rv:* M. *Jv:* B.

For the professional organist and student. International in scope, and the "over all style is newsy with organists' appointments, academic achievements, obituaries, etc. forming the staple." There are usually two to three articles and reviews of church music conferences, books, organ music, choral music, and recordings. Numerous illustrations, about 50% advertising, and a large 13″ x 9″ format.

Down Beat. 1934. bi-w. $7. Dan Morgenstern. Maher Pubns., Inc., 222 W. Adams St., Chicago, Ill. 60606. Illus., adv. Circ: 72,000. Microform: UM.

Indexed: MusicI. *Bk. rev:* 2–3, 300–600 words, signed, critical. *Aud:* Ga, Ac, Jc, Sh, Jh. *Rv:* M. *Jv:* A.

Jazz musicians and fans in 42 countries read *Down Beat,* the top magazine for current coverage of the personalities, the music, the scenes, and the recordings in the jazz world. Issues frequently have a special focus (e.g., "Focus on Piano," Oct. 19, 1967, included "The Natural: A Conversation with Erroll Garner," and "Cheers for Shearing"). There is liberal discussion as to the influence of various persons or groups (e.g., "The Beatles in Perspective"). Of reference value are the many types of discerning reviews, (books, recordings, concerts), some of which are not found elsewhere (e.g., stage band arrangement reviews by George Wiskirchen). A famous music magazine which should enjoy wide support by almost every type of library. Junior high and high school students may find either *Rolling Stone* or *Crawdaddy* more to their taste, and while neither is up to the editorial standards of *Down Beat,* they are more relevant to young people. At any rate, the school librarian who relies solely on the accepted classical music-oriented journals, or the large circulation audio-equipment magazines, is missing the needs of his or her younger charges.

Electronic Music Review. 1967. q. $8. Independent Electronic Music Center, Inc. Trumansburg, N.Y. 14886.

Aud: Sa, Ac, Jc, Ht. *Rv:* M. *Jv:* B.

The purpose of this journal, unlike that of *Source,* is to persuade as much as educate. Directed to the perceptive advocate of electronic music, it first assumes he (one suspects the teacher from high school through college) knows little or nothing about the subject. Consequently, everything is carefully explained—usually by musicians, scholars and scientists. Articles range from a sophisticated how-to-do-it approach to history. The scope is international, and most articles are documented. A useful magazine for any adventuresome library or music center.

Ethnomusicology. 1955. 3/yr. Membership (Non-members, $10.). Frank Gillis. Wesleyan Univ. Press, Middletown, Conn. 06457. Illus., index. Circ: 1,200.

Indexed: MusicI. *Bk. rev:* 4–8, 200–1,200 words. *Aud:* Sa, Ac. *Rv:* H. *Jv:* B.

The basic folk music journal for scholars, not for the younger set. Articles tend to be scholarly, well-documented

and written by experts for fellow experts, e.g., "The Distribution of Sound Instruments in the Prehistoric Southwestern United States." All aspects of the subject, both national and international, are considered. Particularly helpful in libraries for the extensive bibliographies and the book review section, which often features opposing views. Serious students of folk and primitive music will enjoy, but at the average level of interest, a magazine such as *Sing Out* is a better purchase. *Ethnomusicology* is only for the academic or large public library.

Gramophone. 1923. m. $5. Anthony Pollard. General Gramophone Pubns. Inc., 370 Kenton Rd., Kenton, Middlesex, Eng. Circ: 73,000.

Indexed: MusicI. *Aud:* Ga, Ac, Jc. *Rv:* H. *Jv:* B.

To some degree, this is the *American Record Guide* for England. It contains long, critical reviews of the monthly output of classical recordings in the United Kingdom. There are also two or three articles on music and audio equipment. An extremely useful review medium for any library which has more than a moderate-sized record collection.

Guitar Player. 1967. bi-m. $3. L. V. Eastman. Eastman Pubns., 843 The Alamenda, San Jose, Calif. 95126. Illus., adv. Circ: 28,000.

Bk. rev: 5–6, 50 words. *Aud:* Ga, Sh, Jh. *Rv:* L. *Jv:* B.

Gives tips on how to improve the musicians' skills, equipment evaluations, short articles on folk and popular string pickers and general comments on the music scene. Only some 40 pages, but few ads, heavy on illustrations. Includes guitar music scores, and assumes at least a basic knowledge of the instrument. Should be in any general or school collection where there is an interest in the popular guitar—but not for the classical player.

High Fidelity. 1951. m. $7. Roland Gelatt. Billboard Publishing Co., 165 W. 46th St., New York, N.Y. 10036. Illus., index, adv. Circ: 140,000. Microform: UM.

Indexed: AbrRG MusicI, RG. *Aud:* Ga, Ac, Jc, Sh. *Rv:* H. *Jv:* A.

Along with *HiFi/Stereo Review* and *Audio,* one of three general magazines for the informed hi-fi enthusiast and record buyer. Published in several regional editions as well as in a "Musical America" edition ($12/yr). The "Musical America" edition caries 32 extra pages which cover current music performances, music centers and performing artists for those with a special interest in "live" as well as recorded music. *High Fidelity* includes articles about music and musicians written by musicians such as Igor Stravinsky and Glenn Gould, or journalists such as Gene Lees, who contributes outspoken and controversial comments on the recorded scene. Audio equipment reports based on laboratory tests give the latest information on home entertainment electronics, and new trends are given coverage, as evidenced by the newly added section on video equipment for amateurs. The section devoted to critical reviews of recordings is afforded considerable space, and while classical records receive the greatest attention, folk, jazz, and pop music have received wider coverage of late. The difference between this and *HiFi/Stereo* is slight, although some prefer record reviews in the latter. Libraries are advised to try both, or one after the other.

HiFi/Stereo Review. 1958. m. $6. William Anderson. Ziff-Davis Publishing Co., One Park Ave., New York, N.Y. 10016. Illus., index, adv. Circ: 190,000. Microform: UM.

Indexed: MusicI. *Aud:* Ga, Ac, Jc, Sh. *Rv:* H. *Jv:* V.

A popular, useful guide to equipment and recordings for the beginner as well as the knowledgeable user. General articles on music (a series on "Great American Composers," another on the stylistic periods of music, many by distinguished scholars and musicians) are included, all well-illustrated. Many advertisements. Test reports, "Hi-Fi Questions and Answers," and reports on new products adequately cover equipment without allowing this aspect to dominate the magazine. Occasional surveys give a comprehensive view of available equipment, e.g., "Survey of New Stereo Equipment as seen at Fall Hi-Fi Shows." The most important aspect of this periodical is the reviews of all types of recordings, both discs and tapes. Those recordings deemed outstanding (performance, recording, and stereo quality) are indicated with the caption *"Recording of Special Merit."* While the editorial tone is conservative, reviewers such as Eric Salzman dare to criticize cherished idols. See remarks for *Audio* and *High Fidelity*.

The Hill and Dale News. 1961. bi-m. $2.50. City of London Phonograph and Gramophone Soc., 19 Glendale Rd., Southborne, Bournemouth, Hampshire. Illus., adv.

Aud: Ga. *Rv:* L. *Jv:* B.

Containing articles, advertisements, old catalog reprints, discographies, and all manner of material related to the acoustical era of sound recording, 1877–1925, the *News* is written by and for the collector of acoustical records, phonographs, and related items. Content is furnished entirely by Society members, who use the *News* as a medium for exchange of experiences, information, and opinion. Membership accompanies subscription.

Instrumentalist; a magazine for school and college band and orchestra directors, teacher-training specialists in music education, and instrumental teachers. 1946. m. (except July). $6. T. Rohner. Instrumentalist Co., 1418 Lake St., Evanston, Ill. 60204. Illus., index, adv. Circ: 16,500. Microform: UM.

Indexed: MusicI. *Bk. rev:* 3, 100–350 words. *Aud:* Ac, Jc, Ht. *Rv:* M. *Jv:* B.

This practical journal for the music educator deals chiefly with technical problems of teaching and playing the various band and orchestra instruments. (No coverage is given to piano, organ, guitar, and other instruments for which instruction is not generally provided in public schools.) Four articles (called "clinics") in each issue

treat the specific problems encountered by string, woodwind, brass, and percussion instrumentalists. From 10 to 15 articles by music educators and staff writers deal with a wide variety of subjects including bibliographical material, special projects in music schools, and legislation. "The Idea Exchange" (usually 1,000-word essays from readers) and news of new products fit the pragmatic pattern of this periodical. An important and valuable aspect is the annotated new music reviews by John Paynter. According to editorial policy, these reviews are objective, honest and are meant to furnish school directors with reliable and expert guidance. A negative statement is rare since reviews of bad pieces are not published. An obvious selection for any school library where the band is an important consideration.

Inter-American Music Bulletin. 1957. 6/yr. Free. Pan-American Union, Dept. of Cultural Affairs, Music Div., Washington, D.C. 20006. Illus. Circ: 3,000.

Indexed: MusicI. *Aud:* Ga, Ac, Jc, Sh. *Rv:* M. *Jv:* B.

According to its printed statement, the *Bulletin* is published to "complement the more extensive *Boletin Inter Americano de Musica* published by the section in Spanish. It is intended to acquaint English language readers with the music and composers of the Western Hemisphere, musical activities in Central and South America, and activities and movements in contemporary music in America and Europe." There is a conscious stress on modern music. While the bulletin began with lists of festivals and sketches of composers, its tendency of late has been to present more scholarly writings, e.g., "Collecting Techniques with Special Reference to Ballads." Most issues are devoted to one paper and range from 6 to 28 pages. A valuable index published in May 1960 listed periodical articles, by subject, that related to the performing arts in Latin America (110pp). Not only a useful magazine for music collections, but employable in secondary schools and academic libraries to supplement or encourage inter-American studies programs.

Jazz Journal. 1948. m. $6.50. Sinclair Traill. The Cottage, 27 Willow Vale, London W.12. Illus., adv. Circ: 15,000.

Indexed: MusicI. *Bk. rev:* 2–3, 250–300 words. *Aud:* Ga, Ac, Jc, Sh, Jh. *Rv:* M. *Jv:* B.

As of this writing there were more than a dozen magazines devoted entirely to jazz, and six of them are indexed in *Music Index*. Half are published abroad, and while opinion differs, the English *Jazz Journal* is considered by many to be the best of the group. It has wide use in America because of its international coverage, the excellent black and white illustrations, and, most important, the extensive record reviews. The editors make an effort to cover all jazz recordings—regardless of point of issue—of the previous month. In the United States the two best jazz magazines, both of which feature articles and record reviews, are *Jazz and Pop*. (1962. m. $5. Pauline Rivelli. Jazz Press Inc., 1841 Broadway, New York, N.Y. 10023) and *Jazz Report* (1958. bi-m. $3. Paul Affeldt. 357 Leighton Drive, Ventura, Calif. 93001). Any of these are useful additions for the school library where there is an interest in jazz or modern music, and most medium to large public and academic libraries should subscribe to at least one. Where only a single magazine can be chosen to represent modern popular music, the best bet is either *Down Beat, Crawdaddy* or *Rolling Stone,* particularly for secondary schools.

Journal of Church Music. 1959. m. (except Aug.). $4.25. Helen E. Pfatteicher. Fortress Press, 2900 Queen Lane, Philadelphia, Pa. 19129. Illus., adv. Circ: 3,800.

Indexed: MusicI. *Bk. rev:* 2, 300 words. *Aud:* Sa, Ac. *Rv:* M. *Jv:* B.

The purpose "is to help those engaged in the music program to raise the standards of church music so that it adds to the total service." This is accomplished via articles on organ and choral techniques, hymns, and local church activities. Three or four complete anthems are reprinted in each issue. Special issues list suggested music for organ and adult and youth choirs, suggestions on wedding music, and planning the music program. There are an average of three articles per issue, 16 pages of text, 15 pages of music. Illustrations. A specialized music magazine for a specialized audience.

Journal of Music Theory. 1957. semi-ann. $5. Allen Forte. Yale School of Music, New Haven, Conn. 06520. Illus., index. Circ: 1,400. Reprint: Johnson.

Indexed: MusicI. *Bk. rev:* Numerous, long and critical. *Aud:* Sa, Ac. *Rv:* H. *Jv:* B.

A forum for research papers devoted to contemporary and historical theory, e.g., "The Function of the Six-Four Chord in Tonal Music." Important bibliographies appear— "Recent Soviet Articles on Music Theory"—as do extensive, critical book reviews. Of great reference value for music students, scholars and teachers, but only for large collections.

Journal of Research in Music Education. 1953. q. Membership (Non-members, $6.). Allen P. Britton. Soc. for Research in Music Education, Music Educators National Conference, N.E.A. Bldg., 1201 16th St. N.W., Washington, D.C. 20036. Illus., index, adv. Circ: 8,000. Microform: UM.

Indexed: EdI, MusicI. *Bk. rev:* 3–8, 200–1,000 words, signed. *Aud:* Ac, Jc, Ht. *Rv:* H. *Jv:* B.

Research efforts, pertinent in any way to music instruction, are published in this official journal. Efforts range from studies on professional standing—"The Professional Role and Status of Music Educators in the United States"— and changing curriculum ideas to more technical studies and bibliographies. Libraries supporting any research efforts in music education should have this periodical.

Journal of the American Musicological Society. 1948. 3/yr. $10. James Haar. William Byrd Press, 2901 Byrdhill

Rd., Richmond, Va. 23205. Subscriptions to: Otto E. Albrecht, 204 Hare Bldg., Univ. of Pennsylvania, Philadelphia, Pa. 19104. Illus. Circ: 3,000.

Indexed: MusicI. *Bk. rev:* 6–9, 1,000–1,800 words, signed. *Aud:* Sa, Ac. *Rv:* H. *Jv:* B.

Published in conjunction with the University of Pennsylvania Department of Music, this is a scholarly approach to all aspects of music from composers to instruments, but with emphasis on musicology rather than performance. Particularly valuable to music libraries for: "Studies & Abstracts," short, independent articles; bibliographies; an annual list of dissertations in progress, and a lengthy and technical book review section. The latter is edited by Daniel Heartz and the scope is international. A useful magazine for medium to large academic music collections.

Keyboard Jr. 1943. m. (Oct.–May). $.80. Keyboard Jr. Pubns. Inc., 1346 Chapel St., New Haven, Conn. 06511.

Indexed: IChildsMag. *Aud:* Jh, E. *Rv:* M. *Jv:* B.

An eight-page music appreciation bulletin for use in music classes for junior and senior high and possibly some advanced elementary grade students. Each issue features a one- to two-page illustrated articles on a composer, musician, piece of music, orchestra, or type of composition. The writing style is surprisingly adult. Musically ignorant adults might find much of interest here, too. Although small in size, the contents are impressive. The format of unbound pages will prove a librarian's nightmare. The same publisher also issues *Young Keyboard* (1946. m. $.80.), which is similarly indexed and follows the same format and style, although it is somewhat simpler written for ages 4 to 6. One of the few music magazines which can be used in classroom situations with children, and if not in the school library, certainly should be brought to the attention of teachers.

Music. 1966. q. $2. Pergamon Press, 44–01 21st St., Long Island City, N.Y. 11101. Illus.

Bk. rev: 5–10, various lengths. *Aud:* Ht, Et. *Rv:* M. *Jv:* B.

The official journal of the British School of Music Association, which stresses education in the primary and secondary schools. Of limited interest to American or Canadian music teachers, but worth considering for the reviews of recordings and books for both teachers and students. Also useful for articles on composers.

Music and Letters. 1920. q. $5. J. A. Westrup. Music & Letters, Ltd., 44 Conduit St., London W.1. Illus., index, adv. Microform: UM.

Indexed: BritHum, MusicI. *Bk. rev:* Various numbers, lengths. *Aud:* Sa, Ac. *Rv:* H. *Jv:* B.

A British music journal with international coverage of classical music and musicians. Known for scholarship and intelligence in dealing with the complexities of music, past and present. Learned dissertations on styles, contributions by outstanding musicians and subjects of historical significance are included. An important part is the critical reviews of books and new music. While the emphasis is British, it is widely circulated in the U.S., and should be in all medium to large academic libraries.

Music and Musicians. 1952. m. $7.20. Frank G. Barker. Hansom Books Ltd., Artillery Mansions, 75 Victoria St., London S.W.1. Illus., adv. Circ: 17,000.

Indexed: MusicI. *Bk. rev:* 5–10, 200 words, notes. *Aud:* Ga, Ac, Jc. *Rv:* M. *Jv:* B.

Following the same format as other Hansom publications, e.g., *Films And Filming, Dance and Dancers,* this is one of a family of magazines on the arts published by the firm. Although issued in England, it covers music and musicians on an international scale, and is particularly useful for reports on the European scene. A typical issue covers current performers, performances, musical style (both modern and traditional), and a calendar of events. The reviews of musical performances are objective, always fair, and tend to be critical. Book reviews are a minor part of each issue, but Americans will find the survey of current recordings of special value, as emphasis is on English and European releases. The format is noteworthy, primarily because there is an extensive use of illustrations and photographs. Even the non-musician will find much here of interest, and it is a good, general magazine for medium to large music collections.

Musical Educators Journal. 1914. m. (except June, July and Aug.). $5. Charles B. Fowler. Music Educators National Conference, 1201 16th St., N.W. Washington, D.C. 20036. Illus., adv. Circ: 60,000. Reprint: Kraus. Microform: UM.

Indexed: EdI, MusicI. *Bk. rev:* 5–10, 550 words, signed. *Aud:* Ac, Jc, Ht, Et. *Rv:* M. *Jv:* B.

The leading music education journal, which represents music education from grade school through university level. Articles range from philosophy to news of current music activities and developments, research, awards and competitions. Special features are a part of some issues— e.g., "The Tanglewood Symposium—Music in American Society." Sketches illustrate many articles and there is good photo coverage. Each month the cover features an example of musically-oriented fine art. A basic acquisition for all school professional collections. See comments for *American Music Teacher.*

Music Journal; educational music magazine. 1943. m. (Sept.–June). $8. Robert Cumming. Music Journal Inc., 1776 Broadway, New York, N.Y. 10019. Illus., adv. Circ: 22,000. Microform: UM.

Indexed: EdI, MusicI. *Bk. rev:* 2–9, 150 words, signed. *Aud:* Ga, Ac, Jc, Ht. *Rv:* H. *Jv:* A.

One of the best single sources for an overview of contemporary music by outstanding authorities in all fields of music. Often highly controversial articles appear, which

provide the music educator, the student or the general music lover with a knowledge of current thinking on a wide variety of musical topics. Editorials range from polite essays to information about legislation affecting musicians. In addition to announcements and accounts of recent musical happenings, critical reviews by identified writers cover books, records, and music. Highly regarded in music circles, this is useful where there is a growing interest in music and a need is felt to purchase additional general magazines in the field.

The Music Review. 1940. q. $10. Geoffrey Sharp. W. Heffer & Sons Ltd., 3 Petty Cury, Cambridge, Eng. Illus., index, adv. Circ: 800. Microform: UM.

Indexed: BritHum, MusicI. *Bk. rev:* 6–10, lengthy, signed. *Aud:* Sa, Ac. *Rv:* H. *Jv:* B.

The purpose of this British periodical is twofold. It serves as a vehicle for five to six musicological papers and it furnishes exhaustive, critical reviews of books, records and music. The reviews, by identified and competent reviewers, include foreign books and records. Many consider *The Music Review* to be the British parallel to the *Musical Quarterly* in America. Necessary in a college or university with a strong music program but of little interest to the lay person.

Musical Opinion; educational journal. 1877. m. $4.50. Laurence Swinyard. Musical Opinion Ltd., 87 Wellington St., Luton, Beds., Eng. Illus., adv. Circ: 8,000.

Indexed: MusicI. *Bk. rev:* 4–1,100 words, signed. *Aud:* Sa, Ac. *Rv:* H. *Jv:* B.

Another general British music magazine, but primarily limited to classical music with particular emphasis on detailed record reviews, and briefer notice of musical scores. The book reviews, too, are excellent. Although published in England, the magazine tends to discuss music from the Continent as much as in London. Includes a special section for organ enthusiasts. For larger music collections.

The Musical Quarterly. 1915. q. $6. Paul H. Lang. G. Schirmer, Inc., 609 Fifth Ave., New York, N.Y. 10017. Illus., adv. Circ: 5,616. Microform: UM.

Indexed: MusicI, SSHum. *Bk. rev:* 2–4, 2–8 pages, signed. *Aud:* Sa, Ac, Jc. *Rv:* H. *Jv:* A.

A basic journal in all medium to large music collections, this strives to be "a mirror of the world's best musical thought," and serves as a vehicle for the publication of research efforts in the field of serious music. Music students will find it indispensable. A section of about 25 pages called "Current Chronicle" covers events in the U.S. as well as on the international scene. Signed critical book reviews thoroughly explore scholarly books on music, and a quarterly booklist, which is not annotated, covers international publications. Record reviews report in depth on the musical and technical aspects of classical offerings and useful bibliographies are included. Generous use of musical examples as well as charts and photos are useful features. Primarily for all academic and larger public libraries.

The Musical Times. 1844. m. $6. Andrew Porter. Novello & Co., Ltd. 27 Soho Sq., London W.1. Circ: 12,000.

Indexed: BritHum, MusicI. *Bk. rev:* 10–12, 700 words, signed. *Aud:* Sa, Ac, Jc, Ht, Et. *Rv:* H. *Jv:* B.

A general British music magazine, this is written for both the student and the teacher. There are some five, long articles per issue on music, musicians, concerts, instruments, and education. Most of the writing is of a semi-scholarly nature, representing original research. Features include: short news stories; book, record, new music, and concert reviews; a diary of London musical events, and a special section on church and organ music. Approximately one-half of the 96- to 104-page magazine is turned over to advertising. This is somewhat the equivalent of the old *Musical America,* and as one of the best general music magazines published anywhere, should be in all medium to large music collections.

Notes. 1943. q. $9. Harold E. Samuel. Music Library Assn., School of Music, Univ. of Michigan, Ann Arbor, Mich. 48105. Illus., adv. Circ: 3,000.

Indexed: MusicI. *Bk. rev:* 20–25, 600–1,600 words. *Aud:* Sa, Ac, Jc, Sh. *Rv:* H. *Jv:* V.

Devoted primarily to book and record reviews. Many contributors write for the various review sections, all of which are edited by impressive names in the field of music librarianship, such as Kurtz Myers and Ruth Watanabe. Unique is the consensus record review, which covers over 200 discs and which serves as an index to reviews in 19 other periodicals. There also are lists of books and music received. The book list carries one line annotations while the music list is classified according to type and difficulty. Three or four articles furnish essays of interest to both librarians and musicians. Although scholarly in approach, *Notes* strives for comprehensiveness rather than selectivity. A basic requirement for any library, from secondary school through graduate school, where a guide to books, recordings and reviews is an absolute necessity.

Opera News. 1936. irreg. (during opera season); m. (rest of the year). $8. Frank Merkling. Metropolitan Opera Guild, 1865 Broadway, New York, N.Y. 10023. Illus. Circ: 85,000. Microform: UM.

Indexed: MusicI, RG. *Aud:* Ga, Ac, Jc, Sh, Jh. *Rv:* M. *Jv:* B.

During the Metropolitan Opera season, issues deal with the opera that is currently being performed, and include the plot, cast, and historical notes as well as photographs of characters and staging. Monthly issues are more likely to probe history and personalities involved in opera. Signed reports of 250 to 1000 words from various music centers in the U.S. and abroad are a regular future. The principle periodical devoted to opera in the United States, and should be in most libraries.

Perspectives of New Music. 1962. semi-ann. $5. Benjamin Boretz & Edward T. Gone. Princeton Univ. Press, Box 231, Princeton, N.J. 08540. Illus., index, adv. Circ: 2,481.

Indexed: MusicI. *Bk. rev:* 2–4, 1–8 pages, signed. *Aud:* Sa, Ac. *Rv:* H. *Jv:* B.

Published in conjunction with the Fromm Music Foundation, *Perspectives* provides scholarly studies of the new and innovative in serious music, the contributions of various composers to this music, and includes detailed book reviews. Since it is the only periodical in the U.S. that emphasizes new music styles exclusively, its reference value is high for those interested in modern music trends. Research efforts—"Toward a Theory of the Twelve-Note-Class System"—in specialized areas serve the needs of advanced students. Only for larger collections.

Quarterly Check List of Musicology. See Literature Section (*Quarterly Check List of Literary History*).

Rolling Stone. 1967. semi-m. $10. Straight Arrow Publishers, 746 Brannan St., San Francisco, Calif. 94103. Illus., adv.

Aud: Ga, Ac, Jc, Sh, Jh. *Rv:* M. *Jv:* B.

A newspaper format magazine which covers the rock music scene, and which is rapidly becoming a favorite among the younger set. It goes beyond talk about popular music and musicians to talk about what music means to the involved teen-ager or, for that matter, the older listener who enjoys The Beatles, Joan Baez, Bob Dylan, the Jefferson Airplane, etc. Articles are well illustrated, intelligently put together and inevitably serious. The record reviews of both singles and albums are perceptive, quite beyond what is found in most review sections. A regular feature, "The Rolling Stone Interview," consists of a long discussion with a current figure on the scene. Should be included, along with *Crawdaddy,* in any library where current music is of interest.

Sing Out. 1950. bi-m. $5. Irwin Silber. 80 E. 11th St., New York, N.Y. 10036. Illus., adv. Circ: 25,000.

Indexed: MusicI. *Bk. rev:* Various numbers and lengths. *Aud:* Ga, Ac, Jc, Sh, Jh. *Rv:* M. *Jv:* B.

Although the folk music craze comes and goes, it never dies, and this is probably the best single magazine for anyone interested in "singing out." It features interviews with singers, song writers, teachers; articles on the guitar, banjo and autoharp; news and notes on what's happening on the scene; and articles which cover every aspect of folk from traditional to contemporary. Regular columns include: Pete Seeger's "Johnny Appleseed," Israel Young's "Frets and Frails," record reviews, and news of folk festivals. It has added attraction for the player in that each number contains 10 to 15 folk songs, right down to words, music and guitar chords. A first choice for any music-minded high school or junior high library, and worthwhile in medium to large music collections anywhere.

Source; music of the avant garde. 1967. semi-ann. $13. Larry Austin. 330 Univ. Ave., Davis, Calif. 95616. Illus., adv.

Aud: Ga, Sa, Ac, Jc. *Rv:* H. *Jv:* V.

A plastic ringed, 118-page oversized (10″ × 12″) journal, purposely designed to allow for publication of five to eight new music scores. Each is prefaced with a photograph of the composer, explanatory notes and often additional materials such as an interview with John Cage. Beginning with the fourth issue, two long-playing records were included. There are a number of interpretive articles. Typographically it is almost perfect. The content will delight the student or teacher who welcomes innovation, but will be a nightmare for the traditionalist. For a graphic description of the purpose and goals of this remarkable magazine, see a far from sympathetic review by Harold C. Schonberg in *The Sunday New York Times,* (Sept. 24, 1967, p. D19). Should be found in any large or adventuresome music collection in medium to large libraries.

Tempo; a quarterly review of modern music. 1939. q. $2. Colin Mason. Boosey & Hawkes Music Publishers, Ltd., 295 Regent St., London, W.1. Subscriptions to: Boosey & Hawkes Music Publishers, Inc., 30 W. 57th St., New York, N.Y. 10019. Illus., adv.

Indexed: MusicI. *Bk. rev:* 4–6, 750 words, signed. *Aud:* Ga, Sa, Ac. *Rv:* M. *Jv:* B.

Devoted entirely to twentieth century music, this 30- to 40-page English quarterly features articles on modern music, or on certain aspects of a particular composer's work, e.g., "Structure and Concept in Bartok's Sixth Quartet," and "Kodaly—A Personal View." Regular features include perceptive reviews of first performances (in England), grouped record reviews, and book reviews. Illustrations, usually of ballet or opera, and music examples. The articles are well written and, while for the serious student of music, are within the grasp of the interested layman. In view of its coverage and low price, a good periodical for medium to large libraries.

World of Music. 1964. bi-m. $6. Barenreiter-Verlag, Heinrich-Schutz-Alle 29, 3500 Kassel-Wilhelmshohe, Germany. Illus., adv.

Indexed: MusicI. *Bk. rev:* 2–3, 600 words, signed. *Aud:* Sa, Ac, Jc, Sh, Ht, Et. *Rv:* M. *Jv:* B.

A general music magazine published in three languages (with as many columns to the page): English, German and French. The 60- to 70-page journal features three to five main articles on some aspect of world music, e.g., the dance theatre of India, music with or without a public, and music education. However, its main value is the overview, in concise form, of world music festivals, recordings, books, first performances, and a calendar of events. The photographs cover the world, and some are downright exotic. Sometimes the translations are a bit shaky, but the style is literate, and never overly technical. It is a good addition for professional collections in schools, and should be in large public and academic libraries.

MYSTERY AND DETECTIVE STORIES

Alfred Hitchcock Mystery Magazine. m. $6. H.S.D. Pubns., 244 Beach Court, Riviera Beach, Fla. 33404. Illus., adv.

Aud: Ga. *Rv:* L. *Jv:* B.

Although primarily a quick-selling newsstand item, the stories are fair to good, and, needless to add, are not entirely the work of the movie director. Most of them have the surprise ending so loved by Hitchcock, and are written for the reader who is not looking for too many involved situations or sophisticated syntax.

The Armchair Detective. 1967. q. $2. Allen J. Hubin. 3656 Midland, White Bear Lake, Minn. 55110. Circ: 500.

Bk. rev: 5, 250–1,000 words, signed. *Aud:* Ga, Ac, Jc, Sh. *Rv:* M. *Jv:* B.

Without a mystery story in sight, this is a magazine about the genre. The policy is "to publish all types of short material relevant to the mystery-detective-suspense fiction field and of fairly general interest to its fans." Averaging about 33 pages, each issue is of very high quality. Besides feature articles, there are book reviews of old and new books, film reviews, letters and a book exchange page. Ordean Hagen tells how *Who Done It?* came to be written, and G. C. Ramsey discusses the research for his book on Agatha Christie. Most articles are original and the editor welcomes contributions. Librarians will be interested in the annotated bibliographies and checklist material, such as one by James Sandoe on the "hardboiled dick."

Baker Street Journal; a quarterly of Sherlockiana. 1964. q. $4. Julian Wolff. Baker Street Irregulars, 33 Riverside Dr., New York, N.Y. 10023. Illus., index. Circ: 700.

Aud: Ga, Ac, Jc. *Rv:* M. *Jv:* B.

The American counterpart of the English *Sherlock Holmes Journal.* In addition to research articles on Holmes, there are reports on activities of the Baker Street Irregulars and its more than 30 chapters. The tone is serious, and not for anyone who takes a slight view of the glories of Holmes. A valuable feature is the annotated lists of current books and magazine articles on Doyle's hero.

Ellery Queen's Mystery Magazine. 1941. m. $6. Ellery Queen. Davis Pubns., Inc., 505 Park Ave., New York, N.Y. 10022. Illus., adv. Circ: 166,000.

Bk. rev: 10–12, 30–50 words, signed. *Aud:* Ga, Sh. *Rv:* M. *Jv:* A.

Averaging 12 to 15 stories and an occasional article in some 160 pages, this is the best general mystery magazine on the market. Although issued by the master detective, it is not limited to his adventures. On the contrary, it publishes some of the top writers in the field, writers who are familiar to any reader of the genre. There are also a number of "firsts," and a novelette. Detective, suspense, crime, spy and the traditional mystery type fiction are all included.

Each year the best stories are anthologized. The "Best Mysteries of the Month," a monthly book review column by John Dickson Carr, serves as an excellent source of advice for librarians interested in the purchase of mysteries. In view of its relatively high caliber, this magazine may be used in any type of public or senior high school library, particularly where there is a problem with reluctant readers.

The JDM Bibliophile. 1965. irreg. Free. Len & June Moffatt. 9826 Paramount Blvd., Downey, Calif. 90240.

Aud: Ga. *Rv:* L. *Jv:* C.

A unique publication, devoted to listing or tracking down all of the John D. MacDonald magazine stories. The writer himself does not have a complete record because pulp publishers were not in the habit of sending copies to their authors. MacDonald, a well-known mystery writer, has appeared in detective, sports, mystery, western and women's magazines.

The Mystery Lovers' Newsletter. 1968. bi-m. $2. Mrs. Lianne Carlin. P.O. Box 107, Revere, Mass. 02151.

Bk. rev: 2–3, 180 words, signed. *Aud:* Ga. *Rv:* M. *Jv:* B.

One of two fan magazines (see also, *The Armchair Detective*) covering the whole field of mystery, detective and suspense fiction. Each issue consists of about 15 pages of reprinted material, e.g., an interview with Mary Roberts Rinehart, a Margery Allingham checklist, and an annotated list of Raymond Chandler movies.

Sherlock Holmes Journal. 1952. semi-ann. $3. Marquis of Donegall. Sherlock Holmes Soc. of London. The Studio, 39 Clabon News, London, S.W.1.

Bk. rev: 2–3, 400 words, signed. *Aud:* Ga, Ac, Jc. *Rv:* M. *Jv:* B.

Handsomely published, this runs to some 30 pages, all devoted to aspects of Sherlockiana. The tone is scholarly, including some very erudite footnotes. Typical articles: "Sherlock Holmes as a Scientist;" "The Great Use S.H. Made of *Whitaker's Almanack;* "Certain Items on Crime in the *Strand Magazine* for 1894;" "The Origin of the Name, Sherlock" and "Charlie Chaplin in the Stage Role of Billy." There are also news and editorial notes, coverage of the society's meetings, obituaries of famous Sherlockians and a list of society members.

True Detective. 1924. bi-m. $1.50. Macfadden-Bartell Corp., 205 E. 42nd St., New York, N.Y. 10017. Illus., adv. Circ: 300,000.

Aud: Ga. *Rv:* L. *Jv:* C.

The earliest factual detective magazine. It began as *True Detective Mysteries* in 1924, serving as a male companion to Bernard Macfadden's *True Story.* The genre never really caught on—a circulation of 300,000 for any of this type is excellent (this compares with over 2,000,000 for *True Story*). When gangsters were big business during the 1930s, the lurid photographs and jazzed-up facts gave this a boost,

but by the end of World War II they all fell back to a healthy, yet modest circulation. Today's *True Detective* is a rough form of the "new journalism," in which the facts are usually accurate enough, but the material is presented in fictional form. Usually the reader is carried through the story from the point of view of the detective, fact piling upon fact until the crime is solved. Some of this is good to excellent, but the better part is oversimplified and needlessly gory (although no more so than some briefer crime stories in newspapers and *Time* magazine). The emphasis is on murder, and photographs are always included to enlighten the reader. In this same field other circulation leaders include: *Dell's Inside Detective* and *Front Page Detective,* and Fawcett's *Startling Detective* and *True Police Cases.* Although of dubious quality, an argument might be made for including one or two of these in a public library that is attempting to reach an audience other than the well-educated, sophisticated American. Of the group, *True Detective* and *Inside Detective* are probably the best. Librarians, regardless of attitude toward such material, should certainly recognize it exists.

OFFICE AND SECRETARIAL PRACTICES

Indexes and Abstracts

Business Periodicals Index. (For annotation, see Indexes and Abstracts Section.)

From Nine to Five; or thereabouts. 1960. semi-m. $7.50. Marilyn French. The Dartnell Corp., 4660 Ravenswood Ave., Chicago, Ill. 60640. Illus. Circ: 25,000 Microform: UM.

Bk. rev: Occasional. *Aud:* Ga, Jc, Sh. *Rv:* M. *Jv:* A.

Not confined to just the tips and shortcuts, this bulletin-type magazine also offers general interest reading to inspire and inform secretaries and other office personnel. Some issues contain biographical sketches of secretaries to famous people: sketches have included the secretaries of Columnist Sylvia Porter and Senator Charles Percy. Its "Problem Clinic" sometimes raises a lively discussion among readers, pointing out as it does the importance of personality and good human relations in any organization. Also included are suggestions for better work habits and procedures, proper office dress, poise, office etiquette, new products, and news of the professional organizations like The National Secretaries Association and the associations of legal, medical and educational secretaries. Should be of interest to any school where secretarial practices are taught, and to many public libraries.

Junior Secretary. 1966. m. (Oct.–June). Ann M. Merker. Gregg Div., McGraw-Hill Book Co., 330 W. 42nd St., New York, N.Y. 10036. Illus. Circ: 50,000.

Aud: Jh, Sh. *Rv:* L. *Jv:* B.

Published for the "specialized needs of first year secretarial students," it "attempts to fill the need for motivation and additional practice in beginning shorthand and typing skills." Vocational guidance is provided through short, staff-written articles indicating jobs open to girls with secretarial training, and encouraging the development of personality traits helpful in this vocation. Exercises, problems, speed tests, etc., are set up to put some fun into skill development. Short short stories appear in shorthand, with a transcript given. Copy is presented for typing and shorthand tests for which awards are given by Gregg. Produced in small size, on good paper, with a few simple, appealing illustrations, but with rather small type size for the typewritten copy, this would seem a likely prospect to demonstrate to beginning secretarial students the importance of basic skills in secretarial careers. Should be found in secretarial school libraries, and would be useful in high schools with large vocational programs.

Just Between Office Girls. 1950. semi-m. $6. Irene Stone. Bureau of Business Practice, 70 Fifth Ave., New York, N.Y. Illus. Circ: 33,150.

Aud: Ga, Jc, Sh. *Rv:* L. *Jv:* B.

This small brochure-type periodical presents useful and inspirational information to secretaries, stenographers and other office girls. It emphasizes the development of good interpersonal relations at work with such titles as "When You and the Boss Don't See Eye to Eye," "The Snob Snubs Himself," "Women Bosses," and "Your Aggression—And How to Handle It." Regular features include vocabulary quizzes, articles on grammar and typing tips. Useful in high schools, junior colleges or anywhere that commercial courses are offered.

Modern Office Procedures. 1956. m. $12. John B. Dykeman. Industrial Publishing Co., 812 Huron Rd., Cleveland, Ohio 44115. Illus., adv. Circ: 120,000. Microform: UM.

Bk. rev: Notes. *Aud:* Ga, Jc, Sh. *Rv:* M. *Jv:* B.

Practical information for both the office manager and the office employee. Articles such as "The Firing Ordeal," "The Case for Tough Minded Managers," and "How to Combat Noise" appeal to the top and middle manager. Such titles as "How to Form Plurals of Compound Words," "What You Should Know About Carbonless Paper" and "How To Write Small Sums and Percentages" are useful to the student, office manager and secretary. A useful, if not essential magazine, for business and secretarial courses.

The Office; magazine of management, equipment, methods. 1935. m. $6. William R. Schulhof. Office Pubns., Inc., 73 Southfield Ave., Stamford, Conn. 06904. Illus., adv. Circ: 85,000. Microform: UM.

Indexed: BusI. *Bk. rev:* 9–15, 100 words. *Aud:* Sa, Ac, Jc. *Rv:* M. *Jv* B.

Good coverage of many aspects of office practice and management for both the corporate executive and the office manager. Articles on systems analysis, computer programming, equipment, buildings and employee relations. Recently it has emphasized computer applications, often in quite technical language. It has good descriptions of office equipment including a "Readers' Service Card" feature, which provides for mailing further information on products advertised and books reviewed. Occasionally an issue will be devoted to one aspect of office practice, e.g., hospital offices. A valuable magazine for business managers at all levels, and useful in business administration school libraries.

The Secretary. 1942. m. (Sept.–June). $4. Shirley S. Englund. The National Secretaries' Assn., 1103 Grand Ave., Suite 410, Kansas City, Mo. 64106. Illus., adv. Circ: 27,700.

Bk. rev: Notes. *Aud:* Ga, Sh. *Rv:* M. *Jv:* B.

A periodical used to disseminate the news and views of the National Secretaries' Association, which emphasizes the Certified Professional Secretary (CPS) program and examination. This two-day, six-part examination covers personal adjustment and human relations, business law, business administration, secretarial accounting, secretarial skills, and secretarial procedures and is open to non-members as well as members. It is administered annually in May at colleges and universities throughout the United States and Canada by the Institute for Certifying Secretaries, a department of The National Secretaries Association (International). Sometimes, the whole issue is devoted to a special feature such as libraries, equipment purchase, or the male secretary. Recently male secretaries have been accepted for membership, and NSA avoids the slant towards the office "girl" usually found in this type of periodical.

Today's Secretary. 1898. m. (Sept.–June). $5. Ann Merker. Gregg Div., McGraw Hill Book Co., 330 W. 42nd St., New York, N.Y. 10036. Illus., adv. Circ: 175,000. Microform: UM.

Aud: Ga, Sh, Jh. *Rv:* M. *Jv:* B.

Directed to the practicing secretary and to the student preparing for a secretarial career. Several articles in each issue stress the importance of developing and improving skills; in several issues throughout the year, guidance is given on requirements and attributes of various secretarial career areas. Specific experiences are sometimes related to illustrate unusual job opportunities. Tips on grooming, including beauty, dress, and speech are suggested. An extensive "Skill Building" section includes material for practice in Gregg shorthand, transcription, typing speed tests, and vocabulary, spelling, grammar, and usage suggestions. Several regular single-column or one-page departments follow this general theme. The 68- to 76-page format includes black and white photos and drawings for illustration, and a moderate amount of appropriate advertising. A teacher's edition is also available. Used widely in high school and post-high school business education departments and in business schools.

ORNITHOLOGY

Indexes and Abstracts

Biological Abstracts, Canadian Periodical Index, Readers' Guide to Periodical Literature, Subject Index to Children's Magazines. (For annotations, see Indexes and Abstracts Section.)

Audubon Field Notes; devoted to reporting the distribution, migration and abundance of birds. 1947. bi-m. $5. Richard L. Plunkett. National Audubon Soc., 1130 Fifth Ave., New York, N.Y. 10028. Circ: 3,200. Microform: UM.

Indexed: BioAb. *Aud:* Ga, Ac, Jc, Sh. *Rv:* H. *Jv:* B.

A compilation of reports from bird watchers all over the country. The December issue publishes the results of a series of comprehensive breeding bird surveys conducted during the previous nesting season. The April number publishes the results of the annual Christmas bird count, which is perhaps the largest cooperative ornithological endeavor in the world. Should find a place in every library where there is a nearby bird club.

Audubon Magazine. 1899. $8.50. Les Line. National Audubon Soc., 1130 Fifth Ave., New York, N.Y. 10028. Illus., index, adv. Circ: 49,435. Microform: Princeton, UM.

Indexed: BioAb, RG. *Bk. rev:* 5–19, 100–550 words. *Aud:* Ga, Ac, Jc, Sh, Jh, E. *Rv:* H. *Jv:* V.

Audubon, like its parent organization, commands an outstanding place in the ornithology and conservation fields. Articles are written by some of the best known names in the field of nature literature, and are authoritative without being stuffy. The color photography is outstanding, and this, along with the black and white photographs, gives it an added dimension for use in the elementary grades. A regular feature is a book review section, "For the Young Naturalist," which will interest parents, teachers and librarians seeking worthwhile books for children. Because of the National Audubon Society's fight for the preservation of our natural resources, it often finds itself at odds with landowners, industry and government agencies. Thus, the magazine does not present an unbiased viewpoint, but still manages to stay on the side of the angels.

The Society also issues a leaflet of value to elementary and junior high school students. The *Curious Naturalist* gives hints to young readers on what to observe in nature, how to collect, and includes notes on experiments, new books and a questions and answers section. The pamphlet is well illustrated, and features a good layout. A natural companion in the elementary grades to the more advanced *Audubon Magazine.*

The Auk; a journal of ornithology. 1884. q. Membership (Non-members, $6). Robert Mengel. Amer. Ornithologists' Union, P.O. Box 23447, Anchorage, Ky. 40223. Illus., index, adv. Microform: Princeton.

Indexed: BioAb. *Aud:* Sa, Ac, Jc. *Rv:* H. *Jv:* B.

Scholarly in both its scope and its presentation, it publishes original articles containing significant new knowledge about birds, or a new interpretation of existing knowledge. The language is highly technical and the material authoritative. In a section called "Recent Literature," articles in other journals are cited. As much a magazine for the serious bird watcher as for the professional ornithologist, this is a basic item for larger public and academic library collections.

Canadian Audubon. 1939. bi-m. $3. Canadian Audubon Soc., 46 St. Clair Ave., E. Toronto 7, Ont. Illus., adv. Circ: 12,192.

Indexed: CanI, IChildMags. *Bk. rev:* 1–2, one page. *Aud:* Ga, Sh, Jh, E. *Rv:* M. *Jv:* B.

The counterpart in Canada of the *Audubon Magazine,* this features five or six articles on conservation and natural resources. It is well illustrated, and the material is suitable for students in junior high as well as adults. Particular attention is given to younger readers via the monthly features, "Audubon Youth" and "Nature Activities." While the American version is more elaborate, and to be preferred in most schools, *Canadian Audubon* is excellent where a second choice is advisable.

The Colorado Field Ornithologist. 1967. bi-ann. $1.50. Colorado Field Ornithologist, 1895 Alpine, Boulder, Colo. 80301. Illus.

Bk. rev: 1–2, short. *Aud:* Ga, Ac, *Rv:* M. *Jv:* B.

A small, 22-page, offset magazine with some line drawings, this packs a good deal of information in a little space. For example, a chart of birds counted in the 1966 census; articles on local nesting areas and birds; and even a book review. Not a necessary purchase, but should be considered by any library in or about Colorado.

Condor. 1899. bi-m. Membership (Non-members, $6). James R. King. Cooper Ornithological Society, c/o Dept. of Zoology, Washington State Univ., Pullman, Wash. 99163. Illus., charts, maps.

Indexed: BioAb. *Aud:* Sa, Ac. *Rv:* H. *Jv:* B.

A professional ornithology magazine, and the leading source of information on birds of the Pacific and the West. The scholarly papers appeal primarily to the specialist and the advanced student. All libraries in the Pacific Northwest, regardless of type, will want a subscription. In other parts of the country it will only be for large collections.

Massachusetts Audubon. 1917. q. Membership. Wayne Hanley, Massachusetts Audubon Soc., Lincoln, Mass. 01773. Illus., adv. Circ: 19,500. Microform: UM.

Bk. rev: Notes. *Aud:* Ga, Ac, Jc, Sh. *Rv:* H. *Jv:* A.

This slim, little quarterly has an important place in the ornithology literature. While it is directed to New England readers, the articles will interest those who are far from the Atlantic coast. Contributors are generally well known New England naturalists and enthusiastic amateurs, but many articles are published by nationally known or even foreign writers. Should be on every high school periodical list, and is highly recommended for most libraries.

PERSONNEL MANAGEMENT

Indexes and Abstracts

Business Periodicals Index, Education Index, Personnel Management Abstracts, Psychological Abstracts, Public Affairs Information Service. (For annotations, see Indexes and Abstracts Section.)

Management of Personnel Quarterly. 1961. q. $4.50. William H. Price. Bureau of Industrial Relations, Grad. Sch. of Business Admin., Univ. of Michigan, Ann Arbor, Mich. 48104. Illus., adv. Circ: 5,600. Microform: UM.

Indexed: PerManAb. *Bk. rev:* 3, 300 words, signed. *Aud:* Sa, Ac. *Rv:* M. *Jv:* B.

A practical, readable source of information for managers of industrial personnel, with some emphasis on the sociology of manufacturing organizations. Articles (about 2,500 words in length) are nicely balanced between academic and industrial contributors. There is a concerted (and usually successful) effort to make the articles both readable and scholarly. Useful to academic libraries serving schools of business administration and industrial relations.

Personnel. 1919. bi-m. Membership (Non-members, $10). Robert F. Guder. Amer. Management Assn., Inc., 135 W. 50th St., New York, N.Y. 10020. Illus., index. Circ: 58,000. Microform: UM. Reprint: Kraus.

Indexed: BusI, EdI, PAIS, PsyAb. *Bk. rev:* 1–2, 750–1,000 words, signed. *Aud:* Sa, Ac. *Rv:* M. *Jv:* B.

A practical approach to the wide range of problems involved in the management of people. Designed to provide useful guides and insights for all managers, as well as material of particular interest to industrial relations executives. Contributors are from business and industrial organizations, as well as from academic institutions. Especially good for working managers, it has some value also for the student in this and related fields but lacks supporting documentation (charts, diagrams, tables, bibliography, statistics, etc.).

Personnel Administrator. 1948. bi-m. Membership (Non-members, $8). William Largent. Amer. Soc. for Personnel Admin., 52 E. Bridge St., Bevea, Ohio 44017. Adv. Circ: 5,200. Microform: UM. Reprint: Kraus.

Indexed: PAIS, PsyAb. *Bk. rev:* 1–6, 400 words, signed. *Aud:* Sa, Ac. *Rv:* H. *Jv:* B.

A creative approach to better handling of people in the organizational setting, this is of interest to working personnel managers and schools of personnel management. Some recent articles such as "Career Choice Starts at Home," "Unless We Begin Now . . ." (on the career education of women) and "Occupational Changes in the Adult Years" would be of value also to guidance counselors. Its six or seven articles, while generally scholarly, are readable and have practical applications.

Personnel and Guidance Journal. 1952. m. (Sept.–June). Membership (Non-member, $10). Buford Stefflre. Amer. Personnel and Guidance Assn., 1607 New Hampshire Ave., N.W., Washington, D.C. 20009. Adv. Circ: 33,000. Microform: UM. Reprint: Johnson.

Indexed: EdI, PsyAb. *Bk. rev:* 8, 600 words, signed. *Aud:* Sa, Ac, Ht. *Rv:* M. *Jv:* B.

Published by the American Personnel and Guidance Association, this is for the scholar and the teacher. The 10 to 12 articles are primarily the results of research, and not how-to-do-it advice for the counselor. For example: "Counseling Without Assuming Free Will; Improving Prediction of Academic Achievement for Transfer Students." The book reviews are useful for materials in the guidance field.

Personnel Journal; the magazine of industrial relations and personnel management. 1922. m. $8. Arthur C. Croft. The Personnel Journal, Inc., Box 239, Swarthmore, Pa. 19081. Adv. Circ: 12,500. Microform: UM.

Indexed: BusI, PsyAb. *Bk. rev:* 1–2, 500 words, signed and notes. *Aud:* Sa, Ac, Jc. *Rv:* M. *Jv:* A.

The long life of this journal can perhaps be explained by its broad coverage of all aspects of personnel management from scholarly research to popular "this is how we do it" articles. While contributors are both theoreticians from universities and practicing personnel managers, its main appeal would be to working managers. In fact its good book reviews, lists of new books, complete conference calendar, and general coverage of what goes on in the field make it almost a must for anyone in personnel work.

Personnel Psychology. See Psychology Section.

PETS

American Field; the sportsman's newspaper of America. 1874. w. $7.50. William F. Brown. Amer. Field Publishing Co. 222 W. Adams St., Chicago, Ill. 60606. Illus., adv. Circ: 12,000.

Aud: Ga. *Rv:* M. *Jv:* B.

Devoted exclusively to pointing dogs and their sporting activities, this is not a magazine for the average dog lover. Special departments cover game and shooting, fish and fishing, natural history, travel, kennel, field trials, breeding, and everything else pertaining to canine interests. Excellent black and white photographs of winners in various competitions accompany many of the articles.

American Pigeon Journal; devoted to all branches of pigeon raising—fancy, utility and racing. 1912. m. $3.

Frank H. Hollman. Amer. Pigeon Journal Co., Warrenton, Mo. Illus., adv. Circ: 10,000.

Bk. rev: 20–25, 30–50 words. *Aud:* Ga, Sh, Jh. *Rv:* L. *Jv:* B.

Includes illustrations, and some rather fascinating advertising for those involved with pigeons. Articles, a few of which are reprints from other less specialized magazines, cover every aspect of the field: breeding, organizations, shows and displays. Of interest to adults and high school students who see more in a pigeon than a bothersome park pedestrian.

Cats Magazine. 1945. m. $4.50. Jean A. Laux. Graphic House, Washington, Pa. 15301. Illus., index, adv. Circ: 35,000.

Bk. rev: Notes, signed. *Aud:* Ga, Sh, Jh, E. *Rv:* L. *Jv:* B.

Approximately half of the magazine is devoted to cat shows and advertisements of interest to the owners of show cats. The editorial column brings current topics to the attention of all cat owners and solicits their assistance in sponsoring or combatting legislation or humane issues. There are usually five or six signed articles or short stories in each issue. Regular features include poetry, letters and photographs from subscribers, the staff veterinarian's responses to general health questions, the show calendar, and "Aunty and Arabella" (a comic strip). Will appeal to any cat-owner, regardless of age.

Chronicle of the Horse. 1937. w. $1. Alexander Mackay-Smith. Middleburg, Va. 22117. Illus., adv. Circ: 12,303.

Aud: Sa, Sh. *Rv:* M. *Jv:* B.

Primarily a news magazine of horses and racing. Each issue carries regular departments with roundups of both national and international events—racing, stud farms, hunting, horse shows, etc. A good part of the magazine is given over to the last area with a subdivision, "Young Entry," which includes information on horse shows for teen-agers and younger children. Full data is given from the names of winners and horses to precise technical information on each of the entries. As the official publication of some seven equestrian organizations, this deserves a place in any library where the sport is a serious matter. It is not for the casual horse lover or average high school student. See concluding remarks for *Horse Lover's Magazine.*

Dog World. 1916. m. $6. George Berner. Judy Berner Publishing Co., 469 E. Ohio St., Chicago, Ill. 60611. Illus., adv. Circ: 51,752.

Bk. rev: Occasional, short. *Aud:* Ga, Sh, Jh. *Rv:* L. *Jv:* B.

The aim of the "world's largest dog magazine" is to disseminate pertinent information to those interested in pure-bred dogs. Most articles are readily understood by the informed layman who has some knowledge of dog shows, standards and breeding; occasionally more specialized and scientific articles appear. The quality of photographic reproduction is high and the layout good. After the departure of Will Judy as editor-publisher, *Dog World* appeared

to decline in quality of content and size but has since improved again. However, the continuation of a brief article over a spread of two or three pages is objectionable, and at times there are more advertisements than articles to read.

The Horse Lover's Magazine. 1936. bi-m. $3. Dennis Luptak. J Bar D Publishers Inc., P.O. Box 1432, Richmond, Calif. 94802. Illus., adv. Circ: 122,000. Microform: UM.

Aud: Ga, Sh, Jh. *Rv:* M. *Jv:* B.

A general magazine which covers news of anything related to horses. It also discusses ranching hobbies and sports, all written by experts in a popular style. A typical issue will include a biography of a horseman, tips on care, roping, care of stables, 4-H national horse competitions, and various articles on horses in all parts of the world. The magazine is well illustrated and will have strong appeal for anyone, regardless of age, who is remotely interested in horses and riding, and is the best of the three horse magazines in this section.

International Turtle and Tortoise Society Journal. 1966. bi-m. $5. 8847 de Haviland Ave., Los Angeles, Calif. 90045.

Aud: Ga, Sh, Jh. *Rv:* L. *Jv:* B.

Photographs, scholarly but easily followed articles, and obvious enthusiasm point the way to a hobby. "Hatching Tortoise Eggs," "Turtle Trailing," or "About Your Turtle and Tortoise Clubs." Suitable for both adults and children, and useful in those libraries catering to a large contingent of animal enthusiasts.

National Humane Review. 1913. bi-m. $1.50. Eileen Schoen. Amer. Humane Assn., P.O. Box 1266, Denver, Colo. 80201. Illus., adv. Circ: 7,000.

Aud: Ga, Sh. *Rv:* L. *Jv:* B.

Promoting kindness to and care of animals is the primary purpose of the American Humane Association, and this is reflected in its journal. While a good deal consists of reports on activities and members, there are nonsentimental, quite practical articles on the care of pets. The grinding axe, to be sure, is evident in the many reports on the Association's work. May be a trifle beyond elementary school children, but will interest senior high students and many adults.

Our Dumb Animals. 1868. m. $3. Albert G. Governor. Massachusetts Soc. for the Prevention of Cruelty to Animals, 180 Longwood Ave., Boston, Mass. 02115. Illus. Circ: 30,500.

Aud: Ga, Sh, Jh. *Rv:* L. *Jv:* B.

Of interest to those concerned with the welfare of animals, the coverage of this publication is not limited to Massachusetts. The editorial page is devoted to animal topics and takes a positive and non-political stand on all issues that affect animals; sentimentality does not obscure the content. There are about fifteen signed articles by contributors or the staff on timely topics or current legislation, many written in a narrative style. Contains a "Young Readers" section, poetry and well-reproduced photographs; a semi-technical article appears occasionally. Because of the excellent coverage of pets, it is a useful addition to almost any high school library, and should find an enthusiastic audience in public libraries.

Pet Life. 1952. q. $1. Neal Pronek. T.F.H. Publications, Inc., 245 Cornelison Ave., Jersey City, N.J. 07302. Illus., adv. Circ: 250,000.

Aud: Ga, Sh, Jh. *Rv:* M. *Jv:* B.

A general pet magazine with little or no emphasis on technical matters, but which shows concern for the problems, queries and curiosity of pet lovers from children to adults. Practical advice on how to select and care for a variety of animals—fish, birds, dogs, cats, and some strange types not usually found around the home. In fact, some strange creatures show up from time to time in the short, fairly well illustrated articles.

Pet Shop Management. 1947. m. $7.50. Victor W. Hinze. Pet Shop Management, Inc., P.O. Box 109, Fond du Lac, Wis. 54935. Illus., adv. Circ: 10,000.

Aud: Sa, Ga. *Rv:* L. *Jv:* B.

A magazine for a specialized audience, but with considerably wider appeal than might first be suspected. A good number of dollar-making tips are noted in each issue, but there are other articles on dog ownership, ticks, hamsters, etc. *The Annual Directory of Pets and Supplies* sells for $1.

Pure Bred Dogs, American Kennel Gazette. 1889. m. $6. Amer. Kennel Club, 51 Madison Ave., New York, N.Y. 10010. Illus., adv. Circ: 11,000.

Aud: Sa. *Rv:* H. *Jv:* B.

A professional journal for those who breed dogs and take an active part in shows. Primarily consists of detailed news of Club activities and breed clubs throughout the United States. Features on obedience and field trials. Photographs and data on winners will interest younger dog lovers, but on the whole this is not for the amateur or child.

Western Horseman. 1936. m. $5. Dick Spencer. Western Horseman, Inc., 3850 N. Nevada Ave., Colorado Springs, Colo. 80901. Illus., adv. Circ: 186,000.

Aud: Ga, Sh, Jh. *Rv:* M. *Jv:* B.

A magazine devoted to the training, breeding, handling and care of stock horses, i.e., every breed from an Arabian and Palomino to a Quarter Horse and Morgan. More limited in scope than *Horse Lover's Magazine,* it still has wide general appeal. Some attention is given to racing, but the majority of short, illustrated articles cover the type of material of interest to the private horse owner. Regular features include activities at shows, rodeos and sales. Special articles and departments are geared for young

readers, and even those who have difficulty with the text will find the illustrations (and even the advertisements) fascinating. One of the best, general horse magazines for most libraries where there is a demand—and where isn't there?

Another periodical, which covers the same general area, usually with a feature story on a historical horse, is *Horseman, the Magazine of Western Riding.* (1956. m. $4. Cordovan Corp., 7709 Long Point Rd., Houston, Tex. 77018). Again the emphasis is on how-to-do-it, but there is less here for the younger reader, more for the serious amateur and professional. The same firm issues an annual, *Western Rider's Yearbook* ($1), which is well illustrated and primarily for the man or woman who knows something about horses and wishes to learn more. Young people, though, will enjoy thumbing through this one, and at the low price it is worth considering.

PHILOSOPHY

Indexes and Abstracts

British Humanities Index, Catholic Periodical and Literature Index, Chemical Abstracts, Philosopher's Index, Psychological Abstracts, Public Affairs Information Service, Social Sciences and Humanities Index. (For annotations, see Indexes and Abstracts Section.)

American Philosophical Quarterly. 1964. q. $6. (Institutions, $10). Nicholas Rescher. Dept. of Philosophy, Univ. of Pittsburgh, Pittsburgh, Pa. 15213. Circ: 1,200.

Indexed: PhilosI. *Aud:* Sa, Ac. *Rv:* H. *Jv:* B.

Emphasis is on problems under discussion in the contemporary philosophic academy, although occasional articles investigate historical philosophies systems or concepts. The tone of the paper is analytical and the language quite technical. Only for large, specialized collections.

Analysis. 1933. bi-m. $4. Peter Winch. Basil Blackwell, 49 Broad St., Oxford, Eng. Circ: 1,200.

Indexed: PhilosI. *Aud:* Sa, Ac. *Rv:* H. *Jv:* B.

A scholarly journal demanding at least an elementary knowledge of mathematical logic as well as a familiarity with the rhetoric of British analysis and the "ordinary language" schools of philosophy. Articles, by professional philosophers, are very specific, closely reasoned, and are in the nature of contributions to the solution of a problem rather than broad statements of a philosophy. One of the most valuable periodicals (along with *Mind* and the *Australasian Journal*) to students of the field of contemporary British and American empiricism.

Australasian Journal of Philosophy. 1923. 3/yr. $5. A. K. Stout. Australasian Assn. of Philosophy, Philosophy Dept. Univ. of Sydney, Sydney, N.S.W., Australia. Circ: 1,050. Reprint: Kraus.

Indexed: PhilosI. *Bk. rev:* 4-5, lengthy, signed. *Aud:* Sa, Ac. *Rv:* H. *Jv:* B.

One of the leading periodicals of contemporary academic empiricism. The dominant concerns have been with language, logic, and moral philosophy. The techniques of logic have been subordinated to those of explanation of a philosophic argument and do not impose an insuperable barrier to those with a non-technical philosophic background. Generally for the academic audience, but can be enjoyed by the layman with some background in contemporary philosophy.

British Journal for the Philosophy of Science. 1950. q. $9.50. Mary B. Hesse. Cambridge Univ. Press, 32 E. 57th St., New York, N.Y. 10022. Circ: 1,300. Reprint: Kraus.

Indexed: BritHum, PhilosI, PsyAb. *Bk. rev:* 6–8, average 1,000 words, signed, critical. *Aud:* Sa, Ac. *Rv:* H. *Jv:* B.

A highly technical journal of the philosophy and history of science. Papers, by professional philosophers and scientists, deal with such topics as the role of experiment and theory in social and physical science, causality, human and machine logic, etc. There are 10 to 12 abstracts of articles from one or two numbers of the related journals *Methodos* and *Philosophy of Science.* For the sophisticated only, since a knowledge of the physical sciences and mathematics is presupposed. Science and philosophy librarians will find the book reviews of particular value.

Diogenes; an international review of philosophy and humanistic studies. 1953. q. $6. Roger Caillois. Mario Casalini Ltd., 1519 Pine Ave., West, Montreal 25, Que. Circ: 1,500.

Indexed: PAIS. *Bk. rev:* 1–2, lengthy, signed. *Aud:* Sa, Ac. *Rv:* M. *Jv:* B.

Published by the International Council for Philosophy and Humanistic Studies, under the auspices of UNESCO. In addition to the English edition there are French, Spanish and Arabic issues. Articles are by scholars and treat philosophy, politics, geopolitics, history and economics at the theoretical level. The style is lively. Regular features include one or two lengthy book reviews, recent happenings and discoveries in the field of humanities and articles on "current events."

Ethics; an international journal of social, political and legal philosophy. 1890. q. $8. Charles Wegener & Warner Wick. Univ. of Chicago Press, 5750 Ellis Ave., Chicago, Ill. 60637. Circ: 1,700. Reprint: Johnson. Microform: Princeton.

Indexed: PhilosI, SSHum. *Bk. rev:* 3–4, 800–1,000 words, signed. *Aud:* Sa, Ac, Jc. *Rv:* M. *Jv:* B.

Concentrates on the philosophy of law and social policy. Contributors have included social scientists and psychologists as well as philosophers and jurists. Published papers have discussed the theory behind law and policy determination as well as their practice in institutions of varying scope and kinds. Of value both to the specialist and to the intelligent, well-read adult interested in social philosophy.

IPQ, International Philosophical Quarterly. 1961. q. $6.50. (Asia & Africa, $3). Fordham Univ. Press, Bronx, N.Y. 10458. Adv. Circ: 2,000.

Indexed: CathI, SSHum. *Bk. rev:* 1–3, essay, plus several short ones, signed. *Aud:* Sa, Ac. *Rv:* H. *Jv:* B.

Published by the Philosophy Department at Fordham, in collaboration with members of the Philosophy Department at the Berchamans Philosophicum in Belgium, this quarterly has an eclectic base and good credentials. The selection of international contributors shows, among other things, an increasing concern for Asian philosophy. Besides the standard long articles, there is a section called "Contemporary Currents", usually with several selections, which discusses the more recent trends in philosophy, such as critical comparison of Mao Tse Tung's philosophical writings with those of other leading Communist theorists. For college and university libraries.

The Journal of Philosophy. 1904. Fortnightly. $7.50. (Students, $6). Journal of Philosophy, Inc. 720 Philosophy Hall, Columbia Univ., New York, N.Y. 10027. Adv., index. Circ: 3,750. Microform: Canner, UM.

Indexed: PhilosI, SSHum. *Bk. rev:* Occasional, lengthy, signed. *Aud:* Sa, Ac, Jc. *Rv:* H. *Jv:* A.

The leading journal of academic philosophy published in the United States. Displays a heavy emphasis upon logic and the philosophy of science, although it is not exclusively an organ of the schools of linguistic philosophy and logical analysis. Historical articles on philosophers or systems tend to be explications of concepts in relation to current thinking. The necessity for a background in mathematics and science as well as the difficult style make this journal of use largely to the academic audience and advanced student.

The Journal of Symbolic Logic. 1936. q. $17. Alfons Borgers. Assn. for Symbolic Logic, Inc., Box 6248, Providence, R.I. 02904. Circ: 1,600.

Indexed: SSHum. *Bk. rev:* Over 50, 400 words, signed. *Aud:* Sa, Ac. *Rv:* H. *Jv:* B.

A journal of studies in formal logic and the foundations of mathematics. Papers of historical interest are presented, but only when the features of former logical systems have a high degree of relevance to the problems of contemporary logic. Because of its high degree of sophistication, its audience would be restricted to logicians and mathematicians.

Journal of the History of Ideas. See History Section.

Journal of the History of Philosophy. 1963. q. $6.50. Richard H. Popkin. Univ. of California Press, Periodicals Dept., 2223 Fulton St., Berkeley, Calif. 94720. Illus., adv. Circ: 1,000.

Indexed: PhilosI. *Bk. rev:* Various numbers, lengths. *Aud:* Sa, Ac. *Rv:* M. *Jv:* B.

Definitely not for light readers, this is a scholarly journal devoted to the history of Western philosophy. Plato, Locke,

Hegel, and F. H. Bradley, for instance, are the subjects of the four main articles in the July number. Obviously, the focus of the journal is not narrow. Occasional pieces are in foreign languages (the article on Hegel is in German), and notes and book reviews are published regularly. For university and comprehensive public libraries.

Mind; a quarterly review of psychology and philosophy. 1876. q. $4. Gilbert Ryle. Basil Blackwell, 49 Broad St., Oxford, Eng. Circ: 5,000. Microform: Princeton, UM. Reprint: Kraus.

Indexed: BritHum. *Bk. rev:* 5–6, 2000 words, signed, critical. *Aud:* Sa, Ac, Jc. *Rv:* H. *Jv:* A.

Devoted to all aspects of philosophy, although discussions of "ordinary language" and the logic of ethical discourse occupy much space at present. There are papers of historical interest as well as discussions of current philosophic problems. And despite the sub-title, it's now a purely philosophical journal. The book reviews are few, but among the best published in a magazine of this type. Long considered a basic journal for philosophers, it is geared for a professional and academic audience. Along with the American *Journal of Philosophy*, it would constitute the core of any collection in a junior college, college or university where philosophy is taught.

The Monist. 1890. q. $4 (Institutions, $6). Eugene Freeman. Open Court Publishing Co., 1307 7th St., LaSalle, Ill. 61301. Index, adv. Circ: 1,000. Reprint: Kraus.

Indexed: PhilosI. *Bk. rev:* 12–15, 100–200 words. *Aud:* Ga, Ac, Jc. *Rv:* M. *Jv:* B.

Formerly a journal of the philosophy of science, *The Monist* is now more general in character than most philosophical journals. Each issue is devoted to a general philosophical topic set by the editorial board. Papers attempt to explore the current status of the issues posed or to study critically the work of significant philosophers who have dealt with these issues. Except for those rare occasions when the subject is a highly technical one in logic or the philosophy of science, the articles can be enjoyed by the educated adult. An interesting feature is the "Author's Abstracts of Recent Books" section in which the major features of about a dozen recent books are outlined in some 100 or 200 words.

The New Scholasticism. 1926. q. $7. John A. Oesterle. Amer. Catholic Philosophical Assn., Catholic Univ. of America, Washington, D.C. 20017. Circ: 2,500. Microform: UM. Reprint: Johnson.

Indexed: CathI, PhilosI, PsyAb. *Bk. rev:* 10, 1,200 words, signed. *Aud:* Sa, Ac, Jc. *Rv:* M. *Jv:* B.

A journal of wide philosophic interest. Articles, by professional philosophers, are concerned with clarification and solution of contemporary issues as well as historical investigation of the philosophic systems of former metaphysicians. Since the articles are well-written and usually non-technical,

this periodical can be enjoyed by the educated layman as well as the college student working in the field of philosophy. Of especial interest to those concerned with the progress of Roman Catholic neo-realism.

Philosophical Books. 1960. 3/yr. $2. Prof. J. Kemp. Leicester Univ. Press, The University, Leicester, Eng. Circ: 600.

Aud: Sa, Ac, Jc. *Rv:* H. *Jv:* B.

A review medium for current books in philosophy. The reviewers are professionals, which assures competence to judge, but also a necessary bias toward the academy in deciding what is a "philosophical" book. All articles are signed and truly critical, i.e., they investigate the comment upon a book's argument carefully and in detail. The average length of a review is from 750 to 1,500 words and each issue reviews more than a dozen recently published works. A welcome addition to the field of philosophic bibliography. For the professional philosopher and bibliographer who must keep abreast of current publication in the field.

Philosophical Quarterly. 1950. q. $4. G. P. Henderson & Roland Hall. Queen's College, Dundee, Scotland. Index, adv. Circ: 1,300. Microform: UM. Reprint: AMS.

Indexed: BritHum, PhilosI. *Bk. rev:* 16–20, 900 words, signed. *Aud:* Sa, Ac. *Rv:* H. *Jv:* B.

A scholarly journal demanding a knowledge of the language of modern philosophy. Although some papers are historical and expository, the emphasis is upon progress toward the solution of problems which interest professional philosophers. While its difficulty seems to restrict this journal's use to an academic or professional readership, the review section will be of interest to librarians and bibliographers because of its extent and quality.

Philosophical Review. 1892. q. $3. (Institutions, $6). 218 Golden Smith Hall, Cornell Univ., Ithaca, N.Y. 14850. Index, adv. Circ: 3,000. Microform: UM. Reprint: AMS.

Indexed: PhilosI. *Bk. rev:* 10–12, 1,200 words, signed. *Aud:* Sa, Ac, Jc. *Rv:* H. *Jv:* B.

A professional periodical which publishes papers primarily directed towards problems of interest to the contemporary philosophical academy. While not oriented towards the discussion of modern logical techniques, some knowledge of mathematical logic is necessary to the reader who would make adequate use of this journal. Occasional papers of an historical nature are presented. For the academic and professional audience. Librarians and bibliographers will find the number, length and quality of the reviews and comments on new books in the "Discussion" sections of great value.

Philosophical Studies. 1950. 6/yr. (Oct.–June). $3. Wilfred Sellars & Herbert Feigl. Univ. of Minnesota Press, 2037 University Ave., S.E., Minneapolis, Minn. 55455. Circ: 2,000. Microform: UM. Reprint: Johnson, AMS.

Indexed: CathI, PhilosI. *Aud:* Sa, Ac. *Rv:* M. *Jv:* B.

Papers in this journal tend to be shorter than those in most other periodicals devoted to academic philosophy. They are usually addressed to the solution of a specific, limited, problem. Many are in the form of statement and counter-statement—short installments in the philosophic dialogue centered about a specific issue. Since the papers presuppose a detailed knowledge of and interest in the techniques of mathematical logic, the journal's greatest value is to the professional and academic audience.

Philosophy. 1931. q. Membership (Non-members, $6). H. B. Acton. Macmillan (Journals) Ltd., Brunel Rd., Basingstoke, Hants., Eng. Circ: 2,800. Reprint: Johnson, AMS.

Indexed: BritHum, PhilosI, PsyAb. *Bk. rev:* 8–12, 1000 words, signed. *Aud:* Ga, Sa, Ac, Jc. *Rv:* M. *Jv:* A.

One of the few professional philosophy journals which has appeal to the educated layman. Because it is not committed to the viewpoint of any special school, it has remained free from much of the technical jargon which plagues many more specialist publications. Most of the articles are concerned with problems of philosophical theory, but some deal with philosophy from a historical standpoint. In addition to the regular book reviews, there are occasional lengthy review articles. A magazine of professional caliber, written by professional philosophers, but of interest to the educated layman as well as the student of philosophy. Should be found in all medium to large public libraries and most academic collections.

Proceedings of the American Philosophical Society. 1838. bi-m. $5. George W. Corner. Amer. Philosophical Soc., 104 S. 5th St., Philadelphia, Pa. 19106. Circ: 1,200. Microform: Canner, UM. Reprint: Kraus.

Indexed: BioAb, ChemAb. *Aud:* Sa, Ac, Jc. *Rv:* H. *Jv:* V.

Despite the title and sponsor, this comes closer to being a general interest magazine than a specialist's journal. Articles cover every aspect of philosophy, but always in its widest context. Hence, there will be contributions ranging from a discussion of current scientific ethical problems to social history. And while the writing is scholarly, it is written with a touch of style familiar to readers of such publications as *Scientific American* and *The American Scholar.* The magazine deserves a much wider audience, and should be found in more stimulating general reading collections in all academic libraries and large public library collections. The American Philosophical Society also publishes *Transactions of the American Philosophical Society* (9/yr. $6.), which follows the same general approach, yet tends to limit itself to a single monograph of interest. Sometimes the subjects are a bit esoteric, but there are enough of wider appeal that it, too, deserves attention by the same libraries who would consider the *Proceedings.*

Ratio. 1958. semi-ann. $3.90. Stephan Koerner. Basil Blackwell, 49 Broad St., Oxford, Eng. Circ: 500.

Indexed: BritHum, PhilosI. *Bk. rev:* 1–2, 2,000–5,000 words, signed. *Aud:* Sa, Ac. *Rv:* M. *Jv:* B.

A general British philosophical review of interest both to the student and teacher and the educated adult. Occasional articles will demand a knowledge of modern logic. Produces both a German and an English edition. Only for larger, specialized collections.

Review of Metaphysics. 1947. q. $6. (Students, $4; institutions, $7). Richard J. Bernstein. Philosophical Education Soc., Inc., 214 Lyman Beecher Hall, Haverford College, Haverford, Pa. 19041. Circ: 3,400. Microform: UM. Reprint: AMS.

Indexed: PhilosI. *Bk. rev:* 50–75, 160 words, signed. *Aud:* Sa, Ac. *Rv:* H. *Jv:* B.

Its title notwithstanding, this eclectic journal of philosophy does not require its contributors to approve of a particular metaphysical school. The only unifying bond between articles is philosophic relevance and technical competence. While there are occasional historical essays, most articles investigate a topic of current concern to contemporary philosophers. The papers submitted are quite technical, but there is not the obsession with logic, the foundations of mathematics and the philosophy of science which is so common in English-language journals of similar professional caliber. Of great interest to students, librarians and bibliographers will be the "Books Received—Summary and Comments" section, which contains short critical reviews of new books (comments prepared by members of the staff), and the section "Current Periodical Articles—Philosophical Periodicals," which abstracts some 60 to 75 journal articles. For the professional audience.

Revue Philosophique de Louvain. 1894. q. $8.20. Albert Dondeyne. Institut Superior de Philosophie Editions, Kardinal Mercierplein 2, Louvain, Belgium. Circ: 1,800.

Indexed: CathI, PhilosI. *Bk. rev:* 24, 400 words, signed. *Aud:* Sa, Ac. *Rv:* M. *Jv:* A.

A periodical largely of interest to followers of Roman Catholic neo-realism. Presents papers in French by professional philosophers concerning questions of epistemology, ontology, atheism, ethics, and other questions of philosophical import. Of especial interest to the student are the many historical essays concerned with classical and modern philosophers and the great Church metaphysicians. Included in the subscription price is the quarterly supplement, *Répertoire Bibliographique de la Philosophie,* a very valuable bibliography of publications in philosophy and philosophical psychology in all Western languages. The bibliography may be subscribed to separately at $5 per year. The *Revue* is of value mainly to students of philosophy, while the librarian and bibliographer will find the supplementary bibliography of great reference value.

Soviet Studies in Philosophy; a journal of translations from Soviet scholarly sources. 1962. q. $40. Intl. Arts & Science Press, 108 Grand St., White Plains, N.Y. 10601. Index.

Aud: Sa, Ac. *Rv:* H. *Jv:* B.

Translations in full from four Soviet journals, together with occasional entries from other Soviet works. Tends to be broken down into four areas: philosophy of science, social philosophy, history of philosophy and contemporary criticism. The translations are adequate, and the whole is a necessary work for any serious student of philosophy who does not have a ready command of Russian.

Synthese. 1936. q. $13.50. Ed bd. Reidel Publishing Co., P.O. Box 17, Dordrecht, Netherlands. Circ: 1,500.

Indexed: PhilosI. *Bk. rev:* 3–5, 1,500 words, signed. *Aud:* Sa, Ac. *Rv:* H. *Jv:* B.

A very sophisticated journal of philosophy and the logic of science. *Synthese* concerns itself almost exclusively with logic, truth and meaning, linguistic usage and language games. Advanced knowledge of science and mathematics is presupposed. For the professional philosopher, scientist, and mathematician.

PHOTOGRAPHY

Indexes and Abstracts

Applied Science and Technology Index, Art Index, British Technology Index, Chemical Abstracts, Engineering Index, Photographic Abstracts, Readers' Guide to Periodical Literature. (For annotations, see Indexes and Abstracts Section.)

Aperture. 1952. q. $10. Minor White. Aperture, Inc., 168 E. 91st St., New York, N.Y. 10028. Illus. Circ: 3,000. Microform: UM.

Indexed: ArtI. *Bk. rev:* Notes and longer reviews. *Aud:* Sa, Ac, Jc, Sh. *Rv:* H. *Jv:* A.

The leading photography journal for the student of photography as an art. Serious examples of artistic photography are accompanied by essays, comments, poetry, or nothing, as suits the compiler. Format varies from a complete issue devoted to the works, chronology and bibliography of one photographer (e.g., "Paul Caponigro: An Aperture Monograph." Vol. 13, No. 1, 1967) to a rare issue which is all text and includes reviews of books, exhibits and comments. Other issues combine these facets. The photographic works presented range from avant-garde to classical. Articles avoid detailed technical processes and stress the artistic merits of photography. The reproductions usually comprise some 50 or more black and white photos per issue. This, along with *Camera,* represents one of the few photographic magazines that treat the subject as an art form, and should be found in all academic libraries and many public and school collections.

British Journal of Photography. 1854. w. $13. Geoffrey Crawley. Henry Greenwood, 24 Wellington St., London W.C.2. Illus., adv., diag. Circ: 10,380.

Indexed: ChemAb, PhotoAb. *Bk. rev:* Notes and abstracts. *Aud:* Sa, Ac, Jc. *Rv:* M. *Jv:* B.

This British weekly, published on good paper, is intended for all concerned with photography or any of its applications, but is primarily an organ for the professionals. It is international in scope, useful in American libraries. Articles on the press, industrial, medical, scientific, and industrial cinematographic fields appear regularly, as well as news of interest to photographers. There are good equipment and material test reports. A portfolio of a photographer's work is a usual feature (e.g., "My Best Six by Maurice Rowe," by Leslie Sansom, Nov. 3, 1967). The "Cine Digest" gives up-to-date reports on current new books, periodicals and photographic exhibits. There are regular reports from Japan and West Germany. Because of its scope and frequency it is an excellent basic photography journal for larger collections.

Camera. 1922. m. $14. Allen Porter. C. J. Bucher Ltd., Lucerne, Switzerland. Illus., index, adv. Circ: 25,000. Microform: UM.

Indexed: ArtI, ChemAb. *Aud:* Ga, Ac, Jc, Sh. *Rv:* M. *Jv:* V.

One of the best photographic journals published, this is too little known in American libraries. It long ago gained fame among professional photographers and those who study photography as a serious art form. International in scope, it is published in English, French, and German. Contains essays on individual photographers with a liberal sampling of their work. Nudes, landscapes, abstracts, local color shots in excellent glossy reproduction, both color and black and white. Articles of technical interest, though not in the how-to category. "Photo News in Brief" section contains news of latest equipment with current exhibition notices. As each issue covers either a particular school of photography or is an essay on a given photographer or school of photographers, a run of the magazine constitutes an excellent basic history of photography. For a well-balanced photography collection in any type of library, this should be included along with one or two of the more popular do-it-yourself periodicals. Wherever possible, should be side by side with *Aperture.*

Camera 35. 1957. bi-m. $4. Jim Hughes. U.S. Camera Publishing Co., 9 E. 40th St., New York, N.Y. 10016. Illus., adv. Circ: 75,000.

Aud: Ga. *Rv:* M. *Jv:* B.

As the title indicates, this is devoted exclusively to articles (about 10 per issue) on the 35mm camera. Material is prepared by experts and ranges from how-to-do-it articles to more sophisticated reports on photographers and their work. Particularly useful for the accurate, unbiased test reports of cameras and lenses. Many good to excellent black and white photographs and usually at least eight pages of color shots. About one-third advertising. While more specialized than other general magazines such as *Modern Photography* or *Popular Photography,* it is of the same type. Probably a third or fourth choice for smaller collections in public libraries, but of limited use for academic libraries.

Industrial and Commercial Photographer. 1961. m. $5.50. G. H. Wilkinson. Distinctive Pubns., 7 Grape St., London W.C.2. Illus., adv.

Bk. rev: 2, 500–600 words. *Aud:* Sa, Ac. *Rv:* M. *Jv:* B.

The English equivalent of the American professional photography magazine, this deals primarily with the work of individual photographers and the ins and outs of commercial studios. May be useful for advanced students in that there are test reports of new equipment, rather extensive advertisements (about one-half the issue) and an excellent quarterly graphic arts supplement.

Industrial Photography; the magazine that advances technical progress. 1952. m. $6. Arthur H. Rosien. United Business Pubns., Inc., 200 Madison Ave., New York, N.Y. 10016. Illus., adv. Circ: 33,400.

Indexed: ASTI. *Aud:* Sa, Ac. *Rv:* H. *Jv:* B.

Not meant for the amateur, controlled circulation puts this periodical into the hands of working photographers, where they find articles which stress photography as "a major force in explaining man to man." Some articles are fully documented studies while others are primarily staff reports. Each issue usually focuses on a particular topic and is fully illustrated. A valuable reference issue in December lists photographic books, and provides a categorized and annotated guide to bulletins designed to give readers information about photographic equipment, material and services. Useful in college collections where there is serious interest in technical photography.

Infinity. 1952. m. $7.50. Charles Reynolds. Amer. Soc. of Magazine Photographers, Inc., 60 E. 42nd St., New York, N.Y. 10017. Illus., index, adv. Circ: 7,000.

Bk. rev: 1–5, 500 words, signed. *Aud:* Sa, Ac. *Rv:* H. *Jv:* B.

A professional magazine for not only magazine photographers, but for anyone who deals with photography in advertising and art. There are usually two to four articles per issue, which report on technical developments and, more important for the interested layman, the work of individual photographers. The latter feature may highlight either a well-known personality or a newcomer. The black and white and 20 or so color photographs are usually outstanding. One of the basic trade magazines in this area, and of value to the serious photography student. Should be found in larger academic and public library collections.

The Journal of Photographic Science. 1953. bi-m. Membership (Non-members, $10.50). R. J. Cox. Royal Photographic Soc. of Great Britain, 16 Prince's Gate, London S.W.7. Illus., index, adv.

Indexed: BritTech, ChemAb, PhotoAb. *Bk. rev:* Occasional. *Aud:* Sa, Ac. *Rv:* H. *Jv:* B.

The publication of the Royal Photographic Society stresses scientific and technical photography. Scholarly papers read at the Society's meetings as well as important contributions by others are issued. Book reviews, news and reports of meetings, new equipment, and correspondence are included on an irregular basis. Topics presented range from "The Stability of Photographic Processes for Absolute Measurement of Radiation" to "The Washing Power of Water." Not for the general public but valuable to the student of photography or the chemist interested in photographic applications.

Leica Photography. 1932. 3/yr. Free to qualified personnel; others $1. Kenneth Poli. E. Leitz, Inc., 468 Park Ave. S., New York, N.Y. 10016. Illus., adv. Circ: 55,000.

Bk. rev: Occasional. *Aud:* Ga, Sh. *Rv:* M. *Jv:* B.

This is typical of a number of magazines issued for a specific type of camera. It is, however, vastly superior to many of its younger cousins. Included are technical articles, practical articles, and inspirational articles (e.g., "Saturday Afternoon Safari"). Picture spreads by professionals or proficient amateurs are attractively presented on good paper. While this periodical is especially useful for owners of Leica cameras, it has application for others interested in photography as well. Not a first purchase but a good supplement.

Modern Photography. 1937. m. $6. Julia Scully. Modern Photography, 2160 Patterson St., Cincinnati, Ohio 45214. Illus., adv. Circ: 265,000.

Indexed: ASTI, ChemAb, RG. *Bk. rev:* 3–6, 200–500 words. *Aud:* Ga, Ac, Jc, Sh, Jh. *Rv:* M. *Jv:* A.

A substantial staff of informed writers supply the knowledgeable amateur and the professional photographer with the latest picture taking ideas and technical reports. New ideas on composition and techniques are presented through the analysis of the work of top flight photographers. While this periodical stresses the technical aspects of photography, occasional articles by amateurs cover other matters (e.g., "Help Save Our Heritage," by Steward L. Udall). Critical book reviews are a regular feature, as is a list of about 50 booklets which are available from the publisher. The annual guide to the "Top 45 Cameras" furnishes technical data and a critical essay of about 350 words on each camera. Included are the results of various tests run on these cameras by the magazine. Somewhat more advanced than *Popular Photography,* and less specialized than *U.S. Camera.* Of the three for general public and school collections, this would be second to *Popular Photography* and a bit ahead of *U.S. Camera.* In academic libraries it is a first choice. Where photography is meaningful, all types of libraries will subscribe to the trio, and then, hopefully, will go on to the more specialized works.

Officiel de la Photographie et du Cinema. 1952. m. Charles Vandamme, 22 rue Paul Valery, Paris (16e), France. Illus., index, adv. Circ: 150,000.

Bk. rev: 5–6, 250 words, signed. *Aud:* Ga, Ac. *Rv:* M. *Jv:* B.

Due to its emphasis upon photography as an art as well as its technical aspects, this French-language magazine is of special interest to photographers and enthusiasts of photography. Regular features include the calendar of events of activities of the international photographic festivals of photo-clubs and Cine-photo-clubs. News roundups relate the latest technical developments in cameras and equipment. Articles deal especially with coverage of the two professional societies, "Federation francaise de la Photographie" and "Federation Nationale des Societies Photographiques de France." Film is only dealt with briefly in each issue by a single article about a particular film. Particularly pleasing are the striking, double-page photographic spreads of photos selected for the annual international contest. Sometimes there is a portfolio of photos with accompanying poems. A basic international journal, although somewhat too specialized, except for large public and academic libraries.

P.S.A. Journal. 1935. m. Membership (Libraries, $5). Robert L. McIntyre. Photographic Soc. of America, 4707-F N. Paulina St., Chicago, Ill. 60640. Illus., adv. Microform: UM.

Indexed: ChemAb. *Bk. rev:* 1–3, 100–800 words, signed. *Aud:* Sa, Ac. *Rv:* M. *Jv:* B.

A technical journal for the professional. Articles feature new products and methods and are useful to anyone with a strong interest in photography. Included for members are lists of exhibits and competitions, calendars of events, and society news. A correspondence column, "The Diffuser," encourages discussion. A May "Who's Who" issue identifies personalities in the various areas of photography. Only for large collections.

Photo-Cine-Revue. 1888. m. $3.60. Vincent Robert. Editions de Francia, 118 rue d'Assas, Paris (6e), France. Illus., index, adv. Circ: 25,000.

Indexed: ChemAb. *Bk. rev:* Occasional, short. *Aud:* Sa, Ac. *Rv:* M. *Jv:* B.

Directed to much the same audience as *Officiel de la Photographie et Du Cinema,* this emphasizes the technical aspects of photography. Regular features include the "International Photo Revue," news of photo clubs and societies, with emphasis upon the Societé Francaise de Photographie (including a calendar of events), and the latest photographic equipment (cameras, projectors, etc.). Articles often pertain to the audio-visual, and the photographic reportage of events. There are instructional articles of interest to the amateur film-maker-photographer. A substantial portion is devoted to photographs of high artistic quality accompanied by text and criticism. Only for large photographic collections.

Photographic Business and Product News. 1964. m. $4. R. Maschke. Photographic Product News, Inc., 41 E. 28th St., New York, N.Y. 10016. Illus., adv. Circ: 32,000.

Bk. rev: 1–2, 150–200 words, signed. *Aud:* Sa. *Rv:* M. *Jv:* B.

Primarily for the professional commercial, or journalism, photographer, this features methods of improving business as much as pictures. Of some value to the laymen because of the objective analysis of new equipment. Would be equally valuable in business and photographic collections. Only for large public libraries.

Photographic Science and Engineering. 1957. bi-m. Membership (Non-members, $15). T. Howard James. Soc. of Photographic Scientists & Engineers, 1330 Massachusetts Ave., N.W., Washington, D.C. 20005. Illus. Circ: 3,000.

Indexed: EngI, PhotoAb. *Bk. rev:* 2, 200 words, signed. *Aud:* Sa, Ac. *Rv:* H. *Jv:* B.

Somewhat the American equivalent of the British *Journal of Photographic Science.* Usually features six to eight articles of a relatively high technical nature on the application of photography to science and engineering. In addition to the good to fine photographic illustrations, there are regular departments which cover new products, meetings, and biographies and obituaries. Probably the best magazine of its type in the United States, and required for all larger collections, or where there is a specific interest in the subject. The Society also issues *Image Technology* (formerly *SPSE News*), a bimonthly newsletter, and *Abstracts of Photographic Science and Engineering.*

Popular Photography. 1937. m. $6. John Durniak. Ziff-Davis Publishing Co., 1 Park Ave., New York, N.Y. 10016. Subscriptions to: Popular Photography, Circulation Dept., Portland Pl., Boulder, Colo. 80311. Illus., adv. Circ: 430,000. Microform: UM.

Indexed: ChemAb, RG. *Bk. rev:* Notes. *Aud:* Ga, Sh, Jh. *Rv:* M. *Jv:* V.

Designed as a general interest magazine for anyone with a camera who wants to take better pictures, *Popular Photography* claims it is "the most widely read photographic magazine." Articles cover every phase of photography and include many practical hints (e.g., "Camera Overboard and What to do Next" by Norman Goldbert). News of interest to camera bugs include such interesting features as the camera coverage of Luci Johnson Nugent's wedding as well as general coverage of the world of photography. The examples of photography by outstanding photographers, including eight pages in full color, are an inspiration. The hobbyist who takes photography seriously will find it indispensable, and it is probably the best general photographic magazine for school and public libraries, as well as the non-technical collections in academic libraries.

Professional Photographer. 1907. m. $5. Frederick Quellmalz. Professional Photographers of America, Inc., 1090 Executive Way, Oak Leaf Commons, Des Plaines, Ill. 60018. Illus., index, adv. Circ: 20,000.

Bk. rev: 2–3, 50–75 words. *Aud:* Sa. *Rv:* M. *Jv:* B.

This claims to be "the oldest professional photographic publication in the Western Hemisphere." Illustrated articles for the free lance or commercial photographer are geared to help him "become a better businessman, a better technician." About half the contents is technical, the other tips on the trade. Should also have appeal for the serious amateur. Somewhat similar to *Photographic Business,* and only for large public libraries.

U.S. Camera and Travel Magazine. 1938. m. $5. Willard N. Clark. U.S. Camera Publishing Corp., 9 E. 40th St., New York, N.Y. 10016. Subscriptions to: P.O. Box 562, Des Moines, Iowa 50302. Illus., adv. Circ: 200,000.

Indexed: RG. *Bk. rev:* 4–6, short, 1 long. *Aud:* Ga, Ac, Jc, Sh. *Rv:* M. *Jv:* A.

This differs from the two other general photography magazines in that the emphasis is on photographic techniques as they apply to travel, outdoor photography and the esthetic flavor of places, and people. The many how-to-do-it pieces are written by experts, and amateur photographers can understand and profit from the well-illustrated articles. Reports on new products are included and cover some of the less sophisticated models as well as professional equipment. Home movies, sound photography and a section devoted to reader's photos are interesting features. Those devoted to travel are superficial. Jill Hayes regularly contributes a book review, which has strong photographic content. Shorter reviews of books offered for sale by *U.S. Camera* as well as a list of others they carry is a regular feature. Such articles as "What's New in Experimental Films" by Camille J. Cook (March, 1967) indicate a liberal view toward the acceptance of new and pioneering efforts in the field of photography. A good general photography magazine for most libraries.

PHYSICS

Indexes and Abstracts

Applied Science and Technology Index, Biological Abstracts, British Technology Index, Chemical Abstracts, Engineering Index, Mathematical Reviews, Psychological Abstracts, Readers' Guide to Periodical Literature, Science Abstracts, Science Citation Index. (For annotations, see Indexes and Abstracts Section.)

In the main, the journals covered in this section are authoritative research publications sponsored by some outstanding scientific societies; papers included therein have generally been subjected to review by specialists prior to publication and represent high-quality studies. Titles have been limited largely to U.S. and English publications representing general physics journals; a few journals emphasizing applications of physical principles; some foreign titles of historical prominence; and selected periodicals applicable to physics educators, students, and interested laymen. In the case of specialized journals, titles were chosen that represent interdisciplinary publications having applicability to many sciences; specialized journals concerned solely with

the subfields of physics (e.g., nuclear physics) have, of necessity, been excluded. Of course the selection represents a mere fragment of the titles commonly found in academic libraries supporting research interests. Most academic libraries would probably subscribe to many of the prestigious publications of the American Institute of Physics, and to many excellent foreign journals such as *Journal of the Physical Society of Japan, Helvetica Physica Acta, Nuovo Cimento, Annales de Physique, Progress of Theoretical Physics, Zeitschrift für Physik,* as well as to a wide variety of specialized journals, including *Nuclear Physics, Journal of the Physics and Chemistry of Solids,* and *Physics of Fluids,* to name but a few.

Acoustical Society of America. Journal. 1929. m. $27. R. B. Lindsay. Amer. Inst. of Physics, 335 E. 45th St., New York, N.Y. 10017. Illus., index. adv. Circ: 7,000. Microform: UM.

Indexed: BioAb, ChemAb, MathR, PsyAb, SciAb, SCI. *Bk. rev:* 1–2, 300–500 words, signed. *Aud:* Sa, Ac. *Rv:* H. *Jv:* B.

Concerned with all branches of acoustics, this reports on a broad number of topics. Research papers cover such areas as architectural, engineering, and underwater acoustics; music and musical instruments; physiological and psychological acoustics; speech communication; noise and control, and shock and vibration. Studies are both theoretical and experimental and include short "Letters to the Editor," along with some informal technical notes and research briefs. A very complete classified bibliography of current literature on acoustics appears regularly, as do reviews of important U.S. patents of recent issue. Abstracts of papers presented at general meetings of the Society are also published, as well as news of the Society, meetings, and recent developments in the field.

Advances in Physics. 1952. bi-m. $39.20. B. R. Coles. Taylor & Francis, Ltd., Red Lion Court, Fleet St., London E.C.4. Illus.

Indexed: BritTech, ChemAb, EngI, MathR, SciAb, SCI. *Aud:* Sa, Ac. *Rv:* H. *Jv:* B.

The journal aims at long, critical, review articles by experts for experts in areas of current interest in physics. Both theoretical and experimental studies are represented. The 2–3 papers in each issue are usually of monograph length (to nearly 100 pages). An excellent review journal for the researcher. (Included with a subscription to *Philosophical Magazine.*)

American Journal of Physics. 1933. m. $12.50. F. I. Boley. Amer. Inst. of Physics, 335 E. 45th St., New York, N.Y. 10017. Illus., index, adv. Circ: 12,850. Microform: UM.

Indexed: ASTI, ChemAb, EngI, MathR, SciAb, SCI. *Bk. rev:* 9–10, 350–600 words, signed. *Aud:* Sa, Ac, Jc, Ht. *Rv:* H. *Jv:* B.

Published by the American Association of Physics Teachers under the aegis of the AIP, and "devoted to the instructional and cultural aspects of physical science," this fine journal is directed toward physics teachers and students primarily at the college or university level. The entire field of physics and allied sciences are represented; papers and shorter notes vary from the topical and instructional, to those emphasizing the historical and philosophical aspects of the discipline. Brief communications are often concerned with laboratory techniques, new apparatus, instructional uses of such equipment as computers, and the like. Abstracts are also given of proceedings of meetings of the Association, as well as the usual news announcements and personalia. Book reviews are excellent. The diversity and high quality of the material will be of interest to a wide variety of libraries and nonspecialists.

American Physical Society. Bulletin. 1956. m. $12. W. W. Havens, Jr. Amer. Inst. of Physics, 335 E. 45th St., New York, N.Y. 10017. Circ: 25,000. Microform: UM.

Indexed: BioAb, ChemAb, SciAb. *Aud:* Sa, Ac. *Rv:* H. *Jv:* B.

The *Bulletin* consists of abstracts of papers presented at various meetings of the organization or other special symposia of interest; programs or announcements of forthcoming meetings; and a few notices. In addition to its usefulness for news of coming events, the publication has reference value for research libraries, since many of the reports given at meetings are never published elsewhere in the literature.

Annalen der Physik. 1790. irreg. 3v./yr. $25.56. G. Richter & W. Walcher. Johann Ambrosius Barth Verlag, Salomonstr. 18, Leipzig 701, Germany. Illus., index. Circ: 2,100. Microform: Mc. Reprint: Johnson.

Indexed: ChemAb, EngI, MathR, SciAb, SCI. *Aud:* Sa, Ac. *Rv:* H. *Jv:* B.

Some of the most important contributions in science, such as Einstein's early papers, first appeared in this journal, which is one of the oldest physics periodicals still in print. Both theoretical and applied studies are included. International in scope, articles frequently appear in English.

Annals of Physics. 1957. m; semi-m. (Feb., June, Oct.). $21/v. P. M. Morse. Academic Press, Inc., 111 Fifth Ave., New York, N.Y. 10003. Illus., index.

Indexed: ChemAb, EngI, MathR, SciAb, SCI. *Aud:* Sa, Ac. *Rv:* H. *Jv:* B.

A fundamental source for research libraries, this publishes papers "describing original work in all areas of basic physics." Contributions are largely in mathematical and theoretical physics, including some nuclear studies.

Applied Optics. 1962. m. $24. J. N. Howard. Amer. Inst. of Physics, 335 E. 45th St., New York, N.Y. 10017. Illus., index, adv. Circ: 6,500.

Indexed: EngI, SciAb, SCI. *Bk. rev:* 7, 250 words, signed. *Aud:* Sa, Ac. *Rv:* H. *Jv:* B.

Sponsored by the Optical Society of America, the journal is concerned with research papers and short "Letters to the Editor" on the applications of known facts, principles or methods of optics. (More fundamental studies are reported in the Society's other publication, *Journal of the Optical Society.*) All branches of applied optics are covered, as well as other fields related to optics or those employing optical techniques. Frequently, papers may center around one specific subject; some review, historical, or tutorial papers are also published. Featured regularly are detailed reports of meetings; news of the profession; research briefs, and abstracts of pertinent patents.

Bell System Technical Journal. 1922. 10/yr. $7. G. E. Schindler. Amer. Telephone and Telegraph Co., 195 Broadway, New York, N.Y. 10007. Illus., index.

Indexed: ASTI, ChemAb, EngI, MathR, PsyAb, SciAb, SCI. *Aud:* Sa, Ac. *Rv:* H. *Jv:* B.

Although a large bulk of the research papers reported in this journal fall under the realm of electrical engineering, studies include any of the sciences and technologies related to electrical communication, such as applied physics, mathematics, the computing sciences, and the like. Contributors are all from the vast complex of the Bell System, and papers represent the research and engineering efforts explored in their laboratories and concerned with their products and systems. Studies can be very comprehensive, in-depth reports (up to 50 pages in length), and represent high-quality investigations. For physics collections, the publication represents an excellent journal for studies in applications of physical principles.

The Bell System publishes another periodical, *Bell Laboratories Record,* described elsewhere in this book, which reviews, in less specialized language, the current research activities and technological advances in the Bell Laboratories.

British Journal of Applied Physics. 1950. m. $38.40. F. C. Frank. Inst. of Physics and the Physical Soc., 47 Belgrave Square, London S.W.1. Illus., index, adv. Circ: 4,000. Microform: UM.

Indexed: BritTech, ChemAb, EngI, SciAb, SCI. *Bk. rev:* 5–6, 250–500 words, signed. *Aud:* Sa, Ac. *Rv:* H. *Jv:* B.

With its new series (vol. 1, 1968+) the periodical became Part D of the *Journal of Physics* (See annotation, this section). The emphasis in this research journal is on "original work describing applications of basic physical principles." Papers and shorter notes include studies on: properties of materials; applied solid state physics; neutron transport; discharge physics; wave propagation; applications of magnetohydrodynamics. Four to five excellent review articles also appear annually, along with occasional announcements and news.

Canadian Journal of Physics. 1929. semi-m. $12. L. G. Elliott. National Research Council of Canada, Ottawa 7, Ont. Illus., index. Circ: 2,500.

Indexed: BioAb, ChemAb, EngI, MathR, SciAb, SCI. *Aud:* Ac, Sa. *Rv:* H. *Jv:* B.

The publication is a good, general physics journal, and the research papers and short notes represent studies in the various branches of the science. Theoretical and experimental investigations include such fields as atomic and molecular phenomena, physics of the solid state, nuclear physics, and the like. Contributions, largely from Canadian laboratories, may appear both in English and French.

Contemporary Physics; a review of physics and associated technologies. 1959. m. $18.40. G. Noakes. Taylor & Francis, Red Lion Court, Fleet St., London E.C.4. Illus., index, adv. Circ: 2,000.

Indexed: SciAb, SCI. *Bk. rev:* 20, 200 words, signed. *Aud:* Sh, Jc, Ac, Sa. *Rv:* H. *Jv:* B.

A journal that can be read by both nonspecialists and students, ranging from advanced senior high to undergraduates. Interpretive, survey articles by distinguished physicists are written in relatively simple language and encompass, as widely as possible, the entire field of physics. Its scope is not only to provide invited papers, which review highly advanced specialties, but also to supply papers emphasizing basic physical principles underlying new technologies. From time to time some original research papers may also be published. Some issues contain excellent, essay-type book reviews which also serve as tutorials in particular fields. One would hope that this periodical would find its way into many more small collections, particularly junior colleges and even sophisticated high school libraries.

Faraday Society. Transactions and Discussions. See Chemistry Section.

Franklin Institute. Journal. See Science-General Section.

IBM Journal of Research and Development. See Science-General Section.

Journal of Applied Physics. 1931. m. $25. F. E. Myers. Amer. Inst. of Physics, 335 E. 45th St., New York, N.Y. 10017. Illus., index, adv. Circ: 10,000. Microform: UM. Reprint: Johnson.

Indexed: ASTI, ChemAb, EngI, MathR, SciAb, SCI. *Aud:* Sa, Ac. *Rv:* H. *Jv:* B.

"Devoted to general physics and its applications to other sciences, to engineering, and to industry," this important journal publishes research papers and short communications on both new results in experimental or theoretical physics related to applied physics, and on new applications to other scientific disciplines. A special issue published each March covers the proceedings of the Magnetism Conference, sponsored by the AIP. Although it includes brief communications on research of limited scope, preliminary reports of work in urgent need of publication are issued in its sister journal, *Applied Physics Letters* ($15/yr.). Both periodicals are major publications necessary in most academic collections.

Journal of Chemical Physics. 1931. semi-m. $45. J. W. Stout. Amer. Inst. of Physics, 335 E. 45th St., New York, N.Y. 10017. Illus., index. Circ: 6,200. Microform: UM.

Indexed: BioAb, ChemAb, EngI, MathR, SciAb, SCI. *Aud:* Sa, Ac. *Rv:* H. *Jv:* B.

The purpose of this distinguished research publication is "to bridge a gap between journals of physics and journals of chemistry," since "a large and active group is engaged in research which is as much the one as the other." Full-length articles, preliminary communications, and notes of small scope represent studies on spectroscopy, quantum mechanics, thermodynamics, etc.

Journal of Computational Physics. 1966. q. $25. Ed bd. Academic Press, Inc., 111 Fifth Ave., New York, N.Y. 10003. Illus., index.

Aud: Sa, Ac. *Rv:* H. *Jv:* B.

Research articles and short 2-page notes are concerned with techniques "developed in the solution of data handling problems and mathematical equations, both arising in the description of physical phenomena." Papers deal with applications to all of the physical sciences, and studies represent both mathematical and computer techniques.

Journal of Mathematical Physics. 1960. m. $30. E. W. Montroll. Amer. Inst. of Physics, 335 E. 45th St., New York, N.Y. 10017. Illus., index. Circ: 2,900. Microform: UM.

Indexed: MathR, SciAb, SCI. *Aud:* Sa, Ac. *Rv:* H. *Jv:* B.

Interdisciplinary in character, the journal "forms a medium of publication of highly mathematical physics articles and papers on branches of mathematics that are currently or potentially useful for the development of theoretical physics."

Journal of Physical Chemistry. See Chemistry Section.

Journal of Physics. 1968. $194.40. Inst. of Physics and The Physical Soc., 1 Lowther Gardens, Prince Consort Rd., London S.W.7. Illus., index, adv.

Indexed: ASTI, BioAb, BritTech, ChemAb, EngI, SciAb, SCI. *Aud:* Sa, Ac. *Rv:* H. *Jv:* B.

Journal of Physics is the generic title now given to the major research publications of the Institute of Physics and The Physical Society, London. Divided into five parts (Series 2, vol. 1, 1968+), the journal comprises the following publications, each of which may be purchased separately. (See individual titles for annotations.) Section A, *Physical Society. Proceedings (General);* Section B, *Physical Society. Proceedings (Atomic and Molecular Physics);* Section C, *Physical Society. Proceedings (Solid State Physics);* Section D, *British Journal of Applied Physics;* Section E, *Journal of Scientific Instruments.*

Journal of Scientific Instruments. 1922. m. $28.80. Ed bd. Inst. of Physics and The Physical Soc., 1 Lowther Gardens, Prince Consort Rd., London S.W.7. Illus., index, adv. Circ: 5,300. Microform: UM.

Indexed: ASTI, BioAb, BritTech, ChemAb, EngI, SciAb, SCI. *Bk. rev:* 1–2, 200 words, signed. *Aud:* Sa, Ac. *Rv:* H. *Jv:* B.

Section E of *Journal of Physics* (2d series, vol. 1, 1968+). The scope of this journal is "the publication of information on apparatus and associated component parts, techniques and accessories, emphasizing particularly the physical principles involved and quantitative aspects of design and performance." Articles range from review papers and those covering research and design, to brief notes on techniques or preliminary experimental investigations. A short information section supplies details on forthcoming symposia, exhibitions, and the like. Although necessary for any research library, the small academic collection would find its needs sufficiently represented by its American counterpart, *Review of Scientific Instruments* (See annotation, this section).

Optical Society of America. Journal. 1917. m. $30. D. L. MacAdam. Amer. Inst. of Physics, 335 E. 45th St., New York, N.Y. 10017. Illus., index, adv. Circ: 8,500. Reprint: Johnson.

Indexed: BioAb, ChemAb, EngI, MathR, PsyAb, SciAb, SCI. *Bk. rev:* 5, 250 words, signed. *Aud:* Sa, Ac. *Rv:* H. *Jv:* B.

The official publication of the Society is concerned with "experimental or theoretical investigations which contribute new knowledge or understanding of any optical phenomena, principles, or methods." (Studies involving applications of these principles appear in the Society's other research journal, *Applied Optics.*) Research papers and "Letters to the Editor" also include such fields as: spectroscopy; physiological and medical optics; color vision; and colorimetry. In addition to news of the profession, personalia, and the like, the journal also publishes reports and minutes of meetings of the Society.

Philosophical Magazine; a journal of theoretical, experimental and applied physics. 1798. m. $64.50. Nevill Mott. Taylor & Francis, Ltd., Red Lion Court, Fleet St., London E.C.4. Circ: 2,500. Illus., index.

Indexed: ChemAb, EngI, MathR, SciAb, SCI. *Bk. rev:* 6, 250 words, signed. *Aud:* Sa, Ac. *Rv:* H. *Jv:* B.

Originally one of the early, important general science journals, the publication later became concerned with all branches of theoretical and experimental physics. Currently, research papers and correspondence, of a more limited scope, are mostly in the field of solid state physics. Well-written book reviews are limited to research monographs. Its supplement, *Advances in Physics* (see annotation, this section), publishes reviews of current research.

Physical Review. 1893. 72/yr. $100. Ed bd. Amer. Inst. of Physics, 335 E. 45th St., New York, N.Y. 10017. Illus., index. Circ: 8,700. Microform: UM. Reprint: Johnson.

Indexed: ChemAb, EngI, MathR, SciAb, SCI. *Aud:* Sa, Ac. *Rv:* H. *Jv:* B.

Easily one of the world's most important physics journals, this publication of the American Physical Society is devoted to original research contributions in both theoretical and experimental physics. Twelve volumes are published annually, with five monthly issues (per vol.) representing five subject sections. Section I, *Atoms,* includes papers on atoms and molecules, fluids and plasmas; Section II, *Solids (I),* covers atoms and nuclei in matter, collective effects in solids, and magnetic materials; Section III, *Solids (II),* incorporates metals, semiconductors, and insulators; Section IV, *Nuclei,* contains papers on nuclear structure, properties, reactions, and scattering; and Section V, *Particles,* is concerned with elementary particles, fields and relativity. Articles represent full-length studies. Although members of the Society may purchase individual sections, nonmembers must order the full series. A recent "Comments and Addenda" section contains short reports on work already published either in the journal or in *Physical Review Letters.*

Its weekly, sister publication, *Physical Review Letters* ($30.) comprises timely, short communications "dealing with important new discoveries or topics of high current interest." Articles are very brief (1–2 pages). The *Letters* also contains abstracts of papers which will appear in forthcoming issues of the *Review.* Both publications are necessary for all except the smallest academic libraries.

Physical Society. Proceedings. 1874. 30/yr. $139.20. Ed bd. Inst. of Physics and The Physical Soc., 1 Lowther Gardens, Prince Consort Rd., London S.W.7. Illus., index. Circ: 3,000. Microform: UM.

Indexed: ChemAb, EngI, MathR, SciAb, SCI. *Bk. rev:* 10, 250 words, signed. *Aud:* Sa, Ac. *Rv:* H. *Jv:* B.

A major research publication, this journal segmented into three parts when it became *Journal of Physics* A, B, C in its second series (vol. 1, 1968+). All sections comprise authoritative research studies and short "Letters to the Editor." Individual parts may be purchased separately. Section A, *General,* issued bimonthly ($36/yr), is concerned with mathematical physics, general relativity, field theory, low and high energy nuclear physics, plasma studies, optics, and properties of matter. Book reviews are included in this section. Section B, *Atomic and Molecular Physics,* a monthly ($52.80/yr), is primarily devoted to theoretical and experimental spectroscopic studies of atoms and molecules, and studies of gases. Section C, *Solid State Physics,* published monthly ($62.40/yr), contains reports on all aspects of solid state physics and liquid state theory and experiment.

Physics. 1964. bi-m. $40. P. W. Anderson & B. T. Matthias. Physics Publishing Co., 44-01 21st St., Long Island City, N.Y. 11101. Illus., index.

Indexed: SCI. *Aud:* Sa, Ac. *Rv:* H. *Jv:* B.

The approach of this journal is rather unique, since its editors purport to select high quality papers which are worthy of the attention of *all* physicists, regardless of field of specialization. The validity of their argument can be questioned, of course, and, indeed, the editors do admit the presumption involved in this selectivity principle. Nevertheless, research papers are authoritative; all branches of physics are represented, and studies reflect both theoretical and experimental work. Occasionally, review or tutorial articles may be published. Since the scope of the journal is international, papers appear in English, French, or Russian, and, interestingly enough, the Russian articles appear both in English translation and the original language.

Physics Abstracts. See Science Abstracts, "Series A," in Indexes and Abstracts Section.

Physics Teacher. 1963. 8/yr. $5. C. E. Swartz. Amer. Inst. of Physics, 335 E. 45th St., New York, N.Y. 10017. Illus., index, adv. Circ: 8,500. Microform: UM.

Bk. rev: 6, 400–600 words, signed. *Aud:* Ht, Jc, Ac, Sa. *Rv:* H. *Jv:* B.

Another publication of the American Association of Physics Teachers (see also, *American Journal of Physics,* this section), published in cooperation with the AIP. Addressed to "all those who teach introductory physics to the high school student, the junior college or to the freshmen year student," this is particularly commendable to high school teachers. Three to four features in each issue blend authoritative essays on current topics in physics, interviews with scientists, with trends in science education, evaluation of curricula, and other general problems of the educator. Regularly published are brief communications on classroom techniques, lab demonstrations, new equipment, tips on improving existing apparatus; the short reports are geared at a high school level. "Letters to the Editor" can be both technical or informal. The book review section includes, periodically, reviews of films.

Physics Today. 1948. m. $4. R. H. Ellis, Jr. Amer. Inst. of Physics, 335 E. 45th St., New York, N.Y. 10017. Illus., index, adv. Circ: 50,000. Microform: UM.

Indexed: ASTI, ChemAb, EngI, RG, SciAb, SCI. *Bk. rev:* 10, 300–400 words, signed. *Aud:* Sh, Jc, Ac, Ga, Sa. *Rv:* H. *Jv:* A.

Informative, authoritative, yet entertaining, the periodical is an outstanding choice for a generalized, interpretive treatment of the science at any level (layman, student, or professional). Well-written articles by specialists review research; applications to other fields; philosophy and history of the science; trends in education, government, or industry; and problems of the profession. Features may be scholarly and technical, or informal and nontechnical, depending, of course, on the subject matter. The special departments of the magazine serve as a news medium for physicists: detailed reports of technical meetings, activities of societies, personalia, calendars, announcements. Book reviews are excellent, and the section also contains a useful, classified checklist of new physics books. Highly recommended for

any public or high school library that would like to acquire more than a general science periodical.

RCA Review. 1936. q. $4. C. C. Foster. RCA Laboratories, Princeton, N.J. 08540. Illus., index. Circ: 7,500. Microform: UM. Reprint: Johnson.

Indexed: ASTI, ChemAb, EngI, MathR, SciAb, SCI. *Aud:* Ac, Sa. *Rv:* H. *Jv:* B.

Contributions to this journal are from the various divisions of the Radio Corporation of America. Papers, consisting of research reports in all branches of the applied sciences and engineering, are of the high caliber usually associated with scholarly journals and frequently represent detailed studies ranging from 5 to 50 pages in length. Each issue also contains an index of technical publications of the RCA staff which have appeared in other journals. Since many of the investigations fall under the category of applied physics, the quarterly is a valuable choice for academic libraries interested in the applied sciences and their relation to engineering.

Review of Scientific Instruments. 1930. m. $13. J. B. Horner Kuper. Amer. Inst. of Physics, 335 E. 45th St., New York, N.Y. 10017. Illus., index, adv. Circ: 9,300. Microform: UM. Reprint: Johnson.

Indexed: ASTI, BioAb, ChemAb, EngI, PsyAb, SciAb, SCI. *Bk. rev:* Occasional 300–500 words, signed. *Aud:* Sa, Ac. *Rv:* H. *Jv:* B.

The journal is concerned with any type of scientific instrumentation applicable primarily to the physical sciences, and occasionally to the life sciences. Original research papers and some review articles discuss new equipment, novel techniques, or components related to apparatus; short notes are of more limited scope; and letters to the editor comment on work published earlier in the journal. Sections on new materials, components, and equipment describe new products as reported by manufacturers' literature.

Reviews of Modern Physics. 1929. q. $8. L. M. Branscomb. Amer. Inst. of Physics, 335 E. 45th St., New York, N.Y. 10017. Illus., index. Circ: 11,200. Microform: Canner. Reprint: Johnson.

Indexed: BioAb, ChemAb, EngI, MathR, SciAb, SCI. *Aud:* Sa, Ac. *Rv:* H. *Jv:* B.

Scholarly and critical, the review papers published in this distinguished journal (sponsored by the American Physical Society) give authoritative and timely reports on current research problems in all branches of physics. Varying in length from 10 to 50 pages, the articles include the usual comprehensive bibliographies. Brief "Letters to the Editor," which appear occasionally, comment on reviews previously published. The journal is an excellent medium for supplying background material to physicists and advanced students, as well as for providing specialists with accounts of research in their fields.

Royal Society. Proceedings. Series A. See Science-General Section.

Soviet Physics-JETP. 1955. m. $95. Ed bd. Amer. Inst. of Physics, 335 E. 45th St., New York, N.Y. 10017. Illus., index. Circ: 1,400.

Indexed: ChemAb, EngI, MathR, SciAb, SCI. *Aud:* Sa, Ac. *Rv:* H. *Jv:* B.

The periodical is a full translation of *Zhurnal Eksperimental 'noi I Teoreticheskoi Fiziki (Journal of Experimental and Theoretical Physics of the Academy of Sciences of the USSR).* Similar in nature to *Physical Review,* it is one of the leading Russian journals, which publishes significant research papers in all areas of fundamental and experimental physics. Reports represent full-length studies. Shorter papers or important preliminary communications appear semimonthly in its companion journal, *JETP Letters* ($35/yr), a translation of *JETP Pis'ma v Redaktsiyn.*

Soviet Physics-Uspekhi. 1958. bi-m. $45. Amer. Inst. of Physics, 335 E. 45th St., New York, N.Y. 10017. Illus., index.

Indexed: ChemAb, MathR, SciAb, SCI. *Aud:* Sa, Ac. *Rv:* H. *Jv:* B.

Comparable in scope to *Reviews of Modern Physics,* the journal is a complete translation of *Uspekhi Fizicheskikh Nauk (Advances in the Physical Sciences of the Academy of Sciences of the USSR).* Authoritative review papers cover all branches of physics—general, atomic, molecular, solid state and nuclear. Occasionally, some very detailed reports of conferences held in the USSR are included, as well as a few historical or biographical notes tracing the work of some distinguished Soviet physicists. The American Institute of Physics publishes, in translation, several, more specialized, Soviet research journals. *Uspekhi* and *JETP* were selected as representative, high-quality general physics publications.

POETRY

Indexes and Abstracts

Abstracts of English Studies, Index to Commonwealth Little Magazines, Index to Little Magazines, Readers' Guide to Periodical Literature. (For annotations, see Indexes and Abstracts Section.)

Audit/Poetry. 1960. 3/yr. $3. (Libraries, $3.50). George Butterick & Albert Glover. 180 Winspear Ave., Buffalo, N.Y. 14215. Circ: 1,000.

Aud: Ga, Ac, Jc. *Rv:* M. *Jv:* B.

Publishes modern American poets, often those deserving wider attention from a lay audience, yet well known only in limited circles. Occasionally a single issue is given over to the work of one poet, e.g., No. 3, 1967, to Robert Duncan. The selection is careful, the editing superior and the letterpress format good. A basic poetry magazine for any medium to large public or academic collection.

The Beloit Poetry Journal. 1950. q. $2. Ed bd. Box 2, Beloit, Wis. 53511. Circ: 1,100.

Bk. rev: Notes. *Aud:* Sa, Ga, Ac, Jc, Sh. *Rv:* M. *Jv:* B.

An established poetry magazine which leans to the experimental, generally by young, relatively unknown Americans. An occasional translation. Although sometimes uneven in quality, an important showcase for much of today's poetry. Some issues contain "Books in Brief," short unsigned notes on approximately eight current books of poetry. About once a year there is a special Chapbook issue featuring the work of one poet, poems on one subject, poems of one area, e.g., Asia, or poems of one type (concrete), etc. The magazine does much to bridge the generation gap without fanfare, but with solid work. Consequently it may be enjoyed by everyone from the high school student to the dedicated poet and teacher.

Caterpillar. 1967. q. $5. Clayton Eshelman, 10 Bank St., New York, N.Y. 10014. Illus.

Bk. rev: 5–10, various lengths. *Aud:* Ga, Ac, Jc. *Rv:* M. *Jv:* A.

A pocket-sized 100-to 150-page magazine of new American poetry, this is as well printed and illustrated as the contents are edited. Eshelman is a major young American poet and translator who promises to issue this magazine for only three years. As a start he has featured Paul Blackburn, Robert Duncan, Gary Snyder, Cid Corman, Michael Heller and Sam Abrams. Each issue features drawings and or photographs. Some film and political comment, and beginning with the fourth issue, "Notes and Reviews" became a regular feature of the magazine. The poetry reviews are valuable because of the reviewers (particularly the incisive comments of Robert Kelly and Eshelman himself) and the emphasis on lesser known works often overlooked by *Poetry,* or dismissed as unimportant. Apparently, *Caterpillar* will continue to challenge the better established reviews, and in so doing offers libraries an opportunity for reappraisal of many publications. Decidedly liberal, intellectual, and a basic poetry magazine for all public and academic libraries.

Choice; a magazine of poetry and photographs. 1961. irreg. $5/four issues. John Logan & Aaron Siskind. P.O. Box 4858, Chicago, Ill. 60680. Illus.

Aud: Ga, Ac, Jc, Sh. *Rv:* M. *Jv:* B.

Averaging between 120 and 160 pages, printed on excellent paper and nicely designed, this is one of the more striking poetry mags. Poets published have included Blackburn, Simpson, Wright, Bly, Creeley, Dickey and Ammons. Each of the irregularly issued numbers includes from 50 to 60 poets, some well known, others just beginning to break into the circle. In view of its representative coverage of the poetry scene, its fine format, and its solid editing, it serves as an excellent survey of trends in this area. Should be found in any library where there is more than a passing interest in poetry, and is a good choice for high schools.

El Corno Emplumado/The Plumed Horn. 1962. q. Sergio Mondragon & Margaret Randall. Apartado Postal No. 13-546, Mexico 13, D.F., Mexico. Illus. Circ: 3,000.
Bk. rev: 4–10 various lengths, critical. *Aud:* Ga, Ac, Jc, Sh. *Rv:* M. *Jv:* V.

To many critics, this is the leading avant-garde magazine of poetry. Bi-lingual (text in English and Spanish) it is of great value in presenting the best of contemporary North American and South/Central American poets in their native languages as well as in translation (in both directions). Fiction is usually too short and is not up to the mark set by the poetry. Flaunts an irreverent liberal-left, sometimes revolutionary, politic. Each number features exciting line drawings, "comics," or photo-montage, often with satiric power. The letters to the editor are often short essays by some of the leading avant-garde writers. Although not limited in geographic scope (translations from European new poets have been published), it is a most important magazine for those who wish to keep abreast of new poetry within the Americas. Should be found in all libraries where poetry is a consideration. (C.f., the Fall-Winter, 1968–1969, edition of *Tri-Quarterly* magazine, entitled "Contemporary Latin American Literature," containing many Latin American poets, novelists and short story writers.)

Goliards. 1964. semi-ann. 3/yr. Jerry Burns. Goliards Press, P.O. Box 703, San Francisco, Calif. 94101. Illus.
Aud: Ga, Jc, Sh. *Rv:* M. *Jv:* B.

A collection of works by some 50 or more younger poets, primarily of value for the wide range of new talent often introduced for the first time. The poetry is extremely uneven, yet has a fresh quality, a sincerity which will appeal to anyone, any school, any age. Just enough first class work to warrant reading through each issue. Even the most rigid critic is apt to discover a bright new voice. Because of its quantitative approach (120–150 pages) to younger poets, not to mention a good deal of quality, it is a good addition for public, high school and junior college libraries. Universities may want to stick with more accepted versions of the muse.

Intrepid. 1964. q. $3. Allen de Loach. Box 175, Kenmore, N.Y. 14217. Circ: 500.
Aud: Ga, Ac, Jc, Sh. *Rv:* L. *Jv:* A.

A listing of contributors to *Intrepid* would read like a "Who's Who" among contemporary American poets. Tuli Kepferberg, Charles Bukowski, Diane DiPrima, Doug Blazek, Diane Wakoski, Ted Enslin, and Paul Blackburn are only a few of the well-known names who have had poetry published here. Add to this letters or excerpts of

journals by Allen Ginsberg, John Wieners, Peter Orlovsky, Carl Solomon and short fiction by William Burroughs, plus translations of contemporary European poets. The result is an excellent little poetry magazine, which should be one of the first considered for subscription by a library adding in the area of little magazines. Back issues are available from the publisher, but are becoming rare. Stapled mimeo, but better edited and produced than many of the offset magazines in this field. Quarto format.

Journal of Black Poetry. 1966. q. $3.80. Joe Goncalves. 1308 Masonic Ave. #4, San Francisco, Calif. 94117.
Aud: Ga, Ac, Jc, Sh. *Rv:* M. *Jv:* B.

A militant magazine which features poems by Afro-Americans, many written from prisons, slums and streetcorners. As Sanford Berman put it in a review of this magazine in *Library Journal,* the poems "are jubilant, sorrowful, angry, mocking, proud and defiant." While a good deal of the entries are a bit rough both in form and content, the spirit is gold, and there is more control than first evident. In addition to poetry there is a general news section, which includes book reviews, notes on magazines, and personalities. Contributing editors include LeRoi Jones, Larry Neal, Clarence Major and Nazzam Al Fitnah. As one of the few all-Black poetry magazines, this should be found in all libraries where there is social concern. It is an absolute must for high schools with more than one Black student.

Kayak. 1964. q. $3. George Hitchcock. 2808 Laguna St., San Francisco, Calif. 94123. Illus. Circ: 1,000. Reprint: Johnson.
Indexed: LMags. *Bk. rev:* 2–5, 1,500 words, signed. *Aud:* Ga, Ac, Jc, Sh. *Rv:* L. *Jv:* A.

One of the best poetry magazines now being issued in the United States. Its imaginative editor, a poet of taste and imagination, features both traditional and projective verse. Louis Simpson, Gary Snyder, Tom McGrath, David Ignatow, and X. J. Kennedy have printed poetry here. The black and white illustrations, reproduced from nineteenth century books, are an added attraction. The occasional short essay is generally up to the high quality of the poetry. For both teen-agers and adults.

Modern Poetry in Translation. 1965. 3/yr. $1.50. Ted Hughes & Daniel Weissbort. 10 Compayne Gardens, London N.W.6. Circ: 2,600.
Indexed: ComLMags. *Aud:* Ga, Sa, Ac. *Rv:* L. *Jv:* B.

An 18- to 22-page magazine printed on thin stock, this features translations of the best modern poetry now available. The first issues concentrated on French, Scandinavian and German works, with translations by Muriel Rukeyser, Anselm Hollo, Michael Hamburger, and Edward Lucie-Smith. Editor Hughes insists on a literal word-by-word translation, and as only the English version is given it is difficult to judge the merits of the case.

Poet and Critic. 1965. 3/yr. $3. Richard Gustafson. Iowa State Univ. Press, Press Bldg., Ames, Iowa 50010. Circ: 500.

Indexed: AbEnSt. Bk. *rev:* 4–8, 250 words, signed. *Aud:* Ga, Ac, Jc. *Rv:* L. *Jv:* B.

A poetry "workshop-in-print" from Iowa State University. Poems are followed by brief critical comments contributed by other poets appearing in the same issue. Poems and short essays by undergraduates and a few graduate students from other campuses. Some adult contributions. Generally a showcase for the same names, many of whom also appear in *Lyric, Epos,* and *Bitterroot.* Full-page line drawings are a pleasant addition.

Poetry. 1912. m. $12. Henry Rago. 1018 North State St., Chicago, Ill. 60610. Circ: 9,000. Reprint: AMS.

Indexed: RG. *Bk. rev:* 1–16, grouped, signed. *Aud:* Ga, Ac, Jc, Sh. *Rv:* H. *Jv:* A.

The most respected magazine of poetry in the United States, or for that matter, anywhere. Outstanding for experimental and important new poetry. Publishes the work of the complete range of significant poets, from the youngest and least known to the best established. Contains essays on poetry and excellent critical reviews of books of and about poetry. Other special features are "Books Received," notices of poetry prizes, and "News Notes," which contains dates of poetry readings and announcements of new periodicals that are beginning publication. T. S. Eliot once remarked that *"Poetry* has had imitators, but has so far survived them all. It is an American institution." Should be in every library from senior high on up.

Poetry Australia. 1964. bi-m. $6. Grace Perry. South Head Press, 350 Lyons Rd., Five Dock, Sydney, N.S.W., Australia. Circ: 3,000.

Bk. rev: 3–5, grouped, 200 words, signed. *Aud:* Ac, Jc. *Rv:* M. *Jv:* B.

A poetry magazine from Australia with international coverage. Special issues devoted to Canadian, New Zealand, and Australian, poetry. Old and firmly established poets are featured along with some of the younger ones. Poetry tends to the orderly and graceful. Book reviews are similar to those found in *Poetry* (Chicago), but include reviews of German, African, and Scottish poetry as well as some American. Special features include a list of "Periodicals Received" and notices about poetry prizes and workshops.

Poetry Northwest. 1959. q. $3.50. David Wagoner. Parrington Hall, Univ. of Washington, Seattle, Wash. 98105. Circ: 1,500.

Indexed: LMags. *Bk. rev:* Occasional. *Aud:* Ga, Ac, Jc. *Rv:* L. *Jv:* B.

One of the more impressive regional poetry magazines, this gained fame under the editorship of Carolyn Kizer. It has continued to display a remarkable power for discovering new, worthwhile poets. Comparable with *Poetry* (Chicago), although less experimental. Outstanding art-

work by Northwest artists and photographers. A good magazine for all libraries.

Poor Old Tired Horse. 1961. irreg. $3. Ian Hamilton Finlay. Wild Hawthorn Press, Stonypath, Dunsyre, Lanark, Scotland. Illus. Circ: 1,000.

Indexed: ComLMags. *Aud:* Ga, Ac, Jc, Sh. *Rv:* L. *Jv:* B.

A four- to six-page hand-printed little mag, this usually features some aspect of concrete poetry, e.g., No. 24, Concrete Poetry at the 1967 Brighton Festival; No. 23, T. Poem. As one of the leading poets and artists in this field, Finlay often contributes, and other well known poets such as Furnival, Biederman, and Enslin are often featured. The work is outstanding for the illustrations and photographs. Many adults may not catch the drift, but the magazine is a constant delight for the more imaginative teen-ager. A good interest item for high school poetry collections. The leading European concrete journal is *Rot* (7 Stuttgart 1, Hegelstr 14, Germany. 4dm the Number). Each issue is devoted to a particular poet, e.g., Ernst Jandl, Max Bense, Haroldo de Campos.

Priapus. 1962. q. $2. John Cotton. 37 Lombardy Drive, Berkhamsted, Hertfordshire, Eng. Illus. Circ: 350.

Bk. rev: 5–6, grouped, signed. *Aud:* Ac, Jc. *Rv:* L. *Jv:* B.

A 26- to 35-page mimeographed little mag, usually with a colorful cover and frequent color-block illustrations by Rigby Graham. Among regular contributors have been Edward Lucie-Smith, Ted Walker, Jim Burns and Philip Hosbaum. Sometimes has special numbers dedicated to a particular school of poetry.

The Sixties. 1958. irreg. $3/4 issues. Robert Bly. Sixties Press, Odin House, Madison, Minn. 56256. Circ: 2,000.

Aud: Ga, Ac, Jc, Sh. *Rv:* M. *Jv:* V.

The best one-man published and edited poetry magazine in the United States. Since 1958, when the magazine was called *The Fifties,* it has consistently reflected the best in modern poetry as selected by its editor, Robert Bly. Winner of the 1968 National Book Award in poetry, Bly is highly regarded by younger poets and has done much to champion their better efforts in his publication. Equally important, he has issued the original texts and translations of leading European and South American poets. In No. 10, for example, there are poems by Galway Kinnell, Michael Benedikt, Paul Zweig, and a collection of Bly's translations from Norwegian poets. Some book reviews, but these are usually longer essays on aspects of modern poetry. In fact, the quality of the critical writing is exceptionally high, and an excellent source of information on both new and older poets, e.g., "The Collapse of James Dickey," in No. 9. Librarians may find his publishing schedule a bit erratic— there have been only 10 issues in 10 years—but the worth of the magazine far outweighs any inconvenience. It should be found in all types and sizes of libraries, but particularly in senior high schools.

Solstice. 1965. 3/yr. Brian Morse & Steve Bradshaw. 21a Silver St., Cambridge, Eng. Circ: 4,000.

Aud: Ga, Ac, Jc, Sh. *Rv:* L. *Jv:* B.

Solstice now enjoys one of the largest circulations of any small literary magazine in the United Kingdom. Many of the published poets appear here for the first time, while among the established names have been Anselm Hollo, Jim Burns and John Furnival. Has printed supplements presenting new poets of the United States and Latin America. A leader in the publishing of concrete poetry in England. For young adult and adult readers interested in contemporary poetry.

Steppenwolf. 1965. ann. $2. Philip Boatright & Jean Shannon. P.O. Box 55045, Omaha, Neb. 68155.

Aud: Ga, Ac, Jc. *Rv:* L. *Jv:* B.

With admirable restraint, the editors limit themselves to one issue per year. Little known but highly talented poets account for most of the well printed journal. It is his judicious selection that sets Mr. Boatright's apart from many of the other poetry mags, for, as he explains: "We are not very objective, I'm afraid—we think the work we've presented is damn fine writing." It is. A good magazine for any library with an interest in poetry.

Victorian Poetry. See Literature Section.

Wormwood Review. 199. q. $3.50. M. H. Malone. Wormwood Review Press, P.O. Box 101 & 111, Storrs, Conn. 06268. Illus. Circ: 600.

Bk. rev: Various numbers, lengths. *Aud:* Ga, Ac. *Rv:* M. *Jv:* B.

An outstanding magazine whose aim is to "reflect the temper and depth of the human scene." The poems it prints are, almost without exception, good. In fact, there is little about the whole mag that isn't good. A useful addendum is the continuing bibliography of little mags and other items of interest to modern poets and their readers. This bibliography gives short but solid annotations and allots ratings that range from "highly recommended" to "totally panned and damned." Considering the quality of the poetry, as well as the bibliography, this would be especially useful to libraries intent on keeping up with modern poetry.

POLITICAL SCIENCE

Indexes and Abstracts

Abridged Readers' Guide, British Humanities Index, Canadian Periodical Index, Historical Abstracts, Public Affairs Information Service, Readers' Guide to Periodical Literature. (For annotations, see Indexes and Abstracts Section.)

Africa Report. See African Studies Section.

Africa Today. See African Studies Section.

African Forum. See African Studies Section.

American Academy of Political and Social Science.

Annals. 1890. bi-m. Membership (Non-members, $10/yr.). Thorsten Sellin. Amer. Academy of Political and Social Science, 3937 Chestnut St., Philadelphia, Pa. 19104. Illus., adv. Circ: 23,000. Reprint: Kraus. Microform: UM.

Indexed: PAIS, RG. *Bk. rev:* 60–80, 800–1,000 words, signed. *Aud:* Ga, Ac, Jc, Ht. *Rv:* H. *Jv:* V.

Each issue is devoted to a selected topic of current social or political interest. The Academy does not take sides but seeks "to gather and present reliable information to assist the public in forming intelligent and accurate opinions." Sample topics include world population, the realignment in Western and Communist worlds, analysis of national character, and the social goals of American society. An authority in the field is the guest editor of each issue and articles are written at his invitation. Authors include academic experts, writers publishing on the subject, and individuals involved in current research with specialized organizations. The 15 to 20 authoritative articles are from 6 to 10 pages in length. Each presents a different aspect of the topic, so the final result is an interdisciplinary overview of the problem involving material from many of the social sciences. The abstracts preceding each article and the tabular and graphic presentations are both great aids and are very well done. Its reliable, broad, interdisciplinary coverage make it a "must" for all public, university, and high school libraries (in this last case, for teachers and exceptional students).

American Political Science Review. 1906. q. Membership (Non-members, $12). Harvey C. Mansfield. Amer. Political Science Assn., 1726 Mass. Ave., N.W., Washington, D.C. 20006. Adv. Circ: 11,300. Microform: UM.

Indexed: PAIS, SSHum. *Bk. rev:* 50–80, 1,000–1,500 words, signed. *Aud:* Sa, Ac, Jc, Ht. *Rv:* H. *Jv:* A.

Published quarterly by the American Political Science Association, this is a scholarly journal stressing the theoretical rather than the practical phase of political science. A list of doctoral dissertations in political science, classified by subjects, will prove both interesting and valuable to the professionals. There are numerous book reviews of varying length which are particularly valuable for librarians. (See also, *P.S. Newsletter of the American Political Science Association.*)

Asia; a journal published by the Asia Society, New York. 1964. q. $4. Arthur Coake. 112 E. 64th Street, New York, N.Y. Circ: 3,500. Microform: UM.

Indexed: PAIS, *Aud:* Ga, Ac, Jc. *Rv:* M. *Jv:* B.

Both the Asia Society and its journal were founded for the express purpose of increasing American understanding of the Eastern culture and situation in all sectors. The journal takes an uncluttered, non-specialist approach in its articles, for the most part without sacrificing academic rigor. Each issue is devoted solely to five to eight long articles, usually on a number of different subjects such as politics, family life, social organization, industrialization, some point of history, and so on. An occasional issue narrows the spread to a specific country or topic, such as modern India. Worthwhile in both public and academic libraries.

Asian Survey. 1961. 5–6/yr. $8. Robert A. Scalapino. Inst. of Intl. Studies, Univ. of California, 2234 Piedmont Ave., Berkeley Calif. 94720. Circ: 3,000.

Indexed: PAIS, SSHum. *Bk. rev:* Short notes. *Aud:* Sa, Ac, Jc. *Rv:* H. *Jv:* B.

Studies the economic, political and social problems of Asia in its contemporary setting. Five or six scholarly articles appear in each monthly issue, frequently accompanied by charts and tables. The impressive list of contributors—Norman Palmer, Sung Chih Hong, A. G. Noorani, Donald J. Munro—makes *Asian Survey* the outstanding journal on contemporary Asian problems. Although it appears only 5 or 6 times a year, the section entitled "Recent Books on Asia," with very short annotations, provides the scholars and librarians with an excellent source for current literature on Asia. For any public or academic library where there is a need for current information on Asia.

Canadian Journal of African Studies/Journal Canadien des Etudes Africaines. See African Studies Section.

Canadian Journal of Political Science. 1968. q. $10. Canadian Political Science Assn., Univ. of Toronto Press, Toronto 5, Ont.

Indexed: CanI, PAIS. SSHum. *Bk. rev:* 20–25, 250–750 words, signed. *Aud:* Sa, Ac. *Rv:* H. *Jv:* B.

Formerly part of the *Canadian Journal of Economics and Political Science* (1936–67), this consists of general articles on political science both in French and English. A given number of the five to six articles are given over to Canadian problems, but the journal is in no way limited to that country. There are excellent book reviews, covering titles not often found in many similar American publications. A required item for all large collections, and for medium to large Canadian libraries.

China Quarterly. 1960. q. $7.50. Contemporary China Inst. of the School of Oriental and African Studies, London Univ. Subscriptions to: Research Pubns., 11 Nelson Rd., London S.E.10. Circ: 5,000.

Indexed: PAIS. *Bk. rev:* 10–15, 200–250 words, signed. *Aud:* Sa, Ac, Jc. *Rv:* H. *Jv:* A.

A must for any professional mainland "China watcher," this is one of several objective, non-political journals supported by the International Association for Cultural Freedom. Each issue averages 200 closely printed pages, and features seven to eight articles by authorities in international relations, political science, history, economics and law. Material is both current and historical. While issued in England, a good number of the scholars tend to be American specialists. One or two issues a year are given over to a central

topic, as for example "Chinese Communist History and Historiography." The book notes, usually preceded by one or two long essay type reviews, are international in scope. In terms of reference, the journal is particularly useful because of the "Quarterly Chronicle and Documentation." This consists of a chronologically arranged report on Chinese international developments and foreign relations (in two parts), usually based on reports taken from the Chinese press. Required for medium to large academic libraries and for larger public libraries.

Comparative Political Studies. 1968. q. $8. (Institutions, $12). Ed bd. Sage Pubns., Inc., 275 S. Beverly Drive, Beverly Hills, Calif. 90212.

Bk. rev: Various numbers, lengths, signed. *Aud:* Sa, Ac. *Rv:* H. *Jv:* B.

A model statistical approach to political science, with emphasis on material of interest primarily to the teacher and the graduate student. Scope is international, papers are normally by subject experts and require a given amount of background to understand. For libraries the primary value lies in the excellent annotated bibliographies on all facets of political activities.

Congressional Digest. 1921. 10/yr. $10. N. T. N. Robinson. 3231 P St., N.W., Washington, D.C. 20007. Microform: Available from publisher.

Indexed: PAIS, RG. *Aud:* Ga, Ac, Jc, Sh, Jh. *Rv:* H. *Jv:* A.

Not to be confused with the *Congressional Record*, this is a monthly commerical magazine, which considers a current national topic in depth. The style is famous. First there is an objective description of the topic, which is followed by pro and con arguments, usually in the form of partisan speeches, editorials, debates and testimony given in Congress. Those quoted are both authoritative and in the "middle" of the discussion. It's total effect is both lively and informative. A short "Month in Congress" gives a brief news summary of the previous month's activities in the legislature. As this magazine is useful for both the specialist and the generalist, it has wide use in any type library. It certainly should be given priority in school libraries, from junior high on up, where debate or current history is a consideration.

Congressional Quarterly Service. Weekly Report. 1945. w. $120. Thomas N. Schroth. Congressional Quarterly, Inc., 1735 K St., N.W., Washington, D.C. 20006. Circ: 3,000. Microform: UM.

Indexed: PAIS. *Aud:* Sa, Ac, Jc, Sh. *Rv:* H. *Jv:* V.

One of the few journals that can be recommended for all libraries, from high school to academic and public, and should definitely be included in most. Its value lies in the total coverage of all Congressional action or matters related to Congress. Features include: "Congressional Boxscore of Major Legislation," "Presidential Messages," "Committee Action,"—using charts, graphs, and testimony.

The text is authoritative, interesting, factual, and unbiased. Each issue lists roll-call votes of all Congressmen for that week; national politics and elections in comprehensive, objective detail; lobby activities; and studies of major legal issues (related to the Supreme Court). While not constructed for general reading, it is ideally suited for reference work. The annual *CQ Almanac* ($47.50) is a summary index volume, which libraries unable to afford the weekly service should seriously consider.

A Current Bibliography on African Affairs. See African Studies Section.

Current History; the monthly magazine of world affairs. 1922. m. $9. Carol L. Thompson. Current History, Inc., 1822 Ludlow St., Philadelphia, Pa. 19103. Illus., index. Circ: 28,000. Microform: UM.

Indexed: AbrRG, PAIS, RG. *Bk. rev:* 10–20, 200–500 words. *Aud:* Ga, Ac, Jc, Sh. *Rv:* H. *Jv:* V.

One of the best history and international events review magazines now available for the non-specialist. A concerned effort is made to present material in a popular style, but it is usually prepared by noted historians and scholars. The result is an authoritative overview in language grasped by both the high school and college student. Each issue is devoted to a specific area or topic, with about six to ten individual articles on different aspects. There are maps, current documents and speeches (which often may be found in no other source) and book reviews. A magazine for every library.

Current Digest of the Soviet Press. 1949. w. $200. Leo Gruliow. Joint Committee on Slavic Studies, 405 W. 117th St., New York, N.Y. 10027. Illus. Circ: 1,300.

Indexed: PAIS. *Aud:* Sa, Ac. *Rv:* H. *Jv:* B.

For those who do not read Russian, this is the weekly basic source of material from the Soviet press. Approximately one-third of the daily national newspapers, *Pravda* and *Izvestia,* are translated and the contents listing of each is given in full. In addition, selections are taken from some 60 other newspapers and magazines. Where articles are abridged, this is noted, and full bibliographic details are given for each item. The Joint Committee on Slavic Studies is nonpartisan, refrains from comments on works translated, and affords the American student an excellent cross section of Soviet opinion. If libraries cannot afford this service, they should bring it to the attention of any serious student who is relying on *Problems in Communism* or even *Soviet Life* for a picture of Russia today. The *Current Digest* has an index of the same name which is published quarterly as a supplement. The index also includes material from the English-language Soviet magazine, *International Affairs.*

Admittedly, this is an expensive service, but well worth the price for larger libraries. Those with a restricted budget may wish to consider *Reprints from the Soviet Press* (1965. bi-w. Compass Pubns., Inc., Box 69, Cooper Station, New York, N.Y. 10003. Index. Circ: 1,500). This will probably be the first choice of smaller libraries, but no academic library can substitute it for *Current Digest.*

Department of State Bulletin. 1939. w. $10. Madeline S. Patton. Supt. of Documents, Govt. Printing Office, Washington, D.C. 20402. Illus. Circ: 8,400. Microform: Microcard.

Indexed: PAIS, RG. *Aud:* Sa, Ac, Jc, Sh. *Rv:* H. *Jv:* B.

The official weekly record of United States foreign policy. "The Bulletin includes selected press releases on foreign policy, issued by the White House and the Department (State), and addresses made by the President and by the Secretary of State and other officers of the Department, as well as special articles on various phases of international affairs and the functions of the Department." A section entitled "Treaties" gives brief summaries about treaties in which the United States is involved or has an interest. While the reporting is accurate, it is naturally biased in favor of the State Department. In all cases, it should be balanced with other, non-governmental magazines which give divergent views. With this reservation in mind, the *Bulletin* can be used by high school students, as well as in college courses in political science.

East Europe; a monthly review of East European affairs. 1952. m. $5. Francis Pierce. Free Europe, Inc., 2 Park Ave., New York, N.Y. 10016. Illus., index. Circ: 8,500.

Indexed: AmerH, PAIS. *Aud:* Sa, Ac, Jc. *Rv:* M. *Jv:* B.

Primarily a political report on all aspects of government in Communist-controlled East Europe. Contributors are usually scholars, many of them natives of the countries under consideration. The four to five articles per issue are factually authoritative, but the evaluation is often quite biased. There are two other sections: English translations of excerpts from articles appearing in East European journals and newspapers, and short notes on current developments. A few articles are devoted to outstanding literary figures. Best for the graduate student and scholar. Undergraduates and advanced high school students might use this for background material, but *Survey* is better suited for most purposes.

East European Quarterly. 1967. q. $7. Ed bd. Univ. of Colorado. Regent Hall, Boulder, Colo. 80302.

Indexed: HistAb. *Bk. rev:* 7–10, 500–1,500 words, signed. *Aud:* Sa, Ac. *Rv:* H. *Jv:* B.

Focuses attention on the history, politics, economics and personalities of the Baltic, Adriatic, Aegean and Black Sea areas. Usually four to five scholarly papers in English from American, Russian, Hungarian and East European universities. Book reviews cover publications from Europe and the United States. The whole is for the scholar, and primarily for large academic libraries.

Economic Development and Cultural Change. See Economics Section.

Foreign Affairs. 1922. q. Hamilton F. Armstrong. Council on Foreign Relations, Inc., 58 E. 68th St., New York,

N.Y. 10021. Adv. Circ: 58,061. Microform: UM. Reprint: Kraus.

Indexed: PAIS, RG. *Bk. rev:* Extensive notes. *Aud:* Ga, Ac, Jc, Ht. *Rv:* H. *Jv:* B.

As stated by the editors, *Foreign Affairs* seeks to guide American public opinion by presenting divergent ideas and not to represent any one school of thought. It is generally, though not at all times, objective. Topics include social and political issues, economics and, in fact, any aspect of international affairs which would be of interest to the alert layman or student. Fifteen, twenty- to 30-page articles written by the great scholars and journalists of the day—Arthur Schlesinger Jr., Philip Mosely, Bernard B. Fall, Margaret Mead, and Frank Church, to mention a few—make *Foreign Affairs* the prestige journal for political scientists. Along with the brief but critical book reviews appears a section on source materials and a brief biographical sketch of all the contributors. Although scholarly, the articles are written in a style suitable for the non-expert, and should be in every research collection. It is a bit too involved for the average high school student, but would be a first choice for teachers' collections.

Foreign Policy Briefs. bi-m. $1.25. Supt. of Documents, Govt. Printing Office, Washington, D.C. 20402.

Aud: Ga, Ac, Jc. *Rv:* H. *Jv:* B.

A summary approach to foreign affairs as seen via the U.S. Department of State. Comes as a single, fold-out sheet, punched for use in loose leaf binders. Editorial comments are kept to a minimum, and the chief value is that it affords a quick reference check of current U.S. statements, reports and documents on foreign affairs. Quite suitable for both the expert and the layman and senior high schools.

Harvard Journal of Asiatic Studies. 1936. ann. $5/v. John L. Bishop. Harvard-Yenching Inst., 2 Divinity Ave., Cambridge, Mass. 02138. Circ: 750. Microform: B&H, UM. Reprint: Johnson.

Indexed: SSHum. *Bk. rev:* 8–11, 1,000–1,500 words, signed. *Aud:* Sa, Ac. *Rv:* H. *Jv:* B.

This journal is for students and scholars sincerely interested in Asian studies. The articles are for the erudite; the reviews are articles in themselves. Published under the auspices of the Harvard-Yenching Institute, the pioneer in the field of Chinese studies, the journal is edited by experts in the field of Asiatic studies, and written by those most conversant with and knowledgeable in that subject. Bibliographic material is prolific. Six to nine long articles appear in each issue, followed by the reviews and five or six lengthy notices of other publications. Only for large research collections. *Asian Survey* is better suited for the general library collection.

Harvard Journal of Negro Affairs. See Political Science Section.

Headline Series. 1935. bi-m. $4. Norman Jacobs. Foreign Policy Assn., 345 E. 46th St., New York, N.Y. 10017. Illus. Circ: 20,000.

Indexed: PAIS, SSHum. *Aud:* Ga, Ac, Jc, Sh. *Rv:* H. *Jv:* B.

Actually not a magazine, but a booklet that has high reference value for both the adult and student from senior high up. Issued by the nonpartisan Foreign Policy Association, each issue concentrates on a significant international relationship in the current news, e.g., Communism in China, Latin America, the Soviet Union, etc. Includes basic background on the subject, a discussion guide and suggested reading. The magazine is prepared by experts who show a remarkable objectivity in presenting both sides of controversial topics. Maps and charts assist the reader to find his way. A basic work for any high school or college, and for laymen who are preparing talks or leading discussion groups.

Intercom. 1959. bi-m. $5. Miriam C. Miller. Foreign Policy Assn., 345 E. 46th St., New York, N.Y. 10017. Illus. Circ: 16,000. Microform: UM. Reprint: Johnson.

Indexed: PAIS. *Bk. rev:* 50–60, 50–100 words, unsigned. *Aud:* Ga, Ac, Jc, Sh, Ht. *Rv:* H. *Jv:* B.

Primarily a reviewing service, this offers information on new books, pamphlets, films etc. in world affairs. "Memo to Teachers," presents suggestions for curricular resources and teaching projects suitable from senior high school through the first years of college or university. Students will find the magazine helpful because each issue focuses upon one major current area or subject of interest, followed by an up-to-date bibliography. The reporting is objective and nonpartisan. A valuable aid to social studies teachers and leaders of adult discussion groups. Highly recommended for high school, public and college library collections.

International Affairs. 1922. q. 37s. N. P. Macdonald, Royal Inst. of Intl. Affairs, Chatham House, St. James Square, London S.W.1. Circ: 9,000. Reprint: Dawson.

Indexed: BritHum, PAIS, SSHum. *Bk. rev:* 100–200, 50–1,000 words. *Aud:* Sa, Ac, Jc. *Rv.* H. *Jv:* B.

Covers economic social and political topics of international importance. Experts—Kenneth Younger, Leonard Schwartz, Neville Brown, Herbert Feldman, and Saul Rose, to mention a few—contribute timely and interesting articles. The "Reviews," which comprise nearly half of this lengthy periodical, vary in length, but are consistently excellent and are divided into topics for convenience. For the scholars and librarians who need to keep up to date, there is a list of "New Periodicals" and "Other Books-Received." Although basically a college type journal, *International Affairs* could prove of interest and value for the more advanced high school students.

International Affairs (USSR); a monthly journal of political analysis. 1954. $3.50. m. G. V. Bukin, 14 Gorokhovsky Pereulok, Moscow, K-63, USSR.

Indexed: PAIS. *Bk. rev:* 3–6, 500–750 words, signed. *Aud:* Sa, Ac. *Rv:* M. *Jv:* B.

Published by Izvestia in Russian, English, and French for international consumption. It is as biased as it is fascinating. Though it gives its attention to all parts of the world, it is particularly concerned with NATO and other "imperialistic encroachments." It is always presented in an academic style, and is probably often correct in its analyses of interest groups, trade agreements, and so forth. Nonetheless, the opinions expressed in it cannot be divorced from current and potential official policy. Not recommended for anyone without some experience in Kremlin watching.

International Conciliation. 1907. 5/yr. $2.25. Carnegie Endowment for Intl. Peace, United Nations Plaza at 46th St., New York, N.Y. 10017. Circ: 8,000. Microform: UM.

Indexed: PAIS, RG. *Aud:* Ga, Ac, Jc, Sh. *Rv:* H. *Jv:* B.

One of the oldest periodicals devoted solely to the problems of war and peace. Each issue is concerned with a single topic, e.g., the emerging African nations, nuclear arms control, world food, etc., and is written by a specialist in that field. The topic is usually supported by documents and other authoritative evidence. For a number of years, the September issue has been "Issues Before the General Assembly" (of the United Nations) thus offering a preview of the work of the Assembly during the months ahead. The style of writing is scholarly, yet comprehensible to anyone from high school through university or college. An excellent source of background material for speeches, papers and general information. Should be in most libraries, particularly as the price is low and the contents is undiluted with advertising.

International Social Science Journal. See Sociology Section.

Interplay of European/American Affairs. 1967. m. (Oct.–May); bi-m. (June–Sept.). $7. Anthony Hartley. Welkin Corp., 200 W. 57th St., New York, N.Y. 10019. Illus., adv. Circ: 5,000.

Bk. rev: 2–4, 1,000–1,500 words, signed. *Aud:* Ga, Ac, Jc, Sh. *Rv:* M. *Jv:* B.

A journal of opinion that explores the economic, political and social aspects of Europe and America. While the magazine has an international editorial staff the focus is Europe, e.g., "Probing the German Mind," "The Future of Eastern Europe." Writers tend to be professionals. The tone is intellectual, the style relatively popular, the viewpoint objective although on the liberal side. Among the useful features are biographic sketches of leaders, an economic newsletter, and a limited number of in-depth book reviews. Primarily useful to Americans for the European viewpoint. Quite within the grasp of senior high school students.

Journal of Asian and African Studies. See Sociology Section.

Journal of Inter-American Studies. 1959. q. $6. Ione S. Wright. Univ. of Miami Press, Box 8134, Univ. of Miami, Coral Gables, Fla. 33124. Circ: 4,000.

Indexed: PAIS, SSHum. *Bk. rev:* 3–6, 300–600 words, signed. *Aud:* Sa, Ac. *Rv:* H. *Jv:* B.

Published by the Center for Advanced International Studies at the University of Miami, this consists of some five to eight articles on various aspects of Latin American politics, social conflicts and economics. Authors are prominent American scholars, as well as scholars from various Latin American universities. Material is published in the language of the author, although most articles are in English. The journal tends to be relatively objective, although obviously pro-American and anti-Communist. Topical articles often appear, e.g., "Che Guevara, Some Documentary Puzzles at the End of a Long Journey," which are of more than limited interest. A necessary item for anyone concentrating on activities to the south of the United States.

Journal of International Affairs. 1947. semi-ann. $2.75. John H. A. Quitter. School of Intl. Affairs, Columbia Univ., 622 W. 113th St., New York, N.Y. 10025. Circ: 4,000. Microform: UM. Reprint: Johnson.

Indexed: SSHum. *Bk. rev:* 10–12, 275 words, signed. *Aud:* Sa, Ac, Jc. *Rv:* H. *Jv:* B.

Each issue presents an in-depth study of a current topic of international importance. A recent issue, entitled "Theory and Reality in International Relations," presented a study of trends in the theory of international relations, featuring outstanding contributors such as Raymond Aron, Hans J. Morgenthau, Karl K. Deutsch and James N. Rosenau. Besides the excellent book review section, a section of "Books Received" will help librarians and scholars who are interested in building a collection in this area. A much used basic magazine at all levels from junior college through graduate school.

Journal of Modern African Studies. See African Studies Section.

Journal of Political Economy. See Economics.

Journal of Social History. See History Section.

The Journal of Politics. 1939. q. $5. Marian D. Irish. Southern Political Science Assn., Peabody Hall, Univ. of Florida, Gainesville, Fla. 32603. Adv. Circ: 3,250. Microform: UM. Reprint: AMS.

Indexed: HistAb, PAIS, SSHum. *Bk. rev:* 35,900 words, signed. *Aud:* Sa, Ac, Jc. *Rv:* H. *Jv:* B.

"Publishes the results of the latest research in all aspects of political science." Articles are balanced between international politics and American political research. There is no regional bias or emphasis. Aside from the excellent book reviews, a section entitled "Briefer Notices" briefly annotates about 25 other books. "News and Notes" lists appointments, promotions, and obituaries of the Association. Only for large collections, but because of the sponsor may be of wider interest in the Southern states.

Kyklos. See Economics Section.

Latin American Research Review; a journal for the communication of research among individuals and institutions concerned with studies in Latin America. 1965. 3/yr. Membership (Institution, $12). Richard P. Schaedel. Latin American Studies Assn. Subscriptions to: L.A.R., Univ. of Texas Press, P.O. Box 7819, Austin, Tex. 78712. Illus. Circ: 2,500.

Aud: Sa, Ac. *Rv:* H. *Jv:* A.

The basic guide to research in Latin American studies. It is difficult to imagine anyone working in this area who is not familiar with the *Journal*'s impressive coverage. A normal issue is divided into several parts: "Topic Reviews," which consists of four to five articles on research in everything from literacy studies to taxes; "Reports," trends in research and sources; "Current Research Inventory," which makes up the heart of the journal and includes, by university and then subject, all post-doctoral research reported; news on libraries and achives; "Forum," a discussion of current questions. The research reports are divided geographically by areas of the United States, so that over a period of a year every major university is considered. A geographical index locates material by Latin American country. Libraries will find the 10 to 12 pages in each issue given over to archives and libraries particularly useful, as this consists of short notes on 100 or more books, journals, monographs, etc. concerning Latin America. An absolute must for any academic library where there is the slightest interest in Latin American affairs.

Law and Contemporary Problems. See Law Section.

The Middle East Journal. 1946. q. $7.50. William Sands. Middle East Inst., 1761 N St., N.W., Washington, D.C. 20036. Adv. Circ: 2,700. Microform: UM.

Indexed: PAIS, SSHum. *Bk. rev:* 15, 750 words, signed. *Aud:* Sa, Ac. *Rv:* H. *Jv:* B.

The publisher of this journal is a non-profit corporation, "designed to develop among the American people an interest in the Middle East and an appreciation of its history, culture and political and economic affairs." In achieving these ends the Institute takes no editorial stand on problems, but seeks only to give accurate and objective information. From four to five ten-page articles dealing with all possible facets of the Middle East, written by scholars such as Lorne M. Kenny, Robert L. Daniel, Alan D. Crown, Irving Heymont, and Aziz Ahmad, make this a must for research in international political science. A listing of "Recent Publications," arranged by country and topic, and a "Bibliography of Periodical Literature," which lists magazine articles dealing with the Middle East, will prove of value to scholars and librarians. Because of its objective treatment of a major crisis point in the world, this can be recommended for all medium to large academic and public libraries.

Midwest Journal of Political Science. 1957. q. Membership (Non-members, $6). Malcolm E. Jewell. Wayne State Univ. Press, 5980 Cass Ave., Detroit, Mich. 48202. Adv. Circ: 1,355. Microform: UM. Reprint: Kraus.

Indexed: PAIS. *Bk. rev:* 15, 1,500 words, signed. *Aud:* Sa, Ac. *Rv:* H. *Jv:* B.

A general review of political science. While there are articles dealing with the Midwest, the major emphasis is on American government and politics. A high reference value and its readability make this a valuable addition to the academic library, particularly those in the Midwest.

Modern Asian Studies. 1967. q. $9.50. C. A. Fisher. Cambridge Univ. Press, 32 E. 57th St., New York, N.Y. 10022.

Indexed: HistAb. *Bk. rev:* 7–10, 500–1,500 words, signed. *Aud:* Sa, Ac. *Rv:* M. *Jv:* B.

A scholarly British journal, which is concerned "with modern Asian societies as seen from the standpoints of the several social sciences (including human geography and modern history." The four to five articles per issue are thoroughly documented; reviews deal primarily with British books in the area. Only for large libraries.

Near East Report. 1956. bi-w. $7. I. L. Kenen. 1341 G St., N.W., Washington, D.C. 20005. Circ: 12,000.

Aud: Sa, Ac. *Rv:* L. *Jv:* C.

A pro-Israel newsletter of four to six pages, which is useful only in that it gives a definite point of view, and reports accurately enough on matters in Washington, D.C. that have anything to do with the Near East, more specifically the Arab-Israel conflict. Another department, "Viewing the News," touches on aspects of Jewry in other parts of the world, primarily Russia. Only for large collections.

Orbis. 1957. q. $6. Robert Strausz-Hupe. Foreign Policy Research Inst., Univ. of Pennsylvania, 133 S. 36th St., Philadelphia, Pa. 19104. Adv. Circ: 1,600. Microform: UM. Reprint: Kraus.

Indexed: PAIS, SSHum. *Bk. rev:* 5–6, 1,500 words, signed. *Aud:* Sa, Ac. *Rv:* H. *Jv:* B.

"Presents articles dealing with the diplomatic, economic and psychological—as well as the strategic and military aspects of U.S. foreign policy." An outstanding list of contributors, including Dean Acheson, Hobib Bourguiba, Ralph Straus and Edward Teller, lend prestige and depth to this scholarly journal. Such articles as "Sukarno's Fall," and "The World Through DeGaulle's Looking Glass" demonstrate the magazine's diversity and scope. An effort is made to present many sides of the same question, and the magazine complements the better known *Foreign Affairs*. Only for medium to large academic libraries.

P.S. Newsletter of the American Political Science Association. 1968. 4–5/yr. Membership (Non-members, $5). Earl M. Baker. Amer. Political Science Assn., 1527

New Hampshire Ave., N.W., Washington, D.C. 20036. Microform: UM.

Aud: Sa, Ac, Jc. *Rv:* M. *Jv:* B.

As the title suggests, this is literally a "p.s." to the Association's *American Political Science Review*. One issue a year is devoted to a preliminary program description of the annual meeting, and the other numbers incorporate what was the "News and Notes" section of the *Review*. Also, there is now considerably more information on news events, personalities, and data of primary interest only to members. Should be in almost every library that subscribes to the *Review*. Medium to smaller libraries may wish to skip, particularly as *P.S.* goes free to members of the Association, who may be willing to contribute it.

Pacific Affairs. 1928. q. $5. William L. Holland. Univ. of British Columbia, Vancouver, B.C. Index, adv. Circ: 3,360. Microform: UM.

Indexed: PAIS, SSHum. *Bk. rev:* Various numbers, lengths, signed. *Aud:* Sa, Ac, Jc. *Rv:* H. *Jv:* B.

A scholarly magazine that is primarily for the political scientist; touches on all related issues such as economics, sociology, and personalities. The articles are objective, and where a controversial point of view is introduced every effort is made to indicate both sides of the issue. There are excellent book reviews and shorter items of interest to students of the area. While primarily for the specialist, this is still a basic magazine for the college student studying any area touched on by the magazine. Should be in all medium to large collections.

Pan-African Journal. See African Studies Section.

Parliamentary Affairs. 1947. q. $5.60. Ann Dewar. The Hansard Soc. for Parliamentary Government, 162 Buckingham Palace Rd., London S.W.1. Adv. Circ: 2,500.

Indexed: BritHum, PAIS. *Bk. rev:* 3, 500 words, signed. *Aud:* Sa, Ac. *Rv:* H. *Jv:* B.

While particular attention is given to the British Parliament, international affairs are also covered, e.g., "The French General Election of March 1967," and "Elections in the Sudan during the Military Regime." Authoritative and scholarly, the articles will appeal mainly to the advanced student.

Political Quarterly. 1930. q. 42s. William A. Robson & B. Crick. Illustrated Newspapers Ltd., 258 Gray's Inn Rd., London, W.C.1. Microform: UM. Reprint: Johnson.

Indexed: BritHum, PAIS, SSHum. *Bk. rev:* 12, 100 words, signed. *Aud:* Sa, Ac, Jc. *Rv:* H. *Jv:* B.

Considers topical social and political problems from a progressive point of view. The contributors are leading scholars, including Walter Adam, Douglas Allen, Peter Calvocoressi, Ernest Davies, H. S. Ferns, Michael Ryce, and Kenneth Younger. Most issues cover a range of subjects,

but once or twice a year special issues appear on such themes as "Foreigners in Britain," "Parliament," "The Politics of Science," and "Local Government." Primarily (as with *Parliamentary Affairs*) for the academic library with a particular interest in British government.

Political Science Quarterly. 1886. q. Membership (Nonmembers, $6). Sigmund Diamond. Academy of Political Science, Faryerweather Hall, Columbia Univ., New York, N.Y. 10027. Adv. Circ: 9,000. Microform: UM. Reprint: Kraus.

Indexed: PAIS, SSHum. *Bk. rev:* 40, 500 words, signed. *Aud:* Sa, Ac, Jc. *Rv:* H. *Jv:* B.

Published by the Academy of Political Science (which also issues the *Annals*). Covers the broad spectrum of political science in a very thorough and scholarly manner. Lengthy articles are written by scholars such as John P. Windmuller, Robert Rothstein, David Kettler and Rexford Tugwell. A policy of selecting only the leading authorities in their fields is strictly maintained. The book reviews, which cover nearly half of the periodical, deserve special attention because of their scholarly and critical analysis. If only for the reviews, this is of major importance for all academic and large public libraries.

Political Studies. 1953. 3/yr. $7.25. Peter Campbell. Oxford Univ. Press, Press Rd., Neasden, London N.W.10. Adv. Microform: UM. Reprint: Dawson.

Indexed: BritHum, PAIS, SSHum. *Bk. rev:* 150, 700 words, signed. *Aud:* Sa, Ac. *Rv:* H. *Jv:* B.

"Publishes articles and notes on a wide front, including both institutional and theoretical political studies and studies of allied questions in the legal, historical, philosophical, sociological and other fields." The international flavor and a scholarly approach will appeal mainly to the specialist. The book reviews cover nearly two-thirds of the journal and are useful because of their diversity and excellence. A useful supporting item for libraries which take *Political Science Quarterly*.

Presence Africaine. See African Studies Section.

Problems of Communism. 1951. bi-m. $2.50. Abraham Brumberg. Supt. of Documents, U.S. Govt. Printing Office, Washington, D.C. 20402. Illus. Microform: Cannon, UM.

Indexed: PAIS, SSHum. *Aud:* Sa, Ac, Jc. *Rv:* M. *Jv:* B.

Issued by the United States Information Service, this contains thoughtful analyses and significant background information on various aspects of world Communism. Occasionally a whole issue is devoted to a single theme, such as "The Russian Revolution, Some Historical Considerations," which focuses primary attention on those who opted for social alternatives other than Lenin's or Stalin's. All articles are in a scholarly vein, well documented and the author's credentials are given in detail. One lengthy definitive review of a book on communism is usually coupled with several reviews in brief. The reviewers are identified and extensive correspondence in "Notes and Views" indicates that a climate for criticism has been fostered.

Public Opinion Quarterly. See Sociology Section.

Quarterly Check List of Economics and Political Science. See Literaure Section (*Quarterly Check List of Literary History*).

The Review of Politics. 1939. q. $5. M. A. Fitzsimons. Box B, Notre Dame, Ind. 46556. Microform: UM. Reprint: Kraus.

Indexed: CathI, PAIS, SSHum. *Bk. rev:* 10, 1,500 words, signed. *Aud:* Sa, Ac, Jc. *Rv:* H. *Jv:* B.

A Catholic journal interested in the philosophical and historical approach to political realities. The approach to diversified topics makes this an excellent source for Catholic as well as other viewpoints. While most medium to large Catholic academic libraries will want, this is primarily for the larger library.

The Round Table. 1910. q. $6. Leonard Beaton. Round Table Ltd., 166 Picadilly, London W.1. Microform: UM.

Indexed: PAIS, SSHum. *Aud:* Ga, Ac, Jc, Sh. *Rv:* H. *Jv:* B.

Commonwealth problems—economic, race, social, political and educational—are discussed in relation to their international significance. "Canada in the West Indies," "India and the Common Market," and "Nigeria Sinks Into Chaos," all appearing in a single issue, demonstrate its geographical and topical diversity. The short articles, about current and significant problems, make this as valuable to the general reader as to the scholar.

Soviet Studies. See Economics Section.

Stanford Journal of International Studies. 1965. ann. $4. Richard A. Anderman. Stanford School of Law, Stanford, Calif. 94305.

Aud: Sa, Ac. *Rv:* H. *Jv:* B.

A product of interdisciplinary thinking, "designed to contribute to a broad-based approach to international problems." Each annual issue (which may go quarterly) is dedicated to a single theme. The June, 1968 number considered "Foreign Intervention in Civil Strife" and followed the symposium pattern of speakers, commentary and panel discussions. Five areas were considered, from the United Nations and problems of international law and intervention to the U.S. in Vietnam. Each participant is an expert in his field. Of particular value is the concluding, unannotated, subject-arranged bibliography. Of considerable help to any student of the area, and will be welcomed by those seeking background material for papers or debate—not to mention, of course, the interested layman who can turn to

the journal for a well-rounded discussion of a particular problem.

State Government. 1930. q. $5. Frank Smothers. Council of State Governments, 1313 E. 60th St., Chicago, Ill. 60637. Circ: 7,000. Microform: UM. Reprint: Kraus.

Indexed: PAIS. *Aud:* Ga, Ac, Jc, Sh. *Rv:* H. *Jv:* A.

This is a forum where state problems are discussed, an area frequently overlooked in most political science journals. Because of the many areas covered—governmental, political, economic and social—should be of interest to a large public. This popular approach does not reduce the authority or value of the articles. Ramsey Clark, John Cornally, Paul Rand Dixon, Arvo Van Alstyne and Charles L. Decker are examples of the many fine contributors. Easy to read, short articles make it useful for the high school as well as college libraries.

Survey; a journal of Soviet and East European Studies. q. $6. Walter Laqueur & Leo Labedz. Ilford House, 133 Oxford St., London W.1. Circ: 6,500.

Bk. rev: 2–5, lengthy, signed. *Aud:* Sa, Ac, Jc. *Rv:* H. *Jv:* A.

Sponsored by the International Association for Cultural Freedom, this does for the Soviet Union and Eastern Europe what the same organization's *China Quarterly* attempts to do for China. It is one of the top publications in the field, and the contributors are consistently expert, whether the topic is economics, history, politics, or sociology. The 10–15 long articles are likely to range in a single issue over any aspect of East European Studies, from agriculture, technology, and the peasantry to the leaders of the Soviet bloc and the many variations of Marxist theory. Of special note are the occasional issues focused on a single topic. Examples of these were the discussion of the fiftieth anniversary of the Russian Revolution, and a symposium on the more recent variations of Marxism. Excellent for any college or university library or large public library.

UN Monthly Chronicle. 1964. m. $6. United Nations Sales Section, New York, N.Y. 10017. Illus. Circ: 12,000. Microform: UM.

Indexed: AbrRG, RG. *Bk. rev:* 10–12, 150 words. *Aud:* Ga, Ac, Jc, Sh, Jh. *Rv:* H. *Jv:* V.

"Designed to advance public understanding of the work of the United Nations by providing an objective, comprehensive and documented account of the Organization's activities as well as information on its related agencies." This does just that, serving as one of the best single sources for objective news about the United Nations. Includes original articles, documents, speeches and comments. Both sides of most issues are given in full. The book reviews, which appear in the section entitled "Notes of the Month," are UN publications and are merely short annotations. One of the few magazines which should be included in every library. Editions are in English, French, and Spanish.

Vital Speeches of the Day. 1934. semi-m. $8. Thomas F. Daly III. City News Publishing Co., 1 Wolf's Lane, Pelham, N.Y. Circ: 14,000. Microform: UM.

Indexed: RG. *Aud:* Ga, Ac, Jc, Sh. *Rv:* H. *Jv:* A.

As the title implies, this is simply a reprint of important speeches and talks given by social and political leaders. Emphasis is on Americans, and all of the 10 to 15 speeches are published in full, or in excerpts (which is noted). The policy is to cover all sides of public problems. Three words that appear on the cover of the magazine sum up its philosophy nicely: "Impartial—Constructive—and Authentic." A valuable addition for most libraries.

Western Political Quarterly. 1948. q. $5. Ellsworth E. Weaver. Inst. of Government, Univ. of Utah, Salt Lake City, Utah 84112. Adv. Microform: UM.

Indexed: PAIS, SSHum. *Bk. rev:* 30–40, 500 words, signed. *Aud:* Sa, Ac. *Rv:* H. *Jv:* B.

The official journal of the Western Political Science, Pacific Northwest Political Science, and Southern California Political Science Associations, this discusses many international problems as well as local political problems. The June, 1967 issue had the articles "A Comparative Study of Intra-Party Factionalism in Israel and Japan," and "The Life History and Attitudes of Japanese High Court Judges," as well as 14 short articles on the 1966 elections in each western state. Book reviews follow the scope of the magazine, concentrating on general works, but including many of immediate interest to western scholars. Excellent for research on Western United States political problems and should be included in all large libraries.

World Politics. 1948. q. $7.50. Ed bd. Princeton Univ. Press, Princeton, N.J. 08540. Adv. Circ: 3,900. Microform: UM. Reprint: Johnson.

Indexed: PAIS. *Bk. rev:* Reviews, grouped. *Aud:* Sa, Ac. *Rv:* H. *Jv:* B.

Deals primarily with problems in international relations. Academic experts lend authority and prestige to this scholarly journal. The articles tend to stress concepts and theory, and this journal would be of most use to scholars. A review section incorporates a series of book reviews under a single topic. A must for larger libraries, and should be checked regularly by librarians for the books reviewed.

The World Today. 1945. m. $3.50. Margaret Cornell. Oxford Univ. Press, Ely House, Dover St., London W.1. Adv. Circ: 5,000. Microform: UM. Reprint: Dawson.

Indexed: PAIS, SSHum. *Aud:* Ga, Ac, Jc, Sh. *Rv:* H. *Jv:* B.

An English journal which contains about five short, factual articles designed to keep the reader informed on current world problems. A section entitled "Notes of the Month" continues the magazine's policy of presenting only the facts without expressing any particular viewpoint. Authoritative and scholarly, this can be used equally as well by scholars or the interested general public in keeping up-to-date in foreign affairs. An excellent source for librarians in answering questions which require factual and very current information.

PRINTING ARTS AND INDUSTRY

Indexes and Abstracts

Applied Science and Technology Index, Business Periodicals Index, British Technology Index, Chemical Abstracts, Public Affairs Information Service. (For annotations, see Indexes and Abstracts Section.)

American Pressman; a technical magazine devoted to printing. 1890. m. $2.50. Fred Roblin. Intl. Printing Pressmen & Assistants' Union of North America, 1730 Rhode Island Ave., N.W., Washington, D.C. 20036. Illus., adv. Circ: 60,000.

Bk. rev: Notices. *Aud:* Sa, Ac, Jc. *Rv:* M. *Jv:* B.

Directed to union members, with some technical articles on printing, but emphasizing union activities and personnel. Editorials stress education and training in craftsmanship, the importance of labor-management relations, and participation in union activities by all members. Only for large, specialized collections.

Book Production Industry; incorporating Book Industry and Book Production. 1965. m. $10. Paul D. Doebler. Penton Publishing Co., 1213 W. 3rd St., Cleveland, Ohio 44113. Illus., adv. Circ: 10,200. Microform: UM.

Bk. rev: Notices. *Aud:* Sa, Ac, Jc. *Rv:* M. *Jv:* B.

"Published especially for and selectively distributed to editorial, business and production management personnel" in all phases of book and magazine design, publication and manufacturing. Features by professionals or staff are often technical. Coverage includes areas of research, new developments and trends, and is well illustrated with charts and diagrams. "Communication Probe" delves into areas of radical new developments outside of today's immediate publishing concerns that could have meaning for or affect the future of these industries. Only for specialized collections or where curriculum demands.

British Printer; leading technical journal of the printing industry. 1888. m. $6.50. Maclean-Hunter Ltd., 30 Old Burlington St., London W.1. Illus., adv. Circ: 9,396.

Indexed: BritTech. *Bk. rev:* 4, 200 words. *Aud:* Sa, Ac. *Rv:* H. *Jv:* B.

A British-based magazine, this stands well above the average printing trade journal. Many of the articles on machinery, techniques and design will be of interest to bibliographers and students of the history of the book. From time to time particular attention is given to some historical aspect of printing and typefounding. Considered the leading technical journal for printers in Europe, this should be in every large American collection.

Graphic Arts Monthly and the Printing Industry. 1929. m. $7. J. Hartsuch. Graphic Arts Publishing Co., 7373 N. Lincoln Ave., Chicago, Ill. 60646. Illus., adv. Circ: 61,000. Microform: UM.

Indexed: BusI. *Aud:* Sa, Ac. *Rv:* M. *Jv:* B.

Both the technical and management fields of the various areas of graphic arts are covered for management and supervisory personnel, and craftsmen. Graphic arts students will also find the magazine of value. Illustrated news stories on new developments, techniques, and management procedures range from short, explanatory paragraphs to 1,000–1,500 word features. Question and answer departments in various fields (estimating, linecasting, presswork, etc.) give concise, factual answers to questions with sufficient explanatory material to back up the answers. Nearly 65% of the magazine is devoted to advertising. One of the basic journals in the field, and should be in any public or academic library where there is an audience for this type of magazine.

Graphic Arts Progress. 1954. bi-m. $5. Graphic Arts Research Dept., Rochester Inst. of Technology, 65 Plymouth Ave. S., Rochester, N.Y. 14608. Circ: 1,500.

Aud: Sa, Ac, Jc. *Rv:* H. *Jv:* A.

A 24- to 30-page scholarly journal which consists of two parts. The first is a survey article on a given aspect of printing with extensive references, e.g., "The New Character of Ink." The second, more important to libraries, is the "Graphic Arts Index," which closely analyzes the contents of some 150 periodicals under ten major headings, from the printing industry to education. This is a major contribution to bibliographic control and, as such, should be in every library with more than a minor interest in the graphic arts, printing and publishing.

Inland Printer/American Lithographer. 1883. m. $5. Wayne V. Harsha. Maclean-Hunter Pub. Corp., 300 W. Adams St., Chicago, Ill. 60606. Illus., adv. Circ: 18,182. Microform: UM.

Indexed: ASTI, BusI. *Bk. rev:* 6–8, 50–150 words, signed. *Aud:* Sa, Ac. *Rv:* M. *Jv:* B.

For management and production workers in commercial letterpress and offset lithography, this pioneer magazine deals with current problems and possible solutions, new ideas, and creative printing. It would be of value to advanced students in printing and lithography. The approximately eight well-written, technical articles, cover the small shop as well as the large. Monthly features include a newsletter; "New Literature," a listing with brief explanation of catalogs, brochures, guides, etc.; "Book Reviews," and production and equipment. An annual "Buyers' Reference Guide and Directory" for the forthcoming year is included in the December issue. Useful in university and certain special libraries, and public libraries in areas where printing plants are located.

The Journal of Typographic Research. 1967. q. $6. (Institutions, $10). Merald E. Wrolstad. Cleveland Museum of Arts. Subscriptions to: The Press of Western Reserve Univ., 2029 Adelbert Rd., Cleveland, Ohio 44106. Illus.

Bk. rev: 2–3, 300–500 words, signed. *Aud:* Sa, Ac. *Rv:* H. *Jv:* A.

The single best American journal on typography as a scientific and bibliographical concern. Each 100-page issue features illustrated articles on all aspects of typography, from computer developments to studies in use on television, legibility factors and graphic design. Internationally known contributors. The style presupposes background knowledge. There are abstracts of each article in English, French and German. An absolute necessity for any library concerned with bibliography, typography or computer sciences.

Mid-Atlantic Graphic Arts Review. 1960. m. $8. Philip Katcher. North American Publishing Co., 134 N. 13th St., Philadelphia, Pa. 19107. Illus., adv. Circ: 8,000.

Aud: Sa, Ac. *Rv:* M. *Jv:* B.

The editor reports this "is edited for readers in the various graphic arts trade services in the middle Atlantic region exclusively." The average issue usually has some eight or nine feature articles, illustrated with photographs, and a large number of short news stories. Stories, which make up about half of the total space in the book, include in-depth reports on printing markets and how to reach them, creative uses of paper and inks, printing direct mail promotion, profiles of firms and individuals, as well as industry and association news. Useful to libraries in the area covered.

Modern Lithography. 1934. m. $4. Hamilton C. Carson. Modern Lithography, Inc., 4 2nd Ave., Denville, N.J. 07834. Illus., adv. Circ: 10,000. Microform: UM.

Indexed: ChemAb, PAIS. *Bk. rev:* Notes. *Aud:* Sa, Ac. *Rv:* M. *Jv:* B.

Primarily for personnel in the offset-lithographing industry, this magazine's factual but readable features, often written with a note of humor, would be enjoyed by advanced students in the field, as well as by informed laymen. Two to nine articles of 1,000 to 3,000 words by staff and professionals cover all aspects of the industry. Many black and white illustrations aand portraits accompany them. Several issues have carried a special report in one area: color proofing, litho blankets, a history of the National Association of Litho Clubs, etc., with reprints in pamphlet form available. Other departments include news items about plants, personnel, and the Litho Clubs around the country. A basic trade journal for large libraries, or where community interest dictates a subscription.

Printing and Publishing. 1958. q. $1. Printing & Publishing Industries Div., U.S. Dept. of Commerce. Supt. of

Documents, U.S. Govt. Printing Office, Washington, D.C. 20402.

Aud: Sa, Ac. *Rv:* H. *Jv:* B.

A 16- to 20-page publication with emphasis on statistics of printing and publishing, from photo engraving to imports and exports. Several short articles are supported by lengthy statistical tables and data. Of primary value for the student or expert in economics and the printing and publishing industry.

Printing Magazine/National Lithographer. 1894. m. $5. James F. Burns, Jr. Walden, Sones & Mott, Inc., 466 Kinderkamack Rd., Oradell, N.J. 07649. Illus., adv. Circ: 18,200.

Indexed: PhotoAb. *Bk. rev:* Notes. *Aud:* Sa, Ac. *Rv:* M. *Jv:* B.

The "marketing, management, technical, and news journal of the graphic arts." Fifteen or sixteen 500- to 2,500-word technical articles by professionals cover commercial printing. Most issues contain a major report or feature, plus articles on management methods, design, and technological developments. The "National Lithographer" section includes about five of the articles. Directed primarily to the production worker, they tell of ways to overcome common problems or report on actual use of new methods or developments. Several departments include an often critical "Mailbag," a "Newsletter," the editor's "News Commentary," "Business Outlook," "News Highlights," and "Personnel News." Of interest to advanced students and informed laymen.

Pulp and Paper. 1927. w. $5. Charles W. Heckroth. Miller Freeman Pubns., Inc., 370 Lexington Ave., New York, N.Y. 10017. Subscriptions to: 500 Howard St., San Francisco, Calif. 94105. Illus., adv.

Aud: Sa, Ac. *Rv:* M. *Jv:* B.

Contains brief news items on paper from the U.S. and Canada, plus five or six technical articles of 900 to 1,500 words by both staff and professionals. Tables, charts or graphs accompany many of the reports of mill operations, production, management, training, and research features. The "Annual World Review" in July is a definitive report on the pulp and paper industry in every country in the world. Text is a brief introductory article for each country that is followed by the statistical tables. About 150 worldwide advertisers are listed in the index.

Share Your Knowledge Review. 1919. m. Membership (Non-members, $4). John A. Davies. Intl. Assn. of Printing House Craftsmen, Inc., 7599 Kenwood Rd., Cincinnati, Ohio 45236. Illus. Circ: 16,900.

Aud: Sa, Ac. *Rv:* M. *Jv:* B.

"The official monthly publication of the International Association of Printing House Craftsmen, Inc., combined with Craftsmen's Technical Digest." Two to six technical articles are reprints from a number of periodicals. Often an overall theme unites them. News and views of local clubs, and the president's message completes this 16–20 page magazine.

PSYCHOLOGY

Indexes and Abstracts

Biological Abstracts, Index Medicus, Mathematical Reviews, Psychological Abstracts, Public Affairs Information Service, Readers' Guide to Periodical Literature, Social Sciences and Humanities Index. (For annotations, see Indexes and Abstracts Section.)

Adolescence. See Child Care Section.

American Imago; a psychoanalytic journal for culture, science and the arts. 1939. q. $10. Harry Slochower. Assn. for Applied Psychoanalysis, Inc., Wayne State Press, 5980 Cass Ave., Detroit, Mich. 48202. Circ: 750. Microform: UM. Reprint: Kraus.

Indexed: PsyAb, RG. *Bk. rev:* 2–5 per issue, 2–3 pages, signed. *Aud:* Ga, Ac, Jc. *Rv:* H. *Jv:* A.

American Imago applies the non-medical, often popular principles of psychoanalysis to all phases of the arts, science and culture. Each issue deals with a specific topic or individual, and covers the subject with six to eight lengthy, well documented articles. Also included are signed, critical theatre, television and film reviews. While a good deal of the material is of interest to the better educated layman, its primary appeal and audience is the educator, student and the psychologist. It is not a general magazine for most small or medium libraries, but should be an essential item in larger public and academic collections.

American Journal of Psychiatry. 1844. m. $12. Francis Braceland. Amer. Psychiatric Assn., 1700 18th St. N.E., Washington, D.C. 20009. Illus., adv. Circ: 19,500. Microform: Microcard, UM. Reprint: Johnson.

Indexed: BioAb, ChemAb, IMed, PsyAb. *Bk. rev:* Various numbers, lengths, signed. *Aud:* Sa, Ac. *Rv:* H. *Jv:* B.

While a professional journal for practicing psychiatrists and psychologists, the 150 pages often include material of value to students of the behavioral sciences. Articles represent original research and cover all aspects of the profession, from practical problems facing psychiatrists to diagnosis, case histories, and psychiatric education. There are numerous, long book reviews, clinical notes (which often concentrate on the use of drugs), and the usual association news.

American Journal of Psychology. 1887. q. $7. Karl M. Dallenbach. Menzes Hall, Univ. of Texas, Austin, Tex. 78712. Circ: 3,500. Reprint: Abrahams. Microform: UM.

Indexed: BioAb, ChemAb, PsyAb. *Bk. rev:* 5–15, ½ to 2 pages, signed. *Aud:* Sa, Ac, Jc. *Rv:* H. *Jv:* B.

The main emphasis is on experimental psychology. Each issue contains five departments: "Articles," "Minor Communications," "Descriptions of Apparatus," "Notes and Discussions," and "Reviews of Books." There are usually about 12 scholarly articles.

American Journal of Psychotherapy. 1946. q. $14. Stanley Lesse. Assn. for the Advancement of Psychotherapy, 119–21 Metropolitan Ave., Jamaica, N.Y. 10015. Reprint: Abrahams, Johnson.

Indexed: IMed, PsyAb. *Bk. rev:* 10–12, 1–3 pages, signed. *Aud:* Sa, Ac. *Rv:* H. *Jv:* B.

The official organ of the Association. There are usually 10 to 12 articles, about 12 pages long, with extensive bibliographies, as well as case reports on specific problems of patients. One section contains abstracts of current articles in other psychology journals, arranged by subject. There is also a section of abstracts from foreign countries.

American Psychologist (1946. m. $10); **Contemporary Psychology** (1956. m. $10); **Journal of Abnormal Psychology** (1965. bi-m. $10); **Journal of Applied Psychology** (1917. bi-m. $10). **Journal of Comparative and Physiological Psychology** (1908. bi-m. $20). **Journal of Consulting Psychology** (1937. bi-m. $10); **Journal of Counseling Psychology** (1954. m. $10); **Journal of Educational Psychology** (1910. bi-m. $10); **Journal of Experimental Psychology** (1916. m. $20). **Journal of Personality and Social Psychology** (1965. m. $30). **Psychological Bulletin** (1904, m. $20); **Psychological Review** (1894. bi-m. $10). American Psychological Assn., 1200 17th St., N.W., Washington, D.C. 20036.

The basic journals in support of graduate study in psychology, all published by the American Psychological Association, which also issues *Psychological Abstracts* (where all of the above are indexed), and a number of other bibliographic aids. The titles of the journals are self-explanatory, and each is for a particular area. They have several things in common. All articles are prepared for the psychologist or advanced student of the subject. Most are illustrated with charts and diagrams. Few have book reviews. They are authoritative, usually highly technical, and quite beyond the interests and the special talents of the average layman. Conversely, each is apt to carry an article or two of interest to students of related fields such as education, political science, journalism and the like. Thanks, however, to *Psychology Today* and *Trans-Action,* most findings of more than specialized interest inevitably find their way into one of these semi-popular journals. Hence, what remains is a basic set of authoritative periodicals for serious research purposes. All of these titles belong in large academic libraries and in many public libraries where research is important. With the possible exception of the *Journal of Counseling Psychology, Journal of Educational Psychology, Journal of Applied Psychology, Journal of Personality,* and *Contemporary Psychology* none is required for the average public or junior college library.

Behavioral Science. 1956. bi-m. $10. (Libraries, $20). James Miller. Mental Health Research Inst., Univ. of Michigan, Ann Arbor, Mich. 48104. Adv. Circ: 3,800.

Indexed: BioAb, IMed, MathR, PsyAb. *Bk. rev:* 2–3, 2 pages, signed. *Aud:* Sa, Ac, Jc. *Rv:* H. *Jv:* B.

Stresses an inter-disciplinary approach to the problems of behavior. Each issue contains 5 to 10 well-documented articles on general theories and research in the field. A section in each issue is devoted to the use of computers in behavioral science. The book reviews are on books in the field and are critical, and comprehensive. While primarily for the professional, the emphasis on communication makes it of some importance for the general student.

British Journal of Psychology. 1904. q. $16.50. W. Sluckin. British Psychological Soc., Cambridge Univ. Press, 32 E. 57th St., New York, N.Y. 10022. Circ: 2,850.

Indexed: BioAb, BritHum, IMed, PsyAb. *Bk. rev:* 30–90, notes or lengthy, signed. *Aud:* Sa, Ac, Jc. *Rv:* H. *Jv:* B.

Published by the British Psychological Society, this is the English equivalent of the *American Journal of Psychology.* It is particularly valuable for its large book review section, which covers publications in German as well as English. Emphasis is on general psychology, experimental psychology and methods of testing for and measuring psychological variants. A basic work in larger collections.

Bulletin of Art Therapy. See Art Section.

Canadian Journal of Behavioral Science/Revue Canadienne des Science Du Comportement. 1969. q. $7.50. Canadian Psychological Assn. Suite 210/225 Lisgar St., Ottawa, Ontario.

Aud: Sa, Ac. *Rv:* H. *Jv:* B.

Published in English, with short French summaries, articles are primarily theoretical papers, case studies, research reports and practical analyses. Emphasis is on social, abnormal, educational development and child psychology. The material is technical, for the psychologist or advanced student. For larger academic libraries only.

Canadian Journal of Psychology/Revue Canadienne de Psychologie. 1947. bi-m. $10. P. L. Newbigging. Univ. of Toronto Press, Toronto 5, Ontario. Illus. Circ: 2,100.

Indexed: IMed, PsyAb. *Aud:* Sa, Ac. *Rv:* H. *Jv:* B.

The official journal of the Canadian Psychological Association generally contains about 10 articles per issue. Each article is preceded by an abstract and is followed by a resumé and a bibliography. Articles cover all aspects of the field. For larger American and Canadian academic libraries.

Canadian Psychologist. 1951. q. Membership (Nonmembers, $7). Canadian Psychological Assn., 391 Richmond Rd., Ott. Circ: 1,300.

Indexed: PsyAb. *Aud:* Sa, Ac. *Rv:* H. *Jv:* B.

A publication of a group somewhat equivalent to the American Psychological Association. Material is written by and for psychologists and is international in scope, although it more often reports on activities of Canadians. Includes original research and theoretical articles, and a valuable feature: "Abstracts of Research," again closely related to work in Canada. News and official papers of the Association make up the remainder of the journal. The organization also issues the *Canadian Journal of Psychology* which is even more theoretical. Neither journal is necessary in most libraries, although both are invaluable in large academic libraries where there are active departments of psychology.

Contemporary Psychology; a journal of reviews. 1956. m. $10. Gardner Lindzey. Amer. Psychological Assn., Inc., 1200 17th St., N.W., Washington, D.C. 20036. Circ: 10,500. Reprint: Abrahams. Microform: UM.

Indexed: PsyAb. *Bk. rev:* Entire issue. *Aud:* Sa, Ac, Jc. *Rv:* H. *Jv:* A.

This is a journal comprised entirely of long, signed, critical reviews of current books, films and other instructional media in the field of psychology. There are no articles other than an editorial message. The film and instructional media review section is usually 3 or 4 pages long. Basic for librarians who need a substantial collection of books in psychology.

Educational and Psychological Measurement; devoted to the development and application of measures of individual differences. 1941. q. $10. Box 6907, College Station, Durham, N.C. 27708.

Indexed: EdI, PsyAb. *Bk. rev:* Various numbers, lengths, *Aud:* Sa, Ac. *Rv:* H. *Jv:* B.

Primarily a technical magazine for the psychologist and counselor. Averaging some 7 to 12 scholarly articles per issue, contributors cover the use of tests in education, government and industry. Particularly useful for full descriptions of new testing programs. Book reviews vary in number, but are long and detailed.

Existential Psychiatry. 1966. 2/yr. $10. Amer. Ontoanalytic Assn., Suite 5908, Marina Towers, 300 North State St., Chicago, Ill. 60610.

Bk. rev: Various numbers, lengths. *Aud:* Sa, Ac, *Rv:* H. *Jv:* B.

Despite its rather professional title, this journal speaks not only to the specialist but carries interesting non-technical essays on psychology, sociology, theology, philosophy, literature, and the arts for the educated general audience as well. The ethical values of existentialism are always stressed over the medical aspects of psychiatry. Signed critical book reviews, some of them quite lengthy.

Human Organization. See Anthropology and Archaeology Section.

Journal of Applied Psychology. 1917. bi-m. $10. Kenneth E. Clark. Amer. Psychological Assn., Inc., 1200 17th St., N.W., Washington, D.C. 20036. Adv. Circ: 6,200. Microform: UM. Reprint: Johnson.

Indexed: BioAb, PsyAb. *Aud:* Sa, Ac. *Rv:* H. *Jv:* B.

For people interested "in the following broad areas: personnel research; industrial working conditions; research on morale factors; job analysis . . ." Each issue contains about 25 short articles. Subject matter is wide enough to appeal to both the psychologist and the expert in business practices, and personnel.

Journal of Counseling Psychology. 1954. m. $10. Frances P. Robinson. Amer. Psychological Assn., 1200 17th St., N.W., Washington, D.C. 20036. Circ: 3,100.

Indexed: EdI, PsyAb. *Bk. rev:* Various numbers, lengths. *Aud:* Sa, Ac, Jc, Ht, Et. *Rv:* H. *Jv:* B.

A particularly useful journal for the college or school counselor and others working with personnel. Emphasis is on original research and reports, both practical and theoretical, in the field. Particularly good for regular analysis of other research papers. The 15 to 18 articles per issue cover well the whole spectrum of interests of counselors at almost any level. In view of its reliability, authority, and overview of the field, a first choice in medium to large schools where there are counselors or psychologists on the staff.

Journal of Creative Behavior. See Education Section.

Journal of Educational Psychology. See Education Section.

Journal of Learning Disabilities. See Education Section.

Journal of Personality and Social Psychology. 1965. m. $30. William McGuire, Amer. Psychological Assn., 1200 17th St. N.W., Washington, D.C. 20036. Microform: UM.

Indexed: PsyAb. *Aud:* Sa, Ac. *Rv:* H. *Jv:* B.

Highly technical, with articles on recent research on a wide range of subjects. Notes on references and method are uniformly good. Contributors are from nearly all segments of the fields of psychology and sociology, though there is predominance of social psychologists. Volumes cumulate three times annually, with separate indexes, which can make searching time consuming. Only for the college or university library.

Journal of Social Issues. 1945. q. $7. (Institutions, $9). Joshua A. Fishman. Soc. for the Psychological Study of Social Issues, Box 1248, Ann Arbor, Mich. 48106. Illus., adv. Circ: 5,000. Reprint: Kraus. Microform: UM.

Indexed: BioAb, PsyAb, SSHum. *Aud:* Sa, Ac, Jc, Sh. *Rv:* H. *Jv:* A.

Seeks to bring theory and practice into focus on human problems of the group, community, and nation. The goal is to communicate scientific findings in a non-technical manner without the sacrifice of professional standards. Each issue has a guest editor and seven articles on different aspects of a single topic, like bilingualism or cultural change in small communities. Authors are professors or specialists in the field. Extensive bibliographies accompany each article. In the back of the issue are perforated pages of three by five cards giving a full bibliographic citation and an annotation of the articles appearing. Because of the inter-disciplinary and non-technical approach and analysis of current social issues, the journal would be of value to most libraries including high schools.

Journal of Verbal Learning and Verbal Behavior. 1962. bi-m. $35. Endel Tulving. Academic Press, Inc., 111 Fifth Ave., New York, N.Y. 10003.

Indexed: PsyAb. *Aud:* Sa, Ac. *Rv:* H. *Jv:* B.

Concentrates on highly specialized work in the fields of psychology and social psychology. There are anywhere from 20 to 50 articles varying from 2 to 20 pages. Author and subject indexes are issued annually. For experts only.

Literature and Psychology. See Literature Section.

Mental Health. 1940. q. $21. H. L. Freeman. National Assn. for Mental Health, Maurice Craig House, 39 Queen Anne St., London W.1. Illus., adv. Circ: 6,000. Microform: UM.

Indexed: PAIS, PsyAb. *Bk. rev:* 5, 50–500 words, signed. *Aud:* Ga, Ac, Jc. *Rv:* M. *Jv:* B.

This small pamphlet-like magazine gives a rather thorough coverage of events of the National Association for Mental Health in England. Each issue is mainly devoted to one topic, such as alcoholism. An editorial plus about six short articles discuss the topic. A section, "Parliament, Press & Broadcasting," contains brief articles on programs, newspaper articles, and legal actions concerning mental health. Another section, "News & Notes," comments on news of interest to those concerned with what is being done about mental health. Along with book reviews there is a list of recent publications received. Because of its non-periodical character, useful to all larger libraries with psychology holdings.

Mental Hygiene. 1917. q. $8. Henry A. Davidson. The National Assn. for Mental Health, 10 Columbus Circle, New York, N.Y. 10019. Circ: 4,000. Microform: UM.

Indexed: BioAb, IMed, PAIS, PsyAb, RG. *Bk. rev:* Various numbers, lengths, signed. *Aud:* Ga, Sa, Ac, Jc, Ht, Et. *Rv:* H. *Jv:* A.

One of the few psychology directed magazines suitable for laymen and students. All articles are prepared by experts, but are written in a style which can be understood by the average educated reader. Emphasis is on reporting new developments in mental health and is probably of most interest for the authoritative articles on prevention and treatment of various types of mental problems. Social workers and teachers will find much of assistance in understanding given types of personalities, both adult and child, whom they encounter in their work. The book reviews vary in length and number, covering all important titles in the field and related areas; and there are reports of major surveys and other briefer works. A limited amount of space is turned over to activities of the sponsoring agency. For all types of libraries, regardless of size or clientele.

Perceptual Cognitive Development. 1965. bi-m. $20. Frieda Liebow. Box 35336, Preuss Station, Los Angeles, Calif. 90035. Circ: 528.

Indexed: PsyAb. *Bk. rev:* 40 of varying length, signed. *Aud:* Sa. *Rv:* H. *Jv:* B.

Provides a comprehensive ongoing bibliography on perceptual, cognitive, and creative processes. Computer produced in five sections: bibliography, divided by type of materials, which provides the major entry and code numbers for listed items; KWIC index; author's address list, particularly useful for unpublished materials; a list of sources; and a lengthy section of book reviews. Particularly useful at a time when interest and materials on human mental processes are growing rapidly. Necessary for college and university libraries.

Personnel Psychology. 1948. q. $10. John A. Hornaday. Box 6965, College Station, Durham, N.C. 27708.

Indexed: BusI, PsyAb. *Bk. rev:* 12–15, 100–500 words, signed. *Aud:* Sa, Ac. *Rv:* H. *Jv:* B.

Written for and primarily by industrial psychologists, this has wider application than most psychological journals. Articles are useful for anyone doing counseling work, or directly involved with personnel at almost any level of business or in a professional capacity. Teachers may find much of value here, too. While the articles are technical and presuppose at least a basic knowledge of psychology, they touch on problems common in everyday life. In addition to the book reviews, there are surveys of the current literature on personnel psychology. A useful journal for medium to large libraries.

Psychiatry & Social Science Review. 1967. m. $9. Seymour Weingarten. 95 Fourth Ave., New York, N.Y. 10003. Illus., adv. Circ: 22,000.

Aud: Sa, Ga, Ac, Jc, Ht. *Rv:* H. *Jv:* A.

A 32-page illustrated review media which calls upon leading social scientists, psychologists and psychiatrists to write long essay type reviews of major new publications. Contributors have included Paul Goodman, Ernest van den Haag, Edward Glover and Karl Menninger. Some 10 to 12 current books are noted in each issue, usually about a central theme, e.g. children and youth, community action, personality, etc. Other issues are more diversified, some even resorting to articles on a given subject. Somewhat like the

New York Review of Books (only in magazine format) in that books examined are simply springboards for learned essays. Many of the titles are not mentioned or thoroughly reviewed elsewhere. The style is semi-popular, the titles selected of interest to both the specialist and the layman. The end result is both a review and a social commentary on a subject of vital interest. The nice combination of authority with a pleasing, informative approach makes this an excellent item for all medium to large public and academic libraries. It, also, should be in most professional high school collections. (Until Jan. 1, 1969 was a free, controlled circulation publication.)

Psychoanalytic Quarterly. 1932. q. $10. Gerard Fountain. Psychoanalytic Quarterly, Inc., 57 W. 57th St., New York, N.Y. 10019. Adv. Circ: 4,000. Reprint: Abrahams.

Indexed: IMed, PsyAb. *Bk. rev:* 20, 2–5 pages, signed. *Aud:* Sa, Ac. *Rv:* H. *Jv:* B.

A professional journal for psychiatrists. There are generally five to seven fairly long articles (10–30 pages), most with extensive bibliographies. Many articles are case studies or collections of similar cases. There are usually about twenty 2- to 5-page signed, critical reviews of books. Of some interest to students and interested adults, but not necessary to a general collection.

Psychology in the Schools. 1964. q. $12.50. Psychology Press, Inc., 4 Conant Square, Brandon, Vt. 05733. Circ: 1,500.

Aud: Ac, Jc, Ht, Et. *Rv:* M. *Jv:* B.

A semi-popular journal of psychology aimed primarily at teachers from elementary school through colleges. Articles are both by educators and professional psychologists and include a wide variety of material on interpretation, methodology, and research. Useful, too, for counselors. Not a necessity, but a worthwhile addition for larger collections.

Psychology Today. 1967. m. $9. CRM Associates, 1330 Camino Del Mar, Calif. 92014. Illus., adv.

Bk. rev: 4–7, various lengths, signed. *Aud:* Ga, Sa, Ac, Jc, Sh. *Rv:* H. *Jv:* V.

This lively magazine gives intelligent laymen a look at current developments in American psychology while showing the professional what is happening outside his niche. Strikingly illustrated articles do double educational duty: they appeal in their own right and concurrently reflect immediate and historical psychological issues. Thus an article on pain and aggression, dealing with stimulus and response, also explores relationships between animal and human psychology. "The Psychopharmacological Revolution" presents data on the use of drugs in research, in treatment, and in society. An article on amnesia examines the links between the normal and pathological, while a Huxley reprint considers not only genetics and biology, but reflects psychology's continuing interest in utopias. In each article, interplay between specific problems and general concerns highlights a

pithy presentation. The net and cumulative effect is the entertainment and enlightenment of the reader. Along with *Transaction,* one of the best magazines now available to meet need for minimum representation in the behavioral sciences. Highly recommended for all types of libraries from high school through the university, as well as small to large public libraries.

Rehabilitation Record. 1960. bi-m. $1.75. Dorothy Rigdon. Vocational Rehabilitation Administration. Subscriptions to: Supt. of Documents, Govt. Printing Office, Washington, D.C. 20402. Illus. Circ: 7,200.

Indexed: IMed. *Bk. rev:* Notes. *Aud:* Sa, Ac. *Rv:* H. *Jv:* B.

A standard sized, glossy magazine prepared by a government agency to report significant opinions, programs and techniques in the field of rehabilitation of disabled persons. Each article of the usual ten is about 1,500 words long and is illustrated and signed. The magazine also covers research, and training programs for professionals. Of use to guidance departments as well as to those who work in the field of rehabilitation.

Social Sciences and Medicine. See Medical, Nursing and Health Sciences Section.

RADIO, TELEVISION AND ELECTRONICS

Indexes and Abstracts

Applied Science and Technology Index, Business Periodicals Index, Chemical Abstracts, Readers' Guide to Periodical Literature. (For annotations, see Indexes and Abstracts Section.)

Broadcasting. 1931. w. $10. Sol Taishoff. Broadcasting Pubns. Inc., 1735 DeSales St., N.W. Washington, D.C. 20036. Illus., adv., programming. Circ: 32,000.

Indexed: BusI. *Aud:* Sa, Ac, Jc. *Rv:* M. *Jv:* B.

All-inclusive business newsweekly of broadcasting (radio and television), staff-written and edited to serve national and regional advertisers and their agencies; networks; stations; program suppliers; equipment manufacturers; sales representatives; research organizations; governmental bodies and allied phases of the business and art of broadcasting. News concerning TV and radio, government, strikes, and sales are included. Completely reports the Federal Communications Commission's regulations, hearings and legal procedures, discussing all legislation affecting broadcasting. The latest trends, statistics and developments in the field of communications are reported and analyzed for the media and advertising executive. A required magazine where radio and television courses are given, and good for large business collections. The *Broadcasting Yearbook* (1935. $10.) includes 51 separate directories of basic economic, technical and business facts relating to broadcasting and associated arts and services.

CQ; the radio amateurs journal. 1945. m. $5. Cowan Publishing Corp., 14 Vanderventer Ave., Port Washington, N.Y. 11050. Illus., adv. Circ: 98,000.

Aud: Ga, Sh, Jh. *Rv:* M. *Jv:* B.

Somewhat the same in approach and scope as *QST,* this concentrates on "ham" radio, and all related fields. Equipment reports on electronics employed by the amateur, i.e., receivers, antennas, transmitters and almost anything else that comes on the market. The reports are accurate and useful to all amateurs. *QST* covers much the same ground but in more technical fashion. While the publishers claim differences in quality and scope, it is difficult to tell. Like a number of specialized magazines, selection is more a matter of personal bias than objective judgment. Some will prefer *QST* because it is one of the oldest of its type in the field, others will turn to *CQ* for a given feature. What it comes down to for librarians—subscribe to them both, or try one after the other. Both are suitable for anyone involved in the subject from junior high through to the old folks home.

Educational Television International. 1967. q. $15. Pergamon Press, Maxwell House, Fairview Park, Elmsford, N.Y. 10523. Illus.

Aud: Sa, Ac, Ht, Et. *Rv:* H. *Jv:* B.

Includes major articles on educational television in Hawaii, Norway, Singapore, and Plymouth. Features range from production notes to bibliographies. Primarily for the expert, this is an intelligent, international approach to an increasingly important area. Again, a basic magazine for academic libraries supporting educational television curricula, but only for large public libraries.

Electronics Illustrated. 1958. bi-m. $3. Fawcett Pubns., 67 W. 44th St., New York, N.Y. 10036. Illus., adv. Circ: 266,000. Microform: UM.

Aud: Ga, Sh, Jh. *Rv:* M. *Jv:* B.

A popular magazine for the electronic hobbyist of all ages. Emphasis is on amateur radio and on new electronic products. The primary value of the magazine for the younger readers is that it gives detailed, step-by-step instructions for constructing such items as short wave radios, hi-fi sets, and less technical radio equipment. The articles are purposefully non-technical, and well illustrated. Should be both a source of instruction and casual reading for the interested teen-ager or adult.

Electronics World. 1919. m. $6. Ziff-Davis, 1 Park Ave., New York, N.Y. 10016. Illus., adv. Circ: 172,000.

Indexed: ChemAb, RG. *Aud:* Sa, Ac, Jc. *Rv:* M. *Jv:* B.

Unlike *Electronics Illustrated* and *Popular Electronics,* this is primarily for the expert in electronics. It is for adults who have some basic knowledge of the field and are seeking information on technical advances, new products and equipment, and changes in personnel in various plants and government sponsored industries. Of the two magazines,

Electronics Illustrated would be a first choice for all but the larger libraries serving a specialized group of readers.

Ham Radio. m. $5. James R. Fisk, Communications Technology, Inc., Greenville, N.H. 03048. Illus., adv.

Aud: Sa, Ga. *Rv:* H. *Jv:* B.

An amateur radio magazine which is somewhat more technical than either the two standards, i.e., *CQ Magazine* and *QST.* It presupposes a basic knowledge of electronics and an ability to read the many, useful technical diagrams which illustrate each of the ten to twelve articles. One issue, for example, featured such items as "Strip Line Kilowatt for 432 MHz" and "Thermoelectric Power Supplies." There are several regular departments including appraisals of new equipment and products. Will be of primary value to the adult, serious student of the subject. Definitely not a high school magazine, at least at the average level.

NAEB Journal. 1941. bi-m. $6. National Assn. of Educational Broadcasters, Gregory Hall, Univ. of Ill., Urbana, Ill. 61801. Circ: 2,600. Microform: UM.

Aud: Ac, Jc, Ht, Et. *Rv:* M. *Jv:* B.

One of the few objective sources of news and developments in an ever important area of education—educational television and radio. Keeps the reader advised on government financing and activities in the field, and includes both research and pragmatic articles for the teacher who is using educational television and the director of such programs. Even schools without such facilities should enter a subscription, if only to indicate to administrative officials and some teachers what is going on in this major educational field.

Popular Electronics. 1954. m. $5. Ziff-Davis, 1 Park Ave., New York, N.Y. 10016. Illus., adv. Circ: 400,000. Microform: UM.

Indexed: RG. *Bk. rev:* 3–4, 140–200 words, signed. *Aud:* Ga, Sh. *Rv:* H. *Jv:* B.

This is for the amateur, but for a more learned one than envisioned for *Electronics Illustrated.* The features and articles presuppose at least a basic knowledge of ham radio, short wave and electronic equipment. A typical issue may feature articles on careers in the field, a special project complete with detailed diagrams, and a number of departments, from tips and techniques to new products. A considerable amount of advertising.

QST. 1915. m. Membership (Non-members, $6). John Huntoon. Amer. Radio Relay League, Inc., 225 Main St., Newington, Conn. 06111. Illus., adv. Circ: 105,000. Microform: UM.

Indexed: ASTI. *Bk. rev:* Occasional. *Aud:* Sa, Sh. *Rv:* M. *Jv:* B.

The official organ of the League, and one of the oldest radio magazines devoted solely to the interests of the "ham" operator. While the articles are technical, none is beyond the reach of anyone deeply interested in the subject, and the magazine is suitable for the boy in high school as well as for the expert. The writers cover all aspects of ham radio operating, maintenance and information on individual stations and operators. Not an essential item, but it will be welcomed by all adults and students who have more than a passing interest in amateur radio.

Radio Electronics. 1929. m. $6. M. H. Gernsback. Gernsback Pubns., Inc., 154 W. 14th St., New York, N.Y. 10003. Illus., adv. Circ: 158,000. Microform: UM.

Indexed: ASTI, RG. *Bk. rev:* 4, 50 words, unsigned. *Aud:* Sh, Ga, Sa. *Rv:* M. *Jv:* A.

Of interest to electronics students, technicians, and servicemen, as well as the ubiquitous do-it-yourself buffs, the magazine keeps a good balance between practical articles for building new equipment (with an occasional evaluation by the editorial staff), servicing and repairs, and tutorials on new technological advances or refreshers on basic physical principles and mathematical tools. Articles are popularly written; easily comprehensible. Departments include news briefs; "Technotes," tips for the trade; "Service Clinic," data on servicing radio and TV receivers; "Noteworthy Circuits," information on novel circuitry as gleaned from other technical periodicals; and the usual news products, equipment and literature.

RELIGION AND THEOLOGY

Indexes and Abstracts

Abridged Readers' Guide, Catholic Periodical and Literature Index, Index to Religious Periodical Literature, Public Affairs Information Service, Readers' Guide to Periodical Literature, Religious and Theological Abstracts, Social Sciences and Humanities Index. (For annotations, see Indexes and Abstracts Section.)

America; national Catholic weekly review. 1909. w. $8. Thurston N. Davis. America Press, 106 W. 56th St., New York, N.Y. 10019. Adv. Circ: 96,934. Microform: UM.

Indexed: AbrRG, CathI, RG. *Bk. rev:* 5–7, 500 words, signed. *Aud:* Ga, Ac, Jc, Sh. *Rv:* H. *Jv:* A.

Although a Jesuit periodical, this presents a broad variety of topics—national, international, educational, social and political. Articles are written by outstanding Catholics, usually lay personages. The editorial policy represents the new liberal Catholic viewpoint in regard to such topics as birth control, education and civil rights. In addition to weekly book reviews, there is a semi-annual cumulation of book reviews and a good film review section. *America* will give the library an excellent source for one of the many Catholic viewpoints on current social and political problems.

American Jewish Historical Quarterly. See History Section.

American Judaism. 1873. q. $2. Paul Kresh. Union of American-Hebrew Congregations, 838 Fifth Ave., New York, N.Y. 10021. Illus., adv. Circ: 220,000. Microform: UM.

Book rev: Various numbers, lengths. *Aud:* Ga. *Rv:* M. *Jv:* B.

A middle-of-the-road publication of the Reform Jewish movement, which features above average fiction and articles on all aspects of Judaism. While this in no way compares with the more intellectual, more universal *Commentary,* it has wide appeal for the average family. A must for any library serving a Jewish community.

Ave Maria. 1865. w. $8. John Reedy. Ave Maria, Notre Dame, Ind. 46556. Illus., adv. Circ: 50,819.

Indexed: CathI. *Bk. rev:* 1, 1,000 words, signed. *Aud:* Ga, Ac, Jc, Sh. *Rv:* M. *Jv:* B.

One of the oldest Catholic magazines in America, this 32-page paper is issued by the Ave Maria religious order. At one time considered quite conservative, it has taken on a more liberal tone in the past few years. Each issue features five or six articles of 2,000 to 4,000 words, a book review, and photo-essays. Departments include the "Editor's Desk," a page of letters, a four page "Notes and Comments" section (editorials and brief news items) and a page by Edward Fischer, generally dealing with the arts and communication. From time to time, there are long excerpts from books, e.g., Medgar Evers' *For Us, The Living.* The tone is captured by the editor who remarks "We try to offer our readers an examination of events, issues, problems and personalities of the day from a standpoint of religious concern—since we feel that religion has something to say to the times." A good to excellent choice for all Catholic libraries and many larger Protestant and Jewish oriented collections.

The Aylesford Review. See Literary and Political Reviews Section.

Best Sermons. 1966. bi-m. $3. A. R. Roalman. Prol Publishing, 561 Riford Rd., Glen Ellyn, Ill. 60137. Circ: 2,500.

Aud: Sa, Ga. *Rv:* L. *Jv:* B.

According to the editor, this is an "interdenominational" collection of sermons. The issue usually includes two- to four-page messages from a Methodist minister, a rabbi, a priest, and a member of the Princeton Theological Seminary. Topics range from the general to "The Crisis in Catholic Schools." The style is good to excellent; emphasis on objectivity, not emotion.

The Catholic Biblical Quarterly. 1939. q. Membership (Non-members, $6). Catholic Biblical Assn. of America, Catholic Univ. of America, Washington, D.C. 20017. Microform: UM. Reprint: AMS.

Indexed: CathI, RelAb, RelPer. *Bk. rev:* Various numbers, lengths, signed. *Aud:* Sa, Ac. *Rv:* M. *Jv:* B.

This journal serves as a place for the publication of Biblical exegesis from the Catholic point of view. Biblical discussions of one sort or another occupy a good part of the journal, e.g., possible revision of the Church's attitude in the matter of divorce, and the provision of a common-language version of the Bible. In addition to articles, each issue contains a large number of medium-length reviews and a section called "Biblical News", in which events of importance to Biblical scholars are noted. A learned journal in the old-fashioned, somewhat ponderous sense, but indispensable for an understanding of much that is happening in the world of Catholic scholarship.

Catholic Digest. 1936. m. $4. Kenneth Ryan. Catholic Publishing Center of the College of St. Thomas, 2859 N. Hamline Ave., St. Paul, Minn. 55113. Illus., adv. Circ: 625,000. Microform: UM.

Indexed: CathI. *Aud:* Ga. *Rv:* L. *Jv:* B.

A family type magazine which is somewhat the equivalent of *Presbyterian Life,* but aimed directly at Catholics. As the title suggests, it lifts the "best" material from other publications—magazines, books, newspapers—which are not necessarily Catholic. The level of choice is relatively high, but the magazine avoids most controversial or sophisticated, challenging matters. It favors features on travel, hobbies, sports, health, education, and the like. Approximately one-quarter is given over to religious affairs. A solid, pedestrian magazine for the less intellectually motivated Catholic community.

Catholic World. 1865. m. $8. John B. Sheerin. Harristown Rd., Glen Rock, N.J. 07542. Circ: 20,500. Microform: UM.

Indexed: RG, CathI. *Aud:* Ga, Ac, Jc, Sh. *Bk. rev:* 10–15, 250–500 words, signed. *Rv:* M. *Jv:* A.

Published by the Paulist Fathers, this has a thoroughly Catholic orientation, with a questioning and concerned style. Focus is on contemporary social and religious issues, whether or not they are specifically Catholic. Much attention is given to the cases for and against all varieties of dissenters, particularly with situations relevant to the evaluation of Catholic roles in a time of turbulent moral issues. Typical topics are youth, ecumenism, humanism, race, urban problems, and education. Several considered and articulate articles per issue. Recommended for all collections serving users from high school level on up.

Christian Century. See Literary and Political Reviews Section.

Christian Herald. 1878. m. $4. Ford Stewart. Christian Herald Assn., 27 E. 39th St., New York, N.Y. 10016. Illus., adv. Circ: 500,000.

Bk. rev: 8, 50–100 words, signed. *Aud:* Ga. *Rv:* M. *Jv:* B.

An interdenominational Protestant family magazine, this features six to eight major articles on current events, news, and general interest religious and ethical questions. It includes Sunday school lesson background materials, daily devotional features, and an editorial essay. Both photos and drawings are used, and the overall makeup is professional and appealing. As one of the oldest Christian magazines, it boasts a middle-of-the-road, yet realistic approach to both religion and events. It should be in most medium to large libraries where religious material of this type is needed.

Christian Scholar; a journal of Christian higher education. 1917. q. $5. Richard E. Shevell. Div. of Christian Education, National Council of Churches, 475 Riverside Drive, New York, N.Y. 10017. Illus., adv. Circ: 4,000.

Indexed: EdI, RelAb. *Bk. rev:* Various lengths, numbers. signed. *Aud:* Sa, Ac, Jc. *Rv:* M. *Jv:* B.

Directed to teachers and students of higher education, articles discuss the implications of religion and ethics. The tone is scholarly, the interests broad, the bias Protestant, albeit contributors are included from all religious faiths. Of primary interest to church directed schools and those with medium to large theology and education departments.

Christianity and Crisis; a Christian journal of opinion. 1941. Fortnightly. $7. (Schools and foreign nationals, $4). Ed bd. 537 W. 121st St., New York, N.Y. 10027. Circ: 18,000.

Indexed: RelPer. *Aud:* Sa, Ac. *Rv:* M. *Jv:* A.

Although it has a low circulation, this is one of the most respected Protestant periodicals. It is closely associated with the Union Theological Seminary, and has been given an intellectual boost by former Seminary vice-president Dr. Reinhold Niebuhr. As a Christian journal of opinion, it it far beyond the typical religious magazine. As the editor notes, it "explores the implications of Christian faith for the modern world and interprets the significance of 'secular' events for our Christian witness." The articles are clearly written, tend to be in terms an educated layman can understand, and usually number two or three per issue. Many of the journal's former editors are major leaders in the Protestant church, and the influence of the magazine goes quite beyond its subscribers. It should be found in any library where there is the remotest interest in advanced religious opinion.

Christianity Today. 1956. bi-w. $6. Washington Bldg., Washington, D.C. 20005. Circ: 150,000. Microform: UM.

Indexed: PAIS. RG, RelAb, RelPer. *Bk. rev:* 20–30, 150–500 words, signed. *Aud:* Ga. *Rv:* M. *Jv:* B.

A Protestant evangelical magazine which is for conservatives what *The Christian Century* is for liberals. Many consider it the most articulate and significant magazine of its type, particularly under the editorship of Rev. Carl F. H. Henry. However, Henry stepped down in 1968 and the magazine may undergo some changes. Readers who look to the periodical have been described as Protestants who de-emphasize the modern ecumenical movement and prefer a strict and literal interpretation of the Bible. As a balance to theological liberalism, the magazine is a legitimate purchase in any library with more than a small collection of religious periodicals.

Church History. 1932. q. $5. Ed bd. Amer. Soc. of Church History. 321 Mill Rd., Oreland, Pa. 19075. Circ: 1,850.

Indexed: RelAb, SSHum. *Bk. rev:* 31, 150–250 words, signed. *Aud:* Sa, Ac. *Rv:* H. *Jv:* B.

A non-denominational, scholarly journal which considers all aspects of church history. Contributors and editors are representative of the nation's leading theological seminaries and schools—University of Chicago, Harvard, Union Theological Seminary, etc. While a good part of the material is only of interest to theologians, there are occasional articles of broader implications, e.g., a detailed report on the *Christian Century.* In addition to the book reviews and shorter book notes, there is a regular section on "Dissertation Abstracts," business news of the organization, and general information on religion in America and abroad. A basic journal for any medium to large academic library.

The Church Quarterly. 1968. q. Gordon Wakefield. Epworth Press, 25 City Rd., London E.C.1.

Indexed: RelAb, RelPer. *Bk. rev:* 34, 250–500 words, signed. *Aud:* Sa, Ac. *Rv:* H. *Jv:* B.

Until 1968 better known as the *London Quarterly and Holborn Review* (founded 1853); combined with the Anglican *Church Quarterly Review* to become one of the world's leading scholarly theological journals. Contributors are ministers and teachers. About one-half is devoted to the finer points of theology, the other to literature and social considerations. The book reviews are many and outstanding, and the whole is one of the better religious magazines for medium to large academic collections.

Concurrence; a review for the encounter of commitments. 1969. q. $10. Ed bd. Herder & Herder, 232 Madison Ave., New York, N.Y. 10016.

Aud Sa, Ac. *Rv:* H. *Jv:* B.

A philosophical and theological magazine whose purpose is to open conversation between "Christians and atheists, believers and nonbelievers," who share "the common humanistic heritage that binds together all men of good will." The editorial board includes leading scholars of Europe and America, the content reflects a high level of scholarship, and the whole is primarily for the involved student. The first issue, for example, covered such topics as three views of atheism, the second Vatican council, and "Hope as a Problem and Ideal—Legends and Reality." The level of writing is uniformly excellent, and peculiar in that the authors resort to a minimum of footnotes. A required item in larger academic and public libraries.

Critic; a Catholic review of books and the arts. 1942. bi-m. $5. Joel Wells, Thomas More Assn., 180 N. Wabash Ave., Chicago, Ill. 60601. Illus., adv. Circ: 30,000. Microform: UM.

Indexed: CathI. *Bk. rev:* 18, 1,000 words, signed. *Aud:* Ga, Ac, Jc, Sh. *Rv:* M. *Jv:* A.

The Chicago cousin of the New York *Jubilee,* this is equally attractive in approach and format. While addressed to liberal Catholics, it has much broader social and cultural interests. There are usually five to six articles, a short story, a photo story, cartoons, and many illustrations. Writers are among the leading intellectuals (both Catholic and non-Catholic) from the United States and abroad. The book review section, which includes both long and short statements, is considered by many to be one of the best general sources for objective comments on new religious works. Either this or *Jubilee* should be found in most libraries with an above average educated group of users.

Dialogue; a journal of Mormon thought. 1965. q. $6. Eugene England & Wesley Johnson. Dialogue Foundation, P.O. Box 2350, Stanford, Calif. 94305. Circ: 2,500.

Aud: Sa, Ac. *Rv:* H. *Jv:* B.

This publication has as its aim the describing of Mormon culture and the relating of the Mormon experience to everyday life. It is, as its editors say, a journal in which an exchange of opinion is invited on any subject with a bearing on Mormonism. A matter of note is that although *Dialogue* in general puts forward the Mormon viewpoint, it does so with an impartiality that must sometimes seem perilously close to apostasy to conservative-minded Latter-Day Saints. The fact is that *Dialogue's* editors—young Turks of the LDS movement—are determined to show that Mormonism can break out of the solemn stereotype it has acquired for itself over the years. In both content and presentation, this magazine is of enviably high quality.

Ecumenist. 1962. bi-m. Free. Gregory Baum & Kevin Lynch. Paulist Press, 304 W. 58th St., New York, N.Y. 10019. Circ: 19,000.

Bk. rev: 2, 200 words. *Aud:* Sa, Ac. *Rv:* H. *Jv:* B.

A Catholic journal for promoting Christian unity, this is broader in scope than the title implies. As the editor explains: "Since the ecumenical movement in the Christian Churches now focuses on social religious issues—race, poverty, war, etc.—, it concerns itself with these." There are frequent articles on the Jewish-Christian dialogue, some ecumenical news notes and all important documentation in the field. This latter feature, coupled with the fact the magazine is free, makes it a highly desirable reference item for many libraries. In this same area, the World Council of Churches issues two good magazines: *Ecumenical Review* (1948. q. $4. 150 route de Ferney, 1211 Geneva 20, Switzerland) and the *Ecumenical Courier* (1941. bi-m. $5. 475 Riverside Drive, New York, N.Y. 10027). Neither has quite the Catholic emphasis of the *Ecumenist,* but are equally broad in coverage and interests. A large library would want all of these, but medium to large libraries without important religious collections will find the free *Ecumenist* meets most general needs.

Harvard Theological Review. 1908. q. $4. Krister Stendhal. Harvard Univ. Press, 79 Garden St., Cambridge, Mass. 02138. Circ: 1,024. Reprint: Kraus.

Indexed: RelAb, SSHum. *Aud:* Sa, Ac. *Rv:* H. *Jv:* A.

Published by the Harvard Divinity School, this is a non-denominational, scholarly theology journal. It is particularly valuable for the student and educated layman as it covers a wide number of areas, from church history and Biblical studies to the philosophy of religion and science. Contributors are international, albeit a number are drawn from Harvard. The articles are generally quite within the grasp of the well educated reader. In many ways one of the best journals in the field, and a first choice for medium to large libraries seeking material on or related to religion.

Hibbert Journal; a quarterly review of world religions and literal thought. 1902. q. $2.50. Allen & Unwin Ltd., 40 Museum St., London W.C.1. Microform: UM.

Indexed: BritHum, RelAb. *Bk. rev:* Various numbers, 500–1,500 words, signed. *Aud:* Sa, Ac. *Rv:* H. *Jv:* B.

Primarily a scholarly effort to study philosophical implications of Christianity. The scope is international, all periods are covered, and contributors are among some of the world's leading philosophers and theologians. Particularly useful for the long, usually numerous reviews and the notes of current trends in the literature of the field.

History of Religions; an international journal for comparative historical studies. 1961. q. $8. Mircea Eliade, Joseph Katagawa, Charles Long. Univ. of Chicago Press, Chicago, Ill. 60637. Adv. Circ: 960. Microform: UM.

Indexed: RelAb, RelPer. *Aud:* Sa, Ac, Jc. *Rv:* H. *Jv:* A.

The leading journal in this field. Its coverage extends potentially to any past or present religion. The articles are on a high level of scholarship and are sometimes virtually unaccessible without background, but this is eventually a corollary to its excellence. There are about four rather long articles per issue. There are no other features. Excellent for college and university libraries, and necessary for any basic collection on religion.

Intercollegian. 1882. 8/yr. (Sept.–June). $.50. National Board of YMCA's, 291 Broadway, New York, N.Y. 10007. Illus., adv. Circ: 5,000/10,000. Microform: UM.

Aud: Ac, Jc. *Rv:* M. *Jv:* B.

Specifically geared for college and university students, the YMCA publication attempts to demonstrate the importance of the Christian life. The articles and studies are written in an interesting, semi-popular fashion and touch on almost every aspect of religion from sports to international affairs. While this is no intellectual's delight, it has a given amount of appeal for those who take a serious, yet not studious stand on religion.

Interracial Review. See Afro-American Section.

Journal for the Scientific Study of Religion. 1961. semi-ann. Membership (Non-members, $8.50). James Dittes. Soc. for the Scientific Study of Religion, 1200 17th St., N.W., Washington, D.C. 20036. Circ: 2,600. Microform: UM.

Indexed: RelPer. *Bk. rev:* 15–25, varying lengths, signed. *Aud:* Sa, Ac, Jc. *Rv:* H. *Jv:* A.

Despite similarities in the title, this journal takes quite a different, more pragmatic, tack from *Zygon,* and in doing so probably comes closer to accomplishing the goals. Peter Berger, author of *The Noise of Solemn Assemblies* and other sociological studies of religion, is president of the Society, which is reflected in the role played by sociological and psychological studies in the *Journal.* Each of these disciplines has a section, along with sections on history and theory. The book reviews cover nearly everything relevant and are as well done as the rest of the journal. Excellent for any college of university library.

Journal of Bible and Religion. 1933. q. $6. Amer. Academy of Religion, c/o Harry M. Buck, Wilson College, Changersburg, Pa. 17201. Circ: 2,500.

Indexed: RelAb, RelPer. *Bk. rev:* Various numbers, lengths, signed. *Aud:* Sa, Ac, Jc. *Rv:* H. *Jv:* B.

Emphasis here is on scholarly articles of assistance to teachers of the Bible, primarily, although not exclusively, in Christian colleges and universities. The magazine has wider appeal than *Religious Education,* in that it often features studies in related fields such as archaeology and psychology. A useful feature is the abstracts of articles and books in all major areas of religious study. An important journal for the larger library attempting to build a meaningful collection in the area.

Journal of Ecumenical Studies. 1964. q. $8. Leonard Swidler, 1936 N. Broad St., Philadelphia, Pa. Adv. Circ: 4,000.

Indexed: RelAb, RelPer. *Bk. rev:* 30, varying lengths, signed. *Aud:* Ga, Ac, Jc. *Rv:* H. *Jv:* V.

A remarkable journal. It is often technical, always scholarly, yet designed for the general reader. Each article is preceded by a precis, and is supplemented with a special study guide, which is well constructed. Many footnotes, often of help to the layman. The articles cover a wide range of subjects and are contributed by such men as Thomas Merton, Markus Barth, and Hans Kung. The book reviews are excellent. There is a section of abstracts of relevant articles from international sources. Current news notes are included, which cover meetings, studies, and significant events. Needed in any college, university, and public library.

Journal of Religion. 1882. q. $6. J. Coert Rylaarsdam. Univ. of Chicago Press, 5750 Ellis Ave., Chicago, Ill. 60637. Circ: 1,431. Microform: UM.

Indexed: SSHum. *Bk. rev:* 6, 4–14 pages, signed, and book notes. *Aud:* Sa, Ac, Jc. *Rv:* H. *Jv:* A.

Somewhat the American equivalent of the English *Hibbert Journal,* this is more universal in scope, not necessarily limited to Christianity. Articles cover all aspects of religious and theological thought, tend to be scholarly, and are primarily for the student and teacher of theology. There are excellent book reviews and notes of new publications. In that the journal is totally removed from any religious creed, it is one of the best for a general collection where there is any consideration of the social, philosophical or historical implications of religion.

Journal of Religious Thought. 1943. semi-ann. $1.50. John H. Giltner. Howard Univ., Washington, D.C. 20001. Illus., adv. Circ: 800. Microform: UM.

Indexed: INeg. *Bk. rev:* 5–6, 200–400 words, signed. *Aud:* Sa, Ac. *Rv:* M. *Jv:* B.

Not specifically Negro-oriented, but published by a Negro university. The scholarly articles deal with abstract theological as well as more practical approaches to modern-day human problems. Some issues contain editorial comment on recent events. Only for large collections.

Jubilee. 1953. m. $6. Edward Rice. A.M.D.G. Publishing Co., Inc., 168 E. 91st St., New York, N.Y. 10028. Illus., adv. Circ: 50,100.

Indexed: CathI. *Bk. rev:* 8–9, 300 words, signed. *Aud:* Ga, Ac, Jc, Sh. *Rv:* M. *Jv:* A.

A lay-edited Catholic magazine, the editor describes his publication as "one operating on the premise which takes religion seriously and will lead the way in what is happening, not follow in the wake of it." Each issue features seven to eight articles on the new theologians, religious activities, and social and political movements which are in any way connected with religion. There are regular columns, and a highlight is the interview with such personalities as: William Sloan Coffin, Daniel Berrigan, a psychiatrist on the religious possibilities of ESP, a Notre Dame Ph.D. on Pentecostalism, Harvey Cox on Ernst Bloch, etc. There are excellent signed book reviews and cartoons by one whom the editor describes as "a slightly mad Trappist philosopher/poet." While the obvious audience for this liberal magazine is the educated young Catholic liberal, it certainly should be in any library which subscribes to the other more conservative, less intellectual Catholic periodicals.

Motive. 1941. 8/yr. $4. B. J. Stiles. Box 871, Nashville, Tenn. 37202. Illus., adv. Circ: 45,000. Microform: UM.

Bk. rev: 4, 2,000 words, signed. *Aud:* Sa, Ac, Jc, Sh. *Rv:* M. *Jv:* A.

A liberal, Protestant magazine, this is closer to the typical literary review than the average religious publication. Each 55-page issue averages some eight articles on contemporary politics, social sciences, literature, and the arts.

There is some fiction, about six pages given over to poetry, and a number of black and white photographs. In addition to scholarly book reviews, regular departments include film and art reviews. Special issues are given over to such subjects as technology, motion pictures, and even death. While the orientation is literary, there is some emphasis on theology. One of the best general Protestant magazines for the medium to large collection.

National Catholic Reporter. 1964. w. $8. Robert G. Hoyt. National Catholic Reporter Publishing Co., P.O. Box 281, Kansas City, Mo. 64141. Illus., adv. Circ: 88,000.

Bk. rev: 8–10, 1 page. *Aud:* Ga, Ac, Jc. *Rv:* H. *Jv:* V.

One of the most lively, controversial Catholic magazines —in newspaper format, and often referred to as a newspaper. Edited by Catholic laymen (it has no official connection with the Church), the appeal is to the educated readers of almost any faith. Coverage is by no means completely religious oriented, and articles and stories move from civil rights and Vietnam to humor and cartoons by Jules Feiffer. By the end of 1968 it had become so closely identified with the liberal activists that it was officially condemned by the Bishop of Kansas City—St. Joseph diocese. According to *The New York Times* (Oct. 20, 1968 p. 4E) the Bishop asserted "the editors were verging on heresy." (The blow-up seems to have come from articles challenging the perpetual virginity of Mary and papal infallibility.) As a public forum for radical views on birth control, priestly celibacy and other church issues, the magazine has earned a place for itself among all those attempting to reform society in general, and the Church in particular. Articles are by staff members, leading laymen and church leaders from all faiths. The style is semi-popular, similar to what is associated with such lay journals as the *New Republic* or *The Nation.* It has an added value for libraries—a page or more of book reviews in each issue. The short reviews cover about 40 percent religious books, 60 percent general titles. There are also lists of titles and news about publishing. An outstanding religious, socially oriented magazine for most general and academic collections.

New Book Review. See Book Reviews Section.

The Plain Truth. 1934. m. Free. Box 111, Pasadena, Calif. 91109. Circ: 1,290,000.

Aud: Ga. *Rv:* M. *Jv:* B.

Boasting one of the largest free circulations of any politically and socially oriented religious publication, this is a 52-page magazine which averages 20 full-color and five black and white pictures per issue. It is handsomely produced, and according to the publisher is a non-subsidized "world news magazine not controlled by any commercial powers, interests, organizations or forces." However, it is issued from Ambassador College, which places considerable emphasis on Biblical fundamentalism, and Muller (pp. 140–141) classes it with right-of-center interests. It is a good example of a religious voice which takes free swings at Communism, Fascism and, to a degree, Western decadence. Again, according to the editor, the *Plain Truth* "speaks authoritatively—certainly—spiritually. These are opposite approaches to knowledges—opposite goals. Its articles on news, education and social, religious, or scientific issues, bring into focus the real issues facing the world today." A fascinating case of a dedicated religious group which gives an interesting view of world affairs.

Presbyterian Life. 1948. semi-m. $2.50. Robert J. Cadigan. United Presbyterian Church, Witherspoon Bldg., Philadelphia, Pa. 19107. Illus., adv. Circ: 170,000.

Aud: Ga. *Rv:* L. *Jv:* B.

Claiming to be the "nation's largest church affairs magazine," this is family centered. It appeals to the group not touched by more sophisticated magazines such as *Christian Century.* Nevertheless, the content and the style is unpretentious and the format quite professional. It covers topics usually covered by a general magazine—current events, history, music, recreation, home, literature, and, of course theology. It avoids emotionalism, features semi-popular writers, and is middle-of-the-road in social and political affairs. While published specifically for Presbyterians, it will appeal to most Protestants.

Religion in Communist Dominated Areas. 1962. Fortnightly. $10. Paul B. Anderson. International Affairs Commission of the National Council of Churches of Christ in the U.S.A., 475 Riverside Drive, New York, N.Y. 10027. Illus., index. Circ: 2,000.

Aud: Sa, Ac. *Rv:* H. *Jv:* B.

This fairly large offset publication makes available what it calls "authentic information" on Christian activities in the Soviet Union and its satellites. How it does this is to reprint, in translation, news items and articles on church-related matters that have appeared in the Soviet press. Although most of *RCDA's* entries are short, some extend to two or three pages in length. Most, too, are taken from large Soviet publications such as *Pravda* and *Izvestia,* but quite a few come from smaller, less auspicious sources. In a recent issue, for instance, there were reports put out originally by *El Mundo* of Cuba and Liberation Radio, a clandestine Communist radio station in South Vietnam. Of interest in showing how pervasive the Christian influence is, even in parts of the world where it is discounted.

Religious Education. 1906. bi-m. Membership (Nonmembers, $8.50). Randolph C. Miller, Religious Education Assn., 545 W. 111th St., New York, N.Y. 10025. Circ: 4,050. Microform: UM. Reprint: AMS.

Indexed: CathI, EdI, PsyAb, RelAb. *Bk. rev:* Various numbers and lengths, signed. *Aud:* Sa, Ac, Jc, Ht, Et. *Rv:* M. *Jv:* B.

The official publication of the Religious Education Association. Articles are representative of all faiths, and include material on the teaching, history and implications of a religious education. There are often special numbers on various aspects of religion and society and problems besetting the teacher of theology at every level, although emphasis is on colleges and universities. A useful feature is the abstracts of doctoral dissertations in the field. The magazine is useful for the non-theological oriented library in that many articles and frequent special issues touch on topics of interest to anyone remotely involved with today's changing society.

Religious Theatre. See Theatre Section.

Religious Studies. 1965. semi-ann. $9.50. Prof. H. D. Lewis. Cambridge Univ. Press, 32 E. 57th Street, New York, N.Y. 10022.

Indexed: RelPer. *Bk. rev:* Review articles, 8–12 short reviews, signed. *Aud:* Sa, Ac. *Rv:* M. *Jv:* B.

The goal of this journal is to provide space, time and continuity for the discussion of modern religious concepts and questions. It has, naturally a strong theological and philosophical bent, but it devotes considerable space to historical and comparative religious studies, and to the sociology and psychology of religion. The editor welcomes answers to articles, and symposiums presenting differing views of questions are frequent, as in a special section on the ontological argument for the existence of God.

Respond. 1967. irreg. $5. Laymen's League of the Unitarian Universalist Assn., 25 Beacon St., Boston, Mass. 02108. Illus.

Aud: Ga, Sh. *Rv:* L. *Jv:* B.

"The purpose of this magazine is to share events, ideas, concerns that are of significance to the liberal religious community." While the orientation reflects the sponsor—Unitarian—the appeal is general enough to remove it almost entirely from any religious affiliation. An average 50-page issue includes poetry, black and white photographs, and articles on issues of current interest, e.g., "Freedom in Black and White," and "The Paradoxes of Freedom." The writing is scholarly, yet styled for the reader of average education.

Review of Metaphysics. See Philosophy Section.

Saint Louis Quarterly. See Literature Section.

Theological Studies. 1940. q. $5. John C. Murray. Soc. of Jesus in the U.S. I.S.J. Theological Faculties, Woodstock, Md. 21163. Index, adv. Circ: 6,000.

Indexed: CathI, RelPer. *Bk. rev:* Numerous, long, and notes. *Aud:* Sa, Ac. *Rv:* M. *Jv:* B.

This is, as its name implies, a journal devoted to theological matters in general. Its tone is formal but by no means formidable. Recent articles deal with such matters as sin and grace, moral considerations in decision-making and present-day agnosticism. Ecumenism occupies quite a bit of space. Of considerable importance for theological and historical collections.

Theology Digest. 1953. q. $3. Gerald Van Ackeren. St. Louis Univ., School of Divinity, St. Louis, Mo. 63101. Circ: 13,186. Microform: UM.

Indexed: CathI. *Aud:* Sa, Ac. *Rv:* H. *Jv:* B.

Unlike the *Catholic Digest,* this is directed to intellectuals and more particularly those interested in following international trends in religious education, philosophy, and social and political movements. Most of the digested articles come from abroad—Germany, France, Spain, Sweden, etc.—and constitute the best writing of the time. Emphasis is on the Catholic press, but not entirely, and even for the non-religiously oriented student the magazine has much to offer. A good publication for all medium to large libraries seeking a cross section of current religious writing.

Thought. 1926. q. $6.50. Joseph E. O'Neill. Fordham Univ. Press, 441 E. Fordham Rd., Bronx, N.Y. 10458. Circ: 2,300. Reprint: AMS. Microform: UM.

Indexed: CathI, PhilosI, SSHum. *Bk. rev:* 24–30, 600 words, signed. *Aud:* Ga, Ac, Jc. *Rv:* M. *Jv:* B.

This is not a philosophical periodical in the narrow sense, but rather an eclectic Catholic journal of the humanities. The fields of literary criticism, current political affairs and history are covered in scholarly, but eminently readable papers. The numerous, recent book reviews are from a wide variety of fields such as literature, the arts, theology, religion, philosophy, history, etc. Division of the reviews into subject sections makes for ease of use. Because of its many articles relating to such subjects as Catholic reform, religion and secular life, and ecumenism, *Thought* should prove of special interest to educated laymen of all faiths.

The Upper Room. 1935. bi-m. $1. J. Manning Potts. The Upper Room, Board of Evangelism, 1908 Grand Ave., Nashville, Tenn. 37203. Circ: 3,000,000.

Aud: Ga. *Rv:* L. *Jv:* C.

Enjoying the single largest circulation of any Protestant interdenominational evangelical religious publication in the United States, this is also published in 36 languages and 42 editions. Quite rightfully it claims it is "inter-racial and international." The scope and purpose is direct—for each day of the month there is an appropriate scripture reading and prayer. Aside from a few advertisements for religious reading materials, there is little else to distract the reader. Of the close to 1,800 religious publications, *The Upper Room* should offend no one and certainly would be of value to the average reader who may have only a passing interest in either theology or religion, but who seeks comfort from the Bible. Particularly suited for the elderly and the not overly-sophisticated reader. This magazine contrasts sharply with other "best sellers" in the field. The leaders here are two publications of the Watchtower Bible & Tract Society, *The Watchtower* (Circ: 4,300,000) and *Awake* (Circ: 3,950,000). The former promotes the study of the Bible according to principles of the familiar door to door evangelists and the latter is more concerned with gen-

eral activities from government to science. All of these, interestingly enough, outpull Billy Graham's *Decision* (Circ: 3,000,000). There is probably a place for one or a number of these in a library where the community is directed toward a particular faith. But their generally low intellectual content, and highly emotional tone, should give pause to any librarian seeking a well rounded collection. There are other, more objective, thoughtful religious publications.

World Order. 1966. q. $3.50. Muriel Michels. 1 Cove Ridge Lane, Old Greenwich, Conn. 06870. Circ: 4,000.

Aud: Ga. *Rv:* L. *Jv:* B.

The voice of Baha'i faith, a peculiar combination of religion, philosophy, and humanism which has captured the imagination of many. The magazine has a message, makes it in an intelligent fashion, and leaves it to the reader to reach his own decisions. Should interest a good many who are curious about the order.

Zygon; journal of religion and science. 1966. q. $8. Ralph Burhoe. Univ. of Chicago Press, 5750 Ellis Ave., Chicago, Ill. 60637. Microform: UM.

Indexed: RelPer. *Bk. rev:* 2–5, varying lengths, signed. *Aud:* Sa, Ac. *Rv:* M. *Jv:* B.

Expresses two major purposes: to analyze scientifically the nature of religion, and to bring scientific knowledge into positive relation to theology. Subjects of special concern are relativism, evolution, and scientific studies of the nature of man. The motivation is more theological than scientific but it is relevant and enlightening. College and University libraries. (See also, *Journal for the Scientific Study of Religion.*)

ROMANCE LANGUAGES

Indexes and Abstracts

British Humanities Index, Education Index, Social Sciences and Humanities Index. (For annotations, see Indexes and Abstracts Section.)

Bulletin of Hispanic Studies. 1923. q. Geoffrey Ribbans. Liverpool Univ. Press, 123 Grove St., Liverpool, Eng. Circ: 1,000. Reprint: Kraus.

Indexed: BritHum. *Bk. rev:* 10–11, 800 words, signed. *Aud:* Sa, Ac, Jc. *Rv:* H. *Jv:* B.

A scholarly journal devoted to Hispanic languages, literature, and civilization. Text is in England and Spanish, occasionally Catalan and Portuguese. Mainly concerned with studies of Spanish, Portuguese, and Latin American literature, poetry, and drama. Reviews cover books on history, politics and social conditions, as well as language and literature. Special features are occasional "Notes" and "Memoirs." A semi-annual "Review of Reviews" abstracts reviews printed in other significant journals in the field. College and university libraries, as well as larger public libraries.

El Corno Emplumado. See Poetry Section.

El Grito. See Literature Section.

Elle. See Women's Magazines Section.

Foreign Language Review. 1958. q. $1.50. Eugene J. Hall. Foreign Language Review, Inc., 200 Park Ave. S., New York, N.Y. 10003. Illus., adv. Circ: 32,000.

Bk. rev: 5–6, 100–150 words. *Aud:* Ga, Ac, Jc, Sh, Ht. *Rv:* H. *Jv:* B.

As the title implies, the primary purpose of this magazine is to serve as a review of various languages. As such it is useful for the adult who wishes to brush up on a language, or for the student from high school through college. Covers current news events of human interest type from around the world, with corresponding articles in French, German, Latin and Spanish. Quotes by famous persons are given in the five languages (including, of course, English) and there is a section of questions in each language. Book reviews are in English. Illustrations are of places within the countries discussed in each issue.

French Review. 1927. 6/yr. $6. John W. Kneller. Amer. Assn. of Teachers of French, J. Henry Owens, Eastern Michigan Univ., Ypsilanti, Mich. 48197. Adv. Circ: 12,600. Reprint: Johnson.

Indexed: EdI. *Bk. rev:* 25, 450 words, signed. *Aud:* Ac, Jc, Ht. *Rv:* H. *Jv:* B.

Publishes articles of interest to teachers and students of French on the secondary and college levels. Literary studies include critical analyses of literary works and historical and scholarly studies of all periods. Studies of the French language, linguistics, methods of teaching French, and articles of professional interest also appear. Articles in both French and English are of medium length, averaging 10 to 12 per issue. Regular features are professional notes, including lists of dissertations in progress, and society notices and news. The numerous book reviews cover every aspect of the language from texts to scholarly studies. A required magazine for most professional collections in secondary schools, and for all academic libraries.

French Studies; a quarterly review. 1947. q. $7.80. L. J. Austin. Basil Blackwell Ltd., 108 Cowley Rd., Oxford, Eng. Circ: 1,300. Reprint: Johnson.

Indexed: BritHum. *Bk. rev:* 30, 1,000 words, signed. *Aud:* Sa, Ac. *Rv:* H. *Jv:* B.

Publication of England's Society for French Studies. Primarily in French, with four to six articles in each issue covering all aspects and periods of French literature. Extensive book review section with reviews which are thorough, critical, and authoritative. Useful material for all French scholars; college and university libraries.

Hispania. 1918. 5/yr. $8. Irving P. Rothberg. Amer. Assn. of Teachers of Spanish and Portuguese, Prof. Eugene

Saviano, Wichita State Univ., Wichita, Kan. 67208. Adv. Circ: 14,800. Microform: B&H, UM. Reprint: Kraus.

Indexed: EdI, *Bk. rev:* 35, 500 words, signed. *Aud:* Ac, Jc, Ht, Et. *Rv:* H. *Jv:* B.

Devoted to the teaching of Hispanic languages from the elementary to graduate levels. It functions both as a scholarly journal for the advancement of literary and language studies and as a professional bulletin for the diffusion of language instruction methods. The lead articles are scholarly, usually historical and interpretive studies of literature or linguistics. Literary studies cover all periods and forms and are especially strong in very recent Spanish and Latin American authors. Articles are generally of medium length (4,000 words) and the text is in English, Portuguese, and Spanish. Professional and pedagogical departments are: "Shop Talk"—article-length considerations of language programs, teaching methods, and applied linguistics; "Notes on Usage"; "Fact and Opinion"—topics related to Hispanic culture, and "Spanish in the Elementary Schools." Contributors must be Association members. Regular features are society notes, official announcements, film reviews. Of special interest is the section on current events in the Hispanic world and the annual, May issue listing of dissertations in the Hispanic languages and literatures. The Spanish teacher's equivalent to the *French Review,* and just as necessary in all secondary and academic libraries.

Hispanic Review. 1933. q. $7.50. Otis H. Green & Arnold G. Reichenberger. Romance Languages Dept., Univ. of Pennsylvania, Philadelphia, Pa. 19104. Circ: 1,300. Microform: UM. Reprint: Johnson.

Indexed: SSHum. *Bk rev:* 3–12, 700 words, signed. *Aud:* Sa, Ac. *Rv:* H. *Jv:* B.

An esoteric, scholarly journal, with text frequently in Spanish, devoted to research in the Hispanic languages and literatures. Published by the Modern Language Association, Spanish Section, the emphasis is on literature. Includes a "Varia" section with notes that are only somewhat shorter than the articles. The book review section has substantial critical reviews of interest to scholars as well as a "Briefer Mention" section; "Books Received" is an annual feature. Occasional announcements and necrologies. College, university and large, metropolitan public libraries.

Italica. 1924. q. $6. Joseph G. Fucilla. Amer. Assn. of Teachers of Italian, Joseph E. Laggini, Rutgers Univ. New Brunswick, N.J. 08903. Adv. Circ: 1,800. Microform: UM. Reprint: Johnson.

Bk. rev: 5–6, 1,500 words, signed. *Aud:* Ac, Jc, Ht. *Rv:* H. *Jv:* B.

Articles are generally scholarly discussions of Italian literature, covering all periods, but with emphasis on the Renaissance. Critical articles appear occasionally, as do articles on Italian history and art and on linguistics and language teaching. Generally six to eight articles, averaging

3,500 words, appear in each issue. Text is in English and Italian. Regular features are the *A.A.T.I. Newsletter* and a "Bibliography of Italian Studies in America." An interesting indication of the relative popularity of languages in schools can be ascertained by circulation figures, here the lowest of the three major Romance language teaching journals. Obviously only needed in secondary and academic libraries where the teaching of Italian is a consideration, and more than likely this will limit it primarily to larger junior colleges and colleges and universities.

L'Esprit Createur; a critical quarterly of French literature. 1961. q. $3. Box 809, Iowa City, Iowa 52242. Circ: 1,100.

Bk. rev: 3–8, 700 words, signed. *Aud:* Sa, Ac, Jc. *Rv:* H. *Jv:* A.

A journal for the scholar, critic, and "amateur de littérature" interested in the interpretation of French literature. The text is in English and French. Each issue presents five to eight 4,000-word critical analyses of different aspects of the literary production of one author (Balzac, Moliére), or of a movement ("French Manneristic Poetry between Ronsard and Malherbe," "New Directions in the French Novel"). Most of the material is in English, but often with extensive quotes in French, and a knowledge of French is helpful, although not necessary. Covers all periods of French literature. Books reviewed, dealing with the criticism of French literature, are primarily from U.S., French, or Canadian presses. Useful for college and university libraries.

Meridiano; sintesis de la prensa mundial al gusto Espanol. 1942. m. $2.40. Ediciones Joker, San Leonardo 12, Madrid 8, Spain. Subscriptions to: Vernon Hammond, 211 S. Main St., McAllen, Tex. 78501. Illus., adv.

Aud: Ga, Ac, Jc, Sh. *Rv:* L. *Jv:* B.

A combination of *Atlas* and the *Readers' Digest,* this reprints articles from newspapers and magazines throughout the world. The selection, however, is short on controversy, and long on noncontroversial material in the arts, literature, and social sciences. And in view of the base of publication, it is understandably (though not forgivably) reactionary. Nevertheless, it is a good cross section of the world's press, particularly the Spanish press (what there is of it), and is a useful magazine for the advanced, high school Spanish student or for those who want to brush up on their Spanish.

Mundo Hispanico. 1948. m. $7.50. D. Francisco Leal Insua. Av Reyes Catolicos, C.U. Madrid 3, Spain. Subscriptions to: Continental Pubns., 130 S. Bemiston Ave., St. Louis, Mo. 63105. Illus.

Bk. rev: Notes. *Aud:* Ga, Ac, Jc, Sh, Jh. *Rv:* M. *Jv:* B.

A *Life* approach to activities not only in Spain, but in all Spanish speaking countries. Covers aspects of culture, art, literature, history, education, science, and activities of leading personalities. There is little political material. The text is relatively simple, and while the whole is geared for the

Spanish speaking adult, it can be used for both beginners and advanced students in Spanish. There are excellent black and white and color photographs.

Another Spanish language magazine particularly geared for teen-agers rather than adults is *Caminos* (m. Sept.–May. $3. Colegio Americano, Apartado Postal No. 83, Guatamala City, Guatamala). This is issued by the school as a non-profit venture and contains articles and fiction on the culture of Guatemala and all Latin American countries. There is an eight-page insert for beginners, and the whole may be used both by the first year student and the advanced student of Spanish.

Paris Match. 1949. w. $15. 51 Rue Saint-George, Paris (9e), France, Subscriptions to: Continental Pubns., 130 S. Bemiston Ave., St. Louis, Mo. 63105. Illus., adv.

Bk. rev: Notes. *Aud:* Ga, Ac, Jc, Sh, Jh. *Rv:* M. *Jv:* B.

A combination *Life-Time* news magazine which can be useful for both the curious French-reading adult and the advanced student of French in the schools. The emphasis is on current events and personalities, and while primarily limited to the French scene, it also takes in international affairs, particularly in Europe. The many illustrations in black and white and color, the advertisements, and the general tone do much to introduce the student to what life in France is all about. As a popular magazine it is no place, however, to follow the deeper political social issues.

In terms of language courses, other good French magazines are: *Elle* (Woman's Magazines Section), *Realities* (General Magazines Section).

Quinto Lingo. 1964. m. $5. J. I. Rodale & Rita Reemer. Rodale Press, Inc., 33 E. Minor St., Emmaus, Pa. 18049. Illus., adv. Circ: 81,000.

Aud: Ga, Sh, Jh, E. *Rv:* M. *Jv:* A.

The do-it-yourself approach to the learning of language arts, this is a general magazine for the adult or secondary school student wishing to improve his reading skills in the modern languages. The unique format features four columns of identical text, short articles and anecdotes, in German, Spanish, French, and English. The Russian and Italian languages appear in separate departments, each with a column of text and its English translation. Helpful language notes are given for Russian. All articles relate to a monthly topic. The magazine does a good job in presenting vocabulary and grammar in an easily understood manner. The translations are skillfully done, with each of the languages rendered freely and yet parallel to the others. Because of the magazine's limited purpose and the fact that the intrinsic interest of both the articles and the departments lies in the languages, their intellectual content is kept on a superficial level. Among the regular features are: Aesop's Fables in the six languages, with grammatical instruction based on the text; travel; word puzzles in different languages; and special articles, such as summaries of portions of Mario Pei's *Story of Language.*

Quinzaine Litteraire. See Book Reviews Section.

Revista de Estudios Hispanicos. 1967. semi-ann. $4. Univ. of Alabama Press, Drawer 3877, University, Ala. 35486.

Aud: Sa, Ac. *Rv:* M. *Jv:* B.

Devoted to the study of modern Spanish literature and linguistics, the journal also includes essays on the writers of Portugal and Brazil. The articles are in both English and Spanish, and will probably continue to be in the language as written. Where is the hispanic world? Any place where Spanish is now spoken. Bibliographies.

Revue d'Histoire Litteraire de La France. 1894. bi-m. $4. Rene Pomeau. Librairie Armand Colin, 103 bd. St-Michel, Paris 5e, France. Circ: 2,000. Microform: Microcard. Reprint: Johnson.

Bk. rev: 25–35, 500 words, signed. *Aud:* Sa, Ac. *Rv:* H. *Jv:* B.

An important scholarly journal devoted to French literature. With four to ten articles in each issue, it covers all periods, and at least once a year an entire issue is given over to a series of articles on one literary figure (Madame de Stael, Baudelaire). An extensive book review section, with titles primarily from French and other continental presses. The "Bibliography" section is a subject list of books and articles on French literature. While of particular interest to larger academic libraries, the book reviews make it of some value to smaller and medium sized libraries.

Romance Notes. 1959. semi-ann. $4. Urban T. Holmes. Dept. of Romance Languages, Univ. of North Carolina, Chapel Hill, N.C. 27515. Circ: 500.

Aud: Sa, Ac. *Rv:* H. *Jv:* B.

A scholarly journal devoted to signed, short essays concerned with the various Romance languages and literatures. Each issue contains 25 to 35 "Notes," covering the field in breadth as much as in depth. The contributors are primarily U.S. scholars, with a few Canadian and an occasional continental scholar also contributing. The text is in English, French, Italian and Spanish.

Romance Philology. 1947. q. $7.50. Yakov Malkiel. Univ. of California Press, Berkeley, Calif. 94720. Adv. Circ: 1,130. Microform: UM. Reprint: AMS.

Indexed: SSHum. *Bk. rev:* 12–20, 800 words, signed. *Aud:* Sa, Ac. *Rv:* H. *Jv:* B.

A journal of scholarly research concerned with all phases of early Romance literature and Romance linguistics. Articles are long and specialized—usually monographs of 5,000 to 8,000 words—and special interest is with the formative period of the Romance languages, from late antiquity to the early Renaissance. Contributions written in French, Spanish, Portuguese, Italian and German are accepted. Linguistic studies are both descriptive and theoretical, with structural and lexicological studies predominating. Literary research includes textual, interpretive, and bibliographic studies, with emphasis always on the analysis of original texts and source material. The book reviews are excellent

and shorter notes and several review articles are regularly featured.

Romanic Review. 1910. q. $6. Jean-Albert Bede. Columbia Univ. Press, 440 W. 110th St., New York, N.Y. 10025. Circ: 1,300. Microform: UM. Reprint: Kraus.

Indexed: SSHum. *Bk. rev:* 10–22, 800 words, signed. *Aud:* Sa, Ac, Jc. *Rv:* H. *Jv:* B.

A scholarly journal devoted to the entire spectrum of the literature of the various Romance languages. The text is in several languages and occasionally concerned with philosophy or the arts. Each issue contains three to four articles of moderate length, but nearly one-half the journal is given over to review articles and book reviews concerning important single works or a group of related works. Books reviewed are from U.S., British, Canadian, and continental presses. Members of the editorial board frequently contribute both articles and reviews, but other scholars from U.S. campuses also appear.

Table Ronde. 1948. m. S.E.P.A.L., 23 Rue du Renard, Paris (4e), France.

Aud: Sa, Ac. *Rv:* M. *Jv:* B.

A combination French language literary/political review with primary emphasis on literature. A typical number will either concentrate on a given author or form, or offer up a variety of materials on French politics, religion and art. This is one of a number of relatively young French literary periodicals which should find a place in larger academic libraries. John Cruickshank of *The Times Literary Supplement* occasionally reviews both content and editorial changes in a number of French literary magazines. His column is by far the best in English now available for an up-to-date summary of this particular field of periodical publishing, and it should be checked by libraries which have a special interest in the field. See, for example, the *TLS* for Feb. 22, 1968 and Sept. 5, 1968, pp.187 and 951 respectively.

Yale French Studies. 1948. semi-ann. $2. Joseph H. McMahon. W. L. Harkness Hall, Yale Univ., New Haven, Conn. 06520. Circ: 1,000. Microform: UM. Reprint: Kraus.

Indexed: SSHum. *Aud:* Sa, Ac, Jc. *Rv:* H. *Jv:* A.

A journal of literary criticism, comment, and scholarship, with each issue containing brief articles on a particular writer or topic related to French cultural life. All articles are in English and almost exclusively by American scholars. Considers well-known writers such as Proust, Sade, and Camus; topics which have been treated are "Surrealism," "Poetry Since the Liberation," "Structuralism," and "Contemporary Art." Occasional double issues. Because of the subject matter this is a journal which may be used in almost any course or by any student.

Classroom Aids

In addition to the periodicals listed below, the following English-language publications are available in various editions: In French, *House and Garden, Popular Mechanics, Readers' Digest,* and *Vogue;* In Spanish, *Americas, Life, Rotarian,* and *Readers' Digest;* In Italian, *Readers' Digest,* and *True Story. Unesco Courier* is available in all three languages.

Billiken. 1919. w. $4. Editorial Atlantida, Azopardo 579, Buenos Aires, Argentina. Subscriptions to: Vernon Hammond, 211 South Main St., McAllen, Tex. 78501. Illus. Circ: 500,000.

One of the few Spanish-language magazines for children ages 8 to 14, this may be used in Spanish speaking communities and with Spanish courses. The approximately 38 pages are given over to material familiar enough to American youngsters, e.g., games, cartoons, songs, puzzles, comics, profiles, and articles on current activities which have some bearing on the interests of the typical Latin American child. The illustrations are colorful, bold and often more imaginative than found in American counterparts. While a beginner's knowledge of Spanish is needed, the magazine is good for elementary and junior high school classes who have the first section of Spanish behind them.

Caminos. See *Mundo Hispanico,* this section.

Elle. See Women's Magazines Section.

Figaro. See Newspaper Section (Appendix).

Le Monde. See Newspaper Section (Appendix).

Realities. See General Section.

Scholastic Magazines Inc. 50 W. 44th St., New York, N.Y. 10036. Various dates. (during school year). m. $1 to $1.50.

	LANGUAGE LEVEL	INTEREST LEVEL	CIRCULATION
Bonjour	1	E	120,000
Ça Va	1–2	Jh, Sh	42,000
Chez Nous	2–3	Jh, Sh	63,000
Loisirs	3–6	Sh	14,000
Sol, El	1–2	Jh, Sh	90,000
Hoy Dia	2–4	Sh	41,000

See remarks for Scholastic Magazines in German Language Section, Classroom Aids.

The familiar pattern of all Scholastic foreign language classroom papers is followed in the French and Spanish entries. The French issues are particularly winning as they tend to stress popular culture as much as the day-by-day activities of the French people.

SCIENCE—GENERAL

Indexes and Abstracts

Abridged Readers' Guide, Applied Science and Technology Index, Biological Abstracts, British Humanities Index, British Technology Index, Chemical Abstracts, Engineering Index, Historical Abstracts, Index Medicus, Mathematical Reviews, Meteorological and Geoastrophysical Abstracts, Psychological Abstracts, Readers' Guide to Periodical Literature, Science Abstracts, Science Citation Index. (For annotations, see Indexes and Abstracts Section.)

Grouped in this section are publications which encompass, in their scope, more than one branch of science or technology. Periodicals range from scholarly journals, which publish research accounts and reviews in both the physical and biological sciences, to some very popular magazines, which interpret the latest developments in these areas.

The Fall 1968 issue of RQ contains a "compilation of 37 titles in the field of the applied and physical sciences, designed to interpret for the layman new scientific and technical developments and to assist him in his understanding of their significance." This basic list, prepared by the American Library Association's RSD Science and Technology Reference Services Committee, includes brief annotations, and each title is ranked in level of difficulty. (See Appendix for list of titles.) Public libraries may find this bibliography a useful point of departure in accumulating science material for their collections. Many of these titles appear in this section and in more specialized chapters of this book.

Académie des Sciences; comptes rendus hebdomadaires des seances. 1835. w. $210. Gauthier Villars, 55 Quai des Grands Augustins, Paris, France. Illus., index. Circ: 3,100. Microform: MF; Princeton.

Indexed: BioAb, ChemAb, EngI, IMed, MathR, Met&GeoastAb, SciAb, SCI. *Aud:* Sa, Ac. *Rv:* H. *Jv:* B.

Comptes Rendus, an outgrowth of the proceedings of the Academy of Sciences of Paris, established in 1666, is one of the pioneers of the scholarly, general science journals, and its influence on the early development of science was important. All branches of the physical and biological sciences are represented. The journal is issued in three parts, each of which may be purchased separately. Sections A and B (one part) publishes short reports on original research in mathematics and physics; Section C covers the chemical sciences, including such fields as chemical mineralogy and metallurgy; and Section D constitutes research reports in all of the life sciences. Brief notices and news of the Academy are also included.

Advancement of Science. 1939. m. $9. Academic Press, Inc., 111 Fifth Ave., New York, N.Y. 10003. Illus., index, adv. Circ: 2,000. Microform: UM.

Indexed: BioAb, BritHum, BritTech, ChemAb, SciAb. *Bk. rev:* 10, 150–200 words, signed. *Aud:* Sa, Ga, Ac, Jc. *Rv:* H. *Jv:* B.

Sponsored by the British Association for the Advancement of Science, the journal attempts to bring to the attention of scientists significant research in fields other than their own, and to review for interested laymen recent advances in all the sciences and their influence on our society. The tone of the periodical is more scholarly than popular, and the emphasis is on the review or tutorial essay, rather than science in the news, although such items are included. Since every aspect of science and technology is represented —mathematics to medicine, physics to philosophy of science, plastics to psychology—this may be an interesting addition to a general science collection, particularly for junior college and larger public libraries.

American Scientist. 1912. q. $4. Hugh S. Taylor. Soc. of Sigma Xi, c/o Mack Printing Co., 20th & Northampton Sts., Easton, Pa. 18042. Illus., index, adv. Circ: 100,000. Reprint: Johnson.

Indexed: ASTI, BioAb, ChemAb, EngI, IMed, PsyAb, SCI. *Bk. rev:* 50–100, 300 words, signed. *Aud:* Sa, Ac, Jc. *Rv:* H. *Jv:* B.

Published jointly by Sigma Xi, a national honorary science fraternity, and its affiliate, RESA (Scientific Research Society of America) the quarterly is largely comprised of addresses presented at national lectures of these organizations or other noteworthy scientific meetings. All fields of science are represented. Contributions by leading authorities are as specialized as a survey of recent advances in a limited branch of polymer chemistry, or as broad as philosophical musings on the impact of science and technology on our culture. Frequently, essays are written with a historical or biographical approach. In a fairly large book review section, the journal often publishes a lengthy essay-review; and a section entitled "Books Received for Review" supplies a good checklist of publications issued by a large number of publishers. News and notices of Sigma Xi and RESA are also included.

Bulletin of the Atomic Scientists. See Literary and Political Reviews Section.

Endeavour. 1942. 3/yr. Free. T. I. Williams. Imperial Chemical Industries, Ltd., Millbank, London S.W.1 Illus. *Indexed:* BioAb, BritTech, ChemAb, EngI, PsyAb, SCI. *Bk. rev:* 20, 200 words, signed. *Aud:* Sa, Ga, Ac, Jc, Sh. *Rv:* H. *Jv:* A.

The producers of this fine, company-sponsored periodical intend to record and "review the progress of science," and, indeed, they have achieved just this over the past 25 years. They count, among their distinguished contributors, some 30 Nobel Laureates; they cover all the sciences, including behavioral; and their articles reach nearly every type of audience in interest and level of sophistication. Emphasis in the essays may be historical or biographical, may survey an entire field, or may be limited to a highly specialized research review. A good balance between the different disciplines is maintained in each issue. Articles are short and are often elegantly illustrated, frequently with colored plates. Subjects are selected on the basis of timeliness and importance in today's research; moreover, the scope is not limited to British science. The publication is also printed

in French, Spanish, and German. Highly recommended for most libraries.

Environment (Formerly: *Scientist and Citizen*). 1958. 10/yr. $6. V. Brodine. Committee for Environmental Information, 438 North Skinner, St. Louis, Mo. 63130. Illus. Circ: 2,500.

Indexed: RG. *Aud:* Ga. *Rv:* M. *Jv:* A.

Sponsored by an active and concerned citizenry who are involved in understanding environmental pollution caused by technology, the periodical supplies clear, well-documented articles, written by acknowledged specialists for the layman, on these problems. Reports are concerned with any contamination in our skies, waters, foods, etc., whether the conditions exist in our own country or anywhere else in the world; studies have frequently included the effects of nuclear technology. The magazine is not alarmist; rather, it attempts to alert a too-often apathetic public to the imbalance in nature created by our industrial world, and to dangers too often glossed over by our governmental agencies.

Environmental Science and Technology. m. 1967. Membership (Non-members, $7). James J. Morgan. Amer. Chem. Soc., 1155 16th St., N.W., Washington, D.C. 20036. Illus., index, adv. Circ: 10,000.

Bk. rev: 1–2, 600 words, signed. *Aud:* Sa, Ac, Jc. *Rv:* H. *Jv:* B.

"Emphasizing water, air, and waste chemistry," the publication nonetheless contains a good deal of nonspecialist information for interested citizenry concerned with clean water, clean air, and other environmental improvements. About half of each issue is spent on discussions of current activities along these lines—in the government, in industry, in the universities—and the one or two feature articles, written in general language, interpret some new facet of environmental research. The remaining sections of the issue comprise specialized research reports and short communications, a few new product briefs, and meeting announcements.

Experienta. 1945. m. $41.40. Ed bd. Birkhauer Verlag, CH–4000, Basel 10, Switzerland. Illus., index, adv.

Indexed: BioAb, ChemAb, SciAb, SCI. *Aud:* Sa, Ac. *Rv:* H. *Jv:* B.

Although all the pure and applied sciences are represented in this journal which publishes short research reports, the emphasis is on biological and biochemical studies. Important, special supplements, which must be purchased separately, are also issued. Text appears in English, French, German, or Italian.

Franklin Institute. Journal. 1826. m. $22. M. A. Pomerantz. Franklin Inst. of the State of Pennsylvania, 20th & Parkway, Philadelphia, Pa. 19103. Illus., adv. Circ: 3,200. Microform: UM. Reprint: Kraus.

Indexed: ASTI, BioAb, ChemAb, EngI, MathR, SciAb, SCI. *Bk. rev:* 10, 350 words, signed. *Aud:* Sa, Ac. *Rv:* H. *Jv:* B.

Formerly *The Franklin Journal,* which was the second oldest general science journal published in the U.S. The research papers and shorter communications in this publication "devoted to science and the mechanic arts" are now concerned, in large part, with engineering and the entire spectrum of the physical sciences. Also included are addresses presented at the Institute by distinguished scientists.

IBM Journal of Research and Development. 1957. bi-m. $4. E. J. Huibregste. Intl. Business Machines Corp., Armonk, N.Y. 10504. Illus., index. Microform: UM.

Indexed: BioAb, ChemAb, EngI, MathR, PsyAb, SciAb, SCI. *Aud:* Sa, Ac, Jc. *Rv:* H. *Jv:* B.

Sponsor of some of the world's important basic and applied research, the IBM Corporation produces its own journal to describe a part of the original work performed by their scientists and engineers. Included within the scope of the periodical have been papers on chemistry, physics, mathematics, engineering, the computing sciences, psychological reports, and applications to the biological sciences. Papers frequently center around a specific topic or one product of the firm, e.g., the different aspects of control research, or the various facets of science and technology that developed the IBM Selector. Contributions include both lengthy research papers and a few 1- or 2-page communications. Titles of articles by IBM authors that have appeared elsewhere in the literature are also included, as are lists of recent patents. Particularly valuable for any collection in the computing sciences and physics, the journal is recommended for academic libraries.

ISIS; international review devoted to the history of science and its cultural influences. 1913. q. $12. Robert P. Multhauf. Johns Hopkins Press, Baltimore, Md. 21218. Illus., index, adv. Circ: 2,000. Microform: Canner, UM. Reprint: Johnson.

Indexed: BioAb, ChemAb, EngI, HistAb, IMed, MathR, SSHum. *Bk. rev:* 6, 300–500 words, signed. *Aud:* Sa, Ac. *Rv:* H. *Jv:* B.

Founded by the eminent science historian, George Sarton. Long essays and shorter 2- or 3-page research notes represent authoritative, scholarly studies on such topics as anatomical research of the Middle Ages, 15th century astrology, and the like. The publication is also the official journal of the learned History of Science Society, and includes accounts of research in progress, acquisitions of manuscripts, news, notes and correspondence. A separate Critical Bibliography is issued annually for the Society by the University of California Press. Excellent book reviews take up a good portion of each issue.

Journal of Research of the National Bureau of Standards. 1928. Supt. of Documents, Govt. Printing Office,

Washington, D.C. 20402. Illus., index. Circ: 4,000. Microform: Mc, Princeton, UM.

Indexed: ASTI, BioAb, ChemAb, EngI, SciAb, SCI. *Aud:* Sa, Ac. *Rv:* H. *Jv:* B.

Representing research and development undertaken at the various institutes of the National Bureau of Standards, the journal has, for several years, been issued in separate parts, which can be purchased separately. In addition to research papers and an occasional survey article, every section carries selected abstracts of other papers by NBS publications.

Section A, *Physics and Chemistry* (1959. bi-m. $5. C. W. Beckett), covers basic and applied research in most branches of physics and chemistry. Section B, *Mathematical Sciences* (1959. q. $2.75. M. Newman), "presents studies designed mainly for the mathematician and the theoretical physicist, including pure mathematics, mathematical physics, numerical analysis, computation and the preparation of programs for digital computers," etc. Section C, *Engineering and Instrumentation* (1959. q. $2.75. M. Greenspan), "reports research and development results of interest chiefly to the engineer and the applied scientist." Studies cover all aspects of instrumentation and measurements.

Journal of Research in Science Teaching. 1963. q. $10. J. S. Marshall. John Wiley & Sons, 605 Third Ave., New York, N.Y. 10016. Illus.

Aud: Ac, Jc, Ht. *Rv:* H. *Jv:* B.

The journal of the Association for the Education of Teachers in Science and the National Association for Research in Science Teaching. Articles are scholarly, tend to report original research in areas of curriculum change, methodology, student-teacher relationships, new training aids and the like. Although primarily for the science professor in college, it may be used profitably by high school teachers of science and professional educators interested in the area.

Minerva; a review of science learning and policy. 1962. $5. q. Edward Shils. 135 Oxford St., London W.1. Adv. Circ: 1,700.

Indexed: PAIS. *Bk. rev:* 2–3 long review articles, signed. *Aud:* Sa, Ac, Jc. *Rv:* H. *Jv:* A.

A solidly based attempt to provide discussion and debate on topics relevant to the theory and practice of the application of knowledge. It has some of the best intellectual backing of any journal, its advisory editors including Lord Snow and J. Robert Oppenheimer (now deceased). Through its sponsor—the Committee on Science and Freedom—it receives the blessings of such notables as Otto Hahn, and Bertrand Russell. *Minerva's* concerns are many, ranging from education and the concerned academic community to underdeveloped countries and the implications of government sponsorship of research. Each issue has 3–8 articles, sections on various documents and reports, correspondence, and a chronicle of relevant current events. Mandatory for college and university libraries, and excellent for public libraries.

National Academy of Sciences. Proceedings. 1915. m. $20. S. MacLane. National Academy of Sciences, 2101 Constitution Ave., Washington, D.C. 20025. Illus., index. Circ: 5,600. Microform: UM. Reprint: Johnson.

Indexed: BioAb, ChemAb, EngI, IMed, MathR, SciAb, SCI. *Aud:* Sa, Ac. *Rv:* H. *Jv:* B.

The papers in this research journal cover both the physical and biological sciences, although a larger percentage fall within the scope of the biological sciences. Invited papers given at their special symposia are also included, as well as some addresses presented before meetings of the Academy.

Natural History (Incorporating *Nature Magazine*). 1900. m. (Oct.–May); bi-m. (June–Sept.). $7. Robert E. Williamson. Amer. Museum of Natural History, 79th St. & Central Park West, New York, N.Y. 10024. Illus., adv. Circ: 190,000. Microform: UM.

Indexed: BioAb, RG. *Bk. rev:* Various numbers and lengths. *Aud:* Ga, Ac, Jc, Sh, Jh, E. *Rv:* H. *Jv:* V.

Issued by the American Museum of Natural History, this is a popular approach to conservation, anthropology, geography, astronomy—in fact, almost anything of interest to the nature lover. Although the style is semi-popular, the articles are authoritative, and are written by experts who have the facility for being as lucid as they are intelligent. Outstanding photographs give this added value for lower grades. An exceptional magazine for almost all libraries.

Nature. 1869. $48. J. Maddox. Macmillan Journals, Ltd., Little Essex St., London W.C.2. Illus., index, adv. Circ: 15,100.

Indexed: BioAb, BritTechI, ChemAb, EngI, IMed, MathR, Met&GeoAstAb, PsyAb, SciAb, SCI. *Bk. rev:* 10–15, 500 words, signed. *Aud:* Sa, Ac, Jc. *Rv:* H. *Jv:* B.

Similar in scope to *Science,* this British weekly provides news, views, short essays or reviews by leading scientists, and brief studies on original research. Every branch of science is represented. The international coverage of timely developments is larded with interesting and informative editorial comment, some of which discusses social, economic, or political problems. Signed articles vary in levels of technicality from the very general to highly specialized reviews of important scientific endeavors. About 50 "Letters to the Editor," which comprise short research studies, are published in each issue. In addition to good book reviews, a classified checklist of recent scientific books is included regularly. Necessary for research libraries for the original research reports, the journal is an excellent choice for any academic library. (Not to be confused with *Nature Magazine,* an American publication now incorporated into *Natural History.*)

New Scientist. 1956. w. $16. Donald Gould. 128 Long Ave., London W.C.2. Illus., index. Circ: 52,500. Microform: UM.

Indexed: BioAb, BritTech. *Aud:* Sa, Ga, Ac, Jc. *Rv.* M. *Jv:* B.

The intent of this weekly is to provide "lively news presentation with authoritative comment in the world of science." The liveliness is indeed supplied by crisp editorial comment and interpretive news coverage. (Statements on U.S. policies are either provocative or amusing, depending on one's point of view.) And the world of science is well represented by short articles (1 to 2 pages), written both by staff writers and specialists. Features review all types of scientific studies—on sound, sun, sea, social psychology, etc.; international news emerges from academic, as well as industrial, think tanks; language is on a layman's level. The magazine also includes such regular departments as "Tantalizer" (a puzzle) and "Trends and Discoveries" (more spot news culled from the journals). The frills in this periodical are not in the format nor in the illustrations, but in the prose. Recommended for any library which wants to add another magazine with a British flavor, and certainly for any academic collection which needs comprehensive news coverage.

Royal Society. Philosophical Transactions. 1665. irreg. The Royal Society, 6 Carlton House Terrace, London S.W.1.

Aud: Sa, Ac. *Rv:* H. *Jv:* B.

Founded in the 17th century, the Royal Society of London is one of the oldest extant, scientific societies devoted to "improving Natural Knowledge."

Each issue of the *Transactions* is devoted to a single research paper, of monograph length, which represents a definitive and authoritative study. Experimental details or material of a tabular nature are exhaustive.

Series A: Mathematical and Physical Sciences. 1665. irreg. $37. Illus. Circ: 2,000. Microform: Mc. Reprint: Johnson; Kraus.

Indexed: ChemAb, EngI, MathR, SciAb, SCI.

Series B: Biological Sciences, 1665. irreg. $37. Illus. Circ: 1,000. Microform: Mc. Reprint: Johnson; Kraus.

Indexed: BioAb, ChemAb, SCI.

Royal Society. Proceedings. 1832. The Royal Society, 6 Carlton House Terrace, London S.W.1.

Aud: Sa, Ac. *Rv:* H. *Jv:* B.

The *Proceedings* include high quality research papers not exceeding 24 pages.

Series A: Mathematical and Physical Sciences. 1832. irreg. $16/vol. The Royal Society, 6 Carlton House Terrace, London S.W.1. Illus., index. Circ: 3,000. Microform: Mc. Reprint: Dawson.

Indexed: ChemAb, EngI, MathR, Met&GeoAstAb, SciAb, SCI.

Original papers deal with all aspects of the mathematical or physical sciences, and include studies in the applied sciences, such as various branches of engineering. Emphasis is on the mathematical and physical principles underlying the science.

Series B: Biological Sciences. 1832. irreg. $16/vol. The Society, 6 Carlton House Terrace, London S.W.1. Illus., index. Circ: 2,000. Microform: MF. Reprint: Dawson.

Indexed: BioAb, ChemAb, EngI, IMed, SCI.

Research reports cover any aspect of the biological sciences; many studies are theoretical.

Science. 1880. w. $12. P. H. Abelson. Amer. Assn. for the Advancement of Science, 1515 Mass. Ave., N.W., Washington, D.C. 20005. Illus., index. adv. Circ: 139,785. Microform: UM.

Indexed: BioAb, ChemAb, EngI, IMed, Met&GeoAstAb, PsyAb, RG, SciAb, SCI. *Bk. rev:* 10, 300 words, signed. *Aud:* Sh, Jc, Ac, Sa, Ga. *Rv:* H. *Jv:* A.

Serving as a "forum for the presentation and discussion of important issues related to the advancement of science," the periodical is a splendid choice for any library and any audience. Feature articles review developments in all the sciences—physical, biological, behavioral—some with more technical treatment than others, and contributions are always by distinguished specialists. An important section is that devoted to the publication of short reports of original research, much of which falls within the scope of the biological sciences. Departments give thorough coverage. "News and Comment" screens events of the week and airs opinions, including minority voices, on such general topics as legislation affecting the sciences, education, protest movements, trends and philosophies. Detailed digests of important conferences are supplied under "Meetings," and a "Calendar of Events" covers both national and international symposia in every science. Book reviews are excellent. Also issued annually is a "Guide to Scientific Instruments," which serves not only as a buyer's guide, but as a reference tool on new equipment.

Science and Technology. (**Formerly:** *International Science & Technology*). 1962. m. $10. R. Colborn. Conover-Mast Pubns., Inc., 205 E. 42nd St., New York, N.Y. 10017. Illus., adv. Circ: 150,000.

Indexed: EngI. *Aud:* Sa, Ga, Ac, Jc. *Rv:* M. *Jv:* A.

The by-line "for the technical men in management" indicates that the periodical is geared toward non-specialists who seek, in abbreviated form, reviews of new research and development, or state of-the-art in the exploding new technologies, and who need articles in a format that precludes troublesome and highly specialized technical content and vocabulary. (Glossaries are sometimes included to this end.) As such, the magazine might be a good selection for public

libraries, particularly since a large portion of the articles, written by specialists, are directed toward current problems in industrial research and technology, as opposed to straight science. The general tone of the magazine is chatty, interesting, and extremely readable. Features include: interviews with leading scientific personalities; editorials; studies of the literature of science and engineering; and short essays on events or situations in the technical community. For those who wish to plunge deeper into a field, general bibliographies are supplied for the main articles.

Science Digest. 1937. m. $5. R. F. Dempewolff. Hearst Corp., 959 Eighth Ave., New York, N.Y. 10019. Illus., adv. Circ: 150,000.

Indexed: AbrRG, RG. *Bk. rev:* 2, 250–350 words, signed. *Aud:* Ga, E, Jh, Sh. *Rv:* M. *Jv:* C.

A popularization of science, the magazine covers an enormous span of subjects—aerospace, astronomy, biology, electronics, ichthyology, medicine, oceanography, physiology, psychiatry—and often in a single issue. Short, easily read, feature articles (contributed by such astute specialists as Steve Allen, writing on prison reform) may frequently be condensations of books or digests of technical papers. And the emphasis is not only on information, but also on advice: what to do when you feel lonely (psychology); watch out for new deadly spiders (zoology). A good department, though, is that section by Isaac Asimov, who can explain any scientific phenomenon in the most comprehensible terms. Of course, most public libraries are subscribers; yet the publication can also be highly recommended for the waiting rooms of dentists and doctors.

Science Education. 1916. 5/yr. $8. C. M. Pruitt. Univ. of Tampa, Tampa, Fla. 33606. Illus. Circ: 2,000.

Indexed: EdI. *Bk. rev:* 20–30, 150 words. *Aud:* Ac, Jc, Ht, Et. *Rv:* M. *Jv:* B.

Directed to primary and secondary school teachers, and instructors in schools of education. The 10 to 15 articles touch on all aspects of the area, including textbook evaluation. Material is by educators, usually represents original research, and there is a particular emphasis on instructional techniques. While not as broad in scope as *Science Teacher* or *School Science and Mathematics,* it is considerably more scholarly. Should be in larger school libraries, and required in schools of education.

Science Journal. 1965. m. $12. Robin Clarke. Associated Iliffe Press, Ltd., Dorset House, Stamford St., London S.E.1. Subscriptions to: British Pubns., Inc., 30 E. 60th St., New York, N.Y. 10022. Illus., index, adv. Circ: 40,441. Microform: UM.

Bk. rev: 2, 400–600 words, signed; several short, 50 words, unsigned. *Aud:* Jh, Sh, Jc, Ac, Ga, Sa. *Rv:* H. *Jv:* A.

Somewhat comparable to *Scientific American,* the British publication serves to interpret and digest scientific developments and phenomena for the layman. Well-illustrated feature articles explore all branches of science and technology, emphasize the timely (tobacco and lung cancer), as well as the historical (science at the pyramids), and are contributed by authorities. Frequently, an entire issue is concerned with a special subject, such as the food shortage, and the topic is treated from a variety of specialist viewpoints. The periodical also includes news developments, digests from the literature, reports on new patents, and brief, signed reviews of technical meetings. In view of its similarity to *Scientific American*, not a first choice for American libraries, but a useful second choice for larger public and academic libraries.

Science News. 1921. w. $6.50. Warren Kornberg. Science Service, Inc., 1719 N St., N.W., Washington, D.C. 20036. Illus., index, adv. Circ: 90,754. Microform: UM, Mc.

Indexed: AbrRG, RG. *Bk. rev:* Several, 35–40 words, unsigned. *Aud:* Jh, Sh, Jc, Ac, Ga. *Rv:* M. *Jv:* A.

The weekly summaries published in the magazine pertain to timely developments in any of the sciences, as gathered from reports at international meetings, articles from technical journals, recent issues of U.S. patents, and governmental, academic, and industrial news releases. A few 1- or 2-page articles, usually contributed by staff writers, describe, in a little more depth, recent investigations from research laboratories, or supply small tutorials on some scientific phenomena. Facts are well documented, and the prose is extremely readable and appropriately illustrated. Book reviews are descriptive rather than critical; new films, equipment and products are also announced. Recommended for any library seeking quick, popularized, international news coverage in science and technology.

Scientific American. 1845. m. $8. Dennis Flanagan. Scientific American, 415 Madison Ave., New York, N.Y. 10017. Illus., index, adv. Circ: 409,399. Microform: UM, Mc, Micro Photo.

Indexed: ASTI, BioAb, ChemAb, IMed, MathR, RG, SciAb, SCI. *Bk. rev:* 1, 3,000 words, signed; short reviews. 10, 250–500 words, unsigned. *Aud:* Jh, Sh, Jc, Ac, Ga, Sa. *Rv:* H. *Jv:* V.

Surely the periodical needs little introduction to the library world, for the magazine has been interpreting scientific and technological advances and theories to laymen for well over a hundred years. It is by far the best general science publication available. Articles vary in sophistication and experts have stated that some of the more cogent reviews in their own fields have been published here. The general reader, however, will always be able to find material written on his level and directed toward his interests—ranging from research in prehistory to the latest developments in space explorations. The quality is very high, and the contributors are distinguished specialists from both the academic world and industry. Each issue contains a carefully balanced selection from the physical, life, and behavioral sciences, and many articles are beautifully illus-

trated. Special departments include a section on mathematical games; "Amateur Scientist," offering home-type experiments, and "Science and the Citizen," giving brief reviews of research, as gleaned from the more specialized journals. An excellent feature is the main book review, which frequently serves as a tutorial essay in itself. In an age when the lack of communication between specialist and layman is decried, this magazine belongs in every library.

Technology Review. 1899. m. (Nov.–July). $7. J. I. Matthill. Alumni Assn., Massachusetts Inst. of Technology, Cambridge, Mass. 02139. Illus., index, adv. Circ: 30,000.

Indexed: ChemAb. *Bk. rev:* 2–5, 1,500 words, signed. *Aud:* Sh, Jc, Ac, Ga, Sa. *Rv:* M. *Jv:* B.

One would hope that the periodical enjoys a wider circulation than to the homes of M.I.T. alumni. Its emphasis is on reviewing current technological and scientific advances and their impact on our culture: art, education, government, history, industry, philosophy, politics, etc. Feature articles, usually written on a layman's level, are supplied by alumni or faculty. The quality is high, the contributors distinguished, the contents interesting, the graphic work dramatic, and the format good. Special departments cover trends in government, science, news of the Institute, a math puzzle section, and the like. Mention should be made, too, of the well-written book reviews, which are lively, and not necessarily restricted to science. Of course, some issues also contain alumni notes. Recommended for all larger libraries, public and academic alike.

SCIENCE FICTION

Amazing Stories. 1926. bi-m. $2.50. Harry Harrison. Ultimate Publishing Co., Inc., 69-62 230th St., Oakland Gardens, Flushing, N.Y. 11364. Illus., adv.

Bk. rev: 2–3, 500–1,000 words, signed. *Aud:* Ga, Sh. *Rv:* L. *Jv:* C.

One of the earliest science fiction magazines. The stories cover a broad range of subjects other than space travel, e.g., improving secretaries as business machines by selective breeding, the use of hypnosis by a master criminal. These are interesting themes but their development in pulp style will repel some readers. Judged by usual literary standards the magazine does not rate high. Science fiction buffs may not agree with this appraisal.

Analog Science Fact—Science Fiction. 1930. m. $6. John W. Campbell. Conde Nast Pubns., 420 Lexington Ave., New York, N.Y. 10017. Illus., adv. Circ: 80,000.

Bk. rev: 4–5, 500–1,000 words, signed. *Aud:* Ga, Sh. *Rv:* L. *Jv:* V.

This magazine, more than many others, is responsible for the development of science-fiction into a respectable form of writing. John W. Campbell, graduate of M.I.T., took over the editorial reins in the mid-1930's and quickly established a policy related to the rules of logic and science. Pure fantasy was no longer in favor. Each issue now contains an article on some aspect of science—sometimes revolutionary, often rather technical, and most often written by scientists. The editorials are fascinating and thought-provoking. Add to this, accurate book reviews, excellent color covers, and good illustrations, and you have a superior publication by any standards.

Galaxy. 1950. bi-m. $6. Galaxy Publishing Co., 421 Hudson St., New York, N.Y. 10014. Illus., adv.

Bk. rev: 6–10, essay length. *Aud:* Ga, Sh. *Rv:* L. *Jv:* A.

Neither as old nor as famous as *Analog*. This magazine nevertheless has a comparatively large circulation and a good reputation. Story quality is usually good, but can vary from excellent to poor in the same issue. Features include popularized science articles, book reviews, and good cover art.

Gothique. 1967. q. $1.50. Stan Nicholls & Dave Griffiths. 5 St. John's Wood Terrace, St. John's Wood, London N.W.8. Illus., adv.

Aud: Ga. *Rv:* L. *Jv:* B.

An offset, 24-page pocket-sized magazine which attempts to cover all aspects of the Gothic in books, films and magazines. There is more on the film than other areas—and one issue features a nicely illustrated piece on "Hex," a flick built around the black mass. There is usually an interview with an author or director, and comments by the two editors. The magazine is pretty slim, but may have appeal for any serious student of this or wider aspects of science fiction. The same publishers issue another magazine of similar size and format which stresses science fiction and how it is used as a subject for films, illustrators and authors. This is *Stardock* (1968. q. $1.50). Its primary value for Americans is that it touches a few books and flicks not covered by the American based *Science Fiction Times*. However, the latter is to be much preferred, if only for about two to three times the editorial comment and the reviews. *Stardock* is only for the dedicated.

Magazine of Fantasy and Science Fiction. m. $5. Mercury Press, Inc., 347 E. 53rd St., New York, N.Y. 10022.

Aud: Ga, Sh. *Rv:* L. *Jv:* B.

In the literary world, this may be the best known of the S-F mags, unfortunately. The basic problem is the attempt to be literary, which too often fails. Story quality ranges form good to poor, with the good pieces being in the minority. The cover illustration is excellent, and contents include many interesting science articles by Isaac Asimov.

Riverside Quarterly. 1964. q. $1.25. Leland Sapiro. Box 82, University Station, Saskatoon, Sask.

Aud: Ga, Ac, Jc, Sh. *Rv:* L. *Jv:* B.

This is a high-class "fanzine," that is, a magazine intended for the edification and delight of science fiction fans. (Such magazines, incidentally, comprise a large but little-known species, as most are produced by small groups of enthusiasts and distributed mainly to group members.) In format, the *Riverside Quarterly* resembles closely the university literary journal—long articles with footnotes appear, as do reviews, short stories and poems. The big difference, of course, is that here the subject is strictly "little green men." Treatment of this subject, however, is impressively high and entertaining. The result is a fanzine that anyone can pick up with pleasure and perhaps profit. Recent articles include one on T. H. White's *The Once and Future King,* a book with appeal for science-fiction fans; another on what is happening in science-fiction in the Soviet Union, and a third on H. G. Wells' interest in outer-space phenomena. The short stories and poems, some of which are included in each issue, are of literary-journal quality. At the price, the *Riverside Quarterly* is a bargain.

Science Fiction Times. m. $3. Box 515, Washington Bridge Station, New York, N.Y. 10033. Illus.

Bk. rev: 4–6, 500 words, signed, and notes. *Aud:* Ga, Sh, Jh. *Rv:* H. *Jv:* A.

A processed, pocket-sized 28-page report by dedicated enthusiasts on all aspects of science fiction from films and books to annotations of magazines in the field. A typical number features news of science fiction authors, information on activities at the international level, a calendar of events, an index to articles dealing with science fiction (magazines from *Senior Scholastic* to *Playboy* are indexed), a current listing of both hardback and paperback science fiction (no annotations), and five or six long reviews of new titles, plus 20 to 30 short notes on reprints, primarily in paperback. The critics are truly critical, seem to speak from experience. As a guide to a genre this report exceeds almost anything now found in the library world's book review media. Admittedly the format isn't much, but the content is the answer to many a librarian's plea for a reviewing medium in this field. In view of the scope and low price, should be found in any library from junior high through a university where there is an interest in science fiction.

SLAVIC LANGUAGES

Indexes and Abstracts

British Humanities Index, Historical Abstracts, Public Affairs Information Service, Social Sciences and Humanities Index. (For annotations, see Indexes and Abstracts Section.)

Canadian Slavic Studies/Revue Canadienne D'Etudes Slaves. 1967. q. $6. Charles Schlacks, Jr. Dept. of History, Loyola College, Montreal 28, Que.

Indexed: HistAb. *Aud:* Sa, Ac. *Rv:* M. *Jv:* B.

A journal which replaced *Etudes Slaves et Est-Euro-peenes/Slavic and East-European Studies* as Loyola's contribution in the Slavic field. (*Etudes Slaves* continued, but without Loyola's support, as the organ of the Association de Slavistes et de Specialistes Est-Europeenes du Canada de l'Est, 5601, Ave. des Cedres, Montreal 36, Que.) *Canadian Slavic Studies* puts itself forward as a "forum for debate and reflection on the affairs of the Soviet Union and Eastern Europe, before and after 1917," and publishes eastern as well as western views on happenings in the Slavic countries. Good for large Eastern European collections.

International Journal of Slavic Linguistics and Poetics. 1959. irreg. $4.25/number. Ed bd. Prof. D. S. Worth. Dept. of Slavic Languages Univ. of Calif., Los Angeles, Calif. 90024. Illus., adv. Circ: 550.

Bk. rev: 6–10, 2,500 words, signed. *Aud:* Sa, Ac. *Rv:* H. *Jv:* B.

A journal for the presentation of scholarly linguistic studies, generally structural or descriptive analyses of the Slavic languages during all periods of development. Features discussions of Slavic contributions to linguistic science and studies in applied linguistics, especially dialects. Literary studies are usually textual and linguistic. Each issue contains 200 pages, with articles averaging 4,500 words. The text is in English, French, German, and all Slavic languages. There is an international list of contributors.

Russian Language Journal. 1947. q. $6. Vladimir I. Grebenschikov. Michigan State Univ., East Lansing, Mich. 48823. Circ: 500.

Bk. rev: 4–8, 400 words, signed. *Aud:* Ac, Jc, Ht. *Rv:* M. *Jv:* B.

Devoted to research and discussion in modern Russian language and literature, and in methods of teaching Russian in U.S. and Canadian secondary schools and colleges. Intended exclusively for teachers of Russian, its articles concentrate on teaching problems, training, professional matters, and linguistics. Some comparative studies, with emphasis on the Russian language, are presented. Articles are in Russian and English; they average 2,000 words in length. The journal also features reviews of professional journals, information letters on professional activities, announcements of teaching jobs, and a glossary of English and Russian grammar and literary terms.

The Russian Review; an American quarterly devoted to Russia past and present. 1941. q. $7. Dmitri Von Mohrenschildt. Russian Review, Inc., Box 146, Hanover, N.H. 03755. Index, adv. Circ: 1,500.

Indexed: HistAb, PAIS, SSHum. *Aud:* Sa, Ac. *Rv:* H. *Jv:* B.

One of the most prestigious Slavic journals published in the U.S. According to an editorial note, its purpose is "to interpret the real aims and aspirations of the Russian peo-ple, as distinguished from and contrasted with Soviet Communism, and to advance general knowledge of Russian culture, history and civilization." This journal, which began at the time of the Russian entry into World War II, has among its contributors such people as George Kennan, Alexander Kerensky, Vladimir Nabokov, and Alexander Tolstoy. Although much space is given over to political and historical discussion, consideration of general cultural matters is frequent. Of considerable importance to university and large public libraries.

The Slavic and East European Journal. 1943. q. Membership (Non-members, $10). J. Thomas Shaw. Univ. of Wisconsin Press, Journals Dept., Box 1379, Madison, Wis. 53701. Circ: 2,200.

Bk. rev: 15–25, 600 words, signed. *Aud:* Sa, Ac, Jc, Ht. *Rv:* H. *Jv:* A.

The official publication of the American Association of Teachers of Slavic and East European Languages, an affiliate of the Modern Language Association and the Canadian Association of Slavists and East European Specialists. The journal, known previously as *The AATSEEL Bulletin* and *The AATSEEL Journal,* is "devoted to research in language, linguistics, and literature, and to pedagogy." Each issue contains six or eight full-scale articles, a large review section and a section of news and notes concerning AATSEEL matters. Although the journal's appeal is mainly to literature-and-language specialists, there is much for others as well. Recent articles include one on the Russian assessment of Pushkin's achievement, another on Turgenev's opera librettos, and a third on Russian teaching. Of considerable use to large high school, public and university libraries.

Slavic Review; American quarterly of Soviet and East European studies. 1941. q. $12. Henry L. Roberts. Amer. Assn. for the Advancement of Slavic Studies, Columbia Univ., 622 W. 113th St., New York, N.Y. 10025. Circ: 3,200. Reprint: Johnson.

Indexed: PAIS, SSHum. *Bk. rev:* 30, signed. *Aud:* Sa, Ac. *Rv:* H. *Jv:* V.

This journal, which appeared earlier as *The American Slavic and East European Review,* examines matters of interest to Slavicists of every stripe. Although the tone is learned (footnotes burgeon), readability is, on the whole, high. Each issue contains: some half-dozen major articles; a section of notes and comments, in which shorter articles appear; a forum, presenting opinions on journal articles, and a large review section. Each has also "Letters-to-the-Editor" and "News-of-the-Profession" columns. Inclusion is eclectic. Given attention recently have been such subjects as problems of source criticism in Russian history, the education of Russian peasants, and Tolstoy as teacher and prophet. Every university and large public library will want to subscribe to this publication.

Slavonic and East European Review. 1922. semi-ann. $8.40. Ed bd. School of Slavonic and East European Studies, Malet St., London W.C.1. Circ: 1,000.

Indexed: BritHum, SSHum. *Bk. rev:* 20–30, ½ to 1 page, signed. *Aud:* Sa, Ac, Jc. *Rv:* M. *Jv:* B.

Published by the University of London, this is devoted to both the social sciences and humanities. Articles deal with history, literature and social commentary. The detailed, critical reviews cover all aspects of Slavonic studies. A basic journal for academic and junior college libraries with appropriate curricula.

Classroom Aids

Besides the magazine listed below, the *Unesco Courier* is available in a Russian edition, as, of course, is *Sputnik*.

Kometa. m. $1.50 ($1 for 5 or more subscriptions). Scholastic Magazines, Inc., 50 W. 44th St., New York, N.Y. 10036.

See remarks for Scholastic Magazines in the German Language Section, Classroom Aids.

Kometa is geared for both junior high and high school first and second Russian courses. The format follows that of similar Scholastic efforts. The eight pages depend heavily upon photographs and line drawings. There are cartoons, crossword puzzles, and the usual guide to vocabulary used in the issue. Primarily for classrooms and of limited use in the library.

SOCIOLOGY

Indexes and Abstracts

Biological Abstracts, Biological and Agricultural Index, British Humanities Index, Index to Periodical Articles By and About Negroes, Psychological Abstracts, Public Affairs Information Service, Readers' Guide to Periodical Literature, Social Sciences and Humanities Index, Sociological Abstracts. (For annotations, see Indexes and Abstracts Section.)

Adolescence. See Child Care Section.

American Behavioral Scientist. 1957. bi-m. $10/yr. (Institutions, $14). Sara Miller. Sage Pubns., Inc., 275 South Beverly Drive, Beverly Hills, Calif. 90212. Illus., adv. Circ: 3,500. Microform: UM.

Indexed: PAIS, PsyAb, SSHum, SocAb. *Bk. rev:* Numerous notes. *Aud:* Sa, Ac, Jc, Ht. *Rv:* H. *Jv:* A.

Each issue is devoted to a single topic, i.e., the methods and techniques of social research. There are usually eight to ten short articles following an introduction by a guest editor. The authors are specialists in research and clinical work. Topics studied have included social advances in information retrieval in the social sciences, multi-national comparisons of social research, overviews of the relation of environment and behavior, and communication and behavior, and interdisciplinary relationships in political science. The "New Studies Section" is a guide to recent publications in the social and behavioral sciences. The magazine's staff periodically checks over 360 journals and reviews and in each issue lists about 100 new publications selected from these sources with brief annotations. The listing includes books, pamphlets, and articles on sociology, psychology, and the other behavioral sciences. This latter feature makes this a valuable magazine for bibliographers, and frequent articles on communication give it a particular place in library schools.

American Journal of Economics and Sociology. See Economics Section.

American Journal of Sociology. 1895. bi-m. $8. C. Arnold Anderson. Univ. of Chicago Press, 5750 Ellis Ave., Chicago, Ill. 60637. Illus., adv. Circ: 7,200. Microform: Canner, UM. Reprint: Johnson.

Indexed: PAIS, PsyAb, SSHum, SocAb. *Bk. rev:* 25–30, 400–700 words, signed. *Aud:* Sa, Ac, Jc, Ht. *Rv:* H. *Jv:* A.

A professional and scholarly coverage of the most advanced thinking and empirical research in the various fields of sociology and social psychology. Most of the articles are a result of field work and research on specific social problems. The signed, evaluative book reviews and the bibliographic listing of current books received (averaging 200–300 titles) provide the means for keeping abreast with the latest and best American and foreign titles available in sociology and psychology. A valuable feature is the yearly listing of Ph.D.s in sociology and newly started Ph.D. dissertations. Valuable for all academic and larger public libraries.

American Sociological Review; official journal of the American Sociological Association. 1936. bi-m. Membership (Non-members, $10). Norman B. Ryder. Amer. Sociological Assn., 1001 Connecticut Ave., N.W., Washington, D.C. 20036. Illus. Circ: 11,000. Microform: UM. Reprint: Johnson.

Indexed: PAIS, SSHum. *Bk. rev:* 30–50, 800–1,200 words, signed. *Aud:* Sa, Ac, Jc, Ht. *Rv:* H. *Jv:* A.

Similar to the *American Journal of Sociology* in its presentation, research articles on theory and methodology, case studies and field work in all branches of sociology are included along with the official reports and proceedings of the association. Language tends to be technical and theoretical, frequently involving the use of formulas and other symbolic means of representing relationships. There are usually 10 studies per issue; each is from 15 to 20 pages in length. The "Review Symposium" presents 3 reviews on a significant new work in the field. Primarily of interest to professionals in the field.

American Sociologist. 1965. q. Membership (Institutions, $8). Raymond W. Mark. Amer. Sociological Assn., 1001

Connecticut Ave., N.W., Washington, D.C. 20036. Microform: UM.

Aud: Sa, Ac. *Rv:* M. *Jv:* B.

Unlike its sister publication, the *American Sociological Review,* this tends to be more of a professional journal for the membership. Regular features such as the calendar, employment, news of the Association and its members, reports on annual meetings, etc., stress its narrower scope. Conversely, it does present ten to fifteen articles, both theoretical and practical, on aspects of teaching, case work, future trends, the supply and demand of sociologists—to name a few areas. If a choice has to be made for libraries, the *American Sociological Review* would be a first, but for medium to larger academic libraries, both are required.

British Journal of Sociology. 1950. q. $8.30. Terence Morris. Routledge & Kegan Paul, Ltd., Broadway House, 68–74 Carter Lane, London E.C. 4. Illus., adv. Microform: UM.

Indexed: BritHum, PAIS, PsyAb, SSHum. *Bk. rev:* 20–40, 500–600 words, signed. *Aud:* Sa, Ac, Jc. *Rv:* H. *Jv:* A.

Sponsored by the London School of Economics and Political Science, this journal presents scholarly articles ranging over the fields of theoretical and applied sociology. The editors state that there is no attempt to favor any "school center, country, or variety of sociology," and an effort is made to fairly represent social anthropology, social administration, and several relevant areas of history, philosophy and social psychology. Occasionally, in addition to the regular book reviews, there is a 6–8 page review of material on a specific subject such as suicide, race relations in the United States, or alcoholism. Reviews provide greater coverage of British and European publications than do comparable American journals. Of primary value to sociologists and graduate students, although its high standing in the field should insure it a place in academic and large public library collections.

Community. 1941. m. (Sept.–July). $2. Trudi Jenny. Friendship House, 4233 S. Indiana Ave., Chicago, Ill. 60653. Illus. Circ: 5,500.

Indexed: INeg. *Bk. rev:* Notes. *Aud:* Ga, Ac, Jc, Sh. *Rv:* M. *Jv:* B.

A general newsletter on activities at Friendship House, an interracial center in Chicago. Reports on work-study programs in interracial affairs, and usually has one or two longer articles on some current issue. A good part of the magazine is given over to the particular problems of whites and Afro-Americans. While centered in Chicago, the various reports are national and international in scope. The periodical is particularly suited to the lay group which is endeavoring to find non-technical ways of improving interracial harmony in a community. Should be found in all academic libraries, and high school and public libraries where useful.

Comparative Studies in Society and History; an international quarterly. 1958. q. $6. Mouton & Co., P.O. Box 1132, The Hague, Netherlands. Illus., index, adv. Circ: 2,000.

Indexed: SSHum. *Aud:* Sa, Ac. *Rv:* M. *Jv:* B.

Geared for the scholar and advanced student, this journal features articles on problems in history and related fields such as sociology, economics and psychology. It is interested in social organization, the structure of society and explanations of stability and change. The articles are scholarly monographs and include theoretical debate. In view of its close relation to other academic fields, it should be considered a basic addition to all large research libraries.

Current Sociology. 1959. 3/yr. $4.90. Basil Blackwell, 4 Broad St., Oxford, Eng. Circ: 1,227.

Indexed: PAIS. *Aud:* Sa, Ac. *Rv:* H. *Jv:* B. Reprint: Johnson, Kraus.

A publication of the International Sociological Association that is primarily a lengthy annotated bibliography of material in a given subject area. Each issue concentrates on a particular point of interest, is preceded by a "Trend Report" on the topic, and/or several papers of related interest. The main text is both in English and French, the annotations a combination. Coverage is international, and a run of the periodical gives the individual or a library one of the best single sources of information on all major subjects related to sociology, e.g., demography, underdeveloped nations, human organizations, social issues, etc. A basic work for any library or student who has serious interest in sociology.

Family Coordinator; a journal of education, counseling and services. 1952. q. $5. William M. Smith, Jr. National Council on Family Relations, 1219 University Ave. S.E., Minneapolis, Minn. 55414. Illus. Circ: 1,600.

Indexed: SocAb. *Aud:* Sa, Ac, Jc. *Rv:* H. *Jv:* B.

A professional journal for counselors, psychologists and teachers working with marriage and family problems. The articles are written by experts, and are well documented. While much of the material will be of only professional interest, a few articles touch on problems that concern the layman, e.g., birth control, sex education, divorce, and the sexual behavior of adolescents. A few advanced high school students may find the magazine of value, but for the most part it is only for larger academic and public libraries.

Happier Marriage and Planned Parenthood. 1968. q. $.50/copy. Dorothy Whyte Cotton. Parents' Magazine Enterprises, Inc., 52 Vanderbuilt Ave., New York, N.Y. 10017. Illus., adv.

Aud: Ga, Sh. *Rv:* L. *Jv:* B.

Articles on all aspects of marriage such as money problems, in-law relationships, cooking tips, religion, and children. There is also information on planned parenthood.

Authors are professionals, the style is basic, the advice sound. This magazine is more for the adult than the average senior high school student, though it might be of interest to the student who is planning an early marriage. In earlier issues several of the articles were reprinted from *Parents' Magazine,* and apparently this will continue. Hence, libraries already taking the other magazine may hesitate to subscribe. As of this date, only for large libraries with larger budgets.

Human Relations; a journal of studies toward the integration of the social sciences. 1947. q. $12.50. Eric L. Trist. Plenum Publishing Corp., 227 W. 17th St. New York, N.Y. 10011. Illus., adv. Circ: 2,100. Microform: UM.

Indexed: BritHum, SSHum, PAIS, PsyAb. *Aud:* Sa, Ac. *Rv:* H. *Jv:* B.

International in scope, with three editorial committees (Europe, Britain, and the United States). Increasingly concerned with social problems and the "identification of conditions which will render decision making more apposite and social action more effective." There are an average of seven articles per issue, which are either reports on research proposals carried out by the author or extensive monographs based on thorough and extensive reading and rethinking of theory and procedural design. The articles are primarily devoted to the psychological and sociological aspects of group process, systems, interpersonal relations and interaction. Of value to psychologists and social scientists.

International Journal of Comparative Sociology. 1960. 2/yr. $12. K. Ishwaran. E. J. Brill Publishers, Leiden, The Netherlands. Illus., adv.

Indexed: SSHum. *Bk. rev:* 15, 500–700 words, signed. *Aud:* Sa, Ac. *Rv:* M. *Jv* B.

Coverage of world-wide research and developments in sociology. The primary aim is "the furtherance of pure research in the field." The scholarly studies describe and interpret social situations with comparisons to other countries. The evaluative and descriptive reviews submitted by scholars from all over the world provide a sampling of new materials in the field from non-western areas. Occasionally an entire issue is devoted to a single topic, which draws information from different cultures. For example, there have been presentations on the relationship between politics and social change, and kinship and geographic mobility. Primarily for the scholar and college student interested in an international and comparative view of sociology.

International Migration Review. 1964. 3/yr. $4.50. Silvano M. Tomasi. Center for Migration Studies, 209 Flagg Place, Staten Island, N.Y. 10304. Circ: 700. Microform: UM.

Indexed: PAIS. *Bk. rev:* Various numbers and lengths. *Aud*: Sa, Ac. *Rv:* H. *Jv:* B.

Published in cooperation with the Centro Studi Emigrazione in Rome, this is a scientific journal of international scope, studying sociological, demographic, historical, and legislative aspects of migration movements. (It is also a successor to the *International Migration Digest.*) The new title indicates a more original effort of analysis and clarification of issues. Included are papers by specialists, statistics on migration trends, and book reviews covering an unusually high number of titles. Primarily of use to sociologists and other social scientists concerned with this subject.

International Social Science Journal. 1949. q. $7. Peter Lengyel. United Nations Educational, Scientific and Cultural Organization (UNESCO), Place de Fontency, Paris 7e, France. Circ: 3,500 English, 2,000 French. Reprint: Kraus. Microform: UM.

Indexed: PAIS, PsyAb, SSHum. *Aud:* Ga, Ac, Jc, Sh. *Rv:* H. *Jv:* A.

The first part of each issue of this UNESCO publication is a symposium of up to 10 articles, focusing attention on important interdisciplinary efforts, or bringing readers up to date on developments in a particular area. Presentations are aimed at non-specialists and should appeal to scholars, college and high school students and the general public interested in an international survey of the topic. The various social science disciplines are covered in turn. Recent topics have included human rights, the role of science and technology in development, the social science press, the sociology of literary criticism, and modern methods in criminology. Contributors are selected from among specialists on the topic from throughout the world, and there is frequently an extensive selected bibliography of recent materials, relating to the main topic, accompanying the articles. The second part of each issue is entitled the "World of the Social Sciences" and includes the following regular features: statements on the activities of national and international research and training centers and professional bodies, together with listings of new institutions and changes of address; details concerning approaching international conferences in the social sciences, and summary reports of recent important international meetings; a listing of international appointment vacancies for social scientists; and a unique annotated list of documents and publications of the United Nations and specialized agencies of interest to social scientists. There is a "Books Received" section classified by subject headings. The Journal circulates in over sixty countries and is available in an English and a French edition. Recommended for almost all libraries.

Journal of Asian and African Studies. 1966. q. $12. K. Ishwaran. E. J. Brill Publishers, Leiden, Netherlands.

Bk. rev: 10–15, 500 words, signed. *Aud:* Sa, Ac. *Rv:* H. *Jv:* B.

Although issued quarterly, recent practice has been to publish double numbers of some 160 pages twice a year. Issues center on specific subjects of interest to any scholar involved with man and society in developing nations of Asia and Africa, e.g., "Sociology of Japanese Religion," and "Traditional and Modern Institutions in Asia and

Africa." Emphasis is on sociology, but contributors come from other disciplines such as political science history, anthropology and related social sciences. The material represents original research, is well documented, and is an excellent source of reference for the specialist. Not for the undergraduate.

Journal of Conflict Resolution; for research related to war and peace. 1957. q. $7. Elizabeth Converse. Center for Research on Conflict Resolution, Univ. of Michigan, Ann Arbor, Mich. 48104. Illus., adv. Circ: 1,900. Microform: UM.

Indexed: PAIS, PsyAb, SSHum. *Bk. rev:* 2–3, several pages, signed. *Aud:* Sa, Ac. *Rv:* H. *Jv:* B.

Conflict here stands for war, and the sponsoring group publishes articles which consider problems relating to war and to peace. Authors cover a wide spectrum of interests from political science and economics to literature and art. The five to six scholarly articles touch on historical implications of war in all parts of the world. Concerned, as well, with the affects of communication, the magazine should have wide appeal to any serious student of psychology, history, or sociology.

Journal of Human Relations. 1952. q. $4. Ralph T. Templin. Central State Univ., Wilberforce, Ohio. Circ: 350. Reprint: Johnson. Microform: UM.

Indexed: INeg, PAIS, PsyAb. *Bk. rev:* 7–10, 400–1,000 words, signed. *Aud:* Ga, Ac, Jc. *Rv:* M. *Jv:* B.

Approaches human relations from all disciplines in the belief "that the human conditions require the light of every science in order to increase social awareness and to establish more meaningful practical relationships." There are usually eight non-technical articles, of 10 to 12 pages, written by professors and laymen in the fields of literature, philosophy, education, sociology and the other social sciences. Authors have dealt with the necessity of identifying and constructing meaningful national goals, the philosophical groundings of a democracy, human goals and the psychological factors inducing warfare. Occasionally, several articles will present a symposium on various aspects of a topic like poverty. Regular features include: "The Record" —a factual and unbiased study of a controversial matter, such as the Arab-Israeli conflict; "Research Studies and Abstracts"—a brief presentation of a current study; "Human Frontiers"—a short article of theory and thought on frontier questions; "Focus on Human Conditions"—a critical evaluation of trends, programs and habits, etc., and "Contexts of Growth"—articles on educational aspects of human relations. Both the method of presentation and the contents make this suitable for layman as well as students and scholars.

Journal of Marriage and the Family. 1939. q. $12. Marvin B. Sussman. National Council on Family Relations, 1219 Univ. Ave., S.E., Minneapolis, Minn. 55414. Illus., adv. Circ: 7,000. Microform: UM. Reprint: Kraus.

Indexed: PsyAb, SSHum. *Bk. rev:* 8–10, 900–1,000 words, signed. *Aud:* Sa, Ac, Jc, Ht. *Rv:* H. *Jv:* B.

A medium for the presentation of original theory, research, interpretation, and critical discussion on material related to marriage and the family. It is sponsored by the National Council on Family Relations, which seeks to bring together the leaders in research, teaching, and professional service in this field so as to advance the cultural values secured through family relations. Most of the 20 articles per issue are theoretical proposals or reports of research dealing with particular areas of marriage and family relations and are from four to ten pages in length. A regular feature is the "International Department," with three to four articles submitted from overseas. Included also is a book review section. Occasionally, an entire issue is devoted to a single topic, such as the American adolescent in the mid-sixties, the poverty family, and family planning. Of value in larger libraries or specialized sociology, social work, family life, and health collections; of primary interest to scholars and college students and teachers of the above areas.

Journal of Social History. See History Section.

Journal of Social Issues. 1945. q. Joshua A. Fishman. Edwards Brothers, 2500 South St., Ann Arbor, Mich. 48104. Illus., adv. Circ: 5,000. Reprint: Kraus. Microform: UM.

Indexed: BioAb, PsyAb, SSHum. *Aud:* Sa, Ac, Jc, Sh. *Rv:* H. *Jv:* A.

Sponsored by the Society for the Psychological Study of Social Issues, this journal seeks to bring theory and practice into focus on human problems of the group, community, and nation. The goal is to communicate scientific findings in a non-technical manner without the sacrifice of professional standards. Each issue has a guest editor and seven articles on different aspects of a single topic like bilingualism or cultural change in small communities. Authors are professors or specialists in the field. Extensive bibliographies accompany each article. In the back of the issue are perforated pages of three-by-five cards, giving full bibliographic citations and annotations of the articles appearing. Because of the inter-disciplinary and non-technical approach and analysis of current social issues, the journal would be of value to most libraries including high schools.

Law and Contemporary Problems. See Law Section.

Pacific Sociological Review. 1958. semi-ann. $4. John MacGregor. Department of Sociology, Univ. of Oregon, Eugene, Ore., 97403. Illus., adv. Circ: 1,200.

Indexed: SocAb. *Aud:* Sa, Ac. *Rv:* M. *Jv:* B.

Devoted to the publication of research, theory, and methodology in sociology. An average of seven articles per issue range from 6 to 14 pages in length and are generally submitted from the Washington-Oregon-California area. Studies include such topics as: the analysis of membership in voluntary Negro associations; the metropolitan distribution of the older population; a new versus an old theory of deviant behavior; methodological procedures for studying human behavior. Only for large, specialized collections, but should be found in most western academic libraries.

Public Opinion Quarterly. 1937. q. $6. Harwood Childs. Princeton Univ. Press, Box 231, Princeton, N.J. 08540. Adv. Circ: 4,000. Microform: UM. Reprint: Johnson.

Indexed: PAIS, PsyAb, SSHum. *Bk. rev:* 20, 1,000 words, signed. *Aud:* Sa, Ac. *Rv:* H. *Jv:* A.

In a poll-happy country, this is a basic journal. It reports on all aspects of the communication revolution, primarily on how "hot" or "cold" media affect or fail to affect the public. According to the editors, it is "hospitable to all points of view, provided only that the material presented will help readers gain insight into the problems of public opinion." Aside from the lengthy and scholarly articles, there is a section entitled "Current Research" for briefer reports such as case histories and hypotheses, "News and Notes" lists news about professional organizations, awards and grants and personnel and personal notes. "The Polls" reprints current poll results which have significance in public opinion. A basic magazine wherever a sociology, political science or communication course is taught. Should be in all larger public libraries as well.

Public Welfare. 1943. q. $8. Malvin Morton. Amer. Public Welfare Assn., 1313 E. 60th St., Chicago, Ill., 60637. Illus., adv. Circ: 13,000.

Indexed: PAIS. *Bk. rev:* 4–5, 600–800 words, signed. *Aud:* Sa, Ac. *Rv:* M. *Jv:* B.

Devotes attention to public welfare programs, dependent children, the aged, dependent families, administration, staff training, and general welfare. Articles are written by the staff and directors of welfare programs at federal, state and local levels; deans and professors of schools of social welfare, and civic leaders. The 8 to 11 articles are based on the authors' personal, "on-the-job" experiences. Regular features include book reviews of selected new books in the social welfare field; book notes which list many publications of national organizations and publishers; "From Across the Country" which summarizes national and regional activities; and "Message from the Director." While admittedly a specialized approach, the interest in the subject is such that it should be in most medium to large public libraries, certainly in all academic collections.

Psychiatry and Social Science Review. See Psychology Section.

Race; a journal of race and group relations. 1959. semi-ann. $7.25. Simon Abbott. Oxford Univ. Press, Ely House, 37 Dover St., London W.10. Circ: 600.

Indexed: BritHum, PAIS. *Aud:* Sa, Ac, Jc. *Rv:* H. *Jv:* B.

The journal of the Institute of Race Relations of London, it discusses matters of race in generally learned tones, but manages without trouble to be readable as well as informative. Each rather bulky issue contains half a dozen full-

scale articles on such divergent matters as the genesis of segregation, intermarriage, colored immigration to Britain and Negro higher education. A regular feature is the "Quarterly Forum", a section in which articles of lesser scope appear. About half of the available space is devoted to signed book reviews. Most of these are long and detailed. Recommended for academic and public libraries.

Rural Sociology. 1936. q. $8. W. Keith Warner. Rural Sociological Soc. Univ. of Wisconsin, Madison, Wis. Illus., adv. Circ: 2,300. Reprint: Johnson. Microform: UM.

Indexed: BioAg, PAIS, SSHum. *Bk. rev:* 18–25, 600–1,200 words, signed. *Aud:* Sa, Ac, Jc. *Rv:* H. *Jv:* B.

Covers all aspects of rural life in the United States and other countries—including the economic, cultural, social, and demographic components. There are five to seven research articles per issue averaging 8 to 16 pages. These have dealt with migration and settlement patterns; educational and occupational aspirations and achievements; social characteristics of rural peoples and areas; the adoption of agricultural practices; and the relations of rural and urban areas and peoples. The authors are associated with departments of sociology and rural sociology, rural education, or agricultural economics. The "Bulletin Index" is a topical list of new bulletins currently available, and there is a regular listing of recent theses and dissertations on rural sociology. Of value to large sociology and agricultural collections.

Social Casework. 1920. m. $6. Elinor P. Zaki. Family Service Assn. of America, 44 E. 23rd St., New York, N.Y. 10010. Circ: 18,000. Reprint: Kraus. Microform: UM.

Indexed: PsyAb, SSHum. *Bk. rev:* 2–6, 800–1,200 words, signed. *Aud:* Sa, Ac. *Rv:* H. *Jv:* B.

Written for the social worker, this journal pays particular attention to new approaches and techniques for helping children and adults with problems concerning interpersonal relations and social functioning. Authors are the directors of public and voluntary welfare agencies and their professional staff, and the deans and staffs of six schools of social welfare. There are usually five or six brief articles (4 to 8 pages) describing techniques for dealing with clients and other professionals and common problems which arise on the job. Others deal with the role of the social worker in various situations: family courts, marriage counselling, and the training of sub-professional personnel. All are based on personal experience. In addition to the book reviews, the "Have You Seen These?" section regularly lists 10–20 non-reviewed titles with brief annotations. There are occasional editorial notes, classified advertisements and reader comments. Of use in larger libraries and specialized collections for the social worker or student of social welfare.

Smith College Studies in Social Work. 1930. 3/yr. $3. Roger R. Miller. Smith College Sch. for Social Work, Northampton, Mass. 01060. Circ: 1,600.

Indexed: PAIS, PsyAb. *Aud:* Sa, Ac. *Rv:* H. *Jv:* B.

Approximately half of the three to four articles are devoted to reports of investigations based on master's theses and doctoral dissertations submitted to the Smith College School. Presentations are based on the authors' research investigations and practice experiences, but are sufficiently generalized to be applicable to other situations. Papers and reports deal with a range of topics, such as the relevance of ego psychology concepts to social work practice, family relationships, separation problems in children, communication difficulties, identity conflicts, continuity and discontinuity in therapy, and socio-cultural factors related to social work. One issue contains abstracts of all master's theses and doctoral dissertations completed at the school during that year. Also includes a number of papers presented by leading professional and academic specialists in the fields of social welfare and mental health, including social work, psychiatry, and sociology. Of primary interest to larger libraries, and collections related to social work and mental health.

Social Forces; a scientific medium of social study and interpretation. 1922. q. $6. Guy B. Johnson & Rupert B. Vance. Univ. of North Carolina Press, Box 510, Chapel Hill, N.C. 27514. Illus., adv. Circ: 3,500. Reprint: Johnson. Microform: UM.

Indexed: PAIS, PsyAb, *SSHum,* SocAb. *Bk. rev:* 40–50, 400–800 words, signed. *Aud:* Sa, Ac, Jc. *Rv:* H. *Jv:* B.

Brief, scholarly articles report research over the entire range of theoretical and applied sociology. Related subjects include the family, social psychology, regionalism, public opinion and population. Emphasis is placed on the motivation and reasons behind social action, developments and mobility. The theoretical studies have included relating social mobility and such features as job satisfaction; occupational groups and reasons for participation in community activities; and the relation of educational expectations and parents' occupations. There are research notes and comments and short, but numerous book reviews. Of value to most libraries since it deals with the social forces motivating the behavior of the average individual, and of use to the scholar and college student too.

Social Problems. 1953. q. $12. Hyman Rodman. Soc. for the Study of Social Problems, P.O. Box 190, Kalamazoo, Mich. 49005. Illus., adv. Circ: 3,300. Reprint: Johnson. Microform: UM.

Indexed: PAIS, PsyAb. *Aud:* Sa, Ac, Jc. *Rv:* M. *Jv:* B.

Research articles present current data on a full range of social problems. Studies deal with such topics as deviant behavior, comparisons of role behavior and the differences in activities and occupational pursuits between the sexes. A regular feature is the "Review Essay," which provides an overview of information on a particular subject. Since much of the material is clearly presented, college students and informed laymen as well as the professional will find it valuable.

Social Research; an international quarterly of political and social science. 1934. q. $10. Peter L. Berger. Grad. Faculty of Political and Social Science, New Sch. for Social Research, 66 W. 12th St., New York, N.Y. 10011. Circ: 1,800. Reprint: Kraus. Microform: UM.

Indexed: PAIS, SSHum. *Bk. rev:* 6, 800–1,500 words. *Aud:* Sa, Ac, Jc. *Rv:* H. *Jv:* B.

Features articles by economists, philosophers, political scientists, sociologists, and psychologists. The presentations analyze and interpret theories and ideas in the social sciences. Concern is with the role of the intellectual, and the philosophy, theory, and knowledge structure of the social sciences in contemporary society. There are monographs interpreting older theories and historical writings, articles on the structure of knowledge in various social science fields and presentations concerning different philosophical schools and the philosophies and ideologies of important individuals. Recent articles have included analyses of the thought of Weber, Marx, Chardin, Pareto, and Schweitzer. One issue was devoted to contemporary French philosophy. There are usually seven or eight articles ranging from 15 to 20 pages each. A regular feature is the "International Scene of Current Trends in the Social Sciences," which presents translations of social science writings from abroad. Because of its concise presentations of current thought and ideas on old and new situations, theories, and ideologies, it is of value in most libraries and a necessity in larger collections for scholarly and college level use.

Social Sciences and Medicine. See Medical, Nursing and Health Sciences Section.

Social Security Bulletin. 1938. m. $2.75. Josephine Merican. Supt. of Documents, U.S. Govt. Printing Office, Washington, D.C. 20402. Illus. Microform: UM.

Indexed: BusI, PAIS. *Aud:* Ga, Ac, Jc. *Rv:* M. *Jv:* B.

The official publication of the Social Security Administration presents current data and statistics on retirement; health insurance programs; disability insurance; Medicare, Medicaid and other help for the aged; aid for the blind and disadvantaged, and the poverty programs. Authors are associated with the administration's Office of Research and Statistics or are officials with the specialized programs discussed. The two to four articles per issue range from 4 to 6 pages in length. Most of each issue is devoted to a statistical presentation of the administration's current operations, broken down by time period and types of programs. These are cumulated quarterly. Of use in most libraries because of subjects discussed. Necessary in larger collections specializing in social science or related to economics and welfare programs.

Social Service Review. 1927. q. $8. Rachel B. Marks. Univ. of Chicago Press, 5750 Ellis Ave., Chicago, Ill. 60637. Illus., adv. Circ: 4,500. Microform: Canner, UM.

Indexed: PAIS, PsyAb, SSHum. *Bk. rev:* 15–20, 800–1,200 words, signed. *Aud:* Sa, Ac, *Rv:* H. *Jv:* B.

Emphasis is on original research and there are both specialized articles and presentations which "deal more broadly with social issues and problems." Each issue presents six to eight articles ranging from 6 to 15 pages in length. Authors are scholars, faculty, and professionals involved in social service work. Specialized, research designs have included such topics as the policy of the New York City Housing Authority (1958–1961), admissions decisions, and reports on the Midway Research Project. The more general articles deal with issues widely applicable in the field of social work, such as an historical survey of American thought on poverty, the role of voluntary agencies in social work, educating the social worker, interagency coordination, and bureaucratic and professional orientation patterns in social casework. There is a yearly abstracting of PhD dissertations completed in the September issue and a listing of those in progress. The "Notes and Comments" section offers briefer items on current developments in the field.

Social Work. 1956. q. $6. Beatrice Saunders. National Assn. of Social Workers, 2 Park Ave., New York, N.Y. 10016. Adv. Circ: 50,000. Microform: UM.

Indexed: PAIS, PsyAb. *Bk. rev:* 10–15, 300 words, signed. *Aud:* Sa, Ac, Jc. *Rv:* H. *Jv:* B.

"A professional journal committed to improving practice and extending knowledge in the field of social welfare." Editors welcome manuscripts which "yield new insights into established practices, evaluate new techniques and research, examine current social problems or bring serious critical analysis to bear on problems of the profession itself." Authors are professional social workers, educators, administrators, and researchers from government and voluntary agencies. They discuss social problems such as poverty, illegitimacy, chronic illness, methods and techniques used in intervention, and the rationale and ideology underlying social work and its specific programs. Regular features include "Points & Viewpoints," which extends the discussion of controversial matters from previous issues, and "Comments on Currents," which deals with current trends such as the guaranteed minimum income and poverty legislation. Of value to specialized collections in the fields of social work and social welfare, and to practitioners of social work, undergraduate and graduate students, and faculties in allied fields and disciplines such as sociology, psychology, and other behavioral sciences.

Sociological Quarterly. 1960. q. $5.50. Paul J. Campisi. Southern Illinois Univ., Edwardsville, Ill. 62025. Illus., adv. Circ: 1,500.

Indexed: SSHum. *Bk. rev:* 8–12, 500–700 words, signed. *Aud:* Sa, Ac. *Rv:* H. *Jv:* B.

Emphasis is on the theoretical significance of research in the general field of sociology. Articles deal with trends in social thought or an analysis of the ideas and contributions of an individual sociologist. Other studies have dealt with the impact of automation on status and the relation of education and social station. Important for most academic libraries, and since the presentations are not overly technical, it could be used by laymen desiring information on social problems and thought.

Sociological Review. 1908. 3/yr. $4.50. W. M. Williams. The Univ. of Keele, Staffordshire, Eng. Illus., adv. Circ: 1,200. Microform: UM. Reprint: Kraus.

Indexed: BritHum, PsyAb, SSHum. *Bk. rev:* 20–30, 900–1,200 words, signed. *Aud:* Sa, Ac. *Rv:* H. *Jv* B.

A British journal presenting articles on a wide range of general sociological topics, along with short notes on sociological research and critical comments on previous articles. Occasionally pieces summarize work in a particular area, e.g., the role of education in national development, or the positivist movement and the development of English sociology. The five or six research articles cover all areas: the relation of change to demographic factors, the role of ideology in determining behavior, the influence of ecological factors, and comparisons of various matched groups. The book reviews emphasize British publications. Booknotes cover 3 to 12 additional titles with short annotations, while "Books Received" lists 100 to 150 new publications.

Sociology. 1966. q. $9. Michael Banton. Oxford Univ. Press, 37 Dover St. London W.1. Circ: 1,000.

Bk. rev: Numerous, lengthy, signed. *Aud:* Sa, Ac. *Rv:* H. *Jv:* B.

This is the official journal of the British Sociological Association, highly specialized, and of value to American libraries as much for its articles as book reviews. There are usually four to five documented contributions—varying in this issue from a study of toys to compositors. Only for large, specialized collections.

Sociology and Social Research; an international journal. 1916. $6. Martin H. Neumeyer. Univ. of Southern California, Los Angeles, Calif. 90007. Circ: 2,000. Microform: UM. Reprint: Johnson.

Indexed: PAIS, PsyAb, SocAb, SSHum. *Bk. rev:* 10–15, 500 words, signed. *Aud:* Sa, Ac. *Rv:* H. *Jv:* B.

The results of recent research on special aspects of current sociological problems and occasional articles on theory are presented. Coverage is international, with studies made in such countries as New Zealand, South Africa, Iraq, and other nations, as well as the United States. Each issue has about nine 15- to 20-page articles. These include historical surveys and articles on the contributions of individuals, empirical research designs in the area of such social problems as juvenile delinquency, and reports of attitudes toward these problems and programs for their solution. There are also presentations concerning the philosophy of sociology and social theories. Besides book reviews there are shorter, unsigned book notes and a bibliographic listing. Of value in most collections and necessary in larger libraries for use by college students and behavioral scientists.

Sociometry; a journal of research in social psychology. 1937. q. $9. Sheldon Stryker. Amer. Sociological Assn., 1001 Connecticut Ave., N.W. Washington, D.C. 20036. Illus., adv. Circ: 2,000. Microform: UM.

Indexed: PAIS, PsyAb. *Aud:* Sa, Ac. *Rv:* H. *Jv:* B.

Particularly concerned with research which will give the field of social psychology a theoretical structure. Research is generally clearly focused, well-designed, and competently executed. The research designs have studied such aspects of interaction and socialization as the relation of social conformity and attitude changes, the development of similarities between observers and models, and the relation of religious behavior to personality. A specialized journal, only for large social science collections.

Soviet Studies. See Economics Section.

Trans-Action; social science and modern society. 1963. m. (Combined issues Jan.–Feb., July–Aug.) $3.50. I. Horowitz & L. Rainwater. Washington Univ. Box 1043, St. Louis, Mo. 63130. Illus., adv. Circ: 4,000. Microform: B&H.

Indexed: RG. *Bk. rev:* 2–5, 1,000–1,500 words, signed. *Aud:* Ga, Ac, Jc, Sh. *Rv:* H. *Jv:* V.

One of the few sociology-oriented periodicals for all general collections, this contains articles on current sociological discoveries and projects, written for the layman by sociologists, case workers, and nationally known social scientists. It publishes diverse views on subjects of public interest in the fields of government, labor, education, medicine, housing, welfare, law, religion, race relations social service, and politics. Its stated purpose is to further the understanding and use of the social sciences. Many of the articles contain bibliographies. Regular features are: "Roundup of Current Research" and "Book Reviews." A few topics covered in recent issues: "Does Black Power Have a Future?" "The Cash Value of College," "Are Most Professors for the War?" and "Why an Adult's Intelligence Declines." The large editorial board is composed of famous individuals in the social sciences. Recommended for all libraries.

Welfare in Review. 1963. bi-m. $1.75. Supt. of Documents, U.S. Govt. Printing Office, Washington, D.C. 20402.

Aud: Sa, Ac. *Rv:* H. *Jv:* B.

A HEW publication, coming out of the Office of the Administrator, Social and Rehabilitation Service. There are two to four articles per issue on various aspects of current welfare systems. More concern is shown for immediate activity and planning than for matters of more general or speculative nature. The articles are not necessarily by HEW employees, and are by no means representative of an official view. There are, however, two more important reference functions which this journal serves to fill. A regular feature is a list of new publications in the field, government or otherwise. This is indispensable to any library keeping a special collection on the subject. Even more significant is a quite large section on the most current Program and Operating Statistics for Public Assistance. This would be a major source for anyone requiring quantitative data on the disposition of funds and other resources, and on the indices of measurement in current use.

TEENAGE MAGAZINES

Indexes and Abstracts

Readers' Guide to Periodical Literature. (For annotation, see Indexes and Abstracts Section.)

If there is a lack of suitable general children's magazines, much the same may be said for the teen-age group. (i.e., general, not subject magazines, written specifically for the approaching teens or the teen-ager in junior-high and high school.) There are, to be sure, a relatively greater number, but the quality seems to diminish rather than improve. Furthermore, almost all of them are written specifically for the girls who will go on to the heights of the *Ladies' Home Journal* and *Good Housekeeping.* The lack of boy's magazines in this field is amazing. *Boy's Life* may be fine for junior high, but is near a total loss among lads who are growing beards. *Esquire* and *Playboy* would be fine additions to any collection for boys in senior high school, but, admittedly, this may present problems.

Fortunately, by the eighth or ninth grade, the teen-ager is better able to appreciate more fair to good adult general magazines. The wise teen-ager, teacher, parent, or librarian will avoid this section almost entirely. Again, though, for the sake of making sense out of the ratings, they are here only relative to the section, not to this work as a whole.

Allied Youth. 1931. q. $1.50. R. Kelley. Allied Youth, Inc., 1346 Connecticut Ave., N.W., Washington, D.C. 20036. Illus. Circ: 15,000.

Aud: Sh, Jh. *Rv:* L. *Jv:* C.

Directed to the Pat Boone type teen-ager, the main emphasis is on the dangers of this world, particularly those associated with drink. Articles concentrate on the virtues of "a sound mind in a healthy body." No one can argue with this goal, but the approach is somewhat less than sophisticated.

American Red Cross Journal. 1925. m. (Oct.–May). $1. Edgar C. Good, Jr. Amer. National Red Cross, 18th & D Sts., N.W., Washington, D.C. 20006. Illus. Circ: 800,000.

Indexed: IChildMags. *Aud:* Sh, Jh. *Rv:* M. *Jv:* A.

Published for the secondary school membership of the Red Cross, the *Journal* attempts to widen the horizons of service-minded youth on the enormous field of world-wide human need. Its eight to ten articles per issue describe successful individual and group projects, and attempt to promote interest in a wide variety of service activities. Guidance for the high school age group is provided in two ways: by descriptions of some careers in social service, and by thoughtful discussions of the role of today's youth in the society in which he finds himself. Writers, in addition to staff, are mainly Red Cross personnel from various parts of the country, journalists and educators. One or more pages of cartoon humor are included, in the understated vein of today's sophisticated youth. Page layout, general format, illustrations and type size are good to excellent.

Co-Ed. See Home Section.

Datebook. 1957. bi-m. $2. Art Unger. Young World Press, Inc., 71 Washington Pl., New York, N.Y. 10011. Adv. Circ: 150,000.

Aud: Jh, Sh. *Rv:* L. *Jv:* C.

A slick magazine "written for and by teens themselves." Completely oriented to the entertainment world, it contains endless photographs of current celebrities, interviews and stories of the same. Regular departments include gab sessions, diet column, money column, date-lines and a story or two. Bad format and newsprint pages. A poor candidate for a school library.

Dig; the original teen-age magazine. 1955. m. $3. I.D. Pubns., Inc., 9000 Sunset Strip, Hollywood, Calif. 90069. Illus., adv. Circ: 307,000.

Aud: Jh. *Rv:* L. *Jv:* C.

A pulpy and popular approach to the 13- to 17-year-old. Heavy on gossip, heroes, jokes, sayings, and whatever else most girls are supposed to be thinking and talking about. A prize example of what is wrong with many teen-age magazines. The same publisher brings out another magazine of equal calibre, *Fifteen* (Circ: 200,000). Yet, having said all of this, a case might be made for such magazines where the non-reading girl is having trouble because of not being able to relate to the average magazine, even the better ones for her age. If librarians are anxious to at least lure this type of child into the library, something might be said for both *Dig* and *Fifteen*—after all, these circulation figures represent more than passing interest by a good number of the younger set.

For Teens Only. 1962. bi-m. $4/12 issues. Rena Adler. Reese Publishing Co., Inc., 201 Park Ave. S., New York, N.Y. 10003. Illus., adv.

Aud: Jh. *Rv:* L. *Jv:* C.

A magazine of current information on popular TV stars and singing groups, fashions, and beauty tips. Also carries fiction for teens and articles to help the teen be a success. Because of the very nature of the magazine and the lack of treatment of anything of a serious nature, it is not a must in a library.

In Magazine. 1967. m. $4. Edna Rosky. Lisa Pubns., Inc., 30–30 Northern Blvd., Long Island City, N.Y. 11101. Illus., adv.

Aud: Sh, Jh. *Rv:* L. *Jv:* B.

A tabloid type periodical, with such eye-catching titles as "I was a Teen-age Dropout." However, the lead articles which discuss current teen interest—"Good Students Aren't Squares" and "Put Your $$$$$ to Work"—are perceptive, and belie the general appearance of the magazine. Regular features include pen pals, recipe exchange, horoscope, "Dear Doctor," and fiction, usually two stories. Other columns center around the entertainment world; Platter Chatter, movie and T.V. news. A popular personality such as Jean Shrimpton or David McCallum is interviewed each month. Extensive coverage is given to fashion and beauty aids. Should be popular with the 13 to 18 age bracket.

Ingenue. 1959. m. $4. Sylvie S. Reice. Dell Publishing Co., Inc., 250 Third Ave., New York, N.Y. 10017. Illus., adv. Circ: 900,000. Microform: UM.

Bk. rev: Various numbers and lengths. *Aud:* Sh, Jh. *Rv:* L. *Jv:* B.

Published for "sophisticated teens," this is intended for the reader who considers the business of being a girl a serious matter. Fashion and beauty share in importance with guidance on dating, education, career and personal development. Each issue contains upwards of 2 short articles, unsigned. Fiction appears in the form of two or three short stories, generally of good literary quality, by new or lesser known writers, but limited in subject matter to the scope of the articles. The articles on food and decorating are inclined to be superficial. Some interesting poetry by teen agers appears regularly in a contributors' section. A book editor was added to the staff in June, 1966, and he writes an occasional article on what teens are reading, old and new, and, in other issues, his column reviews new books which should be of interest. Illustrations are both color and black and white, and adequate. Page design seems cluttered, following the trend of most magazines of this type intended for mass circulation. A moderate amount of advertising presents teen-age fashions, beauty and grooming products, with a lesser amount of space to advertising of schools and colleges. The popular style of writing assumes an audience of girls in early teens, somewhat younger than that of *Mademoiselle,* and it is to the 14 to 17 age group that it has the strongest appeal.

Miss Chatelaine. 1964. bi-m. $.75 in Canada; $1 elsewhere. Mrs. Doris Anderson. MacLean-Hunter Pubns. Co., Ltd., 481 University Ave., Toronto 2, Ont. Illus., adv. Circ: 150,000.

Aud: Sh, Jh. *Rv:* L. *Jv:* B.

Issued by the same publisher that brings Canadians *Maclean's* and *Chatelaine,* this is a small fashion magazine for girls between 15 and 20 years of age. It is considerably less flamboyant than many similar American magazines, with a good half of it usually given over to colored photographs of fashions. The remainder is an average approach to life and problems via short stories by teenagers, articles about Canadians who have met success, and the usual short reviews of books, films and recording. Hardly required, but a good magazine in Canadian public and school libraries.

Noonmark. 1967. 3/yr. $3. Webster Bull, Phillips Exeter Academy, Exeter, N.H. 03833. Illus., adv.

Aud: Sh. *Rv:* M. *Jv:* A.

Terming itself a "magazine for the creative arts in secondary schools," *Noonmark* is a handsome, well-printed 66-page answer to adults who think the younger generation has gone to hell. On the other hand, some of the stories, articles and poems—all by teen-agers—may only convince the older readers that the revolution is at hand. See, for example, the fine interview about the Columbia revolt with Henry Colman. There is just enough political commentary and a minimum of four letter words to make some wonder what's happening to America's prep schools. Members of the Noonmark Association, by the way, number every leading prep school in the country, and the public high school librarian protecting her charges from life is going to have a hard time explaining why this isn't on the shelves. And it should be, particularly as the editors not only welcome, but call for outstanding literary and artistic contributions from all young people—in private *and* public schools. The graphics, black and white photographs for the most part, are excellent. Some of the literary material is a bit sophomoric (at least to anyone over 21) but it is an honest voice of today's youth, and probably will be appreciated by younger readers. A nice balance for any high school library, and might be considered by schools of education where they are training the teachers of the contributors.

PACE. 1965. m. $4. Pace Pubns., Moral Re-Armament, Inc., 835 S. Flower St., Los Angeles, Calif. 90017. Illus., adv. Circ: 104,000.

Bk. rev: 5, 200 words, signed. *Aud:* Sh. *Rv:* L. *Jv:* B.

Pace is advertised as "64 pages of world wide happenings, photo-journalistic style, news interviews, profiles, and purports to be "the voice of the now-generation." It is for older teenagers and young adults. Editorials generally pose problems and ask questions which serious youth are asking today, "Where are we going, and why?" The moral tone is usually evident. Each issue is composed of 10 to 15 articles, of three to eight pages, all well illustrated with photos and an occasional pictorial chart. Success stories of young individuals account for about 30% of the articles. Most stress the importance of education, training and self-discipline through the examples set by these young achievers and tycoons. Educational, civic and political problems in America, and world problems with which youth is concerned are presented, usually through personalities making the news. Articles on sports, health and fitness follow the same theme of accomplishment. Most articles are signed, many by the staff, others by writers of authority in their own field. The style of writing is fast-paced and geared to modern youth, without resorting to the vernacular or slang. Illustrations are photographic in the "journalistic style" and a few articles are primarily pictorial. Some adver-

tising is included, tastefully done, and geared to the young adult audience. The major drawback, at least for more liberal readers, is the sponsor, who is primarily conservative. The bias against anything or anyone who does not go down the central road of conformity will kill it for sophisticated young people. Otherwise a good magazine for conservative type schools.

Seventeen. 1944. m. $6. Enid A. Haupt. Triangle Pubns., Inc., 320 Park Ave., New York, N.Y. 10022. Illus., adv. Circ: 1,418,978.

Indexed: RG. *Aud:* Jc, Sh, Jh. *Rv:* M. *Jv:* V. Microform: UM.

A slick, fashion-oriented magazine aimed at the teen-age buying public, covering everything that "concerns, excites, annoys, pleases and perplexes the girl between 13 and 19." Each issue is divided into sections emphasizing fashion and beauty, home furnishings and food, reviews of new motion pictures, books and records, and feature articles about the entertainment field. The few serious ones written by guest authors such as Jan Pierce, are practically swallowed up by eye-smashing, double page ads which emphasize either beauty hints or clothes, quite like a youthful version of *Glamour* or *Harper's Bazaar*. The fiction is either humorous, romantic or problem in content. Short story and art contests help keep reader interest alive. Definite appeal for modern youth.

Teen Times. 1945. q. $1. Future Homemakers of America, U.S. Office of Education, Washington, D.C. 20202. Illus.

Aud: Sh, Jh, Ht. *Rv:* M. *Jv:* B.

Primarily for the 13- to 17-year-old girl who participates in the Future Homemakers of America programs. The 20- to 24-page magazine is geared to present news of the organization, groups and individuals. Some information of a practical nature, but this is basically a newsletter. Will interest FHA members, but few other teenagers.

WAY Forum. 1953. bi-m. $2. World Assembly of Youth, 66 rue St. Bernard, Brussels 6, Belgium. Illus., adv. Circ: 30,000.

Aud: Jh, Sh. *Rv:* H. *Jv:* A.

Issued by the coordinating body of the National Youth Councils, which is the major voice for youth associated with the United Nations. The non-partisan nature of reports on youth as related to the world's major problems make this particularly important for a period when young people are more and more aware of a mutual international bond. (Issues are published in English, French and Spanish.) Every number is given over to a central theme, and these have ranged from problems of cities to developments in education. Authors include some of the world's leading figures, who consider the subject from all viewpoints and all applicable places from Asia to North America. The writing style is intelligent, yet geared to the level of a junior high or senior high school student—and not a few college students may profit from the reports. Each article is well illustrated, and the graphics are almost as important as the material. May be used by students for papers, talks, or simply good reading. An excellent balance for the typical daily newspaper or classroom paper, and a required item in almost every junior and senior high library.

Young Ambassador. 1946. m. $2. Ruth I. Johnson. Good News Broadcasting Assn., Inc., Box 233, Lincoln, Neb. 68501. Illus. Circ: 90,000.

Aud: Sh, Jh. *Rv:* L. *Jv:* C.

This is typical of a type of magazine which enjoys a relatively large circulation but is limited for most libraries. *Young Ambassador,* definitely church-oriented, is advertised as a back-to-the-Bible magazine for youth. Interdenominational stories, articles, and special departments are all faith-centered, with lessons for positive Christian living. Puzzles, quizzes, and song of the month are regular features. Because of its strong emphasis on a special type of religious action, this magazine would not be recommended for most school or public libraries.

THEATRE

Indexes and Abstracts

Abstracts of English Studies, British Humanities Index, Catholic Periodical and Literature Index, Education Index, Social Sciences and Humanities Index, Subject Index to Children's Magazines, Readers' Guide to Periodical Literature. (For annotations, see Indexes and Abstracts Section.)

Comparative Drama. 1967. q. $3.50. Clifford Davidson. Dept. of English, Western Michigan Univ., Kalamazoo, Mich. 49001. Illus.

Aud: Sa, Ac. *Rv:* M. *Jv:* B.

Stressing both the international and the interdisciplinary scope of drama, this features four to six articles by scholars. Each contribution is well documented, and there are a few illustrations. Not for the average drama student, but a useful magazine for both large drama history and literature collections.

Creative Drama. 1949. semi-ann. $1. Miriam Cameron. Educational Drama Assn., Stacy Pubns., 1 Hawthorndene Rd., Hayes, Bromley, Kent, Eng. Illus., Circ: 2,000.

Aud: Ac, Jc, Ht, Et. *Rv:* M. *Jv:* B.

A British publication written for teachers of English, speech and drama, or for any teacher who is interested in involving children and young people in the performing arts. The articles are not designed to inform teachers how to teach drama as a literary form, nor help a teacher to plan a theatrical performance. Drama is considered as a method of teaching and learning. The editors feel that "child drama" involves the child in learning in a very personal manner. Educators discuss various ways teachers have used

drama in learning situations and in helping children to make social and behavioral adjustments.

Cue. 1932. w. $8.50. Emory Lewis. Cue Publishing Co., 20 W. 43rd St., New York, N.Y. 10036. Adv. Circ: 240,000.

Aud: Ga. *Rv:* M. *Jv:* B.

A popular, magazine-guide for those who want to go-see-and-do in the big city. In addition to the New York edition, there are editions covering activities in Los Angeles, San Francisco, Chicago and Miami. Included in each week's issue are news, listings and reviews of theatre, movies, TV, FM radio, records, restaurants and night clubs, shopping, resorts and travel, and children's entertainment. Events of the week in the metropolitan area are covered along with concerts, art exhibitions, museums, etc. An advantageous feature is its citing of prices for the diverse activities along with the addresses, and other pertinent information. A useful guide for any library within easy distance of the cities considered.

Drama. 1919. q. $1.50. Ivor Brown. British Drama League, 9 Fitzroy Sq., London W.1. Illus., adv. Circ: 8,000. Microform: UM.

Indexed: AbEnSt, BritHum, SSHum. *Bk. rev:* Numerous, various lengths, signed. *Aud:* Ga, Ac, Jc. *Rv:* H. *Jv:* B.

This British review considers all aspects of theatre including stage management, theatre history, important actors and playwrights. F. W. Lambert's regular article, "Plays in Performance," covers mainly the current scene in Britain. His coverage is evaluative as well as informative. At least one article per issue takes the unpopular side of a controversy. Often as much as a quarter of the periodical is devoted to book reviews. These are some of the best in any drama magazine, short, critical, and frequently humorous. Required for medium to large theatre collections.

Drama Critique. 1958. 3/yr. Membership (Non-members, $4). Hugh Dickinson. National Catholic Theater Conference, John F. Kennedy Center, 1701 Pennsylvania Ave., Washington, D.C. 20006. Circ: 1,200.

Indexed: CathI. *Bk. rev:* 2–7, one page, signed. *Aud:* Sa, Ac, Jc. *Rv:* H. *Jv:* B.

Well written, intelligent discussions of theatre for students of drama. Each issue usually deals with a general topic such as Jewish theatre, playwriting, etc. Articles concern production techniques, the writing of plays and specific dramatists and plays with the emphasis on serious drama. All are usually followed by bibliographies. There is no particular Catholic bias. Material tends to be a trifle esoteric, always scholarly. Not for the casual reader and should only be in larger drama collections.

The Drama Review. 1956. q. $6. Richard Schechner. New York Univ., School of the Arts, Washington Square, New York, N.Y. 10003. Illus., adv. Circ: 14,000.

Indexed: SSHum. *Bk. rev:* Various numbers, lengths. *Aud:* Ga, Sa, Ac, Jc, Sh. *Rv:* H. *Jv:* V.

Anyone from high school student to theatre specialist who wishes to keep-up with modern drama must subscribe to this superior magazine. Within its 180 to 200 well illustrated pages, it covers every aspect of the 20th century theatre. Normally a single issue is given over to a major topic, e.g., "the Black Revolutionary Theatre," "Brecht," and "British Theatre." Contributors range from playwrights and actors to directors and teachers. Almost every major writer on the theatre has appeared at one time or another. Many short plays (a number translated from various languages) are included in full. Emphasis is definitely on the international avant garde, intellectual side of drama, and it is the voice of what has come to be known as the off-Broadway theatre. It definitely is not for the lover of musical comedies and traditional dramas. In view of the concentration on given areas, a run of the magazine offers the best single source of a history of the theatre in our time. Should be found in almost every type of library where drama and the fine arts have any importance.

Drama Survey. 1961. 3/yr. $2.50. John D. Hurrell. Bolingroke Soc., Inc., Box 4098, University Station, Minneapolis, Minn. 55414. Circ: 1,800. Microform: UM.

Indexed: SSHum. *Bk. rev:* Irregular, signed. *Aud:* Sa, Ac, Jc. *Rv:* H. *Jv:* B.

Primarily concerned with the work of serious dramatists rather than popular comedies, musicals, etc. Each issue usually contains seven to nine well written, signed essays, which are studies of plays and playwrights rather than reviews, and pictures of current stage productions. A section at the end of each issue is devoted to current theatre abroad. Most articles are written from a literary viewpoint though with respect for theatrical values. Rarely pedestrian, the essays promote richer understanding of American and foreign drama and dramatists. Bibliographies follow each article. A scholarly, yet highly readable magazine for medium to large collections.

Dramatics; devoted to the advancement of dramatics in secondary schools. 1929. 8/yr. $5. Leon C. Miller. National Thespian Soc., College Hill Station, Cincinati, Ohio 45224. Illus., adv. Circ: 45,000.

Aud: Ht. *Rv:* M. *Jv:* B.

Primarily for drama teachers. Some of the material is suitable for the student, but emphasis is on production and direction of plays, which requires professional ability and training. There are also news items, reports on the theatre and other features which keep the reader advised of current development in both education and the theatre. For high school libraries and large drama collections.

Educational Theater Journal. 1949. q. Membership (Non-members, $10). Francis Hodge. Amer. Educ. Theatre Assn., John F. Kennedy Center for the Performing Arts, 726 Jackson Pl., N.W., Washington, D.C. 20006. Circ: 7,000. Microform: UM.

Indexed: EdI, *Bk. rev:* 5, one page, signed. *Aud:* Sa, Ac. Jc, Ht. *Rv:* H. *Jv:* A.

Primarily for drama teachers in "all areas" and at "all levels," but most articles are geared for colleges and universities. The authoritative articles cover historical aspects of drama, playwrights, drama criticism, design and technical developments, acting and production techniques as well as material concerned with teaching. Regular features include "Broadway in Review" and "News" of the association and its members. Of particular interest to educators are the bibliographies of plays, histories, and textbooks and the annual listing of graduate theses and doctoral work in theatre. Because of its diversity, *ETJ* is of value to anyone, not just instructors, seriously interested in theatre.

First Stage; a quarterly of new drama. 1961/62. q. $4.50. Henry F. Salerno & H. H. Watts. Purdue Univ., Heavilon Hall, Lafayette, Ind. 47907. Circ: 1,500.

Indexed: AbEnSt. *Aud:* Sa, Ac. *Rv:* L. *Jv:* B.

An outlet for the publication of new American and foreign dramatic works. Each issue contains three to six new plays that have never been printed before, nor produced professionally. The plays included are not usually truly experimental works, yet they appear to have been chosen more for their artistic merit than for their show or commercial value. One or two critical editorials or articles usually precede the section of plays. A serious consideration for any large dramatics collection or serious drama student.

Modern Drama. 1958. q. $2. A. C. Edwards. Univ. of Kansas, Lawrence, Kan. 66044. Circ: 2,500.

Indexed: SSHum. *Bk. rev:* Irregular numbers and lengths. *Aud:* Sa, Ac, Jc. *Rv:* H. *Jv:* B.

Presents ten to twelve well written essays concerning drama (since Ibsen), suitable for students and informed laymen. Includes literary discussions of playwrights and plays, dramatic theory, productions, interviews, bibliographies, and state of the art reports. In both content and format *Modern Drama* is similar to *Drama Survey,* but is distinguished from the latter because of the emphasis on 20th century drama.

Modern International Drama; magazine of contemporary international drama in translation. 1967. semi-ann. $4.50. Anthony M. Pasquariello & George E. Wellwarth. Pennsylvania State Univ. Press, Univ. Press Bldg., University Park, Pa. 16802. Circ: 1,800.

Aud: Sa, Ac, Jc. *Rv:* H. *Jv:* A.

A major effort at translating "unjustly neglected modern (that is, 20th century) plays." Each issue contains four to five works by major playwrights of Spain, Hungary, France, Germany, etc. Each is introduced with a brief note about the author, the play and the translator. The translation, with full stage directions, is purposefully adapted for presentation in English but "without any of the author's meaning having been sacrificed in the process." Most works are not obtainable in translation elsewhere, and the editor's efforts represent a major breakthrough for anyone interested in international drama. Should be in all medium to large public and academic drama collections, and will be enjoyed by students and teachers of literature.

New Theatre Magazine; thrice yearly journal of drama and theatre studies. 1959. 3/yr. $3. Neville Denny & Michael Anderson. Univ. of Bristol, 29 Park Row, Bristol 1, Eng. Illus., adv. Circ: 1,500.

Bk. rev: 4–5, short. *Aud:* Sa, Ac. *Rv:* M. *Jv:* B.

Covers theatre practice in England, but frequently offers studies of the work of foreign playwrights such as Ionesco, Williams, and Brecht. Usually a lively editorial concerning the state of British theatre is included. The contributors are primarily members of the university. Along with *Modern Drama* and *Modern International Drama,* an important work for all larger theatre collections.

Playbill; the magazine for theatre goers. 1884. m. $4. Leo Lerman. Amer. Theatre Press, 579 Fifth Ave., New York, N.Y. 10017. Illus., adv. Circ: 1,660,000.

Aud: Ga. *Rv:* L. *Jv:* C.

This is the small magazine the theatregoer often receives as he tries to find his seat. Established in 1884, it is a combination of information about the show at hand and advertising. Editorially it supplies the synopsis and/or scenes and/or musical numbers of a particular play, as well as biographical sketches of the cast. A number of articles relevant to the understanding and enjoyment of theatre are included. The publisher reports that for $20.00 libraries will receive the publication "for every Broadway opening." An offer of dubious value, considering the state of Broadway theatre today.

Players Magazine; serving theatre across America. 1924. bi-m. (Oct.–Aug.). Donald E. Polzin & Byron S. Schaffer. Northern Illinois Univ., University Theatre, De Kalb, Ill. 60115. Illus., adv. Microform: UM. Reprint: AMS.

Aud: Ac, Jc. *Rv:* L. *Jv:* B.

The publication of the National Collegiate Players, this includes three or four short articles which discuss teaching methods and stage techniques. A listing of current plays showing at universities and community theatres appears in the section "Theatre Across America." Addresses of advertisers are grouped together to facilitate the purchase of necessary theatrical paraphernalia. Rarely treats drama as a literary form and includes only the activities of educational groups. Of interest to producers of collegiate theatricals.

Plays; the drama magazine for young people. 1941. m. (Oct.–May). $7. A. S. Burack. Plays, Inc., 8 Arlington St., Boston, Mass. 02116. Adv. Circ: 15,000. Microform: UM.

Indexed: IChildMags, RG. *Bk. rev:* Notes. *Aud:* E, Jh. *Rv:* L. *Jv:* B.

Features eight to ten plays per issue, duly graded from elementary through junior and senior high school. Most of the work is original—usually one act dramas written by women—and the ideas are never particularly imaginative. A few works represent adaptations of better known classics. Some numbers carry skits or puppet programs. Each of the plays is followed by production notes (i.e., number of characters, costumes, time, properties) and there is a limited amount of discreet advertising by the publisher. (A subscriber may produce the plays without writing for permission to the publisher.) The advantage of the magazine is that the work is usually within the abilities of the actors and the teachers, and the themes are traditional, usually humorous, always acceptable for middle and lower grades. However, its use at the senior high level is questionable. Today's high school youth, accustomed to more sophisticated, meaningful drama (even if on television), may take a dim view of the approach of much of the material offered. Conversely, younger children should be delighted. Finally, while the scripts are geared for the children to use, it is not likely to be a magazine they will pick-up and read for pleasure. It is a classroom aid and should be considered as such by librarians. An accepted, useful magazine for elementary and junior high school classes, if not always for the library itself.

Plays and Players. 1953. m. $8. Peter Roberts. Hansom Books Ltd., Artillery Mansions, 75 Victoria St., London S.W.1, Eng. Illus., adv. Circ: 23,000.

Bk. rev: Occasional, signed. *Aud:* Ga, Ac, Jc, Sh. *Rv:* M. *Jv:* B.

Directed primarily towards the British theatre-goer, this presents comprehensive coverage of current London theatrical productions. There are some reports on out-of-town theatres and major plays from New York and Europe. Although not academic, the four to seven reviews are critical and frank, with a pleasing balance between evaluative criticism and photographs of productions. The most valuable feature is the inclusion, in every issue, of the complete text of a new play. Regular features include notes which concern activities and people in theatre, listings of plays running, articles about playwrights, actors or excerpts from books, letters and editorials. Editorials tend to be liberal, but not radical. The quality of the reviews and articles has improved since the publication incorporated *Encore.* Scores high among publications for general coverage of English theatre. Should be a first choice in all medium to large libraries.

Religious Theatre. 1964. Every six to eight months. $2.50. James R. Carlson & Warren Kliewer. c/o James R. Carlson, Florida Presbyterian College, St. Petersburg, Fla. 33733. Circ: 1,000.

Aud: Ga, Ac. *Rv:* L. *Jv:* B.

Directed toward a somewhat scholarly audience, but because each issue contains two or three short plays or one long play, it can be enjoyed by laymen as well. The subject of the plays and articles is always religious, but not in a conventional sense. The dramas deal intelligently, sometimes humorously, with moral questions and questions of God's existence, never offering black and white situations or didactic lessons. Approximately three quarters of each issue contains plays, leaving the rest to editorials and essays, which are signed and often contain references. The contributors are people in theatre, clergy and professional writers. Although published through a Presbyterian college, the plays and articles are not biased. Good for larger public and academic libraries.

Theatre Crafts. 1967. bi-m. $5. Sherwood Arthur. Rodale Press, 33 E. Minor St., Emmaus, Pa. 18049. Illus., adv.

Bk. rev: Notes. *Aud:* Sa, Ac. *Rv:* M. *Jv:* B.

Devoted primarily to professional stage design, costumes, lighting and production innovations. There are usually two or three articles, followed by notes on books, new products and records. Some emphasis on news about personalities in the business. Usually about 50 pages long, with fair to good illustrations; of value to anyone involved with behind-the-scenes activities in theater. It is not for the general public, and is a secondary choice for all but the largest theatrical libraries.

Theatre Design and Technology. 1965. q. $6. Ned A. Bowman. U.S. Inst. for Theatre Technology, 245 W. 52nd St., New York, N.Y. 10019. Illus. Circ: 1,350.

Aud: Sa, Ac. *Rv:* M. *Jv:* B.

Covers news on the construction of theatres and new technical developments. Numbering about seven per issue, articles deal with stage designers and their work, new experiments such as the use of film on stage, lighting and other staging and building problems. A feature, "Reports on Theatre Design as Theatre," offers critical appraisal of the results of the use of new technology and stage craft on particular performances. Other regular features include a bibliography of "Recent Publications on Theatre Architecture" and a summary of "Recent Developments in Technology." An excellent choice for all drama collections.

Theatre Notebook; quarterly journal of the history and technique of the British theatre. 1946. q. $2.40. Ed bd. I. K. Fletcher, 22 Buckingham Gate, London S.W.1. Illus., index, adv.

Bk. rev: 3–4, 1 page, signed. *Aud:* Sa, Ac. *Rv:* H. *Jv:* B.

Directed to scholars and advanced students interested in the history of the British stage. The carefully researched articles, approximately four per issue, cover all types of theatrical memorabilia, including periodicals, theatres, prompt-books, costumes and puppets. There is a useful "Notes and Queries" section. A basic magazine for anyone interested in the history of theatre.

Theatre Research/Recherches Theatrales. 1958. 3/yr. $4. I. K. Fletcher. Intl. Federation for Theatre Research, 22 Buckingham Gate, London S.W.1. Illus.

Bk. rev: 4–6, one page, signed. *Aud:* Sa, Ac. *Rv:* H. *Jv:* B.

The primary value of this publication is that it includes research from all over Europe as well as England and the United States. The five to seven articles concern specific theatres, stage designers, actors, playwrights, etc. Also included are short articles concerning museums, theatre collections and other news of interest to drama historians. The contributors are scholars of drama and professional writers. Articles are in English and one or two in French. Good for active drama collections in larger public and academic libraries.

Variety. 1905. w. $20. Abel Green. Variety, Inc., 156 W. 46th St., New York, N.Y. 10036. Illus., adv.

Indexed: MusicI. *Aud:* Sa, Ac. *Rv:* M. *Jv:* B.

The official newspaper of "show biz," this is as American as mom and apple pie. The language is peculiar to the magazine, and echoes the jargon used up and down broadway. Among journalists it has a reputation for some of the best and snappiest headlines of any newspaper or magazine in the world. Style aside, its main purpose is to report on all aspects of entertainment, although emphasis is on advertising and the business of how much was won or lost. Coverage is world-wide, and its value for the non-business type is the objective, sometimes witty reviews of films, radio, television, theatre, recordings, night clubs and even circus entertainment. In the spring there is a special issue devoted to international films, and a July number reviews the radio-television season. While not a necessary item for small and medium sized libraries, it is a must for larger collections that have anything to do with the arts.

World Theatre. 1950. q. $7.50. René Hainaux. Editions Michel Brient, 64 rue de Saintonge, Paris (3e), France. Illus.

Indexed: SSHum. *Aud:* Ca, Ac, Jc. *Rv:* M. *Jv:* B.

Sponsored jointly by the International Theatre Institute and UNESCO. Presents news and articles concerning the current practice of theatre throughout the world. Anyone interested in theatre can enjoy this periodical because of its non-technical, popular approach. In each issue, the first section is dedicated to a special theme such as "Theatre Architecture," "Production of Greek Tragedy," and "Realism in Drama," or to a particular country. The eight or nine commentaries are written by playwrights, producers, critics, directors and others intimately involved in the theatre. Although there is no in-depth reporting, surveys of small, lesser-known theatre groups as well as the more popular theatres are included. In short, *World Theatre* is an excellent introduction to world-wide theatre.

Yale Theatre. 1968. 3/yr. $4.50. Box 2040, Yale Station, New Haven, Conn. 06520.

Aud: Sa, Ac, Jv. *Rv:* H. *Jv:* B.

Published by the students at the Yale School of Drama, and based on the School's activities, this is not the parochial journal its title might suggest. A wide ranging, beautifully designed periodical, its "true focus is contemporary American theatre. It wants to foster a way of thinking about this theatre that refuses received mythologies and practices which dwindle the heart and numb the imagination." The first issue was devoted to the Greek theatre, and its relevance to modern theatre and society. Contributors include Robert Brustein (Dean of the School) and non-Yale critics Jan Kott and Susan Sontag. Recently, the magazine was rocked by controversy between Brustein and the student editor, who accused Brustein of censorship, a charge which Brustein denied. As a result, two members of the editorial staff quit, and the future of the magazine remains in question. If it continues, it is recommended for all college, university and drama collections.

TRAVEL

Indexes and Abstracts

Abridged Readers' Guide, Readers' Guide to Periodical Literature, Subject Index to Children's Magazines. (For annotations, see Indexes and Abstracts Section.)

Appalachia. See Games and Sports Section.

Arizona Highways. 1925. m. $4. Raymond Carlson. Arizona Highways, 2039 W. Lewis Ave., Phoenix, Ariz. 85009. Illus.
Indexed: IChildMags, RG. *Aud:* Ga, Sh, Jh, E. *Rv:* M. *Jv:* B.

Promotes Arizona and the Southwest as a tourist attraction with many beautiful color photographs of this scenic area. The illustrations account for its wide use in schools. Each issue concentrates on some aspect of life in Arizona past or present that is of broad interest beyond the borders of the state. No advertisements detract from the beauty of this magazine. Correspondence from enthusiastic subscribers indicates its popularity. Obviously a first choice for any library in the area, and for larger school and public libraries where illustrations are as important as text. Although usually recommended on select lists, it is not an essential magazine for any school library, particularly one with a subscription to *National Geographic.* See also other regional magazines, such as *Colorful Colorado.*

Better Camping; the magazine of the open road. 1960. m (Jan.–June); bi-m (July–Dec.). $4. Catherine E. McMullen. Kalbach Publishing Co., 1027 N. 7th St., Milwaukee, Wis. 53233. Illus., adv. Circ: 50,000.
Bk. rev: 2–3, 100–150 words, signed. *Aud:* Ga, Sh. *Rv:* M. *Jv:* B.

Written for family camping enthusiasts. Long, well-illustrated articles spotlight worthwhile recreational areas, and contain maps of scenic hiking and riding trails, and recommended campgrounds. Strong emphasis on good conservation practices. New equipment included in the "Camper's Catalog" section. A valuable aid for the camper and reference librarian is the campground directory found in every issue. "Yearly Index" sent on request. Of the many camping magazines, this is one of the best all around guides for all types of libraries. Tends to put more emphasis on

conservation than *Camping Guide,* less on equipment. On the whole, the choice between the two is mainly a matter of taste, and librarians are advised to try both and gauge their patrons' reactions.

Camping Guide. 1959. 7/yr. $3. George S. Wells. Rajo Pubns., Inc., 215 Park Ave. S., New York, N.Y. 10003. Illus., adv. Circ: 61,251.
Aud: Ga. *Rv:* L. *Jv:* B.

Covers auto, trailer, boat and pack camping for the whole family, and informative articles on where to go, how to do it, outdoor recipes, and news and notes for campers. Some maps and sketches of featured campsites provided. Guides to toll roads, bridges and tunnels, provide useful information for planning camping expenditures. News from the National Campers Association, a rental directory for camping and trailering equipment, and a private campground listing are also included. Many photographs in black and white accompany each article. Choosing between this and *Better Camping* is difficult; see concluding comments for *Better Camping.*

Colorful Colorado, New Mexico, Utah, Wyoming. **(National Edition & Denver Edition).** 1956. bi-m. $3. Donald E. Bower. Merrill G. Hastings, Jr. Press., Colorado Magazine, Inc., 7190 W. 14th Ave., Denver, Colo. 80215. Illus., adv. Circ: Nat'l ed: 101,157; Denver ed: 42,300.
Aud: Ga, Sh, Jh, E. *Rv:* M. *Jv:* B.

Another version of *Arizona Highways,* for another area, and its main purpose is to sell the natural beauty and outdoor recreation of the Rocky Mountain West to both natives and tourists. There are articles of general interest, written by contributors, on the history, art, and natural wonders of this region. Each issue features a section of color pictures showing the scenic beauty of the four state areas of Colorado, New Mexico, Utah and Wyoming. The many black and white and color pictures make this a most attractive magazine. The spring issue is devoted to fishing; the summer issue to camping; the fall issue to hunting; the winter issue to skiing; and the mid-winter issue to general outdoor wintertime activities in the Rocky Mountain West. The national issue, somewhat more geared for a broader audience, will be preferred by libraries. Public and school libraries that subscribe to *Arizona Highways* might look at this as a pleasant alternative, or at least of equal interest.

Desert Magazine. 1937. m. $5. Choral Pepper. Jack Pepper, Palm Desert, Calif. 92260. Illus., adv. Circ: 47,000.
Aud: Ga, Sh, Jh. *Rv:* M. *Jv:* B.

Both a historical and travel magazine, this covers little-known areas of the West. While emphasis is on the desert, it is not exclusively dedicated to these areas. A typical issue will include suggested auto tours—both in regulation cars and in rugged four wheel drive machines—articles on historical points of interest, and a number of black and white photographs. Neither as attractive as *Arizona Highways,* nor as informative as many basic historical western journals, it nevertheless is an excellent second choice for most libraries. Particularly useful in junior high and high schools where there are units on the West and the desert areas.

Discovery Magazine. 1961. q. $2. David L. Watt. Allstate Enterprises, 7435 Skokie Blvd., Skokie, Ill. 60062. Illus., adv. Circ: 520,000.

Aud: Ga. *Rv:* M. *Jv:* B.

A colorful, easy-to-read, house-organ type magazine written for the American motorist by the Allstate Motor Club. Articles usually deal with tourist attractions, national parks and automobile safety. Regular monthly features include "Weekends on Wheels," trips recommended by readers; "Events of the Season," a calendar of events by region, and "Touring with the Editors," brief information on a variety of guidebooks and tourist brochures and where and how to get them. A good magazine for the reader who enjoys touring in an automobile.

Holiday. 1946. m. $5.95. Caskie Stinnett. Curtis Publishing Co., Independence Square, Philadelphia, Pa., 19105. Illus., adv. Circ: 1,083,000. Microform: UM.

Indexed: AbrRG, RG. *Aud:* Ga, Ac, Jc, Sh. *Rv:* M. *Jv:* A.

A popular, mass-circulation magazine for the seasoned traveler and dreamer. Beautifully illustrated, delightful essays describe the history, climate, people, and tourist attractions of famous and little-known places around the world. The arts, theatre, leisure activities, cuisine and fine new books are presented with an international flair. Personal accounts of visits to cities and countries supply an intimate view of the night-life in a gay city or the quiet serenity of a small village. Though designed as a travel guide for the international jet set, this periodical often supplies current political, social, and economic aspects of places covered nowhere else. There are background articles by such eminent contributors as John Dos Passos, John O'Hara, W. H. Auden, and William Golding. A good magazine for almost any type of library, and preferable to either *Travel* or *Venture,* because of its greater literary emphasis.

National Geographic Magazine. See Geography Section.

National Parks Magazine. See Conservation Section.

National Wildlife. See Conservation Section.

Outdoor World. See Conservation Section.

Ranger Rick's Nature Magazine. See Conservation Section.

Sierra Club Bulletin. See Conservation Section.

Trailering Guide. See Automobiles Section.

Travel. 1901. m. $5. Malcolm McTear Davis. Travel Magazine, Inc., Travel Bldg., Floral Park, N.Y. 11001. Illus., adv. Circ: 320,000.

Indexed: RG. *Bk. rev:* 1–2, 500 words, signed. *Aud:* Ga, Ac, Jc, Sh. *Rv:* M. *Jv:* A.

An easy-to-read magazine with black and white and color photos for the tourist who travels around the world or the United States. Each issue features a color section on a country, with a brief sketch of necessary information. All articles are geared for the tourist, but some give historical background of the country. There is usually at least one article of interest to the camping and trailering crowd. Regular monthly features include "New York Notebook," a list of Broadway plays with brief synopses; a calendar of special events around the world; "Roaming the Globe," tidbits of information on different areas, and a camera column. This is considerably less sophisticated than *Holiday,* yet more down to earth in terms of the average traveler and reader. Depending upon the library's audience, it might be a first choice, but on the whole, *Holiday* is preferable in most situations.

Venture—The Traveler's World. 1964. m. $12.50. Curtiss Anderson. Travelventures, Inc., 488 Madison Ave., New York, N.Y. 10022. Illus., adv. Circ: 220,000.

Bk. rev: Notes. *Aud:* Ga. *Rv:* M. *Jv:* B.

A plush, sophisticated travel magazine designed for the American with means, but can be enjoyed as leisure-time reading by most adults. Articles are written by the staff and by guest contributors, and each issue has at least one light-hearted piece written and illustrated by famous writers and illustrators. Throughout the magazine are black and white and color pictures of personalities, art, architecture, and landscape. A separate section gives tourist information on those places covered in the body of the magazine, like restaurants, hotels, shops, a calendar of coming events at concert halls, theatres and museums. Editors recommend travel guides and books about the country. In view of the price, which would allow subscriptions to both *Holiday* and *Travel* (with money left over for bus fare), this is only for those larger libraries with larger budgets.

Wheels Afield. See Automobiles Section.

Wisconsin Tails and Trails. 1960. q. $5. Howard W. Mead, 1722 Baker Ave., Madison, Wis. 53505. Illus. Circ: 10,000.

Indexed: IChildMags. *Aud:* Ga, Sh, Jh. *Rv:* M. *Jv:* B.

The Wisconsin answer to *Arizona Highways,* using much the same type of material, format and approach. Printed on glossy stock, it boasts a number of full color illustrations, four to five articles, special features, and departments which tell of events and personalities in the state. The writing is straight from the Chamber of Commerce, but tempered by good material and competent contributors. While definitely adult fare, it will have appeal, if only because of the illustrations, for the younger set from the upper elementary grades through junior and senior high. Fully as useful as *Arizona Highways,* certainly better for libraries in the immediate Wisconsin area.

VOCATIONS AND VOCATIONAL GUIDANCE

Indexes and Abstracts

Education Index, Public Affairs Information Service. (For annotations, see Indexes and Abstracts Section.)

American Vocational Journal. 1926. m. (Sept.–May). Membership (Non-members, $4). Lowell A. Burkett. Amer. Vocational Assn. Inc., 1025 15th St., N.W., Washington, D.C. 20005. Illus., adv. Circ: 42,000. Microform: UM.

Indexed: EdI. *Bk. rev:* Various numbers and lengths. *Aud:* Sa, Ac, Jc, Ht. *Rv:* H. *Jv:* A.

A magazine of vocational-technical education issued by the American Vocational Association. The six to eight articles are directed to both administrators and teachers and guidance counselors, and include data useful not only for the vocational counselor, but for teachers of business, home economics, industrial arts, agriculture and trade. Material tends to be as theoretical as practical, and there is considerable emphasis on research—a regular feature is a 10- to 20-page report on various research reports submitted by members and chapters. Other features include notes on books, a report of Washington activities, new equipment and aids to teaching, and news of the organization. A first choice for individuals and libraries dealing in this area.

Careers Today. 1968. m. $10. Nicholas H. Charney. CRM Assoc., 1330 Camino Del Mar, Del Mar, Calif. 92014. Illus., adv. Circ: 500,000.

Bk. rev: 2–4, 500 words. *Aud:* Ga, Ac, Jc, Ht. *Rv:* M. *Jv:* A.

A publication by the publishers of *Psychology Today,* which follows many of the same innovative tricks of format, presentation, and yet maintains a high level of accuracy and literacy. The magazine is directed to college graduates, or those about to graduate, who are interested in education and careers. Fully one-third of the first issue concentrated on young people and their immediate problems in colleges and universities. The remainder is given over to opportunities in various types of careers, from banking to general business. It differs radically from the average career magazine in that considerable emphasis is given to the social responsibilities of business, the off-beat graduate who has made it in a different way, and various studies which have broader connotations than simply careers, e.g., a survey by General Electric of what to expect in American society in the next twenty years. In many ways, then, the title is a trifle deceptive. Actually, the magazine will be enjoyed by anyone who takes an interest in the passing American social and economic scene. Should be in all medium to large public and academic libraries, and will unquestionably be of personal interest to high school teachers.

Industrial Arts and Vocational Education; the shop teacher's professional magazine. 1914. m. (Sept.–June). $4. John L. Feirer & Howard E. Smith. Bruce Publishing Co., 400 N. Broadway, Milwaukee, Wis. 53201. Illus., adv. Circ: 26,000. Microform: UM.

Indexed: EdI. *Bk. rev:* 14–16, 100 words. *Aud:* Ht, Et. *Rv:* M. *Jv:* B.

The professional magazine for the instructor at the advanced vocational, high school and elementary school levels. Articles support the need for industrial and vocational courses and give specific advice of a how-to-do-it nature. There is emphasis, too, on how to assist young boys, unique tools and methods, and a number of departments: teacher's notebook, equipment, news in the field, and the short book reviews. A must in any school with an industrial arts program.

Moderator; the magazine for the leading college male. 1962. bi-m. $2./Male college students; $3./others. Sherman B. Chickering, 115 S. 37th St., Philadelphia, Pa. 19104. Illus., adv. Circ: 102,767.

Aud: Ac, Jc, Sh. *Rv:* H. *Jv:* B.

A controlled-circulation magazine directed to college students seeking information on career opportunities. About one-half of each 56-page issue is given over to careers. There is a series of articles on one profession such as banking, or aerospace; a report on career trends, and a shorter summary of careers in other fields such as advertising or government service. The rest of the magazine consists of four general articles, short fiction, cartoons, and features that range from short notes on the lively arts to editorials. Articles are well illustrated and generally concerned with current college interests from the draft to sports. The material is accurate, well written, and convenient—readers are given cards to send to potential employers for more information of specific jobs. Articles are well illustrated and generally concerned with current college interests from the draft to sports. Should be found in all academic libraries, and could be of help to job counselors in senior high schools, although most careers discussed presuppose a university education.

New Generation. (Formerly: *American Child*). 1919. q. $2. Louise Kapp. National Committee on Employment of Youth of the National Child Labor Committee, 145 E. 32nd St., New York, N.Y. 10016. Illus. Circ: 10,000. Microform: UM. Reprint: Abrahams.

Indexed: PAIS. *Aud:* Sa, Ac, Jc, Ht. *Rv:* H. *Jv:* B.

A modest, pamphlet-sized periodical devoted to improving the employment possibilities for young people. Each issue is concerned with a specific topic, i.e. "Office of Economic Opportunity," "The State of Integration versus Segregation," etc. The topic is followed by a dialogue by the authors who have contributed to the issue. For guidance counselors and teachers.

Occupational Outlook Quarterly. (Supplement to Occupational Handbook). 1957. q. $1.25. James J.

Treires. Superintendent of Documents, U.S. Govt. Printing Office, Washington, D.C. 20402. Illus. Circ: 14,700.

Indexed: PAIS. *Aud:* Ga, Ac, Jc, Ht. *Rv:* H. *Jv:* A.

Put out by the United States Department of Labor's Bureau of Labor Statistics. There are usually six to ten articles, from 3 to 6 pages long, often containing many statistics on the employment situation, Job Corps, manpower, and other programs related to education and training. While there are no book reviews, there is a column "Recent Publications on Manpower," that lists free and inexpensive pamphlets on employment. Another feature, "Counseling Aids," lists other Government publications useful in counseling and guidance activities. Helpful to librarians, guidance counselors and job seekers.

The Vocational Guidance Quarterly. 1952. q. $4. Norman C. Gysbers. National Vocational Guidance Assn., 1607 New Hampshire Ave., N.W., Washington, D.C. 20009. Illus. Circ: 13,000. Reprint: Abrahams.

Indexed: EdI. *Bk. rev:* 10–12, various lengths. *Aud:* Ac, Jc, Ht. *Rv:* H. *Jv:* B.

Primarily a method of alerting counselors on new developments in careers. There are 10 to 12 articles on every aspect of guidance, and informative, critical reviews of new books, pamphlets and the like in occupational literature. Also, there are comments on new career films. Useful in high schools, and in any school of education.

Vocations for Social Change. 1967. m. $15 to libraries. Canyon, Calif. 94516. Illus.

Aud: Ga, Ac, Jc, Sh. *Rv:* H. *Jv:* A.

A 50-page mimeographed newsletter dedicated to "encouraging formation of new jobs which implement values more humane than those our present structure reinforces." Issued by a non-profit organization, it lists some 150 employers from the Alabama Committee for Freedom and Peace to the Washington Free Press. Employment opportunities range from architects and writers to librarians and political organizers. Full data is given for each position, along with what is provided in terms of salary and/or meals and housing without salary. Most organizations listed are out to change or improve the world, but while the opportunities are primarily for the dedicated high school or college graduate, there are other jobs for anyone (regardless of background or education) who is eager to help. This is a genuine, unique occupational magazine which will be of tremendous interest to at least a few in high schools, junior colleges and colleges and universities. Also, it should be in most public libraries.

WIT AND HUMOUR

Dublin Opinion; the national humorous journal of Ireland. 1922. m. $5. Charles E. Kelley & Thomas J. Collins. 67 Middle Abbey St., Dublin 1, Ireland. Cartoons. Circ: 12,000.

Aud: Ga, Ac, Jc. *Rv:* L. *Jv:* B.

An Irish magazine of humorous articles, cartoons, verse and brief quotes from the major magazines of the world. It generally succeeds in satirizing everything. Political cartoons and commentary are probably the best. For the student or sophisticated amateur of life in Ireland and Great Britain and for anyone who enjoys intelligent wit and humor.

Harvard Lampoon. 1876. 8/yr. $3. 44 Bow St., Cambridge, Mass. 02138. Illus., adv. Circ: 6,000.

Aud: Ga, Ac, Jc. *Rv:* L. *Jv:* B.

A distinguished representative of college humor, the *Lampoon* continues to be one of the best of its type. While directed to Harvard students and alumni, it can be appreciated by anyone who has at least touched on a college or university campus. Of particular note is the one issue a year given over to spoofing a mass circulation magazine such as *Time:* the entire number is put out in the format of the magazine, right down to departments and pictures. The major difference between the original and the imitation is the content, which is a take-off not only on the magazine but on its readers as well. Should be in every junior college, college and university library, and the special numbers should find their way into all public and school libraries.

Mad. 1953. 8/yr. $5/18 nos. Albert B. Feldstein. E. C. Pubns., Inc., 485 Madison Ave., New York, N.Y. 10022. Circ: 2,000,000.

Aud: Ga, Sh, Jh. *Rv:* L. *Jv:* B.

A comic-strip magazine for the big kids. Although uneven in quality, and at times sophomoric in tone, *Mad* usually has one or two feature strip cartoon stories per issue which are little gems, usually those which satirize radio, television or the movies. Artist Mort Deucker, one of the leading caricaturists in America today (along with David Levine), has developed a style which is unmistakably *Mad's* and as recognizable as Alfred E.—"What me worry?"—Neuman himself. While its satirical point is often blunt, Mad at its best can be, and often is, uproariously funny. For a periodical browsing collection serving readers of high school age and upwards.

Monocle; a leisurely journal of political satire. 1957. irreg. $7.50/10 issues. Victor S. Navasky. 80 Fifth Ave., New York, N.Y. 10011. Illus., adv. Circ: 25,000.

Aud: Ga, Ac, Jc. *Rv:* M. *Jv:* B.

A somewhat more sophisticated approach to the modern scene than *The Realist.* Yet, both drink of the same bitter well, and coverage of the American social and political world is handled with the same irreverent style. As the title implies, the journal is a trifle irregular in publication, but it has become a prize catch for the underground generation which has passed the age of 30. In addition to short, muckraking articles, the editor prints some excellent poetry—with a political slant—and, from time to time, a story. In 1968 the Coordinating Council of Literary Magazines awarded this magazine $2,000 for a symposium on language in America. *Realist* fans will enjoy this as well, and it is a good purchase for the more imaginative collection in any type of library.

Punch. 1841. w. $15. Bernard Hollowood. Punch Pubns., Ltd., 10 Bouverie St., London E.C.4. Circ: 120,000. Microform: B&H, UM.

Bk. rev: 10, 500 words, signed. *Aud:* Ga. *Rv:* L. *Jv:* B.

The best known of all English-language humour magazines. Each issue contains cartoons and humorous essays, often of a political cast, and general satire of British customs and manners. In its sections devoted to activities (theatre, dining, night life) in and around London, it shows itself to be the prototype upon which our American magazines of the *New Yorker* variety are based. While some of the material cannot properly be appreciated by an American audience, *Punch* would seem an excellent choice for browsing collections serving adult and young adult readers.

The Realist. 1958. irreg. $3/10 issues; $5/20 issues. Paul Krassner. The Realist Assn., Box 379, Stuyvestant Station, New York, N.Y. 10009. Circ: 100,000. Microform: UM.

Aud: Ga, Ac, Jc. *Rv:* L. *Jv:* V.

As anti-establishment—any establishment—gadfly, *The Realist* is second to none. It has relentlessly searched out and excoriated stupidity everywhere, be it in the churches, the government or the universities. While displaying a liberal/left politic slant, it has not been slow to satirize the shortcomings of the liberal establishment or its more radical and vociferous offshoots. Although frequently pornographic by conventional standards, *The Realist's* sights are kept dead set on both the follies and the crimes of contemporary man. Despite its obvious appeal to the perennially iconoclastic young, this is actually a magazine for the thinking adult. Don't read it literally (it has never been guilty of what our euphemistic news magazine editors style "factual" reporting), but do take it seriously. A first choice for all libraries.

WOMEN'S MAGAZINES

Indexes and Abstracts

Abridged Readers' Guide, Readers' Guide to Periodical Literature. (For annotations, see Indexes and Abstracts Section.)

Cosmopolitan. 1901. m. $5. Helen Gurley Brown. Hearst Corp., Eighth Ave. at 57th St., New York, N.Y. 10019. Illus., adv. Microform: UM.

Aud: Ga, Ac, Jc. *Rv:* L. *Jv:* B.

Without the nudes, this is often referred to as the woman's *Playboy,* and it concentrates on the world of the young, working, single girl. Helen Gurley Brown, its free-

thinking and very outspoken editor, has taken the rose-colored glasses away from women's magazines, presenting sophisticated, well-written articles and fiction. The unique and often perplexing problems and needs of the employed modern girl are discussed realistically. Beauty, fashion, housekeeping, cooking, decorating, travel, and horoscopes are all represented but with a special twist for the single girl. Cleveland Amory briefly reviews books and Rona Jaffe tours the world to speak out for the working woman. This is the only magazine which presents the "other woman" as the heroine, and sex as it is practiced, not preached. Reaction to the editorial policy has been immediate and heated, and libraries who subscribe to the *Ladies' Home Journal* should consider this for readers who fancy themselves more than the happy little homemakers of the *LHJ* variety. Other libraries who take a dim view of women's magazines altogether can pass by with ease.

Elle. 1957. w. $15. Jean Denys. Regie-Press, 133 Champs-Elysees, Paris (8e), France. Subscriptions to: France Editions et Publications, 229 W. 43rd St., New York, N.Y. 10036. Illus., adv. Circ: 750,000.

Bk. rev: Notes. *Aud:* Ga, Ac, Jc, Sh. *Rv:* M. *Jv:* B.

A French language periodical somewhat the equivalent of *Cosmopolitan, Good Housekeeping* and *Glamour* in one fine mix. Which is to say it has a character of its own, but its range is multiple: fashions, cooking, interior decorating, needlework, gardens, travel, one or two short stories or excerpts from novels, and a few "thought" articles on various aspects of French life. The audience is the teenager and the young married. Primarily of interest to American high school girls and women for the illustrations, and information it gives on what the average French counterpart is about. The advertisements, household lines, and personal products, seem to fascinate even the non-French reader. Interestingly enough, the fashions are not always as "high" as those found in many American magazines. Depending upon the views of the teacher this might be used in advanced French classes. It is a luxury item for libraries in a non-French community.

Family Circle. 1932. m. $.20/no. Robert M. Jones. Family Circle, Inc., 488 Madison Ave., New York, N.Y. 10022. Illus., adv. Circ: 7,000,000.

Aud: Ga, Sh. *Rv:* L. *Jv:* B.

A circulation leader, this inexpensive and practical magazine is purchased and read by almost every woman who enters a supermarket. Food buying and cooking tips, with original ideas for recipes and planning healthful and attractive meals, are simply and sensibly supplied. Articles concerning beauty, fashion, child care, home decorating, creative crafts and health are designed for the middle income homemaker who has little time or money for extravagant and impractical ideas requiring large outlays of both. The information is well presented, pleasantly arranged and easy to use. Though not a subscription magazine, *Family Circle* would be a worthwhile investment for libraries where the periodical budget is small or the income of the patrons is low. See also, *Woman's Day.*

Glamour. 1939. m. $5. Kathleen Johnson. Conde Nast Pubns., Inc., 420 Lexington Ave., New York, N.Y. 10017. Illus., adv. Circ: 1,350,000. Microform: UM.

Aud: Ga, Sh. *Rv:* L. *Jv:* B.

A fashion magazine edited specifically for the young woman, presenting ideas and advice on beauty, grooming, fashion, love, education, decorating, entertaining and health. The whole woman is discussed: her appearance, personality, occupations and surroundings. Articles offer practical though sometimes time-consuming techniques for molding all these facets into a model of glamour and grace. All the material presented displays good taste, creative imagination and a keen eye for beauty. Recognized writers discuss maturing, the business world, travel and the world scene. Regular columns present do's and don'ts of glamour, movie reviews, shopping guides, the "Glamour-scope," and articles on college issues. Definitely, a worthwhile "how-to" magazine. There is little or no controversial material and the editors appear to fear a definite stand on anything this side of fashion. Advertising is excessive, although probably no greater than for other magazines of this type. While not an essential for a library, the large circulation indicates it is of more than passing interest to a number of teen agers and young women.

Good Housekeeping. 1895. m. $5. Wade H. Nichols. Hearst Corp., Eighth Ave. at 57th St. New York, N.Y. 10019. Illus., adv. Circ: 5,750,000. Microform: UM.

Indexed: AbrRG, RG. *Aud:* Ga, Ac, Jc, Sh. *Rv:* M. *Jv:* B.

"The magazine America lives by" is one for the homemaker, and the soon-to-be homemaker. Articles, features, and departments discuss all phases of running a home, raising a family, and keeping in style. Among the well-written features and articles that cover almost every subject, controversial and current political topics appear regularly. The Good Housekeeping Institute studies in its laboratories and in actual use all manner of items submitted for advertising. Those that are accepted for advertising may use the Good Housekeeping Consumers' Guaranty seal. Editorial reports on product types are factual, including possible disadvantages, the do's and don'ts of care. Other Institute departments include food, beauty, needlework, appliances and home care. Health, both mental and physical, is not neglected. Editorial departments include fashion, home decorating articles, features and "The Better Way." Three or four stories, short-short to novelette length are varied in style and content to appeal to a wide audience. Although a far cry from an intellectual challenge, the magazine suits a definite need for women and some teenage girls. Suitable, although not required, for senior high school, academic, and most public libraries.

Gourmet. See Home Section.

Hairdo. 1955. m. $5. Dorothea Zach Hanle. Dell Publishing Co., Inc., 750 Third Ave., New York, N.Y. 10017. Illus., adv. Circ: 500,000.

Aud: Ga, Sh. *Rv:* L. *Jv:* C.

Designed for the young woman, this is the only monthly magazine devoted exclusively to hair fashion and general beauty care. Articles are of the simple "how-to" variety. Through photographs accompanied by brief captions, the original creations of the world's greatest hair stylists are illustrated. Diagrams and uncluttered drawings demonstrate the material discussed in the articles. Unless specifically called for, libraries can pass by.

Harper's Bazaar. 1867. m. $6.50. Nancy White. Hearst Corp., 572 Madison Ave., New York, N.Y. 10022. Illus., adv. Circ: 444,670. Microform: UM.

Indexed: RG. *Aud:* Ga, Ac, Jc, Jh. *Rv:* M. *Jv:* B.

The sophisticated competitor of *Vogue,* there is probably no better known fashion magazine than *Harper's Bazaar.* It is a guide to current trends in clothing, travel and, to a degree, thinking, for the better-than-average educated woman. Each article is copiously illustrated with photographs, many in color. (The photographs represent some of the best work in the United States.) At the "thought" level, there are stories, articles and pieces by celebrities ranging from Bob Dylan to William Burroughs. Men's fashions are touched lightly, and there is usually a rather good travel essay on a country or region which is currently popular. A worthwhile addition for most libraries, regardless of type. The difference between this and *Vogue* is large in terms of competition and views of editorial staff, small in terms of most casual readers. Both are indexed in *Readers' Guide,* both cater to the same dream-like vision of American women and fashion, and certainly one or both should be in most libraries from senior high through the university. Which one is better suited for a particular library is solely a matter of the librarian's taste.

Ladies' Home Journal. 1883. m. $4. John M. Carter. Curtis Publishing Co., Independence Sq., Philadelphia, Pa. 19105. Illus., adv. Circ: 7,000,000. Microform: UM.

Indexed: AbrRG, RG. *Aud:* Ga. *Rv:* L. *Jv:* C.

Among the most popular of women's magazines, this is a nice combination of fiction, how-to-do-it type articles, and advertising. The intellectual content is almost nil, the emotional appeal high. Such features as "Can This Marriage Be Saved?" "Beauty," "Food," and "Fashions and Patterns," indicate the reason for its success. The stories and reprints of short novels are on a level with the regular features. In view of its vast circulation, and its low reference value, it seems to be an unessential magazine for most libraries. Librarians who feel the need to supply this to the women might take a second look at its counterpart such as, *Argosy* and *Playboy.* The rationales for subscribing to one hold for the others as well.

McCall's. 1870. m. $3. Robert R. Stein. McCall Corp., 230 Park Ave., New York, N.Y. 10017. Subscriptions to: McCall St., Dayton, Ohio 45401. Illus., adv. Circ: 8,567,495. Microform: UM.

Indexed: RG. *Bk. rev:* 2–3, 200 words, signed. *Aud:* Ga, Sh. *Rv:* M. *Jv:* B.

Features on fashion and the home form the core of this woman's magazine, which also advises the housewife on child-raising, how to deal with her husband, entertaining, etc. Also includes articles about well-known women, how they got where they are, manage their lives, etc. Thoughtful, sometimes penetrating articles on current newsworthy topics are written for the average woman. Political articles rarely appear. Each issue contains two or three works of fiction, usually romance or about children, and vary from the short-short to novelette length. Such writers as Louis Auchincloss, William Saroyan, James Baldwin, and Truman Capote are among the contributors. One of the monthly features, "Sight and Sound," by Lenore Hershey, reviews films, TV shows, and occasionally operas. As a better woman's magazine, this is suitable for senior high school girls, certainly much more preferable than the *Ladies' Home Journal,* which somehow seems to make almost every high school recommended list.

McCall's Needlework & Crafts. 1935. semi-ann. $3.20/ 2 yrs. Nanina Comstock. McCall Corp., 230 Park Ave., New York, N.Y. 10017. Subscriptions to: McCall St., Dayton, Ohio 45401. Illus., adv. Circ: 2,000,000.

Aud: Ga, Sh. *Rv:* L. *Jv:* B.

A how-to-do-it approach to embroidery and other crafts, this is the biggest seller of its type in the United States. Instructions are detailed and there are complete illustrations. A limited amount of fashion news. Useful for both the beginner and the expert, but most women will want the magazine at home where they can consult it regularly. As it is sold in almost every department store, librarians may want to introduce users to lesser-known publications of the same type.

McCall's Patterns (Formerly: *McCall's Pattern & Home Decorating Fashions*). 1913. 3/yr. $1.80. Phyliss H. Roderick. McCall Corp., 230 Park Ave., New York, N.Y. 10017. Subscriptions to: McCall St., Dayton, Ohio 45401. Illus., adv. Circ: 600,000.

Aud: Ga. *Rv:* M. *Jv:* B.

The lady who likes to sew her own clothes will find here an attractively-modelled assortment of new designs from which to choose. The accompanying prose is pure fashion show. Though selling patterns is the main business of this periodical, it also features instructive articles on how to sew such domestic items as slip covers and drapes. Useful, though not essential, to libraries.

Mademoiselle. 1935. m. $5. B. T. Blackwell. Conde Nast Pubns., Inc., 420 Lexington Ave., New York, N.Y. 10017. Illus., adv. Circ: 676,340. Microform: UM.

Indexed: RG. *Bk. rev:* 2, 150 words, signed. *Aud:* Ga, Ac, Jc, Sh. *RV:* L. *Jv:* B.

While primarily a fashion and beauty magazine, this is unique in that it presents fiction and features with intellectual appeal. It is edited for well-educated, above-average income young women of mid-teens through college age. Its largest number of articles, all well illustrated, cover the areas of fashion and beauty. In its approach to fiction (one or two stories a month) and articles (two or three a month) *Mademoiselle* assumes that its educated readers demand quality. It makes a point of seeking out worthy new writers and has been the first to publish new works by authors of great international stature; Dylan Thomas, Truman Capote, Eugene Ionesco, and Edward Albee are notable examples. Articles cover a wide variety of topics. No subject, from birth control to U.S. policy in Vietnam, is outside its sphere of interests. Decorating, career and educational advice, and some exceptionally good tips on travel are relegated to a lesser position. The column which includes film reviews also discusses other lively arts—music, theater, dance and drama, in a comparative or evaluative way. The entire August issue is devoted to college, and is staffed by guest editors from colleges throughout the country. Illustrations, some colored, are of good quality, and advertising is profuse. A first among women's magazines.

Modern Bride; a complete guide for the bride to be. 1949. bi-m. $3. Ziff-Davis Publishing Co., 1 Park Ave., New York, N.Y. 10016. Illus., adv. Circ: 207,000.

Aud: Ga, Sh. *Rv:* L. *Jv:* C.

This is one of the circulation leaders in a field which boasts almost a dozen titles. The purpose of the publications is to assist the bride from the months to years before she lands the groom, to the wedding, to the honymoon and to the new home. Supposedly after that she takes up another woman's magazine. In addition to tips on home and husband, there are regular columns on emotional problems, etiquette, beauty care, etc. Apparently the real purpose of all these magazines is to serve as a backboard for extensive advertising—advertising which makes marriage a commercial venture. While every woman's magazine covers much the same ground, (e.g. *Good Housekeeping, Mademoiselle, Seventeen,* etc.) none do it with such depth. Probably *Modern Bride* or one of its cousins would be welcomed by many teen-agers and less sophisticated adults, but it is well down the required list, even for a collection devoted solely to women.

Parent's Magazine & Better Homemaking. See Child Care Section.

Redbook. 1904. m. $3. Sey Chassler. McCall Corp., 230 Park Ave., New York, N.Y. 10017. Illus., adv. Circ: 4,465,000. Microform: UM.

Indexed: RG. *Aud:* Ga, Sh. *Rv:* L. *Jv:* B.

During the years this has undergone many editorial changes, but it has emerged as one of the better edited magazines "for young adult women," i.e., senior high school to the late twenties. And, it should be quickly added, not for all senior high school girls, as there is a considerable emphasis on young brides and even younger mothers. Features articles by such experts as Dr. Benjamin Spock and Margaret Mead; "The Young Mother's Story," which consists of real life contributions from readers, and a column on "The Expectant Mother." The tone is definitely middle class. Yet, the magazine prides itself on significant articles on social problems (poverty, race relations, education) and practical advice on everything from the first date to the first child. All of this is laced with good illustrations, short stories and usually a short novel, not to mention the beauty, fashion and cooking hints. Considerably more advanced than *Seventeen, Mademoiselle, Glamour*, etc., and closer to reality than the *Ladies' Home Journal, Good Housekeeping* group. A first choice for small and medium sized public and some high school libraries.

Simplicity Home Catalog. 1967. semi-ann. $1. Simplicity Pattern Co., 200 Madison Ave. New York, N.Y. 10016. Illus., adv. Circ: 700,000.

Aud: Ga, Sh, Jh. *Rv:* M. *Jv:* B.

Each issue offers some 500 garment patterns for all ages of men and women, as well as a selected number of home accessories patterns. The patterns are for both novice and expert. Material for younger girls gives an added dimension for use in junior high and high school courses. News about fabrics and sewing tips in each issue. Another useful magazine issued by the same company, for approximately the same audience, is *Simplicity Fashion Magazine* (1949. 3/yr. $1.50). Here, attention is given to articles on sewing, fashions, fabrics, accessories, etc. Some book reviews. Of the various pattern magazines mentioned here the Simplicity group is probably best suited for junior high and for beginners at the high school level.

True Story. 1919. m. $4. MacFadden-Bartell Co., 205 E. 42nd St., New York, N.Y. 10017. Illus., adv. Circ: 2,200,000.

Aud: Ga. *Rv:* L. *Jv:* C.

With an astounding circulation of over two million, this is the oldest, most typical of the so-called confession or romance type periodicals. The primary audience seems to be the American woman with a limited education or imagination, although at any beauty parlor it may be read by even the college graduate. It is rarely found in libraries, not so much because of the blatant appeal to slush (a good number of women's magazines accomplish the same end), but because it makes no pretenses at being anything other than a thriller and love magazine. While the illustrations exploit sex, the stories inevitably end with a moral: crime or love out of marriage does not pay. In recent years more emphasis has been placed on articles, and there are also a number of departments on home making, child care and even medicine. Imitators such as *True Confessions* (Circ: 586,000, and also a MacFadden publication); *Tan* (Circ: 127,000, for the Negro reader) and *Real Romances* (Circ:

900,000) are rampant. Although considerably alike, each has a distinctive approach. Reaching as they do an audience rarely touched by *McCall's, Cosmopolitan*, and the *Ladies' Home Journal*, they should be seriously considered by any librarian who feels there is a place for the out and out woman's magazine in the collection—particularly by a library serving the lower income or lesser educated areas of the community.

Vogue. 1892. semi-m. (m., May, June, July, Dec.). $10. Diana Vreeland. Conde Nast Pubns., 420 Lexington Ave., New York, N.Y. 10017. Illus., adv. Circ: 444,497. Microform: UM.

Indexed: RG. *Bk. rev:* Notes. *Aud:* Ga, Ac, Jc, Sh. *Rv:* M. *Jv:* B.

Addresses itself to women of every age, and is primarily interested in fashion; what is happening, what will happen, in America and abroad. But it also reports "Fashions in Living," including art, beauty, food, entertainment and travel as well as the people who make things happen. Well known writers such as Truman Capote, Elia Kazan, and Arthur Schlesinger, Jr. contribute, as do such photographers as Richard Avedon and Lord Snowdon. The magazine is beautifully illustrated but over half is devoted to advertising the fashions which it promotes. One of the few women's magazines which has considerable appeal for men. Should be in most libraries along with its competitor, *Harper's Bazaar* (See annotation, this section).

Vogue Pattern Book International. 1915. bi-m. $4.50. Jacqueline Horscher. Butterick Co., Inc., 161 Sixth Ave., New York, N.Y. 10013. Illus., adv. Circ: 424,000.

Aud: Ga, Sh, Jh. *Rv:* M. *Jv:* B.

Emphasis on *haute couture*, i.e., copies of leading American and European designer's latest fashions. Geared for both the beginner and expert, with sewing for all levels. Patterns are carefully explained and detailed. Useful to any woman and girl from junior high on up, but because of the slant on current fashions probably of more interest to the woman under 30.

Woman's Day. 1937. m. $2.40. Geraldine Rhoads. Fawcett Pubns., 67 W. 44th St., New York, N.Y. 10036. Illus., adv. Circ: 7,000,000.

Aud: Ga, Sh. *Rv:* M. *Jv:* B.

Like *Family Circle*, this is usually purchased in the supermarket, but subscriptions are available to libraries. It is a notch more sophisticated than its competitor, and puts heavy emphasis on good taste at a reasonable price. There are articles on fashion, sewing, child care, decorating, beauty, and meal planning. Every issue contains recipes and menus for low cost meals. Most also contain directions for making something, from knitting a skirt to trimming furniture. An excellent regular feature, "Woman at the Wheel," by Julie Candler, talks about cars and equipment and driving from a woman's point of view. A short story is included. To be preferred over *Family Circle*.

Women's Wear Daily; the retailer's daily newspaper.
1910. 5/wk. $20. Earl Dash. Fairchild Pubns., Inc., 7 E.
12th St., New York, N.Y. 10003. Illus., adv. Circ: 64,000.
Microform: NYPL.

Aud: Sa, Ac. *Rv:* M. *Jv:* B.

A tabloid newspaper primarily for department and general women's stores to keep them advised of fashions, prices, buying changes, and personnel. While a specialized trade journal, it has wider appeal because of the play reviews, general stories on fashions and personalities, and a lively style which keeps the modern day woman advised of what she will be wearing (or what she thinks she should be wearing) in the months ahead. A good bit of this is pure froth, or camp, but it apparently has a loyal following. Hardly an essential item for most libraries, yet useful in special and academic libraries where there is an emphasis on fashion, economics, and the home. Men, by the way, who have a strong sense of humor and an interest in the passing American cultural scene, are advised to glance at it occasionally.

Workbasket. See Crafts and Hobbies Section.

APPENDICES

(a) NEWSPAPERS

Every public and academic library should subscribe to the local newspaper, and the daily, or at least Sunday edition of *The New York Times,* America's only national newspaper. A natural third choice would be the *Christian Science Monitor,* and the fourth, a foreign newspaper, preferably an English one. The first two are indispensable; the latter two, a matter of the library's budget.

Senior high school libraries will want to follow a similar pattern, but in junior high schools a first choice will be *The New York Times School Weekly.* Generally, the typical classroom newspaper is no substitute for a good general newspaper (see the Education Section for a discussion of classroom newspapers).

What follows is a select list of newspapers. After the basic titles, the librarian must decide which type of paper is best suited for the community his or her library is serving. And, with a hopeful view about their possible inclusion, this list includes Underground newspapers, both high school and adult.

The best single expository and evaluative guide to both foreign and American newspapers is John Merrill's *The Elite Press: Great Newspapers of the World* (New York: Pitman, 1968). An experienced journalist and teacher, Merrill evaluates the top 40 newspapers of the world; his selection might well constitute a basic list of newspapers for any library going beyond those considered here.

A detailed discussion of foreign newspapers in libraries will be found in Carol Wall's articles, "Foreign Press in U.S. Libraries," published in *Library Journal* (Feb. 1, 1966, pp.638–41).

NEWSPAPER INDEXES

Christian Science Monitor Subject Index. 1960. m. $10/yr; $15/ annual cum. Index, Christian Science Monitor, 1725 King's Rd., Corvallis, Ore. 97330.

A useful index, but not as detailed as the indexes for *The New York Times* or *The London Times.*

New York Times Index. 1913. semi-m. $105; $60/annual cum. N.Y. Times, Times Sq., N.Y. 10036.

Not only does this index the *Times,* but for each major entry there is a short summary of content. Hence, it is a valued reference tool even without the newspaper.

The Times (**London**). 1907. bi-m. $70.56. The Times, Printing House Sq., London E.C.4.

Not as detailed as the *New York Times Index,* but there are as many specific references. The relative infrequency of appearance works against this as an immediate reference tool, but it is excellent for retrospective researches.

Wall Street Journal Index. m. $50/monthly edition; $50/annual cum.; $88/combined svcs. The Journal, 30 Broad St., New York, N.Y. 10004.

Particularly suited for business collections, but as there are numerous feature and general news stories in the paper, the index is also an invaluable reference tool.

GENERAL NEWSPAPERS

Chicago Tribune Magazine. Chicago Tribune. 435 N. Michigan Ave., Chicago, Ill. 60611. Circ: 1,152,000.
Family Weekly. 405 Park Ave., New York, N.Y. 10022. Circ: 5,000,000.
Parade. Parade Pubns. Inc., 733 Third Ave., New York, N.Y. 10017. Circ: 13,000,000.
Sunday. Metropolitan Sunday Newspapers, Inc., 260 Madison Ave., New York, N.Y. 10016. Circ: 21,600,000.
This Week Magazine. United Newspaper Magazine Corp., 485 Lexington Ave., New York, N.Y. 10017. Circ: 12,428,000.

Aud: Ga. *Rv:* L. *Jv:* C.

Some of the largest circulation magazines in the United States are part of the newspaper. Included as an insert in the local paper, normally on Sunday, they are (with the exception of the *Chicago Tribune Magazine*) prepared in the east for national distribution. The editorial content is popular, sometimes touching on matters of importance, but more likely to stress sports, humor, light entertainment, how-to-do-it type information, and sketches of public figures, from politicians to movie stars. All have a number of photographs and illustrations. When controversy is considered, e.g., drugs, crime, racial problems, it is inevitably through the eyes of the moderate viewer. Whereas the *New York Times Magazine* frequently breaks new ground, introduces important writers and subjects, its poor sisters tend to parrot popular opinion. None can be recommended for libraries, except as part of the regular newspaper. It is useful for both laymen and librarians to realize that for a number of readers the Sunday magazine section is one of the few sources of national "opinion" available to them on a regular basis. More important, the local reader should understand that while the magazine may bear the imprint of the town newspaper, it is not a product of the community.

The Christian Science Monitor. 1908. d. (except Sunday & holidays). $24. The Christian Science Publishing Soc., 1 Norway St., Boston, Mass. 02115. Circ: 185,000.

Indexed: Self-index. *Aud:* Ga, Ac, Jc, Sh. *Rv:* H. *Jv:* A.

Next to *The New York Times* this comes as close as any newspaper in the United States to being a national paper. While issued by the Christian Science Society, it is remarkably free of any religious overtones. A single page is given over to church news and opinion. Aside from this, the paper is world famous for its objectivity and thoroughness. If it shuns news of crime and sensational medical events, it contains what might be called essays which summarize and interpret important national and international events of the past several days, as well as sports news, occasional news of the arts, and editorials (which are sometimes instructive). The writing is objective enough to recommend that this paper be read by persons who want to get a new and valuable perspective on events they may be following in detail elsewhere. A third basic newspaper for all size and type of libraries.

Le Figaro. 1826. d. $29 ($149.50/air). 14 Rond-Point, Champs-Elysees, Paris. Circ: 400,000.

Aud: Ga, Ac, Jc, Sh. *Rv:* H. *Jv:* B.

An exceptionally well-written, lively and, for the most part, politically conservative French newspaper. Its average 32-page format follows closely the usual American pattern, complete with advertising. Like its competitor *Le Monde,* it tends to emphasize political affairs, but coverage is not so critical. Conversely, it does cover the world and France in depth, giving special attention to the arts and literature and education. There is more emphasis here on information, less on *Le Monde's* main mission of intellectual opinion. Hence, of the two, the average reader is apt to find more on current news events in *Le Figaro,* particularly those considered less important by its primary competitor. Thanks to the intentionally direct, clear writing it is a good choice for all general newspaper collections, and may be used with advanced French students in high schools.

Grit. 1882. w. $6. Grit Publishing Co., 208 W. Third St., Williamsport, Pa. 17701. Illus., adv. Circ: 1,134,000.

Aud: Ga. *Rv:* L. *Jv:* C.

A newspaper with a general magazine approach, this is subtitled, "the national small-town weekly," and prides itself on offering advertisers a market allegedly not touched by other mass general circulation papers. It has the same general approach and format as many weekly newspapers, strong on short inspirational articles, short on social, political or controversial topics. There is even a sermon, and the firm does not accept alcoholic beverage advertising. Allegedly for the whole family, but strong on items for women with features on food, fashions, beauty hints and the home. Each issue includes many illustrations, general news items, comics, and even a sports section. Of some merit are the continuing reports on activities and progress made in small communities around the country. On the whole, though, the sanctimonious tone is a bit too much for the more sophisticated reader. A last purchase for libraries, albeit patrons who seek entertainment, amusement and not much thought may welcome an introduction to what is obviously a popular publication.

The Guardian. 1821. d. (except Sunday). $38 ($146.00/ air). 3 Cross St., Manchester, Eng. Circ: 285,000.

Bk. rev: Various numbers, lengths, signed. *Aud:* Ga, Ac, Jc. *Rv:* H. *Jv:* A.

The intellectuals' newspaper in England and, to a degree, in the United States, where many readers know it primarily via the *Manchester Guardian Weekly* (which includes major articles and features from the daily edition). Editorially, the policy is independent and liberal. A daily issue devotes a good part of its space to foreign affairs, and boast correspondents in almost every major country. The American representative is Alistair Cooke. British news reflects the interest in both international affairs and the arts. The columnists cover much of the material found in the weekly edition, i.e., music, book reviews, art, political commentary, and the like. More mundane items such as sports, television and radio, women's news and crossword puzzles give it balance. In view of its high level of writing, its consistent policy of calling for political and social reforms, and its many outstanding writers it should be a first choice (along with *The Times* of London) for all academic libraries and for larger public libraries.

Los Angeles Times. 1881. d. $63. Times Mirror Co., Times Mirror Sq., Los Angeles, Calif. 90053. Circ: 840,000.

Aud: Ga, Ac, Jc. *Rv:* M. *Jv:* B.

Now the best newspaper on the West Coast, having replaced the San Francisco *Chronicle* in that position. In terms of other national newspapers, the *L.A. Times* remains a trifle conservative, albeit in the past few years has taken on more of a middle-of-the-road attitude. While it is predominantly the voice of southern California, it speaks for the state in its coverage of political and social matters. A necessary addition for most California libraries, and larger academic and public libraries in the Western states.

Manchester Guardian Weekly. 1919. w. $7 ($10 Air edition). Subscriptions to: 20 E. 53rd St., New York, N.Y. 10022. Circ: 50,000. Microform: UM.

Bk. rev: Various numbers, lengths, signed. *Aud:* Ga, Ac, Jc. *Rv:* H. *Jv:* A.

Along with *Punch* and *The New Statesman,* possibly the best known English publication in the United States. The 24-page airmail, thin-paper format includes both new material and items from the daily *Guardian,* considered to be one of the top ten newspapers in the world. Coverage is international in scope, the viewpoint is liberal British, and the editorials prove that literate opinon need not be dull or pedantic. It is of value for two basic reasons; it alerts Americans to current news sometimes overlooked, underplayed or slanted in a different fashion in the American Press, and it keeps the reader advised of developments in books, politics, art, music, humor—to name a few of the regular features. The whole has the flavor of a somewhat modified cross between *The New York Times Magazine* and the back of *Newsweek.* It excels them both in its brilliant style. Advertisements claim it is the magazine for "lively minds," and this is true whether that mind be in the community served by a public library, college or university. Larger libraries will also wish to subscribe to the daily edition of the *Guardian.*

Le Monde. 1944. d. $37.50 ($146/air). Jacques Fauvet. 5, rue des Italiens, Paris-IXe. Circ: 300,000.

Aud: Sa, Ac, Jc, Sh. *Rv:* H. *Jv:* B.

A highly respected French newspaper. Quoted throughout the world, its sedate, handsomely printed pages contain complete, detailed reporting and analysis of news in France, followed by news from the rest of the world, arranged geographically. Editorials and commentaries are scattered throughout the paper. It has a reputation for being liberal/independent, and so freely critical, when need be, of any government or policy. It covers financial and business news, sports, television, theater, films, and contains a classified section. It sometimes contains transcripts of important speeches (from the peace talks in Paris, for example). This, or other foreign language newspapers, are useful in all medium to large libraries, but serve a particular purpose in high school libraries where a foreign language is being taught. While there are a number of foreign language papers published and written in the United States specifically for classroom use, they fail to serve the same purpose as the newspaper from the country itself.

In mid-1969, the publishers began a special 8-page tabloid, weekly, English edition. This includes the best articles selected from the daily issues, and is somewhat similar in intent to the *Manchester Guardian Weekly* ($20. Subscrip-

tions to: Regie International, 610 Fifth Ave., New York, N.Y. 10020).

The National Observer. 1962. w. $10. Dow Jones & Co., Inc., 11501 Columbia Pike, Silver Spring, Md. 20910. Circ: 451,000.

Bk. rev: 5–10, 300–500 words. *Aud:* Ga, Ac, Jc, Sh. *Rv:* H. *Jv:* B.

A weekly newspaper, run by the publisher of *The Wall Street Journal.* Contains summaries of important national and international news events and stories chosen for wide popular interest, all written in a popularized style. Topics include consumer news, science, education, civil rights, business, politics. Editorials have a conservative cast. This sort of *Time* magazine in newspaper form is often read by those too lazy to read a good daily newspaper. It does contain a great deal of information, and can be read with much profit; but the desire to please will sometimes admit of a certain simplicity and lack of perspective when history becomes unpleasant. The paper does not match "The News of the Week in Review" of the Sunday *New York Times,* when it comes to reporting U.S. foreign policy. Despite its weaknesses, it has a definite advantage over *Time* in that at least the style is straightforward and there is no confusing the conservative editorial bias. Small to medium sized libraries would do well to take this, but only after a subscription to the Sunday *New York Times* and *Newsweek.*

Neue Zürcher Zeitung. 1780. d. $25.50. Falkenstrasse, 11, Zurich, Switzerland. Circ: 240,000.

Aud: Sa, Ac. *Rv:* H. *Jv:* A.

While published in Switzerland, this is the world's leading German language newspaper. In any survey it usually ranks from first to fifth among the world's best newspapers. The judgement is based on a unique approach—it shuns typical reporting, putting particular emphasis on analyses in essay type stories. The writers are in every major world city, give purposefully analytical treatment to political and economic developments. Currency is not as important as background and accuracy. Objectivity is sought for in gathering facts, and the newspaper tends to take a middle-of-the-road stand on questions which require some type of editorial position. It is just as apt to one day come down as hard on anti-Communists as Communists, but it leans towards a relatively conservative line. An average tabloid sized issue of 40 to 60 pages devotes a good part of its space to international news and finance. Unlike *Le Monde,* there is little attention given the arts. A basic—in fact, many consider it *the* basic—newspaper for the library where there is a strong interest in political science and economics.

New York Amsterdam News. w. $10. Powell-Savory Corp., 2340 Eighth Ave., New York, N.Y. 10027.

Aud: Ga, Ac, Jc, Sh, Jh. *Rv:* M. *Jv:* A.

Any collection of newspapers is deficient which does not include this most popular of the nation's Afro-American newspapers. It reports news of interest to, or about, black or Afro-Americans. Business and social news of the five boroughs of New York are prime features; all news bearing on civil rights and urban problems is included. The editorial page includes columns by Bayard Rustin, Roy Wilkins, Whitney Young, Jackie Robinson, and Floyd McKissick, among others. The tone is moderate: in recent issues could be found such little advertisements as: "In Newark, N.J., 400 persons were made homeless by the fires that raged in the rioting that followed Dr. Martin Luther King's death. Who won?" All the features of a daily paper are here: sections on women, sports, entertainment, the classified, and so forth. This is a good supplement to the local paper for any library. It is basic to the library serving Afro-Americans. (For a profile of this newspaper, see J. Kirk Sale's "The Amsterdam News," in the Feb. 9, 1969 *New York Times Magazine.* Sale points out that it is "one of the three or four most respected Negro papers, and the one most often inserted into the Congressional record." Other major Afro-American newspapers include *The Chicago Daily Defender, The Baltimore Afro-American,* and *The Pittsburgh Courier.*)

The New York Times. 1851. d. $75 (Sunday edition, $39). The N.Y. Times Co., 229 West 43rd St., New York, N.Y. 10036. Circ: 635,000 daily; 1,337,000 Sunday.

Indexed: Self-index. *Bk. rev:* Daily and Sunday section. *Aud:* Ga, Sa, Ac, Jc, Sh. *Rv:* H. *Jv:* V.

Daily Edition

Dwight MacDonald once commented that the sure sign of civilization was the ability to pick up the daily *Times* each morning. Towns lacking such service are lost. Libraries can help meet the need.

"To be the accurate, objective newspaper of record. To serve adult needs by being complete in our coverage. To explain, explain and explain again—not in the sense of a primer but in order to fill in the gaps for readers. And, finally, to search for the most talented, the most diligent, the most knowledgeable people for every department." These are the aims of *The New York Times,* according to Turner Catledge, former executive editor promoted to vice president, published in the May 2, 1968 issue. Complete news coverage makes this newspaper the most useful in any size or type of library. It is the only newspaper that prints verbatim the texts of important speeches, statements, and proceedings of news conferences and peace talks. Articles frequently appear which summarize and analyze topics in the news, and sometimes a long article will give a general report on an area, which will not have been called for by any immediate crisis. Reporting is objective; read to the very end of a news story to fill in a picture of what really happened. Each issue contains news of cultural events, a book review, a film review, a theater column by Clive Barnes or Walter Kerr, an exceptional editorial page which

includes columns by James Reston, Tom Wicker, and Russell Baker, a sports section, and a comprehensive business section. In short, for those who would know what is going on in the world, this paper is indispensable. It cannot be replaced, only supplemented.

Sunday Edition

The Sunday edition has the same merits as the daily *Times,* but it is probably the heaviest newspaper published anywhere. It is swollen by separate sections devoted to the news, "Arts and Leisure," "Business and Finance," "Real Estate," "Resorts and Travel," "Sports," classified advertisements, and three sections of particular note: "The News of the Week in Review," *"The New York Times Book Review,"* and *"The New York Times Magazine."* The "Week in Review" contains convenient, well-written summaries of the week's events on all important news fronts, as well as articles on education, law, medicine, science, and religion, editorials, and listings of librarian and teacher job openings. The "Book Review" section is well-known to all who read or deal with books; in addition to the many book reviews, it contains the famed "Best Seller" List. The "Magazine," usually rather thick, contains long articles on all subjects, written by prominent persons, and a good crossword puzzle. Libraries which cannot afford the daily and Sunday edition should at least subscribe to the Sunday issue. It is a must for almost any type library.

St. Louis Post-Dispatch. 1878. d. $37. Pulitzer Publishing Co., 1113 Franklin Ave., St. Louis, Mo. 63101. Circ: 349,000.

Aud: Ga, Ac, Jc. *Rv:* M. *Jv:* B.

Always named among the top ten best-edited newspapers in this country, the *Post-Dispatch* provides excellent news reports in a pleasant, precise format. A daily section called "Editorials—News Analysis and Interpretation" contains a few special news articles and some really good editorial writing, critical and perceptive. There are also syndicated columns by Tom Wicker, Joseph Kraft, and Joseph Alsop. This significant paper has a place in any large newspaper collection, and certainly would be a third choice for libraries within the region.

The Times. d. $48 ($80/air); Sunday, $10.95 ($40/air). Times Newspapers Ltd., Printing House Sq., London E.C.4. Subscriptions to: 201 E. 42nd St., New York, N.Y. 10017.

Indexed: Self-index. *Aud:* Ga, Sa, Ac, Jc. *Rv:* H. *Jv:* A.

Daily Edition

The prestigious British newspaper, which is famous throughout the world for its home and foreign news service. It is written and edited for the educated and for professional people. Like *The New York Times,* it is unsensational, with a neat, precise layout, and headlines of a decent size. The "leader," or editorial, page is particularly well-known, both for the editorials and the letters to the editor (practically a national institution), which are exceptional. The paper, in addition to the worldwide news, contains a large business section, and the usual theater, book, sports, television and radio, and classified sections. This old, traditional, highly influential newspaper should be first choice for any library seeking more than national coverage in the newspaper collection.

Sunday Edition

Some libraries may prefer the Sunday edition ($10.95), which is basically the equivalent of the Sunday *New York Times*. The feature sections on theatre, motion pictures, music, etc., are excellent, noteworthy for contributions by famous English critics, writers and scholars. The magazine is considered one of the best available, both in terms of format (the photography is superb) and content.

The Village Voice. 1955. w. $5. The Village Voice, Inc., Sheridan Square, New York, N.Y. 10014. Circ: 27,800.

Aud: Ga, Ac, Jc, Sh. *Rv:* M. *Jv:* A.

This began as an underground newspaper, but today is one of the more respected journals of opinion and the arts in the country. Although it purports to be the voice of the Bohemian element in Greenwich Village, New York, its scope is much greater, its interests more national and international. It has a particular fascination for the young because it is among the first to report on new activities in the arts, music, theatre and politics. Conversely, the really rebellious young have given it up for the more outspoken, usually less literate, underground newspapers. (In fact, the *East Village Other* began as a counter-voice to the *Village Voice*.) Distinctly liberal in tone, the articles are geared for a sophisticated, above average educated audience. Writers include critics Pete Hammill, Nat Hentoff, Jonas Mekas and Andrew Sarris. There are fascinating cartoonists (Jules Feiffer, for one), photographs and an extremely entertaining classified advertisement section. Those in and around New York value the up-to-date weekly report on current activities, particularly in the Village and off-Broadway. Strongly recommended for all types of libraries, particularly senior high school libraries. On the other hand, it is not the type of newspaper which should be introduced into a rock-bound conservative community.

The Wall Street Journal. 1889. d. (except Saturday & Sunday). $28 (Price varies for regional and air editions). Dow Jones & Co., 30 Broad St., New York, N.Y. 10004. Circ: 887,000.

Indexed: Self-index. *Aud:* Sa, Ga, Ac, Jc. *Rv:* H. *Jv:* A.

Despite its obvious purpose, to give a complete report on today's business, *The Wall Street Journal* offers considerably more for the alert reader. As it must report facts, not opinion or biases, the limited news coverage is the best anywhere. Every issue contains three large absorbing feature articles which start on the front page, on any and all topics—politics, art, science, poverty, business, medicine,

education, the war. The editorial page contains some conservative opinion, another large article on almost any subject, and book and drama reviews, which are quite good. The more general news articles throughout the paper, on legislation being considered in Congress, for example, are recommended to everyone. This newspaper, geared as it is to money-making, is free of cant and ravings often found in local, less sophisticated journals. Among public and academic libraries, it should be the fifth basic choice. Sample copies, too, should be available in high school libraries.

The Washington Post. 1877. d. $54. Washington Post Co., 1515 L St., N.W., Washington, D.C. 20005. Circ: 444,000.

Aud: Ga, Sa, Ac, Jc, Sh. *Rv:* H. *Jv:* A.

Next to the *New York Times,* one of the most widely influential and quoted newspapers in the United States. Liberal in tone, it offers complete news coverage of the Washington scene, frequently breaking stories before any other news service. It is usually one of two or three papers read by the President and every Congressman. Unfortunately, it is not indexed, but it should be found in libraries seeking a broad national coverage. In terms of choice it would follow the *New York Times* and a local newspaper. Recommended for all types and sizes of libraries.

Die Welt. 1946. d. $33. Axel Springer, 36 Kaiser-Wilhelm Strasse, Hamburg, 2, Germany. Circ: Approx. 1,000,000.

Aud: Ga, Ac, Jc, Sh. *Rv:* M. *Jv:* B.

One of the major publications of Axel Springer, who is often accused of holding a virtual monopoly over the German middle-class press. News coverage is more comprehensive than in most European papers, the writing style is clear, and the whole comes close to the average well edited American newspaper. With a circulation of over a million, it tends to be conservative in its approach and during the student revolts of 1968 came under heavy fire from the Left. Nevertheless, it enjoys a good reputation for its international coverage of politics, economics and business. The 20- to 30-page daily boasts more pictures, certainly a more lively layout, than any other European newspaper. The large circulation is due to its wide base of coverage, and if international issues give it a special place abroad, it is welcomed at home for stories on everything from sports and automobiles to stars and education. While intellectually it lags behind the *Frankfurter Allgemeine,* and isn't in the same league as the *Neue Zurcher Zeitung,* it unquestionably serves a real need for the average reader. It can be recommended, too, for advanced high school German classes, although teachers should point out its political attitudes.

UNDERGROUND NEWSPAPERS

There are more than 50 so called "underground" or "hip" newspapers in the United States. They are written by and for the younger generation, usually from the late teens through the late twenties. And, according to a feature article in *The Wall Street Journal* (March 4, 1968, p. 1), they are purchased by "an estimated third of a million Americans, ranging from the 'alienated' among students and the hippies to the merely curious." In order to share advertising and feature writers, the papers have organized the Underground Press Syndicate and the Liberation News Service.

Unlike the general newspaper, they make no claim to objectivity. They do claim, and rightfully so, to feature material, articles and art not found in either the local newspaper or many magazines. Illustrations and stories are not for conservative types.

The following is a representative selection. Sanford Berman, formerly of the University of California, points out that in deciding upon a subscription, librarians should realize that "each underground bears the unmistakable stamp of its editor and locale, but since they're all serviced by UPS and LNS and freely reprint each other's material, a small to medium sized library could well represent the whole genre by subscribing to the one nearest paper plus the *Los Angeles Free Press,* and the *San Francisco Express Times."* Those on the east coast might prefer the *East Village Other,* or *Avatar.*

The initials *J. S.* following annotations are the signature of Jake Sherman, an experienced reporter and journalist, now of the *Albany Times-Union.* The compiler, recognizing his own bias towards the underground press, asked a more objective writer for his opinions and annotations.

The best single guide to the Underground Press is: *Underground Press Guide/Directory.* 1967. q. $1. Joe Korpsak. P.O. Box 46–477, Los Angeles, Calif. 90046. Each issue gives complete bibliographic data on all of the major underground newspapers.

Avatar. $6. bi-w. Brian Keating & Wayne Hansen. Avatar, Inc., 37 Rutland St., Boston, Mass. 02218.

Aud: Ga, Ac, Jc, Sh. *Rv:* L. *Jv:* V.

One of the better and perhaps the best of the underground newspapers, *Avatar* focuses on such issues and phenomena as the Vietnam war, the student revolt, drugs, Zen Buddhism, hippie culture, serious rock music, etc. Also featured is a detailed running account of the paper's battle with Boston and Cambridge authorities, who have sought to ban it on the basis of obscenity. *Village Voice* film critic Jonas Mekas contributes a column on the avant-garde film, while staff members survey non-Establishment theatre in the Boston-Cambridge area. Occasional poetry plus a calendar of events and a substantial section of letters-to-the-editor. What is termed "hard" news is provided by the Liberation News Service, the paper running about two or three pieces per issue. The only underground paper not to appear in tabloid or booklet form, *Avatar* has a bold, easy-to-read page layout and makes extensive use of sketches and photographs. It generally attempts to treat issues seriously and is never scatological purely for its own sake, although face-

tiousness does creep in from time to time. *J.S.* (Note: In the Winter of 1968–69, the paper was issued as a monthly magazine, following a magazine format. The editors may return to a newspaper format later in 1969. Whatever the format, it remains a major voice of the underground/student movement, and should be found in most libraries.)

Berkeley Barb. w. $5. Max Scherr, 2042 Univ. Ave., Berkeley, Calif. 94704.

Aud: Ga, Ac, Jc. *Rv:* M. *Jv:* B.

Thanks to censorship problems with libraries, newsstands and its connection with the Berkeley student dissident elements, this is probably one of the best known underground newspapers. It is often considered the West Coast counterpart of the New York-centered *East Village Other.* It is not necessarily the best, particularly as regards the layout, which seems to be an afterthought. A normal 20- to 25-page tabloid number features the usual left-of-center political news, films, book reviews, cartoons, satirical pieces, and short items on personalities and events. It is particularly strong on the number of photographs—yes, some nudes—it employs (shades of the *Daily News*) and the classified advertisement section, which may run six to ten pages. This latter feature seems to frighten most staid individuals. Anything goes, and almost everything is printed. The December 27, 1968 issue, for example, quoted the *San Rafael Independent Journal* editorial, which pointed out that the classified ads were a bad influence: "It scarcely seems likely that the upbringing of the Sausalito district's children, black or white, would be enhanced by tutelage obtained from these circles." Editorials like this do nothing but boost the readership of the *Barb.* While a second choice for libraries with a collection of underground newspapers, its notoriety may make it a required item in liberal libraries trying to serve the expressed wishes of the college rebels.

Black Panther. See Afro-American Section.

East Village Other. w. $6. East Village Other, Inc., 105 Second Ave., New York, N.Y. 10003.

Aud: Ac, Jc. *Rv:* M. *Jv:* B.

EVO surveys the black revolution, Vietnam, politics, drugs and the East Village scene, but without the depth one would expect from what purports to be a serious hippie journal. The selection of articles seems somewhat arbitrary, and the writing, with the exception of one or two pieces per issue, seems self-conscious and labored. As the emphasis is not on "what happened" but the "total reaction to what happened," the stream-of-consciousness style is in vogue, but this technique is not handled with nearly the skill of the *Village Voice.* Avant-garde art and pop music are handled in columns that are less criticism than half-gossip, half commentary, and an unusual feature is the "HIPpocrates" column, a *Dear Abby* thing by a hippie M.D. who answers questions on the more curious side effects of LSD, marijuana and other drugs. "Wheel and

Deal," the classified ads section, would provide a gold mine of material for a latter-day Kraft-Ebbing. In general, the paper seems more concerned with shocking and taunting the Establishment, than intelligently criticizing it. It has developed an annoying juvenile type of *Mad* magazine approach, typified by the introduction of scatalogical comic strips which are as pointless as they are offensive. *JS*

The Fifth Estate. $3. bi-m. Harvey Ovshinsky & Peter Werbe. Estate Newspaper, Inc., 1107 W. Warren St., Detroit, Mich. 48201.

Aud: Ga, Ac, Jc. *Rv:* L. *Jv:* B.

This is one example of a paper with primary local interest. Issued in Detroit, *The Fifth Estate* fills several pages in each issue with copy from the Liberation News Service but still does an adequate job surveying the hippie and protest scenes in and around its own city. It goes in for the descriptive account of the isolated event and features relatively few interpretive or survey-type pieces. News of national and local politics, draft resistance, the racial situation in Detroit, police brutality, etc. is to be found here, and the general impression is that it's not treated with any particular depth. In the third part of what might have been an engrossing series on life in Castro's Cuba, for example, there is little to suggest the girl who wrote it actually went there. Three jazz records are reviewed, the writing pompous, and one book, the writing meandering. Page makeup is clean but the photography uninspired. In other departments, "HIPpocrates," an underground M.D. (he's syndicated from Berkeley, it turns out), answers some frank questions about sex. There's also some good advice from one Joe Martin on how to "Grow Your Own." *JS*

Logos. m. Communications Unlimited, 3553 A Coloniale, Montreal 18, Que.

Aud: Ac, Jc. *Rv:* L. *Jv:* B.

America has no corner on the "underground press" and north of the border there are a number of such newspapers. One example is *Logos,* organ of the Montreal underground, which calls its reporters "combatants" and describes its purpose as "making Marxism hip, Mysticism op, Maharishi Yogi pop, Canada stop, with Quebec on top." (See also, *The Rebel.*) Analyzing a typical issue, it would appear that the "making Canada stop, with Quebec on top" part receives the bulk of editorial attention. Included in this particular issue are a discussion of "separatiste" groups in Quebec, an attack on NORAD, the U.S.-Canadian anti-bomber defense network ("Are we going to let generals at Colorado Springs call the shots for Canada?"), and a blast at a new housing project in Montreal which is condemned as another application of the "strategic hamlet" theory. These pieces are surprisingly well-written and in no way smack of the glib puerility of the publication's credo. Other topics are the student revolt, exploitation of the workers, news of draft-registers and the underground

cinema. Illustration and photography are clever if at times a bit earthy. This is a worthwhile paper if one is willingly to delve beneath the superficial attempt to be shocking. Part of this will involve not getting too upset over the occasional use of four letter words. *JS*.

Los Angeles Free Press. 1964. w. $5. Art Kunkin. Los Angeles Free Press, 938 N. Fairfax, Los Angeles, Calif., 90046. Circ: 60,000.

Aud: Ga, Ac, Jc, Sh. *Rv:* L. *Jv:* A.

A lengthy article by Mark Lane on CIA links to the Kennedy assassination reflect this paper's policy of using lead pieces by well-known outsiders, when it can. The *Free Press,* otherwise, seeks to keep its readers informed on such matters as war protests, civil rights (both black and Mexican), and Los Angeles area love-ins (particularly when the latter are visited by police). Considerable space is devoted to serious theatre and film criticism, the writers focusing on particular plays and movies in the area rather than on general trends. Plays and films considered are not necessarily underground. Also Lawrence Lipton, one-time chronicler of Venice West, L.A.'s then beatnik enclave, contributes a column on the world scene. There is an extensive classified ad section and a good weekly calendar of cultural events. The work of staff writers tends to be uneven but never flip or designed for shock value, all of which qualifies the *Los Angeles Free Press* as a newspaper and not a put-on. *JS*

National Underground Review. m. $3. National Underground Review, 10 Morton St., New York, N.Y. 10014.

Aud: Ga, Ac, Jc. *Rv:* L. *Jv:* B.

Selected reprints from the underground and collegiate presses from the core of this journal. For instance, there are columns by Thomas Baggio on national politics and black revolutionary Julius Lester on the impending apocalypse. Ernest Thomson contributes a gossip column on Chicago theatre, Thomas Castell on jazz and pop records and Christopher Watson some punch, three-line book notes in the "buy" and "burn" categories. These columnists may not be regulars but something very much like what they do will probably be featured in each issue. The reprints are generally well-written and provocative, but as for the contribution of the people at 10 Morton Street, I'm not too impressed. Theirs' is too obviously a commerical venture. *JS*.

The Paper. w. $.20 issue. Jim Ebert & Jeff Snoyer. Michigan State Univ., Box 367, East Lansing, Mich. 48823.

Aud: Ac, Jc. *Rv:* L. *Jv:* C.

This is an example of an unorthodox school paper which comes close to the "underground" variety and is typical enough of many springing up around the country. *The Paper,* an editorial explains, is a reaction to the Establishment paper on campus, the *State News.* And if the *State News* is really as bad as *The Paper's* editors say it is, then it's high time something was done. That something, however, is not *The Paper*. The problem is that the editors of this sheet have neglected something that no newspaper can be without—content. True, there's the editorial and a decently written book review, but aside from that *The Paper*, it is really nothing more than a compendium of notices for underground goings-on on campus. *JS.*

The Rebel. bi-m. $1.75. c/o S. Gruber. P.O. Box 611, Station H., Montreal 25, Que.

Aud: Ga, Ac, Jc. *Rv:* L. *Jv:* B.

More a magazine than a newspaper (it makes little attempt to deal with "breaking" news), this publication provides a keen insight into the minds of a self-professed group of revolutionaries. It is published by several Americans who have fled to Canada not merely to avoid the draft or because they oppose the Vietnam war, but because they are dedicated to the overthrow of "the U.S. imperialism of which the Vietnam war is only the current manifestation." As such, they hope one day to return to this country to participate directly in the "revolutionary struggle." Topics in a typical issue include violence vs. pacifism, student power, workers, the political situation in Quebec, Canadian complicity in the Vietnam war and specific information on Canadian immigration procedures. Nearly all articles are well-written, of fairly substantial length (1,000–1,500 words), and valuable in that they reflect the mood of potential revolutionaries and the terms in which they think. The tone is serious as opposed to smart-alecky, and it is apparent that these young men are not merely parroting a particular propaganda line but coming to these negative conclusions about the present state of American society on their own. *JS.*

Although adults will think few of the underground newspapers suitable fare for high school students, many of the juniors and seniors think quite differently, and the high schools themselves are developing an underground press movement. This tends to be largely local, but the editors have organized a national service, or clearing house: HIP Service (High School Independent Press), 34 W. 17th St., New York, N.Y. 10011. It has some 25 members, and the number is increasing.

Only two examples of the better high school newspapers are given here (both annotated by Sanford Berman) but Bill Hinchliff of Federal City College, Washington, D.C. sends the names and addresses of seven papers which

local librarians may wish to examine, and others may wish to send for sample copies:

Alton, Ill.—*Common Sense,* 1212 Rock Spring Terrace.

Los Angeles, Calif.—*Insight,* 1620 S. High Pt. St.
                             The Worrier, 1842 Bentley Ave.

Oakland, Calif.—*Student Voice,* 5335 Yuba Ave.

Riverside, Calif.—*It,* 511 Glenhill Drive.

Sacramento, Calif.—*Floyd,* 2710 Montgomery Way.

San Rafael, Calif.—*High Times,* 1817 4th St.

Seattle, Wash.—*The Advocate,* 3707 S.W. Cambridge St.

Free Student. 1968. irreg. $1. 10 issues. 510 Hoover, Los Angeles, Calif. 90004.

Aud: Sh, Jh. *Rv:* L. *Jv:* B.

The ferment, dissatisfaction, and militancy so common to university campuses during the past few years have now boiled over to the high schools, at least in L.A. Issued by High School Students for a Democratic Society, this 4-page tabloid both zestfully and angrily reports local grievances (cases of repression in the classroom and elsewhere), as well as reflecting the posture of radical youth toward larger issues like war, police malpractice, and the draft. Refreshingly knowledgeable and forthright, *Free Student* belongs in all large collections serving educators, parents and young people.

Thought. 1960. q. $1. Richard Taffer. Thought, 275 W. Jamaica Ave., Valley Stream, N.Y. 11580.

Aud: Sh, Jh. *Rv:* L. *Jv:* V.

In many ways this predates the adult underground press—it is going into its seventh year, and seems to be growing both in content and style. The 12-page "open forum is entirely the work of high school students, and is open to all points of view." Material is solicited from throughout the United States, and ranges from attacks on the draft and Vietnam to reprints of pages from censored high school newspapers. There are a few cartoons, poetry and short fiction pieces. The offset printing is a bit crude, but the paper is readable. As the voice of the intelligent, dissident high school student this has no peers. It deserves a place in every junior high and high school library, and in collections in public libraries. Also, those in professional schools of education should be receiving it regularly. It might be noted that there is nothing objectionable here in the way of sex, but it is bound to disturb the adult who still thinks all high school students are reading *Boy's Life* and *Reader's Digest.*

(b) FREE MAGAZINES FOR LIBRARIES

This section includes a sampling of "house" magazines which are available to libraries on a complimentary basis. A house magazine is generally construed to mean a publication of a company or commercial establishment, or an association, commercial or otherwise. These are issued on some regular basis and are generally free to the public. Their main purpose is to promote the interests of the sponsor. Very little, if any, advertising is included.

Library usefulness of this type of publication has been increased in the past decade. By a change in general approach from the frankly promotional, one-sided and sometimes exaggerated picture of the company, to a more factual presentation, public relations value is increased by giving a broader picture of the company, including its history, projections for the future, and its relationship to a much broader field such as public service.

Included here are representatives of this very broad field. (It is estimated that there are 6,000 to 8,000 house magazines being published in the U.S. and Canada.) Variety is shown not only in the industries and interests represented, but also in the format, quality and level of presentation. Some are published for the general reader, some for specialized economic groups, and some for a scholarly audience.

It should be noted that the normal "keys" for indexing, book reviews and audience are deleted. Only a few of the magazines are indexed regularly, and book reviews are incidental. As for audience, all are acceptable for senior high school, junior college, public and university libraries. Some, for illustrations and general interest, may be useful in junior high schools and, in a few cases, elementary grades. This is indicated at the end of the annotation. Selection, then, is more a matter of subject need and budget than any other factor.

As the magazines are free, it is strongly suggested that librarians try a few of them. Those listed here have a substantial circulation, and are indicated as being free to the public and/or libraries. If they serve no purpose, discard and move on to another group. Hopefully, the choice represented by this list will be a good source for any library. If not, librarians may move on to the *Gebbie House Magazine Directory* (6th ed. Sioux City: House Magazine Publishing Co., 1968), which was used in compiling this list.

For additional reading, the librarian is advised to see the excellent article by Wilson Sullivan, "All in the Family," published in the Aug. 12, 1967 *Saturday Review*. Mr. Sullivan points out other magazines not listed here which may also be of value.

It should also be noted that these free magazines are distinct from controlled circulation magazines, which are also free, but sent only to a carefully selected audience, usually one which will respond to the copious advertising. (Adeline M. Smith, High School Librarian, Hoosic Valley Central School, Schaghticoke, N.Y.)

Aerojet-General Booster. 1956. m. A. W. Hessel. Aerojet-General Corp., 9100 East Flair Drive, El Monte, Calif. 91734. Illus. Circ: 10,000.

The Aerojet-General Corp., concerned with aerospace and hydrospace research and development, uses the *Booster* to report uses of its projects and concepts currently under investigation. The four-page leaflet includes five to six short articles. Many of its products are developed and manufactured for NASA, and applications and successful results are explained. One page of "Technology" explains by text and pictures the technical operation of a piece of equipment or power system, ranging from service propulsion system engines for Apollo 4, to new and better police automobiles. A full-page illustration used for the cover is related to one of the articles, and illustrations for other articles consist of photos, diagrams, and drawings.

Aerospace. 1963. q. Gerald J. McAllister. Aerospace Industries of Amer., Inc., 1725 DeSales St., N.W., Washington, D.C. 20036. Illus. Circ: 21,000.

Each issue contains approximately five articles, of 3–6 pages, covering the variety of topics included in the modern aeronautics field. Research and accomplishments are stressed, showing the importance of this industry's contribution to the aerospace program and to national security. A few historical items, current and proposed aircraft models, and areas such as pollution control (in which the industry is cooperating with other agencies) are covered. Illustrations consist mainly of expert drawings, a few photos, and charts where pertinent. High quality paper, artistic page layout and cover designs.

Alcan News. 1960. m. Gloria Menard. Aluminum Co. of Canada, Ltd., Box 6090, Montreal 3, Que. Illus. Circ: 15,000.

Published "as a continuing source of information about developments in the aluminum industry," the rather short (one or two pages) staff-written articles describe a diversity of subjects, including uses of aluminum by transportation industries, housing and other construction, descriptions of appliances and other consumer goods, and accounts of some manufacturing plants and processes. Each 8-page issue contains one article describing some property or potentiality of aluminum from a scientific viewpoint, often with itemized data in chart form. Writing style is popular, and does not require scientific background. Illustrations are mostly black and white photographs of good quality, well selected, and some of the covers are outstanding examples of good color photography. Suitable for junior high libraries.

American Youth. 1960. bi-m. Howard A. Coffin. General Motors Corp., 17390 W. Eight Mile Rd., Southfield, Mich. 48076. Illus. Circ: 1,900,000.

"General Motors sends *American Youth* to newly licensed young drivers with the hope that its articles on driving safety will help to develop further their driving skills." Each issue of this 24 page magazine contains several staff-written articles on driving safety and automobile construction features, which form its main emphasis. Other articles largely are concerned with sports and outdoor activities, and salute outstanding young Americans. The style of writing is geared to modern youth without resorting to slang or the vernacular. Format and arrangement are tasteful and pleasing, with an adequate, but not excessive number of good illustrations.

Aramco World. bi-m. Paul F. Hoye. Arabian American Oil Co., A. Corp., 505 Park Ave., New York, N.Y. 10022. Illus. Circ: 60,000.

Does a colorful job of interpreting the Middle East, and the role of the Arabian American Oil Company there, to the American public. Articles cover historical background material: archaeology, exploration, architecture, etc., in about equal proportion to current matters such as social customs, impact of western civilization on the natives of Middle Eastern countries, technology (oil), and various aspects of science. All material in its 32 pages is presented objectively, but has been selected to show assets and accomplishments of the area, particularly related to petroleum. Articles vary in length, are signed, and often written by authorities in a given field, such as Trevor Christie on archaeology, and William A. Ward on Egyptology. Staff writers of the company cover technological subjects. Superb quality color photographs, as well as black and white photos and other illustrations. This is an excellent source of historical, geographical, cultural and social material on the Arab countries and Middle East in general.

The Attack on Narcotic Addiction and Drug Abuse. 1967. bi-m. Helena Stasiuk. State of New York, Narcotic Addiction and Control Commission, Executive Park South, P.O. Box 8114, Albany, N.Y. 12203.

The Attack "is available for individuals who want to know more about the Narcotic Addiction Control Commission and what it is doing about the drug problem in New York State." Robert Dolins, Assistant Commissioner for Narcotics Education, indicates that requests for subscriptions will be welcomed from outside New York State, and even internationally. News articles, of varying length, fill the 8 to 12 pages of this tabloid size magazine. They cover the commission's education program, with news of community narcotic education centers set up throughout New York State by this agency, and descriptions of rehabilitation programs being carried on by its rehabilitation centers. Emphasis is placed on preventive programs and on rehabilitation efforts. Brief biographies of persons holding positions on the commission, or active in its program, have been included. Articles are well illustrated with photographs, and are written in good, journalistic style. This should be useful to parallel agencies in other states, as well as to students from high school up, interested in the topic of narcotic addiction.

BSCS Newsletter. 1959. 3–4/yr. George M. Clark. The Biological Sciences Curriculum Study, P.O. Box 930, Boulder, Colo. 80302. Illus. Circ: 40,000.

This organization, located at the University of Colorado, reports activities for the improvement of the curriculum in the biological sciences. Each 18- to 32-page issue generally follows a single theme, with several related articles of interest to those concerned with the teaching of the biological sciences on secondary school level. Material relates to methods of presenting new curricula, use of new teaching materials, and reports of successful innovative programs being conducted by secondary schools. Research into the biological curriculum is conducted and reported according to established research procedures. Signed articles are written by staff consultants and school and college faculty and experts in the field. BSCS publications available through commercial distribution, and from BSCS, are listed for the convenience of biology teachers. Photos, diagrams, charts, and drawings are used for illustrations.

Bell Laboratories Record. 1925. m. Free to public, college, and university libraries; $4 to others. B. E. Strusser. Bell Telephone Laboratories, Inc., 463 West St., New York, N.Y. 10014. Illus. Circ: 32,000.

Covers research, equipment development, and systems engineering in the broad field of communications. Each issue contains four or more substantial articles by Bell Lab scientists and engineers. Topics range from the purely scientific to those showing practical applications and improvement of components of communications systems. Presentation is thorough and detailed, and is further clarified by many diagrams and some good quality photos.

Better Farming for Better Living. 1938. q. R. L. Dinnensen. Oliver Corp., 1119 W. Sample St., South Bend, Ind. 46621. Illus.

A variety of farming topics is covered, including proper use of Oliver machinery, new developments and new models, suggestions for maintenance and safety, crop trends, planting, harvesting, etc. Material is staff-written, and a few articles are largely pictorial. Charts and diagrams are used in addition to photos, to good advantage. There is an occasional editorial comment on an issue of importance to farmers, such as proposed legislation. A 2-page women's section includes recipes, suggestions for needlework and various crafts and household arts. The chief interest of this magazine will be to those engaged in agriculture, and to those enrolled in agriculture courses or contemplating it as a career. Suitable for junior high school libraries.

Business of Building. 1947. q. George E. Harper. U.S. Gypsum Co., 101 S. Wacker Drive, Chicago, Ill. 60606. Illus. Circ: 98,000.

Factual articles on building techniques, good design, merchandizing (of United States Gypsum products) and business methods for builders. Quality construction is stressed. New methods and new procedures are introduced. The editorial policy promotes new trends in housing design toward a more aesthetic approach than the stereotyped housing development units. Articles, written by company staff, vary in length from one to three pages and are complemented by good illustrations consisting of photos, floor plans and diagrams. In addition to its usefulness to the industry, this may be of value in secondary and trade school education.

CIBA Review. q. Ed bd. CIBA Chemical & Dye Co., Route 208, Fairlawn, N.J. 07410. Illus., adv.

Each issue is largely devoted to a single theme indicated on the cover. The topic receives thorough coverage, with historical background and a general introduction. Topics relating to textiles cover a broad range. Individual fibers

such as flax are subjects often covered, as are fabric types, clothing motifs of fabric decoration and national or ethnic specializations. The chemistry of textile manufacturing and dyeing is related to such topics as "Radioactivity" and "Sulphur." Presentation is clear and factual, suitable for the intelligent non-specialist. Illustrations, some in color, are of excellent quality, well-placed with relation to the text, and contribute substantially to the value of the magazine. Historically treated topics are illustrated with photos of material from museums, with the source always noted. Photos of modern machine installations, and good clear diagrams are used to illustrate chemical articles and those dealing with manufacturing.

C-I-L Oval. 1932. q. J. F. Cameron. Canadian Industries, Ltd., P.O. Box 10, Montreal, Quebec. Illus. Circ: 90,000.

Published by Canada's largest producer of chemicals and allied products, this is an unusually fine magazine both in content and in format. Each issue has five to eight substantial articles related to the advances of the Canadian chemical industry. Many articles include historical background of the product in addition to the latest manufacturing plants and processes. Occasional articles describe various regions or provinces of Canada, emphasizing progress and improved economic level to which large industries many have contributed. Conservation of Canada's natural resources, modern trends in education, comments on man in modern technological society are other subjects included. "Briefly Stated" is a four-page insert at the center, giving 12 to 15 brief items of interest in the field of chemistry, scholarship awards and related short items. Signed articles are written by qualified persons in the field of industry and education. Illustrations consist mainly of very high quality color photos. Good type and paper, as well as excellent cover photos in color add to the value.

Communities in Action. 1966. q. Office of Economic Opportunity, Public Affairs, Washington, D.C. 20506. Illus.

A government publication which serves as a source of materials for both the layman and the expert. Emphasis is on how to improve the community. Examples are given of successful operations, and techniques for sparking interest are explored. Excellent illustrations.

Connchord. 1958. 3/yr. Daniel J. Hankin. Conn Corp., Elkhart, Ind. 46514.

"Dedicated to the advancement of music education," its 32 pages contain several articles and features which help to promote music in general, with emphasis on public school band participation and instrumental technique. Related material includes a few historical sketches, and the position of the adult amateur. A series, "Profiles in Music," presents a 1-page biographical sketch of a prominent personality in the field of music management, performance, education or composition. Some articles are contributed by music educators and are signed, others are staff-written, and average 2 to 4 pages. "News Briefs" brings to the attention of readers events, scholarships and competitions in which teachers and students will have an interest. Music educators contribute opinions in their letters in "Sounding Board." Illustrations are adequate, format is generally pleasing, and a few of the pages are printed on colored or tinted paper.

Consol News. 1962. bi-m. Leonard S. Gross. Consolidation Coal Co., Inc., P.O. Box 1079, Morgantown, W.Va. 26505. Illus. Circ: 18,500.

A source of general information on coal mining and related industries. News of the various mines and divisions of this company account for at least half of the magazine content, and here the emphasis is on development of new facilities and improvement of others, and on personnel changes, awards, etc. Other articles, of interest to the general reader, show the endeavors of the coal industry to sponsor research, to promote utilization of its waste products, and to combat pollution problems. Safety is often stressed. Also reported are the activities of the company itself in the fields of vocational, technical and mining engineering education: scholarships for higher education in the Appalachian area, the company's training program, and its active recruitment of personnel. Articles average 4 or 5 pages, and illustrations are mostly black and white photos. This will be of some interest where material showing various phases of coal and related industries is needed. Suitable for junior high school libraries.

Cooperation. 1913. q. Public Relations Dept., Kimberly-Clark Corp., Neenah, Wis. 54956. Illus. Circ: 25,000.

A general interest magazine designed to help tell the story of this large manufacturer of paper and paper products. Service-related and human interest articles are included with those describing processes and products, and general industrial management problems and procedures. Subjects have ranged from the position and functions of police forces to the history of Kleenex tissues, and impact of computerization on a large company. Emphasis is placed on people and activities in Kimberly-Clark communities, especially the youthful segment of the population. Staff-written articles are illustrated largely by black and white photos. Suitable for junior high school libraries.

Dodge News Magazine. 1935. m. William Hinds. Dodge Div. of Chrysler Motors Corp., 5436 W. Fort St., Detroit, Mich. 48209. Illus., adv. Circ: 800,000.

A general interest magazine distributed by Dodge dealers to their customers. There are three or four main articles in each issue. The range is very broad, and includes travel, sports, science, performing groups, and personalities, among others. Material presented is of greatest interest to the teen and young adult group, but is not confined too closely to this age group. Main articles are signed, well written, and nicely illustrated with many color and black and white photos. Each issue includes a double-page spread on food, and one on fashions, both interestingly presented and well illustrated. Several short features are included: a "Perfor-

mance Report" on new and experimental models and test results, and letters and short items from readers. A small amount of advertising is included. Suitable for junior high school libraries.

Down to Earth. 1945. q. Lawrence Southwick. The Dow Chemical Co., Midland, Mich. 48640. Illus. Circ: 30,000.

Besides napalm, the Dow Chemical Company manufactures agricultural chemicals, and this is "a review of agricultural and chemical progress for those engaged in agricultural research, extension and instruction in U.S. and Canada." Detailed, technical research reports emphasizing valid research methods include summarized results and references cited. The eight to ten articles are concerned with agricultural problems and successes for which Dow and other chemicals are available or on which this company is continuing research. A few articles discuss other (non-chemical) agricultural topics, and contributions from outside U.S.A. are welcomed. Articles are signed, and credits indicate authors representing the research staffs of the company, universities, the U.S. Department of Agriculture, industrial concerns, and research organizations of wide scope. Black and white photos, charts, diagrams, tables and summaries. In addition to its usefulness in advanced agricultural study, this may have some value to students of chemistry, and may be useful also for demonstrating detailed research procedures and presentation.

Engineering Bulletin. 1952. q. Darrell Thorpe. Govt. Electronics Div., Motorola Inc., 8201 E. McDowell Rd., Scottsdale, Ariz. 85252. Illus. Circ: 12,000.

Highly technical articles in the field of spacecraft and military communications equipment restrict the usefulness of this to those concerned with engineering in this field and to teachers and specializing students. Each of the three or four articles is written by engineers and officials of the several systems and divisions of this corporation. Dan Noble, Vice Chairman of the Board and Chief Technical Officer of the company, writes editorially and very perceptively, in each issue, on the relationship of man to the new concepts of space age technology, and especially to the electronic information processing system. Diagrams constitute the bulk of the illustrations, but a few sketches and photographs are used.

Focus. 1929. semi-ann. J. M. Donovan. Bausch & Lomb, 619 St. Paul St., Rochester, N.Y. 14602. Illus., adv. Circ: 64,000.

Focus is published to explain and promote the use of Bausch & Lomb scientific optical instruments, as well as to promote interest in scientific investigation and research on several levels. Each issue contains about four 4- to 6-page articles, of fairly substantial content, on a level useful in secondary school teaching. Predictions of the impact of new technologies on such things as the office or library of the future are occasionally included. Articles are all signed, and contributors represent science teachers, laboratory personnel and others interested in scientific research throughout the country. "Techniques" by Germain Crossman of the B&L laboratory staff suggests procedures and techniques and helpful tips for persons involved in the teaching of science and in scientific laboratory work in general. The small size (6″ × 9″), neat format, adequate illustrations and minimal advertising contribute to the value of *Focus* as a general scientific periodical.

Ford Times. m. Ray Forrest. Ford Motor Co., American Rd., Dearborn, Mich. 48121. Illus., adv. Circ: 1,500,000.

This pocket-sized, well illustrated magazine is probably one of the better known house organs. It has one of the widest distributions and is geared specifically for the general public, hopefully the Ford buyer. Averaging 30 to 40 pages, it features consistently well written articles on food, travel, automobiles, camping, and outdoor living. There is a minimum of advertising. Many of the articles give background history on a part of the United States, or serve to assist the reader in making plans for a vacation trip. Some of the pieces may be nicely lifted and used in the library's vertical file. The style of writing is purposefully simple, and it is well within the grasp of the junior or senior high school student. A recommended magazine for almost all libraries.

Ford Truck Times. 1952. q. John J. Dabrowski. Ford Truck Times, c/o J. Walter Thompson Advertising, 420 Lexington Ave., New York, N.Y. 10017. Illus. Circ: 2,100,000.

Articles on a wide variety of travel, sports, adventure and general interest topics all include some tie-in with Ford trucks. A few give driving and safety tips for truckers. Advice for campers is associated with information on Ford trucks and truck mounted campers. Each 32-page issue includes about twelve 2- to 3-page articles, and all, except the Ford model promotional pieces, are signed. Good-quality color and black and white photos illustrate all articles. Suitable for junior high school libraries.

Form and Function. 1964. q. George E. Harper. U.S. Gypsum Co., 11 S. Wacker Drive, Chicago, Ill. 60606. Illus. Circ: 18,000.

A "United States Gypsum publication serving architects, engineers and specifiers." Its 16 pages include three to five service-type articles on building techniques and design, and developments in the building materials field that affect design and structural systems of building. Included are noteworthy school and college buildings. An occasional detailed article includes some specifications and detailed descriptions. Construction features where such products as plaster, wallboard, and acoustical materials may be used are emphasized. Staff-written and illustrated with photos, drawings and charts. Subject matter will be of interest to school administrators, developers, and youth selecting a career, as well as the architects, engineers, and building owners for whom it is primarily intended.

Friends. m. Alexander Suczek. Ceco Publishing Co., Department FM, 4–213 General Motors Bldg., Detroit, Mich. 48202. Illus. Circ: 2,300,000.

Published for owners of Chevrolet autos, subscriptions are handled through local dealers. Its purpose is to provide picture articles suggesting points of interest to be visited by automobile (Chevrolet, that is). Subject matter is usually American, with only occasional articles on foreign subjects, and the range of topics includes sports, fashions, travel, human interest, art, music, and theatre, among others. Excellent quality color photography, and some black and white photos are used for illustrations, as well as some commercial art and maps. Suitable for junior high school libraries.

The Grace Log. 1918. q. John A. Murray. W. R. Grace & Co., 7 Hanover Sq., New York, N.Y. 10027. Illus., adv. Circ: 90,000.

An "international industrial concern with chemical, food, petroleum and transportation interests" publishes this magazine. It reflects the very wide spectrum of interests of the company, and only a small amount of it is promotional in tone. Subjects of the 1,000- to 4,000-word articles cover many facets of business and economics, manufacturing processes, research and planning, and new developments related to the firm's products and interests. Travel articles place some emphasis on Latin America. Illustrations are of excellent quality, mostly in color, and especially noteworthy are the industrial process photos. Policy indicates that libraries and schools are a major consideration in editorial planning, and much of the material presented would most certainly be useful, especially in secondary school libraries.

Habitat. 1958. bi-m. E. H. Q. Smith. Central Mortgage & Housing Corp., Canadian Govt., Montreal Rd., Ottawa, Ont. Illus. Circ: 3,400.

Habitat is concerned with describing the housing and living environment of Canadians. Although a bi-lingual (English and French) publication, only a few of the articles appear in both languages. Material is approached mainly from a sociological standpoint, with emphasis on problems of urban growth in relation to population increases. New concepts of multiple unit construction are described. The magazine policy accepts the trend toward larger urban population, and the realization that only through thorough study may some of its attendant problems be solved. Articles, illustrated with black and white photos, run from 2 to 6 pages, and issues vary from 28 to 56 pages. Writing style assumes a serious interest in urban problems, but not necessarily specialized training or education in this field.

Inland News. 1946. q. Jerome A. Schmitt. Inland Steel Co., 30 W. Monroe St., Chicago, Ill. 60603. Illus. Circ: 42,000.

In-depth articles, with clear, well chosen photos, tell the complete story of some of the many facets of the steel industry. Industrial planning, steelmaking developments, and quality control are discussed, with implications for any other industry of similar size. Although limited to 16 to 20 pages per issue, material in these well-written articles will be useful where the overall picture of a large industry is needed. Illustrations are black and white photos in generous quantity. There is a minimal amount of employee news.

International Harvester World. bi-m. free. Gerald D. Hurley. Intl. Harvester Co., 180 N. Michigan Ave., Chicago, Ill. 60611. Illus. Circ: 80,000.

Published by a leading manufacturer of trucks, farm machinery and construction equipment, this presents largely pictorial material. Most issues have a theme, with several related articles. The use of trucks and heavy automotive equipment give glimpses of unusual occupations, enterprises and adventures. Personalities are highlighted: those related to form life, typical native workers in the I–H manufacturing plants in various countries, etc. Illustrations are good quality black and white photographs, and there is no advertising. Material will be of value for a superficial study of life in some foreign countries. Suitable for junior high school libraries.

Lamp. 1918. 4/yr. William L. Copithorne. Standard Oil Co. (N.J.), 30 Rockefeller Plaza, New York, N.Y. 10020. Illus. Circ: 790,000.

While "published primarily for shareholders and employees . . ." and centered around material relating to the oil industry, this has a much wider reader interest. Unusually well illustrated and well written, its chief concerns are information about and interpretation of various facets of company operation: its computer system, and a training program for tanker sea captains, for instance. Other articles are a valuable source of information on aspects of life in many parts of the world. There are travel articles, affairs or celebrations of unusual interest, historical items in the field of transportation, and accomplishments of modern engineering. Its excellent illustrations are almost all colored photographs of remarkable quality, with some sketches, art reproductions, and a few charts.

Kaiser Builder. 1953. m. Free to qualified personnel and libraries. Roger M. Denney. Henry J. Kaiser Co., Engineers Div., 300 Lakeside Drive, Oakland, Calif. 94604. Illus. Circ: 9,500.

A publication of Kaiser Engineers, who "provide consulting, design, engineering and construction services to industries and governments throughout the world," *Kaiser Builder* tells the story and promotes the interests of metallurgical and construction engineering in general. Each issue usually has a theme or a major article of 4 to 5 pages centered around such topics as metal processing, or hydro-electric power plant construction. Some shorter articles are included on similar topics. Of special interest to young people considering a career in this field are articles on "How Engineering Societies Promote Professionalism," as well as its general picture of construction engineering. Articles are staff written, and some are largely pictorial. Illus-

trations are photographs in black and white, plus drawings, diagrams and charts. No advertising.

Maine Line. 1952. bi-m. free. Richard W. Sprague. Bangor & Aroostook Railroad Co., 84 Harlow St., Bangor, Me. 04401. Circ: 6,000.

While primarily published for employees and customers of this northern Maine area, this has much of interest for the general reader. Some aspect of railroading is included in its four to five feature articles per issue, as is material on agriculture or other enterprises indigenous to the area. Solutions to some railroading problems which have been solved by this progressive line, and applications of new equipment to general railroad use, or to use in a northern climate often appear. Safety information figures importantly, offering substantial advice to railroad personnel, and to the general public regarding conduct on railroad property. Unsigned articles range in length, up to about 1,500 words. Several pages of personnel news are included in each issue. Black and white photos of excellent quality illustrate all articles, and the large photo used for the cover pertains to one of the features in the issue.

Mainliner. 1956. m. Norman V. Richards. United Air Lines Exec. Office, P.O. Box 66100, O'Hare Intl. Airport, Chicago, Ill. 60666. Illus., adv. Circ: 350,000.

"For the 27 million travelers who fly the friendly skies of United," *Mainliner* provides a general interest magazine with emphasis on travel, celebrities, and interesting personalities. Material is well selected and copiously and colorfully illustrated. Travel subjects are usually related to areas served by this airline, and include some unusual spots. Signed articles vary in length from 2 to 5 pages, including illustrations, and are written for the general adult reader. The 6 to 8 pages of advertising present auxiliary services such as auto rentals, hotel accommodations, etc. Library usefulness of *Mainliner,* in addition to its general interest matter, will be for the travel articles and excellent illustrations. Suitable for junior high school libraries.

New Jersey Bell. 1927. bi-m. Robert H. Yard. N.J. Bell Telephone Co., Rm. 1705, 540 Broad St., Newark, N.J. 07101. Illus. Circ: 31,000.

Most issues explain a specific job with the phone company, as illustrated by a particular employee. Technological advances and forward-looking applications of new devices are reported and explained, and material on safety, as well as other areas of public service, is included in almost every issue. A few of the five or six articles per issue are signed, and the style of writing is journalistic, with profuse illustrations consisting largely of black and white photos. The greatest value of this magazine for the library will be for career material, and an up-to-date picture of the telephone company.

The Ohio Bell. 1921. bi-m. Norman C. Treadon. The Ohio Bell Telephone Co., 100 Erieview Plaza, Cleveland, Ohio 44115. Illus. Circ: 31,500.

Published "for the information of its employees," *The Ohio Bell* contains material of general interest in addition to news of company personnel. Material follows a theme, with several related articles. Topics increasingly tend to reflect social concern, and often include an attempt at interpretation of the joint responsibility of industrial management and social agencies. An innovation for 1968 is the inclusion of articles in each issue by Ohio educators on topics of current concern. Other material is staff-written, and each issue of this 44- to 48-page magazine presents six to eight general articles in addition to the employee oriented material. Illustrations are largely photos, some colored, and writing style is geared to the general reader.

Ohio Bell Voice. 1953. bi-m. Norman C. Treadon. Ohio Bell Telephone Co., 100 Erieview Plaza, Cleveland, Ohio 44115.

Ohio Bell Voice is characterized by its editors as the "external house organ" of the company, and tends to reflect social concern. The editor further claims that it is quoted by schools, labor unions, churches and even state governments. Topics covered in its ten to twelve articles per issue include telephone company operations of general interest, other manufactures and services prominent in Ohio, and ways in which the modern telecommunication industry serves all types of businesses. A good feature, of wide general interest is "The Heritage of Ohio" appearing in each issue. A fairly long article on local history, it appears to be authoritative (although not documented), and is illustrated with excellent quality color and black and white reproductions of paintings, old prints, etc. Vignettes of unusual service rendered in times of emergency by telephone operators present a human interest angle. Illustrations for articles consist mainly of photographs, some in color, of good quality, and a minimal amount of company advertising is included. This may be useful, beyond Ohio, for a wide sampling of the ways in which the telephone company serves industry and the public. The local history will be of interest generally for students of American history and sociology.

Oil: Lifestream of Progress. q. Peter A. Kozack. California Texas Oil Corp., 380 Madison Ave., New York, N.Y. 10017. Illus. Circ: 50,000.

An excellent 24-page magazine to help interpret the role of petroleum in the modern world. Articles cover a wide variety of topics within the general area of international industry and trade, communications and unusual tourist attractions and events of international interest. Especially valuable for their content and pictures are the articles on what modern engineering is doing to help modernize underdeveloped areas. While there is generally a company tie-in, it is done tastefully and unobtrusively. Editorial tone is uncritical, and emphasis in on achievement and long range planning. Articles are unsigned, and credit for good writing must go to the fine editorial staff. Each of the four articles is profusely illustrated with very good black and white and color photographs, a few sketches and maps and

charts where pertinent. Suitable for junior high school libraries.

Petroleum Today. 1959. q. Robert W. Stock. Amer. Petroleum Inst., 1271 Ave. of the Americas, New York, N.Y. 10020. Illus. Circ: 125,000.

Signed, well-written articles cover topics of general interest on all phases of petroleum and related products and activities. A wide variety is achieved within these limitations, including such aspects as exploration, experimentation and research, background material on localities, related products, operations, and personalities. Length of articles varies, as does relative amount of text to number of illustrations, but all articles are nicely illustrated in black and white and in color, with drawings and sketches, and some beautiful examples of artistic color photography. Suitable for junior high school libraries.

Power Parade. 1947. q. E. J. Baldwin. General Motors Corp., Detroit Diesel Engine Div., 13400 W. Outer Drive, Detroit, Mich. 48228. Illus. Circ: 225,000.

"A magazine for the information and entertainment of users of heavyduty power," its interest extends beyond "users" to those concerned with related industry, to students of industry and social studies, or young people faced with the selection of a career. Road building, major construction projects and marine use of diesel power are frequent subjects. Staff-written articles run from 1 to 6 pages in length, and highlight the performance and desirability of various GM diesel engine models. Value of the material is increased by profuse full-color illustrations of exceptionally high quality. Diagrams and maps are occasionally added to the many color photographs. High quality paper and pleasing type face are other good features. Suitable for junior high school libraries.

The Practicing Veterinarian. q. Allen Baker. The Dow Chemical Co., P.O. Box 512, Midland, Mich. 48640.

A magazine for those raising animals for market, and for scientists and educational institutions concerned with this field. Each issue includes up to twenty articles of varying length, largely staff-written. Featured is valid research on controlled experiments in livestock and poultry feeding and diseases, written by the Dow Company staff, or reprinted from scholarly journals. Successful programs carried out by livestock and poultry raisers, and types of equipment used, are reported in other articles of varying length. Black and white photos, and graphs and charts. Usefulness of this small size, 32-page magazine will be limited to a specialized field, but it is definitely recommended where reader interest warrants it.

Rockwell-Standard News. q. Ernest Rowland. North Amer. Rockwell Corp., Commercial Products Group, Clifford at Bagley, Detroit, Mich. 48231. Illus. Circ: 32,000.

Material includes the area of manufacturing related to trucking and other forms of transportation. Unusual uses of trucks and heavy equipment are shown in domestic and foreign settings. Articles are well written, adequately illustrated, and thorough in their presentation, often including historical background, and must be credited to the editorial staff.

School Product News. 1961. m. Free to school and college executives and administrations; $12 to others. J. Arlen Marsh. School Products News, Industrial Publishing Co., 812 Huron Rd., Cleveland, Ohio 44115.

Provides a service in presenting information on the whole gamut of products pertinent to equipping, servicing and administering a school. Information is presented in short items under one of the sections, "Buyer's Fact File," "Product Briefs," or "Audio-Visuals," which are arranged with no particular continuity, and share all pages about equally with advertising. Included in these sections are audio-visual equipment and storage facilities, playground equipment, furniture and floor coverings, secretarial and teaching supplies, food service needs, and building maintenance equipment and supplies. Data is clear and concise, is factual rather than evaluative, but does not include prices. A few short articles report the installation and/or use of certain products or equipment at a particular school, giving details of the item used. A book review section is included in some issues, evaluating two or three books related to some technical aspect of education, such as the use of new devices or equipment, as well as encyclopedias, atlases, etc., and books on teaching methods and administration. Format is oversized.

Selmer Bandwagon. 1952. 5/yr. Harry Randall. H.&A. Selmer, Inc., P.O. Box 310, Elkhart, Ind. 46514. Illus., adv. Circ: 45,000.

Published by a manufacturer of band instruments as a service to band directors and players, especially at the high school level. Material is of interest primarily to wind instrumentalists. A few historical items appear, relating to specific compositions, old instruments, or unusual musical events. A series on national anthems is especially good. "Careers in Music" is a valuable feature appearing in almost every issue. In 3- to 4-page articles, sound factual information is given by someone engaged in a specific musical career: teaching, performing, managing, or some other area closely allied to music. Selections for various types of performances are often suggested, though scores are, of course, not reproduced. The signed articles vary in length, and content is generally substantial but not so scholarly as to discourage high school students. Illustrations and the general format of the magazine are excellent. Advertising of Selmer instruments is minimal. Suitable for junior high school libraries.

Skyline. 1951. q. Edward A. Herron. North Amer. Rockwell Corp., Aerospace and Systems Group, 1700 E. Imperial Highway, El Segundo, Calif. 90246. Illus. Circ: 110,000.

Concentration on the scientific and technical aspects of the national aerospace program. Some issues have a central theme of current importance to the space program, with several related articles making up the bulk of the 48-page issue. Other material emphasizes pure research, scientific technique, development of new products, and research in areas only loosely related to the aerospace endeavor. Length of articles varies from 2 to 10 pages, all are well illustrated with black and white photos and a few drawings, and a very few articles presented are largely pictorial. Most are signed, some by members of the staff, and all seem to be completely authoritative. Writing style is geared to the adult reader interested in this field, and in some of the more technical articles, vocabulary used assumes some scientific background on the part of the reader. Company tie-in is minimal, and *Skyline* makes a good contribution to the current information available in the aerospace field.

Steelways. 1945. 5/yr. Edw. J. Lally. Amer. Iron & Steel Inst., 150 E. 42nd St., New York, N.Y. 10017. Illus. Circ: 300,000.

This magazine presents in general, a description of the role of steel in economic and social life, and its contribution to progress of the nation. Subject matter covers a wide range of interests, but with some tie-in to the use of steel. This point is stressed in the articles, whether it be the steel machinery used to load and unload an ore boat on the Great Lakes, steel sewing machines used to stitch up costumes for a season of the Metropolitan Opera, or steel building materials in an urban renewal project. News of, and articles directly related to, the steel industry are included in every issue. Writing style is forthright, and directed to the average intelligent reader. Illustrations are generally good, and color photography, on about half of the pages, is of superior quality. Suitable for junior high school libraries.

Surveyor. 1967. q. Free. Michael J. Robinson, Amer. Bureau of Shipping, 45 Broad St., New York, N.Y. 10004.

Although issued by the American Bureau of Shipping, coverage in this beautifully illustrated, 32-page magazine is international. A recent issue, for example, included an article on Brazil's shipbuilding, and a world wide tour of a unique oceanographic vessel. Photo essays move from historical material to current activities in American shipping. Most of the material is non-technical, easily within the grasp of the interested layman, and high school or college student. The black and white illustrations are particularly useful where there is a need for material on ships, ship building, and navigation. Worth a try by almost every type of library.

Think. 1935. bi-m. J. B. O'Connell. Intl. Business Machines Corp., Armonk, New York, N.Y. 10504. Illus., adv. Circ: 160,000.

Probably one of the best known company magazines in the United States (as much for its age as for its title), this is not intended primarily for company employees nor is it an advertising vehicle. The authors are recognized public figures, commissioned to write on topics covering a wide range of problems of modern living. Typical articles examine such topics as the impact of the new technology upon employment and the economy, the information explosion, poverty and overpopulation, trends in higher education, techniques of management, and innovations in science and medicine. The style is good to excellent, the viewpoint conservative to liberal, and there is little evidence of IBM. In view of its scope and relatively high quality it can be recommended for high schools and most public libraries.

Transmission. 1953. q. Frank Barak. Public Relations Dept., Northern Natural Gas Co., 2223 Dodge St., Omaha, Neb. 68102. Illus. Circ: 30,000.

Articles are largely confined to the Northern Plains States, and stress economic and civic problems and progress. Industrial activity of natural gas distributing, as well as other manufacturing education, civic improvement, agriculture and geography of the region, and sports and entertainment are included among the popularly written, profusely illustrated articles. While specifically confined to an eight-state area served by the company, the examples of progress and accomplishment and of civic enterprise may be of interest to communities outside this area which are faced with similar problems. Suitable for junior high school libraries.

Virginia Highway Bulletin. 1934. m. Free to employees, other highway organizations, and on request, to libraries. Floyd H. Mihill. Virginia Dept. of Highways, 1221 E. Broad St., Richmond, Va. 23219. Illus. Circ: 12,000.

A picture for one state which is largely typical of many states. The reader is given an insight into areas of highway planning, the officials involved, and basic principles of highway engineering which might not be obvious to the highway user. Progress reports, with excellent photos for illustration, are included on some of the many arterials and super-highways now under construction in the state. Each issue contains an article of 1 to 2 pages on some aspect of safe driving, stressing human factors such as drinking, and external factors such as weather. Related material is also included, such as the Department's concern for archaeological finds, and occasionally some seasonal material of general interest. Articles are fairly short (500–1,000 words), some are signed, other staff-written, and all are well composed. Purely personal news of department personnel and their families about one third of the magazine's 36 pages. The format is small size (6″ × 9″) with high quality paper and well designed covers.

Ward's Bulletin. 1962. 8/yr. Henry L. Gresham. Ward's Natural Science Establishment, P.O. Box 1712, Rochester, N.Y. 14603; Ward's of California, P.O. Box 1749, Monterey, Calif. 93942. Illus. Circ: 50,000.

One major article, several columns, and news of new products being presented by the company, concentrate a large amount of information into this 8-page leaflet primarily intended for college and secondary school science teachers. An article (up to 2,000 words) written by a company staff member or by an educator or scientist, usually covers the natural history, geology and/or customs of some relatively remote or little known area of the world. "Teacher Workshop Notes" reports seminars and workshops for science teachers which have been held, and summarizes their achievements, and also publishes letters of comment and announcement on such programs of interest to science educators. "Geo-Topics," a signed column, discusses some phase of geology, usually relative to a specific geographical area. Publications and other teaching aids are described, potential uses explained, and prices listed. Small but excellent black and white photos illustrate all material.

Weyerhaeuser Magazine. 1949. 9/yr. Herb Williams. Weyerhaeuser Co., Tacoma Bldg., Tacoma, Wash. 98401. Illus. Circ: 40,000.

Articles cover primarily wood and paper manufacturing and related products, and specific plants and processes in this company's operations. Some interesting aspects of wildlife conservation are brought out, in line with Weyerhaeuser's firmly established policy in the field of conservation. Other material in the five to seven articles per issue, concerning safety, communications and personnel relations and welfare, while specifically illustrating the lumber industry, can readily be related to other large establishments or industries. Regional descriptions of areas of Weyerhaeuser operation are occasionally included. Articles are unsigned and vary in length from 3 to 6 pages, including copious, high quality black and white photos illustrating the text. Those with special interest in the lumber and paper industry and in conservation of natural resources will find useful mtaerial here. Suitable for junior high school libraries.

Weyerhaeuser News. 3/yr. Harry Groom. Weyerhaeuser Co., Tacoma Bldg., Tacoma, Wash. 98401. Illus. Circ: 110,000.

Subject matter centers around the lumber industry and its diversified products in this attractive, larger than average size (11″ × 14″) magazine. A wide variety of related topics is presented: research in the field of soil and mineral surveys, development of new products, uses of wood and derivative products, a few historical items, outdoor sports and industry related problems such as air and water pollution. Large, fine quality illustrations, and choice quality paper add to the attractiveness of the magazine. In addition to the general reader, this will be of special interest to students concerned with, or contemplating a career in forestry or the paper industry.

(c) STANDARDS FOR QUANTITATIVE SELECTION

The American Library Association and its various divisions and committees have consistently worked for improving all types of libraries in the United States. The principal guidelines for librarians, trustees and laymen have been the "Standards," a group of documents which present minimum standards for service. Admittedly, the guidelines are often beyond what libraries have achieved, or are likely to achieve in the next few years. Quite frankly, they are representative of optimum conditions. Yet, they ask no more than the type of service every citizen deserves.

In this series, the most helpful "standards" are those for public libraries and schools—at least in terms of magazine selection. These tend to be relatively exact. Conversely, the criteria for junior college and college collections are considerably more generalized.

What follows are quantitative suggestions from the "standards" as applicable to magazines. Suggestions as to need, preservation, etc., are not included here. Quotes are from the sources, unless otherwise indicated, and all are published by the American Library Association.

(1) *Standards for School Media Programs*, 1969. 66pp.

(2) *Minimum Standards for Public Library Systems, 1966.* 1967. 69pp.

(3) *Interim Standards for Small Public Libraries.* 1962. 16pp.

(4) Standards for Junior College Libraries. *American Library and Book Trade Annual* (1961) N.Y., Bowker, 1960. pp.127–32.

(5) Standards for College Libraries. *College and Research Libraries,* July 1959, pp.274–80.

A. SCHOOL LIBRARIES

(1) "The standards recomemnded for schools of 250 students or over are as follows:

Elementary School (K–6)	40–50 titles includes some adult non professional periodicals)
Elementary School (K–8)	50–75 titles
Junior high school	100–125 titles
Secondary schools	125–175 titles
All schools	In addition: necessary magazine indexes and duplication of titles and indexes as required." *Standards for School Media Programs,* p. 30.)

(2) For teachers, the following are "recommended for the professional collection of books and periodicals in schools of 250 students or over:

Magazines:	40–50 professional titles, with duplication as needed; also *Education Index.*" (*Standards for School Media Programs,* p. 33.)

B. PUBLIC LIBRARIES

(1) "At least one currently published periodical title should be available for each 250 people in the service area." (*Minimum Standards for Public Library Systems.* p.43.)

(2) "Each community library needs a periodical collection which should be maintained as follows:

POPULATION	MAGAZINES AND NEWSPAPERS RECEIVED	BACK FILES TO BE KEPT ACCORDING TO USE AND INDEXING
Under 2,500	at least 25	1–5 years
2,500 to 4,999	25–50	1–5 years
5,000 to 9,999	50–75	1–10 years
10,000 to 24,999	75–100	1–10 years
25,000 to 49,999	100–150	1–10 years"

(*Interim Standards for Small Public Libraries.* p.8.)

Some indication of actual practice is found in the University of Illinois Library School Occasional Papers, No. 61, "Reference Services in American Public Libraries Serving Populations of 10,000 or More" (Processed. Urbana: Univ.

of Illinois Library School, 1961. 22pp). Although now well over 10 years old, the study revealed that the medium number of magazine titles in small public libraries was 61; in medium sized libraries, 153, and in large libraries, 458. And only slightly more than 40 percent took more than a single periodical index, i.e., the *Readers' Guide* (p.9).

C. JUNIOR COLLEGE LIBRARIES

Periodicals constitute an invaluable source of reference for material on many subjects. They should be selected by the librarian, with the assistance of the faculty. The periodical subscription list should be well balanced. It should include titles of lasting reference value as well as journals helpful to the faculty or appealing to the younger college readers.

Junior college libraries should have on their subscription list some outstanding foreign periodicals such as *The Economist, The London Times, Manchester Guardian, Realities,* and the *Times Literary Supplement,* as a guard against provincialism. (*Standards for Junior College Libraries.*)

At this writing the standards for junior colleges have not been revised. Still, a useful survey indicates probable standards for magazine collections: Tanis, Norman E., and Milton Powers, "Profiles of Practice in the Public Junior College Library," *College and Research Libraries* (Sept., 1967. pp.331–336). The authors established a profile which indicated:

(1) "Median Benchmarks for 1963–64. Number of periodicals being received at end of year. . . . 287.

(2) "Seventy-Fifth Percentile Benchmarks for 1963–64. Number of periodicals being received at end of year . . . 372."

D. COLLEGE AND UNIVERSITY LIBRARIES

"The periodicals subscription list should be well balanced and carefully chosen to meet the requirements of students for collateral course reading, to provide in some measure for the research needs of advanced students and faculty, to keep the faculty informed of developments in their fields, and to afford thought-provoking general and recreational reading." (*Standards for College Libraries.* p.277.)

(d) SELECT LISTS

Select Lists for:

Small and Medium Sized Public Libraries
Elementary Schools
Junior High Schools
Senior High Schools
Teachers' Professional Collection
Book Reviews
Basic Science Journals for the Non-Specialist

(1) Entries are given in order of preference of the consultant and the compiler.

(2) Not all subjects are considered, only those of the widest interest.

(3) The lists are suggestive. The librarian must choose on the basis of need, not on this or any other list's suggestions.

(4) All lists quantitatively meet the various standards established by the American Library Association. Qualitatively, the lists represent a balance between what the compiler believes is best and what public taste seems to consider important. At best, this is a compromise—balanced somewhat by comments found in the annotations.

(5) At the end of this section, the reader will find "A Basic List of Scientific Journals for the Non-Specialist" prepared by the ALA. Hopefully this will help to meet an important (and often unmet!) need of the librarian.

(6) Finally, it is strongly urged that anyone using the lists consult them all. A public librarian will find much of value in the school lists, a school librarian should examine the "Teachers' Professional Collection," etc.

SMALL AND MEDIUM SIZED PUBLIC LIBRARIES

AERONAUTICS

Flying, Space World, Aviation Week, American Aviation.

AFRICAN STUDIES

Africa Report, Africa Today, Pan African Journal.

AFRO-AMERICAN

Ebony, Negro Digest, Freedomways, Liberator.

AGRICULTURE

Farm Quarterly, Farm Journal, Successful Farming.

ANTHROPOLOGY AND ARCHAEOLOGY

Antiquity, Archaeology, Current Anthropology.

ANTIQUES

Hobbies, Spinning Wheel.

ARCHITECTURE

Architectural Record, Architectural Forum, Historic Preservation.

ART & DESIGN

Art in America, Artforum, Metropolitan Museum Art Bulletin, Art International.

ASTRONOMY

Review of Popular Astronomy, Sky and Telescope.

ATMOSPHERIC SCIENCE

Weatherwise, Weather.

AUTOMATION

Computers and Automation, Datamation.

AUTOMOBILES

Motor Trend, Autocar, Road and Track, Automobile Quarterly.

BANKING & FINANCE (See also, Business & Industry, and Economics)

Exchange, Financial World.

BIBLIOGRAPHY (See also, Libraries)

Publishers' Weekly, AB Bookman's Weekly.

BIOLOGICAL SCIENCES

Animal Behavior.

BOATS AND BOATING

Boating, Rudder, Yachting.

BOOK REVIEWS

Library Journal and School Library Journal, New York Times Book Review, Booklist & Subscription Books Bulletin, New York Review of Books.

BUSINESS & INDUSTRY

Business Week, Fortune, Forbes, Nation's Business.

CHEMISTRY

Chemistry.

CHILDREN

Children's Magazines.

CHILDREN'S MAGAZINES

See section of this title. Choice depends upon age groups served.

CITIES AND TOWNS

City, National Civic Review.

CLASSICAL STUDIES

Greek Heritage.

CONSERVATION

National Wildlife, Living Wilderness, Sierra Club Bulletin, National Parks Magazine.

CRAFTS AND HOBBIES

See section of this title. Choices other than those that follow depend upon community interests. Popular Science, Popular Mechanics, Craft Horizon.

CRIMINOLOGY AND LAW ENFORCEMENT

Federal Probation.

DANCE

Dance Magazine, Dance Perspectives, Sets in Order.

DISSIDENT MAGAZINES

See section of this title. Choices other than those that follow depend upon community interests. Left of Center: I. F. Stone's Weekly; Right of Center: Human Events; Pacifist: News Notes.

EARTH SCIENCES

Earth Science, Sea Frontiers.

ECONOMICS

Challenge.

EDUCATION

Childhood Education, Education Digest, PTA Magazine, Today's Education, American Education.

Educational News Magazines: The New York Times Student Weekly.

FISHING AND HUNTING

American Sportsman, Outdoor Life, Sporting Times, Field and Stream.

FOLKLORE

Journal of American Folklore, Western Folklore. See also, various regional folklore journals.

FOREIGN LANGUAGE MAGAZINES

See sections of these titles: German Language, Romance Languages, Slavic Languages. Choices depend upon community needs and interest.

GAMES AND SPORTS

See section of this title. Choices other than those that follow depend upon community interests. Sports Illustrated, Sports.

GARDENING (See also, Home)

Flowers and Garden, Plants and Gardens, Home Garden and Flower Grower.

GENERAL MAGAZINES (See also: Literary and Political Reviews, Men's Magazines, Women's Magazines)

Newsweek, New York Times Magazine, New Yorker, Look, Life, Unesco Courier.

GEOGRAPHY

National Geographic, Focus.

HISTORY

American: American Heritage, The American West, American History Illustrated.

General: Horizon, History Today, English Historical Review, The Americas.

HOME

Consumer Reports, Better Homes and Gardens, American Home, Consumer Bulletin, Changing Times, House and Garden.

JOURNALISM

Columbia Journalism Review, Writer's Digest, Editor & Publisher.

LABOR & INDUSTRIAL RELATIONS

American Labor Magazine, Monthly Labor Review.

LAW

Law and Contemporary Problems.

LIBRARIES

Library Journal and School Library Journal, Top-of-the-News, A.L.A. Bulletin, Wilson Library Bulletin.

LINGUISTICS & PHILOLOGY

ETC.

LITERARY & POLITICAL REVIEWS

Emphasis on political/social issues: The Nation, Ramparts, National Review, New Statesman.

Religious oriented political/social: Christian Century (Protestant), Commentary (Jewish), Commonweal (Catholic).

Emphasis on literary/social issues: Harper's Magazine, Saturday Review, Columbia University Forum, American Scholar, Atlantic Monthly, Evergreen Review, Tri-Quarterly.

LITTLE MAGAZINES

The Outsider, The Smith, City Lights Journal.

MATHEMATICS

Journal of Recreational Mathematics.

MEDICAL, NURSING, & HEALTH SCIENCES

Today's Health, World Health, Medical Economics.

MEN'S MAGAZINES

Esquire, True, Playboy, Frontier Times (or any Western magazine listed).

MOTION PICTURES

Film Library Quarterly, Film Quarterly, Film Comment.

MUSIC

High Fidelity *or* Hi/Fi Stereo Review, Downbeat, Crawdaddy, Audio.

MYSTERY & DETECTIVE STORIES

Ellery Queen's Mystery Magazine, The Armchair Detective.

OFFICE & SECRETARIAL PRACTICES

From Nine to Five, Today's Secretary.

ORNITHOLOGY

Audubon Magazine, Massachusetts Audubon.

PETS

See section of this title. Choice depends upon community interests.

PHOTOGRAPHY

Popular Photography, Modern Photography, U.S. Camera, Camera.

PHYSICS

Physics Today.

POETRY

Poetry, The Sixties, Kayak.

POLITICAL SCIENCE

Current History, Congressional Digest, U.N. Monthly Chronicle, American Academy of Political and Social Sciences. Annals, Foreign Affairs, Vital Speeches.

PSYCHOLOGY

Psychology Today, Mental Hygiene, Psychiatry and Social Science Review.

RADIO, TELEVISION AND ELECTRONICS

Radio Electronics, QST, Popular Electronics, Electronics World.

RELIGION & THEOLOGY (See also, Literary & Political Reviews)

Journal of Ecumenical Studies. Catholic: National Catholic Reporter; Protestant: Christianity and Crisis; Jewish: American Judaism. Choosing among the last three would depend wholly upon patrons' desires. No preference is indicated by the order of their listing.

SCIENCE—GENERAL

Natural History, Scientific American, Science, Science News, Science & Technology, Environment, Endeavour.

SCIENCE FICTION

Analog, Science Fiction Times, Galaxy.

SOCIOLOGY

Trans-Action, International Social Science Journal, Journal of Human Relations, Happier Marriage and Planned Parenthood.

TEENAGE MAGAZINES

Eye, Way Forum, American Red Cross Journal, Seventeen, Noonmark.

THEATRE

Drama Review, Plays, Plays and Players.

TRAVEL

Holiday, Discovery, Travel.

VOCATIONS

Careers Today, Occupational Outlook Quarterly, Vocations for Social Change.

WOMEN'S MAGAZINES

McCalls, Harper's Bazaar, Good Housekeeping, Cosmopolitan.

ELEMENTARY SCHOOLS: GRADES K–6

Unless noted, titles listed below are adult. They are considered suitable as much for a lack of proper children's magazines in the subject areas as anything else. Often the textual material is beyond the reading capacities of the child, but may hold his interest because of the subject, illustrations, or format.

Magazines used by teachers with children, not by the children themselves, will be found listed in the Teachers' Professional Collection Section.

AFRO-AMERICAN

Ebony

ASTRONOMY

Review of Popular Astronomy

BOATS AND BOATING

Motor Boating

CHILDREN'S MAGAZINES

See section of this title.

COMICS

See section of this title.

CONSERVATION

Ranger Rick's Nature Magazine (child's title), World Wildlife Illustrated, National Wildlife.

CRAFTS AND HOBBIES

See section of this title. Choices other than those that follow depend upon children's interests. Pack-O-Fun (child's title; usually with adult help), Popular Science.

GAMES AND SPORTS

See section of this title. Choices other than those that follow depend upon child's interests. Sport, Sports Illustrated.

GENERAL

Life, Unesco Courier.

GEOGRAPHY

National Geographic, National Geographic Bulletin (A teacher's aid, but of interest to children), Focus.

HISTORY

American Heritage. Area History magazines specifically for children: Illinois History, The Yorker, Gopher Historian, Badger History.

MUSIC

Young Keyboard (Child's title. See Keyboard)

ORNITHOLOGY

Audubon, Canadian Audubon.

PETS

See section of this title. Choices depend upon child's interests.

SCIENCE—GENERAL

Nature and Science (Child's title), Natural History.

THEATRE

Plays (primarily a teaching aid).

TRAVEL

Arizona Highways, Wisconsin Tales and Trails.

JUNIOR HIGH SCHOOLS: GRADES 7–9

See introduction to Teenage Magazines.

Both the select lists for Elementary Schools and for Senior High Schools should be used in conjunction with any meaningful Junior High school collection.

Unless noted, all titles listed below are adult. Again, magazines used by teachers with children will be found listed in the Teachers' Professional Collection.

AERONAUTICS

Space World, Flying.

AFRO-AMERICAN

Ebony, Freedomways, Negro Digest.

AGRICULTURE

National 4-H News, National Future Farmer, Farm Quarterly.

ART & DESIGN

Art in America, Metropolitan Museum of Art. Bulletin.

ASTRONOMY

Review of Popular Astronomy, Sky & Telescope.

AUTOMOBILES

Hot Rod, Motor Trend, Car and Driver, Automobile Quarterly, Car Craft.

BOATS AND BOATING

Motor Boating, Rudder.

BOOK REVIEWS

The New York Times Book Review

CHILDREN'S MAGAZINES

See section of this title. A few titles listed are suitable for junior high schools.

CLASSICAL STUDIES

Greek Heritage

COMICS

See section of this title.

CONSERVATION

National Wildlife, Living Wilderness, World Wildlife Illustrated, National Parks Magazine.

CRAFTS AND HOBBIES

See section of this title. Choices other than those that follow depend upon child's interests: Popular Science, Popular Mechanics.

DANCE

Dance and Dancing, Sets in Order.

EARTH SCIENCES

Sea Frontiers

EDUCATION

Educational News Magazines: The New York Times Student Weekly.

ENGLISH

Read Magazine (used by teacher with students).

FISHING AND HUNTING

Outdoor Life, Field and Stream.

FOREIGN LANGUAGE MAGAZINES

See sections of these titles: German Language, Romance Languages, Slavic Languages.

GAMES AND SPORTS

See section of this title. Many others, other than those that follow, are suitable for junior high school students: Sports, Sports Illustrated.

GENERAL

Life, Look, Newsweek, Unesco Courier, Atlas.

GEOGRAPHY

National Geographic, Focus.

HISTORY

American Heritage, Horizon. Area History magazines for children: Illinois History, The Yorker, Gopher Historian, Badger History.

HOME

Co-Ed (for this age group).

JOURNALISM

Quill and Scroll (for this age group), Consumer Reports.

LITERARY AND POLITICAL VIEWS

None is entirely suitable for junior high school students' experience or reading level. In more advanced situations, the list for high schools should be consulted.

MATHEMATICS

Mathematics Student Journal

MEN'S MAGAZINES

See section of this title. Depending upon the school, the children's interests, and the attitude of librarian and parent, a few, such as *Esquire, True or Argosy,* may be considered suitable.

MOTION PICTURES

Educator's Guide to Media & Methods, Montage.

MUSIC

Crawdaddy, Sing Out, Guitar Player.

MYSTERY & DETECTIVE STORIES

Ellery Queen's Mystery Magazine

OFFICE & SECRETARIAL PRACTICES

Today's Secretary

ORNITHOLOGY

Audubon Magazine, Canadian Audubon.

PETS

See section of this title. Choices depend upon child's interests.

PHOTOGRAPHY

Popular Photography

POLITICAL SCIENCE

U.N. Monthly Chronicle

RADIO, TELEVISION & ELECTRONICS

Electronics Illustrated, Popular Electronics.

SCIENCE—GENERAL

Natural History, Science News, Scientific American.

SCIENCE FICTION

Analog, Galaxy.

TEENAGE MAGAZINES

See section of this title. Many titles listed here are suitable for junior high schools.

THEATRE

Plays (a teaching aid), Dramatics (a teaching aid).

TRAVEL

Arizona Highways, Holiday, Travel.

WIT & HUMOUR

Mad

WOMEN'S MAGAZINES

See section of this title. Depending upon the school, the children's interests, and the attitude of librarian and parent, a few may be considered suitable.

SENIOR HIGH SCHOOLS

The problem of selection for high school libraries, particularly at the senior high level, is one closer to that familiar to the public and academic librarian. It is not so much a matter of what is available (limited for elementary and junior high libraries) as what to eliminate. Almost all general adult, and a good many specialized adult magazines are suitable for high school students.

Selection seems often to be more a question of what the librarian thinks a boy or girl of this age should read, rather than what the student would choose to read. In most cases the *should* is an acceptable and logical argument, if only it exposes the student to magazines he will not likely find at home or on the local newsstand. Conversely, some attention must be given to the *would read* aspect, particularly for those students lacking the motivation or the intellect to appreciate adult reading at a college or post-college level.

Obviously both the community and the librarian will dictate how liberal or conservative the collection is to be, but there should be a middle ground where more than the tried, true and often dull magazines are displayed. To this end the following selection, while orthodox enough in most respects, takes a few steps towards the recognition that most senior high school students are more interested in their immediate world than the world of the librarian or teacher.

A suggestive study indicates that too frequently the notions of *would* and *should* are generations apart. Here, for example, is a listing of magazines preferred by high school students as contrasted with those ordered by librarians. (Squire, James R. "Student Reading and the High School Library." *School Libraries*, Summer 1967: Charts 5 & 6, pp.15–16.)

School Magazine Subscriptions Compared With Student Magazine Preferences

Libraries (*n* = 91)   Students (*n* = 15,874)

PERIODICAL	RANK ORDER OF FREQUENCY	PERCENT SUB-SCRIBING	RANK ORDER OF PREFERENCE	NUMBER TIMES MENTIONED
Saturday Review	1	99	27	163
Reader's Digest	2	98	6	1,877
U.S. News & World Report	3.5	97	12	575
Newsweek	3.5	97	7	1,616
Science Digest	5.5	96	—	—
National Geographic	5.5	96	9	855
Time	7	95	4	3,212
Popular Mechanics	9	93	26	168

PERIODICAL	RANK ORDER OF FREQUENCY	PERCENT SUB-SCRIBING	RANK ORDER OF PREFERENCE	NUMBER TIMES MENTIONED
Scientific American	9	93	24	176
Saturday Evening Post (Defunct)	9	93	2	4,700
Life	11	92	1	7,455
Atlantic Monthly	12.5	91	—	113
Harper's	12.5	91	—	118
Sports Illustrated	14.5	90	10	850
Popular Science	14.5	90	19	232
Current History	16	85	—	—
American Heritage	17	81	—	—
Theatre Arts (Defunct)	19	80	—	—
Vital Speeches	19	80	—	—
Seventeen	19	80	5	1,988
Look	21	79	3	4,291
Ladies Home Journal	22	73	11	589
McCalls	23	55	8	1,039
Hot Rod	24	48	13	398
Sports	25	25	15	333
Ingenue	26	12	14	338

Fifteen Most Popular Magazines Among Adolescents Compared to School Library Holdings

RANK IN STUDENTS POPULARITY	PERIODICAL	NUMBER OF TIMES RANKED FIRST BY STUDENTS	TOTAL NUMBER OF TIMES MENTIONED BY STUDENTS	PERCENTAGE OF LIBRARIES WITH PERIODICALS
1	Life	4,117	7,455	92
2	Post	1,743	4,700	93
3	Time	1,602	3,212	95
4	Look	1,356	4,291	79
5	Seventeen	892	1,988	80
6	Reader's Digest	632	1,877	98
7	Newsweek	577	1,616	97
8	McCalls	302	1,039	55
9	Sports Illustrated	297	850	90
10	National Geographic	285	855	96
11	Hot Rod	321	398	48
12	Sports	169	333	25
13	Ingenue	120	338	12
14	Ladies Home Journal	111	589	73
15	Playboy	106	264	0

Commenting on these statistics, the author observes that "there is no close correlation between magazines available in school libraries and those they (students) read frequently ... more thoughtful periodicals are seldom selected by students. *Mad Magazine,* in fact, accounted for forty more readers in the survey than either *Harper's* or *Atlantic Monthly.*" (Ibid) The author does not point out the obvious corollary that if *Reader's Digest* is a second choice of librarians, while *Harper's* and *Atlantic Monthly* are both twelfth, the example for teen-agers is a bit dismal. But what is good for the librarian's idea of his public, may not be good for that public's own impressions of its needs. To quote the author:

> "Perhaps a more disturbing result of comparing library magazine collections and student preferences is the number of magazines highly regarded by students not found in libraries. *Seventeen,* ranked fifth by students, is absent from 20 percent of the libraries; *Look,* ranked fourth, is missing from as many. *Hot Rod, Sports,* and *Ingenue,* ranked eleventh, twelfth, and thirteenth in student popularity, are present in only 48, 25, and 12 percent of the libraries. Although there is no evidence to prove that such magazines will provide important literary experiences for students, their absence may indirectly prevent students from becoming interested in any library reading at all." (Ibid)

One solution to the problem of conflicts is for the librarian to query the students as to what magazines they *would* care to read. Balanced with a *should read* approach, many collections will take on a considerably more realistic and meaningful appearance. (An interesting comparison is to compare the change of tastes in both librarians and students. See W. C. Eell's comparative study of some 30 years ago: "Periodicals Received By Secondary School Libraries," *Wilson Library Bulletin,* Nov., 1937.)

AERONAUTICS
Space World, Flying.

AFRICAN STUDIES
Africa Today, African Forum.

AFRO-AMERICAN
Freedomways, Ebony, Negro History Bulletin, Negro Digest.

AGRICULTURE
Farm Quarterly, National 4-H News, Foreign Agriculture, National Future Farmer.

ANTHROPOLOGY & ARCHAEOLOGY
Antiquity, Archaeology, Plains Anthropologist.

ANTIQUES
Hobbies

ARCHITECTURE
Architectural Record, Historic Preservation.

ART & DESIGN
Art in America, Metropolitan Museum of Art. Bulletin, Art-Forum, Handweaver & Craftsman.

ASTRONOMY
Review of Popular Astronomy, Sky and Telescope, Sun at Work.

ATMOSPHERIC SCIENCES
Weatherwise, Weather.

AUTOMOBILES
Hot Rod, Car & Driver, Motor Trend, Autocar, Automobile Quarterly.

BIOLOGICAL SCIENCES
BioScience.

BOATS AND BOATING
Motor Boating, Rudder, Yachting.

BOOK REVIEW MAGAZINES
New York Times Book Review, Book World.

BUSINESS & INDUSTRY
Business Week, Fortune, Forbes.

CHEMISTRY
Chemistry

CHILDREN
Parent's Magazine

CITIES & TOWNS
City

CLASSICAL STUDIES
Greek Heritage

COMICS
See section of this title.

CONSERVATION
National Wildlife, National Parks Magazine, Sierra Club Bulletin, Living Wilderness, Conservationist.

CRAFTS AND HOBBIES
See section of this title. Amost all titles suitable for high schools.

DANCE
Dance and Dancers, Ballet Today, Sets in Order.

DISSIDENT MAGAZINES
Left of Center: CAW; Right of Center: Modern Age; Peace: WIN Magazine.

EARTH SCIENCES
Sea Frontiers, Earth Science.

ECONOMICS

Challenge

EDUCATION

Integrated Education, American Education, Lovejoy's Guidance Digest. Educational News Magazines: The New York Times Student Weekly.

FISHING AND HUNTING

Outdoor Life, Field and Stream, Sporting Times, American Sportsman.

FOLKLORE

Western Folklore

FOREIGN LANGUAGE MAGAZINES

See sections on German Language, Romance Languages, Slavic Languages.

GAMES AND SPORTS

Sports Illustrated, Sports. See section of this title. Almost all are suitable for high school students.

GARDENING

Garden Journal of the N.Y. Botanical Garden

GENERAL (See also Literary and Political Reviews, Teenage Magazines)

Life, Newsweek, Look, New York Times Magazine, New Yorker, Atlas.

GEOGRAPHY

National Geographic, Focus, Canadian Geographical Journal.

HISTORY

American: American Heritage, The American West, American History Illustrated.

General: Horizon, History Today, The Beaver.

HOME

Consumer Reports, Better Homes & Gardens, Co-Ed, American Home.

JOURNALISM

Columbia Journalism Review, Scholastic Editor, Quill & Scroll.

LABOR & INDUSTRIAL RELATIONS

Monthly Labor Review, American Labor Magazine.

LITERARY AND POLITICAL REVIEWS

Emphasis on political/social issues: Ramparts, The Nation, National Review.

Emphasis on literary/social issues: Harper's Magazine, Evergreen Review, Saturday Review, Atlantic Monthly.

LITERATURE

Readers and Writers

LITTLE MAGAZINES

City Lights Journal

MATHEMATICS

Mathematics Magazine, Mathematics Student Journal, Journal of Recreational Mathematics.

MEDICAL, NURSING & HEALTH SCIENCES

Today's Health, World Health, American Journal of Nursing.

MEN'S MAGAZINES

Esquire, True, Playboy, Real West.

MOTION PICTURES

Film Comment, Films and Filming, Montage, Film Quarterly.

MUSIC

Crawdaddy, High Fidelity, Sing Out, Downbeat, Guitar Player, Rolling Stone.

MYSTERY & DETECTIVE STORIES

Ellery Queen's Mystery Magazine

OFFICE & SECRETARIAL PRACTICES

Today's Secretary, From Nine to Five.

ORNITHOLOGY

Audubon Magazine, Canadian Audubon, Massachusetts Audubon.

PETS

See section of this title. Choice depends upon student interest.

PHOTOGRAPHY

Popular Photography, Camera, Modern Photography, Aperture.

PHYSICS

Physics Today, Contemporary Physics.

POETRY

Poetry, The Sixties, Kayak, Caterpillar.

POLITICAL SCIENCE

Current History, Congressional Digest, U.N. Monthly Chronicle.

PSYCHOLOGY

Psychology Today

RADIO, TELEVISION & ELECTRONICS

Radio Electronics, Popular Electronics, CQ.

SCIENCE, GENERAL

Natural History, Scientific American, Science, Endeavour, Technology Review, Science News.

SCIENCE FICTION

Analog, Galaxy, Science Fiction Times.

SOCIOLOGY

Trans-Action

TEENAGE MAGAZINES

General: Way Forum, Noonmark; Girls: Seventeen, Ingenue; Boys: None suitable published—see Men's Magazines.

THEATRE

Plays and Players, Drama Review.

TRAVEL

Holiday, Travel, Arizona Highways.

VOCATIONS

Vocations for Social Change, Occupational Outlook Quarterly.

WIT & HUMOUR

Mad Magazine

WOMEN'S MAGAZINES

McCall's, Glamour, Mademoiselle, Good Housekeeping.

TEACHERS' PROFESSIONAL COLLECTIONS

The titles listed here are professional materials for faculty. They are for both high school and elementary schools. Where primarily for high schools this is indicated by an (H) after the title.

The list is basic, also for most schools of education in junior colleges, colleges and universities.

The list is highly selective, and for the most part limited to publications issued by professional organizations, or to magazines which may be used with children in a classroom situation. It does not include more than a few professional magazines at the academic level, although many of these will be of interest and value to primary and secondary teachers.

The question of organization and building of a total professional collection is discussed in the National Education Association publication, *The Teachers' Library* (Washington, D.C.: N.E.A., 1966. $1.50).

AFRICAN STUDIES

African Image (H)

AFRO-AMERICAN

Journal of Negro Education, Negro Educational Review, Quarterly Review of Higher Education Among Negroes.

AGRICULTURE

The Agricultural Education Magazine (H)

ART & DESIGN

School Arts, Arts and Activities, Art Education, Design.

BIOLOGICAL SCIENCES

The American Biology Teacher (H)

BOOK REVIEWS

See section of this title. See also, Libraries.

BUSINESS

Business Education World (H), Business Education Forum (H), Journal of Business Education (H).

CHEMISTRY

Journal of Chemical Education (H)

CHILDREN

Children, Exceptional Children, Teaching Exceptional Children.

CLASSICAL STUDIES

Classical Journal (H), Classical Outlook (H).

DANCE

Dance Magazine (H)

EARTH SCIENCES

GeoTimes (H), Journal of Geological Education (H).

EDUCATION

See section of this title. The majority of titles are suitable for a professional collection.

ENGLISH

See section of this title. Most titles are suitable for a professional collection.

FOLKLORE

Journal of American Folklore

GAMES AND SPORTS

Scholastic Coach (H), Athletic Journal.

GEOGRAPHY

Journal of Geography

GERMAN LANGUAGE

German Quarterly

HISTORY

American Historical Review (H), Journal of Modern History (H). See also: Social Studies, Social Education. Both listed in Education Section.

HOME

Journal of Home Economics (H), Family Economic Review (H).

JOURNALISM

Columbia Scholastic Press Advisers Assn. Bulletin

LIBRARIES

School Library Journal, Top of the News, School Libraries.

LINGUISTICS & PHILOLOGY

Modern Language Journal, Language Learning (H).

LITERATURE

American Literature (H), Novel (H), Studies in Short Fiction (H).

MATHEMATICS

Arithmetic Teacher (H), Mathematics Teacher (H).

MEDICAL, NURSING & HEALTH SCIENCES

Journal of School Health, Journal of Health, Physical Education, Recreation (listed under Education).

MOTION PICTURES

Educator's Guide to Media and Methods, Audiovisual Instruction, Educational Screen and AV Guide.

MUSIC

Music Educator's Journal, American Music Teacher (H), Instrumentalist.

PHYSICS

Physics Teacher (H), American Journal of Physics (H).

PSYCHOLOGY

Psychology in the Schools, Journal of Counseling Psychology, Psychiatry and Social Science Review.

RADIO

NAEB Journal

RELIGION

Religious Education

ROMANCE LANGUAGES

French Review, Hispania, Italica.

SCIENCE—GENERAL

Journal of Research in Science Teaching (H), Science and Children, Science Teacher (H), School Science and Mathematics.

THEATRE

Educational Theatre Journal (H), Plays, Dramatics.

VOCATIONAL GUIDANCE

See section of this title. Most titles are suitable for a professional collection.

BOOK REVIEWS

Periodicals with the more extensive book reviews of a *general nature* within the subject are listed here. These are not always the best for *specific areas* of the subject, e.g., *Journal of Egyptian Archaeology* would be preferable to *Archaeology* for the specialist. See the Book Review Magazines Section for general reviewing media.

ACCOUNTING

Accounting Review

ADVERTISING

Journal of Advertising Research

AFRICAN STUDIES

Current Bibliography on African Affairs

AFRO-AMERICAN

Bibliographic Survey

AGRICULTURE

Agricultural History

ANTHROPOLOGY

American Anthropologist

ARCHAEOLOGY

Archaeology

ARCHITECTURE

Architectural Forum

ART

Art Bulletin, Art Journal.

ATMOSPHERIC SCIENCE

AUTOMATION

Computers and the Humanities (see Bibliography Section), Computing Reviews.

BANKING & FINANCE

Banker's Magazine, Journal of Finance.

BIBLIOGRAPHY

Papers of the Bibliographical Society of America

BIOLOGICAL SCIENCES

Quarterly Review of Biology

BOOK REVIEW MAGAZINES

See section of same name

BUSINESS

Journal of Business

CHEMISTRY

Journal of Chemical Education

CITIES & TOWNS

New York Magazine, Public Administration Review.

CLASSICAL STUDIES

The Classical Review

CONSERVATION

Defenders of Wildlife News

CRIMES AND CRIMINALS

Federal Probation

DANCE

Ballet Today (see Theatre Section for reviews of modern dance).

EARTH SCIENCES

Journal of Geological Education

EDUCATION

Harvard Educational Review

ENGLISH

English Progress

FOLKLORE

Journal of American Folklore

GEOGRAPHY

Geographical Journal, Geographical Review.

GERMAN LIFE AND LETTERS

Journal of English and German Philology

HISTORY: AMERICAN

American Historical Review, The American West Review, English Historical Review, Historian, History, Journal of American History, Journal of Southern History.

LINGUISTICS & PHILOLOGY

Modern Language Review, English Studies.

LITERATURE

Review of English Studies

MATHEMATICS

American Mathematical Monthly, Mathematical Reviews.

MOTION PICTURES

Film Comment

MUSIC

Notes, Journal of Music Theory, The Music Review.

PHILOSOPHY

Philosophical Books, Review of Metaphysics.

PHYSICS

Physics Today

POETRY

Caterpillar, Poetry, Wormwood Review.

POLITICAL SCIENCE

American Political Science Review, Foreign Affairs, Intercom, International Affairs, Political Science Quarterly, Political Studies, World Politics.

PSYCHOLOGY

American Journal of Psychology, British Journal of Psychology, Contemporary Psychology, Psychiatry & Social Science Review.

RELIGION

New Book Review, Christianity Today.

ROMANCE LANGUAGES

French News, French Studies, Hispania.

SCIENCE—GENERAL

American Scientist, Science.

SCIENCE FICTION

Science Fiction Times

SOCIOLOGY

American Journal of Sociology, American Sociological Review, British Journal of Sociology, Social Forces.

THEATRE

Drama

A BASIC LIST OF SCIENTIFIC JOURNALS FOR THE NON-SPECIALIST

The following, taken from a select list prepared by the American Library Association's Science and Technology

Reference Services Committee, and published in the Fall 1968 issue of *RQ*, includes the Committee's introductory statement and list of titles only; annotations, along with numerical ranking of difficulty, have not been reprinted. Titles which appear in this book have been marked with an asterisk.

"The Science and Technology Reference Services Committee has prepared a compilation of thirty-seven journal titles in the field of the applied and physical sciences, designed to interpret for the layman new scientific and technical developments and to assist him in his understanding of their significance.

The journals appearing on the list range from those containing articles written solely for the layman to others that present an occasional interpretative article and are essentially oriented toward the professional reader. The level of difficulty will vary from journal to journal. The Committee has ranked each by assigning a number, from 1 to 3, signifying the level from the easiest to the most difficult to comprehend." (Prepared by: Elsie Bergland, Antoinette Ciolli, John P. McGowan, Chairman, William L. Page, Margaret Simonds, Richard L. Snyder.)

* Advancement of Science
  Aerospace Technology (now incorporated with *American Aviation)
* American Scientist
* Astronautics and Aeronautics
* Aviation Week and Space Technology
* Bulletin of the Atomic Scientists
* Chartered Mechanical Engineer
* Chemical and Engineering News
* Chemistry
  Electrical World (No longer available to public libraries)
* Electronics
  Electronics & Power
* Electronics World
* Endeavour
* Engineer (London)
* Engineering
* Engineering News-Record
* Fortune
* Geotimes
* IEEE Spectrum
* International Science and Technology (Now titled Science and Technology)
* Journal of Chemical Education
* Mechanical Engineering
* Nature
* New Scientist
* Physics Today
* Popular Electronics
* Popular Science Monthly
* Science
* Science Journal
* Science News
* Scientific American
  Signal
* Sky and Telescope
* Spaceflight
* Technology Review
  Times Review of Industry and Technology

BIBLIOGRAPHY

This selective bibliography is compiled to give the reader an overview of magazines. It is in two parts. The first is a general listing of bibliographies and selection aids. The second lists works arranged under specific, relatively popular subjects. Highly specialized areas are not included in detail.

Titles listed here are not concerned with individual magazines. This would be only to repeat most of what may be found in Schacht's excellent *A Bibliography for the Study of Magazines*.

With few exceptions, entries are limited to titles and articles published after 1960.

A. GENERAL WORKS

HISTORY

Forsythe, David P. *The Business Press in America, 1750–1865*. Philadelphia: Chilton, 1963.

A history of the growth and development of a major type of magazine which is only touched on lightly by other histories. The author hopes to extend his study into the 20th century.

Kronick, David A. *History of Scientific and Technical Periodicals*. New York: Scarecrow Press, 1962.

Mott, Frank Luther. *A History of American Magazines*. 5 vols. Cambridge: Harvard Univ. Press, 1930–68.

The standard history of the American magazine from its beginning until 1930. A cumulative index to the entire five volume set was issued in the concluding volume, published in 1968.

Peterson, Theodore. *Magazines in the Twentieth Century*. 2nd ed. Urbana: Univ. of Illinois Press, 1964.

Takes up where Mott left off, but concentrates primarily on consumer type magazines. Explores the major economic and social implications of the mass magazine.

Wolseley, Roland E. *Understanding Magazines*. Ames: Iowa State Univ. Press, 1965.

The primary purpose of this book is to indicate to the novice the technical and editorial aspects of magazine production. A good part, however, is concerned with the history, and nicely augments both Peterson and Mott.

Wood, James P. *Magazines in the United States*. 2nd rev. ed. New York: Ronald Press, 1956.

A one-volume history of the magazine, from 1741 to modern times. About one-half the work is concerned with the period before 1900. Augments, but does not replace, Mott or Peterson.

BIBLIOGRAPHIES

Gummer, H. M. "Catalogues and Bibliographies of Periodicals." *Journal of Documentation*, Mar., 1956.

More specifically geared for library use, this includes 67 titles. The list was expanded by seven more titles in the *Library Association Record* of October, 1956. Dated, yet moderately helpful.

Magazine Advertising Bureau. *Sources of Consumer Magazine Information*. Mimeographed. 2nd rev. ed. New York: Magazine Center, 1965.

From time to time the Bureau issues pamphlets and lists for anyone dealing with general, commercial magazines: the above, for instance, and a three-page, mimeographed bibliography entitled *Magazine and Magazine Publishing—Bibliography*, published in October, 1967. Specifically, the pamphlet listed here gives information on where to find data on circulation, readership, marketing, rates, costs, etc. While geared for the advertiser and professional journalist, still of great value for the librarian.

Schacht, J. H. *A Bibliography for the Study of Magazines*. Processed. Urbana: Univ. of Illinois, College of Journalism, 1966.

The best general bibliography on magazines. Approximately 400 briefly annotated citations under some 15 broad subject headings. Prepared primarily for a journalism school, the bibliography includes all basic articles of a general nature and many concerned with individual magazines. The author's sources are as multiple as his citations.

DIRECTORIES

Ayer's Directory of Newspapers and Periodicals. ann. Philadelphia: N. W. Ayer & Son, 1880– .

A standard annual guide found in most libraries, this is primarily a state by state, city by city listing of newspapers, but includes all major magazines. Useful for classified lists: Afro-American publications, religious publications, fraternal publications, magazines of general circulation, trade, technical and class publications. The English equivalent to this is *Willings Press Guide* (1871–), which includes basic information on the press of the United Kingdom and the Commonwealth countries. Again, though, emphasis is on newspapers.

Crismond, Linda F. *Directory of San Francisco Bay Area Publishers.* San Francisco: San Francisco Public Library, 1968.

First section is a list of periodical publishers, and there is an index of periodical titles. Although regional, it is of more than regional interest because of the great number of literary and little magazines published in the Bay Area. Several titles not listed in standard guides.

Gebbie House Magazine Directory. Triennial. Sioux City: Gebbie Directory, 1952– .

The basic guide to house organs, this lists some 4,000 house magazines in the United States. Alphabetical by title, with title and geographical index. Particularly useful for libraries with tight budgets. Many of the titles are free.

Koltay, Emery, ed. *Irregular Serials and Annuals: An International Directory.* New York: R. R. Bowker, 1967.

A subject arrangement—with title and subject index—of some 14,500 serials and continuations. Useful to periodical librarians for location of magazine supplements and annuals. Complete bibliographic information.

The Press in . . . Latin America . . . Africa . . . Asia. 3 vols. New York: R. R. Bowker, 1968.

Although primarily a listing, by country, of newspapers, the three volumes are of interest to magazine oriented librarians for one major reason. Each concludes with a section devoted to what magazines (and newspapers) are issued internationally, i.e., *Time, The Economist, Fortune,* etc. Entries include title, where issued, address, circulation, frequency, language, type of readers, format, printing method, price of advertising, and closing date for advertising. Similar information is given for all of the newspapers listed in the main body of the works— some 600 in Latin America, 365 in Africa, and 628 in Asia.

Standard Periodical Directory. Annual. New York: Oxbridge, 1964– .

Concentrates on American magazines. Listed by subject with full bibliographic details, and usually with a brief descriptive note. Title and subject guide.

Standard Rate & Data Media Catalogs. Skokie: Standard Rate & Data Service.

Two Standard publications are relevant here: *Business Publication Rates and Data* and *Consumer Magazine and Farm Publication Rates and Data.* While published primarily for advertisers seeking data on rates, format, circulation, etc., the service is useful for the capsule annotations which precede almost all magazines. The annotations are non-critical, but give an excellent summary of content. The firm publishes a number of other well known services on television, spot radio rates and newspapers, to name a few. Unfortunately, as all of the services are directed to advertisers and publishers, the vast number of scholarly and non-profit journals are not usually listed.

Ulrich's International Periodical Directory. 12th rev. ed. 2 vols. New York: R. R. Bowker, 1967–68.

A two-volume work which covers over 30,000 magazines, here and abroad, in all fields of interest. Arrangement is alphabetical by subject, with a title index. The first volume is devoted to science, medicine and technology; the second to arts, humanities, business and social sciences. Complete bibliographic details for each magazine. Particularly useful for libraries as it indicates in which index or abstracting service the listed magazine is noted. The basic guide to magazines for any library in the United States and abroad. There are also supplements to keep information in the two volumes up-to-date between editions.

Working Press of the Nation, vol. 2, *Magazine Directory.* Annual. New York: National Research Bureau, 1947– .

A three-volume work. The second volume is a guide to magazines. Primarily for advertisers and those actively engaged in the business. Still, the information is often useful to a librarian or a layman seeking unbiased data about a given publication. For purposes of content information, however, not as helpful as the *Standard Rate and Data Media Catalogs.*

Writers' and Artists' Year Book. ann. London: Adam & Charles Black, 1906– .

Contains both English and American magazines which publish material of interest to authors, i.e., fiction, articles, plays, cartoons, poetry, etc. Annotations indicate type of material the magazine uses. Often gives a truer picture of magazine's interests than a normal annotation.

Writer's Market. ann. 1929– . *Writer's Yearbook.* ann. 1930– . Cincinnati: Writer's Digest.

Two market guides, which between them list close to 3,000 periodicals, with data on types of material wanted for publication. Not only useful for free-lance writers, but an invaluable guide to the type of material American magazine publishers are seeking. Both also include editorial features on writing.

UNION LISTS

British Union Catalogue of Periodicals. 4 vols. London: Butterworth, 1955–58.

The four basic volumes locate more than 140,000 titles in 440 British libraries. Quarterly and annual cumulations list magazines which began publication after January 1, 1960. The *World Lists of Scientific Periodicals* is continued in the *British Union Catalogue*.

New Serial Titles: 1950–1960. 2 vols. Washington: Library of Congress, 1961; *1961–65.* 3 vols. New York: R. R. Bowker, 1966.

A continuation of the Union List Serials. Lists by title some 165,000 serials which began publishing as of Jan. 1, 1950 or later. Shows over 6,000,000 locations. Supplemented by monthly and annual volumes.

Union List of Serials in Libraries of the United States and Canada. 3rd ed. 5 vols. New York: H. W. Wilson, 1965.

An alphabetical listing (but without a subject approach) to 156,499 serials held by 956 libraries in the United States and Canada. Complete bibliographic data. Particularly useful for beginning and ending dates of publication, changes in name and, of course, location. Covers period up to December, 1949.

Union List of Serials: A Bibliography. Freitag, Ruth S., compiler. Washington: U.S. Library of Congress, 1964.

A geographical listing—by region and country—of some 1,200 union lists. Takes in separate lists and those published as parts of journals or books.

World List of Social Science Periodicals. 3rd ed. New York: Unesco Pubns. Center, 1966.

A basic annotated list of 1,312 journals published in 92 countries, up to 1963. Full bibliographic description and a 50-to 150-word annotation written "to describe a typical issue of the periodical so as to provide a precise idea of its usual contents." Title, sponsoring organization and subject indexes. Covers periodicals in: sociology, general psychology, anthropology, demography, criminology, economics, political science, public administration, international relations, industrial relations, economic and social history, geography, law.

GUIDES

Fowler, Maureen. *Guides to Scientific Periodicals.* London: Library Assn., 1966.

The best single guide to the vast number of specialized and general lists, directories, bibliographies, etc., in the field of scientific periodicals. Some 1,048 items are arranged by subject, and for each there is a brief annotation.

Toase, Mary. *Guide to Current British Periodicals.* London: Library Assn., 1962.

Brief descriptions of 3,800 British periodicals. Indicates purpose, scope and size of each magazine. Arranged by Dewey Decimal classification, with combined title and subject index.

University of Waterloo. *Reference List.* irreg. Ontario: Univ. of Waterloo Library, 1967– .

Beginning in Nov. 1967 the library commenced the issue of a number of 24- to 30-page pamphlets. Printed from masters produced by an IBM/360, the 14 separate science subject lists range from Astronomy to Nuclear Engineering. Each is divided by form, and there is a section on periodicals. Title and cataloging information only.

White, Carl M. *Sources of Information in Social Sciences.* Totowa: Bedminster Press, 1964.

Although a general guide to the literature of the social sciences, each of the eight chapters includes a listing of basic periodicals. Serves to introduce the reader to magazines in the following areas: social sciences in general; anthropology and business; education, history political science, psychology, sociology.

COMMERCIAL GUIDES

Note: There are a vast number of guides—usually free to libraries—issued by various commercial agencies. The two listed here are representative, and in no way constitute an endorsement of the agencies by the compiler.

F. W. Faxon Library Subscription Agency. *The Faxon Librarians' Guide to Periodicals.* Annual. Boston: F. W. Faxon.

In three sections: alphabetical by title, alphabetical by title with subscription prices; classified list. One of the most complete commercial catalogs (close to 18,000 titles). No annotations, but does include information on indexing.

Franklin Square-Mayfair Subscription Agency. *Periodical Handbook.* Annual. Teaneck: Franklin Square.

An annual which includes an alphabetical list of some 6,000 periodicals, a classified index and then brief annotations for: general interest and farm publications, business and trade publications, and educational, medical and scientific periodicals. The annotations are descriptive and non-critical. Bibliographic information includes price, frequency of self indexing, editor and sometimes indexing services.

CURRENT REVIEWS

Bulletin of Bibliography. 1900– . 3/yr. "Births, deaths and magazine notes: a record of new titles, changed titles, deaths in the periodical world."

Usually simple listing without annotations.

College and Research Libraries. 1939– . m. "New Periodicals of ———." Chicago: Amer. Library Assn.

A bi-annual feature which includes brief critical annotations of 50 to 75 new magazines particularly of value to colleges and universities. Usually appears in September and March issues.

Library Journal. Jan. 1, 1967– . semi-m. "Magazines," ed. by Bill Katz.

A column which covers all magazines, but the humanities, literature and social sciences in particular. The 50- to 100-word annotations are by editor and guest contributors. Signed.

Library Resources and Technical Services. 1955– . ann. "A Survey of Serial Activities During ———."

An annual report which concentrates primarily on bibliographic control, i.e., bibliographies, indexes, abstracts, etc. Little information on new magazines *per se,* yet invaluable for peripheral material.

New Periodicals Report. 1967. m. $7.50. Box 4406, New York, N.Y. 10017.

A four-page newsletter which briefly annotates some 15 to 20 new titles per month. While helpful—it has a cumulative index—most of the titles are covered in more depth, often more critically, in the standard review services.

Small Press Review. 1967– . q. "Magazine Column," by Wally Depew.

A critical survey of new little magazines, both literary and poetry.

Stechert-Hafner Book News. 1945– . 9/yr. "Periodicals and other Serials."

A title listing, with full bibliographic information. No annotations. Useful as a check on new magazines, particularly in the sciences and foreign publications.

Top of the News. 1967– . q. "The Magazine-Rack Children"; "The Magazine-Rack Young Adults."

The single best reviewing medium for new magazines in this age bracket. The feature appears occasionally, and some five to eight new periodicals are critically annotated.

LIBRARIES-MAGAZINE EVALUATION, ORGANIZATION

Bonn, George S. "Methods of Evaluating Science Periodicals." *The Rub-Off,* Sept.–Oct., 1964: 1–3.

While specifically for science magazines, the criteria the author suggests are applicable to almost all types of magazines. His seven point scale should serve as the base for any sound purchasing policy.

Brown, G. H. *Scientific Serials.* ACRL Monograph No. 16. Chicago: Amer. Library Assn., 1956.

While dated in particulars, this remains the basic use study of magazines in mathematics, physics, chemistry, geology, physiology, botany, zoology and entomology. An excellent guide for the student to the methodology of use studies.

Council of National Library Associations. *USA Standard for Periodicals: Format and Arrangement.* New York: U.S. Standards Inst., 1967.

"A guide to aid the manufacturer, the consumer, and the general public," in the organization of bibliographic material in magazines. Includes a basic glossary of terms, and suggestions on arrangement of everything from pagination to supplements. The Institute has also issued standards for indexes and periodical title abbreviations.

"Current Trends in U.S. Periodical Publishing." *Library Trends,* Jan., 1962.

A complete issued devoted to periodicals in various subject areas from the general to agricultural magazines. Among the 13 articles, three are devoted to the economics of publishing and the indexing and abstracting services. Dated, but still useful for basic information.

Davinson, D. E. *A Manual of Practice for Librarians.* 2nd ed. London: Deutsch, 1964.

In 14 brief chapters the English lecturer in librarianship outlines methods of handling periodicals in the small to medium sized library. In general, if not in particulars, the advice is applicable to American libraries. Chapter 13 includes annuals, yearbooks and directories; chapter 14 is a periodicals bibliography by subject, and there is a final general bibliography. Some brief annotations.

Huff, William H. "Periodicals." In *Bibliography: Current State and Future Trends,* ed. Robert B. Downs & Frances B. Jenkins, pp. 62–83. Urbana: Univ. of Illinois Press, 1967.

An overview of present bibliographical control problems of magazines. Particularly good for concise explanations of bibliographies, lists and current thinking.

Osborn, Andrew D. *Serial Publications: Their Place and Treatment in Libraries.* Chicago: Amer. Library Assn., 1955.

A more sophisticated approach than Davinson, and particularly valuable for chapters on cataloging and organization. While dated, the basic information is still extremely useful.

CHILDREN'S AND TEEN AGE MAGAZINES

Amer. Library Assn. *A Basic Book Collection for Elementary Grades.* 7th ed., 1960.

———. *A Basic Book Collection for Junior High Schools.* 3rd ed., 1960.

———. *A Basic Book Collection for High Schools.* 7th ed., 1963.

At the end of each collection there is an annotated list of magazines, usually some 50 to 70 titles. The selection is conservative, the annotations perceptive. Unfortunately, all of the above lists are somewhat dated.

———. "Current art magazines." *Top of the News* 16:31–3. Young adults.

———. "Latest magazine evaluation." *Top of the News* 18:61. Young adults.

———. "Music magazines." *Top of the News* 17:64–6. Young adults; bibliography. Prepared by Magazine Evaluation Committee.

Cundiff, Ruby. *101 Plus Magazines for Schools, Grades 1–12*. 4th rev. ed. Nashville: Tennessee Book Co., 1964.

A frequently revised, briefly annotated list. Alphabetical by title, brief bibliographical information, key to where magazines are indexed. Standard titles.

Dobler, Lavinia. *The Dobler World Directory of Youth Periodicals*. rev. ed. New York: Schulte Publishing Co., 1966.

A listing primarily for advertisers and writers. Gives data on rates paid for articles by some 400 magazines for grades 1–12. Alphabetically arranged under four broad categories: "General," "Religious," "School and classroom," and "Foreign." The some 400 titles are keyed by age or grade group, circulation, average size per issue, and other bibliographic information. Not annotated, although descriptive phrases of two to five words indicate content. Primarily useful as an up-to-date listing.

Field, Carolyn W. "Periodicals That Will Benefit Elementary Children." *Instructor*, Nov., 1963: 56–58.

Discusses periodicals in the elementary school library and the criteria for selecting them. Suggestions of titles, and with thorough annotations.

Gaver, Mary, ed. *Elementary School Library Collection*. Newark: Bro-Dart, 1966.

Reproduces a basic collection on catalog cards, with added information on grade level and notes. Includes a section on periodicals. Standard titles.

Groff, Patrick. "Prediction of the Reading Difficulty of Children's Magazines." *California Journal of Educational Research*, Jan., 1962: 39.

The author outlines criteria for reading levels of 14 children's magazines and compares what the editors consider to be the reading level and what the actual difficulty level is for children. There is some discrepancy, which points up the need of evaluating a magazine in terms of an individual's reading level, not in terms of what a list or an editor claims the level to be for the child.

Horn, Thomas D. "Periodicals for Children and Youth." *Elementary English*, April, 1966: 341–358, 399.

A classified, annotated list of some 150 periodicals. Annotations are primarily descriptive, or indicate use of magazine in classroom. Each is graded, and this is a trifle too broad. Still, one of the best, relatively current lists now available.

Johnson, E. "Hobson's Choice; Or, What Periodicals for Children?" *Top of the News* 20:307–8. Elementary school; some few for high school.

———. "Magazines for Home Purchase." *Top of the News* 21:354. Elementary Magazines.

"Magazines for School Library." *Minnesota Journal of Education*, April, 1960.

Discussion of the titles and of the use of magazines in the school library. Only recommended titles are included, and annotations are full.

Martin, Laura K. *Magazines for School Libraries*. Processed. Frankfort: School Library Services, Kentucky Department of Education. 1967.

A discursive, analytical discussion under 14 broad subject categories of 200 titles for elementary grades through high school. The best study now available. Updates to a degree the author's *Magazines for School Libraries* (New York: Wilson, 1950). The professor of library science at the University of Kentucky is particularly broad in her choice, and shows an understanding of today's youth which is sometimes lacking in lists published by organizations or groups.

"National lists of scientific periodicals." *UNESCO Bulletin for Librarians* 15:91–4. Lists bibliography of periodicals—representative lists. 1961–1963.

"Periodicals for Children and Young People." *School Libraries*, Oct. 1961: 33–35; Jan. 1962: 31–32.

A basic bibliography of selection aids, standards, magazines in the classroom, etc. While somewhat dated, the primary references still are excellent.

Robinson, Eleanor. "Hot Rod Magazines: A Harmless Diversion?" *English Journal*, Jan., 1965: 36.

A teacher takes a dim view of the so-called hot rod magazines in terms of grammar employed. A witty, satirical reply is to be found in the May issue (pp. 483–7) —here the author points up the difference between hope and reality.

Scott, Marian H., ed. *Periodicals for School Libraries*. Chicago: Amer. Library Assn., 1969.

An alphabetically arranged list of 429 magazines for grades K-12. Selection was made by an ALA committee, as were the annotations. Basic data is given for each title, plus an indication of grade level. No indication is made for better or poor quality magazines, but this is often obvious in the annotations themselves. The choices are generally good, and middle of the road.

Squire, James R., and others. "Student Reading and the High School Library." *School Libraries,* Summer, 1967: 11.

A survey of buying policies of librarians in 158 high schools in 45 states. Part of the survey includes periodicals. The findings point up the often unrealistic attitudes of the school librarians as regards what students should read as compared to what magazines the students wish to read. A major survey which should be required reading for all school and public librarians.

Wofford, Azile. *Book Selection for School Libraries.* New York: Wilson, 1962.

Discusses the organization and care of various magazines.

ACADEMIC LIBRARIES

"Eight New York Libraries Survey Their Periodical Holdings," *Library Journal,* March 15, 1963: 1131–32.

Farber, Evan I. *Classified List of Periodicals for the College Library,* 4th ed. Boston: Faxon, 1957.

A dated, yet useful selective listing. Perceptive, critical annotation. Material is arranged by broad subject headings, and recommended titles are so indicated. According to the compiler, a revised edition is scheduled for publication in 1969.

Poteat, Dorothy M. *Basic Materials for Florida Junior College Libraries.* Tallahassee: State Dept. of Education, Jan., 1960. Magazines.

An annotated list of 122 magazines for Florida libraries. Particularly useful as it is based upon holdings of 33 junior colleges in Florida and eleven in states throughout the union.

Welter, Rush. *Problems of Scholarly Publication in the Humanities and Social Sciences.* New York: Amer. Council of Learned Societies, 1959.

A study of the American Council of Learned Societies which surveys some 75 learned journals. The list of learned journals (Appendix E), by broad subjects, constitutes a sound basic collection, although a few have changed names or are no longer published.

AUDIENCES

Who reads what, and why? This should be of primary concern to librarians, and there are a number of articles in this important subject area. None is listed here, as all major ones will be found in Schacht's bibliography, pp. 7–9 and pp. 10–12. An excellent index to such material is *Psychological Abstracts,* and, as Schacht points out, "Journalism libraries often have dozens of studies of audiences of individual magazines," usually conducted by professional services for the publisher.

Ongoing research into audience reactions—at the commercial level—will be found in the standard advertising magazines such as *Media/Scope, Advertising Age,* and *Media Decisions.* The *Journalism Quarterly* and the *Columbia Journalism Review* are the two best sources of scholarly, well researched articles on individual magazines and their audiences.

ECONOMICS OF PUBLISHING

Magazine Industry Newsletter. Business Magazine, Inc., 420 Lexington Ave., New York, N.Y. 10017.

Averaging six to eight pages, this presents information on editorial attitudes, advertising, and circulation of major magazine publishers. The material is in capsule form, and the total a refreshing insight into the magazine business as it is practiced, not as it is plugged.

Peterson, Theodore. "Magazines and the Challenge of Change." *Quill,* Nov. 1965: 44–45.

———. "Magazines Today and Tomorrow." *Quarterly Review of Economics and Business.* Winter, 1964:25–36.

———. "When Magazines Fight Together." Saturday Review, Dec. 12, 1964: 74.

Three representative articles by Peterson, all of which are concerned primarily with the business aspects of the mass circulation, general magazine.

The best single source for current information on the economics of magazine publishing is *Advertising Age* (see Business and Industry Section). Other aspects are treated in several magazines devoted to media advertising, i.e.: *Marketing Communications, Media Decisions,* and *Media Scope. Editor and Publisher* is primarily devoted to newspapers, but does carry information on magazines from time to time. The indexes of the *Wall Street Journal* and *The New York Times* are other current reference aids.

SUBJECT AREA

AERONAUTICS

U.S. Library of Congress. *Aeronautics and Space Serial Publications: A World List.* Washington: 1962. U.S. Govt. Printing Office, 1962.

An unannotated listing of 4,551 titles from 76 countries.

Fry, Bernard M., and Mohrhardt, F. E. *Guide to Information Sources in Space Science and Technology.* New York: Interscience, 1963.

Moore, Patrick. *Space Exploration.* Cambridge: Cambridge Univ. Press, 1958.

AFRO-AMERICAN

Brooks, Maxwell. *The Negro Press Re-Examined.* Christopher Publishing House, 1959.

Primarily a content analysis of major Afro-American newspapers. Magazines are not included. Now dated, yet a useful bibliography.

AGRICULTURE

Boalch, Donald. *Current Agricultural Serials*. Oxford: Intl. Assn. of Agricultural Librarians and Documentalists, 1965– .

A two volume work which lists more than 12,400 serials in agriculture and a good number of related fields. New titles and changes in titles are reported in the *Quarterly Bulletin* of the issuing organization.

ANTHROPOLOGY

International Bibliography of Social and Cultural Anthropology. London: Stevens & Sons, Ltd., 1955– .

Another of the Unesco annual bibliographies which includes periodical articles and is a useful annual checklist of new periodicals.

ARCHITECTURE

Smith, D. L. *How to Find Out in Architecture and Building*. Elmsford: Pergamon Press, 1966.

Chapter 5 is a brief annotated list of periodicals divided by subject. The book is prepared primarily for English librarians, and the majority of titles are British based.

ART

Amer. Library Assn. (Young Adults' Services Division, Magazine Evaluation Committee). "Current Art Magazines." *Top of the News*, May, 1960:31–33.

Art Inst. of Chicago. *Index to Art Periodicals*. 11 vols. Boston: G. K. Hall, 1962.

A retrospective index to over 350 magazines of the 19th and 20th centuries as found in the Ryerson Library. Many of the modern, foreign periodicals are listed in *Art Index*, but several are not. There are plans to issue supplements from time to time to update the index. The basic set is priced at $740.

"Italian Art Periodicals. Romulus." *Apollo* Sept., 1962: 543–44.

Russell, P. "Art Magazines." *Canadian Art* January, March, May, 1965:42, 50, 55, respectively.

BIBLIOGRAPHY

Harvard University Library. *Bibliography and Bibliography Periodicals*. Cambridge: Harvard Univ. Press, 1966.

Widener Library Shelflist No. 7. This is an unannotated list of 19,586 titles which cover bibliographic science. Other shelflists in this series also include periodicals in various subject areas, but are of limited use except as a checklist for large public or university libraries.

Ulrich, Carolyn. *Books and Printing*. Woodstock: William E. Rudge, 1943.

Although now considerably dated, a still useful checklist for periodicals published between 1800 and 1942. Arranged by subject.

BIOLOGICAL SCIENCES

Bottle, R. T., and H. V. Wyatt. *Use of Biological Literature*. London: Butterworth, 1967.

Smith, Roger C. and Painter, Reginald H. *Guide to the Literature of the Zoological Sciences*. 7th ed. Minneapolis: Burgess Publishing Co., 1966.

BOOK REVIEW MAGAZINES

Busha, Charles H. "An Evaluation of Four Book Review Media Commonly Used by Public Libraries. . ." *South Carolina Librarian*, March, 1968:29–34.

A study of promptness of reviewing and how well the *Library Journal, N.Y. Times Book Review, Saturday Review* and *Booklist* meet the needs of librarians.

Perkins, Ralph. *Book Selection Media*. Champaign: National Council of Teachers of English, 1966.

Subtitled "a descriptive guide to 175 aids for selecting library materials," this gives over a single page to each review media, standard list and index. In addition to complete bibliographic information there are short notes on: purpose, scope, type of subject headings, similar tools, special features, and a rather bland two or three line evaluation. Titles are also listed by selection aids for adults, children, college, high school, librarian and teacher-parent. Primarily a neumonic device, as the opinions stated are too general to be meaningful for selection.

Smart, Gary H. "Book Reviewing in American Magazines," *Journalism Quarterly*, Autumn, 1964: 583–585.

A summary of an M.A. thesis which found that book publishers are not overly concerned with book review media. Still, they believe the ten most important reviewing services (i.e., 1963) for their purposes are: *Atlantic, Esquire, Harper's, Nation, New Republic, Newsweek, New Yorker, Reporter, Saturday Review* and *Time*.

BUSINESS

Books for Businessmen. 3rd ed. Arlington: Arlington County Public Library, 1967.

Includes basic indexes, periodicals and newspapers for the medium to large library.

Cahners, Norman L. "There's No Business Like Business," *Saturday Review*, Jan. 9, 1965:73–75.

A brief discussion of the place of the 2,700 esoteric business magazines in the publishing world.

Coman, Edwin T. *Sources of Business Information.* 2nd rev. ed. Berkeley: Univ. of California Press, 1964.

This general bibliography includes a section on American and Canadian periodicals and business publications. Although dated, another useful general guide which includes periodicals is: Marian C. Manley's *Business Information* (New York: Harper, 1955).

Georgi, Charlotte. "How to Keep a Business Library Going. Lesson Number Two." *Library Journal,* Mar. 1, 1968:959–964.

A bibliography. Section 6 lists indexes, section 7 includes selected abstracts, section 8 selected journals and newspapers. Not annotated. See also the same author's "How to Start a Business Library" (*Library Journal,* Mar. 1, 1965).

Harvard Univ. Grad. Sch. of Business Admin., Baker Library. *Printed Catalog of Current Journals.* 2nd ed. Cambridge: 1966.

A simple title listing of periodicals in the Baker Library. No annotations. A companion volume is the *Subject List of Current Journals,* 1966.

———. *Statistical and Review Issues of Trade and Business Periodicals.* Cambridge: 1964.

This is one of the many "reference lists" issued by the Baker Library. An alphabetical list with brief annotations explaining the type of statistical information given. Also helpful in this same series: *Selected Business Reference Sources,* 965.

McNierney, Mary A. ed. *Directory of Business and Financial Services.* 6th ed. New York: Special Libraries Assn., 1963.

In addition to the normal type of business and financial service, lists a number of newsletters and periodicals. Each entry has full bibliographic data and a brief description.

CHEMISTRY

Amer. Chemical Soc. *Searching the Chemical Literature.* (Advances in Chemistry Series No. 30). Washington: Amer. Chemical Soc., 1961.

Committee on Teaching Aids of the Advisory Council on College Chemistry. *Guidelines and Suggested Title List for Undergraduate Chemistry Libraries.* (Serial Publication #12). Washington: 1965.

Contains list of periodicals.

Burman, C. R. *How To Find Out in Chemistry.* 2nd ed. Elmsford: Pergamon Press, 1966.

Chapter on "Periodicals."

Crane, E. J. *Guide to the Literature of Chemistry.* 2nd ed. New York: Wiley, 1957.

Somewhat old, but excellent classified list of periodicals.

Mellon, M. G. *Chemical Publications.* New York: McGraw-Hill, 1963.

Yagello, V. E. "Early History of the Chemical Periodical." *Journal of Chemical Education,* 45: 426–29.

CITIES AND TOWNS

"City Magazines are the Talk of the Town." *Business Week,* Feb. 18, 1967: 184.

CONSERVATION

Person, Ruben L. *Conserving American Resources* 2nd ed. New York: Prentice Hall, 1964.

A periodical listing, pp.484–6.

Syracuse State Univ. College of Forestry. *List of Periodicals in the Library.* Syracuse: Univ. College of Forestry Library, 1963.

A listing from a top forestry school.

DANCE

Belknap, S. Y. *Guide to Dance Periodicals.* New York: Scarecrow Press, 1948– .

An index to some 18 periodicals, which the compiler has taken back to 1931, and is slowly working through to the present. While an index, not a bibliography, it serves as a selection guide, particularly for those magazines not indexed in *Music Index.*

DISSIDENT MAGAZINES

Berry, John. "Public Library Practice in the Selection of Dissident Periodicals." *Library Journal,* Oct. 15, 1964: 3912–17.

A national survey which found that few public libraries subscribe to dissident periodicals.

Goldwater, Walter. *Radical Periodicals in America 1890–1950.* 1st rev. ed. New Haven: Yale, 1966. 51p.

An annotated list of 321 periodicals. Gives dates of publication.

Lasch, Christopher. "The Magazines of Dissent. . ." *The New York Times Magazine,* July 18, 1965: p.10.

A radical looks at *The Nation,* the *National Review, The New Republic* and lesser known magazines of dissent and their impact on America.

Muller, Robert H. *From Radical Left to Extreme Right.* Ann Arbor: Campus Publishers, 1967.

Extensive annotations, many running over a page in length, of 163 radical periodicals being published at the date of issue of this bibliography. Full bibliographic information, comments by editor. The best single guide now available to such magazines. A revised edition is now in the early stages of preparation, and should be available in another year or two.

EARTH SCIENCES

Kaplan, Stuart R., ed. *Guide to Information Sources in Mining, Minerals and Geosciences.* New York: Interscience, 1965.

ECONOMICS

International Bibliography of Economics. London: Stevens & Sons, Ltd., 1952–

An annual that includes both periodicals and periodical articles. Affords one of the best methods of keeping abreast of new economic periodicals. Coverage is international.

Johns Hopkins Univ. *A Selected Bibliography of Economic Reference Works and Professional Journals.* Baltimore: Johns Hopkins Univ., 1956.

Although dated, still useful for basic periodical list and the excellent annotations. One of several continuing lists issued by the Department of Political Economy, many of which have references to periodicals.

Sable, Martin, ed. *Periodicals for Latin American Economic Development, Trade, and Finance: An Annotated Bibliography.* Los Angeles: Univ. of California, Latin American Center, 1965.

A selected list of English and some foreign language periodicals arranged by country. Annotations are descriptive, and there is a broad subject index.

EDUCATION

Bossone, R. M. "Education Journals: An Annotated Bibliography." *Teachers College Journal,* Dec., 1964:134–8.

Camp, William L. *Guide to Periodicals in Education.* New York: Scarecrow, 1968.

A guide for educators who wish to submit articles to periodicals for publication. Some 449 nationally distributed educational magazines are listed, with bibliographic information and data on the type of material required.

Columbia Univ. Teachers College Library. *Periodicals Currently Received.* Columbia Univ., 1968.

A basic alphabetical listing. A useful checklist for larger collections.

Educational Press Assn. of America. *America's Education Press.* Syracuse: Syracuse Univ. School of Journalism, 1926– .

A biennial, classified list of educational publications issued in the United States. Also includes an international list in English, French, and Spanish.

Hanna, N. W. "How to Use Professional Periodicals." *NEA Journal,* Feb., 1967:63–4.

Lins, L. Joseph and Robert A. Rees. *Scholar's Guide to Journals of Education and Educational Psychology.* Madison: Dembar Educational Research Service, 1965.

Similar to Camp, although it covers only 134 journals. Camp is quite sufficient for most libraries.

National Education Assn. *NEA Handbook.* Washington: National Education Assn., 1945–

The annual handbook lists publications of the NEA and also includes a number of periodicals from its 50 departments and units. See also, the annual NEA *Publications Catalog.*

———. *The Teacher's Library.* Washington: National Education Assn., 1966.

Some 150 journals (pp. 180–200) for elementary and secondary school professional libraries are annotated and ranked.

Nicholsen, M. E. "Professional Library," *National Association Secondary School Principals Bulletin,* Jan., 1966:96–106.

Thurmas, R. S. *Annotated Bibliography of Education Periodicals in William Allen White Library.* Emporia: Kansas State Teachers College, 1960.

A good basic list compiled for a teachers college. The annotations make particularly helpful for the medium to large sized library.

ENGINEERING

Burkett, Jack and Philip Plumb. *How To Find Out in Electrical Engineering.* Elmsford: Pergamon Press, 1967.

GAMES AND SPORTS

U.S. Department of the Interior. *Outdoor Recreation: Current Periodicals,* Washington: U.S. Govt. Printing Office, 1964.

Primarily a listing of periodicals with reference to camping, hiking, but some games included.

GENERAL MAGAZINES

Furlong, W. B. "The Cowles Empire Expands." *Saturday Review,* May 11, 1968:71.

A discussion of the magazines and newspaper holdings of the Cowles family.

Goulden, Joseph C. *The Curtis Caper.* New York: Putnam, 1965.

A graphic description of "the life and headline hard times of the Curtis Publishing Company and the *Saturday Evening Post.*" While specifically a history of the *Post,* the work has wider application. It is, in fact, one of the best journalistic studies of general, mass magazine publishing available. A short bibliography.

Magazine Publishers Assn. *Magazines in the U.S.A.* New York: Magazine Publishers Association, 1967. 16pp.

A "propaganda" pamphlet dedicated to the notion that the general consumer "is a basic means of mass communication, distributing an estimated four billion, seven hundred million copies of magazines a year. . . ." An intelligent presentation with a good bibliography.

"Survey Sample: 'Shelter' Magazines," *Columbia Journalism in Review,* Summer, 1964: 32–33.

A survey which indicates what everyone knows: the general home magazine is designed to make the reader want more and more goods.

GEOGRAPHY

Church, Martha. *A Basic Geographical Library.* Washington: Assn. of Amer. Geographers, 1966.

In addition to books, this includes all of the basic journal publications in English.

Clark Univ. Library. *Most Cited Periodicals in Geography,* Worcester: Clark Univ., 1961.

A valuable use study. Primarily, though, for larger collections.

Harris, Chauncey D. *Annotated World List of Selected Current Geographical Serials in English.* Chicago: Univ. of Chicago Dept. of Geography, 1964.

An excellent annotated listing of some 62 serials in English and 56 more in some 28 languages. Useful for both the general and the specialized library. While dated, the basic guide in this field remains Wright and Platt's *Aids to Geographical Research* (Amer. Geographical Soc. Research Series #22. New York: Columbia Univ. Press, 1947).

————. *International List of Geographical Serials.* Chicago: Univ. of Chicago Dept. of Geography, 1960.

A list of serials both current (i.e., in 1960) and no longer being published.

Lock, C. B. M. *Geography, a Reference Handbook.* Hamden: Archon, 1968.

A subject arranged English handbook, with various references to periodicals. No substitute for Harris.

GERMAN LANGUAGE

An evaluative, survey article of the current German magazine scene will be found in Michael Kowal's excellent piece, "The Highbrow Magazines" (*American German Review,* Aug./Sept., 1967: 2–5). For another approach, see Patrick Bridgwater's "Literary Magazines in Germany" (*The Times Literary Supplement,* June 27, 1968:689).

GOVERNMENT PERIODICALS

Guide to U.S. Government Serials and Periodicals. 2nd ed. 4 vols. McLean: Documents Index, 1966.

The first volume, *Current Serials and Periodicals,* is of primary interest because it lists by department and issuing agency all periodicals published by the government. Full bibliographic information, plus a descriptive annotation. Other volumes cover releases, ephemeral publications and a supplement.

Kiraldi, Louis. "Some Problems Selecting Government Periodicals," *RQ* 7:166–68.

The author lists government periodicals indexed by abstracting and indexing services. No annotations.

HISTORY

Boehm, Erich H. *Historical Periodicals.* Santa Barbara: Clio Press, 1961.

The basic list of historical periodicals. Includes brief annotations for 4,500 titles, not only in history but in related areas as well. Scope is international, and arrangement is by area and country.

Perman, D. H. *Bibliography and the Historian.* Santa Barbara: Clio Press, 1968.

A report on the Belmont Conference on bibliographic control. Periodicals, indexes and abstracts are discussed in the first chapter.

HOUSE ORGANS

Tebbel, John. "Business Magazines: A Growing Force." *Saturday Review,* May 11, 1968: 69.

A discussion of the 8,000 or so company magazines published in the United States.

INDEXES AND ABSTRACTING SERVICES

Christianson, Elin B. "Variation of Editorial Material in Periodicals Indexed in Readers' Guide" *ALA Bulletin,* Feb., 1968:173–182.

A detailed discussion of variations in editions of national magazines and the effect on indexing and reference work.

"Science Abstracting Services-Commercial, Institutional, and Personal." *Library Trends,* 16 (No. 3).

An entire issue devoted to the title subject.

U.S. Library of Congress. *A Guide to the World's Abstracting and Indexing Services in Science and Technology.* Philadelphia: National Federation of Science Abstracting & Indexing Services, 1963.

A classified approach to some 1,855 titles. After the classification section, the services are arranged in alphabetical order by title with bibliographical information. There is a subject and country index. This is updated by the various editions of *Ulrich's Internatioanl Periodicals Directory* in the sections on abstracts and abstracting services.

JOURNALISM

Price, Warren C. *The Literature of Journalism*. Minneapolis: Univ. of Minnesota Press, 1959.

Chapter VIII, "Periodicals of the Press."

Wolseley, Roland E. *The Journalist's Bookshelf*. 7th ed. Philadelphia: Chilton, 1961.

Various sections on magazines.

LIBRARY MAGAZINES

Winckler, Paul A. *Library Periodicals Directory*. Brookville: Grad. Library Sch. of Long Island Univ., 1967.

A subject-arranged and annotated list of world-wide library science periodicals. Also includes sections on bibliography, books, and book selection. By far the most extensive, and best list in the field.

Springman, Mary and Betty Brown. *The Directory of Library Periodicals*. Philadelphia: Drexel Press, 1967.

An alphabetical list by issuing agency with a title index. Not annotated. Except for a few titles not covered by Winckler (see above), only required for extremely specialized collections.

LITERATURE

Altick, Richard and Andrew Wright. *Selective Bibliography for the Study of English and American Literature*. 2nd ed. New York: Macmillan, 1963.

Kennedy, Arthur G. and Donald B. Sands. *A Concise Bibliography for Students of English*. 4th ed. Stanford: Stanford Univ. Press, 1960.

Both of the above manuals for students of English include sections on periodicals. The Kennedy work is a particularly useful checklist.

Gerstenberger, Donna. *Second Directory of Periodicals Publishing Articles in English and American Literature and Language*. Denver: Swallow, 1965.

The directory "provides information both for the scholar wishing to submit articles for publication and for the graduate student in English, who may use it as a guide to the extensive publications in English and American literature and language." Arrangement is alphabetical with a title and subject index. Each entry briefly describes the editorial policy and needs of some 400 journals.

Ricks, Christopher. "Learned Journals," *Times Literary Supplement*, March 28, 1968: 324.

A critical, witty essay on the place of literary journals in the world of scholarship.

LITTLE MAGAZINES

Directory of Little Magazines. Paradise: Dustbooks, 1966–

An alphabetical, annotated, annual list of some 600 little magazines. Full bibliographic description and a note on contents. By and large the best single directory available for little magazines. Supplemented by the same publisher's *Small Press Review*.

Hoffman, Frederick J. and Caroline F. Ulrich. *The Little Magazine: A History and Bibliography*. New Jersey: Princeton Univ. Press, 1946.

The standard bibliography and history of the little magazine in the United States, England and Europe. The first half is a history, the second a chronological bibliography with detailed notes on each magazine up to 1945.

Mesiter, Marilyn. "The Little Magazines of British Columbia: A Narrative Bibliography." *British Columbia Library Quarterly* 31 (No. 2):3–19.

A discursive discussion of some major and minor titles. Concludes with a useful list of holdings of the British Columbia Provincial Library and the University of B.C. Library. A more general article is Frank Davey's "Anything But Reluctant: Canada's Little Magazines" (*Canadian Literature*, Summer, 1962): 39–44).

Modern Language Assn. of America. *The Little Magazine and Contemporary Literature*. New York: MLA, 1967.

An almost verbatim publication of a symposium on little magazines held at the library of Congress April 2–3, 1965. Speakers included Reed Whittemore, William Phillips, Karl Shapiro, Allen Tate and scores of little magazine publishers whose remarks from the audience are duly transcribed.

Small Press Review. 1967. q. Paradise, Calif. 95969.

Put together by the editor of the annual *Directory of Little Magazines*, this is an attempt to give a running detailed report on new little mags and books issued from small presses. Coverage is international, and bibliographic information complete. It appears considerably more fullsome than *Trace*. Also, it features a number of articles on little mags.

"The Little Magazine." *The Times Literary Supplement*, April 25, 1968.

An entire issue is devoted to the littles, primarily historical. Also, introduces what has become irregular column in TLS on little magazines by Derwent May.

The Something Newsletter. 1966– . irreg. Something Else Press, 160 Fifth Ave., New York, N.Y. 10010.

Edited and written by the editor and the owner of the Something Else Press, this irregular newsletter normally runs to only four pages, but is an excellent medium for keeping up with the news of the avant-garde press. Dick Higgins also writes lucid essays on topics of current interest such as happenings, "intermedia," and you name it.

Trace. 1952. q. Villiers Pubns., Box 1068, Hollywood 28, Calif.

"The Chronicle," a feature of each issue, traces the birth, death and present status of little mags.

Whittemore, Reed. *Little Magazines.* (American Writers Pamphlet No. 32). Minneapolis: Univ. of Minnesota Press, 1963.

Primarily a historical study of the little and the not so little literary publications.

MATHEMATICS

Lohwater, A. J. "Mathematical Literature," Library Trends, 15:852–67.

Mack, J. D. "A Mathematical Problem." Wilson Library Bulletin, 42:610–13.

May, K. O. "Quantitative Growth of the Mathematical Literature," *Science,* 154:1672–73.

Pemberton, J. E. *How To Find Out In Mathematics.* Oxford: Pergamon Press, 1963.

MOTION PICTURES

Aaronson, Charles S., ed. *International Motion Picture Almanac.* New York: Quigley, 1929–

Includes a section on periodicals, usually with brief annotations.

Samore, Theodore, "The Movies: A Montage of Books and Journals in the Sixties," *Choice* 4:1349–1358.

Primarily devoted to books, but includes a list "For a Basic Collection in this Field." Only two titles annotated.

World List of Film Periodicals and Serials. 2nd ed. Brussels: Cinematheque de Belgique, 1960.

A list of 769 titles with brief annotations. Arrangement is by country. Hopefully there will soon be a new edition as the number of periodicals in this field has grown substantially since 1960.

MUSIC

Watanabe, Ruth T. *Introduction to Music Research.* New Jersey: Prentice-Hall, 1967.

Chapter 17, "Survey of Contemporary Music Periodicals," is an annotated list arranged by broad subject headings. The author discusses each form, e.g., current events periodicals, the scholarly or learned journal, etc., and then gives perceptive annotations. Titles are listed by name and date of first publication. An even more useful list for the small, medium and large music library is the author's "Current Periodicals for Music Libraries" *Notes,* 23 (No. 2): 225–235. Full bibliographic descriptions and annotations are given for the magazines, which are divided first by the size of the library, and then by type of publication. An invaluable list for any type of library.

NEWS AND PICTURE MAGAZINES

Friedrich, Otto. "There are 00 Trees in Russia," *Harper's,* Oct. 1964. pp. 59–65.

An analysis of the fiction which is often passed off as fact and news in the major news weeklies.

Hentoff, Nat. "Review of the Press," *The Village Voice.*

A weekly column on every aspect of the modern newspaper. Hentoff is the closest critic to emulate, and in some ways surpass, the biting criticsm of newspapers by the late A. J. Liebling.

NEWSPAPERS

General

See *Journalism* for magazines dealing with newspapers. See introduction to *Newspaper* section for basic bibliography in the area.

Raskin, A. H. "What's Wrong With American Newspapers." *The New York Times Magazine,* June 11, 1967:28.

A discussion of current newspapers by the assistant editor of *The New York Times.*

Tebbel, John, "Wall Street Publishing Giant." *Saturday Review,* Jan. 13, 1968: 110.

A discussion of Dow Jones' Publications: *Wall Street Journal, The National Observer* and *Barron's.*

Underground

According to an announcement in the January, 1969, *ALA Bulletin* (p. 9): "Librarians can subscribe to all Underground Press Papers . . . for $50 for six months or $100 for the entire year. For more information, write to: Underground Press Syndicates, Bin 1603, Phoenix, Ariz. 85001."

Berman, Sanford. "Where It's At." *Library Journal,* Dec. 15, 1968: 4615.

Brown, Carol and Dan Tatko. "Underground and New Left Press." *Synergy* (San Francisco Public Library), Nov.–Dec., 1968:17.

The editor reports that this will be reprinted in the *Wilson Library Bulletin* sometime in 1969. Excellent for judgements of magazines.

"Making it Underground." *Newsweek,* Mar. 4, 1968:58-9.

Three representative articles on the underground newspaper and its impact on youth—and not a few adults.

Pepper, Thomas. "Underground Press: Growing Rich On The Hippie." *The Nation,* April 29, 1968:569–72.

Romm, E. G. "You Go Underground For 'Inside' Report," *Editor and Publisher.* May 11, 1968:12.

Underground Press Guide. P.O. Box 46477, Hollywood, Calif. 90046.

The first issue of this guide came out in 1967, and consists of a listing, with full address and bibliographic data, on some 80 underground newspapers. Brief editorial statement for each. Sells for $1, with a second edition planned for March, 1968. Another directory, for $2, is available from: Underground Press Syndicate, Bin 1603, Phoenix, Ariz. 85001.

PERSONNEL MANAGEMENT

Forrester, Gertrude. *Occupational Literature*. 1st rev. ed. New York: Wilson, 1964.

Includes annotated periodical information.

Holcomb, James R. "Indispensable: An Up-To-Date Library," *Journal of College Placement*, April, 1963:28–9.

Shartle, Carroll L. *Occupational Information*. New Jersey: Prentice-Hall, 1957.

Pages 366–370 list sources of informational materials, including periodicals. No annotations.

"Use and Appraisal of Occupational Literature." *Personnel and Guidance Journal*, Feb., 1959:441–43.

Some periodicals are listed in 52 sources of occupational information, which are ranked according to their usefulness by 268 guidance counselors.

PHILOSOPHY

U.S. Library of Congress. *Philosophical Periodicals*. Washington: Library of Congress, 1952.

Although dated, this is still a useful annotated list of major periodicals from some 70 different areas of the world. Index of titles.

PHYSICS

Amer. Inst. of Physics. *Check List of Books and Periodicals for an Undergraduate Physics Library* (Pubn. R-195). New York: Amer. Inst. of Physics, 1966.

Keenan, Stella and Pauline Atherton. *The Journal Literature of Physics*. New York: Amer. Inst. of Physics, 1964.

Parke, Nathan Grier. *Guide to the Literature of Mathematics and Physics*. 2nd ed. New York: Dover, 1958.

Yates, B. *How To Find Out About Physics*. Elmsford: Pergamon Press, 1965.

POETRY

Katz, Bill, & Inge Judd and John Pine. "Poetry in Public Libraries." *Library Journal*, June 1, 1968: 2203–2208.

A two-part survey of poetry holdings in libraries. Report is dismal to good.

POLITICAL SCIENCE

International Bibliography of Political Science. London: Stevens & Sons Ltd., 1953–

A useful annual guide to new books and periodical articles. Also serves as a method of checking new periodicals in the field.

PSYCHOLOGY

Garvey, William D. and Belver C. Griffith. *Reports of the American Psychological Association's Project on Scientific Information Exchange in Psychology*. 2 vols. Washington: Amer. Psychological Assn., 1963–65.

An intensive study which includes a considerable amount of reference to use of journals.

Lawler, Edward. "Psychology of the Scientist: IX. Age and Authorship of Citations in Selected Psychological Journals," *Psychological Reports* 12:537.

RELIGION

Marty, Martin E., and others. *The Religious Press in America* New York: Rinehart & Winston, 1963.

A detailed analysis of the Protestant, Catholic and Jewish periodical press. Includes a section on "The Secular Uses of the Religious Press. Unfortunately, lacks an index.

SCIENCE—GENERAL

World List of Scientific Periodicals. 4th ed. 3 vols. London: Butterworth, 1963–65.

A listing of more than 60,000 titles issued between 1900 and 1960. Arrangement is alphabetical by title. The work is continued in the *British Union Catalogue of Periodicals*. A more limited listing is the 13.000 titles included in the U.S. Library of Congress, *A List of Scientific and Technical Serials Currently Received by the Library of Congress* (Washington: National Science Foundation, 1960).

McGowan, John P. "The Periodical Scene: Science Magazines for Laymen." *RQ* 8:3–12.

An annotated list of 37 journals in the field of the applied and physical sciences, "designed to interpret for the layman new scientific and technical developments . . ." The list is annotated and ranked according to difficulty of comprehension. Prepared by the Science and Technology Reference Services Committee of the Reference Services Division, ALA.

Malinowsky, Harold R. *Science and Engineering Reference Sources*. Rochester: Libraries Unlimited, 1967.

Martin, Ralph C. and Wayne Jett. *Guide to Scientific and Technical Periodicals*. Denver: Swallow, 1963.

Similar to Gerstenberger (p. 100) in that it is primarily for writers. Data given on each periodical as regards editorial needs. Arranged under subject headings from general to physical sciences.

"Most-Used Science and Technology Periodicals." *Chemistry & Industry*, June 8, 1963:956.

"Most-Used Science and Technology Periodicals Seen in Study." *Chemical & Enginering News.* May 13, 1963:68–70.

Shank, R. "Scientific and Technical Periodicals." *Library Trends,* 10:390–404.

Strauss, Lucille J. *Scientific and Technical Libraries.* New York: Interscience, 1964.

Appendix contains a good, classified list of periodicals.

SOCIOLOGY

Council on Social Work Education. *Building a Social Work Library; A Guide to the Selection of Books, Periodicals, and Reference Tools.* New York: Council on Social Work Education, 1962.

A useful, classified list, but it lacks an index.

International Bibliography of Sociology. London: Stevens & Sons, Ltd., 1957– .

In addition to new books, this annual includes periodical articles and thus serves as a check on new publications in the field.

TEEN-AGE MAGAZINES

Fuller, Muriel. "Youth Magazines in the United States." *Horn Book,* Feb., 1966:110.

A short, lucid history which includes some magazines for younger children. (See also, additions and corrections in *Horn Book,* June, 1966:368.)

Harris, Dixie. "And This, Dear God, Is What They Read," *Esquire,* July, 1965:50.

A satirical, almost alarmist view of teen age magazines, particularly the movie fan mags. Should be contrasted with Stewart's study (see below).

Peterson, Theodore. "Notes on the Teen-Age Beat." *Saturday Review,* Feb. 13, 1965:76.

A short, objective analysis of some current teen age magazines. Peterson finds that the circulation increases as the quality increases.

Stewart, Janice C. "Content and Readership of Teen Magazines." *Journalism Quarterly,* 41:580–583.

A study which confirms the belief that teen-agers take their magazines much more seriously than adults, and that more sophisticated youths prefer adult periodicals.

THEATRE

Belknap, S. Y. *Guide to the Performing Arts.* New York: Scarecrow Press, 1960– .

An annual index which serves as a selection guide for some 30 to 40 periodicals. Includes music, dance, and films.

Chesire, David. *Theatre.* Hamden: Archon Books, 1967.

Chapter 6 is devoted primarily to English periodicals in the field.

Loney, G. M. "Some European Theatre Publications." *Educational Theatre Journal,* Mar. 1960:16–19.

Stratman, Carl J. *A Bibliography of British Dramatic Periodicals, 1720–1960.* New York: N.Y. Public Library, 1962.

Some 674 magazines are listed chronologically, but there are no annotations. Location of copies in American and British libraries, and a title, place index.

WOMEN'S MAGAZINES

Iversen, William. *The Pious Pornographers.* New York: MB Books, 1964.

See chapter, "The Pious Pornographers," for a man's reaction to *Ladies' Home Journal.*

MacDougall, A. Kent. "Confession Magazine Revenue Keeps Rising. *The Wall Street Journal,* Aug. 2, 1968:28.

A detailed discussion of both the economic and readership impact of the confessional magazine. Throughout are examples of what type of material is acceptable for a given audience, an audience rarely seen in libraries.

Orwell, George. "It Looks Different from Abroad." *New Republic,* Dec. 2, 1956.

A classic essay on the foibles of women's magazines.

St. Code, Ann. "The Decline and Fall of Fashion," *Harper's,* Oct., 1962:134–140.

An analysis of women's fashion magazines, little of which is flattering.

Woodward, Helen. *The Lady Persuaders,* New York: Obolensky, 1960.

One woman looks in detail at women's magazines, and most of what she finds is usually not good. Also, serves as a useful history of the genre.

INDEX